Great Lakes

Ryan Ver Berkmoes

Thomas Huhti

Mark Lightbody

LONELY PLANET PUBLICATIONS

Melbourne • Oakland • London • Paris

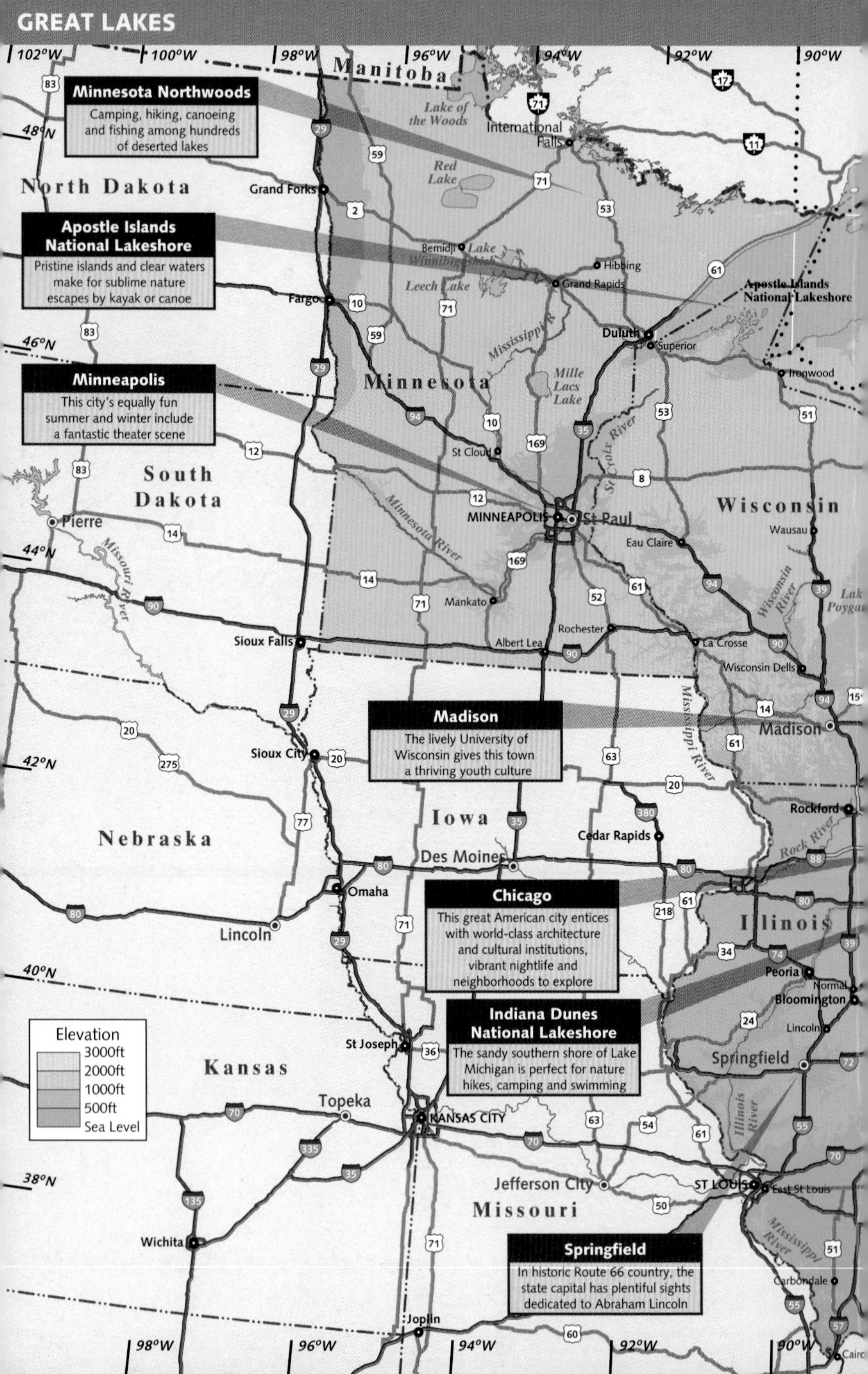
Minnesota Northwoods
Camping, hiking, canoeing and fishing among hundreds of deserted lakes
Apostle Islands National Lakeshore
Pristine islands and clear waters make for sublime nature escapes by kayak or canoe
Minneapolis
This city's equally fun summer and winter include a fantastic theater scene
Madison
The lively University of Wisconsin gives this town a thriving youth culture
Chicago
This great American city entices with world-class architecture and cultural institutions, vibrant nightlife and neighborhoods to explore
Indiana Dunes National Lakeshore
The sandy southern shore of Lake Michigan is perfect for nature hikes, camping and swimming
Springfield
In historic Route 66 country, the state capital has plentiful sights dedicated to Abraham Lincoln
Elevation
3000ft
2000ft
1000ft
500ft
Sea Level
Manitoba
North Dakota
South Dakota
Minnesota
Wisconsin
Iowa
Nebraska
Kansas
Missouri
Illinois
Lake of the Woods
International Falls
Red Lake
Grand Forks
Bemidji
Lake Winnibigoshish
Leech Lake
Hibbing
Grand Rapids
Duluth
Superior
Ironwood
Fargo
Mississippi R
Mille Lacs Lake
St Croix River
St Cloud
MINNEAPOLIS
St Paul
Minnesota River
Pierre
Missouri River
Eau Claire
Wausau
Wisconsin River
Mankato
Rochester
Albert Lea
La Crosse
Wisconsin Dells
Sioux Falls
Mississippi River
Madison
Sioux City
Rockford
Rock River
Cedar Rapids
Des Moines
Omaha
Lincoln
Peoria
Normal
Bloomington
St Joseph
Springfield
Topeka
KANSAS CITY
Illinois River
Jefferson City
ST LOUIS
East St Louis
Wichita
Carbondale
Joplin
102°W
100°W
98°W
96°W
94°W
92°W
90°W
48°N
46°N
44°N
42°N
40°N
38°N

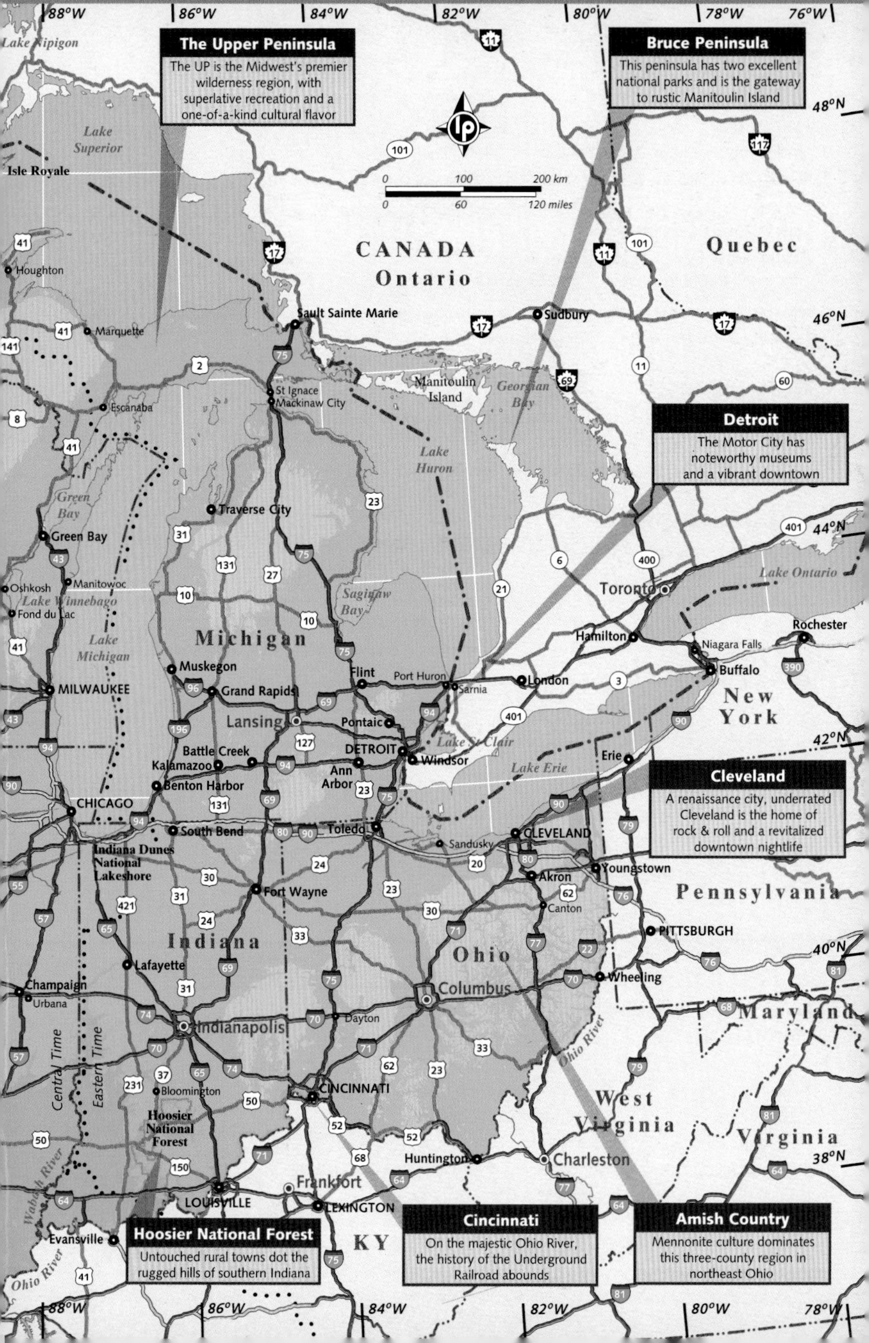
The Upper Peninsula
The UP is the Midwest's premier wilderness region, with superlative recreation and a one-of-a-kind cultural flavor
Bruce Peninsula
This peninsula has two excellent national parks and is the gateway to rustic Manitoulin Island
Detroit
The Motor City has noteworthy museums and a vibrant downtown
Cleveland
A renaissance city, underrated Cleveland is the home of rock & roll and a revitalized downtown nightlife
Hoosier National Forest
Untouched rural towns dot the rugged hills of southern Indiana
Cincinnati
On the majestic Ohio River, the history of the Underground Railroad abounds
Amish Country
Mennonite culture dominates this three-county region in northeast Ohio
0 100 200 km
0 60 120 miles
88°W
86°W
84°W
82°W
80°W
78°W
76°W
48°N
46°N
44°N
42°N
40°N
38°N
CANADA
Ontario
Quebec
Lake Nipigon
Lake Superior
Isle Royale
Houghton
Marquette
Escanaba
Sault Sainte Marie
St Ignace
Mackinaw City
Manitoulin Island
Georgian Bay
Sudbury
Lake Huron
Green Bay
Traverse City
Oshkosh
Manitowoc
Lake Winnebago
Fond du Lac
Lake Michigan
Michigan
Saginaw Bay
Muskegon
Grand Rapids
Flint
Port Huron
Sarnia
London
Lansing
Pontiac
DETROIT
Windsor
Lake St Clair
Battle Creek
Kalamazoo
Ann Arbor
Benton Harbor
MILWAUKEE
CHICAGO
South Bend
Toledo
Sandusky
Indiana Dunes National Lakeshore
Toronto
Lake Ontario
Hamilton
Rochester
Niagara Falls
Buffalo
New York
Lake Erie
Erie
CLEVELAND
Akron
Canton
Youngstown
Pennsylvania
PITTSBURGH
Fort Wayne
Indiana
Ohio
Lafayette
Champaign
Urbana
Columbus
Wheeling
Maryland
Dayton
Indianapolis
Central Time
Eastern Time
Bloomington
Hoosier National Forest
CINCINNATI
Ohio River
West Virginia
Virginia
Huntington
Charleston
Frankfort
LOUISVILLE
LEXINGTON
KY
Wabash River
Evansville

Great Lakes
1st edition – November 2000

Published by
Lonely Planet Publications Pty Ltd A.C.N. 005 607 983
192 Burwood Rd, Hawthorn, Victoria 3122, Australia

Lonely Planet Offices
Australia PO Box 617, Hawthorn, Victoria 3122
USA 150 Linden St, Oakland, CA 94607
UK 10a Spring Place, London NW5 3BH
France 1 rue du Dahomey, 75011 Paris

Photographs
Most of the images in this guide are available for licensing from Lonely Planet Images.
email: lpi@lonelyplanet.com.au

Front cover photograph
Lighthouse on Round Island, Lake Michigan, MI (Stone/Chris Sanders)

Title page photographs
Courtesy of the Library of Congress
Illinois (Russell Lee)
Indiana (John Vachon)
Ohio (Arthur Rothstein)
Michigan (John Vachon)
Wisconsin (Russell Lee)
Minnesota (John Vachon)

ISBN 1 86450 139 1

Printed by The Bookmaker International Ltd
Printed in China

Contents

NORTHERN & CENTRAL ILLINOIS 141

SOUTHERN ILLINOIS 174

FACTS ABOUT INDIANA 190

CENTRAL & NORTHERN INDIANA 195

CHAPTERS
CANADA
Manitoba
Ontario
Quebec
North Dakota
South Dakota
Nebraska
Kansas
Iowa
Missouri
Kentucky
West Virginia
Virginia
Pennsylvania
New York
Lake Superior
Lake Michigan
Lake Huron
Lake Erie
Lake Ontario
Central & Northern Minnesota page 519
Minnesota page 483
Southeastern Minnesota page 488
Eastern & Northern Wisconsin page 452
Wisconsin page 421
Southern Wisconsin page 426
Upper Peninsula page 387
Lake Michigan Shore & the Straits page 359
Lake Huron Shore & the Thumb page 380
Michigan pages 328-329
Southern Michigan page 333
Ontario Shore (Canada) page 412
Chicago page 92
Northern & Central Illinois page 141
Illinois page 87
Southern Illinois page 174
Central & Northern Indiana page 195
Indiana page 191
Southern Indiana page 227
Northern Ohio page 251
Ohio page 248
Central & Southern Ohio page 288
0 100 200 km
0 60 120 miles

The Authors

Ryan Ver Berkmoes

As coordinating author of *Great Lakes*, Ryan researched and wrote the introductory chapters plus those covering Illinois and Indiana. He grew up in Santa Cruz, California, but, too young and naive to realize what a beautiful place it was, left for college in the Midwest at age 17. His first job in Chicago was at a small muckraking publication where, second on a two-person editorial staff, he had the impressive title Managing Editor (the first person was called Editor). After a year of 60-hour weeks, Ryan's first trip to Europe lasted for seven months, confirming his long-suspected wanderlust. During his 13 years living in Chicago, his travels took him to every Great Lake state. His byline has appeared in scores of publications as he's covered everything from wars to bars (he definitely prefers the latter).

In his work for Lonely Planet, Ryan has been author of *Chicago* and *Moscow*, co-author of *Texas, Canada* and *Western Europe* and coordinating author of *Russia, Ukraine & Belarus, Netherlands, Out to Eat London, Britain* and *England*. In the future, Ryan hopes to add more warm weather destinations to the list above. He and his wife, journalist Sara Marley, reside in London near the point of inspiration for noted musician Nigel Tufnel.

Thomas Huhti

A native Wisconsin Cheesehead, Thomas Huhti has spent much of his life in Wisconsin, save for a year of college in Duluth, Minnesota, during which he studied and played a lot of hockey. He ultimately returned to the University of Wisconsin, earning a degree in Linguistics, English and (almost) Chinese. Thomas subsequently fled graduate school to spend a few years on fellowship in East Asia; there he discovered his preference for constant movement and jumpstarted his writing career.

He has researched or written new books and updates of books on China, Thailand, Burma, the Philippines, French Polynesia, Canada, Mexico and the US. When he's not barreling around the world with a backpack, Thomas would rather be shagging fly balls or chasing a loose puck.

Mark Lightbody

Mark has been visiting the USA since early childhood vacations from his Canadian home. He researched and wrote much of the Midwest section for Lonely Planet's *USA*.

He always enjoys meeting his neighbors to the south and seeing more of their country. Mark has traveled in nearly 50 countries, visiting every continent but Antarctica. He continuously works on updating the Lonely Planet *Canada* guide and has worked on the *Papua New Guinea, Australia, Malaysia, Singapore & Brunei* and *Southeast Asia* books.

After growing up in Montreal, he earned an honors journalism degree in London, Ontario. Among his wide range of employment, Mark has worked in radio news and in the specialty graphics trade.

He now lives in Toronto with his wife and two increasingly itchy-footed kids.

FROM THE AUTHORS

Ryan Ver Berkmoes For once the hackneyed phrase 'too many to thank' really applies. I spent a fair amount of my life in the Midwest and friends made over that period were greatly helpful both for information and inspiration. In Chicago, Heidi Kooi, Patricia Sullivan and Gail Orr handled the official end while John Holden and Sue Amati were first among many old pals. Elsewhere in Illinois, Charlotte Doehler in the Quad Cities was a gem and Kim Rosendahl in Springfield was great. Brandon Griffing at Pages For All Ages in Champaign–Urbana was a fine host. In Indiana, John Goss, Lynne Fuller, Greg Bedan and Cheri Wagner at the Indiana Tourism Division in Indianapolis were superb, Ike and Jonesy's notwithstanding. Laura Newton and company in Bloomington were delights. Other big thanks go to Linda Lytle and John Nyberg in Madison, Leigh Ann O'Donnell in Evansville, G Alan Barnett in French Lick, Bruce Shanks at Pioneer Seeds and Tania Campbell. In South Bend, I'm indebted to Kathy McGowan and Fred Ziolkowski at the ND bookstore as well as my many friends, relatives and parents.

Much appreciation goes to the fine people in the LP Oakland office. Eric Kettunen, Mariah 'tube sock' Bear, Kate Hoffman, Michele Posner and Laura Harger all provided guidance and a good deal of friendship as well. Among the many staffers who worked on this book, I am most indebted to Tullan Spitz and Rachel Bernstein for their editing and good humor. Jacqueline Volin, as always, was a treat and is just as good at finding bad syntax as finding a good burrito.

Finally, deep affection to Sara Marley, who's the best discovery I made in the Midwest.

Thomas Huhti Thanks to all the CVB and tourist office folks who go way beyond the call of duty to cheerily point we clueless travelers in the right directions. Thanks to all the travelers who took the time and effort to make friends on boats, in lines, etc. Many thanks to my compadres Mark Lightbody and Ryan Ver Berkmoes for their help and good cheer. And, as always, thanks to Hyeon for being with me even when so far away.

Mark Lightbody I want to sincerely thank all the waitresses, gas station attendants, police officers, museum workers, park rangers, campground hosts and chamber of commerce staff who in so many ways contributed to the Minnesota and Wisconsin sections. Their generosity of time and spirit are much appreciated. Thanks also to Tom Huhti for recommendations, suggestions and advice, and to Ryan Ver Berkmoes for his prompt responses to questions and positive attitude. Lastly, as always, I want to thank Colleen for all manner of assistance and my two kids, Trevor and Ava, who tolerated my impatient outbursts when deadlines were menacing.

This Book

The first edition of *Great Lakes* was edited in Oakland by Tullan 'Spitty' Spitz, Rachel 'F'in B' Bernstein and Jacqueline 'Footloose-and-fancy-freelancer' Volin. Michele 'Don't worry' Posner, Laura Harger and Kate Hoffman provided much-appreciated support and editorial direction. Amelia Borofsky, Susan Derby, Suki Gear and Paul Sheridan proofread the book along with Tullan and Rachel. Ken DellaPenta indexed the book.

The maps were skillfully drawn by lead cartographer Dion 'Smiles' Good and by Kat 'State Symbol' Smith, Connie Lock, Eric Thomsen, Sean Brandt, Chris Gillis, Patrick Huerta, John Spelman and Annette Olson, with oversight from Monica 'We can do that' Lepe and Alex Guilbert. Cartographic kudos are also due Matt DeMartini, Guphy, Heather Haskell, Colin Bishop, Ed Turley and Kimra McAfee.

Ruth 'An old photo would be great here!' Askevold masterfully designed *Great Lakes* and its cover. Beca Lafore popped out brilliant illustration ideas and led the illustration team of Hugh D'Andrade, John Fadeff, Hayden Foell, Rini Keagy, Justin Marler, Jennifer Steffey and Wendy Yanagihara. Jenn Steffey acquired and organized the slides. All this and more took place under the cheerful and watchful eye of Susan Rimerman.

Between 1935 and 1945, the US government commissioned photographers to document various aspects of American life; the photographic title pages for each state and the photographs in scenic-drive text boxes were acquired from the US Library of Congress Farm Security Administration and Office of War photo collection.

Foreword

ABOUT LONELY PLANET GUIDEBOOKS

The story begins with a classic travel adventure: Tony and Maureen Wheeler's 1972 journey across Europe and Asia to Australia. Useful information about the overland trail did not exist at that time, so Tony and Maureen published the first Lonely Planet guidebook to meet a growing need.

From a kitchen table, then from a tiny office in Melbourne (Australia), Lonely Planet has become the largest independent travel publisher in the world, an international company with offices in Melbourne, Oakland (USA), London (UK) and Paris (France).

Today Lonely Planet guidebooks cover the globe. There is an ever-growing list of books, and there's information in a variety of forms and media. Some things haven't changed. The main aim is still to help make it possible for adventurous travelers to get out there – to explore and better understand the world.

At Lonely Planet we believe travelers can make a positive contribution to the countries they visit – if they respect their host communities and spend their money wisely. Since 1986 a percentage of the income from each book has been donated to aid projects and human-rights campaigns.

Updates Lonely Planet thoroughly updates each guidebook as often as possible. This usually means there are around two years between editions, although for more unusual or more stable destinations the gap can be longer. Check the imprint page (following the color map at the beginning of the book) for publication dates.

Between editions, up-to-date information is available in two free newsletters – the paper *Planet Talk* and email *Comet* (to subscribe, contact any Lonely Planet office) – and on our website at www.lonelyplanet.com. The *Upgrades* section of the website covers a number of important and volatile destinations and is regularly updated by Lonely Planet authors. *Scoop* covers news and current affairs relevant to travelers. And, lastly, the *Thorn Tree* bulletin board and *Postcards* section of the site carry unverified, but fascinating, reports from travelers.

Lonely Planet gathers information for everyone who's curious about the planet – and especially for those who explore it firsthand. Through guidebooks, phrasebooks, activity guides, maps, literature, newsletters, image library, TV series and website, we act as an information exchange for a worldwide community of travelers.

Correspondence The process of creating new editions begins with the letters, postcards and emails received from travelers. This correspondence often includes suggestions, criticisms and comments about the current editions. Interesting excerpts are immediately passed on via newsletters and the website, and everything goes to our authors to be verified when they're researching on the road. We're keen to get more feedback from organizations or individuals who represent communities visited by travelers.

Research Authors aim to gather sufficient practical information to enable travelers to make informed choices and to make the mechanics of a journey run smoothly. They also research historical and cultural background to help enrich the travel experience and allow travelers to understand and respond appropriately to cultural and environmental issues.

Authors don't stay in every hotel because that would mean spending a couple of months in each medium-size city and, no, they don't eat at every restaurant because that would mean stretching belts beyond capacity. They do visit hotels and restaurants to check standards and prices, but feedback based on readers' direct experiences can be very helpful.

Many of our authors work undercover; others aren't so secretive. None of them accept freebies in exchange for positive write-ups. And none of our guidebooks contain any advertising.

Production Authors submit their raw manuscripts and maps to offices in Australia, the USA, the UK or France. Editors and cartographers – all experienced travelers themselves – then begin the process of assembling the pieces. When the book finally hits the shops, some things are already out of date, we start getting feedback from readers and the process begins again....

WARNING & REQUEST

Things change – prices go up, schedules change, good places go bad and bad places go bankrupt – nothing stays the same. So, if you find things better or worse, recently opened or long since closed, please tell us and help make the next edition even more accurate and useful. We genuinely value all the feedback we receive. Julie Young coordinates a well-traveled team that reads and acknowledges every letter, postcard and email and ensures that every morsel of information finds its way to the appropriate authors, editors and cartographers for verification.

Everyone who writes to us will find their name in the next edition of the appropriate guidebook. They will also receive the latest issue of *Planet Talk*, our quarterly printed newsletter, or *Comet*, our monthly email newsletter. Subscriptions to both newsletters are free. The very best contributions will be rewarded with a free guidebook.

Excerpts from your correspondence may appear in new editions of Lonely Planet guidebooks, the Lonely Planet website, *Planet Talk* or *Comet*, so please let us know if you *don't* want your letter published or your name acknowledged.

Send all correspondence to the Lonely Planet office closest to you:

Australia: PO Box 617, Hawthorn, Victoria 3122
USA: 150 Linden St, Oakland, CA 94607
UK: 10A Spring Place, London NW5 3BH
France: 1 rue du Dahomey, 75011 Paris

Or email us at: talk2us@lonelyplanet.com.au

For news, views and updates, see our website: www.lonelyplanet.com

HOW TO USE A LONELY PLANET GUIDEBOOK

The best way to use a Lonely Planet guidebook is any way you choose. At Lonely Planet, we believe the most memorable travel experiences are often those that are unexpected, and the finest discoveries are those you make yourself. Guidebooks are not intended to be used as if they provided a detailed set of infallible instructions!

Contents All Lonely Planet guidebooks follow the same format. The Facts about the Country chapters or sections give background information ranging from history to weather. Facts for the Visitor gives practical information on issues like visas and health. Getting There & Away gives a brief starting point for researching travel to and from the destination. Getting Around gives an overview of the transport options available when you arrive.

The peculiar demands of each destination determine how subsequent chapters are broken up, but some things remain constant. We always start with background, then proceed to sights, places to stay, places to eat, entertainment, getting there and away, and getting around information – in that order.

Heading Hierarchy Lonely Planet headings are used in a strict hierarchical structure that can be visualized as a set of Russian dolls. Each heading (and its following text) is encompassed by any preceding heading that is higher on the hierarchical ladder.

Entry Points We do not assume guidebooks will be read from beginning to end, but that people will dip into them. The traditional entry points are the list of contents and the index. In addition, however, some books have a complete list of maps and an index map illustrating map coverage.

There may also be a color map that shows highlights. These highlights are dealt with in greater detail later in the book, along with planning questions and suggested itineraries. Each chapter covering a geographical region usually begins with a locator map and another list of highlights. Once you find something of interest in a list of highlights, turn to the index.

Maps Maps play a crucial role in Lonely Planet guidebooks and include a huge amount of information. A legend is printed on the back page. We seek to have complete consistency between maps and text, and to have every important place in the text captured on a map. Map key numbers usually start in the top left corner.

Although inclusion in a guidebook usually implies a recommendation, we cannot list every good place. Exclusion does not necessarily imply criticism. In fact, there are a number of reasons why we might exclude a place – sometimes it is simply inappropriate to encourage an influx of travelers.

Introduction

The Great Lakes is a surprising region of the United States, even for those who live there. Certainly non-natives often have a skewed vision of this diverse land, thinking that it's merely a boundless cornfield punctuated by the occasional rusting factory.

But these simplistic views are easily altered. How many know that Michigan has 124 lighthouses scattered along its 3200 miles of coast, or that some of the best canoeing in North America is in the parks and forests of Wisconsin and Minnesota? Who would ever guess that Indiana is home to some of America's best beaches and that Ohio boasts a rock music museum second to none? Or that the towns of Madison, Wisconsin, Bloomington, Indiana, and Ann Arbor, Michigan, are home to huge universities and boast scores of cultural and social activities? Finally, how many people stuck on the idea of visiting both coasts overlook Chicago, which with its museums, culture, restaurants and more is one of the world's great cities?

The phrase 'America's Heartland' is used too often, but beneath the cliche there is truth. One of the great presidents – many say *the* greatest – Abraham Lincoln grew up and lived in Indiana and Illinois. A succession of sites in both states not only trace his life, but also give fascinating insight into the lives of early European settlers and 19th-century life. In Canton, Ohio, the birthplace of the National Football League, the Pro Football Hall of Fame honors the country's most popular spectator sport. And what exemplifies the heartland more than the writings of Mark Twain, many of which were set on the legendary Mississippi River, which forms borders for Illinois, Wisconsin and Minnesota?

Small-town America, with its homey charms and simple ways, is exemplified thousands of times over in the six Great Lakes states. Some of the towns, such as those in Indiana's Brown County, are major tourist destinations themselves, but most others wait to be discovered. Old courthouse squares with their proud civic buildings and stolid ring of shops make for fun stops, miles away – literally and figuratively – from the generic freeway interchanges with their ubiquitous fast food eateries. Sometimes the roads themselves are the attraction – finding one of the surviving stretches of infamous Route 66 in central Illinois is an immediate step back in time. It's not hard to empathize with the hopes and dreams of the thousands who drove these narrow, twisting roads in the 1920s in search of better lives.

Away from the highways, towns, farms and cities, many travelers will be most struck by the lakes themselves and the pristine, rugged lands around these inland

seas. Isle Royale, the least visited and most isolated of America's national parks, is a wilderness of moose and wolves, offering weeks of backcountry hiking and coastal exploration. Nearby, Michigan's often forgotten Upper Peninsula is home to many more wilderness lands and waters. And along the Lake Michigan coast of the state are other natural sights, including the Sleeping Bear Dunes National Lakeshore, a vast area of sand and water that figures strongly in Native American lore.

Across the lake, Wisconsin is mostly rural. Its often visited Door County is lined with quaint old fishing towns that now attract those looking for B&Bs. But even here, you can escape the crowds by heading off the coast to remote gems such as Rock Island, a natural wonder, or the stunning Apostle Islands National Lakeshore in the far north. Minnesota boasts of its '10,000 lakes' and with good reason; Voyageurs National Park on the Canadian border is just one shining example in a land that is a dream for anyone wielding an oar.

Finally, the people of the Great Lakes are a fascinating mix resulting from immigration from all parts of the world and the influence of many Native American cultures. The region has been shaped by the communities and beliefs of the diverse peoples – from Scandinavians to Africans, from Latin Americans to Europeans, from Asians to those from other parts of America – who have settled and continue to settle here. What's missing, however, is any kind of attitude; the people of the Great Lakes have a well-deserved reputation for friendliness and openness. This welcoming atmosphere is just another compelling reason to visit the Great Lakes, a region of culture, beauty and charm.

Facts about the Great Lakes Region

HISTORY

The First Immigrants

It is generally accepted that the first people in the Americas came from east Asia, over a land bridge to Alaska across what is now the Bering Strait. The land bridge, called Beringia, occurred when sea levels dropped during the last ice age, between 25,000 and 10,000 years ago. These first immigrants were probably nomadic hunters following large game animals, moving south and east to all corners of the Americas. Impenetrable ice sheets would have made the land bridge impassable during the middle of the ice age (20,000 to 13,000 years ago), so it's thought that the first settlers came across either before the ice peaked or afterward, and then migrated throughout the Americas with remarkable speed. Estimates of the timing of this epic migration vary from as recently as 12,500 years ago to as far back as 70,000 years, but the oldest estimates are largely speculative.

Human artifacts from a site in southern Chile, recently carbon-dated to about 12,500 years old, are among the oldest undisputed evidence of human occupation in the Americas. Many sites in North and South America are said to be older than that, but there is no evidence at all of a progression in the age of artifacts from North to South America, which one would expect if the Americas had been populated by a gradual land migration from Alaska to southern Patagonia.

The most recent prehistoric migration was that of the Inuit people (also called Eskimos), who are thought to have arrived by boat, skirting the edge of the ice fields about 4000 years ago.

Among the earliest inhabitants of North America were the makers of stone tools (probably butchering tools) found near Clovis, New Mexico. These 'Clovis points' have been dated to about 11,000 years ago. Numerous other sites all over the continent have yielded hunting implements almost as old, or possibly older.

After the ice age, there were changes in the climate and environment, and large animals such as the mammoth became extinct. Americans turned to hunting smaller game, fishing and gathering wild berries, seeds, roots and fruits. Agriculture developed, especially as the use of new crops spread north from cultures in the area of modern Mexico. Primitive corn (maize) was cultivated in the Southwest region of what is now the United States from about 3000 BC, and by 500 BC, maize, squash and beans were widespread in the South, East and Midwest.

The Hopewell, a mound-building culture, arose in the Ohio and Mississippi Valleys around 500 BC. Their settlements were characterized by earthen mounds, initially made for defense, but later used as burial sites and temples. These people, with their many towns and well-developed agriculture, had extensive trading links from Lake Huron to the Rocky Mountains and south to Mexico.

The lower Mississippi Mound Builders peaked somewhat later, but declined and disappeared by about 1200 AD. Later, many new Native American groups came to occupy the forest lands in the East, South and Midwest. The remains of mounds can be seen at many sites across the Great

LEE FOSTER

Native American tools from about 1500 BC, at Isle Royale National Park, MI

Lakes region, most notably at Cahokia Mounds in East St Louis, Illinois, and around Chillicothe, Ohio.

The Mound Builders were replaced by various groups of farmers and hunter-gatherers, including the Miami, Illinois, Shawnee and Winnebago. What is now central Illinois had one of the highest concentrations of Native Americans in North America at the time.

European Arrival

The first Europeans were French voyageurs who explored the lakes and rivers, traded for furs with the Native Americans and established missions and forts beginning in the early 17th century. Jean Nicolet searched in vain for the fabled Northwest Passage and in 1634 reached Green Bay. By the late 17th century, the French had established posts around the Great Lakes that were headquartered at Sault Ste Marie. Jacques Marquette began his explorations and efforts to proselytize the indigenous people.

The Ohio Company, a group of British and Virginians, was formed in 1748 to develop more trade with the Indians and to ensure control of the Ohio Valley for the English. Its explorations helped precipitate the French and Indian War (1754–60). The British eventually won over the French, but Native Americans under Pontiac waged war against the British on a 1000-mile front and eventually won a string of victories themselves. This led to London's effectively ceding much of the land west of the Appalachian Mountains to Pontiac and his followers. However this gain for the Native Americans was short-lived: The British had the dynamic Pontiac killed in 1769.

American Expansion

Following the Revolutionary War (1775–83), the area south of the Great Lakes became the Northwest Territories of the new United States of America. It was divided up into administrative districts that led to the creation of the Great Lakes states. (Between 1803 and 1858, each was permitted entrance to the union as a non-slaveholding state once it had adopted a state constitution and reached a population of 60,000.)

New settlers moved rapidly into Ohio, Indiana, Michigan and Illinois in the late 18th century, and a series of conflicts ensued as the Native Americans were progressively displaced by this westward expansion. After the 1803 Louisiana Purchase, the region became the gateway to further expansion west of the Mississippi River, and the War of 1812 consolidated the US border with Canada. Initially, waterways were vital transport routes, greatly enhanced by new canals linking the Great Lakes to the area's river systems. The Erie Canal had opened the region when it allowed cheap transportation of goods from New York City to the Great Lakes port of Buffalo, New York, on Lake Ontario. From there goods were forwarded by boat over all five lakes. Detroit was an early success in this trade; by the late 1830s, 200,000 people a year were passing through the city.

But Chicago, with its 1848 completion of the Illinois and Michigan Canal, which linked the Great Lakes to the Mississippi River and the Gulf of Mexico, soon became the region's hub. It was a center for railroad building as well, with lines radiating in all directions. By 1850 it was the undisputed leading city of what is now the Midwest.

Industries sprang up around the lakes, fueled by local resources of coal, iron and copper. Significantly enhancing their growth were the development of the railroads and the demands of the Civil War (1861–65).

With Native Americans pushed west of the Mississippi for good after the Black Hawk War of 1832, what had been a steady stream of settlers became a flood. Large areas of the region were populated in a short time by homesteaders and farmers, and as you travel around the Great Lakes states today you will find that most towns and cities were established during the short period of 1820 to 1850.

The initial white settlement was mostly by people from the East Coast states. Yankees, with their conservative New England ways, populated a broad swath from northern Ohio to northern Indiana and Illinois right up into Minnesota. Southerners, with their more flamboyant ways, settled in the southern regions of Ohio, Indiana and Illinois. Their influence can still be seen in the ornamented brick buildings in old river towns such as Madison, Indiana.

Immigration & Industrialization

Waves of immigrants were another feature of the growth of the Great Lakes region. European immigrants from Ireland (in the early and mid-19th century), Germany (in the mid- to late 19th century), Scandinavia (in the late 19th century), Italy and Russia (around the turn of the 20th century) and southern and eastern Europe (in the early 20th century) made whole swaths of the region into miniature versions of the lands they left. The Dutch of southwest Michigan, the Poles of northern Indiana, the Germans of Wisconsin and the Scandinavians of Minnesota are examples of groups that dominated certain areas.

While farmers got to work on much of Ohio, Indiana and Illinois, it was loggers who made much of Michigan, Wisconsin and Minnesota. Vast tracts of pine and hardwood fell to the cutters' saws through the late 19th century. Chicago's vital transportation role only added to that city's wealth as millions of logs passed through on their way to feed the needs of America's nonstop westward expansion.

But the real growth of the region began in 1890 with the enormous industrial expansion that swept the shores of the Great Lakes from Cleveland to Chicago. Huge steel plants were built on the southern shores of the lakes at places such as Gary, Indiana, and they were fed by boatloads of iron ore from the Mesabi and other Lake Superior ranges. In 1908 the first Model T rolled off Henry Ford's assembly line. In the next two decades, the Detroit area became the center of America's huge auto industry, which had plants scattered throughout the Midwest and beyond.

All these industries absorbed labor as fast as it arrived. More waves of Europeans were drawn to the Great Lakes region, but even they were not enough, and manufacturers looked to the South. Beginning in 1910, millions of poor southern blacks relocated to the industrial centers of Chicago and Detroit in a movement that came to be known as the 'Great Migration.'

The depression of the 1930s affected the Midwest as much as the rest of the US, but the entire area rebounded with World War II, when every factory and farm was used to its full capacity to feed and fuel the war effort. This prosperity lasted after the war and caused great changes during the 1950s. The growing middle class in the Great Lakes region used its newfound affluence to move out of the cities. Sprawling suburbs were built in rings around every medium and large city, a process that has continued unabated. Meanwhile, the cities were left to the poorer segments of society.

Tough Economic Times

As the 1960s drew to a close, several factors led to rapid changes throughout the region. The Civil Rights movement fermented in the cities, and race riots tore at the fabric of Chicago and Detroit. Increased automation coupled with aggressive competition from Asia and Europe pummeled the auto, steel and other manufacturing industries. Out in the country, consolidation eliminated many family farms, and small towns suffered as their residents moved elsewhere. The recession of the late 1970s was devastating to the Great Lakes region, which gained a new and uncomplimentary name, 'the Rust Belt.'

Rebirth

The 1980s were a time of readjustment. Chicago was one of the first large American cities to benefit from reurbanization. Scores of young professionals discovered the joys of life in the city, as opposed to bland suburban life. Concurrently, block after block of older buildings underwent renovation, transforming from light-manufacturing plants and warehouses into modern offices to serve the growing service economy.

Surviving industries emerged from the brutal economic downturn of the late 1970s with better management and new innovations that allowed them to compete in the

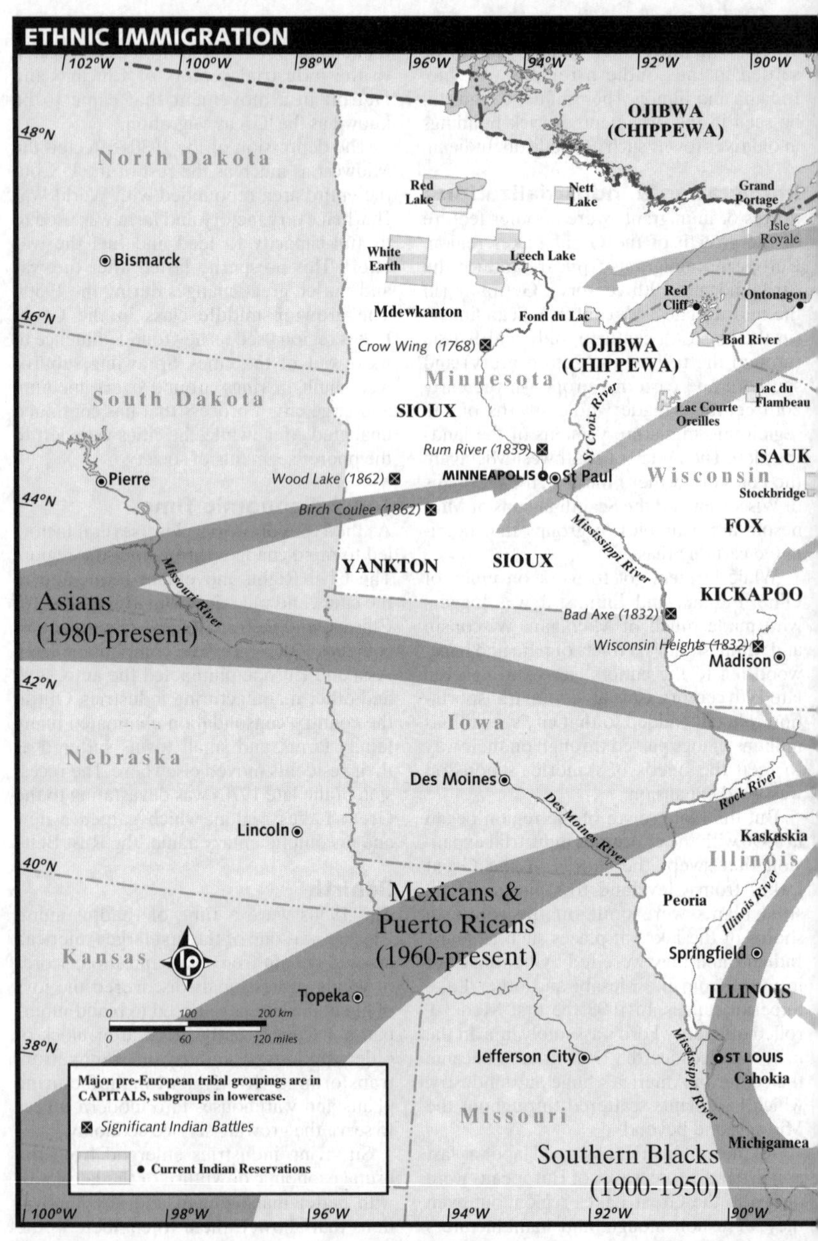
ETHNIC IMMIGRATION
102°W
100°W
98°W
96°W
94°W
92°W
90°W
48°N
46°N
44°N
42°N
40°N
38°N
North Dakota
South Dakota
Nebraska
Kansas
Minnesota
Iowa
Missouri
Wisconsin
Illinois
OJIBWA (CHIPPEWA)
Red Lake
Nett Lake
Grand Portage
Isle Royale
White Earth
Leech Lake
Red Cliff
Ontonagon
Bad River
Mdewkanton
Fond du Lac
Crow Wing (1768)
OJIBWA (CHIPPEWA)
Lac du Flambeau
Lac Courte Oreilles
SIOUX
St Croix River
Rum River (1839)
SAUK
Wood Lake (1862)
MINNEAPOLIS
St Paul
Stockbridge
Birch Coulee (1862)
FOX
Mississippi River
YANKTON
SIOUX
KICKAPOO
Bad Axe (1832)
Wisconsin Heights (1832)
Madison
Bismarck
Pierre
Missouri River
Asians (1980-present)
Des Moines
Des Moines River
Rock River
Lincoln
Kaskaskia
Peoria
Illinois River
Mexicans & Puerto Ricans (1960-present)
Springfield
ILLINOIS
Topeka
0 100 200 km
0 60 120 miles
Jefferson City
ST LOUIS
Cahokia
Mississippi River
Michigamea
Southern Blacks (1900-1950)
Major pre-European tribal groupings are in CAPITALS, subgroups in lowercase.
Significant Indian Battles
Current Indian Reservations
100°W
98°W
96°W
94°W
92°W
90°W

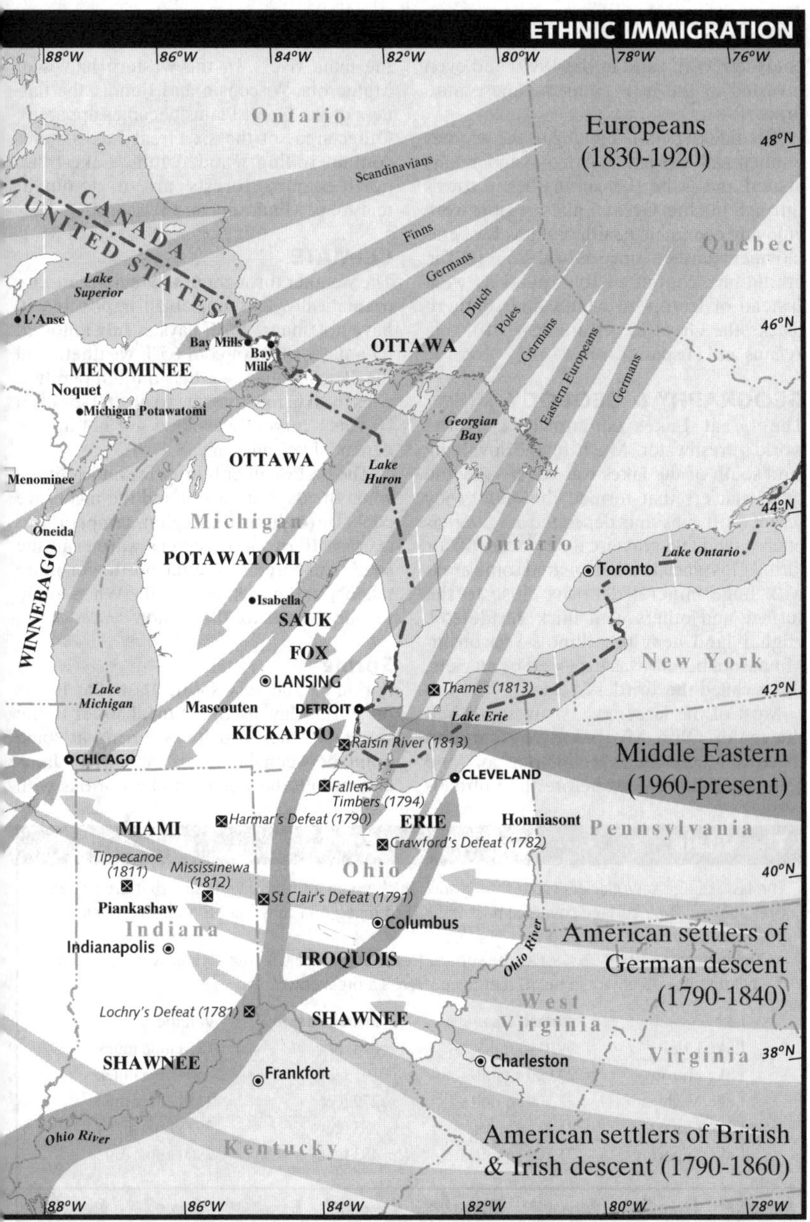
ETHNIC IMMIGRATION
Europeans
(1830-1920)
Scandinavians
Finns
Germans
Dutch
Poles
Germans
Eastern Europeans
Germans
Ontario
Quebec
CANADA
UNITED STATES
Lake Superior
L'Anse
Bay Mills
Bay Mills
OTTAWA
MENOMINEE
Noquet
Michigan Potawatomi
Georgian Bay
Lake Huron
OTTAWA
Menominee
Oneida
Michigan
Ontario
WINNEBAGO
POTAWATOMI
Isabella
SAUK
FOX
Lake Ontario
Toronto
New York
LANSING
Thames (1813)
Lake Michigan
Mascouten
DETROIT
Lake Erie
KICKAPOO
Raisin River (1813)
Middle Eastern
(1960-present)
CHICAGO
CLEVELAND
Fallen Timbers (1794)
Harmar's Defeat (1790)
ERIE
Honniasont
Pennsylvania
MIAMI
Crawford's Defeat (1782)
Tippecanoe (1811)
Mississinewa (1812)
Ohio
St Clair's Defeat (1791)
Piankashaw
Columbus
Indiana
American settlers of German descent (1790-1840)
Indianapolis
IROQUOIS
Ohio River
West Virginia
Lochry's Defeat (1781)
SHAWNEE
SHAWNEE
Charleston
Virginia
Frankfort
Ohio River
Kentucky
American settlers of British & Irish descent (1790-1860)
88°W
86°W
84°W
82°W
80°W
78°W
76°W
48°N
46°N
44°N
42°N
40°N
38°N

world market. Detroit automakers such as Ford, which had been given up for dead, enjoyed record sales in the 1990s and even invested in the now ailing Japanese auto firms.

The tide of people moving to the warmer Sunbelt states (such as Arizona and Texas) abated, and as the 21st century began, towns throughout the Great Lakes region were enjoying economic health and levels of employment unseen since World War II. The ethnic mix continued to expand as well. Instead of European whites and southern blacks, the Great Lakes are now attracting Asians and Hispanics.

GEOGRAPHY & GEOLOGY

The Great Lakes contain 15% of the world's freshwater. Much of the low-lying land south of the lakes was covered by the same glaciers that formed the lakes; they scraped off hills and deposited large areas of clay, sand and gravel, called glacial 'till' or 'drift.' This glacial action created some areas with huge mineral deposits close to the surface and others with thick, fertile soil. Higher land near the Illinois-Wisconsin-Minnesota border was bypassed by glaciers; this is called the 'driftless' region.

Most of the larger rivers run south into the major Ohio–Mississippi system, and these were the area's main transport and communication routes before the railroads arrived in the 1850s. Most of the region's larger cities are on the lakeshores or beside the main rivers. In the western halves of Minnesota, Wisconsin and Illinois, the flatness of the Great Plains becomes apparent. Other areas of the six Great Lakes states contain rolling wooded hills. Lake-filled north-country forests are a dominant feature of Minnesota and Wisconsin.

CLIMATE

The weather throughout the region can vary dramatically. It is not at all impossible to have hot, muggy 90°F days in July followed by a day or two of cool 65°F weather. And the January thaw – when the temperature rises from below freezing to 50°, 60° or even 70°F, is a fervently awaited – if not always dependable – anomaly.

The best weather is in spring and autumn, when the days are warm and the nights are cool. Throughout the region, temperatures average 10 or more degrees warmer in the south compared to the far north. For more talk about the weather, see the When to Go section in Facts for the Visitor.

Spring

Spring can be very short: 'Last year it was on a Tuesday' is the typical joke. If the spring weather, usually occurring at some point between late April and early June, lasts awhile, the season can be glorious, with

The Vitals

The last ice age saw glaciers more than a mile thick gouge out the five basins that are now the Great Lakes. Their surface covers almost 95,000 sq miles, and they hold 6 quadrillion gallons of freshwater, give or take a billion.

The waters represent 95% of all the surface freshwater in the US. If the water were spread over the continental US, it would be 10 feet deep. Here's a breakdown:

lake	surface area	average depth	volume
Lake Erie	9910 sq miles	62 feet	116 cubic miles
Lake Huron	23,000 sq miles	195 feet	850 cubic miles
Lake Michigan	22,300 sq miles	279 feet	1180 cubic miles
Lake Ontario	7340 sq miles	283 feet	393 cubic miles
Lake Superior	31,700 sq miles	483 feet	2900 cubic miles

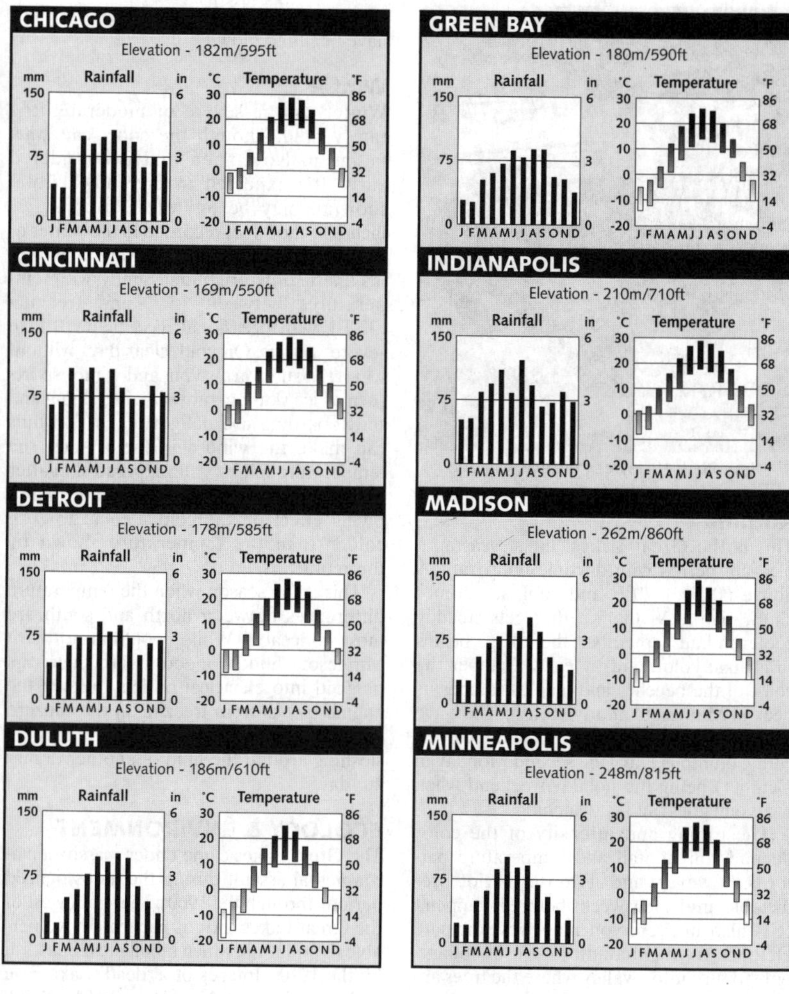

apple and cherry trees in bloom and farmers out tapping maple trees for sap. But if spring is short, it may just come on a Tuesday, to be followed on Wednesday by the heat and humidity of summer.

Summer

Depending on the year, June can be late spring, with some cold, rainy days, or early summer, with balmy temperatures. July and August are warm to hot, with temperatures above 90°F – occasionally above 100°F – and high humidity. The huge volume of water in the lakes, however, means that water temperatures never get really high even in the dog days of summer. The good weather typically lasts into early September.

RICHARD CUMMINS

Navy Pier's Halloween festival, Chicago

Autumn

This is the Great Lakes' finest season, a pleasant period with daytime temperatures above 60°F or 70°F, and cool, sometimes chilly, nights. As the weather gets steadily cooler in late September, the foliage begins to change color, and by early October the color of the beeches and maples reaches its peak in Minnesota and Wisconsin. The wave of color spreads south through mid-October, with Columbus Day (the second Monday in October) being the holiday weekend when everyone goes out leaf watching.

The timing and intensity of the color depends on rainfall and temperature patterns, however, and its onset is not predictable until a few weeks before it happens. It is also uneven; you may travel in late October through country bare of foliage, only to turn into a valley where the trees are ablaze with color.

Harvest time includes fresh pumpkins on sale in the markets and 'pick-your-own fruit' days and cider making at orchards throughout the region.

By November most of the leaves have fallen, but a brief period of 'Indian summer' often brings back a week or so of warmer daytime temperatures. By the end of November it's clear that winter is approaching, and by mid-December the bitter, icy winds have begun to blow.

Winter

Winter can be severe or moderate; it is rarely mild. Though the snow can start falling in November, that is considered early. It's expected in December. Total snowfall may be anywhere from a few inches to the 9 feet recorded in the winter of 1995–96. When it's not snowing, however, it's likely to be bright and sunny, with temperatures between 15°F and freezing (32°F), with occasional days below 0°F in severe winters. On cold, clear days without wind, the sun warms you, and winter sports such as ice skating, snowshoeing, skiing and snowboarding are delightful. Brisk winds can make the wind-chill factor – or, the temperature felt by your exposed skin after taking into consideration the wind's multiplying effect on the cold – equal to 20°F colder than the temperature shown by thermometers.

This is the season when the temperature differences between north and south are most noticeable. While people in northern Minnesota huddle indoors with their cars plugged into electrical outlets to keep the engine blocks from freezing in the subzero temperatures, folks in Cincinnati may be sloshing around the mud of another dreary 40° day.

ECOLOGY & ENVIRONMENT

The Great Lakes came under massive environmental assault during the industrialized periods through the 1960s. The shallowest of the Great Lakes, Erie, is particularly vulnerable to pollution, which killed most of its fish by the 1970s. Images of a 'dead' Lake Erie and a burning Cuyahoga River in Cleveland, in both cases the result of industrial pollution, helped radicalize America's environmental movement. More than 300 chemical compounds have been found in the waters of the Great Lakes. Clean-water laws and billions of dollars spent on treatments and pollution controls may have arrived in the nick of time to save them, and and fish stocks in some places are rebounding.

Even so, the slow outflow of the lakes means they change their water slowly (it takes Lake Superior 180 years to fully replace its water); thus the ecological disasters of the past will not be quickly eradicated. Even where the water is now clean, years' worth of toxic contaminants have built up in lake-bed sediment, rendering bottom-dwelling fish unsafe to eat.

Another major problem for the lakes and their native species has been the introduction of nonnative species, largely via the release of ballast water from ships that have sailed into the Great Lakes from ports elsewhere. The alewife, a nonnative fish, has displaced many of the local species, such as pike, lake salmon and lake trout. The zebra mollusk, Belgian in origin, has caused great havoc, fouling piers and water intakes as well as competing for food with indigenous species.

Another issue involves who exactly controls the water: In 1998 Ontario proposed selling Lake Superior water to Asia, causing outrage in Wisconsin. Just a decade before, this possible sale of water might have been welcomed; the water levels in the lakes reached record highs in the late 1980s, engulfing waterfronts and homes in every state.

The mining operations of Minnesota's Iron Range have produced their share of air and water pollution but have cleaned up their acts since the 1980s. An ongoing issue is how to balance the use of national and state forests between recreation seekers and those extracting timber. Another problem is overfishing by residents and state visitors. The small number of rangers cannot prevent sport anglers from selfishly taking numbers far beyond the legal limits.

The infamous Ohio Valley industrial area produces serious air pollution, some of which migrates as far north as Canada. Acid rain is one result.

Relative to the industrial areas, the farming areas have always seemed environmentally benign. However, there are concerns over pesticide and herbicide use, and groundwater contamination from fertilizers, chemicals and septic tanks. Added to that are the questions and doubts over genetically engineered seeds and crops. In 1999 the use of genetically modified seeds in the region peaked. But by 2000, outcry from Europe and Asia had caused orders for the seeds to fall. If there's no market for these crops, it's likely they will no longer be cultivated.

FLORA & FAUNA

Flora

Campers and hikers might want to keep an eye and nose out for the wild blueberries seen across the northern woodlands. The red pine (also known as the Norway pine) and white pine trees in the region can grow to majestic proportions. Examples of old growth can be seen in the Boundary Waters wilderness area of Minnesota. Also look for pine, spruce and cedar across the northern Great Lakes.

The southern region has a more mixed forest, with deciduous trees such as oak, maple and birch, as well as many evergreens.

Illinois and Indiana still have many of the scores of wildflowers that once carpeted vast areas of the state, such as the prolific pink flowers of wild phlox, lavender dwarf irises, golden black-eyed Susans, orange puccoons and purple-topped blazing stars.

Fauna

Among mammals, white-tailed deer are common in all six states. In fact, despite the best efforts of hunters (and speeding cars), there has been a population explosion. Other ubiquitous critters include small mammals such as squirrels, opossums, raccoons and rabbits.

The north has significant populations of black bear, moose and beaver. Elk, foxes, wolves and bobcats are also present.

Loons, quail, wild turkeys and ringed-neck pheasants are numerous in the grainfields and lakes throughout the region. Songbirds such as American goldfinches, eastern bluebirds and eastern meadowlarks are also common, and ducks and geese darken the skies during the migratory seasons, from September to November and from March to May.

Endangered Species

The huge lake sturgeon is threatened by pollution as well as competition from non-native species.

The wolf, formerly on the endangered list throughout the Midwest, has been 'upgraded' to threatened status in Minnesota, and numbers are increasing. In fact, one sign that this species may have found a way to coexist with humans occurred a few years ago in Chicago when a wolf – 50 miles from its nearest known habitat – made a snack of a poodle near the downtown.

The piping plover and the least tern are two birds on the endangered list that are sometimes glimpsed along the Lake Superior shoreline. The plover is a small, tan shorebird that hops in the sand at the water's edge; the tern is more gull-like in size and can be seen flying over lakes and rivers looking for food. Long Island, in the Apostle Islands, is a breeding zone for the piping plover and has been set aside as a preserve with no visitors permitted. In Michigan, the best spot to see plovers is near Whitefish Point in the Upper Peninsula.

The bald eagle has made a remarkable recovery thanks to the ban on certain pesticides and can be seen in huge numbers along the Mississippi River.

National Parks & Protected Areas

The Great Lakes region does not have a large concentration of national parks. Rather, it has state parks and protected areas, national forests and vast areas of rural countryside that aren't protected as parkland but present great opportunities for escaping the press of the city. Popular examples of the last are Door County, in Wisconsin; the Iron Range and lakelands region of central Minnesota; and the Lake Erie islands of Ohio.

The major national parks and wilderness areas of the Great Lakes region are: the Indiana Dunes National Lakeshore, in Indiana; Sleeping Bear Dunes National Lakeshore, Pictured Rocks National Lakeshore and Isle Royale National Park, in Michigan; Apostle Islands National Lakeshore, in Wisconsin; and Voyageurs National Park and Boundary Waters Canoe Area Wilderness, in Minnesota.

See the National Parks & Protected Areas section in each state's introductory chapter, as well as the regional chapters, for more information.

GOVERNMENT & POLITICS

The US has a federal system with a president and a bicameral congress, consisting of the 100-member Senate and the 435-member House of Representatives. Each of the 50 states has two senators, each serving a six-year term, and a number of congressional representatives in proportion to its population, each serving a two-year term.

The president, whose term lasts four years, is chosen by an electoral college consisting of a number of individual electors from each state equivalent to its number of senators and congressional representatives, who vote in accordance with the popular vote within their state. To be elected, the president must obtain a majority of 270 of the total 538 electoral votes (the District of Columbia, which has no voting representatives in Congress, nevertheless has three electoral votes). The president may only serve two terms of four years each.

See the individual state introductory chapters for details on government and politics in each.

ECONOMY

The Great Lakes region is fertile, producing significant agricultural output, but manufacturing industries have dominated the area since the mid-19th century. The decline of manufacturing, particularly the car industry, in the 1970s caused unemployment and stagnation in many cities. Detroit was especially hard hit. Steel making has since staged a comeback, and that plus light manufacturing, production of high-tech equipment and service-sector advances in fields such as banking, education and medicine have helped the region bounce back to prosperity.

POPULATION & PEOPLE

The Great Lakes region is home to about 46,415,000 people, or about 19% of the US population. The following figures represent the states' populations, ranked by size from largest to smallest:

Illinois	11,435,000
Ohio	10,851,000
Michigan	9,297,000
Indiana	5,552,000
Wisconsin	4,898,000
Minnesota	4,382,000

See the preceding History section for a discussion about the various ethnic groups that compose the Great Lakes region. Although the culture of these groups is still influential in the areas where they once dominated, that influence is waning as younger generations assimilate into broader American culture and new people move in. In South Bend, Indiana, for example, very little remains of the Polish feel that just 20 years ago was quite palpable.

There are Indian nations in Michigan, Wisconsin and Minnesota. They include the Ojibway, Menominee, Mohicans, Ho-Chunk, Oneida, Sioux and Potawatami. Their numbers are small, but many have found a secure financial future in reservation-based casinos, which avoid state laws prohibiting gambling.

EDUCATION

The six states covered by this book are home to many well-regarded public and private universities and colleges. Many are described in the various chapter listings.

The 'Big 10' schools are considered the top public universities. In the six Great Lakes states they are: the University of Illinois, Indiana University, Purdue University (in Indiana), Ohio State University, the University of Michigan, Michigan State University, the University of Wisconsin and the University of Minnesota. Top private universities include the University of Chicago, Notre Dame and Northwestern University (also a Big 10 school). There are also many smaller but still well-regarded private liberal arts schools, such as Oberlin, in Ohio, and Wabash, in Indiana. For more on the Big 10, see Spectator Sports in Facts for the Visitor.

The quality of elementary and secondary public education varies widely in the region, as it does elsewhere in the US. Supported mainly by property taxes, the quality of the schools tends to closely mirror the average property value in their town or area. Impoverished inner city areas are known for having struggling schools, poorly serving students most in need of good public education.

ARTS

The following is a look at the broad themes of the diverse and rich arts culture of the Great Lakes region.

Literature

Chicago Chicago's blustery streets produced a particularly unflinching brand of literature, including Theodore Dreiser's *Sister Carrie* (1900). In many ways, it is the perfect Chicago book: The mean streets of the city rob our heroine of her virtue, but in the best Chicago tradition, she turns this seeming setback into profitable gain. Dreiser's books reflect his views of American society as repressive and hypocritical, which seems to be a common thread among Midwestern writers. *An American Tragedy* (1925) is often considered his best work.

Carl Sandburg's 1916 poem 'Chicago,' merely one in his exceptional collection titled simply *Chicago Poems*, captures a spirit of the city that endures even as the details have changed: 'Hog Butcher for the World, / Tool Maker, Stacker of Wheat, / Player with Railroads and the Nation's Freight Handler; /...City of the Big Shoulders.' Sandburg is still revered throughout much of the state, including his native Galesburg.

Born in Quebec in 1915, Saul Bellow moved to Chicago at age nine and spent most of his life writing in and about Chicago. His high-profile works have won him several prestigious awards, among them the 1976 Nobel Prize for Literature. Bellow's novels focus on the strengths and weaknesses of humanity through the study of flawed figures. They include *Herzog* (1964), *Humbolt's Gift* (1975, winner of the Pulitzer Prize) and *The Dean's December* (1982).

NATIONAL PARKS & PROTECTED AREAS

NATIONAL PARKS & PROTECTED AREAS
88°W
86°W
84°W
82°W
80°W
78°W
76°W
Lake Nipigon
48°N
Isle Royale National Park
Michipicoten Island
Lake Superior
CANADA
Quebec
Grand Island National Recreation Area
Pictured Rocks National Lakeshore
Sault Sainte Marie
46°N
Seney National Wildlife Refuge
Michigan
Hiawatha National Forest
Father Marquette National Memorial
Manitoulin Island
OTTAWA
Nicolet National Forest
Georgian Bay
Lake Huron
Sleeping Bear Dunes National Lakeshore
Huron National Forest
Green Bay
44°N
Ontario
Lake Ontario
Lake Winnebago
Manistee National Forest
Toronto
Horicon National Wildlife Refuge
MILWAUKEE
Michigan
Port Huron
New York
Lake Michigan
Lansing
42°N
DETROIT
Lake Erie
Erie
Illinois & Michigan Canal National Heritage Corridor
Lawnfield-James A Garfield National Historic Site
CHICAGO
Indiana Dunes National Lakeshore
Toledo
CLEVELAND
Perry's Victory & International Peace Memorial
Pennsylvania
Midewin National Tall Grass Prairie
Cuyahoga Valley National Recreation Area
Harrisburg
PITTSBURGH
Indiana
Ohio
40°N
Dayton Aviation Heritage National Historic Park
Columbus
Maryland
Indianapolis
Hopewell Culture National Historic Park
Ohio River
WASHINGTON, DC
William H Taft National Historic Site
Wayne National Forest
West Virginia
CINCINNATI
George Rogers Clark National Historic Park
Hoosier National Forest
Muscatatuck National Wildlife Refuge
38°N
Charleston
LOUISVILLE
Frankfort
LEXINGTON
Wabash River
Lincoln Boyhood National Memorial
Richmond
Ohio River
Kentucky
Virginia
88°W
86°W
84°W
82°W
80°W
78°W

Gwendolyn Brooks became the first African American to win the Pulitzer Prize for her 1949 book of poetry, *Annie Allen*. Her works, which focus on African Americans in Chicago, also include *A Street in Bronzeville*.

Leaving his Chicago Transit Authority bus far behind, former driver Larry Heinemann based his first works on his experiences as a grunt in Vietnam. *Paco's Story* won the National Book Award for Fiction in 1987. His more recent novels have focused on the oddities of contemporary life in the city.

Sara Paretsky's VI Warshawski detective novels at first seem like so much genre fiction, but within the gritty narratives about a woman private investigator in Chicago she weaves her own deep commitment to social justice. A seemingly unstoppable producer of screenplays disguised as books, Chicagoan Scott Turow is known for *The Client* and other legal potboilers. Two extraordinary Illinois-born novelists, Richard Powers (*Gain*, 1998) and David Foster Wallace (*Infinite Jest*, 1996), are among the best American writers working today.

Indiana Indiana venerates the gentle poetry of James Whitcomb Riley (1849–1916) who wrote such bucolic collections as *The Old Swimmin' Hole and 'Leven More Poems* (1883). At the opposite end of the spectrum, fellow Hoosier Kurt Vonnegut satirizes American life in his slapstick novels, which include *Slaughterhouse-Five* (1969).

Ohio Small-town Ohio shaped the writings of Sherwood Anderson (1876–1941). *Winesburg, Ohio* (1919), a series of connected short stories based on the town of Clyde, is considered his greatest work. Nobel Prize–winner Toni Morrison has contributed several rich novels of black life to American literature, including *Song of Solomon* (1977). *Beloved*, a story about ex-slaves, is set outside Cincinnati, Ohio. James Thurber gained fame for his witty writings and cartoons for the *New Yorker* in the 1940s and 1950s.

Michigan Northern Michigan was the summer home for a young Ernest Hemingway. Born in Oak Park, Illinois, Hemingway based many of his early writings on his Michigan vacations. Jim Harrison, author of *Legends of the Fall* (1979) and *Dalva* (1988), is a resident of Michigan's Upper Peninsula. Detroit figures in many of Elmore Leonard's sizzling crime novels, and you can almost hear the Midwestern twang in the voices of characters in books such as *Get Shorty*.

Wisconsin For a more bucolic view of life around the lakes, turn your sights north to Wisconsin and pick up Aldo Leopold's nature-writing classic, *A Sand County Almanac* (1949), or John Muir's *Story of My Boyhood and Youth* (1913). Thornton Wilder won Pulitzer Prizes as a novelist (*The Bridge of San Luis Rey*, 1927) and playwright (*Our Town*, 1938, and *The Skin of Our Teeth*, 1942). His novel *The Eighth Day* (1967) is about Midwestern life around 1900. He was born and raised in Madison, Wisconsin.

Laura Ingalls Wilder (1867–1957), born in Pepin, Wisconsin, along the Mississippi River, wrote many enduring books for children and young people. She is best known for the nine 'Little House' books, based on her experiences growing up in the Midwest in the 1870s and '80s. *Little House on the Prairie* served as the inspiration for pioneer life in the television series of the same name.

North Country (1997), by Howard Frank Mosher, is an entertaining account of the novelist's coast-to-coast trip along the US–Canadian border.

Minnesota Sinclair Lewis (1885–1951) spent his early childhood in Sauk Centre, Minnesota, and used it as the setting in some of his books, including his best-known work, *Main Street* (1920), a satirical portrait of the American small town that drew considerable controversy. *Babbit* (1922) satirizes the American businessman. He received the Nobel Prize in 1930 for his satirical, often critical impressions of American society.

Garrison Keillor was born in Anoka, Minnesota, in 1942. The writer and humorist is best known for hosting the weekly radio show *A Prairie Home Companion*, which includes his immensely popular monologues about life in the fictional town of Lake Wobegon, in Minnesota's lakes district. Many of these segments, full of warm, funny, perceptive stories of everyday life and people, have been collected into short story collections, including *Lake Wobegon Days* and *Leaving Home*.

F Scott Fitzgerald was born in St Paul, Minnesota, in 1896 and lived in the Summit neighborhood while developing his literary reputation. Some of the inspiration for his work about wealthy Americans, immortalized in books such as *This Side of Paradise* (1920), is taken from his life and social circle here.

David Housewright, of the Twin Cities, has written three novels featuring St Paul private investigator Holland Taylor. *Penance* (1995), *Practice to Deceive* (1998) and *Dearly Departed* (1999) are set in Minnesota and Wisconsin. These entertaining, well-written detective stories have been critically praised.

Music

When jazz and blues left New Orleans on Mississippi riverboats, their first stop was Chicago, in the Midwest. New Orleans bandleader King Oliver went to Chicago in 1919 and soon sent home for his star trumpet player, Louis Armstrong. Their presence in town, along with that of the self-styled 'King of Jazz,' Paul Whiteman (whose band included trumpet legend Bix Beiderbecke), inspired local teenager Benny Goodman to form a band of his own. The Association for the Advancement of Creative Musicians, formed in the 1960s, still serves as an incubator for creative jazz.

Gospel composer Thomas A Dorsey came to Chicago in the early 1920s, followed a few years later by gospel's greatest singer, Louisiana native Mahalia Jackson. Another local gospel luminary, Sam Cooke, went on to become an R&B legend.

Chicago became known as the new base of the blues in the late 1940s and '50s, when Muddy Waters, Willie Dixon, John Lee Hooker and other southerners came north and went electric.

Hoochie coochie man Muddy Waters

The Smashing Pumpkins are one of Chicago's better-known modern rock bands, of which there are many. Elsewhere in the Midwest, the cranky R&B genius once again known as Prince and hard-drinking alternative rockers the Replacements helped put Minneapolis on the musical map.

Detroit might be better known as Motown, home of a thousand soul and R&B hits, but its rock streak is wide as well: the Stooges (Iggy Pop's first band), the MC 5 and Ted Nugent all started out in the Motor City.

It must be something they put in those half-dollar-size White Castle hamburgers they eat by the bagful out there, but the music scene in Ohio never gets far from weird: the Breeders and Guided by Voices are as close as Ohio gets to 'pop'; cult bands Devo and Pere Ubu pushed the envelope over the edge.

Architecture

In the mid-19th century, small-scale building was revolutionized by 'balloon-frame' construction – a light frame of standard-milled, 2-by-4-inch timber joined by cheap, mass-produced nails. Developed in Chicago in the 1830s, it provided a fast and economical building method for the rapidly growing cities of the Midwest and the West and is still used today, mainly for houses. Variations on the theme are found throughout the US, notably in California.

After the Civil War, when influential American architects began studying at the École des Beaux-Arts, in Paris, American buildings began showing increased refinement. Beaux Arts married the metal-frame building in Chicago after the fire of 1871. The 'Chicago School' of architects produced the first true skyscrapers and the first 'modern' architecture. Its leading exponent, Louis Sullivan, had studied at both MIT and the École des Beaux-Arts. An intriguing Sullivan survivor is the Carson Pirie Scott department store in downtown Chicago, with ornate metalwork at street level and numerous windows above. It's not far from the historic high-rise Monadnock Building.

Numerous examples of early skyscrapers can be found in Milwaukee, Detroit and Cleveland as well.

Midwestern native Frank Lloyd Wright created an architectural style all his own. Working mainly on private houses, he abandoned all the historical elements of architecture, making each building a unique sculptural form characterized by strong horizontal lines. Wright called them 'prairie houses,' though invariably they were built in the suburbs. Interior spaces flowed from one to another, rather than being divided into rooms, and the inside was connected to the outside via large windows, rather than separated by solid walls. Texture and color came from the materials themselves, not from applied decoration. Wright was innovative in his use of steel, glass and concrete, creating shapes and structures like nothing that existed in the past, and he pioneered panel heating, indirect lighting, double glazing and air-conditioning. See the Oak Park listing in the Northern & Central Illinois chapter for more details.

Wright's influence on modern architecture in Europe bounced back to the US when the Bauhaus School left Nazi Germany to set up here. In America, Bauhaus became known as the International Style, and its principles were practiced in Chicago by architect Ludwig Mies van der Rohe. By using glass 'curtain walls' over a steel frame, the best International Style buildings were able to become abstract shapes – minimalist sculptures on a massive scale. The worst of them are ugly glass boxes. See the Chicago Loop Architecture Walking Tour, in the Chicago chapter, for more architectural discussion.

SOCIETY & CONDUCT

From the vibrant life of Chicago to the relaxed pace of a small town such as Dixon, Illinois, a great difference exists between urban and rural cultures in the Great Lakes. It can be hard to see how Detroit and Traverse City have much in common other than that they are both in Michigan.

Whereas the cities feature all the aspects of life familiar to urban dwellers everywhere – 24-hour culture, a mix of good and bad neighborhoods, a variety of lifestyles, a pervasive feeling of anonymity – rural towns are just the opposite – the streets are quiet by 9 pm, neighborhoods and lifestyles are homogeneous and there's a feeling that everybody knows everybody. If you are from another country, you may not cause notice at all in Chicago, but you might be a sensation in a tiny farm town.

In between large and small cities are the suburbs, those great swaths of houses and strip malls sprawling across the countryside. Although the favored home of America's middle class, the suburbs probably will yield little of interest to the traveler. The bright lights are not matched by culture, and the insular nature of subdivision houses inhibits a sense of community.

RELIGION

The religions practiced in the Great Lakes states generally reflect the backgrounds of the domestic and foreign immigrants who settled there. Roman Catholics predominate, thanks to the large numbers of Irish, Germans, Poles, Italians and others from Roman Catholic countries.

Germans as well as Scandinavians also brought Lutheranism. Europe was the originator of Episcopalianism, Methodism and Presbyterianism and other reformed faiths found in the Great Lakes region.

Baptists in their many variations have their roots in the American South, and large numbers of them came north during the Great Migration. Chicago's gospel music tradition owes its roots to Baptist ceremonies.

The Amish grew out of the Anabaptist movement of Europe in the 1500s in Switzerland. Led by Jacob Amman, they split from the Mennonites in the late 1600s believing them to be following too closely the ways of the world. The Amish left behind European oppression and came to the new world in order to pursue their simple, rural and devout lives. Settling first in Pennsylvania, their growing communities are now found mainly there and in the rural northern regions of Ohio, Indiana and Illinois. Shunning modern tools and conveniences such as cars and radios, the plainly dressed Amish have built prosperous farms and businesses such as furniture manufacturing.

A fair number of Jews live in the region's urban centers, especially Chicago, where there was an influx after WWII. Recently the numbers have been bolstered by immigrating Russian Jews.

LANGUAGE

The Midwest accent has a bit of a nasal twang but is generally one of the most neutral of American accents. However, you will encounter some regional variations. The southern reaches of Illinois, Indiana and Ohio all bear traces of a more southern US accent. In the rural and northern regions of Minnesota you get a distinctive syncopation to speech that was lampooned in the movie *Fargo*.

Fast disappearing are traces of the languages used by the first waves of European immigrants. Even two decades ago you could still hear German, Polish, various Scandinavian tongues and other languages spoken in daily life in many communities. But the passage of time, the death of the immigrant generations, the influence of television and the assimilation of children and grandchildren into US life are quickly eradicating European languages in the region.

Today you are most likely to hear non-English speakers in the immigrant neighborhoods of the largest cities. This is most noticeable in Chicago, where you will find Spanish, Polish, various Asian languages and others in widespread use.

Facts for the Visitor

HIGHLIGHTS

See the Great Lakes map at the front of this book for a graphical presentation of the very best places in the Great Lakes region. Each of the regional chapters also leads with highlights for that area.

Overall, Chicago is a worthy destination in itself. Other interesting cities include Milwaukee, Minneapolis–St Paul and Cleveland. Indianapolis and Cincinnati also have many merits. Don't overlook the smaller cities, especially lively college towns such as Bloomington, Indiana; Ann Arbor, Michigan; and Madison, Wisconsin.

Natural areas abound. Among the best are those in northern Minnesota and Wisconsin, much of northern Michigan and the Upper Peninsula and those in southern Indiana. But again, fascinating areas of natural beauty, such as the Starved Rock area of northern Illinois, occur throughout the region.

There are numerous scenic drives around the Great Lakes; naturally, many have water themes. The circle lake tour around Lake Michigan is a classic, as is the one around Lake Huron. Driving along the Mississippi or Ohio River is also a treat.

SUGGESTED ITINERARIES

There's no 'right' way to see the Great Lakes region, but it can help to have sample itineraries. Modify and combine these to suit your interests. Try to visit cities on weekends and country towns and resorts on weekdays in summer or fall foliage season. That will get you lower prices and fewer crowds.

Less than a Week

Use Chicago as your base, with a day or two of forays into northern Illinois or along Lake Michigan in northern Indiana. To a lesser extent, you can do this from the other major cities and surrounding regions in this book. Alternatively, for outdoor activities, focus on one small area, such as Sleeping Bear Dunes National Lakeshore, in Michigan.

A Week or More

If you have a week or 10 days, you can (after spending several days in Chicago) get a good taste of the area in about a 200-mile radius. Alternatively, you can combine Chicago with any one of the other major cities in this book with time for a few stopovers in between. Or you can truly enjoy the great wilderness areas of the north, such as Apostle Islands National Lakeshore, in Wisconsin, or the vast forests of northern Minnesota.

Two Weeks

This gives you plenty of time to explore two major cities and one large natural area with time for a lot of rural driving to the less-visited small towns. Or, it would allow for any of the routes all the way around any of the Great Lakes, with plenty of side trips thrown in.

A Month or More

If you have four weeks, you can pick three states and explore the highlights of each. If you have longer than that, do the entire book's highlights.

PLANNING

When to Go

The Great Lakes are principally a summer destination, with another busy season when the fall foliage reaches its full color. From mid-July through August, the summer resort areas are very busy, accommodations are fully booked and restaurants are crowded. Perhaps the best time to travel here is between Memorial Day (the last Monday in May) weekend and mid-June, before the local schools close and families hit the road; the early part of September, after the big summer rush but before the 'leaf peepers' (foliage tourists) arrive, is another good time. At these times, and especially during the week, hotels and inns are likely to have rooms available, vacant campsites can be found easily and the hottest restaurants have tables ready without a long wait.

JOHN ELK III

Welcome to Itasca State Park and the land of 10,000 lakes (MN).

JOHN ELK III

Just out of reach of one of five waterfalls in Gooseberry Falls State Park (MN)

JOHN ELK III

Even the downtown has a lake in Minneapolis (MN).

CHARLES COOK
Presque Isle lighthouse (MI)

JOHN ELK III
And then there was light – Lake Vermillion (MN)

JOHN ELK III
Hike, canoe and jump the Minnesota–Wisconsin border in Interstate State Park.

JOHN ELK III
And they call this farm country (MN)

JOHN ELK III
American Gothic, sans wife (MN)

The exception to this would be Chicago, which is a rewarding destination any time of year. The blues clubs, museums, shops and other attractions have much activity and excitement any time of the year.

Remember too that air temperatures can be – and usually are – 10° to 20° warmer in the far south of the Great Lakes region than in the northern reaches of the top three.

Spring (March–May) Cold and snow continue at least until mid-March north of Chicago. Late March brings the beginning of 'mud time,' when the earth thaws.

As mud time continues, the chance of a major snowstorm disappears. Nice balmy days will alternate with cold and miserable ones through mid-May.

Weather in May is usually better, with cool nights and warm days, though cold rain and even a short freak snowstorm are not impossible. If you are planning any outdoor activities, be prepared for very cold temperatures.

Mother's Day, the second Sunday in May, is a commercial celebration that has become the busiest restaurant day of the year – reservations are required everywhere.

The weekend of Memorial Day (the last Monday in May) signals the official start of the summer vacation season. The holiday commemorates US veterans with patriotic parades and ceremonies. Many festivals are held during the three-day weekend. Campgrounds, theme parks, seasonal museums and attractions are all open – and very busy. Make advance reservations for any tourist services (hotel, restaurant, transport) that you may need.

Summer (June–August) Early June is an excellent time to travel in the region. Because schools are still in session, local families do not crowd resort areas, except on weekends. Everything's open, but prices are not yet at the high level they will reach in late July and August. The weather is completely unpredictable: a breathlessly hot few days may be followed by a surprising chill, but mostly the weather is fine.

After mid-June, when schools adjourn, resorts become much busier. You may need to make advance reservations as summer festivals hit their stride in cities and towns across the region. In cities such as Chicago and Milwaukee, it can seem like there is a nonstop succession of world-class outdoor music and cultural events.

Independence Day (July 4) is the USA's biggest patriotic holiday, commemorating the signing of the Declaration of Independence on July 4, 1776. It is celebrated on the actual day with parades, cookouts and fireworks in every town, ranging from the smallest village to the biggest cities.

The eight weeks between the Fourth of July and Labor Day (the first Monday in September) are the high season for tourism in places such as Door County, in Wisconsin; Brown County, in Indiana; and Mackinaw Island, in Michigan. Everything is crowded, and reservations are required for most tourist services.

The weather is at its hottest in August, often with a week or so of 'dog days,' when the temperature exceeds 90° or 95°F in high humidity and everyone, despite the prevalent air-conditioning, complains – except those at the beach. Tourism is at its busiest in August, with prices at their highest. This is also the busiest time for mosquitoes, who feast day and night.

Autumn (September–November) Labor Day (the first Monday of September) honors workers and signals the official end of the summer tourism season. It's the busiest vacation weekend of the season, so advance reservations are essential.

The two weeks after Labor Day are an excellent time to travel. School is in session, so the crowds are gone, but almost all services are still open, and prices drop somewhat. The weather is summerlike, but without the intensity of heat and humidity. Note, however, that many parks, beaches and attractions start to close in September, even while the weather is still good.

Mid-September brings the beginning of foliage season in the far north. Days are still pleasantly warm, but nights are cool. Prices for tourist services rise a bit, and inland resorts see a new surge of visitors. The fall foliage color spreads southward from Canada, often reaching its peak in northern Illinois and Ohio by mid-October.

Columbus Day, celebrated on the second Monday of October, commemorates the landing of Christopher Columbus in the Bahamas on October 12, 1492. On Columbus Day weekend, country inns and other inland lodgings are all booked up well in advance, at high-season prices. Conventioneers often fill many city hotels.

Sunny days are pleasantly warmish ('sweater weather'), but rainy days are chilly; nights are brisk, with frost likely in the northern areas. After Columbus Day, many resorts, attractions and small local museums close for the winter, but enough services stay open to make travel possible. In fact, with a bit of luck, late October can be a wonderful time to travel. Prices for all services are low, the weather is usually agreeable and blazing pockets of fall foliage can be found everywhere except in extreme northern regions.

On Halloween (October 31, not a public holiday), children dress in costumes and go from house to house 'trick-or-treating,' or, looking for sweet treats and (rarely) playing tricks if the treats are not forthcoming.

Early November is much like late October for travel in the region. With fall foliage color gone, the countryside shows a limited palette of gray shades accented with a few browns. Hotel rates and transport fares are often quite reasonable.

Veterans Day (November 11) is a national holiday honoring war veterans. This long weekend marks the opening of the ski season at resorts with snowmaking capabilities.

Thanksgiving, the fourth Thursday in November, is the busiest holiday of the year for travel throughout the US. Millions of people crowd highways, buses, trains and airplanes in order to be with relatives and friends for the dinner that recalls the feast the Pilgrims and their Wampanoag Indian neighbors shared in Plymouth, Massachusetts, in 1621. Peak travel times are the Wednesday just before Thanksgiving Day and the Sunday following it. Avoid traveling on those days if possible. If not, make advance reservations and allow plenty of time for delays.

The Friday after Thanksgiving marks the beginning of Christmas shopping season – shopping districts and malls are packed.

By late November, days are chilly and nights cold; there may be snowfall anywhere in the region.

Winter (December–February) By mid-December, the weather can be bitterly cold, with snowfalls from an inch or two to a foot. If there's freezing weather but no snow, the ice skating can be wonderful on the region's many glacial ponds.

Shopping districts in cities and towns are hectic, thanks to the annual pre-Christmas shopping spree. Stores may do as much business in December as they do in all the other 11 months of the year combined. Chicago is popular with weekend-traveling Midwesterners, and hotels can book up early. Transportation is crowded during the few days before and after Christmas (December 25), which is a national holiday.

New Year's Day (January 1) is also a national holiday. Transportation services are crowded several days before and after New Year's Day, but from January 4 to 14, traveling is easy and relatively cheap. The weather is usually bitterly cold and snowy, though often there is a welcome 'winter thaw,' a few days of surprisingly mild temperatures. In the southern reaches of the region the temperatures can be merely cold, not bitterly cold.

Cross-country skiing, snowmobiling and ice-fishing are the main outdoor activities. Ice skating, both inside and outside, is also popular.

Except for the romantic energies expended around Valentine's Day (the 14th), February is cold and gray, with all seasonal sights and attractions closed.

Maps

The most detailed state highway maps are those distributed – usually free – by state governments. You can call or write the state tourism offices in advance (see Information in the introductory chapters for the states) and have the maps sent out, or you can pick

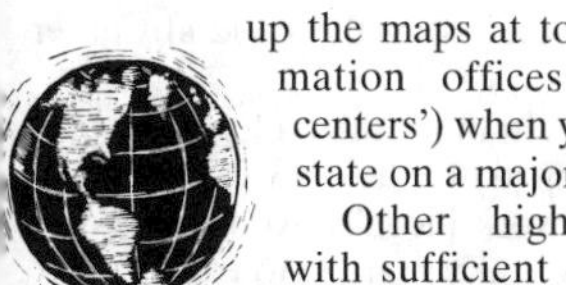

up the maps at tourism information offices ('welcome centers') when you enter the state on a major highway.

Other highway maps, with sufficient detail to be useful for driving, are sold in fuel stations, bookstores, newsstands and some stores and places to stay. These businesses also usually have maps of the local communities.

Local chambers of commerce usually hand out simple maps of their towns. These vary from useless advertisements to very detailed street maps.

Topographical maps from the US Geological Survey (USGS) cover the USA at a scale of 1:24,000, showing every road, path and building (though some of them may be out of date). They are superb close-up maps for hiking or intensive exploration by car. The USGS publishes a variety of other maps, including metropolitan and resort-destination maps at scales between 1:24,000 and 1:100,000, and state topographical maps at 1:500,000.

Information on ordering USGS maps ($4 to $7 each) is now available on the USGS website (www.usgs.gov) or by writing to USGS Information Services, Box 25286, Denver, CO 80225. When you order maps, also request the folder describing topographic maps and the symbols used on them.

For detailed hiking maps, contact the parks on your route for suggestions of good maps and sources.

Atlases If you plan to do a lot of traveling – especially hiking or biking – in a particular state, you may want to get a state atlas. These are also critical for some of the more obscure natural destinations that require careful navigation over poorly marked rural roads.

The Delorme Mapping Company (☎ 207-846-7100, www.delorme.com), PO Box 298, Yarmouth, ME 04096, sells atlases for all the Great Lakes states for $17 each.

What to Bring

If you take prescription medicines regularly, bring a supply of the medicine, not a prescription for it. Doctors are licensed by state, and their prescriptions may not be accepted in any state except the one in which they are licensed. See the Health section for more suggestions.

See Climate in Facts about the Great Lakes Region for climatic charts for key cities in the region. Plan for variations that can be as much as 30° in any direction at any given time and you'll be fine. Otherwise, you can buy anything in the Midwest: camping stores, clothing stores, drug stores and more abound. Often their prices are cheaper than those where you came from.

TOURIST OFFICES

State tourist offices are good general-information sources and are listed in the introductory chapters for each state. State or city convention and visitors' bureaus (often abbreviated CVB) are listed there or with the cities where they are situated. Local tourist offices and visitor centers can not only cheerfully suffocate you with information but also will often help you find accommodations.

VISAS & DOCUMENTS

Passport & Visas

To enter the USA, Canadians must have proof of Canadian citizenship, such as a citizenship card with photo ID or a passport. Visitors from other countries must have a valid passport, and most visitors also require a US visa. Check out the US State Department's Web site for visa information (travel.state.gov/visa_services.html).

There is a reciprocal visa-waiver program in which citizens of certain countries (26 at present) may enter the USA without a US visa for stays of 90 days or less. These countries are Andorra, Argentina, Australia, Austria, Belgium, Brunei, Denmark, Finland, France, Germany, Iceland, Ireland, Italy, Japan, Liechtenstein, Luxembourg, Monaco, the Netherlands, New Zealand, Norway, San Marino, Slovenia, Spain, Sweden, Switzerland and the UK. Under this program you must have a roundtrip ticket that is nonrefundable in the USA, and you are not allowed to extend your stay beyond 90 days.

Other travelers need to obtain a visa from a US consulate or embassy. See Embassies & Consulates, later in the chapter, for a list. In most countries the process can be done by mail.

Your passport should be valid for at least six months longer than your intended stay in the USA, and you'll need to submit a recent photo (37mm by 37mm) with the application. Documents of financial stability and/or guarantees from a US resident are sometimes required, particularly for those visiting from developing countries.

Visa applicants may be required to 'demonstrate binding obligations' – such as a family, a job or enrollment in a university – that will ensure their return home. Because of this requirement, those planning to travel through other countries before arriving in the USA are generally better off applying for their US visa while they are still in their home countries rather than while on the road.

The most common visa is a Non-Immigrant Visitors Visa, B1 for business purposes, B2 for tourism or visits to friends and relatives. A visitor's visa is good for one or five years with multiple entries, and it specifically prohibits the visitor from taking paid employment in the USA. If you're coming to the USA to work or study, you will probably need a different type of visa, and the company or institution to which you're going should make the arrangements. Allow six months in advance for processing the application. For information on work visas and employment in the US, see the Work section, later in this chapter.

The validity period of your US Visitors Visa depends on your citizenship. The length of time you are allowed to stay is ultimately determined by US immigration authorities at the port of entry.

Visa Extensions If you want to stay in the US past the date stamped in your passport, contact the local office of the Justice Department's Immigration and Naturalization Service (INS) *before* the stamped date. In Chicago, call the INS at ☎ 312-353-7335 or ☎ 800-755-0777. The Chicago office is in the Kluczynski Building in the Federal Center at 10 W Jackson Blvd.

If you remain more than a few days past the expiration date, the INS may assume you want to work illegally. At an interview with the INS, you will need to explain why you didn't leave by the expiration date, and you will have to convince the officials you're not looking for work and that you have enough money to support yourself until you do leave. It's a good idea to bring a US citizen with you to vouch for your character, and to bring some sort of proof that you have enough currency to support yourself.

Travel Insurance

A travel insurance policy to cover theft, loss and medical problems is another good idea. It should cover you not only for medical expenses and luggage theft or loss, but also for cancellations or delays in your travel arrangements, and everyone should be covered for the worst possible case, such as an accident that requires hospital treatment and a flight home. Coverage depends on your insurance and type of ticket, so ask both your insurer and your ticket-issuing agency to explain the finer points.

Many travel agencies sell medical and emergency repatriation policies, but these can be relatively expensive for what you get. You'd be well advised to discuss the matter of travel insurance with your health care provider or regular insurance agent for comparison of coverages and costs.

Companies offering various sorts of travel insurance, including health insurance, include the following:

Access America, Inc (☎ 212-490-5345, 800-284-8300, www.accessamerica.com), 600 Third Ave, New York, NY 10116

Tripguard Plus (☎ 800-423-3632, fax 818-892-6576, www.tripguard.com), 16933 Parthenia St, North Hills, CA 91343

Europe Assistance (☎ 0181-680-1234, www.europassistance.com) 252 High St, Croyden, Surrey CR0 1NF, sells travel insurance in the UK

Make sure you have a separate record of all your ticket details or, better still, a photocopy of the ticket. Also make a copy of your insurance policy, in case the original is lost.

Buy travel insurance as early as possible. If you buy it the week before you fly, you may find, for instance, that you're not covered for delays to your flight caused by strikes or other industrial action that may have been in force before you took out the insurance. Insurance may seem very expensive, but it's nowhere near the cost of a medical emergency in the USA. See the Health Insurance section for more information.

Driver's License & Permits

An International Driving Permit is a useful accessory for foreign visitors in the USA. Traffic police are more likely to accept it as valid identification than an unfamiliar document from another country. Your national automobile association can provide one for a nominal fee. It's usually valid for one year.

Automobile Association Card

If you plan on doing a lot of driving in the USA, it might be beneficial to join your national automobile association. Members of the American Automobile Association (AAA) or an affiliated automobile club can get discounts on lodging, car rental and sightseeing admission with membership cards. See the Useful Organizations section, later in this chapter, for more information.

Hostel Card

Most hostels in the USA are members of Hosteling International–American Youth Hostels (HI–AYH). For more information on HI–AYH, see the Useful Organizations and Hostels sections, later in this chapter.

Student & Youth Cards

In most towns – especially ones with lots of students – your student ID card can get you occasional discounts. Museums and attractions outside cities may also give small discounts to students, and you'll need a card to prove you are one.

Photocopies

Before you leave home, it's a good idea to photocopy all important travel documents

HIV & Entering the USA

Anyone entering the USA who is not a US citizen is subject to the authority of the Immigration and Naturalization Service (INS). The INS can keep someone from entering or staying in the USA by excluding or deporting them. This is especially relevant to travelers with HIV (human immunodeficiency virus) or AIDS (acquired immune deficiency syndrome). Though being HIV-positive is not grounds for deportation, it is a 'ground for exclusion,' meaning that the INS can invoke this rule and refuse to admit an HIV-positive visitor to the country.

Although INS officers don't test people for HIV at the point of entry into the USA, they may try to exclude anyone who answers 'yes' to this question on the nonimmigrant visa application form: 'Have you ever been afflicted with a communicable disease of public health significance?' An INS officer may also stop someone who seems sick, is carrying AIDS or HIV medicine or, unfortunately, appears to the official to be from a 'high-risk group' (ie, gay), though sexual orientation itself is not legally grounds for exclusion. Visitors may be deported if the INS later finds that they are HIV-positive but did not declare it.

If you can prove to consular officials that you are the spouse, parent or child of a US citizen or legal permanent resident (green-card holder), you are exempt from the exclusionary law, even if you are HIV-positive or have AIDS.

Immigrants and visitors who may face exclusion should discuss their rights and options with a trained immigration advocate within the USA before applying for a visa. For legal immigration information and referrals to immigration advocates, contact the National Immigration Project of the National Lawyers Guild (☎ 617-227-9727, fax 617-227-5495), 14 Beacon St, suite 602, Boston, MA 02108, or the Immigrant HIV Assistance Project, Bar Association of San Francisco (☎ 415-782-8995), 465 California St, suite 1100, San Francisco, CA 94104.

(passport data page and visa page, credit cards, travel insurance policy, air/bus/train tickets, driver's license, etc). Leave one copy with someone at home and keep another with you, separate from the originals. If your documents are lost or stolen, replacing them will be much easier.

You also can store details of your vital travel documents in Lonely Planet's free online Travel Vault in case you lose the photocopies or can't be bothered with them. Your password-protected Travel Vault is accessible online anywhere in the world – create it at www.ekno.lonelyplanet.com.

EMBASSIES & CONSULATES

Embassies & Consulates Abroad

United States embassies and consulates abroad include:

Australia
Embassy: (☎ 02-6214-5600, www.usis-australia.gov/embassy.html) 21 Moonah Place, Yaralumla, ACT 2600
Consulate: (☎ 02-9373-9200, www.usconsydney.org) Level 59 MLC Center, 19-29 Martin Place, Sydney, NSW 2000
Consulate: (☎ 03-9526-5900, www.usis-australia.gov/melbourne) Level 6, 553 St Kilda Rd (PO Box 6722), Melbourne, VIC 3004
Consulate: (☎ 08-9231-9400, www.usis-australia.gov/perth) St George's Court, 13th floor, 16 St George's Terrace, Perth, WA 6000

Canada
Embassy:(☎ 613-238-4470, 800-283-4356, www.usembassycanada.gov) 100 Wellington St, Ottawa, ON K1P 5T1
Consulate: (☎ 902-429-2485) 2000 Barrington St, Cogswell Tower, suite 910, Halifax, NS B3J 3K1
Consulate: (☎ 514-398-9695) 1155 rue St-Alexandre, Montreal, Quebec H2Z 1Z2
Consulate: (☎ 416-595-1700) 360 University Ave, Toronto ON M5G 1S4
There are also consulates in Calgary, Quebec City and Vancouver.

Finland
Embassy: (☎ 9-171-931, www.usembassy.fi) Itäinen Puistotie 14, 00140 Helsinki

France
Embassy: (☎ 01 43 12 22 22, www.amb-usa.fr) 2 rue Saint-Florentin, 75382 Paris Cedex 08

Germany
Embassy: (☎ 228-339-1, www.usembassy.de) Deichmanns Aue 29, 53170 Bonn
Embassy: (☎ 030-932-0233) Clayallee 170, 14195 Berlin
There are also consulates in Dusseldorf, Frankfurt, Hamburg, Leipzig and Munich.

Ireland
Embassy: (☎ 01-688-7122, www.indigo.ie/usembassy-usis) 42 Elgin Rd, Ballsbridge, Dublin 4

Japan
Embassy: (☎ 3-224-5000) 1-10-5 Akasaka Chome, Minato-ku, Tokyo

Mexico
Embassy: (☎ 5-209-9100, www.usembassy.org.mx) Paseo de la Reforma 305, Colonia Cuauhtémoc, 06500 México, DF
There are consulates in Ciudad Juárez, Guadalajara, Hermosillo, Matamoros, Mérida, Monterrey, Nuevo Laredo and Tijuana.

Netherlands
Embassy: (☎ 70-310-9209, www.usemb.nl) Lange Voorhout 102, 2514 EJ The Hague
Consulate: (☎ 20-575-5309) Museumplein 19, 1071 DJ Amsterdam

Norway
Embassy: (☎ 22 44 85 50) Drammensveien 18, N-0244 Oslo

New Zealand
Embassy: (☎ 9-3003-2724) General Bldg, 29 Shortland St, Auckland

Sweden
Embassy: (☎ 08-783-53-00, fax 660-58-79) Strandvägen 101, S-115 89 Stockholm

UK
Embassy: (☎ 020-7499-9000, www.usembassy.org.uk) 24 Grosvenor Square, London W1A 1AE
Consulate: (☎ 0131-556-8315, fax 557-6023) 3 Regent Terrace, Edinburgh EH7 5BW
Consulate: (☎ 028-90328-239, fax 90248-482) Queen's House, 14 Queen St, Belfast BT1 6EQ

Your Own Embassy

As a tourist, it's important to realize what your own embassy – the embassy of the country of which you are a citizen – can and cannot do.

Generally speaking, it won't be much help in emergencies if the trouble you're in is remotely your own fault. Remember that you are bound by the laws of the country you are in. Your embassy will not be sympathetic if you end up in jail after committing a crime locally, even if such actions are legal in your own country.

In genuine emergencies you might get some assistance, but only if other channels have been exhausted. For example, if you need to get home urgently, a free ticket home is exceedingly unlikely – the embassy would expect you to have insurance. If you have all your money and documents stolen, it might assist in getting a new passport, but a loan for onward travel is out of the question.

Embassies used to keep letters for travelers or have a small reading room with home newspapers, but these days the mail-holding service has been stopped and even newspapers tend to be out of date.

Embassies & Consulates in the USA

Embassies are in Washington, DC. Some countries maintain consulates, honorary consuls or consular agents in Chicago.

Australia
Embassy: (☎ 202-797-3000, fax 797-3168, www.austemb.org) 1601 Massachusetts Ave NW, Washington, DC 20036

Canada
Embassy: (☎ 202-682-1740, www.cdnemb-washdc.org) 501 Pennsylvania Ave NW, Washington, DC 20001
Consulate: (☎ 312-616-1860) 180 N Stetson Ave, Suite 2400, Chicago

Finland
Embassy:(☎ 202-298-5800) 3301 Massachusetts Ave NW, Washington DC 20008

France
Embassy: (☎ 202-944-6200) 4101 Reservoir Rd NW, Washington, DC 20007-2171
Consulate: (☎ 312-787-6657) 737 N Michigan Ave, Suite 2020, Chicago

Germany
Embassy: (☎ 202-298-4000, fax 298-4249, www.germany-info.org) 4645 Reservoir Rd NW, Washington, DC 20007-1998
Consulate: (☎ 312-580-1199) 676 N Michigan Ave, Suite 3200, Chicago

Ireland
Embassy: (☎ 202-462-3939, www.irelandemb.org) 2234 Massachusetts Ave NW, Washington, DC 20008

Japan
Embassy: (☎ 202-238-6700, fax 238-2187, www.embjapan.org) 2520 Massachusetts Ave NW, Washington, DC 20008

Mexico
Embassy: (☎ 202-728-1600, www.embassyofmexico.org) 1911 Pennsylvania Ave NW, Washington, DC 20006
Consulate: (☎ 312-855-1380) 300 N Michigan Ave, Suite 200, Chicago

Netherlands
Embassy: (☎ 202-244-5300, fax 362-3430, www.netherlands-embassy.org) 4200 Linnean Ave NW, Washington, DC 20008
Consulate: (☎ 312-856-0110) 303 E Wacker Drive, Chicago

New Zealand
Embassy: (☎ 202-328-4800, fax 667-5227, www.emb.com/nzemb) 37 Observatory Circle NW, Washington, DC 20008

Norway
Embassy: (☎ 202-333-6000) 2720 34th St NW, Washington DC 20008

Sweden
Embassy: (☎ 202-833-2077) 1501 M St NW, Washington DC 20008

UK
Embassy: (☎ 202-588-6500, fax 588-7850, britain-info.org) 3100 Massachusetts Ave NW, Washington, DC 20008
Consulate: (☎ 312-464-6120) 400 N Michigan Ave, Chicago (☎ 216-621-7674)
Consulate: 55 Public Square (Illuminating Building), Cleveland

CUSTOMS

The US Customs Service allows each person 21 years of age or older to bring 1 liter of liquor and 200 cigarettes duty free into the USA. US citizens are allowed to import, duty free, $400 worth of gifts from abroad; non-US citizens are allowed to bring in $100 worth. Should you be carrying more than $10,000 in US and foreign cash, traveler's checks, money orders and the like, you will need to declare the excess amount. There is no legal restriction on the amount that may be imported, but undeclared sums may be subject to confiscation.

MONEY

Currency

Most of the world knows that the US currency is the dollar ($), divided into 100 cents (¢). Coins are in denominations of 1¢ (penny), 5¢ (nickel), 10¢ (dime), 25¢ (quarter), 50¢ (half-dollar – rare) and $1 (silver dollar – rare). Notes ('bills') are in denominations of $1, $2 (rare), $5, $10, $20, $50 and $100.

Exchange Rates

At press time, exchange rates were as follows:

country	unit		US dollars
Australia	A$1	=	$0.60
Canada	C$1	=	$0.67
euro	€1	=	$0.94
France	FF1	=	$0.14
Germany	DM1	=	$0.48
Japan	¥100	=	$0.95
Mexico	10 pesos	=	US$1
New Zealand	NZ$1	=	$0.47
United Kingdom	UK£1	=	$1.51

Exchanging Money

Cash & Traveler's Checks Only a few banks, mostly in Chicago, are prepared to exchange foreign cash. If you are coming to the US from abroad, you should plan on using your bank cash card (ATM card, cashpoint card, etc) to obtain cash most easily and at the most advantageous rate of exchange. Also plan to use your major credit card (Visa, MasterCard, EuroCard, Access, Diners Club, American Express) often. If you don't have credit cards or a cash card, plan to buy US-dollar traveler's checks before leaving home or upon arrival in the US.

Many banks in small northern towns frequented by Canadian tourists will buy and sell Canadian currency.

ATMs Cash (cashpoint, debit) cards from many banks may be used to obtain cash from automated teller machines (ATMs) and to pay at many hotels, restaurants, stores and fuel stations. There are ATMs everywhere, so you can always get cash. Look for them in or near banks, shopping malls, large supermarkets, airports and train stations, and on busy streets. Most are available for use 24 hours a day. In urban settings, use caution at ATMs after dark. In order for your card to be useful, the bank that issued it must be a member of one of the large interbank card systems such as Cirrus, Interlink, Plus Systems or Star Systems.

Credit Cards Major credit and charge cards are accepted by car rental agencies and most hotels, restaurants, fuel stations, shops and large grocery stores. Many recreational and tourist activities can also be paid for by credit card. The most commonly accepted cards are Visa, MasterCard (EuroCard, Access) and American Express. However, Discover and Diners Club cards are also accepted by a fair number of businesses.

You'll find it hard to perform certain transactions without a credit card. Ticket-buying services such as Ticketmaster, for instance, won't reserve tickets over the phone unless you offer a credit card number, and it's difficult to rent a car without a credit card (you may have to put down a cash deposit of as much as $2000). Even if you prefer traveler's checks and ATMs, it's a good idea to have a Visa or MasterCard for emergencies.

Carry copies of your credit card numbers separately from the cards. If you lose your credit cards or they are stolen, contact the company immediately. The following are toll-free numbers for the main credit card companies:

American Express	☎ 800-528-4800
Diners Club	☎ 800-234-6377
Discover	☎ 800-347-2683
MasterCard	☎ 800-826-2181
Visa	☎ 800-336-8472

Access and EuroCard holders should call the MasterCard number.

Security

Be cautious – but not paranoid – about carrying money. If your hotel or hostel has a safe, keep your valuables and excess cash in it. Don't display large amounts of cash in public. A money belt worn under your clothes is a good place to carry excess currency when you're on the move or otherwise unable to stash it in a safe. Avoid carrying your wallet in a back pocket of your pants – this is a prime target for pickpockets, as are handbags and the outside pockets of day packs and fanny packs (bum bags). See Dangers & Annoyances, later in this chapter, for other cautions to heed.

Costs

The Great Lakes region is among the more inexpensive in the US for travel. Even places such as Chicago are bargains compared to New York or San Francisco. However, what you spend depends on several factors: when and where you travel, how you travel and your age.

Seasonal Costs The Great Lakes' busiest travel seasons are July and August (high summer or in-season), and late September through mid-October (foliage season, also considered in-season). Prices for hotels, transportation and attractions are generally highest at these times.

City vs Countryside Accommodations in cities tend to be more expensive during the week, less expensive on Friday, Saturday and sometimes Sunday nights. In small towns, resorts and the countryside, inns and motels are cheapest during the week, more expensive on weekends. Thus you should plan to visit cities on weekends, and venture out into the country during the week, if possible.

Budget Ranges The most inexpensive way to see the Great Lakes is to camp with a tent, share a rental car among four people, and have picnics for lunch. Traveling this way, your daily budget for food, lodging and transport can be as low as $25 to $35 per person; figure $10 to $15 more per person per day if you plan to spend lots of time in the big cities or resorts. Remember, however, that the weather makes camping practical only from May through mid-October.

Traveling on a mid-range budget, a couple staying in budget motels, eating breakfast and lunch in fast-food places or simple restaurants and dinner in moderately priced little eateries, and getting around by rental car can expect to spend between $60 and $80 per person per day. If you spend lots of time in resorts and cities, your daily costs might be $80 to $100 per person.

For more luxurious accommodations, two people touring in a rental car, staying at luxury-class hotels, motels and inns, and dining as they please should expect to spend $125 to $175 per person per day.

Discounts

At some state tourism information centers are racks of brochures for hotels, motels, inns, restaurants, tours and attractions. Some of these accommodations offer discounts to travelers who present handbills or coupons given out at the information centers. For some lodgings, you must call and make a reservation from the information center to obtain the discount. Also, call the state tourism office for publicity materials, which will be mailed to you and may contain discount coupons for savings on car rentals, lodgings and meals.

Members of organizations such as the affiliates of the American Automobile Association (AAA) and the American Association of Retired Persons (AARP) can often enjoy discounted prices for motels and rental cars, as well as discounts on admission to some attractions. If you are a member of these groups it's always worth asking about discounts. In addition, AAA and AARP membership guides list many of the discounts available.

Families Virtually all hotels and motels allow one or two children to share their parents' room at no extra charge. If a rollaway bed is needed, there may be a charge (often $10 to $20). Usually, children must be younger than 18 years of age. At country inns and B&Bs, however, this policy does not usually apply. In fact, many country inns do not allow young children as guests.

Most activities and attractions – including museums, theme parks, group tours – offer reduced admission charges for children. Some offer special family rates – it's always good to ask.

Some outdoor attractions (concerts, state parks, beaches) charge admission by the car; whether there's one person or seven inside, the charge is the same.

Seniors Older travelers are eligible for discounts at attractions, museums, parks and many hotels, on car rental and train and bus fares and on other items. The age at which discounts apply varies and you must have photo identification as proof of your age. See Senior Travelers, later in this chapter, for more information.

Tipping

Tipping is expected in restaurants and better hotels, and by taxi drivers, hairdressers and baggage carriers. Americans tend to be liberal tippers. (Not giving the appropriate tip may even earn you scorn from the un- or under-tipped service provider.) See the 'Tipping Guidelines' boxed text for details.

Taxes

There is no national sales tax (such as VAT) in the USA. States levy sales taxes, and states and cities or towns may levy taxes on hotel rooms and restaurant meals. Room and meal taxes are not normally included in prices quoted to you, even though (or perhaps because) they may increase your final bill by as much as 11% or 12%. Be sure to ask about taxes when you ask for hotel room rates.

Taxes on transport services (bus, rail and air tickets, gasoline, taxi rides) are usually included in the prices quoted to you. In this book, individual states' tax rates are included in the introductory chapter for each state.

POST & COMMUNICATIONS

There's a post office in virtually every town and village, providing the familiar postal services such as parcel shipping and international express mail. For 24-hour postal information, call ☎ 800-275-8777 or check www.usps.gov. For hours of operation, see Sending Mail. Private shippers such as United Parcel Service (UPS; ☎ 800-742-5877) and Federal Express (FedEx; ☎ 800-463-3339) ship much of the nation's load of parcels and important time-sensitive documents to both domestic and foreign destinations.

Postal Rates

US postal rates are fairly cheap and fairly stable, changing every few years. As of January 1999, rates for 1st-class mail within the USA were set at 33¢ for letters weighing up to 1oz, 22¢ for each additional ounce and 20¢ for postcards.

International airmail rates (except to Canada and Mexico) are 60¢ for a half-ounce

Tipping Guidelines

Bartenders	10% to 15% of the bill
Cinemas, theaters	no tip
Coat checkrooms	75¢ to $1 per coat
Doorman (hotel or restaurant)	$1 at top hotels for calling a cab, getting your car from the parking lot or other direct service
Drivers who handle your luggage	$1 (not required)
Fast-food restaurants	no tip
Fuel station attendants	no tip
Hairdressers, barbers	about 15% of the bill
Hotel housekeepers	$2 to $3 per day
Luggage porters	75¢ to $1 per piece
Restaurant or nightclub servers	15% to 20% of the bill
Taxi drivers	12% to 18% of the fare
Valet parking	75¢ to $1 if attendant brings your car to you

letter and 40¢ for each additional half ounce. International postcard rates are 50¢.

Letters to Canada are 46¢ for a half ounce and 72¢ for a letter weighing up to 2oz. Postcards are 40¢. Letters to Mexico are 40¢ for a half ounce, 46¢ for a 1oz letter and 35¢ for a postcard.

Sending Mail

If you have the correct postage, you can drop your mail into any blue mailbox. However, to send a package 16oz or heavier, you must bring it to a post office. Addresses of many towns' main post offices are given in this book. For the address of the nearest one, call the main post office listed under 'Postal Service' in the US Government section of the white pages telephone directory.

Usually, post offices are open 8 or 8:30 am to 5 pm weekdays; some major post offices in cities stay open until 5:30 or 6 pm. Weekend hours are normally 8 am to noon or 2 pm on Saturday, closed Sunday. In the USA, the post office does not provide telephone service.

Packages must be securely wrapped in sturdy containers to be accepted for international shipment, especially if you expect to insure them. If you want to send a letter or parcel by US Registered Mail, be sure it is sealed with glue or paper tape (not cellophane or masking tape) so that the seams can be stamped with the postmark of the originating postal station.

Receiving Mail

Poste restante is called 'general delivery' in the US. If you're sending (or expecting) mail to be held at the post office in a certain city or town, it should be addressed as follows:

Your Name
c/o General Delivery *(Optional:* Station Name)
Town, State, Zip Code
USA

Mail is usually held for 10 days before it's returned to the sender; you might ask your correspondents to write 'hold for arrival' on their envelopes.

In large cities, it's a good idea to add the optional station name if you know it. If you do not add the ZIP code or station name, your mail will be held at the main station (central post office), which may not be the most convenient one for you, but it will have the longest hours of operation.

When you pick up your mail, bring some photo identification. Your passport is best.

Alternatively, have mail sent to the local office of American Express or Thomas Cook, which provide mail service for their clients.

Telephone

Telephone service is good, convenient and not particularly expensive, but the plethora of private companies, policies and rates is very confusing, even for Americans. Some smaller companies charge much higher rates than the large companies; some charge lower rates.

How to Place a Call All phone numbers within the USA consist of a three-digit area code followed by a seven-digit local number. If you are calling locally, just dial the seven-digit number. From a town in one area code to a town in another, dial ☎ 1 + area code + the number. This method is used, for example, to call from Chicago to nearby Milwaukee, or to California, or to Bermuda or Canada. (To call a nearby city or town within the same area code, you may be able to dial only the last seven digits, or you may have to also dial ☎ 1 + area code.)

For calls to other countries from a public phone, dial the international access code (☎ 011) followed by the country code (check the front of telephone directory if in doubt) and the rest of the number. If for some reason you need operator assistance, dial ☎ 0 and ask for an international operator – but note that your rates will soar (although if you just need a country code you can obtain that information free).

For local directory assistance, dial ☎ 411. For directory assistance outside your area code, dial ☎ 1 + the three-digit area code of the place you want to call + 555-1212. If you don't know the area code, dial ☎ 0 for operator assistance (free of charge).

Area codes for places outside the region are listed in the front of the white pages telephone directory. Be aware that because of skyrocketing demand for phone numbers (for faxes, cellular phones, dedicated Internet lines), some metropolitan areas are being divided into multiple new area codes. These changes are not reflected in older phone books. When in doubt, ask the operator.

The ☎ 800, 888 and 877 area codes designate toll-free numbers within the USA and sometimes from Canada. These calls are free. Numbers that begin with these area codes are fast becoming accessible from abroad, however they are not free when dialed from abroad. Within the US, for toll-free directory assistance, call ☎ 800-555-1212.

Some area codes, including ☎ 550, 554, 900, 920, 940, 976 and others beginning with 5 and 9 designate information services (sports scores, horoscopes, chat lines, phone sex) for which charges – sometimes as much as $2 or $3 per minute – may be levied.

If you're calling from abroad, the international country code for the USA is ☎ 1.

Cost of Calling Local calls cost 25¢ to 35¢ for three minutes or more, depending on the town. Because of the Byzantine rate structure and plethora of phone companies, regional calls (anywhere from 2 miles to 200 miles) are often the most expensive domestic calls, costing from 60¢ to $1 or more per three-minute call. In some cases, it is cheaper to call from Chicago to California than from Chicago to Springfield.

Long-distance domestic calls can cost as little as 9¢ per minute if dialed from a home phone, but will cost more like 25¢ to 75¢ per minute from a public coin telephone. Telephone company credit-card calls may cost several dollars for the first minute, but only 25¢ to 35¢ for subsequent minutes.

The cost of international calls varies by the country called, the telephone used (public or private), the company providing the long-distance service (Sprint, MCI, AT&T and others), the time of day and the day of the week. US rates are generally competitive with, and often cheaper than, public-phone rates in other countries.

For specific rate information, call the operator (☎ 0). Don't ask the operator to put your call through, however, because operator-assisted calls are much more expensive than direct-dial calls. Generally, nights (11 pm to 8 am), all day Saturday and 8 am to 5 pm Sunday are the cheapest times to call (60% discount). Evenings (5 to 11 pm Sunday to Friday) are mid-priced (35% discount). Day calls (8 am to 5 pm weekdays) are full-price calls within the USA.

Paying for Calls Most public telephones in the USA accept only coins (5¢, 10¢, 25¢); some accept credit cards instead. For local and short calls to other points in the USA, using coins is easy enough. However, there are ways to pay for calls that are more convenient than feeding a stack of quarters into the phone.

Some telephones in airports and large hotels allow payment by credit card. There may be a slot to slide your card into, or you may have to punch in your credit card number.

An alternative is phone debit cards that allow purchasers to pay in advance. However, compared to the easy-to-use debit card systems in many other countries, those in the USA are confusing, cumbersome and often expensive.

Purchase a telephone debit card from a convenience store, phone company office, post office or tourist information office. Cards are usually sold in denominations of $5, $10, $20, $40 or $50 and offer calls in the USA for 20¢ to 60¢ per minute, 70¢ to $2 per minute to Canada and the UK, $1 to $2 per minute to Europe, or $2 to $3 per minute to Asian and Pacific countries.

Unfortunately, it is usually impossible to tell how much a call may cost when purchasing a card or how much you have left in your account after you place a call. To learn per-minute call costs, you must call a customer service number (on the card) and ask. When dialing, follow the calling instructions on the card, which usually require that you punch in 35 or so digits altogether. As you talk, your time on the line is deducted from your account.

There are some security issues with phone debit cards. The card often has no magnetic stripe or microchip; instead it just has an account number, so when you use your card in a public place, be careful – you are vulnerable to thieves who will watch you punch in the account number. If given the opportunity, they will memorize it and use your card to make phone calls to all corners of the earth.

In addition, when you purchase a phone debit card, the account number should be covered up (by scratch-off paint or a paper wrapper) to keep it a secret. If the number is exposed to view when you buy the card, you must assume that it has already been used by someone and is worthless.

Not all Canadian telephone calling cards allow for direct dialing from all US locations. Some require calling a Canadian 800 number, from which an operator will make the connection for you. If this number is not on the card, be sure to record it before departure.

You may want to consider Lonely Planet's eKno Communication Card, aimed specifically at independent travelers. It provides budget international calls, a range of messaging services, free email and travel information – though for local calls, you're usually better off with a local card. You can join online at www.ekno.lonelyplanet.com or by phone from the Great Lakes region by dialing ☎ 800-707-0031. To use eKno from the United States once you have joined, dial ☎ 800-706-1333.

Check the eKno Web site for joining and access numbers from other countries and updates on new features and budget local access numbers.

Fax & Telegram

Fax machines are easy to find in the USA, at shipping companies such as Mail Boxes Etc, hotel business-service centers and photocopy services, but be prepared to pay high prices (over $1 a page). Telegrams can be sent from Western Union offices; call ☎ 800-325-6000 for information.

Email & Internet Access

If you want to surf the Net or send the occasional email message, most public libraries have a computer with Internet access. Other options are an Internet café (for worldwide lists of cybercafés, browse www.traveltales.com or www.netcafeguide.com); a copy center (such as Kinko's, which charges about $10 per hour); or a hotel that caters to business travelers. Some hostels even offer Internet access to their guests. The cheapest way to have email access while traveling is to get a free Web-based email account from Hotmail (www.hotmail.com), Yahoo (www.yahoo.com) or Netscape (www.netscape.com) that you can access from any online computer with a browser.

If you're traveling with a computer and modem, you may be able to connect to the Internet from your hotel room. Many hotel phones now have standard RJ-11 jacks labeled 'Data,' into which you can safely plug your modem cord. Before you plug into a regular wall-mounted phone jack, ask if it's connected to a PBX (ie, a private branch exchange, found mainly in big hotels and office buildings). If it is, it may fry your modem. What you want is a normal 'analog' phone jack.

INTERNET RESOURCES

The World Wide Web is a rich resource for travelers. You can research your trip, hunt down bargain airfares, book hotels, check on weather conditions or chat with locals and other travelers about the best places to visit (or avoid).

There's no better place to start your internet explorations than the Lonely Planet Web site (www.lonelyplanet.com). Here you'll find succinct summaries on traveling to most places on earth, postcards from other travelers, and the Thorn Tree bulletin board, where you can ask questions before you go or dispense advice when you get back. You can also find travel news and updates to many of our most popular guidebooks, and the subWWWay section links you to the most useful travel resources elsewhere on the Web.

Web site addresses are given throughout this book for many state and city information services and for many other helpful organizations and businesses.

BOOKS

Most books are published in different editions by different publishers in different countries. As a result, a book might be a hardcover rarity in one country while it's readily available in paperback in another. Fortunately, local bookstores and libraries can search by title or author, so these are the best places to find out about the availability of the following recommendations.

For literature, see that section in the Facts about the Great Lakes chapter.

Lonely Planet

Lonely Planet's *Chicago*; *New York, New Jersey & Pennsylvania*; *USA*; and *Canada* are good supplemental guides for travelers exploring the Great Lakes. Outdoorsy types might want to take a look through *Hiking in the USA* as well.

Guidebooks

It is hoped that the guidebook you have in your hands can provide you with all the information you may need on a first, second or later tour through the Great Lakes. But obviously, no single book can tell all travelers everything they want to know.

Two books, *The Smithsonian Guides to Historic America – The Great Lakes States* and *The Smithsonian Guides to Natural America – The Great Lakes*, are filled with details in these two areas of interest. Also good are the many outdoor activity books from the Mountaineers. *Michigan State Parks* is a good example of their nicely illustrated works.

History & Ecology

Books about the history and ecology of the Great lakes region abound. One of the best single volumes is *Nature's Metropolis*, by William Cronon. A delightful read, it shows how exploitation of the natural resources of the region fuelled its growth, and traces the economic development of Chicago and its influence on immigration and transport.

Other books worth considering include the following:

Atlas of Great Lakes Indian History is a weighty tome with just about everything you could hope to read about the many civilizations that predated the arrival of the Europeans.

Great Lakes Indians: A Pictorial Guide, by William J Kubiak, shows the diverse cultures of these peoples, past and present.

River of Forgotten Days: A Journey Down the Mississippi in Search of La Salle, by Daniel Spurr, is a readable personal account retracing the journeys of the explorer who was one of the first Europeans to encounter the Great Lakes region and its indigenous people.

Where Two Worlds Meet: The Great Lakes Fur Trade, by Carolyn Gilman, is a fine volume that traces the developments in the region after La Salle.

Countering Colonization: Native American Women and Great Lakes Missions, 1630–1900, by Carol Devens, is a scholarly look at the often under-reported role that Native American women played in the relations with early settlers.

Bonfires and Beacons: Great Lakes Lighthouses, by Larry and Patricia Wright, looks at the hundreds of lighthouses past and present that dot the shores of the lakes.

End of an Era: The Last of the Great Lakes Steamboats, by David Plowden, is a nostalgic look at the time during much of the 20th century when the lakes were crisscrossed by fleets of freight and passenger vessels.

A Fully Accredited Ocean: Essays on the Great Lakes is a collection of works highlighting the vastness of these inland seas.

The Great Lakes, by Sharon Katz, is part of a series called Ecosystems of North America, which gives a detailed and scientific yet quite readable view on nature.

FILMS

Chicago has been home to numerous films. In *The Blues Brothers*, possibly the best-known Chicago movie, John Belushi and Dan Aykroyd tear up the city, including City Hall; the scenes with the hapless Nazis in the Pinto were filmed in Milwaukee. *Ferris Bueller's Day Off* is John Hughes' cinematic postcard for the city. In *The Fugitive* Harrison Ford stars as a doctor falsely accused of murdering his wife. The Alfred Hitchcock classic *North by Northwest* includes scenes filmed on location in Chicago (the crop-duster scene is an excellent representation of flat central Illinois). In *The Untouchables* Kevin Costner cleans up Chicago from Al Capone.

Elsewhere in the region, *Breaking Away* was filmed in Bloomington, Indiana, and records the town's Little 500 bicycle race. *Fargo* is a wacko murder-comedy with cartoon versions of northern accents. *Planes, Trains and Automobiles* has John Candy and Steve Martin involved in travel mayhem throughout the Midwest. *Roger and Me* is Michael Moore's mischievous and cutting documentary about General Motors and Michigan's auto industry in general. *Grosse Pointe Blank*, a light comedy with John Cusack and Minnie Driver, is set in that swanky suburb of Detroit.

NEWSPAPERS & MAGAZINES

More than 1500 daily newspapers are published in the USA, with a combined circulation of about 60 million. The newspaper with the highest circulation is the *Wall Street Journal*, followed by *USA Today* and the *New York Times*, which are all available in major cities.

The region's major city newspapers are sold in areas for scores of miles around their home cities. Many smaller cities and large towns have their own local newspapers, published daily or weekly.

Numerous special interest magazines exist, covering various parts of the Great Lakes region. They include *Lake Superior* magazine, *Route 66* magazine, *Outdoor Indiana* and *Chicago*. Check any good magazine rack once you're in the Great Lakes for many more choices.

RADIO & TV

All rental cars have radios, and travelers can choose from hundreds of radio stations. Each station follows a format, which may be to play classical music, country and western, rock and roll, jazz, easy-listening, or 'golden oldies.' FM stations mainly carry popular music. On the AM (middle wave) frequencies, 'talk radio' rules: a more or less intelligent or outrageous radio host receives telephone calls from listeners, makes comments and expresses opinions.

National Public Radio (NPR) features a more levelheaded approach to news, discussion, music and more. NPR-affiliated stations are normally found on the lower end of the FM dial.

You can't visit the Midwest, and especially not Minnesota, without tuning in at least one episode of *A Prairie Home Companion*, Garrison Keillor's nationally celebrated radio program, full of humor, music and stories from the fictitious yet famous town of Lake Wobegon. It's broadcast live every Saturday evening from 6 to 8 pm on probably every NPR affiliate in the Great Lakes region.

Most hotel and motel rooms have color TVs that receive perhaps several dozen channels.

PHOTOGRAPHY & VIDEO

Film & Equipment

All major brands of film are available at reasonable prices. Every town of any size has at least one photo shop that stocks a variety of fresh film, cameras and accessories.

In most towns and tourist centers are shops that can develop your color print film in one hour (more often two or so hours), or at least the same day, for an extra charge. Processing a roll of 100 ASA 35mm color print film with 24 exposures costs about $7 for regular service.

Video Systems

Overseas visitors should remember that the USA and Canada use the National Television System Committee (NTSC) color TV and video standard, which is not compatible with the PAL and SECAM standards used in Africa, Europe, Asia and Australia unless converted. If you buy an NTSC video movie and put it in your PAL or SECAM videocassette player, you'll get only garbled images and sound.

Airport Security

All air passengers must pass their luggage through X-ray machines, which are said to pose no danger to most films. If you'd like to bypass the X-ray scanner, prepare: unpack your film from boxes and plastic film cans and have all the film canisters readily visible in a plastic bag. But you really need to do this only for very high speed film (1600 ASA and above).

TIME

The USA (excluding Alaska and Hawaii) spans four time zones. The Great Lakes region is in two time zones. Ohio and Michigan are on eastern time; Illinois, Wisconsin and Minnesota are on central time. Note that Indiana is always on eastern standard time and never uses daylight saving time. So during the winter, Hoosiers are with the eastern zone and during the warmer months they are with the central zone. The other five states observe daylight saving time. Clocks are set ahead one hour on the first Sunday in April and back one hour on the last Sunday in October.

When it's noon in Chicago, it's 6 pm in London, 1 pm in New York and 10 am in San Francisco.

ELECTRICITY

Electric current is 110 to 120 volts, 60-cycle. Appliances built to take 220- to 240-volt, 50-cycle current (as in Europe and Asia) will need a converter (transformer) and a US-style plug adapter with two flat pins, or three (two flat, one round) pins. Plugs with three pins don't fit into a two-hole socket, but adapters are easy to buy at hardware stores and pharmacies.

WEIGHTS & MEASURES

The USA uses a modified version of the traditional English measuring system of inches, feet, yards, miles, ounces, pounds and gallons. See the inside back cover of this book for a conversion chart.

Here are some easy-to-remember general rules: a yard is slightly less than a meter, and a mile is about 1.6km; a pound is slightly less than half a kilogram; a normal 12oz soft-drink can or bottle holds slightly more than a third of a liter, and a quart of liquid is slightly less than a liter.

More precisely, distances are measured in inches (1 inch=2.54cm), feet (1 foot =30.48cm), yards (1 yard=0.91m) and miles (1 mile=1.61km). Twelve inches equal 1 foot; 3 feet equal 1 yard; 1760 yards, or 5280 feet, equal 1 mile.

Dry weights are measured in ounces (1oz=28.35g), pounds (1lb=453.59g) and tons (1 ton=1016kg). Sixteen ounces equal 1lb; 2000lb equal 1 ton.

Liquids are measured by the fluid ounce (1oz=29.57ml), the cup (1 cup=8oz or 0.24 liter), the pint (1 pint=16oz or 0.47 liter), the quart (1 quart=32oz, 2 pints or 0.95 liter) and the gallon (1 gallon=4 quarts or 3.78 liters). Note that the US pint equals 16 fluid oz, not 20, as in the Imperial (British) system. The US gallon, at 64oz, is 20% less than the Imperial gallon (it takes 1.2 US gallons to make an Imperial gallon). Wine bottles tend to be 70 centiliters or 750 milliliters. Gasoline is dispensed by the US gallon.

The metric system is used in certain situations in the USA. Most commercial products have labels giving their weight, volume or length in metric measure as well as the traditional one. Cars sold in the USA usually have speedometers that are marked in kilometers per hour (km/h) as well as miles per hour (mph).

LAUNDRY

Pricier hotels and motels usually provide valet laundry and dry-cleaning services. Most others have coin machines. You can also find the nearest laundromat (self-service coin-operated laundry) or dry cleaners yourself. Ask a local or check the local telephone directory under 'Laundries – Self-Service' and 'Cleaners.'

TOILETS

Americans have many names for public toilet facilities. The most common name is 'rest room.' Other names include 'ladies' or men's room,' 'comfort station,' 'facility' and 'sanitary facility.' You will find relatively clean public toilets in airports, bars, large stores, museums, state and national parks, restaurants, hotels and tourist information offices. The ones in bus, train and highway fuel stations and rest stops might be clean or might not, but most are still usable. Not all fuel stations have toilets; among those that do, the quality varies considerably. Public toilets in many city parks and other public places have been closed because of criminal misuse.

HEALTH

In an emergency, dial ☎ 911 from almost any telephone for assistance. A very few tiny rural areas require a different number. If you're at all in doubt, dial ☎ 0 and ask the operator for an ambulance.

All cities in the Great Lakes region – even small ones – have hospitals. To find one, look on the highways and roads for the standard hospital symbol, a white 'H' on a square blue background. Many cities also have walk-in clinics where you can show up without an appointment, see a nurse, nurse-practitioner or doctor for a minor ailment or preliminary diagnosis, and pay for it in cash or by credit card.

Make sure you're healthy before you start traveling. If you are embarking on a long trip, make sure your teeth are in good shape. If you wear glasses, take a spare pair and your prescription. You can get new spectacles made up quickly and competently for around $100, depending on the prescription and frame you choose. If you require a particular medication, take an adequate supply. Bring a prescription as well, although the dispensing of prescription medicines is regulated by each state, and a prescription written by a doctor licensed to practice medicine in one state may not be accepted by a pharmacy in another.

No immunizations are needed, unless you are coming to the USA from a country that has experienced a recent cholera or yellow fever epidemic.

Although the potential dangers of some illnesses can seem frightening, in reality few travelers experience anything more than an upset stomach.

Health Insurance

Be sure that you have some form of health insurance that will pay your US medical bills in full should you need medical care while in the USA. Bills for an illness that requires hospitalization can easily exceed $1000 or even $2000 per day, and you will be expected to pay even at publicly supported government hospitals unless you can show that you are destitute.

Some policies specifically exclude 'dangerous activities' such as scuba diving, motorcycling and even hiking. If these activities are on your agenda, avoid that sort of policy.

You may prefer a policy that pays doctors or hospitals directly, rather than making you pay first and claim later. If you have to claim later, keep all documentation from the hospital. Some policies ask you to call collect (reverse charges) to a center in your home country for an immediate assessment of your problem.

Check whether the policy covers ambulance fees or an emergency flight home. If you have to stretch out, you will need two seats, and somebody has to pay for them. For more information on insurance, see Travel Insurance, earlier in this chapter.

Travel Health Guides

For comprehensive health information and advice for travelers, browse the US Centers for Disease Control and Prevention's Web site (www.cdc.gov/travel). Lonely Planet's Web site has lots of good travel health advice (www.lonelyplanet.com/health), and many other travel health sites are listed there. Also try dir.yahoo.com/Health/Travel.

Books on travel health include *Travelers' Health*, by Dr Richard Dawood, a comprehensive, easy to read, authoritative and highly recommended book, but rather large to lug around, and *Travel with Children*, by Maureen Wheeler, which offers basic advice on travel health for young children.

Heat Exhaustion

Dehydration or salt deficiency can cause heat exhaustion, which is characterized by fatigue, lethargy, headaches, giddiness and muscle cramps. Always carry – and drink – plenty of water on long trips. If you are experiencing salt deficiency, salt tablets can help, but adding more salt to your food is better.

Hypothermia

If you plan to camp, hike or canoe in the Great Lakes, remember this: changing weather can leave you vulnerable to exposure. After dark, autumn temperatures can drop from balmy to below freezing, while a sudden rain soaking and high winds can lower your body temperature rapidly. If you must travel alone, especially when hiking, be sure someone knows your route and when you expect to return.

Hypothermia occurs when the body loses heat faster than it can produce it and the body's core temperature falls. It is surprisingly easy to progress from very cold to dangerously cold due to a combination of wind, wet clothing, fatigue and hunger, even if the air temperature is above freezing.

Symptoms of hypothermia are exhaustion, numb skin (particularly toes and fingers), shivering, slurred speech, irrational behavior, lethargy, stumbling, dizzy spells, muscle cramps and violent bursts of energy. To treat mild hypothermia, get victims out of the wind and rain and remove their clothing if it's wet and replace it with dry, warm clothing. Give them hot liquids – not alcohol – and some high-calorie, easily digestible food. Do not rub victims: instead, allow them to slowly warm themselves.

Jet Lag

Jet lag occurs because many of the body's functions (such as temperature, pulse rate and emptying of the bladder and bowels) are regulated by internal 24-hour cycles called circadian rhythms. When traveling long distances rapidly, it takes time to adjust to the 'new time' of the destination; fatigue, disorientation, insomnia, anxiety, impaired concentration and loss of appetite may result. These effects begin to fade within three days of arrival, but there are ways of minimizing the impact of jet lag:

- Rest for a couple of days prior to departure; avoid late nights and last-minute dashes for traveler's checks, passport or other travel necessities.
- Select flight schedules that minimize sleep deprivation; arriving late in the day means you can go to sleep soon after you arrive. For very long flights, try to organize a stopover.
- Avoid excessive eating, and don't drink alcohol during the flight. Instead, drink plenty of noncarbonated, nonalcoholic drinks such as fruit juice or water.
- Make yourself comfortable by wearing loose-fitting clothes and perhaps bringing an eye mask and ear plugs to help you sleep.

Infectious Diseases

Hepatitis Hepatitis is a general term for inflammation of the liver and is a common disease worldwide. Several different viruses cause hepatitis, and they differ in the way that they are transmitted. Symptoms are similar in all forms of the illness and include fever, chills, headache, fatigue, feelings of weakness and aches and pains, followed by loss of appetite, nausea, vomiting, abdominal pain and other more severe symptoms.

Hepatitis A is transmitted by contaminated food or drinking water. Hepatitis B, C and D are spread through contact with infected blood, blood products or body fluids, for example, through sexual contact or through unsterilized needles (see the HIV & AIDS section). Hepatitis B can lead to long-term problems such as chronic liver damage or a long-term carrier state; C and D can also lead to some long-term complications.

There are vaccines against hepatitis A and B, but there are currently no vaccines against the other types of hepatitis. Following the basic rules about food and water (for hepatitis A) and avoiding high-risk situations (for hepatitis B, C and D) are important preventive measures.

Sexually Transmitted Diseases Sexual contact with an infected partner spreads these diseases, including gonorrhea and syphilis (the most common STDs), herpes, hepatitis B and HIV. While abstinence is the only 100% effective preventive, practicing safe sex and using latex condoms can reduce the chance of infection.

Common symptoms of gohorrhea, syphilis and herpes are sores, blisters or rashes around the genitals and discharges or pain when urinating. With some STDs, such as wart virus or chlamydia, symptoms may be less marked or not observed at all, especially in women.

Gonorrhea and syphilis can be cured with antibiotics but can be debilitating if left untreated. Herpes can be treated but not cured. Chlamydia can cause infertility before any symptoms are noticed. If you suspect that you've caught an STD, have an examination and explore your options.

HIV & AIDS Any exposure to blood, blood products or bodily fluids may place you in danger of contracting HIV. In addition to unprotected sex, infection can come from sharing contaminated needles, including needles reused for acupuncture, tattooing or body piercing (a clean-looking needle or tool, or a healthy-looking person, may still be carrying HIV). HIV can also be spread through infected blood transfusions, though the blood supply in the USA is screened and presumably safe. Symptoms may appear only months after infection, so it is impossible to detect a person's HIV status without a blood test.

A good resource for help and information on HIV and AIDS is the US Centers for Disease Control AIDS hot line (☎ 800-342-2437, 800-344-7432 in Spanish, www.cdc.gov). See the boxed text 'HIV & Entering the USA,' earlier in this chapter, for more information.

Cuts, Bites & Stings

Wash all cuts and scratches well and treat them with an antiseptic such as Betadine. When possible, avoid bandages and Band-Aids, which can keep wounds wet.

Bee and wasp stings are usually painful rather than dangerous. However, people who are allergic to them may experience severe breathing difficulties and require urgent medical care. Calamine lotion or a sting relief spray will give relief, and ice packs will reduce the pain and swelling. There are some spiders with dangerous bites, but antivenins are usually available. See Dangers & Annoyances, later in this chapter, for more on Great Lakes pests.

Ticks & Lyme Disease Ticks are parasitic arachnids that may be present in brush, forest and grasslands, where hikers often get them on their legs or in their boots. Adult ticks suck blood from hosts by burying their heads in the skin but are often found unattached and can simply be brushed off.

Deer ticks, which can carry and spread a serious bacterial infection called Lyme disease, are found throughout the Great Lakes. The ticks are usually very small (some as small as a pinhead) and thus are not likely to be noticed casually – you must look carefully for them. A bite from a Lyme disease–infected deer tick may show a red welt and circular 'halo' of redness within a day or two, or there may be no symptoms beyond a minor itch. Also, mild flulike symptoms – headache, nausea, body aches – may or may not follow.

Lyme disease can be treated successfully, but early treatment is essential. If left untreated, it causes mental and muscular deterioration.

The best preventive measures are to wear clothing that covers your arms and legs when walking in grassy or wooded areas, apply insect repellent containing DEET on exposed skin and around ankles and trouser leg openings and always check your body (and especially your child's and pet's bodies) for ticks after outdoor activities.

If a tick has attached itself to you, use tweezers to pull it straight out – do not twist it. If a small chunk of skin comes out along with the head, that's good – you've got it all, and no part of the tick will be left to cause infection. Do not touch the tick with a hot object like a match or a cigarette, because that can cause it to regurgitate noxious gut substances or saliva into the wound. And do not rub oil, alcohol or petroleum jelly on the wound. If you get sick in the next couple of weeks, consult a doctor.

WOMEN TRAVELERS

People are generally friendly and happy to help travelers, but if you are traveling alone, maintain a little extra awareness of your surroundings. The following suggestions should reduce or eliminate the chances of problems, but the best advice is to trust your instincts.

You might want to ask for advice at your hotel or call the visitor's center if you are unsure which areas are considered unsafe, especially when making room reservations.

Avoid situations that leave you vulnerable, and conduct yourself in a commonsense manner: You're more vulnerable if you've been drinking or using drugs than if you're sober, and you're more vulnerable alone than if you're with company. If you don't want company, most men will respect a firm but polite 'no thank you.'

Don't pick up hitchhikers. At night, avoid getting out of your car to flag down help; turn on your hazard lights and display a white cloth outside the driver's-side window or from the radio antenna and wait for official help to arrive. Leaving the hood (bonnet) of your car raised is also a signal that you need assistance.

Some women protect themselves with a whistle, pepper spray or self-defense training. If you decide to purchase a spray, ask which sprays are legal at a local police station; laws regarding sprays vary from state to state. It is a felony to carry defensive sprays on airplanes.

If despite all your precautions you are assaulted, call the police (☎ 911). Many cities have rape crisis centers established to aid victims of rape. For the telephone number of the nearest center, call directory information (☎ 411 or 1 + area code + 555-1212).

The headquarters of the National Organization for Women (NOW; ☎ 202-331-0066, @ now@now.org, www.now.org), 1000 16th St NW, Suite 700, Washington, DC 20036, is a good resource for a variety of information and can refer you to state and local chapters. Planned Parenthood (☎ 212-541-7800, @ communications@ppfa.org, www.plannedparenthood.org), 810 Seventh Ave, New York, NY 10019, can refer you to clinics throughout the country and offer advice on medical issues. Check the yellow pages under 'Social & Human Services,' 'Clinics' and 'Health Services' for local resources.

GAY & LESBIAN TRAVELERS

Gay communities are most visible in the major coastal cities, such as San Francisco and New York, which have the largest gay populations, and in Chicago. When you travel outside of large cities, it is much harder to be open about your sexual preferences. Gay travelers should be careful – holding hands in public might get you bashed.

Large US cities often have a gay neighborhood or area. Some cities have a gay or alternative newspaper that lists current events or at least provides phone numbers of local organizations. Chicago, with its vibrant gay scene, is the center for gay life and culture in the Midwest. In other cities you can usually find at least a few gay bars, clubs or restaurants.

Some good national guidebooks are *The Womens' Traveller*, providing listings for lesbians; *Damron's Address Book*, for gay men; and *Damron Accommodations*, with gay-owned and gay-friendly hotel, B&B and guest-house listings nationwide. All three books are published by the Damron Company (☎ 415-255-0404, 800-462-6654, www.damron.com), PO Box 422458, San Francisco, CA 94142-2458. Ferrari's *Places for Women* and *Places for Men* are also useful, as are guides to specific cities (check out *Betty and Pansy's Severe Queer Reviews* to various cities, available in some bookstores; it's also available online from www.gaymart.com).

Another good resource is the *Gay Yellow Pages* (☎ 212-674-0120, gayyellowpages.com), PO Box 533, Village Station, NY 10014-0533, which has a national edition as well as regional editions.

National resource numbers include the National AIDS/HIV Hotline (☎ 800-342-2437), the National Gay and Lesbian Task Force in Washington, DC (☎ 202-332-6483), and the Lambda Legal Defense Fund in New York City (☎ 212-995-8585) and Los Angeles (☎ 213-937-2727).

DISABLED TRAVELERS

Travel within the USA is becoming easier for people with disabilities. Public buildings (including hotels, restaurants, theaters and museums) are now required by law to be wheelchair accessible and to have available rest room facilities. Public transportation services (buses, trains and taxis) must be made accessible to all, including those in wheelchairs, although compliance with the law is still many years away in places such as Chicago. (Check with the transportation authority in the city you're visiting to find out which lines are wheelchair accessible.) Telephone companies are required to provide relay operators for the hearing impaired. Many banks now provide ATM instructions in Braille. Curb ramps are common, and some of the busier roadway intersections have audible crossing signals.

Large private and chain hotels have suites for disabled guests. Major car rental agencies offer hand-controlled models at no extra charge. All major airlines, intercity buses and Amtrak trains allow guide dogs to accompany passengers and frequently sell two-for-one packages when seriously disabled passengers require attendants.

Airlines also provide assistance for connecting, boarding and leaving the flight – just ask for assistance when making a reservation. (Note: airlines must accept wheelchairs as checked baggage and have an onboard chair available, though some advance notice may be required on smaller planes.) Of course, the more populous the area, the greater the likelihood of facilities for the disabled, so it's important to call ahead to see what is available.

Global Access: A Network for Disabled Travelers (www.geocities.com/Paris/1502/index.html) provides trip advice, lists of guidebooks for the disabled and an excellent variety of links to other websites with similar information.

A number of organizations and tour providers specialize in the needs of disabled travelers. The Society for the Advancement of Travel for the Handicapped (SATH; ☎ 212-447-7284, 347 Fifth Ave, Suite 610, New York, NY 10016), publishes *Open World* magazine, with practical articles on travel in general and good destinations in particular for the disabled.

SENIOR TRAVELERS

When retirees leave the time clock behind and the myriad 'senior' discounts begin to apply, the prospect of rediscovering the USA exerts a magnetic pull for foreigners and the native-born alike. Though the age when the benefits begin varies with the attraction, travelers from 50 years and up can expect to receive cut rates and benefits. Be sure to inquire about such rates at hotels, museums and restaurants *before* you make your reservation.

Visitors to national parks and campgrounds can cut costs considerably by using the Golden Age Passport, a card that allows US citizens age 62 and older (and those traveling in the same car) free admission nationwide and a 50% reduction on camping fees. You can apply in person at any national park or regional office of the US Forest Service (USFS) or National Park Service (NPS), or call ☎ 800-280-2267 for information and ordering.

TRAVEL WITH CHILDREN

Many establishments and services offer discounted fees and fares for children. Age limits for discounts vary. Hotels and motels may count anyone under 18 as a child, though B&Bs rarely offer discounts and may not welcome children at all. At museums, a child may be someone age three to nine, or five to 12. You'll have to ask at each establishment.

Some restaurants offer a limited selection of inexpensive child-friendly foods; ask for the children's menu. Airlines sometimes discount international fares for children's tickets, but these are often more expensive than the cheapest APEX adult tickets. Many buses and tours have discounted children's prices (often 50% lower). Car rental companies provide infant seats for their cars on request.

Various children's activities are mentioned in appropriate places in this book. For information on enjoying travel with the young ones, read Lonely Planet's *Travel with Children*, written by cofounder Maureen Wheeler.

USEFUL ORGANIZATIONS

AAA

The American Automobile Association ('Triple-A'; ☎ 800-222-4357, www.aaa.com) is an umbrella organization uniting a variety of local and regional auto clubs that use the AAA name. Members belong to a certain club and also may use the facilities of any other AAA club in the USA. Clubs have offices in all major cities and many resort towns where they provide useful information, free maps and routine road services such as tire repair and towing (free within a limited radius).

HI–AYH

Hosteling International–American Youth Hostels (☎ 202-783-6161, fax 783-6171, e hiayhserv@HDiayh.org, www.hiayh.org), PO Box 37613, Washington, DC 20013, is the successor to the International Youth Hostel Federation (IYHF). For hostel listings in the USA and Canada, get HI–AYH's official guide, *Hosteling North America*. For a selection of Great Lakes cities with hostels, see the Accommodations section, later in this chapter.

NPS & USFS

The National Park Service and the US Forest Service administer the use of national parks and forests. National forests are less protected than parks, allowing commercial use of some areas (usually logging or privately owned recreational facilities).

In the Great Lakes, Isle Royale is a key national park in the middle of Lake Superior, off the coast of Michigan. The NPS also administers many other sites, from the Indiana Dunes National Lakeshore to the Lincoln Home National Historic Site, in Springfield, Illinois.

Contact the NPS for national park campground information and for reservations: ☎ 800-365-2267, www.nps.gov, National Park Service Public Inquiry, Department of the Interior, 18th and C Sts NW, Washington, DC 20013. You can also contact the parks in this book directly.

Current information about national forests is available from ranger stations or at www.recreation.gov. National forest campground and reservation information is available at ☎ 800-699-6637 or by visiting the reservation Web site (www.reserveusa.com) or writing to the national forests listed in this book.

DANGERS & ANNOYANCES

The USA has a widespread reputation, partly true but also exaggerated by the media, as a dangerous place because of the availability of firearms. The Great Lakes major cities – Chicago, Detroit, Cleveland Minneapolis–St Paul, Milwaukee, Indianapolis – all suffer to some degree from the crimes of pickpockets, muggers (robbers), carjackers and rapists.

As in other cities throughout the world, the majority of crimes takes place in the poorest neighborhoods among the local residents. The signs of a bad or dangerous neighborhood are obvious, and pretty much the same as in any other country.

As for rural dangers, avoid forests – or indeed anyplace where game and hunters roam – during the hunting seasons, especially at dawn and dusk, when game is most active. 'No Hunting' signs are widely ignored and are not a guarantee of safety. Ask locally for details.

Relentless and evidently starving black flies (spring) and mosquitoes (summer) are an unfortunate reality in the northern woods. Those venturing into the forests and lakes must be prepared to battle these pests, as well as the less numerous but downright vicious deerflies and horseflies. Take a strong liquid repellent, such as Muskol (not advisable for kids), and apply as required. For kids, us a repellent such as Off! or others that are marketed for children and sold in drug stores; given that these repellents are not as strong as Muskol, however, parents will have to ensure kids use enough for the repellent to be effective. Some people are allergic to black fly bites (they get nasty swelling), and for them hats with pull-down netting are an option (these are widely available). Bring a tent with fine mesh screening and set it up in open, breezy, dry areas if possible. Light-colored clothing also helps (sort of), as does a smoky fire. By late summer the bugs are gone, making it an ideal time to wet a paddle or hike a trail.

In winter, thin ice is a deadly hazard for skiers and especially snowmobilers. Always err on the side of caution and don't trust anybody's opinion on ice safety other than that of the police and park or forestry officials. Every year people die after crashing through supposedly frozen lake ice.

Winter blizzards can be severe, especially in the north, and roads can become impassable.

Tornados can occur in the summer, and while they're dramatic, your odds of flying off like Dorothy are about the same as for being struck by lightning. Should your odds run out, however, seek below-ground shelter in buildings or, if you're caught on the open road, lodge yourself under a highway overpass.

EMERGENCIES

Most states, cities and towns in the Midwest are connected to the emergency notification system reached by dialing ☎ 911 from any telephone (no money required). Operators who answer 911 calls can dispatch police, fire and medical services.

In areas without 911 service (or if dialing 911 does not work), dial ☎ 0 for the telephone operator, who will connect you to the necessary local emergency service.

LEGAL MATTERS

If you are stopped by the police for any reason, bear in mind that there usually is no system of paying fines on the spot. For traffic offenses, the police officer will explain your options to you. You may be required to accompany the officer to a magistrate to pay the fine.

If you are arrested for more serious offenses, you are allowed to remain silent, entitled to have a lawyer present during any interrogation and are presumed innocent until proven guilty. There is no legal reason to speak to a police officer if you don't wish to. All persons who are arrested are legally allowed (and given) the right to make one phone call. If you don't have a lawyer or family member to help you, call your embassy or consulate. The police should give you the number upon request.

The minimum age for drinking alcoholic beverages is 21. You'll need a government-issued photo ID (such as a passport or US driver's license) to prove your age. Stiff fines, jail time and penalties can be incurred if you are caught driving under the influence of alcohol or providing alcohol to minors.

BUSINESS HOURS

Public and private office hours are normally 8 or 9 am to 5 pm weekdays.

Banks

Customary banking hours are 9 am to 3 pm weekdays, but most banks have extended customer service hours until 5 pm (or even 8 or 9 pm on some days) and on Saturday from 9 am to 2 pm or later. Banks are usually closed on Sunday.

Fuel Stations

Fuel stations on major highways are open 24 hours a day, seven days a week. In small towns and villages, hours may be only from 7 or 8 am to 7 or 8 pm.

Stores & Markets

Most stores are open Monday through Saturday 9:30 or 10 am to 5:30 or 6 pm (usually later in big cities). Many stores are also open 11 am or noon until 5 pm on Sunday.

All cities, and many large towns, have at least a few 'convenience stores,' open 24 hours, which sell food, beverages, newspapers and some household items. Many highway fuel stations, also open 24 hours, have small shops selling snacks, beverages and frequently needed items.

Most city supermarkets stay open from 8 or 9 am to 9 or 10 pm, with shorter hours on Sunday, but some in large cities remain open 24 hours, closing only from Sunday evening to Monday morning for maintenance.

PUBLIC HOLIDAYS

National public holidays are celebrated throughout the USA. Banks, schools and government offices (including post offices) are closed, and transportation, museums and other services operate on a Sunday schedule. Many stores, however, maintain regular business hours. Holidays falling on weekends are usually observed the following Monday.

New Year's Day	January 1
Martin Luther King Jr Day	3rd Monday in January
Presidents' Day	3rd Monday in February
Memorial Day	Last Monday in May
Independence Day (Fourth of July)	July 4
Labor Day	1st Monday in September
Columbus Day	2nd Monday in October
Veterans' Day	November 11
Thanksgiving	4th Thursday in November
Christmas Day	December 25

ACTIVITIES

The Great Lakes region has a wealth of outdoor activities. You won't find great downhill skiing or world-class climbing or surfing, but you will find oodles of opportunities to enjoy the outdoors. The lakes themselves are lined with little inlets, coves and rivers perfect for small watercraft. For all of the activities listed here, the state tourism boards frequently publish special interest guides.

Bicycling

Illinois has bike paths along the Illinois and Michigan Canal Corridor as well as along the Mississippi River, especially around the Quad Cities.

In Indiana, the area around Bloomington is a hotbed of biking thanks to the Little 500, which fosters a bike-friendly culture. The Indiana Dunes National Lakeshore has long-distance trails. In other areas, such as Indianapolis, old railway lines are being turned into bike paths.

South of Cleveland in Ohio is the Cuyahoga Valley National Recreation Area, which features a 20-mile graded multiuse trail along an old canal route.

Michigan has an enormous, visionary plan to cover the entire state with linked trails, most atop converted railroad beds. (It already leads the nation in the number of tracks converted.) Twenty trails currently exist, 12 are under development, and another dozen are proposed for the near future. And this will only cover a fraction of the state. The Rails to Trails Conservancy (☎ 517-393-6022, ⓔ rtcmich@aol.com) has information.

Biking is excellent in Wisconsin, with state trails ranging from 4 to 90 miles long. Two good routes are the Mountain Bay Trail, from Wasau to Green Bay, and the Bearskin-Hiawatha Trail, from Minocqua to Tomahawk. The 40-mile Military Ridge Trail, west of Madison, is popular. See the boxed text 'Ride the Rails,' in Facts about Wisconsin, for information.

Cycling is immensely popular in Minnesota. Routes vary from jaunts around Lake of the Isles, Lake Calhoun and Lake Harriet, in Minneapolis, to trips along the Mississippi to rugged mountain bike paths. The Root River Trail, in the southeastern bluff country, is a favorite. There is an excellent system of state trails to serve all types of riders.

Skiing

Most parks and preserves in the region are good for cross-country skiing. Many public lands also have rental facilities, and Nordic trails abound.

Although hardly alpine, the Midwest does have some downhill ski areas where you can let gravity do the work.

Illinois and Indiana are primarily Nordic ski areas. The Indiana Dunes National Lakeshore is a favorite in winter and on a clear day has stunning views. Many state and national parks groom trails in winter.

Michigan has great skiing, both Nordic and downhill. For downhill skiing, the Traverse City region has decent options, but it's Big Snow Country in the western UP that holds the lion's share. A triumvirate of hills near Ironwood and Bessemer has just about everything folks are looking for. There are more than 40 other ski resorts to choose from. What the hills lack in jaw-drop vertical runs they make up for in copious quality snow.

In Wisconsin two of the best downhill ski centers are Mt Ashwabay, in Ashland, and Whitecap, in Montreal near Hurley.

Major Minnesota downhill centers are Lutsen Mountain, north of Duluth; Spirit Mountain, south of Duluth; and Giant Ridge, Bibwabik. There are other, smaller resorts in virtually every area of the state.

Snowmobiling

Snowmobiling is huge in the region – all those flat and open spaces are excellent for it.

Illinois, Indiana and Michigan all have snowmobiling areas in state parks and forests. A long trail in Illinois follows the Illinois and Michigan Canal.

Wisconsin was one of the world's pioneers in snowmobiling and remains one of the best places to enjoy it, boasting 25,000 miles of trails, with more than a dozen state trails and many more in the state and national forests. Eagle River hosts the World Championship Snowmobile Derby annually.

In Minnesota, there are state-maintained long-distance trails that include International Falls to Tower, 135 miles; Duluth to Grand Marais, 146 miles; and Ely to Coleraine, 159 miles.

Hiking

Virtually all of the national and state forests, parks and preserves have trails.

In Illinois, the Shawnee National Forest has some good longer hikes. Most of the state parks, such as Starved Rock, are good, as is Mississippi Palisades.

Southern Indiana has numerous hikes in its state parks, in Hoosier National Forest and in Muscatatuck National Wildlife Refuge.

The Buckeye Trail is Ohio's famous trail. It reaches all four corners of the state, topping out at 1200 miles. For more information, contact the Buckeye Trail Association (☎ 614-451-4233), PO Box 254, Worthington, Ohio, 43085.

Michigan's spectacular Isle Royale National Park has a trail system that occupies many a book. Pictured Rocks National Lakeshore has a popular backpacking trail and several short day-hike trails. The Porcupine Mountains are hilly, rugged, isolated and rife with wildlife.

Notable Wisconsin hiking areas are Devil's Lake State Park, Kettle Moraine State Forest, Nicollet National Forest, Rock Island and the county parks in the Pembine-Niagara region.

Minnesota's best trail is the renowned Lake Superior Hiking Trail, heading north out of Duluth and running to the Canadian border. The numerous parks along Lake Superior's north shore offer additional spurs to waterfalls and viewpoints. The bluff country of southeastern Minnesota also offers fine walking.

Climbing

There are numerous places that look good for rock climbing in the Midwest, but often it is banned or you need permits. An official rock climbing area is in Ohio's Hocking Hills State Park. The best place in Wisconsin for rock climbing is Devil's Lake State Park, near Baraboo.

Four Minnesota rock climbing centers are Tettegouche and Temperence state parks, on the north shore; Interstate State Park, at Taylor Falls; and Blue Mounds State Park, near Luverne in the state's southwest corner. State park climbing permits are required.

Boating

Boating and summer are synonymous in much of the Midwest. Many of the lakeland resorts rent boats. Minnesota, Wisconsin, northern Illinois and Michigan are dotted with thousands of lakes popular for boating. The Great Lakes themselves are simply great for sailing, and every town of any size on the water has a marina.

Kayaking

The Lake Michigan shoreline in both Illinois and Indiana is popular with kayakers.

The best kayak experience in Michigan is at Pictured Rocks National Lakeshore or

Isle Royale National Park (you can take kayaks on the ferries).

In Wisconsin, the Apostle Islands and nearby mainland shoreline offer superb sea-kayaking, but these waters are not to be trifled with. Get well briefed by an area outfitter before putting in. Sea kayakers also paddle the bay side of the Door County. For inland white water, the Wolf, Pestigo and Menomonee Rivers are good spots.

The north shore of Lake Superior offers good sea kayaking. Voyageurs National Park, in Minnesota, also offers challenging kayaking amid big waters and countless bays. The St Louis River south of Duluth offers white-water opportunities.

Canoeing

It was the way early Europeans explored the area, and it has been both a popular and at times crucial activity ever since.

The Boundary Waters Canoe Area Wilderness, in Minnesota, is one of the best canoeing regions anywhere. Canoe routes with linking portages to suit every level of skill and preference have been mapped out. The Chippewa and Superior National Forests also offer superb canoeing.

In Illinois, the Illinois and Michigan Canal Corridor has developed canoeing areas. Other good spots include most of the rivers, including the Ohio River in the south and even the Chicago River in the north.

Like its neighbor to the west, Indiana has good canoeing in many of its rivers, especially the Blue and White Rivers in the south. The Chain O' Lakes State Park is a delightful place to slip a canoe into the water.

In Ohio, canoeing is sublime in the Mohican State Park area around Loudonville, northeast of Columbus. Rentals and tours are readily available. The Little Miami River has its headwaters in Clark County and flows southwest over 100 miles; it was the state's first federally designated wild and scenic river.

The most popular canoeing river in Michigan is the Au Sable River near Grayling. It runs 120 miles to Lake Huron. Also popular is the nearby Manistee River.

In Wisconsin, excellent flat-water canoeing is available in the Turtle-Flambeau Flowage, near Mercer. Horicon Marsh offers good bird-watching and plant observation. For white water the Wolf and Pestigo Rivers are recommended.

Diving

No exaggeration, Michigan's diving is superlative. Shipwrecks are well preserved in the almost primevally icy waters. The state has designated nine underwater preserves totaling more than 1900 sq miles and comprising hundreds of wrecks. Lots of charters and rentals are found in towns all along the shoreline. See the boxed text 'Shipwreck Diving' in the Facts about Michigan chapter.

Bird-Watching & Wildlife Viewing

Illinois The Illinois River National Wildlife Refuges are a haven for more than 300 species of birds, including many duck and heron species. The area around Alton on the Mississippi River is a winter home for thousands of bald eagles. Much of the open land in the state is the summer home to scores of butterfly species.

Indiana Indiana has many bird habitats. The midsection is especially popular with songbirds. The Muscatatuck National Wildlife Refuge is home to the ominous-looking turkey vulture and the much more lovely Canada goose.

Ohio There's great bird-watching on the Lake Erie Islands. Look for migrating songbirds and nesting bald eagles.

Michigan Given its amazing stretches of littoral landscape and vast carpets of forestland, it's not surprising that Michigan is home to some 200 prime flora and fauna viewing sites. Most in the Lower Peninsula are found along the Michigan and Huron shorelines. One of the country's largest cattail marshes is found in Cheboygan, southeast of Mackinaw City, in the Lower Peninsula. In these parts is a modest elk herd, one of the only east of the Rocky Mountains.

Wisconsin State parks, wildlife preserves and marshes throughout Wisconsin provide excellent bird-watching. Horicon Marsh is known internationally for its spring and autumn migrations of birds and waterfowl. The Crane Foundation in Baraboo breeds and protects these much-threatened species.

The Upper Mississippi National Wildlife Refuge, north of La Crosse, has 270 bird species, including tundra swans. The state and national forests are home to many mammals, including bears, beavers, coyotes, deer, foxes and moose.

Minnesota A prime spot for birders is Hawk Ridge, in Duluth. Near Wabash you can see eagles and tundra swans; you also can see eagles in Chippewa National Forest and along the Mississippi River south of Red Wing. The Tamarac National Wildlife Refuge, near Detroit Lakes, is good all year but especially during spring and autumn migrations. The Boundary Waters Canoe Area Wilderness has thousands of loons. Bear and moose are also plentiful there.

Fishing

With all the lakes and rivers, fishing is a major pastime in the Great Lakes region. From boats, from land, from piers, and in winter from the ice itself, you can observe lines in the water year-round. More than 5 million people a year fish in the Great Lakes.

Much of Illinois is good for bass. Lake Michigan is popular for smelt fishing. The Ohio River in Indiana is loaded with bass and catfish.

In Ohio, the Mohican State Forest has excellent trout fishing. The area around Sandusky is world-class for walleye fishing. The Lake Erie Charter Boat Information Service (☎ 888-675-3474) can help you find a charter with a competent captain.

Fishing is also big in Michigan, with its isolated forests and 11,000 glacial lakes. Bass, perch, pike and trout are plentiful in Michigan's inland lakes.

In Wisconsin the main fish species are walleye, bass, northern pike and muskellunge. The average muskie in the state is 36 inches long and weighs 12lb. Lake Winnebago and the Wolf and Fox Rivers are good walleye waters.

In Minnesota, walleye, excellent on the table, is the number-one sport fish. The southeastern corner of the state offers miles of good trout streams. Lake Superior, with charters available, has salmon and lake trout.

WORK

It is very difficult for foreigners to get legal work in the US. Securing your own work visa without a sponsor – meaning an employer – is nearly impossible. If you do have a sponsor, they should normally assist or do all the work to secure your visa. But an employer has to show that no US national could do the job, a problem when it comes to the kinds of low-paid temporary jobs many long-term travelers prefer. There is illegal work, and as the millions employed this way show, it's not uncommon. But especially for someone on a tourist visa, this is a very risky move. If you're caught you can be immediately deported and then barred from reentering the US for many years.

There are some seasonal jobs in the touristed areas of Michigan and Wisconsin, but the companies involved don't seem to have any problem recruiting students on break.

ACCOMMODATIONS

The Great Lakes region provides an array of comfortable accommodations. In the countryside, the choices range from simple campsites to lavish country inns. In the cities, mid-range and top-end hotels abound, but truly inexpensive accommodations are rare. The most comfortable accommodations for the lowest prices are usually found in that great American invention, the roadside motel.

In order to keep the cost of accommodations down, observe this rule: visit cities on weekends and the countryside during the week. Most city hotels offer low weekend rates for Friday, Saturday and Sunday nights; most country and resort lodgings reduce their rates by 20% to 45% Monday through Thursday.

At the busiest times (July, August and late September through mid-October), you may have to reserve accommodations well in advance. This is particularly true of B&Bs and inns. However, in cities you may also run into special events such as sporting matches or conventions that suck up all available space.

Camping

If you don't bring your own camping equipment, you can buy good supplies at reasonable prices at many places in the Great Lakes. Superstores such as K-Mart and Wal-Mart are everywhere and have low prices on mass-market gear.

You cannot plan to just stop by the road and camp. With few exceptions, you will have to camp in an established campground. Fortunately, the Great Lakes has lots of them. Most of them are full on weekends in July and August, and many fill up during the week as well, so you must reserve in advance or arrive early in the day to give yourself the best chance of getting a site.

Rough camping is permitted in the backcountry of some national forests, but often it must be at established sites; these may have simple shelters and are usually free.

An inexpensive option is the primitive forest site with only basic services: pit (ie, waterless) toilets, cold running water (perhaps from a pump) and fire rings. These are generally found in national forests and cost about $6.

Standard campsites in state and national parks usually have flush toilets, hot showers (for a fee) and often a dump station for RVs. Tent sites are usually shaded and are sometimes on wooden platforms or grass, with plenty of space between sites. These sites cost between $6 and $20. Most government-run campgrounds stay open only during the summer season, from mid-May to early September or late October. For reservations information at national forests, see the Useful Organizations section, earlier in this chapter. For state parks and forests, see the introductory chapters for the individual states.

Private campgrounds are usually more expensive ($13 to $40) and less spacious, with sites closer together and with less shade, but with lots more entertainment facilities. Most of the sites are for RVs and have water and electric hookups and perhaps sewage hookups. A small grassy area without hookups is usually set aside for tent campers, who are distinctly in the minority and pay the lowest rate. Sometimes hot showers are free, sometimes not. Private campgrounds usually have small shops and snack bars for essentials. Recreation facilities are usually elaborate, with playgrounds, swimming, game rooms and even miniature golf courses. Some private campgrounds are open from late May to early September, some from mid-April through November; a few are open all year.

Hostels

Hostelling is not nearly as well developed in the Midwest as it is in Europe or the more touristed parts of the US. Chicago has some hostels and is expected to have a large new one right downtown in the Loop by the summer of 2000. Other cities with hostels include Columbus, Ohio; Madison, Wisconsin; and Minneapolis, Minnesota.

US citizens or residents can join Hostelling International–American Youth Hostels (HI–AYH; ☎ 202-783-6161, fax 783-6171, ⓔ hiayhserv@HDiayh.org, www.hiayh.org), PO Box 37613, Washington DC 20013, by requesting or downloading a membership form and mailing or faxing it in. Membership can also be purchased at regional council offices and at many (but not all) youth hostels. Non-US residents should buy a membership in their home countries. If not, they can still stay in US hostels by purchasing 'Welcome Stamps' for each night they stay in a hostel. When they have six stamps, the stamp card becomes a one-year HI–AYH membership card valid throughout the world.

Motels

Motels range from small, homey, cheap, 10-room places in need of paint and wallpaper to lavish resorts with manicured lawns and gardens, vast restaurants and resort-style facilities. Prices range from $30 to $100 or more. On the highway or on the outskirts of any but the largest cities, you can get a comfortable motel room for $50 to $75. The cheapest motels are invariably the small local ones that are not members of a national chain, which makes it more difficult to find out about them.

Motel rooms often have small refrigerators, and motels always provide free ice for drinks and usually have vending machines for soft drinks and snacks. Many motels have restaurants attached or nearby; if not, most provide a simple breakfast of muffins or rolls, fruit and coffee, often at no extra charge – although the coffee is often weak and the muffins stale. Most motels (excluding the very cheapest) have swimming pools.

Most motels also provide toll-free reservations lines, and the chains have websites. See the Toll-Free & Web Site Directory at the back of this book.

Hotels

City hotels are mostly large and fairly lavish. There are few of the small, inexpensive 'boutique' hotels like those found in London or Paris. Hotel rooms provide similar services to motel rooms but are usually a bit more inclusive. Standard hotel services include restaurants and bars, room service for meals and beverages, and exercise rooms ('health clubs'). Many city hotels set aside several floors as special 'executive' sections, with more elaborate decoration and a central lounge with an attendant.

Prices range from $80 to $200 and up per night, with most between $100 and $150. Weekend discounts and special weekend packages offer significant savings. Be sure to ask about them when you call to inquire about prices and make reservations. Most hotels provide toll-free reservations lines and the chains have websites. See the Toll-Free & Web Site Directory at the back of this book.

B&Bs

In the 1960s, young American tourists flooded Europe and discovered the convenient, congenial and above all, inexpensive B&Bs, *pensions, gasthöfen* and *pensioni*. They took the experience home to America, but, as with most imports to America, it was thoroughly Americanized.

European visitors should be aware that North American bed-and-breakfasts are often not the casual, inexpensive sort of accommodations found on the continent or in the UK. Although they are usually family-run, most B&Bs are like small inns, and they require advance reservations. Some are relentlessly charming, with overwhelmingly frilly decor and theatrically adorable hosts (and pets). Some have the services and amenities of minor resort hotels, and prices to match.

The simpler B&Bs in smaller towns or resorts may charge $60 to $85 for single or double rooms with shared bath, breakfast included. Fancier B&Bs in or near the more popular resorts charge $75 to $150 per night for a room with private bath. At peak times, from mid-July through early September and late September through mid-October, as well as on holiday weekends, prices at the fanciest B&Bs in the most popular resort towns may rise to $175 or even above $200.

B&B rooms vary in size, appointments and conveniences. Most have private bathrooms. Some have air-con and TVs; most do not.

Breakfast may be store-bought cake or muffins and instant coffee; fresh-baked pastries and a selection of fresh-brewed stimulants; a full American-style breakfast of bacon or ham and eggs, toast or muffins, fruit, cereal and milk; or any variation of those. Usually it's pretty good.

In the most popular resort towns, B&Bs may have restrictive policies: a minimum stay of two or three days may be required on weekends; bills may have to be paid in advance by check or in cash (not by credit card); and cancellations may be subject to a processing fee, or worse.

Rental Accommodations

Renting a cottage or condominium for a week or two in the summer vacation areas of the northern Great Lakes region is a popular vacation option, but not particularly easy for those who do not live in the region. There is no central registry of vacation rental properties. The best you can do is contact the local visitors' centers and ask for listings of available properties.

Resorts

Aside from abundant inns, motels, hotels and campgrounds, the northern halves of Michigan, Wisconsin and Minnesota offer a tremendous range of resorts. These holiday centers, generally booked for a week or longer, consist of housekeeping cottages for rent with boats, a beach and activities as part of the package. They range from rustic to deluxe.

FOOD

The introductory chapters for the states describe local specialties. Throughout the Great Lakes you can get a wide range of foods, from the ubiquitous fast-food fare to excellent ethnic cuisines to gourmet delights that take full advantage of local produce.

In major cities you can eat well around the clock; in smaller towns your late-night and off-hours eating choices may be limited to chain coffee shops along the highway. In the smallest of places, be aware that the sidewalks roll up often by 9 pm sharp. Country folk tend to eat early, so don't plan on dining continental style.

That said, there are no shortages of places to fit any budget, even in a large city like Chicago.

Many bakeries, snack shops, cafés and small restaurants in resort areas prepare food to take away. Most supermarkets have delicatessen counters where you can buy cold meats, cheeses, salads, pâtés, dips, spreads and other picnic and quick-meal items.

Vacation cottages and condominiums usually have kitchens or kitchenettes.

DRINKS

Nonalcoholic Drinks

You can get any kind of domestic soft drink or bottled water you'd like anywhere in the Midwest. Tap water is safe to drink virtually everywhere and usually is quite palatable.

Americans are among the world's most frequent coffee drinkers. Traditionally, American coffee is brewed from a light-brown roasted bean and is weaker than that preferred in Europe. Espresso is readily available, as are American versions of other European favorites such as café au lait, cappuccino and caffe latte. True to form, the American versions are often elaborate concoctions with endless variations – vanilla, raspberry or cinnamon flavoring, for instance – but little regard for the quality of the underlying coffee. Still, cities and most larger towns have specialty coffee shops where beans are roasted frequently, ground shortly before brewing and brewed by bean variety or origin, to order.

Tea likewise comes in bewildering variety. It is often served with lemon, unless milk is specified. Herbal teas of many kinds are readily available; decaffeinated tea is also available. Iced tea with lemon is a popular summer drink.

Alcoholic Drinks

The Great Lakes region has vineyards, wineries and craft breweries producing palatable, even excellent, regional vintages and beers.

Beverage Laws The sale of alcoholic beverages is governed by federal, state and

No Smoking

Smoking is prohibited in most public buildings, such as airports, train and bus stations, offices, hospitals and stores, and on public conveyances (subways, trains, buses, planes, etc). Except for the designated smoking areas in some restaurants, bars and a few other enclosed places, you must step outside to smoke. (It's now common to see office workers standing outside near a door to their building, puffing away.)

local laws. See the Information sections of the state chapters for details.

You are not allowed to drink alcohol, even beer, in most fast-food restaurants, such as hamburger, doughnut, pizza or sandwich shops. When in doubt, look for beer advertisements, such as a neon sign in the window, or ask inside.

Public drinking is also often prohibited outdoors – you usually may not take alcoholic beverages to the park, beach or forest trail, or drink on a sidewalk – though if you are discreet and keep bottles out of view, you can usually get away with having wine or beer with your picnic. However at many festivals and other special events public drinking is OK.

Do not have any open alcoholic beverage containers in your car. In some states, the driver may be prosecuted for drunk driving (a serious offense) if any open alcoholic beverage container is found in a car he or she is operating – even if the alcohol is being consumed exclusively by the passengers.

ENTERTAINMENT

The Great Lakes is rich in opportunities for entertainment in music, dance and theater or just hanging out in a bar. Local newspapers often have a section with entertainment listings.

Bars & Clubs

The older industrial cities often have a wide range of bars dating from the days when they were havens for off-the-clock factory workers. Chicago and Milwaukee are examples of cities that now have an astonishing array of bars and nightspots catering to every imaginable taste.

The suburbs often are left with charmless chain bars with manufactured themes. Rural areas can have some real gems – places filled with local color and down-home culture.

Live Music

Most towns have live music venues where local bands play. Large cities such as Detroit, Chicago and St Louis have vibrant local music scenes where you can here anything from rock to blues to jazz and beyond.

Performing Arts

The major cities again have large and well-funded cultural institutions offering classical music, dance, opera and more. Some smaller towns such as Bloomington, Indiana, have very respectable cultural groups thanks to the presence of large universities.

Chicago and Minneapolis both have excellent reputations for theater.

SPECTATOR SPORTS

All the major cities and even some smaller ones such as Green Bay have one or more professional sports teams. Whether they play football, baseball, basketball or hockey, these teams usually generate fierce loyalty from fans.

College football also has a very strong following. The 'Big 10' is the name of the athletic conference of the top schools in the

Midwest. Nine of them are in the Great Lakes region: Northwestern University, the University of Illinois, Purdue University, Indiana University, Ohio State University, the University of Michigan, Michigan State University, the University of Wisconsin and the University of Minnesota. (The 10th is the Pennsylvania State University.) Big 10 football is filled with tradition, and a game at one of the schools in this book should not be missed. A Saturday football game at a Big 10 school – or at Notre Dame, in South Bend, Indiana – is a memorable and for many a classic Great Lakes experience.

Basketball, especially that played in Indiana – even in high school – is a religion to many and another classic Midwestern experience.

SHOPPING

There's no shortage of stuff to buy around the Great Lakes. You can usually tell what the local specialty is in a tourist area by the number of places peddling it – however, don't ever fall for fudge, that perennial tourist treat, as a specialty.

In the north, smoked fish is common and delicious. Other foodstuffs include wild rice in Wisconsin, maple syrup in Illinois and Indiana and anything made with cherries in Michigan.

More lasting items include works by local artists and the antiques and collectibles at the growing number of stores selling such items throughout the six states.

New items can be considerable bargains for people not just from more expensive parts of the US but also from abroad. The old formula is that the worse a strip mall or discount center looks, the better its prices. There are also huge soulless regional malls everywhere, including especially giant ones in Bloomington, Minnesota, and Schaumburg, Illinois. But these indoor malls are mind-numbing and contain the same chain stores found throughout the US.

Non-Americans might be stunned to discover that most American cities have closed down their downtown shopping districts in favor of suburban malls. Notable exceptions include Indianapolis and Minneapolis, which both have large downtown malls, and Chicago, which not only has numerous vibrant neighborhood shopping districts but also one of the best shopping streets in the country: N Michigan Ave.

RICK GERHARTER

Capitalist swine on the Chicago trading floor

RICK GERHARTER

Chicago's not-necessarily-Rapid Transit Authority, the 'el'

JOHN ELK III

Cornfield of dreams in rural Minnesota

JOHN ELK III

A 610-foot ore freighter in Canal Park, Duluth (MN)

RICHARD CUMMINS

RICHARD CUMMINS

RICK GERHARTER

JOHN ELK III

RICK GERHARTER

Don't get dizzy looking at the Great Lakes region's many architectural splendors.

Getting There & Away

AIR

Airports

There are several major international airports in the Great Lakes region; some are hubs for large US airlines. See the Getting There & Away sections of the relevant city listings. The airports listed here are all served by the major US airlines.

Chicago O'Hare International Airport is the busiest airport in the US and has the most international air links in the region. It is a hub for United Airlines and American Airlines, each of which has hundreds of flights to destinations throughout the US and internationally. Many of the world's major international airlines, especially those from Europe, serve O'Hare.

Midway Airport is a smaller facility that is home to several domestic discount carriers.

Other Major Airports Detroit Metropolitan Airport is a hub for Northwest Airlines. It has some international links to Europe and Asia.

Cleveland Hopkins International Airport is a major domestic destination and is served by all the large US airlines.

Cincinnati International Airport is a hub for Delta Air Lines. It has some international flights to Europe.

Lambert–St Louis International Airport, in Missouri, is a hub for TWA. It has some international flights to Europe.

Minneapolis–St Paul International Airport is a hub for Northwest Airlines. It has some international links to Europe and Asia.

Milwaukee, Columbus and Indianapolis have airports that are served with flights from the major cities on both US coasts. Travel to and from other destinations usually requires a change of plane at a large hub airport like those listed previously. Scores of smaller cities and towns around the Great Lakes are served by flights from these hub airports, often on small commuter aircraft.

Airlines

Some of the major airlines operating services to or within the region are Air Canada, Air France, AirTran, American Airlines, British Airways, Canadian Airlines, Continental Airlines, Delta Air Lines, Lufthansa, Northwest Airlines, Southwest Airlines, TWA and United Airlines. See the Toll-Free & Web Site Directory for phone numbers and Web addresses.

Buying Tickets

Airfares in the US range from incredibly low to heights that enter the realm of fantasy. At the time of writing, there were more than a hundred separate roundtrip fares between New York and Chicago, ranging from $154 to $2234. That means some people are paying $154 while others are paying $2234 to fly on the same airplane.

Here's a rough idea of what you can expect to pay for flights using the most

Warning

The information in this chapter is particularly vulnerable to change: Prices for international travel are volatile, routes are introduced and canceled, schedules change, special deals come and go, and rules and visa requirements are amended. Airlines and governments seem to take a perverse pleasure in making price structures and regulations as complicated as possible. You should check directly with the airline or a travel agent to make sure you understand how a fare (and ticket you may buy) works. In addition, the travel industry is highly competitive and there are many lurks and perks.

The upshot of this is that you should get opinions, quotes and advice from as many airlines and travel agents as possible before you part with your hard-earned cash. The details given in this chapter should be regarded as pointers and are not a substitute for your own careful, up-to-date research.

heavily restricted (and therefore cheapest) roundtrip tickets to and from the major Great Lakes airports listed previously:

Major cities within 500 miles	\$150 to \$300
The South and the East Coast	\$250 to \$400
The West and the West Coast	\$350 to \$550

To get an idea of fares, try these online reservations services:

www.bestfares.com
www.counciltravel.com
www.expedia.msn.com
www.statravel.com
www.travelocity.com

In addition, the individual airline Web sites often have Web-only discounts.

Keep in mind that your local travel agent may be able to find you the best deal of all, although because of cuts in airline commissions, many travel agents have been forced to charge small fees for making reservations and issuing tickets. For example, if an agent saves you \$60 on a fare and charges you \$10 for the service, you'll still save \$50. But also note that travel agents may not be able to get you tickets with discount carriers such as Southwest, Vanguard, Frontier and AirTran. For these airlines you'll have to go direct to the carrier.

In the USA, the *Boston Globe, New York Times, Los Angeles Times, Chicago Tribune, San Francisco Examiner* and other major newspapers have weekly travel sections with many advertisements for discounted airfares. Council Travel (☎ 800-226-8624)

Air Travel Glossary

Baggage Allowance This will be written on your ticket and usually includes one 20kg (44lb) item to go in the hold, plus one item of hand luggage.

Bucket Shops Also known as 'consolidators,' these are unbonded travel agencies specializing in discounted airline tickets.

Cancellation Penalties If you have to cancel or change a discounted ticket, there are often heavy penalties involved; insurance can sometimes be taken out against these penalties. Some airlines impose penalties on regular tickets as well, particularly against 'no-show' passengers.

Check-In Airlines ask you to check in a certain time ahead of the flight departure (usually one to two hours on international flights). If you fail to check in on time and the flight is overbooked, the airline can cancel your booking and give your seat to somebody else.

Confirmation Having a ticket written out with the flight and date you want doesn't mean you have a seat until the agent has checked with the airline that your status is confirmed. Until then you could just be 'on request.'

Courier Fares Businesses often need to send urgent documents or freight securely and quickly. Courier companies hire people to accompany the package through customs and, in return, offer a discount ticket that is sometimes a phenomenal bargain. In effect, what the companies do is ship their freight as your luggage on regular commercial flights. This is a legitimate operation, but there are two shortcomings – the short turnaround time of the ticket (usually not longer than a month) and the limitation on your luggage allowance. You may have to surrender all your baggage allowance and take only carry-on luggage.

ITX An ITX, or 'independent inclusive tour excursion,' is often available on tickets to popular holiday destinations. Officially it's a package deal combined with hotel accommodations, but many agents will sell you one of these for the flight only and give you phony hotel vouchers in the unlikely event that you're challenged at the airport.

Lost Tickets If you lose your airline ticket, an airline will usually treat it like a traveler's check and, after inquiries, issue you another one. Legally, however, an airline is entitled to treat it like cash, and if you lose it, it's gone forever. Take good care of your tickets.

and STA Travel (☎ 800-777-0112) have offices in major cities nationwide and may offer good fares.

In Canada, Travel CUTS (www.travelcuts.com) has offices in all major cities and often has fare bargains. The *Globe & Mail* and *Vancouver Sun* carry ads for low fares; the magazine *Great Expeditions*, PO Box 8000-411, Abbotsford, BC V2S 6H1, is also useful.

The travel sections of magazines such as *Time Out* and *TNT* in the UK, or the Saturday editions of the *Sydney Morning Herald* and *The Age* in Australia, carry ads offering cheap fares. STA Travel also has offices worldwide.

The magazine *Travel Unlimited*, PO Box 1058, Allston, MA 02134, publishes details of the cheapest international airfares and courier possibilities.

Return (roundtrip) tickets usually work out to be much cheaper than two one-way fares.

Discount Tickets If you call a major airline and book a same-day roundtrip flight to Chicago from Los Angeles or New York, the fare can be as high as $800 or even more. If you purchase a ticket at least a week in advance and stay over a Saturday night before returning, the roundtrip fare can be as low as $154 to $358.

The rules are complex, but buying as far in advance as possible and staying over a Saturday night usually get you the best fare. Also, certain times of the year are cheaper to fly than others – particularly mid-January through March and October through mid-December, except for Thanksgiving. Also,

Air Travel Glossary

MCO An MCO, or 'miscellaneous charge order,' is a voucher that looks like an airline ticket but carries no destination or date. It can be exchanged through any International Association of Travel Agents (IATA) airline for a ticket on a specific flight. It's a useful alternative to an onward ticket in those countries that demand one and is more flexible than an ordinary ticket if you're unsure of your route.

On Request This is an unconfirmed booking for a flight.

Onward Tickets An entry requirement for many countries is that you have a ticket out of the country. If you're unsure of your next move, the easiest solution is to buy the cheapest onward ticket to a neighboring country or a ticket from a reliable airline that can later be refunded if you do not use it.

Open Jaw Tickets These are return tickets on which you fly out to one place but return from another. If available, open jaw tickets can save you from backtracking to your arrival point.

Point-to-Point Tickets These are discount tickets that can be bought on some routes in return for passengers waiving their rights to a stopover.

Reconfirmation At least 72 hours prior to departure time of an onward or return flight, you must contact the airline and 'reconfirm' that you intend to be on the flight. If you don't do this, the airline can delete your name from the passenger list and you could lose your seat.

Restrictions Discounted tickets often have various restrictions on them, such as advance payment, minimum and maximum periods you must be away (eg, a minimum of two weeks or a maximum of one year), and penalties for changing the tickets.

Standby This is a discounted ticket on which you fly only if there is a seat free at the last moment. Standby fares are usually available only on domestic routes.

Travel Periods Ticket prices vary with the time of year. There is a low (off-peak) season and a high (peak) season, and often a low-shoulder season and a high-shoulder season as well. Usually the fare depends on your outward flight – if you depart in the high season and return in the low season, you pay the high-season fare.

flights on certain days (Tuesday, Wednesday, Thursday, Saturday and Sunday) may be cheaper than others, and flights at certain times (10 am to 3 pm and after 8 pm on weekdays; Saturday after noon and Sunday before noon) may be cheaper as well.

The cheapest tickets are what the airlines call 'nonrefundable,' even though you may be able to get your money (or at least some of it) back under certain circumstances. A good strategy to use when buying a nonrefundable ticket is to schedule your return flight for the latest possible date you're likely to use it. In many cases, an airline will allow you to fly standby at no extra charge if you return earlier than your scheduled flight; but if you want to fly later, you may have to pay a penalty or buy another ticket entirely.

Holiday Periods At holiday times it can be difficult, if not impossible, to get the flights you want unless you plan – and purchase your ticket – well in advance. Holiday times include Christmas, New Year's, Easter, Memorial Day, Labor Day and *especially* Thanksgiving, the busiest travel time of the year in the US. Not only do the planes fill up early during these times, but discount tickets are virtually impossible to find. See When to Go, in the Facts for the Visitor chapter, for more on holiday travel.

Special Fares for Foreign Visitors Just about all domestic carriers offer special fares to visitors who are not US citizens. Typically, you must purchase a booklet of coupons in conjunction with a flight into the USA from a foreign country other than Canada or Mexico. Each coupon in the booklet entitles you to a single flight segment on the issuing airline. However, you may have to use all the coupons within a limited period of time, and there may be other restrictions, such as a limit of two transcontinental flights (ie, flights all the way across the USA).

United Airlines has the most flights in the Great Lakes region, and its program is typical of those offered by major US carriers. Their Visit USA Airpass starts at $380 for three flight segments and must be purchased along with a ticket to the US. You can purchase additional segments for prices that make the program an excellent bargain.

Round-the-World Tickets RTW tickets can be a great deal if you want to visit other countries as well as the USA. Often they work out to be no more expensive – or even less expensive – than a simple roundtrip ticket to the USA, so you get the extra stops for nothing. They're of most value for trips that combine the USA with Europe, Asia, and Australia or New Zealand. RTW itineraries that include stops in South America or Africa can be substantially more expensive. For fliers in search of comfort, business class RTW fares can actually be an excellent value, albeit for prices still higher than economy class.

Official airline RTW tickets are usually put together by a combination of two or three airlines, and they permit you to fly to a specified number of stops on their routes as long as you don't backtrack. Other restrictions are that you must usually book the first sector in advance, and cancellation penalties apply. The tickets are valid for a fixed period, usually one year. An alternative type of RTW ticket is one put together by a travel agent using a combination of discounted tickets.

Most airlines restrict the number of sectors that can be flown within the USA and Canada to three or four, and some airlines even 'black out' a few heavily traveled routes (such as Honolulu to Tokyo). In most cases, a 14-day advance purchase is required. After the RTW ticket is purchased, dates can usually be changed without penalty, and tickets can be rewritten to add or delete stops for $50 each.

From Australia, a ticket that uses United, Lufthansa and Thai, with several stops in the USA, costs about A$2500. A cheap deal with Qantas and Air France flies to Los Angeles, has an open-jaw segment across the USA (enabling you to fly into one city and leave from another), then includes flights from New York to Europe, Asia and back to Australia, for A$1880. There are many other possibilities with Qantas and various partner airlines, ranging from A$1500 to A$3200.

From New Zealand, a ticket via North America, Europe and Asia with Air New Zealand and other airlines costs NZ$2300 and up.

Getting 'Bumped' Airlines routinely overbook flights, knowing that there are always numerous 'no-shows' (people with reservations who do not take the flight). When no-shows leave empty seats, the seats become available to standby passengers. When there are few no-shows and there are more people than seats, the airline must 'bump' excess passengers onto later flights.

If it appears that passengers will have to be bumped, the gate agent first asks for volunteers. Those willing are booked on the next available flight to their destination and are also offered an incentive, which can be a voucher good for a roundtrip flight on the airline – or at least a discount on a flight – at a later date. In extreme circumstances or when faced with a hard bargainer, the airlines may even offer cash, or both cash and a flight pass.

If your schedule is flexible (the next available flight may not be until the next day), getting bumped can be a bonanza: If the airline is desperate or you are hard bargainer, you might get cash or credit for a future ticket and a free room and meals for the night. When you check in at the gate, ask if the plane is oversold and if there may be a call for volunteers. If so, leave your name so you'll get first choice. When it comes time to collect your incentive, keep in mind that you do not have to accept the airline's first offer. You can haggle for a better reward.

Baggage & Other Restrictions

Baggage regulations are set by each airline but usually allow you to check two bags of average size and weight and to carry at least one smaller bag onto the plane. If you are carrying many pieces of luggage, or pieces that are particularly big, bulky, fragile or heavy (such as a bicycle or other sports equipment), check with the airline about special procedures and extra charges.

Your ticket folder usually gives details of items that are illegal to carry on airplanes, either in checked baggage or on your person. These may include weapons, aerosols, tear gas and pepper spray, camp-stove fuel canisters and full oxygen tanks. You may carry matches and lighters on your person, but do not put them in checked luggage.

Smoking is prohibited on all domestic flights within the USA and on most international flights to and from the USA. Most airports in the USA prohibit smoking except in designated areas.

Travelers with Special Needs

If you have special needs of any sort – a broken leg, dietary restrictions, dependence on a wheelchair, responsibility for a baby, fear of flying – airports and airlines can be surprisingly helpful, but you should let them know as soon as possible so that they can make arrangements accordingly. You should also remind them when you reconfirm your booking (at least 72 hours before departure) and again when you check in at the airport.

Guide dogs for the blind must often travel in a specially pressurized baggage compartment with other animals, away from their owners, though small guide dogs may be admitted to the cabin. Guide dogs are not subject to quarantine as long as they have proof of being vaccinated against rabies.

Deaf travelers can ask that airport and in-flight announcements be written down for them.

Children under two years of age travel for 10% of the standard fare (or free on some airlines), as long as they don't occupy a seat, but they usually don't receive a baggage allowance. 'Skycots' may be provided by the airline if requested in advance; these will hold a child weighing up to 22lb (10kg). Children between the ages of two and 12 can sometimes occupy a seat for half to two-thirds of the full fare and do get a baggage allowance. Strollers usually must be checked at the aircraft door; they are returned to you at the door right after the aircraft lands.

Departure Tax

There's a $6 airport departure tax charged to all passengers bound for a foreign destination, as well as a $6.50 North American Free Trade Agreement (NAFTA) tax charged to passengers entering the USA from a foreign country. There may also be smaller airport usage and security fees payable, depending on which airport you fly to or from. Airport departure taxes are normally included in the cost of tickets bought in the USA. If you bought your ticket outside the USA, you may have to pay the tax when you check in for your departing flight.

The USA

Arriving If you are flying direct on an international flight to one of the airports in the Great Lakes region such as Chicago, Detroit or Minneapolis, you will clear immigration and customs on arrival. However, if your flight involves a change of planes at some hub airport such as New York, Washington, DC, or San Francisco, than you will be subjected to those formalities at the first US airport you reach. Your connecting flight will be an internal, or domestic, flight.

As you approach the USA, your flight's cabin crew will hand out a customs and immigration form for you to fill in. Once in the arrivals area, choose the proper immigration line: US citizens or non-US citizens. After immigration, pick up your luggage in the customs area and proceed to an officer, who will ask you a few questions and perhaps check your luggage. The dog sniffing around the luggage is looking for drugs, explosives and restricted agricultural and food products.

If the airport where you enter the US is not your final destination, you must check your luggage again.

See the Customs and Visas & Documents sections in the Facts for the Visitor chapter for other pertinent information.

Leaving You should check in for international flights at least two hours early. During check-in procedures, you might be asked for photo identification, and you will be asked questions about whether you packed your own bags, whether anyone else has had access to them since you packed them and whether you have received any parcels to carry. These questions are for security purposes.

Canada

The major Great Lakes airports receive daily direct and nonstop flights from most major Canadian cities, with Toronto, Montreal and Ottawa having the most frequent service. Carriers include Air Canada, American, Canadian, Delta, Northwest and United. Discount fares range from $200 to $400.

Major Canadian newspapers such as the *Globe & Mail* carry travel agencies' advertisements. The Canadian Federation of Students' Travel CUTS travel agency (www.travelcuts.com) offers low fares and has offices in major cities throughout Canada.

Australia & New Zealand

In Australia and New Zealand, STA Travel is a major dealer in cheap airfares.

Qantas (☎ 13 13 13 in Australia) flies to Los Angeles from Sydney, and Air New Zealand (☎ 0800 737 000 in New Zealand) flies there from Auckland. United (☎ 131 777 in Australia; ☎ 09 379 3800 in New Zealand) flies to San Francisco from Sydney and to Los Angeles from Sydney, Melbourne and Auckland. Connector flights are available to the Great Lakes. Fares are generally around A$2500 (US$1575) to A$2777 (US$1750) roundtrip from Melbourne or Sydney to Chicago.

The UK

The Globetrotters Club (www.globetrotters.co.uk), BCM Roving, London WC1N 3XX, publishes a newsletter called *Globe* that covers destinations worldwide and can help you find traveling companions. Check the free magazines widely available in London – start by looking outside the main railway stations.

Travel Agents Most British travel agents are registered with the Association of

British Travel Agents (ABTA; www.abta.com). If you have paid for your flight through an ABTA-registered agent who then goes out of business, ABTA will guarantee a refund or an alternative.

Besides the many official fares published by the airlines and sold by them and their travel agencies, there are also 'unofficial' bucket shop fares. These seats are sold by the airlines in bulk at a big discount to wholesale brokers, who then sell them to the public and hope to make a profit. If you deal with a reputable shop or agency, these fares can be a good value on the major airlines. Most such fares are nonrefundable (see Discount Tickets earlier in this chapter).

London is arguably the world's headquarters for bucket shops, which are well advertised and can usually beat published airline fares. Two reliable agents for cheap tickets in the UK are Trailfinders (☎ 0171-938-3366, www.trailfinders.co.uk), 46 Earls Court Rd, London W8 6EJ, and STA Travel (☎ 0171-937-9962, www.statravel.co.uk), 74 Old Brompton Rd, London SW7. Trailfinders produces a lavishly illustrated brochure including airfare details.

The very cheapest flights are often advertised by obscure bucket shops whose names haven't yet reached the telephone directory. Many such firms are honest and solvent, but there are a few rogues who will take your money and disappear, only to reopen elsewhere a month or two later under a new name. If you feel suspicious about a firm, don't give them all the money at once – leave a deposit of 20% or so and pay the rest when you receive the ticket. If they insist on cash in advance, go elsewhere. And once you have the ticket, phone the airline to confirm that you are booked on the flight.

Fares & Flights In 1999 some of the lowest airfares in recent memory were available across the North Atlantic. You could easily get a roundtrip economy ticket between London and Chicago for about $300 for much of the year. It remains to be seen if this situation will persist. Normally, expect to pay about $300 during the coldest winter months (except around Thanksgiving and Christmas, when fares soar), $500 during the shoulder months of April, May, September and October and $700 during the peak summer season.

There are nonstop flights between London and the following Great Lakes cities:

Chicago – American (which also serves Manchester), British Airways, United and Virgin Atlantic

Detroit – British Airways and Northwest

Cincinnati – Delta

St Louis – TWA

Minneapolis – Northwest

Continental Europe

Airfares between large European cities and the US generally follow the same pattern as those from London.

All the major European airlines have service to Chicago from their respective hub airports. American and United also have numerous flights between Europe and Chicago. Airlines and the hub airports they serve include the following:

Air France: Paris

Alitalia: Milan

American Airlines: Brussels, Frankfurt, Glasgow, Madrid, Milan, Paris, Stockholm, Zurich

Iberia: Madrid

KLM: Amsterdam

LOT: Warsaw

Lufthansa: Frankfurt, Munich

Sabena: Brussels

SAS: Copenhagen, Stockholm, Zurich

Swissair: Zurich

United: Dusseldorf, Frankfurt, Paris

Nonstop services to other major Great Lakes airports include the following:

Detroit – Northwest: Frankfurt, Paris
Lufthansa: Frankfurt

Cincinnati – Delta: Frankfurt, Paris

St Louis – TWA: Paris

Minneapolis – Northwest: Amsterdam, Frankfurt, Paris

Central & South America

Most flights from Central and South America go via Miami, Dallas–Fort Worth or Los Angeles, although United has nonstop service between Chicago and Buenos Aires and Sao Paulo. American, Northwest and United all have routes to Mexico from their hubs. Mexicana flies between Chicago and Mexico City. Aeromexico and the airlines of the Central American nations (Aeroquetzal, Aeronica, Aviateca, COPA, LACSA and TACA) have flights to either Miami or New York, with connections to the Great Lakes. Fares vary widely on these routes. The nonstop services to and from Mexico City are usually the cheapest.

Africa

Coming from Africa to the Great Lakes region will require flying one of the European carriers to its European hub airport and then transferring to a flight to one of that carrier's Great Lakes destinations, such as Chicago, Detroit or Minneapolis–St Paul. The one exception is South Africa: you can fly direct to New York from Johannesburg and then transfer to a domestic carrier for the remainder of your journey (although that may involve a nettlesome change of airports in New York). Competition for tickets between the Great Lakes region and Africa is thin, so don't expect bargains. You will easily pay $2000 for an economy ticket.

Asia

Hong Kong is the discount-ticket capital of the region, but its bucket shops can be unreliable. Ask the advice of other travelers before buying a ticket. STA Travel has branches in Hong Kong, Tokyo, Singapore, Bangkok and Kuala Lumpur. You can sometimes find bargain airfares for as low as $900 roundtrip from Hong Kong to Chicago, though normal fares are more like $1200. Nonstop services to the Great Lakes include the following:

Chicago – American: Tokyo
JAL: Tokyo
United: Hong Kong, Tokyo

Detroit – Northwest: Osaka, Seoul, Tokyo

Minneapolis – Northwest: Hong Kong, Osaka, Seoul, Tokyo

BUS

Big, comfortable, air-conditioned buses connect most cities and some towns in the USA. However, as the private auto is king, and air service is faster in this big country, bus service is limited. You can get to the Great Lakes by bus from all parts of the USA, Canada and Mexico, but the trip will be long and tedious and ultimately won't be much less expensive than a discounted flight. Bus travel usually makes sense only for those traveling alone, because couples and families can travel more quickly, pleasantly and independently by rental car at about the same expense.

Greyhound

As with planes and trains, Chicago is the region's major hub for buses run by Greyhound (☎ 800-231-2222, www.greyhound.com) the major interstate carrier in the US. Many routes from around the country come through Chicago, and these same routes may well pass through other Great Lakes cities and towns that interest you.

Fares Greyhound frequently offers special travel plans and promotional fares. Following are regular one-way fares and travel times for some sample journeys to the Great Lakes.

route	fare	duration
Seattle to Minneapolis	$97	36 hours
San Francisco to Chicago	$105	46 hours
Los Angeles to Chicago	$104	46 hours
Dallas to St Louis	$81	16 hours
New Orleans to Indianapolis	$113	19 hours
Toronto to Detroit	$44	5 hours
New York to Cleveland	$93	10 hours
Miami to Cincinnati	$102	28 hours

Ameripass This pass, good for unlimited use of Greyhound buses, will make your wallet happy even if your tired butt won't be. A seven-day pass costs $169 for adults, $159 for students, $85 for seniors and children. They are available in numerous permutations up to the marathon 60-day model, which costs $479/439/240. The pass can be purchased at any Greyhound station. If you buy the pass through the Greyhound Web site you have to do so 14 days in advance, but you also save 15%.

An international Ameripass is available for holders of non-US passports. It costs $149/74 adults/children for the seven-day model. This also has numerous permutations, topping out at $429/214 for the 60-day variety, which surely should qualify any user for an advanced degree in American studies, if not sociology or psychology. These passes can also be purchased at Greyhound stations, but if you want the 15% Web discount, you have to buy 21 days in advance.

TRAIN

Visitors from Europe will be appalled at the state of train travel in the US. The quasi-governmental agency Amtrak is the sole provider of interstate service, and it provides very little.

Thanks to penurious government funders, trains in the US are slow and infrequent (Chicago's superb Metra commuter rail system is an exception). But if that keeps most Americans from using trains to get anywhere, it shouldn't stop you. The slow pace of the trains is perfect for sightseeing, and many of the routes run past magnificent scenery. In urban areas, the trains provide a view into residents' backyards, giving you an unvarnished look at how people really live. One thing that's immediately apparent is that Americans keep a lot of crap piled up.

The trains themselves are very comfortable. Lacking speed and frequency, they are filled with amenities to lure people aboard: Dining cars and lounge cars dispense food and drink, and on long-distance trips special sightseeing cars have extra-large windows that encompass part of the roof, to make the good views even better. Sleeping cars come in a variety of sizes and budget levels, and even lowly coach class on long-distance trains has seats roughly equivalent to business-class seats on long-distance flights. The lounge cars are a unique American institution. Selling cheap drinks well into the night, they are filled with convivial former strangers cheerfully chatting each other up.

Reservations

During much of the year it's crucial to have your Amtrak journey reserved well in advance. During the summer, sleeper space and even simple seats are gone weeks in advance. The same situation exists around holidays. Reserve by phone (☎ 800-872-7245), on the Web (www.amtrak.com) or at Amtrak stations.

Fares

Amtrak travel can cost about the same as going by bus; it is slower but a lot more comfortable. Sleeper prices depend on their level of luxury; a basic room for two can cost $150 to $300. These accommodations can be a pretty good deal, because they include all meals, some drinks and other treats, including coffee in bed.

Some sample nondiscounted coach fares and travel times include the following:

route	fare	duration
Seattle to Minneapolis	$112	46 hours
San Francisco to Chicago	$138	52 hours
Los Angeles to Chicago	$138	42 hours
Dallas to Chicago	$127	21 hours
New Orleans to Chicago	$105	20 hours
Toronto to Chicago	$67	12 hours
Boston to Chicago	$81	23 hours
New York to Cleveland	$62	14 hours
Washington, DC, to Cincinnati	$56	15 hours

Discounts The best value overall is Amtrak's Explore America fare. This costs $318 for adults and enables you to travel anywhere you want, with some limitations. Travel must be completed in 45 days, and you are allowed only three stopovers. Additional stopovers can be arranged at extra cost. Your entire trip must be reserved in advance, and the seats are limited, so book as far ahead as possible. Travel between mid-June and late August costs $378.

For non-US citizens, Amtrak offers a variety of USA Rail Passes that must be purchased outside the US (check with a travel agent). Prices vary from high to low season and include the following:

duration	route	high/low season
15 days	national	$425/285
	West Coast	$315/195
	East Coast	$250/205
30 day	national	$535/375
	West Coast	$310/260
	East Coast	$395/255

Amtrak and Via Rail, Canada's national carrier, offer a combined North America Rail Pass that offers unlimited travel for 30 days on the systems of both countries for $645 from June 1 to October 15 and $450 the rest of the year.

Amtrak has a deal with United Airlines by which you can ride the train one way and fly back. This is a great deal, because you can enjoy the scenery on your way to someplace such as Portland, Oregon, but then avoid chugging back through the same sites on your return to Chicago. The special reservations number for this deal, imaginatively called 'Air-Rail,' is ☎ 800-437-3441.

West Coast Trains

Amtrak's three trains between Chicago and the West Coast can be vacation experiences in themselves. They utilize the line's cushy 'Superliner' equipment and have a full range of amenities. Each takes upward of three days and two nights to reach its destination. And don't plan any split-second connections: Amtrak is notoriously late, sometimes by several hours.

The daily *Empire Builder* goes to Seattle and Portland, passing through the northern Rockies and the 'big sky' country of Montana. It serves Milwaukee and Minneapolis and other, smaller, towns.

The daily *California Zephyr* passes through dramatic canyons in both the Rockies in Colorado and the Sierra Nevada in California. It stops in Galesburg, Illinois, before hitting Iowa and also serves Denver and Salt Lake City.

The daily *Southwest Chief* traces the route of the legendary *Super Chief*, once run by the Santa Fe Railroad. It speeds through the painted deserts of New Mexico and Arizona and usually carries Native American guides to point out the sights. It stops in Galesburg and also serves Kansas City, Missouri.

Southern Trains

The daily *City of New Orleans* covers the same route immortalized in the Arlo Guthrie song. It stops in several Illinois cities, including Champaign, as well as Memphis, Tennessee.

The *Texas Eagle* is daily as far as St Louis and then runs thrice weekly to Dallas and San Antonio.

East Coast Trains

The daily *Lake Shore Limited* to New York and Boston makes a dramatic run at dawn along the old Erie Canal and Hudson River (unless it's late; then it's a dramatic mid-morning run). It passes through South Bend, Toledo and Cleveland.

The daily *Capitol Limited* also passes through South Bend, Toledo and Cleveland before turning south for Pittsburgh, Pennsylvania, and Washington, DC. It is augmented by the daily *Pennsylvanian*, a daytime train that follows the same route as far as Pittsburgh. The daily *Three Rivers* travels mostly through rural Indiana and Ohio on its overnight run to New York.

The thrice-weekly *Cardinal* serves Indianapolis, Cincinnati and smaller points on its remarkably pokey run to Washington, DC.

Other Trains

The daily *International* travels through Michigan to link Chicago with Toronto via Kalamazoo, East Lansing, Port Huron and other towns in between. The usual US customs and immigration checks are done aboard the train.

For short-distance Amtrak services within the Great Lakes region, see the Getting Around chapter.

CAR & MOTORCYCLE

Foreign drivers of cars and riders of motorcycles will need their vehicle's registration papers, liability insurance and possibly an international driving permit, in addition to their domestic driver's license. Check with your national motoring organization for details. Canadian and Mexican driver's licenses are acceptable.

Border Crossings

There are numerous border crossings between Canada and the US along the Great Lakes. In Minnesota the main crossings are in the far west, on I-29 into Manitoba at International Falls, and just south of Thunder Bay on Lake Superior.

Michigan's major crossings are I-75 from the Upper Peninsula to Sault Ste Marie, on I-69 and I-94 at Port Huron at the base of Lake Huron and between Detroit and Windsor.

If your papers are in order, taking your own car across the US-Canadian border is usually quick and easy, but occasionally the authorities of either country decide to inspect a car *thoroughly*. Canadian auto insurance is valid in the US – make certain your policy is current before you cross the border. On weekends and holidays traffic at the main border crossings can be very heavy, and there will be a long wait. Avoid these times or try a small, rural crossing.

People with neither Canadian nor American passports can expect the full attention of the immigration and customs officials.

ORGANIZED TOURS

See the Organized Tours section of the Getting Around chapter for details on organized tour possibilities in the Great Lakes region – those tours can be booked from abroad.

Check with a travel agent for word of companies offering packages to Chicago and the Great Lakes from abroad. Although the main focus of group tours to the US has been New York, Florida and California, that is starting to change. The international airlines serving Chicago often have well-priced packages that include hotel accommodations and a rental car.

Getting Around

Without a doubt, the best way to get around the Great Lakes region is by car. The region is large, the highways are good and, as is the case in much of the US, public transportation is not as frequent or as widespread as in some other countries. Still, there are the alternatives of air, train and bus, which may make sense for some routes.

AIR

There are major airports in Chicago, Detroit, Cleveland, Columbus, Cincinnati, Indianapolis, St Louis, Milwaukee and Minneapolis. These are served by large numbers of domestic airlines, and you can usually find competitive fares between them.

Scores more towns and cities have small airports served by the commuter airline affiliates of the big carriers. These airports are noted in the text. Generally, it is much more costly to fly into these airports if you are just trying to get around the Great Lakes region. The cheapest airfare from, say, Chicago to Green Bay is many times more than the cost of driving or the bus fare. Where regional airports can be useful is when you are flying into the Great Lakes region from another part of the US or from abroad. In these cases, the add-on commuter flight from a major hub such as Chicago can add just a few dollars to the price of the ticket.

BUS

Buses go to more places around the region than airplanes or trains, but the routes still leave a lot out, bypassing some prime destinations. Except on the most heavily traveled routes, there may be only one or two buses per day.

Greyhound (☎ 800-231-2222, www.greyhound.com) is the major company covering the Great Lakes. In some cases it contracts out local service to smaller firms, and in a few cases there are competing companies on some routes. These instances are noted in the introductory chapters to the states and in the city listings.

Obtaining reliable Greyhound fare and schedule information can be tricky. Many stops are just that, and the businesses at these locations may know little about the service. Even regular Greyhound stations can prove hard to deal with. Employees often consider simple schedule requests a major chore, or there may be long lines, or both. The Greyhound Web site, however, provides fast and accurate fare and schedule information. When in doubt, try to use that.

It's also worth noting that in small towns, bus stations may really be bus stops at gas stations and convenience stores. In major cities, the stations can be in not-so-savory parts of town and have very limited services.

Also be aware that you won't be able to find bus transportation to most of the national forests or to many interesting small towns, such as Madison, Indiana.

TRAIN

Amtrak (☎ 800-872-7245, www.amtrak.com) service in the Great Lakes centers on Chicago. For getting around the region you have a range of trains. The long-distance trains with famous names, such as the *California Zephyr* and the *Lake Shore Limited* are quite luxurious yet often very affordable. See the Getting There & Away chapter for details.

However, these long-distance trains are often late and are thus poor options for short trips. Amtrak's local trains in the Great Lakes are often a more timely bet for short hops, plus you have the added convenience of going from city center to city center.

Note that Amtrak fares vary as widely as airline fares, so none is listed here. It's always worth checking for various offers with Amtrak, such as weekend or companion deals. Full-fare tickets usually cost a bit more than the bus.

Following are routes in the Great Lakes where Amtrak has at least daily service with short-distance trains. (Other cities, such as South Bend, Indiana, have daily service, but it's exclusively by the long-distance trains.) Selected intermediate stops are also listed.

Chicago to Grand Rapids
Intermediate stops: New Buffalo (Michigan), St Joseph-Benton Harbor, Bangor, Holland, Grand Rapids

Chicago to Toronto
Intermediate stops: Niles (Michigan), Kalamazoo, Battle Creek, East Lansing, Flint, Port Huron

Chicago to Pontiac
Intermediate stops: Niles (Michigan), Kalamazoo, Battle Creek, Jackson, Ann Arbor, Dearborn, Detroit, Birmingham

Chicago to Carbondale
Intermediate stops: Kankakee (Illinois), Champaign-Urbana

Chicago to St Louis
Intermediate stops: Joliet (Illinois), Bloomington–Normal, Lincoln, Springfield, Alton

Chicago to Milwaukee

Chicago to Quincy
Intermediate stops: Galesburg (Illinois)

The short distance trains usually are not as posh as the long-distance trains, but they still are quite comfortable – much more so than the bus, and many have café cars for light meals and drinks.

CAR & MOTORCYCLE

Driving is the best way to see the Great Lakes. If you don't have your own transportation, consider renting a car for at least part of your stay, such as for the time you'll spend outside Chicago. (A car is more a headache than a convenience in Chicago.)

Road Rules

Driving laws are different in each of the Great Lakes states. Generally, you must be 16 years of age to have a driver's license. See each state's introductory chapter for more information.

Most states in the US have passed laws requiring motorcyclists to wear helmets. However, Minnesota, Wisconsin and Illinois have gone against the grain: Motorcyclists don't need (or often wear) helmets in those

Driving Distance (in miles)

	Cairo, IL	Chicago, IL	Cincinnati, OH	Cleveland, OH	Columbus, OH	Detroit, MI	Duluth, MN	Fort Wayne, IN	Green Bay, WI	Indianapolis, IN	Mackinaw City, MI	Madison, WI	Minneapolis, MN	Sault Ste Marie, MI	Springfield, IL	Toledo, OH
Chicago, IL	375															
Cincinnati, OH	361	295														
Cleveland, OH	614	360	253													
Columbus, OH	472	346	111	146												
Detroit, MI	615	262	272	172	202											
Duluth, MN	815	473	768	829	799	759										
Fort Wayne, IN	443	170	165	226	197	176	643									
Green Bay, WI	582	207	502	568	548	490	318	373								
Indianapolis, IN	311	185	110	322	178	305	658	129	392							
Mackinaw City, MI	735	394	544	449	478	293	421	338	258	485						
Madison, WI	519	144	439	512	490	432	329	314	139	332	395					
Minneapolis, MN	767	415	719	765	789	723	154	595	292	610	513	285				
Sault Ste Marie, MI	881	450	621	506	534	349	420	524	285	570	56	422	576			
Springfield, IL	242	202	322	524	390	471	593	332	402	210	571	272	535	652		
Toledo, OH	573	244	210	115	144	62	723	114	451	261	329	389	675	390	432	
Toronto, Canada	859	457	496	303	436	237	886	420	719	515	483	675	956	436	693	309

AMTRAK ROUTES
102°W
100°W
98°W
96°W
94°W
92°W
90°W
Manitoba
Ontario
Lake of the Woods
To Seattle (WA)
Empire Builder
48°N
Grand Forks
North Dakota
Minnesota
Bismarck
Lake Superior
Fargo
Detroit Lakes
Duluth
46°N
Staples
St Cloud
Wisconsin
South Dakota
MINNEAPOLIS
St Paul
Pierre
Wausau
Eau Claire
Wittenberg
44°N
Red Wing
Winona
Tomah
La Crosse
Wisconsin Dells
Portage
Columbus
Madison
42°N
Iowa
Janesville
Beloit
Rockford
Nebraska
Des Moines
Omaha
To San Francisco (CA)
Lincoln
California Zephyr
Creston
Osceola
Ottumwa
Mt Pleasant
Princeton
Kewanee
Galesburg
Burlington
Fort Madison
40°N
Peoria
Macomb
Bloomington-Normal
La Plata
Lincoln
Amtrak and VIA Rail Canada Routes
Connecting Bus Routes
St Joseph
Quincy
Springfield
KANSAS CITY
Illinois
Topeka
Kansas
Lawrence
Independence
Lees Summit
Carlinville
Warrensburg
Sedalia
Hermann
Alton
38°N
Kirkwood
ST LOUIS
Washington
East St Louis
Jefferson City
Centralia
To Los Angeles (CA)
Southwest Chief
Du Quoin
Missouri
Carbondale
City of New Orleans
Texas Eagle
0
100
200 km
0
60
120 miles
To Dallas (TX)
100°W
98°W
96°W
94°W
92°W
90°W

AMTRAK ROUTES
Lake Nipigon
VIA Rail Canada
VIA Rail Canada
Oba
Franz
Quebec
CANADA
UNITED STATES
Sudbury
Michigan
Manitoulin Island
Georgian Bay
OTTAWA
St Ignace
Mackinaw City
Pellston
Petoskey
Walloon Lake
Boyne City
Boyne Falls
Mancelona
Kalkaska
Traverse City
Lake Huron
Washago
Buckley
Mesick
Michigan
Ontario
Green Bay
Cadillac
Appleton
Oshkosh
Manitowoc
Lake Ontario
VIA Rail Canada
TORONTO
To New York City & Boston (MA)
Fond du Lac
Reed City
Big Rapids
Hamilton
Rochester
Lake Michigan
Howard City
St Marys
Niagara Falls
Lake Shore Limited
Rockford
Flint
Lapeer
Port Huron
Sarnia
London
Buffalo
MILWAUKEE
Grand Rapids
Durand
International
Strathroy
New York
Sturtevant
Holland
Lansing
East Lansing
Pontiac
Birmingham
Battle Creek
Royal Oak
DETROIT
Windsor
Bangor
Jackson
Dearborn
St Joseph
Kalamazoo
Albion
Ann Arbor
Erie
Benton Harbor
Glenview
Dowagiac
Lake Erie
CHICAGO
Niles
Pennsylvania
Naperville
Summit
New Buffalo
Elkhart
Toledo
CLEVELAND
Homewood
Michigan City
South Bend
Bryan
To Philadelphia
Joliet
Dyer
Waterloo
Sandusky
Elyria
Youngstown
Hammond-Whiting
Nappanee
Pennsylvanian/ Three Rivers
Dwight
Pennsylvanian
Fostoria
Akron
Kankakee
Rensselaer
PITTSBURGH
Harrisburg
Pontiac
Gilman
Ohio
Lafayette
Rantoul
Wheeling
Capitol Limited
Danville
Champaign-Urbana
Crawfordsville
Columbus
Zanesville
Maryland
Indianapolis
Connersville
WASHINGTON, DC
Mattoon
Cardinal
Hamilton
West Virginia
Effingham
CINCINNATI
Indiana
South Portsmouth
Maysville
Ashland
Huntington
Charleston
Charlottesville
Montgomery
Cardinal
Frankfort
Thurmond
LOUISVILLE
Clifton Forge
Richmond
Kentucky
Virginia
88°W
86°W
84°W
82°W
80°W
78°W
76°W
48°N
46°N
44°N
42°N
40°N
38°N

states. Even so, use of a motorcycle helmet is highly recommended.

Speed Limits The maximum speed limit on most Great Lakes interstate highways is 65mph (but you're likely to find traffic moving at 70mph); some of the interstates near cities have limits of 55mph. On undivided highways, speed limits vary from 30 to 55mph. In cities and towns, they are usually 25 to 35mph, slower near schools and medical facilities.

Speed limits are enforced by police patrolling in marked police cars and in unmarked cars and by 'radar traps' placed so that you won't see them until it's too late. One way to detect a radar trap is to watch the brake lights of the cars ahead of you. If all the drivers ahead put on their brakes as they pass a certain point, it's likely they've seen – too late! – a radar trap. Watch out as well for road signs indicating that speed is being checked by aircraft. In this case a plane times your speed between markers on the road, and then prepositioned police pull you over farther down the line.

The fine for a speeding offense can be well over $100, payable in cash. In some areas the police will demand the cash right there on the spot, and if you don't have it they will haul you off to a little court or police office where you have to try to get the money from an ATM or, worse, by having it wired. This varies by state, and fines can be quite a lot more.

Safety Restraints Rules for seat-belt usage vary by state and are listed in the relevant state chapters. Regardless, your chances of avoiding injury in an accident are significantly higher if you wear a seat belt.

In every state, children are covered by mandatory restraint requirements that are listed in each state's introductory chapters. Older children may be required by law to wear safety belts. Child safety seats are available from car rental firms, sometimes at a small extra charge. In any car equipped with a front-passenger-seat air bag, no child should sit in the front passenger seat. Air bags are designed to protect a full-size, full-weight adult and can seriously injure or kill a small or lightweight person upon inflation – they unfurl at a speed of 200mph. Seat children in the back, and buckle their seat belts for added safety.

Rental

You must be at least 21 years of age (in some cases 25) and have a valid driver's license to rent an automobile. A major credit card is a practical necessity as well. Without one, you may have to put down a cash deposit of up to $2000.

Well-known national car rental companies such as Avis, Budget, Dollar, Hertz, National and Thrifty tend to have higher rates than small local companies but more efficient service. Quality, service and car condition are most variable among the local firms, which often specialize in rentals to people whose own cars are under repair.

National Companies Reservations can be made with the large rental companies – Alamo, Avis, Hertz, Dollar, Budget and others – through a travel agent or by calling the company directly. Local numbers are listed under 'Automobile Renting' in the yellow pages; or see the Toll-Free Directory in this book for 800 numbers.

When talking to the companies, keep asking if there are lower rates. You'd be amazed at what agents can find with a little persistence. Weekly rates for an average-size car with unlimited mileage for well under $200 are not uncommon. However, for these you may have to take the car from an airport location, where the biggest fleets are.

Local Companies You can find rental cars with local rental companies and some automobile dealerships, which often provide good service at cheaper rates than national companies. Most offer free delivery and pickup at the airport or a hotel, unlimited mileage and quality cars. However, the entire process can be time-consuming, especially ferreting out the deals and attending to the details.

Insurance You may want to buy liability insurance when renting a car so that if you hit another car or property, the damage will be paid for. What is not covered is damage to the rental vehicle itself. For this, you have the option to purchase a so-called Collision Damage Waiver (CDW) or Loss Damage Waiver, which may cost between $10 and $16 or more per day, thus significantly increasing the cost of the overall rental. Though it would be foolish to rent without insuring the vehicle in some way, you do not necessarily have to buy the rental company's inflated CDW.

If you own a car registered in the USA, your own auto insurance may cover damage to a rental car; check with your insurance agent to be sure. Some major credit card companies may provide coverage for any vehicle rented with their cards; check your credit card agreement to see what coverage is provided. Note that in case of damage, rental companies may require that you pay not only for repairs, but also normal rental fees for all the time that the rental car is off the road for repairs. Your policy should cover this loss as well.

Saving Money The cheapest rental rates are for the smallest cars, rented from noon Thursday through noon Monday (or for an entire week or more), returning the vehicle to the place of rental (or at least to the city of rental).

You may be offered a choice of 'fuel plans': You can pick up and return the car with a full tank of fuel, or you can pay for the gas that's in the car and return it empty. The full tank is always the better choice. Because it's virtually impossible to return a car empty of gas, you will end up turning over several gallons of fuel to the rental company, which will then try to sell it to the next renter.

RV Rental Most private campgrounds are designed to accommodate recreational vehicles, from camper vans to the largest motor homes. Rentals can cost anywhere from $75 to $125 per day, and because they are large vehicles, they use lots of fuel. In addition, parking them and sleeping in them overnight outside of campgrounds is not allowed in many areas, so you should expect to spend around $20 to $35 per night for a camping place.

Before you decide on an RV rental, read about camping under Accommodations in the Facts for the Visitor chapter. You may find that using a rental car and your own camping gear will not only save you lots of money but also give you a more natural camping experience while saving you from navigating a behemoth of an RV around the roads.

For further information, contact the Recreation Vehicle Rental Association (☎ 703-591-7130, 800-336-0355, fax 703-591-0734, www.rvra.org), 3930 University Drive, Fairfax, VA 22030. Companies that rent RVs can be found in the yellow pages of the phone book under 'Recreational Vehicles – Renting & Leasing,' 'Motor Homes – Renting & Leasing' and 'Trailers – Camping & Travel.'

Fuel

Gas stations can be found everywhere – sometimes on each of the four corners of an intersection – and many are open 24 hours a day. Small-town stations may be open only from 7 am to 8 or 9 pm.

At some stations, you must pay before you pump; at others, you may pump before you pay. The more modern pumps have credit and debit card terminals built into them, so you can pay with plastic right at the pump. (The most modern pumps have little TV screens that blast advertisements in your face as you pump the gas.) At more expensive 'full service' stations, an attendant will pump your gas for you; no tip is expected.

Plan on spending $1.15 to $1.50 per US gallon, more around big cities and for higher-octane fuels. Leaded gasoline is not sold in the US.

Parking

Parking is controlled mostly by signs on the street stating explicitly what may or may not be done. A yellow line or yellow-painted curb means that no parking is allowed there. In some towns, a white line is painted along the curb in areas where you may park.

Safety

To avert theft, do not leave expensive items, such as purses, CDs, cameras, leather bags or even sunglasses, visibly lying around in your car. Tuck items under a seat or, even better, put them in the trunk and make sure your car does not have trunk entry through the back seat; if it does, make sure it is locked. It's a good idea to avoid placing shopping bags or other items in the trunk if you're not going to be moving the car right away. Don't leave valuables in your car overnight.

In winter carrying an ice scraper is essential. Other items you might want to consider are wool blankets and water, in case you are stranded in bad weather that makes immediate rescue difficult.

Breakdowns & Assistance

If your car breaks down and you need help, a few highways in the Great Lakes have Motorist Aid Call Boxes with emergency telephones posted every few miles along the roadside. On other highways, raise the hood (bonnet) of your vehicle and tie a white cloth (such as a handkerchief) to the radio aerial to signal that you need help, and await a police patrol, which often comes within an hour.

The American Automobile Association (AAA; ☎ 800-222-4357, www.aaa.com) provides battery charging, short-range towing, gasoline delivery and minor repairs at no charge to its members and to those of affiliated auto clubs. However, members are still liable for long-distance towing and for major repairs.

BICYCLE

Bicycling is a common sport and means of transport on both city streets and country roads. Several of the larger cities, such as Minneapolis–St Paul and the Quad Cities, have systems of bike paths that make bike travel easy and pleasant. Some towns, such as Indianapolis, have turned disused railroad rights-of-way into bike trails that run for several miles.

It is possible to get around the region by bicycle, but much of the ride would be along major roadways. There are systems of long-distance trails in some states, notably Minnesota, but at present they are too disjointed to form a route through the region. If you're interested in getting around the Great Lakes by bicycle, contact the central tourism office for each state on your itinerary and ask for brochures on biking there.

HITCHHIKING

Hitchhiking is never entirely safe in any country in the world, and we don't recommend it. In the US it is often illegal, and smart, law-abiding drivers do not pick up hitchhikers. Travelers who decide to hitchhike – and drivers who pick hitchhikers up – should understand that they are taking a small but potentially serious risk. People who do choose to hitchhike will be safer if they travel in pairs and let someone else know where they are planning to go.

WALKING

Walking and jogging are popular in the Great Lakes region. More and more trails are being developed. But note that in sprawling suburban areas, walkers are viewed with suspicion. In those areas you may find you're the only one walking, and you also may encounter busy places where there are no sidewalks at all, and you are expected to drive for even short distances.

BOAT

The major boat service in the Great Lakes region is the SS *Badger*, a car ferry linking Manitowoc, Wisconsin, to Ludington, Michigan. It's a four-hour crossing, running daily from mid-May through late October. Call the Lake Michigan Carferry (☎ 888-643-3779, www.ssbadger.com) for reservations, schedules and fares. In 2000 a one-way trip cost $39/36/18 adults/seniors/kids, $47/27 car/motorcycle. There's a discount for taking the 12:30 am trip out of Manitowoc.

This boat can be a real time-saver on going all the way around Lake Michigan in either direction. Keep in mind that Wisconsin, on central time, is an hour behind Michigan, on eastern time.

TRANSPORTATION

Bus & Subway

Chicago has a large and extensive local train and bus network. Other cities and towns have systems that become less useful, the smaller the town. The smallest places have no public transportation at all. Individual city listings have full details.

Taxi

Taxis are useful and common in the largest cities. In smaller cities and towns you will probably have to telephone a cab to pick you up. Ask at a hotel, restaurant or tourist office or look in the yellow pages under 'Taxicabs.' Note that a taxi must be licensed by the city in which you board it in order to pick you up, though some companies are licensed to operate in a number of cities.

Taxi drivers are usually willing to take you just about anywhere if you can afford the fare. For longer trips, this may be about $2.50 or $3 per mile.

City taxis have fare meters, which usually begin at $1.90 and then add a certain price per mile or per fraction of a mile. Extra charges may be added for extra passengers or for driving at night. On top of cab fare, you should add a tip of about 15%. Town taxis may not have meters but will quote you the fare when you call. The same 15% tip is expected.

Standards of service are generally low in big cities, better in smaller towns. Some city drivers speak a limited amount of English. Also, some drivers may not know their city well, but they can usually radio to headquarters and get directions.

Many city taxis are rolling wrecks in which the back seat (where the passenger rides) is separated from the front (driver's) seat by a thick, clear plastic barrier. The passenger can easily be forgiven for feeling as if he or she is in a jail on wheels. Cut into the plastic barrier is usually some sort of hole, chute or sliding door so that the passenger can get money to the driver at the end of the ride. Although this arrangement makes it more difficult for the passenger to rob the driver, it does not hamper the driver from 'robbing' the passenger by taking an unnecessarily long route. For longer journeys that you are able to plan in advance (such as trips to the airport), you may want to hire a limousine instead. The cost is about the same, and the comfort and service far better.

Limousine

A limousine (limo for short) is either an 'executive sedan' (a luxury car such as a Lincoln Town Car or Cadillac El Dorado, or at least a very comfortable full-size sedan) or a 'stretch limo' (an executive sedan that has been lengthened to provide more interior room). A limo takes you anywhere you like at either a predetermined or an hourly rate. Executive sedans are often not much more expensive than regular taxis, but they cannot be hailed on the street – they must be booked in advance. Standards of service and comfort are far higher than those of regular taxis. If you can plan ahead and want a more pleasant ride at a modest increase in price, look in the yellow pages under 'Limousine Service.'

Some shuttle van services use the term 'limo' or 'limousine' for their comfortable – but hardly luxurious – shuttle vans. If luxury matters to you, ask what you're getting when you reserve.

Shuttle Services

In big cities it's also possible to reserve a seat in a comfortable van or minibus that shuttles passengers between the airport and the city center or suburbs. Shuttles hold anywhere from eight to 25 passengers and may serve cities as much as an hour or two away from the airport. Shuttle fares are often less expensive than taxi fares. The shuttle may pick you up at your hotel (or other point), or you may have to meet it at a predetermined stop or station. For the telephone numbers of airport shuttle companies, look in the yellow pages under 'Airport Transportation Service.' Major firms are also in the Getting Around sections for the relevant cities.

ORGANIZED TOURS

Scores of tours are available in the Great Lakes region.

Regional Tours

Regional tours are the way to go if you don't have time to make reservations in many different destinations or don't have a car. In the case of water trips they can put you right on the lakes and rivers, which are often the most interesting parts of the region.

Water Tours Several companies run boats that make stops along the coast of the lakes, where you can join and leave, or along the rivers. There's a myriad of options here, although the steamboats do not quite reach Chicago.

Tour boats on the Great Lakes are starting to proliferate. The Traverse Tall Ship Co (☎ 800-678-0383) offers cruises on Lakes Michigan and Huron aboard large sailing boats that make various stops along the coasts. You can board or leave at any stop along the way.

Clipper Cruise Line (☎ 800-325-0010) has very popular two-week trips between Chicago and Quebec. The American Canadian Caribbean Line (☎ 800-556-7450) has voyages from Chicago all the way to the Atlantic Ocean.

The Delta Queen Steamboat Co (☎ 800-543-1949) has luxurious river cruises aimed at older, well-heeled patrons aboard authentic stern-wheeler riverboats. They make several stops along their routes and go as far south as New Orleans on the Mississippi River (and Minneapolis to the north), Ottawa on the Illinois River and Cincinnati on the Ohio River.

Land Tours Amtrak and most of the airlines have their own tour-company subsidiaries that put together regional tours. Other operators include Allied Tours (☎ 212-863-5100, www.alliedtours.com), which has a large number of itineraries; Discovery Tours (☎ 920-459-2960), which specializes in fly-drive programs where you convey yourself to prearranged accommodations on a preplanned itinerary; and Visit America (☎ 212-683-8082, www.vamerica.com), which has various cultural itineraries.

The 20th Century Railroad Club (☎ 312-829-4500) offers Midwest train tours that cover routes not normally served by passenger trains.

The Nature Conservancy (☎ 703-841-5300), 1815 N Lynn St, Arlington, VA, 22209, offers trips organized by its various regional and city affiliates.

The National Audubon Society (☎ 212-979-3000), 700 Broadway, New York, NY, 10003, offers ecological tours and outings.

White Star Tours (☎ 800-437-2323), 26 E Lancaster Ave, Reading, PA 19607, is a large operator of bus tours aimed at senior citizens. They have several itineraries in the Midwest.

Local Tours

City tours by bus or 'trolley' (actually a bus disguised as a light-rail trolley) are popular in the major cities, tourist towns and resort areas. Most are useful for getting a look at the major sights, though the commentary is often bland. For places on the water, there are often local boat tours. In Chicago, for instance, these tours are a spectacular way to see the city.

Illinois

Facts about Illinois

Great museums, restaurants, and jazz and blues are just some of the joys of Chicago, a good first stop on a Great Lakes tour. The rest of northern Illinois has the fascinating Illinois and Michigan Canal Corridor and the quaint and touristy Galena.

Historic Route 66 crosses the state, giving great views of the flat farmlands of central Illinois. Springfield, the capital, is filled with sites connected to the man many consider the greatest American president ever, Abraham Lincoln.

The Mississippi River forms the state's western border. This fabled river runs past St Louis, the dominant city in Missouri, which should be on anybody's downstate Illinois itinerary. Nearby prehistoric Indian sites rival the pyramids in Egypt for their archaeological importance.

Southern Illinois is influenced by another important river, the Ohio. Shawnee National Forest offers getaways into the woods and hikes far from the crowds.

Illinois Facts

Nickname Land of Lincoln

Population 11,435,000 (6th largest)

Area 56,400 sq miles (24th largest)

Admitted to Union December 3, 1818 (21st state)

Road Information Contact the Illinois State Police (☎ 312-814-2834).

Road Rules Seat belts are required for people in the front seat, and for everyone in the car when the driver is under 18. Child seats are required for kids under 4. Motorcyclists are not required to wear helmets.

Taxes Statewide sales tax is 6.25%; cities may charge additional taxes at their discretion.

History

Thousands of prehistoric mounds in Illinois are evidence of early civilizations that not only used tools and pottery, but also had developed religious beliefs. When Europeans arrived, beginning in the early 17th century, there were Algonquian-speaking peoples in the southern and western portions of the state who had been displaced by Iroquois and other groups expanding from the north. French missionaries and traders explored the region via the Mississippi and Illinois Rivers and moved on to Lake Michigan, where they founded forts and villages in the late 17th century. After periods under the control of France, Britain and Virginia, Illinois became part of the Northwest Territory in 1787, and new settlers were able to acquire public land. It was proclaimed the Illinois Territory in 1809 and admitted as a state in 1818.

In the state's first years, pioneer farming settlements grew across Illinois. In the 1820s the completion of canals linking Lake Michigan with the eastern states stimulated growth in the north, especially Chicago. New roads, steamboats and railroads facilitated further settlement of Illinois and the plains to its west. That led to conflict with the Indians, culminating in the 1832 Black Hawk War and the forced removal of Indians to areas west of the Mississippi.

Many early settlers were from the South and favored slavery, but there were

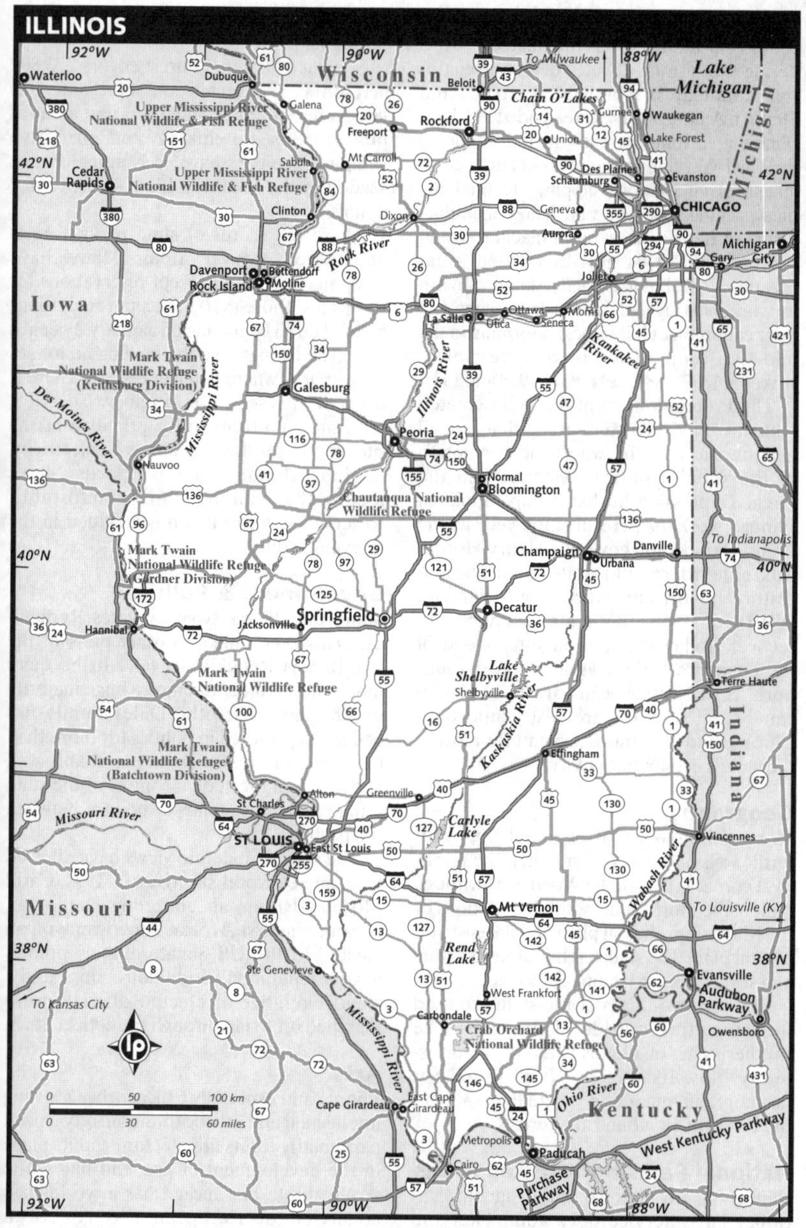
ILLINOIS
92°W
90°W
88°W
42°N
40°N
38°N
Wisconsin
Iowa
Missouri
Kentucky
Indiana
Michigan
Lake Michigan
Waterloo
Dubuque
Galena
Beloit
To Milwaukee
Chain O'Lakes
Gurnee
Waukegan
Lake Forest
Union
Rockford
Freeport
Mt Carroll
Sabula
Upper Mississippi River National Wildlife & Fish Refuge
Upper Mississippi River National Wildlife & Fish Refuge
Cedar Rapids
Clinton
Dixon
Des Plaines
Schaumburg
Evanston
CHICAGO
Geneva
Aurora
Rock River
Davenport
Bettendorf
Rock Island
Moline
Joliet
Gary
Michigan City
La Salle
Utica
Ottawa
Seneca
Morris
Kankakee River
Mark Twain National Wildlife Refuge (Keithsburg Division)
Mississippi River
Illinois River
Galesburg
Des Moines River
Peoria
Nauvoo
Normal
Bloomington
Chautauqua National Wildlife Refuge
Champaign
Urbana
Danville
To Indianapolis
Mark Twain National Wildlife Refuge (Gardner Division)
Springfield
Decatur
Hannibal
Jacksonville
Mark Twain National Wildlife Refuge
Lake Shelbyville
Shelbyville
Kaskaskia River
Terre Haute
Effingham
Mark Twain National Wildlife Refuge (Batchtown Division)
Alton
St Charles
Greenville
Missouri River
Carlyle Lake
ST LOUIS
East St Louis
Vincennes
Wabash River
Mt Vernon
To Louisville (KY)
Rend Lake
Ste Genevieve
Evansville
Audubon Parkway
West Frankfort
To Kansas City
Carbondale
Crab Orchard National Wildlife Refuge
Owensboro
Mississippi River
Ohio River
East Cape Girardeau
Cape Girardeau
Metropolis
Paducah
West Kentucky Parkway
Cairo
Purchase Parkway
0 50 100 km
0 30 60 miles

abolitionists here too. The state's internal conflict on the issue was articulated in 1858 during the historic debates between senatorial candidates Abraham Lincoln and Stephen A Douglas. Despite divided loyalties, Illinois contributed greatly to the Union in the Civil War and in the process emerged as an industrial state, developing steelmaking, meatpacking, distilling, and heavy manufacturing of items such as farm machinery and railroad cars. This growth created great private wealth, but it also led to labor activism as workers struggled against low wages and poor conditions. Unions began forming in the mid-19th century, and there were violent strikes in 1877, 1886, 1894, 1904, 1908 and 1919.

The Prohibition era of the 1920s created a lucrative illegal alcohol trade that funded gangsterism and the wholesale corruption of the state's political system. Then the Great Depression hit hard – up to half of Illinois' workers were unemployed. In the 1930s, Democratic governor Henry Horner was able to rebuild state finances and restore honest and efficient government. WWII enabled the state economy to recover. Today the state maintains one of the country's highest agricultural outputs; pork, corn and soybeans are most significant. Coal and oil are also important. Chicago and its suburbs account for most of the state's economic activity.

Geography

Most of Illinois is flat or undulating, with fertile soils of glacial till (or, drift). The northwest corner is part of the Wisconsin 'driftless' region; the more scenic south has sections of the Mississippi alluvial plain and the east gulf coastal plain. The state has hundreds of rivers and seven separate drainage basins.

The top two-thirds of the state are used for agriculture outside of the cities. The southern part of Illinois is the most consistently hilly. Its thin soil is ill-suited for farming, and minerals coal and fluorspar are the basis for economic life here.

National Parks & Protected Areas

Illinois has no national parks, but the National Park Service does administer the Lincoln Home National Historic Site, in Springfield.

Shawnee National Forest covers 273,800 acres in the bottom portion of the state. It is largely undeveloped and offers vast areas of hilly forests for hiking and primitive camping. See the Shawnee National Forest section in the Southern Illinois chapter for details.

There are scores of state parks, forests and other natural areas. Many have camping, but not all accept reservations for campsites. Those that do accept reservations by mail do so beginning on January 2 of each year. The listings give the mailing addresses of the parks where you can reserve. There is no central reservation number. Costs for campsites run from $6 for primitive hiking sites to $11 for drive-in sites with electricity.

Many Illinois state parks also have lodges that can be quite comfortable. Reservation information is included in the relevant listings.

Government & Politics

Statewide, Illinois typically votes Republican. However, unlike in other parts of the US, Illinois Republicans tend to be quite moderate. Democrats enjoy a huge majority in Chicago, where the Daley family has been a major force in politics for more than half a century, and they do reasonably well in the rest of the state – control of the state senate and house tends to bounce between the parties.

The state's moderate views have allowed for some electoral surprises. In 1992, Carol Moseley-Braun, an underdog Democrat, became the first African American woman elected to the US Senate. Illinois politics have a reputation for dubious ethics, and a steady number of elected officials were marched off to jail through the 20th century.

Arts

Illinois, and especially Chicago, has a strong intellectual and artistic tradition, recognized particularly for its architecture and its place in the development of jazz and blues. The Art Institute of Chicago has a world-class collection of European and American paintings. Chicago is also home to more professional theaters than any other city in the US.

Illinois has been home to writers as diverse as Ernest Hemingway, Saul Bellow and Carl Sandburg.

Information

The Illinois Bureau of Tourism (☎ 800-226-6632, www.enjoyillinois.com) is at 620 E Adams St, Springfield, IL 62701. State welcome centers are situated near the state borders on all the interstate highways.

Except for the touristy region around Galena, much of the state should be accessible to travelers without reservations throughout the year. The exceptions are the many state parks near major cities. Chicago can be busy year-round, but that's part of its excitement.

Liquor is sold every day; the bars usually close by 3 am, but some stay open as late as 5 am.

Special Events

The Illinois State Fair, held in Springfield every August, features horse racing, famous entertainers, prize pigs and all the other events that make for a classic state fair. Jazz legend Bix Beiderbecke got his start in Davenport in the 1920s; the town holds a jazz festival (☎ 319-324-7170) in his honor every July. And there's a Blues Heritage Festival in St Louis, MO on Labor Day Weekend.

Chicago has scores of special events. See the Chicago chapter for details.

Food & Drinks

Illinois grows a large percentage of the food consumed in America. Much of it consists of staples that are reflected in the menus. Expect lots of pork, beef, corn, wheat and other mainstays of the larder. All those farms also mean lots of dairy products. A milk shake from a roadside diner is perfect on a summer day.

Summer and fall bring harvests of all kinds, and at roadside stands and country markets you can find fruit such as strawberries and apples, as well as all manner of vegetables: beans, squash, tomatoes and more. Corn, fresh from the field and cooked on the cob, is one of life's simple pleasures.

Chicago is known for thick pizza, ribs and hot dogs. It is also home to scores of excellent ethnic restaurants, reflecting its diverse population.

Getting There & Around

Chicago has two major airports. Central and Southern Illinois are served by Lambert–St Louis International Airport and by regional airports in Springfield, Champaign and Peoria.

Greyhound buses link most major centers in the state and connect to neighboring states as well.

Amtrak has several lines in Illinois that radiate from Chicago. Many of them are partially funded by the state.

Interstate highways crisscross the state. I-57 runs nearly the length of the state, I-55 links Chicago and St Louis and I-80 is the main east-west route in the US. I-90 and I-94 head north into Wisconsin, the latter via Milwaukee.

On weekdays the expressways (as the highways are called locally) are jammed during the morning and evening rush hours for 30 miles around Chicago. Don't expect things to be much better during the rest of the day, either.

Chicago

• **pop 2.8 million**

Chicago is, quite simply, a great city. It has great art, great architecture, great music, great shopping and great food. Its short history has seen it emerge as a leader in fields as diverse as architecture, blues music, nuclear physics and commodity trading.

Although Chicago has a gritty, hard-working reputation, it spent the 1990s gussying itself up. Huge planters have sprouted like weeds in the medians of streets throughout the city, and thousands of trees have been planted. The Loop – once a desert after hours – is now the city's fastest-growing residential neighborhood, with a burgeoning nightlife scene.

Highlights

- Discovering Loop architecture
- Experiencing the wonders of the Museum Campus
- Walking along the lake
- Strolling the neighborhoods of the North Side
- Listening to blues in a club
- Devouring Chicago pizza

The city's charm isn't just downtown, however. Great rewards await those who explore Chicago's many neighborhoods, each with its own personality and culture. Taken together, the city's attractions are more than a vacation in themselves.

HISTORY

Native Americans in the region can be traced back to 1000 AD. In the late 17th century, the dominant tribe in the region, the Potawatomi, gave the name 'Checaugou' to the area around the Chicago River mouth. The linguistic roots of the name are hazy; some say it means 'wild onion,' others 'skunk.'

In 1779 Quebec trader Jean Baptiste Point du Sable established a fur-trading store on the north bank of the river. After the Louisiana Purchase, in 1803, the US government built Fort Dearborn here as a wilderness outpost.

The last Indian resistance was crushed in the 1832 Black Hawk War, and all the remaining Indian lands in Illinois were appropriated, including the lands of the Potawatomi in Chicago. Five years later, Chicago incorporated as a town, with 4170 residents. When the Illinois and Michigan Canal opened in the 1840s, shipping began to flow through Chicago from the Caribbean to New York, traveling via the Great Lakes and the St Lawrence Seaway. In 1851 the Illinois Central Railroad was given land to establish freight yards, and Chicago was soon the transportation hub of the US.

The first steel mill opened in 1857, and immigrants flooded in to take jobs in industry and the railroads. The population had reached 100,000 by 1860. Five years later the first stockyards opened. In 1871, the Illinois and Michigan Canal was deepened so that the flow of the Chicago River was reversed: It began to flow south, taking the city's sewage down the river instead of into the lake, where it had caused outbreaks of typhus.

On October 8, 1871, much of the city burned to the ground in the great Chicago fire (see 'Don't Look at Me – It Was the Cow'). The whole inner city was destroyed, and 90,000 were left homeless. This disaster enabled the city to replace wide areas of substandard housing and create space for modern industrial and commercial buildings. The next year, Montgomery Ward founded the first mail-order company, a business that was to spawn many imitators, including Sears, Roebuck & Co.

The city's industrial workers had begun to organize as early as the 1860s, and for the next 50 years there were a series of strikes and protests, many of them violent and brutally suppressed by police. The 1894 Pullman strike was put down by legal injunctions that effectively made strikes illegal in the USA for the next 30 years.

The Union Loop Elevated rail system was completed in 1897, defining the boundaries of the city center and making it feasible to commute from outer suburbs. Despite political corruption and embezzlement, more civic improvements were made in the early 20th century, and immigration swelled the population to more than 2 million by 1910. In addition, hundreds of thousands of blacks from the American South moved to Chicago, lured by industry's demand for labor. This later came to be known as the Great Migration.

In the 1920s, Prohibition led almost immediately to the infamous period of gangsterism and to even more widespread corruption. In the middle of the devastating depression, after the murder of Mayor Anton Cermak, the Democratic Party machine gained control of city politics and maintained it for the next 50 years.

The city grew strong during WWII; its population peaked in 1950, then started to decline as residents moved to outer suburbs and other states. Despite some improvements, the postwar period was dominated by corruption scandals, Civil Rights protests and the fiasco of the 1968 Democratic Convention, when the local police went on a nationally televised rampage against protestors calling for an end to the Vietnam War and other evils. Starting in the 1970s, traditional industries declined severely: The stockyards and South Shore steel mills closed, and smaller factories moved to the suburbs or Southern states. Many others simply went out of business.

Longtime mayor Richard J Daley, who presided over the city with an iron fist during the tumultuous 1960s, died in 1976, leaving a political vacuum that lasted until

Chicago Firsts

Not every Chicago invention has been as significant as steel-framed skyscrapers (1885) or hospital trauma rooms (1966). Many others have had far-reaching social impact, if only on the palate or wallet.

1893: Cracker Jack The candy-coated popcorn, peanuts and a prize are still a popular snack.

1893: Zipper People have been groping for them ever since.

1920s: One-Way Ride Gangster Hymie Weiss receives credit for deducing the role cars could play in dispatching rivals. Some historians give this important credit to 'Dingbat' Obierta.

1930: Hostess Twinkie Rumors that the very first one is still as fresh as the day it was extruded are thought to be apocryphal.

1930: Pinball Bally is still a large local company.

1947: Spray Paint Municipalities have been cleaning it off official surfaces ever since. Chicago even banned the sale of spray paint within city limits a few years ago.

1955: McDonald's The first one was actually opened in Des Plaines by Chicagoan Ray Kroc. More than 21,000 branches have opened in 103 countries since. The original store is now a free museum (☎ 847-297-5022), 400 Lee St, with erratic hours.

1968: 'Police Riot' This term was used in a government report on police behavior at the Democratic National Convention, when marauding cops beat up protesters, reporters and anyone else who got in the way.

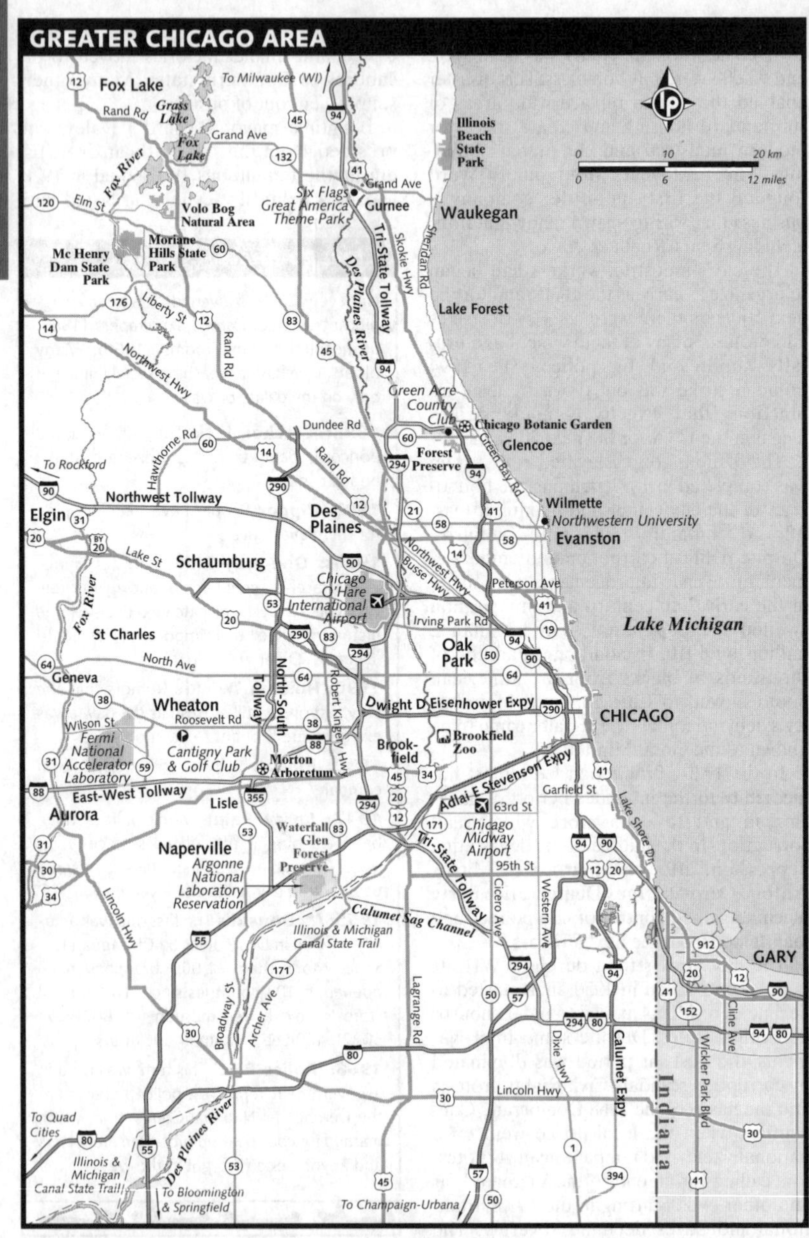

GREATER CHICAGO AREA
0
10
20 km
0
6
12 miles
Fox Lake
Grass Lake
Fox Lake
Rand Rd
Grand Ave
Fox River
To Milwaukee (WI)
Illinois Beach State Park
Elm St
Volo Bog Natural Area
Moriane Hills State Park
Mc Henry Dam State Park
Six Flags Great America Theme Park
Grand Ave
Gurnee
Waukegan
Tri-State Tollway
Skokie Hwy
Sheridan Rd
Des Plaines River
Liberty St
Rand Rd
Northwest Hwy
Lake Forest
Green Acre Country Club
Chicago Botanic Garden
Glencoe
Green Bay Rd
Dundee Rd
Hawthorne Rd
Rand Rd
Forest Preserve
To Rockford
Northwest Tollway
Elgin
Des Plaines
Wilmette
Northwestern University
Evanston
Lake St
Schaumburg
Northwest Hwy
Busse Hwy
Fox River
Chicago O'Hare International Airport
Peterson Ave
Irving Park Rd
St Charles
Lake Michigan
Oak Park
North Ave
Geneva
North-South Tollway
Robert Kingery Hwy
Wheaton
Dwight D Eisenhower Expy
CHICAGO
Roosevelt Rd
Wilson St
Fermi National Accelerator Laboratory
Cantigny Park & Golf Club
Morton Arboretum
Brookfield
Brookfield Zoo
Adlai E Stevenson Expy
East-West Tollway
Lisle
Aurora
Garfield St
63rd St
Chicago Midway Airport
Lake Shore Dr
Waterfall Glen Forest Preserve
Naperville
Argonne National Laboratory Reservation
95th St
Tri-State Tollway
Lincoln Hwy
Calumet Sag Channel
Cicero Ave
Western Ave
Illinois & Michigan Canal State Trail
GARY
Broadway St
Archer Ave
Lagrange Rd
Dixie Hwy
Calumet Expy
Cline Ave
Wickler Park Blvd
Indiana
Lincoln Hwy
To Quad Cities
Des Plaines River
Illinois & Michigan Canal State Trail
To Bloomington & Springfield
To Champaign-Urbana

Don't Look at Me – It Was the Cow

For more than 125 years, legend has had it that a cow owned by a certain Mrs O'Leary kicked over a lantern, which ignited some hay, which ignited some lumber, which ignited the whole town. The image of the hapless heifer has endured despite official skepticism from the start. Now that story may have been milked for the last time.

Richard Bales, a lawyer and amateur historian, has spent years examining the case from every angle. His conclusion is that Bessie was a victim of circumstance. It seems that Mrs O'Leary's barn was shared by a neighboring family. Each day Daniel 'Peg Leg' Sullivan dropped by to feed his mom's cow. Bales' evidence, gathered from thousands of pages of postinferno investigations, indicates that 'Peg Leg' accidentally started the fire himself and then tried to blame it on the bovine. After all, if you had just burned down what was then the fourth-largest city in the US, who would *you* blame?

The Chicago City Council has accepted Bales' version of the story; in 1997 the cream of Chicago politics passed a resolution officially absolving the O'Leary family of blame. Of course, for proponents of the cow story, this revision is nonsense, and during the 1999 cow craze (see 'Holy Cow!'), the bovine in front of the Chicago Historical Society was shown kicking over a lantern.

Harold Washington was elected as Chicago's first black mayor, in 1983. This set off years of unseemly wrangling that often had racial overtones but which also resulted in much-needed reforms. More political turmoil followed Washington's death in 1987. However, the election of another Daley, Richard M, in 1989, coincided with relative prosperity for Chicago. More inclusive than his father, Daley and his city government have been more sympathetic to minorities and have tried to tackle intractable problems, such as the appalling public schools.

Michael Jordan and the winning Chicago Bulls were a metaphor for Chicago in the 1990s, when the city successfully hosted the opening of the 1994 World Cup and held a peaceful Democratic Convention in 1996. But everything hasn't changed: A 1998 federal undercover sting netted a half dozen of the local representatives called aldermen, proving that corruption never goes out of style.

ORIENTATION

The intersection of Madison and State Sts in the Loop is the center of Chicago's logical street-numbering system. As you go north, south, east or west from here, each increase of 800 in street numbers corresponds to 1 mile. At every increase of 400 there is a major arterial street. For instance, Division St (1200 N) is followed by North Ave (1600 N) and Armitage St (2000 N). If you tell a local to meet you at 800 West and 3200 North, he or she will show up at the corner of N Halsted St and W Belmont Ave.

The central downtown area is the Loop, and beyond it, Chicago is a city of neighborhoods, some with vague boundaries, others precisely defined. Much of Chicago is a 'side' – North, West, South, etc. Using the Loop as the center of a pie you can figure out which side is which, although borders can be fuzzy. The Near North Side includes River North and the Gold Coast, north of the river from the Loop to around North Ave and Lincoln Park. From there the North Side runs all the way to Evanston, encompassing Lincoln Park and other favored neighborhoods. To the west of the North Side is, sensibly enough, the Northwest Side, an area that begins around the Kennedy

Expressway and extends west. The true West Side is a pie-shaped swath with the Stevenson Expressway as its southern border. The border between the West and Northwest Sides is ill defined and depends on the neighborhood allegiance of whomever you ask. The South Side is basically everything south of the Loop and the Stevenson. There's a little Southwest Side down by 95th St and Evergreen Park, and there's even a tiny East Side near the Indiana border.

Maps

Maps are widely sold at hotels, drugstores, and newsstands. Rand McNally's *Chicago* is the most popular, but it doesn't show El lines or stations and is better for driving than walking or touring. Besides the maps in this book, Lonely Planet publishes a laminated city map for Chicago that shows both streets and the El.

INFORMATION

Tourist Offices

The main Visitor Information Center is in the Chicago Cultural Center (☎ 312-744-2400, TTY 312-744-2947), just to the left as you enter at 77 E Randolph St at Michigan Ave. They have hundreds of brochures and booklets, and maps of varying quality. The staff will endeavor to answer your questions as well. The center is open 10 am to 6 pm weekdays, 10 am to 5 pm Saturday, 11 am to 5 pm Sunday.

A second location, the Chicago Visitor Center in the Water Tower Pumping Station (same telephone numbers as previous), 163 E Pearson St at Michigan Ave, is quite impressive. Besides the usual plethora of

Capone's Chicago

Al Capone was the mob boss in Chicago from 1924 to 1931, when he was brought down on tax evasion charges by Elliot Ness, the federal agent whose task force was given the name 'The Untouchables' because its members were supposedly impervious to bribes. (This wasn't a small claim, given that thousands of Chicago police and other officials were on the take, some of them raking in more than $1000 a week.)

Capone came to Chicago from New York in 1919. He quickly moved up the mob ranks and took control of the city's South Side in 1924. He expanded his empire by making 'hits' on his rivals. These acts, which usually involved thousands of bullets shot from submachine guns (or, 'Tommy guns'), were carried out by Capone's lieutenants. Capone earned the nickname 'Scarface' because of the large scar on his left cheek, the legacy of a dance-hall fight.

Prohibition fueled the success of the Chicago mob. Not surprisingly, the citizens' thirst for booze wasn't eliminated by government mandate, and gangs made fortunes dealing in illegal beer, gin and other intoxicants. Clubs called 'speakeasies' were highly popular and were only marginally hidden from the law, an unnecessary precaution, given that crooked cops usually were the ones working the doors. Commenting on the hypocrisy of a society that would ban booze and then pay him a fortune to sell it, Capone said: 'When I sell liquor, they call it bootlegging. When my patrons serve it on silver trays on Lake Shore Drive, they call it hospitality.'

It can be hard to find traces of the Capone era in Chicago. The city and the Chicago Historical Society take dim views of Chicago's gangland past, with nary a brochure or exhibit on Capone or his cronies (though the CHS bookstore does have a good selection of books). Many of the actual sites have been torn down; what follows are some of the notable survivors.

Capone's Chicago Home At 7244 S Prairie Ave, this home was built by Capone and mostly used by his wife, Mae, son 'Sonny' and other relatives. Al preferred to stay near the Loop, where his vices were. The house looks almost the same today.

brochures, you'll find helpful employees, a good café, a sitting area with a fireplace, free chilled water, free treats for dogs (!) and a store selling genuine Chicago souvenirs, such as old voting machines that let you vote as often as you want. You can also tour the historic old pumps in the basement. The center is open 7:30 am to 7 pm daily.

The center with the longest hours is the Illinois Marketplace Visitor Information Center, 700 E Grand Ave at Navy Pier. It's open 10 am to 9 pm Sunday to Thursday, 10 am to midnight Friday and Saturday.

For information in advance about events such as festivals and exhibitions, contact the Chicago Office of Tourism branch at the Chicago Cultural Center (☎ 312-744-2400), 78 E Washington St, Chicago, IL 60602.

For information geared toward meetings and conventions, try the Chicago Convention and Tourism Bureau (☎ 312-567-8528, 312-567-8500 for an automated system that will fax you information you request), 2301 S Lake Shore Drive, Chicago, IL 60616.

Money

ATMs The vast majority of ATMs in Chicago operate under the 'Cash Station' moniker. You will find them almost everywhere. The Cash Station network is linked up with Cirrus and Plus, the two largest ATM networks worldwide. They'll also accept MasterCard or Visa for cash advances provided you know your PIN.

Currency Exchange You will notice garishly lit 'currency exchanges' on many street corners. They are not what you might think. They are primarily for people without bank accounts who 'exchange' their 'currency' in

Capone's Chicago

Holy Name Cathedral At 735 N State St, this was the scene of two gangland murders. North Side boss Dion O'Banion was gunned down in his floral shop at 738 N State in 1924 after he crossed Capone. In 1926 his successor, Hymie Weiss, died in a hail of Capone-ordered bullets emanating from a window at 740 N State. Both had tried to rub out Capone, who returned the favor far more effectively.

St Valentine's Day Massacre Site In perhaps the most infamous event of the Capone era, seven members of the Bugs Moran gang were lined up against a wall in a garage by mobsters dressed as cops and gunned down. After that, Moran cut his losses and Capone gained control of Chicago's North Side vice. The garage at 2122 N Clark St was torn down in 1967 to make way for a retirement home. The building just south remains. A house used as a lookout by the killers stands across the street, at 2119 N Clark St.

The Green Mill This tavern (☎ 773-878-5552, 4802 N Broadway) was one of Capone's favorite nightspots. During the mid-1920s the cover for the speakeasy in the basement was $10. You can still listen to jazz in its vintage setting today.

Mt Carmel Cemetery Capone is now buried in this cemetery on Roosevelt Rd at Wolf Rd in Hillside, west of Chicago. He and his relatives were moved here in 1950 from Mount Olivet Cemetary, on the Far South Side, a less classy resting place than Mt Carmel. Al's simple gray gravestone is concealed by a hedge; it reads 'Alphonse Capone, 1899–1947, My Jesus Mercy.' It has been stolen and replaced twice. Capone's neighbors include old rivals O'Banion and Weiss.

For a guided tour of many of these sights, along with enthusiastic amateur theatrics, try **Untouchable Gangster Tours** (☎ 773-881-1195). Using an old school bus, two actors lead the tour, taking people for a ride that's part show, part history. It's $22 for adults, $16 for children; reservations required.

Chicago for Children

Chicago can seem like a big mean city to kids, but it doesn't have to. Almost all the museums have installed special areas aimed at entertaining, amusing and even (don't let this one slip) educating them. Here are some of the major sites that work at being kid friendly (see the main text for full information):

Chicago Children's Museum – on Navy Pier, an obvious place to start, followed by the rest of the pier itself

Art Institute of Chicago – features an excellent hands-on art area

Field Museum of Natural History – dinosaurs everywhere!

Lincoln Park Zoo – with a special children's area where the kids can commune with rodents

Museum of Science and Industry – a perennial favorite

Chicago Academy of Sciences – lots of new interactive environmental exhibits

RICK GERHARTER

Lincoln Park Zoo

return for services such as money orders or check-cashing. If you slip your German marks, French francs or other currency under the bulletproof divider at a currency exchange, they will come sliding right back, possibly with an ill-tempered tirade from the clerk.

To exchange your foreign currency you need a Foreign Exchange Broker. There's one in the arrivals area at Terminal 5, the international terminal at O'Hare.

In the city itself there are a few choices; call to check hours before setting out. American Express has exchange services that favor its cardholders or people carrying its brand of traveler's checks: (☎ 312-435-2595) 122 S Michigan Ave; (☎ 312-435-2570) 625 N Michigan Ave; and (☎ 773-477-4000) 2338 N Clark St, in Lincoln Park.

World's Money Exchange (☎ 312-641-2151), 6 E Randolph St above Walgreens, has the largest selection of foreign currency, accepting bills from 120 countries.

Don't expect good rates from these places, but do expect high fees.

Taxes You will encounter a thicket of taxes as you spend money in Chicago. Sad for the visitor, many of the taxes are aimed right at you, since you can't vote for (or against) the local politicians who impose them. The basic sales tax is 8.75%. The hotel tax is 14.9%. The car-rental tax is 18%.

Post

The following three post offices have a full range of services and accept general delivery mail. Try to avoid them at lunchtime on weekdays, when they are swamped.

Main Post Office (☎ 312-654-3895) 433 W Harrison St, Chicago, IL 60607

Loop Station (☎ 312-427-4225) 211 S Clark St, Chicago, IL 60604

Fort Dearborn (☎ 312-644-7603) 540 N Dearborn St, Chicago, IL 60610

Telephone

The city has two area codes, with more soon to come as the proliferation of pagers, faxes and Internet connections sops up the available supply of numbers. The area code ☎ 312 serves the Loop and an area bounded roughly by 1600 North, 1600 West and 1600 South. The rest of the city uses area code ☎ 773. The northern suburbs are area code ☎ 847, those close to the west and the south ☎ 708, and the far west suburbs ☎ 630

Email & Internet Access

The Chicago Public Library (see the Libraries section later in this chapter) has numerous computers at its branches throughout the city where you can surf the Net for free.

Internet Resources

The proliferation of Chicago Web sites is mind numbing. A good starting place is the city's official site (www.ci.chi.il.us/Tourism), with hundreds of pages listing all types of information, plus long-range calendars of events. The *Chicago Sun-Times* site (www.suntimes.com) is easy to navigate to find listings for the latest entertainment and events.

Newspapers & Magazines

Chicago has a long tradition of newspapers and is one of the few American cities still to have separately owned and competing major dailies. On Friday both papers publish comprehensive guides to current entertainment and events.

The *Chicago Sun-Times* concentrates most of its resources on coverage of the city. The paper is known for its columnists, including Robert Feder, Bill Zwecker and famous movie critic Roger Ebert.

The largest newspaper in the Midwest, the *Chicago Tribune* is known for having good writers who are experts in their areas of coverage, and it has a fair amount of foreign and national news from its bureaus worldwide. The Sunday *Trib* weighs in at several pounds and has more than a million readers.

With daily circulation down to 20,000, the *Chicago Defender* gives little hint about the pivotal role it once played in the black community, not just in Chicago but across the nation (see 'The Great Defender').

Each Thursday two free weeklies hit the streets. The *Reader* is a mammoth four-section tabloid listing virtually everything going on in town, from theater to live music to offbeat films to performance art. Navigating your way through this behemoth can take hours.

The other weekly, *New City*, is a nimbler and hipper publication. By no means complete, it lists major goings-on of interest to younger, more 'alternative' readers.

The *Windy City Times* is the city's best gay and lesbian weekly, with local, national and entertainment news. Also look for the *Chicago Free Press* and *Out Guide*, both weekly and free.

Streetwise is a monthly paper sold by the homeless and others down on their luck.

Chicago is a monthly magazine filled with feature articles and culture coverage. For visitors, the magazine's greatest value lies in

The Great Defender

After World War I the *Chicago Defender*, founded in 1905 by Robert S Abbot, was the most important black newspaper in the country and the most popular newspaper among Southern blacks.

A complex distribution system, which included Pullman sleeping-car porters throwing bundles of papers off at every stop, meant each week's edition was read by hundreds of thousands of African Americans. So effective was the *Defender* that racist whites, fearing the paper's influence, murdered its readers and tortured its distributors.

The paper played a pivotal role in the Great Migration, the movement of millions of Southern blacks to Chicago and other northern cities in the 1910s. Abbott knew that the influx of thousands of blacks into the city would increase the community's clout – and by sheer numbers alone, it did. Abbott, the city's first black millionaire, reveled in the Great Migration. By 1929, the *Defender*'s circulation was 230,000. After Abbott's death in 1940, however, the paper's influence steadily declined. Today it is but a shadow of its former self.

its massive restaurant listings. The scores of expert reviews are up to date and indexed by food type, location, cost and more.

Radio

Once you're caught in the Chicago area's terrible traffic, you'll want something on the radio. The following stations might be of interest:

WMAQ – 670 AM, news and traffic reports every 10 minutes

WGN – 720 AM, middle-of-the-road chatter with lots of farm reports

WLS – 890 AM, talk radio with lots of paranoid blabbermouths

WBBM – 780 AM, news and traffic reports every 10 minutes

WBEZ – 91.5 FM, the National Public Radio affiliate

WXRT – 93.1 FM, a rock station with an eclectic playlist

WFMT – 98.7 FM, classical

Travel Agencies

In addition to the American Express branches listed under Currency Exchange, you can try Council Travel (☎ 312-951-0585, ⓔ councilchicago@ciee.org), at 1160 N State St. They specialize in budget and student travel.

Bookstores

There are hundreds of bookstores in the city. Check the yellow pages for complete listings of special-interest stores for everything from religion to socialism.

For serious fiction, you can't touch Barbara's Bookstores, (☎ 312-642-5044) 1350 N Wells St in Old Town, and (☎ 312-222-0890), near the entrance to Navy Pier.

Sandmeyer's Bookstore (☎ 312-922-2104), 714 S Dearborn St, in the heart of the Printer's Row neighborhood, emphasizes fiction and architecture.

The Seminary Cooperative Bookstore (☎ 773-752-1959), 5757 S University Ave, is the bookstore of choice for several University of Chicago Nobel Prize winners. The store carries more than 100,000 academic and general titles.

The goal of The Savvy Traveller (☎ 312-913-9800), 310 S Michigan Ave near the Art Institute, is to carry every travel-related title in print. They also sell gadgets such as electricity converters, luggage and atlases. There are two Rand McNally travel stores (☎ 312-332-2009), 150 S Wacker Drive and (☎ 312-321-1751), 444 N Michigan Ave.

There are two good gay and lesbian–focused bookstores: Women & Children First (☎ 773-769-9299), 5233 N Clark St in Andersonville and Unabridged (☎ 773-769-9299), 3251 N Broadway in Lake View.

If you're in search of a new book, also stop by the following:

Afrocentric Book Store
(☎ 312-939-1956) 234 S Wabash

57th Street Books
(☎ 773-684-1300) 1301 E 57th St in Hyde Park

Brent Books & Cards
(☎ 312-364-0126) 309 W Washington St

Michigan Ave Brent Books
(☎ 312-920-0940) 316 N Michigan

Libraries

The Harold Washington Library Center (☎ 312-747-4300), 400 S State St on the block bounded by Congress Parkway and Van Buren St, is a huge free library. You can while away hours wandering its nine floors; the main collections begin on the 3rd floor. The library is open Monday 9 am to 7 pm; Tuesday and Thursday 11 am to 7 pm; Wednesday, Friday and Saturday 9 am to 5 pm; Sunday 1 to 5 pm. You can also call and get the location nearest you of one of the scores of branches across the city.

The Newberry Library (☎ 312-943-9090) 60 W Walton St between Clark and Dearborn Sts, is a research facility geared toward scholars. Its 1.5 million volumes cover specialties such as the Italian Renaissance, cartography and genealogy. After registering at the front desk, visitors may browse.

The Gerber-Hart Library (☎ 773-883-3003), 3352 N Paulina in Lake View, is one of the nation's oldest and largest gay and lesbian libraries.

Universities

The Chicago area has plenty of universities and colleges. The four major campuses are:

The University of Illinois at Chicago
(☎ 312-996-7000) with 30,000 students and a sprawling campus south of the Eisenhower Expressway and west of S Halsted St

DePaul University
(☎ 773-325-7000) a Catholic institution with 5000 students at its main campus in Lincoln Park on W Fullerton Ave, and several buildings in the Loop

Northwestern University
(☎ 847-491-3741) a private university with more than 10,000 students; the main campus is in Evanston, the law and medical schools in Streeterville, east of N Michigan Ave

University of Chicago
(☎ 773-702-1234) a private institution known for its graduate programs; it has more than 7000 students at its Hyde Park campus

Cultural Centers

The Chicago Cultural Center (☎ 312-744-1424), 78 E Washington St, was once the Chicago public library. Now it's an amalgam of a number of draws, such as an art gallery, the Museum of Broadcast Communications, a visitor information center, a special events venue, and a public space where you can get a muffin and coffee and chill out for a while.

Laundry

Laundries in the Spincycle chain are all over town. They are clean, air-conditioned and have TVs. A call to ☎ 312-578-2233 will tell you the branch closest to you.

Toilets

You shouldn't have a problem finding a place to go. Try department stores, large bookstores, hotels, fast-food joints, bars, train stations and other large public places. There's usually some facility that's not too vile at the parks and beaches.

Medical Services

Northwestern Memorial Hospital (☎ 312-908-2000), 233 E Superior St east of N Michigan Ave, is the most convenient to the Near North and Gold Coast. If your condition is not acute, call first, because they also have a clinic that can see you in a more timely and convenient manner than if you wait in the triage line in the emergency room here or at Cook County Hospital.

The Howard Brown Health Center (☎ 773-871-5777), 945 W George St near the Diversey El stop, specializes in treating lesbians and gay men.

If you are broke and have no insurance, head to Cook County Hospital (☎ 312-633-6000), 835 W Harrison St, one block south of the Medical Center El stop on the Blue Line. If your problem is not life threatening, you may wait 12 hours or more. However, if you have been shot, stabbed or injured in a horrific accident, you will come here by ambulance and will receive excellent trauma care; this is where the concept was invented. The TV show *ER* is based on this place.

Emergency

Dial ☎ 911 for police, fire or ambulance services.

For any disaster on the lake, call the Coast Guard at ☎ 847-729-6190.

To report a picked pocket or other minor crime for which speedy police response is useless, dial ☎ 312-746-6000. You will need a police report in most cases to file for an insurance claim.

The Chicago Rape Victim Emergency Assistance 24-hour hot line is ☎ 312-744-8418.

Useful Organizations

Horizons (☎ 312-929-4357, 6 pm to 10 pm), 961 W Montana St, is a good social service agency for gays, lesbians and bisexuals, offering counseling and a crisis hot line. They can make referrals to social service agencies and provide many other services as well. You can reach the Chicago Area Gay & Lesbian Chamber of Commerce at ☎ 888-452-4262.

For AIDS- and HIV-related questions, try the AIDS Foundation of Chicago (☎ 312-922-2322), 411 S Wells St, suite 300, or the Illinois AIDS Hotline (☎ 800-243-2437).

The Mayor's Office for People with Disabilities (☎ 312-744-6673, TTY 312-744-7833) is a good starting point for referral information on questions about the availability of services.

Dangers & Annoyances

Parts of Chicago are as safe as you'll find in any American city; other parts are virtual killing fields, with several murders a day. There were 697 murders in 1998, more than recorded in all five boroughs of New York City. Fortunately, there is little reason for you to go to the unsafe parts of the city, although you should be aware of their existence – not just for your own safety, but so that you have a balanced image of Chicago.

The kind of crime you should be most aware of in Chicago is the same type that exists throughout the world: pickpockets, purse or jewelry snatching, auto break-ins and bike stealing. Basically, if you leave something accessible to crooks, they will try to steal it.

Unsafe Areas Unless noted otherwise, the areas written about in this book are reasonably safe during the day. At night the lakefront, major parks (with the exception of Grant Park during any kind of festival or concert) and certain neighborhoods (especially south and west of the Loop) can become bleak and forbidding places. The Loop, Near North, Gold Coast, Old Town, Lincoln Park, Lake View and Wrigleyville neighborhoods are generally safe at night, especially on the busy commercial streets.

Be aware that neighborhoods can change in just a few blocks. Four blocks west of N Clark St in the Gold Coast and south of Old Town lie the Cabrini-Green housing projects, which are very unsafe.

Use your common sense. If a neighborhood, street, El station or any other situation doesn't seem right or worries you, don't stick around.

Women Travelers You will be safe alone in the parts of the city considered generally safe, though exercise a degree of caution and awareness of your surroundings. The El is normally safe, even at night, though you might want to seek out the busier cars. Or take one of the buses that parallel many train lines.

THE LOOP

The Loop is the historic center of the city, drawing its name from the elevated tracks that circle it. It's a fascinating place to walk around, and its buildings constitute a virtual textbook of American architecture. During the daytime it hums with shoppers, office workers and tourists. At night things used to get much quieter, but recently there have been numerous signs of life after dark: Old theaters have been reborn and historic office buildings have been converted to condos and hotels. It's now Chicago's fastest-growing residential neighborhood.

On Thursday night the city runs a program called 'Downtown Thursday Night' that features performances, longer hours at museums and stores and specials at bars and restaurants.

Art Institute of Chicago

One of the world's premier museums, the Art Institute of Chicago (☎ 312-443-3600), Adams St at S Michigan Ave, has a collection that spans 5000 years of art from around the globe. Sculpture, textiles, painting and furniture are just a few of the wide-ranging media represented. The museum's collection of Impressionist and Postimpressionist paintings is second only to collections in France. Here's a brief rundown of the types of art you'll find: African and ancient American art; American art from the 17th century through 1955; ancient Egyptian, Greek and Roman art; architecture; Chinese, Japanese and Korean art, beginning 5000 years ago; European decorative arts since the 12th century; European painting and sculpture from 1400 to 1800; 19th-century European painting; photography; prints and drawings; textiles; 20th-century painting; and sculpture. The main entrance is the original 1893 Allerton Building, where Adams St meets Michigan Ave. The bronze lions flanking the steps are Chicago icons. Open 10:30 am to 4:30 pm weekdays (Tuesday till 8 pm), 10 am to 5 pm Saturday, noon to 5 pm Sunday and holidays; closed Thanksgiving and Christmas. Admission is a recommended $8 for adults, $5 for children (free on Tuesday). Technically you can give less, but nobody does.

Museum of Broadcast Communications

This museum (☎ 312-629-6000), at 78 E Washington St in the Chicago Cultural Center, is dedicated to Chicago's pioneering role in American radio and television. Famous local moments are also replayed, including the Kennedy–Nixon debate of 1960, which many argue contributed to Nixon losing the election, because on television his shifty eyes and heavy beard made him look like a crook. The museum also has rooms where visitors can watch videotapes. Open 10 am to 4:30 pm Monday to Saturday, noon to 5 pm Sunday, closed major holidays; free (the fee for unlimited videotape viewing is $2). There are also many galleries with temporary exhibits of art.

The Four Seasons

Russian-born artist Marc Chagall loved Chicago and donated this grand mosaic in 1974. Using thousands of bits of glass and stone, he portrayed six scenes of the city in hues reminiscent of the Mediterranean coast of France, where he kept his studio. The work is on view in the plaza just south of the BankOne building, at S Dearborn and W Monroe Sts.

Chicago Loop Architecture Walking Tour

The Loop is a festival of important, beautiful and interesting architecture. Just by walking its streets for about half a day, you can trace the development of modern architecture in Chicago, the US and worldwide. This walking tour (see map on page 107) can be completed in less than two hours. You can explore the public spaces of most buildings during office hours on weekdays. Weekend entrance is much more problematic. Note that the proper names for some buildings are actually their addresses.

Start at the entrance to the Sears Tower observation deck, on W Jackson Blvd, just west of S Franklin St, two blocks from the Quincy El stop.

Sears Tower By some factors still the world's tallest building (233 S Wacker St; see 'Tower Envy'), this 110-story tower, completed in 1974, consists of nine structural square 'tubes' that rise from the building's base, two stopping at the 50th floor, two more ending at the 66th floor, three more calling it quits at 90 stories and two stretching to the full height. Sears is now based in the suburbs, and this building contains a mix of tenants.

Join the mobs on the Skydeck (☎ 312-875-9696), whose entrance is on the W Jackson Blvd side of the block-size building,

Tower Envy

The Sears Tower was the undisputed size champ in the tallest-building category until the 1996 opening of the Petronas Towers in Malaysia. But the matter wasn't that simple. The 88-story Petronas Towers were shorter than the Sears Tower until two 111-foot decorative towers were added, topping the 110-story Sears Tower by 20 feet.

Civic boosters licked their erectile wounds until the Council on Tall Buildings and Urban Habitat, the international group that certifies tall buildings, came to the Sears Tower's rescue. In 1997 the council expanded the categories of tallest buildings from one to four:

- height to structural or architectural top
- height to the highest occupied floor
- height to the top of the roof
- height to the top of the antenna

Under this scheme, Petronas wins the first category, Sears takes the second and third and the taller of New York's World Trade Center towers garners the fourth. So, thanks to the Council on Tall Buildings and Urban Habitat, Chicago and the Sears Tower still win two out of four.

Meanwhile, hopes are high for a proposed 2000-foot tower for a site at 7 S Dearborn St. Although financing for the $600 million, 108-story project is uncertain, local boosters hope it will soon bring the undisputed title of world's tallest building back to the city.

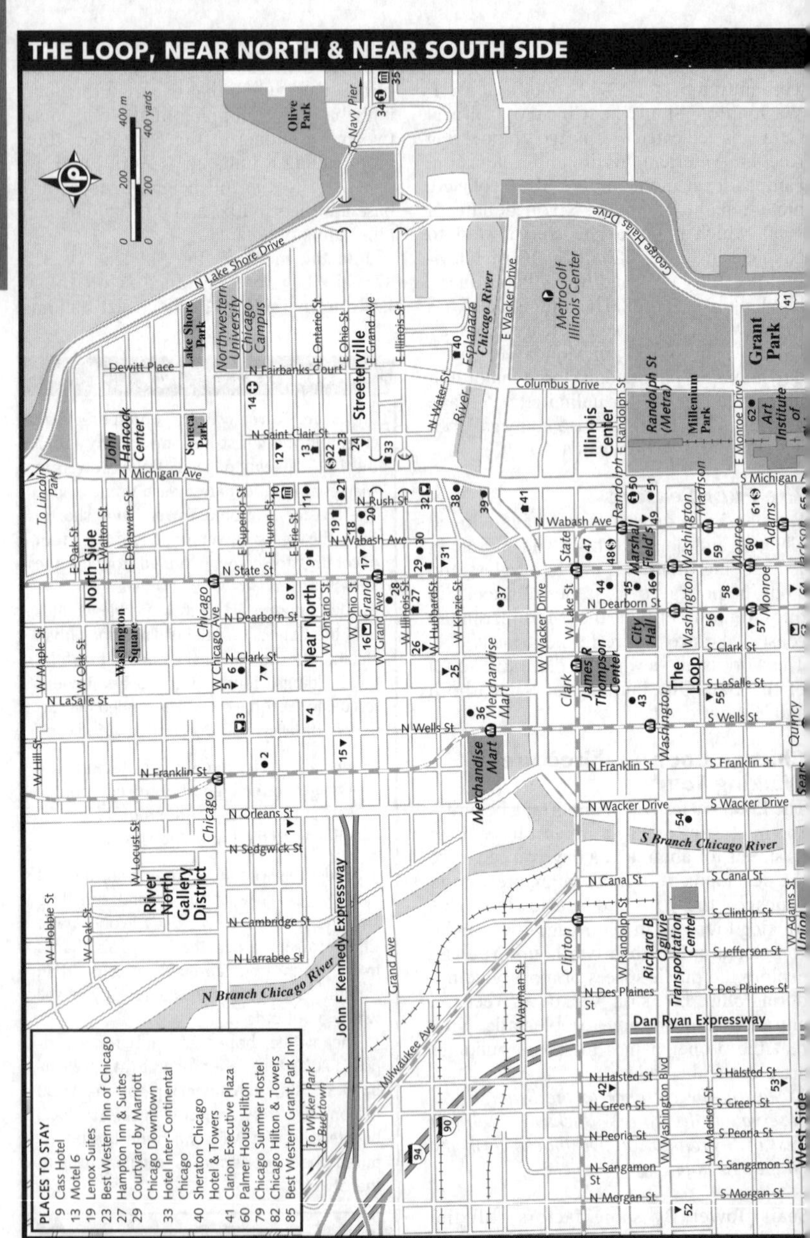
THE LOOP, NEAR NORTH & NEAR SOUTH SIDE
0 200 400 m
0 200 400 yards
PLACES TO STAY
9 Cass Hotel
13 Motel 6
19 Lenox Suites
23 Best Western Inn of Chicago
27 Hampton Inn & Suites
29 Courtyard by Marriott Chicago Downtown
33 Hotel Inter-Continental Chicago
40 Sheraton Chicago Hotel & Towers
41 Clarion Executive Plaza
60 Palmer House Hilton
79 Chicago Summer Hostel
82 Chicago Hilton & Towers
85 Best Western Grant Park Inn
Olive Park
To Navy Pier
N Lake Shore Drive
Lake Shore Park
Northwestern University Chicago Campus
Dewitt Place
John Hancock Center
Seneca Park
N Michigan Ave
To Lincoln Park
North Side
Washington Square
Near North
Streeterville
Chicago River
Esplanade
MetroGolf Illinois Center
George Halas Drive
E Wacker Drive
Columbus Drive
Illinois Center
Randolph St (Metra)
Millenium Park
Grant Park
Art Institute of Chicago
Marshall Field's
City Hall
James R Thompson Center
The Loop
Merchandise Mart
River North Gallery District
N Branch Chicago River
S Branch Chicago River
John F Kennedy Expressway
Dan Ryan Expressway
Richard B Ogilvie Transportation Center
Milwaukee Ave
Grand Ave
To Wicker Park & Bucktown
West Side
N Wabash Ave
N State St
N Dearborn St
N Clark St
N LaSalle St
N Wells St
N Franklin St
N Orleans St
N Sedgwick St
N Cambridge St
N Larrabee St
N Wacker Drive
N Canal St
N Des Plaines St
N Halsted St
N Green St
N Peoria St
N Sangamon St
N Morgan St
S Clark St
S LaSalle St
S Wells St
S Franklin St
S Wacker Drive
S Canal St
S Clinton St
S Jefferson St
S Des Plaines St
S Halsted St
S Green St
S Peoria St
S Sangamon St
S Morgan St
W Randolph St
W Washington Blvd
W Madison St
W Adams St
E Monroe Drive
E Randolph St
Washington
Madison
Monroe
Adams
Quincy
Clinton
Clark
State
W Lake St
W Wacker Drive
W Kinzie St
W Hubbard St
W Illinois St
W Grand Ave
W Ohio St
W Ontario St
W Chicago Ave
W Oak St
W Maple St
W Locust St
W Hill St
W Hobbie St
W Wayman St
E Ohio St
E Ontario St
E Grand Ave
E Illinois St
E Erie St
E Huron St
E Superior St
E Delaware St
E Walton St
E Oak St
N Rush St
N Fairbanks Court
N Saint Clair St
N Water St
Chicago
Grand
Sears
Union
90
94
41

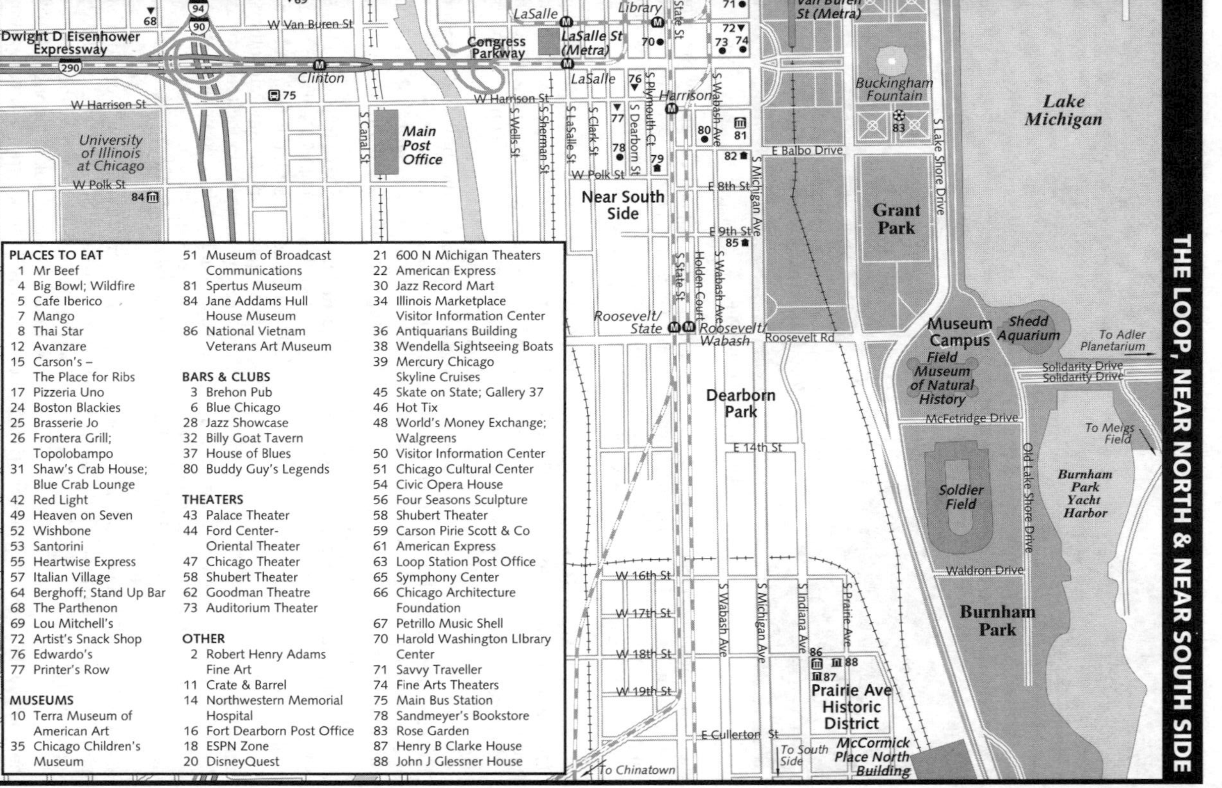
THE LOOP, NEAR NORTH & NEAR SOUTH SIDE
Lake Michigan
Shedd Aquarium
Museum Campus
Field Museum of Natural History
Soldier Field
Burnham Park
Burnham Park Yacht Harbor
Grant Park
Buckingham Fountain
Dearborn Park
Near South Side
Prairie Ave Historic District
McCormick Place North Building
Main Post Office
University of Illinois at Chicago
Dwight D Eisenhower Expressway
Congress Parkway
To Adler Planetarium
To Meigs Field
To Chinatown
To South Side
PLACES TO EAT
1 Mr Beef
4 Big Bowl; Wildfire
5 Cafe Iberico
7 Mango
8 Thai Star
12 Avanzare
15 Carson's – The Place for Ribs
17 Pizzeria Uno
24 Boston Blackies
25 Brasserie Jo
26 Frontera Grill; Topolobampo
31 Shaw's Crab House; Blue Crab Lounge
42 Red Light
49 Heaven on Seven
52 Wishbone
53 Santorini
55 Heartwise Express
57 Italian Village
64 Berghoff; Stand Up Bar
68 The Parthenon
69 Lou Mitchell's
72 Artist's Snack Shop
76 Edwardo's
77 Printer's Row
MUSEUMS
10 Terra Museum of American Art
35 Chicago Children's Museum
51 Museum of Broadcast Communications
81 Spertus Museum
84 Jane Addams Hull House Museum
86 National Vietnam Veterans Art Museum
BARS & CLUBS
3 Brehon Pub
6 Blue Chicago
28 Jazz Showcase
32 Billy Goat Tavern
37 House of Blues
80 Buddy Guy's Legends
THEATERS
43 Palace Theater
44 Ford Center-Oriental Theater
47 Chicago Theater
58 Shubert Theater
62 Goodman Theatre
73 Auditorium Theater
OTHER
2 Robert Henry Adams Fine Art
11 Crate & Barrel
14 Northwestern Memorial Hospital
16 Fort Dearborn Post Office
18 ESPN Zone
20 DisneyQuest
21 600 N Michigan Theaters
22 American Express
30 Jazz Record Mart
34 Illinois Marketplace Visitor Information Center
36 Antiquarians Building
38 Wendella Sightseeing Boats
39 Mercury Chicago Skyline Cruises
45 Skate on State; Gallery 37
46 Hot Tix
48 World's Money Exchange; Walgreens
50 Visitor Information Center
51 Chicago Cultural Center
54 Civic Opera House
56 Four Seasons Sculpture
58 Shubert Theater
59 Carson Pirie Scott & Co
61 American Express
63 Loop Station Post Office
65 Symphony Center
66 Chicago Architecture Foundation
67 Petrillo Music Shell
70 Harold Washington LIbrary Center
71 Savvy Traveller
74 Fine Arts Theaters
75 Main Bus Station
78 Sandmeyer's Bookstore
83 Rose Garden
87 Henry B Clarke House
88 John J Glessner House

RICK GERHARTER

Looking up in the Loop

where on a rare, truly clear day you can see for 40 to 50 miles – as far as Indiana, Michigan and Wisconsin. You reach the top after a 70-second elevator ride in the world's fastest elevators. Open 9 am to 11 pm daily from March through September, 9 am to 10 pm daily the rest of the year; $8/5 adults/children.

Walk east on Jackson until you reach the intersection of S LaSalle St.

Chicago Board of Trade The original 1930 tower (141 W Jackson Blvd; designed by the firm Holabird & Root), fronting LaSalle St, is a classic 45-story Art Deco skyscraper topped with a statue of Ceres, the Roman goddess of agriculture.

Turn north on LaSalle.

Federal Reserve Bank These buildings (230–231 S La Salle St) were constructed in 1922 and 1924. Their major exterior difference is that the federal building has Corinthian columns, while its sibling's are Ionic. The Bank of America has a 2nd-floor public banking area that would do any Roman god proud.

The Rookery The 1885–88 Rookery (209 S LaSalle St) is one of Chicago's most beloved buildings. The original design, by the firm Burnham & Root, surrounds a spectacular atrium space that was remodeled in 1907 by Frank Lloyd Wright.

190 S LaSalle St New York architect Philip Johnson's sole contribution to Chicago (1987) bows heavily to long-gone Chicago architectural gems. The lobby, with its vaulted ceiling covered in gold leaf, is designed to impress the building's lawyer tenants and overwhelm their clients.

Walk two blocks east on W Adams St to the intersection of S Dearborn St.

Marquette Building Above its massive base, the 1893 Marquette (140 S Dearborn St) is really an E-shaped building facing north. Sculptured panels by Tiffany and others, above the entrance and in the lobby, recall the exploits of French explorer and missionary Jacques Marquette.

Turn south on S Dearborn St.

Chicago Federal Center (on Dearborn St between Adams St and Jackson Blvd) Ludwig Mies van der Rohe gave this complex his signature austere look in his original 1959 design. The 30-story Dirksen Building was completed in 1964 and followed in 1974 by the 42-story Kluczynski Building. The post office, finished the same year, completes the troika. *Flamingo* (1974), a bright red sculpture by Alexander Calder, offers a counterpunch to Mies' ebony palette.

Monadnock Building Really two structures, an 1891 northern portion and an 1893 southern addition, this building (53 W Jackson Blvd) can be considered the Lourdes of the Loop for architecture buffs on a pilgrimage. The original portion of the building was constructed entirely with load-bearing walls that are six feet wide at the base. Working with brick, architects Burnham & Root fashioned a free-flowing facade from base to cornice that becomes almost sensuous around the bottoms of the window bays. The addition was built with a then-revolutionary metal frame that avoided the thick base walls.

Fisher Building The main structure of this yellowish terra-cotta-clad building (343 S Dearborn St) was completed in 1896. The exterior boasts a playful menagerie of shells, fish, crabs and other sea creatures.

Turn east on W Van Buren St.

Harold Washington Library Center Robustly traditional, with details derived from many classic Chicago forms, this 1991 building (400 S State St) was the winner of an architectural contest voted on by the public. Note the whimsical copper roof details, including studious-looking owls.

Turn north on State St and walk 2½ blocks.

Palmer House Hilton Designed by Holabird & Roche and completed in 1927, this luxury hotel (17 E Monroe St) is the fourth to bear the name of former owner Potter Palmer. His Francophile wife Bertha's tastes were responsible for the ornate French lobby.

Carson Pirie Scott & Co When the major part of this building (1 S State St) was completed in 1906, critics said it was too ornamental to serve as a retail building. You be the judge as you admire Louis Sullivan's superb metalwork around the main entrance, at State and Madison Sts. The rest of the building is clad simply in white terra-cotta.

Chicago Building This 15-story 1904 building (7 W Madison St) is typical of many designed by the firm Holabird & Roche throughout the Loop during the late 19th and early 20th centuries. The windows fronting State St are classic Chicago style: two narrow sash windows on either side of a larger fixed pane.

Reliance Building Built in the early 1890s by Burnham & Root, the Reliance Building (32 N State St) is like a breath of fresh air. Its lightweight internal metal frame supports a glass facade that gives the building a feeling of lightness, a style that didn't become universal until after WWII. Narrowly avoiding demolition – a common fate for Chicago's architectural gems – the Reliance has been restored and is now the luxurious Hotel Burnham.

RICK GERHARTER

The Reliance Building

Other Buildings of Note

BP-Amoco Building, 200 E Randolph St, three blocks east of Michigan Ave

If it weren't in the aesthetic desert of Illinois Center (a vast collection of truly ugly buildings), the 80-story Amoco Building (1973) – Chicago's second tallest in overall height – might get some respect. It is covered in 43,000 panels of granite.

Wrigley Building, 400 N Michigan Ave at the river

The most photographed building in town was designed with a Hollywood flair: The white terra-cotta actually was cast in six shades, which brighten the closer they move to the top, ensuring that the building pops out of the sky whether it's high noon or midnight. It was designed and built between 1919 and 1924.

Tribune Tower, 435 N Michigan Ave, across from the Wrigley Building

The self-proclaimed World's Greatest Newspaper was never one to let modesty get in the way of bombast. When it announced an architectural competition in 1922 for a new headquarters, the requirement was for 'the most beautiful office building in the world.' The winning entry borrowed elements of Gothic cathedrals such as flying buttresses and applied them to a skyscraper.

Around the base are the Tribune Tower Rocks. Eccentric owner Colonel Robert McCormick both collected and had his overworked reporters send rocks from famous buildings and monuments around the world. See how many you recognize. Continuing the tradition, in 1999 the Tribune added a moon rock brought back by Apollo 15. It's in the main lobby.

John Hancock Center, 875 N Michigan Ave at Chestnut St

Perhaps the most recognizable Chicago high-rise, the 100-story, 1127-foot Hancock Center combines, from bottom to top, shopping, parking, offices, condos, tourist attractions and broadcast transmitters. This 1969 building muscles its way into the sky atop a series of cross-braces.

Marshall Field & Co Covering an entire block, Marshall Field's (111 N State St) was built in five stages between 1892 and 1914. On the State St side, the soaring ground-floor retail spaces are topped by Tiffany skylights.

Chicago Theater This 3800-seat theater (175 N State St) is a grand example of the movie palaces of the 1920s. Its architects, Rapp & Rapp, cut their teeth on the 1921 commission and went on to design scores of theaters that increasingly came to resemble fantastic wedding cakes.

Turn west on W Lake St and walk one block under the El structure, which dates from 1897. At N Dearborn St turn south and walk one block, then walk west on W Randolph St.

Richard J Daley Center The 31-story Daley Center (1965; on Dearborn St between Washington Blvd and Randolph St) is home to scores of county courtrooms that have ceilings two floors high. The plaza on the south side is the scene of regular performances and protests. It also hosts 'The Picasso,' the name given by locals to this officially untitled Picasso work. The huge sculpture is made out of Cor-Ten steel (the same material that clads the Daley Center) and is a bird, dog, woman – you decide.

County Building & Chicago City Hall Serving two government bodies, this 1911 Holabird & Roche building (121 N LaSalle St) is adorned with 75-foot columns that were a challenge to construct and support. City Hall constitutes the western half.

James R Thompson Center This bulbous 1986 building (100 W Randolph St) has been controversial from the start, not just

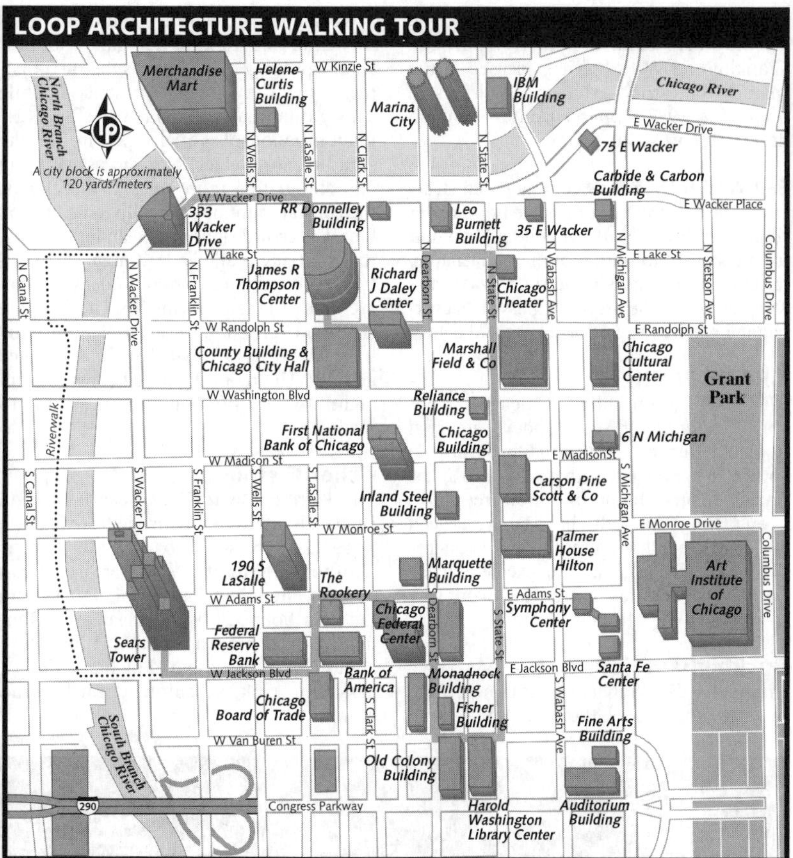

for its shape but for its all-glass design. Architect Helmut Jahn thought the structure should be a metaphor for open government and left off doors, ceilings and walls from interior offices. The effect was to produce a vast greenhouse filled with overheated bureaucrats. Improved air-conditioning has lowered temperatures, and everybody loves the soaring atrium lobby. The sculpture of blobs out front is *Monument with Standing Beast*, by Jean Dubuffet.

Cut through the Thompson Center and exit onto N LaSalle St. Walk north to W Wacker Drive and the Chicago River.

Marina City Look east along the river to the twin 'corncob' condominium towers of this mixed-use complex, located on the north bank of the river between Dearborn and State Sts. Designed by Bertrand Goldberg in 1967, it derives its name from the boat marina built into the structure at water level.

Walk west along Wacker Drive.

Merchandise Mart Completed in 1930 as a wholesale store for Marshall Field & Co, the Merchandise Mart was converted into commercial space by the Kennedy family, who purchased it in 1945. Its 4.1 million sq feet, on the north bank of the river between Franklin and Wells Sts, are encased in the massive limestone exterior. The less said about the 1977 Apparel Center, immediately to the west, the better.

333 Wacker Drive This curving green structure (1983) is the most popular Loop tower to emerge from the 1980s building boom. It is a masterful utilization of the odd triangular site on the curve in the river. Water and sky play across the mirrored glass in an ever-changing kaleidoscope of shapes and colors.

GRANT PARK

This park, often called 'Chicago's front yard,' suffered for years under municipal neglect. But an ambitious program to spruce it up, begun in the early 1990s, has done wonders. Hundreds of new trees have been planted, sidewalks have been replaced and Buckingham Fountain has been repaired. Grant Park is now an excellent place both to visit and travel through on your way to and from the Museum Campus.

Buckingham Fountain

Impressive Buckingham Fountain is twice the size of its model, the Bassin de Latone at Versailles. The central fountain is meant to symbolize Lake Michigan, the four water-spouting sea creatures the surrounding states. The fountain presents a subtle show rather than randomly spraying its 1.5 million gallons. Like so much in life, the spray begins small. Each successive basin fills, stimulating more jets. At the climax, the central fountain spurts up to its full 150 feet. The crowd sighs in awe and is thankful that smoking is allowed. At night the fountain is illuminated by colored lights that are timed to match its moods. The fountain is turned on from 10 am to 11 pm daily from May 1 to October 1. It climaxes once an hour. The mood lighting begins at 8 pm nightly, with 9 pm being the best time to see it.

Other Highlights

The **Petrillo Music Shell**, near E Jackson Blvd, is home to many music festivals. The **Rose Garden**, south of the fountain, is another highlight. A major extension called **Millennium Park** is taking shape in the area bounded by Michigan Ave, Randolph St and Monroe Drive. It will feature a music pavilion designed by Frank Gehry, a skating rink, a sculpture garden and more.

RICHARD CUMMINS

Buckingham Fountain's hourly extravaganza

MUSEUM CAMPUS

The Museum Campus is a recent Chicago creation that brings together institutions devoted to land, sea and sky. A pedestrian underpass makes the campus either a 15-minute walk east from the Roosevelt El stop or a longer, but very enjoyable, sojourn through Grant Park from the Loop. Alternatively, the No 146 bus makes the run from N Michigan Ave and State St in the Loop.

Field Museum of Natural History

Mummies, Native American artifacts, stuffed animals, dinosaurs and more dinosaurs are part of the 20 million artifacts in the collections of the Field Museum (☎ 312-922-9410), at Roosevelt Rd and Lake Shore Drive. Entrances on the north and south sides lead to the dramatic 300-foot-long, two-story-high Stanley Field Hall. Exhibits radiate off this space and include Africa, which attempts to capture the scope of the continent by taking visitors from the streets of Dakar to Saharan sand dunes; Inside Ancient Egypt, which re-creates an Egyptian burial chamber on three levels; and the Dinosaur Hall, with its real and replica skeletons of a range of the beasts who measure their age in the tens of millions. Open 9 am to 5 pm daily except on Thanksgiving, Christmas and New Year's Day; $7/4 adults/children.

John G Shedd Aquarium

The world's largest assortment of finned, gilled, amphibious and other aquatic creatures swims within the marble-clad confines of the Shedd Aquarium (☎ 213-939-2438), 1200 Lake Shore Drive. The centrally located coral reef tank is home to 500 tropical fish, from placid nurse sharks to less neighborly moray eels. The Oceanarium holds a controversial exhibit of 1200lb beluga whales, which were plucked from their Arctic homes and brought to Chicago. Open 9 am to 6 pm daily from June through August; 9 am to 5 pm weekdays, 9 am to 6 pm weekends from September through May; closed Christmas and New Year's Day. Entrance to the entire place costs $11/9 adults/children. For advance-purchase tickets (and to reserve the best Oceanarium times) call ☎ 312-559-0200. On Thursday the original building is free, but you need a reduced-price ticket ($6/5) for the Oceanarium.

Adler Planetarium & Astronomy Museum

On the lake at the end of Solidarity Drive, the Adler Planetarium and Astronomy Museum (☎ 312-922-7827) has a new wing with a digital sky show that allows such cataclysmic phenomena as supernovas to be replicated. Interactive exhibits allow you to simulate cosmic events such as a meteor hitting the earth. Before this major bummer occurs, take advantage of the great lake and city views, both inside and outside. Open 9 am to 5 pm weekdays (till 9 pm Friday), 9 am to 6 pm weekends; open till 9 pm Thursday from late May through early September; closed Thanksgiving and Christmas. Admission is $3/2 adults/children (free Tuesday); the must-see sky shows are another $3 each.

RICHARD CUMMINS

Adler Planetarium

BURNHAM PARK

Just south of the Museum Campus is Burnham Park. The huge hulk across McFetridge Drive from the Field Museum is **Soldier Field**. Built from 1922 to 1926, the oft-renovated edifice is better looking outside than in, which is the reason the Bears are in a perennial battle to win not just a game but a new taxpayer-subsidized football stadium.

The planes overhead come from nearby **Meigs Field**, used almost exclusively by corporate jets. The **Burnham Park Yacht Harbor** completes this increasingly bucolic picture. Nearly ruining it is **McCormick Place**. Called the 'mistake on the lake' for its destruction of prime open space on the lake, this convention center (☎ 312-791-7000) is nevertheless an economic engine for the city's hotels, restaurants, shops and airlines. The 2.2 million sq feet of meeting space are spread over three halls. It's easy to get a cab to McCormick Place, but much harder to get one leaving at, say, 5 pm. Use the 23rd St Metra train station, hidden in the lowest level of the North Building. Trains to and from the Randolph St and Van Buren St stations, in the Loop, are frequent ($1.75).

NEAR SOUTH SIDE

A hundred years ago the best and worst of Chicago mingled freely south of the Loop. Millionaires lived cheek by jowl with prostitutes. Today the entire area, called the South Loop or Near South Side, is undergoing a renaissance. It resurged in the 1980s with the success of the Dearborn Park development, on the site of the old Santa Fe rail yards south of Polk St to 15th St, now home to 15,000 people; and the emergence of Printer's Row, along S Dearborn St from Congress Parkway south to Polk St, as a gentrified district of converted lofts. The Central Station neighborhood is being built on the old Illinois Central yards, east of Michigan Ave and south of Roosevelt Rd.

The Roosevelt El stops on the CTA Red and Green Lines serve the north end of the neighborhood. Otherwise, the No 3 King Drive bus starts at Chicago Ave and N Michigan Ave and stays on Michigan all the way south to Roosevelt Rd, where it shifts one block east to Indiana Ave and covers the length of the neighborhood. The area is improving, but the streets can be quite bleak and empty at night.

The **Spertus Museum** (☎ 312-922-1769), 618 S Michigan Ave, juxtaposes aspects of Jewish life and religion to convey the diversity of both. The Zell Holocaust Memorial presents oral histories from survivors who emigrated to Chicago, as well as the names of Chicagoans' relatives who died. Open 10 am to 5 pm Sunday to Wednesday, 10 am to 8 pm Thursday, 10 am to 3 pm Friday; $5/3 adults/children (free on Friday).

The **Prairie Ave Historic District** is all that remains of a once-rich area that was abandoned by the swells more than a century ago. Surviving mansions include the **John J Glessner House** (☎ 312-326-1480), 1800 S Prairie Ave, and the **Henry B Clarke House**, at 1855 S Indiana Ave. Combined tours of both houses are given at 1, 2 and 3 pm Wednesday to Sunday; $8.

The **National Vietnam Veterans Art Museum** (☎ 312-326-0270), 1801 S Indiana Ave at 18th St, displays the art of Americans who served in the military during the Vietnam War. The collection presents works both pastoral and disturbing. Open 11 am to 6 pm Tuesday through Friday, 10 am to 5 pm Saturday, noon to 5 pm Sunday, closed holidays; $5. Cafe V serves innovative and healthful food.

NEAR NORTH

West of N Michigan Ave between the river and Chicago Ave there was an assortment of warehouses, factories and association headquarters until the 1970s. Thereafter the neighborhood known as River North rapidly changed, as the grimy industrial remnants were swept away and replaced with galleries, trendy shops, hotels and the highest concentration of restaurants in the city.

The neighborhoods north of the river to Chicago Ave, known collectively as Near North, have several distinct areas. Most people are already familiar with **Gold Coast** and the upscale shopping heaven of

N Michigan Ave, called the **Magnificent Mile**. Just west of here is an area now dubbed **North Bridge**, which is rapidly filling up with theme restaurants and amusements. On the weekends and all summer long the sidewalks crawl with Chicagoans and out-of-towners visiting the place of the moment. They usually leave with bulging stomachs and even more bulging bags from the gift stores.

The area east of Michigan Ave is named **Streeterville** and is home to hotels, expensive high-rise condos and offices.

Terra Museum of American Art

Amid the commercial confines of the Mag Mile, this modest museum (☎ 312-664-3939), 666 N Michigan Ave, displays an overview of American art since 1800. The collection includes lesser works by James Whistler, John Singer Sargent, Mary Cassatt and others, including a passel of works by Andrew Wyeth. Special exhibitions focus on American artists. Open noon to 8 pm Tuesday, 10 am to 5 pm Wednesday to Saturday, noon to 5 pm Sunday; $5/3.00 adults/children (free Tuesday).

DisneyQuest

DisneyQuest (☎ 312-222-1300), 55 E Ohio St, has five floors of virtual reality games simulating everything from fantasy settings to roller coasters. All this technological wonder doesn't come cheap: a limited card good for just a few games costs $16, an unlimited card costs $32 for everyone over age seven. The tills are open 11 am to 11 pm daily (until midnight Friday and Saturday). Next door, the Disney Corporation has an outlet for another one of its brands: **ESPN Zone** (☎ 312-644-3776), 43 E Ohio St. Here there's a collection of bars and video games aimed at the same couch-potatoes who watch the cable sports channel. For those able to make it off the BarcaLounger, the place is open 11 am until after midnight daily.

Navy Pier

Navy Pier (☎ 312-595-7437) is more than a half mile long and was once the city's municipal wharf. During the 1990s, $200 million in public money was spent turning it into a combination amusement park, meeting center and food court. A visit here can easily consume half a day, much of it spent wandering the great length. Grab a free map at the entrance. The views from the very end are excellent, and there's no charge to just wander around or get wet in the fun and creative fountains.

There are knickknack shops and lots of places to eat, from McDonald's to expensive sit-down restaurants. The new **Chicago Shakespeare Theater** (see the Entertainment section later in this chapter) adds a bit of class.

Designed to challenge the imaginations of kids age one through 12, the colorful and lively **Chicago Children's Museum** (☎ 312-527-1000), near the main entrance, has numerous politically correct exhibits on topics such as recycling. Open 10 am to 5 pm Tuesday

Holy Cow!

In June 1999, a herd of more than 300 life-size fiberglass cows hit the streets of Chicago. The bovines were bolted into sidewalks throughout the Loop and Near North and struck a chord in a city where millions of cows once met their deaths in the old stockyards. Each of the plastic-horned critters sported a unique look courtesy of a local artist or designer, an idea that the city had borrowed from a similar display in Zurich in 1998. Among the variations, one was painted purple, another covered with artificial grass and another with a back leg mechanized to kick over a lantern. Chicagoans embraced the cows; some cheerfully argued the artistic merits of their favorites while others tried to see all 300. By the end of the summer the cows had become a major tourist attraction. When the herd was corralled for good in October and auctioned off for charity (a few can still be seen lurking around), the Mayor's Office of Special Events had but one beefy problem: how to top the cows in 2000.

RICHARD CUMMINS

Navy Pier, more than half a mile of views, food and entertainment

through Sunday, on Monday from June to September and on some school holidays; $6.

The 150-foot **Ferris Wheel** ($3 per ride) moves at a snail's pace, but that's good for enjoying the views. A variety of performers appear through the summer at the **Skyline Stage** (☎ 312-595-7437), a 1500-seat rooftop venue with a glistening white canopy.

Navy Pier is about a 15-minute walk east from N Michigan Ave. CTA bus No 29 State runs on State St through the Loop until it takes a right on Illinois St in River North. The lakefront bike path goes right past the entrance. There's also a free shuttle service in one of those silly fake trolleys along Grand Ave and Illinois St between State St and the pier. The pier is open 10 am to 10 pm Sunday through Thursday, 10 am to midnight Friday and Saturday. Note that individual restaurants and attractions may have different hours.

NORTH SIDE

North of North Ave begins the area known as the North Side, encompassing Old Town and Lincoln Park, as well as several other neighborhoods.

Water Tower

It's hard to believe that the 154-foot Water Tower, 806 N Michigan Ave, a city icon and focal point of the Mag Mile, once dwarfed all the buildings around it. Built in the late 1860s, the Water Tower and its associated building across the street, the Pumping Station, were constructed with local yellow limestone in a Gothic style popular at the time. This stone construction and lack of flammable interiors saved the two in 1871, when the great Chicago fire roared through. The complex was obsolete by 1906, and only concerted public outcry saved it from demolition. The Pumping Station now houses the Chicago Visitor Center.

Museum of Contemporary Art

The collection at this contemporary art museum (☎ 312-280-2660), 220 E Chicago Ave, includes Franz Kline, René Magritte, Cindy Sherman and Andy Warhol. The displays are arranged to show the gradual blurring of the boundaries between painting, photography, sculpture, video and other media. Open 11 am to 6 pm Tuesday to Sunday (Wednesday till 9 pm), closed Thanksgiving, Christmas and New Year's Day; $7/4 adults/children (free Tuesday).

John Hancock Center

The world's tallest mixed-use building, the John Hancock Center, 875 N Michigan Ave, is the third-tallest overall in Chicago, at

1127 feet. The plaza below street level has a nifty fountain whose curtain of water muffles traffic noise above. The Observatory (☎ 312-751-3681) is less crowded than the Sears Skydeck and has better views. Open 9 am to midnight daily; $7/5.

Gold Coast

Home to some of the city's wealthiest people, the Gold Coast area along Lake Shore Drive north of Oak St was once filled with mansions. Surviving examples are at 1308–1312, 1355 and 1365.

There are two good adjoining beaches on the lakefront. At the north end of Michigan Ave, less than five minutes from the Water Tower, is fabled **Oak St Beach**, the closest real beach to a major business and shopping district in the US and a place to see and be seen, attracting its share of silicon-enhanced chests and abs. **North Ave Beach** is popular for volleyball and has a curving breakwater with postcard-perfect views of the city.

Old Town

Once a simple neighborhood of wood houses, Old Town was one of the first in the city to gentrify in the 1960s. The old wood houses have been fixed up and modified in ways their builders never would have imagined. But those are the lucky ones; many other simple old homes have been demolished by greedy owners whose replacement houses fill the lots to bursting in all their extravagance. The area bordered by North Ave, Wells St, Lincoln Ave, Armitage and Larrabee Sts is safe and filled with architectural surprises.

Lincoln Park

Chicago's most popular neighborhood, named for the park it abuts, is alive day and night with people in-line skating, walking dogs, pushing strollers and driving in circles for hours looking for a place to park. The humble origins of most of the blocks away from the lake have been lost under the waves of renovation and gentrification that began in the mid-1970s. Notable highlights are few, but the entire neighborhood, which stretches roughly from North Ave north along the lake to Diversey Parkway and west to Clybourn and Ashland Aves, is a pleasant place to stroll and sample some of the scores of eateries and bars.

Lincoln Park Proper

At 6 miles in length, this is Chicago's largest park. Its 1200 acres stretch north from North Ave to Diversey Parkway, where they narrow along the lake and continue until the end of Lake Shore Drive. There are paths for walking, riding and skating, and ponds where you can rent paddleboats.

The museum of the **Chicago Historical Society** (☎ 312-642-4600), 1601 N Clark St at North Ave, is devoted to Chicago's development and history. The roles of immigration and industry are addressed, as are the problems of slums and the lives of the rich. Special exhibitions are the museum's strong point. Open 9:30 am to 4:30 pm Monday to Saturday, noon to 5 pm Sunday, closed major holidays; $5/3 adults/children (free Monday).

The **Lincoln Park Zoo** (☎ 312-742-2000) is one of Chicago's most popular attractions not just because admission is free, but also because of its wide range of exhibits, featuring 1600 animals on a compact 35-acre setting. The official address is 2200 N Cannon Drive, but in reality it is easily reached from most parts of the park; there are entrances to it on all sides. The zoo recently completed a major rebuilding program that includes the Regenstein Small Mammal–Reptile House, a real stunner. Other popular critters include the gorillas, lions, penguins and elephants. Food has been upgraded as well, and there are several nice cafés. Open 9 am to 5 pm daily.

Near the zoo, the **Lincoln Park Conservatory** (☎ 312-742-7736) has rotating displays of seasonal plants and a permanent display of large ferns. Open 9 am to 5 pm daily; free.

The new home of the **Chicago Academy of Sciences** (☎ 773-549-0606) is across Fullerton Ave from the north side of the zoo. Among the exhibits in the building known as the Peggy Notebaert Nature Museum are exhibits showing how many different wild animals live in urban Chicago,

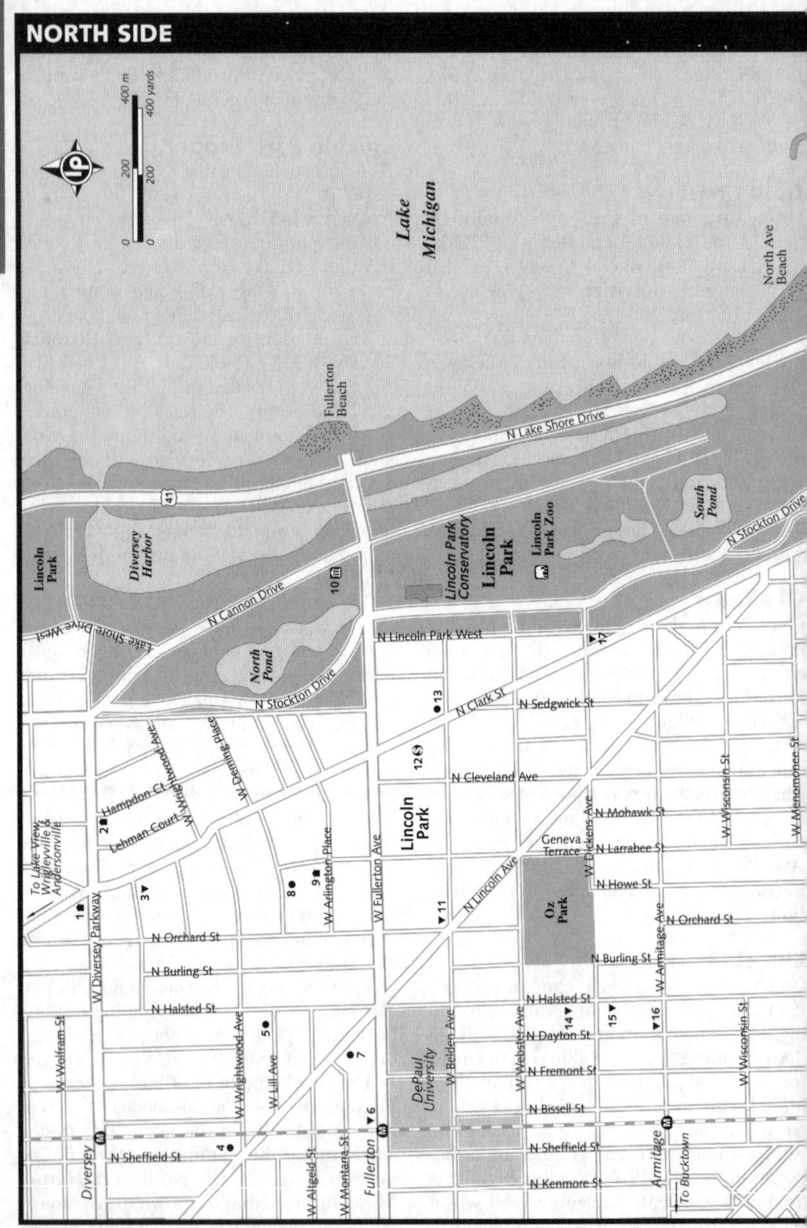
NORTH SIDE
0
200
400 m
0
200
400 yards
Lake Michigan
North Ave Beach
Fullerton Beach
N Lake Shore Drive
41
Lincoln Park
Diversey Harbor
Lake Shore Drive West
N Cannon Drive
10
North Pond
N Stockton Drive
Lincoln Park Conservatory
Lincoln Park
Lincoln Park Zoo
South Pond
N Stockton Drive
N Lincoln Park West
17
13
N Clark St
N Sedgwick St
12
N Cleveland Ave
Hampdon Ct
W Wrightwood Ave
W Deming Place
Lehman Court
2
To Lake View, Wrigleyville & Andersonville
Lincoln Park
N Mohawk St
Geneva Terrace
N Larrabee St
W Dickens Ave
N Howe St
W Wisconsin St
W Menomonee St
8
9
W Arlington Place
W Fullerton Ave
3
1
W Diversey Parkway
11
N Lincoln Ave
Oz Park
N Orchard St
N Orchard St
W Armitage Ave
N Burling St
N Burling St
N Halsted St
N Halsted St
14
15
16
W Wolfram St
W Wrightwood Ave
5
W Lill Ave
7
W Belden Ave
W Webster Ave
N Dayton St
N Fremont St
W Wisconsin St
DePaul University
6
N Bissell St
4
N Sheffield St
N Sheffield St
Diversey
W Altgeld St
W Montana St
Fullerton
N Kenmore St
Armitage
To Bucktown

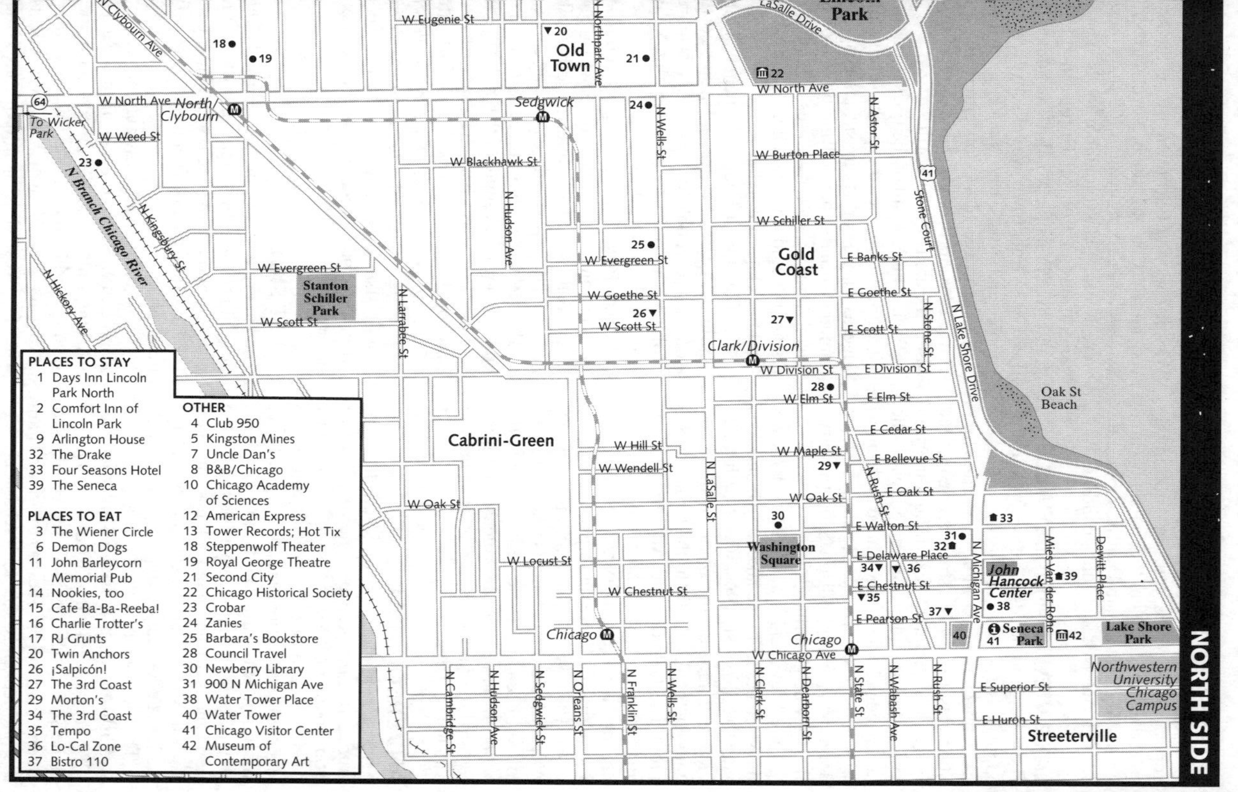
NORTH SIDE
Oak St Beach
N Lake Shore Drive
Stone Court
N Stone St
N Astor St
LaSalle Drive
Park
W North Ave
Old Town
Gold Coast
Cabrini-Green
Streeterville
Clark/Division
Sedgwick
North/Clybourn
Chicago
Washington Square
John Hancock Center
Seneca Park
Lake Shore Park
Northwestern University Chicago Campus
Stanton Schiller Park
N Branch Chicago River
To Wicker Park
Dewitt Place
Mies Van der Rohe
N Michigan Ave
N Rush St
N Wabash Ave
N State St
N Dearborn St
N Clark St
N LaSalle St
N Wells St
N Franklin St
N Orleans St
N Sedgwick St
N Hudson Ave
N Cambridge St
N Larrabee St
N Kingsbury St
N Hickory Ave
N Northpark Ave
W Eugenie St
W Blackhawk St
W Evergreen St
W Goethe St
W Scott St
W Schiller St
W Burton Place
W Division St
W Elm St
W Maple St
W Oak St
W Chicago Ave
W Hill St
W Wendell St
W Chestnut St
W Locust St
W Weed St
N Clybourn Ave
E Banks St
E Goethe St
E Scott St
E Division St
E Elm St
E Cedar St
E Bellevue St
E Oak St
E Walton St
E Delaware Place
E Chestnut St
E Pearson St
E Superior St
E Huron St
PLACES TO STAY
1 Days Inn Lincoln Park North
2 Comfort Inn of Lincoln Park
9 Arlington House
32 The Drake
33 Four Seasons Hotel
39 The Seneca
PLACES TO EAT
3 The Wiener Circle
6 Demon Dogs
11 John Barleycorn Memorial Pub
14 Nookies, too
15 Cafe Ba-Ba-Reeba!
16 Charlie Trotter's
17 RJ Grunts
20 Twin Anchors
26 ¡Salpicón!
27 The 3rd Coast
29 Morton's
34 The 3rd Coast
35 Tempo
36 Lo-Cal Zone
37 Bistro 110
OTHER
4 Club 950
5 Kingston Mines
7 Uncle Dan's
8 B&B/Chicago
10 Chicago Academy of Sciences
12 American Express
13 Tower Records; Hot Tix
18 Steppenwolf Theater
19 Royal George Theatre
21 Second City
22 Chicago Historical Society
23 Crobar
24 Zanies
25 Barbara's Bookstore
28 Council Travel
30 Newberry Library
31 900 N Michigan Ave
38 Water Tower Place
40 Water Tower
41 Chicago Visitor Center
42 Museum of Contemporary Art

a computer lab where visitors can solve environmental problems and one of those trendy rooms where you can walk among butterflies. Open 10 am to 5 pm daily (until 8 pm Wednesday, and until 6 pm June through August); $6/3 adults/children.

LAKE VIEW & WRIGLEYVILLE

These neighborhoods have become just as popular as Lincoln Park to the south, but are younger and have more of an edge. Specific sights are few, but strolls along Halsted St, Clark St, Belmont Ave or Southport St, where the mundane is mixed with the trendy, edgy and unusual, can be both entertaining and surprising. Halsted St from Belmont Ave to Addison St is the city's main gay neighborhood.

Lake View begins at Diversey Parkway and stretches from the lake to Ashland Ave. Near Addison St, what was North Lake View has adopted the name of the Cubs' stadium, thanks mostly to the efforts of Realtors. The Belmont and Addison El stops serve the area well, with able bullpen support from the Diversey, Wellington, Southport and Sheridan stops.

At 1060 W Addison St at Clark St, **Wrigley Field** draws tourists who pose year-round under the classic neon sign over the main entrance. See the Spectator Sports section later in this chapter for details about watching a game.

ANDERSONVILLE

Once a neighborhood of Swedish immigrants, the blocks surrounding Clark St from about 5000 North through Bryn Mawr Ave have become popular with young professionals and various creative types. There are numerous cafés and unusual shops along Clark St. The Berwyn El stop on the Red Line is a 10-minute walk east of Clark St. The No 22 Clark bus also cuts through the heart of Andersonville.

The permanent collection at the small **Swedish-American Museum Center** (☎ 773-728-8111), 5211 N Clark, focuses on the lives of the Swedes who originally settled Chicago. Open 11 am to 4 pm Tuesday to Friday, 11 am to 3 pm weekends; $2/1 adults/children.

WICKER PARK & BUCKTOWN

Ground zero for the trendy and vibrant Wicker Park and Bucktown area is the six-way intersection of Damen, North and Milwaukee Aves. For more than 100 years these were working-class neighborhoods where generations of Central European immigrants lived in simple wood-frame homes. In the 1980s, Bucktown was discovered by yuppies and artists, who quickly gentrified the area on the blocks on either side of Damen Ave north of the railroad tracks that bisect the area at 1800 North.

Wicker Park, south of the tracks and surrounding the namesake park, retains an edge, as yuppies, artists, musicians, Hispanic immigrants and others all mix in a mostly harmonious manner. Cafés, exquisite restaurants and dives peddling brain tacos for a buck line Milwaukee Ave.

The Blue Line El stop at Damen will put you in the heart of the area. Farther north along Damen, public transportation is more problematic. A cab ride from the Near North will cost about $6.

Wicker Park, a triangular park south of the Damen El stop, is the focus of the neighborhood, where buffed bods walk pedigreed dogs past retirees playing chess.

The **Nelson Algren House**, a three-flat building one block south of the park at 1958 W Evergreen St, is where the writer created some of his greatest works about gritty life in the neighborhood. His novels *Never Come Morning* and *The Man with the Golden Arm* are Chicago classics. You can't go in, but you can admire the house from the street.

WEST SIDE

The flat expanse west of the Loop and affluent lakefront is a patchwork of ethnic neighborhoods, urban renewal, blight, gentrification and a lot of sleepy areas that defy description.

The area west of Milwaukee Ave, the Loop and S Halsted St has always been a working-class area. Neighborhood names such as Greek Town, Little Italy and others reveal the origins of their early residents. The far West Side neighborhoods that radiate out from W Madison St, such as Lawndale, are some of the worst in the city.

The **University of Illinois at Chicago** already has 30,000 students and continues to grow. Its sprawling campus is spreading in all directions from its core, south of the Eisenhower Expressway and west of Halsted St.

Rather than focusing on Poles in America, the **Polish Museum of America** (☎ 773-384-3352), 984 N Milwaukee Ave at Augusta Blvd, focuses on Poles in Poland. Open 11 am to 4 pm daily, closed on major Catholic holidays; $3. The Division El stop on the Blue Line is three blocks north of the museum on Milwaukee Ave.

Jane Addams Hull House (☎ 312-413-5353), 800 S Halsted St, recalls the life and work of Jane Addams, who won the Nobel Peace Prize in 1931. The house, along with the 1905 dining hall, is what remains of a sprawling complex where poor immigrants once could come for food, a bath and various literacy courses. Displays and a 15-minute slide show document the struggle for social justice waged by Addams, Hull House supporters and others. Open 10 am to 4 pm weekdays, noon to 5 pm Sunday; free.

PILSEN

Pilsen has been the first stop for immigrants to Chicago for more than a hundred years. First it was the Czechs, who gave the neighborhood its name (Pilsen is the second-biggest town in the Czech Republic). Later it was home to Poles, Serbs and Croats. In the 1950s Hispanics began arriving in great numbers, drawn by the low rents for both residential and commercial space, which encouraged small business.

Today the streets pulse with the sounds of salsa music, the cries of food vendors with carts and the chatter of a thousand conversations. The focus of the area is 18th St, with its scores of taquerias, bakeries and small shops selling everything from devotional candles to the latest CDs from Mexico.

Founded in 1982, the vibrant **Mexican Fine Arts Center Museum** (☎ 312-738-1503), 1852 W 19th St, is in a renovated and expanded old field house in Harrison Park,

Nobel Peace Prize–winner, Jane Addams

about a five-minute walk from the 18th St El stop. The large exhibition spaces are used for temporary exhibits of work by Mexican artists. Open 10 am to 5 pm Tuesday to Sunday; closed most holidays; free.

CHINATOWN

The charm of Chinatown can best be enjoyed by wandering its streets and browsing in the many small shops and restaurants. Wentworth Ave south of Cermak Rd is the retail heart of the neighborhood, southwest of the Prairie Ave Historic District. The fanciful **On Leong Building**, 2216 S Wentworth Ave, is worth a look. This area is easily reached by the El – ride the Red Line to the Cermak stop and you're one block east of Wentworth Ave, the traditional heart of the neighborhood.

SOUTH SIDE

The South Side has had a tough time since WWII. Whole neighborhoods vanished as crime and blight drove residents away. Housing projects created impoverished enclaves where community ties were broken and gangs held sway. Some areas survived the damage, and redevelopment here now aims to promote mixed-income communities.

The **Illinois Institute of Technology** is noted for the 22 campus buildings designed by Ludwig Mies van der Rohe, which reflect his much copied 'International Style' of architecture, which combines simple metal frames painted black with glass and brick infills. Crown Hall, 3360 S State St, is the classic suspended black-glass box. The Bronzeville-IIT El stop is close by.

The neighborhoods radiating from 35th St and Martin Luther King Drive are together named **Bronzeville** and were the center of Chicago's black culture from 1920 until 1950 – comparable to Harlem in New York. Shifting populations, urban decay and troubled public housing led to its decline, and visitors should be cautious here. Many of the area's grand houses have been restored, especially on Calumet Ave between 31st and 33rd Sts. Note the Frank Lloyd Wright row houses at 3213–19 S Calumet St. The Pilgrim Baptist Church, 3301 S Indiana Ave, was an early home of gospel music and has a vast, opulent interior. Other significant buildings are in miserable condition. The area is best visited by day.

HYDE PARK

University of Chicago

At the prestigious University of Chicago, the heart of the Hyde Park enclave, graduate students outnumber undergrads and some 70 Nobel Prizes have been won. The bookish residents give the place an insulated, pleasant, small-town air. A highlight of the mostly Gothic campus is the imposing **Rockefeller Memorial Chapel**, E 59th St and S Woodlawn Ave.

From the Randolph St and Van Buren St stations in the Loop there is frequent commuter train service on the Metra Electric Line. The 55th-56th-57th St station is convenient for much of Hyde Park and the campus ($1.95).

The university's **Oriental Institute Museum** (☎ 773-702-9521), 1155 E 58th St, displays artifacts from ancient Egypt, Mesopotamia and the Near East. Open 10 am to 4 pm Tuesday to Saturday, noon to 4 pm Sunday; free.

The **David & Alfred Smart Museum** (☎ 773-702-0200), 5550 S Greenwood Ave, has the university's fine-arts collection, with works by Henry Moore and Rodin. Open 10 am to 4 pm Tuesday to Friday (until 9 pm Thursday), noon to 6 pm weekends; free.

Museum of Science & Industry

The Museum of Science and Industry (☎ 773-684-1414), at 57 S Lake Shore Drive on the lakefront, is a vast and confusing yet equally fascinating place that was the Palace of Fine Arts at the 1893 Columbian Exposition. Highlights include the Apollo 8 command module, a WWII German submarine, a replica of a coal mine and an excellent exhibit on scientific imaging. Open 9:30 am to 5:30 pm daily (till 4:30 pm weekdays from September to May); $7/4 adults/children (free Thursday). There's an IMAX theater as well, which costs extra.

Other Attractions

Frank Lloyd Wright's Prairie Style is epitomized in the **Robie House** (☎ 773-702-8374),

Birthplace of the Bomb

At 3:53 pm on December 2, 1942, Enrico Fermi looked at a small crowd of men around him and said, 'The reaction is self-sustaining.' The scene was a dank squash court under the abandoned football stadium in the heart of the University of Chicago. With great secrecy, the gathered scientists had just achieved the world's first controlled release of nuclear energy. More than one sigh of relief was heard amid the ensuing rounds of congratulations. The nuclear reactor was supposed to have been built in a remote corner of a forest preserve 20 miles away, but a labor strike had stopped work. The impatient scientists went ahead on campus, despite many who thought the thing might blow up and take a good part of the city with it. Places such as Los Alamos, New Mexico, and Hiroshima and Nagasaki, in Japan, are more closely linked to the nuclear era, but Chicago is where it began. The bronze sculpture *Nuclear Energy*, a half block north of E 57th St on S Ellis Ave, marks the exact spot.

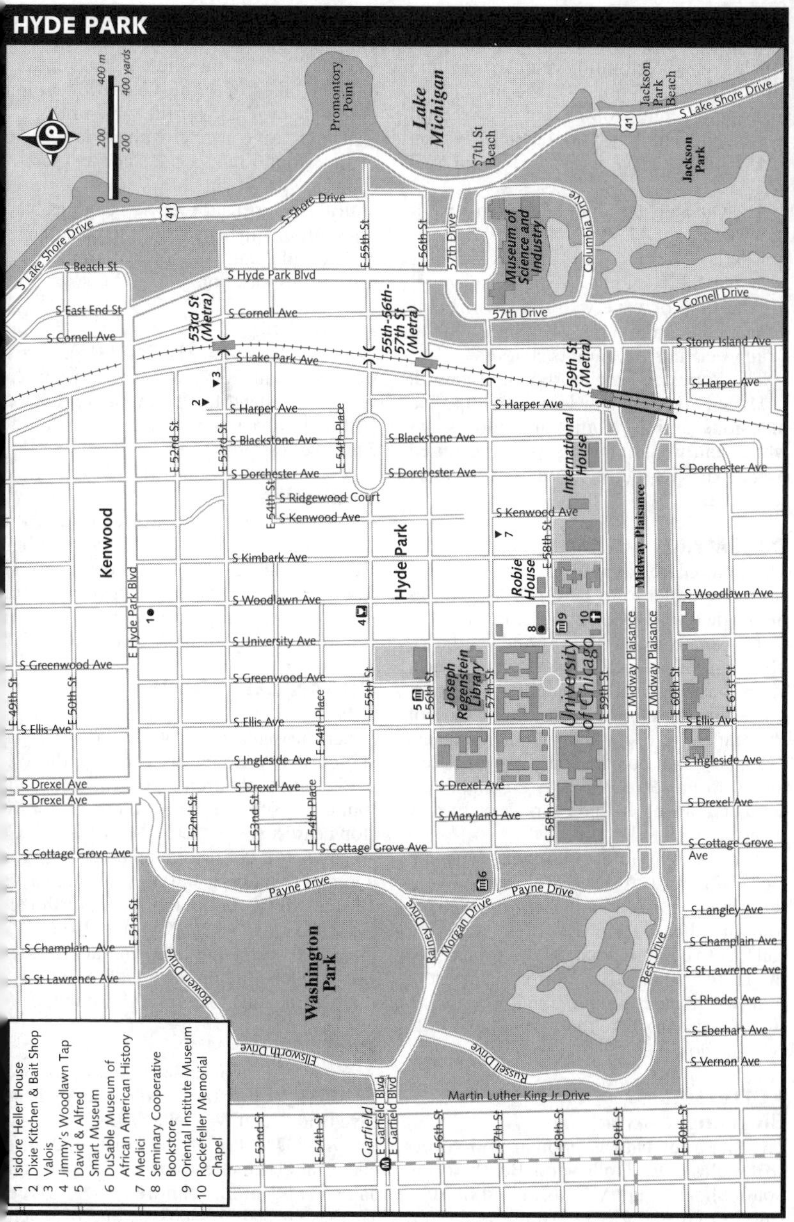
HYDE PARK
0 200 400 m
0 200 400 yards
1 Isidore Heller House
2 Dixie Kitchen & Bait Shop
3 Valois
4 Jimmy's Woodlawn Tap
5 David & Alfred Smart Museum
6 DuSable Museum of African American History
7 Medici
8 Seminary Cooperative Bookstore
9 Oriental Institute Museum
10 Rockefeller Memorial Chapel
Lake Michigan
Promontory Point
57th St Beach
Jackson Park Beach
Jackson Park
Museum of Science and Industry
Kenwood
Hyde Park
Washington Park
University of Chicago
Joseph Regenstein Library
Robie House
International House
Midway Plaisance
53rd St (Metra)
55th-56th-57th St (Metra)
59th St (Metra)
Garfield
S Lake Shore Drive
S Shore Drive
S Hyde Park Blvd
E Hyde Park Blvd
S Cornell Ave
S Lake Park Ave
S Harper Ave
S Blackstone Ave
S Dorchester Ave
S Ridgewood Court
S Kenwood Ave
S Kimbark Ave
S Woodlawn Ave
S University Ave
S Greenwood Ave
S Ellis Ave
S Ingleside Ave
S Drexel Ave
S Maryland Ave
S Cottage Grove Ave
S Beach St
S East End St
S Stony Island Ave
S Cornell Drive
57th Drive
Columbia Drive
Payne Drive
Rainey Drive
Morgan Drive
Best Drive
Russell Drive
Ellsworth Drive
Bowen Drive
Martin Luther King Jr Drive
E Garfield Blvd
S Langley Ave
S Champlain Ave
S St Lawrence Ave
S Rhodes Ave
S Eberhart Ave
S Vernon Ave
E 49th St
E 50th St
E 51st St
E 52nd St
E 53rd St
E 54th St
E 54th Place
E 55th St
E 56th St
E 57th St
E 58th St
E 59th St
E 60th St
E 61st St
E Midway Plaisance

5757 S Woodlawn Ave, with its long, low lines and leaded-glass doors and windows. Much-needed restoration is under way, and tours (11 am to 3 pm; $8) take in only the living and dining rooms, but they're still worthwhile. The 1897 **Isidore Heller House**, 5132 Woodlawn Ave, is also by Frank Lloyd Wright.

The **DuSable Museum of African American History** (☎ 773-947-0600), in Washington Park at 740 E 56th Place, has artworks by and exhibits on black Americans, covering the time of slavery to the Civil Rights era. Open 9 am to 5 pm weekdays, noon to 5 pm weekends; $2/1 adults/children.

The **Kenwood** neighborhood, just north of Hyde Park, has many large and imposing mansions and is a mix of middle-class whites and wealthy blacks. It's best toured by car, since its sights of interest are widely scattered.

PULLMAN

The millionaire railroad car manufacturer started a model town here in 1880, but his dream died with a violent strike in 1894. The factory finally closed in 1981 and was horribly damaged in a 1998 fire. Plans are now afoot to reconstruct the building as a transportation museum. The southern part of Pullman, where craftsmen and managers lived, has been bought up by people determined to preserve it. North Pullman, with simpler housing for laborers, is only now being appreciated.

The lovely **Hotel Florence Museum** (☎ 773-785-8181), 11111 S Forrestville Ave, is the center of preservation efforts. Walking tours are offered many days of the week, but call first to confirm hours. Metra trains go to the 111th St/Pullman station, in the heart of Pullman, 13 miles south of the Loop ($2.75). If you're driving, take the 111th St exit from I-94 and go a half mile west.

ACTIVITIES

Bicycling

The lakefront path is popular and covers 18½ miles from Hollywood Beach to the South Shore Country Club, at 71st St. Bike Chicago (☎ 800-915-2453), at Navy Pier, rents bikes for $8 an hour and $30 a day. They offer free tours of the lakefront every weekday at 1:30 pm whether you rent one of their bikes or bring your own. In-line skates are available for the same prices.

If your visit coincides with the last Friday of the month, rent a bike and be part of Chicago's Critical Mass (www.chicago criticalmass.org), an event that brings bicyclists through the city streets to promote bicycling and the use of bicycles as a means of urban transportation.

Ice Skating

Skate on State (☎ 312-744-3315), across from Marshall Field's, has skating from November through March. You can rent skates ($3) and drink hot chocolate from 9 am to 7 pm. Admission is free.

Swimming

Lakefront beaches have lifeguards from late May through early September. However, you can swim at your own risk whenever you want, depending on what you think of the temperature. The water in August is usually in the 70s Fahrenheit.

ORGANIZED TOURS

Bus

American Sightseeing (☎ 312-251-3100) has standard two-hour bus tours of the city ($16/8 adults/children). You can catch the tour at any of a variety of hotels; call for the stop nearest you. Chicago Motor Coach Co (☎ 312-666-1000) uses double-decker buses and makes pickups and drop-offs all day at 10 stops in the Loop and Near North ($1[illegible] for a daylong ticket). Chicago Trolley Co (☎ 312-663-0260) has dinky imitation street cars that let you hop on and off at the city's main attractions ($16 for a daylong ticket).

Boat

Mercury Chicago Skyline Cruises (☎ 312-332-1353), at the south end of the Michigan Ave Bridge, and Wendella Sightseeing Boats (☎ 312-337-1446), at the north end, offer identical 90-minute tours of the river and lake ($14/7 adults/children). Ugly Duck Cruises (☎ 630-916-9007) is one of several

Streetwalking

Wandering the streets of Chicago is one of the city's greatest pleasures. Doing so in the Near North is one of the easiest places to start – it's fun and fascinating and you won't need any guidance there; just start walking. The maps in this book will guide you and the number of routes is infinite.

Following are four ideas to help you get started. Use these routes as starting points. Wander off them in any direction and see what you find.

Wells St & Lincoln Ave The walk north from Division St to Diversey Parkway covers the heart of Old Town and Lincoln Park in 2.3 miles.

Clark St The 3.4-mile trek north from North Ave to Irving Park Rd goes from the gentrified Lincoln Park neighborhood through lively Lake View and Wrigleyville.

Lincoln Park Start where Dearborn St ends at North Ave and head north; when you reach Diversey Parkway, head east to the lake and you can keep going all the way to Hollywood Ave, 1.7 to 5.4 miles. This is the most bucolic long walk in the city.

The Loop to the Museum Campus Take S Michigan Ave south from Madison St to Roosevelt Rd and east to the Museum Campus, 1.8 miles. This walk encompasses the grandeur of Michigan Ave, Grant Park and the museums.

competing companies operating at Navy Pier. Their cruises along the lakefront start at $16. Both companies operate year-round, except when the waters may be covered with ice (roughly from November to March).

Shoreline Water Taxi (☎ 312-222-9328) offers a handy and scenic water shuttle between the Sears Tower, Navy Pier and Shedd Aquarium; the boats operate 10 am to 6 pm daily from June to September and cost $6/3 adults/children one-way.

Architectural

For a choice of excellent architectural tours by bus or boat, contact the Chicago Architecture Foundation (☎ 312-922-3432), which also has a wide range of walking tours starting at $8 (call for other prices). Offices are at 224 S Michigan Ave and in the John Hancock Center, 875 N Michigan Ave.

Cultural

The city's Office of Tourism (☎ 312-742-190) offers highly worthwhile neighborhood tours that explore areas of the city far from the normal tourist haunts. The tours, which generally last an afternoon and can include lunch, narration by a historian or interaction with some notable locals, cost $30; call for details and reservations.

SPECIAL EVENTS

Dates of special events can shift from year to year, so if any of these events are essential to you, confirm the dates with the Chicago Office of Tourism (☎ 312-744-2400).

February

Black History Month – displays and live events take place all month at Navy Pier.

March

St Patrick's Day Parade – a Chicago institution that snakes south on Dearborn St from the river, dyed green for the occasion; look to see which politicians are jostling to be at the very front – that's the best part.

June

Chicago Blues Festival – this highly regarded three-day festival takes place in Grant Park on the first weekend of the month.

Chicago Gospel Festival – the best gospel music floats for an entire weekend over Grant Park.

Gay and Lesbian Pride Parade – this fabulously celebratory spectacle parades through Lake View, usually on Belmont Ave and Broadway to Lincoln Park.

July

Taste of Chicago – an enormous festival that closes Grant Park for the 10 days leading up to Independence Day; there's lots of greasy food and live music, with fireworks on July 3rd.

August

Chicago Air and Water Show – the latest military hardware flies past the lakefront from Diversey Parkway south to Oak St Beach.

Chicago Jazz Festival – loads of national and local groups play, usually the last weekend of the month in Grant Park.

September

Viva! Chicago – this Latin music festival takes place in Grant Park, usually mid-month.

October

Chicago International Film Festival – scores of films compete during this weeklong event, which every year produces some sleepers and some stinkers.

November

Magnificent Mile Lights Festival – 600,000 lights fill the trees on N Michigan Ave through January.

Neighborhood Festivals

From May through September, just about every neighborhood has a street festival on one weekend. Check with the Mayor's Office of Special Events to see what's on where (☎ 312-744-3315).

PLACES TO STAY

There is a myriad of lodging choices in Chicago, from world-class five-star hotels on N Michigan Ave to hostels far from the center. Your budget and your choice of neighborhood in which to lay your head should help you decide among them.

As the most popular convention city in the US, Chicago is well served with hotels. More than a hundred of all types can be found in the **Loop**, **Near North** and **North Side**, offering more than 28,000 rooms. The conventions can attract tens of thousands of visitors, who fill up even the most remote places to stay and pay top dollar for the chance to do so.

The rates listed are the normal midweek rates. Use them for comparison purposes only, since they can vary widely. There are frequent weekend or special rates, so it is worth checking what deals are on offer for the dates you want to visit.

Beware of a nasty surprise you will find on your bill: The hotel tax is an ugly 14.9%.

Loop area hotels are convenient to Grant Park, the museums and the central business and financial districts. They are usually no more than a 15-minute walk to River North and N Michigan Ave (and for those hotels near the river, much less).

In the **Near North** you can't go a block in any direction without finding a hotel. This is the neighborhood to stay in if you want to be near the center of Chicago's tourist action. Eating, drinking, shopping and entertainment are all here.

The hotels and inns in **Lincoln Park and North** are often cheaper than the big ones downtown and place you near a lot of the city's best nightlife. Daytime pleasures at the museums and in the **Loop** and **Near North** are a short El or bus ride away.

Hotels near **O'Hare** International Airport don't offer any price advantage over those downtown, and you're stuck in the suburbs around O'Hare. The hotels in Rosemont are mostly linked to an enclosed pedestrian walkway leading to the Rosemont Convention Center, a growing collection of buildings hosting trade shows and fairs for collectors of limited-edition plates and the like.

Budget

Hostels constitute the cheapest accommodations in Chicago. As in many towns summer is the best time for availability of hostel rooms.

Loop Area During the summer the ***Chicago Summer Hostel*** *(☎ 312-327-5350 fax 312-327-4287, e hiayhchicago@aol.com 731 S Plymouth Court)* is one block west of State St near the Harrison El station. It is a good choice that's fairly central, in the Printer's Row district in the South Loop. The 1897 building was restored in 1986 when the area became gentrified. Typically open from early June to early September the dorm-style accommodations have two to three beds per room. Rates are $16 for HI cardholders, $19 for everybody else. MasterCard and Visa are accepted. A new, huge year-round hostel *(☎ 312-360-0300, fax 312-360-0313, @ hichicago2000@aol.com, 24 E Congress Parkway)* will be open in the Loop as of 15 June 2000.

Near North The ***Cass Hotel*** *(☎ 312-787-4030, 800-787-4041, fax 312-787-8544, www.casshotel.com, 640 N Wabash Ave)* has simple, small rooms. The location, however, is excellent. Singles/doubles start at $64/69. Those accustomed to the ratty roadside outlets of ***Motel 6*** *(☎ 312-787-3580, 800-621-8055, fax 312-787-1299, 162 E Ontario St)* will be surprised at the budget hotel chain's Chicago offering. Once a French-style hotel in a building from the 1930s, it even has flowers in the lobby. But the rooms are utilitarian and begin at $79/89 a single/double.

Lincoln Park & North North of downtown, near Loyola University, the ***Chicago International Hostel*** *(☎ 773-262-1011, fax 773-262-3673, @ chicagohostel@hotmail.com, 6318 N Winthrop St)* is three blocks south of the Loyola El stop on Sheridan, then two blocks east. It's housed in a 1960s building and its location is safe enough, but you're far from the action: The El takes at least 35 minutes to get you to the **Near North**. A bed in the three- to six-person rooms is $13. Doubles with bath are $40. It's open year-round.

In the heart of Lincoln Park, ***Arlington House*** *(☎ 773-929-5380, fax 773-665-5485, www.arlingtonhouse.com, 616 W Arlington Place)* is a hostel with an excellent location one block west of Clark St. Within the classic brick building, your room may be less than ideal if it's one of the basement four-, six- or seven-bed dorms. The hostel is open year-round, 24 hours a day. IYHF cardholders pay $17 for a bed, others $20. MasterCard and Visa are accepted. Private rooms may be available – ask when you reserve.

The ***Comfort Inn of Lincoln Park*** *(☎ 773-348-2810, 800-221-2222, fax 773-348-1912, 601 W Diversey Parkway)* is about five minutes' walk from Lincoln Park and the lake. There's free parking and free breakfast. Rates start at $75/85 for basic singles/doubles.

Near the busy intersection of Clark St, Diversey Parkway and Broadway, the ***Days Inn Lincoln Park North*** *(☎ 773-525-7010, 888-576-3297, fax 773-525-6998, 646 W Diversey Parkway)* is above one of the North Side's gazillion coffee bars. Basic singles/doubles start at $84/94 and include breakfast.

Hyde Park The ***International House*** *(☎ 773-753-2270, 1414 E 59th St)* is a half block west of the 59th St Metra stop, in a 1932 Gothic building on the University of Chicago campus. Accommodations are in single rooms with shared bath. The rate is $36, but be sure to call first. They accept MasterCard and Visa. Note that if you don't plan to focus your stay on Hyde Park or the university, you'll spend a lot of time on trains to and from the Loop.

O'Hare The ***Excel Inn of O'Hare*** *(☎ 847-803-9400, 800-367-3935, fax 847-803-9771, 2881 Touhy Ave)*, in Elk Grove Village, is a simple motel in the town that likes to boast that it's America's largest industrial park. Singles/doubles start at $67/73, and the hotel offers free shuttle service to and from the airport. There are many other budget motels in this area.

Mid-Range

Loop Area The ***Best Western Grant Park Inn*** *(☎ 312-922-2900, 800-472-6875, fax 312-922-8812, 1100 S Michigan Ave)*, three blocks from the Roosevelt El stop, is not much to look at inside or out. It's close to the Museum Campus, though, and about a mile from McCormick Place. Rates range from $89 to $167 single/double, and there are frequent specials.

Built in 1927, the ***Palmer House Hilton*** *(☎ 312-726-7500, 800-445-8667, fax 312-917-1707, 17 E Monroe Drive)* is on the block bounded by State St, Adams St and Wabash Ave. As in many hotels of its era, the Hilton's 1639 rooms vary greatly in size, so ask for a big one when you check in. Up one

Chicago B&Bs

Chicago has finally caught on to the bed-and-breakfast concept. Bed & Breakfast/Chicago (☎ 773-248-0005, 800-375-7084, fax 773-248-7090, www.chicago-bed-breakfast.com), 607 W Deming Place, Chicago, IL 60614, books rooms at more than a hundred B&Bs throughout the city, most of them in the Gold Coast, Old Town and Lincoln Park areas. The units run the gamut, from bedrooms in upscale old graystones to whole apartments in elevator buildings where you are left to your own devices. The minimum stay is usually two nights. The service provides you with a list of B&Bs based on your desires for price, location and proximity of the owners. Rates for singles and doubles range from about $75 to $250. This is an excellent opportunity to experience life in the more interesting neighborhoods.

flight on an escalator, the lobby is the stunning feature of the place; there's enough gilding to cover several lesser establishments. Rooms normally start at $107/132 single/double and rapidly increase.

The best thing about the ***Clarion Executive Plaza*** *(☎ 312-346-7100, 800-621-4005, fax 312-346-1721, 71 E Wacker Drive)* is its location, right on the river. Rooms in front have excellent views of the Near North. Otherwise, this older hotel is undistinguished. Rates range from $109 to $199.

Near North & Gold Coast One of the best values off Michigan Ave is the ***Best Western Inn of Chicago*** *(☎ 312-787-3100, 800-557-2378, fax 312-467-1665, 162 E Ohio St)*. The building is old and the rooms aren't fancy, but you can't beat the location. Its rooms, costing from $99 to $189, are favorites with tour groups.

The ***Seneca*** *(☎ 312-787-8900, 800-800-6261, fax 312-988-4438, 200 E Chestnut St)*, on the Gold Coast, has the feel of a well-maintained older apartment complex from the 1920s. Accommodations range in size from one room to large suites. Room rates begin at $115, and there are frequent specials.

Don't be fooled by the fact that the ***Courtyard by Marriott Chicago Downtown*** *(☎ 312-329-2500, 800-321-2211, fax 312-329-0293, 30 E Hubbard St)*, at State St, has rooms with good work areas for travelers needing to pound away at the laptop. There's also a sundeck, whirlpool and indoor lap pool. Accommodations start at $129 for singles, $149 for doubles.

The ***Hampton Inn and Suites*** *(☎ 312-832-0330, 800-426-7866, fax 312-832-0333, 11 W Illinois St)*, at Dearborn St, is relatively new and boasts an indoor pool and free breakfast in addition to its comfortable rooms, which range from $139 to $169 single/double.

The location and prices of the ***Lenox Suites*** *(☎ 312-337-1000, 800-445-3669, fax 312-337-7217, www.lenoxsuites.com, 616 N Rush St)* are hard to beat. Some of the suites are barely bigger than one room, but others are sizable and can easily accommodate families. Rates start at $139.

Lake View & Wrigleyville Location, location, location. Between Clark St and the El, the ***City Suites Hotel*** *(☎ 773-404-3400, 800-248-9108, fax 773-404-3405, 933 W Belmont Ave)* definitely has it. You won't go hungry or thirsty or get bored in this locale. The same company, Neighborhood Inns of Chicago (www.cityinns.com) also operates two other stylish North Side hotels. ***The Willows*** *(☎ 773-528-8400, 800-787-3108, fax 773-528-8483, 555 W Surf St)* is west of Broadway near Lincoln Park. The lobby is small; the rooms are big and traditionally decorated. The ***Park Brompton Inn*** *(☎ 773-404-3499, 800-727-5108, fax 773-404-3495, 528 W Brompton St)* is close to Wrigley Field and the Halsted Ave gay scene. Rooms at all three hotels start at $99.

O'Hare The ***Holiday Inn O'Hare International*** *(☎ 847-671-6350, 800-465-4329, fax 847-671-5406, 5440 N River Rd)*, in Rosemont, has indoor and outdoor pools and all the other amenities of this venerable chain, including free shuttle service to and from the airport. Prices for rooms average $140.

Top End

Loop Area When it was built in 1927, the ***Chicago Hilton and Towers*** *(☎ 312-922-4400, 800-445-8667, fax 312-922-5240, 720 S Michigan Ave)* was the largest hotel in the world, with close to 2000 rooms. A $225 million renovation in the mid-1980s brought that total down to a still huge 1543. The public spaces are exquisitely grand, reaching a crescendo in the gilded ballroom, which is modeled after one at Versailles. Singles range from $165 to $260, doubles from $185 to $290.

Near North The ***Hotel Inter-Continental Chicago*** *(☎ 312-944-4100, 800-628-2112, fax 312-944-3050, 505 N Michigan Ave)* has a split personality. The older portion, on the south side, dates from 1929 and holds an indoor swimming pool with a beautiful mosaic. Just north, the cheesy aluminum addition is definitely second-class. When reserving and checking in, be sure to go for the classic side. Rates range from $189 to $289.

The best of the monster convention hotels is the ***Sheraton Chicago Hotel and Towers*** *(☎ 312-464-1000, 800-233-4100, fax 312-329-6929, www.sheratonchicago.com, 301 E North Water St)*. All 1206 rooms have excellent views, and the hotel's lower level is on the parklike River Esplanade, which runs east from Michigan Ave. Rates start at $275, but there's often a plethora of deals.

Gold Coast The grandest hotel in Chicago, the ***Drake*** *(☎ 312-787-2200, 800-553-7253, fax 312-787-1431, 140 E Walton St)*, at Michigan Ave, is ageless. The hotel has a commanding location at the head of Michigan Ave and is convenient to Oak St Beach. Rooms are very quiet. The public places are suitably grand, and the restaurants and bars many notches above the norm. Room rates begin at $275. Suites cost much more, depending on the level of opulence.

The ***Four Seasons Hotel*** *(☎ 312-280-8800, 800-332-3442, fax 312-280-7585, 120 E Delaware St)* is high up in the 900 N Michigan building and is commonly considered the best hotel in Chicago. Each of the 343 rooms is unique, because the rugs and other decor are all handmade. Needless to say, there's an indoor pool, health club, whirlpool, sauna and just about anything else spa-related short of a mud bath. To be king or queen for a day, you'll pay $395 a single, $435 a double, or more.

O'Hare The ***O'Hare Hilton*** *(☎ 773-686-8000, 800-445-8667, fax 773-601-2873)* is right in the middle of O'Hare, across from Terminals 1, 2 and 3. Underground tunnels link up with the terminals, the shuttle tram and the CTA. There is an indoor pool. Rates start at $175 for the large, sound-proofed rooms.

PLACES TO EAT

Visitors to Chicago regularly cite its restaurants as the city's top draw, ahead of other virtues such as museums or shopping. And these people aren't stupid. The breadth of dining options at all price levels is breathtaking; some of the most innovative chefs in America are working in Chicago kitchens.

Reservations at more expensive places are always a good idea, although not all places accept them. If you are staying in a hotel with a concierge, ask him or her to make your reservations for you. Concierges can often get you in to full places or secure reservations at places that don't 'officially' accept them.

The places to eat are grouped by neighborhood and, within each section, listed in roughly ascending order of price.

Loop Area

Most Loop eateries are geared toward the lunch crowds of office workers, but given the burgeoning nightlife and residential character of the area, more and more places are catering to diners well into the night. If your desires lean toward fast food, you'll be well served, with scores of chain outlets dotting every block. Note that most of the places here are closed on Sunday.

LaSalle St bankers can try to lower their blood pressure at ***Heartwise Express***

(☎ *312-419-1329, 10 S LaSalle St)*, whose entrance is off Madison. Very slick, with the trappings of a fast-food joint, the menu offers veggie burgers for $4 and bags of carrot sticks for 75¢.

The sign surrounded by lightbulbs is the best feature of the ***Artist's Snack Shop*** *(☎ 312-939-7855, 410 S Michigan Ave)* in the Fine Arts Building. Otherwise, it's an updated diner with a better-than-usual selection of coffee and beer.

A good casual outlet south of the Loop is ***Edwardo's*** *(☎ 312-939-3366, 521 S Dearborn St)*. It serves justifiably famous stuffed spinach pizza, as well as thin-crust models, sandwiches and salads. Everything is fresh and cheap.

Visit New Orleans without the travel expense at ***Heaven on Seven*** *(☎ 312-263-6443, 11 N Wabash Ave)* on the 7th floor (surprise!) of the Garland Building. Louisiana shrimp po' boys ($10), jambalaya ($10) and more are served up every lunch hour to mobs of people. To get a seat, drop by before 11:45 am or after 1:30 pm. They close at 4 pm.

History abounds at the ***Berghoff*** *(☎ 312-427-3170, 17 W Adams St)*, where the building and the restaurant both date from 1898. The menu carries old-world classics such as sauerbraten and schnitzel, but it also features modern treats such as swordfish Caesar salad ($10). Next door, the ***Stand Up Bar*** (same phone number as the Berghoff) has changed little in a century. Sandwiches ($5) are served from a buffet line at lunch, and frosty mugs of Berghoff beer line the bar.

It's three restaurants in one at the ***Italian Village*** *(☎ 312-332-7005, 71 W Monroe Drive)*. ***La Cantina*** is a casual supper club with regional specialties such as cannelloni ($12) and seafood. The namesake ***Village*** serves old-style cuisine such as mastacholli with sausage ($14). ***Vivere*** is at the high end of the village, both in price and cuisine. The menu is a high-minded interpretation of standards such as veal scalloppine, joined by unusual numbers such as bass-filled squid-ink pasta ($17).

Printer's Row *(☎ 312-461-0780, 550 S Dearborn St)* provides fresh pairings of primarily Midwestern foods. Venison direct from the woods and fish direct from the rivers are featured nightly. The menu changes with the seasons, but always expect to spend at least $40 a head before drinks for a memorable dinner.

Near North

Literally hundreds of restaurants dot the area from the river through the Gold Coast. From family-run snack bars to overhyped international theme cafés, from cheap vegetarian to haute cuisine, you can find it all.

Juice will run down your arms at ***Mr Beef*** *(☎ 312-664-5496, 660 N Orleans St)*. The $4 Italian beef sandwiches are a local classic complete with long, spongy white buns that rapidly go soggy after a load of the spicy beef and cooking juices has been ladled on.

Thai Star *(☎ 312-951-1196, 660 N State St)* features excellent and inexpensive food served on plywood tables in a charmless corner location. Palate-scorching curries are the specialty, none costing more than $5.

Happy diners look like kids in a candy store as they ponder their little plates of tapas at ***Cafe Iberico*** *(☎ 312-573-1510, 739 N LaSalle St)*. The wide-ranging menu averages $4 to $6 per plate. Tables sprawl through several tiled rooms.

Big Bowl *(☎ 312-787-8297, 159 W Erie St)* ladles up big bowls of Asian noodles. Wheat noodles with shrimp, black beans and snow peas are $9; barbecued chicken and noodles in broth are $8.

Boston Blackies *(☎ 312-938-8700, 164 E Grand Ave)* is one of the best of the usually excellent Greek-owned coffee shops serving up platters of burgers and sandwiches made with top-notch ingredients. The cheddar oozes out like volcanic magma under the chives and bacon bits on the $5 potato skins.

The legend of Chicago-style pizza was started by Ike Sewell on December 3, 1943 at ***Pizzeria Uno*** *(☎ 312-321-1000, 29 E Ohio St)*. The well-worn building has been gussied up to resemble the franchised branches, but the pizza still tastes best here. The $13 classic lands on the table with a resounding thud and can feed a family of four.

The smell of baking baguettes hits you on the way into ***Mango*** *(☎ 312-337-5440, 712 N Clark St)*. An American bistro with a European accent, it serves food as fresh and lively as its name suggests. Entrées rarely top $17, making a meal here an excellent value.

Carson's – The Place for Ribs *(☎ 312-280-9200, 612 N Wells St)* is a dream for cardiologists with cash-flow problems. Huge piles of fall-off-the-bone baby-back pork ribs are the specialty at this Chicago classic. Coleslaw, fries and rolls are mere sidelights to the main attraction, which costs $15.

At ***Wildfire*** *(☎ 312-787-9000, 159 W Erie St)* a huge grill, rotisserie and wood-burning oven roast shrimp, prime rib, steak and ribs. Portions are generous, and prices hover in the $17 range – not bad for this comfortable and welcoming place sharing an address with the Big Bowl.

At ***Frontera Grill*** *(☎ 312-661-1434, 445 N Clark St)*, chef-owner Rick Bayless has achieved celebrity status with his fresh variations inspired by south-of-the-border fare. Hot tortillas made near the entrance hold tacos al carbón, which are filled with charred beef and grilled green onions ($7). You can have an incomparable meal here for less than $20. Next door, at the more formal ***Topolobampo*** (same phone number as Frontera Grill), Bayless lets his creativity flow unfettered by cost restrictions. The menu changes almost nightly; be prepared for a memorable experience.

Avanzare *(☎ 312-337-8056, 161 E Huron St)* is a swank and cosmopolitan Italian nightspot in a contemporary building with high ceilings. A perennial favorite and a dish that launched the restaurant's reputation is the tortellini with smoked chicken ($18). On nice days the outdoor café serves lunch with a lighter, cheaper menu in a pleasant, shrubbed setting.

Shaw's Crab House *(☎ 312-527-2722, 21 E Hubbard St)* has some of Chicago's best seafood. The crab cake appetizer and the key lime pie make good bookends to the meal, which will run about $30 a person. The adjoining ***Blue Crab Lounge*** has oysters on the half-shell in an open and appealing bar area.

Brasserie Jo *(☎ 312-595-0800, 59 W Hubbard St)* serves wonderful food from Alsace, the French region near Germany that is the birthplace of owner Jean Joho. The service is as bright and cheery as the decor. Expect to pay at least $30 per person here.

Gold Coast

Loads of restaurants crowd the streets of this affluent neighborhood, which is the first primarily residential neighborhood on the North Side as you head away from the Loop.

The 3rd Coast *(☎ 312-664-7225, 29 E Delaware Place)* is a stylish café that buzzes morning, noon and night. The people-watching from the sidewalk tables is so good that people pile on the layers to extend the season into November. A second Gold Coast location *(☎ 312-649-0730, 1260 N Dearborn St)*, doesn't quite have the same cachet but is more relaxed.

Lo-Cal Zone *(☎ 312-943-9060, 912 N Rush St)* is a veggie and budget haven in the midst of the Gold Coast's ritziest shopping. It offers twists on its namesake calzones, as well as veggie burgers, funky burritos and other healthy treats for less than $5.

Open 24 hours, ***Tempo*** *(☎ 312-943-4373, 1 E Chestnut St)* is good around the clock. Omelets, BLTs, soups, salads and more are moderately priced and above average in taste.

Bistro 110 *(☎ 312-266-3110, 110 E Pearson St)* has country French food that's heavy on earthy flavors. Shortly after you sit down you're given a sliced baguette, accompanied by roasted heads of garlic to spread on it. The roasted vegetable plate is heavily herbed and has surprises such as wild mushrooms – a favorite with vegetarians. Entrées average about $14, a good price for the experience.

Widely regarded as the best steak house in a town with a lot of competition, ***Morton's*** *(☎ 312-266-4820, 1050 N State St)* makes no compromises in its quest for the title. The meat is aged to perfection and displayed tableside before cooking. See that half a cow? It's the 48oz double porterhouse. You'll feel like you've bought the whole cow after you see the prices, so see if you can get someone else to pay.

Old Town & Lincoln Park

Wells St in Old Town is lined with scores of places north from Division St. Lincoln Park bursts with restaurants, especially on Halsted and Armitage Sts, Lincoln Ave and Clark St.

Demon Dogs *(☎ 773-281-2001, 944 W Fullerton Ave)* is directly under the Fullerton El stop and is a shrine for the band Chicago. The cheap menu is short and celebrates another local institution, the Chicago-style hot dog: The poppy-seed bun is steamed, and the condiments, such as onions, cucumbers and celery salt, are piled on high.

The ***Wiener Circle*** *(☎ 773-477-7444, 2622 N Clark St)* reaches its frenetic and chaotic peak at about 4 am, when the bars let out. Mobs of patrons clamor for cheap charburgers and char-dogs to satisfy their munchies. The cheese fries make a perfect grease-soaking companion. At ***Nookies, too*** *(☎ 773-327-1400, 2114 N Halsted St)*, a full complement of eggs, waffles and sandwiches is on hand. It's open 24 hours on Friday and Saturday and is a popular brunch spot.

RJ Grunts *(☎ 773-929-5363, 2056 N Lincoln Park West)* will take you right back to the swinging '70s, when Lincoln Park emerged as the young singles' neighborhood of choice. The fruit and vegetable bar and burgers are still the mainstays at this place, which makes a good lunch spot after a visit to the zoo.

John Barleycorn Memorial Pub *(☎ 773-348-8899, 658 W Belden Ave)*, at Lincoln Ave, is vast and comfortable, just like its menu, which offers moderately priced burgers, tuna melts, potato skins and the like. There's lots of outdoor seating in summer.

If you plan on kissing anyone after dinner at ***Cafe Ba-Ba-Reeba!*** *(☎ 773-935-5000, 2024 N Halsted St)*, make certain they've dined with you. The garlic-laced sauces are worth licking the dishes for at this rambling, multiroom tapas bar. The menu changes daily and prices are about $5 a plate.

One of the most popular eateries in Old Town is ***¡Salpicón!*** *(☎ 312-988-7811, 1252 N Wells St)*. Ceviche (raw fish marinated in lime juice) starts at $7 and includes versions made with lobster. Chiles rellenos ($13) have been raised to an art. Create bright colors in your head by trying some of the 60 tequilas.

Twin Anchors *(☎ 312-266-1616, 1655 N Sedgwick St)* doesn't take reservations, so you'll have to wait outside or around the bar, but the wait is worth it for the ribs ($18). The ambience is like a supper club from the '50s and is authentic right down to the neon-lit bar and the almost all Sinatra jukebox.

At ***Charlie Trotter's*** *(☎ 773-248-6228, 816 W Armitage St)* the eponymous owner modestly says his dream is to run the finest restaurant in the world. It's a goal he's meeting with a slew of culinary awards from experts, including French ones. There is no regular menu, no signature dish. Rather there is an ever-changing lineup of dishes shaped by the seasons and the inspiration and ingenuity of Trotter and his artful staff. Diners are given a choice of the $70 prix fixe vegetarian menu or the $90 grand menu. Wines are selected from a 45-page list and a 40,000-bottle cellar.

Lake View & Wrigleyville

Another restaurant-rich part of town, this area of the North Side offers a huge variety of eateries whose quality – but not prices – match that found closer to the center of town. Clark St between Belmont Ave and Irving Park Blvd is lined with every kind of place to eat imaginable.

If you want to become a part of the vibrant local theater scene, the best place to go is ***Coffee Chicago*** *(☎ 773-477-3323, 3323 N Clark St)*. At any table you might find actors studying scripts, directors making casting decisions and a few hard-luck cases deciding that its time to chuck it all for another stint temping in the Loop.

Ann Sather's Restaurant *(☎ 773-348-2378, 929 W Belmont St)*, serves platefuls of reasonably priced diner chow in stylishly friendly surroundings. Famous for breakfast are the warm and gooey cinnamon rolls worth a trip themselves.

Obviously, with a slogan like 'Love animals, don't eat them,' you don't go to the ***Chicago Diner*** *(☎ 773-935-6696, 3411 N Halsted St)* for a steak. Large portions of fresh vegetarian food are the rule here. Breakfast tofu omelets for $6 are a hit. Vegans take note: Even the pesto for the pasta can be had without a lick of cheese.

At ***Arcos de Cuchilleros*** *(☎ 773-296-6046, 3445 N Halsted St)* the bar is long, the room is narrow and the furniture is dark wood. Small plates of tapas average $5 each. Don't keep track of how many pitchers of tangy sangria you drink; just keep ordering.

It doesn't look like much from the outside and actually looks worse inside, but ***Moti Mahal*** *(773-348-4392, 1031 W Belmont St)* serves excellent Indian food. The 'Big Mix' combines a lot of everything – curries, tikkas and more – and tops the price list at $13. It's just about impossible to spend more per person.

Leona's *(773-327-8861, 3215 N Sheffield St)* takes customer service very seriously and the sandwiches, salads and various entrées are huge. The pizza is justifiably famous; a medium for two runs about $10. If there's a lengthy wait when you arrive, they give you lots of red wine to help pass the time.

Mia Francesca *(☎ 773-281-3310, 3311 N Clark St)* is one of scores of small family-run Italian bistros in the city. It is also one of the most popular. The frequently changing handwritten menu features earthy standards such as caper-laced rigatoni siciliana for $10.

Some of the best Thai food in the city can be found at ***PS Bangkok*** *(☎ 773-871-7777, 3345 N Clark St)*. The various fish tanks indicate the long list of seafood dishes, many of them the elaborate kind found at banquets in Thailand. Prices are in the $8 neighborhood for simple dishes but escalate rapidly for the seafood creations.

The wooden boat in the window hints at the fish-dominated menu at ***Matsuya*** *(☎ 773-248-2677, 3469 N Clark St)*. This is one of the best-value Japanese restaurants in town and has a lengthy, moderately priced and unusual sushi menu. Less adventurous types will be happy with the teriyaki-marinated grilled fish. There are at least a dozen more Asian places within a block or two.

There's a taste of Africa at ***Addis Abeba*** *(☎ 773-929-9383, 3521 N Clark St)*. The foods of Ethiopia are served in heaping portions that feature lots of legumes, grains, spices and vegetables. Prices are cheap – you'll be out of Africa for $10 a head.

Bistro Zinc *(☎ 773-281-3443, 3443 N Southport Ave)* has classic French cooking at fair prices – about $12 an entrée; the steak au poivre is $17. The atmosphere is boisterous and trendy, just like many of the other places along this stretch of Southport Ave, which is best reached by the Southport El stop.

Andersonville

Kopi, A Traveler's Cafe *(☎ 773-989-5674, 5317 N Clark St)* is a casual coffeehouse with a pile of pillows on the floor and a wall of travel books in back. They have piles of some of the most esoteric free weeklies in town, as well as travel magazines and brochures galore. The bulletin board has ads from people looking for trekking partners for Kazakhstan and the like.

Andie's *(☎ 773-784-8616, 5253 N Clark St)* is an upscale Middle Eastern restaurant with prices that are delightfully downscale. Discerning Andersonville locals flock here for smooth, garlicky hummus and more. If you somehow manage to spend $15 a person, you'll either be drunk, bloated or both.

Wicker Park & Bucktown

Scores of restaurants in all price ranges line Damen Ave. The attitude is cocky at ***Merlot Joe*** *(☎ 773-252-5141, 2119 N Damen Ave)* – sort of like Bordeaux meets the Bronx. The affordable choices feature that staple of budget menus in Paris, couscous, for $9. The tree-shaded porch is open in summer.

Soul Kitchen *(☎ 773-342-9742, 1576 N Milwaukee Ave)* has big, bright dishes drawn from the South. Sweet and crunchy pecan-coated catfish is $12. This highly recommended corner spot is an excellent example of the kinds of innovative restaurants found in this neighborhood.

Classic French food at nonclassic prices (read: cheap) is the winning combination at ***Le Bouchon*** *(☎ 773-862-6600, 1958 N Damen Ave)*. This quaint little spot, which flies the tricolore over the street, is often packed with neighborhood types who know a bargain when they bite it. The pepper steak and frittes are très bon at $14. Other favorites, from escargot to chocolate mousse, are listed on the short menu.

West Side

You can reach the following places via buses running west on the streets where they're located, but a short cab ride will be much easier.

The best burrito in the world is at ***Tecalitlan*** *(☎ 312-384-4285, 1814 W Chicago Ave)*. Weighing more than a pound and costing $5, the carne asada burrito is one of the city's best food values. The many other Mexican staples on the menu are all cheap and good.

Immediately west of the Loop and close to Union Station, ***Lou Mitchell's*** *(☎ 312-939-3111, 565 W Jackson St)* draws hordes for breakfast and lunch. Whether it's omelets hanging off the plates, fluffy flapjacks, crisp waffles or anything else on the long menu (most items are $4 to $6), you can expect perfect preparation with premium ingredients.

Southern cooking makes good – very good – at ***Wishbone*** *(☎ 312-850-2663, 1001 W Washington Blvd)*. The perfect corn muffins set the tone for a menu of spicy classics such as blackened catfish, fried chicken and baked ham. Breakfasts come with hot, fresh buttermilk rolls. Prices are low: $6 to $8 will get you loads of chow, even at dinner.

The culinary pick of the Halsted St Greektown strip is ***Santorini*** *(☎ 312-829-8820, 800 W Adams St)*, at the corner of Halsted St. Fish, both shelled and finned, honor the legacies of Greek fishermen. The room is boisterous yet cozy, thanks in part to the large Aegean fireplace. Everything, from the bread to the baklava, goes down swimmingly.

The ***Parthenon*** *(☎ 312-726-2407, 314 S Halsted St)* has anchored Greek Town for three decades. The amount of saganaki set ablaze here may be a principal factor in global warming. You can escape with a feast for less than $15.

Red Light *(☎ 312-733-8880, 820 W Randolph St)* is one of several trendy dinner spots in a once-seedy neighborhood. It serves up Chinese fare that isn't anything like the fortune-cookie standard. The lo mein noodles are fantastic, but like everything else on the menu, only for those of high means.

Chinatown

There are scores more restaurants in Chinatown than the ones listed here. Wanderers will be rewarded by discovering little noodle shops seemingly transplanted from China.

Phoenix *(☎ 312-328-0848, 2131 S Archer Ave)* rises above the old veterans of Chinatown with excellent fresh food prepared by chefs direct from Hong Kong. Midday sees an endless parade of dim sum issuing forth on trolleys from the kitchen. On Sunday the parade is lengthier yet. Dinner entrées range from $9 to $16.

An enduring Cantonese-style restaurant, ***Emperor's Choice*** *(☎ 312-225-8800, 2238 S Wentworth St)* is known for excellent seafood and service to match. Lobster is at the center of the menu and many of the tables. Prepared in a number of ways, it stars in several prix fixe meals that average $25 a person.

Hyde Park

At ***Valois*** *(☎ 773-667-0647, 1518 E 53rd St)* the motto is 'See your food.' The cafeteria standards here include long-steamed vegetables, hot beef sandwiches and good, fresh biscuits. Everything is cheap and hearty. The regulars run the gamut of Chicago denizens from number-crunching Nobel Prize winners to rock-crunching ditch diggers.

Medici *(☎ 773-667-7394, 1327 E 57th St)* is widely popular because of its thin-crust pizza, sandwiches and salads, which average $7. After your meal, check out the vast bulletin board out front. It's the perfect place to size up the character of the community and possibly find the complete works of John Maynard Keynes for sale cheap.

Dixie Kitchen and Bait Shop *(☎ 773-363-4943, 5225 S Harper Ave)* serves soulful standards such as sweet potatoes and black-eyed peas. The main events are both uptown and downtown: shrimp in garlic, blackened catfish and country fried steak. Prices are as cheap as the faux rummage-sale interior.

South Side

Given that 40% of Chicago's population is African American, it makes sense that soul food places are common. Many are little more than storefronts serving take-out buckets of wings, rib tips and macaroni and cheese. ***Army and Lou's*** *(☎ 773-483-3100, 422 E 75th St)*, near Martin Luther King Drive on the Far South Side, is several cuts above the norm. Fried chicken, catfish, collard greens, sweet potato pie and all the other classics are here at prices that are good for your soul. If you've never had soul food, start at this warm and welcoming Chicago classic. Come in a car or cab.

ENTERTAINMENT

You can find something to do in Chicago virtually around the clock. Most bars and clubs close at 2 am every night except Saturday, when they close at 3 am. But many stay open until 4 am nightly and 5 am Saturday.

The theater, classical music and blues are all world class. The professional sports are hot. To find out what's going on turn first to the weekly newspapers – the *Reader* and *New City* – followed by the Friday entertainment sections in the *Sun-Times* and *Tribune*.

Bars

The long winters mean that for decades Chicagoans have pursued their social lives indoors. There are bars for virtually every mood and personality. These listings run north to south.

The ***Hop Leaf*** *(☎ 773-334-9851, 5148 N Clark St)*, just south of Foster in Andersonville, has the best selection of beer in the city and is a fine place to just hang out.

The ***Ginger Man*** *(☎ 773-549-2050, 3740 N Clark St)*, in Wrigleyville, has a huge and eclectic beer selection and numerous pool tables. The crowd is edgy and arty, and this is one of the best places in a long strip of Clark St bars.

Roscoes *(☎ 773-281-3355, 3354 N Halsted St)* is one of many gay and lesbian bars on the stretch of Halsted St between Lake View and Wrigleyville. Within this very friendly corner pub you'll find a tasty menu, a beer garden and dancing.

A refined and classy place, ***Pops for Champagne*** *(☎ 773-472-1000, 2934 N Sheffield St)*, in Lake View, has numerous champagnes by the glass, 140 more by the bottle and scores of excellent wines as well.

At the north end of Bucktown, ***Quenchers*** *(☎ 773-276-9730)*, at the corner of Fullerton Ave and Western Ave, is another place offering a good range of brews, as well as one of the most charming staffs around.

The ***Brehon Pub*** *(☎ 312-642-1071, 731 N Wells St)*, in River North, is a fine example of the corner saloons that once dotted Chicago.

Only the dimmest of rubes tries to order fries at the ***Billy Goat Tavern*** *(☎ 312-222-1525, 430 N Michigan Ave)*, a Near North cathedral of grease, smoke and rousing conversations. The place has qualified as a tourist attraction ever since it was immortalized by John Belushi on *Saturday Night Live*, and it's still the gathering spot for local journalists who think the best finish to any edition comes out of a tap.

In Hyde Park, ***Jimmy's Woodlawn Tap*** *(☎ 773-643-5516, 1172 E 55th St)* is where University of Chicago types debate weighty questions in an intellect-rich but bar-poor neighborhood.

Dance Clubs

The club scene in Chicago ranges from hip, snooty places where admittance is at the whim of some dullard at the door to casual joints where all you do is dance.

Club 950 *(☎ 773-929-8955, 950 W Wrightwood Ave)* is a veteran club in Lincoln Park that has kept its edge for more than 20 years with a mixture of techno and British and American dance music.

The neighborhood and music are postindustrial at ***Crobar*** *(☎ 312-413-7000, 1543 N Kingsbury St)*, west of Old Town. The cavernous interior is a stylish mix of materials intercepted on their way to the metal recycler. The crowd consists of yuppies gone punk for the night and punks who will never go yuppie.

Feeling lost, lonely, antisocial? ***Berlin*** *(☎ 773-348-4975, 954 W Belmont Ave)*, in Lake View, caters to virtually everyone. The crowd is as mixed as the music.

Live Music

There's more music being played any night of the week in Chicago than you could ever listen to, even if you had a year. Cover charges vary from free to $25 or more depending on the day, the act and the venue.

Jazz & Blues In a city that has played a pivotal role not just in jazz and blues but in the genres they have engendered, such as rock, it would be foolish not to sample some of this vibrant scene. The following listings are organized from north to south.

Kingston Mines *(☎ 773-477-4646, 2548 N Halsted St)*, in Lincoln Park, has two stages, which means that somebody's always on. The club's popularity means they get big names.

Look for the Pabst signs in the window to find ***Blue Chicago*** *(☎ 312-642-6261, 736 N Clark St)*, in the Near North. The blues is mainstream and the talent lives up to expectations.

At ***Jazz Showcase*** *(☎ 312-670-2473, 59 W Grand Ave)*, owner Joe Segal presides over an elegant Near North club that caters to jazz purists.

The ***House of Blues*** *(☎ 312-923-2000, 329 N Dearborn St)*, in the Marina City complex, has major blues and rock acts. Given the fame of this chain, there's no surprise that T-shirt buying opportunities abound.

You're likely to find the namesake at ***Buddy Guy's Legends*** *(☎ 312-427-0333, 754 S Wabash Ave)*, in the South Loop. Look for top national and local groups playing in this no-nonsense, cavernous space.

The ***New Checkerboard Lounge*** *(☎ 773-743-3335, 423 E 43rd St)*, on the South Side, is just what you would expect from one of the most well known blues clubs in town. Take a cab – they'll call you another when you leave.

Rock Bands on the verge of superstardom regularly play ***Metro*** *(☎ 773-549-0203, 3730 N Clark St)*, in Wrigleyville, formerly a classic theater.

Double Door *(☎ 773-489-3160, 1572 N Milwaukee Ave)* is known for classic and hard rock by performers as diverse as clean-cut Marshall Crenshaw and the many post-punk groups spawned in Wicker Park (remember the Smashing Pumpkins?).

Music at the ***Empty Bottle*** *(☎ 773-276-3600, 1035 N Western Ave)*, west of Bucktown, spans the styles from funk to punk. The progressive, hip bands reflect the crowd.

Classical Music & Opera Performances of the Chicago Symphony Orchestra and the Lyric Opera of Chicago are sold out each year to subscribers. However, even the most devout fans don't make every performance. Check with the box offices, or hang around outside the venue about 30 minutes before curtain: More often than not some besuited swell will offer to sell you a pair of tickets usually at face value.

The supernova of the Chicago cultural scene, the ***Chicago Symphony Orchestra*** *(☎ 312-294-3000, 220 S Michigan Ave)* enjoys lavish support locally. Their home, the former Orchestra Hall, has become the Symphony Center thanks to a substantial reconstruction.

One of the top opera companies in the US, the ***Lyric Opera of Chicago*** *(☎ 312-332-2244, 20 N Wacker Drive)* performs in the grand old Civic Opera House. Their repertoire is a shrewd mix of old classics and much more modern and daring work.

Classical music for the masses is performed four nights a week for most of the summer at the Petrillo Music Shell, in Grant Park at Jackson and Columbus Drives between the Art Institute and the lake. The free performances by the ***Grant Park Symphony Orchestra*** *(☎ 312-819-0614)* span the classical genre, from opera to Broadway and 'pop.'

Theater

Chicago theater is lively and well respected by both Broadway and Hollywood – representatives from each make regular talent raids on the city. There are usually several dozen shows running at any time, staged by companies ranging from huge and professional to ones featuring principals freshly graduated from college.

Buying Tickets Ticket prices for shows range from $5 for small shows to $35 or more for main companies. Most average in the $15 to $25 range.

The League of Chicago Theaters operates Hot Tix booths, where same-day tickets to participating shows are sold at half price. The lineup varies every day and is usually best early in the week. Weekend tickets are sold beginning on Friday, and Hot Tix also sells full-price tickets. City locations include 108 N State St, across from Marshall Field's; 163 E Pearson St, in the Chicago Visitor Center; and 2301 N Clark St, in Tower Records. You can call to see what's on offer (☎ 900-225-2225), but the calls cost a discount-nullifying $1 a minute.

Major Companies The city's oldest professional theater group is also its most prestigious: ***Goodman Theatre*** *(☎ 312-443-3800, 200 S Columbus Drive)*, at the rear of the Art Institute, presents five works a year, a mixture of classics and new pieces.

Steppenwolf Theater *(☎ 312-335-1650, 1650 N Halsted St)*, an ensemble group, helped put Chicago theater on the map when it won a Tony Award in 1985 for regional theater excellence.

With a grand new theater opened on Navy Pier in 1999, the ***Chicago Shakespeare Theater*** *(☎ 312-595-5600)* has reached the big time with its works by the Bard.

Small Companies The following are just a few of the many companies active locally: In Wrigleyville, ***Annoyance Theater*** *(☎ 773-929-6200, 3747 N Clark St)* specializes in goofy and tasteless send-ups of modern culture. ***Live Bait Theater*** *(☎ 773-871-1212, 3914 N Clark St)* was founded in 1987 and performs dramatic works often written by the principals. The South Side ***Black Ensemble Theatre*** *(☎ 773-769-4451, 4520 N Beacon St)* performs original works about the lives of African Americans.

Venues The Loop is now home to a growing collection of grandly restored theaters. They include the ***Palace Theatre*** *(☎ 312-902-1500, 151 W Randolph St)*, the ***Ford Center – Oriental Theatre*** *(☎ 312-902-1400, 24 W Randolph St)*, the huge ***Auditorium Theater*** *(☎ 312-902-1500, 50 E Congress)*, the ***Chicago Theater*** *(☎ 312-443-1130, 175 N State St)* and the ***Shubert Theater*** *(☎ 312-977-1700, 22 W Monroe St)*.

In Old Town, the ***Royal George Theatre*** *(☎ 312-988-9000, 1641 N Halsted St)* has three theaters in one building west of Old Town.

Cinemas

There's no shortage of first-run cinemas throughout the city, including ***600 N Michigan*** *(☎ 312-255-9340)*, which despite its name is really off Rush St. Check the papers to see what's playing and where.

Among the many venues for offbeat, foreign and classic films are the ***Fine Arts Theaters*** *(☎ 312-939-3700, 418 S Michigan Ave)*, in the Loop, and the wonderfully restored ***Music Box Theater*** *(☎ 773-871-6604, 3733 N Southport Ave)* in Wrigleyville.

Comedy

Second City *(☎ 312-337-3992, 1616 N Wells St)*, a Chicago must-see in Old Town, has staged more than 80 revues, usually sharp and biting commentaries on life, politics, love and anything else that falls in the crosshairs of its rapid-fire, hard-hitting wit. ***Second City ETC*** *(☎ 312-642-8189, 1608 N Wells St)*, in the Pipers Alley complex, is the troupe's second company. Its work is often more daring, as actors try to get noticed and make the main stage.

The mere presence of Second City fuels the dreams of would-be comedians all over the city. Improvisational clubs litter the North Side like the broken dreams of funny people doomed to forever cutting up for their coworkers. First among the improvs, ***Improv-Olympic*** *(☎ 773-880-0199, 3541 N Clark St)*, in Wrigleyville, features professional performers who respond to input – useful, scatalogical, etc – from the audience. ***Zanies*** *(☎ 312-337-4027, 1548 N Wells St)*, in Old Town, regularly books big-name national comedians familiar to anyone with a TV.

SPECTATOR SPORTS

Chicagoans are deeply loyal to their sports teams, despite the teams' mixed results in competition. Attending a game is a real part of life in the city. Each of the teams, its stadiums and its fans have unique traditions that enrich the experience.

The Chicago Cubs (☎ 312-831-2827) have been dropping games at the corner of Addison and Clark Sts for more than 80 years, all the while filling Wrigley Field and Wrigleyville with fans. Few experiences in Chicago can equal an afternoon at Wrigley. The bleacher seats have a manic culture all their own. Because of the good attendance, Cubs tickets can be hard to find. Scalping is illegal and you'll feel like you're doing a drug deal if you try to buy tickets on the street. Wrigley Field is one block west of the Addison El stop on the Red Line. Parking stinks.

The White Sox (☎ 312-831-1769) are second fiddle to the Cubs in almost every category except for their die-hard fans' loyalty. The team's stadium, Comisky Park is a widely derided early-1990s effort tha has a mountainous upper deck, and it churlish owner, Jerry Reinsdorf, provoke boos wherever he goes. But at least it's eas to get tickets. The stadium is a short wall from the Sox-35th station on the Red Lin and the 35-Bronzeville-IIT station on th Green Line. The neighborhood is safe o game days, when it is flooded with cops.

'Rebuilding' is the kindest euphemism that can be used to describe the Chicag Bulls (☎ 312-559-1212) since Michael Jorda retired in 1998. After five championshi seasons they promptly became the wors team in basketball when MJ left for othe fame and Nike fortune. The Bulls play o the West Side in the United Center, 190 W Madison. The CTA runs special buses to th games, mostly from th Loop. Cab rides fron the Loop and Nea North cost about $5 and parking is plentiful The neighborhood is no really safe enough to d much walking.

The Chicago Bear (☎ 847-615-2327) spen the 1990s disappointin fans with perenniall flaccid play. Still, th faithful are hopeful tha they will one day regai the dominance of the National Football League tha they enjoyed decades ago Games are played at Soldie Field, south of the Museum Campus. From the Loop it' a 30-minute walk. Metr trains from Randolph S Station stop at nearby Roo sevelt Rd Station ($1.75) the Roosevelt CTA El stop are a half mile west.

The Chicago Blackhawk (☎ 312-559-1212) usuall manage to make the Nationa Hockey League playoffs onl to make a quick exit in the early rounds. The team plays at the United Center, 1901 W Madison St. The season runs from October to April. Transportation and parking information is the same as for the Bulls.

SHOPPING

From N Michigan Ave to the neighborhoods, there's a wide range of stores, big and small. Outside the Loop, most stores are open seven days a week. In the Near North stores close by 8 pm, earlier elsewhere.

Where to Shop

The Loop Recently, the Loop has undergone a rebirth, and numerous national retailers have moved in to serve the daytime office workers and the growing population of condo dwellers. State St and Wabash Aves are lined with stores big and small. Note that many are closed on Sunday.

The grandest old department store in the country, Marshall Field's (☎ 312-781-1000) is a full block in size, between Randolph St, Wabash Ave, Washington Blvd and State St, with 10 floors of designer clothes, furnishings, gifts, housewares and much, much more.

Carson Pirie Scott & Co (☎ 312-641-7000), 1 S State St, has lived in the shadow of Marshall Field's since it opened in 1899. Architecturally, it's a gem. Its goods are moderately priced, and the selection among its six floors is good.

N *Michigan* Ave The Greater North Michigan Avenue Association likes to claim that the 'Magnificent Mile,' or 'Mag Mile,' as it's widely known, is one of the top five shopping streets in the world. It's hard to argue with that. Only the south end, toward the river, is a bit thin in retail, and that is changing with the vast Nordstrom development just south of the Marriott.

Water Tower Place (☎ 312-440-3166), 835 N Michigan Ave, is in many respects an anomaly. Its popularity with out-of-towners and tourists is inexplicable, since its collection of stores can be found at any mainstream mall in the nation. There's a Marshall Field's (☎ 312-335-7700) among its stores, which number more than a hundred.

Another huge vertical mall is 900 N Michigan Ave (☎ 312-915-3916), featuring a Bloomingdale's (☎ 312-440-4460) and high-end shops such as Gucci (☎ 312-664-5504) and Mondi (☎ 312-943-5449).

Within the stunning, almost transparent, white Crate & Barrel (☎ 312-787-5900), 646 N Michigan Ave, are modestly priced functional and stylish kitchen goods, along with sleek and comfortable furniture.

Gold Coast Designer boutiques sprout like mushrooms on the tony blocks just west of Michigan Ave. They sprout so thick on the single block of Oak St between Michigan Ave and Rush St that you'd think it was a decayed log.

Lake View & Wrigleyville North from Belmont Ave you'll find the kind of colorful, irreverent, wild and kinky shops you'd expect in a gay neighborhood. The Woolworth of the strip is Gay Mart (☎ 773-929-4272), 3457 N Halsted St, which sells toys, novelties, calendars, souvenirs, you name it.

Near Belmont Ave are several stores serving full-on punks and teens simply interested in manifesting rebelliousness. On weekend days the sidewalks are jammed with rich teens from the North Shore, black-clad Goths with blond roots and the rest of the Lake View diaspora.

The Alley (☎ 773-525-3180), 3218 N Clark St, is a vast emporium based on counterculture and pop trends, selling everything from head-shop gear to human-size dog collars.

What to Buy

Antiques Chicago is a magnet for antiques and collectibles buyers. You will find clusters in the blocks around the Merchandise Mart in River North, along the stretch of Lincoln Ave north from Diversey Ave to Irving Park Ave and along Belmont Ave west from Ashland to Western Aves.

The Antiquarians Building (☎ 312-527-0533), 159 W Kinzie St, has rare items from five continents in 22 shops.

Fine Art River North has a concentration of big-name galleries, but you can also find plenty of galleries in Wicker Park and Bucktown near the intersection of Damen and North Aves.

Openings are held on Friday evenings – usually the first Friday of the month – with the first Friday after Labor Day being the start of the season. To try to make sense of the Chicago art scene, pick up the free *Chicago Gallery News* at most galleries.

Richard Gray Gallery (☎ 312-642-8877), 875 N Michigan Ave, suite 2503, in the John Hancock Center, exhibits works by 20th-century greats from Miró to Nancy Graves. In the same building, Alan Koppel (☎ 312-640-0730), suite 2850, also has a contemporary focus.

Robert Henry Adams Fine Art (☎ 312-642-8700), 715 N Franklin St, shows works by pre–World War II American impressionist, regionalist and modernist painters. This is one of more than 60 galleries concentrated in this area.

Music Earwax (☎ 773-772-4019), 1564 N Milwaukee Ave in Wicker Park, has a polyglot selection of music from the US and around the world, including thousands of selections that would never make the racks of mainstream places.

Serious jazz and blues aficionados flock to Jazz Record Mart (☎ 312-222-1467), 444 N Wabash Ave in the Near North. This is the place to go to complete your Bix Biederbecke collection.

The Symphony Store (☎ 312-435-6421), 220 S Michigan Ave, is where the Chicago Symphony Orchestra sells a large selection of CDs, tapes and albums of their performances all over the world.

Outdoor Gear The smell of leather hits you in the face as you walk into Uncle Dan's (☎ 773-477-1918), 2440 N Lincoln Ave in Lincoln Park. A big selection of hiking boots and gear is augmented by camping supplies and many brands of backpacks.

Souvenirs Selling souvenirs a few cuts above the generic T-shirt, ashtray, refrigerator magnet standard is the Chicago Architecture Foundation (☎ 312-922-3432), 224 S Michigan Ave, heaven for anyone with an edifice complex.

Another good bet is to join the crowds thronging the Art Institute Store (☎ 312-443-3535), 111 S Michigan Ave, which has poster and postcard versions of popular works from the museum's collection. There's another branch (☎ 312-482-8275) in the 900 N Michigan mall.

GETTING THERE & AWAY

Air

Chicago is served by two main airports. O'Hare International (ORD) is the world's busiest hub. Midway (MID) is much smaller and is primarily served by discount carriers.

O'Hare International Airport Sixty-five million passengers a year – one quarter of the population of the United States – pass through O'Hare each year, continuing Chicago's historic role as a US transportation hub. Each day flights depart to 284 cities worldwide.

The place is huge. Domestic flights and the international departures for domestic airlines depart from Terminals 1, 2 and 3. All international arrivals, as well as departures for most non-US airlines, are in Terminal 5.

The terminals and the main long-term parking lot are linked by a people mover system, which runs 24 hours a day. Short-term parkers can use the main parking garage, a vast facility where the fee starts at $3 and increases by $1 an hour thereafter. Daily fees at the long-term parking lots are $12 in Lot E and $8 in Lot F.

City-run information booths are located in the baggage claim areas of Terminals 1, 2 and 3. In Terminal 5 the desk is between the two customs exits. The employees are not only polite but often enthusiastic. Many speak a range of languages. Unless you are familiar with Chicago, it's worth visiting these booths for advice and armloads of maps and brochures.

The terminals boast a full range of services: ATMs, bookstores, and even some rather interesting cafés, such as one in Terminal 1 run by the famous Berghoff restaurant in the Loop. Terminal 2 has a large

:hildren's play area and a branch of the Museum of Broadcast Communications.

Midway Airport Home to cut-rate carriers such as Southwest Airlines, Midway has a suitably low-rent ambience. The facility dates from the 1950s. Unless your flight is late, you won't have to spend much time here, and that's good. A city information center is at the confluence of Concourses A and B in the main terminal. There's an ATM, a newsstand, a café and a bar often filled with drunken yahoos.

Airlines Airlines serving Chicago include those on the list following. Note that especially at Midway, scheduled service by low-fare airlines changes frequently. Also, most of the following airlines have at least one city ticket office; United and American have scores. These are handy places for working out complex itineraries. Check the yellow pages for their addresses.

The letter M following the airline name indicates an airline serving Midway. The letters M, O indicate an airline serving both airports. See the Toll-Free & Web Site Directory at the back of the book for phone numbers.

Air Canada
Air France
America West Airlines (M, O)
American Airlines
American Trans Air (M)
British Airways
Canadian Airlines
Continental Airlines (M, O)
Delta Air Lines
Frontier Airlines (M)
Japan Airlines
KLM
Lufthansa
Mexicana Airlines
Northwest Airlines (M, O)
SAS
Southwest Airlines (M)
TWA
United
US Airways
Vanguard (M)

Bus

The striking, modern main bus station (☎ 312-408-5980), often referred to as 'the Greyhound station,' is at 630 W Harrison St between Des Plaines and Jefferson Sts. The Clinton El stop on the Blue Line is two blocks away.

Greyhound (☎ 312-408-5980) has buses to all points on the compass. Sample fares with service frequency and travel time include the following:

destination	cost	travel time	frequency
Detroit	$27	7 hours	5 per day
Cleveland	$35	7½ hours	8 per day
Indianapolis	$30	4½ hours	10 per day
St Louis	$30	6 hours	7 per day
Minneapolis	$63	10 hours	8 per day
Milwaukee	$14	2 hours	10 per day

Train

Chicago is the hub for Amtrak's national and regional service. Trains depart from Union Station, 210 S Canal St between Adams St and Jackson Blvd. The station is a grand old structure that was carefully restored a few years ago. The steps in the main waiting concourse were used for a memorable scene in the movie *The Untouchables*. The Clinton El station is two blocks south; the Quincy El station is three blocks east across the river.

Amtrak has long-distance service from Chicago to points on both coasts. See the regional Getting There & Away chapter for details. Short-distance trains serve Detroit (3 daily, 6 hours), St Louis (3 daily, 6 hours) and Milwaukee (6 daily, 1½ hours). Fares vary widely depending on season, and advance purchase bargains are available.

Car & Motorcycle

Interstate highways converge on Chicago from all points of the compass. None is especially scenic or otherwise recommended, although if you are coming from the east, follow the Indiana Toll Rd all the way to the border and then spring for the $2 for the Chicago Skyway. You'll save a good 30 minutes or more, compared to curving around on I-94. On all the roads, try to avoid arriving or departing during the worst weekday rush hours, from 6 to 9 am and 4 to 7 pm.

GETTING AROUND

Public transit in Chicago is not bad by American standards. This is one of the few American cities you can fully enjoy without a car. In fact, having a car in Chicago would seriously *detract* from your enjoyment.

To/From the Airport

O'Hare The CTA offers frequent El service on the Blue Line to and from the Loop ($1.50). Unfortunately, the O'Hare station is buried under the world's largest parking garage. Directional signs are variously marked as 'CTA,' 'Rapid Transit' and 'Trains to City.' The fare ride takes about 45 minutes.

Note that the El trains are not designed for people with luggage, and the stations downtown have few escalators and fewer elevators, so be prepared to schlep your bags.

Airport Express has a monopoly on van services between the airport and downtown. The fare is $16 per person, plus the usual 10% to 15% tip. Once downtown you may get driven around for a while as others are dropped off.

The drive to the Loop on the Kennedy Expressway can take 30 to 90 minutes. Cabs cost about $30 to the Loop (plus tip).

Midway The CTA El Orange Line goes to Midway from the Loop elevated tracks. A very long walkway connects the airport terminal to the station. The ride to and from the Loop takes 35 minutes.

The Airport Express van charges $12 per person (plus tip) to and from downtown.

To reach the city from Midway, drive north on Cicero Blvd for 2 miles, until you reach the Stevenson Expressway (I-55). Veer right and head northeast into the city. Depending on traffic it should take 20 minutes to one hour.

The taxi fare to the Loop is about $20 plus tip.

CTA

The Chicago Transit Authority (CTA) is the underfunded public transportation system serving the city. It consists of the El trains and buses.

Bus drivers, El conductors and station attendants may give you detailed and friendly transit advice or they may tell you to bug off. At best you'll be able to wrangle one of the good free maps. Otherwise, call ☎ 836-7000 preceded by the area code of whatever area of Chicago you are in – ☎ 312, 708, 847, 630 or 773.

Fares The single fare on a bus or the El is $1.50. You pay your fare with Transit Cards, which are bought from vending machines in every El station for any value between $3 and $100. Note that for every $10 in value you put on the card, you actually get credit for $11. There are also 24-hour passes good for unlimited use on the system for $5, seven-day passes for $20 and 30-day passes for $75. Transfers between buses and El cost 30¢, which is deducted from the card as you go through the El turnstile or board the bus. Transfers between most El lines are free.

On the buses you can pay your fare in exact change and cash (buses accept dollar bills) and buy a transfer good for another ride on the bus or the El, or you can use your transit card. (You cannot buy a transit card on the buses, however.)

So what happens when your card has some useless amount like 60¢ left on it? You add value to the card using one of the vending machines. Children younger than seven ride free. Those seven to 11 ride at half price, but you have to prove their age to the bus driver or station attendant, which is a hassle.

The El The CTA likes to call its train service 'Rapid Transit.' But everybody just calls it the El, whether the specific service they are referring to runs above ground, below ground or somewhere in between. The view from the elevated tracks can be spectacular.

There are seven color-coded lines on the El: Red, Blue, Purple, Orange, Brown

Green and Yellow. Most visitors should be able to use the system for almost all their transit needs, the exception being those going to Hyde Park, certain areas of Lincoln Park near the lake and the area east of N Michigan Ave that includes Navy Pier.

During the day you shouldn't have to wait more than 15 minutes for a train. At night and on weekends, service varies. The Red Line and the Blue Line between the Loop and O'Hare operate 24 hours a day, but other lines and many stations may not run or may be closed.

Buses CTA buses go almost everywhere, but they do so on erratic schedules. The bus stops are clearly marked with signs on poles showing which routes stop there, but little else. Buses make frequent stops and don't go very fast. At rush hour you'll have to stand, and during the summer many are not air-conditioned.

The following routes are of use to visitors and run from early in the morning until late in the evening.

No 22 Clark – runs north on Dearborn St until Oak St and then on Clark St all the way to the north end of the city; this is a good bus for getting to the parts of Lincoln Park such as the zoo.

No 29 State – runs on State St through the Loop and River North, then east on Illinois St to Navy Pier; these buses have large 'Navy Pier' signs on their fronts.

No 146 Marine-Michigan – runs from the Berwyn El stop in Andersonville south along the lakefront all the way to N Michigan Ave; it transits the Loop via State St, then cuts through Grant Park to the Museum Campus. This is a very tourist-friendly route.

Disabled Travelers Most of the El is inaccessible. If you do find a station with an elevator, make doubly sure that there's also one at your destination. You can get from O'Hare to the Clark and Jackson stations on the Blue Line in the Loop. From Midway, the Orange Line Library, Washington and Clark stations are accessible in the Loop. Half the CTA buses are not equipped with wheelchair lifts. Call to find out which buses or stations are accessible.

Metra

A web of commuter trains running under the Metra banner serves the 245 stations in the suburbs surrounding Chicago. The trains are clean and have two levels, with the second offering tight seating but better views.

Some of the Metra lines run frequent schedules seven days a week; others operate only during weekday rush hours. The Metra information line is an excellent service that can tell you what combination of CTA, Metra and Pace (a very limited suburban bus service) can get you from where you are to where you want to go. The information number is ☎ 836-7000, preceded by the area code of whatever area of Chicago you are in – ☎ 312, 708, 847, 630 or 773.

Short trips start at $1.75 and go to $5 or more for long journeys. Tickets are on sale from agents and machines at major stations. If you board at a small station where nobody is on duty you can buy the ticket without penalty from the conductor on the train.

Metra's 12 lines depart from four stations ringing the Loop:

Union Station, 210 S Canal St between Adams St and Jackson Blvd – In addition to Metra services, all Amtrak trains depart from here. Metra trains go southwest to Brookfield and on to Aurora on the busy BNSF line. The Heritage Corridor service to Joliet, the South West service to Orland Park, the North Central service to Antioch and the Milwaukee District services to Elgin and Fox Lake also depart from here.

Richard B Ogilvie Transportation Center, 500 W Madison St at Canal St – Formerly called Northwestern Station. Trains go north to Waukeegan and Kenosha, northwest to Crystal Lake and Harvard and west to Geneva on the frequent Union Pacific services.

Randolph St Station, below street level at Randolph St and Michigan Ave – This station is in the midst of a multiyear reconstruction that has reduced amenities to a bare minimum. Besides the frequent Metra Electric service to Hyde Park, Pullman and on to South Chicago and University Park, the station is the terminus for the South Shore trains to the Indiana Dunes and South Bend.

LaSalle St Station, 414 S LaSalle St between Congress Parkway and Van Buren St – Trains regularly depart for Joliet on the Rock Island District line.

Car & Motorcycle

In most cases, once you are in the city, you can forget about your car. Whether it's for the day or for a week, park it and forget it. Better yet don't bring it. Parking expenses will rapidly eat through your wallet.

Parking Trying to park your car will soon make you wish it would be stolen. In the Loop and Near North there are plenty of parking garages, but they charge $15 a day or more.

In the Near North area most streets have parking meters, which average 25¢ for 15 minutes. In the neighborhoods the parking may be free, but there may be some sort of permit scheme in effect that bars you from parking.

Rental If Chicago is your first stop on a tour of the Midwest, wait to pick up a rental car until you are ready to leave the city. All the major car rental companies have outposts at the airport and in the city. For the best deals, you may have to go to the airport to pick up your car from one of the vast lots. See the Getting Around chapter and the Toll Free & Web Site Directory at the back of the book for details on car rental companies.

Taxi

Taxis are easy to find in the Loop and north through Wrigleyville. Raise your arm and one will promptly cut a few cars off to pick you up. In other parts of the city you can either call a cab or face what may be a long wait for one to happen along. The major cab companies are Yellow Cab (☎ 312-829-4222) and Flash Cab (☎ 773-561-1444).

Fares are $1.50 when you enter the cab and $1.20 for each additional mile; extra passengers are 50¢ per passenger. Drivers expect a 10% to 15% tip.

Many cab drivers are people new to the US job market and may have limited English skills and knowledge of the city, so it's best to know the address and cross-street of your destination.

Bicycle

Curbs are the highest mountains you'll find in Chicago, but other obstacles exist. Chicago streets, while flat, are not terribly accommodating: Bike lanes don't exist, except in a couple of places where they have become de facto double-parking zones, and many streets are just wide enough for speeding traffic and parked cars.

Northern & Central Illinois

The farther you get from Chicago, the more rural and countrified Northern Illinois becomes.

Close to Chicago are numerous sights that make for good day trips. The Illinois & Michigan Canal Corridor makes a good exit from the city and a good way to get to scenic Starved Rock State Park. Galena has many charms that are better seen when not obscured by tourists. The Mississippi River dominates the terrain in the west and is a good place to start the drive south.

Highlights

- Hitting the sand at Illinois Beach State Park
- Following the Illinois & Michigan Canal Corridor
- Hiking Starved Rock
- Driving Historic Route 66
- Sampling all four Quad Cities
- Exploring Lincoln's Springfield

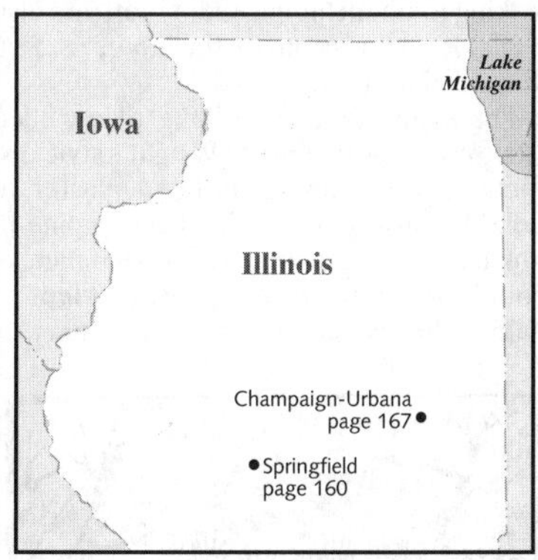

Greater Chicago Area

The rich prairie responsible for much of Chicago's original wealth is by its very grain-growing nature not the most invigorating of destinations. In fact, one of the biggest complaints of people living in Chicago is the dearth of exciting weekend getaways.

Still, the surrounding area is not devoid of interest. The following destinations can provide a good counterpoint to your time in Chicago and are good places to stop if you are motoring off someplace else. Frank Lloyd Wright and Ernest Hemingway fans in particular will enjoy Oak Park; there are some surprisingly good rural hikes within an hour's drive of the Loop.

OAK PARK

• pop 54,000

Oak Park is the place to go to make a Frank Lloyd Wright pilgrimage. For 10 years – from 1898 until 1908, when he took a surprise trip to Europe (see 'He Was Not Morally Up to Snuff') – Wright worked and lived in a studio in Oak Park. Strolling the streets of this pleasant old town is like stepping back into one of those 1950s TV sitcoms, with all its bland bucolic charm. Native son Ernest Hemingway was unmoved, though – he called Oak Park a 'village of wide lawns and narrow minds.'

Frank Lloyd Wright Sights

Wright's work is sprinkled throughout the town and is easily visited. The Oak Park Visitors' Center (☎ 708-848-1500), 158 Forest Ave at Lake, boasts helpful, plain-talking volunteers and provides a wide variety of information. Ask for the architectural walking tour brochure that comes with a useful map. The center is open 10 am to 5 pm daily.

Staff at the **Frank Lloyd Wright Home & Studio** (☎ 708-848-1976), 951 Chicago Ave, offer tours of the complex, the neighborhood and other Wright-designed homes between 11 am and 3 pm daily. Self-guided walking tours, including audio tours, are also available. Admission to the home is $8/6 adults/children.

The studio is a fascinating place, filled with the details that made Wright's style distinctive. Note how he molded plaster to look like bronze and stained cheap pine to look like rare hardwood. Always in financial trouble, spendthrift Wright was adept at making the ordinary seem extraordinary.

The trademark style of Frank Lloyd Wright

The studio's bookstore has mountains of Wright-related paraphernalia. Unfortunately, all the books seem to have been written by supplicants, sycophants and adoring relatives.

One block away, the **Moore House**, 333 N Forest Ave, is Wright's bizarre interpretation of an English manor house. Tours depart from the front of the house when enough people have gathered, noon to 4:30 pm on weekends from April to October.

Oak Park honors another famous local – despite the crack about the lawns – at the **Ernest Hemingway Museum** (☎ 708-848-2222), 200 N Oak Park Ave. There are displays about his middle-class Oak Park background and his innocent years before he went off to find adventure. Other exhibits follow the rest of his life, focusing on his writings in Spain and during World War II. The museum is open 1 to 5 pm Thursday to Sunday (from 10 am Saturday) and costs $6/5. Admission includes admittance to **Hemingway's Birthplace**, 339 N Oak Park Ave, where you can see his first room. 'Papa' was born here in 1899 in the home of his maternal grandparents.

Getting There & Away

The CTA Green Line and the Metra Union Pacific West Line serve Oak Park from Chicago with frequent and fast service. The CTA offers the more interesting ride; also see the CTA section in the Chicago chapter. On either line, exit at the Oak Park stop, walk north one block on Oak Park Ave to Lake St, turn left, and walk west on Lake to the visitors' center, which is five minutes from the Oak Park stop.

By car, take I-290 west, exiting north on Harlem Ave; take Harlem north to Lake St and turn right.

EVANSTON

• pop 73,000

A clean, pleasant place 14 miles north of the Loop, Evanston combines sprawling old houses with a compact and very walkable downtown shopping district. Much of the town is dominated by Northwestern University, whose influence is felt in many ways.

The Methodists who founded the town in 1850 would be happy to see that today it is still hard to buy a beer here, a lingering effect of both the Methodist ethos and a rule once passed by Northwestern that forbade the sale of alcohol within 4 miles of campus.

Northwestern University

Lacking the grand vision of its rival, the University of Chicago, the Northwestern University (☎ 847-491-7271) campus holds more interest for its faculty and students than for visitors.

The campus was founded in 1851 and has more than 10,000 students. The undergraduate arts and sciences programs are especially strong. Music and drama students can be found working throughout the Chicago creative community, which means that NU itself doesn't have the same sort of campus cultural scene you find at, for example, Indiana University.

The medical, legal and business graduate programs are all among the top five of their kind in the nation. All three are located in Chicago's Streeterville neighborhood.

Sports The less said on the topic of sports, the better. The Wildcats football squad had a brief moment of glory in the 1990s. But they soon returned to their traditional spot as doormats for the Big 10, laboring under the pejorative 'Mildcats' moniker, among

'He Was Not Morally Up to Snuff'

Oak Park may be home to a good portion of Frank Lloyd Wright's legacy, but you can't accuse locals of glossing over his checkered reputation. That Wright was 'not morally up to snuff' was an observation made by a woman who worked in Oak Park's official visitors' information center. She had a variety of cutting comments about the acerbic and philandering Wright, who one day didn't go home to his wife and six kids at his Oak Park studio because he was on his way to Europe with Mamah Borthwick Cheney, the wife of a client.

Born in Wisconsin in 1867 and always a prodigy, Wright went to Chicago in 1887 to work for Louis Sullivan as a drafter. But in 1893 that relationship ended when Sullivan found out that Wright was moonlighting and not cutting the firm in on the profits.

After his European escapade in 1908, Wright worked from studios on a Wisconsin farm, where he lived with Cheney, although he was still married to his first wife. Public condemnation was harsh. On Christmas Day, 1911, Wright held a press conference to explain his infidelity, proclaiming that he, as a 'thinking man,' did not have to follow the rules of 'the ordinary man.'

In 1914, a deranged servant murdered Cheney. Wright found consolation with Miriam Noel, who had sent him a letter of sympathy. They married in 1923 and divorced in 1927. In 1928 Wright married his third and final wife, Olga Ivanovna, with whom he had had a child in 1925.

Wright spent most of his later years working at his home in the Arizona desert, where he died in 1959 at the age of 90. His personal life notwithstanding, Wright was already rightfully recognized as the most original of all American architects when he died.

While some of Wright's best-known projects are in New York, Chicago and California, many important examples of his work can be viewed and visited in Wisconsin. See the Madison, Racine and Wisconsin Dells sections in the Southern Wisconsin chapter.

On the same day that the visitors' center staffer passed moral judgement, a touring architect outside the Moore House offered the following anecdote about his own run-in with the tart-tongued Wright: 'I was 19 and going to a small architecture school back east. Wright came and spoke. Afterwards I tried to speak to him, because I admired him. He looked at me and said, "You'll never be an architect, because you go to school in a shoe factory." Then he hit me with his cane and drove away.'

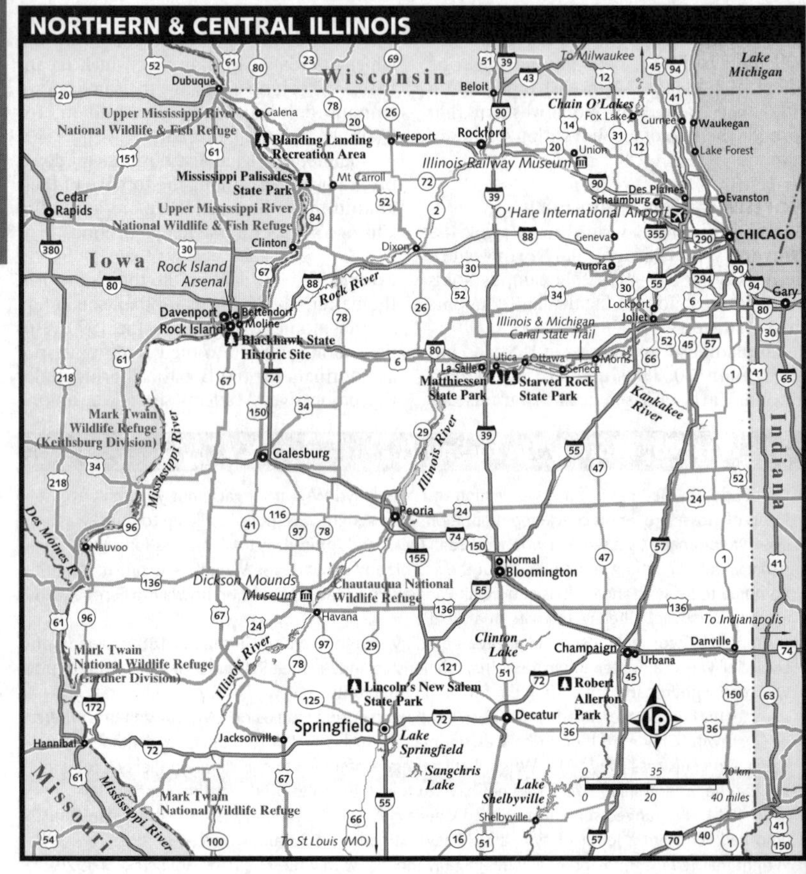

others. They've never developed the traditions that make games at other Big 10 schools such fun. Tickets (☎ 847-491-2287) are always available for the fall home games at Ryan Stadium, 1501 Central Ave, a short walk from the CTA Central El stop on the appropriately shaded Purple Line. In fact games here are more like a big high school game.

Other Northwestern athletic pursuits are not much grander – these men and women are truly here for their brains – although the fencing squad is said to be pretty good.

Mitchell Indian Museum

The lives of Native Americans in the Midwest, both past and present, are documented in this large regional museum (☎ 847-475-1030) in Kendall College at 2600 Central Ave. Artwork, including pottery, textiles, clothing, baskets and quilts, show aspects of the Indians' daily existence. Special displays let visitors handle traditional everyday objects, such as the stone tools used to make cornmeal. You'll never eat a corn tortilla so nonchalantly again – making one is wrist-killing work. Many

Native Americans who live in the area take an active role in the displays, temporary exhibitions and lectures that the museum hosts. The museum is open 10 am to 5 pm (until 8 pm Thursday, noon to 4 pm Sunday, closed Monday); $3/2.

Getting There & Away

During rush hour you can ride the CTA Purple Line Evanston Express to and from the Loop. At other times, ride the Red Line to Howard and transfer to a Purple Line local. Also see the CTA section in the Chicago chapter. The Davis stop is in the heart of town and gown. Alternately, you can take the Metra Union Pacific North Line from Northwestern Station, in the West Loop ($3 one-way). The drive north from Chicago on Sheridan Rd is especially scenic.

NORTH SHORE

Chicago's northern suburbs on the lake are pleasant and gracious places that are worth every dollar the residents pay in property taxes. Quiet yet urbane, they became popular in the late 19th century with the carriage set, who were sick of Chicago's fires, riots, tainted water and other big city excitement.

If you have a car, a Sunday drive any day of the week through the North Shore communities provides a glimpse of the beautiful homes and stately gardens. Head north from Chicago on Lake Shore Drive. When it ends, turn right on Sheridan Rd, drive north through Rogers Park to Evanston and you're on your way on a classic 30-mile drive following Sheridan through towns that include Kenilworth, Wilmette, Winnetka, Glencoe, Highland Park and the apex of the drive and of social standing, Lake Forest. Just be sure to watch the signs, as Sheridan twists and turns. Return via the Edens Expressway (I-94).

Baha'i House of Worship

You may have seen this huge white-domed edifice as you flew over Wilmette on the way in. Completed in 1953 by members of the Baha'i faith, a Persian sect, the temple is a glistening white showplace and one of seven major Baha'i houses of worship worldwide. The grounds in summer are ablaze with flowers, providing colorful contrast to the white cement.

Wilmette is the last stop on the CTA Purple Line. Catch an express in the Loop during rush hours, or take the Red Line to Howard and transfer to the Purple. The temple is a short walk east from the Linden El station.

Chicago Botanic Garden

The garden (☎ 847-835-5440) is actually in tony Glencoe, at 1000 Lake-Cook Rd, a half-mile east of the Edens Expressway (I-94). Featuring thousands of plants in 20 distinctive settings on 385 acres, the facility is run by the Chicago Horticultural Society. There is a tram tour of the site, but come on, it's not that big and what better way to explore gardens than on foot? Among the leafy sights you'll see are a prairie garden, an herb garden, a Japanese garden and a rose garden. Frequent demonstrations show you how to try to replicate the gardens at home. For fun, assign each member of the group a letter and see who can find the most plants beginning with that letter. For instance, the letter G will garner geraniums, grapes, ginkgo trees, gourds and, of course, grass.

The garden is open 8 am to dusk daily. Admission is free, but you'll suffer from the suburban scam of charging $6 for parking, since the only people likely to walk there are those out of gas. Public transport is not an easy option.

Gurnee

• pop 14,000

Hold on to your stomach at **Six Flags Great America** (☎ 847-249-1776), a 300-acre amusement park that's part of the national chain. Rides are the emphasis here and the names – such as Shock Wave and Viper – should tell you what to expect. There's no gold ring for those who guess the theme of the Giant Drop. Anyone less than 54 inches tall is kept away from the wild rides; children are instead sent packing to the marketing-driven Camp Cartoon Network and Looney Tunes. The park opens at 10 am and closes, according to a complex schedule, between 5 and 10 pm. The season runs mid-April to October 31 and varies between being open daily and only weekends. Admission and unlimited rides cost $35/18. Take the Grand Ave exit off I-94.

Marathon runners will feel at home at **Gurnee Mills** (☎ 847-263-7500), an endless outlet mall in Gurnee, 40 minutes north of the city at the Grand Ave exit off I-94. Everything is cheap, cheap, cheap at the outlet stores run by national chains and brands such as Ann Taylor, the Gap, Panasonic, Maidenform and about 200 others. But before your bargain hormones go into overdrive, consider the ugly secret of many of these places: No longer do they sell their own top-notch merchandise or T-shirts that inexplicably ended up with three sleeves. Instead, to protect their own retail stores and resellers, these 'outlet' stores often sell lower quality merchandise produced specifically for the bargain-hunting masses. A final note: If you weary of the chase and sit down in one of the rest areas, a TV will urge you to get back up and shop.

Lake Forest

• pop 3000

The toniest of the status suburbs is also the farthest north. Its downtown is a gracious place to wander, having been built in 1916 to designs inspired by English market towns, with other European influences. Considered by many to be the first suburban shopping area, its influences are hard to detect in your average strip mall.

The reward for a Sheridan Drive cruise, Lake Forest is about 45 minutes to an hour north of the city, depending on traffic. The Metra Union Pacific North Line has frequent service right to the heart of downtown ($4 one-way).

Illinois Beach State Park

Just north of Waukegan, Illinois Beach State Park (☎ 847-662-4811), Lake Front, Zion, 60099, has 6 miles of the remaining lake dunes in Illinois. It's a good alternative to the crowded sands of the Indiana dunes, although some will be put off by the Zion nuclear power plant that bisects the beach.

Campsites with electricity and hot showers cost $11 a night. Back from the shore, there is good hiking in the marshland.

DES PLAINES

• pop 54,000

This is where it all began, billions and billions of burgers ago. The **McDonald's Museum** (☎ 847-297-5022), 400 Lee St, is housed in the very first outlet Ray Kroc built back in 1955. The corporation is still based in the Chicago area (Oak Brook) and this site is a place of corporate pride. There's a video presentation and lots of mementos and original equipment. However, the hours are somewhat less reliable than the preparation time of your fries and it's best to call first to confirm.

BROOKFIELD ZOO

With 2500 animals and 215 acres, **Brookfield Zoo** (☎ 708-485-2200), 8400 W 31st St, can easily gobble up an entire day. Much more commercially oriented than Chicago's Lincoln Park Zoo, it boasts several special attractions, some of which cost extra.

Because most visitors use the North Gate and tend to hit the attractions closest to it first, you can avoid some of the crowds by starting in the southern part of the zoo and working back north. You'll soon find that the exhibits have names invented by the marketing department. Some highlights follow.

Really three exhibits, the **Fragile Kingdom** includes an indoor African desert scene, an indoor Asian rain forest scene and an outdoor collection of big cats. The desert scene has the feel of an Indiana Jones movie set and includes jackals, monitor lizards and naked mole rats.

The largest indoor exhibit at the zoo is **Tropic World: A Primate's Journey**. It is divided into three areas representing rain forests in South America, Asia and Africa. Frequent showers douse the animals but spare the visitors. Check out Ramar, a male gorilla who was brought to the zoo in 199 to improve its flaccid breeding program

Sadly, Ramar has been a major letdown, ignoring the simian charms of a succession of potential mates.

If walking with bats is your idea of a nightmare, skip the **Australia House**. Otherwise, the exhibit is well worth a stop. Couch potatoes and other critters with low metabolic rates will identify with the perpetually snoozing wombats.

Upstairs at the **Seven Seas Panorama** is the 2000-seat amphitheater, where you can see trainers putting dolphins through their paces. Downstairs, visitors can see the dolphins for free through the underwater viewing windows. Watch the dolphins looking through windows into the kitchen where their meals are prepared.

Habitat Africa! is built on five acres and set in a mythical African game reserve called Makundi National Park. The level of detail used to create the exhibit is most effective in the kopje area, which represents a rocky outcrop rising from the African savanna.

The **Living Coast** models a portion of the coast of Chile and Peru where the world's driest desert meets one of the ocean's richest breeding grounds. Sharks, turtles, penguins and 60 other species live in and around the huge tank of water.

The zoo is open 9:30 am to 5:30 pm daily from May to September (10 am to 4:30 pm other times). Admission is $6/3. On Tuesday and Thursday October to March admission is free. Parking is $4.

The Hollywood train station is near the main entrance and is served by frequent trains on the Metra BNSF line from Chicago's Union Station ($3 one-way). By car the zoo is 14 miles from the Loop. Go west on the Eisenhower Expressway (I-290) to the 1st Ave exit, then south to 31st. Follow signs to the zoo.

SCHAUMBURG

• pop 69,000

Schaumburg has long been the butt of jokes made by smug city dwellers. And why not? Completely given over to unfettered development, it is home to soulless subdivisions and the only chains you won't find here are those that are bankrupt.

The heart of this supposed city is **Woodfield Mall** (☎ 847-330-1537) where the cheery motto is 'Shop Happily Ever After.' Boasting that it has the largest amount of retail space in the world (the Mall of America nightmare, in suburban Minneapolis, is bigger but much of its space is devoted to a Peanuts amusement park), it has more than 300 stores, scores of restaurants, big department stores and an ocean of a parking lot. In fact the latter is often crowded with idling charter buses that bring in legions of shoppers from all over the Midwest, often passing mall after mall with the same stores in order to reach Woodfield. Don't come here unless you're doing a sociological study on the wonders of a Brobdingnagian retail monster.

Schaumburg is at the junction of the Northwest Tollway (I-90) and I-290.

NORTHWEST

Volo Bog Natural Area

One of the most unusual habitats in Illinois is at the Volo Bog Natural Area (☎ 815-344-1294). A large lake, left behind from the last ice age 12,000 years ago, is slowly being filled in and consumed by insatiable, creeping moss. This geologic horror movie is the only one in the Midwest and is home to a number of rare plant and animal species. There's a short nature trail and on weekends experts are on hand to make sense of the whole mossy mess. From Volo, go north on US Hwy 12/Hwy 59 to Sullivan Lake Rd and turn west, following signs to the parking lot.

Illinois Railway Museum

One of the best museums of its kind in the US, the Illinois Railway Museum (☎ 815-923-4000) has more than 200 acres of historic trains from the mid-1800s to the present. There are steam, diesel and electric locomotives, and passenger and freight cars, many of which are protected by large sheds. As you walk around, you'll see many of the hundreds of volunteers who keep the place going. With little provocation they'll happily relate story after story about the equipment. (They'll also tell you their great fear: that soon, unfettered development will

The Illinois Railway Museum tracks 150 years of trains.

bring the first subdivisions to this location, 60 miles from Chicago.)

Admission times are widely variable, but the grounds generally are open at least 10 am to 4 pm April 1 to October 30; call to confirm. Weekends May to September, steam trains run over 9 miles of track. When the trains are running, admission is $8/6. At other times it's less and, on weekdays in April and May and from mid-September to October 31, the museum is free. Take the exit for US Hwy 20 and Marengo off the Northwest Tollway (I-90), then drive north for 4½ miles to Union and follow signs.

Rockford

• pop 139,000

This old manufacturing city on the Rock River absolutely marks Chicago's farthest influence. From here it is rural all the way to the Mississippi.

The must-see sight is the **Time Museum** (☎ 815-398-6000), located in the Clock Tower Resort. Ignore the rooms but check out this remarkable assemblage of clocks from around the world. The collection includes everything from odd German timepieces with springs right through an atomic clock that uses atoms' pulses to regulate itself. It's open a very punctual 10 am to 5 pm Tuesday to Sunday; $3/2. It's at the junction of the US Hwy 20 business route and I-90 at 7801 E States St.

Rockford is also the start of one of the best drives in the state. The 43-mile stretch of Hwy 2 that goes south to Dixon follows a beautiful stretch of the Rock River. It's a good drive any time of year, as each season can add its own appeal.

WESTERN SUBURBS

Cantigny

• pop 52,000

Colonel Robert R McCormick was one of America's best screwball millionaires. A newspaper publisher along the lines of William Randolph Hearst, he was editor of the *Chicago Tribune* from 1914 until he died in 1955. Under his leadership, the *Tribune* became a powerful and idiosyncratic newspaper, the apex of an empire that included radio stations, ships, real estate and more.

A staunch conservative, McCormick used his newspaper to trumpet his political beliefs. He vilified President Franklin Delano Roosevelt during the 1930s and apologized for Adolf Hitler right up until the Nazi dictator declared war on the US. He also tirelessly promoted his idea for a huge convention center on the city's unspoiled lakefront. The paper continued the campaign after McCormick's death and steamrolled politicians into supporting the project by threatening to publish unfavorable articles about them. The resulting McCormick Place has been dubbed 'The Mistake on the Lake,' since there were vast tracts of city land elsewhere that could have been used for the center.

For insight into the colonel, you can't miss a visit to **Cantigny** (☎ 630-668-5161) in Wheaton. Cantigny includes a large herb garden; the colonel's mansion, filled with artwork provided by his two wives; and a rather large and complex museum devoted to the exploits of the US Army's First Division, the force that gave McCormick his title. The grounds are open 9 am to dusk Tuesday to Sunday, the mansion 10 am to 4 pm. Admission is free, but it costs $5 to park.

Morton Arboretum

• pop 20,000

A private nature preserve on more than 1500 acres, the **Morton Arboretum** (☎ 630-719-2400) combines a wide variety of terrain and trees. The settings range from manicured shrubs, to special plantings of trees not native to the area and long stretches of local forest and prairie. Many trees are marked with small informational signs.

There are 25 miles of trails, but a realistic circular path covering most of the preserve runs for 6 to 7 miles. Plan your course using the map you receive at the entrance. Parts of the arboretum are quite hilly, with paths that feel pleasantly rural. However, large sections of the park seem to have been designed with autos rather than walkers in mind. Many people tour the entire location without once leaving their car, a situation befitting the park's suburban location. It's fairly quiet in the middle, but toward the edges there's noise from I-88 and other busy roads. And there are those constantly touring automobiles....

The arboretum is open 7 am to 5 pm daily, until 7 pm April to October. It's 25 miles west of Chicago on Route 53, just north of I-88. This is a car-only trip. Admission is $7 per car ($3 on Wednesday).

Geneva & St Charles

These two towns on the Fox River are major weekend destinations. Both Geneva and St Charles have nicely restored downtowns and a plethora of antique shops. Geneva has the advantage of being accessible via the Metra Union Pacific West Line from Chicago ($5, 70 minutes). Everything else out here is along Hwy 31.

Both towns are very walkable and have not only antique shops, but also entire emporiums devoted to fudge, potpourri, aromatherapy goop, fragile straw flower arrangements and all the other goodies that make your trip to a cute town so profitable for the local merchants. Oh, and did we say fudge?

The Geneva Chamber of Commerce (☎ 630-232-6060), PO Box 481, 60134, and the St Charles Convention & Visitors' Bureau (☎ 630-377-6161), 311 N 2nd St, 60174, can provide lists of the ever-growing number of B&Bs.

One of the major draws to the area is the **Kane County Flea Market** (☎ 630-377-2252), which draws hundreds of dealers selling everything from junk to rare curios. It's held noon to 5 pm Saturday and 7 am to 5 pm Sunday the first weekend every month. The market is in the fairgrounds off Randall Rd, between Geneva and St Charles.

SOUTHWEST SUBURBS

Waterfall Glen Forest Preserve

The 2200-acre Waterfall Glen Forest Preserve completely surrounds the **Argonne National Laboratory**, where research is done on nuclear bombs. The setting has some of the most diverse scenery in the area, including a waterfall, a deep limestone ravine, prairie, woods, marsh and a pond.

In the past the site supplied the limestone used for Chicago's Water Tower and was the location of a nursery where trees were grown for Lincoln Park. Although the lab is in the middle, it's almost impossible to see. It doesn't even glow. On the south side of the preserve is a large field popular with people flying radio-controlled planes.

The main hiking trail is one of the area's most beautiful walks; it is also – by local standards – hilly and strenuous. The 9-mile loop is an excellent way to explore the site. Maps are usually not available, so study the large one posted at the parking lot. The main trail is marked by brown plastic posts with orange circles. Follow them carefully, because it's easy to miss a turn and end up amid apartments or houses. The best way to proceed from the parking lot is counter-clockwise, so that you'll get through the less interesting terrain first, saving the lake for the end. About 4 miles into the hike, the trail follows some old limestone walls under a thick canopy of trees.

The park is 9 miles southwest of Chicago, off Cass Ave, 1½ miles south of the Cass Ave exit off I-55. The trailhead is at the large map adjacent to the main parking lot.

Illinois & Michigan Canal Corridor

Dubbed a National Heritage Corridor, this linear park is administered by the National Park Service and encompasses 41 towns, 11 state parks and scores of historic sites.

The I&M Canal resulted from a desire for a waterway to link the Mississippi River basin with the Great Lakes, making it possible to ship goods by boat from the eastern US to New Orleans and on to the Caribbean. In 1836 the first shovelful of dirt was turned, and during the next 12 years, thousands of

Gambling

Riverboat gambling began in Illinois in 1991. In the years since, the entire motif has turned out to be a sham: The boats stopped leaving port in 1999 and are nothing more than small, somewhat cramped casinos. Meanwhile, deals are being cut in the legislature to allow regular casino gambling on land. This would save casino-hungry yet landlocked Rosemont the effort of digging a big moat.

There's no mistaking riverboat gambling in Illinois for that found in the mega-casinos of Nevada. Still, during an average month $1.23 billion dollars is dropped into slot machines statewide and another $180 million is wagered at tables. Many of the customers are retirees lured to the 'boats' by cheap bus rides. But there's no question about who really wins: The average visitor to a riverboat casino leaves about $50 poorer.

The following casinos are all within an hour of Chicago. Unless you get a bus ride, expect to drive. Now that the sham of 'riverboat' gambling has been admitted, the floating casinos are open almost 24 hours a day and you can enter and exit as you wish; no longer do you have to wait for 'sailings.'

Empress Casino Joliet The *Empress* (☎ 888-436-7737), on the Des Plaines River near the confluence of I-55 and I-80 in Joliet, is a North African spectacle, with obelisks flanking the entrance, that looks like an extremely loose approximation of an Egyptian palace. The *Empress I* and *Empress II* are nearly identical sleek, modern-looking vessels. The boats are decorated simply and almost devoid of windows.

Harrah's Joliet Casino Harrah's boats (☎ 800-427-7247) are quite different from each other. The *Northern Star* is a modern yachtlike craft. The *Southern Star II* resembles an old riverboat complete with a big, working paddle wheel on the rear. Plans are afoot to build a regular casino on land by 2001.

Hollywood Casino Aurora The Hollywood Casino's boats (☎ 800-888-7777), *City of Lights I* and *II*, have a riverboat look, without the paddle wheels. Inside, the gaming areas are rather opulent, with a brightly colored decor that reflects the Hollywood theme.

mmigrants, primarily Irish, were lured to Chicago to work on the 96-mile course.

After it opened in 1848, the constant flow of goods through Chicago propelled the city's economic development. In 1900 it was supplemented by the much deeper Chicago Sanitary & Ship Canal, which, besides being a much more navigable waterway, became Chicago's de facto drainpipe.

Competition from railroads and other waterways caused the I&M Canal to molder for most of the 20th century. The establishment of the park in 1984 has spurred restoration and development of the I&M Canal's remaining sites and of some of the historic towns along the route.

The I&M Canal and related sights are a car-only trip. Most are easily accessible from Chicago off I-55 and I-80.

Orientation & Information The Heritage Corridor driving route can be hard to follow, and the sites are greatly dispersed. It's a good idea to get some of the available free maps in advance so you can plan your itinerary – the trip can easily fill a day. One bonus: Most sites are free.

The Heritage Corridor Visitors' Bureau (☎ 815-727-2323, 800-926-2262), 81 N Chicago St, Joliet, 60431, is a local agency that has information on the parks as well as food and lodging details for the region.

The Illinois & Michigan Canal Heritage Corridor Commission (☎ 815-740-2047), 200 W Eighth St, Lockport, 60441, is the source for all the excellent National Park Service brochures and maps of the corridor. The one devoted to archaeology is especially good. They also know when various

Gambling

Grand Victoria Casino Operated by Circus Circus Enterprises – one of the largest casino operators in Las Vegas – the Grand Victoria (☎ 847-888-1000), on the Fox River in downtown Elgin, is a floating behemoth. Almost all of the 1200 gambling positions are on one deck, giving the casino a spaciousness that approaches that of some Las Vegas casinos.

The following two casinos in Northwest Indiana still have to abide by that state's rules requiring them to weigh anchor. They also close by 3 am every night.

Trump Casino High-volume New York developer and self-promoter Donald Trump has found tough odds with his big-ticket casino (☎ 888-218-7867). It's in a remote part of Gary, Indiana, reachable by I-90 (take the Cline Blvd/State Road 912 exit and go north 3 miles). He's imperiously renamed the location 'Buffington Harbor' to camouflage the Gary connection, but gamblers seem to prefer the looser rules in Illinois.

Empress Casino Hammond Developers dug a big hole, filled it with water and plopped a boat into it. Voila! Riverboat gambling in Hammond! Just off US 41, the Empress operation (☎ 888-436-7737) seems to be biding its time until the Indiana legislature can be swayed to allow it to build some huge casino on land.

information centers along the canal are open. This center is open 10 am to 5 pm Wednesday to Sunday.

ILLINOIS & MICHIGAN CANAL STATE TRAIL

Already 61 miles in length, the Illinois & Michigan Canal State Trail runs from I-55 in the east, to LaSalle in the west. The path follows the canal and is ideal for biking, hiking and snowmobiling. You can also wilderness camp along the length of the canal. For many activities, such as snowmobiling and camping, advance registration is required at one of three information centers. The centers also have information about the portions of the canal suitable for canoeing. Call for details:

Gebhard Woods State Park (☎ 815-942-0796)
Channahon Access (☎ 815-467-4271)
Buffalo Rock State Park (☎ 815-433-2224)

LOCKPORT

A good place to start the tour is the town of Lockport, 33 miles southwest of Chicago. The town of 10,000 is itself historic, having been bypassed by most development in favor of much larger Joliet, to its south. The center of Lockport is in the National Register of Historic Places. It is home to the **I&M Canal Museum** (☎ 815-838-5080), 803 S State Rd, housed in the original 1837 home of the canal commissioners. The museum is open 1 to 4:30 pm daily; admission is free. It has all the maps and brochures you didn't get in advance, as well as displays about life along the waterway when more flowed by than just the odd fallen leaf.

The surviving Lock No 1 is the highlight of the 2½-mile **Gaylord Donnelley Canal Trail**, which follows the canal through town and has several exhibits along the way.

MORRIS

The Kankakee and Des Plaines Rivers join near Morris. This is the location for **Goose Lake Prairie State Natural Area** (☎ 815-942-2899), which contains the largest surviving portion of tall-grass prairie in Illinois. The plants, which early pioneers likened to a ocean of color, grew up to 10 or more feet i height and blossomed in waves through th growing season; what little survives is sti worth seeing. A visitors' center explains th unique ecology of the prairie, and on week ends a naturalist is usually around for ques tions. The area is on Jugtown Rd, which off Lorenzo Rd that reaches I-55 on the eas and Hwy 47 in the west.

SENECA

A small town on Route 6 off I-80, 65 mile from Chicago, Seneca is home to the **Senec Grain Elevator**, a fascinating affair tha towers over the canal, which at this point little more than a muddy ditch. Completed i 1862, the 65-foot building is one of the olde survivors from the early grain industr Check with the Heritage Corridor Commis sion for hours and be sure to get a copy c the heavily illustrated Park Service brochur explaining the workings of the place.

Near Seneca, **Marseilles** is famous toda as the site of the National Weather Servic tornado warning radar and for its 'quain downtown, which has become home to cluster of antique stores and cute cafés.

OTTAWA

The **Illinois Waterway Visitors' Cent** (☎ 815-667-4054) is off Dee Bennett Rd an Route 178, some 88 miles from Chicag The Starved Rock Lock, a major point c the waterway that replaced the I&M Cana is the focus of its several exhibits and its ob servation deck. The center is open 9 am 8 pm daily June to September, 8 am to 5 p other times.

Ottawa itself has a nice downtown an plenty of services such as supermarket There are large numbers of motels at exit 9 off I-80 and Hwy 23. The ***Ottawa In*** *(☎ 815-434-3400, fax 815-434-3904, 30 Columbus St)* has an indoor pool and plea ant rooms from $40/45.

UTICA

A charming small town, Utica has found itse a profitable place near the end of the I&

Canal zone and across the river from Starved Rock State Park. It's a good place for a stroll.

Items used by the people who lived and worked near the I&M Canal are on display at the **LaSalle County Historical Society** (☎ 815-667-4861) at Mill and Canal Sts. It's open noon to 4 pm Friday to Sunday (also Wednesday and Thursday June to September) and costs $1/50¢.

Starved Rock Inn *(☎ 815-667-4238)* is at Hwys 6 and 178 and has rustic cabins that cost $45.

Patti's Pancake House *(☎ 815-667-4151, 704 Clark St)* specializes in yummy flapjacks like banana-walnut and pumpkin-pecan ($5). ***Duffy's Tavern*** *(☎ 815-667-4324)* is across from the museum and serves inexpensive burgers and more at lunch and dinner daily.

STARVED ROCK STATE PARK

One of the most popular parks in Illinois, Starved Rock State Park (☎ 815-667-4726), PO Box 509, 61373, is a mile south of Utica. More than 2000 acres of wooded bluffs feature 18 canyons carved through the limestone during the last ice age. After heavy rains there is a waterfall at the head of each canyon. Some 15 miles of hiking trails wander through the park, and there are spectacular views from the highest bluff. You can rent canoes for paddled jaunts on the Illinois River and the canyon waterways, and go on guided nature tours. There are seasonal canoe, horse, bike and ski rentals.

The park takes its name from the legend that a band of Illinois were trapped during battle with the Ottawa atop the park's 130-foot sandstone butte and starved to death.

The park visitors' center is open 9 am to pm daily June to September and 1 to 4 pm daily (from 10 am weekends) at other times. It has full information on the many rental opportunities as well as the various hiking trails and other park features. Although very crowded on summer weekends, you can always leave the crowds behind by hiking beyond Wildcat Canyon, which is less than a mile east of the main parking area. Less than a mile from this point is La Salle Canyon, which has a waterfall that turns into a glistening ice fall in the winter.

Camping in the park gets very popular; sites with electricity cost $11. The ***Starved Rock Lodge*** *(☎ 815-667-4211, 800-868-7625, fax 815-667-4455, ⓔ srlodge@ivnet.com)* is right in the park and is both rustic and modern at the same time. Comfortable rooms start at $68/75; cabins start at $69. The park is off Hwy 178 across the river from Utica.

MATTHIESSEN STATE PARK

Matthiessen State Park (☎ 815-667-4868) is just across Hwy 178. It has dramatic limestone cliffs and chasms formed by water runoff to the river. There are hiking, skiing and equestrian trails and it is often less crowded than Starved Rock. There is no camping.

Northwestern Illinois

GALENA

• pop 3600

Named for the Latin word for lead ore, Galena grew rich after the federal government authorized mining in the area in 1807. The lead boom during the first half of the 19th century saw over 800 million pounds of lead shipped out of Galena. Most of it left in boats that traveled the Galena River to the Mississippi 3 miles away. The wealth that poured into the town was reflected in the grand mansions lining the hills and the fine shops on Main St. Federal, Greek Revival, Second Empire and Queen Anne were just some of the architectural styles used.

After the lead ran out, Galena ran out of gas. Relegated to an economic backwater, the town and its fine architecture hibernated for 100 years until the inevitable occurred: An antique store opened and a few people came, a boutique opened and more people came, a B&B opened and still more people came, then a fudge shop opened and the buses came.

To get an idea of what Galena used to look like, stand on a corner on Main St and squint your eyes to block out the ice cream shops and teddy bear emporiums. Under the tourist gloss, Main St retains its historic charm. In some of the surviving gritty bars you'll find locals whose incomes aren't tied to the tourist boom and who will provide entertaining and profane commentary on what it's like to, say, get stuck driving behind large sedans of antique shoppers.

Galena is well worth a stop, but avoid summer and fall weekends when traffic moves more slowly than caramel apples on a hot day. On any day, take to the steps that lead up from Main St to find quiet streets that still feel like they're hibernating.

Galena is well-suited for walking. A pedestrian bridge links the two sides of the Galena River. Mountain Bike Rental (no phone), 517 S Main St, rents bikes for $25 a day.

Information

The Visitors' Information Center (☎ 815-777-4390, 877-444-5850, www.galena.org) is in the Old Train Depot across the river from the center at 101 Bouthillier St. It's open 9 am to 5 pm (from 10 am Sunday and until 7 pm Friday and Saturday June to September). They will find you rooms for busy weekends.

Things to See & Do

The **Galena Jo Davies County Historical Society & Museum** (☎ 815-777-9129), 211 S Bench St, has the usual local exhibits and a good model showing the complex geography of the county. It's open 9 am to 4:30 pm daily and admission is $4/3. One of the best ways to see Galena is by the **walking tours** offered by the historical society at 11 am Saturday May to October. The tours leave from DeSoto House Hotel lobby (see Places to Stay) and cost $5. You can also arrange tours at other times.

The **Old Market House** (☎ 815-777-2570) is on Market Square and was built in 1845. The dignified building hosts rotating local exhibits and is open 9 am to 5 pm daily.

Town boosters took some of their lead profits and gave local-boy-made-good and Civil War hero Ulysses S Grant a fin Italianate house. Today it's the **US Gran State Historic Site** (☎ 815-777-3310), 50 Bouthillier St, and it has items left ove from his on and off post-Civil War residenc (he had to leave every so often to do thing like go to Washington and be president). It' open 9 am to 5 pm daily and admission is b donation.

Places to Stay

The best place to camp is down the Missis sippi at the ***Blanding Landing Recreatio Area***; see Mississippi River, later in thi chapter.

About 3 miles east of town, the ***Gran Hills Motel*** *(☎ 815-777-2116, 9372 Hwy 20* has a pool and basic rooms with nice view of the hills for $35/45.

The ***Main St Inn*** *(☎ 815-777-3454, fa 815-777-6621, 404 S Main St)* is a forme cigar factory that's been converted int a hotel, with rooms starting at $75. Re stored in the 1980s, the ***DeSoto Hous Hotel*** *(☎ 815-777-0090, 800-343-6562, 23 S Main St)* first opened its doors in 185 and has been a landmark ever since. Toda rooms start at $75.

Not every stately home in Galena is B&B, it just seems that way. The visitor center can help you find one. ***Brierwrea Manor*** *(☎ 815-777-0608, ⓔ briew@galen link.net, 216 N Bench St)* is close to Main S and offers the typical Galena B&B exper ence: friendly owners, good and heart breakfast and a quiet room that starts at $9 a night.

Places to Eat

Locals meet at ***Emmy Lou's*** *(☎ 815-77 4732, 200 N Main St)*, which has the town best pancakes ($2) and other unadorne foods in a bright unadorned old-fashione coffee shop.

The Log Cabin *(☎ 815-777-0393, 201 Main St)* is another place loved by loca Lunch specials such as a hot beef sandwic are less than $5 and as one discerning lon time resident said, 'the pork chops are th best ever.'

Right up at the high end, the ***Eldorado Grill*** *(☎ 815-777-1224, 219 N Main St)* has creative Southwestern cuisine, much of it prepared with organic local ingredients; be ready to spend about $30 a person.

Getting There & Away

Greyhound inexplicably stops half a mile east of town at the R&L Gas Mart on US Hwy 20. This is fairly inconvenient as the little stretch of road you have to traverse is quite steep and narrow and has no sidewalks. There's one bus a day to/from Chicago ($33, 4 hours).

River Cruises (☎ 800-331-1467, @ twilight@galenalink.net) runs two-day roundtrip journeys on the Mississippi between Galena and Le Claire, Iowa, near the Quad Cities. Passage aboard the steamboatlike *Twilight* costs from $240 and includes meals.

MISSISSIPPI RIVER

On the Illinois side, Hwy 84 south from Galena forms part of the Great River Road, the route that follows the Mississippi River the length of Illinois. However, for pure driving and viewing pleasure, US Hwy 52 on the Iowa side between Dubuque and Sabula is considered the better option.

The US Army Corps of Engineers (☎ 800-645-0248), as part of its management of the river, has developed lots of small campgrounds and recreation areas along the river that are usually fairly remote and unvisited; call for details.

Blanding Landing Recreation Area

Placid Blanding Landing (☎ 815-591-2326) is typical of the many small Corps of Engineers facilities along the Mississippi. There's a boat landing, an excellent shower and toilets, and ***camping*** *(☎ 877-444-6777 for reservations only)* with sites with electricity ($12) and without ($10). It's also a haven for transportation nuts since a major railway passes on the east side and the busy Mississippi lines are on the west side. There are some good walks on the lonely country roads and a fun café about a mile away that you pass on the way in.

Reaching Blanding Landing from Galena is a challenge, however. The 13-mile drive is a scenic test of your sign-reading skills. From Galena, take Blackjack Rd to Pilot Knob Rd, following the small signs for 'campground' or 'recreation area.'

Mississippi Palisades State Park

For more than a thousand years, Native Americans lived in the area north of today's Savanna, 32 miles south of Galena on Hwy 84. The limestone bluffs contain caves that gave good shelter and the Mississippi was teeming with fish, making the area hospitable for habitation. Today the area is preserved in Mississippi Palisades State Park (☎ 815-273-2731). Camping and hiking are the activities of choice in these 2500 acres. Over 13 miles of trails, some quite rugged, lead from the river flood plains up to the crests of the Palisades through dense forest.

Camping is very popular and the park does not accept reservations. There are 241 sites with vehicle access. Those with electricity cost $11, and $8 without. There are also three serene areas for primitive camping ($6) that are about a half-mile walk from the nearest parking.

Mt Carroll

• pop 3800

This is the kind of place where you expect to find a dog asleep in the road. Mt Carroll is a bit like what Galena was like when everybody was still bemoaning the loss of lead. Lined with historic buildings, the town hasn't made many itineraries, yet.

Eleven miles west of Savanna on US Hwy 52, Mt Carroll's main drag is Hwy 78, which passes through a registered National Historic Site for several blocks. Many of the houses have small plaques out front explaining their significance. Many are on Broadway, Clay and Main Sts. The **Owen P Miles Home**, 107 W Broadway, is a solid brick house from 1873. It is sometimes open for tours and has local information. There's no phone, so drive by and see if anyone's home.

The ***Mt Carroll Café & General Store*** *(☎ 815-244-1700, 314 Main St)*, across from the Carroll County Court House (☎ 815-244-9171), is open 6 am to 8 pm daily and has local information. It also has a mean hot turkey sandwich for $4.

Dixon

• pop 15,000

At the southern end of the scenic stretch of Hwy 2 from Rockford, Dixon is just beginning to realize the opportunities inherent in its status as a childhood hometown of Ronald Reagan, the 40th US president.

Another president, Abraham Lincoln, was stationed here during his time in the army during the Black Hawk War in 1830. The predictable **Lincoln Statue** is on the site of the old fort, on the north bank of the gushing Rock River between Galena and Peoria Sts.

The Dixon Area Chamber of Commerce (☎ 815-284-3361) is right on the south bank of the river at 74 S Galena Ave. These folks are repositories for information on the region and are open 9 am to 5 pm weekdays.

A very modest two-story wood structure, the **Ronald Reagan Boyhood Home** (☎ 815-288-3404), 816 S Hennepin Ave, is what Reagan called home after his family moved to Dixon from nearby Tampico in 1920, when he was 9 years old. The inside has been restored to reflect that era and it's easy to see that whatever else you might say about him, Reagan wasn't born with a silver spoon in his mouth. There's a photo of a strapping high-school-age Reagan in his lifeguard duds that definitely reveals a certain star quality (well, at least B-movie star quality). The house and adjoining visitors' center are open 10 am to 4 pm daily (from 1 pm Sunday, and weekends only in February and March). Admission is free.

Places to Stay & Eat Out of town at I-88, the ***Super 8*** *(☎/fax 815-284-1800, 1800 S Galena Rd)* is a recent, tree-less construction and is perhaps a tad pricey at $44/46.

Right downtown, the ***Peoria Avenue Iced Cream Co*** *(☎ 815-288-8086, 116 S Peoria Ave)* is a real ice cream parlor with cones from $1. Closed Sunday, it has lunch salad and sandwiches.

Quad Cities

Really four cities in one, Rock Island (po 40,500) and Moline (43,200) are on the Illi nois side of the Mississippi and Davenpor (95,400) and Bettendorf (52,700) are on th Iowa side.

Their histories are linked and center o the Mississippi, farming and manufacturing Rock Island has always been an importan facility for the US government; it was major prison during the Civil War, a conflic precipitated in part by local slave Dred Scot who unsuccessfully sued for his freedom Moline is the home of John Deere, the hug farm implement manufacturer. All fou towns were important river ports during th steam boat era.

Today the metropolitan sprawl shoul be thought of as one area, as it benefit from the collective interest of all fou towns.

Rock Island, the town, is the city on th banks of the river; Rock Island Arsenal i the island in the river. East Moline adjoin Moline and its residents would love for th area to be known as the 'Quint Cities,' bu that seems most unlikely.

Information Coming from the west, th Mississippi Valley Welcome Center (☎ 319 289-3009) has a good view of the river and i open 8:30 am to 4:30 pm daily (until 8 pr May to mid-October). It has vast amount of regional information and is at I-80 ex 306 and US Hwy 67 in LeClaire, Iowa.

The Mississippi River Visitors' Cente (☎ 309-794-5338) is also packed with infor mation and has the advantage of being righ over a lock on the river, so you can watc the huge barges go up and down. It i located at the southern end of Rock Islan Arsenal at Arsenal Bridge.

The Moline Visitors' Center (☎ 309-788 7800) is open 8:30 am to 5 pm weekdays an will help find accommodations. It's in th old train depot at 2021 River Drive.

The *River Cities' Reader* is a free alterna-ive weekly that has entertainment and vent listings.

ROCK ISLAND ARSENAL

'his was the site of Fort Armstrong where he Mesquakie and Sauk Native Americans atefully signed the 1832 treaty opening the American West to settlement after the Black Hawk War.

The US has used the island as a military actory to produce ordnance since the 1870s. **Colonel Davenport's Home** (☎ 309-786-7336) s the oldest structure, having been built for s namesake, an officer at Fort Armstrong in 833. It's open noon to 4 pm Thursday to unday, but call to check the hours; $3/2.

The **Rock Island Arsenal Museum** (☎ 309-82-5021) has more than 1000 guns, many of which were manufactured at the arsenal. 'here are also displays of the island's history. t's open 10 am to 4 pm daily and is free.

During the Civil War, the Union used the sland as a prisoner of war camp. The first ontingent of Confederates arrived in December 1863 to find that the Union Army adn't actually built a prison. Left outside in he Midwestern winter, over 1000 prisoners ied by spring. A **cemetery** recalls this ugly hapter, which was typical of POW treatment by both sides.

BLACK HAWK STATE HISTORIC SITE

'his 207-acre wooded site is on the Rock River upstream of its confluence with the Mississippi. In the 1700s it was one of the argest Native American villages in North America. The two tribes, the Sauk and Mesquakie, sided with the British in the Revolution and in 1780 American troops ventured this far west to destroy the village. In 812, the tribes, again siding with the British, ot their revenge and eliminated the 400 American troops in the area. Things were ettled for good in 1832 with the Black Hawk reaty. The Black Hawk State Historic Site ☎ 309-788-9536) has hiking trails through ees and a museum that's open 9 am to 5 pm aily (closed at 4 pm and on Monday and uesday, November to February).

Iowa

Bill Bryson always says 'I was born in Iowa, somebody had to be.' But really the state makes a fine companion to northern Illinois, and if it weren't for the Mississippi you would not know where one quit and the other began.

Nickname: Hawkeye State, for the prairie flower

Population: 2,853,000 (30th largest state)

Area: 56,275 sq miles (26th largest)

Admitted to Union: December 28, 1846 (29th state)

Information The Iowa Division of Tourism (☎ 512-242-4705, 800-345-4692), 200 E Grand Ave, Des Moines, IA 50309, has tourist information.

Taxes Statewide sales tax is 5%.

Road Rules Seat belts are required for people in the front seat of the car as well as child seats for children under three; children three to five must wear seat belts. Motorcyclists are not required to wear helmets.

JOHN DEERE PAVILION

Moline is home to Deere & Company, makers of the ubiquitous green and yellow farm tractors, harvesters, farm implements and very expensive lawn mowers beloved by well-heeled suburbanites. The company began in a rural Illinois blacksmith shop in 1837 when John Deere fashioned a new kind of plow. It caught on and the company later moved to Moline, where its worldwide operations are centered.

The John Deere Pavilion (☎ 309-765-1000) is a giant glass hall where Deere products past and present are displayed with the same care as that used by a jeweler. Sparkling under the lights, these gems are much, much bigger than a jeweler's wares, but equally expensive. A corn harvester will set you back a mere $250,000. There are lots of misty-eyed farmers here caressing the tractors and hanging out next door at the **John Deere Store** (☎ 309-765-1007) where you can buy a green hat for $8 (chewing tobacco not included). The store is slick and part of the disturbing trend in which people pay billion-dollar corporations top money to help market their products. The pavilion is at 1400 River Drive and is probably the sole thing of interest in downtown Moline. It's open 9 am to 6 pm weekdays, to 5 pm Saturday and 12:30 to 5 pm Sunday.

CASINOS

The waters are alive with gambling boats in both states. *Jumer's Casino Rock Island* (☎ 800-477-7747) is on the Rock Island waterfront. The *President Casino* (☎ 800-262-8711) is in downtown Davenport and the *Lady Luck Casino* (☎ 800-576-5825) is at State Street Landing in Bettendorf. The Iowa boats are open around the clock; the Illinois boat closes in the early morning.

SPECIAL EVENTS

Jazz legend Bix Beiderbecke got his start in Davenport in the 1920s. The town holds a jazz festival (☎ 319-324-7170) in his honor every July.

PLACES TO STAY

The ***Camelot Campground*** *(☎ 309-787-0665)* has two lakes, a playground, a store and more with sites starting at $12. It's at 2311 78th Ave W, off Hwy 92.

In downtown Bettendorf, the ***Twin Bridges Motor Inn*** *(☎/fax 319-355-6451, 221 5th St)* is a simple motel-style place with basic rooms from $30/40. Out on the interstates, the ***Excel Inn*** *(☎ 309-797-5580, fax 309-797-1561, 2501 52nd Ave)* is one of several chain places at exit No 5 at the junction of I-74 and I-280 in Moline. Basic rooms cost $39/44.

In downtown Rock Island, the ***Four Points Sheraton*** *(☎ 309-794-1212, fax 309-794-0852)* is at 3rd Ave and 17th St and is close to the entertainment neighborhood called the District. Comfortable rooms start at $79. Near the tractors in downtown Moline, ***Radisson on John Deere Commons*** *(☎ 309-764-1000, fax 309-764-1710, 141 River Drive)* is part of the Deere Pavilio complex and has business traveler-friendl rooms from $79.

Davenport's downtown has the ***Radisson Quad City Plaza Hotel*** *(☎ 319-322 2200, fax 319-322-9939, 111 E 2nd St,* probably the nicest hotel in the are Rooms are $85. One of the most interestin places to stay is ***The Abbey*** *(☎ 319-355 0291, fax 319-355-7647)* which is on a hill i Bettendorf overlooking the river at 14th S and Central Ave. Posh rooms in the forme monastery start at $80.

PLACES TO EAT

All four towns have oodles of places fo food and drink. The following places ar each in neighborhoods with numerou choices.

All Kinds of People *(☎ 309-788-256 1806 2nd Ave)* is in the District in Roc Island and serves good sandwiches, salac and hot entrées like meat loaf at lunch. Th coffee bar, which has a selection of gay per odicals, is open until 11 pm. ***Blue Cat Bre Pub*** *(☎ 309-788-8247, 113 18th St)* is one c several Quad Cities microbreweries. It has huge menu with lots of pastas, salads an sandwiches. Most everything is less tha $12. It's also in the District.

Wise Guys Pizza *(☎ 319-326-1532)* is local institution in the very walkab neighborhood of East Davenport Villag in Davenport. A large garlic barbecu chicken pie goes for $19. ***The Doc*** *(☎ 319-322-5331, 125 S Perry St)* is on th riverfront in Davenport. Finely prepare steaks and seafood are served here prices that average $20.

ENTERTAINMENT

The District in Rock Island is a six-squar block area by the water that has a score pubs, cafés, restaurants and clubs. It roughly bounded by 1st and 4th Aves an 17th and 19th Sts.

Rock Island Rapids *(☎ 309-794-983 1721 2nd Ave)* has live local rock, blues an country bands nightly.

·ETTING THERE & AWAY

)uad City Airport (☎ 309-764-9621) is in ⁄Ioline on Airport Rd off I-74 and I-280. ·ervice by the following airlines includes (see he Toll-Free & Web Site Directory at the ·ack of the book for contact information):

ccess Air – Los Angeles, New York

irtran – Atlanta

merican Eagle – Chicago

orthwest Airlines – Minneapolis

rans World Express – St Louis

nited Express – Chicago, Denver

he main bus terminals are at the airport nd at 304 W River Drive in downtown)avenport. Greyhound (☎ 309-757-7155) as five buses daily to/from Chicago ($28, hours). Burlington Trailways (☎ 319-322-876) has one bus daily to/from Champaign $33, 4½ hours).

River Cruises (☎ 800-331-1467, twilight@alenalink.net) runs two-day roundtrip ›urneys on the Mississippi between Le laire, Iowa, near the Quad Cities and ;alena. Passage aboard the steamboatlike *wilight* costs from $240 and includes neals.

·ETTING AROUND

.ocal bus service in the Quad Cities is pro-ided by Metrolink on the Illinois side ☎ 309-788-3360), Davenport Citibus (☎ 319-88-7954) and Bettendorf Transit (☎ 319-44-4085). The three systems link their routes nd schedules and have daily service. ⁄Ietrolink bus No 20 links the airport and ownttown Moline, a local transit hub.

The Channel Cat Water Taxi (☎ 309-788-360) links Davenport, Bettendorf and ⁄Ioline with hourly boats daily from May to ·eptember. All-day tickets are $4.

The Quad Cities have an impressive etwork of bike paths and trails. Many ›llow both banks of the Mississippi. The)uad Cities Bicycle Club (☎ 319-344-2805) as maps and details. Wolfe's Village Bike hop (☎ 319-326-4686), 1018 Mound St in ast Davenport Village, rents bikes for $17 day.

Central Illinois

The rolling prairies of central Illinois were mostly settled by pioneers in the 1820s. The land was carved up into farms over a relatively short period and most of the towns were incorporated between 1820 and 1940.

Springfield is the major city, with not only the state capital but also numerous important Abraham Lincoln sites. He spent most of his adult years as a lawyer and politician in central Illinois and the region is rife with related sites. Back east, the joke may be that every other rock bears the inscription 'Washington slept here' but in central Illinois you'll soon think that every town bears the inscription 'Lincoln spoke here.'

The region has numerous medium-size cities, such as Bloomington and Decatur, that don't have a lot of visitor interest beyond a few old homes. But there's interest in the land itself and following old Route 66 is a great way to see life on the farm.

SPRINGFIELD

• pop 109,000

The state capital, with its fine architecture, has a serious obsession with Abraham Lincoln, who practiced law and politics here from 1837 to 1861. Its Abe-related sites offer an in-depth look at the man many consider the greatest of US presidents and his turbulent times. The great irony is that the same town that venerates Honest Abe has been home to some of the greatest backdoor deals and cons ever perpetrated by the Illinois state legislature. The state is building a major new Lincoln museum and library that's set to open by 2003.

Springfield was chosen as the state capital in 1837 not because of its natural beauty – it has none – but because it is near the middle of Illinois. Chicago is 210 miles north on I-55.

Information

The Springfield Convention & Visitors' Bureau (☎ 217-789-2360, 800-545-7300, www.springfield.il.us/visit), 109 7th St, is

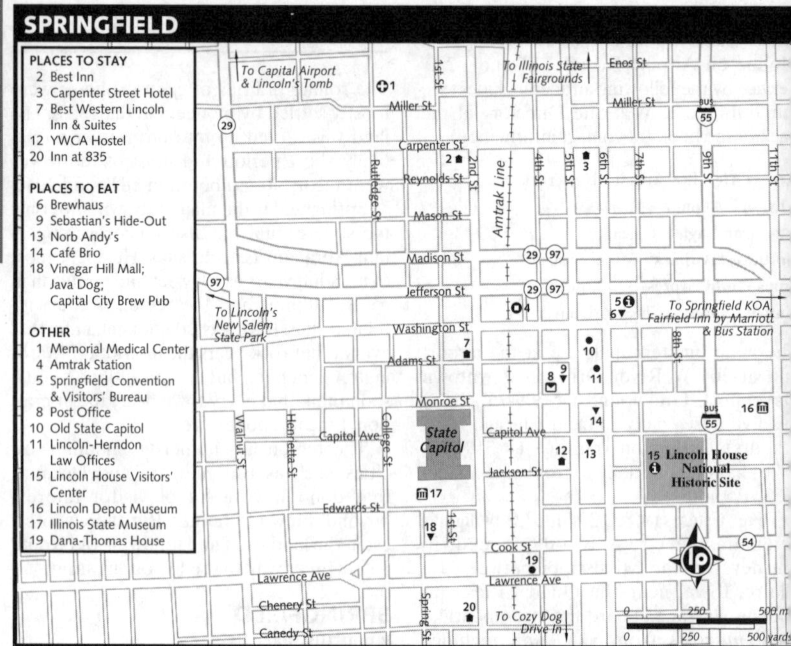

open 8 am to 5 pm weekdays. Outside of these hours, the Lincoln Home Visitors' Center, 426 7th St, has lots of local information and maps; see Lincoln Sights, below, for more information.

There's a post office (☎ 800-275-8777) at the corner of Monroe and 4th Sts that's open 8 am to 5:30 pm weekdays.

Java Dog (☎ 217-522-6882), two blocks south of the capitol in the Vinegar Hill Mall at 107 Cook St and Spring St, has free Internet access for anyone who buys a drink such as a double cappuccino ($2). The muffins are good, too.

The *Illinois State Journal-Register* is the local daily. The best entertainment and event listings are in the weekly *Illinois Times*.

Memorial Medical Center (☎ 217-788-3000), 800 Rutledge St, is a major hospital.

Lincoln Sights

Abraham and Mary Lincoln lived at 8th and Jackson Sts from 1844 to 1861, then moved to the White House. This house is part of th **Lincoln House National Historic Site** (☎ 217 492-4150), a growing collection of histori and authentic buildings set on streets a they would have looked in Lincoln's time Lincoln bought the home for $1500, a goo year's salary at that time for a lawyer lik himself. Mary expanded it and brought it u to her standards, which were always mor refined than her former-pioneer husband.

Today, the house appears much like it di when Lincoln lived there. Restorers hav been especially aided by an illustrated *Ne York Times* article on the home life of Ab that ran when he was elected, proof that suc stories are truly evergreen. You'll also notic the small size of the furniture, sized for th average person at the time. At 6 feet 4 inche Lincoln usually ended up sitting on the floo reading rather than enduring such 'comforts

For a free tour, visitors must first obtain ticket at the Lincoln Home Visitors' Cente (see Information), where you can look a

CHARLES COOK

CHARLES COOK

nois treasures include gorgeous national forests and historic Lincoln sites.

CHARLES COOK

nestone cliffs and canyons grace Illinois' Matthiessen State Park.

RICK GERHARTER

ank Lloyd Wright's home and studio, Oak Park (IL)

RICHARD CUMMINS

Baha'i temple, near Wilmette (IL)

RICHARD CUMMINS

Chicago's 900 N Michigan Ave

RICK GERHARTER

Urban bicyclists reach Critical Mass on the Chi-town streets.

PETER PTSCHELINZEW

The city's signature on the Lake Michigan shore

RICHARD CUMMINS

Chicago Lighthouse from Navy Pier

RICK GERHARTER

Chicago's got flavor!

displays and a 20-minute film while you wait – it gets crowded and on peak summer weekends the line can extend for hours, so go early. There is an excellent bookstore filled with Lincoln tomes. Many of the other buildings are open for visits and the area can easily consume a few hours. The visitors' center is open 8:30 am to 5 pm daily (until 6 pm April to September).

A short walk northwest, the **Lincoln-Herndon Law Offices** (☎ 217-785-7960), 209 6th St, is the restored building where Lincoln practiced law with his partner and close friend William Herndon from 1844–53. Tours leave 9 am to 5 pm daily (until 4 pm November to March) and cost $2/1 adults/children.

Lincoln's immortal line, 'A house divided against itself cannot stand…' was delivered in the **Old State Capitol** (☎ 217-785-7691), near 6th and Adams Sts, in the days before the Civil War. Here, detailed tours outline his early political life, which included the dramatic Lincoln-Douglas debates in 1858. It's open 9 am to 5 pm daily (until 4 pm November to March) and accepts donations. The library is a major repository of Lincoln papers.

In 1861, the newly elected Lincoln departed for Washington at the train station at 10th and Monroe Sts, which now houses the **Lincoln Depot Museum** (☎ 217-544-8695), recalling his moving farewell address as he left for Washington and the presidency. It's open 10 am to 4 pm daily April to September and is free.

After his assassination, Lincoln's body was returned to Springfield, where it lies today – the impressive **Lincoln's Tomb** sits in Oak Ridge Cemetery (☎ 217-782-2717),

The Tall Man in the Tall Hat

Despite being president for only four years, Abraham Lincoln (1809–1865) left a legacy as profound as that of any American. Time seems only to add to his near deification. His poor rural childhood in Indiana and self-schooling in Illinois fuel the notion that greatness, and the presidency, can be anybody's. His historic Illinois debates with political opponent Stephen Douglas, in which he argued against slavery, have made him a lasting symbol of justice. He led the country through its civil war managing to preserve the young nation's unity. With his writings and speeches, most famously the Gettysburg Address, the democratic ideal became one of America's most cherished principles. When he was shot in Washington, Lincoln was the first president to be assassinated, unspooling what has become another, albeit ignominious, thread through American politics.

2 miles north of downtown off Walnut St (Hwy 29). The gleam on the nose of Lincoln's bust, created by visitors' light touches, indicates the numbers of those who pay their respects here.

Other Sights

The colossal **State Capitol** (☎ 217-782-2099), at 2nd St and Capitol Ave, offers free tours around the sumptuous interior from 9 am to 3 pm daily. The 405-foot-tall building is open for much longer hours when the legislature is in session. Watch your pocket when the politicians are about.

The **Illinois State Museum** (☎ 217-782-7386), at Spring and Edwards Sts, features Illinois artwork and Native American exhibits. A perennial school-group stop, it's best seen if you have an extraordinarily long wait for a Lincoln house tour. It's open 8:30 am to 5 pm daily (from noon Sunday) and is free.

Route 66 – The Ultimate Scenic Drive

LIBRARY OF CONGRESS

The classic highway from Chicago to Los Angeles is known through legend, song (Bobby Troup sang 'Get Your Kicks on Route 66') and novel (John Steinbeck called it 'The Mother Road, the road of flight, and the Glory Road to the Land of Second Chance'). Now almost totally superseded by I-55, various sections of the old road, which cuts diagonally across the state, and its associated Americana survive in towns bypassed by the interstate.

For much of its length in Illinois, Route 66 originated as a bureaucratic concept rather than a purposely built road. Starting in 1926, it was cobbled together from existing roads that were then slowly improved to reflect their new status. When you try to retrace the road today you have to be aware of which era's Route 66 you want to follow. The Illinois Department of Transportation makes a good map, *Illinois Historic Route 66*, showing the various routes through the years. Most tourist offices along the route have copies.

On the road itself, you'll find brown 'Historic Route 66' markers with one of three eras noted: 1926–30, 1930–40 and 1940–77; '77 was when the route was officially replaced by I-55.

If you're starting the trip in Chicago, you might want to stop by the Road Trip Travel Store (☎ 773-388-8338), 3758 N Southport Ave, in the Wrigleyville neighborhood. They have truckfulls of Route 66 memorabilia and books. Otherwise start right downtown at Jackson Blvd and Lake Shore Drive and head west to Ogden Blvd, which becomes US Hwy 34.

At Summit you have to hop on I-55; at Bolingbrook you can stay on I-55 following the pre-1940 route or join Hwy 53, the later and more authentic road. The routes combine and you're back on I-55, although you can see the post-1940 road being used as a frontage road on the west side.

At the town of Normal, 145 miles from Chicago, take exit No 167 and head downtown to the original **Steak 'n Shake** (☎ 309-452-0095, 1219 S Main St) burger joint. Back on I-55, the post-1940 Route 66 is now the frontage road on the east side.

The **Dixie Truckers Home** (☎ 309-874-2323) is right at the exit for McLean. Besides solid chow you can pile on your plate from the buffet, this otherwise typical truck stop has a whole gallery of

The 1904 **Dana-Thomas House** (☎ 217-82-6776), 301 Lawrence St, was one of rank Lloyd Wright's first 'Prairie style' ouses. It is the result of an interesting cretive collaboration between the brilliant but rrogant Wright and Susan Lawrence urner, a young local widow who dared to e different, and whose house turned archictural notions of the time on their ears. ntique collector and former governor Jim hompson has devoted enormous energies to funding the house's restoration inside and out. Tours are offered 9 am to 4 pm Wednesday to Sunday. The suggested donation is $3/1.

Special Events

The Illinois State Fair (☎ 217-782-6661) is an event as huge as the championship hogs on display during its 10-day run every mid-August. The fairgrounds are north of the center and are bounded by Sangamon Ave

Route 66 – The Ultimate Scenic Drive

Route 66 photos. It's also a good place to get insight into the lives of truckers. The display of high sodium meals you can heat in the cab of your truck should forever dispel any romantic notions about life on the open road.

Take I-55 another 12 miles south to Lincoln. The oldest portions of Route 66 passed through this unremarkable town, named in 1853 in honor of a circuit judge of such integrity that he was called 'Honest Abe.' Then little known, Lincoln christened the town by spitting watermelon seeds on the ground. A delightful watermelon sculpture now marks the spot at Sangamon and Broadway Sts.

Back on I-55 you parallel the last Route 66 all the way to Springfield. See the Springfield section, later in the chapter. On the north side, **Shea's Truck Covers** (☎ 217-52-0475), 2075 N Peoria Rd, has a Route 66 museum begun in the days when Bill Shea operated a Texaco station.

South of Springfield, Route 66 diverges. The post-1930 version follows I-55 and from Divernon almost to Litchfield is the straight-as-an-arrow frontage road on the west side of the Interstate.

The more atmospheric route south is along Hwy 4, which closely follows the 1926–30 edition of Route 66. This part of Illinois is flat as a board, and fans of *North by Northwest* will get itchy watching for malevolent crop dusters. Watch for the historic Route 66 signs leading you off Hwy 4, especially near the sleepy farm towns of **Thayer**, **Virden** and **Nilwood**. These minor detours take you on surviving concrete sections of the original road that rigorously followed the original plot lines of the land. There's not a diagonal stretch to be found as you ladder-step your way southwest. You can almost imagine the convoys of Model Ts rattling past the farmhouses. On weekends, you'll likely pass lots of car collectors out for a cruise in their vintage autos.

At **Nilwood** (don't blink) some of the original brick road is visible.

You can cut nine miles east at Gillespie on Hwy 16 to the post-1930 portion of Route 66 in **Litchfield**. Here you can snuggle up for a nostalgic night at **Route 66 Motel Court** (☎ 217-324-2179, 703 N Old Route 66) where classic roadside lodging charm starts at $30 a night. The **Ariston Café** (☎ 217-324-2023) on S Old Route 66 has the sort of classic dishes that have fed generations of happy travelers, such as fried chicken, pork chops and liver and onions (all less than $9).

South of here, the various editions of Route 66 are all over the map like water in a river delta and you'll need the state map to make sense of it. St Louis is 300 miles from Chicago, with lots of stops t is a classic two-day historic Route 66 drive.

and Peoria Rd. In addition to the prize porkers, there's horse racing, big-name bands, a huge slide and lots more. The best halls are the ones showing off winning crafts and produce from the thousands of farms dotting the state.

Places to Stay

Camping There are 200 sites at ***Lincoln's New Salem***, 20 miles northwest of Springfield (see Around Springfield, later in the chapter). ***Springfield KOA*** *(☎ 217-498-7002)* has RV sites and amenities include a pool. It's about 7 miles southeast of town off Hwy 29 at 4320 Koa Rd in Rochester. Sites start at $14.

Downtown The ***YWCA Hostel*** *(☎ 217-522-8828, fax 217-522-8820, 421 Jackson St)* has rooms for $15 a person with shared facilities and a kitchen.

The ***Best Inn*** *(☎ 217-522-1100, fax 217-753-8589, 500 1st St)* has a pool and comfortable rooms from $45/49 single/double. The ***Best Western Lincoln Inn & Suites*** *(☎ 217-523-5661, fax 217-523-5675, 101 Adams St)* has different sized rooms that start at $48/52. It's in a restored seven-story building.

Carpenter Street Hotel *(☎ 217-789-9100, 888-779-9100, 525 6th St)* is relatively new and has rooms designed for business travelers that cost $59/64.

The pick of the downtown places is the ***Inn at 835*** *(☎ 217-523-4466, 888-217-4835, fax 217-523-4468, www.innat835.com, 835 2nd St)* which is a B&B-style place without the frumpiness. It has large decks where you can sip your complimentary evening wine and top-notch breakfasts. Rooms are $100 to $135.

Interstate 55 Area Most chain motels known to humankind cluster around exit Nos 92 to 96 off I-55. This is typical strip mall country and not worth bothering with unless downtown is full. The ***Fairfield Inn by Marriott*** *(☎/fax 217-793-9277, 3446 Freedom Drive)* is typical and has a small indoor pool and modern rooms from $53/56.

Places to Eat

Cozy Dog Drive In *(☎ 217-525-1992)* on th southern outskirts at 2935 6th St, has bee operating since 1948 and is a Route 6 legend. It's a cheap, friendly, funky plac with all sorts of memorabilia. The hous specialty is its version of the corn dog (a ho dog dipped in batter and deep-fried, yum!

The following places are all downtow Many serve the local specialty 'horseshoe,' filling, artery-clogging fried meat sandwic covered with melted cheese.

The ***Brewhaus*** *(☎ 217-525-6399, 617 Washington St)* is a good place for horseshoes ($. at lunch and has a good selection of be until late. ***Norb Andy's*** *(☎ 217-523-7777, 51 Capitol Ave)* is a haven for wheeling an dealing. You can see deals being cut ov hearty and moderately priced sandwiches steaks at lunch and dinner (closed Sunday)

The Vinegar Hill Mall, a restored com mercial building at 107 Cook St and 1st St, home to the ***Capital City Brew Pub*** *(☎ 21 753-5725)* which has the usual burgers an other bar food to go with its seasonal bee ***Café Brio*** *(☎ 217-544-0574, 524 Monroe S* has interesting and upscale Mexican fa with lunches for $6 and dinners around $1 It has vegetarian items and the weeke brunch is always a hit.

Sebastian's Hide-Out *(☎ 217-789-898 221 5th St)* has excellent and carefully pr pared steaks and seafood that average $1 at dinner (closed Sunday). It also has a ni lounge downstairs with live jazz som nights.

Getting There & Away

Air Springfield's Capital Airport (☎ 21 788-1060), 1200 Capital Airport Drive, is 3 miles northwest of downtown via Walnut (Hwy 29). American Eagle and Unit Express each have a few commuter flights day to O'Hare International Airport Chicago. United Express also has fligh catering to bureaucrats to Chicago's Mei Airport near the Loop. Trans World Expre flies to St Louis. See the Toll-Free & W Site Directory at the back of the book f airlines' contact information.

Bus Inconvenient for tourists, the bus station, 2351 Dirksen Parkway, is 2½ miles southwest of the center. Greyhound (☎ 217-544-8466) service includes:

destination	cost	travel time	frequency
Champaign	$16	2 hours	4
Chicago	$39	5 hours	5
St Louis	$26	2 hours	4

Train Amtrak (☎ 800-872-7245) has the most convenient service with three trains daily between Springfield and Chicago (3½ hours) and between Springfield and St Louis (3 hours). The trains' other stops include Alton and Joliet. The historic station is right downtown at Washington and 3rd Sts.

Getting Around

Springfield Mass Transit District (☎ 217-522-5531) operates buses mostly for the benefit of state bureaucrats and other workers scattered about town. There are no buses to useful places such as, say, the bus station or airport. Should you take a bus, the fare is 75¢.

For taxis, try Lincoln Yellow Cab (☎ 217-522-7766) and Airport Cab (☎ 217-789-2629).

AROUND SPRINGFIELD

New Salem

Lincoln lived here from 1831 to 1837. He arrived a penniless ex-farmboy who had been doing odd jobs around the region. While here, he began to set a course for his life. He was elected to the Illinois legislature; he studied to become a lawyer; and he broadened his general knowledge as local postmaster, a job that allowed him to read the variety of information sources that passed by in the mail.

Lincoln's New Salem State Park (☎ 217-632-4000) is a reconstruction of the village as it was when Lincoln lived there. An authentic building, Onstot Cooper Shop is where Lincoln sat at nights reading. There are over 20 other buildings that were used by New Salem's peak population of 25 families. Pioneer skills such as log splitting and blacksmithing are among the many demonstrations. The village has a pretty location on a bluff overlooking the Sangamon River and in the summer there are trips on the replica riverboat *Talisman* ($3).

The entire village is a worthwhile stop that can eat up an entire day. But be warned that April and May are peak months for teeming masses of screaming school groups. There is a demonstration of today's culinary skills at ***McDonald's***, New Salem's kid-friendly caterer. The village is open 9 am to 5 pm daily March 1 to October 31 and 8 am to 4 pm other times. Admission is a suggested $2/1 donation. An outdoor theater (☎ 217-632-5440) stages various historical productions at night mid-June to late August.

The historic site has ***camping*** for tents and RVs for $11 a night. New Salem is 20 miles northwest from Springfield via Hwys 125 and 97.

Dickson Mounds

Another 24 miles beyond New Salem on Hwy 97, Dickson Mounds State Museum (☎ 309-547-3721) is centered on the 1000-year-old burial mounds of pre-historic Native Americans. This fertile valley near the Illinois River has long been used by farming peoples and the museum here has in-depth and well presented displays on their cultures. The 15-minute multimedia program is a good place to start your tour.

The top floor of the modern building has an outdoor observation deck from which there are excellent views out over the preserved mounds in the surrounding valley. The building itself was built atop a mound that was excavated and open for viewing until 1992 when it was closed due to public pressure to respect the burial site. The museum is open 8:30 am to 5 pm daily and is free. There is a small café. The site is off County Rd 1050 N, 4 miles north of Havana on Hwy 97.

Chautauqua National Wildlife Refuge

The US Fish & Wildlife Service has a string of refuges along 124 miles of the Illinois River. Many are not accessible, but the

Chautauqua National Wildlife Refuge, near Havana, is one of the more reachable. It has an observation deck, headquarters (☎ 309-535-2290) and a half-mile nature walk that explains the diverse habitat. It also has ducks, geese, ducks, geese, and more ducks and geese. The whole series of refuges are major hostelries for migratory waterfowl. There are also eagles keeping a close watch on the fish. Reaching the refuge will require eagle eyes: Take the main paved county road that exits Havana north for 8½ miles and watch as its name changes with each twist and turn. Turn north on County Rd 1950E and watch for the refuge sign.

Decatur

• pop 84,000

This is the town where soybeans go to die. Food behemoth Archer-Daniels-Midland has vast operations here, including several soybean-processing plants. Decatur's farm roots go back to its founding in 1829.

The **Macon County Historical Society Museum Complex** (☎ 217-423-4919), 5580 N Fork Rd, has a number of representative buildings from Decatur's past that include an 1855 log house and an 1863 rural school. It's open 1 to 4 pm Tuesday to Sunday and costs $2/1.

HANNIBAL (MISSOURI)

• pop 18,000

This would probably still be a sleepy Mississippi riverside town (100 miles upriver from St Louis) were it not for its association with Mark Twain, and the town milks his novels for all they are worth. The Hannibal Visitors' & Convention Bureau (☎ 573-221-2477) is at 505 N 3rd St and is open 8 am to 5 pm daily (shorter weekend hours in winter). The town is just across the river by US Hwy 36 from the hardly used I-72.

Reread the books and then visit the **Mark Twain Boyhood Home & Museum** (☎ 573-221-9010), 208 Hill St, which has 16 commissioned Norman Rockwell paintings illustrating classic scenes. It's open 8 am to 6 pm daily June to September, 10 am to 4 pm the rest of the year. Admission is $6/3 adults/children. The whitewashed fenc made famous in the line, 'Does a boy get chance to whitewash a fence every day? stands alongside. The Tom and Huck statu is at the foot of Cardiff Hill, known a 'Holiday Hill' in the books.

Burlington Trailways (☎ 800-992-4618 operates two buses a day to/from St Loui ($14, 2½ hours).

Places to Stay & Eat

Campers can settle in at the ***Injun Jo Campground*** *(☎ 573-985-3581, info@clem landing.com)*, 4 miles south of town off U Hwy 61 at 14113 Clemens Drive. It has kiddie park and tent sites for $12 and R sites for $16.

The ***Econo Lodge*** *(☎/fax 573-221-1490)* i just west of the river bridge at 612 Mar Twain Ave (US Hwy 36). Basic rooms sta at $25/30.

Honeymooners will revel in the luxury o the historic, Gothic-looking ***Garth Woodside Mansion*** *(☎ 573-221-2789, 11069 Nev London Gravel Rd)*, with its canopy bed and gourmet breakfasts. Rooms cos between $77 and $107.

Mark Twain Dinette *(☎ 573-221-530 400 N 3rd St)* has a classic drive-in as well a inside table service and a cheap menu.

CHAMPAIGN–URBANA

Champaign (pop 36,000) is separated fro Urbana (36,000) by the dotted line down th middle of Wright St. There are occasiona efforts to give the two places separate identi ties, such as a misguided scheme to officiall refer to them as Urbana–Champaign, bu they are really just one place that also in cludes the little area of Savoy on the sout side. Note that the towns do occasionall declare their identities by having sma streets suddenly change names at the borde

Champaign–Urbana's claim to fame i the University of Illinois, the huge stat school that attracts students from not jus the state but all over the world. Like s many Midwestern college towns, the regio benefits greatly from having the university vibrant culture and activities.

Information

The Champaign–Urbana Convention & Visitors' Bureau (☎ 217-351-4133, 800-369-6151, www.cupartnership.org), 1817 S Neil St in Champaign, is open 9 am to 5 pm weekdays.

There's a post office (☎ 800-275-8777) at 508 S Sixth St in Champaign. It is open 7:30 am to 5:30 pm weekdays and 7:30 am to 1 pm Saturday.

You can usually find a free terminal within the bustling confines of the Illini Union (☎ 217-333-INFO) at 1401 W Green St in Urbana.

It's hard to imagine a better bookstore than Pages for All Ages (☎ 217-351-7243) in the Savoy Plaza shopping center at Curtis and Dunlap Rds (US Hwy 45) in Savoy. This large independent operation beats the superstore chains at their own game with a café, vast selection and enthusiastic staff. It's open 9 am to 11 pm daily (9 pm Sunday).

The *New-Gazette* is the local daily newspaper. The *Daily Illini* is the free daily published by U of I students. The *Octopus* is a free alternative weekly that's the pick of the litter for entertainment and events listings.

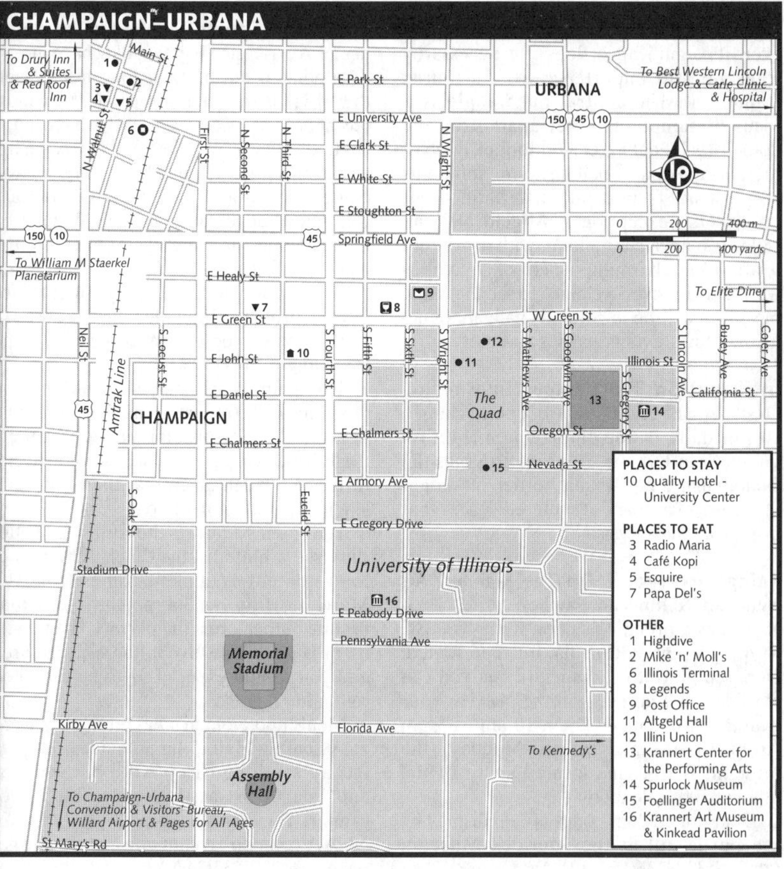

Carle Clinic & Hospital (☎ 217-383-3311), 611 W Park St in Urbana, is a large health facility with emergency services.

University of Illinois

Begun in 1867 as the Illinois Industrial University, today the University of Illinois (☎ 217-333-1000) has 36,000 students and is a leading research center for agriculture, veterinary science, engineering and computer science. In fact the U of I can claim to be one of the founders of the Internet. The earliest Web browsers and other critical software were all written here.

A Big 10 school, the U of I is one of the Midwest's most important schools. However, its significance does not necessarily translate into importance from a tourist standpoint. The central **quadrangle** is a focus of campus life. Yet apart from the domed 1907 **Foellinger Auditorium**, none of the 200 university buildings are standouts and instead, form a rather disharmonious group. One exception is **Altgeld Hall**, an 1896 Romanesque building with a 132-foot tower. One charming aspect of a campus walk is it gives you a chance to see the many messages written in colored chalk announcing meetings, events, parties and more.

Information The Campus Information Desk (☎ 217-333-INFO) is open 9 am to 10 pm daily in the Illini Union, 1401 W Green St in Urbana. The campus spans the Champaign and Urbana border of Wright St. Visitors can park at metered spaces that display a blue sticker.

Things to See & Do The **Krannert Art Museum & Kinkead Pavilion** (☎ 217-333-1860) has a broad collection from 4000 BC to the present. All media are represented, from sculpture to ceramics. In fact you can consider an hour spent in the place as your own Art 101 course. Open 10 am to 5 pm (from 2 pm Sunday, closed Monday), the museum is free. It's located south of the quad at 500 E Peabody.

Dem bones, dem bones are on display by the bottle-full at the **Spurlock Museum** (☎ 217-333-2360), 1301 W Green St in Urbana, the display case as it were for the natural history departments. It's open 9 am to 4:30 pm weekdays and 2 to 5 pm Sunday and is free.

The prettiest part of the U of I is 17 miles away from Champaign in Monticello. **Robert Allerton Park** (☎ 217-244-1035) is a 1500-acre outdoor research facility that's beautifully landscaped and has hiking trails and cross-country skiing. *Octopus* readers voted it their favorite place for – illegal – outdoor sex. It is open 8 am to sunset daily and is free. Take I-72 exit No 166, then Hwy 105 to Allerton Rd.

Spectator Sports Named for the state's namesake tribe, the Fighting Illini have mostly disappointed during their long history and their Big 10 record is not good. Their most recent year of success was 1983, which ended comically after U of I alum and *Playboy* magazine publisher Hugh Hefner invited the entire team to a raucous party before their Rose Bowl appearance. Possibly drained by their libations at the Playboy mansion, the team was beaten 45-9 by UCLA.

Given the mediocre play, tickets are never a problem. Individual tickets cost $14 to $27 and can be bought before the game by calling ☎ 217-333-3470.

The games are played in Memorial Stadium, a 78,000-seat arena that suffered a disastrous 'modernization' in 1985. Among the fiascoes was the installation of artificial turf, a real laugh given that the U of I is a leading agricultural school.

The games feature the antics of Chief Illini, see 'Chuffed at the Chief.' A better bet for game entertainment comes from the Marching Illini, a 360-person band that usually outperforms the players. The majority of U of I alums live in the Chicago area and you should expect I-57 to be thronged right after a game.

Men's and women's basketball is played at Assembly Hall, a large, modern domed facility south of Kirby Ave between First and Fourth Sts at the southern edge of campus. The teams have done pretty well in NCAA competition but you can usually get tickets (☎ 217-333-3470).

William M Staerkel Planetarium

Champaign–Urbana's *other* college, Parkland College, has a good planetarium (☎ 217-351-2446) at 2400 W Bradley Ave in Champaign near I-57. Close to 8000 stars are projected onto a 50-foot dome during the 45-minute shows, presented at 7, 8 and 9:30 pm Friday and Saturday night. Admission is $4/2.

Places to Stay

Accommodations in Champaign–Urbana are dispersed throughout the two communities and along the three interstate highways. You might be able to get a ticket to a football game, but don't expect a room at an inn on home football weekends. Unfortunately there is no hostel or cheap summer housing for non-students.

The ***Red Roof Inn*** *(☎ 217-352-0101, fax 217-352-1891, 212 W Anthony Drive)* is a typical unit of this good-value chain. Basic rooms cost $36/41 single/double. The motel is right in the middle of chain-store land at exit No 182B off I-74 in Champaign.

Plusher digs can be found nearby at the ***Drury Inn & Suites*** *(☎/fax 217-398-0030, 905 W Anthony Drive)* which has free breakfasts, a pool and large rooms for $65/75. The tall hotel is at exit No 181 off I-74.

In Urbana, the ***Best Western Lincoln Lodge*** *(☎ 217-367-1111, fax 217-367-8233, 403 W University Ave)* has decent rooms in a well-maintained older property that has a pool. Rooms cost from $49/55.

Near the campus, ***Quality Hotel – University Center*** *(☎ 217-384-2100, fax 217-384-2298, 302 E John St)* is easy to find; it's the 21-story round structure that can politely be described as 'siloesque.' Rooms are $61/65. The ***Illini Union Guest Rooms*** *(☎ 217-333-1241, fax 217-333-0804, 1401 W Green St)* overlook the quad. Guests have access to campus facilities and rooms cost $65/72.

Places to Eat

Green St near the campus in Champaign is lined with cheap eateries aimed at students. Downtown Champaign is another good place for wandering around and eating.

Chuffed at the Chief

The University of Illinois mascot is Chief Illiniwek, who supposedly takes his name from an old Native American word meaning 'they are men.' A fixture at football and basketball games, the chief prances about the sidelines doing faux native dances and other routines designed to inspire the crowd. This has not earned him universal acclaim, especially from many Native Americans. A locally produced film, *In Whose Honor?*, focuses on crusaders' efforts to have the chief sent packing. In the meantime, the chief's outfit comes from the non-Illinois Sioux and the university's chief propaganda – cognizant of the controversy – is riddled with words like 'respect' and 'dignified.' Nowadays, when the chief performs, the screams from the stands seem as much intended as a message to the anti-chief forces as voices in support of the players.

Esquire *(☎ 217-398-5858, 106 N Walnut St)* is a friendly bar and grill with a nice patio and a fine pork chop sandwich ($4). The deep-fried broccoli would seem to have its health benefits negated. The crunches underfoot are peanut shells.

Nearby, textbooks litter the tables at ***Café Kopi*** *(☎ 217-359-4266)*, downtown at 109 N Walnut St. It's like somebody's funky, comfy living room where you can sit around chatting, reading or staring all day. It has lots of baked goods and interesting numbers like the 'hummus and eggplant experience' ($5). There's a juice bar and a real bar and it's open 7 am to midnight.

An unreconstructed Urbana classic, the inexpensive ***Elite Diner*** *(☎ 217-384-7300, 210 E Elm St)* is authentic right down to the last stainless steel panel. Breakfast is served around the clock and the bread pudding is sublime.

Top seafood is flown in daily to ***Kennedy's*** *(☎ 217-384-8111, 1717 S Philo Rd)* in Urbana's Sunnycrest Mall. The menu depends on what's fresh, but the salmon seared on the wood-burning grill is always excellent ($13). ***Papa Del's*** *(☎ 217-359-7700, 206 E Green St)* serves gut-busting monster Chicago-style pizza, as well as thinner crust pies. A favorite with townies and students, the prices are low (large, $14).

A real find in downtown Champaign is ***Radio Maria*** *(☎ 217-398-7729, 119 N Walnut St)*, which has an ever-changing menu served in a light and open stylish dining room. The dishes tend toward fusions of those from warmer climes like the Caribbean and the Mediterranean and there's always a vegan choice or two. Expect to pay at least $15 a person.

Entertainment

The top downtown venue, ***Highdive*** *(☎ 217-359-4444, 51 Main St)* squeezes 400 people in for live music from top local bands playing rock to country-punk. The cover varies depending on who's playing.

Down a Champaign alley, ***Mike 'n' Moll's*** *(☎ 217-355-1236, 105 N Market St)* is an Irish place with an Irish music jam every Sunday and a nice patio, and without a cover charge.

Legends *(☎ 217-355-7674, 522 E Green St)* is typical of the college bars along this strip. It has lots of beer specials and cheap burgers and other bar grub.

Krannert Center for the Performing Arts *(☎ 217-333-6280, 500 S Goodwin Ave)* is literally the U of I's Lincoln Center – both this expansive facility and the New York institution had the same architect. The university's theater, opera, dance and music departments all stage performances through the year; ticket prices vary widely.

Getting There & Away

Illinois Terminal, 45 E University Ave, is an impressive new transportation center in downtown Champaign that combines facilities for all train and bus services. There is a cab stand as well.

Willard Airport (☎ 217-244-8600) is south of town off US Hwy 45. Four commuter airlines link the region to their respective hub airports (see the Toll-Free & Web Site Directory at the back of the boo[k] for airlines' contact information):

American Eagle	Chicago O'Hare
Northwest Airlines	Detroit
US Airways Express	Pittsburgh
Trans World Express	St Louis

Greyhound (☎ 800-231-2222) has seve[ral] daily buses to Chicago ($18, 3 hours). Illin[ois] Swallow (☎ 217-373-5035) runs one bus [a] day to/from Peoria ($13, 2 hours) and In[]dianapolis ($25, 3 hours).

Amtrak (☎ 800-872-7245) has one short distance train daily to/from Chicago (2½ hours) and Carbondale (3 hours) as well a[s] the daily passage of the *City of New Orlean[s]* between Chicago and New Orleans.

Getting Around

Cabs to/from Willard Airport cost $10. Bluebird Charter Coach (☎ 800-400-5500) run[s] scheduled services to Chicago's Midway an[d] O'Hare airports ($30). Call for pick-up loca[]tions, schedules and reservations.

The Champaign–Urbana Mass Transi[t] District (☎ 217-384-8188) runs the loca[l] buses. Fares are 75¢ and there is dail[y] service until midnight and later. Most loca[]tions close to the U of I are served and th[e] main transfer center is at Illinois Terminal.

Corky's Cab (☎ 217-352-3121) is one o[f] many local taxi firms.

BLOOMINGTON–NORMAL

Another twin town, Bloomington (po[p] 52,000) and Normal (37,000), is divided b[y] Franklin Ave, noteworthy for having Illinoi[s] State University at one end and Illinoi[s] Wesleyan at the other. Three interstate[s] converge on the cities and you're bes[t] to stay on them, as Bloomington–Norma[l] focuses more on its major industries such a[s] car production than on luring in tourists. See 'Route 66 – The Ultimate Scenic Drive'

PEORIA

• pop 114,000

The town was one of the later places devel[]oped on the Illinois prairie, not incorporate[d] until 1845. In the late 1800s Benjamin Holt and Daniel Best founded companies that were to merge and produce products that literally changed the face of the world. Their breakthrough product was a 1908 tractor that instead of using wheels – which tended to get sucked into the muck – used a track around gears that allowed the tractor to roll along on its own never ending track. It resembled a caterpillar and the company soon adopted the name for itself. Its bulldozers and earthmovers can be found leveling mountains, building roads and more worldwide.

As Caterpillar has gone, so has Peoria. The recession of the 1980s was tough for both. Caterpillar's record of labor relations has not been good either; it had two lengthy strikes in the 1990s and there is widespread fear that the company, like so many of its jobs, will head south.

Besides bulldozers, Peoria is also part of the national conscience as expressed by the phrase 'Will it play in Peoria?' This originated with old Vaudeville performers who wondered if gags would fly with Peoria audiences, who were thought to represent average Americans. Betty Friedan, author of the ground-breaking 1963 *Feminine Mystique*, is another famous product of Peoria and often said that growing up in such an 'average' place helped her understand American society all the better.

Information

The Peoria Area Convention & Visitors' Bureau (☎ 309-676-0303, 800-747-0302, www.peoria.org) has a visitors' center (☎ 309-672-2860) on the riverfront open 11 am to 4 pm Tuesday to Saturday and from noon Sunday. It's at the base of Main St on the river in an area that is slowly being restored by fits and starts.

The Peoria Library (☎ 309-497-2000), 107 NE Monroe St, has free Internet access. The *Peoria Journal-Star* is the daily newspaper. *The Alternative Times* is the free biweekly newspaper for lesbians and gays in central Illinois.

Things to See & Do

As one longtime resident said, 'There used to be so much here.' And by all accounts she's right. But suburban malls and suburban flight have sucked the life out of downtown Peoria. The riverfront has some touristy restaurants but at night things are very quiet.

GP Transit (☎ 309-676-4040) offers **tours** of some of the city's nice old neighborhoods and buildings on one of those dopey faux trolleys. But the tours themselves are not dopey and are narrated by Peoria Historical Society members. Call for schedules; typically it costs $5 and tours operate on assorted days May to November.

You can take yourself on your own tour by driving **Grand View Drive**, which is just north of downtown and is aptly named for its views of the broad Illinois River and the splendid homes that line it.

Ten miles west of downtown Peoria, **Wildlife Prairie Park** (☎ 309-676-0998) attempts to recreate the flora and fauna of Illinois at the time of the arrival of the first pioneers. Animals on display in natural settings include wolves, black bears, river otters and badgers. Despite the fact that a top employee was unable to answer the question, 'What's worth seeing here?' the park does a good job of trying to convey Illinois before it was plowed under for corn and soybeans. Run by the Chicago area's Brookfield Zoo, the park is open 9 am to 6:30 pm daily May to September and 9 am to 4:30 pm other times (closed January and February). Admission is $5/3. Take I-74 exit No 82 and drive south following signs to Taylor Rd.

Places to Stay & Eat

The chains huddle around the suburban interchange of I-74 and US Hwy 150. The ***Super 8*** *(☎ 309-688-8074, fax 309-688-8284, 4025 War Memorial Drive)* has the usual basic rooms for $48/54.

Downtown, the choice digs are in the renovated ***Hotel Pere Marquette*** *(☎/fax 309-637-6500, 800-447-1676, 501 Main St)* which has been welcoming guests since the 1920s. Elegant rooms start at $94/104.

Fun ***Sully's Irish Pub*** *(☎ 309-674-0238, 121 SW Adams St)* is one of several bar and grills downtown. It is famous for its 'King Tenderloin' hubcap-size sandwich ($5).

Up the hill, ***One World*** *(☎ 309-672-1552, 1245 W Main St)* prints its mission statement on its menus. Besides the verbiage pledging good coffee, enlightenment and more, it has moderately priced fine baked goods, lots of veggie items and, well, good coffee. On the river, ***Crooked Waters Brewery & Pub*** *(☎ 309-673-2739, 330 SW Water St)* has good views and good beer. It has a large menu that averages less than $10.

Getting There & Around

Eight miles from town, the Greater Peoria Area Airport (☎ 309-697-8272), 6100 W Everett McKinley Dirksen Parkway, has commuter airline links to Chicago, Detroit, St Louis and Denver.

Peoria Charter Coach (☎ 309-688-9523, 800-448-0572) runs four daily buses to/from Chicago's O'Hare and Midway airports ($25). These buses also stop at the River CTA El station, which may be the best connection to Chicago as there is no direct bus service. Call ☎ 309-697-9000 for details on the infrequent bus services to/from Bloomington and Champaign.

The local bus operator is GP Transit (☎ 309-676-4040). Fares are 75¢ and route No 7 links the airport and downtown.

GALESBURG

• pop 34,000

Known as the birth and burial place of poet and Lincoln biographer Carl Sandburg, Galesburg has done a fine job of restoring its historic downtown and makes a good stop off I-74.

The Galesburg Area Convention and Visitors' Bureau (☎ 309-343-1194, www.galesburg.org/visitors), 292 E Simmons St, is open 8:30 am to 5 pm weekdays. The excellent free booklet *Galesburg, Eight Self-Guided Walking Tours* gives details about the historic homes and buildings in and near downtown. That booklet and other brochures are widely available at restaurants around town and at the train station.

The most famous old house is the **Carl Sandburg State Historic Site** (☎ 309-342-2361), 313 E Third St. Sandburg was born in the house in 1878. Through his childhood he lived in a series of homes in the immigrant neighborhood. Another fine freebie available at the historic site and elsewhere details Sandburg-related locations throughout town using excerpts from his autobiography *Always the Young Strangers*. The house is a good example of how typical families lived in the late 1800s; it's open 9 am to 5 pm daily. Entrance is by donation.

Pretty **Seminary St** is has many restored old buildings, cafés and other businesses that make a stroll a pleasure. Nearby, the **Galesburg Railroad Museum** (☎ 309-342-9400), 423 Mulberry St, is housed in an old Pullman car and recalls the area's history as a center of several important rail lines. It's open noon to 5 pm Tuesday to Sunday June to September and by appointment other times. Entrance is by donation. If the train bug bites, head across the street to **Depot Hobby Shop** (☎ 309-342-9323), 180 S Seminary St, a large and friendly shop filled with model trains.

Places to Stay & Eat

Check with the visitors' center for the latest list of B&Bs operating in historic homes. The ***Ramada Inn*** *(☎ 309-343-9161, fax 309-343-0157, 29 Public Square)* is right downtown, has an indoor pool and rooms from $50/55.

The ***Landmark Café & Crêperie*** *(☎ 309-343-5376, 62 S Seminary St)* has hearty breakfasts, lots of filled crepes, veggie choices and more for less than $10 a person. The ***Seminary St Pub*** *(☎ 309-343-1038, No 105 S)* has a classic horseshoe bar and friendly bartenders.

Getting There & Away

The tidy train station, 225 S Seminary St, is right near downtown. Amtrak (☎ 800-872-7245) has service to/from Chicago (3 hours) on its daily train to/from Quincy. The long-distance *California Zephyr* and *Southwest Chief* also stop on their respective journeys between Chicago and Northern California and Los Angeles.

NAUVOO

• pop 1100

In the far west of the state on a pretty Mississippi River promontory, Nauvoo's pastoral location belies a tragic past. It was founded in 1839 by Joseph Smith, the leader of the Church of Jesus Christ of Latter-Day Saints (commonly called Mormons). Having been persecuted throughout the east, Mormons flocked to Nauvoo – which is Hebrew for 'beautiful place.' They industriously got to work building their idea of a utopian community and in just five years they'd built a town, laid out a huge temple and were planning a university. The tragedy struck when Joseph Smith and his brother Hyrum were murdered by an anti-Mormon mob in nearby Carthage.

The Mormons abandoned Nauvoo and fled west yet again, this time to end up for good in the locust-ridden desert of Utah. Their town moldered for over a century, and was eventually settled by wine-making Germans.

Today, Nauvoo is in the midst of a multi-decade restoration process that's being funded by Mormons, the state of Illinois and others. Various organizations operate visitors' centers and offer tours of the buildings in their care, all of which are, refreshingly, free. The three main operations are:

LDS Visitors' Center (☎ 217-453-2237), at Main and Young Sts – Operated by the Mormon church, tours of 24 buildings, including the Brigham Young home, leave from here. Open 8 am to 9 pm daily June to September (until 5 pm other times).

Joseph Smith Historic Center (☎ 217-453-2246), 149 Water St – Operated by a branch of the Mormon church, tours include the Joseph Smith Homestead and Smith's grave, which was rediscovered in 1928. Open 9 am to 5 pm daily (from 1 pm Sunday).

Nauvoo State Park (☎ 209-453-2512), PO Box 426, 62354, just south of town off Hwy 9 – The park has a good museum of local history and a restored Mormon home later used by vintners; open 1 to 5 pm May to October.

Nauvoo State Park has ***camping***. Sites with/without electricity cost $10/7. The 1840s ***Hotel Nauvoo*** *(☎ 217-453-2211, fax 217-453-6100, 1290 Mulholland St)* offers eight comfortably updated rooms starting at $40. Its restaurant, like others, specializes in hearty pioneer fare like ham and biscuits ($6).

Southern Illinois

In much of Southern Illinois, you're closer to Memphis, Tennessee, than you are to Chicago. This gives the region a Southern accent that is far removed from the flat farmlands of Northern Illinois. The often steep and rugged hills alone set the southernmost area apart and much of this region is part of the Shawnee National Forest, a vast area with many opportunities for outdoor activity.

Farther north, the land is shaped by rivers. Illinois Hwy 3 follows the Mississippi River in the west and the flood-prone Wabash River, which forms the border with Indiana, is kept in check with complex dams and dikes.

The major city is St Louis, which is across the border in Missouri but dominates the low-lying region around it. The city is a fascinating mix of the new and old and is a good place to soak in that last bit of urban culture before you venture into Southern Illinois, where cities and towns of interest are few and far between.

Highlights

- Exploring the St Louis riverfront
- Pondering the Lewis & Clark legacy at the convergence of the Mississippi & Missouri Rivers
- Learning about Cahokia Mounds
- Hiking the Shawnee National Forest
- Following the Ohio River

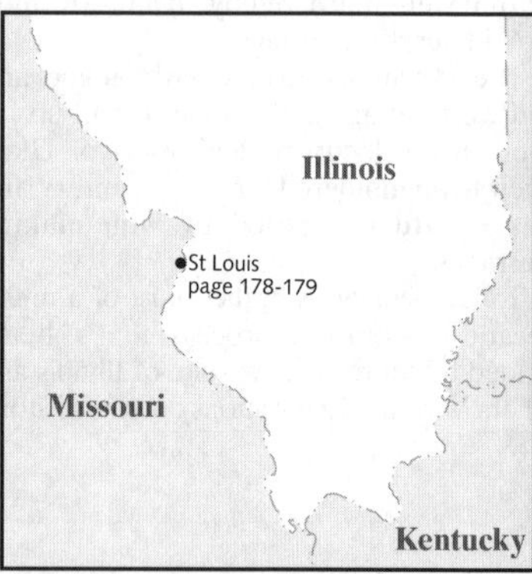

St Louis (Missouri)

It was inevitable that one of the frontier's earliest outposts would be established at the junction of the country's two mightiest rivers, in the center of the continent, and at a point accessible from New Orleans. Fur trapper Pierre Laclede chose the site in 1764, and settlers and trappers followed. When the railroad link was completed in 1857, there was a further influx of settlers, mostly Europeans, and by the 1870s the population had swelled to 300,000.

The 1904 Louisiana Purchase Exposition underlined the city's importance as an innovator and growth center on the edge of the 'frontier.' Today St Louis is a major automobile manufacturer, has vibrant aerospace and aircraft industries and is headquarters to many large multinational corporations. There always seems to be some sort of

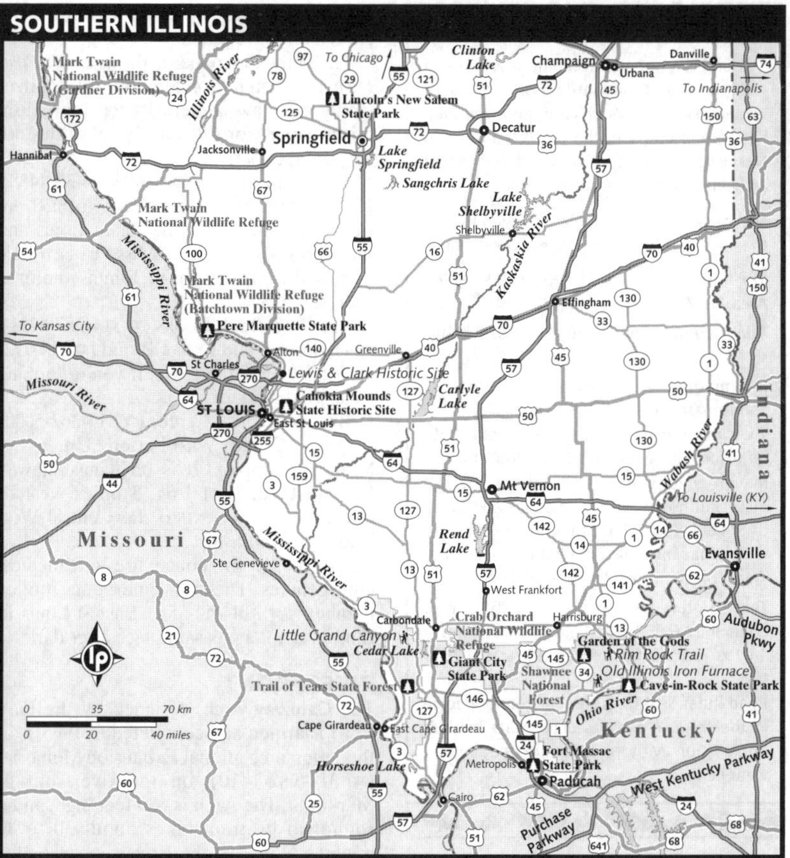

special event going on in St Louis – check the calendar. On Labor Day weekend, St Louis hosts the Blues Heritage Festival.

The giant Gateway Arch symbolizes St Louis' role as 'Gateway to the West' – all that lies west of the Mississippi – and interstates radiate from the city. Many modern explorations of the West are likely to start in this vibrant entrepôt.

ORIENTATION

The landmark Gateway Arch is in the riverside park called the Jefferson National Expansion Memorial. Just north is Laclede's Landing Historic District (see later in the chapter). There is plenty of parking near Memorial Plaza; there's more parking on the levee. The cheapest is on Laclede's Landing, a short walk from the Arch.

The downtown area is west of the riverfront, along Market St; here you will find the shopping and restaurant enclave of Union Station.

Neighborhoods of particular interest to visitors are Forest Park; University City Loop; Grand South Grand; the Hill, one of

Missouri

Missouri is a popular destination, as it has a good mix of urban attractions, areas of wilderness, the Mississippi and Missouri Rivers, and Branson, the Ozarks' answer to Nashville. St Louis is known for its great archway and its blues music scene.

Nickname: Show Me State – derived from the legendary skepticism of early residents

Population: 5,460,000 (16th largest state)

Area: 69,710 sq miles (19th largest)

Admitted to Union: August 10, 1821 (24th state)

Information The Missouri Division of Tourism (☎ 314-751-4133, 800-877-1234, www.missouritourism.org), PO Box 1055, Jefferson City, MO 65102, has tourist information centers in Hannibal (Hwy 61, two miles south of Hwy 36 junction) and north of St Louis (off I-270 at the Riverview exit).

For road information, contact the Dept of Transportation (☎ 573-751-2551).

Taxes Statewide sales tax is 4.225%; in St Louis it is 6.85%. St Louis also charges a 14.1% lodging tax and a 5.97% rental car tax.

Road Rules Seat belts are required for people in the front as well as child seats for kids under four. Motorcyclists are required to wear helmets.

the best dining areas in town (known for its Italian ambience); charming Central West End; the Ville, the most significant of the African American neighborhoods; and Soulard, the restaurant and club enclave, south of downtown.

INFORMATION

The St Louis Convention & Visitors' Commission (☎ 314-421-1023, 800-916-0092, www.explorestlouis.com) visitors' center (☎ 314-241-1764), 308 Washington Ave, is open 9:30 am to 4:30 pm daily. The free weekly alternative newspaper *The Riverfront Times* is packed with the usua entertainment listings.

The daily newspaper is the *St Louis Post Dispatch*. You'll wonder how the Pulitze family can have America's top journalisn prizes named for them *and* publish this no very good paper.

The main post office (☎ 314-436-4458) 1720 Market St, is open 7 am to 8:30 pn weekdays. The area code for St Louis an the surrounding part of Missouri is ☎ 314 Across the Mississippi in Illinois the are code is ☎ 618.

Visit Left Bank Books (☎ 314-367-6731) 399 N Euclid, and Planet Proud (☎ 314-772 4528), 3194 S Grand Ave, if you're lookin for a good read.

Barnes Medical Center (☎ 314-362-5000 is part of the Washington Universit Medical Complex. It is on Kingshighwa Blvd just north of I-64, 3 miles west o downtown. It is next to the Central Wes End MetroLink stop.

Dial ☎ 911 for police, fire and medica emergencies. The non-emergency polic number is ☎ 314-444-5555. East St Louis, i Illinois, is not a pleasant place after dark.

RIVERFRONT

The **Gateway Arch**, designed by the Fin Eero Saarinen and completed in 1965, is i the Jefferson National Expansion Memoria (☎ 314-982-1410), on the riverfront a Market St. The Arch is 630 feet high, and roundtrip by tram takes about 30 to 4 minutes. Note that the Arch is a beacon fo crowds and can get jammed. It is ope 8:30 am to 9:30 pm daily June to Septembe and 9:30 am to 5:30 pm the rest of the yea Admission is $4/2 adults/children.

Underneath the Arch is the high-concep **Museum of Westward Expansion**, with ex hibits covering Lewis and Clark, the Plain Indians and buffalo soldiers. It is huge bu emphasizes form over function, so you ma find there's actually less there than meet the eye. It's open the same hours as the Arc and is free. The IMAX theater presentation ($6/14 for one/three attractions) are amon the other diversions.

The 1839 Greek Revival **Old Courthouse Museum** (☎ 314-425-6017), where the famed Dred Scott case was first tried, is a couple of blocks from the Arch. It's open 8 am to 4:30 pm daily; free. The courthouse is often the centerpiece of Arch photos.

The **waterfront** is no longer a bustling cargo area, and the old warehouses have been demolished or renovated. **Laclede's Landing Historic District** (named after St Louis' founder) is a shopping and entertainment precinct just north of historic (and closed) Eads railway bridge.

Gateway Riverboat Cruises (☎ 314-621-4040) operates paddle steamers moored nearby daily from June to September and weekends for two months before and after summer. Rides cost $9/4 adults/children for a one-hour narrated tour. Nearby is the garish floating President Casino on *The Admiral* (☎ 314-622-3000). And just across the river is the very faux steamboat *Casino Queen* (☎ 618-874-5000).

FOREST PARK

This superb, landscaped 1300-acre park is open 6 am to 10 pm daily. On the grounds is the **St Louis Art Museum** (☎ 314-721-0072), on Art Hill, built for the 1904 World's Fair. It has a magnificent 30,000-piece collection from all parts of the world. It's open 10 am to 5 pm Wednesday to Sunday and 1:30 to 8:30 pm Tuesday.

Also on the grounds are the **St Louis Zoo** (☎ 314-781-0900), at 1 Government Drive, with its 'Jungle of the Apes Tropical Rainforest' and 'Big Cat Country.' It's open 9 am to 5 pm daily and while nominally free, charges extra for many attractions.

The **History Museum** (☎ 314-746-4599) has more exhibits on Western expansion as well as on famed aviator and eccentric Charles Lindbergh. It's open 9:30 am to 5 pm Tuesday to Sunday.

OTHER ATTRACTIONS

A visit to the world's largest brewery can be a horrifying experience for anyone who likes beer with qualities such as, say, flavor. The massive **Anheuser-Busch Brewery** (☎ 314-577-2626), at 12th and Lynch Sts, has free tours 9 am to 5 pm (closed Sunday). You can browse the merchandise in 'Bud World,' see the home of the world-famous Clydesdales, and learn all about how their ubiquitous brew is concocted. They also give out free samples, but really, shouldn't they pay you?

The **Scott Joplin House** (☎ 314-533-1003), at 2658A Delmar Blvd, celebrates Joplin's contribution to ragtime music – his 'Entertainer' was revived as the theme music for the 1973 movie *The Sting*. It's open 10 am to 4 pm (closed Sunday) and admission is $2/1.

The **International Bowling Museum & Hall of Fame** (☎ 314-231-6340), 111 Stadium Plaza, celebrates the spare-time activity that was once called 'the opiate of the suburbs.'

For the Kids

Apart from the zoo and the 'floating McDonald's' at the waterfront, there are several attractions that children will enjoy. **Grant's Farm** (☎ 314-843-1700), on Gravois Rd, has an 1856 cabin built by Ulysses S Grant and lots of diversions for kids. It's open 10am to 3pm Thursday to Sunday (also open Tuesday and Wednesday June to September, closed November to March); free.

The **Magic House – St Louis Children's Museum** (☎ 314-822-8900), 516 Kirkwood Rd, has all the hands-on favorites. It's open noon to 5:30 pm (closed Monday) and costs $5. The **St Louis Science Center** (☎ 314-289-4444), 5050 Oakland Ave in Forest Park, offers kids the chance to build their own arch in the free hands-on exhibit galleries. It's open 9 am to 5 pm (until 9 pm Friday and Saturday) and costs $7/5 adults/children.

The 1845 **Eugene Field House & Toy Museum** (☎ 314-421-4689), 634 S Broadway, birthplace of the famous children's writer, has a great collection of toys. It's open 10 am to 4 pm Wednesday to Saturday, noon to 4 pm Sunday and costs $3/50¢.

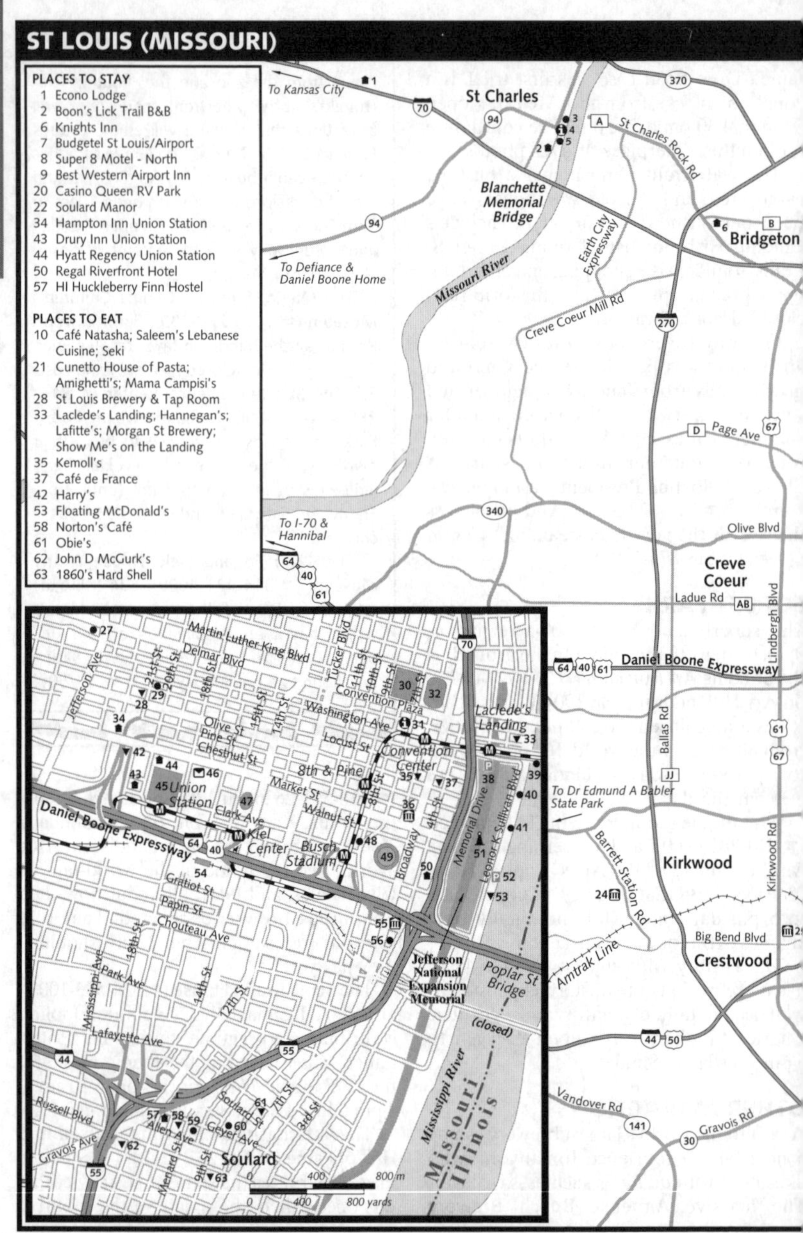
ST LOUIS (MISSOURI)
PLACES TO STAY
1 Econo Lodge
2 Boon's Lick Trail B&B
6 Knights Inn
7 Budgetel St Louis/Airport
8 Super 8 Motel - North
9 Best Western Airport Inn
20 Casino Queen RV Park
22 Soulard Manor
34 Hampton Inn Union Station
43 Drury Inn Union Station
44 Hyatt Regency Union Station
50 Regal Riverfront Hotel
57 HI Huckleberry Finn Hostel
PLACES TO EAT
10 Café Natasha; Saleem's Lebanese Cuisine; Seki
21 Cunetto House of Pasta; Amighetti's; Mama Campisi's
28 St Louis Brewery & Tap Room
33 Laclede's Landing; Hannegan's; Lafitte's; Morgan St Brewery; Show Me's on the Landing
35 Kemoll's
37 Café de France
42 Harry's
53 Floating McDonald's
58 Norton's Café
61 Obie's
62 John D McGurk's
63 1860's Hard Shell
To Kansas City
St Charles
St Charles Rock Rd
Blanchette Memorial Bridge
Earth City Expressway
Bridgeton
To Defiance & Daniel Boone Home
Missouri River
Creve Coeur Mill Rd
Page Ave
Olive Blvd
To I-70 & Hannibal
Creve Coeur
Ladue Rd
Lindbergh Blvd
Daniel Boone Expressway
Ballas Rd
To Dr Edmund A Babler State Park
Barrett Station Rd
Kirkwood
Kirkwood Rd
Big Bend Blvd
Amtrak Line
Crestwood
Vandover Rd
Gravois Rd
Martin Luther King Blvd
Delmar Blvd
Jefferson Ave
Tucker Blvd
Convention Plaza
Washington Ave
Olive St
Pine St
Chestnut St
Locust St
Laclede's Landing
Convention Center
8th & Pine
Market St
Walnut St
Union Station
Clark Ave
Kiel Center
Busch Stadium
Broadway
Memorial Drive
Leonor K Sullivan Blvd
Gratiot St
Papin St
Chouteau Ave
Park Ave
Mississippi Ave
Lafayette Ave
Jefferson National Expansion Memorial
Poplar St Bridge
(closed)
Mississippi River
Missouri
Illinois
Russell Blvd
Gravois Ave
Allen Ave
Geyer Ave
Soulard St
Soulard
Menard St
0 400 800 m
0 400 800 yards

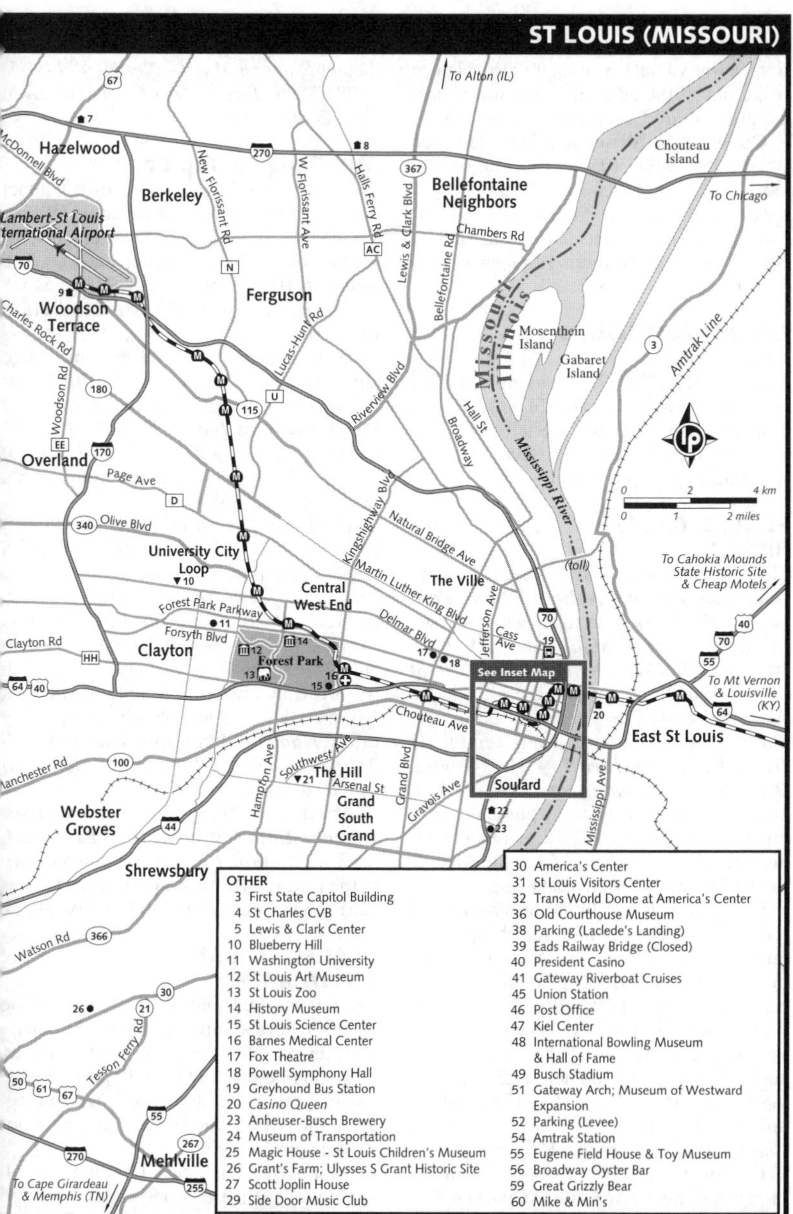
ST LOUIS (MISSOURI)
To Alton (IL)
Chouteau Island
To Chicago
Hazelwood
McDonnell Blvd
Berkeley
New Florissant Rd
W Florissant Ave
Halls Ferry Rd
Lewis & Clark Blvd
Bellefontaine Neighbors
Chambers Rd
Bellefontaine Rd
Lambert-St Louis
ternational Airport
Ferguson
Woodson Terrace
Charles Rock Rd
Lucas-Hunt Rd
Riverview Blvd
Missouri
Illinois
Mosenthein Island
Gabaret Island
Amtrak Line
Hall St
Broadway
Mississippi River
Woodson Rd
Overland
Page Ave
Olive Blvd
Kingshighway Blvd
Natural Bridge Ave
0 2 4 km
0 1 2 miles
To Cahokia Mounds State Historic Site & Cheap Motels
University City Loop
Central West End
Martin Luther King Blvd
The Ville
(toll)
Forest Park Parkway
Delmar Blvd
Jefferson Ave
Cass Ave
Forsyth Blvd
Clayton Rd
Clayton
Forest Park
See Inset Map
To Mt Vernon & Louisville (KY)
Chouteau Ave
East St Louis
Manchester Rd
Southwest Ave
Hampton Ave
The Hill
Arsenal St
Grand Blvd
Gravois Ave
Soulard
Mississippi Ave
Webster Groves
Grand South Grand
Shrewsbury
Watson Rd
Tesson Ferry Rd
Mehlville
To Cape Girardeau & Memphis (TN)
OTHER
3 First State Capitol Building
4 St Charles CVB
5 Lewis & Clark Center
10 Blueberry Hill
11 Washington University
12 St Louis Art Museum
13 St Louis Zoo
14 History Museum
15 St Louis Science Center
16 Barnes Medical Center
17 Fox Theatre
18 Powell Symphony Hall
19 Greyhound Bus Station
20 Casino Queen
23 Anheuser-Busch Brewery
24 Museum of Transportation
25 Magic House - St Louis Children's Museum
26 Grant's Farm; Ulysses S Grant Historic Site
27 Scott Joplin House
29 Side Door Music Club
30 America's Center
31 St Louis Visitors Center
32 Trans World Dome at America's Center
36 Old Courthouse Museum
38 Parking (Laclede's Landing)
39 Eads Railway Bridge (Closed)
40 President Casino
41 Gateway Riverboat Cruises
45 Union Station
46 Post Office
47 Kiel Center
48 International Bowling Museum & Hall of Fame
49 Busch Stadium
51 Gateway Arch; Museum of Westward Expansion
52 Parking (Levee)
54 Amtrak Station
55 Eugene Field House & Toy Museum
56 Broadway Oyster Bar
59 Great Grizzly Bear
60 Mike & Min's

Open 9 am to 5 pm daily (from noon Sunday) the museum pins you for an admission charge of $5/3. You might also want to strike out to the adjoining museum honoring the St Louis Cardinals baseball team.

Out west, the **Museum of Transportation** (☎ 314-965-7998), 3015 Barrett Station Rd, has a large and impressive collection of historic trains. Take the Manchester Rd exit from I-270 and go west 2 miles to Barrett Station Rd and turn south. It's open 9 am to 5 pm daily and costs $4/2.

ORGANIZED TOURS

Tour companies include Gateway City Tours (☎ 314-721-8687), charging $20 for a city tour, and the Greater St Louis Black Tourism Network which specializes in local black history (☎ 314-865-0708). Call to schedule a pick-up and tour.

PLACES TO STAY

Budget

There are no campgrounds close to the city center. ***Dr Edmund A Babler State Park*** *(☎ 314-458-3813)* is 20 miles west of town ($5 to $12); the ***Casino Queen RV Park*** *(☎ 800-777-0777, 200 Front St, East St Louis)* is in Illinois right across from the Arch and costs $25. The only true budget place is the tidy and relatively central HI ***Huckleberry Finn Hostel*** *(☎ 314-241-0076, ✉ huckfinn@mindspring.com, 1904 S 12th St, Soulard)*. It's handy to many pubs and clubs but in a rough area; $15/18 members/nonmembers. Take bus No 73 from the Arch or the Union Station MetroLink stop.

Cheap motels are found around the interstate cloverleaves and get cheaper the farther you get from the Arch; there are many across the Mississippi in Illinois (especially at the I-55, I-70 and I-255 junction). The largest St Louis congregations are around I-270 exits 16 (Page Ave) and 17, and in dodgy Bridgeton near I-270 exit 20B (along St Charles Rock Rd). The comfortable ***Knights Inn*** *(☎ 314-291-8545, 12433 St Charles Rock Rd)* charges $35 per double.

On (or just off) I-270, choose from the pleasant ***Budgetel St Louis/Airport*** *(☎ 314-731-4200, 318 Taylor Rd)* in Hazelwood (from $35/42 singles/doubles) or the predictable ***Super 8 Motel – North*** *(☎ 314-355-7808, 2790 Target Drive)* in Ferguson ($41/43 singles/doubles).

Mid-Range & Top End

Most of the B&Bs are out of town; contact Bed & Breakfast Inns of Missouri (☎ 800-213-5642), 204 E High St, Jefferson City, MO 65101-3207, for more information. The ***Soulard Manor*** *(☎ 314-664-9738, 2346 S 13th St)* is a historic 1890 Victorian villa ($55 to $125).

There is a cluster of reliable mid-range chains around the airport (I-70, exit No 236) in Woodson Terrace, including the ***Best Western Airport Inn*** *(☎ 314-427-5955, 800-872-0070, fax 314-427-3079, 10232 Natural Bridge Rd)* which is a low-rise motel with a pool. It charges $65/70.

The ***Regal Riverfront Hotel*** *(☎ 314-241-9500, 800-325-7353, fax 314-241-6171, 200 S 4th St)* is superbly positioned, and some rooms have views straight through the Arch (all rooms $99). ***Drury Inn Union Station*** *(☎ 314-231-3900, 800-378-7946, fax 314-231-3900, 201 S 20th St)* is a good value for both its location and fine Italian restaurant (rooms start at $96). Nearby is similarly priced ***Hampton Inn Union Station*** *(☎ 314-241-3200, fax 314-241-9351, 2211 Market St)* which has a pool.

Another notch up is the classy ***Hyatt Regency Union Station*** *(☎ 314-231-1234, fax 314-923-3970, 1 St Louis Union Station)*, in the restored Romanesque station. Rooms start at $115 weekends and $180 weekdays

PLACES TO EAT

Riverfront

The floating ***McDonald's***, nestled below the Arch (there's an uncanny similarity between the Arch and the golden arches how soon before McDonald's pays to have the big one painted yellow?), is a must – when the river traffic passes, you can try not to toss your $4 lunch.

At nearby Laclede's Landing are all manner of touristy eateries, most in restored warehouses. These include ***Hannegan's*** *(☎ 314-241-8877)*, for swordfish and prime rib; ***Lafitte's*** *(☎ 314-241-3202)*, for burgers and pasta; ***Morgan Street Brewery*** *(☎ 314-231-9970)*, for microbrews, finger-food appetizers, pasta and gourmet burgers; and ***Show Me's on the Landing*** *(☎ 314-241-3245)*, a 'Florida beach-style' place known for its chicken wings and chili ($5 to $7).

There is an eclectic mix of restaurants downtown. The ***Café de France*** *(☎ 314-231-2204)* at the corner of Olive and 4th Sts, has a prix fixe menu ($29 for three courses, or $21 before 6 pm and after 9 pm). ***Kemoll's*** *(☎ 314-421-0555, 211 N Broadway)* is in the Metropolitan Square Building and consistently satisfies lovers of fine Italian food.

West of Union Station, ***Harry's*** *(☎ 314-421-6969, 2144 Market St)* is worth a visit for its carefully prepared American dishes. ***St Louis Brewery & Tap Room*** *(☎ 314-241-2337, 2100 Locust St)*, has a good range of microbrews and innovative pub grub. They deserve support for their efforts to provide an alternative to that *other* local brew.

Soulard

St Louis' French quarter has a wealth of moderately priced restaurants and pubs. The best is ***John D McGurk's***, at 12th St and Russell Blvd, with a wealth of interesting entrées, an outdoor garden and Irish music most nights – it's consistently voted St Louis' best pub.

You can get Cajun and Creole food at ***Norton's Café*** *(☎ 314-436-0828, 808 Geyer Ave)* and at ***1860's Hard Shell Café & Bar*** *(☎ 314-231-1860, 1860 S 9th St)* which has music nightly. ***Obie's*** *(728 Lafayette Ave)* has vegetarian specialties.

The Hill

Here you'll find some of the best Italian food in St Louis, all at reasonable prices. Try ***Cunetto House of Pasta*** *(☎ 314-781-1135, 5453 Magnolia Ave)* for veal dishes and pastas; ***Amighetti's*** *(☎ 314-776-2855, 5141 Wilson Ave)* a traditional bakery and café; and ***Mama Campisi's*** *(☎ 314-771-1797, 2132 Edwards St)* for delicious toasted ravioli.

University City Loop

Especially along Delmar Blvd, University City Loop has many eateries. ***Café Natasha*** *(☎ 314-727-0419, No 6623)* serves cheap Persian and vegetarian dishes. ***Seki*** *(☎ 314-726-6477, No 6335)* offers bento-box lunches ($6) and other Japanese dishes.

Saleem's Lebanese Cuisine *(☎ 314-721-7947, No 6501)* claims to be 'where garlic is King,' which tells you what to expect from its fine, moderately priced Middle Eastern cuisine.

ENTERTAINMENT

St Louis is dubbed the 'Home of the Blues,' and a number of musical legends – Miles Davis, Chuck Berry and Tina Turner – got their start here. It was also the home of ragtime master Scott Joplin.

Bars & Clubs

Most of the restaurants and pubs described above in Laclede's Landing and Soulard are archetypal drinking holes. Cover charges at clubs range from free to $10 or more depending on the artist and night.

Great music clubs abound in Soulard. The ***Great Grizzly Bear*** *(☎ 314-231-0444, 1027 Geyer Ave)* has bluesy appearances by the Billy Peek Band and Soulard Blues Band (no cover). ***Mike & Min's*** *(☎ 314-421-1655, 925 Geyer Ave)* has great food and features classic St Louis blues.

Also good are ***Broadway Oyster Bar*** *(☎ 314-621-8811, 736 S Broadway)* which has a Cajun menu and regular blues and R&B bands, and the ***Side Door Music Club*** *(☎ 314-231-3666, 2005 Locust St)* which offers alternative rock music.

Blueberry Hill *(☎ 314-727-0880, 6504 Delmar Blvd)* has two rooms full of memorabilia: one dedicated to Chuck Berry, the other Elvis (who has left the building). It hosts local and touring bands and serves great burgers, soups and salads.

Performing Arts

The 1929 ***Fox Theatre*** *(☎ 314-534-1111, 527 N Grand Blvd)* features concerts, dance and Broadway productions. ***Powell Symphony***

Hall *(☎ 314-534-1700)*, nearby, is the home of the St Louis Symphony Orchestra.

SPECTATOR SPORTS

They're sports mad in St Louis. Busch Stadium (☎ 314-421-2400), 250 Stadium Plaza, is a baseball shrine to the Cardinals (15-time National League champs), whose fortunes have risen with the steroid-driven exploits of slugger Mark McGwire.

The Rams, St Louis' NFL team (☎ 314-425-8830), play downtown at Trans World Dome at America's Center. The St Louis Blues (☎ 314-622-2583) play professional ice hockey at Kiel Center.

GETTING THERE & AWAY

Lambert–St Louis International Airport is the home base of TWA, which has services to all major US cities. The airport is also served by the other major airlines, including Southwest, with frequent service to Chicago's Midway Airport. The airport is 12 miles northwest of downtown, connected by limousine ($9/15 one-way/return), bus, taxi ($20) and the MetroLink light-rail system. See the Toll-Free & Web Site Directory at the back of the book for airlines' contact information.

The Greyhound bus station (☎ 314-231-4485) is at 1450 N 13th St, though some buses stop at the airport. Seven buses depart for Chicago daily ($30, 6 hours) and five head to Indianapolis ($28, 4½ hours).

The Amtrak station (☎ 314-331-3300) is at 550 S 16th St. There are three trains daily to Chicago ($26, 6 hours). Other less frequent services link St Louis to Kansas City, Dallas and New Orleans.

GETTING AROUND

The Bi-State Transit System (☎ 314-231-2345, 618-271-2345 in Illinois) runs local buses and the MetroLink ($1.25, transfers 10¢, children half-price). The MetroLink is an expanding tram system that runs in a subway downtown. The line goes west to the airport and east to East St Louis. An extension will go as far as Belleville, Illinois, from 2000.

Taxicabs include Laclede (☎ 314-652-3456) and Yellow (☎ 314-361-2345); $3 first mile, $1 each extra mile.

Around St Louis

ST CHARLES (MISSOURI)

This pleasant 19th-century river town, 20 miles northwest of St Louis and across the Missouri River (see the St Louis (Missouri) map), is now almost a suburb – and a good alternative to staying in St Louis. St Charles was founded in 1769 as Les Petites Côtes (the Little Hills) by the French fur trader Louis Blanchette.

The St Charles Convention & Visitors Bureau (☎ 314-946-7776, 800-366-2427), 230 S Main St, has information about accommodations and the showboats and floating casinos that cruise the river. You can get here on the Bi-State Transit System (☎ 314-231-2345) from St Louis.

St Charles has a large, picturesque, historic nine-block downtown with the **first state capitol building** (St Charles became state capital in 1821) and the nearby historic 26-block **Frenchtown** neighborhood has an interesting museum.

St Charles was a base for the Lewis and Clark Expedition in 1804. Lewis and Clark heritage days are reenacted in the third week of May. The **Lewis & Clark Center** (☎ 314-947-3199), 701 Riverside Drive, has many interesting exhibits. It's open 10:30 am to 4:30 pm daily and costs $1/50¢ adults/children.

Five miles west of the small town of **Defiance**, on the west bank of the Missouri south of St Charles, is the four-story Georgian-style Daniel Boone Home (☎ 314-987-2221). The frontier legend lived here off and on from 1803 until his death in 1820. It's open 9 am to 5 pm daily March 15 to November 30 and 11 am to 4 pm weekends the rest of the year. Admission is $6/3.

Places to Stay & Eat

There are budget chain places along I-70 (exits 227, 228 and 229), including the good-value ***Econo Lodge*** *(☎ 314-946-9992, fax 314-724-7266, 3040 W Clay St)*. Rooms start at $40/46 singles/doubles, and it's 3 miles away from St Charles' downtown.

The more expensive ***Boone's Lick Trail B&B*** *(☎ 314-947-7000, fax 314-946-2637*

1000 Main St) is downtown and has doubles with nice river views from $85.

There's a good selection of restaurants here, as St Charles is a popular weekend destination for St Louis' citizens. ***Lewis & Clark's American Restaurant*** *(☎ 636-947-3334, 217 S Main St)* has outdoor dining and an extensive menu at reasonable prices. For French food, there's the top end ***Reserve 1867*** *(☎ 314-949-3888, 201 N Main St)*, known for its roast pheasant and delectable pâtisseries.

CAHOKIA MOUNDS STATE HISTORIC SITE

An ancient site that's been compared in significance to the Great Pyramids of Egypt and Teotihuacán in Mexico, the Cahokia Mounds were part of a complex city built by the most advanced civilization north of Mexico from 700 to 1400 AD. The mounds are a UN World Heritage Site.

The park (☎ 618-346-5160) covers 2200 acres of the once 6-sq-mile city. Cahokia was the name of the Native Americans living here at the time of the first French contact in the late 1600s, but who actually built the mounds is unknown. What is known is that about 20,000 people lived here at the city's peak in the year 1200, which was a population greater than London's during the same period.

The site preserves 68 of the original 120 mounds, the highest, **Monks Mound**, rises to 100 feet in four terraces. Excavations have uncovered '**Woodhenge**,' a circle of poles used for highly accurate solar observations and date keeping.

An excellent **interpretive center** helps explain the mounds through dioramas and interactive displays. The site is open 8 am to dusk daily and is free. The interpretive center is open 9 am to 5 pm daily and suggested donations are $2/1. The site is just east of Hwy 111 south of its junction with I-55/70. Not far from here, modern humans are building their own mounds: huge garbage landfills that dwarf Monks Mound.

LEWIS & CLARK HISTORIC SITE

This neglected little site is close to the point where, on May 21, 1804, Captain Meriwether Lewis and Captain William Clark set out on their epic exploration of North America to the Pacific Ocean and back. There is a good view of the confluence of the Mississippi and Missouri Rivers and what must be one of the most unattractive memorials around. The site is off Hwy 3, 2 miles north of I-270.

ALTON & AROUND

• pop 32,900

One of the old river towns, Alton dates from 1814. It was the scene of the last Lincoln–Douglas debate on October 15, 1858. Today it is cleaning up its riverfront with nice parks and boasts the attractive, unique Clark Bridge, a 1994 cable-stay span across the Mississippi.

The Alton Visitors' Center (☎ 618-465-6676, 800-258-6645, www.altoncvb.org) is open 8:30 am to 5 pm weekdays and 9 am to 3 pm weekends. It's at 200 Piasa St, across from **Alton Belle Casino** (☎ 800-336-7568).

Downtown Alton still has a sleepy air about it. There are more than 40 **antique shops** between George and State Sts. A plaza commemorates the **Lincoln–Douglas Debate Site** at Landmarks Rd and Broadway.

A 93-foot lighted monument dominates Alton Cemetery on Monument Ave just east of downtown. It's a memorial to **Elijah P Lovejoy**, a local newspaper publisher who was murdered in 1837 by a mob after he published articles condemning slavery.

Alton's most noteworthy resident was Robert Pershing Wadlow, who at 8 feet, 11½ inches was the **world's tallest person**. When he died from an infection at age 22 in 1940, over 10,000 townsfolk turned out for his funeral. A life-size model of him sits on the campus of the Southern Illinois University Dental School, on College Ave just east of Main St above the old town.

Pere Marquette State Park

Overlooking the confluence of the Illinois and Mississippi Rivers, Pere Marquette State Park (☎ 618-786-3323), PO Box 158, Grafton, 62037, is on the site reached by explorers Father Jacques Marquette and Louis Joliet in 1673. The park is an excellent place to see the large numbers of bald eagles that winter here and along the river to Alton, 17 miles to the south along the very scenic Hwy 100.

Places to Stay & Eat

Pere Marquette State Park *camping* is reservable by mail. Sites with electricity are $11, without $8. The *lodge (☎ 618-786-2331)* has an indoor pool and conference center and costs $67/82 for nice rooms.

In Alton, the ***Super 8*** *(☎ 618-465-8885, fax 618-465-8964, 1800 Homer Adams Parkway)*, on Hwy 111, 2 miles east of US Hwy 67, has basic and good-value rooms from $48/54.

Downtown, ***Tony's*** *(☎ 618-462-8384, 312 Piasa St)* has a respectable menu of steaks and pasta with most dishes less than $12. The adjoining ***Third St Café*** has pleasant sidewalk seating and a good beer selection.

Getting There & Away

Three Amtrak (☎ 800-872-7245) trains stop daily in each direction between Chicago (5 hours) and St Louis (1 hour). The station is on the edge of town at 3400 College Ave.

Far Southern Illinois

At the southern end of the state, there is a portion of the Ozark Mountains as well as swampy lowlands around the confluence of the Mississippi and Ohio Rivers. The area is rural and not highly fertile, with industry providing a few coal-mining jobs. Shawnee National Forest covers a large portion of the region.

Many of the natural sights are reached by roads that are small and not well marked. Good local maps, available at gas stations, are essential.

WEST FRANKFORT

• pop 8500

This simple town in the heart of Illinois coal country is a fitting location for the National Coal Museum (☎ 618-937-2481). The world's only deep coal mine open to the public allows visitors to descend in cage elevators 600 feet below the surface into a labyrinth of tunnels. Retired miners demonstrate equipment, show how air was tested after the canaries were retired and with very little prodding will offer fascinating insights into one of the most difficult and least safe professions in the US. Tours depart on the hour 9 am to 4 pm (closed Monday) and cost $10/8. The mine is 5.6 miles east of I-57 exit No 65 just off Hwy 149 at 1941 S Logan Rd.

STE GENEVIEVE (MISSOURI)

This tiny town, 60 miles south of St Louis was the first permanent settlement in Missouri (settlement occurred between 1725 and 1750). French influences are evident in the architecture of buildings such as the Bolduc House, the Bolduc-Le Meilleur House and La Maison Guibourd-Valle. The **Historical Museum** (☎ 573-883-3461), at the corner of Merchant and 3rd Sts, has many relics relating to the town's heyday ($2). The **Great River Rd Interpretive Center** (☎ 573-883-7097), 66 S Main St, has displays on the Mississippi River and a video on local history. Ste Genevieve is linked to Illinois by a river ferry that connects with County Rd 12, which leads to Hwy 3.

CARBONDALE

• pop 27,000

This modest city is the largest in the region. It draws its name from the importance coal mining has played locally. Its other claim to fame is Southern Illinois University, which holds raucous celebrations every Halloween at the end of October. The city proper is not a haven of sights and is actually heavily dominated by railroad yards. The Associated Artists Gallery (☎ 618-457-4743), 213 S Illinois Ave, sells the works of scores of artists who live up in the surrounding hills.

The Carbondale Convention & Tourism Bureau (☎ 618-529-4451, 800-526-1500), 111 S Illinois Ave, is open 9 am to 5 pm weekdays.

Places to Stay & Eat

The state parks in the region have excellent campgrounds; see State Parks, later in this chapter.

The ***Super 8*** *(☎ 618-457-8822, fax 618-457-4186, 1180 E Main St)* has basic rooms from $37/42. The ***Best Inn*** *(☎ 618-529-4801, fax 618-529-7212, 1345 E Main St)* is right in the middle of the chain strip by University Mall. There is a pool and the comfortable rooms are a good deal at $39/42.

Mary Lou's Grill *(☎ 618-457-5084, 114 S Illinois Ave)* is the kind of stick-to-your-ribs place that made America great – or at least fat. Inexpensive homemade cream pies, real biscuits and gravy lead the caloric assault. It's open 7 am to 2 pm.

Cooper Dragon Brewing Co *(☎ 618-549-3219, 700 E Grand St)* brews 14 different beers a year. It has a fine, moderately priced bar with snacks and frequent shows by live bands.

Getting There & Away

Greyhound (☎ 618-549-3495), 404 S Illinois Ave, has services that include three buses departing for Chicago daily ($53, 7 hours) and three that head to St Louis ($39, 3 hours).

The Amtrak *City of New Orleans* (☎ 800-872-7245) stops here in the dead of night as it travels between Chicago and New Orleans. The station is at 401 S Illinois Ave near the Greyhound stop. There is also a daily short-distance train to/from Chicago (5½ hours).

CAPE GIRARDEAU (MISSOURI)

Around 1733, one Jean Giradot established a trading post along this then-remote part of the Mississippi; the steamboats started to roll past in 1835. The town, 115 miles downstream from St Louis, is now one of the most pleasant escapes imaginable.

The Cape Girardeau Convention & Visitors' Bureau (☎ 800-777-0068), PO Box 617, 63702, has information. The town is across the river from McClure and Hwy 3 in Illinois.

The **Cape River Heritage Museum** (☎ 573-334-0405), 538 Independence St, tells the story of the town and its river associations. It is open a bit sporadically – 11 am to 4 pm Wednesday, Friday and Saturday – and costs $1/50¢.

Some 10 miles north on Hwy 177 is **Trail of Tears State Park** (☎ 573-334-1711), a beautiful region that belies its sad past as part of the Cherokees' forced march to Oklahoma (see Trail of Tears State Forest under State Parks, later). It makes a good companion to the state forest across the river in Illinois; see State Parks below.

SHAWNEE NATIONAL FOREST

Made up of more than 270,000 acres, Shawnee National Forest covers much of the farthest south region of Illinois. A natural and wild area, it was initially settled in the mid-1800s by farmers who soon found that the land couldn't support crops because it was easily eroded. In the 1930s the federal government bought up scores of these failed homesteads to create the forest. The hills abound with both Native American and pioneer sites that are now protected and there are more than 250 miles of hiking trails.

Shawnee's headquarters (☎ 618-253-7114, 800-699-6637, www.fs.fed.us/r9/shawnee), 50 Hwy 145 S, 62946, is in a large new building in Harrisburg, northeast of the forest. For information, phone or write the Forest Supervisor. The office is open 8 am to 4:30 pm daily June to September (weekdays only other times). It has lots of good material on the sprawling forest, including details on the many diverse recreation areas, and sells topographic maps.

Garden of the Gods

Ancient ocean sediment has been exposed in this park and various weathering and ice ages have created a fantasyland of weathered rocks, many in unusual shapes that have been given names such as Camel Rock, Anvil Rock and Monkey-Face Rock. Several miles of trails link the geologic oddities. The parking lot is reached by a small road off Karbers Ridge Rd, which turns off of Hwy 34, 8 miles south of its junction with Hwy 145. Watch for the signs.

Rim Rock Trail

Barely a mile long, this trail traverses an especially scenic part of the forest. Signs along the path point out features that include native hardwoods, a cedar plantation and the remains of an old Indian settlement. The

Pounds Hollow Lake Recreation Complex is here and has camping, swimming, rental boats and a snack stand. The area is 2 miles west of Hwy 1 and 10 miles north of Cave-in-Rock, a riverfront town.

Little Grand Canyon

One of the forest's most interesting areas is reached by a 3.6-mile loop hiking trail that passes high limestone bluffs and comprises hill prairies, wetlands and old-growth oak and hickory forests. The parking lot is 10 miles west of Carbondale over County Rd 1100 N and Farm Rd 346. Follow signs and be prepared to make lots of inquiries on the curving, barely improved roads.

Old Illinois Iron Furnace

From 1837, this rudimentary furnace smelted ore for the US government. It supplied iron used as armor plating for the Union Navy's battles on the Mississippi during the Civil War. The site today is very quiet and is an interesting place to contemplate the noises that would have been echoing off the surrounding bluffs 150 years ago.

From the junction of Hwy 34 and 146 near Rosiclare, take the farm road that heads due north; it's almost 3 miles to the furnace. As always in the tangle of small forest roads, watch the signs.

Camping

Shawnee National Forest has 12 developed campgrounds. Most are unattended, quite remote and have limited services: Not many have hot showers or hook-ups. Reservations are not accepted, so you'll just have to show up and see what's available. Rates are $5 a night at most. Call the main information number (☎ 618-253-7114, 800-699-6637) for more information. ***Pharaoh Campground*** is at the Garden of the Gods and has 12 simple sites. ***Pine Ridge Campground*** is at the Pounds Hollow Recreation area and has 76 tent and RV sites as well as hot showers.

STATE PARKS

Giant City State Park

The 'giants' here are huge sandstone cubes that rise from canyons. Giant City State Park (☎ 618-457-4836), 336 Church Rd, Makanda 62958, also is the site of an area fortified with stones thought to have been used by Native Americans in the area around 700 AD. The Fern Rocks Nature Preserve has rare plants such as French's shooting star and large flowering mint. Visitors' center rangers can explain the geologic formations, and there is boating and swimming.

Campsites with electricity cost $11 a night. Remote backpacking tent sites cost $6 a night. The ***Giant City Lodge*** *(☎ 618-457-4921)* has a classic 1930 main building and 34 rustic but comfy cabins from $49 per night. The restaurant is renowned for its steaks.

The park is 12 miles south of Carbondale on US Hwy 51.

Trail of Tears State Forest

During the winter of 1838–39, the US government forced 10,000 Cherokee Nation people to march from their homes in the east some 800 miles west to present-day Oklahoma. Blocked from crossing the Mississippi by ice, the Cherokee had very poor shelter in the snow and over 4000 died before they finally reached the end.

Called 'Trail of Tears' after the name commonly applied to the march, the state forest (☎ 618-833-4910), 3240 State Forest Rd, Jonesboro, 62952, has more than 4[illegible] miles of trails over the rugged terrain. There are no developed campsites; you must obtain a camping permit in advance by calling or writing the Park Superintendent. The forest is 5 miles northwest of Jonesboro, bisected by Union Forest Rd, which connects with Hwys 3 and 127.

Cave-in-Rock State Park

If you want an advance look at this spectacular park (☎ 618-289-4325), PO Box 338, Cave-in-Rock, 62919, rent the 1962 John Ford cornball classic *How the West Was Won*. As Debbie Reynolds heads down the Ohio River with her family, bandits hidden in the namesake feature of the park raid the boat, only to be driven off by James Stewart. Other than details such as Reynolds' freshly coifed hair, the incident reflects the reality of this stretch of the Ohio in the early 1800s

Forest to River: Driving the Shawnee

LIBRARY OF CONGRESS

You won't see many other people on this roughly 110-mile trip that can fill a half-day or more. The trip begins in Harrisburg and ends in Metropolis, although you can do it in reverse. Sights in bold are listed in detail elsewhere in the chapter.

Head south from Harrisburg on Hwy 34 past tiny Herod, turn east on Karbers Ridge Rd. Watch for the signs to **Garden of the Gods**. Continue east and stay left at the fork in the road for Cadiz. Signs will mark the entrance to **Rim Rock Trail** at the Pounds Hollow Lake Recreation Complex. If you decide to hike here, this might be a good place for a picnic.

Drive two miles east to Hwy 1 and turn south, driving to **Cave-in-Rock State Park** near the Ohio River. The town of Cave-in-Rock, on the river, is a good place for supplies.

Head west on Hwy 146, a classic two-lane road through the rolling farmland and bluffs. You can take a detour to the river to see Tower Rock, whose 160-foot cliff is the highest on the Illinois side of the Ohio. Watch for the signs near diminutive Peters Creek.

Right before Elizabethtown, watch for the signs that direct you over small farm roads to **Old Illinois Iron Furnace**. Continue on over the small roads south to Rosiclare where there is a small park on the river, another good picnic spot. This part of Illinois and Kentucky is the US center for fluorspar mining, a mineral-rich rock used for chemical and glass production. You might spot veins of the sometimes-translucent rock on the sides of exposed cliffs. Trivia buffs will thrill to know that fluorspar is the official mineral of Illinois.

Continue back on Hwy 146 to Golconda, a very small town where you can see traces of its former river port wealth in the oldest buildings. This was a crossing point for the Trail of Tears.

Leave Hwy 146 at Golconda and follow the small county roads through nearly non-existent Bay City and on to the Smithland Locks & Dam. Unwieldy river barges pass through the twin locks here, some of the biggest run by Army Corps of Engineers. A visitor's center provides views and information.

Continue 2½ miles south to New Liberty and turn west for the straight 10-mile drive to Brookport. From here you join US Hwy 45 to **Metropolis**.

Today the bandits are long gone but the 5-foot-wide cavern still has the same weeping view. A ***campground*** has tent nd RV sites for $10 a night. The ***lodge*** ☎ *618-289-4545)* has comfortable duplex abins that start at $60 a night. The ***restaurant*** serves meals of hearty Southern food t moderate prices. The park is just off Iwy 1.

Fort Massac State Park

Illinois' first state park (☎ 618-524-4712), 1308 E 5th St, Metropolis, 62960, was dedicated in 1908. The location on the Ohio River has a much longer history, having been the location of a French fort in 1757. The Americans built the larger Fort Massac on the same location in 1794 and used it until 1814 to fend off the British and the

Spanish from the south. Portions of this latter fort have been reconstructed at the park, which also has canoeing, boating, hiking and other activities.

The ***campground*** has sites with electricity for $11 and tent sites for $8. The fort museum is open 10 am to 5:30 pm.

METROPOLIS

• pop 6700

This small river city has done a commendable job of milking its fictional claim as the home town of Superman, who, you may recall, worked as reporter Clark Kent in 'Metropolis.' Here, to 'leap tall buildings in a single bound,' the man of steel need clear just two stories.

I-24 passes just east of Metropolis and connects with Paducah, Kentucky, across the Ohio River and with I-57 to the north. Fort Massac State Park is near the center. The Metropolis Chamber of Commerce (☎ 618-524-2714, 800-949-5740) is at 604 Market St.

The **Super Museum** (☎ 618-524-5518), 517 Market St, has items associated with the Kryptonite-adverse guy, from the original comic book through the Christopher Reeve movies to the latest TV show. It's open 9 am to 7 pm daily;$3.

The ***Days Inn*** *(☎/fax 618-524-9341, 141 E 5th St)* is one of several modest chain lo cations between exit No 37 on I-24 an downtown. The typical motel rooms start a $35/44.

CAIRO

• pop 4800

Cairo's interesting history doesn't necessar ily make it worth a detour, even if it is at th confluence of the Ohio and Mississipp Rivers.

During the Civil War it was the stagin ground for General Ulysses S Grant's inva sion of the South. For the next 100 years th narrow, low-lying peninsula devoted itself t industry. Lately the town has fallen on har times, its high dikes casting all too ominou a shadow.

The **Old Customhouse** (☎ 618-734-1019) 1400 Washington Ave, is an impressive 186 Romanesque government building. Its dis plays are a mixed bag bu include one of Grant's desk. It's open 10 am to 3 pm week days and is free.

At the very southern end o both Cairo and the state, **Fort Defiance State Park** was the locatio of Grant's fort. It's dominated b a flood-proof concrete structur meant to be a steamboat that pro vides views of the two great rivers a they merge on their course to Ne Orleans and the Gulf of Mexico.

Indiana

Facts about Indiana

Though Indiana is not a hugely popular destination in itself, the state's position at the 'crossroads of America' means that many travelers pass through heading east and west or north and south.

The capital city, Indianapolis, is famous as the home of the world's oldest and most publicized car race, the Indianapolis 500. It also is home to several good museums and is a short drive from the popular covered bridges west of the city in Parke County.

Northern Indiana's premier attraction is the Indiana Dunes, which feature mile after mile of beaches as well as unique habitats and natural areas. South Bend has some good regional museums and the popular Notre Dame campus.

South of Indianapolis, Bloomington is an ideal small city with great culture, thanks to Indiana University. Nearby Brown County is home to many artists and Columbus is a virtual playland of modern architecture.

Hoosier National Forest occupies large swaths of the southern region. Its limestone hills hold many beautiful hikes as well as fascinating caves for exploration. The part of Indiana along the Ohio River has many historic river towns such as Madison, one of the state's gems.

Indiana Facts

Nickname The Hoosier State

Population 5,552,000 (14th largest)

Area 36,291 sq miles (38th largest)

Admitted to Union December 11, 1816 (19th state)

Road Information For road information, contact the Indiana State Police (☎ 317-232-8248).

Road Rules Seat belts for people in the front and child seats for kids under four are required. Motorcyclists are required to wear helmets.

Taxes Statewide sales tax is 5%. Local communities may levy additional food and lodging taxes of 1% to 5%.

History

Prehistoric mound-building cultures once occupied much of Indiana, and archaeological sites can be seen mostly in the central and southern part of the state. Tribes of the Algonquian language group occupied most of Indiana when the first Europeans arrived.

French fur traders used the state's waterways as early as the mid-17th century, and by 1679 they had charted a water route between the Great Lakes and the Mississippi River system, forging a tenuous link across their North American empire. The French established several forts to protect this route; the town of Vincennes, on the lower Wabash River, is the only surviving permanent settlement from this era.

The British acquired the area in 1763, following the French & Indian War, and they immediately proclaimed it an Indian territory to limit the expansion of the Eastern colonies. In the Revolutionary War, rebels from Kentucky overcame the British and their Indian allies, ensuring that the lands northwest of the Ohio River became part of the new USA.

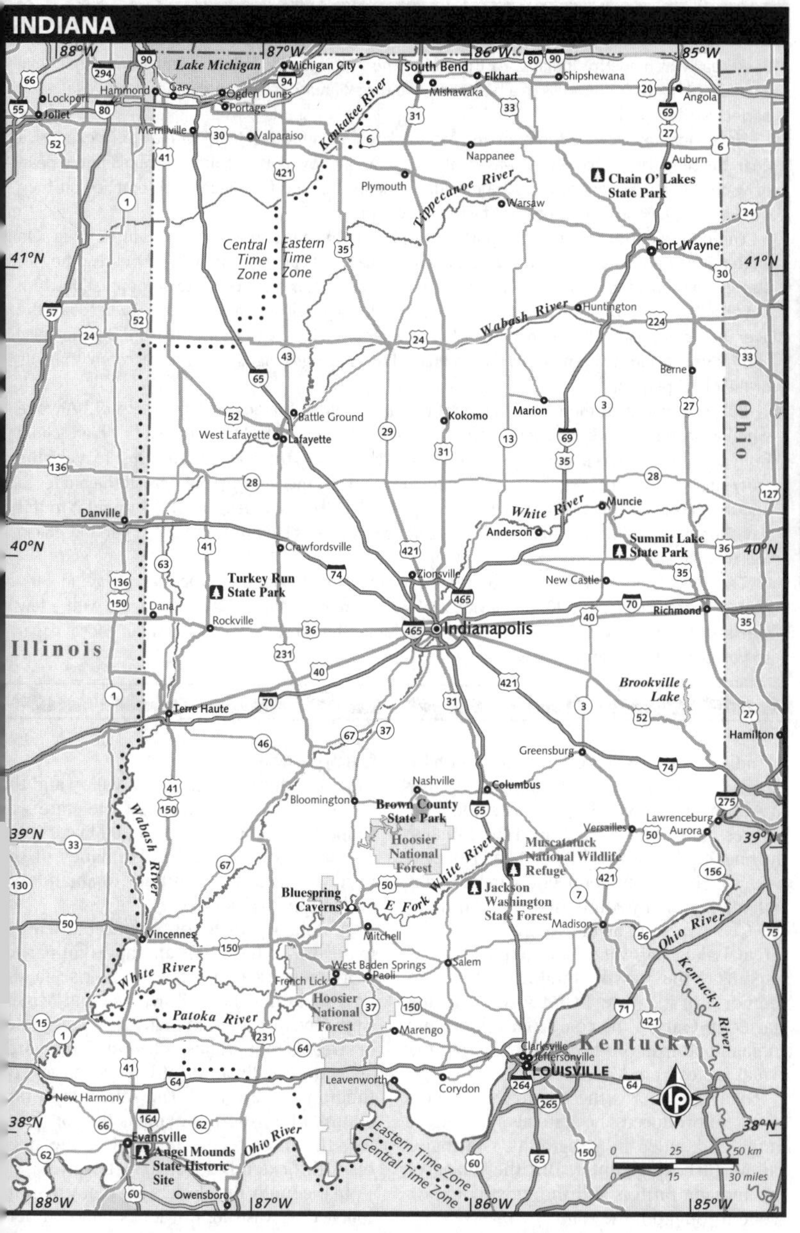
INDIANA
Lake Michigan
Michigan City
South Bend
Elkhart
Shipshewana
Mishawaka
Angola
Lockport
Hammond
Gary
Ogden Dunes
Portage
Joliet
Merrillville
Valparaiso
Kankakee River
Nappanee
Auburn
Plymouth
Tippecanoe River
Warsaw
Chain O' Lakes State Park
Central Time Zone
Eastern Time Zone
Fort Wayne
Huntington
Wabash River
Berne
Marion
Kokomo
Battle Ground
West Lafayette
Lafayette
Ohio
Muncie
White River
Anderson
Danville
Summit Lake State Park
Crawfordsville
Zionsville
New Castle
Turkey Run State Park
Dana
Richmond
Rockville
Indianapolis
Illinois
Brookville Lake
Terre Haute
Hamilton
Greensburg
Nashville
Columbus
Bloomington
Brown County State Park
Lawrenceburg
Versailles
Aurora
Hoosier National Forest
Muscatatuck National Wildlife Refuge
Bluespring Caverns
Jackson Washington State Forest
E Fork White River
Madison
Ohio River
Vincennes
Mitchell
Salem
West Baden Springs
French Lick
Paoli
Kentucky River
Hoosier National Forest
Patoka River
Marengo
Clarksville
Jeffersonville
Kentucky
LOUISVILLE
Leavenworth
Corydon
New Harmony
Evansville
Angel Mounds State Historic Site
Ohio River
Eastern Time Zone
Central Time Zone
Owensboro
88°W
87°W
86°W
85°W
41°N
40°N
39°N
38°N
0 25 50 km
0 15 30 miles

INDIANA

Hoosier Hysteria

Basketball was made for Indiana. At the end of the 19th century, folks in a small town could nail a couple of hoops to the walls of a barn, find five boys of reasonable coordination, and voila! – the perfect winter sport.

Since most towns were too poor and too small to field a football team with all of its expensive gear, the simplicity of basketball was ideal. Plus as an indoor sport, it could be played in the dead of winter when farmers couldn't be outside working. Isolated farm kids could practice on their own, aiming balls at a peach basket tacked onto a post.

Through the 20th century, the sport had a place in Indiana's soul unmatched in America. On winter Friday nights all over the state, convoys of cars still converge on high school field houses and gymnasiums that can hold the student body many times over. Entire town populations turn out and the names of 16-year-old players are bandied about like local superstars. Even today, the average Hoosier can rattle off names such as Homer Stonebreaker, Oscar Robinson, Damon Baily, Larry Bird and Judi Warren. Many towns erect statues or signs highlighting the accomplishments of their best players.

But no name holds more awe than that of Bobby Plump, the boy who hit 'the shot.' Anyone who has seen the movie *Hoosiers* knows the story: A tiny basketball team from a tiny high school from a tiny town beats every huge team in the state and wins the championship. Just to make the story line Hollywood perfect, a short kid named Plump hits the winning shot right at the buzzer to end the game. Of course it was all true, it happened in 1954 and people still talk about it to this day. Plump, now almost retired, still sells insurance and owns Plump's Last Shot, a bar and grill in Indianapolis.

The high school basketball season runs November to late February. The playoffs are in early March. Teams play about 20 games, most of which are on Friday or Saturday nights with a few weekday nights thrown in. If you're in Indiana during this time, check the listings in a local paper so you can attend a bit of Hoosier Hysteria.

Indiana was first settled from the south by farmers from Kentucky (including the family of Abraham Lincoln). Expanding settlement and resulting conflicts displaced the Indians; the final battle was fought in 1811 at Tippecanoe. The Kentucky connection meant that Indiana had many southern sympathizers in the Civil War but, as elsewhere around the Great Lakes, the war's main impact was its impetus to the growth of industrial towns in the north of the state. In 1906, steel-making started in Gary, using coal from Illinois and Indiana and iron ore transported across the Great Lakes from Minnesota.

Today, Indiana is the country's number-one steel producer. The state also has oil refining and, aided by geography, is a major rail and trucking center. But the image of the Indiana farm is still the most common scene throughout the state.

Geography

Indiana is in the Ohio River Valley and th Great Lakes basin. Much of the state wa shaped by the last ice age, 10,000 years ag Glaciers scoured the flat farmlands of th north, scooped out hundreds of small lake and left hills of debris.

A notable but hardly noticeable featur in northwest Indiana is an important part o North America's waterways: A rise in th land separates the St Lawrence and Missis sippi River systems. In many cases, the wate in streams that are just a few hundred yard apart eventually flows into the ocean severa thousand miles apart. The other importan feature of northern Indiana is the soil; poss ibly the most fertile in the US, the dee black dirt extends down 40 feet or more.

In the south, the glaciers left many hills un touched. A vast area of limestone, souther

CHARLES COOK

CHARLES COOK

e tranquil beauty of Indiana Dunes National Lakeshore

PETER PTSCHELINZEW

orse-drawn ploughs and buggies mark Amish country around Shipshewana (IN).

CHARLES COOK

mes Dean was here (still is), Fairmont (IN).

CHARLES COOK

Notre Dame's Golden Dome (IN)

THOMAS HUHTI
Cleveland's reborn downtown

THOMAS HUHTI
The Rock & Roll Hall of Fame & Museum, Cleveland (OH)

THOMAS HUHTI
Cincinnati and the Roebling suspension bridge (OH)

THOMAS HUHTI
Rural living in Ohio's Amish country

THOMAS HUHTI
The Lake Erie Islands (OH)

ndiana features chasms, caves and other dramatic features.

National Parks & Protected Areas

The Indiana Dunes National Lakeshore is the crown jewel of the state's protected areas. With the Indiana Dunes State Park, it protects dozens of miles of some of the best beaches on the Great Lakes. The Hoosier National Forest, in the south, has many developed areas including some of the largest and oldest deciduous trees left in the Midwest.

The state has numerous parks, forests and reserved areas. Many have various concessions offering services such as canoe rentals.

Who's a Hoosier?

Since the 1830s, the people of Indiana have been known by the odd moniker 'Hoosiers.' Everyone wants to know what the heck the nickname means. Well, here is the definitive explanation – sort of, maybe. One theory is that early settlers knocking on a door in the region were met with 'Who's yere?', which soon became 'Hoosier.' Another notion is that the early rivermen were so good at pummeling or 'hushing' their adversaries that they got reputations as 'hushers.' Then there's the one about a foreman on the Louisville and Portland Canal whose name was Hoosier and who preferred to hire his workers from Indiana. They were soon known as Hoosier's men. More likely, others say, pioneers walking into a tavern on a fight-filled Saturday night would find a torn, displaced body part and say 'Whose ear?'

In a more academic vein, the word hoozer, from an early dialect in England's Cumberland District, was evidently used in the 19th-century South to describe woodsmen or hillbilly types. In any case, the word is now well entrenched and thought to have only honorable attributes, although take care to pronounce it as locals do. With a solid overlay of nasally twang, stretch the 'oo' in hoo for at least a beat followed by a lower 'sier' that should have a nice soft 'z' rumble.

Most also have campsites that can range from those with full hookups for $13 to primitive sites for $5. There is no central reservations facility and phone reservations are not accepted. See the listings for the addresses of the parks that accept campsite reservations; at these parks, mail reservations are accepted beginning March 1 each year. Requests should be sent to the desired park along with a deposit equal to one night's fee per site plus an additional $1 per site.

Government & Politics

Indiana is a politically moderate state. Both Republicans and Democrats have had nearly equal luck in statewide elections. The state senate and house have been held at various times by majorities of both parties.

Arts

There is a concentration of artists around Brown County, south of Indianapolis near Bloomington. Indianapolis itself is home to a fine art museum and symphony. In the north, many people prize the Amish crafts such as quilts on sale around Shipshewana.

Information

The state Division of Tourism (☎ 800-289-6646, www.indianatourism.com), 1 N Capitol St, suite 700, Indianapolis, 46204, has state welcome centers located near the state borders on all the interstate highways.

No alcoholic beverages are sold on Sunday; try to buy some beer from the big display in the supermarket and you will be denied. Most bars close by 3 am.

Special Events

April

Little 500 Bicycle Race – a premier event in Bloomington and an excuse for a week of parties and events

May

Indianapolis 500 – the famous car race held Memorial Day weekend in Indianapolis, preceded by a month of special events and celebrations

August

Indiana State Fair – a classic example of the genre, held in Indianapolis

September

Penrod Arts Fair (☎ 317-923-1331) – Indianapolis hosts the state's largest art fair

October

Parke County Covered Bridge Festival – celebrates the dozens of photogenic river spans scattered about the county

Food & Drinks

Indiana's foodstuffs revolve around what's grown, which is almost everything. The summer and fall harvest seasons feature almost every kind of fruit and vegetable imaginable. There is a wine-producing region along the sunny banks of the Ohio River.

Getting There & Around

Indianapolis has a major airport well linked to the rest of the US. Regional airports in South Bend, Fort Wayne and Evansville provide connections to airline hubs. Chicago and Louisville both have airports that serve the nearby parts c Indiana.

Greyhound Bus links the major cities t Indianapolis. However many smaller town have no bus service at all.

Amtrak runs a minimal service fror Chicago though Indianapolis to the eas The South Shore Line provides a handy lin between South Bend and Chicago via th dunes.

I-94 passes through northwest Indiana o its route between Chicago and Detroit. Th Indiana Toll Road runs east and west acros the north and is designated I-80 and I-9(Although drivers were told the road woul become free after the original constructic bonds were paid off, the tolls have simpl gone up ($4.65 across the state) and th money plowed back into a never-endin series of cosmetic improvement projects.

Indianapolis is a highway hub. I-65 rur from Gary south through Louisville, I-7 runs east-west and I-74 goes to Cincinnati.

entral & Northern Indiana

ndianapolis

pop 814,000

dianapolis, the capitol of Indiana and its rgest city, lives up to its billing as the 'cross-ads of America.' Four interstates and veral other important Midwestern roads nverge on the town. This emphasis on ads makes Indy, as many call it, a fitting lo-tion for the annual Indianapolis 500, one the most storied events in auto racing. The owntown is a vibrant mix of new museums, ghtlife and sporting venues, all watched ver by the solemn dome of the Indiana ate capitol.

ISTORY

ne location of Indiana's capital, on flat rnfields in the geographical center of the ate, was the result of a legislative compro-ise in 1820 between agricultural and indus-al regions. The city became a natural hub r road and rail transport, but the lack of vigable waterways limited development heavy industry. However, by 1900 it had come an urbane place with cultural insti-tions, paved streets and a tram system.

The city had many early car makers that ere soon eclipsed by the Detroit giants. eir legacy was a 2½-mile rectangular test ack that was used in 1911 for the first In-anapolis 500 race (won at an average eed of 75mph). The lack of heavy industry oved a bit of a blessing because after orld War II, the local economy developed ound more technological pursuits such as ectronics and pharmaceuticals.

Managing the rapidly expanding suburbs s given a twist unique in US politics with e emergence of the 'Unigov' system, ich combines the functions of the city vernment with those of surrounding arion County. This allows for more cohe-e planning rather than the urban versus burban conflict common elsewhere. This

Highlights

- Visiting Notre Dame
- Sniffing the basketballs at New Castle
- Seeing Indy's many museums
- Kicking the sand at Indiana Dunes National Lakeshore
- Smelling burning rubber at the Indianapolis 500
- Driving backroads at Crawfordsville

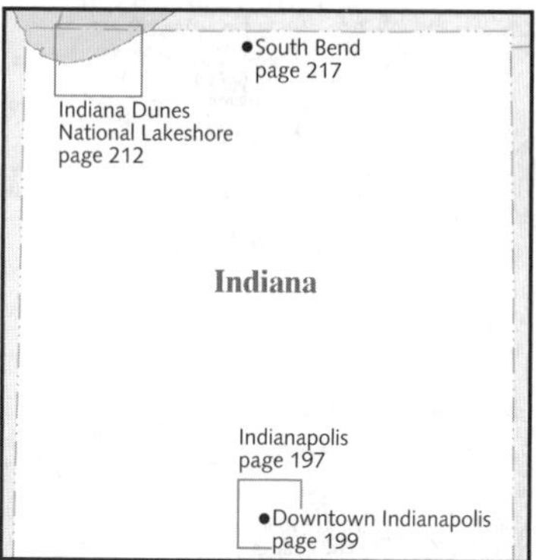

CENTRAL & NORTHERN INDIANA

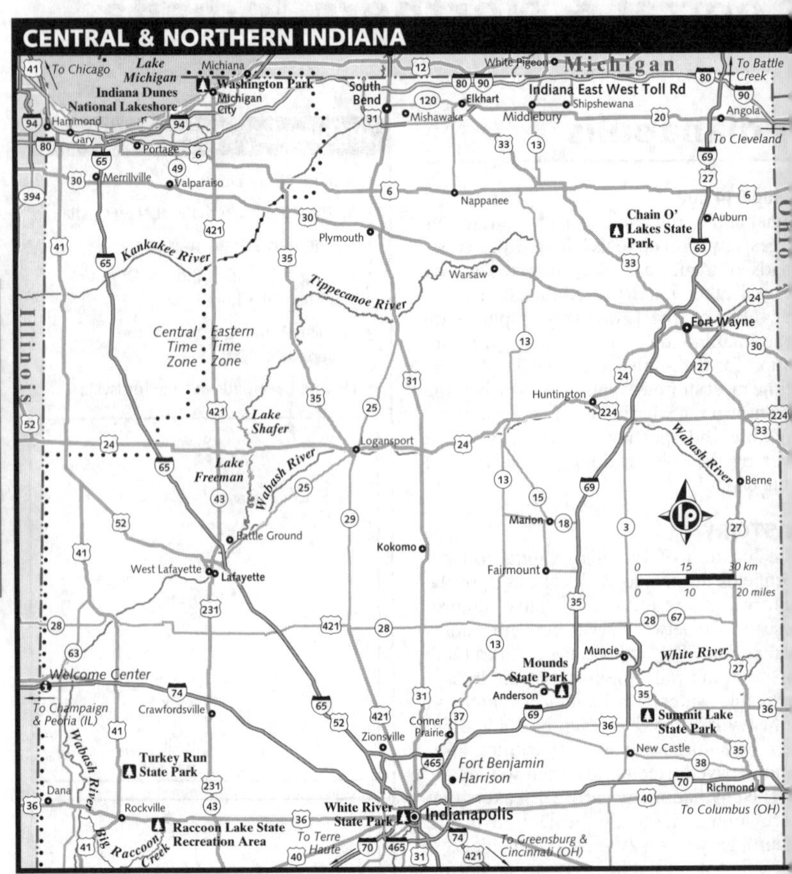

has also given Indy a local government that's especially conservative by American urban standards.

Indianapolis' downtown was redeveloped in the 1980s and '90s with a new sports stadium, museums and shopping complexes. Many downtown commercial buildings around the Circle Centre retail and entertainment complex have thoughtfully retained their original facades.

ORIENTATION

Indianapolis is geometrically laid out, not unlike Washington, DC, with diagonal avenues superimposed on a grid layou Everything radiates out from the massiv Monument Circle. Meridian St divides th east-west designations. The old Broa Ripple district, at 62nd St and College St miles north of the center, contains sever blocks of restaurants, bars and interestir shops. It was the high school hangout local boy David Letterman. College St ar Meridian St (US Hwy 31) link Broad Ripp to downtown.

Chicago is 183 miles northwest of I dianapolis and Louisville is 124 miles sou on I-65. Cincinnati is 112 miles southeast

74. St Louis is 254 miles west on I-70 and South Bend is 139 miles north on tortuous US Hwy 31.

Maps

The free *Downtown Indianapolis Official Map* is excellent and widely available at hotels and the visitors' center; see Information, below.

Odyssey Map Store (☎ 812-635-3837), 902 N Delaware St, has a huge selection of local, Indiana and Midwestern maps, including detailed topographical maps. They're open 10 am to 4 pm (closed Sunday).

INFORMATION

The Indianapolis City Center (☎ 317-237-5200, 800-468-4639, www.indy.org), 201 S Capitol Ave on the corner of Georgia St, is open 10 am to 5:30 pm weekdays, 10 am to 5 pm Saturday and noon to 5 pm Sunday. It has the usual wealth of materials as well as a huge model of the downtown with buildings that light up when you press buttons.

The main post office (☎ 317-464-6374), 125 W South St, is open 7:30 am to 5:30 pm weekdays. ATMs abound throughout the city.

The Indianapolis–Marion County Public Library (☎ 317-269-1700), 40 E St Clair St,

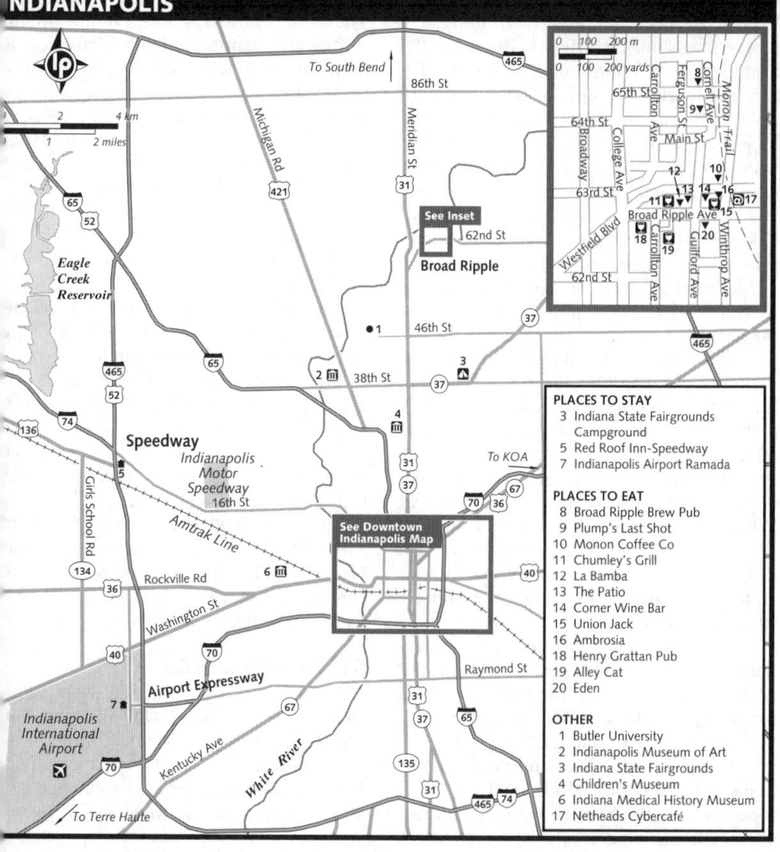

INDIANA

has free Internet access. It's open 9 am to 9 pm weekdays, 9 am to 5 pm Saturday and 1 to 5 pm Sunday.

Netheads Cybercafé (☎ 317-257-6635, www.netheads.com), 1011 E Westfield Blvd in Broad Ripple, is a stylish place with Internet access for $6 an hour and lots of good coffees, cakes, etc. It's open until at least 11 pm daily.

The *Indianapolis Star* is the big local daily newspaper. Don't look here for hip coverage. In fact its deeply conservative convictions are on display on the masthead, which carries a Biblical quote. *Nuvo* is the alternative weekly. It's widely available and the main source for entertainment and events listings. *Indianapolis Monthly* is a glossy magazine that runs features on the homes of local luminaries, such as TV weather forecasters. On the last Tuesday of the month, gay and lesbian travelers should look for the *Word* for news and views. For organization listings and nightlife tips, another gay and lesbian freebie is *Outlines*.

Just about all the malls have chain bookstores; see the Shopping section for details. Downtown, Bookland (☎ 317-639-9864), 137 W Market St, has an excellent selection of out-of-town newspapers and foreign magazines.

Indiana's major learning institutions are scattered elsewhere in the state. The main local school is Butler University (☎ 317-940-8000), 4600 Sunset Ave near the Broad Ripple neighborhood. It has 3500 students and the full range of arts and science degrees. Right downtown, just north of White River State Park, Indiana University–Purdue University Indianapolis (☎ 317-274-7711) is a combined campus of the two state universities, focusing on graduate studies and research.

Downtown there are few self-service laundries. Fortunately, most of the cheaper accommodations have coin laundries. If it's really important, ask before checking in.

Clarian Health Partners (☎ 317-274-5000) is an enormous agglomeration of hospitals at the junction of I-65 and 21st St. It incorporates the Indiana University, Riley and Methodist hospitals.

The Indianapolis Gay and Lesbia Switchboard (☎ 317-251-7955) takes cal from 7 to 11 pm daily.

Dial ☎ 911 for police, fire and medic emergency. The rape crisis line is ☎ 317-25 7575. The Indiana Victim Assistance Ne work is ☎ 317-546-4826.

Like most American cities, Indianapol has a ring of scruffy neighborhoods aroun its core. Although crime is not a majc problem, it's always wise to exercise cautio and have a feel for a neighborhood befo you go wandering about. The downtown an Broad Ripple are generally safe for visitor

DOWNTOWN

There are construction cranes aplent throughout central Indianapolis. Look fc more additions to the list of sights below.

At Monument Circle, the city center marked by the jaw-dropping 284-fo Indiana limestone **Soldiers & Sailors Mon ment**, surmounted by the 30-foot statue 'Miss Victory.' A free observation deck the base of the statue is open 11 am to 7 p Wednesday to Sunday. There are plans open a museum here as a tribute to Civ War soldiers.

Also on the circle are the 1916 **Hilbe Circle Theatre** and the 1857 **Christ Churc Cathedral**, with its Tiffany glass windows.

You can't miss the **RCA Dome** (☎ 31 262-3452), 100 S Capitol St, where 63,0 fans can watch the Indianapolis Colts pla football under a vast fiberglass dome. Tou are given at 11 am and 1 pm Monday to Sa urday and cost $5/4 adults/children.

The **Scottish Rite Cathedral** (☎ 317-26 3100), 650 N Meridian St, is a 1929 Tudc Gothic wonder. The tower rises 212 feet ar contains a large carillon. It's open 10 am 3 pm weekdays; free.

STATE BUILDINGS

The gorgeous, restored 1880 **state capit** (☎ 317-233-5293) is at 500 W Washington S The Renaissance Revival building has great stained glass window in the rotund You can take a self-guided tour that tak about 30 minutes. If the legislature is session, you will see various snappily dress

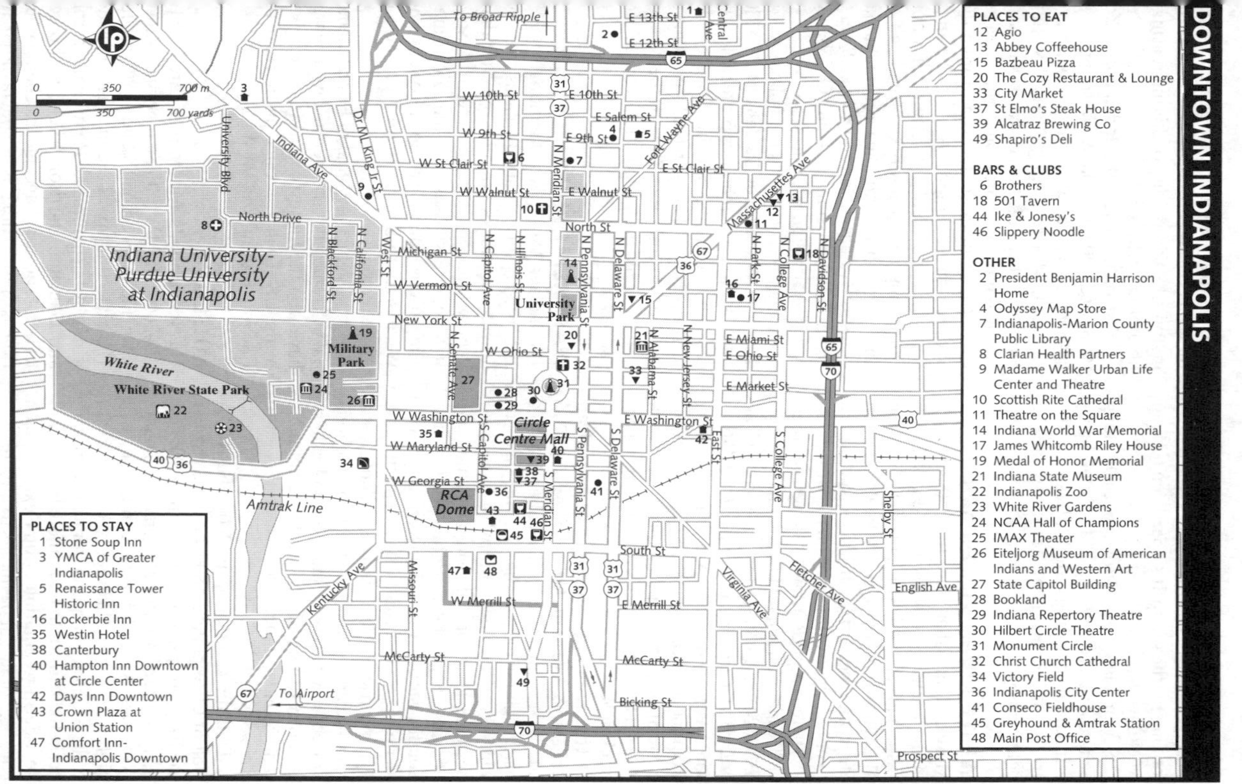
DOWNTOWN INDIANAPOLIS
PLACES TO EAT
12 Agio
13 Abbey Coffeehouse
15 Bazbeau Pizza
20 The Cozy Restaurant & Lounge
33 City Market
37 St Elmo's Steak House
39 Alcatraz Brewing Co
49 Shapiro's Deli
BARS & CLUBS
6 Brothers
18 501 Tavern
44 Ike & Jonesy's
46 Slippery Noodle
OTHER
2 President Benjamin Harrison Home
4 Odyssey Map Store
7 Indianapolis-Marion County Public Library
8 Clarian Health Partners
9 Madame Walker Urban Life Center and Theatre
10 Scottish Rite Cathedral
11 Theatre on the Square
14 Indiana World War Memorial
17 James Whitcomb Riley House
19 Medal of Honor Memorial
21 Indiana State Museum
22 Indianapolis Zoo
23 White River Gardens
24 NCAA Hall of Champions
25 IMAX Theater
26 Eiteljorg Museum of American Indians and Western Art
27 State Capitol Building
28 Bookland
29 Indiana Repertory Theatre
30 Hilbert Circle Theatre
31 Monument Circle
32 Christ Church Cathedral
34 Victory Field
36 Indianapolis City Center
41 Conseco Fieldhouse
45 Greyhound & Amtrak Station
48 Main Post Office
PLACES TO STAY
1 Stone Soup Inn
3 YMCA of Greater Indianapolis
5 Renaissance Tower Historic Inn
16 Lockerbie Inn
35 Westin Hotel
38 Canterbury
40 Hampton Inn Downtown at Circle Center
42 Days Inn Downtown
43 Crown Plaza at Union Station
47 Comfort Inn-Indianapolis Downtown
0 350 700 m
0 350 700 yards
To Broad Ripple
To Airport
Indiana University-Purdue University at Indianapolis
White River State Park
White River
Military Park
University Park
Circle Centre Mall
RCA Dome
Amtrak Line
Massachusetts Ave
Fort Wayne Ave
Indiana Ave
Virginia Ave
Fletcher Ave
Kentucky Ave
University Blvd
North Drive
Dr ML King Jr St
N Meridian St
S Meridian St
N Illinois St
N Capitol Ave
S Capitol Ave
N Senate Ave
N Pennsylvania St
S Pennsylvania St
N Delaware St
S Delaware St
N Alabama St
N New Jersey St
East St
N Park St
N College Ave
S College Ave
N Davidson St
Shelby St
English Ave
Prospect St
E Washington St
W Washington St
W Maryland St
W Georgia St
South St
Missouri St
W Merrill St
E Merrill St
McCarty St
Bicking St
West St
N California St
N Blackford St
Michigan St
W Vermont St
New York St
W Ohio St
E Ohio St
E Miami St
E Market St
North St
E Walnut St
W Walnut St
E St Clair St
W St Clair St
E 9th St
W 9th St
E 10th St
W 10th St
E Salem St
E 12th St
E 13th St
Central Ave

lobbyists looking to peddle influence. The shabbily dressed folks are journalists looking for the scoop. It's open 9 am to 4 pm weekdays; free.

Surrounding the capitol, especially along Senate Ave, are legions of other stolid governmental buildings that attest to the growth in government despite what the politicians say.

WHITE RIVER STATE PARK

More buildings than trees, this 250-acre park in the center of downtown is loaded with sights and can easily consume a day in itself. The eastern entrance is off W Washington St. A nice pedestrian bridge spanning the river links with attractions on the west bank.

There is a pleasant walk along a restored 1870 canal. You can rent paddleboats (☎ 317-632-1824) and take to the water for $12 an hour. The park visitors' center (☎ 317-634-4567) is in a restored pump house dating from the 19th century when this was the industrial center of Indianapolis. It's open 8:30 am to 5 pm weekdays and 10 am to 4 pm weekends.

The **Eiteljorg Museum of American Indians & Western Art** (☎ 317-636-9378), 500 W Washington St, seems almost out of place this far east in the US. But take advantage of the philanthropy of local businessman Harrison Eiteljorg and enjoy one of the city's best sights. Inside the Southwestern-style building are major collections of all forms of art depicting the American West. There is an excellent American Indian exhibit and works by Georgia O'Keeffe, Charles Remington and others. It's open 10 am to 5 pm Tuesday to Saturday (and Monday June to August) and noon to 5 pm Sunday; $5/2.

Due for completion in 2000, the **NCAA Hall of Champions** (☎ 800-735-6222) is near the Eiteljorg and will be adjacent to the new headquarters for the National Collegiate Athletics Association. The museum will highlight accomplishments of American college athletes in sports from badminton to basketball to football. Although there will be video presentations, don't expect much coverage of illegal payments to athletes.

An **IMAX theater** (☎ 317-233-4629) shows its big-screen magic at 650 W Washington St. Admission to this increasingl ubiquitous sight is $8/5.

West of the river, the **Indianapolis Zo** (☎ 317-630-2001), 1200 W Washington S has more than 320 species in a cageless, ye confined, 64-acre setting. Natural setting represented include the African savanna, a Asian temperate forest and the Amazo River (think of the latter as a drop-in-the bucket representation). Among the high lights are the elephants, many of whor enjoy painting. Their works provide an in teresting contrast to such recent huma styles as Brutalism. The zoo is open 9 am t 5 pm daily (closing at 4 pm October t April). Admission is a pricey $10/6.

Next to the zoo, a variety of plants are o display at **White River Gardens** (☎ 317-63(2001). Various greenhouses protect the flor from the elements and there are regula themed displays. It's open the same hours a the zoo and costs $6/4. At both the zoo an the gardens they also nick you $3 fo parking.

WAR MEMORIALS

The **Indiana World War Memorial** (☎ 317-232-7615) is set on various plazas over fiv downtown blocks bounded by Meridiar Pennsylvania, St Clair and New York Sts. A 100-foot obelisk rises from the central are The various exhibits are open 9 am to 5 pr Wednesday to Sunday (until 7 pm June t August); free.

A new sight, the **Medal of Honor Memorial** will remember the men and women wh have won the highest award for valor give by the US. It will be located just north of th Eiteljorg Museum off West St.

MUSEUMS

The **Indianapolis Museum of Art** (☎ 317-920-2660), 1200 W 38th St, is north of dowr town and is set among 52 acres of garden The collection spans the eras and include works by big names like Rembrandt, Turne and Gauguin. Harrison Eiteljorg also co lected African art and his excellent collec tion is here. There is a special area fo ndiana artists. The museum has various afés and shops and on many days there is ive music. It's open 10 am to 5 pm Tuesday o Saturday (until 8:30 pm Thursday) and oon to 5 pm Sunday; free.

Also north of downtown, the **Children's Auseum** (☎ 317-924-5431), 3000 N Meridian t, offers the usual big-screen cinema and ineractive exhibits, as well as dinosaur dislays, Egyptian tombs, an exhibit on African torytelling and a miniature railroad. The nuseum is open 10 am to 5 pm daily (closed Aonday September to May) and costs $8/4. he museum is also open (and free!) 5 to pm the first Thursday each month.

Much less conventional is the **Indiana Aedical History Museum** (☎ 317-635-7329), 045 W Vermont St, with incisive exhibits n 19th-century techniques. It's open 10 am o 4 pm Wednesday to Saturday.

The **Indiana State Museum** (☎ 317-232-637), 202 N Alabama St, includes good dislays on early black settlement after the Civil War. It also has lots of state memorailia such as Bobby Plump's high school acket and a number of paintings by TC Steele. It is housed in the old Indianapolis ity hall and is open 9 am to 4:45 pm daily from noon Sunday); free.

The **President Benjamin Harrison Home** ☎ 317-631-1898), 1230 N Delaware St, is one mile north of downtown and was the ongtime home of the 23rd US president. Built in 1875, it shows that Harrison and his amily knew how to live in the best genteel Victorian manner. Open 10 am to 3:30 pm from noon Sunday); $5/1.

LOCKERBIE SQUARE

Beginning in the 1970s, a group of 'urban pineers' swam against the suburban tide and egan buying and restoring these lovely Vicorian wooden homes in a neighborhood ounded roughly by New York, East, Davidon and Michigan Sts. Pick up a walking tour rochure from the main visitors' center owntown and then make the 10-minute valk west to Lockerbie's narrow cobbletone streets, gas lamps and old oaks.

The **James Whitcomb Riley House** ☎ 317-631-5885), 528 Lockerbie St, was the residence of the poet the last two decades of his life from 1893 to 1916. It is open 10 am to 3 pm (closed Monday). Landmark Tours (☎ 317-639-4646) offers neighborhood tours.

Two blocks west, the restored old commercial strip of diagonal Massachusetts Ave has many cafés and clubs.

ACTIVITIES

The Indianapolis Greenways program (☎ 317-327-7431) links 175 miles of asphalt, limestone and natural trails within the city. Car-free, they are excellent for bicycling, running and walking. The White River trail starts downtown and goes to Broad Ripple where it meets up with the Monon trail. This former railway line stretches north into rural Hamilton County and runs south from Broad Ripple to the Indiana State Fairgrounds.

Bicycle Garage (☎ 317-253-7433), 1079 Broad Ripple Ave, usually has bikes for rent. Call for details.

SPECIAL EVENTS

May

Indianapolis 500 (☎ 317-291-4090), Indianapolis Motor Speedway, Speedway Indiana – much of the month prior to the Memorial Day race is filled with special events such as time trials, parades, parties and other activities for people who have a thing for the smell of exhaust and tires.

August

Indiana State Fair (☎ 317-927-7500), Indiana State Fairgrounds, 38th St and Fall Creek Parkway – mid-month, one of the great state fairs, with the finest critters and produce Indiana's farmers can raise, big name entertainment and more greasy food than you can imagine

September

Penrod Arts Fair (☎ 317-923-1331) – set throughout town, Indiana's largest art fair brings together artists from all over the Midwest

PLACES TO STAY

Downtown lodgings may offer discounts on weekends (sometimes you can find specials for $69), but everything is full and costs much more in May.

Camping

The closest camping is the ***Indiana State Fairgrounds Campground*** *(☎ 317-927-7510, 1202 E 38th St)*, where bleak sites cost $10, or $14 with hookups. There's a ***KOA*** *(☎ 317-894-1397, 800-562-0531)* about 20 miles east of town in Greenfield. Expect the usual range of amusements and sites from $14.

B&Bs

The ***Stone Soup Inn*** *(☎ 317-639-9559, 1304 N Central Ave, www.stonesoupinn.com)* is a positively delightful place in a restored mansion not far from Lockerbie Square. Rooms are quite luxurious and start at $75 a night. The owners have other inns nearby.

Hotels & Motels – Budget

Downtown The ***YMCA of Greater Indianapolis*** *(☎ 317-634-2478, 860 W 10th St)* is a short city bus ride from downtown and has good facilities and simple rooms from $25, plus a very few at $35 with private bath. There is one floor for women, the rest is men-only; there are no coed rooms. The place is usually full of long-term tenants except in summer, when the lack of air-con makes the rooms very warm.

Days Inn Downtown *(☎ 317-637-6464, fax 317-637-0242, 401 E Washington St)* has the usual basic units from $56/69 single/double on weekdays.

Beltway Look for cheap motels off I-465, the freeway that circles Indianapolis. The basic ***Dollar Inns*** are generally the cheapest, and are numerous in all directions of the I-465 beltway. They usually have a pool and access to some sort of cheap fast food. The rooms cost about $40 and are not places you'll want to linger during your waking hours. Among the many, there are locations at: Speedway West and I-465 *(☎ 317-248-8500, 6331 Crawfordsville Rd)*; I-465 and US Hwy 40 *(☎ 317-486-1100, 623 W Washington St)*; and I-65 at Lebanon *(☎ 317-482-9190, 1280 W Hwy 32)*.

Seeing the Checkered Flag

To join the 450,000 spectators at the annual Indianapolis 500 the last weekend in May, you will need to book about 51 weeks and six days in advance (☎ 800-822-4639, ✉ tickets@brickyard.com). Tickets cost from $30 to $140. Remember, hotel rooms will also have to be reserved and prices will be high. For packages, call ☎ 800-556-4639.

To use the parking lot in the middle of the Indianapolis Motor Speedway, where the most raucous partying occurs, you'll need to arrive at about 5:30 am on race day. Nearby Speedway residents allow people to camp on their front lawns for about $15/person per night on race weekend. Race regulars show up the day before and secure a choice lawn campsite so they will be ready to join the crowds at dawn.

Even if you can't make race day, it's worth noting that the course is alive with activity through the entire month of May and it's often fairly easy to get tickets to the qualifying and time trials that determine from what position cars will start.

The rest of the year, it's worth checking out the **Hall of Fame Museum** (☎ 317-484-6747), 4790 W 16th St, which features 75 racing cars, including former Indy 500 winners and a bus tour of the track (at a very sedate 37mph). The museum is right in the middle of the racetrack and you get there via a tunnel. It's open 9 am to 5 pm daily and costs $3/1 plus $3 for the bus ride.

Hotels & Motels – Mid-Range

There are a few good moderate choices downtown. Otherwise there are scores of places on I-465.

Downtown In the historic district, the ***Lockerbie Inn*** *(☎ 317-636-7527, 345 N East St)* is a small lodge with four rooms that start at $79. It is convenient to many of downtown's sights.

The ***Renaissance Tower Historic Inn*** *(☎ 317-261-1652, fax 317-262-8648, 230 E 9th St)* is a restored residential hotel where every room (from $85) has a kitchenette. These rooms are an especially good value if you have four people.

The ***Comfort Inn – Indianapolis Downtown*** *(☎ 317-631-9000, fax 317-631-9999, 530 S Capitol Ave)* is near the RCA Dome and has a small pool. Rooms are $89/99.

The ***Hampton Inn Downtown at Circle Center*** *(☎ 317-261-1200, fax 317-261-1030, 105 S Meridian)* is in the restored Chesapeake Building – an unusual venue for this modern chain. Rooms are $94/104.

Speedway Not far from the Indianapolis Motor Speedway, ***Red Roof Inn – Speedway*** *(☎ 317-293-6881, fax 317-293-9892, 6415 Debonair Lane)* is at the junction of I-465, I-74 and US Hwy 136. Simple but decent rooms are $56/61.

Airport Right by the terminals, the ***Indianapolis Airport Ramada*** *(☎ 317-244-3361, fax 317-241-9202)* has a heated indoor pool where you can swim away flight stress. Rooms are $109/119.

Hotels & Motels – Top End

The best hotels are all downtown.

The ***Crown Plaza at Union Station*** *(☎ 317-631-2221, fax 317-236-7474)* has some accommodations in restored Pullman railroad cars. Rooms start at $130 and cost much more in the train. In the regular building be careful not to end up in a room with a view of a wall.

The Westin Hotel *(☎ 317-262-8100, fax 317-231-3928, 50 S Capitol Ave)* maintains the usual high standards of this business-oriented chain. Very comfortable rooms start at $175. Ask about weekend deals.

The classiest place is the ***Canterbury*** *(☎ 317-634-3000, fax 317-634-3000)*, 123 S Illinois St, where renovated rooms with antique furnishings start at $200 for European-style grand luxury.

PLACES TO EAT

Downtown

At lunch it's hard to beat the incredible range of cheap eats at ***City Market*** *(☎ 317-634-9266)*, two blocks east of Monument Circle on Market St. The buildings date from 1886.

A little out of the center, ***Abbey Coffeehouse*** *(☎ 317-269-8426, 771 Massachusetts Ave)* is where local actors and other types hang out, read the newspaper all day over one cup of coffee and maybe spring for one of the many baked goods that include fine focaccia sandwiches ($5).

Shapiro's Deli *(☎ 317-872-7255, 808 S Meridian St)* is a local institution. On weekdays at breakfast and lunch you'll find a selection of local politicians and journalists chowing down on the homemade soups, good pastrami sandwiches ($6) and decent bagels.

Bazbeaux Pizza *(☎ 317-636-7662, 334 Massachusetts Ave)* is a long-time local favorite. It has excellent thin-crust pizzas ($14 for a large) and more than 50 toppings. Get anything with garlic.

Alcatraz Brewing Co *(☎ 317-488-1230, 49 W Maryland St)* is hardly local, but what do you expect in the chain-laden Circle Centre Mall? The beer is brewed on the premises and is quite good. The sandwiches and other greasy delights are all dependable.

The Cozy Restaurant and Lounge *(☎ 317-638-2100, 20 N Pennsylvania St)* is a casual place with steaks and pasta for under $15. The Wisconsin cheese soup wins raves. It's also a good place for drinks and has pool tables and darts.

Agio *(☎ 317-488-0359, 635 Massachusetts Ave)* is a stylish place serving good Italian food in this increasingly hip neighborhood near downtown. Expect to spend about $15 to $20 per person, before drinks.

If you can afford it, don't miss ***St Elmo's Steak House*** *(☎ 317-635-0636, 127 S Illinois St)*. Since 1902 it has been serving up the very best in steaks, which although not cheap, are worth every penny of their $25-plus prices. The shrimp cocktail has a nearly atomic sauce that will be orgasmic to any fan of horseradish. The wine list is equally impressive.

Broad Ripple

Choices abound and you can do well just by wandering around and looking for something that grabs your fancy. On warm summer nights almost every place has outdoor tables where the quiet and the bug noises can almost make you think you're in the country.

The ***Monon Coffee Co*** *(☎ 317-255-0510, 920 E Westfield Blvd)* has various coffee drinks (extra large regular to go, $2) and baked goods. It's open until 10 pm weekends.

La Bamba *(☎ 317-466-9805, 840 Broad Ripple Ave)* makes fresh burritos (steak $4) as big as your head. You can take out or eat in the charm-free dining area. It's open until well after midnight.

Plump's Last Shot *(☎ 317-257-5867, 6416 Cornell Ave)* has pitchers of beer and a long menu of burgers ($7), sandwiches and other treats you'd expect from a classic bar and grill. What sets this place apart, besides the extra large deck, is that it is owned by Bobby Plump, a genuine Indiana icon; see 'Hoosier Hysteria' in Facts about Indiana.

The ***Broad Ripple Brew Pub*** *(☎ 317-253-2739, 842 E 65th St)* evokes the feel of an English pub but the beers are colder and compared to your average plonkish bitter, much better. It offers lots of veggie items including black bean burgers ($6) as well as pizzas ($8) and more.

Ambrosia *(☎ 317-255-3096, 915 E Westerfield Blvd)* has a nice Old World Italian feel. Garlicky bruscetta ($5) and penne alla melanzane ($13) are favorites.

The ***Corner Wine Bar*** *(☎ 317-255-5159, 6331 Guilford Ave)* has a huge wine list, with many served by the glass in this refined setting. The menu leans French, with pâtés, cheese plates, salads and various entrées for about $20 a person.

ENTERTAINMENT

TicketCentral (☎ 317-624-7430, 800-965-2787) is a nonprofit centralized source for tickets to all the city's cultural attractions and events.

Bars & Clubs

Downtown ***Ike & Jonesy's*** *(☎ 317-632-4553, 17 Jackson Place)* is a raucous downtown joint with dancing, high jinks and more, plus a good beer selection. The underwear hanging from rafters should tell you that this isn't the place for a quiet martini.

Alcatraz Brewing Co and ***The Cozy Restaurant & Lounge***, both listed under Places to Eat, above, are good places for a beer.

Slippery Noodle *(☎ 317-631-6974, 372 S Meridian St)* at South St behind Union Station, was once a whorehouse and is the oldest bar in the state, not to mention one of the best blues bars in the country. There's live music nightly, and it's cheap – great stuff.

Brothers *(☎ 317-636-1020, 822 N Illinois St)* is a friendly gay bar with a limited menu and frequent karaoke.

501 Tavern *(☎ 317-632-2100, 501 N College Ave)* is a gay leather bar near Lockerbie Square.

Broad Ripple You can bar-hop in Broad Ripple, especially on its namesake avenue. In addition to the places below, ***Plump's Last Shot*** and the ***Broad Ripple Brew Pub*** are good for hanging out with pals for a few.

The cheapest beer can be found down an alley at the appropriately named ***Alley Cat*** *(☎ 317-257-4036, 6267 Carrollton Ave)*. Your feet might stick to the floor, but the cheap booze should keep you from noticing.

Chumley's Grill *(☎ 317-466-1555, 83[illegible] Broad Ripple Ave)* is typical of the string of neighboring bars. It's packed with frat boys and sorority girls who gobble up high-fat finger food while guzzling some pints of the 99 different beers.

Union Jack *(☎ 317-257-4343, 924 Broad Ripple Ave)* is vaguely British – although the food is better and cheaper – and has a good line-up of porters and other brews.

Cross the Irish Sea from above for the ***Henry Grattan Pub*** *(☎ 317-257-6030, 745 Broad Ripple Ave)*, which is almost serious and pours a good Guinness.

Eden *(☎ 317-475-1588, 6235 N Guilford Ave)* is a dance club that the bouncer described as 'a little bit of the real world in Indy.' He meant that it's a bit like a New York City club of the early '90s with dancing to house and techno on three levels. The cover is a non-NYC $3 on weekends.

The Patio *(☎ 317-255-2828, 6308 Guilford Ave)* has live rock most nights, except on Saturday night when it's a retro disco.

Classical Music

The ***Indianapolis Symphony Orchestra*** *(☎ 317-236-2040)* performs at Hibert Circle Theater on Monument Circle. The 87-piece professional orchestra has gained a national reputation. Ticket prices start at $12 and climb quickly.

Indianapolis Opera *(☎ 317-239-1000)* performs at Clowes Memorial Hall on the Butler University campus at 250 E 38th St.

Theater

Indiana Repertory Theatre *(☎ 317-635-5252, 140 W Washington St)* stages edgy and mainstream performances using local and big-name actors. The season runs from October to May.

Theatre on the Square *(☎ 317-637-8085, 627 Massachusetts Ave)* is the local equivalent of off-Broadway. Look for new and unfamiliar works here.

The ***Madame Walker Urban Life Center & Theatre*** *(☎ 317-236-2099, 617 Indiana Ave)* is a long-established venue for African American performing arts – jazz, dance, theater, movies, etc. It's worth visiting just to see the unusual African Egyptian decor. They also have an art gallery.

SPECTATOR SPORTS

Stolen in the dead of night from Baltimore in the 1980s, the Indianapolis Colts (☎ 317-239-5151) have found a happy home in Indy by the simple expediency of winning. Fans flock to the RCA Dome – despite its gloomy dome atmosphere – to see the Colts play on fall Sundays. The most expensive tickets are always sold out but you might get some of the $10 nosebleed ducats.

Venerable Market Square Arena awaits the wrecking ball and Indy's new home for basketball is the Conseco Fieldhouse, a huge new palace at Georgia and Pennsylvania Sts that's meant to evoke the atmosphere of a classic Indiana high school stadium. Of course no high school ever charged $45 per ticket as the NBA's Indiana Pacers (☎ 317-239-5151) do.

More tax dollars have found their way into Victory Field, the new home of the Indianapolis minor league baseball team, the Indians (☎ 317-269-3545; tickets from $6). The stadium has loads of fan-friendly features such as a grassy hill for picnics, and it is located right downtown at West and Maryland Sts.

SHOPPING

It's a suburban mall in the city, but Circle Centre (☎ 317-681-8000) has played a big role in the downtown revival, so who's to quibble? Well, maybe those who can't find their way in through the forest of restored storefronts, which look open but are mere facades for the walled mall within. Department stores include Nordstrom (☎ 317-636-2121). Most of the chain stores in those malls you passed on the way into town are here as well. The stores are open 10 am to 9 pm Monday through Saturday and noon to 6 pm Sunday. The many bars and restaurants are open later.

There are other stores out in the air throughout downtown. Numerous interesting little shops with vintage clothing, old comic books and just plain oddball items can be found in Broad Ripple.

GETTING THERE & AWAY

Air

Indianapolis International Airport (☎ 317-487-9594) has the misfortune of being operated by BAA, the airport company that takes over second-rate airports and turns them into third-rate shopping malls. Where Indy airport once had comfy waiting areas there are now fast-food outlets and knickknack shops peddling ties and socks. The windows are now lost behind a sea of retail. Don't hope for a seat either. Remarkably uncomfortable plastic benches are now the norm – unless you'd like to purchase something and use one of the nice food area seats.

That said, you won't want to linger here. Fortunately a full compliment of airlines are ready to whisk you away. Airlines with service at Indy include American Eagle, America West, Continental, Delta, Northwest, Pro Air, Southwest, TWA, United and US Airways.

Bus

The Greyhound station (☎ 800-231-2222), 350 S Illinois St at South St, beside the old Union Station building, has frequent buses to many Midwestern cities. Some examples:

destination	cost	travel time	frequency
Bloomington	$17	1 hour	1
Chicago	$30	4½ hours	10
Cincinnati	$18	2 hours	7
Louisville	$17	2 hours	8
St Louis	$28	4½ hours	5

Illinois Swallow Lines (☎ 217-352-4234) has one bus a day to and from Champaign ($25, 3 hours) and Peoria ($38, 6 hours).

There is also scheduled van shuttle service from Indianapolis International Airport to Bloomington and Lafayette. See those cities' Getting There & Away sections for details.

Amtrak

The Amtrak terminal (☎ 317-263-0550, 800-872-7245) is in the bus station. Service is meager. Six trains a week leave Chicago at about 8 pm arriving in Indy after 1 am ($32). In the opposite direction, the bizarre schedule has trains leaving at about 4:30 am for a 10 am arrival. Three times a week, the trains to/from Chicago are *The Cardinal*, a long-distance train that serves Indianapolis on its run between Chicago and Washington, DC (from Indy, $62).

GETTING AROUND

To/From the Airport

Taxis downtown cost $19. Shared limos cos $6. Local bus No 8 links the airport to/fron downtown. Going to the airport, AAA Hoosier Cab (☎ 317-685-1111) will take yo there from downtown for a flat $13 if yo pre-arrange.

Bus & Taxi

Local transport is provided by IndyGo bu (☎ 317-635-3344), but service is limited o weekends. Fares cost $1 and transfers ar free. There is a big marketing push fo 10-ride tickets that cost $10, such a deal! Bu No 18 links Broad Ripple with downtown.

The IndyGo Transit Store, 139 E Ohio S has schedules and sells tickets. Most buse stop here as well as in front of the capito building and along Maryland St by th Circle Center Mall.

Reliable cab companies include Ted' Taxi (☎ 317-291-5168) and Yellow Ca (☎ 317-487-7777).

Car & Motorcycle

Downtown Indianapolis seems to hav more parking lots than trees. There is als street parking, which is both cheaper an much less hassle than either the high-rise o underground lots.

The major rental car firms all have office at the airport and in the city. See the Tol Free & Web Site Directory at the back o the book for a list of car rental firms' tele phone numbers.

Around Indianapolis

The following central Indiana places are al easy day trips from Indianapolis. Or you ca visit them on your way to someplace else.

ZIONSVILLE

• pop 5300

Twenty miles north of downtown Ind Zionsville is a well preserved small tow hat is just about to be swallowed up by sub-rbia. In the meantime the savvy residents iave created no shortage of gift, curio and nickknack shops to attract the weekend iordes in their SUVs. From I-495 take the JS Hwy 421 exit and go north to Hwy 334. Turn and go west right into town. Or, just ollow the Ford Explorer.

CONNER PRAIRIE

Every school kid in central Indiana has been to Conner Prairie (☎ 317-776-6006), a econstruction of an 1836 pioneer village hat's like no pioneer village ever was. Think nstead Disney meets *Little House on the Prairie*. In Prairietown Village, an entire tory line is presented: While Mrs Whitaker nakes a quilt, the locals enjoy a good time buying dry goods from her husband, George the store owner…Jeremiah Hudson inds that some people are intolerant of his abolitionist views…Samuel Hastings, a war veteran, has fallen on hard times and needs nelp…It's all enough to make you tune in next week or at least visit again; the actors' story line changes regularly at Conner Prairie.

In addition to the running drama, there are areas where you can find out how hard t was to raise a barn, keep house and otherwise live before people had the idle time to go to places like this.

How you react to this elaborate show depends on your tolerance for schmaltz. If you like schmaltz, you'll love the place. If you don't, you'll find yourself wishing for an epidemic of milk fever to break out and clear away a lot of these 'pioneers,' just as it egularly did 200 years ago.

There's an elaborate gift store in the lobby of the huge entrance building and numerous acclaimed cafés and restaurants inside (where the milk is definitely safe to drink). Conner Prairie is open 9:30 am to 5 pm Tuesday through Saturday and 11 am to 5 pm Sunday April 1 to November 30 (closed Tuesday in November). Admission is $10/6. Take I-69 north to exit 5 then north on SR 37 then follow signs.

ANDERSON

• pop 60,000

This city on I-69, 39 miles northeast of Indianapolis, is worth a stop for anyone interested in the still-poorly understood prehistoric Native American cultures. **Mounds State Park** (☎ 765-642-6627), 4306 Mounds Rd, 46017, includes 10 mounds from the Hopewell people. Built 2000 years ago, the large earthworks – one of the rings was 360 feet in diameter and six feet high – were probably used for solar observation as well as ceremonial purposes.

The park is on a nice stretch of the White River. An outside operator, Kate's Canoe Rentals (☎ 812-273-5915) organizes trips on the water. There are 75 ***campsites*** with electricity ($11). The park is just west of town on Hwy 232.

NEW CASTLE

• pop 18,000

This otherwise typical central Indiana town is notable because it's home to the **Indiana Basketball Hall of Fame** (☎ 765-529-1891). This impressive facility has just about everything you could hope to find pertaining to the state's remarkable passion for basketball (as played by teenagers).

Besides famous old balls and musty old nets, there are some good displays. There is a talking model of famed coach John Wooden giving a 'pep' talk. Given his huge winning record, Wooden's, well, wooden style makes an interesting contrast to the chair-throwing nonsense of another famous Indiana coach, Bobby Knight. As you check out the Hall of Fame area, you might notice the absence of women. The answer is that players aren't eligible until 25 years after they played in the state finals and the first women's state finals were in 1976.

The museum is open 10 am to 5 pm Tuesday to Saturday and from noon to 5 pm Sunday. It's on Trojan Lane just off Hwy 3; admission is $3/1. Visible from the museum is New Castle High School where the Trojans play in the largest high school field house in Indiana. It seats over 5000, or 30% of the town.

EAST TO OHIO

US Hwy 40 is lined with **antiques dealers** west to Knightstown and east all the way to Richmond.

In Fountain City, **Levi Coffin State Historic Site** (☎ 765-847-2432) is the restored 1839 Federal-style home of Levi and Catherine Coffin, who helped more than 2000 slaves escape to freedom in Canada through the Underground Railroad. Quakers, the Coffins were the models for the characters of Simeon and Rachel Halliday in *Uncle Tom's Cabin*. House tours include the 2nd-floor hiding place. The home is open 1 to 4 pm Tuesday to Saturday June to September and Saturday only the rest of the year. The site is 6 miles north of I-70 on US Hwy 27.

Five miles northeast on Fountain City in the rolling hills is the otherwise unremarkable hill that's **Indiana's highest point** at 1257 feet.

PARKE COUNTY

These gently rolling farmlands bill themselves as 'the covered bridge capital of the world.' And with 32 bridges scattered about its narrow, two-lane farm roads, it may actually have a legitimate claim.

The Parke County Tourist Information Center (☎ 765-569-5226) is just east of Rockville on US Hwy 36. This is the logical first place to stop in the county, as they have free driving-tour maps that show how to find and visit the bridges. The center is open 9 am to 4 pm daily from June to September and generally weekdays only the rest of the year, although during the October leaf-viewing season the whole operation cranks into overdrive. Note that even if the center is closed, they leave a rack of the maps outside. In October the place crawls with tourists for its Covered Bridge Festival, which coincides with the leaf change.

There are five color-coded tour routes: red, brown, blue, black and yellow. Each will take about 90 minutes or longer. The yellow is considered the most scenic, while the brown is the most popular because it hits the highest concentration of bridges.

Note that the tours are not wonderfully signposted. The style of signs has changed through the years and, due to weathering there will be times when you can't tell if the marker is red, brown or black. Also the roads aren't all charming little two-lane paved jobs. Many are fairly rough dirt roads that won't be in great shape after a bout of the frequently bad Indiana weather.

Finally, the invasion of bridge-o-philes may not be appreciated by every resident. One summer day, just about every bridge bore large spray-painted graffiti that expressed the kind of profane sexual longings common among tortured adolescents. The graffiti was strategically placed; tourists were having a hard time standing in such a way that both blocked the markings and allowed a pretty picture to be taken for the folks back home.

Just west of the visitors' center, **Billie Creek Village** (☎ 765-569-3430) is a fairly low-key reconstruction of a pioneer village. It's worth about a 30-minute stroll. Better are summer weekends when there are special shows. We saw a meeting of historical farm tool and tractor restorers and collectors. It was fascinating to learn how things have changed for family farmers over the last century. The village is open 9 am to 4 pm daily. Admission is $4, more during special events.

If you're continuing west on US Hwy 36 at Dana near the Illinois border, the **Ernie Pyle State Historic Site** (☎ 765-665-3633) preserves the birthplace of one of the great war correspondents of all time. Eschewing the flash of headquarters during World War II Pyle covered the war from the front lines and through the eyes of typical soldiers. His stories were written with an honesty that won him the affection of the men he covered. Pyle was killed during the Battle of Okinawa in 1945. His description of how he worked is simple yet timeless advice for any budding journalist: 'I sit and talk and listen. Later I go and sit at the typewriter. Maybe for a long time.' The house is open 9 am to 5 pm Tuesday to Saturday and 1 to 5 pm Sunday (closed January and February); free.

Places to Stay

Parke County is an easy day trip from Indianapolis or Bloomington. However if you want to stay here there are a couple of choices in Rockville. ***Parke Bridge Motel*** *(☎ 765-569-3525, fax 765-569-0317, 304 E Ohio – US Hwy 36)* is a decent place with pretty rooms from $25/30. ***Billie Creek Village & Inn*** *(☎ 765-569-3430, fax 765-569-3582)* is adjacent to the attraction of the same name. It has a pool and the modern motel-style rooms start at $59. You can splurge and splash out for the $79 whirlpool suite.

TURKEY RUN STATE PARK

Just 65 miles west of Indianapolis, this large state park (☎ 765-597-2635) has many and varied recreation areas. But the real attraction is the **Rocky Hollow Falls Nature Preserve**, a bizarre area of natural phenomena reached by a pedestrian suspension bridge from the main park area.

Among large hemlock trees, enormous blocks of limestone – much larger than humans – have fallen from canyon walls to create a scene that would do proud a demented Cubist. The perspectives are all askew and you might find yourself starting to walk at funny angles. You can regain your balance on some of the park's 15 miles of trails.

Turkey Run has a small ***campground*** ($11, electricity) that is often full. The ***Turkey Run Inn*** *(☎ 765-597-2211, 877-500-6151)* is typical of the rustic inns in many Indiana state parks. Room prices vary by time of year, from $49 to $159.

GREATER LAFAYETTE

The cities of Lafayette (pop 44,000) and West Lafayette (26,000) are separated only by the Wabash River and for all intents and purposes are one place. Purdue University is in West Lafayette. It is the main reason for a stop in the area.

Orientation & Information

I-65 between Gary and Indianapolis bisects Lafayette.

The Greater Lafayette Convention & Visitors' Bureau (☎ 765-447-9999, www.lafayette-in.com) is at 301 Frontage Rd in Lafayette.

The Purdue University Visitors' Information Center (☎ 765-494-4636) is on campus on Northwestern Ave. It's open 8 am to 5 pm weekdays and 8 am to 4 pm Saturday. Call in advance to reserve a free guided tour.

Von's Book Shop (☎ 765-743-1915), 315 W State St, is one of the country's great independent bookstores. It has a huge stock and smart enthusiastic employees. It's in the strip of bars, restaurants, copy shops and other college-related businesses right by the campus.

Purdue University

More people have graduated with bachelor's of engineering degrees from this renowned school of 35,000 students than any other place in the US. The aeronautics department has produced 21 US astronauts including the first and last people to walk on the moon, Neil Armstrong and Gene Cernan.

The campus, founded in 1869, is not a pretty place. The core buildings around the **Purdue Mall** have a bit of Gothic and brick charm. But mostly the campus and its 140 buildings look like they were designed by a bunch of engineers who built for the ages with lots and lots of concrete.

Spectator Sports You have to love the highly appropriate name for Purdue's sports teams: the Boilermakers. Purdue's football team has generally had above average success in the Big 10 and they've had a lot of success against their non–Big 10 rival, Notre Dame.

Football games are played in 67,861 seat Ross Ade Stadium. Tickets (☎ 765-494-3194) are generally sold out but scalpers will come through for you. The games are loud and rowdy affairs. One of Purdue's mascots is a replica steam engine called the 'Boilermaker Express,' which charges around the sidelines after scores. The 350-person All-American Marching Band is one of the loudest around and employs an eight-foot diameter drum. Purdue's arch rival for state bragging rights is Indiana University. The Boilermakers record against the Hoosiers is 60-34-6. Each year's winner gets possession of the Old Oaken Bucket, a trophy that's just that.

Purdue's men's and women's basketball squads are also respectable. They play in dungeonlike Mackey Arena. Gene Keady, the men's coach, is not as well known nationally as arch rival IU's notorious Bobby Knight, but he has the better stats for in-state play: Purdue led IU 12 to 9 games during the 1990s.

Places to Stay & Eat

The chain motel and restaurant ghetto is in Lafayette off I-65 (exit No 172) at Hwy 26. The budget choice is the ***Knight's Inn*** *(☎ 765-447-5611, fax 765-449-4996, 4110 Hwy 26 E)* which has 111 rooms around a small pool. Prices start at $34/39.

Comfort Suites *(☎ 765-447-0016, fax 765-447-9980, 31 Frontage Rd)* has an indoor pool and large rooms/suites. Rates start at $69/74, which includes breakfast. In West Lafayette, the ***Travelodge*** *(☎ 765-743-9661, fax 765-743-8253, 200 Brown St)* is not far from State St and the campus. Basic rooms are $45/50.

Right on the campus in the Purdue Memorial Union, the ***Union Club Hotel*** *(☎ 765-494-8900, 800-320-6291)*, on the corner of State and Grant Sts, has 172 nice rooms and access to the university's many athletic facilities. The Union has numerous restaurants and cafés.

Entertainment

Purdue's students sadly agree that there are really only two college bars in town. ***Harry's Chocolate Shop*** *(☎ 765-743-1467, 329 W State St)* has nothing to do with candy but everything to do with cheap beer. The ***Boiler Room*** *(☎ 765-746-5700)* is a sweat box of dancing and drinking. Both places are open until about 2 am.

After football games, one of the most popular places for people to go to party is Chicago, 121 miles north.

Getting There & Away

Lafayette Limo (☎ 765-497-3828) has service from the Greater Lafayette area to Indianapolis International Airport nine times daily. Vans leave every two hours from the airport beginning at 6:30 am and cost $19 one-way and $33 roundtrip. Call for reservations and Lafayette pick-up times and locations.

Greyhound (☎ 765-742-7925), 200 N 2n St in downtown Lafayette, has service tha includes these cities:

destination	cost	travel time	frequenc
Chicago	$30	3 hours	3
Indianapolis	$17	1½ hours	3

Northern Indiana

Except for the area around the dunes o Lake Michigan, northern Indiana is nc blessed with great natural beauty. Much o this part of the state is barely rolling farm land. But the city of South Bend has number of interesting places such as th University of Notre Dame, and the Amis country adds interest.

NORTHWESTERN INDIANA

Seen by most visitors as a gray and brow blur outside the car as they whiz along I-8 or the Indiana Toll Road, much of northwes Indiana suffers from the side effects of bein the center of steel production in the U Towns such as Hammond, Whiting and Eas Chicago bear all the environmental scars c their heavy industry. Most Chicagoans kno of Whiting only as a place that makes th news for its chemical plant explosions.

Gary is the most blighted of all. company town built in the early 20t century by US Steel, it is a center of povert decay and desolation. Crime is a majo problem and it's not really a place to visi unless you're a sociology student. Gar native, pop star and oxygen fanatic Micha Jackson is not known for his frequent visi to his childhood home at 2300 Jackson S (the street was named for Andrew the pres ident long before Michael was born). H family has long since moved to sunnie (read: California) climes since the Jackso Five gave their first performance at Gary Roosevelt High School in 1965.

Gary has tried to gamble its way to pros perity by giving out casino licenses, but s far the results are mostly visible in fresh

From Seeds Grow Seeds

On a sweltering summer day a dull roar emanates from the Pioneer Hi-Bred International seed company's factory, which sits like a vast defense plant on the outskirts of Plymouth, a town in the heart of the northern Indiana farm belt.

In all directions the fields are covered with fast-growing stalks of corn. Their growth literally explodes under the Hoosier sun and at night when things get quiet you can hear snaps and pops echoing off the fields. But here at Pioneer, they're already getting ready for next year's crop. The huge roar comes from the array of machines that take truckloads of corn grown for seeds and remove the kernels to be grown in a year's time. It's a highly technical and complex task run with military precision that matches the plant's no-nonsense exterior. The corn being grown for seed is all hybrids, meaning that two different strains of corn are planted together so that a third hybrid strain will result carrying the desired traits from both. It's a process that's been going on for generations. The corn that Abe Lincoln's family raised grew to heights of 18 feet. Today's corn grows to less than half that, putting its energy into cobs rather than stalks.

It's critical work and it's also labor intensive. Corn is self-pollinating, so to prevent this, hundreds of laborers are hired for the hot, sweaty and messy work of chopping the pollen-laden tops – or tassels – off the rows of plants designated as the pollen receptors. They earn $200 a week for this and the prime labor market is teenagers on summer vacation.

Once the corn matures it is monitored by computer, and at the optimal level of ripeness it is harvested from the fields and brought to the Pioneer plant where it is inspected, dried, graded, bagged and stored for the next year. From field to warehouse takes about four days and is a process largely watched over by technicians at computers who control the enormous, roaring machines.

The biggest concern is that some of the 40 different types of corn hybrid will be mixed up. They have various traits that make varieties suitable for differing soil, water and other growing conditions. A farmer who mistakenly got dry-field corn for his boggy land might well defect to Pioneer's competition and their 40% market share would start to wilt.

When you're driving around northern Indiana, you can spot the seed plants by looking for corn where every four out of five rows has had its tassels removed. But you won't see a lot, because 26,000 acres of seed corn produces enough seeds for 2.6 million acres of corn.

Pioneer's Plymouth plant (☎ 219-842-8267) offers free tours during much of the year; these require one or two days' notice. The best time is when the hybrid seed corn is being harvested and processed, usually in late July or early August, a few weeks ahead of the regular crop. Look for the serious red and beige complex on US Hwy 30, about three miles west of the junction with US Hwy 31.

INDIANA

paved roads; see 'Gambling' in the Northern & Central Illinois chapter.

The steel mills that line the Lake Michigan shore – a location chosen for the ease of access for boats filled with raw materials from the Iron Range in Minnesota – are enormous temples of industry. Their blast furnaces have a primordial quality and the enormous presses dwarf the soul and send synapses atwitter. Unfortunately, typical American liability fears coupled with little regard for public relations means that the mills are mostly off limits. The closest you can come to experiencing some of their awe is on an Amtrak or South Shore train that travels on tracks bisecting some of the plants.

LTV Steel does offer occasional tours (☎ 219-391-2226) that are worth looking into. You'll have the chance to see the entire steel-making process from the raw taconite pellets through the final roll of galvanized sheet metal.

INDIANA DUNES

The Indiana Dunes are the notable scenic exception in northern Indiana and are easily the most scenic part of the state. The more than 15 miles of sandy beaches and dunes were formed by the prevailing winds of Lake Michigan. On a windy day you can place an obstacle on the beach and watch a dune form behind it. Behind the sands, there are large areas of woods and wetlands, major wildlife habitats.

Preserving the dunes, which today stretch about 21 miles east from Gary to Michigan City, has always been a struggle. The occasional vast and stinky steel mill amid the bucolic beauty shows which way the struggle has frequently gone. Initial attempts to have the area named a national park in 1913 flopped under pressure from industry. Indiana scored the first success in 1923 with the creation of Indiana Dunes State Park near Chesterton. The construction of what was then the world's largest steel mill, on prime dunes at Burns Harbor by Bethlehem Steel in the 1950s, solidified public pressure to save the remaining stretches. Activist Dorothy Buell and Illinois Senator Paul Douglas led the fight, which resulted in the creation of the Indiana Dunes National Lakeshore in 1966. In the decades since, the designation has also effectively saved the dunes from full-scale real estate development. The areas where this had occurred in the 1950s and early '60s give some idea of the horrors that could have spread.

Today the entire area is hugely popular on summer days when people from Chicago to South Bend flock to the shores for good swimming and general frivolity. Most don't take the time to explore the area's diverse natural wonders where hikes offer escape from the crowds. Other times of year, the lake winds and pervasive desolation make the dunes a moody and memorable experience. You may well hear the low hum of the 'singing sands' caused by the zillions of

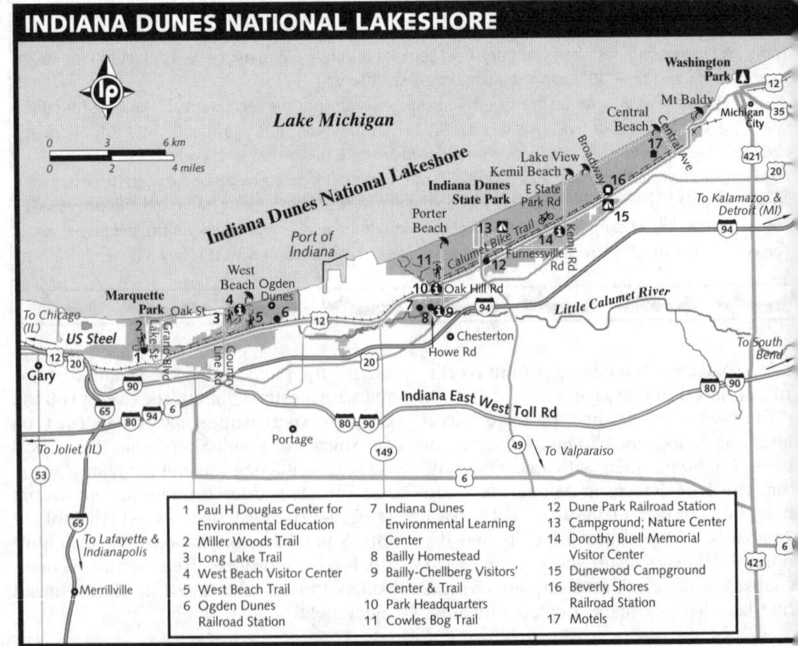

grains of sand hitting each other in the wind.

Indiana Dunes National Lakeshore

Administered by the National Park Service, this area encompasses much of the surviving dunes east and west of the state park. It also preserves large areas of wetlands and woods up to 2 miles behind the shoreline.

Orientation US Hwy 12 follows an old pioneer trail that linked Forts Dearborn and Wayne, which became Chicago and Fort Wayne, respectively. The two-lane road passes near virtually all of the park's major sites and is quite scenic in many parts. It carries the name Dunes Hwy for much of its length in the park. I-94 links Chicago with Detroit and passes just south, and a few miles farther south is the Indiana Toll Rd (I-80/90) which has exits at Portage (No 31) and Chesterton (No 39).

Information The Dorothy Buell Memorial Visitors' Center has a section on the park's flora and fauna. It is open 9 am to 5 pm daily and is located on Kemil Rd just off US Hwy 12 near Beverly Shores. The official and free map is up to the usual excellent park service standards.

For advance information, write: Superintendent, Indiana Dunes National Lakeshore, 11 N Mineral Springs Rd, Porter, IN 46304, or call ☎ 219-926-7561.

Beaches Obviously anywhere there are dunes there's beach, but only certain areas are developed. Swimming is allowed anywhere along the national lakeshore and on busy days, a short hike away from the folks clogging up a developed beach will yield an almost deserted strand. Developed beaches with lifeguards in summer, restrooms and concessions include:

Central Beach – This is a good place to escape the crowds.

Kemil Beach – Right in the middle of a 10-mile stretch of beach. You can get away from the crowds by walking a mile or two east.

Mt Baldy Beach – By far the busiest beach and the one closest to Michigan City, it has the highest dunes with namesake Mt Baldy offering the best views all the way to Chicago from its 120-foot peak. Don't look east or you'll see the environmental travesty of downtown Michigan City's coal-powered electric plant and huge cooling tower.

West Beach – West is one of the best beaches because it is less crowded than the others and it has a number of nature hikes and trails.

Hiking The park service has done a good job of developing trails through a range of terrains and environments.

Bailly-Chellberg Visitors' Center & Trail – This major site is away from the beaches; a nature trail winds through the forest, whose diversity continues to astound botanists. Among the plants growing here are dogwood, Arctic berries and even cactus. The 1¾-mile trail passes restored log cabins from the 1820s and a farm built by Swedes in the 1870s.

Cowles Bog – This nicely varied 4-mile walk combines marsh and dunes.

Miller Woods Trail – The trail is a combination of dunes, woods and ponds and is home to the Paul H Douglas Center for Environmental Education (☎ 219-926-7561) which has day programs.

West Beach – The walk around inland Long Lake is a classic wetlands walk.

Other Activities Much of the park area is good for biking, although US Hwy 12 can get very busy and has narrow shoulders. However the Calumet Bike Trail runs west from near Michigan City almost to the Chelberg Farm. Cross-country skiing is popular in the inland areas, especially along the trails described above.

Indiana Dunes State Park

On summer days, Indiana Dunes State Park (☎ 219-926-1952), 1600 N 25 E, Chesterton, IN 46304, is jammed with people hitting the beach from all over the region. Several tall dunes are popular with people who like to climb to the top, roll all the way down and then say hello to their lunch.

During the summer there are hot dog stands and other amenities of varying merit. Unlike the national lakeshore,

Indiana regulates where you can swim and where you can't. Fido and Bud are unwelcome: Dogs and alcohol are verboten.

Away from the mobbed beaches, the park has many secluded natural areas. The hiking can be excellent. Some highlights among the numbered trails:

- 2 – Good for spring flowers and ferns and popular with cross-country skiers
- 4 – Passes through dunes that are in the process of being colonized by black oak trees
- 8 – Surmounts three of the highest dunes with the reward of great views

In winter cross-country skiing is very popular and there is a ski rental facility near Wilson shelter.

The park is at the end of Hwy 49, which going south has interchanges with US Hwy 12, US Hwy 20, I-94 and the Indiana Toll Road (I-80/90). The beaches are open daily, usually from 9 am to sunset. The park itself is open 7 am to 11 pm April to September and 8 am to 10 pm the rest of the year. Admission is $2 to $5 per person depending on day and season.

Places to Stay

Camping The national lakeshore has the ***Dunewood Campground*** *(☎ 219-926-7561, ext 225)* 2 miles east of the Buell Visitors' Center right off US Hwy 12. There are 54 sites for vehicles and 25 more pleasant walk-in sites for tents. None of the sites have electricity or hook-ups. The campground is open April 1 to October 31 and costs $10 a night per site. There are no reservations; sites are assigned first-come, first-served. Summer weekends are very tight, but other times are not normally a problem. The nearest beach is an easy one-mile walk.

The state park's ***campground*** *(☎ 219-926-1952)* has 118 sites with electricity ($11) and 168 tent sites ($7). There are full showers, bathrooms and a grocery. There is also a youth tent camp with a full range of juvenile high jinks on offer.

Sand Creek Campground *(☎ 219-926-7482)*, in Chesterton, is reached from Hwy 49 on the evocatively named County Rd 1050 N to 350 E. It's popular with familie and others looking for amusements more amusing than the nature trails in the park campgrounds. There are hayrides, a pool video games and more. There is a range o sites, those with full hook ups cost $18 a night, those with a simple tent pad are $14 For those who find the warm summe breezes a bit too natural, portable air conditioners can be rented for $2 a night.

Motels There are two simple but pleasan motels at the eastern end of the nationa lakeshore just inside the Michigan City cit line. Both are on West Dunes Hwy (US Hwy 12). The rates listed are for summer expect bargains off-season.

Blackhawk Motel *(☎ 219-872-8656, fa 219-872-5427, No 3651)* has showers only but you can plunge into the pool. Room start at $35. There are no points for guessin the owners' names at ***Al & Sally's Mote*** *(☎ 219-872-9131, No 3221)*. They have a pool, a playground and nice grounds Rooms start at $40/50 single/double.

Getting There & Away

Train Trains on the South Shore Line (☎ 800 356-2079) depart frequently from Randolph St Station in Chicago. The key stops fo the parks and beaches are Ogden Dunes ($6 70 minutes), Dune Park ($6, 79 minutes) an Beverly Shores ($7, 85 minutes). Trains als come west from South Bend, which is 5 minutes from Beverly Shores.

Major sights within a 2-mile walk of eac station include:

Beverly Shores – Lake View and Kemil Beache Dunewood Campground, Dorothy Buell Visi tors' Center

Dune Park – Indiana Dunes State Park, Cowle Bog Trail

Ogden Dunes – West Beach

Car & Motorcycle There is parking at al the beaches, trails and sights listed above But on a warm weekend, the parking lots just like the patches of sand closest t same – are stuffed to capacity and the acces roads are just as coagulated as the hideous cheese on those snack bar nachos.

MICHIGAN CITY

• pop 34,000

Michigan City was founded in 1675 by French explorer Father Jacques Marquette. It stagnated along as a minor lake port until the 1900s, when numerous small manufacturers set up shop. One of the more notable was Jaymar, makers of 'Sans-a-Belt,' a line of slacks for middle-aged men with ever-increasing waistlines.

Michigan City is also notable as the home of the maximum-security Indiana State Penitentiary, a very grim-looking fortress close to downtown where Indiana still executes the occasional luckless con. Signs in the blocks around the prison warn against picking up hitchhikers, although why anyone would willingly stop for a frantically running person in an orange jumpsuit is a mystery.

Aside from the prison – and a horribly situated and horrible-looking coal-fired power plant right on the lakeshore downtown – Michigan City has tapped into the lucrative recreational trade and has spiffed itself up a bit of late.

LaPorte County Convention & Visitors' Bureau (☎ 219-872-5055, 800-634-2650), 1503 S Meer Rd, 46360, has local information.

Prime Outlet Mall

Michigan City's heritage is recalled at Prime Outlet Mall (☎ 219-879-6506), 601 Wabash St, where you can see lots of folks wearing Sans-a-Belt slacks. This sprawling place has 135 stores, including outlets of Brooks Brothers, Eddie Bauer, Anne Klein, Nine West, Polo/Ralph Lauren and Reebok. Bargain shoppers jam the sidewalks year-round making this place the town's leading attraction by far. The mall is open 9 am to 9 pm daily (until 6 pm Sunday).

Washington Park

This sandy downtown park (☎ 219-873-1506), right on the shoreline, is an extension of the dunes. There's a beach, lookout tower, tiny maritime museum and a band shell that has concerts on Thursday night in summer. From April to October there are admission charges: $2 weekdays and $4 weekends. Parking is limited and the streets, for about a half-mile in all directions of the park, are festooned with 'no parking' signs and patrolled by ravenous tow trucks.

Places to Stay & Eat

You can stay at the places listed for the national lakeshore, earlier, or at one of the thicket of chain motels out by I-94 at Exit No 34, 4 miles south of town on US Hwy 421. Typical is the ***Knight's Inn*** *(☎ 219-874-9500, fax 219-874-5122, 201 W Kieffer Rd)* with basic rooms from $40.

Fast-food horror abounds out at the interstate. In town, ***Basil's Tratorria*** *(☎ 219-872-4500, 521 Franklin St)* has good and cheap pasta dishes for $7, although they didn't get it when we asked if the place was named after the herb or Mr Fawlty.

Getting There & Away

The South Shore Line (☎ 800-356-2079) from the Randolph St Station in downtown Chicago makes frequent daily runs to the 11th St Station in Michigan City ($7 one-way, 1 hour, 40 minutes). Less frequent trains also come west from South Bend (45 minutes).

SOUTH BEND

• pop 106,000

South Bend is named for its geographic location on the meandering St Joseph River, which from this point heads north into Michigan and the lake. One of its earliest residents was Edward Sorin, a Catholic priest who set up a small mission for both the Potawatami Native Americans and early settlers. The institution grew and is now America's leading Catholic university, Notre Dame.

South Bend's other historical roots are in industry. The Studebaker brothers, Henry and Clement, started a blacksmith shop in 1852 that grew into an industrial empire that prospered for 100 years. Joseph Oliver made numerous improvements to the traditional farm plow and in the late 19th century his Oliver Plow Works could not keep up with demand from farmers worldwide and especially in the deeply fertile lands of northern Indiana.

The post-WWII years were not kind to South Bend. Its traditional industrial base suffered and was nearly dealt a deathblow when Studebaker – the town's leading employer – collapsed in the early 1960s. At the same time, officials who can most politely be described as 'boneheads' decided to tear down most of South Bend's dignified downtown. The thought was that new buildings would be redeveloped on the sites of the old. Instead, the businesses and stores moved far from the center, mostly to neighboring Mishawaka (population 46,000). Here they developed a modern retail area collectively known as 'Grape Road,' which is an aesthetic purgatory, even by the usual low standards of American commercial strips.

South Bend, after the millennium, is back on its feet. Notre Dame, Indiana's No 2 tourist attraction after the Indianapolis Motor Speedway, is the largest employer and the economy is now diversified into several sectors.

Orientation

South Bend is the major city of a region known as Michiana, made up of north central Indiana and the neighboring area of Michigan. South Bend is bisected by the Indiana Toll Road (I-80/90). US Hwy 31 heads south to Indianapolis. A bypass loops around the west side of town, but unless you're in a hurry it's worth passing through the center where most of the main attractions are within a 15-minute radius.

Notre Dame is on the north side of town just east of US Hwy 31/33.

Information

Tourist Offices The South Bend Mishawaka Convention & Visitors' Bureau (☎ 219-234-0051, 800-828-7881, www.michiana.org), 401 E Colfax St, 46634, has the usual piles of local info. They have an unstaffed location at the Michiana Regional Airport.

Post & Communications The main post office (☎ 219-282-8400), 424 S Michigan St, is downtown and is open 8 am to 5:30 pm weekdays and 8 am to 1 pm on Saturday.

The downtown St Joseph County Public Library (☎ 219-282-4630), 304 S Main St, is an excellent facility that also has free Internet access. It's open 9 am to 9 pm Monday to Thursday and 9 am to 6 pm Friday and Saturday. On Sunday it's open 1 to 5 pm.

Media The *South Bend Tribune* (☎ 219-235-6161) is the local daily that covers the entire Michiana region. *The Observer* is the free daily student-run newspaper of Notre Dame and St Mary's College, the neighboring all-women's school. It is the place to look for listings of campus cultural events. *Liquid Magazine* is an edgy free monthly newspaper covering the Michiana entertainment scene.

Bookstores In 1999, Notre Dame went from having one of the worst college bookstores in the country to one that is among the better. The Hammes Notre Dame Bookstore (☎ 219-631-6316) is near the Main Gate on Notre Dame Ave and is open 9 am to 11 pm daily (from 11 am Sunday). Besides academic tomes they have a large selection of general interest titles on the main floor in a plush and café-equipped setting that would do a chain store proud. Most visitors, however, will head for the second floor, which caters to the desires of misty-eyed fans. Here just about anything imaginable is for sale in the school colors of blue and gold.

Medical Services St Joseph's Medical Center (☎ 219-259-2431), 801 E LaSalle St, is between Notre Dame and downtown.

University of Notre Dame

One of America's best-known schools, the University of Notre Dame (☎ 219-631-5000) claims it would like its fame to come from its academics, but since it's the only university whose football team has an exclusive and highly lucrative national TV contract, the question is really who's fooling whom?

The legends around Notre Dame's Fighting Irish football squad are many. The 194

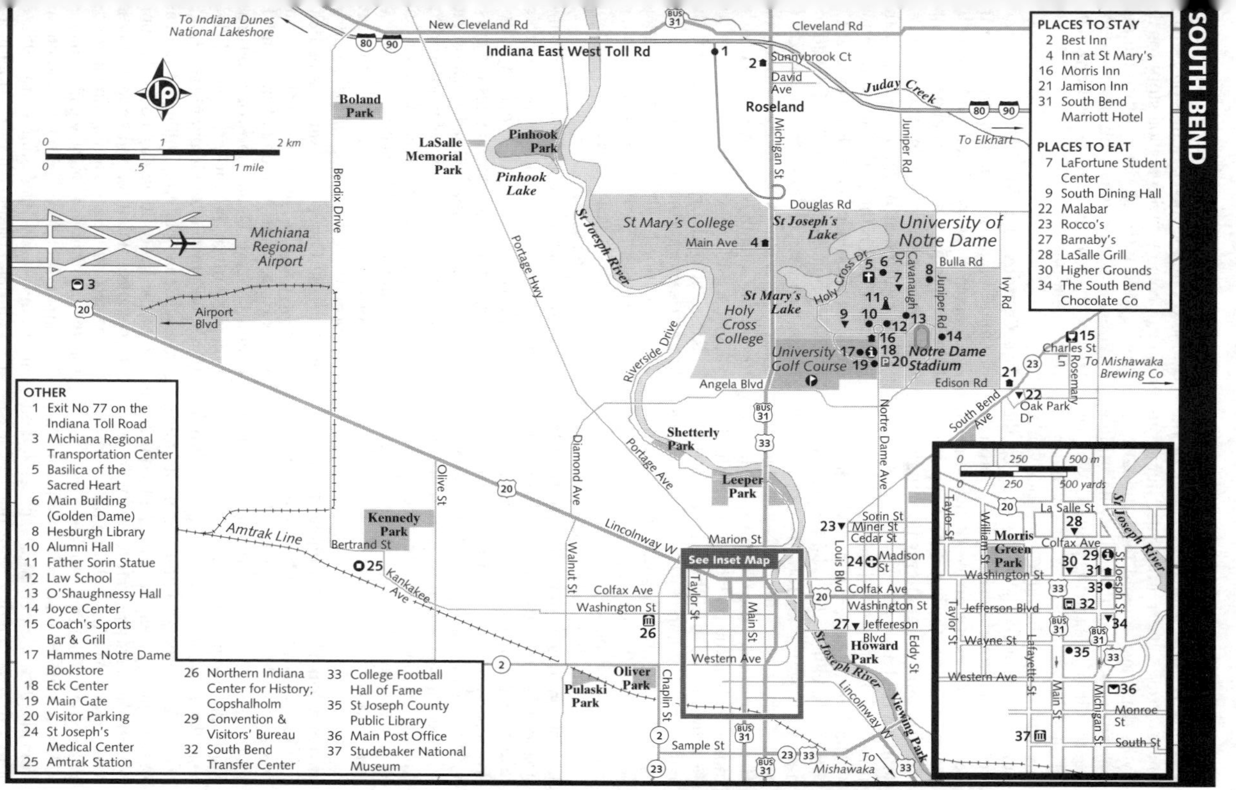
SOUTH BEND
PLACES TO STAY
2 Best Inn
4 Inn at St Mary's
16 Morris Inn
21 Jamison Inn
31 South Bend Marriott Hotel
PLACES TO EAT
7 LaFortune Student Center
9 South Dining Hall
22 Malabar
23 Rocco's
27 Barnaby's
28 LaSalle Grill
30 Higher Grounds
34 The South Bend Chocolate Co
OTHER
1 Exit No 77 on the Indiana Toll Road
3 Michiana Regional Transportation Center
5 Basilica of the Sacred Heart
6 Main Building (Golden Dame)
8 Hesburgh Library
10 Alumni Hall
11 Father Sorin Statue
12 Law School
13 O'Shaughnessy Hall
14 Joyce Center
15 Coach's Sports Bar & Grill
17 Hammes Notre Dame Bookstore
18 Eck Center
19 Main Gate
20 Visitor Parking
24 St Joseph's Medical Center
25 Amtrak Station
26 Northern Indiana Center for History; Copshalholm
29 Convention & Visitors' Bureau
32 South Bend Transfer Center
33 College Football Hall of Fame
35 St Joseph County Public Library
36 Main Post Office
37 Studebaker National Museum
To Indiana Dunes National Lakeshore
New Cleveland Rd
Cleveland Rd
Indiana East West Toll Rd
Sunnybrook Ct
David Ave
Roseland
Juday Creek
To Elkhart
Juniper Rd
Michigan St
Boland Park
LaSalle Memorial Park
Pinhook Park
Pinhook Lake
Bendix Drive
Portage Hwy
St Joseph River
Douglas Rd
St Mary's College
St Joseph's Lake
University of Notre Dame
Main Ave
Bulla Rd
Holy Cross Dr
Cavanaugh Dr
Ivy Rd
St Mary's Lake
Holy Cross College
University Golf Course
Notre Dame Stadium
Angela Blvd
Edison Rd
Charles St
Rosemary Ln
To Mishawaka Brewing Co
Oak Park Dr
South Bend Ave
Michiana Regional Airport
Airport Blvd
Riverside Drive
Shetterly Park
Leeper Park
Portage Ave
Diamond Ave
Olive St
Nortre Dame Ave
Kennedy Park
Bertrand St
Amtrak Line
Kankakee Ave
Lincolnway W
Marion St
See Inset Map
Walnut St
Colfax Ave
Washington St
Taylor St
Main St
Western Ave
Sorin St
Miner St
Cedar St
Louis Blvd
Madison St
Jeffereson Blvd
Howard Park
Eddy St
Viewing Park
Oliver Park
Pulaski Park
Chaplin St
Sample St
To Mishawaka
La Salle St
William St
Morris Green Park
Jefferson Blvd
Wayne St
Lafayette St
St Joseph St
Monroe St
South St
0 1 2 km
0 .5 1 mile
0 250 500 m
0 250 500 yards

movie *Knute Rockne All American* was both a sanitized and idealized account of the famous coach's life. It propagated numerous myths that have entered the national consciousness, such as that of dying athlete George Gipp's plea to the team to 'Win one for the Gipper.' Needless to say, much of this highly enjoyable film – whether you're laughing at it or crying with it – reflects the Hollywood touch. The young Ronald Reagan uses every ounce of his corn-fed charm to sanitize the life of the Gipp, in real life probably a gambler who caught his death of cold after passing out in the snow at the end of a night of drinking.

The Notre Dame Victory March, more commonly called the 'Fight Song,' is instantly recognizable from its lyrics, which begin, 'Cheer, cheer for old Notre Dame...' The team name, the Fighting Irish, was chosen by Rockne both because it reflected the ethnic makeup of the team in the 1920s and because he hoped its colorful connotations would dispel the nickname that had been given to the school by many of its opponents, 'the Papists.'

There are 7800 undergraduate students and 2500 graduate students at Notre Dame. Its top programs, business and engineering, reflect the pragmatic character of the place. Women were first admitted in 1972 and now, thanks to an open admission policy, often comprise a majority of their class. Annual tuition and associated costs easily top $30,000 and 75% of the students receive some form of financial aid.

Information The Eck Center (☎ 219-631-5726) is the school's visitors' center. Staffed by eager students, the building has displays about the University and is open 9 am to 5 pm daily (from 11 am Sunday). It is located near the university's Main Gate on Notre Dame Ave. Free 90-minute campus tours leave from here daily at 11 am and 3 pm. For $25 you can have a private tour any time you want. Even if you're exploring on your own, pick up one of the free campus maps.

Visitor parking is across Notre Dame Ave from the Eck Center. Most academic and administrative buildings are open at least from 8 am to 6 pm when school is in sessio and fewer hours when school is out. Unles you can come up with a good story for th guards, don't try to drive onto campus although the less you look like student trying to sneak in cartons of booze, th better your odds.

The Campus The Notre Dame campus i one of the prettiest outdoor spaces in northern Indiana. **St Mary's Lake** and **St Joseph' Lake** are tree-lined and surrounded by path that make for lovely walking year-round.

The focal point of the campus and th emblem of ND is the Main Building, know to all as the **Golden Dome**. Built in 1879, th five-story building reopened in 1999 after lavish two-year restoration. The inside c the dome features 12 murals about th legend of Columbus that were painted b Vatican artist Luigi Gregori.

Right next door, the **Basilica of th Sacred Heart** was completed in 1892 and ha a lush interior brightly lit through staine glass windows. The 10 am Sunday mass features the full musical efforts of a large choi backed by a huge organ.

Away from the dome and the church, large central space leads south to Notr Dame Ave. A **statue** of the university' founder, Father Sorin, dominates the crossing point with the **South Quad**, the most picturesque of the many quads. Standing in th middle of the quad near Father Sorin an facing south, the buildings on either side c the Notre Dame Ave circle are the **La School** on the left and **Alumni Hall**, a dorm on the right. Other fine examples of 193(collegiate Gothic include Morrissey an Lyons Halls at the west end of the quad. I contrast, Notre Dame's postwar constru tion was often lackluster. When Fran Lloyd Wright saw **O'Shaughnessy Hall**, 1952 academic building hulking at the ea end of the quad, he was asked his opinio His response: 'Plant ivy and hope it grows.

The second-tallest building on campus the 1963 **Hesburgh Library**, which is name for Father Theodore Hesburgh, the chari matic university president from 1952 t 1987 and photogenic pal of presidents an

›opes. It has great views from its 11th floor, ›therwise it's another huge hulk. However, ts south face is part of Notre Dame football ore thanks to the huge mural formally ıamed *The Word of Life*, but known to one ınd all as *Touchdown Jesus*. Visible from the ootball stadium, Christ's arms are raised in ı manner quite similar to that used by refer-ees to signal a touchdown. For the record, he statue of Moses on the campus side of he library is called *No 1 Moses* because of ıis outstretched finger.

At the southeast end of the campus, **Jotre Dame Stadium** underwent a signifi-ant expansion in the mid-1990s. Across uniper Rd, the large double-domed **Joyce Center** has displays of sports memorabilia ›n the second floor.

pectator Sports The Fighting Irish hold ›ooks full of records for collegiate football: nost national championships (8), most Heisman Trophy winners (7), etc. But its ecent record has not been so impressive. Its ast national championship was for the 1988 eason and the 1990s were marked by mar-ginal success and increasing fan discontent. The coach, Bob Davie, is an amiable chap vho often seems as addled as his players.

That said, don't expect to walk up to the icket window and buy a ticket. That hasn't ıappened since 1966, the last time a game vasn't sold-out. There isn't even a sure-fire vay of trying to get tickets, since those that ıre available are sold on a lottery basis to he school's 100,000 alumni.

The only way into the stadium for most ND fans without an assured source is hrough scalping, the technically illegal but olerated practice. Ignore the preying calpers you see along the streets up to 2 niles from campus and wait until you are at ›ne of the gates. Here you'll have your best hance of finding some well-heeled alum vho will part with an extra ticket for face alue or less. Even if you have to pay extra, he team's recent performance means that ou won't pay more than $5 above the $35 ace value. Of course if ND returns to its vinning ways, add a few zeros to the above stimate.

The games themselves are well worth the effort just for the charged atmosphere. The mascot, a person dressed as a leprechaun, cavorts about the field, the student section screams for the entire four hours and if ND misses something simple like an extra point attempt, many of the more devout fans around you will display the pulse-quickening signs of an imminent coronary.

Before a game, there is a strong tradition of 'tailgating' in the parking lots that ring the outskirts of the campus. You'll see everything from a few weenies on a grill washed down by cheap beer to swells sipping champagne and enjoying the delights of fully catered spreads. Try to make friends with these folks.

Thanks to the men's basketball team's steady decline since their heady winning days under colorful coach Digger Phelps two decades ago, you can always get tickets to games at the Joyce Center (☎ 219-631-7354). But why watch their sad efforts when you can see the women's team, which for the last decade has been one of the top programs in the country?

Other Attractions

Hoping to benefit from its proximity to Notre Dame, the downtown **College Football Hall of Fame** (☎ 219-235-9999), 111 S St Joseph St, is an oddly static place that somehow manages to capture the schmaltz of collegiate football but none of the excitement. Many of the displays are lifeless plaster portraits of inductees with little information on the talents that gained them admission. The hall is something of a local political football – sorry – owing to the fact that attendance won't cover its costs and tax money has had to be used to keep it afloat. A financial lifeline from Pepsi has resulted in the odd insertion of Pepsi products in some displays. It's open 10 am to 7 pm daily June to December and until 5 pm the rest of the year; admission is $9/4.

Easily South Bend's best but often overlooked attraction, the **Northern Indiana Center for History** (☎ 219-235-9664), 808 W Washington St, is a large and impressive museum documenting the area's rich past. It is the official repository for Notre Dame history and has many exhibits relating to the area's industrial heritage. There is a good humanist bent to many of the displays; a reconstructed typical worker's home from the 1920s is near the parking lot. The museum is linked to **Copshaholm**, the mansion of the wealthy Oliver family. The house is a fascinating study of how 'that' half lived. The museum is open 10 am to 5 pm Tuesday to Saturday and from noon Sunday. There are frequent tours of the Oliver mansion. Admission to both is $8/4.

The legacy of one of South Bend's claims to fame is preserved at the **Studebaker National Museum** (☎ 219-235-9714), 525 S Main St. Studebaker cars were admired for their style and engineering. Unfortunately, Studebaker talents did not extend to accounting and the business died in the early 1960s. This large downtown museum holds scores of the company's products and is open 10 am to 5 pm Tuesday to Saturday and from noon Sunday; $5/3.

Places to Stay

On home football weekends, prices for accommodations soar and unless you made reservations many months in advance, the closest rooms will be 30 or more miles away. Another tight time is during the mid-May graduation weekends for ND and St Mary's.

Camping Notre Dame no longer allows people in RVs to arrive days before a football game and camp out – they decided people were having just too much fun. But enterprising home owners around the campus allow people to park and camp on their properties. Your best bet is to drive around the streets just east of campus and look for signs. There is no tent-friendly campground close to South Bend.

Motels & Hotels The ***Best Inn*** *(☎ 219-277-7700, fax 219-277-7700, 425 Dixie Hwy N)* is one of many budget chains on this stretch of the US Hwy 31/33 just north of ND and near exit No 77 of the Indiana Toll Road (I-80/90) in an area called Roseland. Rates for the pleasurable rooms are $45/48 single/double. You can walk to campus in about 30 minutes.

The ***Inn at St Mary's*** *(☎ 219-232-4000, fax 219-289-0986, 53993 US Hwy 31/33 N)* is on the St Mary's College campus right across from ND. Comfortable rooms start at $91 a night.

On the east side of Notre Dame, the ***Jamison Inn*** *(☎/fax 219-277-9682, 1404 N Ivy Rd)* is within sight of the stadium. These condo units have kitchens and living rooms and can be a good value at prices from $80 a night plus $10 per person.

Right on the ND campus at the end of Notre Dame Ave, the ***Morris Inn*** *(☎ 219-631-2000, fax 219-631-2017)* shares the unfortunate architectural heritage of some of the campus' less heralded buildings but has an unbeatable location. Fairly basic rooms cost $85/95. For football weekends and graduation the rates are $150, but the old alumni joke is 'first comes conception then comes a reservation' at the Morris Inn for the unborn offspring's estimated commencement date. The ***South Bend Marriott Hotel*** *(☎ 219-234-2000, fax 219-234-2252, 123 N St Joseph St)* is downtown and has good views of the St Joseph River. Rates start at $89/99.

Places to Eat

On campus, ND has the usual collection of collegiate cafés and fast fooderies, mostly in the ***South Dining Hall*** and ***LaFortune Student Center***. But for a gracious experience ($14), try the ***Morris Inn Dining Room*** *(☎ 219-631-2000)*.

Downtown there are two coffee bars. ***Higher Grounds*** *(☎ 219-282-2552, 109 W Washington St)* has good coffee and bad over-priced food. It's where you'll find South Bend's disaffected youth who dream of tattoos and escape to California; their mothers can be found nearby at the ***South Bend Chocolate Co*** *(☎ 219-287-0725, 122 S Michigan St)* where they dream about anything but the calorie content of their luscious cakes.

Barnaby's *(☎ 219-288-4981, 713 E Jefferson Blvd)* is a local institution known for its fabulous thin-crust pizza (large special, $13) and unreconstructed 1960s interior.

Just up the hill toward campus, ***Rocco's*** *☎ 219-233-2464, 537 N St Louis Blvd)* is ven more of an institution. After home ames, the line of alums craving the cheap nd good Italian family fare runs down the lock.

East of campus, the ***Malabar*** *(☎ 219-282-977, 1640 South Bend Ave)* has decent ndian cuisine including lots of vegetarian pecialties.

The ***LaSalle Grill*** *(☎ 219-288-2012, 115 V Colfax Ave),* South Bend's best restau-ant, has an ever-changing menu that re-ects the seasons and what's fresh locally. Regular features are thick steaks that verage $20.

ntertainment

Both the ND administration and South Bend politicians have tried to emulate the Dean Warmer character in the movie *Animal House* by banning fun. Well at least t seems that way. Scores of collegiate bars ave been closed and the local police regu-arly raid the remaining bars and off-campus arties where some hapless underage tudent has just taken her first sip of beer.

Coach's Sports Bar & Grill *(☎ 219-277-678)* is on the South Bend Ave commercial trip east of campus at No 2046. It's an en-irely typical sports bar with lots of greasy ood and big-screen TVs.

A better bet is the ***Mishawaka Brewing Co*** *(☎ 219-256-9993, 3703 N Main St, Mishawaka)* all the way east in the horrific Grape Rd area. The home-brewed beer is ex-ellent and the usual burger-fare pretty good.

Getting There & Away

Michiana Regional Transportation Center ☎ 219-282-4590) is an enlightened surprise: t combines the airport, bus station and South Shore train station in one modern fa-ility. It's 3 miles west of downtown on Lincoln Way (US Hwy 20).

Air Frequent flights connect South Bend with the hub airports of all the major air-nes. There is especially frequent service to/ rom Chicago where you can connect to ights to points worldwide. The local carri-ers and nonstop destinations include American Eagle (Chicago), Continental Express (Cleveland), Delta (Cincinnati), Northwest (Detroit), Trans World Express (St Louis), United Express (Chicago) and US Airways Express (Pittsburgh).

Bus Greyhound's (☎ 219-287-6541) services include:

destination	cost	travel time	frequency
Chicago	$26	2 hours	4
Cleveland	$55	5½ hours	3
Detroit	$43	6 hours	4
Indianapolis	$37	3 hours	5

Train For once the train is a good non-car alternative. The South Shore Line (☎ 219-233-3111) runs between the Randolph St Station in Chicago and the Michiana transportation center five times weekdays and nine times weekends (2 hours 40 minutes, $9). The train's stops include Gary, the Indiana Dunes stations and Michigan City.

Amtrak (☎ 219-288-2212), 2702 W Washington Ave, has a forlorn outpost by itself in a cinder block building on South Bend's west side. Three trains stop daily in each direction between Chicago and East Coast points that include Boston, New York and Washington, DC. See the Getting There & Away chapter for details. These trains are not recommended for getting between South Bend and Chicago, as those tickets are costly and the trains often run very late.

Car & Motorcycle Exit No 77 on the Indiana Toll Road (I-80/90) is most convenient for South Bend and ND. Plan on two hours travel time between South Bend and Chicago during non-rush hour periods.

O'Hare & Midway Airport Connections Many people forgo the commuter plane connections between flights to Chicago's O'Hare International Airport and South Bend. The vagaries of the weather alone cause many disruptions.

The cheapest option is to combine the Chicago CTA El with the South Shore Line.

The combined fare is $11, but there's also a 10-minute walk between stations in Chicago and it's a hassle if you have luggage.

United Limo (☎ 219-674-7000) is actually a bus company that runs between the ND campus, the Michiana transportation center and Midway and O'Hare airports. But the ride is not a good deal at $28/52 one-way/roundtrip and the buses take almost three hours to reach O'Hare.

If you're driving, you can make the trip in about 2¼ hours outside of rush hour.

Getting Around

Cabs from the transportation center to downtown or ND shouldn't cost more than about $10. Try Michiana Taxi at ☎ 219-233-4040.

Transpo (☎ 219-233-2131) is the local bus operator. The various bus lines converge on the South Bend Transfer Center at Main and South Sts downtown. There is half-hourly service to the Michiana transportation center and ND via downtown. Fares are 75¢. They have limited Saturday service and nothing on Sunday.

AROUND SOUTH BEND

Elkhart

• pop 44,000

The center of America's recreational vehicle and 'manufactured homes' (read: mobile homes or trailers) industry, Elkhart is also a major producer of band instruments. It's 15 miles east of South Bend on US Hwy 20 and is 3 miles south of exit No 92 on the Indian Toll Road (I-80/90).

Elkhart's role as a major rail switchin yard on the main Chicago to New York ra line is the focus of the **National New Yor Central Railroad Museum** (☎ 219-294-3001 721 S Main St, a small place downtown. Th collection looks at the history of the fable railroad – long since gobbled up by large companies – and places it in a local contex It's open Tuesday to Friday 10 am to 2 pm Saturday 10 am to 4 pm and from noo Sunday. Admission is $2. Author Ryan Ve Berkmoes' grandfather was station maste for many years at Elkhart's train statio across the tracks from the museum.

Amish Country

East and south of Elkhart, the towns o Middlebury and Shipshewana are reache via US Hwy 20. South, Nappanee is accesse on Hwy 19. All of these places are in th heart of Indiana's Amish communities. It not uncommon to see horse-drawn buggie on the small roads and the large and wel maintained Amish farms dot the landscap Note that Amish-owned businesses ar closed Sunday.

Tidy **Shipshewana** (population 500) the most interesting of the Amish towns. is home to the **Menno-Hof Mennonite Amish Visitors' Center** (☎ 219-768-4117), serious place that documents the Amish ex perience and is housed in a structure bui

PETER PTSCHELINZEW

Road signs reflect reality near Shipshewana.

y locals using traditional techniques. This is good first stop and is open 10 am to 5 pm closed Sunday).

Nearby is the scene of one of the Iidwest's largest markets, the **Shipshewana uction** (☎ 219-768-4129). Every Tuesday nd Wednesday from May to October, over 000 vendors set up stalls selling everything om the useful to the useless. Year-round, it the scene of livestock and hay auctions on Vednesday and horse auctions on Friday.

Other days – except Sunday – the town's w square blocks are home to a number of mish general stores, food markets, bakries, cafés and curio shops selling locally nade craft items and the coveted quilts.

IORTHEASTERN INDIANA

ort Wayne

pop 173,000

t the confluence of the St Joseph (still nother one) and St Mary's Rivers, which eet to form the Maumee, Fort Wayne was n early French trading post from 1690. The aders and the local Native Americans, the Iiami, co-existed until the British arrived in 760 and threw the French out. Three years ter Chief Pontiac sent the Brits packing nd the area again became a trading center.

The town owes its name to General Mad' Anthony Wayne, a Revolutionary Var figure who defeated the Miami Indians fter two previous American expeditions ad failed. Fort Wayne was established and apidly became an important post in the merican expansion westward.

Today, Indiana's second largest city is eavily industrialized and there are numerus automotive and machine tool manufacurers. Fort Wayne optimistically calls itself e 'City of Attractions,' but other than an nportant Lincoln museum, nothing here is verly compelling. However the city has one a good job of landscaping the banks nd parks along the flood-prone local rivers.

nformation The downtown Fort Wayne-llen County Convention & Visitors' ureau (☎ 219-424-3700, 800-767-7752), 021 S Calhoun St, is eager to help. It is pen 8 am to 5 pm weekdays.

I-69 passes the city to the west and together with Hwy 469 forms a beltway around Fort Wayne. The junction with the Indiana Toll Road (I-80/90) is 43 miles north and Indianapolis is 122 miles south.

Lincoln Museum One of the most significant museums devoted to Abraham Lincoln in the country, the Lincoln Museum (☎ 219-455-3864), at 200 E Berry St, is a must-see for anyone interested in the 16th president. It has a signed copy of the Emancipation Proclamation, which Lincoln used to declare the South's slaves free. Numerous video and film presentations trace Lincoln's life from his southern Indiana childhood through his time as president. The museum was started by the Fort Wayne-based Lincoln National Life Insurance Co in 1905 with one picture donated by their namesake's only surviving son, Robert Todd Lincoln. The museum is open 10 am to 5 pm Tuesday to Saturday and noon to 5 pm Sunday; $3/2.

Other Downtown Sights Within easy walking distance of each other are several sights worth quick visits if you're downtown. The **Allen County–Fort Wayne Historical Museum** (☎ 219-426-2882) is in the old 1893 city hall. There is a special section on the Erie–Wabash Canal, once the nation's largest and a major reason the area grew to industrial prominence. Open 9 am to 5 pm Tuesday to Friday, noon to 5 pm weekends, admission is $2.

The **Fort Wayne Museum of Art** (☎ 219-422-6467), 311 E Main St, has more than 1300 pieces, thanks largely to the patronage of local machine tool and automotive part tycoons. It's open 10 am to 5 pm Tuesday to Saturday and noon to 5 pm Sunday; $3/2.

A breath of greenhouse air right downtown, the **Foellinger–Freimann Botanical Conservatory** (☎ 219-427-6440), 1100 S Calhoun St, has plants from around the world. The 'talking tree' exudes a rather wooden charm. It's open 10 am to 5 pm daily (from noon Sunday); $3/2.

Fort Wayne Children's Zoo More than 1200 critters roam their spaces at this 42-acre zoo (☎ 219-427-6800), 3411 Sherman Blvd. Among the highlights are Indonesian orangutans and a large Australian area with kangaroos, Tasmanian devils and a barrier reef aquarium, mate. The zoo is northwest of the center in Franke Park. It's open 9 am to 5 pm daily (check for closing times in winter); $5/3.

Special Events The Three Rivers Festival is held every August and features balloon races, parades, music, dancing, fireworks and more.

Places to Stay & Eat Exit No 111 off I-69 at the junction with US Hwy 27 and Hwy 3 is pockmarked with chain motels. The name says it all at the ***Economy Inn*** *(☎ 219-489-3588, 1401 W Washington Center Rd)* where basic rooms cost $33/43.

Business travelers like the ***Courtyard by Marriott*** *(☎ 219-489-1500, fax 219-489-3273, 1619 W Washington Center Rd)*, which has the usual amenities and an indoor pool. Rooms start at $69.

Downtown, with its concentration of sights, is a good place to stay. The ***Fort Wayne Hilton*** *(☎ 219-420-1100, fax 219-424-7775, 1020 S Calhoun St)* is linked up to the Grand Wayne Convention Center. Its rooms with the usual three-star amenities are quite reasonable at $49/59.

Ziffle's Ribs *(☎ 219-493-1222, 6340 E State Blvd)* is a long-time favorite with locals. Family-owned, it has top-notch baby back ribs and perfectly crispy fries for $12.

Getting There & Away Fort Wayne International Airport (☎ 219-747-4146) is served by the commuter carrier affiliates of all the major US airlines. The airport is 8 miles southwest of downtown on Hwy 1. Cab rides to the center cost $18.

Greyhound (☎ 219-423-9525), at 929 Lafayette St downtown, has services to the following places:

destination	cost	travel time	frequency
Chicago	$39	5 hours	2
Cleveland	$48	6 hours	2
Detroit	$39	4 hours	2
Indianapolis	$27	4 hours	2

Lakefront Lines (☎ 800-638-6338) runs on bus a day to and from Columbus, Ohio ($3 4 hours).

Chain O' Lakes State Park

About 20 miles northwest of Fort Wayn Chain O' Lakes State Park (☎ 219-63 2654), 2355 E 75S, Albion, 46701, include 11 lakes set on 2678 acres. The park is a pa adise for canoeists and small boaters: eig of the lakes are interconnected and th calm is preserved by the ban on any moto larger than small electric trolling motors.

The lakes here were once huge blocks ice left behind after the last ice age 10,0 years ago. The melt-waters produced kett lakes, as these 11 are called.

The park has concessions that rent boat canoes and paddleboats. There are 41 ***campsites***, ranging from those suitable f vehicles and with electrical hookups ($11) t some quiet and remote primitive tent sit ($5). There are also 18 simple ***family cabi*** available year-round for $55 a night. Th park is off Hwy 9 just north of US Hwy 33.

Auburn

• pop 9400

The highlight of this small farming town the **Auburn Cord Duesenberg Museu** (☎ 219-925-1444). Auburn was once th home of the Auburn Automobile Co, whic made these fabled luxury brands. Th company's 1930 Art Deco showroom hol the museum, which will interest anyone fa cinated by cars or design. The collectio comprises over 100 cars produced from th late 1800s through Auburn's peak years the 1920s and on to the present. It's ope 9 am to 5 pm daily and admission is $7/5.

Huntington

• pop 16,000

The highlight of this otherwise typic town – and one well worth a detour – is th **Dan Quayle Center & Museum** (☎ 219-35 6356), 815 Warren St, right in the town center. America's 44th vice preside Quayle grew up in town and his elementa school – where he presumably learned ho to spell 'potato' – is right across from th ıuseum, which is in a restored building. The xhibits span Quayle's life and there are lots f charming photos of the always genial ıan at the golf course, at dinners, on vaca-on, etc. There is a wall of media quotes bout Quayle as vice president, all along the nes of 'he's smarter than you think.' erhaps most telling is the placement of a hoto of the 1988 vice-presidential debate, here he was trounced by his opponent, enator Lloyd Benson: It's in the men's oom. The museum staff are a friendly lot – ne said, 'People come in all the time with rong feelings about Dan and we just nod ur heads and smile.'

The museum also has a large area evoted to the office of US vice president, ıcluding displays on all five VPs who came om Indiana. But you'll look in vain if you ant the source of the legendary quote bout the office, '[It's] not worth a pitcher of arm spit.' (Answer: John Nance Garner, 'S vice president 1933 to 1941.) The ıuseum is open 10 am to 4 pm Tuesday to aturday and 1 to 4 pm Sunday. There's a ıggested donation of $3.

OUTH TO INDIANAPOLIS

his is the heart of farm country. Sights not ertaining to corn, soy beans or hogs are w and scattered widely.

Iarion

pop 33,000

Vice place to raise a family' propaganda side, it's not hard to see why James Dean as so happy to leave this town for the bright ghts of Hollywood. Marion is a nice place, ıt unless you're a Dean fanatic, there's little draw you here. On the other hand, if the ar of films such as *East of Eden* and *Rebel 'ithout a Cause* is your passion, then you'll vel in the numerous locations here associ-ed with Dean's childhood.

The Marion/Grant County Convention & isitors' Bureau (☎ 765-668-5435, 800-662-74), 217 S Adams St, 46952, has a handy ap listing scores of Dean-related sights.

The **James Dean Birthsite** is now a field; e house that once stood at the corner of ourth and McClure Sts is dead, having been torn down. A sidewalk star marks the correct corner.

Neighboring Fairmont (population 3100) has more Dean sites. **Fairmont High School**, 203 E Washington St, is also dead, having closed in 1986. Dean attended here from 1945 to '49. Not far away is the **James Dean Gravesite** for the star who is, of course, dead, having been killed when he wrecked his car in California at age 24 on September 30, 1955. The site receives thousands of visitors annually and is in Park Cemetery, a half mile north of Hwy 26 on County Rd 150E.

The **James Dean Memorial Gallery** (☎ 765-948-3326) is an unintentional monument to all the people who have made money off Dean since his death. Rooms of memorabilia include collections of memorial plates, coffee mugs, chewing gum collectable cards and much, much more. One wonders what the enigmatic star would have made of all this. The gallery is open 10 am to 6 pm daily; $4.

Marion is 7 miles west of I-69, exit No 64 on Hwy 18. Fairmont is just west of I-69 exit No 59.

Kokomo

• pop 45,000

Known mostly for its stoplights, which each day frustrate thousands of motorists as they try to traverse the city on US Hwy 31, Kokomo boasts lots of fast-food places that provide respite from the traffic.

The **Automotive Heritage Museum** (☎ 765-454-9999) recalls the many automotive companies, such as Rambler, DeSoto, Muntz and Hupmobile, that once made cars in the Kokomo area. Long gone – because of industry consolidation as opposed to the traffic – the cars retain their appeal. This large museum in a failed discount store does a good job of telling the stories behind the cars. It's open 10 am to 5 pm daily and admission is $5.

The same building at 1500 N US Hwy 31 houses the Kokomo-Howard County Visitors' Bureau (☎ 765-457-6802, 800-837-0971), open 9 am to 5 pm weekdays.

Twelve miles north of town on US Hwy 31 is the **Grissom Air Museum**. Housed at a former US Air Force base, the open-air museum has an impressive collection of famous US military aircraft including the B-25, B-47, F-4 and massive EC-135. Run by volunteers, the museum is open 7 am t sunset daily and is free. A building on th grounds with smaller exhibits is open 10 a to 4 pm Tuesday to Saturday and is also fre

;outhern Indiana

ɔuth of Indianapolis, Indiana has much to ·ward the traveler with a few days to spend. ℓoomington and Columbus are perfect ·ils to the more typically charmless small merican towns and cities. There are vast ıral areas dotted with mountains and ılleys carved by ice age runoff, pock-arked by caves and hollows in the porous nestone. The hiking in these areas is excel-nt. Along the Ohio River you can trace e routes of the first European settlers, en-ɔuntering small towns little changed in ore than 100 years.

Highlights

- Hanging in Bloomington, a great college town
- Pondering the architecture in Columbus
- Driving the backroads of Hoosier National Forest
- Reliving Abe Lincoln's childhood at the Lincoln Boyhood National Monument
- Driving along the Ohio River

ℓLOOMINGTON

pop 61,000

classic American college town, Blooming-n has amenities and pleasures far greater an its population would suggest. Indiana niversity's 35,000 students add a vibrancy ıat is matched by the school's strong eater and cultural programs. The town ;elf is compact and walkable; you can ·rget your car while you're here, a delight itself. In recent years the city has garnered est place awards' from magazines as verse (and telling) as *Bicycling*, *Vegetarian ïmes* and *Psychology Today*. These acco-des merely prove what you'll discover, that ℓoomington should be at the top of your ;t of Indiana destinations.

·rientation

ıdiana University (IU) sprawls eastward ɔm Indiana Ave. Kirkwood Ave, which is ıed with student bars and restaurants, ıks the campus to the courthouse and ℓoomington's central Downtown Square. ıdianapolis is 50 miles north on Hwy 37. ɔlumbus is 38 miles east on scenic Hwy 46.

ıformation

ıe Monroe County Visitors' Center · 812-334-8900, 800-800-0037, fax 812-334-;44) is north of the town center at 2855 N ʼalnut St, which branches off Hwy 37 when

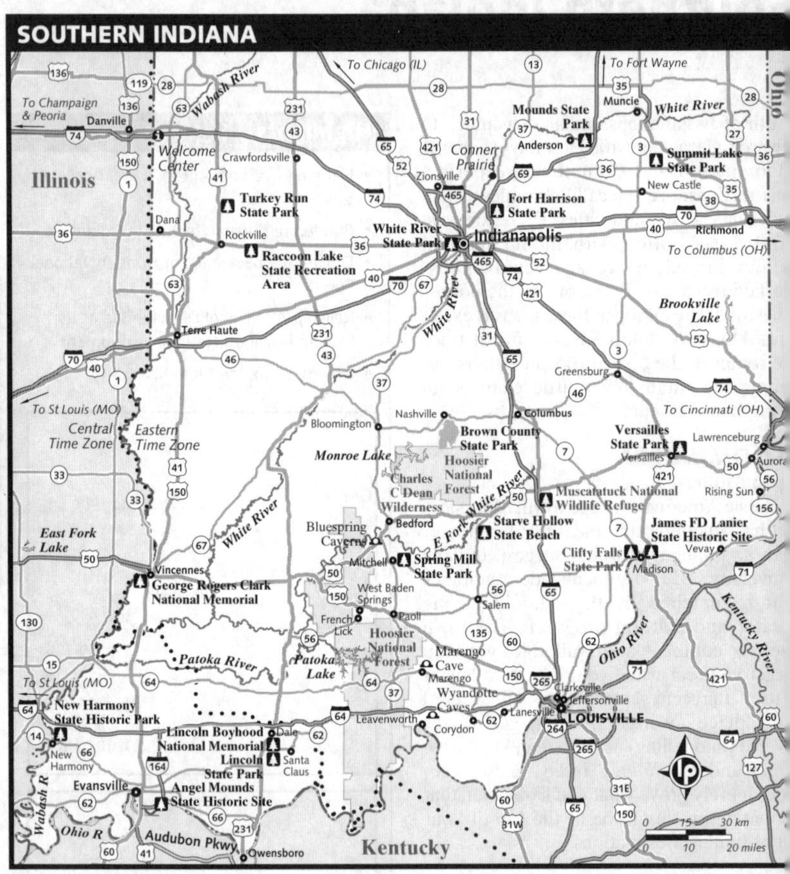

you're coming from the north. Open 8 am to 5 pm weekdays and 10 am to 4 pm Saturday April to October (10 am to 3 pm other times) as well as 10 am to 3 pm Sunday year-round, it's a well-stocked and helpful place with tons of information. It even has a free phone for local calls.

The IU Visitors' Information Center (☎ 812-856-4648) is across from the main entrance at the corner of Kirkwood and Indiana Aves. It offers campus tours and is open 10 am to 6 pm weekdays, 10 am to 5 pm Saturday and noon to 4 pm Sunday.

Both the alternative weekly *Bloomin ton Independent* and the top-notch *Indian Daily Student* have good entertainment an events listings.

The post office (☎ 812-334-4030), 206 4 St at Washington St, is open 8 am to 5:30 p weekdays.

The Monroe County Public Libra (☎ 812-349-3050), 303 E Kirkwood Ave, h free Internet access and is open 9 am 9 pm weekdays (until 6 pm Friday), fro 9 am to 5 pm Saturday and 1 to 5 p Sunday. The campus' Indiana Memori nion (☎ 812-855-4352) is a large facility at's open 24 hours daily and has free Inter-et access, ATMs, cheap fast food and more.

Because this is a university town, it ould be no surprise that there are nu-erous bookstores. Three ring Downtown quare: Book Corner (☎ 812-339-1522), 0 N Walnut St, is good for newspapers nd maps; Caveat Emptor (☎ 812-332-95), 112 N Walnut St, has lots of new and sed books in ramshackle piles; and oward's (☎ 812-336-7662), 111 W Kirk-ood Ave, has a large general collection uarded by cats. The IU Bookstore (☎ 812-55-4352), in the Indiana Memorial Union, as a large store with the expected aca-emic tomes as well as just about anything u could want in the school colors of red d white. One Stop Travel Shop (☎ 812-3-2772) is at 411 E 4th St.

Campus Laundry (☎ 812-339-0880), 202 7th St, is open 8 am to midnight daily.

Bloomington Hospital (☎ 812-336-6821), 1 W 2nd Ave, is a full-service regional spital.

Call ☎ 911 for police, fire or medical nergencies. For non-emergency police atters, call ☎ 812-339-4477. For Rape ictim Assistance, call ☎ 812-336-0846.

diana University

J (☎ 812-855-0850, 800-937-3448) is the ly Big 10 school to have a forest – **Dunn's oods** – right on the main quad. Most of e buildings are built with local limestone, hich gives the place a suitably sedate and ademic air. Although the campus occu-es a vast area, the main sights are in the re area between Indiana and Hwy 45/46. verything to see at IU is free.

The area around the woods is the **Old escent**, where you'll find the best of the iginal buildings. Using the Romanesque **udent Building** (1906) as a north point, me of the notable buildings going around e crescent in a clock-wise direction are: rreted **Maxwell Hall** (1894), **Kirkwood Hall** 901), **Lindley Hall** (1903), Gothic **Rawles ll** (1923), Art Deco **Bryan Hall** (1936) and othic **Franklin Hall** (1907). Pick up the excellent map and walking-tour brochure from the IU Visitors' Information Center.

IU Art Museum Designed by IM Pei, the angular structure foreshadows his later East Gallery at the National Gallery in Washington, DC. The museum (☎ 812-855-5445) is in the heart of the campus and is a 'teaching museum,' meaning that the collection gives a good overview of art through the ages. Beyond this, the museum concentrates on African art and pre-Columbian and 20th-century sculpture. It's open 10 am to 5 pm Wednesday to Saturday and from noon Sunday.

Mathers Museum Permanent and changing exhibits at the Mathers Museum (☎ 812-855-6873), 416 N Indiana Ave, highlight IU's strong anthropology department and give a good view of the history and culture of civilizations worldwide. It's open 9:30 am to 4:30 pm (from 1 pm weekends, closed Monday).

Lilly Library You can see works ranging from Shakespeare to Spiderman in the hushed viewing rooms of the Lilly Library (☎ 812-855-2452) in the center of campus. Among the historic works here are a Gutenberg bible, original James Whitcomb Riley manuscripts and the personal papers of Sylvia Plath. It's open 9 am to 6 pm weekdays (until 1 pm Saturday).

Monroe County Historical Society Museum

There's much more to Bloomington than the IU eggheads. The history museum (☎ 812-332-2517), 202 E 6th St, looks at the early European settlers, the limestone industry (see 'Cutters') and local ecology. Open 10 am to 4 pm (from 1 pm Sunday, closed Monday); free.

Monroe Lake

Indiana's largest lake is a reservoir 6 miles south of Bloomington. The Indiana Department of Resources (☎ 812-837-9546) operates several recreational facilities that offer

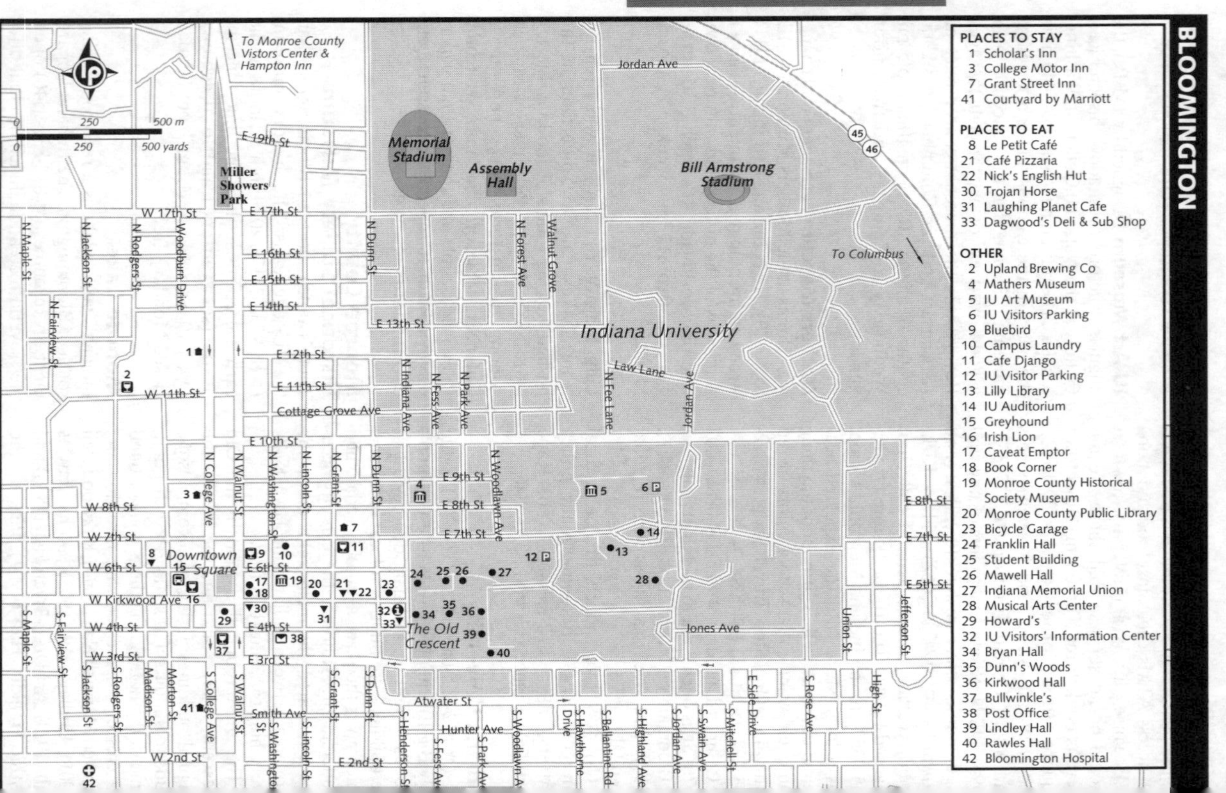
BLOOMINGTON
PLACES TO STAY
1 Scholar's Inn
3 College Motor Inn
7 Grant Street Inn
41 Courtyard by Marriott
PLACES TO EAT
8 Le Petit Café
21 Café Pizzaria
22 Nick's English Hut
30 Trojan Horse
31 Laughing Planet Cafe
33 Dagwood's Deli & Sub Shop
OTHER
2 Upland Brewing Co
4 Mathers Museum
5 IU Art Museum
6 IU Visitors Parking
9 Bluebird
10 Campus Laundry
11 Cafe Django
12 IU Visitor Parking
13 Lilly Library
14 IU Auditorium
15 Greyhound
16 Irish Lion
17 Caveat Emptor
18 Book Corner
19 Monroe County Historical Society Museum
20 Monroe County Public Library
23 Bicycle Garage
24 Franklin Hall
25 Student Building
26 Mawell Hall
27 Indiana Memorial Union
28 Musical Arts Center
29 Howard's
32 IU Visitors' Information Center
34 Bryan Hall
35 Dunn's Woods
36 Kirkwood Hall
37 Bullwinkle's
38 Post Office
39 Lindley Hall
40 Rawles Hall
42 Bloomington Hospital
Indiana University
Bill Armstrong Stadium
Memorial Stadium
Assembly Hall
Miller Showers Park
Downtown Square
The Old Crescent
To Columbus
To Monroe County Vistors Center & Hampton Inn
500 m
500 yards

›oating, fishing, hiking and various sports as vell as a nature center. Although not a ıatural feature, Monroe Lake has some ɪuiet coves away from the summer crowds.

Walking Tours

Besides the walking tours of IU, there are ight historic walking-tour brochures of Bloomington available for free from the Monroe County Visitors' Center.

The Little 500

Begun in 1950, the legendary Little 500 ☎ 812-855-9152) is the top collegiate cycling vent in the US. Each year in mid-April eams of male competitors ride 50 miles in 00 laps around a quarter-mile cinder track t Bill Armstrong Stadium; women ride 100 aps. Participants must be full-time IU students, but the race and related parties and pecial events draw people from all over the Midwest. The race was immortalized in the 979 Oscar-winner *Breaking Away*.

Places to Stay

Camping There is camping at more than 00 sites at ***Monroe Lake*** *(☎ 812-837-9546)*. The campgrounds are scattered around he lake and range from sites with full ookups ($11) to more primitive sites good or tents ($5).

B&Bs The ***Grant Street Inn*** *(☎ 812-334-2353, 00-328-4350, fax 812-328-4350, 310 N Grant t, www.grantstinn.com)* is ideally located ear the campus. The comfortable rooms, omplete with excellent breakfast, start at 65. Try to get one with a porch. ***Scholar's nn*** *(☎ 812-332-1892, 800-765-3466, fax 812-35-1490, 801 N College Ave)* has rooms in a estored 1892 brick mansion from $75. It lso has an excellent restaurant (see Places › Eat, below).

Motels & Hotels A relative bargain right owntown, the ***College Motor Inn*** *(☎ 812-36-6881, 509 N College Ave)* has very basic ooms for $30/40 single/double.

You can stay on campus at the ***IMU Hotel*** *(☎ 812-856-6381, 800-209-8145)* in the ndiana Memorial Union. The rooms are modern and comfortable and start at $72/82.

The ***Courtyard by Marriott*** *(☎ 812-335-8000, fax 812-336-9997, 310 S College Ave)* is downtown. It has a pool and rooms good for business travelers that start at $79.

Otherwise, there's a thicket of motels north of town near the junction of Walnut St and Hwy 45/46, but you're far away from the action in a suburban hell that negates the joys of Bloomington. If you must, you might try the ***Hampton Inn*** *(☎ 812-334-2100, fax 812-334-8433, 2100 N Walnut St)* which has all the standard chain charm and rooms from $61/73 single/double.

Places to Eat

A college town means lots of cheap college chow. Pizza and burritos dominate the low end, but there are also some excellent places for profs and for when parents come to town.

Things are funny, not lonely, at the ***Laughing Planet Café*** *(☎ 812-323-2233, 322 E Kirkwood Ave)*, and beyond the good cheer it has a long vegetarian menu of burritos ($3), salads and vegan specials. Downstairs there is a coffee bar and a big patio.

Dagwood's Deli & Sub Shop *(☎ 812-333-3000, 116 S Indiana Ave)* speaks for itself. Near the main IU entrance, it's open until 2 am.

The ***Trojan Horse*** *(☎ 812-332-1101, 100 E Kirkwood Ave)* holds no surprises except for the deep-fried dill pickles ($2). Otherwise the classic Greek menu has all the standards from gyros ($4) to moussaka ($12).

Nick's English Hut *(☎ 812-332-4040, 423 E Kirkwood Ave)* is popular before and after football and basketball games. It's a dark-wood institution known for its stromboli ($7), burgers ($6) and more. They sell beer by the pound rather than the glass.

Another long-standing favorite for game days is ***Café Pizzaria*** *(☎ 812-332-2111, 405 E Kirkwood Ave)* which has been serving thin-crust pies (large combo, $15) since 1953.

Got a date? Head to the vaguely romantic but very friendly ***Le Petit Café*** *(☎ 812-334-9747, 308 W 6th St)* where the changing French menu features classics like steak au poivre ($15).

Cutters

Scores of buildings around the world are faced with Indiana limestone, including New York City's Empire State Building, Chicago's Tribune Tower and many in Washington, DC. Famed for its ability to be easily worked while being resilient to the elements, the luminous gray stone is mined at quarries between Bloomington and Bedford.

A major part of the local economy, limestone quarrying has employed generations of people in the area. Many spent their younger days swimming in the deep pools formed at abandoned quarries. The 1979 movie *Breaking Away* looks at four local boys searching for life beyond limestone. Derisively called 'cutters' by snooty IU students, the boys turn to the Little 500 bicycle race as a means out.

Visit the **Land of Limestone** (☎ 812-275-7637), a small but worthwhile free exhibition inside the Oakland City University building, 405 I St. It's open 8 am to 5 pm daily.

Bloomington's best food is dished up at the ***Scholar's Inn*** *(☎ 812-332-1892, 801 N College Ave)*. Excellent gourmet fare made from local ingredients is served up in a casual setting. Expect to pay $20 or more per person. In summer, dine on the huge patio.

Entertainment

Bars & Clubs Kirkwood Ave is lined with bars. ***Nick's English Hut*** (see Places to Eat) is popular for a beer or three. Just past Downtown Square, ***Irish Lion*** *(☎ 812-336-9076, 212 W Kirkwood Ave)* has a classy wooden interior, an ambitious dinner menu and well-poured Guinness ($5 per half-yard). It's open until 2 am.

Excellent beer is on tap at the ***Upland Brewing Co*** *(☎ 812-336-2337, 350 W 11th St)*, a microbrewery with a limited menu that's open daily until 11 pm.

Inside a purple house, ***Café Django*** *(☎ 812-335-1297, 116 N Grant St)* has live jazz on weekend evenings. ***Bluebird*** *(☎ 812-336-2473, 216 N Walnut St)* has live ban almost nightly.

Bullwinkle's *(☎ 812-334-3232, 201 College Ave)* is a gay cocktail lounge wi frequent live music.

The ***IU Auditorium*** *(☎ 812-855-1103)* the major performing arts facility featurir big name touring productions and top-lev work from the school's performing ar departments.

The ***Musical Arts Center*** *(☎ 812-85 7433)* is home to performances by the I Ballet Theater and the IU Opera Theater.

Spectator Sports

You know a football program is troubl when it offers all sorts of discount tick schemes (☎ 812-855-4006). The IU Hoosie are perennial Big 10 doormats and studen and alumni will tell you that the team slogan: 'What it takes to win' should b rewritten as a question. Games are playe at Memorial Stadium and tickets cost rather high $26.

But if the football team comes up shor the men's basketball team doesn't. The I squad is a regular contender for the NCA title. Their games in Assembly Hall a always sold out (hope for scalpers), but you can get in you will be part of an almo manic atmosphere. Of course some of th mania comes from IU's notorious longtim coach Bobby Knight. Thanks to his chai throwing, hysterical outbursts, he's bee called 'bad boy', 'enfant terrible' and mor although 'jerk' will suffice.

Getting There & Away

Bloomington Shuttle Service (☎ 812-33 6004, 800-589-6004) has nine van shuttl daily to/from Indianapolis Internation Airport. Reservations are recommende and the cost is $19 one-way, $32 roundtrip

Greyhound (☎ 812-332-1522) has but single bus each afternoon to/from I dianapolis ($14) from its storefront at 409 Walnut St.

Getting Around

Your feet are your best way around dow town Bloomington and the IU campu

Cutters rule, frat boys don't, in film classic *Breaking Away.*

loomington Transit (☎ 812-336-7433) operates local buses) the surrounding eighborhoods. A ngle ride costs 75¢.

Competing with 5,000 students for arking isn't easy. IU as several visitors' arking lots (☎ 812-55-9848) that charge es. The most central) the campus is ehind the Indiana Memorial Union off th St. Another is ehind the IU Art Museum and is ccessible from 10th t. Away from the ampus, parking on loomington's streets isn't normally a roblem.

If you want to take advantage of Bloomigton's reputation for good bicycling, try e Bicycle Garage (☎ 812-339-3457), 507 E irkwood Ave, to see if they have any bikes r rent.

ASHVILLE

pop 900

ome 50 miles south of Indianapolis and a ere 18 miles east of Bloomington on Hwy 6, Nashville is the place to go for people oking for a 'nice Sunday drive.' As such, n an autumn weekend when the leaves are color, the sidewalks are filled with hordes f day-trippers choking down the ubiquious fudge while ducking in and out of the arrens of antique, curio and craft shops at are ably backed up by local artists' galries. Much of the retail action takes place n Main and Van Buren Sts.

The Brown County Convention and Visirs' Bureau (☎ 812-988-7303, 800-753-255), PO Box 840, 47448, will provide lots f local information as well as sell you a anvas shopping bag ($10) you can stuff ith curios and fudge. The **Brown County rt Guild** (☎ 812-988-6185) displays the work of local artists; many items are sized just right for your new canvas shopping bag. It's in the old Minor House on Van Buren St, one block south of Main St.

At night there's fun at numerous venues. The ***Brown County Playhouse*** *(☎ 812-988-2123, 70 S Van Buren St)*, stages performances by IU's drama department June through October. The ***Little Nashville Opry*** *(☎ 812-988-2235)*, on Hwy 46 just west of town, has live country music most weekends.

BROWN COUNTY STATE PARK

Indiana's largest park, popular Brown County State Park (☎ 812-988-6406), PO Box 608, Nashville, 47448, is just south of Nashville with entrances off of Hwy 46. There are many trails among the hills; one of the best is the **Ogle Hollow Nature Preserve Trail**. This rugged trail is only a mile in length but is a good way to see the rare yellowwood tree with its fragrant blossoms.

The park has more than 400 ***campsites*** with electricity ($11) and 24 tent-only sites ($7). The rustic ***Abe Martin Lodge*** *(☎ 812-988-4418, 877-265-6343)* has rooms from $55. Family cabins that sleep several people cost $89 a night and are available year-round, including in winter when they are popular with cross-country skiers.

COLUMBUS

• pop 32,000

For architecture buffs, this town at the confluence of three small rivers is a veritable theme park of design and buildings. More than 50 buildings showcase the work of notable architects, including Henry Weese, Richard Meier, IM Pei and Cesar Pelli. This enormous commitment to innovative design began in 1950 when the charitable arm of the main local employer, Cummins Engine Works, offered to pay the design fees for public buildings if distinguished architects were used. According to the *New York Times*, 'As groups of buildings by distinguished architects go, there is no place in the United States like Columbus, Indiana.'

The town is on US Hwy 31, just east of I-65, some 46 miles south of Indianapolis. As you enter town you can't miss the North Christian Church (1964) with its soaring spire designed by Eero Saarinen.

Greyhound's anemic twice-daily Indianapolis service ($13, 1 hour) stops at 406 Washington St downtown.

Information

The Columbus Visitors' Center (☎ 812-378-2622, 800-468-6564, fax 812-372-7348, www.columbus.in.us) should be your first stop in town. This is where tours depart from. It also has much local and regional information and displays on local buildings and history. The center is open 9 am to 5 pm Monday to Saturday year-round and 10 am to 4 pm Sunday March to November.

Viewpoint Books (☎ 812-378-9677) is locally owned and has an excellent selection of books about Columbus, on everything from architecture to humor. An especially good read is *The Faces Among Us*, a delightful look at local characters by Harry McCawley, an editor for *The Republic*, the local daily newspaper. The store is downtown in the Commons Mall at 3rd and Washington Sts.

Organized Tours

One- and two-hour bus tours leave from th visitors' center every day it is open. Thes are the best way to see the many buildin scattered throughout the town. The short tour ($7/3 adults/children) concentrates c the center. The longer tour ($10/5) cove the many buildings on the outskirts.

You can also pick up a driving-tour ma that allows you to cover most of the sites b car in about three hours. However yo won't have the benefit of expert comme tary provided by tour leaders.

After you've driven about town, tak time to wander the streets of the restore old downtown in the blocks around the vi itors' center. The **Bartholomew County Ve erans Memorial**, at Jackson and 2nd Sts, an especially moving example of its kin Excerpts from letters written home by loc people who later died in battle are carve into the stones. It's impossible not to be a fected by the words of Marvin Monroe, wh died in Vietnam in 1968.

Places to Stay & Eat

There's a passel of chain places out by th junction of I-65 and Hwy 46. The cheapest the ***Knights Inn*** *(☎ 812-378-3100, fax 81 378-3080, 101 Carrie Lane)* with basic room from $45/50.

Ruddick–Nugent House *(☎ 812-37 1354, 800-814-7478, fax 812-379-1357, 12 16th St)* is a B&B in an old mansion breathtaking proportions about a mile fro the center of town. Rooms start at $65.

Right downtown, the ***Columbus In*** *(☎ 812-378-4289, fax 812-378-4289, 445 5 St)* has 39 charming rooms ($90/100) in th former city hall.

Becker's Root Beer *(☎ 812-372-2466)*, the corner of Union and 25th Sts, is a original 1950s drive-in that makes its ow root beer (large $1.05). ***Zaharako's*** *(☎ 81 379-9329, 329 Washington St)* is an old-tim ice cream parlor that makes its own h fudge. It's open 10 am to 5 pm (close Sunday).

The ***Columbus Bar*** *(☎ 812-372-5252, 3 4th St)*, a classic bar and grill with a lo

ɪenu, makes quite a bit of its own food, in-
uding a pungent garlic coleslaw. The pork
ɪnderloin sandwiches ($5) are the size of
isbees.

ɅADISON

pop 12,000

ɪere's one of Indiana's gems. A major port early in the 19th century, Madison 'as Indiana's largest town in 1850. Railɔads and a decline in its other industries ɪeant that Madison went into hibernation ɔr the next century. This means that it is ne of the best-preserved towns in the ɪidwest. Block after very walkable block is lined with historic buildings; 133 blocks are on the National Register of Historic Places. Although increasing in popularity, Madison still is not overrun by tourist hordes and maintains a slightly somnolent air.

Madison is at the junction of US Hwy 421 and Hwy 56. It is almost 100 miles from Indianapolis and has no scheduled bus service.

The Madison Visitors' Center (☎ 812-265-2956, 800-559-2956, www.visitmadison.com), 301 E Main St, is open 9 am to 5 pm weekdays, 9 am to 3 pm Saturday and 10 am to 3 pm Sunday year-round.

Route of the Steamboats

LIBRARY OF CONGRESS

This 57-mile stretch of Hwy 56 follows a portion of the Ohio River that once was choked with the steamboat traffic between Cincinnati and the Mississippi River. Small towns such as Madison prospered through the mid-1800s when railroads drained the river of traffic and the port towns of affluence. For the past 150 years, this rural area has been the center of Indiana tobacco production; you'll see the plants with their huge leaves and the large curing barns where the leaves are hung out to dry.

Begin the drive near the Ohio border at **Aurora**. Somewhat restored, there are some good cafés and a floating bar. Numerous B&Bs dot the hillside. The Dearborn County Convention Visitors' & Tourism Bureau (☎ 812-537-0814, 800-322-8198, fax 812-537-0845, www.dearborncvb.org) can provide accommodations information.

Eight miles west, **Rising Sun** is just barely rising from a long sleep. The 1842 courthouse is the oldest in continuous use in the state.

Swiss people settled **Vevay** and it's been playing on this ever since. Once a wine region, the unfortunately bitter vintages (bad soil) have been long replaced by another vice, tobacco. The downtown is good for a wander but the ice cream shops have arrived, so beware. There are loads of B&Bs; the Switzerland County Welcome Center (☎ 812-427-3237, 800-435-5688), 209 Ferry St, has details. It's in the Hoosier Theater, a preserved 1837 hall with music on some Saturdays.

The drive concludes in Madison.

Historic Buildings

Madison's buildings represent a range of architectural styles; Federal, Italianate, Queen Anne and Greek Revival are just some of the styles represented. Many houses, stores and old factories are open for visits at various times, check with the visitors' center for details. Most tourable buildings – including those below – are open roughly 10 am to 4 pm daily.

Easily the star among many, the **James FD Lanier State Historic Site** (☎ 812-265-3526), 511 W First St, is a Greek Revival mansion (1844) with an octagonal cupola on the roof, broad views of the Ohio River and many examples of the finely detailed wrought ironwork found throughout the town.

The **Shrewsbury-Windle House** (☎ 812-265-4481), 301 W First St, is another fine Greek Revival mansion (1849). Look for the 3-story freestanding spiral staircase. Proving that all doctors' offices have out-of-date magazines, the **Dr William D Hutchings Office & Hospital** (☎ 812-265-2967), 120 W Third St, is a time capsule of Victorian medicine. Once the workplace of the namesake owner, it was closed after his death in 1903 and not reopened until 1967.

Clifty Falls State Park

Clifty Creek and its tributaries have formed a series of waterfalls totaling 381 feet as they cut through limestone and bedrock on their way down to the Ohio River. Within the park (☎ 812-265-1331), 1501 Green Rd, 47250, there are good views from the many bluffs but the best way to see the craggy rockfaces is along the 2-mile No 2 hiking trail, which follows the creek beds. The park is immediately west of Madison on Hwy 56.

Places to Stay & Eat

Clifty Falls State Park has ***camping***. Some of the 59 ($5) sites have electricity. The park also has ***Clifty Inn*** *(☎ 812-265-4135, 877-925-4389)* which has million-dollar views from its comfortable $59 rooms.

Most of Madison's visitors are day-trippers and the town has its own sedate charm after dark. ***Crescent House*** *(☎ 812-265-4251, 617 W Main St)* is typical of the many sma one- or two-room B&Bs along the tre shaded streets. The ***Historic Broadwa Tavern & Hotel*** *(☎ 812-273-6467, 31 Broadway)* was built in 1834. Simple roon start at $75 and they have a good restaura with steaks and seafood ($15) and friendly bar.

The ***Thomas Family Winery*** *(☎ 812-27 3755, 208 E Second St)* has an excellent de that sells picnic supplies to go with the good Riesling. On most Saturday nigh they have live music.

In Aurora, along the way from Columbu to Madison (see 'Route of the Steamboats' take a break at the ***Wild Duck Café***, a b moored on the river. A bit farther in Risir Sun, feel like a steamship magnate l staying at the riverfront ***Empire Hou*** *(☎ 812-438-4064, 800-313-1996, 114 S Fro St)* which was built in 1816 and has roon from $55.

LOUISVILLE AREA (KENTUCKY)

The world-famous Kentucky Derby Louisville's big annual event, on the fir Saturday in May. For the rest of the year, th Louisville area is a nice place to stop, a cu tural and industrial center with some class Americana.

There is a rather fun rivalry betwee Louisville on the Kentucky side of the riv and towns on the Indiana side of the Oh River, which call themselves 'the sunny sic of Louisville.' Clarksville and Jeffersonvil are small towns with good river views ar some decent accommodations options.

Louisville prospered after railroa arrived in 1850. Industry expanded after th Civil War, and Louisville competed wi Cincinnati as the prime port on the bu Ohio River.

Orientation & Information

Louisville's old downtown is a compact gr beside the Ohio River – actually, it's besic the I-64 freeway now. The main restaura and nightlife strip is Bardstown Rd, runnir southeast from downtown. A series pretty parks (laid out by Frederick La

)lmsted in the 1890s) encircle the city, long with an inner (I-264) and outer I-265) ring road. The helpful Convention nd Visitors' Bureau (☎ 502-582-3732, 800-92-5595, www.gotolouisville.com), 400 S st St, has maps and lots of local informa-.on. It's open 8:30 am to 5 pm weekdays, am to 4 pm Saturday and 11 am to 4 pm unday.

The George Rogers Clark Memorial ridge is the local link between Jeffersonille and downtown Louisville. The very elpful Southern Indiana Visitors' Center ☎ 812-280-5566, www.sunnysideoflouisville org) is painted a sunny shade of yellow and open 9 am to 6 pm daily (from noon unday). It is at 305 Southern Indiana Ave etween Exit 0 on I-65 and the Clark ridge.

Kentucky is on Eastern Time, so from lovember to March it will be one hour ter than in Indiana.

Kentucky Facts

Kentucky is a wonderful combination of the American South, North, East and West. It combines mountains and forests with some of the most beautifully manicured rural landscapes imaginable.

Nickname: Bluegrass State

Population: 3,910,000 (24th largest state)

Area: 40,411 sq miles (37th)

Admitted to Union: June 1, 1792 (15th)

Information The Kentucky Department of Tourism (☎ 800-225-8747, www.tourky.com), PO Box 2011, Frankfort KY, 40602, has tourist information.

Taxes Statewide sales tax is 6%. In Louisville there is a 12% lodging tax.

Road Rules Seat belts are required for all people in the car and child seats for kids under 40 inches tall. Motorcyclists are required to wear helmets.

'hings to See & Do

)n Kentucky Derby day, **Churchill Downs** acetrack, 3 miles south of downtown, is the ıost important place in the country. The urprisingly interesting **Kentucky Derby Auseum** (☎ 502-637-7097), at Gate 1 on :entral Ave, has displays on horses, jockeys nd mint juleps, a 360° audiovisual on the ace, and a tour of the facilities. It's open am to 5 pm daily; $6/2 adults/children. For etails of spring and fall race meetings, as vell as Derby Week events, call ☎ 502-636-400. On Derby Day, $30 gets you into the 'addock party scene if you arrive by 6 am, ut you won't see the race. For reserved eats, you have to book years ahead.

The handsome, neoclassical **Speed Art Auseum** (☎ 502-634-2700), 2035 S 3rd St, has good selection of art and is open 10:30 am ɔ 4 pm daily (from noon Sunday); free.

It's hard to miss the **Louisville Slugger Auseum** (☎ 502-588-7228), 800 W Main St – ɔok for the 120-foot baseball bat leaning gainst the building. The manufacturing lant here makes regulation wooden baseall bats for all major and minor league layers. Entry ($5/3) includes exhibits, a plant tour and a collection of baseball memorabilia. It's open 9 am to 5 pm (closed Sunday).

Across the river in Indiana, the **Falls of the Ohio State Park** (☎ 812-280-9970), 201 W Riverside Drive in Clarksville, is one of the largest exposed fossil beds in the world. There are more than 600 species encased in limestone and there is an impressive visitors' center, open 9 am to 5 pm daily (from 1 pm Sunday); $2/1. The **Howard Steamboat Museum** (☎ 812-283-3728), 1101 E Market St, has models and artifacts of the riverboat era. It's open 10 am to 3 pm (closed Monday) and costs $4/2.

Organized Tours

Joe & Mike's Pretty Good Tours (☎ 502-459-1247) are fun 3-hour adventures that cost $20. *Belle of Louisville* (☎ 502-574-2355), a 1914-era sternwheeler, offers sightseeing cruises from the end of 4th Ave. Itineraries vary and tickets are from $10.

Places to Stay

In Clarksville, ***Louisville Metro KOA*** *(☎ 812-282-4474, 800-562-4771, 900 Marriott Drive)* has tent/RV sites for $18/24 and some cabins. ***Emily Boone Guest Home*** *(☎ 502-585-3430, 102 Pope St)*, offers an idiosyncratic option, especially for bicycling tourists. It's a shared home and it's essential to call first ($10 per person, plus chore).

Downtown accommodations are pricey. ***Travelodge*** *(☎ 502-583-2629, fax 583-2629, 401 S 2nd St)* is nothing special at $65 a double. Nicer is ***Club Hotel by Doubletree*** *(☎ 502-585-2200, fax 502-584-5657, 101 E Jefferson St)*, with an indoor pool and business traveler facilities. Rooms start at $89.

Cheaper options are across the river in Indiana. The ***Econo Lodge*** *(☎ 812-288-6661, fax 812-288-5923, 460 Auburn Ave)* is one of several cheap chain properties around the junction of I-65 and Hwy 131 in Clarksville. The ***Ramada Inn*** *(☎ 812-284-6711, fax 812-283-3686, 700 W Riverside Drive, Jeffersonville)* is not itself pretty, but has pretty views of the river. Rooms are $72/82 single/double.

Places to Eat

Downtown eateries are mainly for office workers' lunches. ***Luigi's Pizzeria*** *(☎ 502-589-0005, 702 W Main St)* is a good choice for pizza and pasta in the old part of town. One of the best restaurants is ***Timothy's*** *(☎ 502-561-0880, 826 E Broadway)* with top-notch steaks and seafood from around $15.

Schimpff's Confectionery *(☎ 812-283-8367, 347 Spring St)* is a fine old soda fountain and sweets shop in historic downtown Jeffersonville. It's open 10 am to 5 pm weekdays and until 3 pm Saturday. A few blocks away, ***Kingfish Restaurant*** *(☎ 812-284-3474, 601 W Riverside Drive)* is part of a good local chain of fish restaurants and has great views.

Entertainment

The free weekly *Leo* lists gigs and entertainment. The prime performance venue, ***Kentucky Center for the Arts*** *(☎ 502-562-0100, 5 Riverfront Plaza)*, has theater, classical and popular music performances and a good sculpture collection. The 1928 ***Palace Theater*** *(☎ 502-583-455, 625 4th Ave)*, is great ornate venue for theater and concert

O'Malley's Corner *(☎ 502-589-3866*, downtown at 2nd and Liberty, offers sep rate spaces for country, rock, disco and th piano bar ($3). ***The Connection*** *(☎ 502-58 5752, 130 Floyd St)* is a popular mixed ga dance club.

Getting There & Around

Louisville International Airport (☎ 502-36 6524), 5 miles south of town on I-65, ha good domestic connections. Get there b cab ($14) or local bus No 2.

The Greyhound station (☎ 502-58 3331), 720 W Muhammad Ali Blvd, just we of downtown, is a hub for service. Destin tions include:

destination	cost	travel time	frequen
Chicago	$38	6 hours	7
St Louis	$31	6 hours	6
Indianapolis	$17	2 hours	8
Cincinnati	$20	2 hours	13

Local buses are run by TARC (☎ 502-58 1234), based at the Union Station depo 1000 W Broadway. Fares are $1 and a dow town shuttle service is free. Bus No 73 link downtown Louisville with Jeffersonville.

HOOSIER NATIONAL FOREST

Covering more than 195,000 acres in tw distinct parts, Hoosier National Forest dom inates much of the hilly central part southern Indiana. It includes develope recreation parks as well as remote wilde ness areas.

Most of the forest is second growth th has thrived since the federal governme began buying up scores of failed pione farms early in the 20th century. One of th few places left where you can see the eno mous walnut, oak, beech and other tre that once dominated this part of the US is the **Pioneer Mothers Memorial Forest**, small 88-acre plot that avoided the ma logging elsewhere. Many of the trees a hundreds of years old and their size – som are more than four feet in diameter – w amaze anyone who is used to only seeing relatively young second-growth trees. Look for a small parking area a mile south of Paoli on Hwy 37.

Information

The forest headquarters (☎ 812-275-5987) is right off Hwy 37 at 811 Constitution Ave in Bedford. Open 8 am to 4:30 pm weekdays, the office has reams of park information and the staff help you make sense of these huge tracts of land. There is also a rack in the parking lot filled with general information when the office is closed.

For reservations at the campgrounds, call the National Forest Service at ☎ 800-280-2267.

Hiking

There are 239 miles of trails throughout the forest. A memorable time for a hike is in the fall when the rolling hills are painted a riot of reds, oranges and browns.

At the **Hemlock Cliffs Recreation Area**, the grounds are deeply shaded by hemlock trees. A 2-mile loop trail follows a deep limestone canyon back to a waterfall and a prehistoric rock shelter. To reach the parking lot and entrance, follow Hwy 37 for 3 miles north from I-64 then turn west on a small county road and follow signs.

Lakes Indian & Celina

A longer and more bucolic trail is also off Hwy 37, 2 miles south of St Croix and I-64.

INDIANA

Southern Indiana Scenic Drives

The rolling hills of southern Indiana hold some lovely drives on curvy two-laners. Though not crowded most of the year, when the leaves turn colors you'll find you have company.

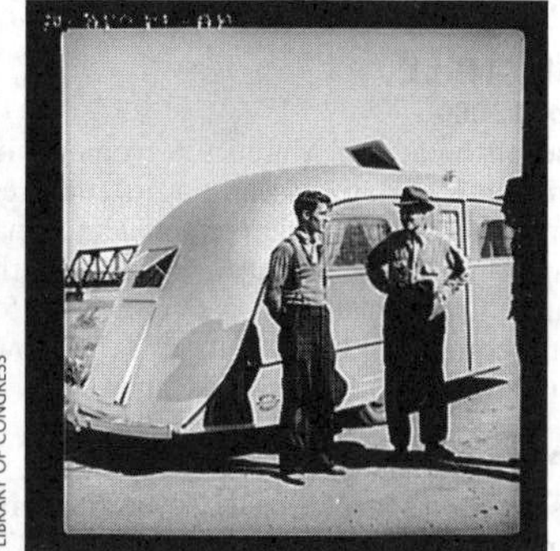

LIBRARY OF CONGRESS

US Hwy 421 – Greensburg to Versailles It's 28 miles from Greensburg, with its tree-topped courthouse and square with delightful retail artifacts, to Versailles. Reward yourself with a stop at Versailles State Park (☎ 812-689-6424) for camping, hiking and swimming.

Hwy 7 – Columbus to Madison Passing through farmlands, you get an idea of the hopeful vistas that greeted the first Europeans. At North Vernon take a 10-mile detour west on US Hwy 50 to Muscatatuck National Wildlife Refuge (☎ 812-522-4352), with its many nature trails amid the wetlands and woods.

Hwy 135 – Nashville to Corydon Driving the full 120-mile winding length of this small road can easily take an entire day. North of Story, the vistas could be postcard cliché's but they're real. Starve Hollow State Beach (☎ 812-358-3464), near Vallonia, has camping and a large reservoir.

Hwy 62 – Lanesville to Dale Glaciers from the last ice age never reached this far south but their runoff waters did, leaving behind carved canyons, steep hills and the Swiss cheese of caves through the soft limestone. Corydon is a good stop and Leavenworth has a sweeping view of a horseshoe curve on the Ohio River.

The 12-mile loop trail passes Lakes Indian and Celina, which are good for fishing and boating. There are special interpretive nature trails as well.

There are more than 63 campsites (☎ 812-547-7051), some with connections and others quite rural, that start at $9 a night and are open from mid-April to December.

Charles C Dean Wilderness

This is Indiana's only federally designated wilderness area. Covering 13,000 acres in an area equidistant from Bloomington and Bedford, the area is one of the few places in the forest that is far enough away from developed areas to be truly quiet. Scores of trails wind through the rolling hills, but the best marked is the 43-mile **Hickory Ridge Trail**, popular with both hikers and horse riders.

There is a free primitive campground with pit toilets near the center of the wilderness area. Small roads heading north from Norman Station off Hwy 58 lead into the forest and go close to the campground. Follow the signs and inquire locally.

FRENCH LICK

• pop 2100

Evocatively named, French Lick is really named after a French trading post and salt lick that stood in the area prior to the town's founding in 1811. Locals found some fortune beginning in the mid-1800s by marketing the sulphery water from its springs. Fame came from toothsome local boy Larry Bird, who made a fortune playing basketball despite detractors who regularly yelled, 'Hick from French Lick!' wherever he played.

The town makes a good base for exploring the Hoosier National Forest and is dominated by two enormous hotels, relics of the early 1900s when French Lick was a popular summer resort for the upper classes.

The **West Baden Springs Hotel** (☎ 317-639-4534) has been miraculously restored but is not actually open for lodgers. However, you can tour the building, with what was once the world's largest domed atrium, and its lovely grounds. Tours are given at 10 am to 3 pm daily April to November and at 1 pm Wednesday to Sunday the rest of the year. They cost $10, but don't feel you need to stick with the well-meaning but pedantic guides once you're on the grounds. The hotel is just off Hwy 56 in West Baden Springs, which abuts French Lick.

The ***French Lick Springs Resort*** *(☎ 812-936-9300, 800-457-4042, www.frenchlick.com)* is the still-operating huge old resort. Right out of *The Shining*, hundreds of rooms sprawl through the rambling old buildings that feature several bars and restaurants, pools and a health spa. Located in the center of town, often you can snag a room at the resort in the off-season for the bargain rate of $59 a night.

Out in front of the resort along Hwy 59 the **Indiana Railway Museum** (☎ 812-936-2405) has a nice selection of old trains around the beautiful old limestone railroad station; free. On weekends they offer 20-mile train rides into the beautiful surrounding mountains for $8/4 adults/children.

MITCHELL

• pop 3000

The birthplace of Mercury astronaut Gus Grissom is as down-to-earth as its late, great famous son. A touching **memorial** and small display of Grissom's artifacts are in the Mitchell Municipal Building (☎ 812-849-2151) at the corner of 6th and College Sts. The town is at the crossroads of Hwys 37 and 60.

SPRING MILL STATE PARK

Just east of Mitchell on Hwy 60, this large park (☎ 812-849-4129), PO Box 376, Mitchell, 47446, features caves, a restored pioneer village, a lake, a nature center and more. You can easily spend a day here; it's worth making a special effort to see **Donaldson Woods**, another nicely preserved remnant of old-growth forest. A nature trail winds around numerous sinkholes, the result of this porous limestone land.

A park museum to Gus Grissom features a Gemini spacecraft but suffers from obvious neglect. There's ***camping*** and a nice rustic ***inn*** (☎ 812-849-4081) where rooms cost from $49 to $89 per night.

CAVES

There are more than 700 caves under the porous limestone of southern Indiana. Some are several miles in length and feature dramatic stalactites and stalagmites that grow less than an inch every 100 years. Many of the caves are easily visited.

Bluespring Caverns Park

Water from the White River has been hollowing out caverns at the Bluespring Caverns Park (☎ 812-279-9471) for centuries. In 1940, nature pulled the plug on a pond and the water drained away underground, leaving the entrance to these caves that's used today. Much of the cave tour is aboard a boat equipped with lights. The caverns are open 9 am to 5 pm daily May to November; $9. From Bedford, go south on US Hwy 50 for 5 miles and look for the signs.

Marengo Cave

Wildly popular in summer, Marengo Cave is a marvel of flowing stone forms on an enormous scale that surely would have charmed the Spanish architect Antoni Gaudi. There is a range of tours from those suitable for all ages to actual spelunking expeditions where you can get good and dirty while wearing a neat helmet with a light. The park is open 9 am to 5 pm daily (until 6 pm in June to August) and tour prices start at $10/5. It's just north of Marengo on Hwy 64.

Marengo is also the home for canoe trips on the **Blue River**, a spring-fed stream that passes many wild areas and numerous caves as it flows from Fredricksburg to the Ohio River. Cave Country Canoes (☎ 812-365-2705) offers a range of canoe and kayak tours of the river ranging from two hours to two days.

Wyandotte Caves

Run by the state, the Wyandotte Caves (☎ 812-738-2782) are part of the **Wyandotte Woods State Recreation Area** and are certainly the least commercialized of the major caves open to the public. The caves cover many miles of large and small chambers. Tours last from 30 minutes ($4/2) to a six-hour endurance test ($12, no children under 12 allowed). The caves are 5 miles east of Leavenworth on Hwy 62.

CORYDON

• pop 2700

The archetypal Indiana small town, Corydon has a historic main square and is on scenic Hwy 62, which is especially pretty to the east. The Corydon Chamber of Commerce (☎ 812-738-2137, 888-738-2137), 310 Elm St, is open erratic hours but has lots of local and regional information.

The **Corydon Capitol State Historic Site** (☎ 812-738-4890) is right on the main square in the shadow of the imposing courthouse. Built of local blue limestone, the small building was the capitol until 1825. It's open 9 am to 5 pm (from noon Sunday, closed Monday); free.

Corydon has numerous places to stay. There's a thicket of modern motels at exit 105 on I-64 where Hwy 135 crosses. These include the ***Hampton Inn*** *(☎ 812-738-6688, fax 812-738-6699, 2455 Landmark Ave NE)* with nice rooms from $60. Much more atmospheric are the ***High Ridge Log Cabins*** *(☎ 812-732-8802)*, 12 miles south of Corydon off Hwy 135. Each all-wood cabin goes for $58 a night.

LINCOLN SITES

Abraham Lincoln's family moved to Indiana from Kentucky in the dead of winter 1816 when he was 7. Here he spent the next 14 years of his life, a time he later recalled as 'pretty pinching times.'

The **Lincoln Boyhood National Memorial** (☎ 812-937-4541) is a fascinating and not very visited place administered by the National Park Service. There is an excellent visitors' center with artifacts from Lincoln's young life. The spot where the Lincolns had their farm has been re-created with log buildings and crops. From May to September, specialists demonstrate the everyday techniques pioneer families used to survive, a dicey proposition at best. Nearby is the grave for Lincoln's mother Nancy, who died in 1818. His sister Sarah is buried a short distance away.

The site is open 8 am to 5 pm daily; $2. It is 2 miles east of US Hwy 231 and Hwy 62 off Hwy 162.

Right near the entrance to the memorial, **Lincoln State Park** (☎ 812-937-4710), PO Box 216, Lincoln City, 47552, has additional sites related to Lincoln that include the remains of the mill where he would sit, reading voraciously, while the family's thin crops were ground into wheat. A musical play, *Young Abe Lincoln*, has been running for enough years to bring tears to the eyes of a Broadway producer. The show (☎ 812-937-4493, 800-346-4665) is presented nightly in an outdoor amphitheater mid-June to September. The park also has ***camping***. Sites with electricity cost $11, tent sites cost $5. There are 10 simple ***cabins*** for $33 a night. Entrance to the park is $2.

EVANSVILLE

• pop 127,000

Right on the Ohio River, Evansville has done a good job of beautifying its downtown river walk. The town grew rich during the steamboat era and lately Evansville has been busily restoring its extensive architectural heritage.

Orientation & Information

Evansville is at the end of I-164, a spur that runs 20 miles south from I-64. It is also the junction of Hwy 66 that runs west to New Harmony and Illinois and scenic Hwy 62 which runs east to the Lincoln sites.

The Evansville Convention & Visitors' Bureau (☎ 812-421-2200, fax 812- 421-2207, 800-433-3025, www.evansvillecvb.org) is located in the historic Pagoda building on the river and is open 10 am to 7 pm daily.

Historic Buildings

The visitors' bureau has a good range of free publications on Evansville's historic neighborhoods and buildings. The simply titled *Historic Evansville* is filled with good walking tours. Among the buildings not to miss are the **Old Vandenburgh County Courthouse** at Fourth and Vine Sts, the **Willard Library** at 21 First St and the **Evansville Municipal Market** at First Ave an Lloyd Expressway.

The **Reitz Home Museum** (☎ 812-426 1871), 224 SE First St, is an 1871 Frenc Second Empire mansion open for tour 11 am to 3:30 pm (closed Monday); $5.

Angel Mounds

About 1000 to 3000 people lived on thi fertile site for more than 250 years begin ning around 900 AD. Archeologists have re constructed part of the village and there i an excellent new visitors' center (☎ 812-853 3956) and nature trails. This state histori site is open 9 am to 5 pm Tuesday to Satur day and from noon Sunday. The entire plac is closed January and February. Admissio is by donation. East from Evansville, tak the Covert Ave/Hwy 662 exit off I-164 an follow the signs.

Places to Stay & Eat

The ***Comfort Inn*** *(☎ 812-477-2211, 5006 Morgan Ave/Hwy 62)* has simple room near the center from $59. The ***Starkey In*** *(☎ 812-425-7264, 800-580-0305, fax 812-425 7333, 214 SE First St, www.starkeyinn.com* is right downtown near the river. The re stored 1850 mansion has five comfortabl rooms from $85.

Located in an 1890 building, ***Gers Bavarian Haus*** *(☎ 812-424-1220, 2100 W Franklin St)* is in a historic and walkabl old neighborhood. The German cuisine i hearty and you get piles of tasty chow fo less than $10. Just up the street, ***Sportsman's Billiards & Grille*** *(☎ 812-422-0801 2315 W Franklin St)* is a friendly place wit sidewalk tables, a fine beer selection an terrific cheeseburgers for $3. It's ope until 3 am.

The best place to sample (or stomach the local specialty of, yes, brain sandwiche is 10 miles west of town at the ***Dogtow Tavern*** *(☎ 812-423-0808)*. You can debate as locals do – whether pork or beef brain are best at this roadhouse on Old Hender son Rd. There are more familiar choices o the menu, but everyone says the smar choice is the brains ($5).

·etting There & Away

·vansville Regional Airport (☎ 812-421-400) has commuter airline links to Chicago ·nd St Louis.

Greyhound (☎ 812-425-0309) has one ·us a day to Indianapolis ($30, 3 hours).

The Metropolitan Evansville Transit ·ystem (METS; ☎ 812-423-4856) runs local ·uses that cover the city. The fare is 75¢.

·EW HARMONY

pop 800

·n the Wabash River, south of I-64, charm-·ng New Harmony is the site of two early ·ommunal-living experiments and well ·orth a visit. In the early 19th century, a ·erman Christian sect, the Harmonists, de-·eloped a sophisticated town here while ·waiting the Second Coming. Later the land ·as acquired by the British utopian, Robert ·wen. Even today the residents all seem to ·ear tranquil smiles.

Learn more at the free Athenaeum Visi-·ors' Center (☎ 812-682-4474), open 9 am to · pm daily April to October and much ·horter hours other times. New Harmony ·etains an air of contemplation, if not other-·orldliness, which you can experience at its ·ewer sites, such as the almost Far Eastern, ·emple-like Church With No Roof and the ·abyrinth, a sort of maze symbolizing the ·pirit's quest. Walking tours of the lovely old ·own are given when the Athenaeum is ·pen; tours start at $6.

There is camping at ***Harmonie State ·ark*** *(☎ 812-682-4821)*, three miles south of ·own off Hwy 69. Fully equipped sites are $11. The ***New Harmony Inn*** *(☎ 812-682-4491)* is in the center and has rooms from $75/85.

VINCENNES

• pop 20,000

Once a French colonial fort, Vincennes sits astride the Wabash River at the junction of US Hwys 41, 50 and 151. A typical small Indiana town, its claim to fame happened well over 200 years ago.

In 1779, a lieutenant colonel in the American revolutionary army, George Rogers Clark, was holed up for the winter on the Mississippi River with 170 men in what was then called the Illinois Country. Word reached him that most of the British army in the west was spending the winter at the old French fort in Vincennes. Leading his men on a miserable journey across frozen swamps, Clark arrived at the fort on February 23. Needless to say, the British – who had expected to spend their months trying to stay warm and keep the bugs out of their biscuits – were surprised and after a short confrontation, surrendered.

This victory had far-reaching implications for the young USA: It doubled its size by gaining the entire Great Lakes region. This gave the US the farmlands needed to feed its fast-growing population.

The National Park Service oversees the **George Rogers Clark National Historical Park**, a small museum (☎ 812-882-1776) and a rather showy memorial building (1933) that has paintings and a good audio tour. The site is open 9 am to 5 pm daily; $2.

Ohio

Facts about Ohio

As a major industrial state, Ohio is associated with both the rise and fall of US manufacturing and with the resurgence and renewal of many Rust Belt cities. Those driving across the Buckeye State (a buckeye is a type of horse chestnut) may be surprised to find that much of it – a *lot* of it – is also farmland. Cleveland's Rock & Roll Hall of Fame & Museum is a major attraction, as are, to a lesser degree, the summer resorts and fun spots on the Erie lakeshore. The world's largest concentration of Amish is in three of Ohio's southeastern counties.

The classic Depression-era Works Progress Administration's *Ohio Guide* dubbed Ohio the 'Barometer State' – a non-pejorative reflecting the state's grand cross-section of US culture, so much so that national marketers use certain Ohio communities as test areas. This ability to feel the national pulse is perhaps why seven Ohioans have resided in the White House.

Ohio Facts

Nickname Buckeye State

Population 11,016,710 (7th largest)

Area 41,222 sq miles (35th largest)

Admitted to Union February 19, 1803 (17th state)

Road Information The Ohio Highway Patrol has an Emergency Hotline (☎ 800-525-5555) to report car accidents, breakdowns, and especially, drunk drivers. For road conditions, call ☎ 888-264-7623 or view the Department of Public Safety's Web site (www.dot.state.oh.us) for updates.

Road Rules Motorcyclists under age 18 must wear a motorcycle helmet. Radar detectors are permitted in private vehicles. Seat belts are mandatory for both driver and front-seat passenger; child restraints are required for children under age four or less than 40lb.

Taxes State sales tax is 5.5%. Communities have the option of tacking on a hotel room tax, usually between 5% and 7% more, along with local sales tax. Few neglect to.

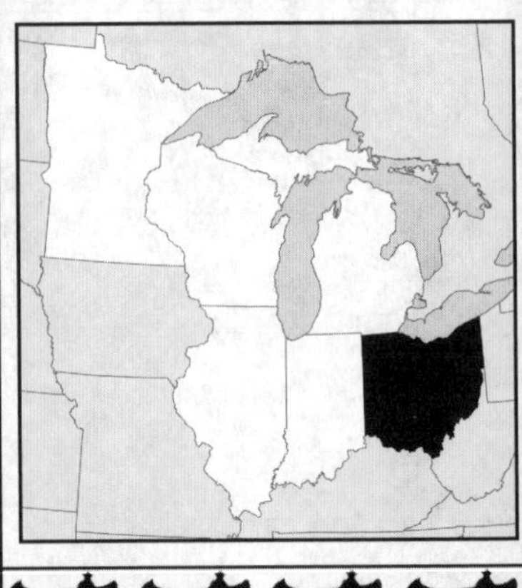

History

After the Revolutionary War opened the way for westward expansion, Ohio was one of the first areas to be settled; the town of Marietta, along the Ohio River bordering West Virginia, was established in 1788. After several clashes, the local Indians were decisively beaten at the 1794 Battle of Fallen Timbers. A growing number of immigrants – particularly Germans, but also Irish and Swiss – arrived starting in the early 19th century.

In 1832, the completion of the Erie–Ohio Canal between Lake Erie and the Ohio River gave the state excellent transport connections that, combined with abundant local resources, enabled a number of its cities to become early centers of industry. By 1850, Ohio had the third-largest population in the country.

Many soldiers from Ohio fought in the Civil War, including Generals Sherman and Grant, though many in the state's south pledged allegiance to the Confederacy. Ohio's industry grew as part of the Union war machine, and after the war, many blacks from the South came to cities such as Cincinnati, Cleveland and Toledo.

Home to huge industrial plants, Ohio became a center for organized labor and it experienced several significant strikes and disputes. Growth in the 20th century was well below the national average, as the state bore the brunt of big recessions in the 1930s and 1970s. The '90s brought more diversity and prosperity to Ohio's cities, and the massive steel industry of the north has recovered.

Geography

Geographically, Ohio is a bit of everything. In the north and west it's classic Great Lakes Midwestern (read: 'farms with a Great Lakes view'), bordered by Lake Erie and portions of Michigan and Indiana. However, as the map rolls to the east the beginnings of the hills of West Virginia indicate Appalachia. To the south, the epic 400-mile-plus-long Ohio River border is the gateway to the South.

Northern Ohio is dominated by the presence of Lake Erie, which can act as a moderating influence on the region's weather. Commonly heard on weather broadcasts is 'cooler/warmer near the lake.' Lake effect snowfall is common for littoral communities, while inland towns get none at all.

National Parks & Protected Areas

Ohio has an extensive system of 74 nature preserves to protect rare or endangered species of flora and fauna. These offer an excellent chance to experience ecosystems that existed prior to large-scale human occupation and that are now being restored. The Department of Natural Resources Division of Natural Areas and Preserves (☎ 614-265-6561) publishes a thorough, helpful glossy brochure listing each preserve and detailing visitor facilities, landscape types and notable features. (Most state visitor centers should have the brochure.) This is a good resource for birders. If you're really keen on exploring, you can get a wire-bound 111-page guidebook ($15) to the system. Write to the division at 1889 Fountain Square Court, Columbus, OH 43224.

Ohio gets kudos for its state parks and forests system; there are no entrance fees. Most of the 72 parks and 19 forests also have good campgrounds; these range in price from $8 to $20. At selected locations you can rent camping equipment, RVs, cottages, houseboats or tepees. Eight state parks even have resort lodges with posh amenities. For Rent-A-Camp sites, reservations are taken for up to a year in advance, beginning on March 1 the year of travel. The Ohio State Parks Information Center can be reached via the Department of Natural Resources (☎ 614-265-6561), 1952 Belcher Drive, Columbus, OH 43224. Check out the Web site at www.dnr.state.oh.us.

The state park system has an extensive network of hiking trails, the majority of which can be tackled as day hikes. Two major backpacking trails are maintained in the state forest system: Shawnee (60 miles) and Zaleski (23 miles). The Buckeye Trail is the state's jewel. It originally linked Mentor Headlands Beach on Lake Erie to Eden Park in Cincinnati. It has since been extended to all four corners of the state, topping out at 1200 miles. For more information, contact the Buckeye Trail Association (☎ 614-451-4233), PO Box 254, Worthington, OH 43085, or check out www.buckeyetrail.org.

With Lake Erie to the north and the mighty Ohio River along the entire southern border, not to mention hundreds of rivers and lakes in the middle, it's not surprising that water sports are a major draw in Ohio. You can do pretty much anything at all on Lake Erie *except* use a canoe (it's too dangerous). Near the Lake Erie Islands region, the walleye fishing is world famous. Charter boats leave from many ports along the lakefront. The Ohio Division of Wildlife (☎ 614-265-6300) produces an excellent newsletter on Ohio fishing, especially on Lake Erie. Inland, canoeing is sublime in the Mohican State Park area around Loudonville, northeast of Columbus. Rentals and tours are

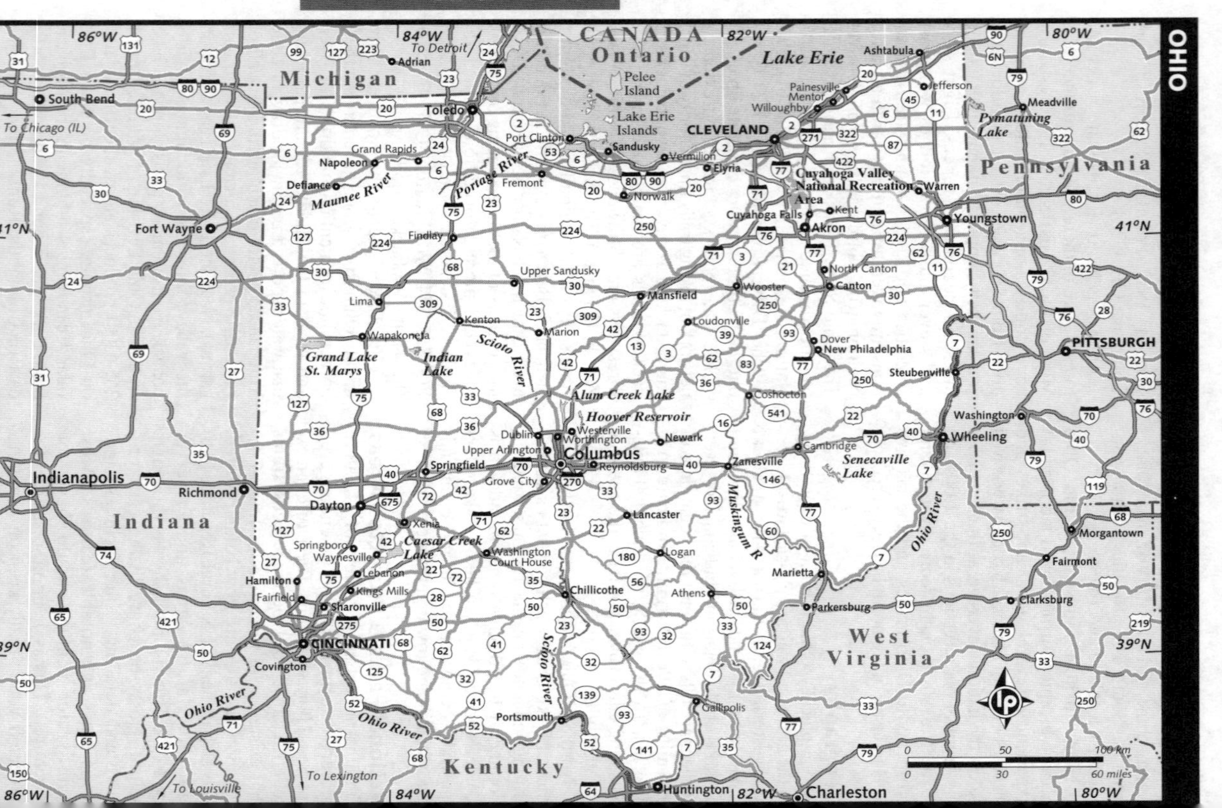
OHIO
Lake Erie
CANADA
Ontario
Pelee Island
Lake Erie Islands
Michigan
Pennsylvania
West Virginia
Kentucky
Indiana
PITTSBURGH
Meadville
Pymatuning Lake
Youngstown
Warren
Jefferson
Ashtabula
Painesville
Mentor
Willoughby
CLEVELAND
Elyria
Vermilion
Sandusky
Norwalk
Port Clinton
Fremont
Portage River
Toledo
To Detroit
Adrian
Grand Rapids
Napoleon
Defiance
Maumee River
Cuyahoga Valley National Recreation Area
Cuyahoga Falls
Kent
Akron
North Canton
Canton
Wooster
Dover
New Philadelphia
Steubenville
Washington
Wheeling
Morgantown
Fairmont
Clarksburg
Ohio River
Senecaville Lake
Cambridge
Coshocton
Zanesville
Muskingum R
Marietta
Parkersburg
Athens
Logan
Lancaster
Newark
Hoover Reservoir
Alum Creek Lake
Loudonville
Mansfield
Upper Sandusky
Marion
Kenton
Findlay
Lima
Wapakoneta
Indian Lake
Grand Lake St. Marys
Scioto River
Westerville
Worthington
Columbus
Reynoldsburg
Dublin
Upper Arlington
Grove City
Springfield
Xenia
Caesar Creek Lake
Washington Court House
Chillicothe
Gallipolis
Huntington
Charleston
Portsmouth
Dayton
Springboro
Waynesville
Lebanon
Kings Mills
Sharonville
CINCINNATI
Fairfield
Hamilton
Covington
To Lexington
To Louisville
Richmond
Indianapolis
Fort Wayne
South Bend
To Chicago (IL)
80°W
82°W
84°W
86°W
41°N
39°N
0
50
100 km
0
30
60 miles

readily available. These are also some of the best trout fishing waters anywhere.

Some of the best bicycling in Ohio is in the Cuyahoga Valley National Recreation Area south of Cleveland.

Government & Politics

Ohio is very evenly split between Democratic and Republican supporters. This progenitor of presidents has a sometimes-heard slogan, 'mother of presidents.'

Arts

Cleveland and Cincinnati have two of the finest groupings of museums and arts venues in the US; the Cleveland Symphony Orchestra is one of the most-recorded orchestras anywhere. Ohio may be most special not for major cultural draws such as Cleveland's world-renowned orchestra, but for the gems in mid-size cities, such as the art museums in Dayton and Toledo. Amish-crafted quilts and furniture from the state have been featured in Smithsonian Institution exhibits.

Information

The state's Office of Travel & Tourism (☎ 800-282-5393) is at PO Box 1001, Columbus, OH 43266. On the Web site (www.ohiotourism.com) you can make room reservations, though the network isn't large yet. There are 13 additional Ohio Visitor Centers at major entrance points along interstate highways.

Special Events

Some of Ohio's special events are:

February

BockFest – late in the month, or in early March, this outdoor festival celebrates the arrival of Cincinnati-made Bock beers and Bockwurst sausages

April

Cincinnati Flower Show – the downtown explodes in an artist's palette of color with displays by green thumbs from around the country

May

Cincinnati May Festival – an annual choral celebration dating back more than 125 years

Quilt National – folk quilt displays offer a unique opportunity to experience the heritage of Midwestern immigrant groups (held in Athens every other year; through September)

July

Gold Star ChiliFest – enjoy country music and Cincinnati's signature spicy food

Rib Fest – Columbus' German Village hosts a lively festival for carnivores and jazz aficionados

US Air and Trade Show – Dayton hosts one of the region's most impressive festivals, in which thousands of aircraft are displayed on the ground and perform in the air

August

German Village Oktoberfest – Columbus' may not rival Munich's in scope, but it's fun and lasts through September

Ohio State Fair – north of downtown Columbus, this is one of the US' largest, with something for everyone from agricultural exhibits to carnival sideshow

September

Ohio Heritage Days – Mansfield celebrates Ohio's early pioneer days, with a nod to local boy Johnny Appleseed

Ohio River Sternwheel Festival – Marietta fetes the crucial period in Ohio River history when it was the country's first 'highway' to the unexplored west

Ohio Swiss Festival – a fine chance to take in the Amish culture of Sugarcreek and beyond

Popcorn Festival – held in Marion, it's a tongue-in-cheek but fascinating look at a local agricultural linchpin, popping corn

October

Covered Bridge Festival – head to Jefferson in Ashtabula County to celebrate a waning Midwestern architectural highlight

Ohio Sauerkraut Festival – Waynesville's one-of-a-kind event reveals the area's Teutonic legacy and offers plenty of hearty food, antiquing and music

Oktoberfest – Cincinnati hits the streets to honor its German heritage and drink beer

Food & Drinks

In Cincinnati, try *goetta* ('gedda'), a kind of sausage patty made from minced pork and beef, spices, and usually oatmeal. Cincinnati also has what most recall about a trip to

Ohio – Cincy chili: meat sauce, spiced with chocolate and cinnamon, over spaghetti with beans, cheese and onions. Cleveland is known by foodies for its seemingly endless ethnic neighborhoods, each with a distinctive cuisine. In the northeast, hearty Amish cooking will always leave you full. Along Lake Erie, Ohio vintners make some very good wines.

Getting There & Around

Cincinnati is a major US air hub; Cleveland, surprisingly less so. Flights from Cincinnati are usually on time, but they aren't cheap – flying and out of Columbus tends to be cheaper.

Greyhound has an extensive network in Ohio. It also subcontracts routes with Lakefront Trailways (☎ 800-331-5009).

Amtrak operates along Ohio's northern half from Chicago on its way to the East Coast. From Cincinnati, rails head west to Indianapolis and Peoria, Illinois, and east to Washington, DC. There are also Amtrak bus routes from Cincinnati to Columbus, Cleveland and Pittsburgh.

A unique way to enter or exit Ohio is via ferry from Pelee Island, Ontario. Note immigration regulations before boarding. The Island Rocket (☎ 519-724-2469) makes the run the fastest.

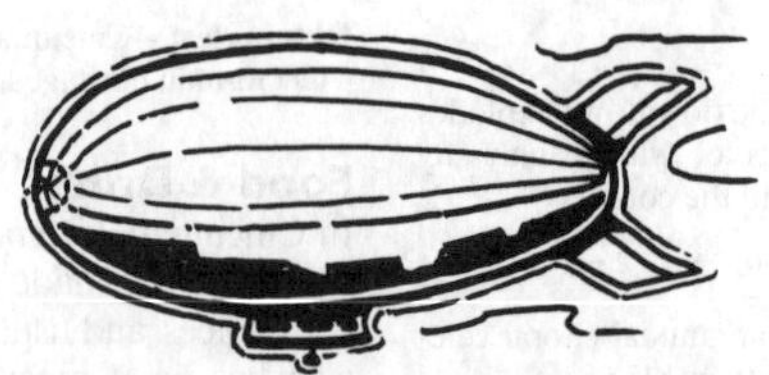

Northern Ohio

Interstate 70 bisects Ohio into roughly equal-size north and south chunks. The northern section is the part that stands out when looking at a map, since its northern boundary is eye-catching Lake Erie. The big lake does have its draws. Toledo – which is oft-neglected – is at the western edge. The Lake Erie Islands are prime vacation and walleye-fishing land. East of Cleveland is Ohio's original resort area, Geneva-on-the-Lake, and the Western Reserve, in which Ashtabula County and its covered bridges are sublime.

Inland, the Akron–Canton region is the state's industrial and population base, and home to the National Football League's Hall of Fame. Central Northern Ohio has the state's best canoeing, near Loudonville. The area east of there is simply called Amish Country, as it's the nation's highest density of Mennonite culture.

Highlights

- Cleveland, a great sports town and home to the Rock & Roll Hall of Fame & Museum
- The Lake Erie Islands, peaceful respites a short ferry ride from the mainland
- Holmes, Wayne and Coshocton counties, the world's highest concentration of Amish culture, set amid rolling hills
- Ashtabula County's covered bridges
- The Pro Football Hall of Fame in Canton, birthplace of the NFL
- Penny candy and fantastic lake views in Geneva-on-the-Lake

Cleveland & Vicinity

CLEVELAND

pop 495,820

To best encapsulate Cleveland's struggle with image, a cliché: What a difference a decade makes. Well, it's taken a bit longer than that, but you get the idea.

Long unfairly derided by Americans, Cleveland was an afterthought at best, an easy target at worst – its nickname was the 'Mistake on the Lake.' Whenever the then-woeful Cleveland Indians baseball team played, those in other Rust Belt cities in economic and social swoon held banners aloft on national television reading, 'At least we ain't Cleveland.'

Cleveland reached its nadir in the 1970s, when its Cuyahoga River was so chemically polluted that it caught fire and the decline of its traditional industries led to urban decay and severe social problems. To close out the

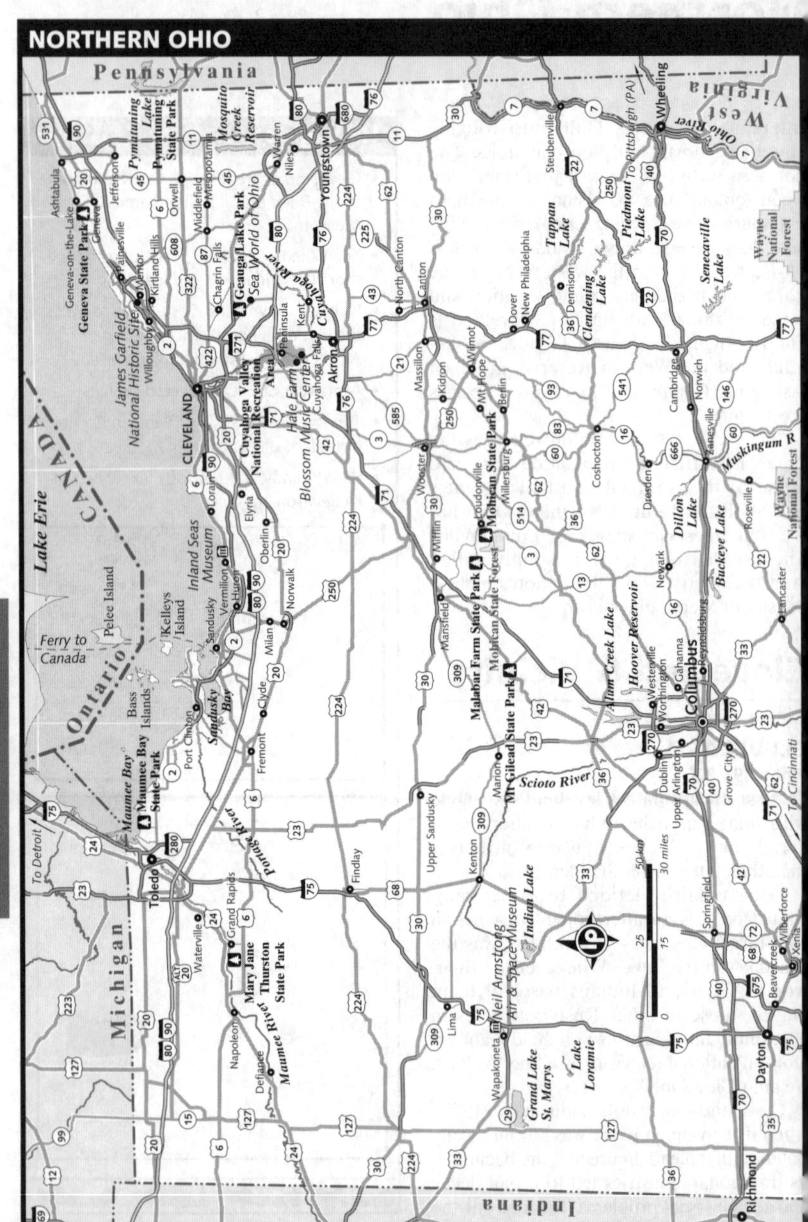
NORTHERN OHIO
Pennsylvania
Lake Erie
CANADA
Ontario
Michigan
Indiana
West Virginia
Ferry to Canada
To Detroit
To Pittsburgh (PA)
To Cincinnati
Pelee Island
Kelleys Island
Bass Islands
Maumee Bay
Maumee Bay State Park
Sandusky Bay
Port Clinton
Sandusky
Huron
Vermilion
Inland Seas Museum
Lorain
Elyria
Oberlin
Norwalk
Milan
Clyde
Fremont
Toledo
Waterville
Grand Rapids
Mary Jane Thurston State Park
Napoleon
Defiance
Maumee River
Portage River
Findlay
Upper Sandusky
Kenton
Lima
Wapakoneta
Neil Armstrong Air & Space Museum
Indian Lake
Grand Lake St Marys
Lake Loramie
Marion
Mt Gilead State Park
Scioto River
Mansfield
Malabar Farm State Park
Mohican State Forest
Mohican State Park
Loudonville
Mifflin
Wooster
Kidron
Millersburg
Mt Hope
Berlin
Wilmot
Massillon
Canton
North Canton
Akron
Cuyahoga Falls
Hale Farm
Blossom Music Center
Cuyahoga Valley National Recreation Area
Peninsula
Kent
Cuyahoga River
CLEVELAND
James Garfield National Historic Site
Willoughby
Mentor
Kirtland Hills
Painesville
Geneva-on-the-Lake
Geneva State Park
Geneva
Ashtabula
Jefferson
Pymatuning Lake
Pymatuning State Park
Orwell
Middlefield
Mesopotamia
Mosquito Creek Reservoir
Chagrin Falls
Geauga Lake Park
Sea World of Ohio
Warren
Niles
Youngstown
Steubenville
Wheeling
Ohio River
Dover
New Philadelphia
Tappan Lake
Dennison
Clendening Lake
Piedmont Lake
Senecaville Lake
Wayne National Forest
Cambridge
Norwich
Zanesville
Muskingum R
Coshocton
Dresden
Dillon Lake
Buckeye Lake
Roseville
Newark
Lancaster
Hoover Reservoir
Alum Creek Lake
Westerville
Gahanna
Reynoldsburg
Worthington
Columbus
Dublin
Upper Arlington
Grove City
Springfield
Wilberforce
Xenia
Beavercreek
Dayton
Richmond
0 25 50 km
0 15 30 miles

ecade, the city became the first since the ;reat Depression to default on its finances. Jrban renewal started in the 1980s, and the erelict waterfront areas became an attrac-ve restaurant and shopping precinct. Three 990s developments also had a large impact. . new baseball stadium, Jacobs Field ('the ake'), became the focus of civic pride (a si-nultaneous resurgence of quality baseball lso helped). The Cleveland Browns football eam, the cornerstone of local pride – if not eligious belief – was spirited away by its wner to Baltimore. But, amazingly, a 'new' 'rowns team was returned to the city – to a ew stadium – by the NFL in 1999 ('Cleve-nd *is* football' was the refrain from the eague offices). The splendid, eye-catching akefront gem, the Rock & Roll Hall of ame & Museum, brought the city interna-onal attention.

Today Cleveland is a unique blend of arly architecture and gentrified neighbor-oods, with enough urban grit and grime to dd an edgy ambience. The city garners udos for quality of life and tourism; *Money* nagazine even rated it the second-best place) live in the Midwest. And the new self-ppointed informal city slogan, taken from ne lyrics of a bar band's local anthem, is 'Cleveland Rocks!'

History

Cleveland's progenitor, Moses Cleaveland vith the 'a'), arrived in the early 1790s as a epresentative of the Connecticut Land 'ompany, a group of investors speculating n 'western' lands. He hung around long nough to strike a deal with the local Six 'ations Native American tribes: His group ould settle only the east bank of the Cuya-oga River, and the tribes could remain on ne west side. The Six Nations got to keep neir land longer than most native tribes efore the settlers reneged on their deal, nostly because many early transplants from ne East Coast came, looked around at the narshy, mosquito-filled land, and left; sur-eyed in 1796, four years later it had pre-sely two residents.

Cleveland really took off after the Erie–Ohio Canal was completed in 1832, linking Lake Erie to the Ohio River. Using iron from the upper Great Lakes and coal trans-ported along the Ohio River, Cleveland became one of the biggest US steel produc-ers by the end of the Civil War. This eco-nomic output increased even more during and following World War I and began to draw huge numbers of immigrants; prior to World War II two-thirds of the city's inhabi-tants were foreign-born or had at least one foreign-born parent. The city later diversi-fied into production of all sorts of machin-ery, textiles, clothing and chemicals and became a center of trade unionism and so-cially progressive policies. Industrial wealth bankrolled cultural aspirations, too, and the city still surprises with its world-class museums and performing arts.

Orientation

Cleveland's main attractions cluster around downtown and University Circle to the east. Superior, Prospect and Euclid Aves are the main streets and these link the downtown with University Circle, a grouping of museums, restaurants and places to stay. East and west street designations begin at Ontario St. All streets using numbers run north to south; you'll likely get to know E 9th St, as it takes you to the lakefront and most of its attractions. When confused, re-member that Lake Erie is the northern boundary.

The *Greater Cleveland Official Visitors Guide,* available from either information office listed below, has an OK Greater Cleve-land map and a quite good downtown map.

Information

Tourist Offices The Convention and Visi-tors Bureau of Greater Cleveland (☎ 216-621-7981, 800-321-1004) is at 3100 Terminal Tower, 50 Public Square. It maintains an in-formal information desk in the lobby of the Terminal Tower; you can get brochures and maps from the helpful staff. It's closed week-ends. There is also a tiny office (☎ 216-621-2218) in the Flats on Old River Rd, open 11 am to 7 pm daily in summer. The airport also has an information desk. Cleveland has a 'Touch Cleveland' system of map kiosks; the

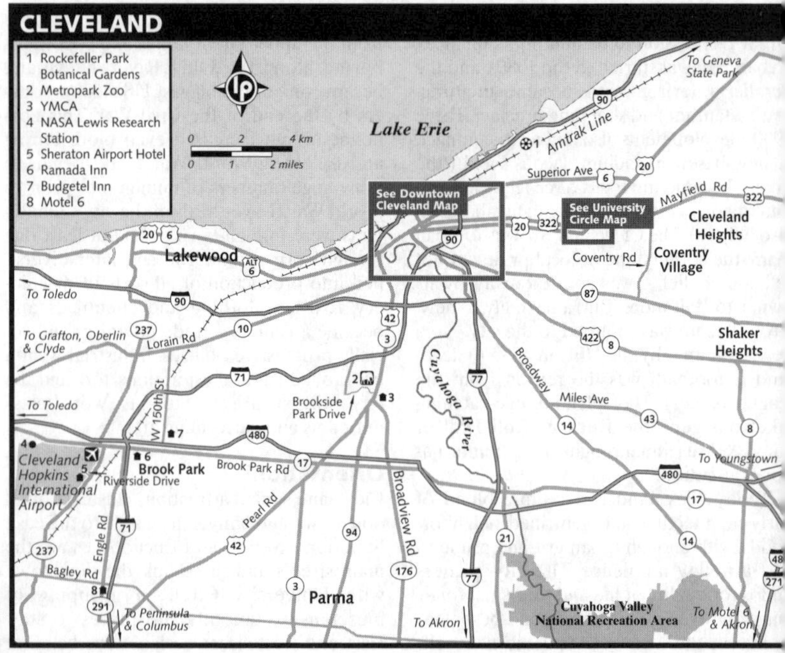

handiest locations are in the baggage claim area of the airport, Playhouse Square Center, the Powerhouse along the West Bank of the Flats and the Rock & Roll Hall of Fame. The Convention & Visitors Bureau's Web site (www.travelcleveland.com) is extensive.

Money Currency can be exchanged at the airport, directly across from the Food Court, or at Key Bank, 127 Public Square, or Star Bank, 1350 Euclid Ave.

Cleveland levies a 14.5% hotel room tax.

Post In the Federal Building, near the southwest corner of Lakeside Ave and E 9th St, you'll find a post office; another is in the Arcade at 401 Euclid Ave.

Fax, Email & Internet Access Kinko's is a copy shop on E 9th St, south of Rockwell Ave. You can send faxes and log on to the Internet from here for $12 per hour or 20¢ per minute.

Bookstores Many of Cleveland's book stores are beyond the downtown area and in the suburbs. On the west side, try S Steps Down Bookstore (☎ 216-566-889 at 1921 W 25th St. If you're headed east, h Appletree Books (☎ 216-791-2665) 12419 Cedar Rd, Mac Back's paperback (☎ 216-321-2665) at 1820 Coventry Rd Cleveland Heights or K&M Books (☎ 21 283-1647) at 16969 Chagrin Blvd in Shak Heights. Farther east in Hudson is th Learned Owl (☎ 330-653-2252) at 2 Main St.

Gay & Lesbian Travelers The Clevelan Lesbian & Gay Community Center, 66 Detroit, runs a hot line (☎ 216-651-5428 Both the *Free Times* and *Scene* give listin about local events.

Medical Services If you're in need of car the Lutheran Hospital (☎ 216-696-4300) at 1730 W 25th St, near West Market.

edia The *Cleveland Plain Dealer* – the 'D' – is Ohio's largest and probably most fluential newspaper and the only major ily left in town. You can glean some information on local events, restaurants and ghtlife in it in the Friday edition, but for uch more of this type of information, nsult the free local weeklies, *Cleveland ee Times* and *Scene*.

angers & Annoyances Visitors should ke care after dark in most parts of the city her than the Flats and waterfront areas. void going east of 40th St in downtown, eyond University Circle in the Euclid Ave cinity. There's nothing of interest anyway. lsewhere, the Ohio City and Tremont eas are potentially unsafe.

owntown

ne visitor information center along Old iver Rd has an excellent free fold-out ochure with seven **walking tours** of the rious downtown districts and their historal and architectural highlights. It's open am to 7 pm weekdays, May through Sepmber, 11 am to 4 pm the rest of the year.

ublic Square Cleveland's center is Public quare, with the conspicuous Terminal ower and Tower City Center office and opping complex. The 42nd-floor observaon deck ($2) is open 11 am to 4:30 pm, May rough September, 11 am to 3:30 pm weekds only the rest of the year. A block northst, don't miss the 1890 **Arcade**, with its vely period wrought iron, glass skylights d terrazzo floors. Three blocks southeast the Square are **Jacobs Field** baseball adium, where 42,000 fans flock to see the dians play, and the **Gund Arena**, a basketll, hockey and entertainment venue. An closed walkway runs to Jacobs Field and und Arena from Tower City Center. Tours Jacobs Field (☎ 216-420-4200) are popular d leave from the Team Shop every half ur from 10 am to 2 pm Monday through turday; $5/3 adults/children.

e Flats On the west side of downtown d once a riverfront industrial area, the Flats has been reborn as Cleveland's nightlife zone. Factories and warehouses have been recycled into bars, restaurants and clubs, with an emphasis on catering to 20- and 30-somethings. The riverside patios are pleasant, set around and beneath the old iron bridges; a half-mile boardwalk connects venues. Water taxis shuttle across the Cuyahoga River in the evening.

Lakeside & Rock & Roll Hall of Fame

North of downtown, on the Erie lakeshore, the **Great Lakes Science Center** (☎ 216-694-2000) gives a good account of the lakes' environmental problems, with hands-on exhibits and an Omnimax theater. The indoor tornado is particularly cool. Major traveling exhibitions are also shown. Hours are daily from 9:30 am to 5:30 pm year-round. Admission is $8/5 adults/children each, $11/8 adults/children for both. The glittering, silvery new Cleveland Browns football stadium is next door.

Also near the lake, the renowned **Rock & Roll Hall of Fame & Museum** (☎ 216-781-7625, 800-493-7655), One Key Plaza, is more than a collection of rock star memorabilia. IM Pei's architecture features towers, a pyramid and a phonograph-style entrance; its one-of-a-kind look has become to some the image of Cleveland. Be sure to see the numerous handwritten lyrics, notes and personal letters. Innovative, interactive multimedia exhibits trace the history and social context of rock music and the many performers who created it. Changing displays begin with rock's roots and originators and carry through to Madonna and various contemporary artists, simultaneously creating a historical record and fan nostalgia. The newest exhibit, which was nearing completion as this book was being researched, is devoted solely to hip-hop.

One huge, pitch-black room projects video music highlights of enshrinees in nearly perfect and – *warning* – loud sound; some folks have wound up spending hours in the dark, just listening, watching, and grinning. A café is also on site and you may need it, just to decompress from all the stimulation. Why is

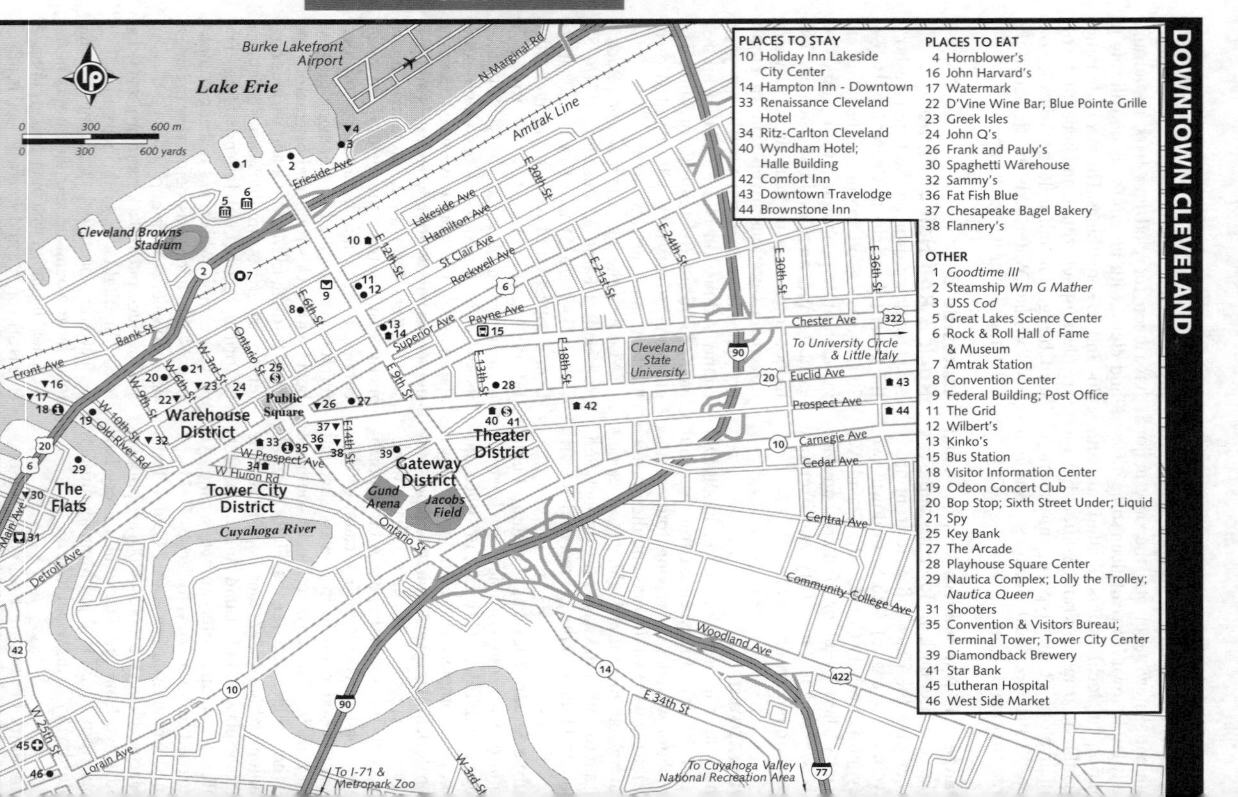
DOWNTOWN CLEVELAND
PLACES TO STAY
10 Holiday Inn Lakeside City Center
14 Hampton Inn - Downtown
33 Renaissance Cleveland Hotel
34 Ritz-Carlton Cleveland
40 Wyndham Hotel; Halle Building
42 Comfort Inn
43 Downtown Travelodge
44 Brownstone Inn
PLACES TO EAT
4 Hornblower's
16 John Harvard's
17 Watermark
22 D'Vine Wine Bar; Blue Pointe Grille
23 Greek Isles
24 John Q's
26 Frank and Pauly's
30 Spaghetti Warehouse
32 Sammy's
36 Fat Fish Blue
37 Chesapeake Bagel Bakery
38 Flannery's
OTHER
1 Goodtime III
2 Steamship Wm G Mather
3 USS Cod
5 Great Lakes Science Center
6 Rock & Roll Hall of Fame & Museum
7 Amtrak Station
8 Convention Center
9 Federal Building; Post Office
11 The Grid
12 Wilbert's
13 Kinko's
15 Bus Station
18 Visitor Information Center
19 Odeon Concert Club
20 Bop Stop; Sixth Street Under; Liquid
21 Spy
25 Key Bank
27 The Arcade
28 Playhouse Square Center
29 Nautica Complex; Lolly the Trolley; Nautica Queen
31 Shooters
35 Convention & Visitors Bureau; Terminal Tower; Tower City Center
39 Diamondback Brewery
41 Star Bank
45 Lutheran Hospital
46 West Side Market
Burke Lakefront Airport
Lake Erie
N Marginal Rd
Amtrak Line
0 300 600 m
0 300 600 yards
Erieside Ave
Cleveland Browns Stadium
Lakeside Ave
Hamilton Ave
St Clair Ave
Rockwell Ave
Payne Ave
Superior Ave
Chester Ave
To University Circle & Little Italy
Euclid Ave
Prospect Ave
Carnegie Ave
Cedar Ave
Central Ave
Community College Ave
Woodland Ave
E 34th St
E 12th St
E 20th St
E 24th St
E 21st St
E 30th St
E 36th St
E 6th St
E 13th St
E 18th St
E 9th St
E 14th St
Cleveland State University
Bank St
Front Ave
Ontario St
W 3rd St
W 6th St
W 9th St
W 10th St
Old River Rd
Public Square
Warehouse District
W Prospect Ave
W Huron Rd
Tower City District
Gateway District
Theater District
Gund Arena
Jacobs Field
The Flats
Main Ave
Cuyahoga River
Detroit Ave
W 25th St
Lorain Ave
To I-71 & Metropark Zoo
To Cuyahoga Valley National Recreation Area

OHIO

e museum in Cleveland? Because it's the ometown of Alan Freed, the disc jockey who opularized the term 'rock and roll' in the rly 1950s, and because the city lobbied hard nd paid big. The whole complex is hugely opular (deservedly so); avoid weekends and olidays. Hours are 10 am to 5:30 pm daily 0 am to 9 pm Wednesday), though some ex- bits don't open until 11 am. Admission is eep – $15/12 adults/children. For parking, e lot across the highway in front of the en- ance is cheapest.

Just east of the Rock & Roll Hall of Fame Museum sits the hulking steamship *Wm G ather*, once a mighty Great Lakes freighter, ow retired as a walk-through museum. ou can explore from down deep into the olds all the way up to the stately dining oms. The engine room is absolutely mon- rous. Hours during the summer are 10 am 5 pm Monday through Saturday, noon to pm Sunday; $5/3 adults/children.

Farther east from here sits the USS *Cod*, retired WWII submarine that still has vir- ally all of its original equipment and a ell-preserved air of wartime under tight nditions. The guides served aboard subs ring WWII. With its tiny portholes and eep ladders, this is not for the claustropho- c nor the physically challenged. Hours are om 10 am to 5 pm daily; $4.

niversity Circle

bout 5 miles east of downtown, there's a uster of museums starring the **Cleveland useum of Art** (☎ 216-421-7340), 11150 E lvd, with its excellent collection of Euro- ean paintings, as well as African, Asian and merican art. Of particular note is the ex- nsive medieval armor collection. The café the museum is quite good. Hours are am to 5 pm Tuesday to Sunday (10 am to pm Wednesday); free.

US history is revealed at the **Western serve Historical Society** (☎ 216-721-5722), 825 E Blvd. On the ground floor is a story museum focusing on early settle- ents in northeast Ohio and, in particular, e swank early dwellings of the city's well- -do. On the lower level is the Crawford uto-Aviation Museum, with its comprehensive collection of old cars and planes. Hours are 10 am to 5 pm Monday to Saturday, noon to 5 pm Sunday; admission is $7/5 adults/children.

Several other museums of interest are in the vicinity. The **Museum of Natural History** (☎ 216-231-4600), 1 Wade Oval Drive, has dinosaur and Indian exhibits – it even has a piece of 'Lucy,' the most famous fossil in history. It's open 10 am to 5 pm daily, with longer hours Wednesday; admission is $7/5 adults/children.

The **Health Museum** (☎ 216-231-5010), 8911 Euclid Drive, has over 150 exhibits, some hands-on. You won't soon forget the talking transparent woman. Hours are 9 am to 5 pm Monday through Friday, 10 am to 5 pm Saturday, noon to 5 pm Sunday. This isn't to be confused with the **Dittrick Museum of Medical History** (☎ 216-368-3648), 11000 Euclid Ave, which features early medical technology. Hours are 10 am to 5 pm weekdays; free.

The **African American Museum** (☎ 216-791-1700), 1765 Crawford Rd, rounds out the list with its exhibits on the local history of African Americans, who comprise the largest population in central Cleveland. Other exhibits trace African culture from ancient Egypt through the African diaspora. Exhibits highlight contributions to US culture from African Americans. It's open 9 am to 5 pm weekdays, 11 am to 3 pm weekends. The Greek-influenced, art-deco interior of **Severance Hall**, at 11001 Euclid Ave, is worth seeing even if you don't hear the acclaimed Cleveland Orchestra (the ticket office is also here). Just east of the Cleveland Museum of Art are the **Cleveland Botanical Gardens**, which contain nearly 10 acres organized into a half-dozen separate gardens, including a Japanese garden. The grounds are open dawn to dusk daily.

The **Center for Contemporary Art** (☎ 216-421-8671), 8501 Carnegie Ave, offers a consistently challenging array of modern art in changing exhibitions. Hours are 11 am to 6 pm Tuesday through Thursday, 11 am to 9 pm Friday, and noon to 5 pm weekends; free.

See Getting Around for local bus information to University Circle.

Other Areas

The **Metropark Zoo** (☎ 216-661-6500), 3900 Brookside Drive, about 5 miles south of downtown, features a rain forest environment that includes thunderstorms, waterfalls and tropical insects. A highlight is the 2-acre reserve on which a pack of gray wolves lives. Hours are 9 am to 5 pm daily; $7/4 adults/children. During the summer, the No 20C 'Zoo Bus' runs hourly from Public Square; with a valid bus ticket, your admission is halved.

Cleveland's Metropark system is one of the nicest in the country. Locals dubbed it the 'Emerald Necklace,' as it's composed of 14 linked parks that make up 19,000 acres, with over 100 miles of trails. Local visitor information centers have trail maps.

It would be easy to while away a day at the **West Side Market** (☎ 216-664-3386), W 25th St at Lorain Ave. This sprawling, two-block complex dates from the 1920s and still harks back to those days with row after row of 180 local vendors selling it *all* here fruits, vegetables, meats, dairy, fish, cigar pizza, imports, candy, whatever. There ar 10 bakeries alone. Hours are 7 am to 4 pr Monday through Wednesday and 7 am t 6 pm Friday through Sunday.

Located just west of the Clevelan Hopkins International Airport at 2100 Brookpark Rd, the **NASA Lewis Researc Station** (☎ 216-433-2000) is one of NASA' most vital research and development site Exhibits focus on aeronautics, satellites, an the history of the US in space. Tours take i developing and testing areas; lots of demor strations keep it lively. The complex is ope 9 am to 4 pm weekdays, 10 am to 3 pm Sa urday and 1 to 5 pm Sunday; free.

James Garfield, the 20th president of th US, is interred near famed industrialist Joh D Rockefeller at **Lakeview Cemetery**, 1231 Euclid Ave. A handful of other minor histo ical celebrities are also found here. Som may have misgivings about touting a ceme

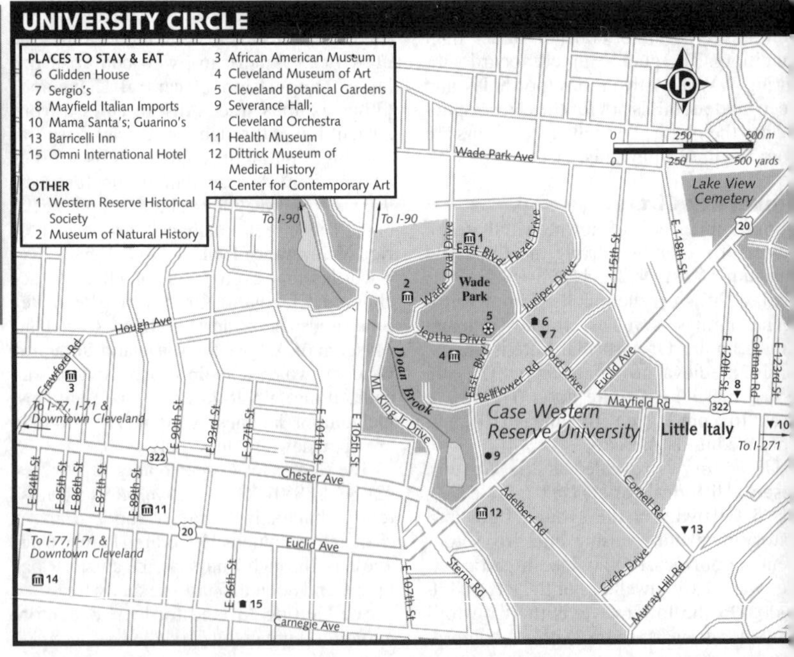

ry as a tourist sight, but it is well-known for s distinctive memorials and well-designed arden spots. Hours are 9 am to 4 pm daily.

The remnants of the wealthy Rockefeller mily's Cleveland estate have been made to a civic park. The **Rockefeller Park otanical Gardens** are known for four acres f diverse garden displays. A large greenouse showcases exotic species. Hours are) am to 4 pm daily; free.

The **Coventry Village** neighborhood, ased along Coventry Rd at Mayfield Rd, is small, relaxed district of alternative shops, staurants, etc. The Big Fun store at No 327 is sure to bring a smile.

rganized Tours

ne most popular local tours are the onend two-hour tours aboard **Lolly the Trolley**, ost of which start at the Powerhouse, at e Nautica Complex on the West Bank. he longer tour travels along the harbor ear the Rock & Roll Hall of Fame & useum, proceeds through the downtown, e Warehouse District, the Flats, Ohio City stretch of lovely Victorian homes), West de Market, Playhouse Square and Univerty Circle. It stops once, at the Rockefeller rk Greenhouse.

Tours run daily May through October. onday to Saturday two-hour tours leave at 30 am and 2 pm (Friday and Saturday in mmer also have a 6 pm tour), with a oneour tour at 12:30 pm; Sunday there's a o-hour tour at 1 pm and a one-hour tour 3:30 pm. November through April tours n only Friday and Saturday, with a twoour tour at 2 pm and a one-hour tour at :30 pm. The two-hour tour costs $12/7 ults/children; the one-hour tour costs $8/5.

Cleveland also has two water-borne tours. ehind the Rock & Roll Hall of Fame & useum sits the *Goodtime III*, which offers me half-dozen options, the most popular of ich are the two-hour lake and river tours 13/8 adults/children), offered at noon and m Monday through Saturday, with an adional 6 pm tour Friday and Sunday, midne through Labor Day. In early June and e September limited trips are offered. ere are also dance cruises, daily luncheon cruises, and Saturday night dinner dance cruises. Reservations are necessary for the latter two. Call ☎ 216-861-5110.

Located in the Flats district adjacent to the Nautica complex is the *Nautica Queen*, a similar boat that offers lunch ($22/12 adults/children) and dinner ($39/21) cruises Monday to Saturday. Prices given are Monday through Thursday; they increase Friday and Saturday. Sunday features a popular brunch cruise ($27/12) along with an additional dinner cruise ($34/17).

You can also get an eagle-eye view. The T&G Flying Club (☎ 216-241-2321), under the control tower at Burke Lakefront Airport, just east of the harbor and Rock & Roll Hall of Fame & Museum, offers halfhour flights for $45 per person; $60 for two or three people.

Places to Stay

Budget The closest campground is ***The Maples*** *(☎ 216-926-3700)*, on Hwy 83 a quarter mile south of Hwy 303 in Grafton, southwest of the city. It offers tent and RV sites and a beach. Much better is ***Geneva State Park*** *(☎ 216-466-8400)*, 50 miles west of the city on the Lake Erie shoreline. Sites ($18) are allocated on a first-come, firstserved basis, and there are RVs for rent at $55; reservations are accepted.

Near Peninsula, about 22 miles south of Cleveland, is the HI ***Stanford House*** *(☎ 330-467-8711, 6093 Stanford Rd)*, sitting peacefully in the wooded Cuyahoga Valley National Recreation Area. It charges members $12, plus $2 for sheets. The fine old farmhouse is surrounded by trails; watch for deer. Call for directions, which are a little tricky: From Cleveland, take I-77 south and Route 303 east to Peninsula, but note that there's no exit off I-77, so you have to jog north a bit on I-271.

The ***YMCA*** *(☎ 216-749-2355, 3881 Pearl Rd)*, south of downtown, takes men only and is mainly rented by the week or longer. The cost for one night is $34.

The best area for budget motels is southwest of Cleveland's center, near the airport in the Brook Park district, off I-71 or I-480. ***Motel 6*** *(☎ 216-234-0990, fax 440-234-3475)*,

7219 Engle Rd at the corner of Bagley Rd, charges about $40/46 for singles/doubles. ***Budgetel Inn*** *(☎ 216-251-8500, 4222 W 150th St)*, costs slightly more. Others (some of which are a little dubious and might rent by the hour) can be found nearby along Brookpark Rd. There is a second, newer ***Motel 6*** *(☎ 330-467-9189, fax 330-467-9189, 311 E Highland Rd)*, near the intersection of Hwy 8 and I-271, southeast of downtown some 20 miles, in a good location for the Cuyahoga Valley National Recreation Area (see Around Cleveland, later in this chapter), with rates similar to the Motel 6 above.

Downtown, cheap accommodations are minimal. The best value is ***Comfort Inn*** *(☎ 216-861-0001, fax 216-861-0001, 1800 Euclid Ave)*, which has singles from $80, depending on day and events. The bus station is a short walk away. This hotel, incidentally, was for most of the century *the* swinging hotel where all visiting celebrities holed up; not so anymore, though it is a decent place. ***Downtown Travelodge*** *(☎ 216-361-8969, 3614 Euclid Ave)* is similar. A bit farther from downtown is the ***Brownstone Inn*** *(☎ 216-426-1753, 3649 Prospect Avenue)*, a Victorian mansion with rooms and a kitchenette. Rooms with shared bath start at $65/75 single/double; those with private baths start at $85/95.

Mid-Range Again, the rule of thumb is – the farther you creep from downtown, the cheaper you'll find the rooms. University Circle has the lion's share of bed and breakfasts, which qualify as most of Cleveland's mid-range lodging options. Private Lodgings, Inc (☎ 216-321-3213) is a private referral service arranging for bed and breakfast stays in local homes (it also offers the service around the state).

In the University Circle, the lodging of choice is the ***Glidden House*** *(☎ 216-231-8900, 1901 Ford Drive)*, built in 1910 by heirs to the Glidden Paint Co fortune. There are eight luxury suites and a newer guest wing. Rates start at around $85 single/double. A restaurant and pub are in the old carriage house.

The most reasonable rates in downtown itself are found at a couple of spots. The well-located ***Holiday Inn Lakeside Ci[ty] Center*** *(☎ 216-241-5100, 1111 Lakesi[de] Ave)* has singles/doubles starting at arou[nd] $105. You'll also find a health club and restaurant/lounge. Similar rates are fou[nd] at the ***Hampton Inn-Downtown*** *(☎ 21[6]-241-6600, 1460 E 9th St)*, which also has health club.

Ramada Inn *(☎ 216-267-5700, 139[.] Brookpark Rd)* is just about 2 miles east [of] the Cleveland Hopkins Internation[al] Airport. It offers several travel packages [to] local sights. There's also a bar-restaura[nt] and a health club. Rates are $100/105 sing[le/] double.

Top End Take your pick of a doz[en] premium-priced digs downtown. If you'[re] planning to avail yourself of Clevelan[d's] Playhouse Square, the ***Wyndham Hot[el]*** *(☎ 216-615-7500, fax 216-615-3355, 12[.] Euclid Ave)* is worth considering; it is own[ed] in part by the foundation that overse[es] Playhouse Square and offers packages [of] lodging and theater tickets. You can relax [in] the heated pool or work out in the heal[th] club. Rates top out at $148.

In University Circle, a nod to the ***Om[ni] International Hotel*** *(☎ 216-791-1900, f[ax] 216-231-3329, 2065 E 96th St)*, sitting adj[a]cent to the Cleveland Clinic. The hotel has lovely atrium featuring artwork by Oh[io] artists. The dining room, Classics, is also w[ell] regarded. Rates are $165.

The venerable ***Renaissance Clevela[nd] Hotel*** *(☎ 216-696-5600, fax 216-696-3102, [.] Public Square)* is Cleveland's longest reig[n]ing posh hotel. The site has seen hotels as [far] back as 1815; the present edifice was built [in] 1918. Numerous renovations – includi[ng] using white marble from the quarry whe[re] Michelangelo's *David* was taken – ha[ve] made it the very definition of sybaritic. Ra[tes] are rather reasonable at $180, given t[he] regal atmosphere and lengthy list of extra[s].

The ***Ritz-Carlton Cleveland*** *(☎ 216-62[.] 1300, fax 216-623-0515, 1515 W 3rd St)* h[as] perhaps the best location, opposite t[he] Tower City complex, attached to a row [of] more than 100 shops and restaurants. T[he] main underground rail lines all conver[ge] re and you can take an enclosed walkway Jacobs Field and the Gund Arena. The t of amenities is staggering and should be, ven the cool $210 room rate.

If you need to stay at the airport, the ***eraton Airport Hotel*** *(☎ 216-267-1500, '00 Riverside Drive)* is as close as you'll t, actually within the property limits of e airport (you still need to take the shuttle n). Rates are $150/160 single/double.

laces to Eat

owntown ***Chesapeake Bagel Bakery*** *40 Euclid Ave)* has bagel sandwiches and nall coffees big enough to make you glad u didn't order the large.

Frank and Pauly's *(☎ 216-575-1000, 200 ıblic Square)* is very central and serves pious southern Italian cuisine (main urses from $6); when you enter, the red-d-white-checked tablecloths and tubular eel padded chairs are something straight t of a mafia movie. The food is the real al. In Terminal Tower, the ***Hard Rock afé*** serves up its home-style American od with good old-fashioned rock and roll; trées start at $6.

Excellent Greek food can be had at ***Greek les*** *(☎ 216-861-1919)*, on the corner of W h St and St Clair Ave. The feta-spinach pie good; it also offers an array of seafood. ıtrées start at $7. Not far away to the west ***D'Vine Wine Bar*** *(☎ 216-241-9463, 836 W Clair Ave)*, with over 80 wines and two zen beers; they serve a tapas menu (from). ***Fat Fish Blue*** *(☎ 216-875-6000, 21 ospect Ave)* has the coolest name in town d serves up real Louisiana crawdads, po-ys (submarine sandwich), steaks and other you traditional favorites (main courses ɔm $7). It also is a solid blues venue.

Shandong-style Chinese food ($10 and main course) in an upscale atmosphere is und at ***La Cuisine*** *(☎ 216-241-8488, 1228 ıclid Ave)* in the Halle Building.

The ***Blue Pointe Grille*** *(☎ 216-875-7827, 0 W St Clair Ave)* is a trendy little bistro th excellent steaks and seafood (main urses from $13).

Flannery's *(☎ 216-781-7782, 323 Prospect e)* is a pub and restaurant with an Irish slant and occasional evening entertainment. ***John Q's*** (☎ 216-861-0900), right downtown at 55 Public Square, is a classic steakhouse ($20 main course). For seafood, ***Hornblower's*** *(☎ 216-363-1151, 1151 N Marginal Rd)*, a converted barge, is a local fave ($10 to $20 main course) with its commanding views of Lake Erie. Reservations are a good idea on weekends.

The Flats Straddling the Cuyahoga River at the west edge of downtown, there are several places for a meal and more for a drink. ***John Harvard's*** *(1087 Old River Rd)* makes its own good beer (sample five for $5) and offers food superior to standard pub grub. More expensive and with a fine riverfront location, the enormous ***Watermark*** *(☎ 216-241-1600, 1250 Old River Rd)* specializes in seafood ($12 and up for main courses) and is so popular they've even started their own dinner river cruises. ***Sammy's*** *(☎ 216-523-5560, 1400 W 10th St)* is perhaps Cleveland's most creative contemporary American cuisine eatery and is particularly famed for its seafood raw bar. It isn't cheap; entrées hover around the $20 range.

Across the river, the Nautica Complex's two main buildings house a number of raucous eateries, including the ***Rock Bottom Brewery & Restaurant*** *(☎ 216-623-1555)* and a ***TGI Fridays*** *(☎ 216-621-1993)*. The ***Spaghetti Warehouse*** *(☎ 216-621-9420, 1231 Main Ave)* serves low to moderately priced pasta dishes in a colorful atmosphere; a $6 cram-in-all-you-can buffet draws crowds.

University Circle Fusion cuisine with a Brazilian base (main courses from $12) is at University Circle's best-known eatery, ***Sergio's*** *(☎ 216-231-1234, 1903 Ford Drive)*; live music is offered in summer. In the Omni International Hotel, ***Classics***, serving continental cuisine (main course from $12), is probably the most romantic dining spot in town.

If somebody else is paying, try the ***Barricelli Inn*** *(☎ 216-791-6500, 2203 Cornell Rd)*, serving creative continental food at creative prices (main courses from $20).

The early-20th-century brownstone mansion has cozy parlor rooms for diners.

Italian food is well-represented in the area, much of it inexpensive. Several pleasant blocks for strolling, plus restaurants, cafés and a bakery, are found in the Little Italy area, along Mayfield Rd a few blocks east of Euclid Ave near University Circle. Friendly ***Mayfield Italian Imports***, No 12018, serves excellent fresh entrées and authentic sandwiches at good-value prices. Copious amounts of inexpensive home-style Sicilian are served at the popular eatery ***Mama Santa's*** *(☎ 216-231-3100)*, No 12305, a spirited place (main courses from $7). Virtually next door is the more upscale ***Guarino's***, *(☎ 216-231-3100)*, No 12309, operating since 1918. The southern Italian style food (main courses from $8 to $13) is served in a decidedly Victorian atmosphere.

Entertainment

Downtown The ***Diamondback Brewery*** *(☎ 216-771-1988, 724 Prospect Ave)* regularly has contemporary music and jazz. The ***Playhouse Square Center*** *(☎ 216-241-6000, 1501 Euclid Ave)* hosts theater, opera and ballet, and there are five other live theaters around town.

The Flats This is the area for clubs, dancing and lively bars. On the West Bank, these are all housed in two early 20th-century refurbished buildings – the Powerhouse and the Sugar Warehouse, collectively referred to as the ***Nautica Complex***. The Powerhouse contains an improv comedy club, a cacophonic TGI Fridays restaurant, the popular Howl at the Moon Saloon (there's plenty of howling at their dueling baby grand pianos), a brewpub, and, should you fall short of cash, a well-placed ATM. Up the boardwalk at the glass-enclosed Sugar Warehouse you'll find a few bars and clubs, including Shooter's Waterfront, another filled-to-capacity bar. Panini's Bar & Grille has huge sandwiches popular after all the carousing. An upscale billiards hall is also on site.

On the East Bank, the ***Odeon Concert Club*** across from the visitors' information center brings in a wide variety of moderately well-known popular music acts, h hop to heavy metal retreads. Any number watering holes can be found in the vicini and it is a popular pub run indeed.

University Circle The acclaimed Clev land Symphony Orchestra holds its seas (August to May) at ***Severance Hall*** *(☎ 21 231-1111, 11001 Euclid Ave)*, near Unive sity Circle. It's been said that this is t world's most-recorded orchestra. It al performs in summer at the ***Blossom Mus Center***, in the Cuyahoga Valley Nation Recreation Area.

Warehouse District At the corner E 9th and St Clair Ave, ***Wilbert's*** specializ in blues, as does ***Fat Fish Blue***, downtov (see Places to Eat). ***The Grid*** *(☎ 216-62 0113, 1281 E 9th St)* is a gay dance venu The entire block of W 6th St north of Clair Ave is a happening spot. Not one b two jazz clubs – ***Bop Stop*** and ***Sixth Stre Under*** – are found here, as well as a cig bar and ***Liquid***, a hip café-cum-dance plac Across the street from these, ***Spy*** is hard peg – you might get a Browns football gan party, you might get a '70s night, you mig get swing dance lessons.

Spectator Sports

Cleveland is a serious sports town and h three modern downtown venues. T beloved Indians play baseball at Jacobs Fie (☎ 216-420-4200) from April to October. T 'Jake' was the first 'new-old' stadium major league baseball and is an absolu treasure, architecturally speaking, with nod to stadiums of the early 20th century a fan-friendly seating and amenities. Ticke are hard to come by, depending on who is town to play the Indians, but give it a try.

Some argue that football defines the ci even more than does baseball; the Clevela Browns have one of the most storied fra chise histories in the NFL. In 1999 the Brow football team was resurrected after its own took the previous incarnation to Baltimo the fans howl in their 'Dawg Pound' again brand-new Cleveland Browns Stadium besi the Great Lakes Science Center.

The NBA Cavaliers (☎ 216-420-2000) ıd WNBA Rockers (☎ 216-263-7625) play ısketball at nearby Gund Arena. The umberjacks minor-league hockey team ıares the arena.

etting There & Away

ir Cleveland Hopkins International irport (☎ 216-265-6030) is 11 miles south-est of town. Serving the terminal are Air anada/Air Ontario, American Airlines, merica West, Continental, Delta, North-est, Southwest, TWA, United and US irways. Without question, the best airline ith service to the Great Lakes is on lidwest Express, a Milwaukee-based airline hich has superb service and all-leather, ısiness class seats, all for not much more ıan other airlines. See the Toll-Free & Web te Directory at the back of the book for rlines' contact information.

us The bus station (☎ 216-781-0520), ɔwntown at 1465 Chester Ave, has fre-ıent Greyhound connections to Pitts-ırgh, Pennsylvania ($19, 3 hours), Chicago 35, 7 hours) and New York ($76, 9½ ɔurs). Within the state, buses leave regu-rly for Columbus ($18, 2 hours), Cincin-ıti ($35, 5 hours), Toledo ($19, 2½ hours) ıd other towns.

rain Daily trains leave the Amtrak ation (☎ 216-696-5115, 800-872-7245), ɜar the waterfront at 200 Cleveland lemorial Shoreway, across from the Great akes Science Center, for Pittsburgh ($30, hours), Chicago ($57, 7 hours), Washing-n, DC ($65, 11 hours) and New York 75, 11½ hours). To get to Detroit you ave to disembark at Toledo and take a ɔnnecting bus. No trains link Cincinnati ıd Cleveland; you have to take the bus. he station is open only when trains arrive ıd depart, usually late at night.

etting Around

he Regional Transit Authority (RTA; 216-621-9500 for 24-hour information) as a fairly comprehensive local bus and ain system. The Tower City main station is connected via walkways to Jacobs Field and Gund Arena. The RTA maintains a customer service center in the BP building at 315 Euclid Ave.

To/From the Airport There are easy connections to the airport on the local Regional Transit Authority Red Line train ($1.50). An airport shuttle ($9) departs from the lower level baggage claim No 6 and hits major downtown hotels.

Bus Local buses cost $1.25, or 50¢ for a weekday local loop service. From Public Square the Outer Loop runs to Cleveland Memorial Shoreway, just south of the lakefront attractions. The Center City Loop connects the west side of downtown, near the Flats, as far east as E 18th St.

Departing from University Circle station the 'Circlelink' shuttle runs to the Cleveland Botanical Gardens, the Cleveland Museum of Art, and the Cleveland Museum of Natural History.

Train The Waterfront Line connects the major waterfront attractions, the Flats and Tower City Center; with a valid pass or transfer, you also get great discounts at major attractions (like $3 off admission to the Rock & Roll Hall of Fame & Museum and $1.50 off a combination museum and Omnimax Theater ticket at the Great Lakes Science Center) or certain restaurants and organized tours. The Waterfront Line runs from 6:56 am to 11:48 pm.

The Blue and Green Lines run to the eastern suburbs. The Red Line links the airport to University Circle starting at 3:39 am; the last train leaves the airport at 10 pm.

A single journey train ticket costs $1.50 and *any* ticket is also good for four hours on the Waterfront Line; ask about a day pass if you're going to do a lot of riding.

Boat The *Holy Moses* water taxi connects both banks of the Cuyahoga River in the Flats district during the summer. Tuesday to Sunday a boat crosses from the Main Ave Dock, just behind the information center on

Old River Rd, to Panini's Dock on the West Bank, or to the Nautica Dock when concerts are taking place. Friday and Saturday another trip departs from Fado's Irish Pub, just to the north of the information center, crossing to Shooter's, another pub on the West Bank. Hours are 6 pm to 1 am Tuesday to Thursday, noon to 2 am Friday and Saturday, and noon to midnight Sunday. The fare is $3 one-way, $1.50 if you show a valid local bus or train ticket.

Car Parking is scarce and expensive downtown; metered spots on the street are very tough to get. In the more plentiful parking garages, daily rates run from $5 to $10. Surface lots are often a little cheaper than garages.

Prepare for sticker shock if you rent a car at the airport; various 'fees' can tack on up to 30% more than you expected to pay.

Taxi Cabs are around $2 flagfall for the first quarter-mile and come out to about $3 for the first mile. They sit waiting at Public Square. Yellow Cab (☎ 216-623-1500) is one of many.

AROUND CLEVELAND

Mentor

This town some 20 miles east of Cleveland was the home of James A Garfield, the 20th president of the US. **Lawnfield–James A Garfield National Historic Site** (☎ 440-255-8722) was his estate prior to leaving for Washington, DC. A massive renovation of the 30-room mansion's ornate interiors was finished in 1999. A carriage house that served as his campaign office is now a visitors' center. Hours are 10 am to 5 pm Monday to Saturday, noon to 5 pm Sunday. The visitors' center is free; the house costs $5/4 adults/children.

Sea World

The most-hyped attraction southeast of Cleveland is the ever-popular Sea World of Ohio (☎ 216-562-8101), 25 miles away off Hwy 43 in Aurora. People plunk down their money just for a chance to get splashed by Shamu (a trademarked killer whale name). You'll also find waterski shows, up-clos views of sea life and an exhibit center fea turing changing interactive exhibits. Hour are 10 am until dusk (or whenever they ca get everybody out) daily, late May throug early September. Admission is a stee $31/23 adults/children. Oh, and it's $4 fo parking. Mid-May through early Septem ber, an express bus runs to Sea World fro the Van Aken Rapid Station every 3 minutes; with a valid bus ticket, your admis sion is reduced by $4.

If that isn't enough to wear out parent also right here is the **Geauga Lake Amuse ment Park** (☎ 330-562-7131), a high-octan place that draws thrill-seeking types with i suspending looping coaster, one of a hal dozen in the park. A water complex has wave pool and endlessly cool water slide Hours are 11 am to 10 pm weekdays, noo to 10 pm weekends, late May through Se tember. Admission is $25/12 adults/childre

Cuyahoga Valley National Recreation Area

This is a gem located some 23 miles sout east of downtown Cleveland. It cove 33,000 acres along the serpentine course the Cuyahoga ('crooked') River betwee Akron and Cleveland. Most come to use th outstanding 20-mile graded, multius **Towpath Trail**, a path right next to the riv formerly used by horses towing barge More than 100 miles of other trails twi through the region, including a woode section of the 1200-mile Buckeye Trail. Cleveland Metroparks **multiuse trail** para lels the recreation area; a trailhead is foun just west of Hwy 8 along Hwy 303.

Information A number of visitors' cente or supplies stores, in remodeled origin dwellings, highlight the region's history ar the many outdoor activities available her All but one are found along the Towpa Trail. The main Canal Visitor Center found approximately 5 miles southeast the I-77 and I-480 junction; this one has th most exhibits. Ten miles south is the Bost Store (☎ 216-524-1497), which rents bicycl and sells supplies. Seven miles south of he the Hunt Farm Visitor Center, built on an ld farmstead. One mile west of the intersecon of Hwys 8 and 303 is the Happy Days isitor Center – slow down, it's easy to miss.

hings to See & Do The park is sublime. he **Blossom Music Center**, a natural amhitheater on 800 acres, is the summer ome of the Cleveland Symphony Orchesa – it also attracts popular music artists – nd the acoustics are nearly perfect. The **uyahoga Valley Scenic Railroad** offers twoour train rides ($11/7 adults/children) rough the valley from Independence to eninsula. Two trips depart Wednesday rough Sunday, June through August, eekends only the rest of the year; daily ips are also offered when fall colors arrive, sually mid-October.

The **Hale Farm and Village**, 5 miles south f Peninsula near Bath, is a restored – and orking – 1848 village, with costumed ocents demonstrating blacksmithing, maple rup making and other skills. It's open 10 am 5 pm Tuesday through Saturday, noon to pm Sunday, late May through October 31. dmission is $9/6 adults/children.

The village of **Peninsula**, 2 miles west of wy 8 along Hwy 303, is the hub and most opular trailhead. Four miles southwest of eninsula along Riverview and Everett Rds a picturesque **covered bridge**.

laces to Stay No camping is allowed in e recreation area. The village of Boston, 2 iles north of Peninsula, has a youth hostel; e Cleveland's Places to Stay section for etails. East of Peninsula along Hwy 303, en south on Akron–Cleveland Rd will ring you to a number of cheap ***motels***, me of which charge as little as $35 for a ouble.

berlin

Vest of Cleveland approximately 45 miles, berlin is an attractive, old-fashioned ollege town with fine architecture by Cass ilbert, Frank Lloyd Wright and Robert enturi, as well as many other fine prerved houses. **Oberlin College** was founded the same time as the town and its presence dominates. In 1837 four women were matriculated into its regular program of study, making it, they claim, the world's first coeducational college. Later, it would be a leader in accepting African American students. The college has an excellent free art museum and its music conservatory offers a full schedule of events throughout the year.

You're limited to one place to stay here, and it's not cheap. The ***Oberlin Inn*** *(☎ 440-775-1111, 7 N Main)* is right on campus and does have good rooms. Singles/doubles are $80/90. There are plenty of sandwich places around.

Lake Erie Shore

THE WESTERN RESERVE

In the free-for-all that was US expansion, eastern cities laid claim to enormous tracts of uncharted territories in the 'western frontier.' Realizing the ongoing chaos, the US government reined in the madness. Connecticut agreed to give up a major portion of its claims and instead 'reserved' a stretch of land along its own latitudinal lines stretching to the Cuyahoga River. 'New Connecticut,' and later the Western Reserve, was intended as compensation to Connecticut citizens who had suffered during the Revolutionary War. It's a region of anachronistic small towns, wineries, Ohio's best covered bridges, the state's original Lake Erie resort town, and a tiny Amish enclave. Along Lake Erie, US 20 links many picturesque communities; along the original route of the Oregon trail, this highway accesses lots of what the Western Reserve has to offer.

Ashtabula

Nestled along Lake Erie near the Pennsylvania border, Ashtabula is the seat of a county famed for covered bridges. Before you go out bridge-hunting, give the town some time. It's got a great museum and nice water views. The **Great Lakes Marine Memorial Museum** (☎ 440-964-6847), overlooking the harbor at 1071 Walnut Blvd, is an outstanding local museum. Loads of exhibits

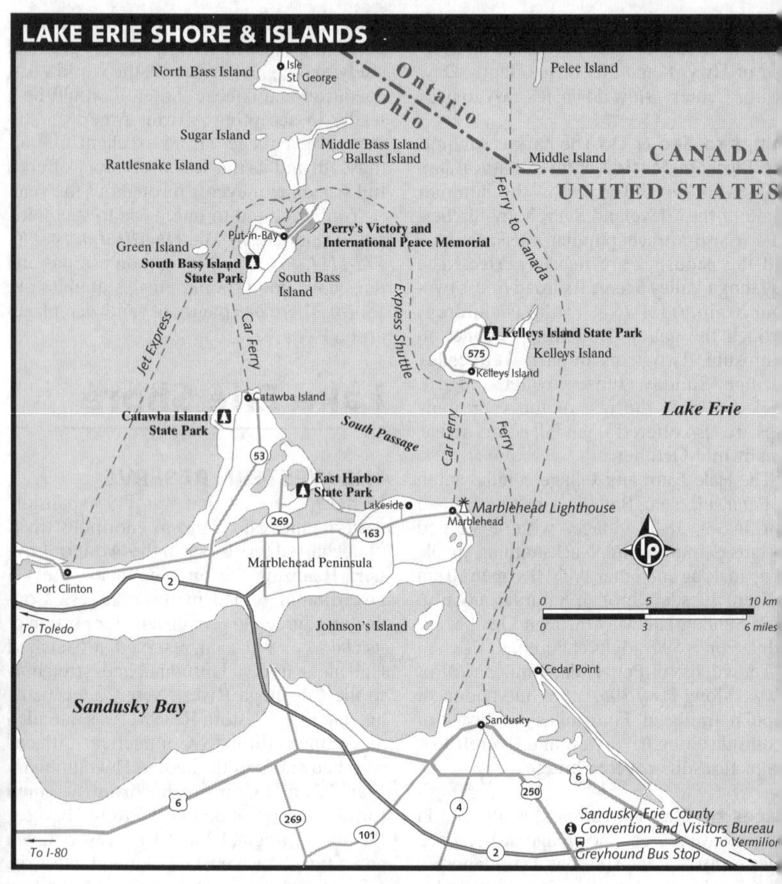

and memorabilia fill a former lighthouse keeper's residence. You can peer into the radar screens of a restored pilot's house. Best of all is the amazing working scale model of a Hulett ore unloader (device that moved massive piles of ore into carriers) – built by hand by a retired local dock worker. Hours are noon to 6 pm Friday to Sunday, Memorial Day weekend through Labor Day; free.

Up the street the **Hubbard House** (☎ 440-964-8168) was a terminus on the Underground Railroad. It has been refurbished with period furnishings and antiques. Hours are the same as the marine museum; adm sion is $3/1 adults/children.

Cedars Motel *(☎ 440-992-5406, 2015 Prospect Rd)* is centrally located along U 20. Its clean, redone rooms cost $45/ single/double. A number of motels are the vicinity. Cheaper motels can be fou south of town at the exits off I-90.

East of Hwy 45, the ***Covered Brid Pizza Parlor*** *(4861 North Ridge W)* is ju that. An original 1862 covered bridge, it w moved here and made into a restaura (main dishes from $4); two others are al pizza joints in the county.

Greyhound (☎ 440-992-7550) is at 1819 E ospect Rd and has regular buses to Clevend and Akron ($20, 3½ hours).

eneva-on-the-Lake

pop 21,500

top Lake Erie 25 miles west of the Ohio–ennsylvania border, Geneva-on-the-Lake as Ohio's first resort town, and in many ays it hasn't changed since its early days. enny candy and old-fashioned cotton ndy stands vie for tourist dollars with achronistic putt-putt courses, and the dging options have a real retro feel. Vhen making reservations, don't confuse is place with Lake Geneva, Wisconsin, as any people have done.)

The visitors' information center (☎ 440-6-8600, 800-862-9948) is right along the ain street in town.

What to see is the gorgeous lakefront enery. What to do is get in touch with your ner kid at **Erieview Amusement Park**, full classic old rides. Across the street is the untry's oldest mini-golf course, dating om 1924.

Note that any place to stay in the area oks up well in advance. For camping, west town, ***Geneva State Park*** *(☎ 440-466-8400)* s a prime waterfront location and sites for 8, or $30 if you need to rent all equipment.

Downtown, ***Uncle Tom's*** *(☎ 440-466-8791, 75 Lake Rd)* is a classic place, a family siness lodging visitors since the 1930s. It s cottages and myriad motel rooms, some th cooking facilities. Basic rooms are $40 d options and prices go up from there to 50 per week for a lakefront cottage.

The local institution for food is ***Eddie's rill***, along the main drag. Since the 1940s is has been the place for hot dogs, burgers d ice cream. It's so popular that the little and has grown to a half-block-long enterise and now commands a huge parking t across the street. A number of pubs ong the main street have good food and e entertainment.

esopotamia

is dot on the map is the center of Ohio's cond-largest concentration of Amish. The town has a lovely public square flanked by imposing Victorians and the **End of the Commons General Store**, a bulk goods store where you can get to-die-for root beer and Amish knickknacks.

SANDUSKY

• pop 21,700

Its natural harbor formed by an 18-mile bay, one of the largest on the Great Lakes, the town of Sandusky has long been a port for boats on Lake Erie and the inland rivers. At one point it battled Cleveland to be the northern terminus of the Ohio and Erie Canal; it lost out on that, but was made the terminus of Ohio's second railroad, bringing industry to town. Manufacturing is still Sandusky's economic linchpin, but in summer the place fills with tourists heading to the popular destinations of the Bass Islands and Kelleys Island, not to mention a phenomenally popular amusement park.

Information

The Sandusky–Erie County Convention & Visitors Bureau (☎ 419-625-2984, 800-255-3743) is on US 250, a mile north of the Hwy 2 intersection. It's fully loaded with area information; free telephones are linked to local lodgings.

Downtown

Sandusky features some 19th-century architecture; the **Follet House**, at the corner of E Adams and Wayne Sts, is now a museum (free), but it was once a stop for escaping slaves on the Underground Railroad. Most popular is the **Merry-Go-Round Museum** (☎ 419-626-6111), right on the public square a block from the dock. In a magnificent old post office, its working carousel is an explosion of color. You also can watch carvers restore old carousel horses on site. Hours are 11 am to 5 pm Monday to Saturday and noon to 5 pm Sunday from late May through early September, with reduced hours the rest of the year; $4/2 adults/children.

Cedar Point

The big daddy locally is the Cedar Point amusement park (☎ 419-627-2350), which has a dozen roller coasters, ranging from historic wooden trestle types to the latest, fastest, highest and scariest ones that suspend their riders upside down from twisting tracks. The Magnum XL-200 roller coaster has been voted the best roller coaster in the world, according to the knowledgeable readership of *Inside Track*, a coasterphile magazine. There aren't any Mickey Mouse themes or educational overtones; it's just a lot of fun.

The park is open every day May to September ($33/29/9 adults/kids/little kids). The surrounding area includes a pleasant beach, a water park and a slew of tacky, old-fashioned tourist attractions.

Organized Tours

The *Goodtime I* (☎ 419-625-9692) runs al day island-hopping cruises to Kelleys an Middle Bass Islands. It departs at 9:30 a and returns at 6:30 pm. The fare is $22/1 adults/children. You may also opt for raucous Friday night party boat.

Places to Stay & Eat

The best camping is found on the Er shore north of Port Clinton (see Lake Er Islands, later in this chapter). Th ***Rodeway Inn*** *(☎ 419-626-6852, 102 Cleveland Rd)* offers rates of $55 singl double, though it charges more on weel ends. Lots of motels line roads coming int

Ashtabula County Covered Bridges

LIBRARY OF CONGRESS

Ashtabula County has one of Ohio's largest concentrations of covered bridges, 16 in all (not all are still in use). Jefferson, 10 miles south of Ashtabula, is the focal point for two tours. The short circuit takes in five bridges; a longer version visits 11. Both routes cover nearly 70 miles and can take two-plus hours, or, if you like to linger, all day. Road conditions vary, but a lot of gravel sits out there. A map outlining this tour is available from any county visitors' information center, including the Ashtabula Area Chamber of Commerce (☎ 440-998-6998), 4536 Main Ave, Ashtabula. Directional signs are posted but beware: One or two are missing, so be prepared to backtrack if you think you have missed a turn somewhere. Jefferson also hosts the annual Covered Bridge Festival the second full weekend in October.

To get started, head east out of Jefferson along E Jefferson St. Three miles out of town you'll probably whiz right past the turnoff to the newest covered bridge in the county, still being worked on in 1999, along Netcher Rd. Backtracking to S Denmark Rd, another 3 miles brings you to the white 1890 **S Denmark Rd Bridge**, now bypassed but still accessible by the side of the road.

Continue east to Hwy 193, turn left, travel to Hwy 167, turn right and continue to Stanhope-Kelloggsville Rd. A right turn on gravelly Caine Rd leads, after 7 miles, to the **Caine Bridge**, built in 1986 for the county's 175th birthday celebration.

Go east on Caine Rd to Hwy 7. Turn left and travel 2 miles to Graham Rd. Turn left and continue to the **Graham Bridge** (6 miles total from the previous bridge). This old gray monster now lies aging gracefully by the roadside; it's a favorite picnic spot.

OHIO

›wn, but keep in mind that nothing comes ıeap in summer. (Even usually dirt-cheap *'otel 6 (☎ 419-499-8001)* at the junction f I-80/90 and US 250 charges $79 in ımmer!)

The ***Radisson Harbour Inn*** *(☎ 419-627-500, 2001 Cleveland Rd)* occupies a nice aterfront location and has an indoor pool, fitness center, a children's activity center ıd a 24-hour dining room. High season ıtes are $130 single/double.

Coffee Temptations *(137 E Water St)* ›rves coffee and inexpensive sandwiches ;4), muffins, bagels and juices. Get big ɜrch sandwiches and fresh fish to take ˌway at ***DeMore's*** *(302 W Perkins Ave)*.

Getting There & Away

The local Greyhound stop (☎ 419-625-6907) is near the intersection of Hwy 2 and US 250, on the north side of the road. It has connections to Cleveland ($12, 1½ hours) and other cities.

Amtrak (☎ 800-872-7245) makes a stop at the corner of Depot St and Hayes Ave. Trains depart daily for points east and west: Chicago ($46, 5 hours), Cleveland ($10, 1½ hours).

Sandusky is a departure point for Pelee Island, Ontario, via Pelee Island Transportation (☎ 800-661-2220); the crossing takes two hours and costs $14/7 adults/children. The quicker speedboat Jet Rocket (☎ 419-627-1500) makes the trip in less than half

Ashtabula County Covered Bridges

Travel west to Stanhope-Kelloggsville Rd. Turn right and continue north to Root Rd, a total of 4 miles. The **Root Bridge** is a lattice-type built in 1868 (don't worry, it's been updated).

The going gets weird here, with a few signs missing. Go west on Root Rd to gravel Reger Rd. Going north, bear left at a Y-intersection, then straight on Caleb Ave and follow signs to Hwy 84. At the intersection of Hwy 84 and Hwy 7 turn left and travel to South Ridge Rd. Turn right; this is a rutted section. There's no sign for your next right turn along Middle Rd; total distance from the previous bridge is 8½ miles. Here you'll find a lovely 136-ft-long bridge in a deep dell.

Head south to Hatch Corners Rd, turn left and travel about 5 miles to the **State Rd Bridge**, a massive bridge made from 97,000 sq feet of southern pine and oak. It also has a window running its entire length (to see oncoming traffic).

The next one's basically impossible to find as no signs exist. Heading north along State Rd, Keefus Rd, and Amboy Rd some 3½ miles *should* bring you to the **Creek Rd Bridge**. If you get lost, try to find US 20, from which you should be able to find Amboy Rd. Head west along US 20, then south to Hwy 193, which leads you to Kingsville. A pit stop is warranted, so have a pizza at the **Covered Bridge Pizza Parlor,** one of three restaurants built out of retired county bridges (fare from $4).

Continue south on Hwy 193 to Gageville-Monroe Rd, and turn right. The **Benetka Rd Bridge**, dating from 1900, should be 11½ miles from the previous bridge. If you go north along Benetka Rd to Dewey Rd and turn left, you'll come to **Olin Bridge**, another oldie, dating from 1873.

You're almost home. Continue west to Rockwell Rd. Turn left, then make a right on Plymouth Ridge Rd and drive until you come to State Rd (it's a different one from the previously mentioned State Rd). This joins up with US 46 and continues south to Griggs Rd. Turn left and go to Giddings Rd. Make a right: The final bridge, the **Giddings Rd Bridge**, was built in 1995.

From here you can head right back into Jefferson by continuing south on Giddings Rd.

the time; it costs $15/5 adults/children. The same speedboat company also makes a run to Kelleys Island.

Getting Around

The Sandusky Transit System (☎ 419-627-0740) has a summer shuttle bus ($2) that serves the downtown with area hotels, attractions, boat lines, and Cedar Point. It operates Friday evening, 8 am to midnight Saturday, and 9 am to 7 pm Sunday.

AROUND SANDUSKY

Vermilion

The **Inland Seas Museum** (☎ 440-967-3467), 480 Main St, has two floors chock-full of paintings, clippings, and memorabilia from Great Lakes shipping history. There's a good exhibit on diving. You can also take the wheel at a restored pilot's house. Hours are 10 am to 5 pm daily. Admission is $5/3 adults/children.

Milan

Nine miles south of Sandusky, little Milan hacked out a canal to Lake Erie in the early 19th century and made itself into one of the nation's largest wheat shippers. But it's really on the map as the birthplace of Thomas Edison, the genius inventor of the incandescent light bulb and phonograph, among many other things. The **Thomas Alva Edison Birthplace** (☎ 419-499-2135) has a collection of rare Edison artifacts, including early inventions and family mementos. The museum is open 10 am to 5 pm Tuesday to Saturday and 1 to 5 pm Sunday, June to August, lesser times February through May; $5/2 adults/children.

OHIO

LAKE ERIE ISLANDS

Native American pictographs have been found on these islands, which were inhabited by Iroquois when the French first arrived. In the War of 1812's Battle of Lake Erie, Admiral Perry met and defeated the enemy English fleet near South Bass Island. His victory ensured that all the lands south of the Great Lakes became US, not Canadian, territory. The islands were exploited for timber and later planted with grapevines. Today, the nearby mainland gets very bus[y] and isn't particularly attractive, but th[e] islands have remained largely unspoile[d] even though tourism is now the main indus[try], so much so that in summertime if yo[u] plan to take a vehicle over to the islands, yo[u] must provide written evidence of a lodgin[g] reservation. There's great bird-watchin[g] here as well.

Kelleys Island

Once the site of numerous limestone qua[r]ries, this quiet green island is now a popula[r] weekend getaway. A thriving vineyard i[n]dustry has also risen on the island.

Call the chamber of commerce (☎ 41[9-]746-2360) for accommodations informatio[n].

Things to See & Do Due east of the ferr[y] landing is **Kelleys Mansion**, a mansion bui[lt] by one of the island's original European se[t]tlers, Addison Kelley. The freestandin[g] spiral staircase is interesting. Nearby on [a] limestone boulder are pictographs fro[m] Native Americans, who used the island as [a] hunting ground.

On the north side of the island is **Glaci[al] Grooves State Memorial**. The area is th[e] largest example of glacial grooving in th[e] world. The 400-foot by 35-foot grooves a[re] the result of the Wisconsin glacier, dating t[o] some 30,000 years ago.

Places to Stay & Eat Arrive early to get [a] campsite at ***Kelleys Island State Par[k]*** *(☎ 419-797-4530)*; a site costs $15, and yo[u] can rent all camping gear for $30. Th[e] Village, the small commercial center of th[e] island, has places to eat and shop, as well a[s] a couple of pubs. The ***Kelleys Island Win[e] Tasting Room and Bistro***, northeast of th[e] docks, has wine tasting and casually upsca[le] fare.

Getting There & Around Access to th[e] island is by frequent ferry from Sandusky o[r] Marblehead. Among the numerous opera[tors] is Kelley Island Ferry Boat Line (☎ 888-225-4325), which leaves from th[e] dock in Marblehead ($10/17 person/car). For a few dollars more, the Jet Rock[et] peedboat (☎ 419-627-1500) from Sandusky uts the crossing time by more than half. hort flights from Sandusky ($24) are an ption. The Express Shuttle (☎ 800-245-538) connects Kelleys Island with Put-in-Bay on South Bass Island ($6/1 adults/hildren).

You'll have no trouble finding a bicycle o rent; they're everywhere you look for bout $15 per day.

outh Bass Island

Another popular destination in summer is outh Bass Island, when Put-in-Bay ecomes a party town and the rest of the sland becomes a haven for camping, fishing, iking and swimming.

The chamber of commerce (☎ 419-285-832) has information on lodging, which tarts at $60 in summer and books up early. You need proof of lodging to bring a vehicle ver in summer.

hings to See & Do A singular attraction **Perry's Victory and International Peace Memorial**. The 352-foot Doric column commemorates Perry's win in the Battle of ake Erie. On September 10, 1813, Commodore Oliver Hazard Perry's ragtag fleet f nine thrown-together ships defeated a British flotilla not far off Put-in-Bay. It was ne first naval victory for the young US, which had not had much luck during the War of 1812. You can climb up to the observation deck for a view of the battle site – and, on a good day, Canada. The fee is $3 for dults, free for children 16 and under.

West of Perry's Memorial on Langram Rd, **Stonehenge Estate** is an early 1800s armhouse and a cottage housing an erstwhile winepress and period furniture. Admission is $4/2 adults/children.

Caves line the islands. The world's largest eode can be found at **Crystal Cave**, part of which is used by Heineman's Winery. A winery tour – with a tasting – costs $4.

The **Tour Train** offers one-hour narrated ours ($8/2 adults/children) of the island.

laces to Stay & Eat The ***South Bass sland State Park*** campground *(☎ 419-797-4530)* fills up early ($16), but you can reserve a campsite at the private campground ***Bass Isle Resort*** *(☎ 419-285-6121, 800-837-5211)*.

A plethora of lodging exists, but in summer it books up very early. East of the Miller Boat Line on Langram Rd, the ***Bird's Nest Motel*** *(☎ 419-285-6119)* is among the cheaper options, with doubles from $65. A restored 1863 home and erstwhile boardinghouse for fleet officers, ***Ashley's Island House*** *(☎ 419-285-2844, 557 Catawba Ave)* has 10 guestrooms from $70, but is much more expensive Friday and Saturday.

Put-in-Bay has plenty of places for eating. Most feature concoctions of lake perch or walleye and have evening entertainment. Outside of seafood, ***Pasqual's*** in Village Park has Italian food (main dishes from $5).

Options for imbibing are unlimited for such a small island; most are in Village Park. Many visitors first quaff a brew at the distinctively domed red ***Round House Bar***, but the world's longest bar is at the ***Beer Barrel Saloon***, with 160 bar stools and nearly 60 beers on tap. Entertainment is constant during the summer here.

Getting There & Around Most ferries to South Bass Island leave from Port Clinton or Catawba Island (not really an island), north of Port Clinton, on the mainland. Miller Boat Line (☎ 419-500-2421) is the main one, with hourly auto and passenger ferries to Put-in-Bay ($5/10 passenger/auto) and fewer trips to Middle Bass Island ($6/13 passenger/auto) from Catawba Point; reservations may be necessary depending on the time of year. The Jet Express (☎ 888-245-1538) ($10/2 adults/children) runs regularly from Port Clinton. From Sandusky, the Jet Rocket speedboat (☎ 419-627-1500) serves both islands, saving a drive up the peninsula ($11/4 adults/children).

There are taxis ($2 anywhere) on South Bass island, but bicycling is the best way to get around; cars, in fact, are a hassle. Bicycles rent for $3 per hour or $18 per day. Pesky – and ubiquitous – little golf carts are another option; they start at $8 per hour.

The Lime Kiln bus ($1) operates between the Miller Ferry Dock and downtown.

Middle Bass Island

Middle Bass Island is a popular day trip by ferry from South Bass. The medieval-looking Lonz winery is the big attraction. A ferry ($7 roundtrip) makes the trip daily from South Bass. A winery tour costs less than $2.

PORT CLINTON

You'll probably have to at least pass through Port Clinton to get to the islands (two ferries depart from the docks here). There's not a lot to see here but it has many motels and restaurants. Six miles northeast on the shoreline of the peninsula are two state parks, only one of which, ***East Harbor State Park*** *(☎ 419-734-4424)*, has camping ($12).

MARBLEHEAD

At the very tip of the Lake Erie peninsula is flyspeck-size Marblehead, a ferry departure point for the islands. Also here is **Marblehead Lighthouse**, a 50-foot signal dating from 1822. Eighty-seven steps lead to the top. Admission is $2.

The little community of **Lakeside** just to the west is an anachronism, one of the largest and last remaining chautauquas on the Great Lakes. These summertime arts and cultural centers once flourished in the late 19th and early 20th centuries. The historic Victorian village is a vacation resort that still provides a series of music performances, lectures and seminars. You can camp or lodge in an inn ($65 and up single/double). Just to enter the village costs $2 for a two-hour pass.

TOLEDO

• pop 312,170

Toledo is actually in the consciousness of Americans, thanks to the TV show *M*A*S*H*; local hero Jamie Farr's character, Corporal Klinger, maniacally tried – in every episode – to escape the army and return to Toledo. But this awareness hasn't seemed to translate into let's-pull-off-the-interstate-between-Cleveland-and-Detroit.

It warrants a visit, though, to its worth Toledo Museum of Art, an awesome arra of ethnic eateries, and America's mos famous minor league baseball team (se 'Household Names').

History

A decisive military victory against Nativ American tribes in 1794 forced them to ced most lands to the US government. White se tlement was sparse initially and those wh did come mostly fled when the War of 181 broke out. The town became embroiled i what came to be known as the 'Toledo Wa of 1835–36, a nearly bloody spat with Michi gan over state boundaries. The states' militia faced off in Toledo and undertook sporadi raids on each other; damage was limited t symbolic thieving of state flags and the lik Prisoners were taken and ultimately, Presi dent Andrew Jackson had to intervene. Th end result was that Toledo remained part c Ohio, but Michigan got most of what is no its Upper Peninsula. Toledo's prime locatio along Lake Erie also brought shipping; it' one of the busiest and most important por on the Great Lakes.

Information

The Greater Toledo Convention & Visitor Bureau (☎ 419-321-6404, 800-243-4667) i downtown at 401 Jefferson Ave inside th SeaGate Convention Center. It doesn have much information; the Web sit (www.toledocvb.com) has more.

Kinko's (☎ 419-535-5679) has a branch a 3111 W Bancroft St, about 4 miles west c the downtown. Rates are $12 per hour o 20¢ per minute.

Reading Railroad (☎ 419-882-4944) a 6600 Sylvania Ave, northwest of town, is good bookstore.

The Weekly is a free weekly with overview of local nightlife.

Toledo Museum of Art

Professional museum associations regar this museum (☎ 419-255-8000), 2445 Monro St, west of downtown, as one of the top 1 in the US. Exhibits cover every period bac to ancient Egypt and include hundreds c ıasterworks by artists such as El Greco, ‹ubens, Rembrandt, Monet, van Gogh and 'icasso. Sculpture, glassware, furniture, ilverware and graphic arts are also on isplay. The museum café is good. Hours are 0 am to 4 pm Tuesday to Saturday, until 0 pm Friday, 11 am to 5 pm Sunday; free.

:OSI Toledo

'he Center of Science and Industry COSI) is a hands-on science education ıuseum (☎ 419-244-2674) featuring eight xhibition areas, a high-wire bicycle, a irtual sports arena and a Simulator Theater. On the corner of Summit and Adams Sts, hours are 10 am to 5 pm Monday to Saturday, noon to 6 pm Sunday; $7/5 adults/children.

SS *Willis B Boyer*

At International Park on the opposite bank of the river from downtown, this former freighter sailed the Great Lakes for six decades. Now a museum, it's been refurbished right down to the captain's wheel, the obligatory photo op. Hours are 10 am to 5 pm, noon to 5 pm May through September; $5/3 adults/children.

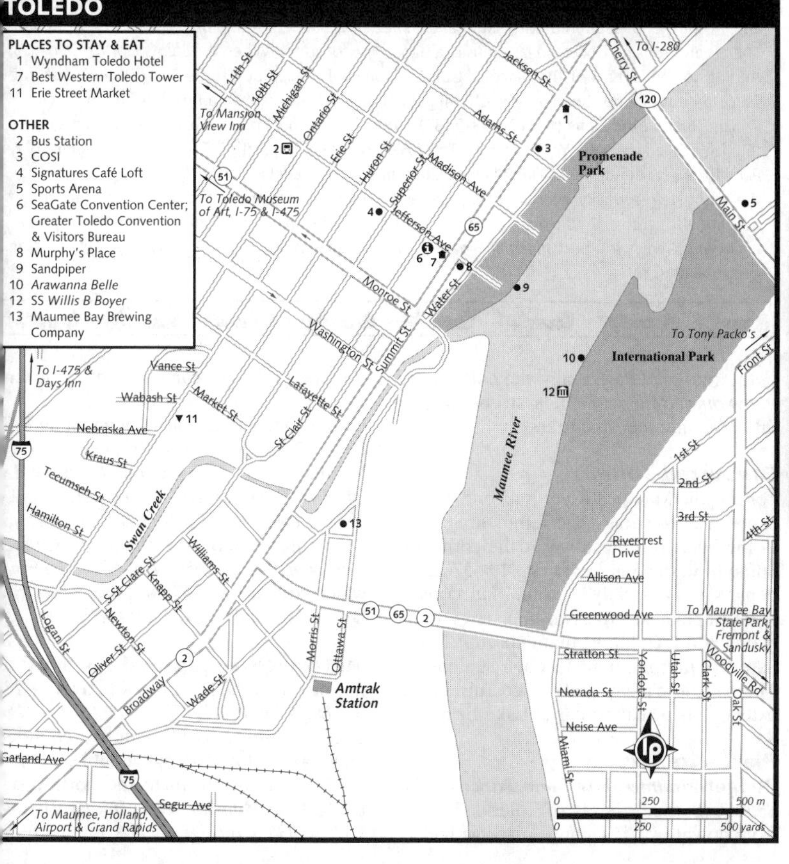

Household Names

For over a decade, the television 'dramedy' *M*A*S*H* was a cultural institution for Americans, an invulnerable number-one show. One of the show's main characters was Corporal Max Klinger, played by Toledo native Jamie Farr. Klinger was the Korean War's version of the novel *Catch-22*'s Yossarian, comically pretending to be insane to avoid the madness of war and get home. Only Klinger, instead of plotting to escape to Sweden, decided to do it by dressing in women's clothing. The running gag of Klinger, chest hair sticking out of a white nurse's uniform, shocking a wounded soldier lying in the hospital, was used a hundred times in the show and never once did Americans tire of it.

Klinger's maniacal windmill-chase occurred weekly; he would flee the camp, staggering down the road in high heels, and the military police would dutifully retrieve him. Brought before the commanding officer, he would collapse in a heap and rave about Toledo. It brought national attention to two Toledo institutions: Tony Packo's and the Toledo Mud Hens.

Tony Packo's (☎ 419-885-4500, 1902 Front St) is across the Maumee River from downtown Toledo in the Hungarian community of Birmingham. Since 1932 it's been *the* place for great chili and hot dogs in an unpretentious atmosphere. Originally take-out only, it now has a dining room and a full menu peppered with Hungarian specialties like stuffed cabbage (entrées from $5). There's also rousing Dixieland jazz music (a dance line forms for 'When the Saints Go Marchin' In'). Adding to the legend of the place, astronaut Donald Thomas took some Tony Packo's hot dog sauce on not one but two space shuttle flights and even autographed a hot dog bun in space.

The **Toledo Mud Hens** (☎ 419-893-9483) is possibly the most famous baseball team in America that isn't called the New York Yankees. The AAA-affiliate of the Detroit Tigers, the Mud Hens play April through September at Ned Skeldon Stadium in Maumee. Like other minor league ball clubs, the team stages wacky events during games to draw crowds and it's great fun for families. If nothing else, grab a Mud Hens T-shirt or hat, the coolest souvenir in Ohio. The Mud Hens perennially win surveys for 'best sports nickname,' in no small part due to that war-weary cross-dresser, Corporal Klinger.

International Park is also the port for the *Arawanna Belle*, a replica stern-wheeler that gives summertime tours.

Organized Tours

Touring the Maumee River is a good way to experience Toledo. At the Jefferson St dock in the heart of downtown at the corner of Summit St, the *Sandpiper* (☎ 419-537-1212) departs for a variety of tours and cruises. Most popular are the two-hour river tours ($10/5 adults/children) that depart at 10 am Saturday morning June through September. There are also picnic and sunset cruises. One extended trip heads out into Lake Erie.

Places to Stay

Budget ***Maumee Bay State Park*** *(☎ 419-836-7758)* is northeast of Toledo, 7 miles from downtown. It's a huge place with electric sites ($16); you can also rent rustic tent cabins ($32).

Most budget lodging is found along I-47 far west of downtown, in the village c Maumee. Best is the ***Cross Country In*** *(☎ 419-891-0880, 1704 Tollgate Drive)* on U 20 just east of I-75. Good rooms cost jus $35/40 single/double. Another ***Cross Countr Inn*** *(☎ 419-866-6565, 1435 E Mall Drive)* which costs a few dollars more, is north c here in Holland, at exit 8 off I-475.

Mid-Range & Top End Just north o downtown at the junction of I-75 and I-28C the ***Days Inn*** *(☎ 419-729-1945, 1821 E Manhattan Blvd)* has rooms with free continen tal breakfast for $50 single/double.

Close to downtown to the northwest i the historic ***Mansion View Inn*** *(☎ 419-244 5676, 2035 Collingwood Ave)*, a Quee ınne B&B with rooms starting at $90 ingle/double.

A handful of pricey hotels are found in ıe city center. The ***Best Western Toledo*** ***'ower*** *(☎ 419-242-8885, fax 419-242-1337, 41 N Summit Ave)* is where you'll find the ıeapest of these. There's a pool, sauna, exrcise room, and restaurant with views of ıe city. Singles/doubles start at $99.

Rooms at the ***Wyndham Toledo Hotel*** *☎ 419-241-1411, fax 419-241-8161, 2 Summit t)* have great river views, along with an ıdoor pool. Room rates during the week re high at $135 single/double, but they lummet on weekends.

'laces to Eat

'or information about Toledo's main eatery, 'ony Packo's, see 'Household Names.'

Thursday to Sunday the ***Erie Street*** ***Iarket***, southwest of downtown, boasts a undred vendors selling produce, crafts and ood. You'll find cheap coffee boutiques, akeries, delis and food stands, even Amish elling pies. The produce sellers are there aily.

Some dining exists downtown, but many ateries are found far west of downtown long Monroe St. The ***Beirut*** *(4802 Monroe t)* has Lebanese and Italian food, along ith some vegetarian options (entrées from 7). ***JD Wesley's*** *(☎ 419-841-7594, 5333 Ionroe St)* is an elegant French bistro erving lunch and dinner Tuesday to Friday, inner only on weekends.

If you are lodging in Maumee, in the iolden Gate Shopping Center the ***Golden*** ***'ing*** *(☎ 419-893-7111)*, Anthony Wayne 'rail at Conant St, has award-winning 'hinese food (main dishes from $7).

Aside from Tony Packo's, Toledo resients would probably pick ***Mancy's*** *(☎ 419-76-4154, 953 Phillips Ave)*, in north Toledo, the local restaurant of choice. Since the 920s it has been the regional place for eaks and seafood (entrées from $10). eservations are necessary.

ntertainment

couple of places offer entertainment owntown. One block north of the SeaGate Convention Center, ***Signatures Café Loft*** *(513 Jefferson Ave)* has rock and R&B acts Thursday to Saturday. ***Murphy's Place*** *(151 Water St)* has jazz nightly. A lively place is ***Major Oliver's Pub***, inside the Maumee Bay Brewing Company at 27 Broadway Ave in a historic structure. It has live music on weekends.

Spectator Sports

For information on the Toledo Mud Hens, see 'Household Names.' The Toledo Storm (☎ 419-691-0200) is a minor-league affiliate of the Detroit Red Wings hockey team. They drop the puck at the Sports Arena, 1 Main St, on the other side of the river from downtown.

Getting There & Away

Toledo is served by mostly commuter shuttles at the Toledo Express Airport (☎ 419-865-2351).

Greyhound (☎ 419-248-1498) is at 811 Jefferson Ave, north of the SeaGate Convention Center and within walking distance of downtown. It has daily connections to Dayton ($24, 3 hours), Cleveland ($19, 2 hours), Indianapolis ($49, 5 hours) and Detroit ($10, 1 hour).

Amtrak (☎ 419-246-0159), 415 Emerald St, runs trains daily between Chicago, Cleveland and the East Coast that stop in Toledo. Sample fares are Chicago ($46), Cleveland ($20) and New York City ($86). To go north into Michigan, Amtrak has Thruway bus connections to Detroit and Ann Arbor.

Getting Around

The Toledo Area Regional Transit Authority (TARTA) (☎ 419-243-7433) has service to all points in town but not to the airport. A good option is the downtown trolley (25¢) that circles the downtown area noon to 2 pm. For a ride to the airport, try Black & White Cab (☎ 419-478-8866).

AROUND TOLEDO

Grand Rapids

Approximately 35 miles southwest of Toledo, this small town is the site of a historic reconstruction of a portion of the Miami and Erie Canal. **Providence Metropark** (☎ 419-535-3058), US 24 at Hwy 578, has an original mill – the Isaac Ludwig Mill – with costumed guides. Most people come for a canal ride through old lock No 44 aboard a mule-drawn boat. Boats operate 10 am to 4 pm Wednesday to Friday, 11 am to 5 pm weekends May through October; $4/2 adults/children.

The Bluebird (☎ 419-878-2177) is a scenic tour train that operates between Grand Rapids and Waterville, 20 miles to the northeast. The railroad operates May through October on a varied schedule, generally weekends; $8/5 adults/children.

Mary Jane Thurston State Park *(☎ 419-832-7662)* is 1 mile west of town on Hwy 65, with good riverside sites ($8).

Fremont

Thirty-five miles southeast of Toledo, Fremont was the home of Rutherford B Hayes, the 19th president of the US and Ohio's first three-term governor. The **Hayes Presidential Center** (☎ 419-332-2081), at Hayes and Buckland Aves, is a 25-acre estate where he lived with his family (they're interred in a granite tomb on the grounds). The six gates on the wrought-iron fence originally hung around the White House. The site consists of the family mansion and a museum; tours leave every half-hour. If nothing else, the grounds are lovely and full of trails that were originally used by Native Americans traveling from the Great Lakes to the Ohio River. The center is open 9 am to 5 pm Monday to Saturday, noon to 5 pm Sunday. A combination ticket for both is $9/3 adults/children.

Clyde

East a handful of miles from Fremont on Hwy 20 and surrounded by farmland is Clyde, which bills itself as the USA's most famous small town. It got that way when *Winesburg, Ohio*, by native son Sherwood Anderson, was published in 1919. It didn't take long for the unimpressed residents to figure out where the fictitious town really was. Stop at the Clyde Museum (☎ 419-547-9330), in the old church on Buckeye St. A few doors down is the library, which has an extensive Anderson book collection.

Central Northern Ohio

LIMA

South of Toledo some 70 miles, Lima is a sleepy town that had its 15 minutes of fame when John Dillinger got into a shootout with a local sheriff, mortally wounding him; it led to a nationwide dragnet and Dillinger's eventual demise.

High school football appears to be the thing that rouses the locals most. The **Allen County Museum** (☎ 419-222-9426), 620 W Market St, and **MacDonnell House** (☎ 419-222-9426), nearby, contain items relevant to local history. The latter, an elegant Victorian redone in period style, costs $2 to tour.

To browse books, visit Readmore Bookstore (☎ 419-225-5826) at 217 Flanders.

A slew of cheap motels line the intersection of I-75 and Hwy 309, including a ***Motel 6*** *(☎ 419-228-0465, 1800 Harding Hwy)*, with rooms from $36. More luxurious options are at the junction as well.

Downtown's best attraction, ***Kewpee Hamburgers***, at the corner of Elizabeth and Market Sts, is what people pull off the interstate to wander downtown for. Since the 1930s this place has been frying up 'sliders,' delicious hamburgers ($1). They also serve great pies. A line of cars backs up from the drive-through window around the block pretty much all day.

Lima's intercity bus stop (☎ 419-224-7781) is at 2995 Harding Hwy (Hwy 309) at a cemetery headstone store (seriously), but you're in the middle of nowhere here.

AROUND LIMA

Eight miles south of town off I-75 at exit 111, near the town of Wapakoneta, is the **Neil Armstrong Air and Space Museum** (☎ 419-738-8811), which explores not just Armstrong but the history of flight from as far back as French attempts at ballooning

.ots of planes and space vehicles related to \rmstrong and his Gemini and Apollo missions are on site. Kids love the Astroheater's **space ride** experience. Hours are :30 to 5 pm Monday to Saturday, noon to pm Sunday; $5/1adults/children.

MARION

The pleasant town of Marion is approximately 40 miles north of Columbus via busy JS 23. The steam shovel was developed in Marion and huge earth movers and heavy nachinery with the name emblazoned on hem rolled out of the town's Marion Steam Shovel Plant for places all over the globe. This is now overshadowed by more northrn Ohio presidential history. Warren G Harding, the 29th president of the US, pubished a newspaper in Marion from 1884 until his presidential victory in 1920.

Greyhound has a depot at 137 S State St. Buses leave for Cleveland ($36, 6 hours) nd Columbus ($10, 1 hour).

Things to See

Warren G Harding's home is now a state historic site, the **President Harding Home and Museum** (☎ 740-387-9630) at 380 Mt Vernon Ave. The house appears exactly as it did when Harding gave his famous 'Front Porch Campaign' speeches; he was probably the ast political candidate who never left home. A press house in back is now a museum. Hours are 9:30 am to 5 pm Wednesday to aturday, noon to 5 pm Sunday, Saturday before Memorial Day weekend through Labor Day weekend, lesser times otherwise n September and October. Admission is $3/1 dults/children.

A mile southeast of here at the junction of Delaware Ave and Vernon Heights Blvd s a 10-acre greenway comprising the **Harding Memorial**, a circular monument of white marble housing the coffins of Harding nd his wife.

Of a completely different bent, you might lso stop by the **Wyandot Popcorn Museum** (☎ 740-387-4255), 169 E Church St. Yes, hat's right, a popcorn museum. You'll see a itschy collection of antique popcorn machines, wagons and even a Model T popcorn truck. It's open 1 to 4 pm Wednesday to Sunday May through October, 1 to 4 pm weekends the rest of the year; free.

A Writer's Writer

Though hardly a household name even in literary circles, Sherwood Anderson (1876–1941) is considered a revolutionary force in American fiction. The publication of *Winesburg, Ohio*, his collection of connected short stories based on events and characters in Clyde, startled both critics and the public with its form and subject matter and ushered in a new era of realism. It's considered his most important work.

Anderson's stories are not moved forward by action and plot but are based on the emotions of the characters. He was a major influence on Thomas Wolfe, John Steinbeck, William Saroyan, Henry Miller, Norman Mailer, Studs Turkel, William Faulkner and Ernest Hemingway, the latter two of whom he assisted in first getting published. His unconventional life has led to his reputation as a symbol of those who reject materialism and middle-class values, replacing them with loyalty and devotion to the principles of art.

Other Anderson books include *Many Marriages*, *Dark Laughter* and the autobiographical *Sherwood Anderson Memoirs*. His Virginia grave marker is etched with the words 'Life, not Death, is the Great Adventure'; not a bad motto for the traveler, either.

Places to Stay

Twelve miles east of town is ***Mount Gilead State Park*** *(☎ 419-946-1961)* at 4119 Hwy 95, with camp sites from $6. In town, the ***Harding Motor Lodge*** *(☎ 740-383-6771, 1065 Delaware Ave)* offers good access to the Harding Memorial. Singles and doubles are $45.

MANSFIELD

Mansfield, midway between Columbus and Cleveland along I-71, is famous mostly for being the birthplace of Johnny Appleseed,

THOMAS HUHTI

Marion's monument to President Warren G Harding

that prolific planter of apple trees. Besides planting his trees, he also played a part in defending the city during the War of 1812. The city is a major crossroads in northern Ohio. In 1996, the US Conference of Mayors declared Mansfield the Most Livable City in the US.

Readmore Bookstore (☎ 419-756-9311) is worth a visit at 1456 Lexington Ave.

Greyhound (☎ 419-524-1111) is at 74 S Diamond St and has a few buses daily to Columbus ($11, 1 hour) and Cleveland ($15, 2 hours) among other destinations.

Things to See & Do

North of the junction of Park Ave and Main St is the three-block Carrousel [sic] Square, a very modestly gentrified section of downtown where you'll find most of the restaurants and shops. Also here is **Carrousel Park** (☎ 419-522-4223), 75 N Main St, an indoor wooden horse carousel, the first one built in the US since the 1930s. A ride costs 60¢. Nearby on Fourth St is Carrousel Magic!, a workshop where you can watch the carousel figures being carved. Admission is $3/1 adults/children.

North of downtown near the intersection of Hwy 545 and US 30 is a somewhat creepy attraction. The **Ohio State Reformatory** (☎ 419-522-2644) wouldn't normally be considered for a tour, but ever since Hollywood filmed *The Shawshank Redemption* and *Air Force One* here, it's been popular. Tours are given 1 to 4 pm Sunday, May through October; reservations are necessary. Admission is $7.

A mile west of downtown on Park Ave **Kingwood Center** (☎ 419-522-0211) is a 47 acre floral exhibit and cultural center. More than 40,000 tulips grow in the display gardens. Nature trails wind through the grounds.

Places to Stay & Eat

The best camping is found in the ***Mohican State Forest***, 15 miles to the southeast which has sites for $10. ***Malabar Farm State Park*** *(☎ 419-892-2784)* has camping ($6 and an HI ***youth hostel*** *(☎ 419-892-2055)* smack dab in the center of the 914 acres open January 16 through December 16 Rates are $14 for HI members. One private triple is available for $30. In town the mos entrally located motel is ***191 Park Place Iotel*** *(☎ 419-522-7275, 191 Park Ave)*, just a ew blocks west of downtown. Singles/ loubles are $40/55 and there's a good estaurant. A cheaper motel is a couple of locks east.

Right on Park Ave near these two motels s the always crowded ***Mr T's***, a 24-hour iner with cheap breakfasts ($3). There are couple of brewpubs with extensive menus, ncluding ***J Fred Schmidt's Packing and Brewing Company*** *(120 N Main St)*, in Carousel Square.

AROUND MANSFIELD

Malabar Farm State Park

'en miles southeast of Mansfield on Hwy 9, this is a working farm that's part of the Ohio State Park network. The 914-acre state belonged to novelist Louis Bromield (winner of the 1926 Pulitzer Prize for *Early Autumn*), who returned from Paris to is Mansfield home at the outbreak of World War II. He spent his years here conducting agricultural research and promoting conservation. The 32-room mansion is illed with period furniture and antiques. The park is open 10 am to 5 pm daily late May through early September, closed Monday thereafter; $3, $4 with wagon tour of the farm.

Loudonville

Fifteen miles southeast of Mansfield, Loudonville is the canoeing center of Ohio, thanks to a stunning gorge along the Mohican River. The gorge can be seen in its mmensity in **Mohican State Park** (free) outh of town; the park itself touches the orthern boundary of the Mohican State Forest, which has great camping, gorgeous winding roads and a fire tower or two to cramble up. If you're looking to get on the iver, at times it seems Loudonville has nore canoe liveries than people. Expect to ay between $11 and $20 per day for a basic anoe or kayak rental. Right in the heart of own is the Loudonville Canoe Livery ☎ 419-994-4161) which has rentals and trips rom a half-day to three days, along with ampsites (you can rent gear).

COSHOCTON

Located at the confluence of the Tuscarawas, Walhonding and Muskingum Rivers, Coshocton grew as a key point along the Ohio and Erie Canal. The main draw is its fully restored canal town, the only one in Ohio.

At the northwest end of Coshocton, just off Hwy 16/83, **Roscoe Village** is a fully restored canal port with 23 original village buildings. Some function as living museums and require an admission ticket; others have been converted to specialty shops or restaurants. The lock has been restored and a horse-drawn boat floats along the canal on hour-long trips. Tours are given daily 10 am to 3 pm; $10/5 adults/children. Boat tours run daily 1 to 5 pm in summer, lesser times spring and fall; $5/2 adults/children.

East of town are a couple of campgrounds. ***Forest Hill Lake Campground*** *(☎ 740-545-9642, 52176 Hwy 425)* has sites for $15; to get there follow US 36 east, then go north on Hwy 10 to Hwy 425 and turn east. The junction of Hwy 541 and Hwy 16/83 has a couple of decent budget motels. The ***Roscoe Motor Inn*** *(☎ 740-622-8736, 421 Whitewoman St)* has large rooms for $39/45 singles/doubles.

The ***Roscoe Village Inn*** *(☎ 740-622-2222, 200 N Whitewoman St)* is at the south end of the historic district. This casually upscale place has good rooms filled with Amish furniture. Singles/doubles cost $100.

Roscoe Village has a number of dining options. ***The Old Warehouse*** *(☎ 740-622-4001)* is an 1830s storehouse that has a menu of soups, salads, sandwiches and steaks (entrées from $6). It also features live entertainment.

DRESDEN

Seventeen miles southwest of Coshocton, diminutive Dresden bills itself as 'Basket Village USA,' thanks to the Longaberger Basket Company. The company, 3 miles north of Dresden near the junction of Hwys 16 and 60, opened its **Longaberger Homestead** (☎ 740-322-5588), a sort of utopian synthesis of retail sales and family fun, in late 1999. The founding family's former home is now a museum and the largest

19th-century barn in Ohio, relocated here and turned into a museum–craft mall. There are activities for kids, and adults can learn how to make a basket. Trams shuttle back and forth between here and the main plant, where you can watch basket makers at work. You'll find lots of food options – the ***Homestead Restaurant*** has excellent home-style food at great prices (main dishes from $6). Musical performances are offered at outside tents. Hours are 8 am to 6 pm Monday to Saturday, noon to 5 pm Sunday March through December, reduced hours during other months; free.

Back in the village, Dresden is chock-full of shops, restaurants and B&Bs. Its sole attraction is the Dresden Basket, on the corner of Main and 6th Sts; at 23 feet high, 11 feet wide and 48 feet long, it's known as the world's largest basket. Well, perhaps it was,

THOMAS HUHTI

Proof that you're in 'Basket Village USA'

but the corporate offices of Longaberge Basket Company in Newark, 16 miles west o Dresden, are now housed in a 7-story basket For real.

AMISH COUNTRY

Ohio's Amish communities are clustere among farming villages roughly an hour' drive south of Cleveland. Wayne, Holme and Tuscarawas Counties have the USA' densest Amish concentration, followed b areas in Pennsylvania, Indiana and Wiscon sin. (Another Ohio concentration is foun in the Western Reserve east of Cleveland, i the little communities of Mesopotamia an Middlefield.) Horse-drawn buggies carryin traditionally clothed families are frequentl seen and area shops sell homemade craft and foods. Some travelers are as aghast a the staggering number of belching tou buses as they are intrigued by the Amis culture. Note that Sundays are days of re flection in Amish country and everythin pretty much comes to a stop (except for th caravans of buggies heading for church i the morning).

Though at times it seems every dwellin in northeastern Ohio has been converted t a B&B, there might still be a crunch for bed in mid-summer. Or, you may be baffled b the sheer weight of choices. Amish Countr Reservations (☎ 330-674-7005, 800-606 9400), a centralized reservations service, ca walk you through it.

If you show up on Sunday, you may g hungry. Most restaurants shut down; eve your B&B might provide only a continenta breakfast.

Berlin

The heart of Amish country is Berlin, 3 miles southwest of Canton. On Hwy 7 north of the junction with Hwy 39 is th requisite stop for any visitor to Amis Country. The **Mennonite Informatio Center** (☎ 330-893-3192) contains *Behalt*, 265-foot-long cyclorama detailing Mennon ite history, from 15th-century Switzerland t their subsequent diaspora in search o freedom for their Anabaptist beliefs. Yo can often meet the artist, Heinz Gaugel, o

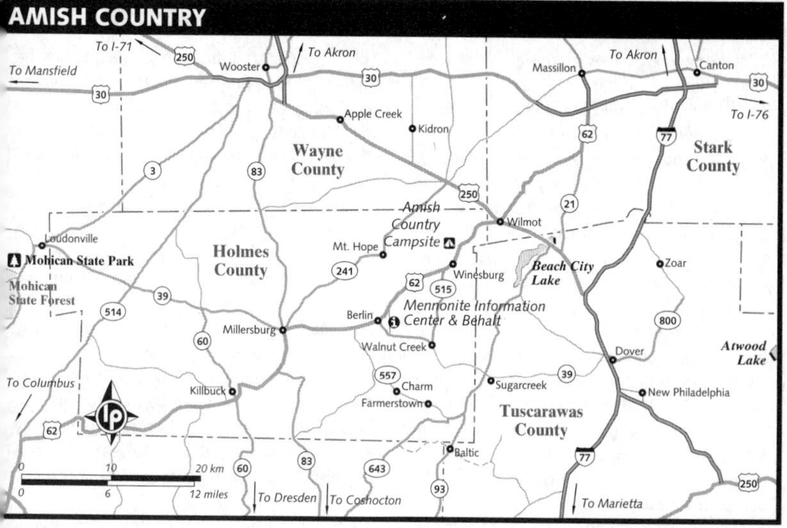

ɪaily tours. These half-hour tours cost $6/3 dults/children. There's also a 15-minute ideo synopsis of the history of the local ommunity. The bookstore takes up half the omplex and carries virtually everything in rint on the Amish. Hours are 9 am to 5 pm Monday to Saturday.

East of Berlin on Hwy 38, the **Amish arm** offers tours and buggy rides. You can alk through the farmhouse; kids can visit nd touch the animals. Hours are 10 am to pm daily, until 6 pm Saturday; fares vary. dmission is $4, with buggy rides costing $2.

laces to Stay & Eat For campers, 6 miles ortheast of Berlin on Hwy 62, just past Vinesburg, ***Amish Country Campsite*** *(☎ 330-359-5226)* has tent or RV sites for $14. he cheapest room options include tourist oms (similar to a room in a B&B, but ithout the meal), most of which have rivate bath. ***Mattie's Tourist Rooms & Vengerd's Country Lodging*** *(☎ 330-359-969)*, next to Amish Country Campsite, has ngles/doubles for $37/40 and a fully quipped apartment for $35. West of town on Hwy 39, the ***Berlin Village Inn*** *(☎ 330-893-861)* has gorgeous views and rooms well worth the $45/50 single/double price. Right in Berlin, ***Sommerset Tourist Rooms*** *(☎ 800-337-6414)* has singles/doubles from $50.

In Berlin there's a plethora of places to eat. Best bet: Grab some Amish bread from ***Der Bake Oven*** (so busy they've got a drive-through window) at the corner of Hwy 39 and US 62, then buy some fresh-ground Amish peanut butter and fresh fruit preserves at ***Nature's Food Market*** on the square for the best PB&J sandwich you've ever had. The ***Berlin Cafe*** on the square has excellent, healthful soups, salads, sandwiches, and, especially, chili (main dishes from $4). The coffee's also worth a stop. There's live entertainment Friday and Saturday. Next door is an old-fashioned soda fountain. The place for atmosphere – and locals – is ***Boyd & Wurthman Restaurant*** on Main St, with home-style food. Depending on the day, you might get the Amish specialties of ham loaf or 'wedding steak,' ground meat in a mushroom sauce (main dishes from $5).

Charm

Charm is off the beaten path (for these parts anyway). **Guggisberg Cheese** (☎ 330-893-2500), 5060 Hwy 557, lets you watch

The Gentle People

They know themselves as 'the gentle people,' 'the plain people' or, intriguingly, 'the quiet in the land.' There are perhaps 125,000 Amish in North America, though precise numbers aren't known. Most originally settled the US East Coast – Lancaster, Pennsylvania, is the place many Americans associate with the Amish – but beginning in the early 19th century, some began migrating westward and today a third of all Amish reside in Ohio. So pervasive is the culture that even McDonald's in Ohio's Amish Country have 'Swissburgers' (the Amish are Swiss in origin).

People often confuse the Amish and the Mennonites; indeed the groups are spiritually connected. Mennonites, Dutch Protestants who split with the church over the subject of baptism in the 16th century, fled to other European nations, including Switzerland. A further subsplit occurred in the late 1600s; one conservative faction took the name Amish after its leader, Jacob Ammann, and settled in America during the 18th century.

It's nearly impossible to summarize all the different Mennonite and Amish subgroups, mostly because each community follows its own version of the *Ordnung*, or way of life (or, simply, the rules). This sometimes severe social code is the crux of all Amish culture. It's based on two overriding keys: separation and obedience. Any outside influence is considered to be a contamination, hence the more conservative Amish don't do things such as use electricity. Failure to obediently follow the *Ordnung* can result in a person being shunned, a practice that leads to years of persecution and which most outsiders (they call all non-Amish 'English,' 'high people' or 'Yankees') completely misunderstand.

It's the electricity and motorized vehicle avoidance that most baffles non-Amish. Some use it, some don't. Some will use it if it isn't 'theirs.' Some drive. And not even all buggy drivers who look Amish are Amish. More conservative sects are called Old Order – the majority – and these are the ones who refuse to use electricity or phones. Though some Amish accept rides – and some locals bristle when pleas for rides and phone use become too frequent – most Amish use hired drivers (usually 45¢ to 60¢ per mile).

cheese makers at work 8 am to 2 pm weekdays. Across the street, the ***Chalet in the Valley*** *(☎ 330-893-2550)* has an extensive menu of Swiss, Austrian and Amish food (entrées from $6) and a popular Sunday buffet. You can hear Swiss music depending on the night. Another county institution is the ***Homestead Restaurant***, also along Hwy 557, which has been dishing out solid country fare since the 1930s and, in more than a few humble opinions, the best pie to be found in Amish Country.

Kidron

For many, Kidron, just north of Hwy 250 on Hwy 52, is a highlight of Amish Country. Every Thursday the **Kidron Auction** takes place at the livestock barn. Literally hundreds of buggies will be lined up along the roadside at the 155-foot hitching post, and flea market rings the barn. It's great fun Across the street, **Lehman's Store** simpl must not be missed. For a half-century it' been the Amish community's main purveyo of products for a self-sufficient lifestyle. It' grown so large that it had to take over a erstwhile cow barn. Room after room i filled with modern-looking appliances tha use no electricity. Stuff your great grandparents used can be purchased nev here. It even has a huge collection of retr metal advertising signs. It's almost imposs ble to leave without buying something.

Adjacent to the auction, the **Kidron Sonnenberg Heritage Center** is a good twc story museum and gallery coverin Mennonite culture. Hours are 11 am t 3 pm Tuesday, Thursday, and Saturday, Jun

The Gentle People

Amish families can choose to send their kids to a public school or to one of the 100 or so one-room schoolhouses with an Amish woman, aged 16 or older, as the teacher. They learn English and German (to read the Bible); Pennsylvania Dutch is spoken at home. Many Americans resent that Amish pay no Social Security tax, but then again, they don't receive Social Security payments, either, and they do pay all other taxes.

Non-Amish farmers can learn much from their gentle neighbors. During the Great Depression of the 1930s and again during the continuing family farm crisis in the Midwest, the Amish fared better than most 'English' farmers. Their refusal to use credit left them debt-free and solvent, and when they did encounter troubles, the entire community pitched in to help them. Added to this is a do-it-yourself ethic that has resulted in incredibly beautiful woodworking and quilt-making, two home industries that have really helped the Amish establish an economic livelihood to buttress farming.

Etiquette The Amish are friendly and genuinely happy to have guests. Don't translate this into touristic overindulgence with the camera. The Amish view a photograph as a potential for graven images (a biblical taboo) and, worse, self-pride.

More important – *Slow down when driving*. Most roads are hilly, winding and barely wide enough for two cars; there's not much room for you, the pickup headed toward you and a buggy. Always assume that there's a buggy with a family just beyond the crest of the next hill.

Auctions An excellent opportunity to see the Amish outside of farm tours is at an auction, where farmers go to sell livestock, hay, produce and delicious pies. The regional schedule is: Monday, Sugarcreek; Tuesday, Farmerstown; Wednesday, Mt Hope; Thursday, Kidron; Friday, Sugarcreek.

The Thursday auction in Kidron is sublime. First take in the auction and adjoining flea market, then wander, mouth agape, through Lehman's store across the road from the livestock barn.

Tours Amish Heritage Tours (☎ 330-893-3232) has a dozen tour options, most costing $25 to $30 per person.

nrough September. October through May 's closed Tuesday. A recommended $4 do-ation is worth it.

Aillersburg

Aillersburg, west of Berlin on Hwy 83, is the ast 'Amishy' town in Amish country, but it oes have cheap places to stay and a useum. The local attraction is the **Victo-an House** (☎ 330-377-4572), along Hwy 83 ist east of the town square. This 28-room ueen Anne looks like it did in 1902, the ear it was built. All the antiques were onated by county residents. Hours are 1:30) 4 pm Tuesday to Sunday, May through October; $3.

Downtown the historic ***Hotel Millers-urg*** *(☎ 330-674-1457, 35 W Jackson St)* was uilt in 1847 and was brought back to life in the 1980s. Today you can get a basic room with a twin bed for $37; bigger rooms cost $60 to $65 for a double. Since they don't drink alcohol, you probably won't find local Amish in the popular tavern and dining room on the ground floor. Southeast of town on Hwy 310, the ***Cricket Hill Cabin*** *(☎ 330-674-1892, 6109 Hwy 310)* is a romantic restored cabin with one bedroom, a Jacuzzi and a fireplace; it's in a great location. High season weekend rates are $115 per night, less at all other times.

Ask for directions to ***Miller's Bakery*** *(☎ 330-893-3002)*; it's a local favorite.

Sugarcreek

The real treat in Sugarcreek is riding the **Ohio Central Railroad** (☎ 330-852-4676). Its real chugging transport steam (or sometimes diesel) trains also take passengers on regional tours. From Sugarcreek there is a daily tour to Baltic, 5 miles south, and the network has grown to include a number of routes, including special 'fall foliage' and 'murder mystery' excursions. Times vary but generally run May through October. Fares range from $10 to $100.

In the Dutch Valley complex, **David Warther Carvings** (☎ 330-852-3455) is the workshop of a fifth-generation Swiss expert ivory carver from a legendary family of carvers. The work focuses on maritime subjects and the detail is remarkable – even the rigging on the ships is ivory. Hours are 9 am to 5 pm Monday to Saturday. Admission is $4 for adults.

The **Alpine Hills Historical Museum** (☎ 330-852-4113) on the square has an excellent (and large) collection of local historical artifacts, including a complete replica of an 1890 cheese-making house and an Amish newspaper shop. A 10-minute slide presentation on the Amish and cheese making airs in the small theater. Hours are 10 am to 4:30 pm Monday to Saturday, April through November, with increased hours July through September; free.

Amish Country Bus Tours (☎ 330-852-4299), at 110 W Main St in Sugarcreek, offers 1½-hour tours of Amish country. They depart four times daily 10 am to 4 pm Monday to Saturday, May through October, fewer trips in March, April, and November. The cost is $7/4 adults/children.

Walnut Creek

Between Sugarcreek and Berlin just north of Hwy 39, Walnut Creek is a nice respite from the hordes of Berlin. The **Amish Flea Market** is an amazing place. You can find new or used (sometimes ancient) knickknacks, crafts, quilts, produce, antiques, delicious baked goods and just about anything else imaginable. Over 170 booths are set up 9 am to 5 pm Friday and Saturday, April through November.

Just north of town along Hwy 515, **Yoder's** (☎ 330-893-2541) is an Amish farm that has buggy and hay rides, a petting zoo and farm tours. Hours are 10 am to 5 pm, Monday through Saturday, mid-April to October. Tours are $3/2 adults/children; buggy rides are $2/1.

Country Coach, Inc (☎ 330-893-3636) offers regional narrated tours. Tours depart at 9 am and noon Monday to Saturday and last about 2½ hours; $15/8 adults/children.

Walnut Creek has a wider range of lodgings than the rest of Amish Country. Right in town, the ***Inn at Walnut Creek*** *(☎ 800-262-7181, 4869 Olde Pump St)* has rooms from $80 weekends in summer, down to half that in the off-season. Four suites cost $1[illegible] more and have their own kitchens.

Southeast of Walnut Creek ***Marbeyo B&B*** *(☎ 330-852-4533, 2370 Hwy 144)* is a moderately priced B&B on a 100-acre farm. It has rooms for $55 and up. The woodwork is exquisite and rooms tastefully decorated at ***Oakridge Country Inn*** *(☎ 330-893-3811, 4845 Milo Drive)* just south of town off US 39. Each room features a patio and kitchenette. Rates are $75 single/double in high season.

Southwest of town off Hwy 114 and Hwy 135, the ***Miller Haus B&B*** *(☎ 330-893-3602)* sits on the highest part of 23 acres and may be the quietest place in Ohio. Its nine rooms range from $99 to $119 and there's a lovely sitting area and dining room combo.

For food, ***Der Dutchman*** along Hwy 515 offers great Amish and American fare (entrées from $7); the view from the veranda is alone worth the visit.

CANTON

• pop 85,000

Twenty-five miles south of Akron, Canton is a shrine for the gridiron-obsessed. This was the birthplace of the National Football League (NFL), and that perhaps explains the rabidness with which Ohioans pursue their football.

The Canton–Stark County Tourist Information Center (☎ 330-452-0243) is located directly behind the Pro Football Hall of Fame's parking area and has lots of information. Its Web site (www.visitcanton.com) has more tips.

'ro Football Hall of Fame

he very popular Pro Football Hall of Fame ☎ 330-456-8207), with its football-shaped ɔwer, is Mecca for football nuts who enter, nimated, like little kids on Christmas ıorning, and exit, eyes glazed over like a ıted Homer Simpson. Most find the actual Iall of Fame a bit tedious, and scurry imıediately to the amazing GameDay tadium, a multi-media football experience. Iigh-definition TV with digital sound is rojected onto an enormous 20-foot by 42-ɔot Cinemascope screen; all this while the eating platform rotates. Other exhibits are articipatory – you can see adults practially holding themselves back from pushing ttle kids aside to play. It's right off I-77 on ıe north side of town. Hours are 9 am to pm daily late May weekends through arly September, 9 am to 5 pm daily the rest f the year; $10/6 adults/children, or $25 per ımily.

)ther Things to See

xiting left, then right, out of the Pro Football Iall of Fame, puts you on a lovely riverside rive, full of joggers, in-line skaters and geese. ollow the signs until you reach the **McKinley lational Memorial**. William McKinley, the 5th president of the United States, was a 'anton resident for most of his life. This 30-cre complex has at its center a raised monuıent with the tomb containing the x-president and his wife. If you can handle ıe steps, you can get a fine view of Canton. .djacent to the memorial, the McKinley Iuseum is akin to a hands-on scientific disɔvery museum; there are 55,000 sq feet of ience experiments and animated exhibits. Iuseum hours are 9 am to 6 pm Monday to aturday, noon to 6 pm Sunday late May to arly September, 9 am to 5 pm the rest of the ear. Admission is $6/4 adults/children.

The **Canton Museum of Art** (☎ 330-452-)96) is housed in the Cultural Center for ıe Arts (see Entertainment). Its galleries mphasize the work of Ohio artists, espeally 19th- and 20th-century watercolorists nd ceramists. Hours are 9 am to 5 pm eekdays; $3/1 adults/children.

In North Canton is the unique **Hoover Historical Center** (☎ 330-499-0287), 1875 Easton St NW, the Victorian farmhouse home of WH Hoover, founder of the country's preeminent vacuum cleaner manufacturer. It may sound pedestrian, but the collection of antique vacuum cleaners is fascinating. Hours are 1 to 5 pm Tuesday to Sunday; free.

Places to Stay

See Akron's Places to Stay section for the nearest camping facility. North Canton is the best place for cheap lodging (and is near the airport). There's a ***Motel 6*** *(☎ 330-494-7611, 6880 Sunset Strip Ave NW)* at exit 111 off I-77, with singles/doubles from $42/46 in summer, cheaper the rest of the year. Two miles south there's a ***Super 8*** *(☎ 330-837-8880, 242 Lincoln Way)* with similar rooms and rates about $10 higher.

For a mid-range place, ***Best Suites of America*** *(☎ 330-499-1011, 4914 Everhard Rd)* is close to the Super 8, at exit 109 off I-77. This all-suite motel has a pool and minor work-out facility. The rates of $70/80 single/double aren't bad. Plenty of other options are in the vicinity.

Downtown the only option is the ***Hilton*** *(☎ 330-454-5000, fax 330-454-5494, 320 Market Ave S)*. It has a very good restaurant, an indoor pool, a health club and a sauna. Singles/doubles cost $75/85.

Places to Eat

One exit south of the Pro Football Hall of Fame on I-77 and always packed is ***The Stables*** *(☎ 330-452-1230, 2317 13th St NW)*. Taking full advantage of its proximity to the Hall of Fame, this converted 1900 horse barn features a five-ton, handcarved redwood football statue right in the dining room. The food ranges from burgers to seafood and wood-fired pizzas (main dishes from $7); the ambiance is upscale sports bar.

Canton's most unique eatery is the ***365th Fighter Group*** *(☎ 330-494-3500, 4919 Mt Pleasant Rd)*, adjacent to the Akron–Canton Airport, north of town. It's a restaurant-cum-museum full of World War II memorabilia in a building reminiscent of a farmhouse from Suffolk, England (where the group was stationed in World War II). Swing and big band get people dancing. It's popular for steaks and seafood (entrées from $10) and offers a Sunday brunch. While eating, you can put on headphones hooked up to the control tower and listen in on the controllers talking to the pilots.

Downtown there's not much, and nothing budget save for a few cheap but unremarkable greasy spoons or sandwich shops. However, if you've got some extra coins, ***Bender's*** *(☎ 330-453-8424)*, at the corner of 2nd St and Court Ave SW, is a 1902 tavern and a Canton original. Fresh seafood is the center of the creative American cuisine – this is one of the few places to find Prince Edward Island (Canada) oysters in the Great Lakes region. Dinner is pricey at $13 or more per entrée but lunches are a little cheaper.

Entertainment

Canton has a cultural center housing all of the area's arts disciplines. The ***Cultural Center for the Arts*** *(☎ 330-627-2282, 1001 Market Ave North)* is home to the Canton Symphony Orchestra, Canton Ballet, Player's Guild and others, and has a regular schedule of offerings throughout the year.

Getting There & Away

The Akron–Canton Regional Airport (☎ 330-499-4059) is 11 miles south of Akron; it's served by six regional shuttles: Continental, Delta-ComAir, Northwest Airlines, United Express, US Airways and Air Tran Airways. See the Toll-Free & Web Site Directory at the back of the book for airlines' contact information.

The Greyhound station (☎ 330-456-7323) is at 819 Market St S with buses to Akron ($6, 35 minutes) and Wheeling, West Virginia ($21, 2½ hours), among other places.

AKRON

Underpopulated until BF Goodrich established the first rubber plant here in 1869, Akron, 30 miles south of Cleveland, was once the rubber capital of the US. It still produces more than half the country's tir and over 50,000 different rubber produc Americans are aware of the city – durin practically every televised sporting eve the Goodyear blimp *Spirit of Akron* is fe tured prominently.

The Akron–Summit County Conventic and Visitors Bureau (☎ 330-374-7560) is 77 E Mill St, inside the convention cente Its Web site (www.visitakron-summit.or has information as well.

See Canton's Getting There & Awa section for airport information. The Gre hound station (☎ 330-434-9185) is at 78 Grant St. Regular departures include Clev land ($6, 40 minutes), Canton ($6, 3 minutes) and Ashtabula ($20, 2½ hours).

Things to See

For insight into Yankee ingenuity, vis downtown's **Inventure Place & Invento Hall of Fame** (☎ 330-762-4463), 221 S Broa way, which has lots of exhibits to inspire i ventiveness, such as one that traces Thom Edison's creations from idea through rea ization. Hours are 9 am to 5 pm Monday Saturday, noon to 5 pm Sunday; $8/6 adult children. North of here, **Quaker Square** is th renovated former home of the Quaker Oa Company. Its distinctive mill architectu now houses specialty shops and restauran One block north the **Akron Art Museu** (☎ 330-376-9185) is small but has good di plays, traveling exhibitions, and a sculptu garden. Hours are 11 am to 5 pm daily; fre

Frank A Sieberling, the rubber baro founder of Goodyear, spent part of h fortune on the **Stan Hywet Hall & Garde** (☎ 330-836-5533), 714 N Portage St, note for its Tudor Revival architecture, antiqu and gardens. Hours are 9 am to 6 pm dai April 1 through January 1; reduced hou the rest of the year.

Goodyear World of Rubber (☎ 330-79 7117), 1201 E Market St, provides a overview of the rubber industry, with exhibi heavy on Goodyear products. Films descrit the tire manufacturing process. Hours a 8 am to 4:30 pm Monday to Friday; free.

The **Summit County Historical Socie** (☎ 330-535-1120), 550 Copley Rd, overse o historic homes opposite each other ng Copley Rd. The John Brown Home s the residence of the famed abolitionist o led the 1859 raid on Harper's Ferry. Its ferings include photographs, an old canal at, a captain's quarters and changing exbits. Across the street, the Perkins ansion is an 1830s stone edifice built by e son of Akron's founder. Hours are 1 to pm Tuesday to Sunday February to Dember. A $5 admission covers both houses.

aces to Stay

n miles south of town along Manchester d, ***Portage Lakes State Park*** *(☎ 330-644-20)* has cheap camping ($9).

Lots of cheap motels are found north of kron in Cuyahoga Falls, and it's in a prime ot for visiting the Cuyahoga Valley Nanal Recreation Area. The ***State Road Inn*** *330-928-1111, 1709 State Rd)* has singles/ ubles for as low as $35.

The interstate arteries surrounding downwn have any number of mid-range places, cluding the ***Days Inn South*** *(☎ 330-644-04, 3237 S Arlington Rd)*, at exit 120 off 7, near the airport. There's a tiny pool and me rooms have kitchenettes. Singles/ ubles cost $55.

The rooms are round at the ***Hilton*** *330-253-5970, fax 330-253-2574, 135 S oadway Ave)* in Quaker Square, downtown, because the hotel was built in the original silos of the Quaker Oats Company. This posh place has a heated indoor pool and good restaurants within its complex. Singles/doubles are $110/120.

Places to Eat

Downtown Quaker Square has a couple of casual restaurants, one housed in an old railroad car. The ***Spaghetti Warehouse*** *(510 S Main St)* has copious amounts of inexpensive Italian food (entrées from $5). South of here ***Jillian's*** *(363 S Main St)* is a lively eatery that has a sports bar feel. The above-average bar food (from $5) runs the gamut from burgers to eats prepared by tableside hibachi chefs.

Away from downtown, ***Tangier*** *(☎ 216-376-7171, 532 W Market St)* is a regional legend for its blend of Middle Eastern, continental and American cuisine – some vegetarian options – and for its live entertainment. The act is often a Las Vegas-style cabaret, but on a recent visit it was, bizarrely, a retread late–'70s southern funk rock band. Entrées start at $9.

Entertainment

The ***Carousel Dinner Theater*** *(☎ 330-724-9855, 1275 E Waterloo Rd)* is the largest professional dinner theater in the US and has a full slate of Broadway musicals. Prices vary with each production.

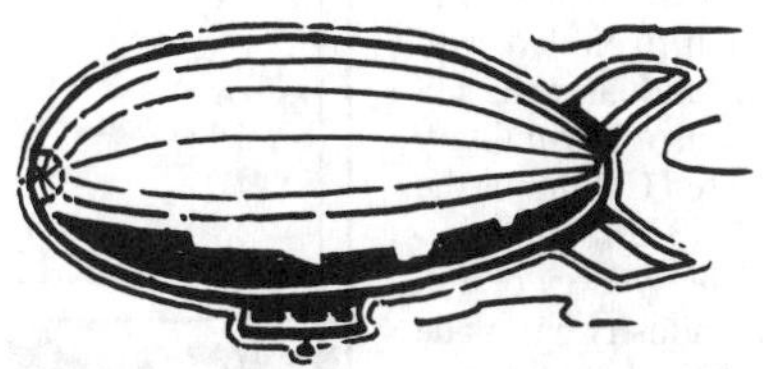

Central & Southern Ohio

Central Ohio

COLUMBUS

• pop 633,000

Columbus, the state capital, is Ohio's largest city, a fact that rarely fails to surprise visitors impressed by the subdued charm of the place. (The city's perfectly apt official tourist slogan is, 'Surprise, it's Columbus.') It is also a major center for education, research and commerce. Clean, spacious streets, quite unlike the downtown funk of Cleveland, give it a prosperous air. Miles of sprawling suburbs surround the high-rise downtown, but the 60,000 students of Ohio State University (OSU), plus those of five other colleges, give the city a youthful vitality.

History

Columbus was born of politics. It didn't yet exist when some backroom political maneuvering in Zanesville and Chillicothe – between which the government seat had wandered for nine years after statehood in 1803 – gave the nod to Columbus' now-western suburb of Franklinton, mostly due to its central location. Columbus arose on the east bank of the Scioto River and, with its freshly platted streets, soon attracted enough settlers to displace Franklinton as seat of power. The capitol's construction – then a tiny two-story structure – was finished in 1816 after being delayed by the War of 1812. (The next building constructed was a prison.)

Columbus really grew following the completion of the Ohio and Erie Canal in 1831 and the National Road in 1833, crucial commercial transport links to the rest of the eastern US. The population exploded with the arrival of the railroads and later the US Army, which used the city as a key military center. The legislature granted Columbus the Ohio State University in 1873, essentially cementing the city's future. The synergy of university research with local industry has made Columbus the economic hotbed of Ohio.

Highlights

- Columbus, the capital and a university town, with great ethnic neighborhoods
- Cincinnati, the Queen City and gateway to the South, a classic Ohio River town
- The Hocking Hills Region, an incredible variety of geology and topography
- Lovely scenic drives and mysterious residuals of Hopewell culture around Chillicothe
- Riparian scenery and river history along the hundreds of miles of Ohio River roadway
- Fascinating aviation history of Dayton, home of the Wright brothers

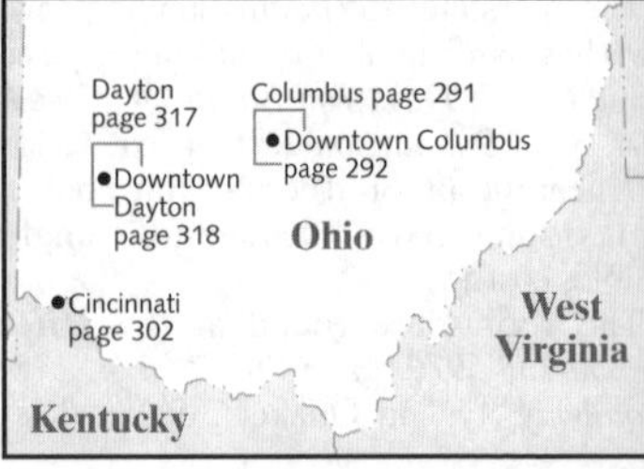

OHIO

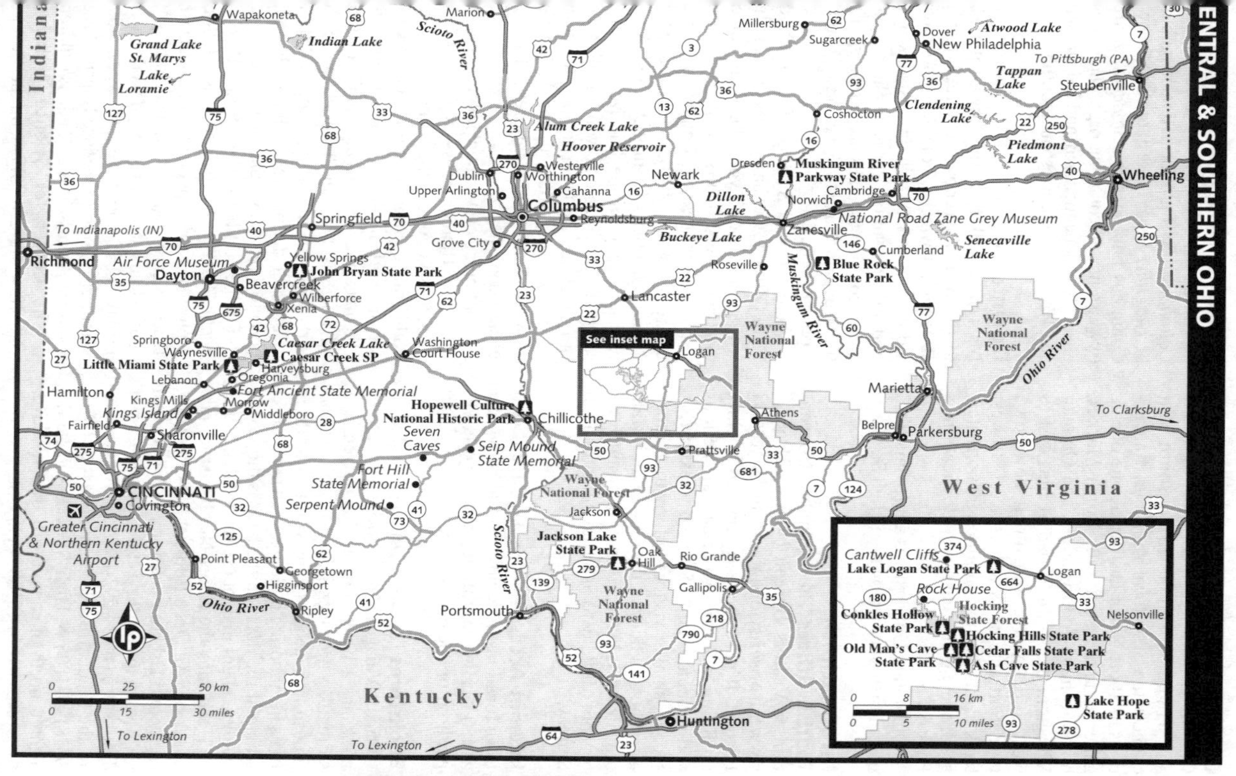
CENTRAL & SOUTHERN OHIO
Indiana
To Indianapolis (IN)
Richmond
Dayton
Air Force Museum
Springfield
Yellow Springs
John Bryan State Park
Beavercreek
Wilberforce
Xenia
Caesar Creek Lake
Caesar Creek SP
Harveysburg
Oregonia
Fort Ancient State Memorial
Morrow
Middleboro
Waynesville
Little Miami State Park
Springboro
Lebanon
Kings Mills
Kings Island
Sharonville
Hamilton
Fairfield
CINCINNATI
Covington
Greater Cincinnati & Northern Kentucky Airport
Point Pleasant
Higginsport
Georgetown
Ripley
Ohio River
To Lexington
Kentucky
Portsmouth
Serpent Mound
Fort Hill State Memorial
Seven Caves
Seip Mound State Memorial
Hopewell Culture National Historic Park
Chillicothe
Washington Court House
Grove City
Upper Arlington
Dublin
Worthington
Westerville
Gahanna
Columbus
Reynoldsburg
Hoover Reservoir
Alum Creek Lake
Marion
Scioto River
Indian Lake
Wapakoneta
Grand Lake St. Marys
Lake Loramie
Newark
Buckeye Lake
Dillon Lake
Lancaster
Roseville
Dresden
Zanesville
Norwich
Cambridge
Muskingum River Parkway State Park
National Road Zane Grey Museum
Cumberland
Blue Rock State Park
Muskingum River
Coshocton
Millersburg
Sugarcreek
Dover
New Philadelphia
Atwood Lake
Tappan Lake
Clendening Lake
Piedmont Lake
Senecaville Lake
Steubenville
To Pittsburgh (PA)
Wheeling
To Clarksburg
Ohio River
Wayne National Forest
Marietta
Belpre
Parkersburg
West Virginia
Athens
Nelsonville
Logan
See inset map
Prattsville
Jackson
Jackson Lake State Park
Oak Hill
Rio Grande
Gallipolis
Huntington
Scioto River
Cantwell Cliffs
Lake Logan State Park
Rock House
Hocking State Forest
Conkles Hollow State Park
Hocking Hills State Park
Old Man's Cave State Park
Cedar Falls State Park
Ash Cave State Park
Lake Hope State Park
0 8 16 km
0 5 10 miles
0 25 50 km
0 15 30 miles
OHIO

Orientation

Columbus has three main arteries: Front and High Sts run north to south and connect the downtown with tourist attractions in Short North District, a zone of chic galleries and restaurants; North Market, home to more food vendors; and German Village in the south. Broad St runs east to west and has the remaining downtown tourist attractions as well as access to west bank sights. North-south designations start at Broad St; the east-west delineation is High St.

Ohio State University is approximately 3 miles north of downtown on High St.

Information

Tourist Offices The Columbus Convention & Visitors Bureau (☎ 614-221-6623, www.SurpriseItsColumbus.com) is at 90 N High St. It publishes a specialized booklet outlining African American attractions and is open 9 am to 5:30 pm weekdays. A second, smaller visitors' information office is on the 2nd floor of the City Center Mall, downtown at 111 S 3rd St, open from 10 am to 9 pm Monday to Saturday, noon to 6 pm Sunday.

Internet Access Kinko's has three downtown locations. The most central is the one at 180 N High St. Internet access costs $12 per hour or 20¢ per minute.

Bookstores The Book Loft, 631 S 3rd St, in German Village, is hard to believe. Every nook has a book here, as this warren of a store takes up the entire interior of an enormous old mansion along with two or three of its neighboring buildings. You need to get a map at the door; on the back is the store's own excellent map of German Village.

Head into the Short North district and check out An Open Book (☎ 614-291-0080), a gay and lesbian bookstore, at 761 N High St. Also to the north, visit the Wexner Center Bookstore (☎ 614-292-1807), 30 W 15th Ave, or the Student Book Exchange (☎ 614-291-9528) at 1806 N High St. Kids will be delighted north of campus at Cover to Cover (☎ 614-263-1624), 3560 N High St.

Media The *Columbus Dispatch* is publishe mornings. Check out the free weeklie *Columbus Alive* for information on nightlif or *The Other Paper* for restaurants. Stonewa Columbus publishes the *Stonewall Journ* (www.stonewall-columbus.org). *Outlook* is biweekly, independent gay and lesbian pape and *Word is Out!* is a lesbian monthly.

Downtown

It's a short walk from the City Center Ma to the recently renovated Greek Reviv **state capitol**, which is notable for *not* havin a dome. Over $100 million was sunk into mid-90s renovation, sprucing the exterio and decorating the halls in period style. Fre tours depart 9 am to 3 pm and 11 am t 4 pm weekends.

Across Broad St, the 40-story **Rhode State Office Tower** has an observation dec with grand views; if you take a tour you ca also gain access to the state Supreme Cour

Nine blocks east, the **Columbus Museu of Art** (☎ 614-221-4848), 480 E Broad St, h several galleries of European and Amer can art, heavy on the Old Masters, and sculpture garden, along with traveling exh bitions. Hours are 10 am to 5:30 pm Tuesd to Sunday (until 8:30 pm Thursday). Admi sion is $4/2 adults/children; Thursd evenings are free.

Continuing east a couple blocks, and th north, the **Thurber House** (☎ 614-464-103 77 Jefferson Ave, is the erstwhile home author and cartoonist James Thurber, know for his work in the *New Yorker* magazi His magazine cartoons and family memor bilia are displayed in this house, which fe tured prominently in his stories. Litera celebrities often give readings. Hours a noon to 4 pm daily; admission is free.

On the east bank of the Scioto River, t *Santa Maria* (☎ 614-645-8760) is a full-sca replica of Christopher Columbus' flagsh Docents garbed in 15th-century clothing le tours. Hours are 10 am to 5 pm Wednesday Friday, 11:30 am to 6 pm weekends summer; its hours are reduced April, May a October. Admission is $4/2 adults/children.

The **Center for Science & Indust** (COSI; ☎ 614-228-26774), on the west ba

OHIO

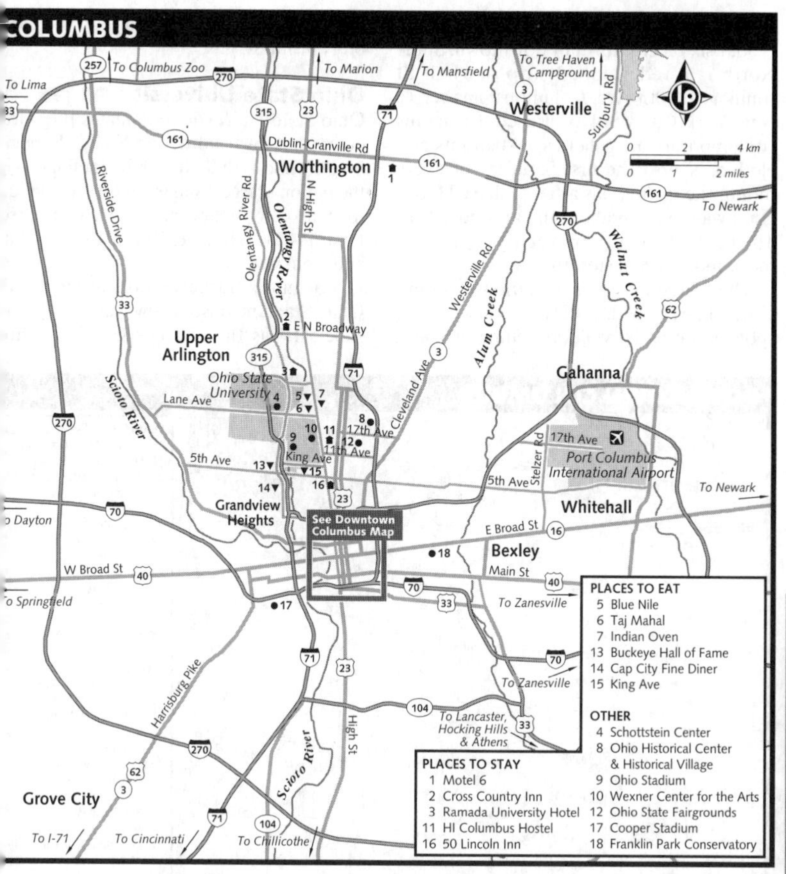

the Scioto River in a huge new complex ›ened in October 1999, is an interactive ıuseum that's great for kids (but not solely r them). Innumerable exhibits and experıents focus on all the sciences. It's a treat, pecially the exhibit that allows you to ride high-wire tricycle 20 feet off the ground. ours are 10 am to 5 pm Monday to Satury, noon to 6 pm Sunday. Admission is $8/6 ıults/children, or $28 per family.

erman Village & Brewery District

half dozen blocks south of downtown is e remarkably large, all-brick German Village, a restored, 200-acre 19th-century neighborhood. Since 1960, it has grown into the largest privately funded restoration project in the country. The German Village Society (☎ 614-221-8888), 588 S 3rd St, has more information. The neighborhood is one of the city's gay and lesbian enclaves. The village's **Oktoberfest** is very popular.

The adjacent Brewery District once had seven major breweries but now consumes more brew than it produces, and several buildings have been converted to restaurants and bars.

Short North & North Market

About six blocks north of downtown, Short North is a redeveloped strip of High St running to 10th Ave. Columbus' answer to New York City's SoHo district, it contains contemporary art galleries, restaurants and clothing shops. The first Saturday of every month the district has a fun Gallery Hop, a good way to learn about the art and artists. To the north is the university area, with many more casual storefronts.

The contiguous North Market is an enclosed market with a host of casual eating spots and over 40 vendors selling produce, meats, cheeses and seafood. You can ent on N Front St.

Ohio State University

Ohio State University dominates the nort ern part of town, bordering N High St begi ning around 12th St. It should dominate – i the nation's largest single campus; the guid tours take two hours and leave from Enars Hall, 154 W 12th Ave, Room 131, at 10 a and 2 pm weekdays.

Catching a Buckeyes football game at t Ohio Stadium (also known as 'the Hors shoe'; it was the nation's first horsesho

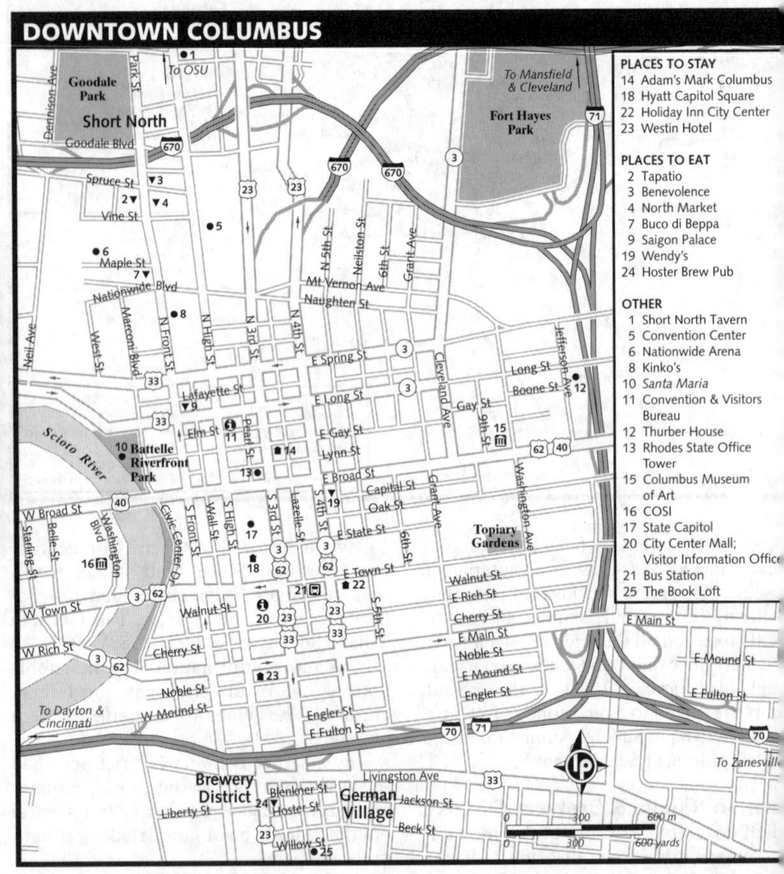

aped stadium and is distinctive for having ıd dormitories actually built into its west le) would capture OSU in all its frenetic ory, but good luck getting tickets. Or forget e game and visit nearby Buckeye Grove, ıere they plant a tree for every All-merican player. The Buckeyes are also a g Ten power in basketball (they advanced the semifinals of the national tournament recently as 1999) and their home, the rome Schottstein Center, is the Big Ten's gest arena. The Buckeye Hall of Fame (see aces to Eat) is a requisite stop for the ıngry sports-inclined fan; you can get a eal, occupy yourself in an enormous game om, wander about gazing at more than a ntury of OSU sporting memorabilia or en pick up some OSU garb.

If you'd rather not overdose on sports, so on campus is the Hopkins Hall Gallery, th art exhibits, and the Chadwick Arbore-m, off Fyffe Rd, is a nice place for a stroll. ıe acclaimed **Wexner Center for the Arts** 614-292-3535), N High St and 15th Ave, is op-notch mixed media cultural attraction. museum displays visual arts; music and eater performances are offered. Hours are am to 6 pm, Tuesday to Sunday; $3.

orthern Columbus

though it gets little promotion, the **Ohio storical Center and Ohio Village** (☎ 614-7-2300), well north of downtown Colum-s off I-71 at 17th Ave (or take the No 8 s), is a highly recommended, excellent story museum that could take three hours see. For those planning to tour the state's ıthern Hopewell Indian sites, a visit here invaluable. Ohio Village is a reconstruc-n of a 19th-century Ohio village staffed costumed docents. Hours are 9 am to om Wednesday to Saturday, from 10 am 5 pm Sunday, open April through No-mber. Admission is $5/1 adults/children.

Farther north, the **Columbus Zoo and uarium** (☎ 614-645-3550), north on Hwy 7 off I-270, is the nation's third-largest o. It's famous as the birthplace of the first rilla to be born in captivity. The pachy-rm complex is the world's largest indoor phant exhibit. Hours are 9 am to 5 pm daily, with extended hours Memorial Day to Labor Day; $7/4 adults/children.

Eastern Columbus

At 1777 E Broad St, **Franklin Park Conservatory and Botanical Garden** (☎ 614-645-8733) has 12,000 sq feet of architecturally unique greenhouse containing nine distinct climates. The garden is made up of 30 acres and features a Japanese garden, a victory garden and a 5-acre landscaped Grand Mallway. Hours are 10 am to 5 pm Tuesday to Sunday, until 8 pm Wednesday. Admission is $4/2 adults/children.

Special Events

July

Columbus Rib Fest – crowds come to chow down on ribs and listen to national jazz artists (☎ 614-225-6922)

August

Ohio State Fair – the granddaddy of Ohio festivals, one of the nation's largest state fairs is held off I-71 between the 11th and 17th Ave exits (☎ 614-644-4012, 888-646-3979)

Places to Stay

Budget The nearest campground is ***Tree Haven Campgrounds*** *(☎ 740-965-3469, 4855 Miller Rd)*, 11 miles northeast of Columbus (on I-270) in Westerville. A site is $18 for two people.

The convenient and central HI ***Columbus Hostel*** *(☎ 614-294-7157, 95 E 12th St)* is a friendly and well-run hostel in a house rumored to have been designed by Frank Lloyd Wright; even the manager isn't sure. Dormitory beds cost $12/15 members/nonmembers; family rooms are also available. Women may not want to walk alone in the area after dark.

Cheap chain motels are clustered near the I-270 ring road, where the main highways intersect. ***Motel 6*** has four locations: The most central and costly is 15 minutes north of downtown at 1289 E Dublin–Granville Rd *(☎ 614-846-9860, fax 614-431-0272)*; singles/doubles cost $42/48.

In the vicinity of Ohio State University, the ***Cross Country Inn*** *(☎ 614-291-2983, fax*

614-291-4082, 1445 Olentangy Rd) is good value at $43/48 single/double.

Mid-Range Downtown, the ***Holiday Inn City Center*** *(☎ 614-221-3281, fax 614-221-2667, 175 E Town St)* has a heated pool and rates from $65 single/double. Very good value is ***Adam's Mark Columbus*** *(☎ 614-228-5050, fax 614-228-5050, 50 N Third St)*, with some finely appointed rooms. There's also a heated pool. Rates are $79/99 single/double.

Farther north and well located for the university, the ***Ramada University Hotel*** *(☎ 614-267-7461, fax 614-263-5299, 3110 Olentangy River Rd)* has good rooms, some with whirlpools and good river views. Rates are $80 single/double.

In German Village, there are three B&Bs, including ***Gaslight Inn*** *(☎ 614-621-9112, fax 614-224-5340, 499 City Park Ave)*, at $85 for a double. The restored, century-old ***Westin Hotel*** *(☎ 614-228-3800, fax 614-228-7666, 310 S High St)*, formerly the Great Southern Hotel, was once the most opulent joint in town. The lobby features original artwork. Rates are $95 single/double.

Top End Between downtown and the university, ***50 Lincoln Inn*** *(☎ 614-291-5056, fax 614-291-4924, 50 E Lincoln St)*, about a mile north of downtown, is a historic, early 20th-century brick dwelling with cozy, modern rooms. Rates are $100/110 single/double.

Close to the capitol, the ***Hyatt on Capitol Square*** *(☎ 614-228-1234, fax 614-469-9664, 75 E State St)* has large rooms and a good restaurant; some of the rooms have whirlpools. Rates are $200/220 single/double.

Places to Eat

Downtown The first link in the ***Wendy's*** *(257 E Broad St)* hamburger chain is downtown, at the corner of 55th St. It looks as it did in 1969 and has become a museum of sorts to the corporation and to its aw-shucks founder Dave Thomas (of television ubiquity). Adjacent is a ***Tim Horton's***, a Canadian staple for fresh, cheap doughnuts.

Saigon Palace *(☎ 614-464-3325, 114 N Front St)* is a casual Vietnamese eatery with good daily specials including some vegeta ian items (entrées start at $6). E Gay St h several restaurants.

German Village & Brewery Distri These neighborboods have some gre places to eat and prices aren't bad at som ***Katzinger's Deli*** *(☎ 614-228-3354, 475 S 3 St)*, the local landmark, was the first pla Bill Clinton came when in Columbus; probably had as much trouble as everyo else making up his mind with the min boggling array of sandwiches (all betwe $4 and $10). ***Thurman Café*** *(183 Thurm Ave)* is an unpretentious little place wi great old-fashioned booths and hu burgers (main dishes from $5).

Top-end ***Lindey's*** *(☎ 614-228-4343, 169 Beck St)* is in a fine gentrified structure a serves excellent steaks, seafood and pas (entrées from $8).

The ***Hoster Brew Pub*** *(☎ 614-228-606* open daily, is in the Brewery District at t corner of S High St and E Hoster St; it ha creative American menu (entrées from $ The ***Columbus Brewing Co*** *(☎ 614-46 2739, 525 Short St)* serves standard pub fa as well as steaks and wood-fired pizz (main courses from $8).

Short North & North Market The ***Nor Market*** *(☎ 614-463-9664)*, on Spruce St the Short North area, has all manner fresh foods and numerous prepared me under one roof in a converted warehouse decent East Indian lunch costs just $4 ***Flavors of India***. The bedrock to the No Market is ***Frank's Diner*** *(☎ 614-621-2233* retro eatery (entrées from $4). ***Pasta*** serves homemade pasta dishes from arou $5. Just north of the market, then right on Swan St, ***Benevolence*** is a small deli w great vegetarian soups and salads (from $

Short North district begins north North Market. A more ambitious veget ian restaurant is found at the north end Short North. ***King Avenue*** *(☎ 614-294-82 247 King Ave)* has a huge menu and ma vegan choices (entrées from $5). Plenty other options exist, including ***Tapa*** *(☎ 614-221-1085, 491 N Park St)*, a fusion aribbean and Latin American cuisine ntrées from $8).

Between North Market and downtown, ***uca di Beppo*** *(☎ 614-621-3287, 343 N ·ont St)* is probably the best deal you'll find Columbus. This southern Italian restau-.nt has lines out the door nightly and for ›od reason; you cannot possibly eat all the ıtstanding food that is put in front of you ›astas from $7, other entrées from $12).

niversity Area The area around OSU ong N High St offers you everything from [exican to Ethiopian food, plus numerous ıality coffee and bagel cafés. The 2200 and 300 blocks of N High St boast several ıteries. Both the ***Indian Oven*** *(2346 N igh St)* and ***Taj Mahal*** *(☎ 614-294-0208, ²47 N High St)* serve excellent Indian food nain dishes from $8). The former offers ›me vegetarian choices. The ***Blue Nile*** *☎ 614-421-2323, 2361 N High St)* has tradi-ɔnal Ethiopian food and a lunch buffet ntrées from $7).

Flanking the university on the west side the Mecca, to which scarlet-and-gray clad uckeye faithful come to celebrate any ›orts event. The ***Buckeye Hall of Fame*** *☎ 614-291-2233, 1421 Olentangy River Rd)* an enormous place to eat, with heaps of merican-style food (main dishes from $7). ɔu can watch the Buckeyes play in a huge ljoining entertainment complex with a ır, or just wander around looking at more an a century's worth of proud OSU ath-tic achievement. You can be sure no other S university sports hall of fame (not that any have one) would have its own free let parking.

One block south the ***Cap City Fine Diner*** *☎ 614-291-3663, 1299 Olentangy River Rd)* a retro-chic eatery – a diner with a hip at-ude. Eclectic American reigns here, and s always packed (entrées from $8).

ntertainment

here there are students, there are bars, ıd North High St anywhere around the ıiversity is pretty much the Strip. Plenty of ıb-run opportunities would commence ɔm here.

In Short North, the ***Short North Tavern*** *(674 N High St)* is a landmark with live music Friday and Saturday. At least half a dozen decent other clubs with regular music can be found in a six-block stretch to the north.

The Brewery District is an up-and-coming place for nightlife. In addition to the breweries listed in Places to Eat, ***Howl at the Moon*** *(450 S Front St)* is a raucous joint with dueling baby grand pianos. You never know who's going to start hammering away. A handful more bars are within a two-block radius.

The ***Columbus Association for the Performing Arts*** *(☎ 614-469-1045)* has a regular schedule of music, dance and theatrical performances throughout Columbus venues. The stately Ohio Theater, directly across from the capitol building at 77 E State St, is the site of many, as is the Wexner Center for the Arts (see Ohio State University).

Spectator Sports

The Columbus Blue Jackets (☎ 614-540-4625) joined the National Hockey League in 2000 in their new Nationwide Arena, between downtown and the North Market. The Columbus Crew (☎ 614-292-6330), Ohio's not-very-successful professional soccer team, started playing in a new stadium on the Ohio Expo Center grounds in June 1999; it is the US' first professional soccer stadium. The Columbus Quest women's basketball team (☎ 800-340-3626) plays at the convention center on N High St. The Columbus Clippers (☎ 614-462-5350) are the AAA minor league affiliate of the New York Yankees and play at Cooper Stadium, southwest of town off I-70 via W Mound St.

But most Columbus residents follow their Buckeyes, competing in NCAA Division I-A athletics. The football team garners the most slavish devotion Saturday afternoons, but the school is generally top tier in every sport. Contact the ticket office (☎ 614-292-2624) as far in advance as possible; football tickets are hard to get.

Getting There & Away

Air The airport is 7 miles east of downtown and is fairly popular for its low fares. If you're heading to Ohio, check into flying here instead of Cleveland or Cincinnati. Columbus is connected nonstop to 33 US and Canadian cities.

Bus The Greyhound bus station (☎ 614-221-2389), 111 E Town St near the corner of 4th St, has frequent buses to Cincinnati ($16, 2 to 3 hours), Cleveland ($18 to $21, 2½ to 4½ hours), Dayton ($11, 1½ hours), Pittsburgh ($21, 3 hours) and Chicago ($48, 7 to 11 hours, depending on departure time).

Getting Around

The Central Ohio Transit Authority (COTA; ☎ 614-228-1776) runs the local buses (the fare is $1.10). COTA runs a great shuttle trolley (25¢) along High St that allows you to visit Short North district, North Market, German Village and Brewery District.

Taxi fares average around $14 from downtown. COTA has service as well. From High St downtown take the No 2 (E Main to James Rd) line, cross Main St, stand on James Rd next to the BP gas station and take the No 92 (James Rd to Port Columbus).

Taxis cost $2 at flagfall with $3.25 the first mile, decreasing with additional miles.

For once, it's fairly plentiful and cheap, averaging $5 all-day in parking lots and garages.

AROUND COLUMBUS

Newark

• pop 45,000

Twenty-seven miles east of Columbus, Newark, named after the New Jersey city, is more or less the geographic center of Ohio. Like Lancaster, to the south, it was a non-player until the town was linked to the Ohio & Erie Canal, at which point it became a major node on the waterway, attracting industry, commerce and lots of settlers.

Note that no public transportation exists to Newark.

Things to See Newark is best known for its inhabitants predating East Coast migration. **Mound Builders State Memorial** (☎ 740-344-1920), southwest of the intersection of Hwys 16 and 79, preserves just one section of a number of local prehistori Native American mounds. The highligh here is a mound 1200 feet in diameter. O site is the Ohio Indian Art Museum, whic has displays on prehistoric Native America art and on the disparate mound-buildin cultures in Ohio. Other earthwork memor als are nearby. The museum is open 9:30 a to 5 pm Wednesday to Saturday, noon t 5 pm Sunday and holidays, Memorial Da weekend through Labor Day. During Sep tember and October it's open 9:30 am t 5 pm Saturday and noon to 5 pm Sunda The site is free; the museum costs $3/ adults/children.

The **National Heisey Glass Museu** (☎ 740-345-2932), at the corner of Sixth an Church Sts, displays over 4500 pieces c glassware, molds, glassmaking tools an factory designs from noted glassmaker A Heisey. His work dates from 1896 to 195 Hours are 10 am to 4 pm, Tuesday to Satu day, 1 to 4 pm Sunday; admission is $2 fc adults. At the corner of Sixth and Main S the **Licking County Historical Societ** (☎ 740-345-4898) has three restored 19t century homes to tour. Times vary but a usually 1 to 4 pm; free.

Places to Stay Six miles west in Granvill the ***Lazy R Campground*** *(☎ 740-366-438 2340 Dry Creek Rd)* has tent and RV sit for $18. The ***Holiday Inn*** *(☎ 740-522-116 733 Hebron Rd)* in Heath, southwest Newark, was completely renovated in 199 so the rooms are nice. Singles/doubles sta at $50 – pretty good value.

Zanesville

• pop 27,000

In the late 18th century, pottery-quality cl was discovered in the vicinity of Zanesvil and by the mid-18th century, the city w known as the pottery capital of the US vestige remains but an artists' colony it not). In 1810 it was designated the capit but later lost out because it was a few mil too far from the geographic center of t state. Most folks come to the town tod because it was the birthplace and boyho home of Western novelist Zane Grey.

rientation & Information Zanesville's -bridge across the Muskingum River is stinctive; you'll know it when you're on it. 's one of the only bridges in the world here you can cross and still be on the same de of the river.

The Muskingum County Convention and isitors Bureau (☎ 740-455-8282) is at 205 orth Fifth St, a few blocks from the river.

ings to See & Do A couple of blocks om the visitors' bureau at Zane's Landing ark, the *Lorena* stern-wheeler offers river urs along the Muskingum River. Tours epart three times daily June to August, eekends only September and October. ckets are $5/2 adults/children.

In the north of town at 620 Military Rd e **Zanesville Art Center** (☎ 740-452-0741) as European and Asian art exhibits but is interest mainly for its Midwestern ramic displays. Hours are 10 am to 5 pm esday to Friday, 1 to 5 pm weekends; free.

aces to Stay & Eat Six miles southeast ong Hwy 60 is ***Blue Rock State Park*** *614-674-4794)*, which has campsites for $6.

Zanesville's cheaper lodging is found rtheast of town along I-70. The ***Red Roof n*** *(☎ 740-453-6300, 4929 E Pike)* is at exit 0 and has basic singles/doubles for $47. ere is a heated pool.

Downtown, ***The Dining Car*** *(☎ 740-453-07, 231 Market St)* is a casual and inexpenve lunch spot (choices from $4) with mple soups, salads and sandwiches in an d railroad car. ***Zak's*** *(☎ 740-453-2227)*, a ock away on Third St, is a lively Americanajun joint with a nice patio (entrées om $6).

etting There & Away The Greyhound ation (☎ 740-454-2901) is at 375 Fairbanks . Four buses each day go to Columbus hour, $13); two daily make the run to heeling, West Virginia (1½ hours, $19).

ational Road Zane Grey Museum

is excellent museum (☎ 740-872-3143) is miles east of Zanesville along I-70. It houses artifacts pertaining to Zanesville native and Western novelist Zane Grey in one wing, but the second wing, tracing the development and construction of the US' first 'interstate,' the National Road, is more fascinating. Constructed from Cumberland, Maryland, west to Illinois, it still exists as US 40. A 136-foot-long diorama is well worth the visit. Hours are 9:30 am to 5 pm Monday to Saturday, noon to 5 pm May through September. Admission is $5/1 adults/children.

Roseville

Approximately 10 miles south of Zanesville is the center of pottery in Ohio, if not the Midwest; at one time, nearly 50 potteries were in production in a 4-mile radius from Roseville. The **Ohio Ceramic Center** (☎ 800-752-2604), 1 mile south of Roseville on Hwy 93, is a five-building complex comprised of a museum, workshops, studios and display galleries. History of pottery is the overall theme, with displays from a variety of periods. Hours are 9:30 am to 5 pm Wednesday to Saturday, noon to 5 pm Sunday; admission is $2/1 adults/children.

Southeast Ohio

LANCASTER

• pop 34,000

Approximately 25 miles southeast of Columbus, Lancaster was founded in 1797 and at one point considered itself a prime spot for the state house and legislature (not many agreed). It really took off in 1836 when the Lancaster Lateral Canal was dug to connect the town with the Ohio & Erie Canal. Today it's a snug, hilly town with some fine architecture around its central square.

Greyhound has connections to and from Columbus ($10) and Cincinnati ($28) once daily on Lakefront Trailways. The bus stops at McDonald's at 1401 N Memorial Drive. See the Toll-Free & Web Site Directory at the back of the book for contact information.

Information

The Lancaster & Fairfield County Visitors and Convention Bureau (☎ 740-653-8251) is at 109 N Broad St and has lots of local maps and brochures for the sights in town. You can also pick up a narrated walking tour tape for the downtown.

Things to See

Lancaster has a few sights located within a block of each other. The **Sherman House** (☎ 740-687-5891), 137 E Main St, was the birthplace of the Sherman family, which produced Civil War hero General William T Sherman, and John Sherman, who wrote the Sherman Anti-Trust Act. Next to their house, another fine old home was being renovated into the Decorative Arts Center of Ohio and should be open by the time you read this. A block north, the **Georgian** (☎ 740-654-9923), 105 E Wheeling St, is an 1832 Federal-style mansion renovated and furnished in period style. Both homes are open 1 to 4 pm Tuesday to Sunday April 1 through mid-December. A combination ticket costs $4/2 adults/children.

Places to Stay & Eat

One highlight in Lancaster is ***Shaw's Restaurant & Inn*** *(☎ 614-654-2477, 123 N Broad St)*, a historic inn where rooms cost $55/65 single/double and are worth it – in part because most motels worth staying at in town charge fairly high prices. The restaurant offers casually upscale French country- or American-style cuisine at decent prices (entrées from $10).

For those of more modest means, Main St has several low-cost food options, including ***Four Reasons Bakery & Deli***, serving a host of sandwiches (from $4).

OHIO

AROUND LANCASTER

Between Columbus and the West Virginia border in southeastern Ohio is one of the state's most picturesque regions, the **Hocking Hills**. Although you can view a lot of the area from your car window, don't forget to get out and hike around. You may discover it's worth staying in the area for a night or two. Besides the ubiquitous campgrounds (for information, see 'Hocking Hills Scenic Drive'), the ***Inn at Cedar Falls*** *(☎ 614-385-7489, 21190 Hwy 374)* has cozy, antique-filled rooms in a barn-like buildin the dining room is an 1840s double lc house and much of the food comes from th organic gardens on site. There are als cabins. Rooms cost $70/90.

ATHENS

• pop 21,000

With a population of 21,000, plus 19,000 st dents, Athens makes a lovely stop and good base for seeing the southeaster region. Situated where US 50 crosses US 3 it's set among wooded hills and is bu around the Ohio University campus, whic makes up half the town. The downtown trim, with solid, unpretentious early-19t century architecture. The university's pre ence gives the town an edge and vibrancy.

The Visitor Center (☎ 614-592-181 www.athensohio.com) is at 667 E State St. good bookstore is the Athens Book Cent (☎ 740-592-4865) at 753 E State St.

The Oasis Coffeehouse, 70 Universi Terrace, is the local stop for Lakefront Tra ways, which subcontracts some routes fro Greyhound. Getting to Columbus takes 1 hours and costs $20. See the Toll-Free & W Site Directory at the back of the book f Lakefront Trailways' contact information.

Things to See

The university *is* the thing to see. Stop the OU Visitor Center for brochures on tw self-guided campus tours. The **Kenne Museum of Art** has permanent galleries ar a gallery for traveling exhibits. The unive sity also has two theaters and a full schedu of summertime dramas.

The ponderously named **Dairy Ba Southeastern Ohio Cultural Arts Cent** (☎ 740-592-4981), 8000 Dairy Lane, h regular arts and crafts exhibitions in adc tion to its wonderful biennial Nation Quilt Show.

Places to Stay & Eat

There are inexpensive motels on the ou skirts, such as ***Budget Host*** *(☎ 740-594-229 fax 740-594-2295)* on Route 50 W, which h good rooms for $34/37 single/double. Adj cent to Ohio University, the ***Ohio Univers*** *n* (☎ *740-592-6661, fax 740-592-5139, 331 chland Ave)* is the best place in town. It's t a pool and restaurant. Singles/doubles e $90.

Just wander along Court St and you'll d something you like to eat. There are nu-erous student bagel cafés and lots of pubs)hio University is well-known nationally r its partying student body). ***Dalt's Diner***, so here, is an absolute classic; try the tato soup. You can get a full stomach for . Just off Court St on Mill St is the excellent ***Casa Nueva***, best described as creative Southwestern and Mexican, heavy on vegetarian items (entrées from $6).

CHILLICOTHE

• pop 22,000

Chillicothe was the capital of the Northwest Territory but very nearly didn't join the Union. The territorial leader, General Arthur St Clair, was bitterly opposed to the territory becoming a state, and the struggle featured flare-ups of mob violence until, finally, Ohio

Hocking Hills Scenic Drive

Around Lancaster start driving southeast on US 33. Soon the hills begin and before you know it – pastoral respite from Ohio's many urban centers and suburban sprawl. Turn right on Hwy 374 and you're soon at the stunning heights and gorges of Cantwell Cliffs, part of the wonderful **Hocking Hills State Park** (☎ 614-385-6841). This 231-acre region of streams, waterfalls, sandstone cliffs and cavelike formations is an excellent area to explore in any season – if you can avoid getting impossibly lost on the labyrinthine county roads. Naturalists will love the place, as virtually every flora and fauna checklist item in the Midwest can be found here. There are other state parks, miles of hiking trails, abundant campgrounds and cabins to rent.

From Cantwell Cliffs, Hwy 374 takes a hugely circuitous route to **Rock House**, whose name indicates the geology. The highway bends south to eventually reach **Conkle's Hollow**, a jaw-drop beautiful place and well worth a couple of hours of trekking. Two rim trails trace a 200-foot-deep gorge – not for acrophobes! For the fainthearted, an easy trail follows the bottom of the gorge past numerous waterfalls. There's even a state forest rappelling area nearby.

Hwy 374 eventually somehow conjoins with Hwy 664 into the heart of the park, **Old Man's Cave**, where you'll find the visitors' center and a short trail to the granddaddy cave locally. Lots of trails branch out through the park from here, though be aware that serious flooding in early 1999 washed several out and they can be dangerous. (A massive rebuilding project is adding many new trails and bridges.) The center also provides information on camping in the park. Basic sites are $14 and you can rent a site with equipment for $32; there are also popular state park cabins ($100 per day, $480 per week).

Continue south on Hwy 374 and you'll get more falls and caves at **Cedar Falls**; by trail from Old Man's Cave it's only 2½ miles. Hwy 374 ends at Hwy 56, where you turn right to come to the second-most popular spot in the park, **Ash Cave**, 700 feet long and nearly 100 feet high.

If you're still not bushed, head east along Hwy 56. Hydrophiles can head for **Lake Hope State Park**. Train lovers should bend northward along Hwy 278 to Nelsonville, where the historic Hocking Valley Railway offers short trips ($11) on weekends that are popular with autumn leaf-peepers.

For those who are heading back toward Lancaster on US 33, there's a cool little place with an old-fashioned soda fountain in Logan.

OHIO

joined the US in 1803 with Chillicothe as its capital (it would later be moved to Zanesville before winding up in Columbus).

At the corner of N Paint and W Water Sts sits a little tourist information caboose (☎ 740-775-0900) open 10 am to 4 pm weekdays. The Chamber of Commerce (☎ 740-702-7677) also has information.

The Greyhound station (☎ 740-775-2013) is at 61 N Bridge St and has buses throughout the state, including Portsmouth ($1, 1 hour) and Cincinnati ($33, 5 hours).

Things to See & Do

The visitor information caboose has brochures for a self-guided **walking tour** of the historic downtown. An exhaustive overview of local history is found at the **Ross County Historical Society Museums** (☎ 740-772-1936), 45 W 5th St. There are a few buildings at the site, including a reconstructed log house. Exhibits include early Chillicothe and Hopewell culture. Hours are 1 to 5 pm Tuesday to Sunday April through August, weekends only after that. Admission is $2/1 adults/children.

Just beyond the northern border of the city along Hwy 104 next to a prison, er, correctional facility, is the **Hopewell Culture National Historic Park** (☎ 614-774-1125), the site of Mound City, one of the greatest concentrations of Hopewell Indian burial mounds discovered. The largest mound here is 13 acres. The visitors' center has archaeological displays and shows a film about the mound groupings. Trails wind around the 125-acre grounds. Hours are 8:30 am to 6 pm daily Memorial Day weekend through Labor Day, until 5 pm otherwise. Park admission is $2/free adults/children; it's free for everyone January through March.

Shawnee leader Tecumseh

Chillicothe's largest tourist attractio in the summer is the **Tecumseh** outdo drama at the Sugarloaf Mounta Ampitheatre (☎ 740-775-070 7 miles northeast of tow The rousing spectac traces the life of th eponymous Shawne leader. A buffet dinn ($8/5 adults/childre and a small Native Ame ican museum (free) are al options. The show goes on 8 pm Monday to Saturday mid-Jur through Labor Day weekend. Ticke are $15/6 adults/children.

Places to Stay & Eat

Central and inexpensive is the ***Chilli cothe Inn*** *(☎ 740-774-2512, 24 Bridge St)* along the business route US 23. Good singles/doubles a $30/35. Chillicothe has lots of B&B from cheap to expensive. The ***Chilli cothe B&B*** *(☎ 740-772-6848, 202 S Pai St)* is in the 1864 home of an early in dustrialist. Singles/doubles are $40/5 Another historic dwelling houses th ***Greenhouse B&B*** *(☎ 740-775-5313, E 5th St)*, a gorgeous 1894 mansion. Single doubles are $60/70.

Bangkok Palace *(870 N Bridge St)* h Thai food (with Chinese overtones; entré from $6). Most popular is ***Harvest Restaurant & Cellar Lounge*** *(9 S Paint St* in a historic downtown building. Class American fare (main dishes from $6) is th rule here; it also has a good beer selection

AROUND CHILLICOTHE

West of Chillicothe, US 50 bobs pleasant up and down between hills, farms and woo lands. Sixteen miles out at a roadside stop the large **Seip Mound**, another Hopewe legacy. Farther along, follow Route 41 sout which is even prettier, as it meande through a small Amish community who buggies often can be seen. A stop at the **Fo Hill State Memorial** is worthwhile. In a larg natural area with numerous hiking trails an a gorge, it is one of the best-preserve

OHIO

[opewell hilltop enclosures in the state. It is ɔw believed to have been a significant cer-nonial site rather than a fort. There is also small museum here.

Farther southwest is perhaps the most ıptivating of all the regional Indian sites. n Hwy 73, 4 miles northwest of Locust rove, the **Serpent Mound** is the largest figy mound in the USA and one of the ıost finely represented of all the zoomor-hic mounds. It's over 450 yards long and as a beautiful serpentine shape ending in a rcle, and has given rise to various interpre-ıtions. A museum exhibits artifacts from ıe site, and an observation tower gives a ɔod perspective on the design. Admission ı this National Historic Landmark is $5.

If you continue west along US 50 instead f bearing south on Hwy 41, after a few iles you'll come to **Seven Caves**, a 65-acre ilderness park highlighted by seven caves. aniel Boone supposedly spent time as a risoner of the Shawnee in a now-vanished llage on the grounds. It's got an ambitious pography of creeks, waterfalls and cliffs; ails snake throughout the park. Hours are am to dusk daily. Admission is $10/5 dults/children.

outhwest Ohio

INCINNATI

pop 336,000

significant industrial and commercial ɛnter, Cincinnati seems smaller than it ppears on a map. The Tri-State area in-udes Kentucky, Indiana and Ohio, and res-ents include this region in their concept of ıe city; this spread out area pushes it into ɛcond place population-wise in Ohio, but it ırely feels that crowded. The cliche of 'big ty with small-town feel' is actually appro-riate here. The downtown is compact and ith little effort you can reach – even on ot – lovely hills overlooking the downtown nd Ohio River. There is no major lure nless you count cheerful typicality – sociol-gists have ranked Cincinnati one of the ation's most 'typical' cities, by whatever sta-stical or demographic measure. It was also rated as the best city in America in which to live by *Places Rated Almanac* in 1994 and generally is in the top 20 of any such ratings. Winston Churchill purportedly called it 'the most beautiful inland city in the country.' Visitors to town may find a wander through one of its well-preserved 19th-century neighborhoods and a meal or two make a pleasant stop. There are also many cultural attractions to consider and a couple of sections of the downtown are experiencing a revival of sorts.

History

Founded in 1788, soon after the Revolutionary War, Cincinnati was one of the first US cities west of the Allegheny Mountains. At this time the Ohio River was the principal transport route, and Cincinnati became a base for wars against the Indians and a transport center for the rich agricultural hinterland. The introduction of steamboats on the river and the completion of the Miami-Erie Canal made it even more important as a gateway to the expanding frontier. It soon became Ohio's largest city, and a huge influx of German and Irish immigrants pushed the population above 160,000 by 1860. The many meat works earned Cincinnati the nickname 'Porkopolis' and provided enough leftover lard for Procter & Gamble to become one of the world's largest soap makers.

Though in many respects a northern industrial city, Cincinnati had plenty of Southern sympathizers in the mid-19th century because of its proximity and connections to the South. Nevertheless, the city became a center for the antislavery movement, an important station on the Underground Railroad and a home of abolitionist writing and publishing. (This occurred to such an extent that in 1999 the city was named the site of the National Underground Railroad Freedom Center, to be opened on Elm St, hopefully as early as 2002. The center will be a museum and research facility on the history of slavery.) The Civil War was a boost to Cincinnati's industries, but later the city suffered from corruption, maladministration and a decline in its river transport role as the

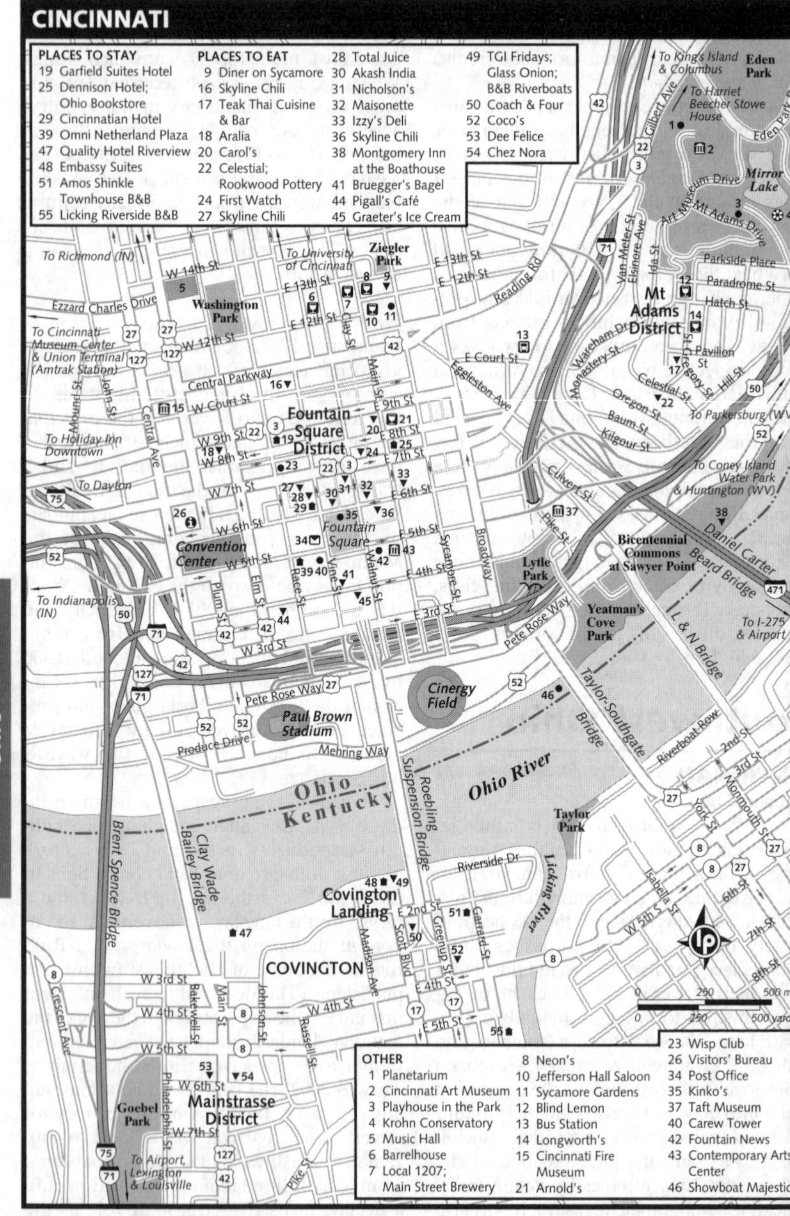
CINCINNATI
PLACES TO STAY
19 Garfield Suites Hotel
25 Dennison Hotel; Ohio Bookstore
29 Cincinnatian Hotel
39 Omni Netherland Plaza
47 Quality Hotel Riverview
48 Embassy Suites
51 Amos Shinkle Townhouse B&B
55 Licking Riverside B&B
PLACES TO EAT
9 Diner on Sycamore
16 Skyline Chili
17 Teak Thai Cuisine & Bar
18 Aralia
20 Carol's
22 Celestial; Rookwood Pottery
24 First Watch
27 Skyline Chili
28 Total Juice
30 Akash India
31 Nicholson's
32 Maisonette
33 Izzy's Deli
36 Skyline Chili
38 Montgomery Inn at the Boathouse
41 Bruegger's Bagel
44 Pigall's Café
45 Graeter's Ice Cream
49 TGI Fridays; Glass Onion; B&B Riverboats
50 Coach & Four
52 Coco's
53 Dee Felice
54 Chez Nora
OTHER
1 Planetarium
2 Cincinnati Art Museum
3 Playhouse in the Park
4 Krohn Conservatory
5 Music Hall
6 Barrelhouse
7 Local 1207; Main Street Brewery
8 Neon's
10 Jefferson Hall Saloon
11 Sycamore Gardens
12 Blind Lemon
13 Bus Station
14 Longworth's
15 Cincinnati Fire Museum
21 Arnold's
23 Wisp Club
26 Visitors' Bureau
34 Post Office
35 Kinko's
37 Taft Museum
40 Carew Tower
42 Fountain News
43 Contemporary Arts Center
46 Showboat Majestic
To King's Island & Columbus
Eden Park
To Harriet Beecher Stowe House
Eden Park Drive
Mirror Lake
Art Museum Drive
Mt Adams Drive
Parkside Place
Paradrome St
Hatch St
Mt Adams District
Pavilion St
St Gregory St
Hill St
To Parkersburg (WV)
To Coney Island Water Park & Huntington (WV)
Gilbert Ave
Van Meter St
Elsinore Ave
Ida St
Reading Rd
Wareham Dr
Monastery St
Celestial St
Oregon St
Baum St
Kilgour St
E Court St
Eggleston Ave
To Richmond (IN)
To University of Cincinnati
Ziegler Park
E 13th St
E 12th St
W 14th St
Washington Park
Ezzard Charles Drive
To Cincinnati Museum Center & Union Terminal (Amtrak Station)
W 12th St
Central Parkway
Clay St
Main St
Mound St
John St
Central Ave
W Court St
To Holiday Inn Downtown
To Dayton
W 9th St
W 8th St
W 7th St
W 6th St
W 5th St
Fountain Square District
E 9th St
E 8th St
E 7th St
E 6th St
E 5th St
E 4th St
E 3rd St
W 3rd St
Fountain Square
Convention Center
Plum St
Elm St
Race St
Vine St
Walnut St
Sycamore St
Broadway
Culvert St
Pike St
Lytle Park
Bicentennial Commons at Sawyer Point
Daniel Carter Beard Bridge
To I-275 & Airport
Yeatman's Cove Park
L & N Bridge
Pete Rose Way
To Indianapolis (IN)
Cinergy Field
Paul Brown Stadium
Produce Drive
Mehring Way
Taylor-Southgate Bridge
Riverboat Row
2nd St
3rd St
Ohio
Kentucky
Ohio River
Roebling Suspension Bridge
Monmouth St
York St
Taylor Park
Brent Spence Bridge
Clay Wade Bailey Bridge
Riverside Dr
Licking River
Isabella St
6th St
7th St
8th St
W 5th St
Covington Landing
E 2nd St
Scott Blvd
Greenup St
Garrard St
COVINGTON
Madison Ave
E 4th St
E 5th St
W 3rd St
W 4th St
W 5th St
W 6th St
W 7th St
Crescent Ave
Bakewell St
Main St
Johnson St
Russell St
Philadelphia St
Goebel Park
Mainstrasse District
To Airport, Lexington & Louisville
Pike St
0 250 500 m
0 250 500 yards

OHIO

ailways expanded. Greater Cincinnati now as a wide manufacturing base. It's also a ıajor coal port and cultural center.

›rientation

'ountain Square is the nucleus of the down-ɔwn, which has Central Parkway and Third t as its north and south boundaries; ʾentral Ave and Sycamore St are the east-ʼest dividing lines. The downtown is then urrounded by hills on three sides. The hills f the Mt Adams and Eden Park Districts, ·oth east of downtown, proffer lovely views nd cultural and gastronomic attractions.

The Ohio River (and the I-71 freeway) is ·n the south side and the first thing you otice is that from downtown Cincinnati it ure doesn't seem to exist; access is hin-ered by the mess of roads around Ft Wash-ıgton Way. There has been much rancorous ebate over whether to redevelop the ripar-an stretches into citizen-friendly green paces, but so far no luck, especially now hat the new Paul Brown Stadium – where he Cincinnati Bengals football team will ·lay – sits in a previously developable site.

The Over-the-Rhine (OTR) neighbor-ood (originally a German enclave) is the ortion of Main St and streets north of ʾentral Parkway, an urban distress zone hat has been experiencing a renaissance.

Driving is little problem in the downtown rea. The streets are in a grid pattern, and he numbered streets run east–west, using 'ete Rose Way near the river as a starting oint. Vine St demarcates east–west streets.

Five interstates pass through the city. 'hey're only as bad traffic-wise as any ther US metropolitan area, but special ıention goes to I-75, a major US north-ɔuth artery, which is perpetually white-nuckle crowded.

The Visitors' Bureau has good, free maps t their main office and at a Fountain quare kiosk.

nformation

ourist Offices The Cincinnati Conven-on & Visitors' Bureau (☎ 513-621-2142) is t 300 W 6th St, at the corner of Plum St. In ummer there are information booths in Fountain Square and the Museum Center. Pick up a free walking-tour brochure. The 6th St office is open 9 am to 5 pm, Monday through Friday. The bureau's Web site (www.cincyusa.com) is good.

Money & Post Cincinnati's local sales tax totals 6%. The city hotel tax is 10%; in Kentucky it's 8.2%. The downtown post office is at 525 Vine St.

Email & Internet Access To log on, visit Cincinnati's first Internet café, Sitwells (☎ 513-281-7487) at 404 Ludlow Ave next door to the Esquire theater (arthouse) in the Gaslight district (see the University of Cincinnati Entertainment section, later in the chapter). Heading north on Vine St will take you in the general direction of the University of Cincinnati, but call for directions so you don't get lost; Sitwells merits a visit.

Kinko's has a copy shop at 51 E 5th St, in Fountain Square. Internet access costs $12 per hour or 20¢ per minute.

Media The *Cincinnati Enquirer* comes out in the morning and on Sunday; the *Cincinnati Post* is the afternoon paper. The free local weekly is *City Beat*, with the city's best overview of restaurants and nightlife. The *Greater Cincinnati GLBT News* is the city's monthly gay paper. The *Ohio Gay People's Chronicle*, which is circulated statewide, also covers Cincinnati; it's free and distributed weekly.

Bookstores Cincinnati has some good ones. The Ohio Bookstore (☎ 513-621-5142), 726 Main St, where the Dennison Hotel is (see Places to Stay), is a pleasantly aged used book shop that is the best place for any detailed Cincinnati books. At the corner of 5th and Walnut Sts, Fountain News (☎ 513-421-4049) has an excellent selection of international media, and its coffee bar is tops in Cincinnati for people-watching.

West of downtown in Northside you'll find Crazy Ladies Bookstore (☎ 513-541-4198), 4039 Hamilton Ave at the corner of Blue Rock. For over twenty years, Crazy

Ladies has been specializing in books by, for and about women. Call for directions; it's worth the trip. Pink Pyramid (☎ 513-621-7465), 907 Race St, also focuses on gay and lesbian publications.

Another great independent store with a comprehensive inventory (including a great children's section), an author reading series and a café is Joseph-Beth (☎ 513-396-8966) at 2692 Madison Rd in the Hyde Park neighborhood. For kids' books, in the same area, try Blue Marble (☎ 513-731-2665) at 3054 Madison Rd. Call for directions for both.

Visit Mt Adams Bookstore (☎ 513-241-9009) at 1101 Gregory St, or New World Bookshop (☎ 513-861-6100) at 336 Ludlow Ave, if you find yourself in these neighborhoods. Farther afield, there's The Bookshelf (☎ 513-271-9141) at 7754 Camargo Rd, The Open Book (☎ 513-931-4433), 8537 Winton Rd and Montgomery Book Company (☎ 513-891-2227), at 9917 Montgomery Rd.

Gay & Lesbian Travelers In addition to several publications and bookstore resources (see Media and Bookstores above), you might find the Cincinnati G&L Switchboard (☎ 513-591-0222) to be helpful; it's a recorded, navigable line. The Gay & Lesbian Community Switchboard (☎ 513-221-7800) provides tips for travelers. Also, there's a community Web site at www.GayCincinnati.com.

Dangers & Annoyances The Over-the-Rhine neighborhood may be gentrified, but not too long ago it was not a place to go at night. Take care in nearby areas. The area between the train station, Union Terminal and downtown is also to be avoided.

Downtown

The center of downtown is **Fountain Square**, where people congregate around the fancy old 'Spirit of the Waters' fountain. At the corner of the square, Carew Tower has a great view from its 49th-floor observation deck ($2; open daily) and a fine art-deco interior – its ceramics are from the celebrated local Rookwood pottery. West of the square, the Skywalk system of elevated walkways links hotels and shops in a 20-block are around the convention center.

East of the square is the big postmoder Procter & Gamble building, with its attrac tive gardens, and the **Contemporary Ar Center** (☎ 513-721-0390), 115 E 5th St, 2n floor, which has changing exhibits of ever form of modern art. It's open 10 am to 6 p Monday through Saturday, Sunday fror noon to 5 pm and costs $4/2 adults/childre free to those 12 and younger. Its 1990 sho of Robert Mapplethorpe's photograph sparked a national controversy over feder funding for the arts. A few blocks farthe east, have a look in Lytle Park at the statu of Lincoln bearing the burdens of offic then continue to the **Taft Museum** (☎ 51 241-0343), at 316 Pike St. The handsom 1820 mansion has a notable collection c Chinese porcelain and European painting Hours are 10 am to 4 pm daily. It costs $ but is free Wednesday.

Northwest of Fountain Square distric the **Cincinnati Fire Museum** (☎ 513-62 5553), 315 W Court St, is a good bet for kid in the downtown area. Lots of origin equipment – some over a century old – ca be viewed, touched, even climbed on. Cir cinnati's firehouses originated the slidir pole now associated with fire stations an were the first to use fire engines. It's ope 10 am to 4 pm Tuesday to Friday, noon 4 pm weekends. Admission is $5/3 adult children.

Beyond Downtown

Just north of downtown, beyond Liberty S is the 1852 **Findlay Market**, chock-full c produce, meat, dairy and flower vendors. It great for people-watching and photo ops.

Northeast of downtown at 2950 Gilbe Ave in Walnut Hills, the **Harriet Beech Stowe House** (☎ 513-632-5120) is where th author of the novel *Uncle Tom's Cabin* live with her family. Some original furnishing can be viewed, as well as exhibits on slaver It's open 10 am to 4 pm, Tuesday to Thur day; free. Also to the northeast is th **William Howard Taft National Historic Si** (☎ 513-684-3262), 2038 Auburn Ave. Th Greek Revival building was the birthplac of the 27th president of the US and features original furnishings and family heirlooms. It's open 10 am to 5 pm daily; free.

Two miles northwest of downtown, the **Cincinnati Museum Center** (☎ 513-287-7000), at 1301 Western Ave, is in a classic Art Deco train station. The 1933 Union Terminal, which was listed on the National Register of Historic Places in 1972, is still used by Amtrak. The Cincinnati History Museum features a side-wheel river steamboat and lots of exhibits on the city and the region. More geared toward kids is the Museum of Natural History, with an excellent exhibit on the ice age that shaped the Great Lakes region, and a limestone cave with real bats. An Omnimax theater rounds out the sites. The building looks a little like Darth Vader's helmet, and its interior has magnificent murals designed by artist Winold Reiss. The museums are open 10 am to 5 pm Monday through Saturday, 11 am to 6 pm Sunday. Omnimax has films roughly on the hour; there are some evening shows but it varies seasonally. A combination ticket for both museums and the Omnimax theater costs $12. The museums are free for the last half hour of each day, but parking costs another $3.

University of Cincinnati Area

You'll feel a distinctly academic flair in the Corryville district, near the University of Cincinnati. There are a few trendy clubs, coffeehouses and cafés. If you're interested in architecture, visit the university's College of Design, Architecture, Art and Planning headquarters, the controversial Aronoff Center for Design & Art, designed by Peter Eisenman. See if you can find the stairwell (or anything else) amid all that drywall.

Check out nearby 100-acre **Burnet Park** and its hiking trails. Near the campus at 2615 Clifton Ave is the **Hillel Jewish Student Center** (☎ 513-221-6728), with exhibits on Judaica from the Midwest. Hours are 9 am to 5 pm Monday to Thursday, 9 am to 3 pm Friday; free. Jewish culture is examined in great detail at the **Skirball Museum, Hebrew Union College Jewish Institute of Religion** (☎ 513-221-6728), farther north at 3101 Clifton Ave. Exhibits, photographs and

Harriet Beecher Stowe, abolitionist, author & Cincinnati resident

memorabilia focus on the Jewish diaspora, immigration, the Holocaust, the Torah and other topics. Most attention is riveted on a Dead Sea Scroll urn. Hours are 11 am to 4 pm Monday to Thursday, 2 to 5 pm Sunday; free.

Riverside

South of the city center, the elegant 1876 **Roebling Suspension Bridge** was a forerunner of John Roebling's famous Brooklyn Bridge in New York. To the west is the brand new Paul Brown Stadium for the Cincinnati Bengals football team. Going east, you reach Cinergy Field, surrounded by a mess of freeways and parking lots, and the public boat landing, home to the showboat *Majestic* (see Entertainment). Then there's the riverfront walk, which goes through several parks, including Bicentennial Commons at Sawyer Point, with whimsical monuments and flying pigs.

Mt Adams & Vicinity

Hilly **Mt Adams**, east of downtown, is a 19th-century neighborhood of narrow, winding streets with galleries, bars and restaurants. The views alone are worth the trip. You can walk from the Taft Museum to Mt Adams, though there are a lot of busy streets and highways between them. The best route is to follow E 6th St, cross the bridge and then look for the stairs that must

THOMAS HUHTI

Cruises reveal the Ohio & Kentucky shores near the 1876 Roebling Suspension Bridge.

be climbed. It takes about 30 minutes, but walking is a good idea because driving there is no picnic.

Farther out in lovely Eden Park, the **Cincinnati Art Museum** (☎ 513-721-5204) has the city's best collection, with an emphasis on Middle Eastern and European art. Hours are 10 am to 5 pm Tuesday to Saturday, noon to 6 pm Sunday. Admission is $5/free adults/children, free to all on Saturday. A **planetarium** is nearby. The **Krohn Conservatory** (☎ 513-421-4086), also in the park, is a vast greenhouse with rain forest, desert flora and superb seasonal flower shows. Hours are 10 am to 5 pm daily, and it costs $2.

Covington (Kentucky)

You can walk across the Ohio River to Covington, Kentucky, a sort of suburb of Cincinnati. Right by the south end of the Roebling Suspension Bridge, Covington Landing has a number of floating bars and tour boats. There is a good historic riverfront walk east of the bridge. Further gentrification is ongoing. Nearby, Covington's attractive **Mainstrasse** was a 19th-century German neighborhood, and its main street is now given over to shops and pubs.

Special Events

Cincinnati's German heritage has insured a healthy respect for beer. There's a huge Oktoberfest each year and a celebration of the issue of the winter beer. The city hosts many other events throughout the year, including a blues and jazz fest, flower show and an fair on Hyde Park Square. For more information on beer and other festivals, see 'Bock-to-Bach Festivity in Cincinnati's Over-the-Rhine.'

Organized Tours

The most popular way to get onto the Ohio River is on a tour from **BB Riverboats** (☎ 606-261-8500), which offers one-hour sightseeing tours ($9/8 adults/children) as well as breakfast, lunch and dinner cruises; schedules vary wildly so call for that day's sailings. Boats depart from Covington Landing, next to the Roebling Suspension Bridge, on the Kentucky side.

Places to Stay

Budget There's a dearth of budget accommodations, and the central downtown hotels are gorgeous but pricey. Main St at 7th St has a couple of serious dives, like th

Bock-to-Bach Festivity in Cincinnati's Over-the-Rhine

A celebration of Cincinnati's proud German American heritage, the annual BockFest takes place over a long weekend in late February or early March, with the festivities including a Renaissance costume parade through the historic Over-the-Rhine district, live music throughout the thriving Main St Entertainment District and plenty of potent Bock beer, savory Bockwurst sausages and live goats.

Live what?...A little beer history is in order. According to brew guru Michael Jackson (www.beerhunter.com), Bock beer dates back to 17th-century Bavaria, where Catholic monks would brew the heavy, malty potable to 'nourish' themselves during the Lenten season when they had to refrain from solid food. According to one prominent legend, the best Bock in those days came from the town of Einbeck, whose name was slurred – perhaps under the influence of the product itself – into 'Em Bock,' dialect for 'a billy goat.' The name stuck, and ever since, the goat has been the unofficial mascot of Bock beer – a fitting one in another sense, since at 7.5% to 13.7% alcohol by volume, Bock packs a mean kick!

Cincinnati's BockFest typically gets underway with a Friday evening parade led by a goat-drawn cart bearing the first barrel of locally brewed Bock beer. Civic luminaries and the reveling masses don whimsical Renaissance costumes for the festive stroll, which starts at historic Arnold's Bar & Grill on downtown E Eighth St, then heads up Main St into Over-the-Rhine, passing by the district's abundance of new pubs, nightclubs and restaurants, as well as Main St mainstays such as Japp's and Kaldi's Coffeehouse (which also has a goat for a mascot – hmm...). The parade winds up on Twelfth St with an outdoor blessing of Cincinnati-made Bock beers and Bockwurst sausage, followed, in another Bock-inspired twist of the tongue, by live performances of music by JS Bach.

After all that walking, it's time to eat and drink. The celebration continues in 'Sausagefest' at Grammer's on Liberty St, Cincinnati's oldest German restaurant, with a wealth of Bock and Bockwurst on hand, plus live entertainment by local bands. Bock is in no short supply anywhere on Main St, where most of the restaurants and clubs pour the mighty brew in honor of the season.

Friday night at BockFest is also a great time to discover one of Main St's other popular activities, the Final Friday gallery walk (usually on the last Friday of each month). Rechristened the 'Bock Around the Block Gallery Walk' for this event, the monthly walk is a free, evening open house in Over-the-Rhine's numerous art galleries and workshops, including the Marta Hewett Gallery and the Pendleton Art Center. Many of the boutiques and craft shops on Main St also stay open late on gallery walk nights, adding to the general festivity.

BockFest continues through the weekend, with much more food and drink on Saturday and additional Bach concerts on Sunday morning. For dates and other information on the annual BockFest, call the BarrelHouse Brewing Co at ☎ 513-421-2337.

Cincinnati offers a number of other festivals throughout the year, including: the Cincinnati May Festival (beginning mid-May), a choral gathering dating back more than 125 years; Taste of Cincinnati (late May), which purports to be the nation's longest-running culinary arts festival; the Gay Pride parade (usually in June, see www.GayCincinnati.com for more information); the Gold Star ChiliFest (mid-July), serving up country music and spicy food, including Cincinnati's curious contribution to American cuisine, chili on spaghetti; and another great celebration of beer and other things German, Oktoberfest-Zinzinnati (mid-September), featuring live music, more than 50 food vendors and grown men in *lederhosen*! For more information on these and other Cincinnati events, visit the Cincinnati Convention & Visitors Bureau Web site at www.cincyusa.com, or call ☎ 800-246-2987.

– Matthew Campbell

Dennison Hotel *(☎ 513-241-7035, 716 Main St)*, but it's generally full on a permanent basis.

For budget motels near downtown, look in the Uptown area along Central Parkway; exit at Hopple St, a few miles north of downtown along I-75. Rates vary with the month (they're highest in summer), and weekends cost more. Try ***Budget Host*** *(☎ 513-559-1600, fax 513-559-1616, 3356 Central Parkway)* with rooms at $49/57 single/double, or for a little more money, ***Days Inn*** *(☎ 513-599-0400, fax 513-559-9662, 2880 Central Parkway)*, with rooms at $55/60 single/double.

Near the airport, there is a ***Motel 6*** *(☎ 606-283-0909, fax 513-953-3190, 7937 Dream St)*, with rates from $33/37 single/double. ***Motel 6*** has two other options, far north of downtown in Sharonville, around 20 miles away. The cheaper one *(☎ 513-772-5944, fax 513-772-2680, 2000 E Kemper Rd)* is found near the Hwy 747 exit off I-275; rooms can dip as low as $29/32 single/double here. East of here on I-275 at the US 42 junction is a slightly more expensive one *(☎ 513-562-1123, fax 513-563-8242, 3850 Hauck Rd)*, a good option if you're planning to go to the King's Island Amusement Park (see Around Cincinnati).

Mid-Range Mid-range is a relative term in downtown Cincinnati, and everybody ratchets prices up during the summer. The ***Holiday Inn Downtown*** *(☎ 513-241-8660, fax 513-241-9057, 800 W 8th St)* has a restaurant, lounge and swimming pool. Its rates usually hit the $95 range for a single/double; however, depending on when you reserve and for what dates, it has been known to offer steep discounts, sometimes as low as $69.

A good idea is to stay in Covington, Kentucky, a short drive (or walk) across the river. A handful of B&Bs are well located and substantially cheaper than downtown Cincinnati options. The best spot belongs to the ***Amos Shinkle Townhouse B&B*** *(☎ 606-431-2118, fax 606-491-4551, 215 Garrard St)*, just east of the Roebling Suspension Bridge. This lovely manor, built in 1854, has rooms in the erstwhile carriage house as well as the main house. Rates are $69/79 single/double Another historic dwelling is the ***Lickin Riverside B&B*** *(☎ 606-291-1200, 51 Garrard St)*, an 1868 Greek Revival. Rate are a bit higher at $99 single/double.

Covington Landing, just west of the Suspension Bridge, has a couple of hotels wit superb views and not outrageous prices The ***Quality Hotel Riverview*** *(☎ 606-491 1200, fax 606-491-0326, 668 W 5th St)* is a exit 192 off I-75. The rooms aren't huge bu they are well-maintained. There's also pool, a whirlpool, and a restaurant/lounge Rates are $89 single/double. East of her the ***Embassy Suites*** *(☎ 606-261-8400, fa 606-261-8486)* is impressive but much mor expensive.

For mid-range prices very close to th airport, ***Residence Inn*** *(☎ 606-282-7400, fa 606-282-1790, 2811 Circleport Drive)* is a apartment-style hotel with one- and two bedroom units, the latter having fireplaces Rates are $104 single/double.

Top End The 1920s-era ***Omni Netherlan Plaza*** *(☎ 513-421-9100, fax 513-421-4291, 3 W 5th St)* is an ornate Art Deco monumen comprising part of the Carew Tower, th tallest building in Cincinnati. The hote offers a health club, an indoor pool, a sauna whirlpool and two dining rooms, one o which, Orchids, is outstanding – especiall for its Sunday brunch. Rates are $125 single double.

The 1882 ***Cincinnatian Hotel*** *(☎ 513 381-3000, fax 513-651-0256, 601 Vine St)* is a equally magnificent French Second Empire style building. It definitely offers a more in timate luxury than any of the mega-hotel downtown. It also has a sauna and ton restaurant offering Continental cuisine Rates are $210 single/double.

If you find the prices a tad steep, th lobbies are still worth a look.

If restored elegance isn't exactly wha you're looking for, the ***Garfield Suite Hotel*** *(☎ 513-421-3355, fax 513-421-3729, Garfield Place)* offers one, two and three bedroom suites, with private balconies an kitchens, along with a weight room. Rate are $175 single/double.

'laces to Eat

)owntown For cheap eats downtown, try he ***food court*** in Carew Tower or ***Izzy's)eli*** *(☎ 513-721-4241, 819 Elm St; ☎ 513-41-6246, 610 Main St)*, the latter of which ıas outstanding corned beef. ***Bruegger's ʒagel*** *(☎ 513-421-2320)*, at the corner of /ine and E 4th Sts, serves bagels kettle-ıoiled on the premises with a choice of 12 ream cheeses and other toppings, plus ;ood coffee. ***Total Juice*** *(☎ 513-784-1666, 31 Vine St)* has a large array of wraps (in-luding vegetarian) and healthful juices and moothies. At any of the places above you an get a light meal for less than $5.

You'll see in-line skaters next to Armani-lad executives at the place to power-ıreakfast (it also serves lunch) – ***First Vatch*** *(☎ 513-721-4744)*, near the corner of Valnut and 7th Sts. It has basic egg-centric ıreakfasts and more creative specials, in-luding some healthful options (entrées rom $6).

Rock Bottom Restaurant & Brewery *☎ 513-621-1588)* is in Fountain Square and ıas a straightforward American lineup of andwiches, salads and steaks (entrées rom $7).

Carol's *(☎ 513-651-2667, 825 Main St)* is ıften touted for its cabaret act and night-ıme spirit, but the food's great too, with op-level pub grub and some vegetarian ıptions (entrées average less than $10). 'lus, it serves until 1 am.

Nicholson's *(☎ 513-564-9111, 625 Walnut t)* is a Scottish–style tavern with British, ontinental and American cuisine (main ourses start under $10); the patios are great laces to relax. The tavern features over 70 ingle-malt scotches.

A few Indian eateries are found down-own, including ***Akash India*** *(☎ 513-723-300, 24 E 6th St)*, specializing in northern ndian cooking (specials from $6). Sri ankan food in a very cozy setting is at ***ıralia*** *(☎ 513-723-1217, 815 Elm St)*, with rguably the most creative curries in town most main courses under $10). Afternoon ea is served Tuesday to Saturday.

For something fancier, ***Pigall's Café*** *☎ 513-651-2233, 127 W 4th St)* has nostalgic French decor but an innovative American menu ($20 per entrée). A chic diner in a converted railcar in the Over-the-Rhine neighborhood, ***The Diner on Sycamore*** *(☎ 513-721-1212,1203 Sycamore St)* features well-made dishes from sandwiches to creative contemporary (main courses from $10). The best restaurant downtown is ***Maisonette*** *(☎ 513-721-2260, 114 E 6th St)*, nationally famous for its French haute cuisine and extensive wine list. It's expensive and formal, and you'll need reservations.

Another celebrated Cincinnati eating experience is ***Graeter's Ice Cream*** *(☎ 513-381-0653)*, at 41 E 4th St downtown and 10 other locations. The only thing better is the beautifully tiled ***Rookwood Ice Cream Parlor***, in the Cincinnati Museum Center – don't miss it.

Riverside Locally famous are the barbecued ribs at the ***Montgomery Inn at the***

Local Flavor

A breakfast specialty is *goetta* ('gedda'), a fried patty of ground pork, ground beef, bay leaf, salt, pepper, cornmeal or oatmeal and special ingredients varying from chef to chef.

But one simply mustn't depart the Queen City without tasting *the* local specialty, five-way chili. That is: meat sauce (spiced with chocolate and cinnamon) over spaghetti and beans, garnished with cheese and onions. You can get it three-way or four-way – based on the number of toppings – but what the hell, go the whole way; life's an adventure. **Skyline Chili,** with inexpensive outlets all over town and the state, has been in the chili game since 1949. The one at 1007 Vine St, on the corner of W Court St, is a total experience at noon on weekdays. Aficionados may want to sample a bowl at **Camp Washington Chili,** where the city's fave food first touched a palate. It's northwest of town (take I-75 a few miles north), in the middle of nowhere at the corner of Colerain and Hopple Sts.

Boathouse *(☎ 513-721-7427, 925 Eastern Ave)*, by the river.

Just across the Suspension Bridge at Covington Landing are a few restaurants right atop the water, including a ***TGI Fridays***, a boisterous, family-style place that's part of a national franchise, and the more formal, dinner-only ***Glass Onion*** *(☎ 606-491-6692, 1 Madison Ave)*, with very creative Continental cuisine (main courses from $15).

Mt Adams East of downtown, this district has unequivocally the most superb views. Housed in a historic former pottery factory, ***Rookwood Pottery*** *(☎ 513-721-5456, 1077 Celestial St)* is casual, with a menu from burgers to seafood (entrées from $10). Some guest tables are in former firing kilns.

The ***Teak Thai Cuisine & Bar*** *(☎ 513-281-7000)* serves excellent Thai food in a lovely setting (entrées from under $10). It's wonderful eating on the patio.

Also in Mt Adams is the ***Celestial*** *(☎ 513-241-4455, 1071 Celestial St)*, an elegant French restaurant with a view to die for and exquisite food and service (main courses from $20). Reservations are required.

Covington Covington's main drag retains its German original name – Mainstrasse. It's mostly good for strolling and shopping, but a couple of nice eateries are pleasant for a meal or, in the evening, live jazz. ***Chez Nora*** *(☎ 606-491-8027, 530 Main St)* is a relaxing corner bistro/bar with lighter fare such as salads, soups and sandwiches (most main courses under $10), and good daily specials. The martinis are also huge. ***Dee Felice*** *(529 Main St)* has Cajun food (entrées from $10) and the place gets rollicking with Dixieland jazz.

Closer to the Roebling Suspension Bridge are a couple of good restaurants. ***Coco's*** *(☎ 606-491-1369, 322 Greenup St)* is a subdued two-level place with a vaguely Southwest USA feel. You'll find eclectic contemporary American cuisine with daily pasta specials (main courses from $10). Right in front of the bridge is a long-time local institution, ***Coach and Four*** *(☎ 606-431-6700, 214 Scott Blvd)*, whose dark interiors are reminiscent of a tony private club. Again, more experimental American dominates the menu, but steaks and such are also found (entrées from $10). Friday and weekends, make a reservation.

Entertainment

Downtown Downtown, ***Arnold's*** *(☎ 513-421-6234, 210 E 8th St)*, is a tavern dating from 1861, with food, drink and live jazz and other music. Another hot entry in the local jazz scene is the ***Wisp Club*** *(19 Garfield Place)*, excellent since it features live music nightly ($4 and up). See Places to Eat for details on entertainment at ***Carol's***.

At the public landing east of Cinergy Field, the showboat ***Majestic*** (☎ 513-241-6550) is one of the country's last riverboat theaters and stages performances during its season, usually Wednesday to Sunday, April through October.

Over-the-Rhine The city's most happening nightlife is probably in the Over-the-Rhine neighborhood, mostly along Main, Vine, and Sycamore Sts north of Central Parkway. An urban blight zone in the late '80s, it's experiencing a renaissance (but still take care, especially if you've been celebrating). In addition to those listed here, you will doubtlessly stumble on many, many more. Enjoy! The cornerstone is the ***Jefferson Hall Saloon*** *(1150 Main St)*, with a regular slate of obscure or well-known rock or blues acts. A block north on Main St is the ***Main St Brewery***, the city's original brew pub and the one that really started the rejuvenation of the district. It has a restaurant but is really known for live music. A personal fave is ***Local 1207***, virtually next door at 1207 Main St; it's another original and you've got to love the impossible stage situation – really makes you work for your music. Around the corner on E 12th St, ***Neon's*** has R&B, blues and even swing, but mostly fits the niche for martinis, scotches and cigars.

Barrelhouse *(22 E 12th St)* is another brew pub that's joined the fun in the neighborhood. It's got a great copper bar, good pizza and lots of live music.

Southeast of here, ***Sycamore Gardens*** *(1133 Sycamore St)* is one of the larger concert venues for lots of different music.

The acoustically excellent ***Music Hall*** *☎ 513-721-8222, 1241 Elm St)*, is the city's lassical music venue, where the symphony rchestra, pops orchestra, opera and ballet old their seasons. This is not a very good eighborhood, so be cautious and park earby.

Iniversity of Cincinnati Area In Coryville near the University of Cincinnati, ***ogart's*** *(2621 Vine St)* is one of the mustlay places for most every mid-level rock and, and some superstars, too. Soon to ave live music, ***Sitwells*** *(☎ 513-281-7487)* n Ludlow St (any UC student can point ou in the right direction) is a great place to o for a coffee, beer, something to eat (vegtarians can find something here), live oetry and the like. It's a hotbed of counterulture. A Cincinnati standard for coffee or Guinness over a game of chess or peoplevatching is the ***Highland Coffee House*** *☎ 513-861-4151, 2839 Highland Ave)*. Again, sk a student-type for directions, and wear our black turtleneck.

Mt Adams In Mt Adams, look for the ***lind Lemon*** *(936 Hatch St)*, a gem of a ar with lots of history, atmosphere and ood live music. ***Longworth's*** *(1108 St Gregory St)* is also very comfortable, with leasant outdoor tables. To enjoy a view f the city's twinkling lights from a small eck perched on a steep Mt Adams hillide, see if you can find the unpretentious ***City View Tavern*** *(☎ 513-241-8439, 403 Oregon St)*.

A popular summertime activity is a visit o the ***Cincinnati Playhouse in Eden Park*** *☎ 513-421-3888)* for theatrical perforiances. Shows are held daily except Monday; matinees are held Wednesday and veekends (September through June).

Covington Landing At Covington Landing ıst across the Roebling Suspension Bridge, alf a dozen lively places attract young rowds – good on a hot night when there's a reeze off the river. Covington's Mainstrasse ve music venues are highlighted in Places o Eat.

Spectator Sports

The Cincinnati Reds (☎ 513-421-5337) are direct descendants of the Cincinnati Red Stockings, the country's first professional baseball team, still revered for decades of championship-caliber baseball. They play at aging Cinergy Field (formerly called Riverfront Stadium). The Cincinnati Bengals are the city's pro football team (☎ 513-621-3550); they were not so fortunate win-wise in the 1990s. Paul Brown Stadium, west of Cinergy Field, is the new home to the Bengals.

Shopping

Downtown Cincinnati has a good number of quality art galleries. Fourth St no longer dominates the scene as it once did, though it is still central. Many galleries are springing up along Main St in the Over-the-Rhine neighborhood, north of Central Parkway.

Getting There & Away

Air Tourists are always shocked when they arrive at the airport and are greeted by 'Welcome to Kentucky.' The Cincinnati-Northern Kentucky International Airport (☎ 614-239-4083) lies 12 miles southwest of downtown on the Kentucky side of the Ohio River. It's a huge, important air crossroads; Delta (see Toll-Free & Web Site Directory at the back of the book for contact information) has made the airport its hub. It has also been ranked number one for ontime arrivals for many years. Cheaper tickets into Ohio, however, can usually be found via Columbus, two hours away (the Columbus airport actually advertises its flights in Cincinnati newspapers).

Bus The Greyhound bus station (☎ 513-352-6012), 1005 Gilbert Ave, is within a mile of downtown. There are regular buses to Louisville, Kentucky ($20, 2 hours), Frankfort, Kentucky ($28, 8 hours), Indianapolis ($17, 2½ hours), and Charleston, West Virginia ($58, 7 hours). Within the state, buses run to Dayton ($12, 1½ hours), Columbus ($15, 3 hours) and Cleveland ($35, 5 hours).

Train The beautiful Amtrak station (☎ 513-651-3337), at the Cincinnati Museum Center,

1301 Western Ave, has three trains a week departing at 1:55 am to Indianapolis ($34, 3½ hours) and Chicago ($67, 8 hours), and at 5:55 am to Washington, DC ($104, 14 hours), via Kentucky and West Virginia. Tickets purchased in advance are cheaper – sometimes significantly. Unfortunately, no trains connect Cincinnati with Cleveland.

Boat The anachronistic-looking *American Queen* and *Delta Queen* replica paddleboats steam along the Mississippi and Ohio Rivers. Out of Cincinnati three- to seven-day tours are offered to St Louis (Missouri), Pittsburgh (Pennsylvania), Memphis and Nashville (Tennessee). Trips to and from Pittsburgh stop in Maysville (Kentucky), Marietta (Ohio), and Wellsburg (West Virginia). En route to St Louis, a stop is made in Madison (Indiana). Various package tours are offered, but base fares are $660 for the lowest-class, three-day tour and go up to a cool $9170 for a two-week sybaritic cruise. Fares include room, meals and entertainment.

The Ohio River is a mighty river, so it's appropriate that a ferry still operates. West of Cincinnati approximately 9 miles along US 50 you can hop the Anderson Ferry ($2.75 per car, 50¢ per bicycle) to Constance, Kentucky. It's not convenient, but it would let you avoid I-75, and it would be a cool way to get to the airport, which is 3 miles away from Constance.

Getting Around

To/From the Airport TANK (Transit Authority of Northern Kentucky; ☎ 606-331-8265) has airport service on its 2X route (75¢) from downtown Cincinnati stops from 5:15 am to 11:19 pm. Jet'port Express (☎ 513-767-3702) has a shuttle that departs the airport for primary downtown hotels every 30 minutes from 6 am to 11 pm. Rates are $12 one-way, $16 roundtrip.

Taxis charge a flat fee of $22 between downtown Cincinnati and the airport; they'll take one to four passengers (or grudgingly take five). Taxis also have flat fees to many other locations outside the city center.

Bus Queen City Metro (☎ 513-621-4455 runs local commuter buses daily, wit reduced routes on Sunday. Rates rang from 65¢ to 95¢, depending on time of da and which county you're in. The popula Downtowner (25¢), Route 79, runs every 1 minutes from 10:30 am to 2:30 pm weekday and loops around the downtown via Mai St, Central Parkway and Plum St. There ar plenty of stops.

TANK (☎ 606-331-8265) has route throughout Northern Kentucky from th downtown. Fares are 75¢. Transfers fron Metro to TANK cost 40¢.

Taxi Cabs are around $2 for flagfall an then $1.25 to $1.50 per mile; there's a $ minimum. You can find them at majo hotels or call Yellow Cab (☎ 513-241-2100)

Parking You've got to love a city that give you free parking at its meters, albeit only fo the first 10 minutes, if you just have to run i and take care of an errand (just twist th knob). Drive around the downtown parking lots and garages vary wildly in pric from $4 to $12 all-day. (Those on the nort side of Fountain Square tend to b cheaper.) Streetside parking enforcemen officials seem to be omniscient.

AROUND CINCINNATI

King's Island

A number of family amusement centers ar found in the area but King's Island (☎ 513 573-5800), 25 miles north at I-71 exit 24, i the area's top attraction. It has the famou 'Beast' roller coaster (the world's longes wooden roller coaster), several other adren aline generators, its own water park and little Eiffel Tower. The newest ride, the Face Off roller coaster, is the park's 12th, whic ties a world record for most coasters; thi lovely little type-T overloader generate five g's of force as it flips you six times. Th astonishingly large complex – no, city state – is not unlike an airport in scope, a you'll discover if you drive there.

The park opens at 9 am, but the staff wi restrain those boisterous young ones fron he rides until 10 am; if staff can round veryone up, the park closes around 10 pm. 'he season generally runs mid-April hrough late October. Admission is $35/20 dults/children. On-site is also a venue for nusical performers that draws some big ames. Show tickets may cost extra.

.ebanon

pop 11,000

Northeast of Cincinnati 30 miles via I-71 is his attractive small town seemingly taken rom a Norman Rockwell painting. Some of)hio's finest extant dwellings are found in .ebanon's neighborhoods.

hings to See The Lebanon area in the 9th century had one of the largest concenrations of Shakers in the US; the Shakers vere a sect that seceded from the Quakers, o-called because of their trembling when in he throes of religious ecstasy. A good haker exhibit is found at the **Warren County Historical Society Museum** (☎ 513-32-1817) a few doors down from the Golden Lamb Inn (see Places to Stay & Eat elow). A restored village green is excellent, vith storefronts recreated in great detail. It's pen 9 am to 4 pm Tuesday through Saturay, noon to 4 pm Sunday; $3.

Also in Lebanon is the **Glendower State Memorial** (☎ 513-932-1817), three blocks outh of the junction with Hwy 123 on US 2. This restored 1836 Greek Revival is furished in its original state. Hours are noon to pm Wednesday to Sunday, first Wednesday n June through Labor Day. Admission is $3.

The **Turtle Creek Valley Railroad** (☎ 513-933-8016) departs from its depot down the hill from the Golden Lamb Inn for hour-long train tours. Trains run April to November, but most go May through October, when two tours per day leave Wednesday and Friday to Sunday. The fare is $9/5 adults/children.

An eerie peace prevails at **Fort Ancient** (☎ 513-932-4421), 7 miles to the southeast via Hwy 350. Some of the Midwest's best preserved Hopewell earthworks are located within the park's 775 acres. Easy nature trails trace the mound works and link up to the statewide Buckeye Trail and transcontinental North Country Trail. The interpretive center has well-designed interactive exhibits. Open 10 am to 8 pm daily Memorial Day weekend through Labor Day. Admission is $5/1 adults/children.

Places to Stay & Eat It's a fabulous inn and restaurant – Ohio's oldest, you'll hear incessantly, dating from 1803 – but the ***Golden Lamb Inn*** (☎ 513-932-5065) along S Broadway, the main drag, is a tourist attraction in itself. Apparently, all major US historical figures and their mothers have lodged here. An extensive collection of Shaker furniture and related items are on display. If you wish to stay, rates are $70/80 single/double weekdays; they rise on weekends. For dining, reservations are always a good idea.

Waynesville

• pop 1800

This diminutive village 9 miles northeast of Lebanon was founded in 1796 and soon

The Hopewell & Their Enduring Mysteries

The Hopewell Indian culture that flourished in the Ohio Valley region was named after the farmer's field where its remnants were first unearthed. Despite being relatively unknown today, they had developed a sophisticated village-based society in which successful agriculture and management allowed for artistic and complex spiritual pursuits. Most intriguing are the Hopewell's internment rites and elaborate burial mounds, many of which remain. Finely worked artifacts indicate that they had far-flung trading relationships and influence. What spelled the decline of the Hopewell and the emergence of the Mississippian culture is not known.

became home to large numbers of Quakers; at one point it had the only Quaker boarding school in the US. But what brings everyone to Waynesville today – by the busload – is antiquing. Nearly 100 antique shops and art galleries are found, amazingly enough, in a village all of five blocks long. Show up the second weekend in October for the **Ohio Sauerkraut Festival**, feting that sour Teutonic delicacy; a huge arts and crafts fair runs concurrently.

Three miles southeast of town on Hwy 73 is Caesar Creek Lake. In Harveysburg on the east side of the lake, the **Ohio Renaissance Festival** has performers and guides in 16th-century garb demonstrating the folkways of old England. Some 150 artisans are on site. The festival runs eight weekends late August through October. Admission is $14/7 adults/children.

The entire circumference of Caesar Creek Lake is subsumed by **Caesars Cree Lake State Park** (☎ 513-897-3055). Wate recreation is the key here, thanks to a Army Corps of Engineers' impoundmen on the west end of the lake. At the dam is visitors' center detailing the Corps' role i water management. Southeast of the dam i a recreated pioneer village with two doze 19th-century structures relocated here; fre

Southeast of Waynesville just across th Little Miami River is the village of Corwir where there's a major trailhead for the **Littl Miami Trail**. This 65-mile multiuse trail fror Milford to Springfield runs alongside th Little Miami River through picturesqu scenery. You can rent bikes in Corwin c Oregonia, 5 miles south. The placid Littl Miami River is popular for canoeing The **RiversEdge Outfitters** (☎ 937-862-4540

Ticket to Ride

As every book on the subject says, the Underground Railroad was neither underground, nor was it a railroad. But it was secretive, a subculture. The Underground Railroad was a loosely organized network of routes, safe houses ('stations') and hosts ('conductors') willing to risk imprisonment, all in the hopes of defeating the greatest evil – slavery.

The Underground Railroad is one of the most misunderstood aspects of the antebellum antislavery movement. Having reached the level of folklore in US culture, its history is now equal parts mythology and fact. Intrigued travelers will come to a reputed abolitionist town (sometimes it seems *every* town in the northeastern and mid-central US claims to have been a hotbed of abolition) and ask to see the 'rails.' Any new homeowner who discovers a dormant root cellar assumes it was a holding cell for escaped slaves. To be fair, certain local networks were so well organized as to not have to keep records and the world will never know how they helped the cause.

Prior to the (technical) 'emancipation' of African Americans subsequent to the Civil War, it's hard to be sure of just how many slaves attempted escape. Conservative figures put the number at roughly 125,000; top-end claims say more than a million. Most attempted to flee north; the cliche about following the north star is true. However, conduits did also flow south into Mexico and the Caribbean. The most fascinating example of a southern destination is the swamps of southern Florida, where escaped slaves were embraced by the Seminole Indians, who were also fighting foreign incursion. If you think about it, any slave who escaped his or her owner since the late 17th century was a 'passenger' on the famed railroad; it wouldn't be until the great US expansion westward that someone glommed onto the railroad metaphor.

Nor was the northern US any sort of nirvana (in the north the abolitionist movement was never more than a very vocal minority, for example). Despite Ohio's opposition to slavery, it was bound by the Fugitive Slave Act of 1850 – the passage of which is arguably the darkest moment in US history – to return all slaves to their owners and hand over for federal prosecution every person

OHIO

at 3928 Hwy 48 offers trips and rentals ($17 per canoe).

Places to Stay & Eat A family ***campground*** in Caesars Creek Lake State Park has 287 shaded or open sites with full electric hook-ups ($15). The ***Creekwood Motel*** (*☎ 513-897-1000, 401 Main St*) is central and features Amish furniture. Rates are $55/60 single/double.

Antiquing is an aerobic sport, and there's plenty of stick-to-your-ribs home-style food in the village to refuel. The local favorite is ***Der Dutchman Restaurant***, a few blocks downhill from the main drag on US 42. Copious portions of Amish country cooking is the norm here ($7 and up main portions), served up family dinner style. If you use the Little Miami Trail, in Oregonia is the lovely ***Little River Café***, serving casually creative food in a converted farmhouse (entrées from $6).

Springboro

• pop 6600

Eight miles west of Waynesville, Springboro is a blip on the map and often gets overlooked by travelers barreling past on I-75. But if you're into historical structures, it's worth a quick stop. This tiny village had nearly 30 Underground Railroad 'depots' within its limits. Local shops or the Chamber of Commerce along Hwy 741, the town's sole street, have copies of a good walking tour brochure outlining all the local historical structures.

Springboro is also home to **LaComedia** (☎ 800-677-9505), 765 W Central Ave, a first-rate dinner theater. It's famous for its brunches (usually Wednesday and Thursday)

Ticket to Ride

who had abetted a slave's escape. This would lead thousands of blacks to flee across the border at Detroit into Ontario, Canada, which, along with the rest of the former British empire, had abolished slavery. Coincidentally, 1850 was also the year in which Harriet Tubman, the famed former slave, worked to free her first slave, the first of hundreds.

Although the Fugitive Slave Act exemplified the influence that southern states held prior to the Civil War, it harmed the slave owners more than it helped. Prior to its passage, abolitionism was a passionate, if not well-organized, movement (among whites at least). After its passage, any fence-sitters had their minds made up for them. (Heretofore most had bristled at but tolerated the Southern states' right to count every five African Americans as three persons in census counts.) Celebrity antislavery activists boasted about abetting slaves, but lesser-known abolitionists rotted in jail for bearing witness to evil.

Ohio, with its 440-mile river border with slaveholding states Kentucky and West Virginia, was on the northern end of the first of two routes traveled by runaway slaves. During the 1830s many former slaves became famous for conducting nocturnal forays into Kentucky to find and bring escaped slaves safely across the river. One could spend a lifetime in Ohio experiencing the history of the Underground Railroad. Highlights include the little town of Springboro, north of Cincinnati, where virtually every local dwelling was used to aid slaves. In the north, the community of Oberlin was perhaps America's most ardent abolitionist community and also the site of the first integrated US college. Northeast of Dayton is the National African American Museum; and, eventually, Cincinnati will be the home of the National Underground Railroad Freedom Center. In little Ripley, along the Ohio River southeast of Cincinnati, the wealthy owner of the Rankin House supposedly helped over 2000 slaves escape; this was also where freed slave John Parker surreptitiously crossed the Ohio River here nights, with armed slave hunters patrolling both shorelines, and helped hundreds reach the promised land.

and buffet, featuring a sweet potato soufflé par excellence.

DAYTON

• pop 173,000

Dayton is a nondescript city, of interest primarily to aviation enthusiasts, who know it as the home of the Wright brothers. This is the place where they developed the world's first engine-powered plane. The downtown is not exactly thriving, but the city has a certain charm to it. A couple of downtown districts are highly gentrified with hip bistros, shops and clubs. There are plenty of attractions, including a new baseball stadium that is already bringing life to the city center, and it's got (arguably) the best restaurants per capita in Ohio. You'll also find a noticeably high quotient of genuine friendliness.

History

Dayton sits at a fork of the Miami Valley, a crucial conduit for Native Americans and, later, Civil War armies traveling from Lake Erie to what is now Kentucky. Native Americans were astonished that early settlers wanted to settle the flood-prone plain, but dams and canals eventually tamed the waters enough to allow for construction of a canal to Cincinnati, and following that, the Miami and Erie Canal to Lake Erie. The National Road (US 40) brought major industries and commerce (the road now passes through Vandalia, north of Dayton). Dayton's early industries got off to a fast start in 1879 when local resident James Ritty invented the 'mechanical money drawer' – the precursor to the cash register. The company would eventually become the NCR Corporation. This inventiveness lured other designers and Dayton's industries have been credited with inventions as humble as the electric automobile starter and as important as the airplane.

Orientation

Dayton's downtown is bordered by the Great Miami River to the west and north. Its streets are in a grid backing off the river. Numbered streets run roughly northeast to southwest but are referred to as east and west. Jefferson, Main and Ludlow Sts ar the main cross streets to these. Drivin around downtown is very straightforward with few one-way street traps.

Overzealous marketers have divide Dayton into designated neighborhoods. Th one of interest for travelers is Oregon Historic District, a gentrified little enclave eas of Jefferson St along Fifth St.

Information

The Visitors' Bureau (☎ 937-226-8211 www.daytoncvb.com) is on the ground floo of the Convention Center, downtown at E Fifth and S Main Sts. It has loads of infor mation – best of all is a map showing the lo cation of every restaurant in the county.

No Internet access facilities can be foun downtown. The closest is a Kinko's at 113 Brown St. Internet access is $12 per hour o 20¢ per minute. It's south of the Orego Historic District along Brown St.

Impact Weekly is a free weekly with run downs on local activities and nightlife.

If you're in need of a good read, stop in a Book Friends (☎ 937-461-4466) in th downtown area at 19 E Second St. Civil Wa buffs should visit the Morningside Book shop at 260 Oak St.

A referral service (☎ 937-208-3463) is op erated by several Dayton hospitals to hel find the nearest local treatment center.

Dayton Art Institute

Considered one of the nation's finest mid-siz arts institutes, the Dayton Art Institut (☎ 937-223-5277), 456 Belmonte Park N, i Dayton's top downtown attraction. The hold ings contain 12,000 objects from every con ceivable style; permanent exhibits includ African, American, Asian, modern American European, Oceanic and pre-Columbian ar You're guaranteed a major national travelin exhibit whenever you come, and the museum also has a wonderful Experiencecenter, hands-on art education annex. Regular jaz concerts ($6) are held at the museum, as we as classical and gospel music choir perfor mances. It's open 10 am to 5 pm daily (unt 9 pm Thursday) every day of the year, an amazingly, it's free. A nice café is also on sit

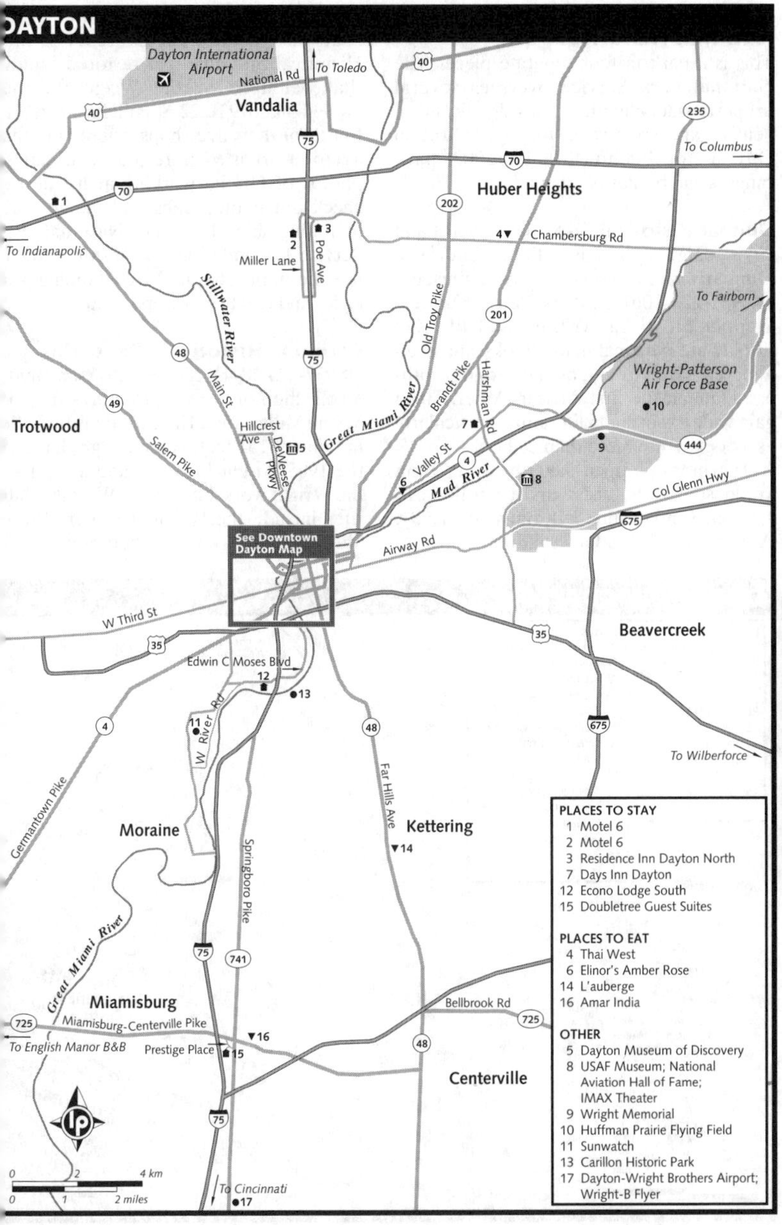
DAYTON
Dayton International Airport
National Rd
To Toledo
Vandalia
To Columbus
Huber Heights
To Indianapolis
Miller Lane
Poe Ave
Chambersburg Rd
Stillwater River
Old Troy Pike
To Fairborn
Brandt Pike
Harshman Rd
Wright-Patterson Air Force Base
Main St
Trotwood
Hillcrest Ave
DeWeese Pkwy
Great Miami River
Salem Pike
Valley St
Mad River
Col Glenn Hwy
See Downtown Dayton Map
Airway Rd
W Third St
Beavercreek
Edwin C Moses Blvd
W River Rd
Far Hills Ave
To Wilberforce
Germantown Pike
Moraine
Kettering
Springboro Pike
Great Miami River
Miamisburg
Bellbrook Rd
Miamisburg-Centerville Pike
To English Manor B&B
Prestige Place
Centerville
To Cincinnati
4 km
2 miles
PLACES TO STAY
1 Motel 6
2 Motel 6
3 Residence Inn Dayton North
7 Days Inn Dayton
12 Econo Lodge South
15 Doubletree Guest Suites
PLACES TO EAT
4 Thai West
6 Elinor's Amber Rose
14 L'auberge
16 Amar India
OTHER
5 Dayton Museum of Discovery
8 USAF Museum; National Aviation Hall of Fame; IMAX Theater
9 Wright Memorial
10 Huffman Prairie Flying Field
11 Sunwatch
13 Carillon Historic Park
17 Dayton-Wright Brothers Airport; Wright-B Flyer

Dayton Aviation Heritage National Historical Park

This is a park in four separate pieces. The National Park Service oversees several properties detailing Dayton's significant inventive and creative history (see Around Dayton for the fourth). By 2003, park rangers will be stationed at all.

Dunbar Historical Site Poet, novelist and Civil Rights activist Paul Laurence Dunbar's family home is now a museum (☎ 937-224-7061), 219 N Paul Laurence Dunbar St, to his writings and life. On display are personal items, books, and even a bicycle given to him by the Wright brothers. Dunbar, the first African American to gain wide exposure in literature, particularly as a poet, wrote more than 20 books.

The house is open 9:30 am to 4:30 pm Wednesday to Saturday and from noon to 4:30 pm Sunday, June 1 through August 31. Admission is $3/1 adults/children.

Wright Cycle Company A quarter-mi southeast of the Paul Laurence Dunb Historical Site, this is a restored buildi that belonged to the Wright brothe (☎ 937-443-0793), 22 S William St. It's t fourth of their five shops. There is nothi aviation-oriented here, but you can s photos of Orville working at his desk check out photographs and memorabili including bicycles. The National Pa Service has ambitious expansion plans f this site, hoping to purchase adjoining pro erties and create a visitors' center.

Carillon Historical Park This pa (☎ 937-293-2841), 2001 S Patterson Blvd, a collection of historic structures from t Miami Valley area. The carillon is the talle in Ohio at 151 feet. The highlight has to the 1905 Wright Flyer III and a replica the Wright workshop. Other Wright-relat sites include the Wright Brothers Bicyc Shop and the Wright Brothers Hangar, wi

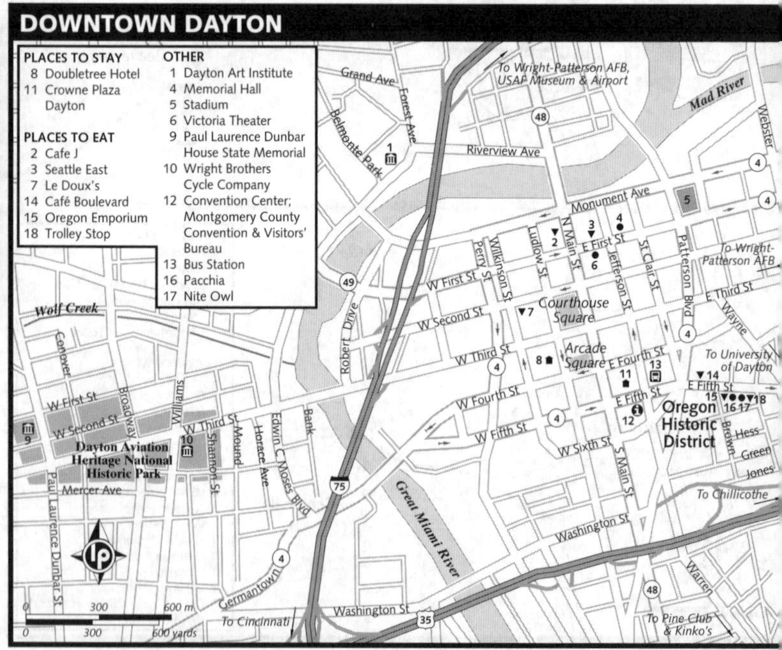

ɪe original flying 'B' plane, or at least most f it. Sixty percent of the plane is original – nly the original canvas that covered the ings couldn't be retained. The park is pen 9:30 am to 5 pm Tuesday to Saturday, oon to 5 pm Sunday May 1 through ctober 31; $2/1 adults/children. Incidenlly, the only flying 'B' plane (a copy) in xistence is at the Dayton–Wright Brothers irport (☎ 937-885-2327), south of own, on Springboro Pike. Rides in the eplica can be arranged if you make an ppointment.

ʌuseum of Discovery

ʌt 2600 DeWeese Parkway north of downown, this is a fun stop-off for kids and their olks. Interactive exhibits are aplenty, but ids especially like the Eco-Trek, allowing aipses through different ecosystems, from esert to ice age tundra. Wild Ohio is a ini-zoo of native Ohio fauna. There's also planetarium. Hours are 9 am to 5 pm Monday to Saturday, noon to 5 pm Sunday. ʌdmission is $5/2 adults/children.

pecial Events

n late July, the Dayton International ʌirport hosts the United States Air and rade Show (☎ 937-767-1274), drawing nore than 100,000 people to watch air perormances by the likes of the US Navy's lue Angels. There are flight-related exibits on the ground.

laces to Stay

udget Eighteen miles east of Dayton ear Yellow Springs, ***John Bryan State ark*** *(☎ 937-767-1274, 3790 Hwy 370)* has tes for $14.

Motel 6 has two locations north of town. he first one *(☎ 937-898-3606, 7130 Miller ane)* is just off I-75 at exit 60; rates are 29/33. The second one *(☎ 937-832-3770, 212 S Main St)* is actually in Englewood and convenient to the airport. Singles/doubles ost $36/41. The ***Days Inn Dayton*** *(☎ 937-36-8083, 1891 Harshman Rd)* is close to the JSAF Museum. Singles/doubles cost $35/42.

South of Carillon Historical Park, the ***cono Lodge-South*** *(☎ 937-223-0166, 2140 Edwin C Moses Blvd)* has singles/doubles from $40 with a free continental breakfast.

Mid-Range & Top End Most of Dayton's mid-range hotels lie north or south of town along I-75. To the south, at exit 44 off I-75 in Miamisburg is ***Doubletree Guest Suites*** *(☎ 937-436-2400, fax 937-436-2886, 300 Prestige Place)*. This all-suite hotel has singles/doubles from $104 (less on weekends) and all suites have a coffeemaker, two TVs and two telephones. Miamisburg also has the ***English Manor B&B*** *(☎ 937-866-2288, 505 E Linden Ave)*, a 1924 brick manor. Rates are $75 single/double.

Eight miles or so along I-75 to the north, near the Little York Rd exit, is a string of motels, including the ***Residence Inn Dayton North*** *(☎ 937-898-7764, 7070 Poe Ave)*, which has excellent suites and lofts from $100.

The downtown area has mostly top-end places. The ***Crowne Plaza Dayton*** *(☎/fax 937-890-9995, 33 E Fifth St)* is opposite the convention center and has rooms and some suites from $120/135 single/double.

To the north near Arcade Square, the ***Doubletree Hotel*** *(☎ 937-461-4700, fax 937-224-9160, 11 S Ludlow St)* in a historic building, is the newest hotel in Dayton (opened in 1999). A host of amenities are offered. Rates are $110 single/double.

Places to Eat

Downtown For breakfast ***Café J*** on N Main St between Monument Ave and First St is a funky little place. It smacks of a retro hotel lobby and serves straight-up diner fare for reasonable prices (specials from $4). It hosts popular Mimosa Saturdays. Above average sandwiches and soups are found just east of here at ***Seattle East*** *(33 E First St)*, where you can get a sandwich from $4.

Le Doux's at the corner of Second and Wilkinson Sts has Cajun food and live zydeco or blues Friday and Saturday night (entrées from $6).

Oregon District The central Oregon District, based along E Fifth St east of Jefferson St, has a small, concentrated and eclectic mix of stores, bars and restaurants. You'll find excellent coffee at ***Oregon Emporium*** *(410 E Fifth St)*; it also serves microbrewed beers and light meals (options from $4). Vegetarian options are found at the fun tavern ***Trolley Stop*** *(530 E Fifth St)*, along with an eclectic menu (main dishes from $5) and live music. Across the street the trendy ***Café Boulevard*** *(☎ 937-824-2722, 329 E Fifth St)* is best described as a French bistro with a fusion complex (entrées from $9); there are also some vegetarian options.

South Landmark of them all in Dayton is the venerable ***Pine Club*** *(1926 Brown St)*, near the University of Dayton campus. The interior is dark, and it looks like the carpet is the 1947 original. The place stubbornly eschews accepting reservations and credit cards. But the steaks and conviviality are enough to have kept George Bush (when he was president) waiting in line like everybody else. Entrées start at $10.

South of town in Kettering is what may just be Ohio's best restaurant. ***L'Auberge*** *(☎ 937-299-5536, 4120 Far Hills Ave)* serves an eclectic continental cuisine with a menu that changes throughout the year. It offers a nearly perfect synthesis of service, atmosphere and food, according to even the snootiest foodies. It has won every culinary award there is. Twice. There is also a more casual café with outdoor dining. Entrées are from $20.

If you go south all the way to Miamisburg you can find good Indian food at ***Amar India*** *(☎ 937-439-9005, 2759 Miamisburg–Centerville Rd)* if you can withstand the strip-mall hell it's located in (main dishes from $8).

North If you're lodged in the northern stretches along I-75, you're close enough to warrant a visit to ***Thai West*** *(☎ 937-237-7767, 6118 Chambersburg Rd)* in Huber Heights, southwest of the junction of I-70 and Hwy 201. The Thai food's great (main dishes from $9), as is the seafood, and it offers a few vegetarian dishes.

At 1400 Valley St in the historic Old North Dayton district, ***Elinor's Amber Rose*** *(☎ 937-228-2511)* serves up dishes of home style German and Eastern Europea cuisine (entrées from $11).

Entertainment

Live music is found at virtually ever nightspot along E Fifth St. Jazz music i offered along with trendy food at ***Pacchi*** *(410 E Fifth St)*; you'll hear jazz to blues t lots of reggae at ***Nite Owl*** *(430 E Fifth St)*.

The elegant ***Victoria Theater*** *(☎ 937-22 3630)* is a stunning 1866 Victorian theate that holds regular performances by th Dayton Symphony Orchestra, Dayto Ballet and Dayton Opera, along wit touring national Broadway shows and loc theater troupes. ***Memorial Hall*** *(☎ 937-22 9000)* is another venue for local arts. Bot are in the northern part of downtown, alon E First St.

Spectator Sports

The Dayton Bombers (☎ 937-775-4747) ar a member of the East Coast Hockey Leagu and play games at the Ervin J Nutter Cente in Fairborn. The Dayton Dragons (937-22 2287), a minor league baseball team, play i a downtown stadium.

Getting There & Away

The Dayton International Airport (☎ 93 454-8200) is 10 miles from downtown an has 80 flights daily to 15 hubs. Every majc airline flies through.

The Greyhound bus station (☎ 937-22 1608) is central at the corner of E Fifth an Jefferson Sts. Regular service is offered t Columbus ($11, 1½ hours), Cincinnati ($1 2 hours), Indianapolis ($28, 2 to 5 hour and Toledo ($24, 3 hours), in addition t other destinations.

Getting Around

Dayton has one of the country's fine public bus systems. One of the innovators electric tram transport in the early 20t century, Dayton brought the technolog back in the 1990s. By the time you read thi the entire fleet will be electric-powere Dayton's Regional Transit Authorit

☎ 937-226-2244) oversees routes througha:t the county. A number of lines reach farang places such as the United States Air ɔrce (USAF) Museum at the Air Force ase. Fares are $1/50¢ adults/children.

The *Wright Flyers* are a system of maɔgany and brass simulated streetcars (25¢) at operate 10 am to 6:30 pm (until midght Friday and Saturday night), Monday Saturday, May through September. They ak a number of local attractions.

ROUND DAYTON

SAF Museum & National viation Hall of Fame

ıe huge USAF Museum (☎ 937-255-3286), the Air Force base, 6 miles northeast of wn, offers about 200 historic aircraft. Fasciating exhibits on many aspects of aviation e its premier attraction. It's got everything om a Wright exhibit, a Sopwith Camel VWI fighter plane) and a Stealth Bomber to tronaut ice cream, military propaganda and e world's largest aerial camera. An Aviation all of Fame lets you walk through exhibits out the biggest names in aviation history. xpect a visit to take three or more hours ome food is available). And don't miss the nex, with its collection of presidential anes – there's a free shuttle bus over to the angar. An IMAX theater with a six-story reen shows brainthumping films. The west attraction is the MovieRide Theater, a ght simulator. Overall, many have said it's e most thrilling experience in Ohio.

The site is open 9 am to 5 pm daily and is e. The IMAX theater shows movies every our and costs $6/4 adults/children. ayton's RTA has public transport.

'right Brothers Memorial Upon rerning from Kitty Hawk, North Carolina, ter their successful flight, the Wright others built a storage hangar for their ane at Huffman Prairie Flying Field, now part of Wright–Patterson Air Force Base, t far from the USAF Museum. The ngar you'll see is a replica. At the field is a onument honoring the brothers. To gain mission, get a pass at the USAF Museum.

Sunwatch

South of town is Sunwatch (☎ 937-268-8199), 2301 W River Rd, a replica and interpretation center of a Fort Ancient Indian village, of interest to scientists for their advanced solar observations. The Fort Ancient Indians inhabited the Ohio Valley about 800 years ago. The village has been reconstructed and the dwellings can be toured. The site is open 9 am to 5 pm Tuesday to Saturday, noon to 5 pm Sunday, April through November. Admission is $4/3 adults/children.

National Afro-American Museum & Cultural Center

Twenty-one miles southeast of Dayton in Wilberforce, this museum and cultural center (☎ 937-376-4944) traces the black experience in American life with an extensive exhibit on the growth of the Civil Rights movement from World War II to the 1970s called 'From Victory to Freedom,' among other displays and artifacts. Hours are 9 am to 5 pm Tuesday to Saturday, noon to 5 pm Sunday; $4/2 adults/children. The town of Wilberforce was also the site of the country's first African American university, Wilberforce University, begun by the Methodist Church in 1856 to aid freed slaves.

Along the Ohio River

Southern Ohio is dominated by one jewel – the Ohio River. Stretching for over 400 miles, it is the demarcation line for Ohio's border with Kentucky and West Virginia. Early Native Americans referred to it as 'great water' and European settlers made use of it as a major water highway during westward expansion. Travelers are often surprised to find so little development along the riparian stretches, save for Marietta and perhaps a few other towns. It's a somnolent yet picturesque drive, with plenty of side trip options. Along the way you'll find loads of campgrounds and unpretentious bed and breakfasts.

POINT PLEASANT

President Ulysses S Grant was born in a small frame house in this village 15 miles southeast of Cincinnati along US 52. The home is done in period detail and open 9:30 am to 5 pm Wednesday to Saturday, noon to 5 pm Sunday; admission is $1. There's a nice park across the street.

GEORGETOWN

• pop 3500

Another 20 miles and already there's a side trip! At Higginsport, you have a couple options. You can take a ferry ($5) into Kentucky, or you can continue tracing the life of President Grant by driving another 11 miles or so north to Georgetown along Hwy 221, where there are two points of interest regarding Grant. At 219 E Grant Ave the **Grant Boyhood Home** (☎ 937-378-4222) was where the Grant family moved when the future president was a young boy. Some of the artifacts in the house are original. Hours are 9 am to 5 pm Monday to Saturday, Memorial Day weekend through Labor Day; free. A few blocks away is the **Grant Schoolhouse**, where young Ulysses learned his three Rs. Hours are noon to 5 pm Wednesday to Sunday, late May to early September.

RIPLEY

• pop 1750

Ripley was a major point on the Underground Railroad and after the Civil War a group of freed slaves founded Africa, a now-gone village across the river in Kentucky. The road climbs an incredibly steep bluff to the **Rankin House** (☎ 937-392-1627), a state memorial to Reverend John Rankin, a passionate abolitionist who helped transport some 2000 slaves northward, including, if local history is to be believed, the original Eliza, from the novel *Uncle Tom's Cabin*. Hours are noon to 5 pm Wednesday to Sunday, late May to early September, weekends only during the rest of September and October; $2/1 adults/children.

Ripley is also home to the **Ohio Tobacc Museum** at the Ripley Tobacco Warehous farther east. There's an annual Tobacco Fe tival in August.

PORTSMOUTH

• pop 23,000

Portsmouth, 95 miles east of Cincinnati, the first town of any size along the riv road. It is one of two along the river th lays claim to being the 'Mural City.' Murali Robert Dafford has lined the Portsmou floodwall with 36 of 55 eventual murals very valuable ones – detailing local histor Look for cowboy movie star Roy Roge and Jim Thorpe (member of both the pr baseball and football halls of fame), th greatest athlete the US has ever produce they're both local boys. South of Wheeler burg, 12 miles from Portsmouth, th **Greenup Dam** can be toured – it's great watch barges locking through – but it's a cessed from the Kentucky side.

One of Ohio's three sections of th **Wayne National Forest** lies to the east. It got a free campground and eight trails tota ing 132 miles. Nothing decent is chea motel-wise. The ***Super 8*** *(☎ 740-353-888 4266 US 23)* is 5 miles from downtown ar has singles/doubles from $49/54.

The Greyhound station (☎ 740-353-226 is at 3102 Sciota Trail; north to Chillicot takes an hour and costs $10.

GALLIPOLIS

• pop 4760

Gallipolis (guh-lahp-oh-LEES) is a litt gem of a town. French settlers founded th town in 1790 – hence the name – but th county's heritage is very much Welsh, to The local visitors' bureau, 45 State St, h brochures outlining a Welsh culture drivi tour of the area (Oak Hill, 30 miles we has a **Welsh museum**). In the attracti Gallipolis downtown, **Our House** is a r stored 1819 tavern which entertain French general Lafayette, a Revolutiona War hero. One block east the **French A Colony** is an arts center in a proud o mansion; it maintains several art exhibits. block north and another west is the **Ar**

eater, a lovingly restored opera house ilt in 1895.

About 30 miles away, traveling west of allipolis on US 35 and south on Hwy 279 ill bring you to ***Jackson Lake State Park*** *(☎ 614-682-6197)*, which has sites for $6. If u're really hard up you can camp at the allia County Junior Fairgrounds closer to wn.

Just north of downtown along Hwy 7 is e ***William Ann Motel*** *(☎ 740-446-3373, 8 2nd Ave)*, a nice place and close enough walk downtown. It's got singles/doubles r $40/45.

On the square downtown ***City Perk*** has od coffee and inexpensive smoothies, lads and sandwiches; you can eat for der $5.

There is no bus service to Gallipolis.

ARIETTA

pop 15,000

arietta was the first settlement in the orthwest Territory. Lots of Huck Finn references fly about this place, and for good ason. With a gentle somnolence, sternheeler paddleboats every which way and chitecture not unlike 19th-century Hannil, Missouri, it is Ohio's truest river town.

The helpful Washington County Conven-n and Visitors Bureau (☎ 740-373-5178, 0-288-2577, www.rivertowns.org) is down-wn at 316 3rd St.

Greyhound doesn't have a bus station. It s a flag stop at the corner of Putnam and d Sts, near the Convention and Visitors reau office. To Canton takes 2½ hours d costs $26. See the Toll-Free & Web Site rectory at the back of the book for Grey-und's contact information.

ings to See & Do

e **Ohio River Museum** (☎ 740-373-3750) at 601 Front St. You can't miss it for the acefully worn *WP Snyder Jr* docked arby, which retired in 1955 with the honor having been the last working sterneeler towboat on the Ohio River. Inside, Ohio River in all its historical imporce is examined with scale dioramas, a all theater and lots of models. Special emphasis is put on paddleboats. Hours are 9:30 am to 5 pm Monday to Saturday, noon to 5 pm Sunday, May through September; it's open reduced hours March through April and October through November; $5/1 adults/children.

The early history of Marietta and the Northwest Territory is explored at the **Campus Martius Museum** (☎ 740-373-3750), 601 2nd St. The sole surviving building from the original settlement is housed here, along with a huge Conestoga wagon. Hours and admission are the same as the Ohio River Museum.

Probably the most popular attraction in Marietta are the melodramas aboard the *Becky Thatcher* (☎ 740-373-6033), a 1926 sternwheeler showboat. Performances are given nightly in July and August, sporadically mid- to late June. Ticket prices vary but are usually around $12.

Across the Muskingum River is historic **Harmer Village**, an eye-catching little enclave of original architecture and quaint – but not too quaint – shops and restaurants. Also here are two little museums. The Harmar Station Model Railroad Museum ($5) has 20 trains running simultaneously. Butch's Cola Museum is a pack rat's delight of old Coca Cola memorabilia.

Under the Washington Street Bridge near the Ohio River Museum is the landing for the *Valley Gem* (☎ 740-373-7862), a sternwheeler with a slate of river tours, including dinner and autumn colors tours. Basic tours leave five times Tuesday to Sunday and cost $5/3 adults/children. You can take a **trolley tour** (☎ 740-373-7937) April through October on an incredibly complex schedule. Basically, Thursday to Sunday you can get a tour (but not always). Fares are $8/5 adults/children.

Places to Stay

The nearest camping would be at the ***municipal fairgrounds*** *(☎ 740-373-7937)*, at exit 1 off I-77. Free primitive camping (no water) is found 10 miles or so northeast in the Wayne National Forest at two ***campgrounds*** along Hwy 26.

Choices are limited for cheap motels. Head east along Pike St to the junction with I-77. The ***Knight's Inn*** *(☎ 740-373-7373, 506 Pike St)* offers singles/doubles for $45/50. A ***Super 8*** *(☎ 740-374-8888, 46 Acme St)* is across the street in Washington Square Center and has similar rates. Along Pike St are a number of mid-range options, including a ***Holiday Inn*** *(☎ 740-374-9660, 701 Pike St)*, which has singles/doubles starting at $65.

Downtown the ***Lafayette*** *(☎ 740-373-5522, 101 Front St)* is a historic grand dame. Its singles/doubles for $65 are a pretty good value considering the location. The hotel has lots of package deals. The dining room is popular and has a good lunch buffet and Sunday brunch.

Places to Eat

The ***Bridgewater 1*3*0*** *(130 Front St)* is a coffee bar with a bistro complex. It has great salads, wraps and sandwiches, many for under $5. There's also a more substantial entrée menu featuring chicken, pastas and seafood. Vegetarians aren't forgotten here.

Across the street the ***Marietta Brewing Company*** has pretty standard pub grub. The burgers, sandwiches, and salads are good (from $5) and it's a popular pizza place.

Tampico *(221 2nd St)* has an extensi menu of good Mexican food, including a fe vegetarian options (main dishes from $5).

STEUBENVILLE

From here most travelers turn westward head for Amish Country, or to the nort west for Canton. Steubenville is locat nearly 110 miles northeast of Marietta. Li Portsmouth, it's famous for an extensive s of downtown **murals** detailing local histo more are being added all the time. Also Steubenville is the **Welsh Jaguar Classic C Museum** (☎ 740-283-9723), which contai 20 classic cars, from rare Jaguars to 196 muscle cars. Hours are noon to 6 pm dai admission is $3.

The local ***Super 8*** *(☎ 740-282-4565, 15 University Blvd)* has basic rooms from $ single/double. The ***Jaggin' Around Resta rant & Pub*** at the corner of 5th and Was ington Sts is in a 1930s Art Deco buildi and has a menu of soups, salads, deli sar wiches and steaks (main dishes from $6).

The bus stop is at 219 N 3rd St, at t R&K Browse & Buy (☎ 740-283-378 Buses to Canton take six hours and c $28; to Wheeling, West Virginia, it takes minutes and costs $10.

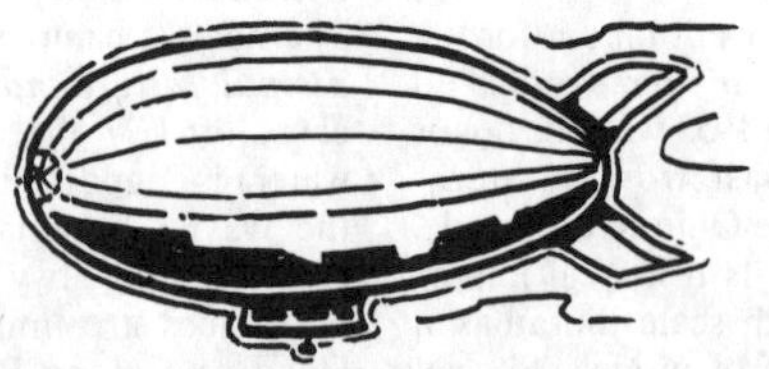

Michigan

Facts about Michigan

The Great Lakes are in the heart of the Midwest, and in the heart of the Great Lakes lies Michigan. Surrounded by four of the five lakes (Superior, Michigan, Huron and Erie), Michigan is a pair of peninsulas featuring 3200 miles of shoreline (secon only to Alaska), the most extensive fres water sand dunes in the country and 11,0 inland lakes. Stand anywhere in the sta and you are never more than 6 miles from Great Lake, inland lake or blue-ribbo trout stream.

Michigan's state park system of 96 park with more than 14,000 campsites, ranks fir in the country for total number of sites. Ad almost 5000 more sites in its national an state forests, and it's easy to understand wh camping holidays are a time-honored trad tion in Michigan. If you have transportatic and a tent, Michigan can be an extreme scenic and affordable place to visit fro May to October.

Michigan Facts

Nickname The Wolverine State

Population 9,773,000 (26th largest)

Area 58,216 sq miles (23rd largest)

Admitted to Union January 26, 1837 (26th state)

Road Information There's no central number for highway condition reports but the state's Department of Transportation Web site (www.mdot.state.mi.us) has information. Radar detectors are permitted, and helmets for motorcyclists are required.

Road Rules Seat belts are mandatory for all front-seat passengers and for all minors ages 16 and under. Children ages one to four years may use a seat belt in the backseat but must be in a safety seat in the front of the car, as must babies ages one and younger. Motorcyclists are required to wear helmets.

Taxes Statewide sales tax is 6%.

History

Easy travel on the Great Lakes has led to long and colorful history in Michigan. The is evidence of prehistoric copper mining the Upper Peninsula and on Isle Roya Remains of Hopewell ceremonial sites ha been found near Grand Rapids. When t first European explorers arrived in the mi 17th century, the region was already settl by five major Indian tribes: the Ojibw Ottawa, Miami, Potawatomi and Huron (Wyandot).

The state's first European settlemer Sault Sainte Marie, was founded by Fren Jesuit Pere Jacques Marquette in 16 making it the third-oldest city in the US Pere Marquette founded St Ignace in 16 and, in 1701, the French explorer Antoi de La Mothe, Sieur de Cadillac, establish Detroit in a strategic position betwe Lakes Erie and Huron.

In 1763 the French settlements we taken over by the British, who, during t Revolutionary War, used Michigan as a ba for instigating Indian raids against t upstart colonists. The British also built a f on Mackinac Island in 1780. Its location the straits between Lake Michigan, La Huron and the St Marys River, which flo om Lake Superior, made it one of the ost important ports in the North Ameri-ın fur trade. The small island was also the te of one of the most infamous moments Michigan's history. After the colonials ok over Fort Mackinac diplomatically, the ritish recaptured it during the War of 1812 y secretly landing in the middle of the ight and dragging a cannon up a bluff verlooking the stockade. When the US arrison awoke the next morning and saw hat was aimed at them, they gave up ithout firing a single shot.

After the Erie Canal was completed in 325, Michigan experienced its first major ave of settlers. Thanks to the newly cut etroit–Chicago Rd and the federal gov-nment's sale of Michigan land for $1.25 an cre, the state endured an era of 'Michigan ever' when its population jumped from 00 in the early 19th century to more than 0,000 by 1840. During this period, many f the state's major cities – Kalamazoo, attle Creek, Jackson, Grand Rapids and ansing – were founded.

By 1835 Michigan had become populated ough to qualify for statehood, but Con-ess delayed due to a boundary contro-ersy with Ohio over a sliver of land that cluded Toledo. Both states eventually lled out their militias in the so-called oledo War, but, fortunately, there was no oodshed. When Michigan gave up claims the city, it was awarded both the lion's are of the Upper Peninsula and state-ood, becoming the 26th state, in 1837.

When the automobile industry took off the early 20th century, Michigan thrived the benefits of its success. The industry ominated the state until the mid-1970s, hen automation and competition from pan and Europe caused its rapid decline. ichigan has since worked hard to diversify economy. Agriculture is very important the state; Michigan is a leading producer navy beans, apples and cherries. Forestry oducts, tourism and natural gas produc-on also bring in significant revenue.

But the manufacture of passenger cars d transportation equipment still accounts r 27% of the annual gross state product, and the 'Big Three' – General Motors (GM), Ford and Daimler–Chrysler – maintain world headquarters in or near Detroit (Daimler–Chrysler's is now technically a US headquarters, since Chrysler merged with the German company Daimler–Benz in the 1990s).

Geography

Passing through the middle of Michigan is the 45th Parallel, the halfway point between the Equator and the North Pole. The Lower Peninsula is shaped like a mitten and is 285 miles from north to south and 195 miles from east to west. This half of the state features a topography of low rolling hills in the south, a 1200- to 1500-foot plateau in the north and lovely sand dunes along the Lake Michigan shore. Detroit is a bit of a geographical oddity; it actually lies north of Ontario, and it is the only city in the contiguous US that looks south to Canada.

The rugged and lightly populated Upper Peninsula (UP) is more rectangular in shape and stretches 325 miles from east to west. The two peninsulas are connected by the Mackinac Bridge, over the Straits of Mackinac (pronounced 'Mackinaw').

The southern half of the Lower Peninsula is predominantly agricultural land surrounding the urban sprawl of the state's largest cities. The rest of Michigan is well forested: The northern half of the Lower Peninsula features hardwoods with a mix of pine; red and white pine are dominant in the UP. On the whole, about three-quarters of the state's trees are hardwoods, resulting in spectacular October colors that rival those in the country's New England region.

National Parks & Protected Areas

Michigan has three national park units – Isle Royale, Sleeping Bear Dunes and Pictured Rocks – to go along with its excellent state park system. Isle Royale is one of the most isolated and least visited national parks – a wonderful gem for backcountry hiking. Gazing at a map of Michigan, it's remarkable how much of the state is verdant – green denoting county, state or (mostly) federal forest. In fact, the lion's share of

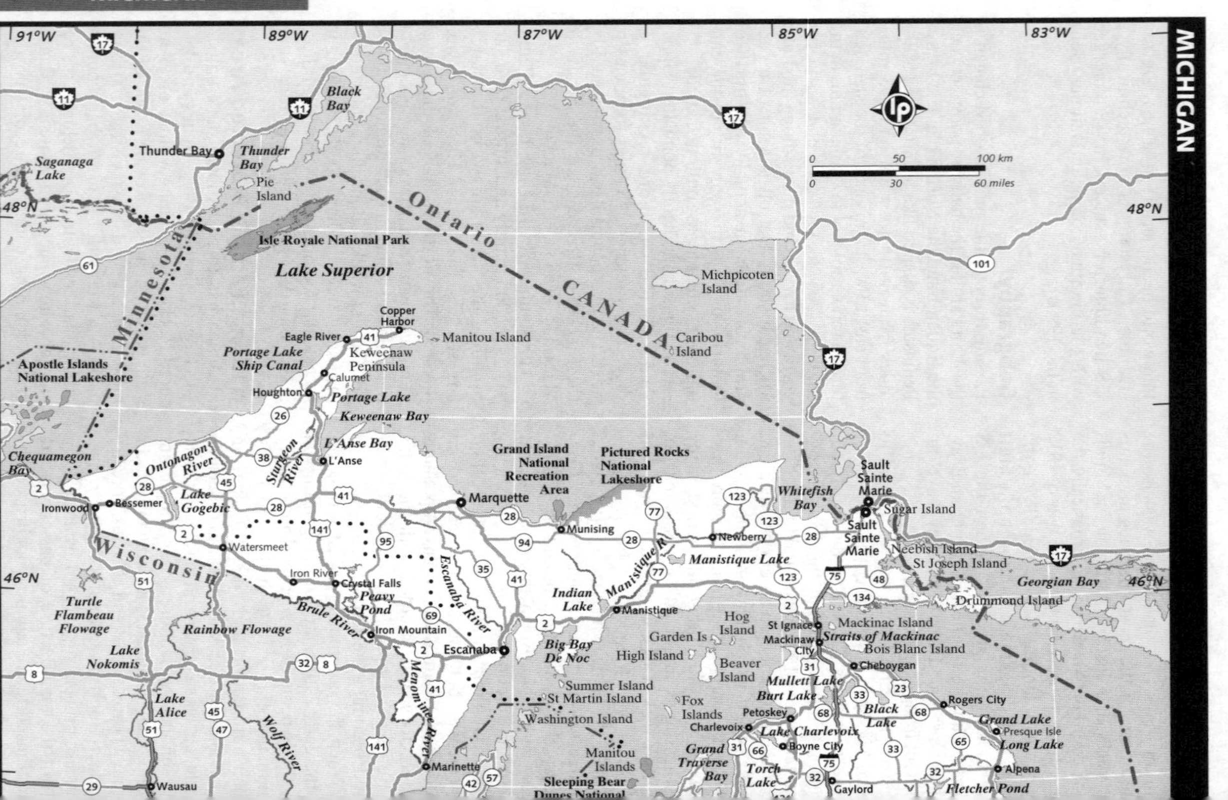
MICHIGAN
100 km
60 miles
91°W
89°W
87°W
85°W
83°W
48°N
46°N
Ontario
CANADA
Minnesota
Wisconsin
Lake Superior
Isle Royale National Park
Thunder Bay
Black Bay
Pie Island
Saganaga Lake
Manitou Island
Michpicoten Island
Caribou Island
Copper Harbor
Keweenaw Peninsula
Eagle River
Calumet
Portage Lake
Keweenaw Bay
Portage Lake Ship Canal
Houghton
L'Anse Bay
L'Anse
Sturgeon River
Apostle Islands National Lakeshore
Chequamegon Bay
Ironwood
Bessemer
Ontonagon River
Lake Gogebic
Watersmeet
Iron River
Crystal Falls
Peavy Pond
Brule River
Iron Mountain
Menominee River
Marinette
Escanaba River
Escanaba
Marquette
Grand Island National Recreation Area
Munising
Pictured Rocks National Lakeshore
Indian Lake
Manistique
Manistique R
Manistique Lake
Newberry
Big Bay De Noc
Summer Island
St Martin Island
Washington Island
Garden Is
High Island
Hog Island
Beaver Island
Fox Islands
Manitou Islands
Sleeping Bear Dunes National
Charlevoix
Grand Traverse Bay
Torch Lake
Petoskey
Lake Charlevoix
Burt Lake
Mullett Lake
Boyne City
Gaylord
St Ignace
Mackinaw City
Straits of Mackinac
Mackinac Island
Bois Blanc Island
Cheboygan
Black Lake
Rogers City
Grand Lake
Presque Isle
Long Lake
Alpena
Fletcher Pond
Whitefish Bay
Sault Sainte Marie
Sugar Island
Neebish Island
St Joseph Island
Drummond Island
Georgian Bay
Rainbow Flowage
Wolf River
Lake Alice
Wausau
Lake Nokomis
Turtle Flambeau Flowage

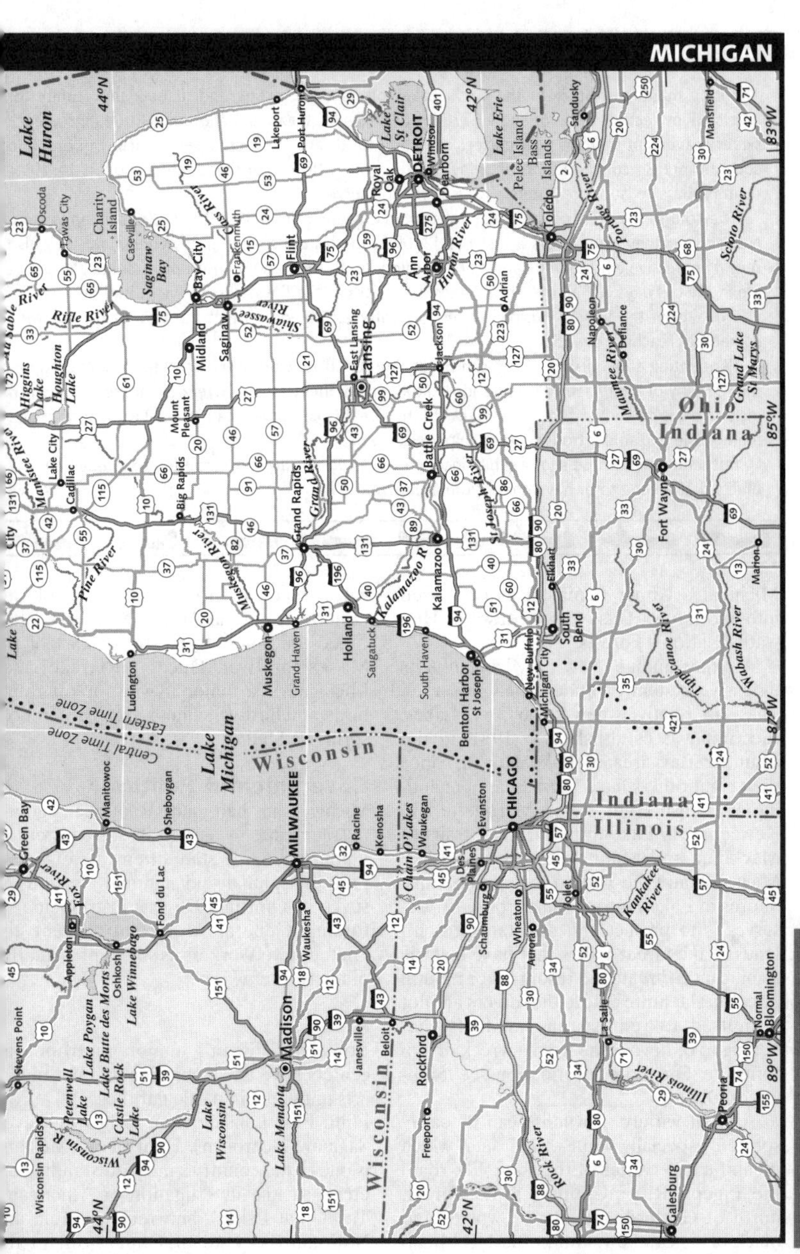
MICHIGAN
Lake Huron
Saginaw Bay
Charity Island
Lake Michigan
Lake Erie
Lake St Clair
DETROIT
Windsor
Dearborn
Royal Oak
Port Huron
Lakeport
Flint
Ann Arbor
Lansing
East Lansing
Jackson
Battle Creek
Kalamazoo
Grand Rapids
Holland
Saugatuck
Grand Haven
Muskegon
Ludington
South Haven
Benton Harbor
St Joseph
Saginaw
Bay City
Midland
Mount Pleasant
Big Rapids
Cadillac
Lake City
Houghton Lake
Higgins Lake
Oscoda
Tawas City
Caseville
Frankenmuth
Adrian
Toledo
Sandusky
Pelee Island
Bass Islands
Defiance
Napoleon
Mansfield
Fort Wayne
Marion
South Bend
Elkhart
New Buffalo
Michigan City
CHICAGO
Evanston
Des Plaines
Schaumburg
Wheaton
Aurora
Joliet
La Salle
Peoria
Normal
Bloomington
Galesburg
MILWAUKEE
Racine
Kenosha
Waukegan
Waukesha
Madison
Janesville
Beloit
Rockford
Freeport
Green Bay
Manitowoc
Sheboygan
Fond du Lac
Oshkosh
Appleton
Stevens Point
Wisconsin Rapids
Lake Winnebago
Lake Mendota
Lake Wisconsin
Castle Rock Lake
Petenwell Lake
Lake Poygan
Lake Butte des Morts
Chain O'Lakes
Ohio
Indiana
Illinois
Wisconsin
Eastern Time Zone
Central Time Zone
Huron River
Shiawassee River
Grand River
Kalamazoo R
St Joseph River
Muskegon River
Pine River
Rifle River
Cass River
Manistee River
Maumee River
Portage River
Scioto River
Grand Lake St Marys
Tippecanoe River
Wabash River
Kankakee River
Illinois River
Rock River
Wisconsin R
Fox River
44°N
42°N
83°W
85°W
87°W
89°W

Shipwreck Diving

The long maritime history of the Great Lakes offers a fascinating and unique opportunity for divers. Shipwrecks line the offshore portions of Lakes Michigan, Superior and Huron, and the icy waters have kept them in near perfect condition for divers. Nowhere else on earth can one find such an intense concentration of shipwrecks – from 17th-century wooden schooners to 20th-century massive 'superfreighters' – so superbly preserved.

The cold freshwaters of the Great Lakes hold anywhere from 3000 to 10,000 sunken vessels. Not only do they offer divers a first-hand look at the history of maritime architecture, they also reveal impressively preserved cargoes of clothing, food, tools and utensils, providing a glimpse at life in the old days. Of all the Great Lakes, Superior has the finest wreck diving, both in quantity and quality of the wrecks. Visibility averages between 30 and 40 feet throughout the summer, sometimes reaching over 50.

Penetrating sunken shipwrecks can be dangerous. It requires special certification and equipment. Many of the full-service dive shops in the region offer classes in wreck diving, some of which include dives on some of the best wrecks in the Great Lakes. Divers can thus take advantage of a memorable and safe introduction to shipwreck diving.

But remember: These sites are historical preserves. Divers are not permitted to remove any artifacts that belong to or have come from a shipwreck.

Michigan's Upper Peninsula is organized into enormous tracts of the Ottawa or Hiawatha National Forests.

Another unique draw to Michigan is its extensive system of underwater preserves. These are relatively new in the Great Lakes; the first was established in 1981, in the Thunder Bay area of Lake Huron. Since then eight others have been created including: Whitefish Point, Alger, Marquette and Keweenaw in Lake Superior; the Straits of Mackinac and Manitou Passage in Lake Michigan; and the Thumb area and Sanilac Shores in Lake Huron. The purpose of preserves is to protect and maintain bottomlands of the Great Lakes that have historic significance, threatened resources or natural or cultural features. Note that divers are not permitted to remove any artifacts that belong to or have come from a wreck or historic site. For more information see 'Shipwreck Diving.'

A great variety of wildlife can be easily spotted, especially white-tailed deer, which inhabit every corner of the state. Elk roam the Pigeon River Country State Forest, north of Gaylord, and moose, wolves and black bears can be found in the UP. Michigan is renowned for its brown, brook an[d] rainbow trout; the Au Sable River is ofte[n] called the 'finest trout stream east of th[e] Mississippi River.' Due to the Great Lake[s] Michigan is a major flyway for migratin[g] birds, and bird-watching is excellent in bot[h] spring and fall.

Government & Politics

Michigan has had many Republican gover[-]nors, but due in part to its long history o[f] unionization, the state often votes Democ[-]ratic in regional and national elections. A strike in Flint in 1936 was instrumental i[n] forcing General Motors to accept th[e] United Auto Workers as sole representativ[e] of the workers.

Arts

Lower Michigan's major metropolita[n] centers have an astonishing number of fin[e] arts museums, in particular those in Detroi[t,] Flint, East Lansing, Ann Arbor and eve[n] Saginaw. Dearborn's Henry Ford Museu[m] is one of the country's most outstanding ex[-]ercises in the investigation of American[a.] The Great Lakes Shipwreck Museum an[d] National Ski Hall of Fame, both in th[e]

Jpper Peninsula, are must-see museums. Near Traverse City, Interlochen Center for he Arts is a respected cultural events enter, rivaling Detroit, Ann Arbor, and Grand Rapids for music, dance and other rts attractions.

nformation

The Michigan Travel Bureau (☎ 888-784-328), PO Box 3393, Livonia, MI 48151, will end you a free travel guide and a road map o the state; you can also check its Web site www.michigan.org). The West Michigan Tourist Association (☎ 616-456-8557, 800-42-2084), 1253 Front Ave, Grand Rapids, MI 49504, publishes the free *West Michigan Travel Guide*, which describes accommodaions, attractions and visitor facilities in the vestern half of the Lower Peninsula. The Jpper Peninsula Travel and Recreation Asociation (☎ 800-562-7134, 906-774-5480), PO Box 400, Iron Mountain, MI 49801, pubishes a similar guide for the UP.

For a guide to the Michigan state park ystem, contact the Michigan Department of Natural Resources, Parks & Recreation Division (☎ 517-373-9900), PO Box 30257, Lansing, MI 48909. It's best to reserve a ampsite in advance during the summer at ny of the state parks by calling ☎ 800-447-757. All state parks charge a $4 per vehicle daily fee in addition to any camping costs. Even if you only spend a week, consider etting a $20 annual state park vehicle pass; vith 96 parks, odds are you'll visit more han five in a week.

Special Events

anuary

North American International Auto Show (☎ 248-643-0250) – mid-month, attracting car buffs from around the country to this show in Cobo Hall, one of the most prestigious car shows in the world

ebruary

UP 200 Sled Dog Race – held in Marquette, as close to an Alaskan experience as you'll get

April

Blossomtime – an explosion of color in St Joseph

May

Tulip Time – no surprise – a town named Holland specializes in acres of tulips

June

Summer Arts Festival – all summer in Interlochen, with world-renowned cultural performances

Cereal Festival and World's Longest Breakfast Table – Battle Creek's celebration of the bedrock of its economic history

Freedom Festival (☎ 519-971-5111) – late June in Windsor and Detroit, highlighted by the largest fireworks display in North America, over the Detroit River

July

National Cherry Festival – Traverse City, 'Cherry Capital' of the world, serves 'em up

Chicago-to-Mackinac Yacht Race – one of the only races of its kind and more than a hundred years old

August

National Blueberry Festival – sweetness and blueberries in South Haven

Michigan State Fair (☎ 313-369-8250) – in Detroit, celebrations of the state's agricultural heritage

Upper Peninsula State Fair – Yoopers special 'state' fair, in Escanaba

Ford Montreaux–Detroit Jazz Festival – famous performers liven up Detroit

Festival of Native America – a gathering of many Native American tribes in St Ignace, through September

Michigan Womyn's Music Festival (☎ 231-757-4766), 2½ hours north of Grand Rapids, the largest lesbian music festival in the US

September

Mackinac Bridge Walk – an opportunity to walk the Mighty Mac, offering amazing vistas of two Great Lakes

Montreux–Detroit Jazz Festival (☎ 313-963-7622) – a four-day festival over Labor Day weekend in Hart Plaza, the largest free jazz festival in North America, attracting local and international jazz artists and more than half a million fans.

October

Fall Color Tours – held statewide October through November

Food & Drinks

Great Lakes fish is prime Michigan cuisine. It's getting harder and harder to find the delectable lake perch, but trout and salmon are still common, as is the ubiquitous whitefish. Cedar-planked whitefish is a specialty. Consider the smoked variety of any of these – it makes good picnic food.

Virtually every Michigan community in the Lower Peninsula specializes in one form of fruit or another; cherries, apples and blueberries are the most commonly seen.

In the Upper Peninsula, pasties are the food of choice. These meat-and-vegetable filled pockets are compact, dense and a great deal.

Michigan also has a large number of wineries, mostly in the northern half of the Lower Peninsula. All welcome visitors for tasting.

Detroit offers more varieties of ethnic cuisine in its neighborhoods than you can count; its Greektown is the most accessibl of the ethnic enclaves and is a vibrant hu to the downtown.

Getting There & Around

Detroit's airport is a major hub (especiall for Northwest Airlines) and as such man travelers come through Michigan one way o another. Amtrak trains serve the state fron Chicago up the Lake Michigan shoreline. I also runs to Port Huron (from where you ca enter Canada) via Battle Creek, Lansing an Flint; still another line operates fron Chicago to Detroit. Greyhound and India Trails – along with one or two subcontracte ride services – cover most of the state, thoug often late at night in smaller towns. Uniqu ways to enter Michigan include via ferr from Manitowoc, Wisconsin, to Ludingtor Michigan, and from Grand Portage, Minne sota, to Houghton or Copper Harbor, via Isl Royale National Park.

Southern Michigan

outhern Michigan is dominated by urban enters. Michigan's heartland is a 20-county egion that lies at the center of the Lower 'eninsula, south of US 10 and away from ne Great Lakes shore lines. It includes rban areas, farm fields and suburbs conected by a network of interstates (I-94, -96, I-69 and I-196) and US highways. On our way north don't necessarily forsake nese cities; some of them are attractive and ave their own charm.

)ETROIT

pop 1,014,000

ince its 1950s heyday when Detroit was ome to more than 2 million residents, the ity has suffered some hard times. The city as been considered a national symbol of rban decay, the center of the so-called Rust Belt; its population has slipped to around a nillion. So few tourists spend time in the ity that in 1998 the Detroit Convention & 'isitors Bureau closed its information enter.

But thanks to the car industry boom of ne mid-1990s, Detroit is now staging a teady comeback. It's not a Chicago or even Cleveland, but the Motor City is culturally ich. Detroit's population is 80% black, naking it a national center for African American culture. One of the more famous ttractions is the city's Motown Museum vhere Stevie Wonder first played, and it's orth your while to spend an evening at ne of the many music clubs scattered nroughout the city.

Detroit and southeastern Michigan are egions of vivid contrasts. While some parts f Detroit are depressing displays of urban light, cities such as Birmingham and West Bloomfield make Oakland County, just orth of Detroit, one of the richest counties n the United States. Wealthy, too, is the Grosse Pointe area, just east of the city, vhich was featured in the 1997 film *Grosse 'ointe Blank*, starring John Cusack and Minnie Driver.

Highlights

- Detroit, the Motor City, birthplace of muscle cars and Motown
- Lansing and East Lansing, the former the capital, the latter home to large Michigan State University
- Ann Arbor, a busy, lovely Big Ten campus with lots of life and lots of sights
- Battle Creek, home of a working museum dedicated to southern Michigan's other product – cereal
- Kalamazoo, an underappreciated college town with an excellent museum of military aircraft
- Jackson, home of the Michigan Space Center

History

At the turn of the 20th century, Detroit was a medium-size city of 285,000 known as a center for manufacturing horse-drawn carriages and bicycles. Thanks in part to the massive iron and copper mines in the Upper Peninsula, cheap transport on the Great Lakes and enterprising souls such as Henry Ford, the Dodge brothers and the Fisher brothers, Detroit quickly became the motorized vehicle capital. Ford in particular changed the fabric not only of Detroit, but also of US society. He didn't invent the automobile, as so many mistakenly believe, but he did perfect the assembly line method of production and became one of the first industrialists to use mass production. The result was the Model T, the first car that the USA's middle class could afford.

The car industry was crippled by the Great Depression, but WWII restored prosperity as Michigan led the nation in the production of military equipment. Among other things, war work in Detroit's converted car factories attracted blacks from the South to a city that was already ethnically diverse. Racial tensions in Detroit led to a riot in 1943 that took 34 lives, and in 1967, during the height of the civil rights struggle, a second riot left 43 dead and blocks of the city smoldering. The car industry foundered again in the 1970s, and the city suffered as many residents – especially whites – moved to the suburbs.

The election of Detroit's first two black mayors (Coleman Young in 1974 and Dennis Archer in 1993), coupled with the prosperity of the car industry in the 1990s, has done much to heal the city's wounds.

Orientation

The heart of Detroit is Hart Plaza, at the foot of Woodward Ave, where in 1701 Antoine de la Mothe Cadillac built Fort Pontchartrain. Woodward Ave, the city's main boulevard, heads north from the plaza all the way to Pontiac (in the 1950s, cruisin' Woodward in a souped-up Dodge or Chevrolet was a common summer pastime in the Motor City).

Just east of Hart Plaza, dominating the Detroit skyline, is the massive Renaissance Center, GM's world headquarters. Just east of the 'Ren Cen' is Rivertown, a former warehouse district on Atwater St that now holds some of the city's finest nightclubs. Detroit's liveliest area is Greektown, on Monroe St just off I-375, which is lined with Greek restaurants and bakeries. Head south via the Detroit–Windsor Tunnel or Ambassador Bridge to reach the Canadian city of Windsor, another lively spot at night. For the best overview of the downtown area hop on the People Mover (see Downtown).

Information

Tourist Offices The Detroit Convention & Visitors Bureau (☎ 313-202-1800, 800-338-7648) no longer has a tourist center in the downtown area. You can call the bureau's 24-hour Metro Detroit Info-line (☎ 888-658-8500) though not knowing its three-digit codes for various subjects is quite an impediment to successfully using the hot line. Look on its Web site (www.visitdetroit.com) for a list of local activities, entertainment, golf courses, shopping, tours, restaurants and transportation options.

Email & Internet Access Kinko's is a copy shop on the ground floor of the Renaissance Center. It has Internet access for $12 per hour or 20¢ per minute.

Media Pick up a copy of *Metro Times*, distributed free throughout southeast Michigan; it's the best guide to Detroit's arts, music and nightclub scene. It also has a pretty decent listing of (though no information on) restaurants. *Real Detroit Weekly* is an upstart competitor; it has a good rundown on nightlife but also no restaurant information at all. Detroit has two dailies, the *Detroit Free Press* and the *Detroit News*.

Medical Services Harper Hospital (☎ 313-745-8303) is the closest hospital to downtown, south of the Cultural Center area, between Woodward Ave and I-75.

Dangers & Annoyances Travelers should avoid some areas in Detroit, such as 12th St (where the 1967 riots began). The bus station area is also somewhat dicey.

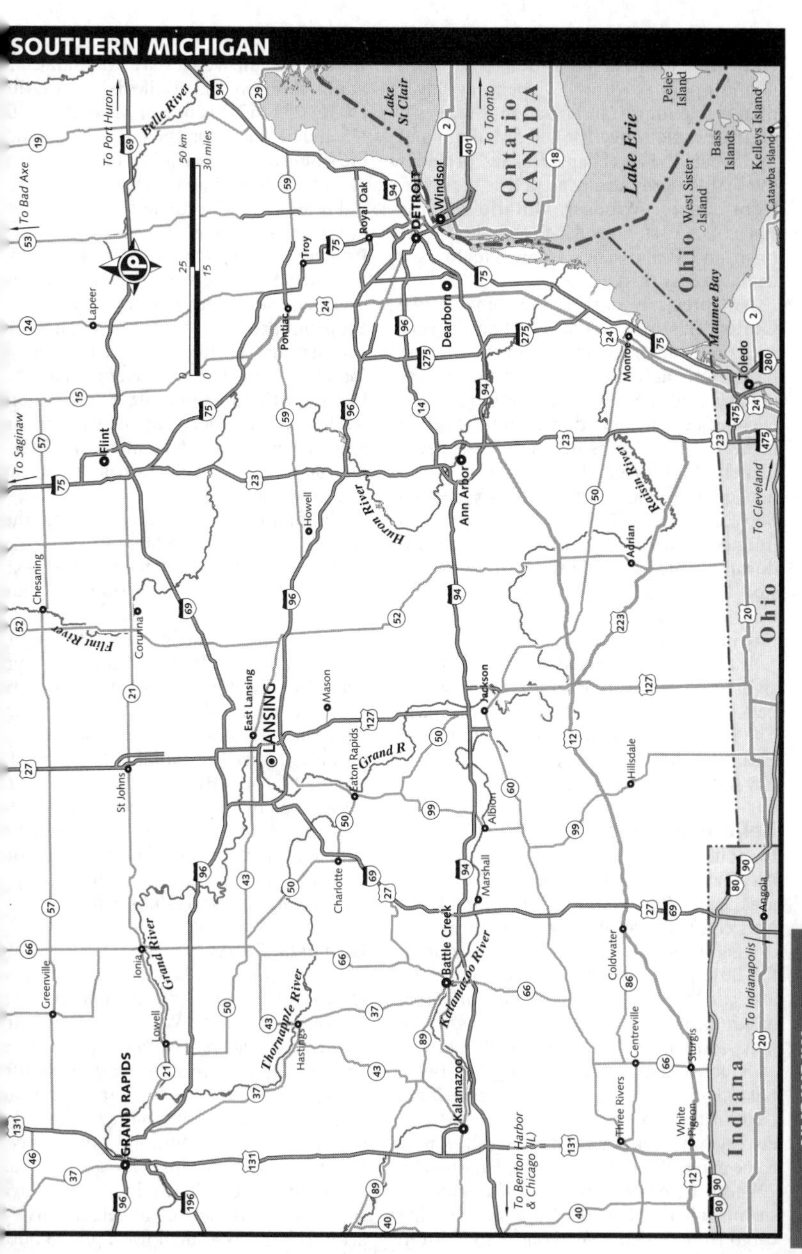
SOUTHERN MICHIGAN
To Bad Axe
To Port Huron
Belle River
To Saginaw
Flint
Lapeer
Chesaning
Flint River
Corunna
East Lansing
LANSING
St Johns
Greenville
Ionia
Grand River
Lowell
GRAND RAPIDS
Hastings
Thornapple River
Charlotte
Eaton Rapids
Grand R
Mason
Howell
Huron River
Pontiac
Troy
Royal Oak
DETROIT
Dearborn
Windsor
Lake St Clair
To Toronto
Ontario
CANADA
Lake Erie
Pelee Island
Bass Islands
Kelleys Island
Catawba Island
West Sister Island
Ohio
Maumee Bay
Toledo
Monroe
Ann Arbor
Raisin River
Adrian
To Cleveland
Jackson
Hillsdale
Albion
Marshall
Battle Creek
Kalamazoo River
Kalamazoo
Coldwater
Centreville
Three Rivers
Sturgis
White Pigeon
Angola
To Indianapolis
Indiana
To Benton Harbor & Chicago (IL)
50 km
30 miles
0
25
15

Downtown

Detroit's elevated rail system was more political pork – tax money spent lavishly – than viable mass transportation. But a ride on the **People Mover** (☎ 800-541-7245) and its 2.9-mile loop is cheap (50¢) and provides the best view of the city as well as the riverfront and the Windsor, Ontario skyline. Each of its 13 stations, which include Greektown and Renaissance Center, features a distinctive work of art.

Not precisely pork is the **Renaissance Center**. This one was an elephant, a very white one, upon its completion. It was the largest privately financed operation in US history, and a $400 million failure when clients failed to materialize and the white flight to the suburbs didn't reverse itself. General Motors' purchase of it as its world headquarters has given it a much needed boost, and gradually it's beginning to do its intended job of revitalizing the central downtown. It's actually fun getting impossibly lost in the four 39-story towers on the way to the observation deck ($4), which provides incredible views.

If the day is nice, you can enjoy the lively riverfront scene at **Hart Plaza** or along pedestrian-friendly Washington Boulevard. The boulevard terminates at Grand Circus Park, the delineator of downtown, with a few statues and a fountain.

Belle Isle & Vicinity

Detroiters' favorite place to escape is **Belle Isle**, 2½ miles northeast of the downtown area at E Jefferson Ave and E Grand Blvd. You can while away an afternoon by just driving its 5-mile loop road, stopping at all the little parks and attractions. Among the attractions on the 981-acre island park are a nature center with educational trails, and a kids' zoo where an elevated path lets you walk above the animals roaming free (well, not *that* free!). The interesting **Dossin Great Lakes Museum** (☎ 313-852-4051) has fine displays on Great Lakes shipping. Out front is the anchor from the *Edmund Fitzgerald*, a 729-foot freighter sunk in a Lake Superior storm on November 10, 1975. It was carrying cargo from Superior, Wisconsin, to Detroit; all 29 men aboard were lost. Hours ar 10 am to 5 pm Wednesday to Sunday; $2/ adults/children. The Belle Isle Aquariu (☎ 313-259-1176) is one of the oldest in th US and has more than 50 tanks with aquat life from around the world. Hours are 10 a to 5 pm daily; $2/1 adults/children.

From the road to Belle Isle, travel east miles or so along E Jefferson Ave t **Pewabic Pottery** (☎ 313-822-0954), 10125 Jefferson Ave. This workshop-cum-museu was begun by potter Mary Chase Perr Stratton around the turn of the 20t century, and its impressive tiling can b found in virtually every major building i Detroit, as well as in quite a few nation landmarks. A gallery rotates exhibits an you can watch potters at work. This i Detroit's one-of-a-kind (albeit not chea souvenir place.

Continuing east another 2 miles, the turning east on Dickerson St to Lenox Av brings you to **Fisher Mansion** (☎ 313-33 6740), 383 Lenox Ave, an ornate – ma have used more vulgar terms – mansio built by a bon vivant, Roaring-'20s auto i dustry millionaire. 'Eclectic' comes to min when looking at it, but it's hard to deny th exquisite artistry that went into every inc from stained glass to rare black waln parquet floors. The building today is als home to the Bhaktivedanta Cultur Center, run by the International Society f Krishna Consciousness. A vegetari restaurant is on the second floor. Mansio tours are offered four times daily Friday t Sunday and cost $6/4 adults/children.

Cultural Center

One place the People Mover doesn't go Detroit's Cultural Center, a neighborhoo clustered around Woodward Ave an Kirby Ave. Diego Rivera's mural *Detro Industry* fills a room at the **Detroit Institut of Arts** (☎ 313-833-7900), 5200 Woodwar Ave, and reflects the city's blue-collar labo history. All that automobile money ce tainly allowed the institute to purchas some fine art. It's an incredibly larg complex and the list of priceless works o art is as large as a small town phone boo

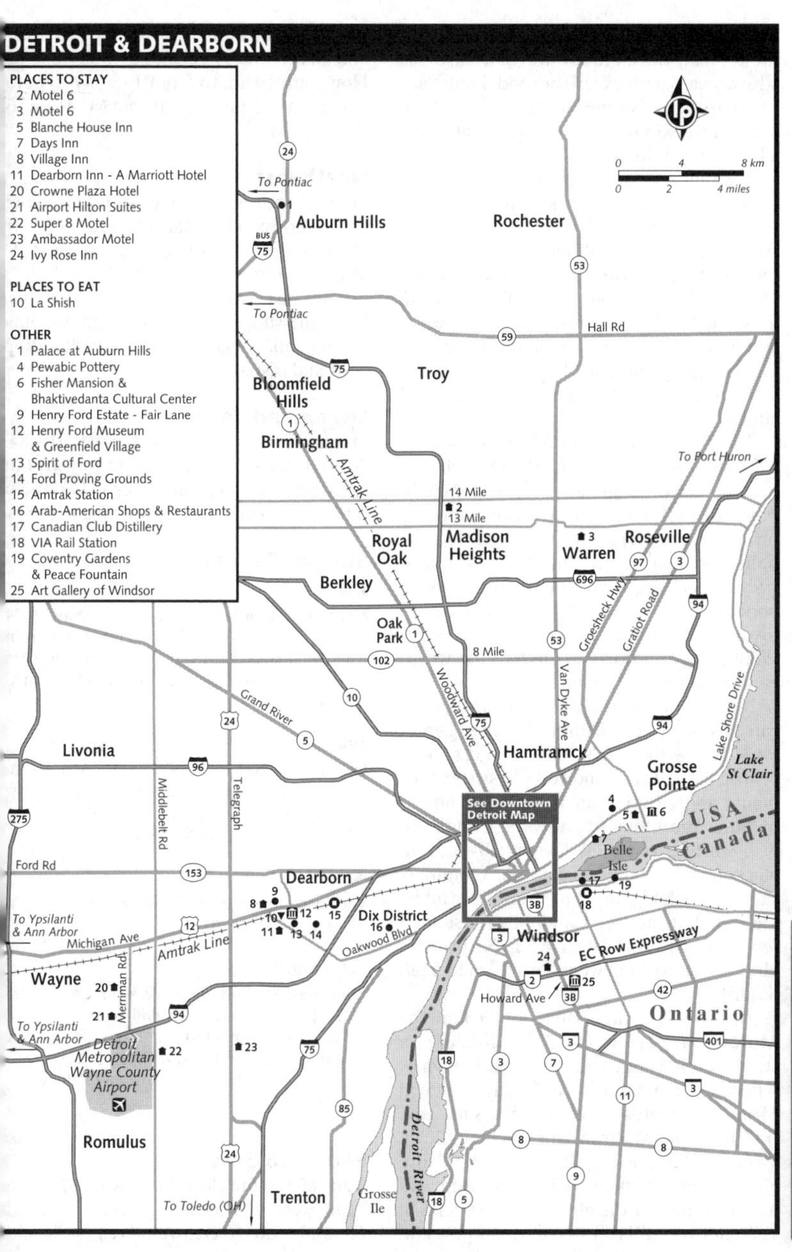
DETROIT & DEARBORN
PLACES TO STAY
2 Motel 6
3 Motel 6
5 Blanche House Inn
7 Days Inn
8 Village Inn
11 Dearborn Inn - A Marriott Hotel
20 Crowne Plaza Hotel
21 Airport Hilton Suites
22 Super 8 Motel
23 Ambassador Motel
24 Ivy Rose Inn
PLACES TO EAT
10 La Shish
OTHER
1 Palace at Auburn Hills
4 Pewabic Pottery
6 Fisher Mansion & Bhaktivedanta Cultural Center
9 Henry Ford Estate - Fair Lane
12 Henry Ford Museum & Greenfield Village
13 Spirit of Ford
14 Ford Proving Grounds
15 Amtrak Station
16 Arab-American Shops & Restaurants
17 Canadian Club Distillery
18 VIA Rail Station
19 Coventry Gardens & Peace Fountain
25 Art Gallery of Windsor
To Pontiac
Auburn Hills
Rochester
Hall Rd
Troy
Bloomfield Hills
Birmingham
Amtrak Line
To Port Huron
14 Mile
13 Mile
Royal Oak
Madison Heights
Warren
Roseville
Berkley
Groesbeck Hwy
Gratiot Road
Oak Park
8 Mile
Woodward Ave
Van Dyke Ave
Lake Shore Drive
Grand River
Livonia
Hamtramck
Grosse Pointe
Lake St Clair
Middlebelt Rd
Telegraph
See Downtown Detroit Map
USA
Canada
Belle Isle
Ford Rd
Dearborn
To Ypsilanti & Ann Arbor
Michigan Ave
Amtrak Line
Dix District
Oakwood Blvd
Windsor
EC Row Expressway
Wayne
Merriman Rd
Howard Ave
Ontario
Detroit Metropolitan Wayne County Airport
Romulus
Detroit River
Trenton
Grosse Ile
To Toledo (OH)
0 4 8 km
0 2 4 miles
MICHIGAN

the museum is generally regarded as one of the top half-dozen in the world. It also has a lovely café with excellent food. Hours are 11 am to 4 pm, Wednesday to Friday, 11 am to 5 pm weekends; tours are given at 1 pm; $4/1 adults/children.

The full-scale model of slaves chained up on an 18th-century slave ship and the door to Martin Luther King's Birmingham, Alabama, jail cell will leave you chilled at the **Museum of African American History** (☎ 313-494-5800), at 315 E Warren. The museum has been growing over the years and now is the largest one in the US detailing African American history. Hours are 9:30 am to 5 pm Tuesday to Sunday; $5/3 adults/children.

The **Detroit Historical Museum** (☎ 313-833-1805), Kirby Ave and Woodward Ave, traces Detroit's growth from a Native American settlement to a major manufacturing center. Here's where you'll find the obligatory exhibit detailing the auto industry (it's smaller than you'd think) and a popular mock-up of a 19th-century downtown street. Hours are 9:30 am to 5 pm Wednesday to Friday, 10 am to 5 pm weekends; $3/2 adults/children.

Next to the Museum of African American History is the **Detroit Science Center** (☎ 313-577-8400), 5020 John R St. It's a kid-centric place, with hands-on physics experiments and exhibits on technology, not to mention the Omnimax theater. Hours are 9:30 am to 2 pm weekdays, 12:30 to 5 pm weekends; $3/2 adults/children; Omnimax shows cost $4. More kid-friendly exhibits are found at the free **Children's Museum** a few blocks northwest at 67 E Kirby Ave. Hours are 1 to 4 pm weekdays, 9 am to 5 pm Saturday.

At 2648 W Grand Blvd, you'll find the **Motown Museum** (☎ 313-875-2264), a string of large homes that became known as 'Hitsville USA' after Berry Gordy launched Motown Records here in 1959. Stars that rose from the Motown label include Stevie Wonder, Diana Ross, Marvin Gaye, Gladys Knight and Michael Jackson. Gordy and Motown split for the glitz of Los Angeles in 1972, but you still can step into Studio 4 and see where the Four Tops, Smokey Robinso[n] and many others recorded their first hit[s]. Hours are 10 am to 5 pm Tuesday to Satur[day], noon to 5 pm Sunday and Monday; $6/[...] adults/children.

Northeast

Detroit's cultural melting pot is best exper[i]enced at **Eastern Market**, said to be th[e] oldest farmers' market in the country. O[n] Tuesday and Saturday, the large halls a[t] Gratiot Ave and Russell St are filled wit[h] bartering shoppers and vendors; surround[ing] the open market are specialty shop[s,] delis and restaurants.

Organized Tours

Diamond Jack River Tours (☎ 313-843-7676) departs from Hart Plaza for two-hou[r] cruises on the Detroit River ($12) aboar[d] retired Mackinac Island, Michigan, ferries.

Special Events

January

North American International Auto Show (☎ 248-643-0250) – Mid-month, car buffs from aroun[d] the country arrive for this show in Cobo Ha[ll,] one of the most prestigious car shows in th[e] world.

June

Freedom Festival (☎ 519-971-5111) – Windsor an[d] Detroit team up in late June for this festiva[l] highlighted by the largest fireworks display [in] North America, over the Detroit River.

August

Michigan State Fair (☎ 313-369-8250) – This is th[e] largest fair in the state.

September

Montreux–Detroit Jazz Festival (☎ 313-96[...]-7622) – A four-day festival over Labor Da[y] weekend in Hart Plaza, the largest free jazz fe[s]tival in North America, it attracts local an[d] international jazz artists and more than half [a] million fans.

Places to Stay

Budget For the closest public campgroun[d] head west of Pontiac on Hwy 59 to th[e] ***Pontiac Lake Recreation Area*** (☎ *248-66[...]*

020), where a site costs $11 per night plus a aily $4 vehicle entry permit.

Accommodations, other than glitzy hotels nd questionable flophouses, are scarce in he downtown area. ***Park Avenue Hostel*** *☎ 313-961-8310, 2305 Park Ave)* is near the ity's lively Theater District, but not near nough for some travelers, and it's $12 a ight. The nearest HI hostel is ***Country Grandma's Home Hostel*** *(☎ 734-753-4901)* n New Boston, southwest of Detroit and 10 niles from Metro Airport. You must call in dvance ($10/13 members/nonmembers), nd there is no public transportation – to the irport nor the city center.

A mile east of the Belle Isle bridge is the ***Blanche House Inn*** *(☎ 313-822-7090, 506 Parkview Drive)*. Rooms in the Victorian B&B begin at $65 per double.

Shorecrest Motor Inn *(☎ 313-568-3000, 00-992-9616, 1316 E Jefferson Ave)* is six blocks northeast of Hart Plaza and has ingles/doubles for $58, not a bad deal at all or the location. Northeast of here is a ***Days nn*** *(☎ 313-568-2000, 3250 E Jefferson Ave)* vith singles/doubles from $64. Other motels nd hotels are being developed around ere, probably in response to a slew of new asinos in development.

Affordable motels abound in the Detroit uburbs. If you're arriving from Metro Airport, head for Middlebelt Rd, Telegraph Rd or Merriman Rd and take your pick. ***Ambassador Motel*** *(☎ 734-287-8686, 11811 Telegraph Ave)* in Taylor, east of the airport, as $40 doubles. ***Motel 6*** has five locations n the suburbs; the closest to downtown Detroit is in Madison Heights *(☎ 248-583-500)*, on 14 Mile Rd across from the Dakland Mall, with rooms from $37/42 ingle/double. Another is in Warren *(☎ 810-26-9300)*, at 13 Mile Rd and Van Dyke Rd; ooms are $32/38 single/double. ***Super 8 Motel*** *(☎ 734-946-8808, 9863 Middlebelt Rd)* in Romulus, has rooms for $48/54.

Mid-Range Downtown, ***Hotel St Regis*** *☎ 313-873-3000, fax 313-873-2574, 3071 W Grand Blvd)* has large, comfortable rooms rom $110 single/double during peak times, ut $80 rooms are not unheard of here.

In Greektown, the ***Atheneum Suite Hotel*** *(☎ 313-962-2323, 800-772-2323, fax 313-962-2424, 1000 Brush St)* has rooms with separate living areas and great restaurants on site. Rates of $110 single/double are reasonable for a downtown location.

The best location of any mid-range lodging is that of the ***Doubletree Hotel*** *(☎ 313-222-7700, fax 313-222-6509, 333 E Jefferson Ave)*, opposite the Renaissance Center. This stylish place has a heated indoor pool and racquetball and tennis courts. Rooms top out at $130 single/double.

Near the airport, choices are nearly limitless. The ***Crowne Plaza*** *(☎ 734-729-2600, fax 734-729-9414, 8000 Merriman Rd)* has some rooms whose balconies overlook the elegant lobby. The rooms are well appointed. Rates are $130 but drop sharply (by nearly 40%) Friday and Saturday when business travelers are gone.

Top End The local landmark in lodging has to be ***Hotel Pontchartrain*** *(☎ 313-965-0200, fax 313-222-6509, 2 Washington Blvd)*, opposite Cobo Hall. This historic hotel is still in good shape despite retaining its air of the past. New touches include a pool, health club and business services. Rooms are $150 single/double.

The most commanding views of any hotel in Detroit – if not Michigan – are certainly found in the ***Westin Hotel*** *(☎ 313-568-8000, fax 313-568-8146)* inside the Renaissance Center. It has nearly 1400 rooms and is the tallest hotel in the world, which gives you an idea of the epic size of the Ren Cen itself. There is a heated indoor pool and health club. Of the hotel's three dining rooms, the revolving one at the top is most popular. Rooms are $180/200 single/double.

At the airport, the units at ***Airport Hilton Suites*** *(☎ 734-728-9200, fax 734-728-9278, 9555 Merriman Rd)* are even larger than most. Ask for one facing the courtyard. There is also a heated pool. Rooms are $145/155 single/double.

Places to Eat

Restaurants in Detroit and throughout southeast Michigan reward their ethnically

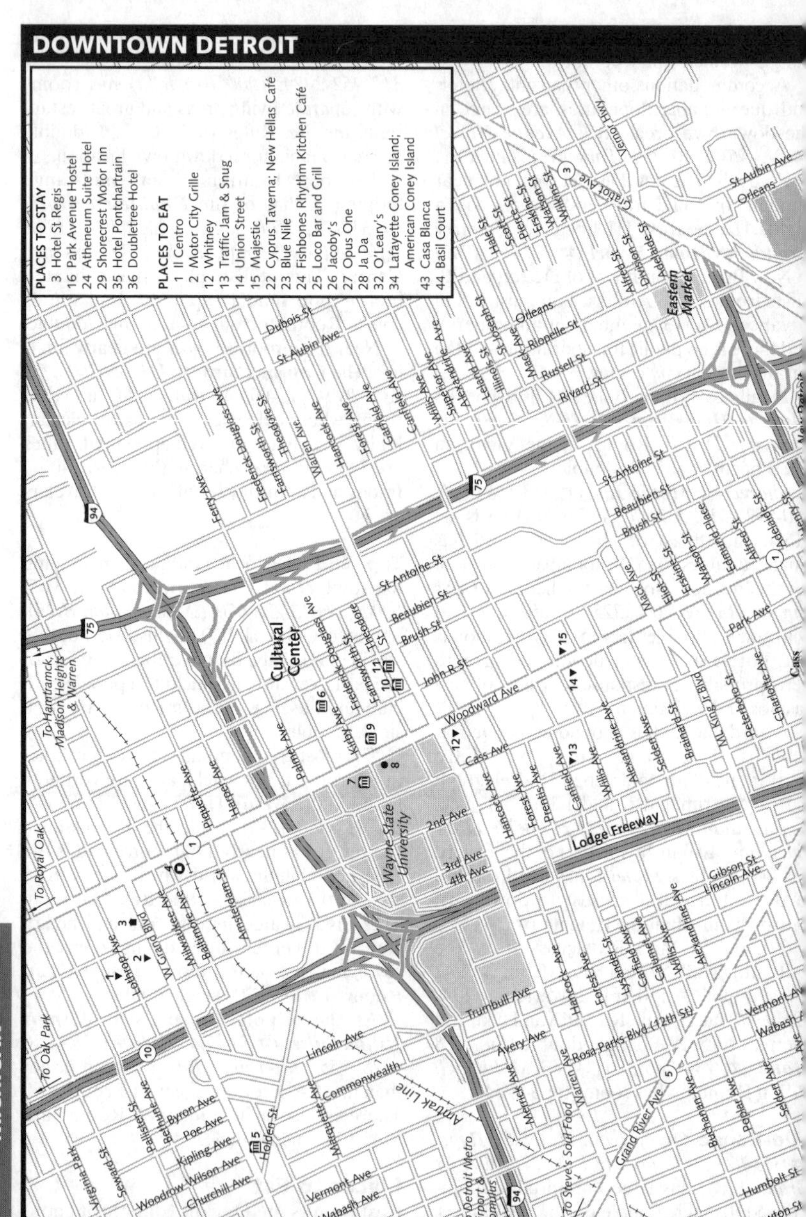

DOWNTOWN DETROIT
PLACES TO STAY
3 Hotel St Regis
16 Park Avenue Hostel
24 Atheneum Suite Hotel
29 Shorecrest Motor Inn
35 Hotel Pontchartrain
36 Doubletree Hotel
PLACES TO EAT
1 Il Centro
2 Motor City Grille
12 Whitney
13 Traffic Jam & Snug
14 Union Street
15 Majestic
22 Cyprus Taverna; New Hellas Café
23 Blue Nile
24 Fishbones Rhythm Kitchen Café
25 Loco Bar and Grill
26 Jacoby's
27 Opus One
28 Ja Da
31 O'Leary's
34 Lafayette Coney Island; American Coney Island
43 Casa Blanca
44 Basil Court
Cultural Center
Wayne State University
Eastern Market
Lodge Freeway
Amtrak Line
To Hamtramck, Madison Heights & Warren
To Royal Oak
To Oak Park
To Detroit Metro Airport & Romulus
To Steve's Soul Food
Woodward Ave
Cass Ave
Grand River Ave
Gratiot Ave
Vernor Hwy
Trumbull Ave
W Grand Blvd
Rosa Parks Blvd (12th St)
ML King Jr Blvd

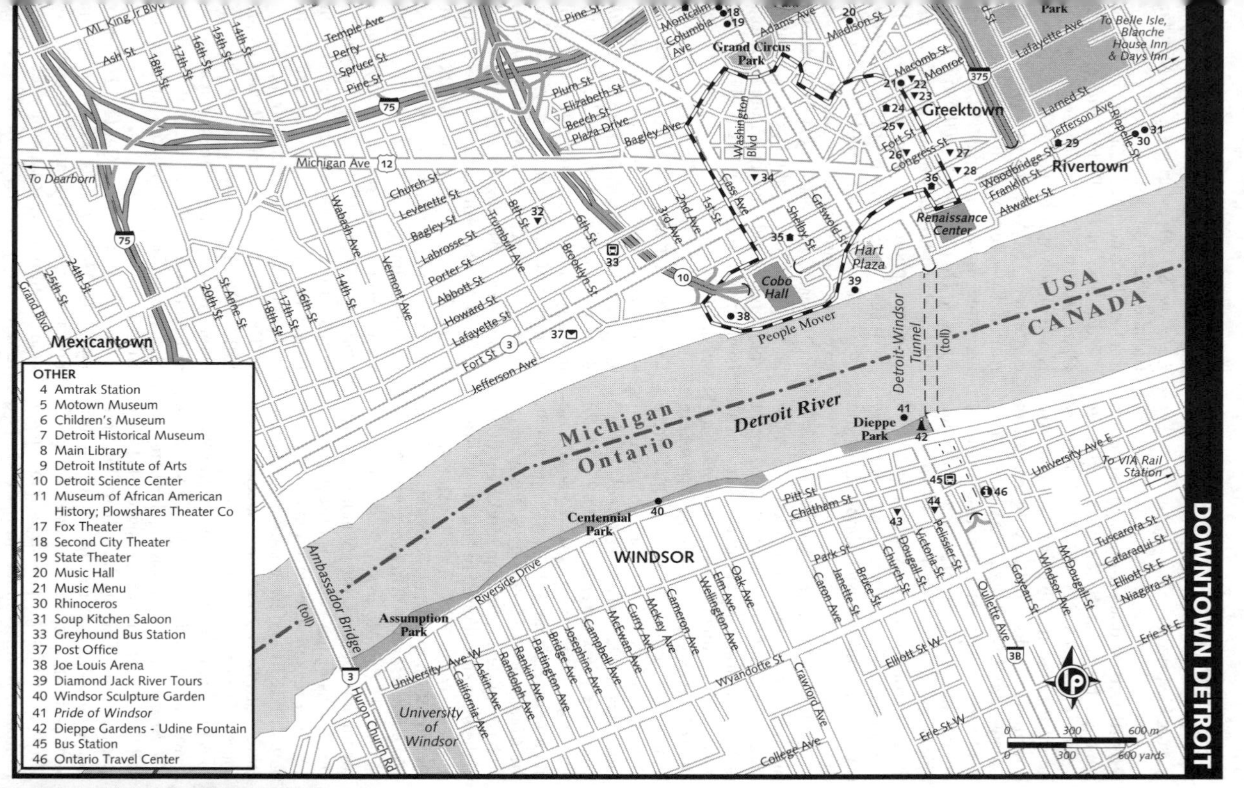
DOWNTOWN DETROIT
USA
CANADA
Michigan
Ontario
Detroit River
Detroit-Windsor Tunnel
(toll)
Ambassador Bridge
WINDSOR
Greektown
Rivertown
Mexicantown
Grand Circus Park
Hart Plaza
Cobo Hall
Renaissance Center
People Mover
Dieppe Park
Centennial Park
Assumption Park
University of Windsor
To VIA Rail Station
To Belle Isle, Blanche House Inn & Days Inn
To Dearborn
Michigan Ave
Jefferson Ave
Washington Blvd
Riverside Drive
Ouellette Ave
Huron Church Rd
University Ave E
University Ave W
OTHER
4 Amtrak Station
5 Motown Museum
6 Children's Museum
7 Detroit Historical Museum
8 Main Library
9 Detroit Institute of Arts
10 Detroit Science Center
11 Museum of African American History; Plowshares Theater Co
17 Fox Theater
18 Second City Theater
19 State Theater
20 Music Hall
21 Music Menu
30 Rhinoceros
31 Soup Kitchen Saloon
33 Greyhound Bus Station
37 Post Office
38 Joe Louis Arena
39 Diamond Jack River Tours
40 Windsor Sculpture Garden
41 Pride of Windsor
42 Dieppe Gardens - Udine Fountain
45 Bus Station
46 Ontario Travel Center
0 300 600 m
0 300 600 yards

diverse, working-class patrons with authentic dishes served in large portions at very reasonable prices.

Downtown Middle-of-the-night appetites are taken care of at the legendary ***Lafayette Coney Island*** (*☎ 313-964-8198*), open 24 hours at Lafayette Blvd and Michigan Ave downtown. It does battle with ***American Coney Island*** (*☎ 313-961-7758*), its fiercest rival and right next door, also open 24 hours. Coneys – a wiener sausage with chili, onions, mustard and other items – are something Detroiters take very seriously.

Inside the Renaissance Center are a few soup places and sandwich shops where you can eat for less than $5.

Lively Greektown, of which Monroe St is the nucleus, is downtown Detroit's main drag of food and entertainment, lined with a dozen restaurants and Greek bakeries. The best of the bunch is ***New Hellas Cafe*** (*☎ 313-961-5544, 583 Monroe St*), where flaming cheese and the cry of 'Opa!' are a Detroit tradition. Many of those who don't think this is Detroit's best Greek say it's found at ***Cyprus Taverna*** (*☎ 313-961-1550*), next door, a tad more upscale (both have main courses from $7). Across the street, the ***Blue Nile*** (*☎ 313-964-6699, 508 Monroe St*) has real-deal Ethiopian food, right down to the *injera* bread used in lieu of tableware (entrées from $10). The most popular restaurant on the street, however, might be ***Fishbones Rhythm Kitchen Cafe*** (*☎ 313-965-4600, 400 Monroe St*), in the same corner complex as the Atheneum Suite Hotel. This Cajun eatery is always packed, for good reason. The bayou cuisine is supplemented by a few creative items and there's always a good daily special (main courses from $9).

A number of bar-and-grills serve up spirit as well as food. ***Jacoby's*** (*☎ 313-962-3334, 624 Brush St*) is a two-story German-style hall that's been in business since 1904. Vegetarians won't find much to their liking but the atmosphere is rousing. Only at this Sunday brunch could you have a Bloody Mary with banana pancakes and *wiener schnitzel*. Main courses start at $7. Two blocks north and one block east, the ***Loc Bar & Grill*** (*☎ 313-965-3737, 454 Lafayette St*) serves up great Tex-Mex far (main dishes from $6).

One block north of E Jefferson Ave an a block east of the People Mover track ***Opus One*** (*☎ 313-961-7766, 565 Larned S*) is one of downtown's best eateries. Eclecti contemporary American cuisine (entrée from $20) is very well done. The interio are done in soothing pastels. Across th street, ***Ja Da*** (*☎ 313-965-1700, 546 E Larne St*) has down-home ribs and soul food in chic atmosphere (main courses from $11).

West of downtown proper is ***O'Leary*** (*☎ 313-964-0936, 1411 Brooklyn St*), a coz airy Irish teahouse and restaurant appropr ately located in a district called Corktow Scrumptious fresh baked goods are avai able; lunches and dinners feature tradition Irish fare (entrées from $6). High tea is als served daily.

Cultural Center The Cultural Center are sports a number of good eating choice Ever popular is the ***Majestic*** (*313-833-970 4120 Woodward Ave*). The heart of th menu is Middle Eastern but it rarely limi itself to just that (main courses from $8 Across the street, ***Union Street*** (*☎ 313-83 3965, 4145 Woodward Ave*) is usuall packed to the gills, often with studen letting their visiting parents foot the bill. It heavy on pasta items but there's a goo variety (main courses from $8). Two block west of Woodward from here, ***Traffic Jam Snug*** (*☎ 313-831-9470, 511 W Canfield S*) brews its own beer and changes its men frequently. Expect hearty American far and good chili (main courses from $8).

Three blocks north, the ***Whitney*** (*☎ 31 832-5700, 4421 Woodward Ave*) is this area choice for fine dining. Housed in a majesti old mansion, it serves elegant America fare; the seafood is top-notch (main course from $17).

North of Cultural Center, ***Il Centr*** (*☎ 313-872-5110, 670 Lothrop St*) ha upscale southern Italian food, much of heart-healthy, made by a local chef of som repute (main courses from $10). A bloc outh in the architecturally significant 'isher Building, the ***Motor City Grille*** *☎ 313-875-4700, 3011 W Grand Blvd)* is a ood bet for steak and seafood (main ourses from $12).

Vestern Detroit The best southern-ooking cuisine is at ***Steve's Soul Food*** *☎ 313-894-3464, 8443 Grand River)* in vestern Detroit, serving 10 meats and 10 ides daily. Barry Sanders, former football unning-back great of the Detroit Lions, rders the smothered chicken here, and)iana Ross has been known to send her haufeur for carryout.

Mexicantown is along Bagley St, offering iexpensive, authentic Mich-Mex food at ***'ochmilco*** *(☎ 313-843-0179, No 3409)* and ***:l Zocala*** *(No 3400)*.

Iorthern Detroit Detroit's Polish com-unity is centered around the city of Ham-amck, where Pope John Paul once erformed Mass. At ***Under the Eagle*** *☎ 313-875-5909, 9000 Joseph Campau)*, you an dig into stuffed cabbage, pork goulash nd pierogi for less than $7.

Keep heading north on the Lodge reeway to reach Oak Park, the heart of)etroit's Jewish district. Among the many elis and bagel shops is ***Bread Basket Deli***, a shopping center on Greenfield Rd etween 10 Mile and 11 Mile Rds. You'll ave to wait for a table, but the corned-beef andwiches, salads and matzo ball soup are utstanding.

North of here, Main St in Royal Oak is a vely spot with outdoor cafés and offbeat ightclubs. Practically next door to each ther are ***Mongolian Barbecue*** *(☎ 248-398-560, 108 E 5th St)* where you watch a chef ook your meal on an open grill, and ***Mr B's*** r ribs, hamburgers and a brew. Around e restaurants and bars are several coffee iops. Skip Starbucks and head for ***Brazil***.

ntertainment

ars & Clubs ***Atwater Block Brewery*** *☎ 313-393-2337, 237 Joseph Campau)* is in a rn-of-the-20th-century factory in the ware-ouse district east of central downtown.

Clubs for local blues and jazz include ***Rhinoceros*** *(265 Riopelle)* and ***Soup Kitchen Saloon*** *(1585 Franklin)*, both in the Rivertown area; this district was really be-coming gentrified and a host of casinos were opening in 1999. Downtown, Monroe St (and the rest of Greektown) is a good bet for nightlife. ***Music Menu***, just west of the Cyprus Taverna Restaurant, is a Cajun eatery with daily blues, rock or jazz. North-east of downtown in Hamtramck district, ***Attic Bar*** *(11667 Joseph Campau)* is a true blues bar where customers take over the piano when a band isn't around.

Performing Arts Nightlife in Detroit centers on the revived Theater District along Woodward Ave, anchored by the ***Fox Theater*** *(☎ 313-396-7600)*. Built in 1928 and gloriously restored in 1988, the Art Deco icon attracts some of the best acts passing through the city. Next door is ***Second City Theater*** *(☎ 313-965-2222)*, modeled after Chicago's famous comedy club. Still farther south, the ***State Theater*** *(☎ 313-961-5450)* is an Italian Renaissance structure pre-dating the Fox Theater; it too draws in a wide variety of national acts.

Just south of the new sports stadiums, ***Music Hall*** *(☎ 313-963-2366)* calls itself the 'Dance Capital of Mid-America.' Virtually every night a drama, dance, opera, or jazz performance takes place.

In the same complex as the Museum of African American History, ***Plowshares Theatre Company*** *(☎ 313-872-0279)* is Michigan's only African American profes-sional theater company.

Spectator Sports

The Palace at Auburn Hills (☎ 248-377-0100) hosts the men's Detroit Pistons and the women's Detroit Shock basketball teams. The Detroit Red Wings – 1997 and 1998 Stanley Cup winners – play hockey at Joe Louis Arena (☎ 313-396-7544), though it is almost impossible to get tickets. (Detroit is known as Hockeytown, USA, after all.) Con-sider seeing the Detroit Vipers, members of the bruising International Hockey League, at the Palace of Auburn Hills.

The Detroit Lions (☎ 248-335-4131), the town's National Football League team, and Detroit Tigers (☎ 313-962-4000), the Major League Baseball team, are building side-by-side downtown stadiums. Baseball fans everywhere rued the closing, in 1999, of Tiger Stadium ('The Corner') where legends such as Babe Ruth and Ty Cobb used to swat home runs. The city hopes to convert the upper decks to luxury condos and put a park and plaza in the field. Not as many will miss the Lions' old haunt, the Pontiac Silverdome, since ground was broken for new Ford Field in 1999.

Getting There & Away

Air Detroit Metropolitan Wayne County Airport (Metro Airport), 18 miles southwest of Detroit, is the primary regional air center, offering direct flights to most major cities in the country. Northwest Airlines (☎ 800-225-2525) uses Detroit as a major hub and routes many of its European flights through Metro Airport, making it easy for overseas travelers to spend some time in Michigan before moving onward.

Bus The Greyhound bus station (☎ 313-961-8011) is at 1001 Howard St at the Lodge Freeway. Greyhound provides service to more than 40 cities throughout Michigan, including destinations in the UP, as well as to other Midwest states. Sample one-way fares out of Detroit include

destination	cost	travel time	frequency
Toledo	$10	1 hour	16
Cleveland	$21	3½ to 5 hours	10
Chicago	$26	5 to 9 hours	9
Battle Creek	$19	3 to 5 hours	6
Lansing	$15	2 to 3½ hours	6
Mackinaw City	$51	9 hours	1

Train The Amtrak station (☎ 313-873-3442, 800-872-7245) is at 11 W Baltimore at Woodward Ave. There are trains daily to Kalamazoo ($29), Battle Creek ($26) and Chicago ($36). The Chicago-bound train stops in Ann Arbor. Battle Creek is a junction; from here you could switch to trains (or buses) to Eas Lansing, Flint, and Port Huron, though this i time-consuming and rather costly. You als can head east on Amtrak, but you'll first b bused to Toledo. A one-way fare to New Yor is $94.

Getting Around

See the Downtown section, earlier in th chapter, for information on the Peopl Mover rail service.

To/From the Airport Commuter Trans portation (☎ 313-941-3252, 800-351-546(and Jet Port (☎ 800-552-3700) are amon the many airport shuttle companies a Metro Airport's terminals. It's $19 pe person to anywhere in downtown Detroit.

Bus Local bus service in Detroit is handle by the Detroit Dept of Transportation (DO Buses; ☎ 313-933-1300), offering limite service to the suburbs. A fare is $1.25; tran fers cost 25¢. Suburban Mobility Authori for Regional Transportation (SMAR Buses; ☎ 313-962-5515) handles bus servic in southeast Michigan with connections Detroit. The fare is $1.50; transfers cost 25¢.

Red trolley-buses (50¢) run from the Re naissance Center to Grand Circus Park dail

Taxi Cabs cost $1.40 at flagfall and aroun $1.50 per mile. Checker Cab (☎ 313-96 7000) is the largest company.

Parking Not much exists on the street, bu you'll find a plethora of surface lots an garages; avoid the latter, as they can go a high as $12 for just a few hours.

DEARBORN

This is the city that Henry Ford built, an today Dearborn is home to the world head quarters of the Ford Motor Company. It now best known for the extensive museu founded by and named for Henry.

But Dearborn isn't just about cars. Visito are often surprised when they happen upo the Dix neighborhood, east of Dearborn automotive attractions near Melvindal ver 90% of this thriving neighborhood lled with shops and restaurants is Arab; reet signs are in both Arabic and English.

Dearborn sites appear on the Detroit & earborn map.

enry Ford Museum : Greenfield Village

en miles west of downtown Detroit, the enry Ford Museum & Greenfield Village ☎ 313-271-1620) is at 20900 Oakwood lvd. Keep in mind that the museum and e village are separate attractions with sep-rate admissions; to see both takes at least a ood part of a day.

The museum's main attraction is 'The utomobile in American Life,' an homage car culture that also offers a social history f 20th-century America. There's also a vast ollection of vehicles, furnishings, fashions, phemera and Americana, everything from e first neon-trimmed McDonald's arch to complete diner from the mid-1940s.

Adjacent Greenfield Village features xtant buildings shipped in from all over the ountry, reconstructed and restored in this utdoor museum. They include Thomas dison's laboratory from Menlo Park, Henry ord's birthplace and the Wright brothers' ycle workshop. Most of the buildings ontain displays and exhibits and are staffed y guides in period costume. By the time you ad this, the largest IMAX theater in the ate should be open; the $15 million facility ill be the only one in Michigan capable of rojecting both two- and three-dimensional lms. In 1999 the excellent Michigan Café pened. It has a menu devoted to the cuisine nd ingredients of Michigan; Dearborn's ummus is first on the list.

Hours are 9 am to 5 pm daily, though reenfield Village buildings shut tight nuary through April. Entry to either the illage or the museum costs $13; for $22, ou can get a combination ticket good for vo days. Seriously consider the two-day cket. This is one of the finest museum omplexes in the country and spending nything short of a full day here will result a rush job.

Other Car Sights

But wait, you're just getting started on the car thing. Adjacent to the Henry Ford Museum, the **Automotive Hall of Fame** (☎ 313-240-4000) highlights every major contributor to the culture of cars, and that's a lot of people. Rotating exhibits are featured along with hands-on activities. Hours are 10 am to 5 pm daily; it's closed Monday, November 1 through late May.

Across the street from the museum and village at 1151 Village Rd – and within sight of the Ford Proving Grounds – is the gearhead's delight, **Spirit of Ford**, an interactive technology education center that takes you behind the scenes of making a Ford car, from research and design right through manufacturing and testing. Engineering kiosks allow you to design your own car; then you can strap in and take a ride on a test vehicle simulator. You definitely don't need to be a kid to enjoy this museum. Hours are 9 am to 5 pm daily; $9/7 adults/children.

If you're not yet exhausted, **Henry Ford Estate-Fair Lane** (☎ 313-593-5590) on the campus of the University of Michigan at Dearborn, off Evergreen St, is a National Historic Landmark. Eight cars including Ford's first vehicle, the quadricycle, are on display in the garage. Just as intriguing is the power plant, designed by Ford and Thomas Edison, that allowed the estate to produce its own power. Trails wind through gardens and extensive grounds. Tours depart hourly 10 am to 3 pm Monday to Saturday and every half-hour 1 to 4:30 pm Sunday; $6. Take to just the trails for $2.

After spending all day immersing yourself in the car culture of the USA, head to the **Ford Wyoming Drive-In** (☎ 313-846-6910) for the night. This is the largest drive-in theater in the Midwest, featuring eight screens showing eight different films and attracting more than 2000 cars and some 6000 moviegoers on the weekend. This is US car culture at its finest. Tickets are $3 per adult. From I-94 in Dearborn, take exit 210 and head north on Wyoming Ave to reach the drive-in.

Places to Stay & Eat

No shortage of options exists here, though most aren't cheap. The ***Village Inn** (☎ 313-565-8511, 21725 Michigan Ave)* is centrally located, well-kept and fairly cheap at $42/45 for a large single/double. Luxury is found at the ***Dearborn Inn-A Marriott Hotel** (☎ 313-271-2700, 20301 Oakwood Blvd)*, with spacious rooms and a host of elegant cottages on a large wooded estate. Rates are $165/175 single/double in summer.

Michigan Ave is lined with Middle Eastern restaurants and it's hard to recommend one since they're all so good. The Lebanese ***La Shish** (22059 Michigan Ave)* is one of the local faves (main courses from $8).

Getting There & Away

Coming from Detroit, Amtrak makes a stop in Dearborn on the way to Chicago; the train station is within walking distance of the Henry Ford Museum and Greenfield Village. SMART buses also serve the town (see Detroit's Getting Around section).

ANN ARBOR

Trendy Ann Arbor is home to the University of Michigan, the 'Harvard of the Midwest,' top 10 in virtually every academic field (and athletic competition). College athletics fans know the city well. Home to the maize-and-blue enthused, otherwise known as Michigan Wolverines fans, a football game on a Saturday afternoon here will not soon be forgotten. Ann Arbor ('A-squared' in local parlance) is an attractive, vibrant community that oozes a particular free spirit; in the Midwest it's similar to Madison, Wisconsin, as both are islands known for their tolerance of somewhat off-center culture.

Information

The Ann Arbor Convention & Visitors Bureau (☎ 800-888-9487, www.annarbor.org) is at 120 W Huron St, next to the bus station. Call ☎ 734-763-4636 for University of Michigan information; alternately, stop by the main information desk on the 1st floor of the Michigan Union, 530 S State St, or the desk in the lobby of Pierpont Commons, 2101 Bonisteel Blvd.

There are loads of free newspapers de-tailing local nightlife. *Current* is a dense fre monthly magazine that provides excellen listings for all types of entertainment. Th student paper, the *Michigan Daily*, also ha events listings; it's available for free in heap all over campus.

For books, try Shaman Drum Booksho (☎ 734-662-7407), 311 S State St, or Jour neys International (☎ 734-665-4407), 10 April Drive, suite 3.The flagship Border store (from which the chain grew) is at 61 E Liberty St.

University of Michigan

The university provides many of the town' top attractions, including the fine **Kelse Museum of Archaeology** (☎ 734-764-9304 434 S State St, with nearly 100,000 artifact from ancient Egypt, Greece and Rom Hours are 9 am to 4 pm weekdays, 1 to 4 pn weekends; free.

The **University of Michigan Museum o Art** (☎ 734-764-0395) is at 525 S State St an has galleries with artwork from Africa, Chin Japan, and 20th-century America, along wit European art from the 15th through 19t centuries. There is also a room of works o paper. Hours are 10 am to 5 pm Tuesday t Saturday, noon to 5 pm Sunday; free.

The **Ruthven Exhibit Museum of Natura History** (☎ 734-764-0478), 1109 Geddes Av is home to the most popular dinosaur col lection in Michigan. It also has exhibits o Native Americans in Michigan, state fauna and planetarium shows every Saturday an Sunday. Hours are 9 am to 5 pm Monday t Saturday, noon to 5 pm Sunday. Admissio is free; planetarium shows cost $3/2 adult children.

East of here, on Geddes Ave, is the beau tiful and free **Nichols Arboretum**, with nic gardens and nature trails that wind down t the Huron River. Plantheads also like th university's **Botanical Gardens** (☎ 734-998 7061), 1800 N Dixboro Rd, with an indoo conservatory of exotics and marked natur trails. It's open daily.

Music fans will enjoy the **Stearn Musical Collection** (☎ 734-764-4389), 110 Bates Drive, which displays more tha

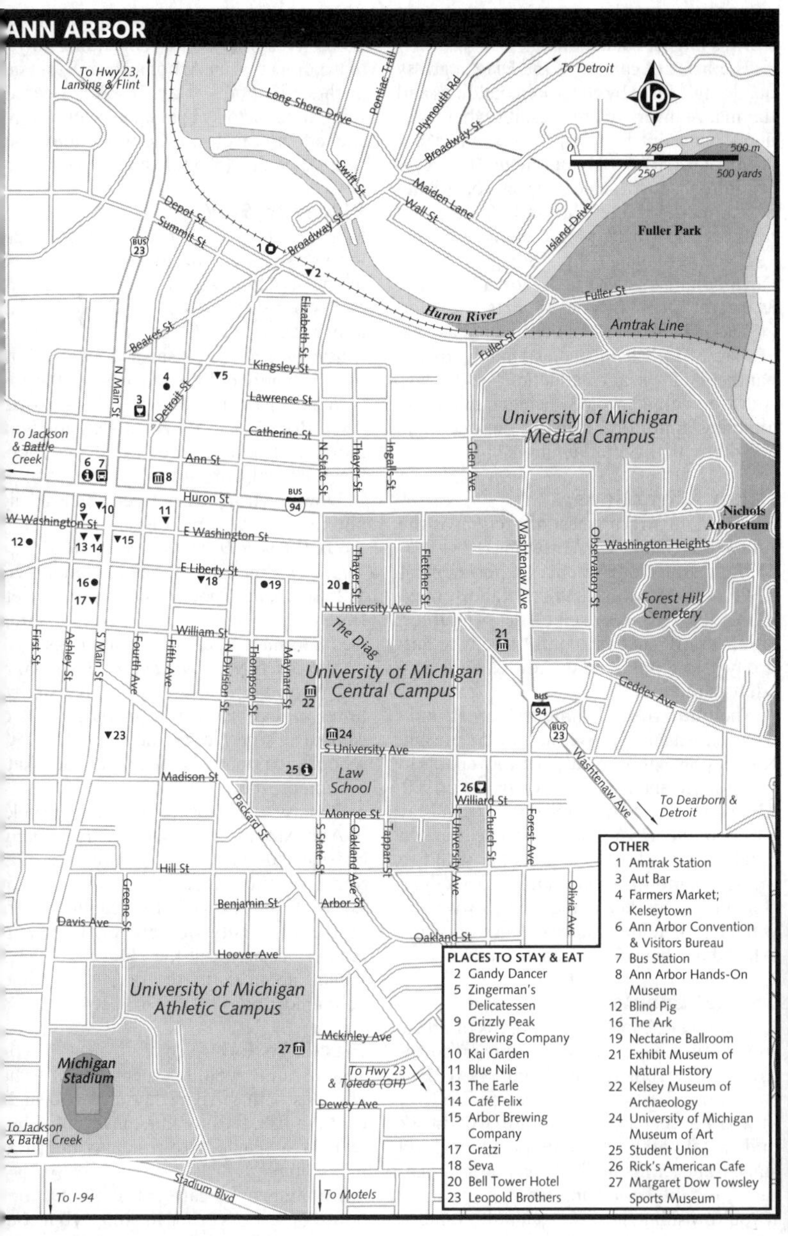
ANN ARBOR
To Hwy 23, Lansing & Flint
To Detroit
To Jackson & Battle Creek
To Dearborn & Detroit
To Hwy 23 & Toledo (OH)
To Jackson & Battle Creek
To I-94
To Motels
Long Shore Drive
Pontiac Trail
Plymouth Rd
Broadway St
Swift St
Maiden Lane
Wall St
Island Drive
Depot St
Summit St
Fuller Park
Fuller St
Huron River
Amtrak Line
Beakes St
Kingsley St
Lawrence St
Catherine St
Ann St
Huron St
W Washington St
E Washington St
E Liberty St
William St
N University Ave
The Diag
Elizabeth St
N State St
Thayer St
Ingalls St
Glen Ave
Washtenaw Ave
Observatory St
Fletcher St
Washington Heights
Nichols Arboretum
Forest Hill Cemetery
University of Michigan Medical Campus
University of Michigan Central Campus
Law School
S University Ave
Willard St
Monroe St
Geddes Ave
N Main St
Detroit St
First St
Ashley St
S Main St
Fourth Ave
Fifth Ave
N Division St
Thompson St
Maynard St
Madison St
Packard St
S State St
Oakland Ave
Tappan St
E University Ave
Church St
Forest Ave
Olivia Ave
Hill St
Greene St
Benjamin St
Arbor St
Davis Ave
Oakland St
Hoover Ave
University of Michigan Athletic Campus
Michigan Stadium
Mckinley Ave
Dewey Ave
Stadium Blvd
0 250 500 m
0 250 500 yards
PLACES TO STAY & EAT
2 Gandy Dancer
5 Zingerman's Delicatessen
9 Grizzly Peak Brewing Company
10 Kai Garden
11 Blue Nile
13 The Earle
14 Café Felix
15 Arbor Brewing Company
17 Gratzi
18 Seva
20 Bell Tower Hotel
23 Leopold Brothers
OTHER
1 Amtrak Station
3 Aut Bar
4 Farmers Market; Kelseytown
6 Ann Arbor Convention & Visitors Bureau
7 Bus Station
8 Ann Arbor Hands-On Museum
12 Blind Pig
16 The Ark
19 Nectarine Ballroom
21 Exhibit Museum of Natural History
22 Kelsey Museum of Archaeology
24 University of Michigan Museum of Art
25 Student Union
26 Rick's American Cafe
27 Margaret Dow Towsley Sports Museum

2000 musical instruments – one of the world's largest collections.

The heart of campus is the **Diag**, a grassy quadrangle lined by classroom buildings and the main university libraries; it's where students hang out between classes, and it's a good place to cool your heels. The **Law School**, on a quadrangle of its own on S State St, was modeled after England's Oxford and features a spectacular high-ceilinged library.

If you're making the pilgrimage to Michigan Stadium, that Mecca of football fans, the **Margaret Dow Towsley Sports Museum** (☎ 734-747-2583), east of the stadium at 1000 S State St in Schembechler Hall, holds the pantheon of Michigan athletics. The displays show the dominance of Michigan in college athletics. Hours are 11 am to 5 pm weekdays and on football Saturdays; free.

Other Attractions

One of Ann Arbor's best attractions is the **Ann Arbor Hands-On Museum** (☎ 734-995-5437), a four-floor science experiment at 220 E Ann St. More than 250 hands-on exhibits let kids test scientific principles. Hours are 10 am to 5:30 pm Tuesday to Saturday, 1 to 5 pm Sunday. Admission is $6/4 adults/children.

The **Ann Arbor Farmers Market**, held between 4th and 5th Aves and Catherine and Kingsley Sts, has been the place for vendors to sell produce and handmade crafts since 1900. It's open Wednesday and Saturday from May 1 to November, Saturday only thereafter. On Sunday there's usually a crafts fair with live music, demonstrations and storytelling. Behind the market is the Kerrytown mall, with many boutiques, and a greengrocers' and fish and butcher counters on its 1st floor.

Special Events

In late July of each year, hundreds of artists from around the country converge on downtown Ann Arbor for the Summer Art Fair (☎ 734-662-3382). Visitors swarm in to look at and buy paintings, sculpture, woodwork and metalwork, and vendors set up food stands and crafts stalls. Live music is featured, too. Make lodging reservations early if you're visiting the city around this time.

Another annual event (famed or infa mous across the country, depending on you viewpoint) is Ann Arbor's Hash Bash, hel each April Fools' Day. It takes over th Diag at noon; folks light up in celebration c the city's smack-on-the-wrist marijuan possession fine ($25 for small amounts).

Places to Stay

Most budget (that's a relative term) lodgin is found south of downtown along S State S at the junction with I-94. Trusty ***Motel*** *(☎ 734-665-9900, 3764 S State St)*, south of th interstate, is somewhat more expensive tha it usually is at $45/50 single/double, but th price is typical of local lodging. Northeast c the interstate, ***StudioPLUS*** *(☎ 734-997-762 3265 Boardwalk St)* is an extended-sta motel with kitchenettes in all the room Singles/doubles are $60.

Downtown are a half dozen hotels, all hig mid-range or top end. Elegant rooms are a the ***Bell Tower Hotel*** *(☎ 734-769-3010, 300 Thayer St)* on campus. Singles/doubles co $125/135. Ann Arbor also has plenty of prett B&Bs; the Convention & Visitors Burea (see Information) can give you listings.

The ***Michigan League*** *(☎ 734-764-317 911 N University Ave)* is a university-ru hotel in a pretty brick building right o campus; it's perfect for anyone visiting th school and popular among academics. Rate are comparable to the Bell Tower's.

It's easy to find low-priced summer suble in Ann Arbor – check the *Michigan Daily* classified ads and bulletin boards on campu Some of the cheapest are in fraternit houses. If you're enrolled at a summer cours at the university or here on universit related business, call the Housing Office t inquire about dormitory or Student Unio accommodations (☎ 734-763-3164).

Places to Eat

Just as one would expect, Ann Arbo abounds with great restaurants and nigh clubs. In fact, the city's first tavern was bui in 1824, a year before residents built the first school.

Looking for a latte? There's a coffee house on every corner in Ann Arbor. ***Ca*** *elix*, at the corner of Main and Washington ts, is great. Its cathedral ceilings and warm oods give it a comfortable air. The coffee's xcellent and there's a relatively inexpen-ve menu of omelettes, soups, and sand-iches (from $4).

Zingerman's Delicatessen *(422 Detroit t)* is often regarded as one of the finest elis in the Midwest. For eclectic vegetarian re (vegan available), go directly to ***Seva*** *314 E Liberty St)*, heavy on Southwestern nd Mexican. There are excellent daily nch specials for around $5.

Kai Garden *(116 S Main St)* has excel-nt (and health-conscious) pan-China fare, long with some creative Taiwanese dishes. few vegetarian items are found as well rom $6). Enjoy Ethiopian cuisine (from 8) at ***The Blue Nile*** *(221 E Washington)*.

The 300 block of Main St has a number f casual places with trendier – and ricier – fare, heavy on Italian cuisine. In an ld theater, ***Gratzi*** *(☎ 734-663-5555, 326 S lain St)* has good Italian food and a great tmosphere (entrées from $10). Two blocks orth, then west on Washington, is ***The arle*** *(☎ 734-994-0211, 121 W Washington t)*, featuring provincial French and Italian uisine (entrées from $15) and one of lichigan's best wine lists. Live jazz is ffered regularly.

The ***Gandy Dancer*** *(☎ 734-769-0592, 401 epot)*, one of Ann Arbor's most legendary ateries, is housed in the 1886 Michigan entral Railroad station (Amtraks still under past while you eat) and retains the legance of the period. It's famous for fresh eafood and steaks; the enormous Sunday runch is fabulous.

ntertainment

ock, blues, and rhythm and blues fans have host of venues to choose from. ***Rick's merican Cafe*** *(611 Church St)* is the largest lub, and it's always packed. The ***Blind Pig*** *208 S 1st St)* has lots of blues and reggae. he most eclectic music in town is at ***The Ark*** *316 S Main St)*, where you simply never now what kind of music will be on tap. The ***lectarine Ballroom*** *(510 E Liberty St)* is the ost centrally located dance club.

Live music and handcrafted beer are found at the ***Arbor Brewing Co*** *(300 Detroit St)* (food from $6). A block away at 120 W Washington St, ***Grizzly Peak Brewing Company*** has more pub grub at similar prices. An only-in-Ann-Arbor entry is ***Leopold Brothers*** *(529 S Main St)*, which, when opened in late 1999 or early 2000, was to be the first 'environmentally sustainable' brewery, making organic German-style beers. A greenhouse will also be on site. The ***Del Rio*** *(122 W Washington St)* is a cozy locals' pub, brick-walled, trimmed with old leaded windowpanes and very dark inside. It has Mexican snacks in addition to lots of brews on tap.

Ann Arbor is a center of Midwestern gay and lesbian life. One key local nightlife spot for the scene is the ***Aut Bar***, at 4th and Catherine Sts, which hosts a leather party on the last Friday of each month. It's mostly a guys' bar, but gay women visit, too. The Nectarine (see above) also draws lots of gay patrons.

Restored to the grandeur of its first years, the landmark ***Michigan Theater*** *(603 E Liberty St)* is both a cinema (showing classic and art-house films) and a live-music venue. Its calendar hops year-round.

For information on the campus' jammed calendar of events – concerts, plays, read-ings, etc, many low-cost or free – contact the Major Events Office (☎ 734-9358) or visit it in room No 3401 of the Student Union.

Spectator Sports

Michigan athletics are popular. Getting a football ticket isn't realistic unless you're lucky enough to catch a student selling a ticket. Scalpers may well ask $100 per ticket for important football games. But Michigan has highly ranked teams in most men's and women's sports, and tickets for other events may be available from the university ticket office (☎ 734-764-0247). The stadium itself is at the corner of Main and Stadium Sts.

Getting There & Around

Amtrak (☎ 734-994-4906) stops at 325 Depot St in Ann Arbor between Chicago and Detroit; to Chicago ($41) takes four hours.

Michigan vs OSU

Of all college football rivalries, Michigan versus Ohio State is a step above any other, a ferocious rivalry matching any alumni-fueled fury at which much more than victory is riding on the game. It is not an exaggeration to say that if a coach goes 9–3 at one of these schools, his job is in jeopardy; most other schools would have celebratory fits. And it's not uncommon for a coach to be on the hot seat just for losing to that bitter arch enemy. Some have traced this enmity, somewhat tongue-in-cheek, back as far as the 'Toledo War' of 1835–36 (see Toledo in the Northern Ohio chapter) – what else could explain such martial fervor?

Michigan and Ohio State have for most of modern memory been the two top dogs in the toughest conference in college football, the Big 10. (Penn State, another powerhouse, is excluded since they joined the Big 10 only in the last decade.) In fact, from 1968 till the mid-'90s, when parity to be seen, pretty much the only Big 10 game that was nationally anticipated during the September–November schedule was Michigan vs OSU, since it would likely decide the Big 10 championship, a trip to the Rose Bowl (the 'granddaddy of all bowl games') and, more than once, a national championship. Things reached their peak beginning in 1969 when Michigan hired Bo Schembechler to go against his old coach, Woody Hayes, the latter still something of a deity in Columbus. For the next seven years one or the other would take the Big 10 title, and only in 1971 did they not finish one–two. Considering the talent turnover in college athletics, this is amazing. Since 1935, the Michigan versus OSU game decided the Big 10 crown no fewer than 32 times, and 18 times the game pitted No 1 versus No 2 in the national rankings. Ohio State has had a particularly bad luck streak in the '90s, going 1–7–1 against Michigan (don't tell Buckeye fans I told you...), including a disastrous defeat in 1995, when OSU was ranked No 2. A couple of years later, Ohio State had a national crown in its sights, was upset by Michigan State at home and, still with a shot at redemption and a Rose Bowl trip against Michigan, again was sent packing. (Then again, OSU fans say, look at their '90s record against Michigan's powerhouse baseball team.)

You'll not soon experience anything like the walk to Michigan Stadium, listening to 10,000 boom boxes pumping out 'Hail to the Victors.' Nor, for that matter, will you soon forget the vision of 110,000 people pumping their fist on every 'victory' in the song during the game or of one half of the stadium shouting 'Go!' while the other thunders 'Blue!' in response. The venerable old place actually *creaks*.

Columbus, Ohio, has its own traditions and football-oriented sights. Visit Ohio Stadium, the first horseshoe-shaped football stadium in the US. It was actually built with student dormitory rooms into its west side. Also stop by the nearby Buckeye Grove, where a tree is planted for every Ohio State All-American player. The week before the match against Michigan, thousands attend a senior class–only last tackling practice called Senior Tackle; local gendarmes have curtailed another tradition of toilet-papering the campus the Thursday night prior to the game. At 5 am the day of the game, Columbus pubs on High Street open for their amazing 'Kegs and Eggs' meals and it's here that student fervor can become a bit much for non-sports fans. The OSU band is among the country's best and the halftime show's dotting of the 'i' by a sousaphone player – a ceremony honoring a dedicated senior – akin to winning an Academy Award.

If you go to the game, expect to start bidding at $100 from a ticket scalper if you're lucky to find one available (be careful – counterfeiting has been a plague). The best place to watch the game on TV in Columbus is in front of the Holiday Inn near the stadium; Heineygate is a huge tailgate party with an enormous TV. In Ann Arbor, try Touchdown Cafe at 1220 S University Ave or Rick's American Cafe at 611 Church St.

The bus station (☎ 734-662-5511) is at 116 Huron St. Buses go to Detroit ($9, 1 to ½ hours) and Toledo ($19, 3 hours).

The Ann Arbor Transportation Authority ATA; ☎ 734-996-0400) is located at 331 S h St, where you can get maps and schedes. It has been voted the number-one midze transit authority in the US. Fares are ¢ for adult, 35¢ for kids.

LINT

is town is a historic stop for labor-history iffs and anyone who sympathizes with the ight of the workers. During the Depression, December of 1936, workers at a Flint eneral Motors plant began a sit-in strike to rce management to recognize their right to ganize. This action was contagious, inspiring orkers at several area plants to stage sit-ins. January, GM called in the police, who, med with tear gas, stormed the factories. hirteen workers were wounded in this ent, know as the Battle of the Running ulls, and Michigan Governor Murphy called the National Guard – to protect the orkers from the police. With the support of esident Roosevelt, Murphy forced GM and her auto companies to officially recognize e United Auto Workers and come to the rgaining table. By this time – February 11, 37 – workers who had started the original strike had been in the plant for almost a month and a half. As singer Billy Bragg says, 'There is power in a union.'

In more recent times, a recession and declining auto sales in the 1980s forced massive layoffs in Flint's local auto plants. The city received dubious national attention when native son and irreverent gadfly Michael Moore made his first documentary film *Roger and Me* about the economic swoon. Funny but disquieting, it followed Moore in his quixotic attempt to ask the chairman of General Motors a few simple questions. The movie studio financing the film wanted to host the premiere in Flint but, alas, all the movie theaters had closed. Flint is making a comeback, however, and is worth a stop if only for the great Sloan Museum detailing the area's rich automotive history (see below).

The Flint Area Convention & Visitors Bureau (☎ 810-232-8900) is at 519 S Saginaw St. Its Web site is www.flint.org.

Things to See & Do

The excellent **Sloan Museum** (☎ 810-760-1169), 1221 E Kearsley St, has a lengthy walk-through exhibit that examines in great detail the rise of Flint as a powerful automobile manufacturing center. It gives the good with the bad and is as educational as any museum piece in the state. Hours are 10 am to 5 pm weekdays, noon to 5 pm Sunday; $4/3 adults/children.

The United Auto Workers grew out of labor organizing in Flint.

The **Flint Cultural Center**, a campus of six separate museums or performance centers located east of the downtown and I-475 and I-69 spur, definitely warrants a stop. The Institute of Arts (☎ 810-234-1695), 1120 E Kearsley St, has a collection of over 6500 pieces; exhibits rotate regularly. Hours are 10 am to 5 pm Tuesday to Saturday, noon to 5 pm Sunday; free. Good for families is the Longway Planetarium (☎ 810-760-1181), 1310 E Kearsley St, with its daily star shows and Friday and Saturday laser light shows. Hours are 9 am to 4 pm weekdays, noon to 4 pm weekends. Admission is $6 though some weekends the displays are free.

Northeast of town at exit 13 off I-475, the **Genesee Recreation Area** (☎ 810-736-7100) has numerous bike trails, beaches, a campground and picnic areas. Admission is free. Also here is the Crossroads Village, a restored late 1860s village with over 30 reconstructed buildings. On the grounds are a carousel, Ferris wheel, and hay and boat rides. Most popular are the hour-long rides along the Huckleberry Railroad, pulled by an old steam engine. Hours are 10 am to 5 pm weekdays, 11 am to 6 pm weekends; $9/6 adults/children.

Places to Stay & Eat

There are budget places west of town off I-75 at the junction with Miller Rd, including a ***Motel 6*** *(☎ 810-767-7100, 2324 Austin Pkwy)* with singles/doubles for $40/44. You've got two pervasive food options in Flint: coneys and burgers. Coneys, so loved in Detroit, may be even more so in Flint. You'll find no fewer than a dozen places serving the special sausage, including the four Flint locations of ***Angelo's Coney Island & Grill*** *(1816 Davison Rd)*. Many coney places are open 24 hours. Then there's one of the most famous burger places in Southern Michigan – ***Bill Thomas' Halo Burger*** *(800 S Saginaw St)*, a local fixture since the 1920s.

Getting There & Away

The Flint Bus Terminal (☎ 810-232-1114) is at 615 Harrison St; to Oscoda, a town on Lake Huron, takes three hours and costs $17. Amtrak (☎ 810-234-2659) is at 1407 S Port St. The train to Port Huron takes a bit more than an hour and costs $12.

CLD Transport Systems (☎ 810-659-7436) runs shuttles to the Lansing and Detroit airports. Call for a reservation.

LANSING

• pop 127,000

In 1847, when Lansing was chosen as Michigan's state capital, it was little more than a wilderness hamlet. In the 20th century, as the home of GM's Oldsmobile division, Lansing suffered through the same automotive hard times in the 1980s as did Detroit and Flint. But due to its status as the seat of state government, the capital city has done a better job of reviving itself and now makes for an interesting stop for visitors. Adjacent East Lansing is a college town, home to Michigan State University.

Information

The Greater Lansing Convention and Visitors Bureau (☎ 517-487-6800, 888-252-674[illegible], www.lansing.org) is north of downtown, off Hwy 27 at 1223 Turner St. It's a bit tricky to find.

East Lansing Sights

A classic college town, East Lansing is home to MSU, the arch rival of Ann Arbor's University of Michigan. It's a far more interesting campus to visit, including the **Kresge Art Museum** (☎ 517-355-7631), at Auditorium and Physics Rds, which displays artwork from every continent as far back as 500[illegible] years. Hours are 9:30 am to 4:30 pm Monday to Wednesday and Friday, noon to 8 pm Thursday, and 1 to 4 pm weekends.

The natural and historic displays at the **MSU Museum** (☎ 517-355-2370), near Beaumont Tower, have an emphasis on the Great Lakes but there are many exhibits on world cultures. And, of course, dinosaurs. Hours are 9 am to 5 pm weekdays, 10 am to 5 pm Saturday, noon to 5 pm Sunday.

The **MSU Children's Garden** (☎ 517-35[illegible]-6692) is one of two gardens along Bogue St and one of three on campus. This one is behind the Plant and Soil Science Building. It's fully accessible and has a tree house built out of tree limbs, a garden house and theme gardens. At the corner of Bogue St and Service Rd are the **MSU Horticulture Gardens**. Adjacent to the MSU main library the **WJ Beal Botanical Gardens** is the oldest rden of its type in the US, with more than 00 species.

Michigan State takes athletics seriously, o. The Spartans won the men's basketball tional championship for the second time in e 1999–2000 season and are perennially nked in the top twenty nationally in football and ice hockey. The football crowds are rticularly boisterous; in fact, too boisterous times – MSU students have been known riot over simple things like limiting serving urs in bars. Tickets (at least for decent ats) are generally scarce for football and sketball, depending on the quality of the ponent. For ticket availability, contact the SU athletic ticket office (☎ 517-355-1610).

All museums and gardens are free and cated on the MSU campus, south of Grand ver Ave. East Lansing, the town proper, is the north side of Grand River Ave.

nsing Sights

ee tours are offered every half hour 10 am 4 pm Monday to Saturday at the **State pitol Building** (☎ 517-373-2353), which minates the downtown area at the head Michigan Ave.

Far more interesting and also free is the arby **Michigan Historical Museum** 517-373-3559), at 712 W Allegan. This te museum features 26 permanent galies, including a replica UP copper mine at you can walk through, a 1920s street ene and a three-story relief map of the te. Hours are 9 am to 5 pm weekdays, 1 to m weekends; free.

East of the Capitol along Museum Drive a number of attractions. See the first dsmobile and other vintage cars at the **RE ds Transportation Museum** (☎ 517-372-22), overlooking the Grand River just off chigan Ave. Hours are 10 am to 5 pm nday to Saturday, noon to 5 pm Sunday;

Nearby is the **Michigan Museum of Surying** (☎ 517-484-6605), the only surveying seum in the US. It's open 8 am to noon d 1 to 5 pm weekdays; free. Also nearby a renovated old warehouse is the **Impresn 5 Science Center** (☎ 517-485-8116), a nds-on science education museum. Hours are 10 am to 5 pm Monday to Saturday, noon to 5 pm Sunday; $5/3 adults/children.

Linking downtown Lansing with MSU is Lansing's **River Trail**, which extends 7 miles along the shores of Michigan's longest river, the Grand. The paved path, popular with cyclists, joggers and in-line skaters, links a number of attractions, including a children's museum, zoo and salmon ladder.

A rare opportunity to see a car being built up close is found at the **Lansing Auto Assembly Plant** (☎ 517-885-9676), off the Saginaw Hwy at Stanley St. This is the home of the Pontiac Grand Am, Buick Skylark and Chevrolet Cavalier, among others. Reservations are necessary.

Places to Stay

The closest campground is found off US 127/ I-496 at Jolly Rd. The ***Lansing Cottonwood Campground*** *(☎ 517-393-3200, 5339 S Aurelius Rd)* is mostly an RV place, but they'll take tents ($14). Close to here, along Cedar St, exit 104 off I-96, is a grouping of motels, including ***Super 8*** *(☎ 517-393-8008, 910 American Rd)*, with singles/doubles from $40.

At the junction of Hwy 43 and I-69 west of town is another grouping of mostly midrange chain places, but also a ***Motel 6*** *(☎ 517-321-1444, 7326 W Saginaw Hwy)*, with singles/doubles for $40/44.

Downtown, the most centrally located is the ***Radisson Hotel*** *(☎ 517-482-0188, 111 N Grand Ave)*, within shouting distance of the Capitol. It's got an indoor pool, sauna, whirlpool and exercise room. Singles/ doubles are $100.

In East Lansing nothing's inexpensive. ***Travelodge*** *(☎ 517-337-1621, 2736 E Grand River Ave)* has been known to dip as low as $45 for a single/double, but it's usually higher.

Places to Eat

Lansing The downtown area is full of nondescript Greek restaurants; most of the city's best restaurants are clustered around the head of Michigan Ave. One that stands out is ***Parthenon*** *(☎ 517-484-0573, 227 S Washington Square)*, which has great Greek food and more capitol lawyers and bureaucrats in it than one could imagine (main dishes from $8). If you've got a picky family, head for ***Clara's*** *(637 E Michigan Ave)*, a casual place in a Victorian train depot. Its dense, 16-page menu of American fare has something for everybody (main dishes from $6).

East Lansing E Grand River Ave is a good place to start for eating or imbibing. ***Healthy Foods of India*** *(547½ E Grand River Ave)* has vegetarian and non-vegetarian curries (from $6). ***Michaelangelo's*** *(213 E Grand River Ave)* has southern Italian cuisine with lots of veggie options (from $8). If there is an East Lansing landmark, it's ***Beggar's Banquet*** *(☎ 517-351-4540, 218 Abbott Rd)*, a casually upscale place decorated by local artists and full of people trying to be seen (entrées from $8).

Getting There & Away

The Amtrak depot is just west of the football stadium at 1240 Harrison Rd in East Lansing. One train a day goes to Chicago ($37, 3½ hours) or Port Huron.

The bus station (☎ 517-332-2569) is at 420 S Grand Ave in Lansing, in the CATA terminal (see below); Lansing's depot (☎ 517-482-0673) is at 310 W Grand River. Lots of buses depart for Ann Arbor ($13, 1½ hours), Battle Creek ($8, 1 hour) and other destinations.

Getting Around

Capital Area Transportation Authority (CATA; ☎ 517-394-1000) has excellent coverage between Lansing and the MSU campus on lots of buses. Their main center is at the corner of S Grand Ave and Lenawee St, four blocks southeast of the Capitol. CATA's basic fare is $1; 25¢ with a valid college ID. Route 20 links Amtrak to MSU's main highlights. A number of routes run between Lansing and East Lansing; the primary one is route 1X, which starts at the transportation center. There's also a SafeRide program, offering rides throughout East Lansing on weekend evenings from midnight to 3 am.

GRAND RAPIDS

• pop 190,000

The second-largest city in Michigan, Gra Rapids is best known for office-furnitu manufacturing, a conservative Dutch Refor attitude and the fact that it's only 30 mil from Lake Michigan's Gold Coast. Dow town Grand Rapids is a bustling, lively ar split by the Grand River – thus the cit name. It's home to two outstanding museun both on the river's west bank, and a diver selection of restaurants and nightlife.

Information

Downtown, the Grand Rapids Visitor Infc mation Center (☎ 800-678-9859, www.vi grandrapids.org) is at 134 Monroe Ma catercorner from the Amway Grand Pla Hotel.

Four Friends Coffee House (☎ 616-45 5356) is at 136 Monroe Center and h email access.

On-the-Town is an outstanding (a dense) free monthly arts, culture and ent tainment monthly. Less useful, *Music Rev* is a free weekly distributed throughout W Michigan.

Things to See & Do

The **Gerald R Ford Museum** (☎ 616-45 9263), on the north side of Pearl St, is de cated to the country's only Michigand president, who was also the USA's or nonelected president. Ford stepped into t Oval Office after Richard Nixon and vice president, Spiro Agnew, resigned in d grace. It's an intriguing period in US histc and the museum does an excellent job covering it. Hours are 9 am to 5 pm dai $3/free adults/children.

Nearby on Pearl St is the striking **V Andel Museum Center** (☎ 616-456-396 dedicated mostly to the history of Gra Rapids and west Michigan, though the fi thing you'll notice is an enormous finba whale skeleton. There are good exhibits the Native Americans of Michigan. Ki can ride an operational carousel (50 Hours are 9 am to 5 pm daily; $5/2 adu children.

If you're not museumed out, the **Grand apids Art Museum** (☎ 616-831-1000), 155 ivision St N, has a 6000-piece collection ostly emphasizing 19th- and 20th-century t. There are usually good traveling exbits. Hours are 11 am to 6 pm Tuesday to ınday; $3/1.

The *Grand Lady* (☎ 616-457-4837) is a ern-wheel riverboat that makes sighteing tours ($10) along the Grand River eekends at 1:45 pm June through Septemer. A whole list of lunch and dinner cruises also offered.

pecial Events

late August, the city pays tribute to Michan's main industry with the Grand Rapids rand Prix (☎ 616-336-7749). They close own half the city streets for it and you can el the asphalt rumble from a half-mile vay as the cars roar by.

Two and a half hours north of Grand apids, Hart hosts the annual Michigan 'omyn's Music Festival (☎ 231-757-4766) August. The festival is the largest lesbian usic festival in the country.

laces to Stay

or camping, head south 15 miles on US 131 d follow the signs to ***Yankee Springs ecreation Area*** *(☎ 616-795-9081)*, which so features the most popular mountainking trails on the west side of the state. Afrdable motels, along 28th St on the south de of the city, include ***Econo Lodge*** *(☎ 616-2-2131, 5175 28th St SE)* and ***Motel 6*** *616-957-3511, 3524 28th St SE)*, both of hich have singles/doubles from around $35.

Downtown Grand Rapids has some good id-range options. The ***Days Inn*** *(☎ 616-5-7611, 310 Pearl St)* has a restaurant, unge and exercise room. Singles/doubles art at $60. A number of lovely B&Bs are und in the Heritage Hill District, includg the ***Peaches B&B*** *(☎ 616-454-8000, 29 ay St SE)*, a huge Georgian with a weight om. Rates are $88 single/double.

The ***Amway Grand Plaza*** *(☎ 616-774-00, 800-253-3590, 187 Monroe Ave)* is an egant hotel, a delicate synthesis of classic and modern. Two restaurants on site are well regarded. If you've got the money, this is the place to stay. Singles/doubles are $99.

Places to Eat

At night, head to ***Grand Rapids Brewing Company*** *(3689 28th St SE)*, one of a half dozen brew pub-restaurants in Grand Rapids, with a diverse menu (items from $7). Perhaps the most popular eating and nightlife option is the ***B O B*** (see Entertainment, below).

Gaia *(209 Diamond St SE)* is near downtown and is famous for its coffee and oversize fresh-baked cookies. Modest vegetarian selections are offered ($4 and up). The Italian-with-French-undertones ***Bistro Bella Vista*** *(44 Grandville Ave SW)* has creative entrées (from $5) and good service.

The ***Rhythm Kitchen Cafe*** *(125 Ottawa Ave NW)* starts with Cajun food, then lets itself go with lots of other options (items from $7), along with a full slate of blues acts.

Entertainment

B O B *(20 Monroe Ave NW)* is the 'Big Old Building' and has three floors of everything imaginable – folk, rock, swing dancing, comedy, billiards and five restaurants. Clubs come and go quickly, but ***Intersection Lounge*** *(1520 Wealthy St SE)* in Eastown has been around the longest. It has local nobodies followed up by almost-major players from every musical genre.

DeVos Hall (☎ 616-742-6600) at Monroe and Lyon Sts is home to the Grand Rapids Ballet, Grand Rapids Symphony, Opera Grand Rapids and the Broadway Theatre Guild.

Getting There & Around

The Kent County International Airport (☎ 616-336-4500) is served by nine commuter airlines with direct flights to a dozen Midwestern cities and Toronto.

The Amtrak depot (☎ 800-872-7245) is at the corner of Market and Wealthy Sts, southwest of downtown and near the river. Daily trains to Chicago ($33) depart at 7:45 am and take three hours.

The bus station (☎ 616-456-1700) is at 190 Wealthy St SW, one block east of the Amtrak depot. Regular buses head to Detroit ($23; 3½ hours) and Kalamazoo ($8; 1 hour).

Daily from 11 am to 3 pm, the local bus service's free *DASH* bus runs every three minutes along a loop of Monroe and Ottawa Aves. Route 15 ($1.25) serves the airport.

JACKSON

Thirty miles south of Lansing on US 127, Jackson has a huge, popular park, **Cascades at Sparks Foundation County Park**, southwest of the city limits; it's got a long waterfall and six fountains discharging water in a variety of patterns. Most people stop off at the **Michigan Space and Science Center** (☎ 517-787-4425) on the grounds of Jackson Community College, 2111 Emmons Rd, southeast of town. This impressive museum houses a real Apollo 9 lunar module, a Gemini capsule and lots of memorabilia from space flights. Some exhibits are hands-on; you can climb into one space capsule. A theater shows films on space exploration. Hours are 10 am to 5 pm Tuesday to Saturday, noon to 5 pm Sunday May through Labor Day, reduced hours the rest of the year; $4/3 adults/children.

BATTLE CREEK

To an American, 'Battle Creek' conjures the image of breakfast cereal. Home of Kellogg's Company, purveyors of famed corn flakes, Battle Creek got its start thanks to the company. The company's start is worth noting, too. Battle Creek was the site of the Seventh Day Adventist Church's Western Health Institute, a system of sanitariums and spas (opened in 1866) designed to promote health through a regimen of hydrotherapy, exercise and vegetarianism. Dr John Harvey Kellogg, a church member, made h contribution to dietetics by developing healthful cereal flake to counterbalance tl average American's breakfast intake of lar butter, eggs and fried meats. The rest is co porate history.

Sojourner Truth

The Battle Creek–Calhoun Count Visitor & Convention Bureau (☎ 616-96 2240, www.battlecreekvisitors.org) is at W Jackson St, but they don't have much the way of printed information.

Things to See & Do

One can't help but notice **Kellogg's Cere City USA** (☎ 616-962-6230), 171 W Michiga Ave, what with a giant Tony the Tiger (tl cartoon character who represents Kellogg Frosted Flakes – *'They're Grrrreat!')* smilin down on the city center. It's a look at tl production of corn flakes – from assemb line all the way through marketing – in hands-on way. Three theaters show a dizz ing array of cereal-oriented films. Hours a 10 am to 5 pm daily in summer, close Monday the rest of the year. Admi sion is $7/5 adults/children.

Battle Creek was also the home ardent abolitionist Sojourner Trut a freed slave who passionate spoke out against slavery an possibly, assisted escaping slav on the Underground Railroa She's buried in Oak Hill Cem tery, 255 South St. A memori sculpture to the Undergrour Railroad is adjacent to tl Kellogg House, betwe Capital Ave and Division St

Exercise was the key health for Mr Kellogg, so Batt Creek's got parks aplenty. **Line Park** is an 11-mile chain of par and waterways linked by a pav path; it's a good spot for bikin You can access it at the Unde ground Railroad Sculptu Wander in **Leila Arboretum**, 72-acre arboretum a fiv minute drive west of dow town, designed after sever famous European gardens.

In early June, Battle Creek fetes its in-
ıstrial heritage with **Cereal Days**, including
e World's Longest Breakfast Table.

laces to Stay

ght miles west of Battle Creek on Hwy 96, e ***Fort Custer National Recreation Area*** *616-731-4200)* has campsites for $12. ıdget places can be found south of town at it 97 off I-94; from downtown take Capital ve SW. ***Motel 6*** *(☎ 616-979-1141, 4775 ckley Rd)* has rooms from $33/37 single/ uble. There's also a ***Super 8*** *(☎ 616-979-28, 5395 Beckley Rd)* for slightly more.

Right downtown, the ***McCamly Plaza otel*** *(☎ 616-963-7050, fax 616-963-4335, 50 pital Ave SW)* is a very good luxury choice th a lengthy list of amenities. The well-pointed rooms cost $110/120 single/double.

laces to Eat

rcadia Brewing Company *(103 W Michi-n Ave)* makes British-style ales and has a enu dominated by good wood-fired pizzas d daily specials (main dishes from $7). cross the street, ***Pierre Lamborghinis-n's*** is a half-block-long deli with a huge ray of fresh breads, meats, cheeses, soups d more; grab the fixings and have a picnic der Tony the Tiger on the grounds of real City.

Close to being a local institution, ***Clara's the River*** *(☎ 616-963-0966, 44 N cCamly St)* is a casual family place in a Vic-rian train depot. The menu is as thick as a one book and runs the gamut from nachos fried rice (main dishes from $5).

etting There & Around

e nearest airport is east of Kalamazoo e Kalamazoo's Getting There & Away ction). Amtrak (☎ 616-963-3351) is at 104 pital Ave SW. Battle Creek is a major rail ıction in Michigan. Trains go to Chicago 35, 2½ hours) and Detroit daily. The bus ation (☎ 616-963-1537) is in the same mplex and has buses to Chicago ($18, 4½ urs) and Detroit ($19, 3½ hours) daily.

A free trolley circulates the downtown ery 20 minutes from 10 am to 3 pm onday to Saturday, June through October.

KALAMAZOO

Michigan's city with the coolest name (said to come from the Potawatomi word 'Kikalamazoo,' which meant 'rapids at the river crossing,' or 'boiling water') has agriculture and industry as economic linchpins, but it's hardly an industrial or cow town. Nor is it plain, as poet Carl Sandburg memorialized the town in a poem, an image that stuck for many people. Kalamazoo has charm. There's an offbeat, university-town feel, due to the presence of Western Michigan University. The downtown is modestly gentrified and there are a few worthwhile attractions and above-average restaurants.

Orientation & Information

Downtown Michigan Ave is the main east-west street; Park St is the main north-south road. Three blocks east of Park St, bisected by Michigan Ave, is the Kalamazoo Mall, a pedestrian-only zone of shops that's a good place to start in Kalamazoo.

Downtown, the Kalamazoo County Convention and Visitors Bureau (☎ 616-381-4003, www.kazoofun.com) is at 346 W Michigan Ave; there's another little tourist office at exit 78 off I-94.

Kinko's copy shop is at 1550 W Michigan Ave; Internet access is $12 per hour or 20¢ per minute.

The *Kalamazoo Express* is a free weekly with overviews of nightlife. Just east of the Convention and Visitors Bureau, the Michigan News Agency is an enormous shop with literally thousands of magazines and titles of local interest.

Things to See

The **Kalamazoo Valley Museum** (☎ 616-373-7990), 230 N Rose St, east of the mall, is comprised of separate interactive learning centers. The main center has a 2300-year-old mummy, its most popular exhibit. OPUS, a 14-foot-tall robot, is the world's first fully interactive museum theater 'conductor' – creating a multimedia display as audience members contribute topics. There's also a planetarium and a theater that simulates a trip to the moon. Hours are 10 am to 6 pm Monday to Saturday (until

9 pm Wednesday), 1 to 5 pm Sunday. Each center costs $3/2 adults/children.

Two blocks south of the visitors center, the **Kalamazoo Institute of Arts** (☎ 616-349-7775), 314 S Park St, has a museum focusing mainly on 20th-century art, including some Michigan artists, along with a make-your-own-art center. Hours are 10 am to 5 pm Monday to Saturday, 1 to 5 pm Sunday; free.

At exit 78 off I-94, on the south side of the airport, the **Aviation History Museum** (☎ 616-382-6555) is called the Air Zoo. Visitors can get up close to 50 vintage planes, including modern F-14 Tomcats; flight demonstrations take place daily. On sunny days, flights are available in an antique Ford Tri-Motor. Kids will like the open cockpit (they can climb in) and the flight simulator. Hours are 9 am to 6 pm Monday to Saturday (9 am to 8 pm Wednesday), noon to 6 pm Sunday; $10/5 adults/children.

Places to Stay

For camping, the ***Kalamazoo County Fairgrounds*** *(☎ 616-383-8776)* is south of Business Hwy 94 on Lake St. Budget lodging can be found at a ***Motel 6*** *(☎ 616-344-9255, 3704 Van Rick Rd)* at exit 78 off I-94, which has rooms from $38/42 single/double. Closer to downtown, the ***Knight's Inn*** *(☎ 616-381-5000, 1211 Westnedge Ave)* has rooms from $45 single/double. To get there, head north from exit 76B off I-94.

Stuart Avenue Inn *(☎ 616-385-3442, 229 Stuart Ave)*, west of downtown, is actually separate Victorian residences in a historic district, surrounded by lovely gardens. Rooms start at $60/70 single/double.

Downtown, the ***Radisson Plaza Hotel*** *(☎ 616-343-3333, fax 616-381-1560, 100 W Michigan Ave)* is a full-service luxury hotel with rooms from $90 single/double.

Places to Eat

South of the Kalamazoo Mall, the friend ***Fishel's Jewish Deli*** *(410 S Burdick St)* is longstanding place with delicious corned be sandwiches that are arguably the best in t state (half sandwiches from $5). Eight sou and fresh-baked breads are available daily ***The Soup Kitchen*** *(150 S Kalamazoo Mal* where you can get a meal for less than $5.

Near the Radisson Hotel is ***Café Gulist*** *(105 E Michigan Ave)*, whose Kurdish own fuses Turkish, Armenian and Lebanese fo wonderfully (entrées from $6).

Webster's, in the Radisson Plaza Ho (see Places to Stay), is one of southe Michigan's best restaurants. For fine dinir ***Josephine's*** *(601 S Burdick)* serves elega country French cuisine (entrées from $1 The wine list is extensive.

Entertainment

A number of nightclubs are in town, mos catering to the university crowd. ***Harve on the Mall*** *(416 S Burdick St)* books ro acts. ***Keggers*** *(109 W Lovell St)* is a dan spot, with everything from '70s night techno. Inside the Kalamazoo Brewing C the ***Eccentric Cafe*** *(355 E Kalamazoo Av* has a variety of live music.

The venerable ***Civic Theatre*** *(☎ 616-34 1313, 404 S Burdick St)* is home to most Kalamazoo's cultural performances.

Getting There & Away

The Kalamazoo–Battle Creek Airport is Portage Rd, just south of I-94 east of tow It's served by commuter flights on six airlin Amtrak (☎ 616-341-1841) is at 459 N Burdi and has trains east and west daily; to Chica ($33) takes two hours. The bus station (☎ 61 343-2502) is in the same complex as Amtr and has buses to Detroit ($25, 4 hours) a Battle Creek ($5, 45 minutes).

.ake Michigan Shore & the Straits

his is Michigan's Gold Coast, a 300-mile oreline featuring sand, surf and incredible nsets best watched while sitting atop a wering sand dune. Dotting the west coast Michigan are small towns that boom uring the summer tourist season, lots of oreline parks and endless stretches of each.

ARBOR COUNTRY

retching north from the Indiana state line ong Lake Michigan 24 miles, Harbor ountry is not a singular entity, but rather a ring of communities from Michiana in the uth to Sawyer in the north (and Three aks inland). Chicagoans use it mostly as a uick getaway spot, and as such, you can kpect extraordinary prices. There's not a hole lot to see and do unless you like an-quing or lounging in sybaritic inns and &Bs.

hings to See & Do

hopaholics will love the area, with innu-erable craft stores, antique shops and art alleries everywhere. Along S Whittaker St New Buffalo, the **New Buffalo Railroad Auseum** has a miniature train display and arious artifacts of the old train depot.

Three Oaks, inland 3 miles along US 12, the closest thing to a hub of activity in ese parts. The **Vickers Theatre** (☎ 616-756-522, 6 N Elm St) is a restored vaudeville ouse which has an offbeat schedule of lms – from classic French films to current rt films. There's an art gallery too. Also ere is the fun **Three Oaks Spokes Bicycle Auseum** (☎ 616-756-3361) with its antique icycle displays. You can rent a bike here to ead out into the Backroads Bikeway, a ystem of country on- and off-road routes at's well worth a day.

North of Sawyer, the **Cook Energy Infor-ation Center** (☎ 800-548-2555) is sort of e PR wing of the nearby Cook Nuclear lant. It offers 45-minute tours through ree theaters with presentations on nuclear

Highlights

- Charlevoix & Petoskey, two quaint resort towns filled with well-to-do vacationers
- Traverse City, the Cherry Capital of the World, central to exploring the Leelanau and Old Mission Peninsulas
- Saugatuck, a popular artists colony with great dining and shopping and one of the best beaches in the Great Lakes
- Tumbling down giant dunes or camping on offshore islands at Sleeping Bear Dunes National Lakeshore
- Mackinac Island, the isle that time forgot, where cars are banned and sunsets are sublime

MICHIGAN

energy. The lobby has a variety of displays. If you do nothing else here, hike the dune trails along the lake. Hours are 10 am to 5 pm, Tuesday to Sunday; free.

Places to Stay

Warren Dunes State Park *(☎ 616-426-4013, 12032 Red Arrow Hwy)* is in Sawyer and has campsite rates of $15. The dunes here are incredible – so high that hang gliders use them for takeoffs. The cheapest motel options will be found along I-94 in New Buffalo, including the ***Grand Beach Motel*** *(☎ 616-469-1555, 19189 US 12)*, where you may get lucky and find a double for less than $50.

But high prices are the rule. Union Pier has some excellent luxury choices. The ***Inn at Union Pier*** *(☎ 616-469-4700)* has a superb lakefront location. The rooms have porches and Swedish fireplaces. Singles/doubles start at $125.

Places to Eat

The ***General Store of Three Oaks*** has a funky 1920s soda fountain serving up great malts and phosphates, along with penny candy. For cheap breakfast and lunch specials ***Rosie's***, a diner along N Whittaker St in New Buffalo, has good diner fare (main dishes from $4). Along the highway in Lakeside, ***Blue Plate Café*** has organic coffees, a juice bar and light, healthful breakfast and lunch (main dishes from $4). Locals favor ***Miller's Country House*** along the highway in Union Pier. It's a casually upscale place with seafood, steaks, ribs, some lighter fare and creative specials with seating in a nice wooded garden (entrées from $7). Chic ***Kent's*** along W Buffalo St in New Buffalo has pricier contemporary American cuisine with vegetarian options (entrées from $10).

Getting There & Away

New Buffalo has no bus depot, but the Indian Trails bus will stop. You just have to wait at the flag-stop (presently the Comfort Inn) and wave it down. To Benton Harbor it takes 30 minutes and costs $6.

Amtrak trains stop along Whittaker St on their Grand Rapids–Chicago run; to Chicago it takes 90 minutes and costs $15. Note that there's a time change; Illinois is a hour behind Michigan.

ST JOSEPH & BENTON HARBOR

These two sister communities couldn't b more different. Thriving St Joseph is a pic turesque little second-home spot fo tourists; over the bridge, Benton Harbor is ghost town – forlorn if not finished alto gether. St Joseph's downtown is lined wit upscale shops and restaurants, and there ar great parks and beaches.

Things to See & Do

There are two attractions within walkin distance of St Joseph's little downtown. Th **Krasl Art Center** (☎ 616-983-0271), 707 Lak Blvd, has three display areas that feature variety of disciplines. The permanent collec tion emphasizes outdoor sculpture; ther are some nice folk art exhibits too. Hour are 10 am to 4 pm Monday to Thursday an Saturday, 10 am to 1 pm Friday, and 1 t 4 pm Sunday; free.

Three blocks away is the **Curious Kid Museum** (☎ 616-983-2543), an interactiv museum highlighted by the costumes kic get to wear. Activities range from appl picking to hot air balloon flying. Hours ar 10 am to 5 pm Wednesday to Sunday; $4.

In April (sometimes early May), th **Blossomtime Festival** is one of Michigan' oldest festivals.

Places to Stay & Eat

Lodging is pretty reasonably priced in S Joseph. The ***Best Western Golden Lin Lodge*** *(☎ 616-983-6321, 2723 Hwy 63)* ha basic singles/doubles from as low as $35/5(A slew of cheap options is also found alon West I-94, south of town, toward Harbo Country.

For pricier digs, the ***Boulevard In*** *(☎ 616-983-6600, 521 Lake Blvd)* has super views and large suites for $100/125 single double. There's also a very good bistro her for alfresco dining.

Downtown ***Caffe Tosi*** *(516 Pleasant St* has good coffee along with simple, healthfu breakfast and lunch (from $4). Occasiona guest chefs prepare fixed-price dinne

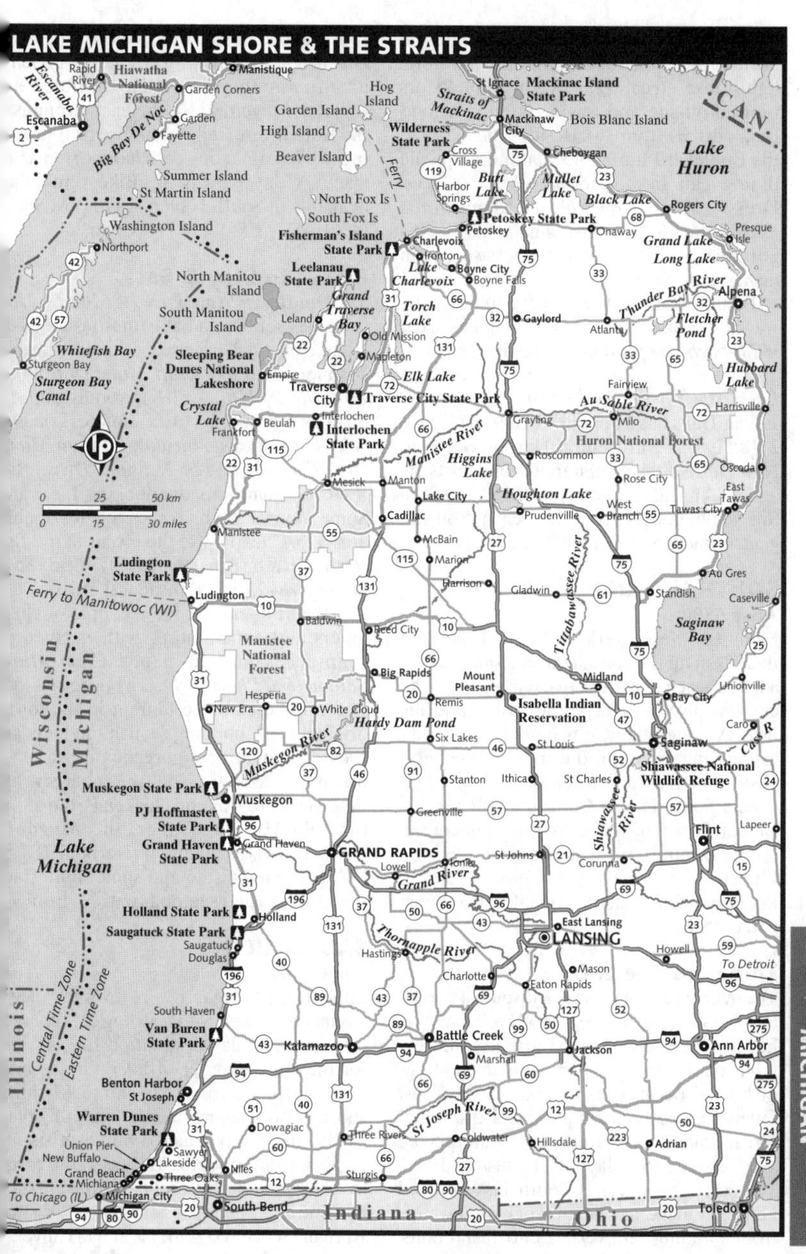
LAKE MICHIGAN SHORE & THE STRAITS
Escanaba River
Rapid River
Hiawatha National Forest
Manistique
Garden Corners
Escanaba
Big Bay De Noc
Garden
Fayette
Summer Island
St Martin Island
Washington Island
Northport
Hog Island
Garden Island
High Island
Beaver Island
Ferry
North Fox Is
South Fox Is
Fisherman's Island State Park
Leelanau State Park
North Manitou Island
South Manitou Island
Leland
Whitefish Bay
Sturgeon Bay
Sturgeon Bay Canal
Sleeping Bear Dunes National Lakeshore
Empire
Crystal Lake
Frankfort
Beulah
Interlochen
Interlochen State Park
Traverse City
Traverse City State Park
Grand Traverse Bay
Old Mission
Mapleton
Elk Lake
Torch Lake
Lake Charlevoix
Charlevoix
Ironton
Boyne City
Boyne Falls
St Ignace
Straits of Mackinac
Mackinac Island State Park
Mackinaw City
Bois Blanc Island
CAN
Wilderness State Park
Cross Village
Harbor Springs
Burt Lake
Mullet Lake
Cheboygan
Black Lake
Rogers City
Lake Huron
Petoskey State Park
Petoskey
Onaway
Presque Isle
Grand Lake
Long Lake
Thunder Bay River
Alpena
Gaylord
Atlanta
Fletcher Pond
Hubbard Lake
Fairview
Au Sable River
Harrisville
Grayling
Milo
Huron National Forest
Manistee River
Higgins Lake
Roscommon
Oscoda
Rose City
East Tawas
Tawas City
Mesick
Manton
Lake City
Houghton Lake
West Branch
Prudenville
Cadillac
Manistee
McBain
Marion
Ludington State Park
Ferry to Manitowoc (WI)
Ludington
Harrison
Gladwin
Tittabawassee River
Au Gres
Standish
Caseville
Saginaw Bay
Baldwin
Reed City
Manistee National Forest
Big Rapids
Mount Pleasant
Midland
Unionville
Bay City
Isabella Indian Reservation
Hesperia
New Era
White Cloud
Remis
Hardy Dam Pond
Caro
Cass R
Muskegon River
Six Lakes
St Louis
Saginaw
Shiawassee National Wildlife Refuge
Wisconsin
Michigan
Muskegon State Park
Muskegon
Stanton
Ithica
St Charles
Shiawassee River
PJ Hoffmaster State Park
Greenville
Lapeer
Flint
Lake Michigan
Grand Haven State Park
Grand Haven
GRAND RAPIDS
Lowell
Ionia
Grand River
St Johns
Corunna
Holland State Park
Holland
Saugatuck State Park
Saugatuck
Douglas
Thornapple River
Hastings
East Lansing
LANSING
Howell
To Detroit
Charlotte
Mason
Eaton Rapids
Illinois
Central Time Zone
Eastern Time Zone
South Haven
Van Buren State Park
Kalamazoo
Battle Creek
Marshall
Jackson
Ann Arbor
Benton Harbor
St Joseph
Warren Dunes State Park
Dowagiac
St Joseph River
Three Rivers
Coldwater
Hillsdale
Adrian
Union Pier
New Buffalo
Grand Beach
Michiana
Sawyer
Lakeside
Three Oaks
Niles
Sturgis
To Chicago (IL)
Michigan City
South Bend
Indiana
Ohio
Toledo
0 25 50 km
0 15 30 miles

MICHIGAN

evenings. The ***Lighthouse Depot***, at the north pier, is a brewpub built into a historic lighthouse structure. It's got eight beers brewed on site and a wide variety of food (main dishes from $6). Besides the bistro in the Boulevard Inn, somewhat more upscale dining can be found in several places. Dressy casual is the rule at ***Clementine's*** *(1235 Broad St)*, overlooking the harbor. It's got steaks and seafood as a base (main dishes from $12).

Benton Harbor doesn't have much in the way of food, but it does have – no joke – a ***car wash-barbecue joint*** along the main road.

Getting There & Away

Indian Trails has a depot (☎ 616-925-1121) at 2412 Hwy 139 in Benton Harbor. South to New Buffalo takes 30 minutes and costs $6.

The Amtrak depot is at 410½ Vine St in St Joseph, not far from the beach. You can get to Chicago or Grand Rapids.

SOUTH HAVEN

• pop 5500

Many travelers overlook South Haven on their dash up the coast. Too bad, since it's got a killer beach and attractive harbor area. The city has always been known for producing fruit. Among others, it is one of the world's leading blueberry producers; the Blueberry Festival in mid-August is loads of fun.

The South Haven Convention & Visitors Bureau (☎ 616-637-5252) is at 415 Phoenix St.

Greyhound stops at the South Haven Utilities Center (☎ 616-639-9600), 1210 Phoenix Rd. To Kalamazoo takes two hours and costs $14.

Things to See & Do

The **Michigan Maritime Museum** (☎ 616-637-8078), at the bridge along Dyckman Ave, has a variety of historical artifacts and exhibits on the area's history, with an emphasis on boats. Lots of boats. Of note are the Coast Guard rescue boats and a good display of Great Lakes maps. Hours are 10 am to 5 pm Wednesday to Sunday; $3/2 adults/children.

Across the water is South Haven's Old Harbor Village, a collection of extant waterfront buildings converted into restaurants, shops and lodging. Much more fun is th ***Blueberry Store*** downtown at 525 Phoeni it's an entire shop devoted to the little berr

South Haven is also the east terminus c the Kal-Haven Trail, a multiuse trail stretch ing to Kalamazoo on a converted trai track. A day pass is $2. Bike rentals ar available in South Haven at Outpost Spor (☎ 616-637-5555), 114 Dyckman Ave.

Places to Stay & Eat

The ***Van Buren State Park*** *(☎ 616-637-278* is 4 miles south and has campsites for $12.

Like everywhere else, nothing is cheap i summer. The ***Lake Bluff Motel*** *(☎ 616-68 1305, 76648 11th Ave)* has rooms that ca drop as low as $50 for a double. Loads c B&Bs are in town, including ***Yelton Man*** *(☎ 616-637-5220, 140 N Shore Drive)*, tw Victorian mansions overlooking the wate Some rooms have balconies. Singles/doubl are $125. Cheaper are the rooms at the ***La Resort B&B Inn*** *(☎ 616-637-8943, 86 Shore Drive)*, owned by a local artist.

Along Phoenix St are a couple of chea diners and coffeehouses with inexpensiv soup and sandwich menus. ***Clementine Saloon*** *(500 Phoenix St)*, is a boisterous loc watering hole and restaurant in the town original bank building (which the bank st uses). The interior is gorgeous, down to th original pressed tin. The fare is burgers an sandwiches to ribs and chicken (from $6). the Old Harbor Village, the ***Magnol Grille*** is housed in an old riverboat. It's g lots of Cajun cuisine and some more trad tional steaks and seafood (entrées from $7

SAUGATUCK

• pop 1000

This Lake Michigan resort town in Allega County is known for its strong arts comm nity, as a popular destination for gays an for the large number of B&Bs in the are Every little town on the Lake Michiga shore is popular in summer, but this pla can be absolutely crushed with tourists.

An unstaffed visitor kiosk is at the corn of Culver and Butler Sts with maps ar brochures. The Convention & Visito Bureau (☎ 616-857-1701) is at 350 Culver S

hings to See & Do

he best thing to do here is also the most af-
ɔrdable. Jump aboard the **Saugatuck Chain erry** ($1), and the operator will pull you ːross the Kalamazoo River. On the other de climb the stairs to the grand views at ıe top of Mt Baldhead, a 200-foot sand une. Race down the north side to beautiful **val Beach**, where MTV once filmed a ımmer beach party show (and called it one f the top five beaches in the world).

Southeast of the information kiosk, at the ridge to Douglas, sits the *SS Keewatin*. This ld steamship is now a floating museum and reserved almost perfectly as it was in its eyday in the early 1900s. Hours are):30 am to 4:30 pm; $5/3 adults/children. hree miles north of downtown, **Dunes tate Park** is a gorgeous place, and usually mazingly devoid of people.

Otherwise, the Saugatuck routine is to ound the pavement visiting the 100 shops, ɔutiques and art galleries. That is, if you ın get in the door with the crowds.

The *Star of Saugatuck* (☎ 616-857-4261) a stern-wheel paddleboat that offers tours n the Kalamazoo River and Lake Michi- an. The tour schedule varies a lot, but in ımmer it goes up to five times per day om 11 am to 8 pm; $9/5 adults/children.

laces to Stay & Eat

he closest campground is the private ***augatack RV Resort*** *(☎ 616-857-3315, 473 Washington St)*, southwest of I-196, here you can get a tent site for $25.

Friday and Saturday in summer you can ɪrget about budget lodging. Off nights you ın usually scare something up in the $60 ınge somewhere, including the ***Pines lotel*** *(☎ 616-857-5211, 56 S Blue Star Hwy)* ıd the ***Shangri La*** *(☎ 616-857-1453, 6190 lue Star Hwy)*.

Most of the town's B&Bs are in century- ld Victorian homes and range from $70 to 150 a night per couple. Try the charming ***ay Side Inn*** *(☎ 616-857-1870, 618 Water)*, a former boathouse with an outdoor ıb, or ***Twin Oaks Inn*** *(☎ 616-857-1600, 227 riffith St)*, with seven rooms from $70 to 00 per night.

The ***Loaf and Mug*** *(☎ 616-857-2974, 236 Culver St)* has great (and cheap) breakfasts ($3), sandwiches ($4) and soups; their specials are always creative. Off Water and Hoffman Sts the ***Water St Cafe*** has a healthful eclectic menu, heavy on Mediterranean (main dishes from $6).

For an evening of fine dining, ***Toulouse*** *(☎ 616-857-1561, 248 Culver St)* has superb French country cuisine in a romantic garden setting (entrées from $14).

Entertainment

The ***Red Barn Playhouse*** *(☎ 616-857-7707)* has musicals and dramas throughout summer. In town, a few places have live entertainment, including ***Coral Gables***.

HOLLAND

• pop 31,000

Given the name, it's not hard to guess the heritage of most of this town's citizens. Holland is an attractive town 10 miles north of Saugatuck and home to the majority of Michigan's Dutch, descendants of Dutch religious secessionists who fled Holland in the late 1840s. The town has a massive tulip garden operation, delftware potteries, and two wooden-shoe factories, all of which can be visited. Holland is currently considering redeveloping its Windmill Island into an authentic Dutch-style village – a residential and business area radiating from its nucleus, a church atop a small rise.

The well-stocked and helpful Holland Area Convention and Visitors Bureau (☎ 800-506-1299) is at 272 E Eighth St.

Things to See & Do

Northwest of downtown, **Windmill Island** is dominated by the 230-year-old DeZwaan Windmill, the only authentic Dutch windmill in the US. Around it spreads a 30-acre park full of canals, tulips (and more tulips), a carousel, traditional 'klompen' dancers and reconstructions of Dutch houses. Hours are 9 am to 6 pm Monday to Saturday, May through October, reduced hours otherwise; $6/3 adults/children.

Dutch culture can also be experienced at the **Dutch Village** (☎ 616-396-1475) north of town. More tulips, more canals and more dancing. Hours are 9 am to 5 pm daily, May through October; $7/5 adults/children.

Downtown, the **Holland Museum** (☎ 616-392-6740), 228 W 9th St, has exhibits detailing Dutch settlement in western Michigan. Delft pottery displays are the most interesting. Hours are 1 to 4 pm Friday and Saturday, May through September; $3.

Holland really explodes in color during its **Tulip Time Festival** in mid-May.

Places to Stay & Eat

Seven miles west of town on Lake Michigan, ***Holland State Park*** *(☎ 616-399-9390)* has campsites for $15. The ***Lakeshore Resort and Motel*** *(☎ 616-335-5355, 1645 S Shore Drive)* is probably the least expensive place you'll find in town, with singles/doubles from around $50.

There are quite a few B&Bs in town. The ***Dutch Colonial*** *(☎ 616-396-3664, 560 Central Ave)* has singles/doubles from $60.

The ***Queen's Inn*** is at the Dutch Village and surprisingly, it's the only place in town to get authentic Dutch food, here served by waitstaff in costume. Downtown at 8th St and Central Ave, ***Cafe Konditorei*** has coffee, soups (such as Austrian Steak soup), salads, pasta and panini specials for reasonable prices. ***Alpenrose*** *(4 E 8th St)* has Austrian and Continental cuisine, with some vegetarian choices (dishes from $10).

Getting There & Around

The bus depot (☎ 616-396-8664) is at 171 Lincoln Ave. A direct bus to Muskegon takes 35 minutes and costs $9. Amtrak stops at 250 E 7th St; to Grand Rapids takes 45 minutes and costs $5.

Dial-A-Ride (☎ 616-355-1010) is a phone-in public transportation system. Call them and tell them where you want to go; fares will be between $1.25 and $2.

GRAND HAVEN

• pop 12,000

Touristy Grand Haven is filled with travelers heading directly to **Grand Haven State Park** (☎ 616-798-3711), with 182 sites ($15) along a great beach; campers are unfortunatel squashed into a loud and tiny area. The par is connected to the downtown restaurant bars and shops by a scenic 2½-mile-lon boardwalk along the Grand River. Th same boardwalk also takes you past th **Tri Cities Historical Museum** in an old rai road depot; it's got a variety of items detai ing local history and old railroad engines ou front. Between Grand Haven and Mu kegon is **PJ Hoffmaster State Park** (☎ 61 798-3711), offering 293 sites ($15), th interesting Gillette Sand Dune Natur Center and a 10-mile trail system, several which are along Lake Michigan.

Besides the two state parks mentione above, the cheapest motels are found alon S Hwy 31, including the ***South Shore Mot*** *(☎ 616-842-7720, 805 S Hwy 31)*, which ha rooms for around $45 single/double, highe weekends. Centrally located, the ***Harb House Inn*** *(☎ 616-846-0610, 114 S Harbc Drive)* looks historic but it's relatively nev it's got great views, cozy rooms, and rate from $125 single/double in high season.

Pavilion's Garden Wharf Deli *(16 Wash ington St)* has great deli-style sandwiche and a good veggie burger, among othe veggie items (choices from $4).

Greyhound and Indian Trails run out the bus station (☎ 616-842-2720) at 440 Ferry St. To Holland ($8) takes 20 minute A trolley ($2) runs about Grand Have during the summer.

MUSKEGON

• pop 40,000

Although it was once billed as the 'Lumb Queen,' rapacious clearcutting practice doomed Muskegon-area forests. But th city's proximity to Lake Michigan began draw tourists following WWII. Since it's n *right* on Lake Michigan, Muskegon ofte gets overlooked, but it's a friendly, attracti place. Enormous amounts of green spac and a couple of good attractions make worth a stop.

The Muskegon County Convention ar Visitors Bureau (☎ 800-250-9283), at 610 Western Ave, has lots of printed informatio

'hings to See & Do

⁄luskegon has some excellent architecture ı its downtown districts, thanks to the ımber barons trying to outbuild each other. 'wo of the state's finest examples are the **łackley & Hume Historic Sites** (☎ 231-722-278), at 6th and Webster Sts. The homes are pen for tours noon to 4 pm Wednesday to unday; $3/free adults/children.

Lumber wealth also provided the artwork ow housed in the **Muskegon Museum of ‚rt** (☎ 231-720-2570), considered to have ne of the finest art collections in the ⁄lidwest. Hours are 10 am to 5 pm Tuesday ɔ Friday, noon to 5 pm weekends; free.

On the west side of Muskegon Lake sits JSS *Silversides* (☎ 231-755-1230), a decoated World War II submarine open for ɔurs. The sub was famed as one of the top hree subs in number of ships sunk. A mar:ime museum sits adjacent. Hours are 0 am to 5:30 pm daily June through Sepember, shorter hours otherwise; $4/3 dults/children.

'laces to Stay & Eat

łorth of Muskegon is ***Muskegon State Park*** *☎ 231-766-3480)*, with 183 sites in two ampgrounds and 12 miles of trails through ugged, wooded dunes. Camping is $15 a ight.

The ***Seaway Motel*** *(☎ 231-733-1220, 631 ⁄orton St)* has singles/doubles from $45. 'he ***Super 8*** *(☎ 231-733-0088, 3380 Hoyt St)* as similar rates. The ***Port City Victorian nn*** *(☎ 231-759-0205, 1259 Lakeshore)rive)* is an 1877 Queen Anne with nice ooms starting at $65 single/double.

The ***City Café*** *(411 West Western Ave)*, in ıe lower level of the Frauenthal Center for ıe Performing Arts, is an Italian and French istro with creative soups, salads and sand⁄iches for reasonable prices (from $5). ***The tation Grill***, off the intersection of Broad⁄ay Ave and Henry St, has interiors that ɔok just like a 1940s gas station (dishes from 5). Muskegon's institution is ***Tony's Club*** *☎ 231-739-7196, 785 W Broadway Ave)*, with thick menu of steaks, seafood and their ımous Greek dishes (entrées from $9).

Getting There & Around

The Muskegon County Airport (☎ 231-798-4596) is southwest of town; three airlines operate shuttles to Chicago, Milwaukee and Detroit. The bus station (☎ 616-722-6048) is at 351 Morris St; to Holland ($9) takes 35 minutes. The city of Muskegon's transportation company operates trolleys (25¢) that make a circuit of the downtown attractions; the South Beach Trolley goes to PJ Hoffmaster State Park.

LUDINGTON

Travelers mostly know Ludington as the port of the SS *Badger*, the steam ferry to and from Manitowoc, Wisconsin (the only shore-to-shore car ferry service left on Lake Michigan). The town is worth a bit of time itself, with a nice lakefront beach park and a few attractions.

Things to See & Do

Three miles south of downtown sits **White Pine Village** (☎ 231-843-4808), a reconstructed lakefront village dating from the 1840s. Twenty buildings comprise the site and among them are a small maritime museum and lumbering museum. Hours are 11 am to 5 pm Tuesday to Saturday, mid-June to late September, lesser times in May and October; $5/4 adults/children.

The largest state park and one of the most popular along Lake Michigan is **Ludington State Park** (☎ 616-843-8671), with almost 300 campsites ($15), an excellent trail system and miles of beach. To its north is **Nordhouse Dunes**, a 3000-acre federally designated wilderness with its own trail system. You enter Nordhouse Dunes through the Lake Michigan Recreation Area, a US Forest Service campground several miles south of Manistee.

One of the most unusual backpacking trips in the Lower Peninsula is the 20-mile hike between Manistee and Ludington along the undeveloped beaches of these large parks, overnighting in Nordhouse Dunes. Stop at the Manistee Ranger District (☎ 616-723-2211), south of Manistee on US 31, for maps and information.

Places to Stay & Eat

Camping at Ludington State Park (see Things to See & Do) would be the most logical first option. A dozen or so lodgings are found in and around town. The ***Blue Spruce Motel*** *(☎ 231-843-9537, 109 N Ferry St)* is off the main street, quiet and furnished with Amish hickory chairs and rockers. Ferry customers get a discount. Singles/doubles cost $45; note that this place doesn't accept credit cards.

A handful of average greasy spoons are found along the main street and outside town, heading toward US 31. A number of casual eateries overlook the marina, including ***PM Steamers*** *(502 W Loomis St)*, with a moderately ambitious menu of pastas, poultry, steak and freshly caught seafood (main dishes from $9).

Getting There & Away

The car ferry *SS Badger* (☎ 888-643-3779, www.ssbadger.com) sails between Ludington and Manitowoc, Wisconsin, daily from mid-May through late October. The four-hour trip saves a heap of time on the journey around Lake Michigan. One-way fares cost $39/36/18 adults/seniors/kids, $47/27 car/motorcycle.

SLEEPING BEAR DUNES NATIONAL LAKESHORE

This national park stretches from north of Frankfort nearly to Leland, on the Leelanau Peninsula. Stop at the park visitors' center (☎ 616-326-5134, 800-365-2267 for campsite reservations), at the corner of Hwys 72 and 22 in Empire, for information and trail maps. The visitors' center is open 9 am to 6 pm daily, late May through early September, 9 am to 4 pm the rest of the year.

The park now levies a $7 entrance fee, valid up to seven days.

Things to See & Do

The **Sleeping Bear Point Coast Guard Station** is an interesting maritime museum in Glen Haven, north of Empire; USCGS lifesaving squads demonstrate lake rescue methods every afternoon. You can drive or cycle **Pierce Stocking Scenic Drive**, a 7-mile, one-lane road that passes stunning Lak Michigan views (open 9 am to 10 pm – or half-hour after sunset – April through Nc vember). The most popular attraction, espe cially with kids, is **The Dune Climb** alon Hwy 109 just south of Glen Haven, wher you trudge up the 200-foot dune and the run or roll down.

Backpackers should head to Leland an catch the 10 am ferry, daily except Tuesda and Thursday ($20 roundtrip), over to **Nort Manitou Island** for an overnight wildernes hiking adventure ($5 camping) on its 2 miles of organized trails. Take a fishing pole the smallmouth bass fishing is great. **Sout Manitou Island**, also reached by a 10 ar ferry, has three organized campgrounds ($5 and some sights, including a 100-foot ligh house. The western shallows off Sout Manitou Island are part of the Manito Passage Underwater Preserve and attrac divers. (For more information on the pre serve and diving, check out www.deq.stat .mi.us/shipwreck/manitou.html.) Ferry rese vations for both trips can be made by callin ☎ 231-256-9061.

Many streams and rivers in the vicinit allow for canoeing and kayaking. Gle Arbor has rentals ($13).

You could sneeze and miss little Lelanc If you're not heading to the Manitou Island you can still stop off and wander about th restored **fishing village** on the harbor. Thes 19th-century fish shanties now house a co lection of shops and restaurants.

Places to Stay & Eat

The park maintains two large campground ***Platte River Campground***, south c Empire, and ***DH Day***, near Glen Haver where sites cost $10 to $19 per night. Thes campgrounds are very popular, so get ther early to stake out a site! The park also offer two backcountry campgrounds with 11 site ($5). If they are full, head east toward Tra verse City along US 31 and try one of th half dozen state forest campgrounds tha are sign-posted along the road.

Within the park, Glen Arbor and Empir have a few motels and especially B&B Outside the park confines Leland has man

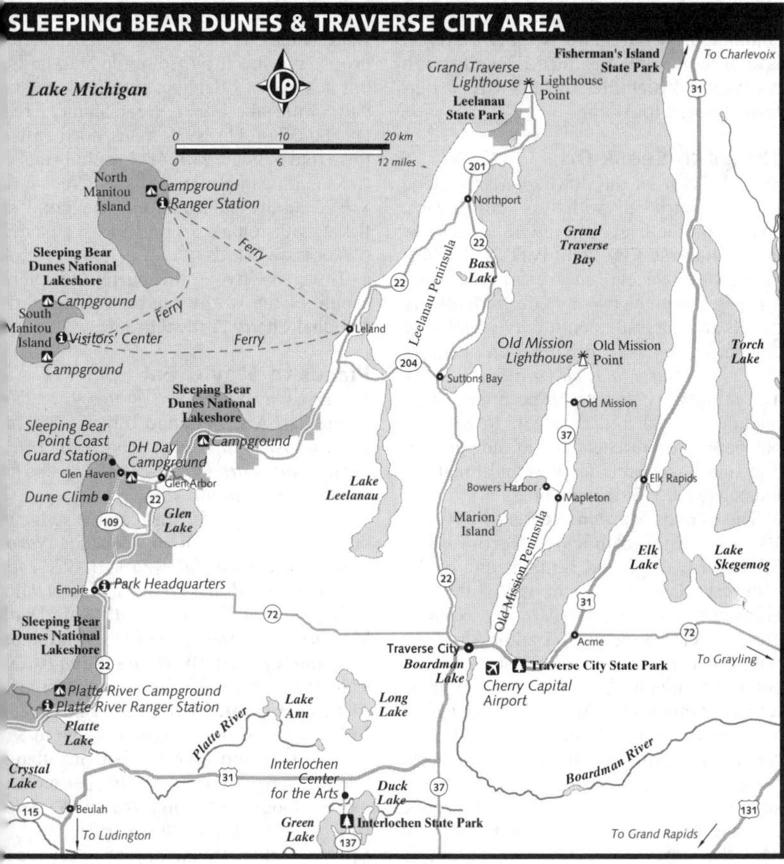

ıore options, but these will be very expen-ive. The ***Leelanau Country Inn*** *(☎ 231-228-060, 149 E Harbor Hwy)* is 6 miles south of ꜀eland. It's very well regarded for its ꜀eafood and Midwestern country cooking, ıd it also has moderately priced rooms: 45/55 for a single/double.

In Leland itself the ***Falling Waters Lodge*** *☎ 231-256-9832)* has the best location, ·verlooking the harbor and restored village. 'he rooms are good and you pay for the omfort – up to $135 per double in high eason. Leland has a few simple seafood ꜀staurants along the waterfront. ***Cove***, also on the harbor, has some creative seafood options (entrées from $10). The whitefish is legendary at ***Bluebird***, on the main drag; folks have been eating it up since 1927.

TRAVERSE CITY

• pop 15,000

Michigan's Cherry Capital is the largest city in the northern half of the Lower Peninsula. In recent years the urban sprawl has alarmed residents, but tourists find Traverse City safe, beautiful and fun, with lots to see and do.

Stop at the Traverse City Visitor Center (☎ 800-872-8377), downtown at the corner of Grandview Parkway and Union St, for a complete list of lodgings. *Northern Express* is a free weekly produced locally with overviews of nightlife. Traverse City is perfectly located for skiing.

Things to See & Do

Two blocks from the downtown area along US 31 is **Clinch Park**, with its beautiful beach. Nearby on the East Arm of Grand Traverse Bay is **Traverse City State Park** (☎ 616-922-5270), with 700 feet of sugary sand and swimming. Between the two are dozens of resorts, motels and parasail operators. For a relaxing day on the bay, take an afternoon or sunset sail on *Tall Ship Malarbar* (☎ 616-941-2000). The cruises last two to three hours, often include a meal and cost $30 to $38 per person; there are cheaper morning cruises. The ship is available for bed and breakfast lodging ($100/175 single/double).

The **Dennos Museum Center** (☎ 231-922-1055) is on the campus of Northwestern Michigan College and contains one of the Midwest's largest collections of Inuit art. Hours are 10 am to 5 pm Monday to Saturday, 1 to 5 pm Sunday; $2/1 adults/children. South of Traverse City is one of the state's cultural highlights. South of town the **Interlochen Center for the Arts** (☎ 231-276-6230), a summer camp and boarding high school for artistic kids, features regular musical performances ($7 and under). It hosts a summertime festival of cultural events, drawing professional performers from all over the world. More water recreation is found south of here at **Interlochen State Park** (☎ 231-276-9511), where there are some of the few remaining stands of virgin pine trees in Michigan.

Winding through the city and along the bay is the **Traverse Area Recreation Trail** (TART for short), an 11-mile paved path. At Brick Wheels (☎ 616-947-4274), 736 E 8th St, you can rent a road bike, mountain bike or inline skates and then jump on the trail outside. Rentals are around $12 to $15 per day.

If you're visiting in winter, Traverse City is near several great **skiing** areas, including virtually unlimited cross-country options. Sugar Loaf (☎ 800-952-6390) is 18 miles northwest of town and borders Sleepin Bear Dunes. It boasts a 500-foot vertica drop – not much by Colorado standards but it is one of Michigan's steepest, and th view of the lakeshore is great. Shanty Cree (☎ 800-678-4111) is 36 miles northeast c town and is huge, with 41 downhill runs o two separate mountains. Shanty Creek cos $36/22 adults/children for a weekend li ticket, with rentals around $40 per day fc skis or snowboards.

Traverse City, as the purported cherr capital of the world, celebrates during th **National Cherry Festival** in July.

Places to Stay & Eat

Traverse City State Park *(☎ 616-922-5270* on the East Arm of Grand Traverse Bay, ha 343 campsites that cost from $15. ***Inter lochen State Park*** *(☎ 231-276-9511)* also ha campsites for around $15.

Traverse City has considerable lodging but they are often full on weekends. ***North western Michigan College*** *(☎ 231-922-140 1701 E Front St)* has rooms in East Hall i the summer for $25 a night with shared bat Motels on the other side of US 31 are mo moderately priced. The ***Budgetel Inn*** *(☎ 23 933-4454, 2326 US 31)* has rooms starting $40; rooms at ***Mitchell Creek Inn*** *(☎ 23 947-9330)*, near the state park, begin at $4

Resorts overlooking the bay are ubiqu tous and range from $90 to $160 per night. modest lodge and motel, ***Ranch Rudolp*** *(☎ 231-947-5072, 6841 Brownbridge Rd)* is a prime location. Rooms are $68 to $165 yea round. Downtown, the ***Park Place*** *(☎ 23 946-5000, 300 E State St)* is a renovate historical landmark with premium rooms fc premium prices – $135 single/double.

Pick up fresh produce and baked gooc at the Saturday morning ***farmers marke*** held along Boardman River not far fro the visitor information center. Downtow the ***Omelette Shoppe*** *(124 Cass St)* has e cellent omelettes and fritattas, includin some vegetarian choices (from $5). ***Mack inaw Brewing Company***, along State S has a soup, salad, sandwich and stea menu (items from $7); it's heavy on th brisket. ***Apache Trout Grill*** *(13671 W Ba* hore Rd) has one of the most eclectic nenus. A variety of whitefish dishes is lways available and, in hunting season, a vild game menu appears (main dishes rom $10). For something completely different, the ***Grand Traverse Dinner Train*** (☎ *888-933-3768)* wends through the ountryside for lunch and dinner tours $45 to $65).

Many fine restaurants are peppered hroughout the two-peninsula area, particuarly in Suttons Bay and Bowers Bay.

Getting There & Around

The Cherry Capital Airport (☎ 231-947-250), southeast of town, is served by four huttle airlines with trips to Minneapolis, Milwaukee, Detroit and Chicago.

The intercity bus station (☎ 231-946-180) is at 4233 Cass Rd, in the Bay Area Transit Authority complex. Buses go to Grand Rapids ($20, 3½ hours); faster buses go to Mackinaw City ($20, 2 hours).

The Bay Area Transit Authority (☎ 231-941-2324) operates local public transport. Regional Ride (☎ 888-228-7743) operates a ide service through the adjoining sixounty region.

TRAVERSE CITY AREA

Mission Peninsula

The most popular scenic drive is to head north from Traverse City on Hwy 37 for 20 miles to the end of **Mission Peninsula**. Along the way, stop at the Chateau Grand Traverse or Chateau Chantel winery and sample a chardonnay or pinot noir. If you purchase a bottle, you can enjoy it on the **Lighthouse Park** beach at the end of the peninsula with the waves licking your toes. Hungry? Visit the boisterous ***Old Mission Tavern*** on the way back, a rousing stop. Or veer off toward the water and into Bowers Harbor, where the ***Bowers Harbor Inn*** has excellent planked whitefish dishes.

Suttons Bay & Northport

Suttons Bay, 15 miles north of Traverse City, is button cute and a good place to stretch the legs at a few galleries. It's even better for food. A couple of places really stand out. ***Cafeliss*** *(420 St Joseph Ave)* has a creative menu filled with Indian entrées and lots of vegetarian choices (main dishes from $9). One of the region's most intimate restaurants is ***Hattie's*** *(111 St Joseph Ave)*, which emphasizes regional ingredients in its creative American fare (entrées from $14).

Northport, 26 miles north of Traverse City, is where Hwy 22 bends back inland. Continuing northward leads to two units of **Leelanau State Park**. The southern unit has great trails and a view of North Manitou Island. The northern unit has a rustic campground ($6) with great views and the popular **Grand Traverse Lighthouse**; $2/1 adults/children.

Grayling

Fifty miles east of Traverse City, Grayling is the epicenter for Lower Michigan's canoe and kayak aficionados. A half dozen streams and rivers meander through the area; the granddaddy is the wild and scenic **Au Sable River**, named after a game fish once prevalent in these waters (until overfishing doomed the species). The river runs through the eponymous state forest. Paddlers will find 14 state forest campgrounds in the county (around $8) and even more liveries offering canoe and kayak rentals. The Grayling Area Visitors Council (☎ 800-937-8837) has lists of all outfitters. Some avid paddlers decry the crowds that now regularly appear on weekends and decamp for Gaylord, farther north, but the Manistee River nearby Grayling has far fewer people. Rates vary from $15 to $40 for a basic four-hour tour; many local outfitters also offer overnight trips.

CHARLEVOIX

• pop 3090

Charlevoix has long been known for its exclusive, swank (and private) resort clubs, built one after another in the 19th century – each to outdo the ones that came before. Today it is a trim, attractive place, and an easy place to spend an afternoon wandering around. The city sits on a promontory where Lake Michigan flows into Lake Charlevoix via a channel. Roads lead to white sand beaches or to yacht-crammed marinas. Sailing tours ($25/15 adults/children) leave three times daily on Sunshine Charters (☎ 231-220-4418).

The town is also used as an access point to **Beaver Island**. Beaver Island was an Irish settlement until the late 1840s, when a Mormon colony was founded by 'King' James Strang, who had formed a splinter group from the Brigham Young Party. Wise mainland authorities left the cult to its own devices – save for one bloody skirmish – and ultimately Strang was assassinated by a follower, at which time the Irish returned. This is the only time a sovereign held sway within mainland US borders. Missing Beaver Island wouldn't exactly ruin you vacation, but it's got a sedate charm to it. A few museums – including one dedicated t the Mormon group – are on the island, a are a lighthouse and a wildlife researc station. Mountain bikes can be rented at th dock on the island for around $20.

Back downtown, an architectural tour is highlight. In the 1920s local resident Ea Young began building distinctive loca dwellings with huge boulder facades. Local call them 'mushroom homes' due to thei rounded tops. He averaged nearly a buildin a year, 30 in all, including a few notabl hotels and restaurants. Boulder Park is a area home to several of these buildings

Charlevoix to *Mackinaw City* – Scenic Drive

You basically can't go wrong from Charlevoix to Mackinaw City. US 31 runs along the Lake Michigan shoreline and is superb. An inland jaunt isn't all that bad either.

Leaving Charlevoix, you face a choice. The first option is to head due south on Hwy 66 for 6 miles or so to little Ironton, where you can take the indescribably cool little **Ironton Ferry** ($2) across an arm of Lake Charlevoix.

Since 1876 one form of cable-guided ferry – all of three cars fit on it – or another has crossed the 100 yards of Lake Charlevoix's South Arm, from April through November. The crossing takes only five minutes, and it saves 18 miles of driving. The ferry became internationally famous when *Ripley's Believe It or Not* featured it for its captain, 'who travelled 10,000 miles but was never more than 1000 feet from home.'

Gourmets may wish to branch off Hwy 66 via Hwy 65 south to **Ellsworth**, a tiny village with perhaps the highest number of reputable restaurants per capita in the Great Lakes. Haute cuisine to the extreme is found at legendary **Tapawingo** (☎ 231-588-7971), where prix fixe dinners start at $28. Only slightly less famous, **Rowe Inn** (☎ 231-588-7351) has outstanding seasonal cuisine and an astonishingly good wine cellar. For those more gourmand than gourmet, **Susie's** is a more casual café with an old-fashioned soda fountain. It calls itself 'Ellsworth's *other* restaurant' where, despite the low prices, in some humble opinions its desserts are just as much to die for as the more well-known neighbors'.

LIBRARY OF CONGRESS

ferred to en masse as the 'mushroom stone ttages.'

Charlevoix is a good base for Ernest emingway fans. See 'Charlevoix to Macki-aw City – Scenic Drive.'

laces to Stay & Eat

othing's dirt-cheap in Charlevoix. But 5 iles southwest of town, ***Fisherman's Island ate Park*** (*☎ 231-547-6641*) has $6 camp-tes in a rustic location, perched on 5 miles f undeveloped Lake Michigan shoreline. on't swim here, due to the treacherous cur-nts. Southeast of town, ***Young State Park*** *☎ 231-582-7523)* has good campsites for $15. he ***Lodge Motel*** *(☎ 231-547-6565, 120 Michigan Ave)* has singles/doubles from around $45, though rates may be higher in peak times. The ***Weathervane Inn*** *(☎ 231-547-9955, 111 Pine River Lane)* is one of those Earl Young homes. It has a nice riverside location and singles/doubles for $100.

The downtown has a few popular pubs with basic pub grub. ***The Village Pub*** right on US 31 also has live bands. A block north, ***Sweet Sam's*** has great coffee, with beans roasted to suit. You'll find fusion, nouvelle, eclectic and any other kind of eatery in town. ***Whitney's Oyster Bar*** is a local landmark for quaffing and seafood. Once totally destroyed by fire, it was rebuilt with pieces from an English lithographer's shop and a

Charlevoix to Mackinaw City – Scenic Drive

Whichever route you choose, head for **Boyne City**, at the southeast end of Lake Charlevoix. This anachronistic town at the bottom of Lake Charlevoix is the site of one of Michigan's original ski resorts and is the beginning of Hemingway country. Ernest Hemingway spent his formative years summering around this lake, and he continued to vacation here well into his adult life.

Bear north along the winding County Rd 71, and you pass through Young State Park and its campground. Three miles farther leads to **Horton Bay** and more Hemingway nostalgia. He was married in a local church and the Horton Bay General Store houses Papa memorabilia. Look for photographs of the writer from his days in the community and the Salem cigarette ad that featured him.

Hop northward back to US 31, through Petoskey, to Hwy 119. A side tour westward is obligatory along what may be Michigan's most picturesque road. It certainly is one of the most challenging. Called the 'Tunnel of Trees,' it's a narrow, ribbony strip smothered by dense trees above. (It's so narrow, in fact, that despite its appeal for bikers, it's something of a suicide mission – and drivers will find that attempting to avoid cyclists is dangerous too.)

The next 27 miles take a long time. When you're finally expelled from the tunnel in Cross Village, you'll probably be exhausted from gripping the wheel. And hungry. Luckily, one of the most delightful restaurants in Lower Michigan is here. You can't help but notice **Legs Inn**, what with the stovepipe legs sticking out of the roof. Walking in, the visual business continues with carvings, antlers, animal heads – among other things – poking out from everywhere. It's all courtesy of the original owner, Stanley Smolak, a Polish immigrant who settled here and was befriended by local Native Americans. Inspired by their carvings, he began whittling and collecting. The Polish food is wonderful, too, with hearty platters of *golabki* (cabbage roll), *kielbasa* (sausage) and a delicious *zurek* (a sausage, egg and potato soup). The dining room extends into a wonderful garden.

From Cross Village, you can follow the signs along county roads up to windswept Wilderness State Park and its hiking and campground. Mackinaw City is 8 miles to the east.

boat fantail. Lots of seafood is found here, with intriguing options such as oyster stew (main dishes from $12).

For gourmet eats in the area, see 'Charlevoix to Mackinaw City – Scenic Drive.'

Getting There & Away

The *Beaver Island Ferry* (☎ 231-547-2311) has one to four trips daily ($31/16 adults/children) to the island; it also offers island tour packages. Autos may be taken ($104). Reservations are a good idea. Island Airways (☎ 231-448-2326) offers 20-minute flights ($65) to the island.

PETOSKEY & HARBOR SPRINGS

Tucked away inside Little Traverse Bay, Petoskey and Harbor Springs are where Michigan's upper crust maintains summer homes. The downtown areas of both cities have gourmet restaurants and high-class shops, and the marinas are filled with 30-foot yachts and sailboats. The gentrified Petoskey marina area, connected to downtown thoughtfully by underground walkways, is the home of the **Little Traverse Historical Museum** (☎ 231-347-2620), which has a large exhibit on Ernest Hemingway, whose family vacationed nearby in summer. He recuperated after World War I in Petoskey. Hours are 10 am to 4 pm Monday to Saturday; $1. The **Gas Light District** is a beautifully restored section of Petoskey, lined with shops and restaurants.

The local intercity bus stop is the Book Stop (☎ 231-347-4400) at 301 W Mitchell St. To Traverse City ($12) takes two hours.

Places to Stay & Eat

Between Petoskey and Harbor Springs along Hwy 119 is ***Petoskey State Park*** *(☎ 231-347-2311, 800-447-2757 for reservations)*, with a beautiful beach and 150 campsites ($15 a night). You must reserve a site in advance to stay at this very popular park. Rockhounds love the park, scouring for Petoskey stones, Michigan's state stone, which isn't a stone at all but dead coral.

For lodging, the ***Coach House Motel*** *(☎ 231-347-2593, 2445 Charlevoix Ave)* is as close to budget as you'll get. Singles/doubles in high season cost $50. The best lodgin option is ***Stafford's Perry Hotel*** *(☎ 231-347 4000)*, right in the center of the Gas Ligh District. Rates in this lovingly restored 189 inn are not bad at $75 single/double. Take look at a number of rooms, as there is som variety.

The outstanding ***Grain Train*** *(42 Howard St)* features natural and organi vegetarian foods (items from $5). To mak its breads it uses only well water, sea sal and organic wheat – superb with veggi soup. You can make your own stuff wit fixings from ***Syman's General Store*** a fe blocks away on Howard St. You'll find ove 150 cheeses, wines, smoked fish and fin Milwaukee sausages. With that lovel marina area, it's picnic time.

STRAITS OF MACKINAC

This region between the Upper and Lowe Peninsulas features a long history, miles c beach and lots of attractions. Spanning th Straits of Mackinac is the 6-mile-lon **Mackinac Bridge**, known locally as 'Bi Mac.' The $1.50 toll is worth every penny, a the views from the bridge, which includ two Great Lakes, two peninsulas and hun dreds of islands, are second to none in Mich igan. Photo opportunities are better on th Mackinaw City side.

Mackinaw City

• pop 875

At the south end of the Mackinac Bridge bordering I-75, is Mackinaw City, a tack tourist town with a gift shop and fudg kitchen (fudge is Northern Michigan's mos famous product) on every corner. Mackinaw City is best known as one of two depar ture points for Mackinac Island, but it doe have a couple of interesting attractions.

Right next to the bridge (the visitors center is actually beneath the bridge) i **Colonial Michilimackinac**, a National His toric Landmark that features a recon structed stockade first built in 1715 by th French. Docents garbed in period costume display skills of the time. Most popular ar the military reenactments (parades an musket firing) and cannon firings. Hours ar

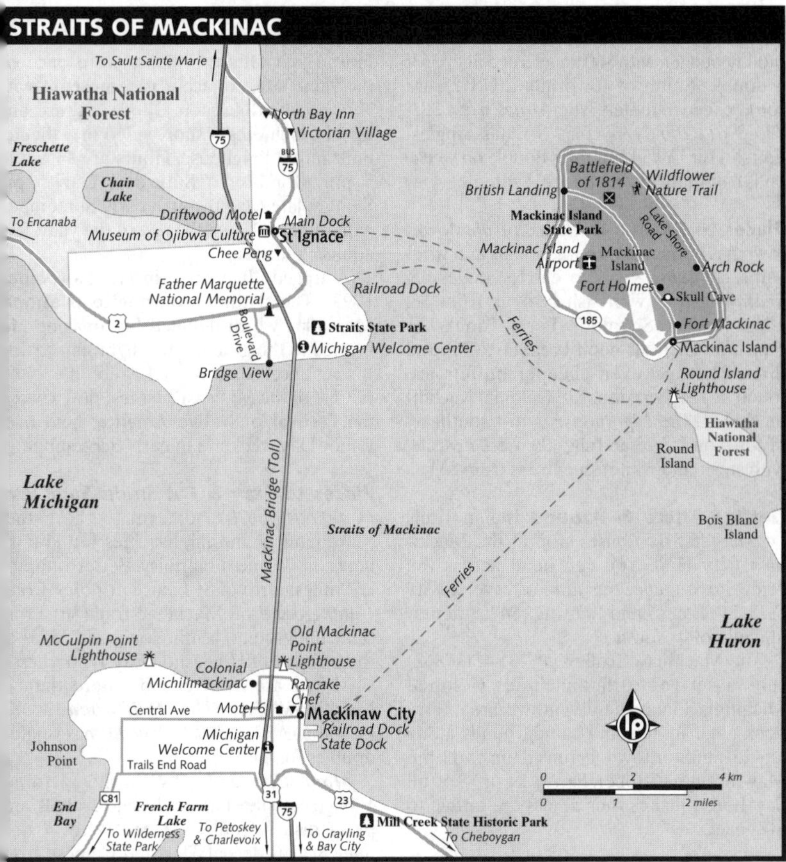

am to 6 pm daily mid-June through late August, shorter days the rest of the year. Admission is $8/5 adults/children.

Some 3 miles southeast of the city on US 23 is **Historic Mill Creek**, with historic displays and demonstrations, an 18th-century sawmill and nature trails. The mill is the oldest in the Great Lakes. Hours are the same as Colonial Michilimackinac. Admission is $6/4 adults/children.

If you plan to spend a few days at the Straits, purchase a Mackinac combination ticket ($15), which will provide entry to Fort Mackinac on Mackinac Island along with Historic Mill Creek and Colonial Michilimackinac.

Places to Stay If you have a tent, skip the high-price accommodations for a scenic campsite at ***Wilderness State Park*** *(☎ 231-436-5381)*, 8 miles west of town via County Rd 81. The 8286-acre park has 250 sites ($15), some overlooking the Straits, a nice beach and hike-in cabins for rent. Heading south on US 23 and Hwy 108, you'll find a few other private – and cramped – campgrounds.

The only things that outnumber the fudge shops in Mackinaw City are motels, which line I-75 and US 23. Between Memorial Day and Labor Day none of these is even remotely budget, with $60 an average figure for a double. South of town along US 23 are some cheaper motels. The ***Motel 6*** *(☎ 231-436-8961, 206 N Nicolet St)* has singles/doubles for $39/50, but rates double on weekends from June through early September.

Places to Eat The ***Wilderness Cafe*** downtown has homemade soups, breads and wild-game chili, and you can eat for under $5. ***Scalawags*** has whitefish baskets from $6. Close to the Shepler's Ferry Line, ***The Pancake Chef*** has good breakfast ($6) and dinner buffets; even cheaper buffets are found at ***The Fort*** opposite Colonial Michilimackinac. ***The Lighthouse*** is just southeast of town on US 23 and slightly more upscale, with steak and whitefish entrées from $11.

Getting There & Around Indian Trails (☎ 517-725-5105) buses stop at the Mackinaw City Hall. You can head across the bridge to St Ignace or south to Traverse City ($15, 2½ hours) and Lansing ($47, 8 hours) and all points south.

The Mackinaw Trolley (☎ 231-436-7812) runs a set route that includes Colonial Michilimackinac, the downtown area, ferry docks, and motels and campgrounds along US 23 south of town. It runs 8 am to 11 pm May through October. Fare is $1 or $3.50 all day. It also makes runs across the bridge to St Ignace.

St Ignace

• pop 2580

At the north end of the Mackinac Bridge is St Ignace, the second-oldest settlement in Michigan – Pere Jacques Marquette founded a mission here in 1671. This is also an access point for Mackinac Island.

You'll pass a huge Michigan Welcome Center (☎ 906-643-6979) with racks of brochures as soon as you've paid your bridge toll. A city visitors center is downtown near the Museum of Ojibwa Culture.

Things to See & Do In St Ignace, check out the **Museum of Ojibwa Culture & Marquette Mission Park**, where the famous Jesui priest, missionary and explorer is buried Huron and Ottawa villages were once o the same site. Adjacent is a museum wit very good exhibits on Ojibwa culture an history, including a short video in a theate built into a longhouse. Hours are 11 am t 5 pm Monday to Saturday, 1 to 5 pm Sunday, late May through early September with reduced hours the rest of the year; $2/ adults/children.

A tragedy happened in late November 1999. The **Father Marquette Nationa Memorial**, which detailed his amazing life burned to the ground after lightning struck It's yet uncertain if it will be rebuilt.

One of the Midwest's largest powwows i the **Festival of Native America**, held ove Labor Day weekend in early September.

Places to Stay & Eat ***Straits State Par*** *(☎ 906-643-8620)*, adjacent to the Fathe Marquette Memorial, has sites for $14; it' next to I-75 and a bit noisy. Better campin is 2 miles north of St Ignace at ***Foley Cree Campground***, off Mackinac Trail ($6). Fro the campground, a mile-long trail leads t the beaches of Horseshoe Bay Wilderness.

Motels are a bit cheaper here than i Mackinaw City. The ***Driftwood Mote*** *(☎ 906-643-7744, 590 N State St)* has singles doubles for $40/44.

Madd Chadder's Deli in the Victoria Village complex has sandwiches, salads, an pasta dishes from $5. ***Chee Peng*** *(416 N State St)* has decent Thai and Chinese fro $7. Popular is the ***North Bay Inn*** *(1192 N State St)*, 3 miles north of the bridge. Th cheap breakfast buffet ($4) is good, but it' mostly popular for its Friday night seafoo buffet and Saturday night prime rib buffe (each $13).

Getting There & Away Indian Trail (☎ 906-643-9861) stops at George's Bod Shop, 448 N State St, and has buses south t Mackinaw City, Lansing ($38, 8½ hours and Traverse City ($16, 3 hours). To g north to St Ignace, call Indian Trails; th company often subcontracts with a privat shuttle service for this run.

Mackinac Island

• pop 475

From either St Ignace or Mackinaw City, you can catch a ferry to Mackinac Island, Michigan's first tourist destination and today its best-known one. The British built a fort on top of the famous limestone cliffs in 1780 and then fought with the Americans for control of it during the War of 1812. In 1875 the federal government preserved Mackinac Island as the country's second national park, only three years after Yellowstone was dedicated, but handed it back to Michigan in 1895.

But the most important date on this 2000-acre island was 1898 – the year cars were banned to encourage tourism. Today all travel on the island is by horse or bicycle; even the police use bikes to patrol the town. The crowds of tourists (known on the island as Fudgies) can be crushing at times, particularly on summer weekends. If at all possible, and if funds allow it, spend a night on Mackinac Island; the real charm of this historic place emerges after the last ferry leaves at 6 pm.

One last thing: Never, ever pronounce the 'c.' It's *mack-in-aw*, not *mack-in-ack*. It's kind of a delicate issue.

Things to See & Do Overlooking the downtown area from a commanding position is **Fort Mackinac** (☎ 906-847-3328), one of the best-preserved military forts in the country. Several buildings are furnished in period detail. (Some of the exhibits show a whimsical, clever side.) Above the general store is a new, labyrinthine walk-through exhibit on the entire history of the island; it's excellent. There are regular military demonstrations and popular cannon firings. Hours are 9 am to 6 pm daily June through September, reduced hours May and October: $8/5 adults/children. A $15 combination ticket gives you access to Mackinaw City's museums.

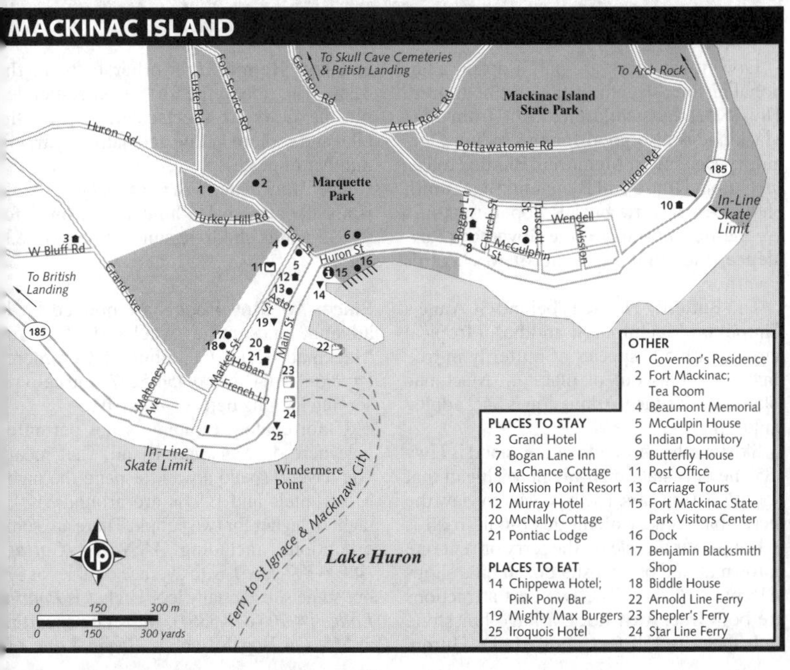

THOMAS HUHTI

Looking over Mackinac Island from Fort Mackinac

Downtown, there are half a dozen additional historic structures that can be toured. The $8/5 adults/children ticket from Fort Mackinac is also good for the Indian Dormitory, Beaumont Memorial, Biddle House, McGulpin House and Benjamin Blacksmith Shop. Less historic but also open for tours Wednesday mornings is the **Governor's Residence**, the summer home of Michigan's governor.

The **Butterfly House** is behind St Anne's Church on McGulpin St and has a tropical garden with 500 species of butterfly in free flight. It seems out of place on Mackinac Island, but it's nice. Admission is $4/2 adults/children.

Skirting the shoreline of the island is Hwy 185, the only state highway in Michigan that doesn't permit cars. The best way to view the incredible scenery along this 8-mile road is to bring your bicycle on the ferry or rent one in town at one of almost a dozen bike shops ($15 per half day). The two best attractions are both free: **Arch Rock**, a huge limestone arch that sits 150 feet above Lake Huron, and **Fort Holmes**, the 'other fort' on th island. The ride to the fort is a knee-bende but the views are spectacular. Hop off th bike and explore hiking and nature trails in number of places.

The *Mackinaw Breeze* (☎ 906-643-0241 is a sailboat with 1½-hour island tours fc $25/15 adults/children; sunset tours are $3 for all.

Places to Stay Rooms are booked far i advance on summer weekends. Call th Mackinac Island Chamber of Commerc (☎ 906-847-6418, 800-454-5227) for help re serving lodging before you arrive.

Unfortunately, camping is not permitte anywhere on Mackinac Island. That mean you have to spend a wad to spend the nigh Most hotels and B&Bs are around $120 night or higher for two people. There are som exceptions, including ***McNally Cottag*** *(☎ 906-847-3565)*, with average doubles at $7 but some substantially less. Higher is ***Pontia Lodge*** *(☎ 906-847-3364)*, with rooms startin at $65. On Bogan Lane is ***Bogan Lane In***

☎ 906-847-3439), with four rooms beginning $70 for two people. Also check ***La Chance ottage*** *(☎ 906-847-3526)*, a 30-room tourist ome a short walk from downtown on Huron , with doubles for $80 per night.

If money is less of an object, you've got *ts* of options. Downtown, the ***Murray otel*** *(☎ 906-847-3360)* has not unreason-le rates of $94/119 single/double in high ason. The ***Mission Point Resort*** *(☎ 906-17-3312)* might have the best location on e island, east of town and away from the adding crowds. Singles/doubles are $160.

And then, there is the ***Grand Hotel*** *☎ 800-334-7263)*, the largest resort in the orld and certainly among the most exclu-ve. This city-state has not only jaw-oppingly priced rooms (from a cool $300 r day, including two meals) but also a ozen restaurants, a famed 660-foot porch, d afternoon tea ($16). Such is the wking that there's now an admission fee 10) just to walk around.

laces to Eat The best-known eateries on ackinac Island are the dozen ***fudge shops***, hich use fans to blow the tempting aroma the freshly made confection out onto uron St. Taste it, but don't gorge; Mack-ac Island fudge is heavy and rich.

A couple of throwback ***burger joints*** are Main St, and you'll find an absolute preponderance of sandwiches on local pub menus. Also on Main St, the ***Chippewa Hotel***'s dining room has superlative views, even if the service is spotty. Its ***Pink Pony Bar*** has great pub grub and, if nothing else, this is the local hot spot for imbibing. At the other end of the street, the ***Iroquois Hotel*** has a much more upscale menu (from $12) and awesome views.

If you purchase a ticket to the fort, you can lunch at the ***Fort Mackinac Tea Room***, whose outdoor tables feature a million-dollar view of the downtown area below and the Straits of Mackinac. The food here is excellent.

Getting There & Around Three ferry companies – Arnold Line (☎ 800-542-8528), Shepler's (☎ 800-828-6157) and Star Line (☎ 800-638-9892) – operate out of both Mackinaw City and St Ignace and charge about the same rates: $13.50 roundtrip per adult and another $5.75 per bicycle. Times vary depending on the season; call for more information.

Once you're on the island, horse-drawn taxis will take you anywhere, even on a private tour ($15 per person per hour). If you want to rent your own horse, it's $25 per horse for the first hour, $20 thereafter. Bikes are available for rent everywhere you look ($4 to $10).

Lake Huron Shore & the Thumb

East of Mackinaw City, US 23 traces along the edge of Lake Huron nearly 200 miles before it rejoins the interstate whoosh approaching Bay City, the gateway to Michigan's 'Thumb' region – so-called because the Lower Peninsula is said to resemble a mitten, and this sticks out like a you-know-what. The Thumb shoreline drive along Hwy 25 adds an additional 150 or so miles to the trip and ends in Port Huron, where you can enter Canad or bend south toward the Motor City.

Highlights

- River Road Scenic Byway, a 22-mile traipse along the Au Sable River, with insights into the region's water and timber heritage
- Presque Isle, with two outstanding lighthouses and rustic hiking
- Rogers City, home to PH Hoeft State Park, one of Lake Huron's most beautiful, and close to the Lower Peninsula's only major waterfall
- Midland, which sports the heritage of Dow Chemical money, including Dow Gardens and the Alden B Dow Home & Studio, one of the most intriguing architectural highlights in Michigan

CHEBOYGAN TO BAY CITY

Cheboygan

• pop 5010

Cheboygan was one of the major lumberin towns along the Lake Huron coast. The co struction of a lock to connect Lake Hurc and the Cheboygan River to a chain c lakes stretching inland some 40 mil brought the first tourists. The 'Inland Wate way,' as it's called, is still a popular spot fc pleasure crafts.

Indian Trails buses stop at the Nor Country Inn (☎ 231-627-3129), 1355 Mac Ave. The ride to Flint takes six hours an costs $30.

Things to See East of the US 23 bridg across the Cheboygan River, **Gordon Turn Park** has a nice lighthouse and lakefro views (you can see the Mackinac Bridge Its best feature is an enormous catta marsh, and a prime spot for nesting birds. boardwalk leads to an observation towe Downtown, the **Opera House** (☎ 231-62 5841), 403 N Huron St, constructed in 187 with lumber money, was ravaged by fire couple of times but has been restored to i former beauty. Guided tours ($1) are avai able 1 to 4 pm daily June through Augus East of downtown is the **Cheboygan Coun Historical Museum** (☎ 231-627-9597), 404 Huron St, filled with local artifacts; it's fu mostly because it's in the old jail an sheriff's house. It's open 1 to 4 pm wee days, May through October; free.

Places to Stay & Eat The ***Birch Ha Motel*** *(☎ 231-627-5862)* is north of town c US 23; it has singles/doubles for $30/3 Chain motels are found on Hwy 27. F food, ***Kretchman's Koffeehaus Kafe*** c Main St near the bridge is a local favori for pastries, quiche, potpie and good coff (main dishes from $4). Overlooking tl ıver west of here, the ***Boathouse*** *(106 Pine ŧ)* is a steak and seafood place and a ɛputed former hideout of the 1920s Purple ìang of Detroit (entrées from $15).

ꞩogers City & Vicinity

Jorthwest of Rogers City along US 23 near Forty Mile Point) is a picturesque ghthouse and beach. The partially recon-ꞔructed pilothouse of a ship lies aging racefully in the yard. Rogers City itself is a usy, friendly place. It's home to the largest **mestone quarry** in the world and you can heck it out from an observation area south f downtown along Business Rte 23. Not far way is **PH Hoeft State Park** (☎ 517-734-543) with good ship watching.

Around Onaway, southwest of Rogers City, is the **Sinkhole Area**, a 2600-acre zone haracterized by freak karst geology. It's losed to motorized vehicles and offers some ilderness recreation; if you go, take a ompass and know how to use it. Closer to ꞩogers City, 11 miles west on Hwy 68 is **Ocqueoc Falls**, the largest in Lower Michi-an. A series of rapids, the 'falls' will leave ou unimpressed if you've seen the UP's cas-ades, but it's a nice spot nonetheless. Near ere is Clear Lake State Park, with a trail ystem.

Indian Trails stops at the Rogers City Motel (see Places to Stay & Eat). To Flint akes five hours and costs $27.

laces to Stay & Eat Since motels are on ıe expensive side, ***camping*** at Clear Lake tate Park south of Ocqueoc Falls on scenic Iwy 33 is the best option. You can also amp at ***PH Hoeft State Park*** *(see above)* ɔr $11 a site. Most motels are along N Bradley Highway (US 23), including the ***ꞩogers City Motel*** *(☎ 517-734-3707, 220 Bradley Hwy)*, where you can get a double ɔr around $45.

Head for the great ***Nowicki's Sausage hoppe***, where you can get outstanding rilled sausage, soups with homemade ɔodles and salads (items from $3) or to ***he Lighthouse***, right downtown, for urgers, steaks and pizza (main dishes rom $5).

Presque Isle

Nearly 15 miles southeast of Rogers City, a turnoff leads to the scenic little Presque Isle area. You'll find two lighthouse museums here. The **Historic Old Lighthouse Park** ($2/1 adults/children) has Civil War cannons, recovered ships, bells and a keeper's house. Up the road is the interesting **Presque Isle Lighthouse Park** ($2 to climb the tower), a restored keeper's house and lighthouse, along with excellent trails along the lake.

South of here is Presque Isle village. Continue through the village to the **Besser-Bell Natural Area**, along a horribly rutted dirt road. More lakefront hiking is here, and of interest along this trail is a ghost lumbering town. The whole is eerie and cool.

Alpena

• pop 11,000

Alpena is the largest town along the Huron shore north of Bay City and probably the least touristy. It's a bit surprising that so many settlers stuck around, considering its isolation. When the township was surveyed in 1839, the whole township site was offered instead of wages – and not one worker took the offer. Later, the town arose around flour and lumber mills.

Indian Trails stops at Lud's Hamburgers (☎ 517-356-6899), 1223 State Ave. To Bay City takes three hours and costs $17.

Things to See & Do The **Jesse Besser Museum and Planetarium** (☎ 517-356-2202), 491 Johnson St, has exhibit areas on local history and a variety of arts and science programs. The main piece in the collection is a 60,000-piece collection of Native American artifacts. Hours are 10 am to 5 pm Tuesday to Saturday, noon to 5 pm Sunday; $2/1 adults/children. Not far from here is **Island Park**, a gorgeous city park and wildlife sanctuary (bird-watching is wonderful). It has great nature trails and an established canoe route.

Downtown in a historic district, the **Thunder Bay Theatre** (☎ 517-354-2267) is a year-round troupe that performs musicals and dramas.

Offshore, the Thunder Bay Underwater Preserve contains the remains of nearly 80

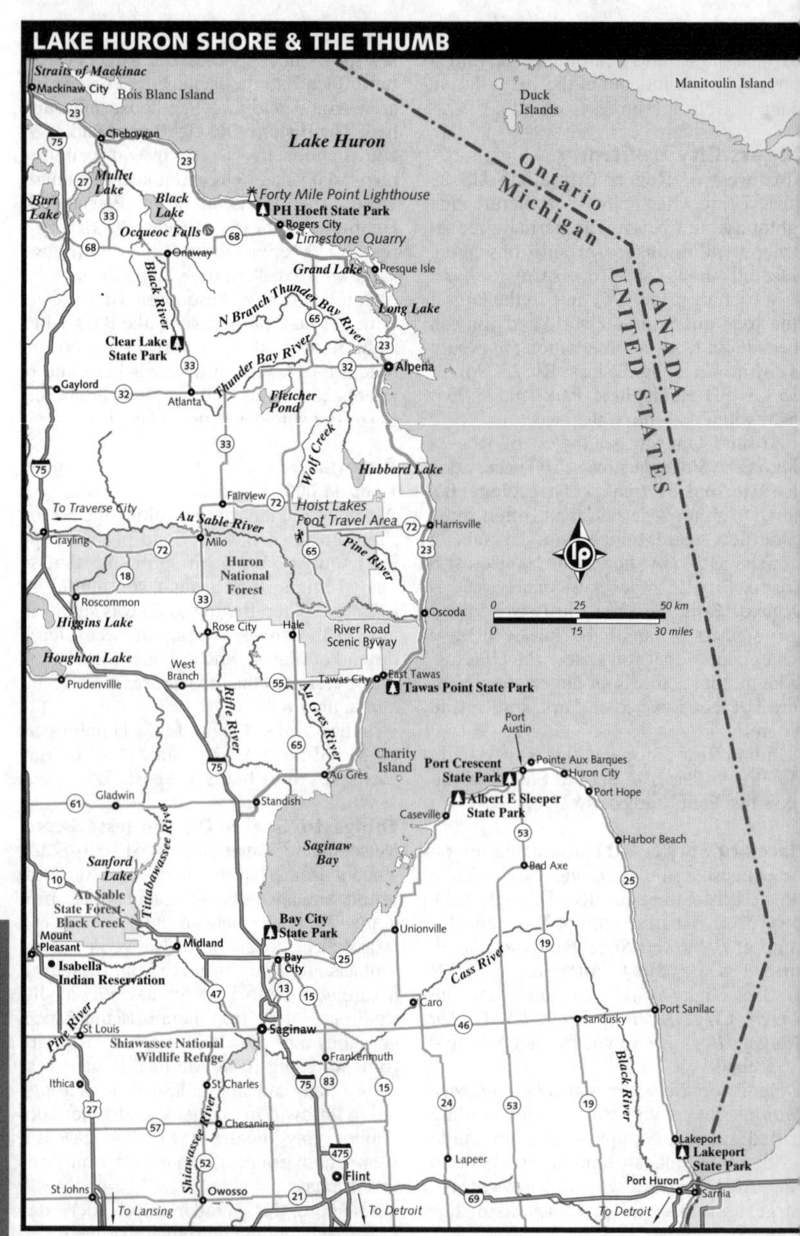
LAKE HURON SHORE & THE THUMB
Straits of Mackinac
Mackinaw City
Bois Blanc Island
Duck Islands
Manitoulin Island
Lake Huron
Cheboygan
Mullet Lake
Burt Lake
Black Lake
Ocqueoc Falls
Forty Mile Point Lighthouse
PH Hoeft State Park
Rogers City
Limestone Quarry
Onaway
Grand Lake
Presque Isle
Ontario
Michigan
CANADA
UNITED STATES
Black River
N Branch Thunder Bay River
Long Lake
Clear Lake State Park
Thunder Bay River
Alpena
Gaylord
Atlanta
Fletcher Pond
Wolf Creek
Hubbard Lake
Fairview
Hoist Lakes Foot Travel Area
To Traverse City
Au Sable River
Harrisville
Grayling
Milo
Pine River
Huron National Forest
Roscommon
Oscoda
0 25 50 km
0 15 30 miles
Higgins Lake
Rose City
Hale
River Road Scenic Byway
Houghton Lake
West Branch
Prudenville
Tawas City
East Tawas
Tawas Point State Park
Rifle River
Au Gres River
Port Austin
Charity Island
Port Crescent State Park
Pointe Aux Barques
Huron City
Au Gres
Port Hope
Albert E Sleeper State Park
Gladwin
Standish
Caseville
Tittabawassee River
Saginaw Bay
Harbor Beach
Sanford Lake
Bad Axe
Au Sable State Forest-Black Creek
Bay City State Park
Unionville
Mount Pleasant
Midland
Isabella Indian Reservation
Bay City
Cass River
Caro
Port Sanilac
Pine River
St Louis
Saginaw
Sandusky
Shiawassee National Wildlife Refuge
Frankenmuth
Black River
Ithica
St Charles
Chesaning
Shiawassee River
Lapeer
Lakeport
Lakeport State Park
Flint
Port Huron
St Johns
Owosso
Sarnia
To Lansing
To Detroit
To Detroit

MICHIGAN

ssels that sank in and around the rocky chipelago. Thunder Bay Divers (☎ 517-6-9336) has charter trips.

laces to Stay & Eat The ***Dew Drop Inn*** *517-356-4414, 2469 French Rd)* is north town along US 23. Singles/doubles cost 0. Look at a few rooms since there is a riety. For food, burgers are a big thing cally. ***Lud's*** *(1223 S State St)* and ***The Owl afe*** *(121 W Chisholm St)* are the two best; e former has ⅓lb monsters. Downtown ***hn A Lau Saloon & Steakhouse*** *(414 N cond St)* is a brewpub and steak joint in a storic complex (main dishes from $8).

scoda

pop 1000

scoda, at the mouth of the Au Sable River, is long been a recreation base. Even while was churning out millions of feet of mber, the vast tracts of the Huron National Forest to the west drew trout fanatics id paddlers. Backpacking is great in the ,000-acre **Hoist Lakes Foot Travel Area**, rthwest of Oscoda where Hwys 65 and 72 eet. Over 20 miles of trail snake through nse aspen and hardwoods forest. A pass 3) must be purchased for certain areas in e national forest. Stop at the Huron ores Ranger Station (☎ 517-739-0728), 61 North Skeel Rd, for maps and information on the Huron National Forest.

Stop by in September for the tons-of-fun ul Bunyan Days and the Michigan ainsaw Carving Championship. Call the hamber of Commerce (☎ 517-739-7322) r more information.

Indian Trails buses stop at the Aspen otor Inn (☎ 517-739-9152). The ride to int takes three hours and costs $17.

wwas City

pop 2880

wwas City is made up of East Tawas and e larger Tawas City, both stretching out r what seems like forever along the lake. shing is a huge draw here – both on Lake uron and on inland lakes. There is a hisrical museum in Tawas City but the real aw is Tawas Point, an oddly shaped peninsula east of East Tawas. **Tawas Point State Park** (☎ 517-362-5041), at the tip, includes a 2-mile beach and some of the best birdwatching in Michigan. ***Camping*** is $15. A lighthouse (not open to the public) is opposite the beach.

Indian Trails stops at the Tawas Motel on US 23.

BAY CITY & SAGINAW

Bay City and Saginaw are separated by 10 miles, but it's hard to tell sometimes because of suburban sprawl. Bay City is the better known of the two, being the hometown of Madonna. There's enough of interest to spend an afternoon here.

The Saginaw County Convention & Visitors Bureau (☎ 800-444-9979) is at 901 S Washington Ave. In Bay City, the Bay Area Chamber of Commerce (☎ 517-893-4567) is at 901 Saginaw St.

The Indian Trails bus depot (☎ 810-753-5454) in Saginaw is at 511 Johnson St downtown. In Bay City, the depot (☎ 810-893-6589) is at 1124 Washington Ave.

Things to See & Do

Saginaw has a lovely Japanese garden complete with an almost one-of-a-kind (for the US) tea house. The **Japanese Cultural Center** (☎ 517-759-1648), 527 Ezra Rust Drive, was a gift from Tokushima, Saginaw's sister city in Japan. A full tea ceremony is performed every second Saturday; $6. Hours are 9 am to 4 pm Tuesday to Saturday; tea house tours are given every half hour noon to 4 pm in summer; $3. The gardens are free.

On the campus of the Saginaw Valley State University is the **Marshall M Fredericks Sculpture Gallery** (☎ 517-790-5667), 2250 Pierce Rd. Fredericks is a renowned sculptor whose work you may have seen in Detroit; the *Spirit of Detroit* sits at the City County Building. Hundreds of pieces are in the collection both inside the museum and outdoors in a garden. Hours are 1 to 5 pm Tuesday to Sunday; free.

Bay City is pleasant enough to just stroll around the downtown or along the lovely **riverwalk**; especially if you're lucky enough to see a massive freighter come floating by. The local historical society gives $5 trolley tours of downtown architecture and history. Of the impressive downtown architecture, none is more distinctive than the grand **Bay City City Hall** (☎ 517-894-8147), 301 Washington Ave. Built in 1894, this Romanesqu structure has a 125-foot clock tower th dominates the skyline. Weekday afternoon go to the 4th-floor Planning Office and po litely ask to climb up the tower. Afte signing a liability waiver – those stairs ar

River Road Scenic Byway – Scenic Drive

Oscoda is the eastern terminus of a wonderful scenic and historical side trip – the River Road Scenic Byway, mixing lovely national forest and Au Sable river scenery with half a century's logging history. It's only 22 miles from Oscoda to Hwy 65 north of Hale, but it could easily take most of a day if you take in all the area has to offer.

Just a mile or so out of town you pass by the **Eagle Run Cross Country Trail**, a short nature trail next to the Au Sable River. If you want to canoe the Au Sable River, Oscoda Canoe Rental (☎ 517-739-9040) is at 678 River Rd here and has canoes and kayaks for rent ($18 to $22 per trip). Six miles west of Oscoda is the first obligatory stop. From its Foote Dam dock, the *River Queen* paddleboat (☎ 517-739-7351) departs one to two times daily June to mid-October for two-hour narrated tours of the Au Sable River. Fare is $10/5 adults/children.

A couple of miles west is **Old Orchard Park**, the first of three USFS campgrounds along the road. South of here along Wells Rd is gorgeous scenery at the **Tuttle Marsh Wildlife Area**. At the approximate halfway point of the scenic road is the highlight. **Lumberman's Monument** is the site of a USFS visitors' center with a memorial statue to the early loggers of the area. The center also has interpretive displays. Certain areas within the Huron National Forest require a $3 fee, and this office sells passes year-round. The center commands a grand view of the Au Sable River from a high vantage point and a great interpretive trail descends to the river from here. A **campground** is also here. The monument is also one trailhead for the **Highbanks Trail System**, a backcountry network of trails totaling 7 miles from Iargo Springs to the west with Sidtown to the east. (No camping.) South of Lumberman's Monument 4 miles along Monument Rd is the **Corsair Trail Complex**, a system of trails totaling 26 miles. A $3 fee is required here.

A mile or so west of Lumberman's Monument is a memorial to canoeists. An additional mile west is **Iargo Springs**. A stairway descends 150 feet down to the Au Sable River, where several springs and small waterfalls gurgle from the banks. The scene from the top of the stairway is impressive.

Two or so miles west is an informational kiosk on the fascinating history of the area – settlement, logging and its effects, and the role hydropower played in restoring the river's forested areas.

From here, Hwy 65 heads south to Hwy 55, and Tawas City and the big lake are 15 miles to the east.

:eaky – you can get some great views of ıe area from the top.

North of Bay City at the foot of Saginaw ·ay is the **Bay City State Recreation Area** ☎ 517-667-0717), close to the Bay City tate Park and linked via trails. There are reat beaches and a huge coastal marsh. A isitors' center has wetlands exhibits, bird bservation areas and regularly scheduled ducational talks. Admission is $4.

'laces to Stay & Eat

aginaw has budget lodging at the junction f I-75 and Hwy 46, including a ***Rodeway nn*** *(☎ 517-753-2461, 3425 Holland Rd)*, here you can get a single/double for $45/55, r for much less on Friday and Saturday. aginaw also has one of the most elegant &Bs in this part of the state. The ***Montague nn*** *(☎ 517-752-3939, 1581 S Washington ve)* is not far from the Japanese Cultural enter and has 17 rooms with rates ranging om $65 to $180. The dining room is also ell regarded.

For cheap lodging in Bay City, Hwy 13 Euclid Ave) off Hwy 25 has a few dirt-cheap ut OK motels, like the ***Delta Motel*** *(☎ 517-84-4490, 1000 S Euclid Ave)*, which has ngles/doubles for less than $30 sometimes.

Downtown Bay City has plenty of casu-lly upscale eateries. One local institution is ***rampa Tony's*** *(1108 Columbus Ave)*, a ery casual Italian place with pizza, pasta, aked casseroles and huge banana splits items from $4). Better – it's open until mid-ight. ***Krzysiak's*** *(1605 Michigan Ave)* has ood Polish food. On the west side of the iver Bay City has a few good pubs and afés along Midland St, including the ***Here-ord & Hops*** *(☎ 517-891-4677, 804 Midland t)*, a popular brew pub and grill-your-own-teak joint (main dishes from $7).

ROUND BAY CITY & SAGINAW

rankenmuth

pop 4330

rankenmuth is kind of a shock to the ystem if you don't know what to expect. ust 11 miles southeast of Saginaw, it's likely he most popular tourist trap you've never eard of. It's at once kitschy but lovely, overcrowded but appealing. All for what? Chicken and Santa Claus.

Coming into town along Hwy 83, the first thing you'll see is **Bronner's Christmas Wonderland** (☎ 517-652-9931), if not the world's largest Christmas store then certainly the most ostentatious (in a fun way). Stop in here at 25 Christmas Lane – the parking lots alone must be able to handle 500 buses – and wander the store, itself the size of four football fields. Everything you could possibly relate to Christmas is whirring, blinking, or flashing. Hours are 9 am to 9 pm Monday to Saturday, noon to 7 pm Sunday.

The downtown area of Frankenmuth is a piece of eye candy right out of Bavaria. And everyone who comes here is aiming for either ***Bavarian Village Restaurant*** *(☎ 517-652-2651, 713 S Main St)* or ***Zehnder's*** *(☎ 517-652-6337, 730 S Main St)*, both of which are famed in Michigan for their copious farm-style smorgasbord chicken dinners. You can also get German food, but who does that? Stories vary as to what started the whole craze, but these two do it so well they both have expanded into massive resorts, replete with golf courses. And 'Frankenmuth-style' is now a trademark! Starve yourself before stopping in.

Otherwise, Frankenmuth offers boat tours ($6/3 adults/children) on the Cass River, a couple of OK museums, and lots of shops on the ersatz Bavarian main strip.

Midland

• pop 38,000

Dow Chemical Co is the mainstay of this town 15 miles west of Bay City. Don't let the imagery of a petrochemical town put you off from visiting – it's a picturesque city with numerous excellent sights.

The Midland County Convention & Visitors Bureau (☎ 517-839-9901) is downtown at 300 Rodd St.

Michigan's official architect laureate was Alden B Dow, a student under Frank Lloyd Wright and the designer of some of Michigan's most famous buildings. The **Alden B Dow Home & Studio** (☎ 517-839-2744), 315 Post St, is regarded as important an architectural work as anything in the US; like

Wright, Dow believed in the synthesis of nature and design and this is a stellar example. Tours ($10/5 adults/children) are given twice Friday and once Saturday; reservations are a must. (Brochures for self-guided tours of downtown architecture are available from the visitors information office.) Just southeast of here are the **Dow Gardens** (☎ 800-362-4874), 100 acres of flowers, trees and shrubs with lovely walking trails winding throughout; open 10 am to sunset. Adjacent is the **Midland Center for the Arts** (☎ 517-631-5930), with interactive exhibits and displays on art, science and history, along with a performing arts theater; 10 am to 6 pm. Admission is $5/2 adults/children for both, or $3/2 adults/children separately.

It is possible to tour the **Dow Chemical Company** (☎ 517-636-8659), but you must reserve in advance for the free 2½-hour tour.

Fifteen miles west of town near Sanford, the ***Au Sable State Forest – Black Creek*** *(☎ 517-826-3211)* has primitive campsites for $4. Lodging is not cheap in Midland. The most centrally located is the ***Ashman Court Hotel*** *(☎ 517-839-0500, 111 W Main St)*, with an excellent riverfront location. Rooms are $79/89 single/double. The restaurant here is the best downtown.

The Greyhound stop is at H&L Coin-a-matic (☎ 517-832-1627), 416 E Ellsworth Ave. The drive to Bay City takes 30 minutes and costs $7.

THE THUMB

Hwy 25 heads east out of Bay City and alternates heartland agrarian stretches with Great Lakes vista. The word 'charming' comes to mind for most towns along the way. It's noticeably less congested than the Lake Huron coast to the north. Most of the sights don't come until the tip of the Thumb, near Port Austin.

Thumb Area Transit (TAT; ☎ 517-269-2121, 800-322-1125), operating out of Bad Axe, is a dial-in ride service ($1). The problem is that it operates only in Huron County, at the tip of the thumb, but it's the only public transport there is.

Caseville to Port Austin

After Caseville, it seems that every mil brings another reason to pull off the road Nine miles northeast of Caseville, the **Huro County Nature Center – Wilderness Arbore tum** (free) has nearly 300 acres of san ridges and shallow swales. Not far to th north, more dunal topography is found a **Albert E Sleeper State Park** (☎ 517-856 4411), named after the man who founde Michigan's state park system. Four miles o trails follow old dune ridges and both we lands and hardwood forest. Campsites ($15 are on the south side of the road. Ye another state park is 10 miles northeast **Port Crescent State Park** (☎ 517-738-8663 on the site of what was once a lumbe boomtown. Campsites ($15) here have view of either Lake Huron or the Pinnebo River. Canoes are available at a livery nea the park entrance.

Port Austin

• pop 800

Very near the tip of the Thumb, Port Austi is an unpretentious town that's often calle Michigan's best place to watch either sunset or a sunrise.

North of town, **Pointe Aux Basques** wa for a long time a getaway resort communit for the well-heeled of Detroit. A lighthous still stands in a park. In Port Austin, th most popular activity is to head out on *Mis Port Austin* (☎ 517-738-5271), a charte fishing boat that has five-hour fishing tou ($30 with poles); there are usually two trip a day June through August.

Besides the campgrounds to the south west, the ***Blue Spruce Motel*** *(☎ 517-738 8650, 8527 Lake St)* has basic singles/double from $45; it also has cabins for $65. Th ***Garfield Inn*** *(☎ 517-738-5254, 8544 Lake S* is on the National Register of Historic Place and has lovely rooms for $75/80 single double. President James A Garfield was re portedly a regular visitor, thus the name.

For food, the ***Sportsman's Inn*** has ½l perch dinners. ***Finan's*** has an old-fashione soda fountain. (Both have food from $4. The ***Garfield Inn's restaurant*** *(see above)* i highly regarded, with a popular Sunda runch ($6). Casually upscale dining is ound at the ***The Bank*** *(☎ 517-738-5353)*, vith outstanding fish dishes (entrées from 8). ***The Farm*** *(☎ 517-874-5700, 699 Pt Cresent Rd)* has good heartland cuisine, using resh seasonal vegetables and ingredients main dishes from $9).

luron City

'he best known of the Thumb's attractions what's left of Huron City 6 miles east of 'ort Austin. A once bustling lumber town, luron City was ravaged twice by fire. The emaining buildings are now housed along lwy 25 in the **Huron City Museum** (☎ 517-28-4123). Extant buildings include a US 'oast Guard lifesaving station, an inn and a og cabin. The jewel in the crown is the louse of Seven Gables, the lavish original ome of Huron City's founder. The family ccupied the house for nearly a century, and 's been maintained almost exactly as it vas, providing an excellent glimpse into ocal history. The 10-acre complex is open 0 am to 5 pm Thursday to Monday, July 1 rough early September. Admission to the useum *or* mansion is $6/3 adults/children; ombination tickets are available.

Continuing toward the lake from here, here is a nice municipal ***campground*** ($15) nd lighthouse/museum.

'ort Hope

even miles south of Huron City, Port Hope in the middle of the Thumb Area Under-'ater Preserve, an offshore accumulation of early a dozen large shipwrecks. Most are accessible to novices, but a good spot is outh of town.

larbor Beach

ifteen or so miles south of Huron City, larbor Beach is known as the birthplace nd home of Frank Murphy, one-time ayor of Detroit, governor of Michigan, Atorney General of the US and – how he ade his mark – US Supreme Court Justice. le wrote famously liberal dissenting opinons decrying the 'legalization of racism' ith the internment of Japanese Americans uring WWII. He wrote strenuously on labor's right to strike, refusing to send troops during Flint's 1937 sit-down strike. His home and law office, a short walk away, are now a museum. Hours are 10 am to 5 pm Thursday to Sunday.

Port Sanilac

Port Sanilac has the **Sanilac County Historical Museum and Village** (☎ 810-622-9946), a grouping of historic structures including the 1875 Loop-Harrison House, a well-maintained Victorian with most of its original furnishings. Hours are 11 am to 4:30 pm Tuesday to Friday, noon to 4:30 pm weekends, mid-June through mid-September; $6/2 adults/children. Offshore is the **Sanilac Shores Preserve**, with nine wrecks lying in fairly shallow waters. Four Fathoms Diving (☎ 810-622-3483) has charter trips.

Port Huron

Port Huron is the largest town on the Lake Huron shoreline and one of Michigan's oldest settlements. Fort St Joseph was established here in 1686 to protect the French fur trade. It lasted only two years before the garrison gave up and moved to Mackinac Island. It would be a century more before French settlers from Detroit settled around the mouth of the Black River.

Information A Michigan Welcome Center (☎ 810-984-2361) is located west of town off I-69. Near the base of the original Blue Water Bridge to Canada sits the Blue Water Area Convention & Visitors Bureau (☎ 800-852-4242), 520 Thomas Edison Pkwy, a very with-it and helpful organization. The old depot housing the CVB has displays on Thomas Edison, Port Huron's most famous resident.

Things to See & Do Port Huron is linked to Sarnia, Ontario, by the Blue Water Bridge, a popular entry point into Canada. A second Blue Water Bridge has been constructed right next to the first to speed up the flow of traffic. The bridges are, somewhat uniquely, jointly owned by Canada and the US. North of the bridges stands the **Port Gratiot Lighthouse**, off limits except for rare occasions.

South of the bridges in Pine Grove Park sits the retired USCG lightship *Huron*, the only lightship designated a National Historic Landmark. It spent nearly four decades guiding ships through the narrow dredged channel of Lake Huron. Hours are 1 to 4:30 pm Wednesday to Sunday, July through August, weekends only May, June and September; $2. Downtown at the corner of Sixth and Court Sts is the **Port Huron Museum** (☎ 810-982-0891), with a little bit of everything. It's heavy on marine exhibits and Thomas Edison memorabilia. Hours and admission are the same as the lightship.

The *Huron Lady II* (☎ 810-984-1500) has two-hour St Clair River tours ($11/6 adults/children) one or two times daily, including evening tours.

Places to Stay & Eat For camping, ***Lakeport State Park*** *(☎ 810-327-6265)* is 11 miles north on Hwy 25 with sites for $14. The cheapest motel lodging is found along I-94 west of downtown at the Water St or Lapeer Rd exits. ***Knights Inn*** *(☎ 810-982-1022, 2160 Water St)* is at exit 274 off I-94 and offers singles/doubles from $45. The ***Thomas Edison Inn*** *(☎ 810-984-8000, 500 Thomas Edison Pkwy)* overlooks the S Clair River in a quiet location not far fror the Blue Water Bridges. Singles/double are $89 and the hotel has a full list o amenities.

Downtown ***Bangkok Star*** *(421 Beers S* has good Thai food and daily specials (fror $6). Also downtown is the precious ***Dian Sweet Shoppe*** *(307 Huron Ave)*, an old fashioned soda fountain serving basic sanc wiches. It was built in 1926 and hasn changed a bit. The ***Fogcutter*** *(☎ 810-98 3300, 511 Fort St)* sits atop the People's Ban Building and has superb views to go with i creative seafood and heartland fare at nc unreasonable prices (entrées from $9).

Getting There & Around There isn't a intercity bus service. Amtrak is downtow at 2223 16th St and has daily service west t Chicago and east to Toronto. The trip t Flint takes a little more than an hour an costs $12.

The Blue Water Trolley (10¢!) operate along a fixed route taking in all major sigh and the visitor information center. It's great deal. Hours are 10:45 am to 5 pı Tuesday to Saturday.

Upper Peninsula

\ third of the state lies in this rugged, vooded and isolated region. There are only ·5 miles of interstate highway in the Upper 'eninsula (UP) and a handful of cities, of vhich Marquette (population 22,000) is the argest and most interesting. Between the ities are miles of undeveloped Great Lake horelines (Huron, Michigan and Superior); cenic two-lane roads; small rural towns; nd lots of rustic campsites, many of them in he Hiawatha and Ottawa National Forests, he three state forests and the 23 state arks. A palpable individualism character- zes the populace of the UP (Yoopers); it is n many respects a world wholly different rom Lower Michigan, spiritually as much s physically.

You can drive across the UP, from the Aackinac Bridge to Ironwood, on the Wis- onsin border, in less than six hours. Or you an just as easily spend two weeks here, amping, hiking, canoeing and viewing some f the more than 200 waterfalls that dot the orthern Michigan landscape. Do take your ime, as it's indeed a precious place.

.AKE MICHIGAN SHORE & VISCONSIN BORDER

)rummond Island

The Upper Peninsula is off most tourist paths n Michigan, and Drummond Island, which is ctually on Lake Huron, is even farther off. Many Michiganders aren't even aware of it.) The largest US island on the Great Lakes, it is nore than two-thirds state owned.

From St Ignace, the UP's access point for he Lower Peninsula, it's a 16-mile jaunt orth along the tedium of I-75, then a lovely ·0 miles eastward along Hwy 134. Rustic ampsites are found along the way at ***De Tour State Park*** (☎ *906-643-8620*) in Cedarville. Cedarville is also the conduit to he 36 rocky outcroppings comprising the .es Cheneaux Islands archipelago, used for enturies by Native Americans and Euro- ean fur traders to flee the wrath of Lake Iuron storms. Cedarville has a charming

Highlights

- Isle Royale, the most isolated and least visited national park, worth weeks of backcountry exploring with the moose and wolves
- Pictured Rocks National Lakeshore, an isolated stretch of spectacular shoreline featuring lovely geological formations
- Marquette, an attractive small city used as a comfortable base camp for exploring the rugged Huron Mountains to search out Michigan's moose
- Keweenaw Peninsula, home to some of the US' most well-preserved mining-era architecture

maritime museum with boat models and boat paraphernalia, along with a boat-building shop mock-up. You won't find much else of interest around unless you happen to show up in August, when there's a wonderful antique boat festival.

Twenty-four miles east of Cedarville at De Tour village, a ferry ($10 car and driver) is the only way over to Drummond Island. It runs hourly April through December, much less frequently other times.

Once on Drummond Island, you're left to your own devices. And that's the whole draw to the rugged, isolated place, with all that public verdancy itching to be explored. The only 'attraction' of any sort is ***Woodmoor*** *(☎ 800-999-6343)*, a gorgeous private resort that once belonged to the Domino's Pizza food giant, which used it as a corporate retreat. Today it's a luxury resort best known for its championship golf course, the Rock. Rates are around $100 for lodging in the summer. If you're of less impressive means, some two dozen more modest lodging options exist. ***Annie's Attic*** *(☎ 906-493-5378, 525 Humms Rd)* has rooms with private or shared bath in either a carriage house or a renovated log cabin. Rates start at $45 single/double.

Hiawatha National Forest – East

From the Mackinac Bridge, you can head miles west on US 2 and stop at the St Ignace Ranger District office of the Hiawatha National Forest (☎ 906-643-7900). This visitors center can provide a wealth of information

Yooper Pride

The denizens of Michigan's Upper Peninsula – Yoopers – are individuals isolated from, and not always on speaking terms with, the rest of the state. This at times has less to do with geography than attitude.

It's easy to blame the lay of the land; Copper Harbor, on the Keweenaw Peninsula, is a hell of a long way from Lansing or Detroit and the I-94 population (and power) corridor. Others blame the fact that the UP wasn't even supposed to be part of Michigan. It was only because of the 'Toledo War' of 1835–36 (see Toledo in the Northern Ohio chapter) that most of the UP was given to Michigan. Many legislators who agreed to give up Toledo and the Lake Erie shoreline did so grudgingly, feeling that the UP was a 'poisoned wasteland.' Some residents are still so isolated that the US Census Bureau has to send out its canvassers in four-wheel-drive vehicles and, especially, snowmobiles.

Some Yoopers now feel that the UP is not much more than an afterthought to Lower Michigan, especially when it comes to doling out state resources. The 'trolls' (as some Yoopers derisively call anyone who lives 'below' the Mackinac Bridge) come up for summer vacation, then ignore the region the other 11½ months. Many roads – and we're not talking 'wilderness rural' here either – of the UP weren't paved until the 1980s; some residents first got indoor plumbing about the same time. You couldn't even make a direct call to the Upper Peninsula from Detroit until the late 1970s. This was easy enough to deal with while the copper and iron mines were humming along gloriously (producing tax wealth, incidentally), but once mineral companies began pulling out, the differences between the Brobdingnagian-size peninsulas began to surface. Hey, the UP even holds its own state fair, if that gives you any indication of the feelings.

Now and again a tongue-in-cheek secessionist movement will start up. In the 1970s a few symbolic 'takeovers' of the Mackinac Bridge took place. Others prefer to capitalize on the tourist dollar: If we have to tolerate the trolls for only half the year, they say, it ain't so bad. Still others are rabidly anti-Lower UP and still dream of the ultimate goal – secession and formation of the 51st state, known as 'Superior' or 'Huronia,' including portions of northern Wisconsin and of northeastern Minnesota, an idea that was actively bandied about in the early 19th century.

UPPER PENINSULA

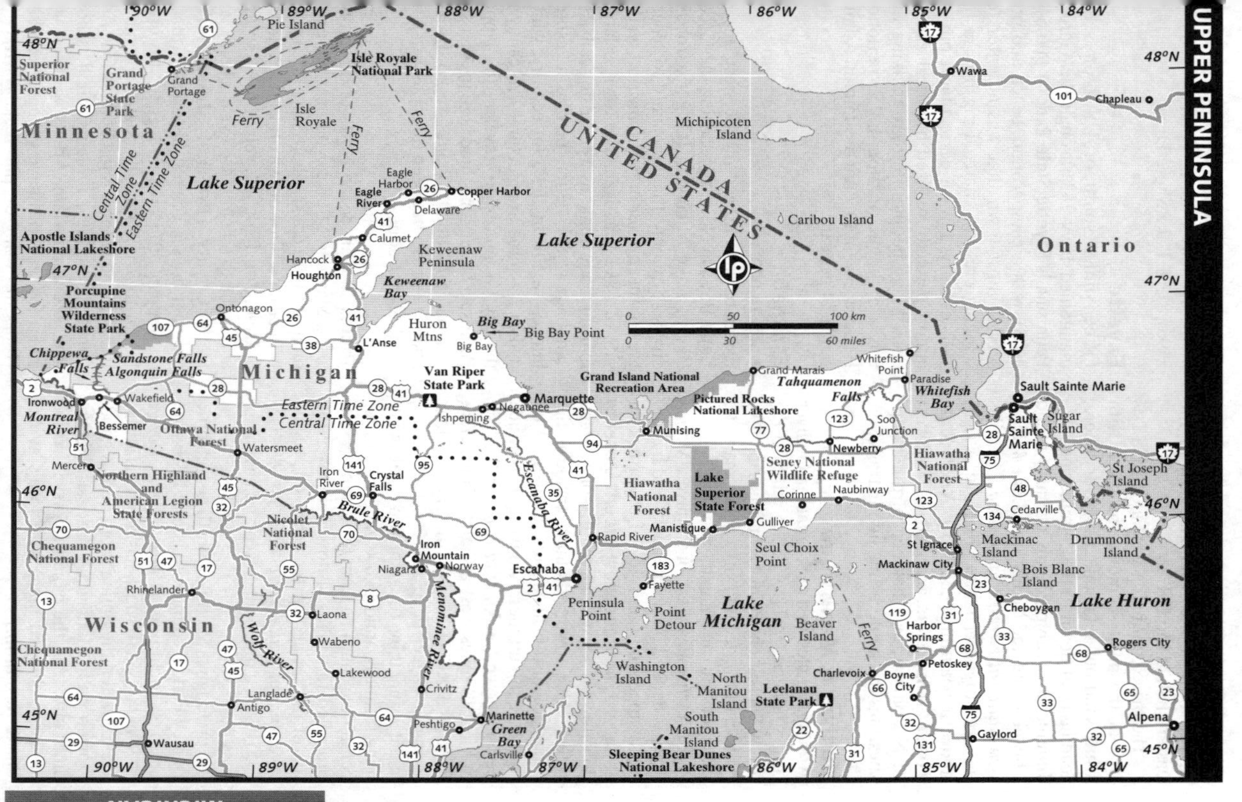

MICHIGAN

about camping, hiking, canoeing and scenic drives along Lake Michigan and in the eastern half of the UP.

The drive continuing west along US 2 is one of the most scenic in the state, with white-sand pullouts appearing everywhere, leading right down to the shimmering lake. Innumerable campgrounds are also found between here and Manistique. ***Lake Michigan National Forest Campground***, 18 miles west of St Ignace, has 38 wooded sites right above a beautiful beach. ***Big Knob State Forest Campground***, accessed off US 2 west of Naubinway, also has beachfront campsites, plus three interesting hiking trails.

Gulliver & Manistique

Around 50 miles west of St Ignace in Gulliver bear southeast on Hwy 432, 5 miles to the lovely **Seul Choix Point Light**. Built in 1895, it's been converted into an excellent maritime museum. You can climb the tower ($2).

Thirteen miles west of Gulliver, Manistique is flanked by smokestacks and has the oddly appealing pungency of papermaking about it. The **Imogene Herbert Museum** downtown is housed in a century-old cottage with a brick tower adjoining; inside is the usual local historical detritus. It's open 10 am to 4 pm in summer. Manistique is much better known for *Kitch-iti-Kipi*, or the 'Big Spring,' 12 miles west at **Palms Book State Park** (☎ 906-341-2355). This crystal clear spring is 45 feet deep and 200 feet across, and it's something to see brown trout swimming furiously amid 16,000 gallons of water per minute churning from the depths. A self-propelled raft takes visitors right over the top of the spring. On the other side of the lake, ***Indian Lake State Park*** *(☎ 906-341-2355)* is on a mile-long beach and has campsites for $15.

For lodging, 22 miles northeast in little Blaney Park, a couple of historic B&Bs are options, including ***Blaney Park Lodge*** *(☎ 906-283-3883)*, which has rooms as low as $35 in winter; the dining room here is good. Downtown in Manistique, order straight-up diner fare, read the papers and swill coffee in classic chipped mugs with locals at ***Jax Bar & Restaurant***.

Buses make midnight – or worse – sto[p] at the Holiday Fuel & Food (☎ 906-34[…]-2796), 813 E Lake Shore Drive.

Fayette

Fifteen miles south of US 2 on sem[i-]maintained Hwy 183 through the Gard[en] Peninsula is **Fayette State Park** (☎ 906-64[…]-2603), with a campground, beach and pr[e-]served ghost town that was a center f[or] smelting ore into charcoal pig iron in th[e] 19th century. It's an eerie place, but a[n] almost perfectly realized historical experi[-]ence. Many people go away thinking th[is] was a highlight of their UP experienc[e.] Hours are 9 am to 7 pm in summer. Admi[s-]sion is $4 per car.

Escanaba

• pop 14,000

Escanaba sits perched on the west side [of] Little Bay De Noc, approaching the Gre[en] Bay of Lake Michigan. It's got a robu[st] diverse economy thanks mainly to havi[ng] the only deepwater-ore shipping port on th[is] side of Lake Michigan. The town is larg[er] than anybody thinks as well. Historically, E[s-]canaba was the beneficiary of aweso[me] lumber wealth in the 19th century, whi[ch] makes for some architectural eye candy [in] the city. Of interest to travelers, the Upp[er] Peninsula State Fair is held here in August.

Don't forget that 15 miles west of Esca[n-]aba you cross between the Eastern an[d] Central time zones.

Things to See & Do North of downtow[n] along Sheridan St takes you near the eno[r-]mous iron-ore docks, where ships are load[ed] with taconite. Downtown off Ludington A[ve] is **Ludington Park**, a lovely littoral stret[ch] and home to a lighthouse ($1 to climb) a[nd] Delta County Historical Museum. Th[e] museum houses general historical artifac[ts] on shipping, iron ore and logging. It's ope[n] 11 am to 7 pm June through Septembe[r;] free. Also downtown is the **Bonifas Fine Ar[ts] Center**, housed in a former Catholic scho[ol] gym and auditorium. Artists work on si[te] and a few galleries have changing exhibi[ts.] Hours are 10 am to 5 pm weekdays; free.

MICHIGAN

East of Escanaba is the Stonington Penin-ula, at the bottom of which is the **Peninsula oint Lighthouse**, whose 40-foot tower can e climbed (free). It's only a couple of miles s the crow flies from Escanaba, but the total ip around the bay is around 20 miles. nother attraction is **Little Bay de Noc ecreation Area**, which has virgin hemlock ines, a nice beach and a great campground or information call the Rapid River ranger ation at ☎ 906-474-6442) with sites for $10.

laces to Stay & Eat Dozens of mom-nd-pop and chain motels line US 2 both est and northeast of town, including the ***orway Pines Motel*** *(☎ 906-786-1000)* ortheast of town, where you can get a ecent single/double for $37/47.

Drury Lane Bakery & Café *(906 Luding-on Ave)* has great Finnish baked goods. The wedes also make an appearance with the ***wedish Pantry*** *(819 Ludington St)*, serving xcellent basic Swedish fare, including omemade *limpa*, a type of pastry (items rom $4). Three blocks from here ***Hereford nd Hops*** *(624 Ludington Ave)* is a grill-our-own-steak joint in a historic local uilding. Five miles west of town on US /41, ***Dell's Supper Club*** is a classic supper lub; the salad bar ($5) is worth the trip.

etting There & Away Escanaba is some-ning of a UP junction for Greyhound and s subcontracted ride services. The bus tation is in the Delta Transit Station ☎ 906-789-7030), 2901 27th Ave N. Buses eave only in the wee hours of the morning. o Iron Mountain ($13) takes an hour; to Ailwaukee ($34) takes seven hours.

ron Mountain

ust over 50 miles to the west of Escanaba ia US 2, Iron Mountain is an interesting lace to visit, with lots of affordable motels nd good restaurants. It's one of the few UP ommunities where the Finnish influence is ess obvious; here, the Italians set up camp nd have kept their presence known.

hings to See & Do Probably owing to he giddy heights, the local constabulary won't try to stop you from inching yourself up the **Pine Mountain Ski Jump**, where skiers set a US record of 400 feet. As the leaves turn it's a phantasmagoric, if not somewhat shaky, scene from the top.

East of town to Norway, then south along US 8 (follow the signs) brings you to the very impressive **Piers Gorge**, where 19th-century timber workers called 'tie-hacks' battled the elements to somehow ram millions of feet of logs through a churning gorge along the Michigan–Wisconsin border. Trails follow the course of the gorge and make for a great day trip. Go white-water rafting at Piers Gorge with Argosy Rafting Adventures (☎ 715-251-3886; $20 per person). Or, as the billboards *incessantly* scream in the UP, ride an underground train into an iron-ore mine at **Iron Mountain Iron Mine** (☎ 906-563-8077), 8 miles east on US 2. Hours are 8 am to 6 pm in summer, reduced hours through late October; $6/3 adults/children.

Much closer to town, the **Cornish Pump and Mining Museum** (☎ 906-774-1086) is just a couple of blocks off US 2 (follow the signs). The highlight is one of the most massive steam engines in North America, extraordinary in size. You'll also find a WWII glider display. Hours are 9 am to 5 pm Monday to Saturday, noon to 4 pm Sunday, May through October; $4/2 adults/children.

Places to Stay & Eat The ***Lake Antoine Motel*** *(☎ 906-774-6797, 1663 N Stephenson Ave)* has rooms for around $34, or rent a cabin on the Menominee River at ***Edgewater Resort*** *(☎ 906-774-6244)*.

Bimbo's *(314 E Main St)* is a highlight of the UP. A tavern with a blue-collar feel, it has indescribably good porketta (roasted pork) sandwiches ($3) Wednesday to Saturday (it regularly roasts its own pig). You'll also find other from-scratch Italian food, and it's all in a friendly atmosphere.

For more substantial Italian, ***Fontana's*** *(115 S Stephenson Ave)* is an excellent Italian eatery and steakhouse (entrées from $9).

Getting There & Away Greyhound (☎ 906-779-9537) stops at Crispigna's Party Store, 710 Norway St. Buses arrive and

The National Dish in Yooperland

Ten minutes in Michigan's Upper Peninsula and it's apparent there are two things of note, food-wise: whitefish (understandable, given the geography) and something called 'pasty.' Pasties are basically meat and vegetable pies brought into US culture by European immigrants; the Cornish get all the credit, but other ethnic groups had them too. Pasties were the perfect food for miners – they were incredibly filling and practical to carry. A true pasty sticks to your ribs like nothing else. Traditionally pasties were very basic, using flour, beef, potatoes, carrots, and onions – real Yooper pasties included rutabaga, that distinctively flavored tuber. Today you'll find other (sometimes questionable) ingredients: turkey, tofu and salsa, among other things.

One thing to note: Pasty is meant to rhyme with 'nasty,' never 'tasty.'

My Grandma's Pasty Recipe

2½ cups flour
¾ cup vegetable shortening
1 teaspoon salt
8 tablespoons cold water
1 pound coarse ground beef chuck roast
4 medium potatoes, finely chopped
1½ medium onions, chopped
1½ cups rutabaga, diced
1½ cups carrots, diced

Directions For the crust, cut shortening into flour with pastry blender. Gradually add water to make soft dough. Divide into four sections. Roll each section to the size of a dinner plate.

For filling, thoroughly mix meat and vegetables. Place ¼ of mixture on half section of dough. Dot with butter (one teaspoon per pasty). Season to taste. Fold uncovered portion of dough over filled side. Crimp edges. Place on cookie sheet. Bake at 375 degrees for 1½ hours. Yield: four servings.

Mom's Cheating Method To cut the preparation time in half, grind all vegetables and mix with meat. Roll dough for pie pan. Place half the filling mix in a pie pan. Cover with crust. Cooking temperature and time remain the same.

– Thomas Huhti

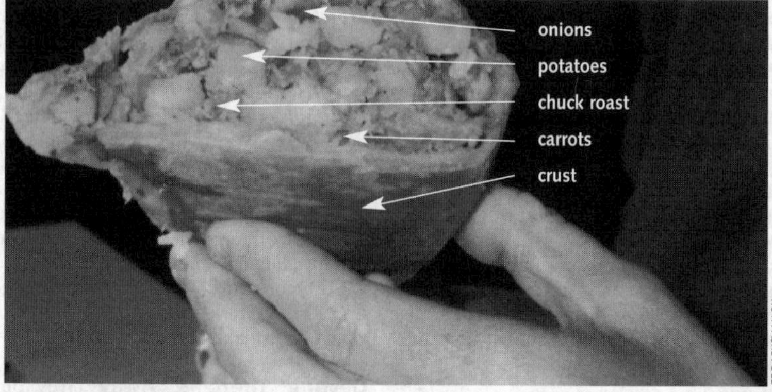

RUTH ASKEVOLD

MICHIGAN

epart at inconvenient hours. To Escanaba $13) takes an hour; to Ironwood ($23) ikes three hours.

ron River

on River started up near the end of the nining heydays and despite its somewhat rim demeanor from US 2, it has an attraction worth stopping for. If you can get to 'aspian, a couple of miles to the south, ou'll find the **Iron County Museum** (☎ 906-65-2617), with old mining paraphernalia uch as the Caspian Head Frame and a reconstructed village of buildings representng mid-19th-century mining life. Best of all ; the interactive exhibit exploring local nines and mine families. You'll also find a ice wildlife art gallery and exhibits detailng songwriter Carrie Jacobs Bond (she vrote 'I Love You Truly'), who was the nine-doctor's wife. Hours are 9 am to 5 pm Monday to Saturday, 1 to 5 pm Sunday, ummertime; $5/3 adults/children.

West of Iron River, ***Lake Ottawa Campround** (☎ 906-265-5139)* is part of the Ottawa National Forest and has basic campites for $5 and up. West of downtown, the ***ron River Motel** (☎ 906-265-4212)* has very partan rooms from around $30 single/ouble. Downtown an ***AmericInn** (☎ 906-65-9100)* provides more upscale lodging.

Mouth-watering Italian food is also found n Iron River. ***Alice's Café***, on US 2, has resh-made pasta dishes that seem simple ut are truly to die for; the breadsticks alone re worth a trip. East of town in Crystal Falls ***lub Felix*** is a bistro with a chef trained by he Culinary Institute of America. The food ; unpretentious but definitely above verage (main dishes from $9).

Greyhound stops at two places: next to he Iron Inn Motel (☎ 906-265-5111), 211 W 'ayuga St and a flag stop at the Citgo gas tation at the corner of US 2 and County Rd \. Bus times are not optimal. To Escanaba $22) takes two-plus hours.

Vatersmeet

his town is a one-flashing-traffic-light kind f place. No real attractions are here, but he **Ottawa National Forest Visitor Center** (☎ 906-358-4724) on Old US 2 can provide information on the Sylvania Wilderness, a 21,000-acre rugged tract perfect for backwoods exploring ($4 permits required). Plunked within the million acres of the Ottawa National Forest, the area is also a boundary waters for the Wisconsin River with over 300 lakes and 240 streams, including the Cisco Chain, a gemlike string of 15 isolated lakes. Waterfall hunting is also a favorite pastime; the center has maps. Campgrounds are ubiquitous.

Ironwood & Bessemer

You're entering Big Snow Country, an unofficial second name for these parts of the far western section of the UP. Because of its proximity to the most massive of the Great Lakes, Superior, the stretch from Ironwood northeast all the way up to the tip of the Keweenaw Peninsula gets absolute tons of snow – 300 inches per winter before anyone bats an eye. As such, it's a prime skiing and snowmobiling center.

Things to See & Do Blackjack Ski Resort (☎ 800-848-1125) and Big Powderhorn Mountain (☎ 800-501-7669), both east of Ironwood in Bessemer, offer good alpine skiing, along with snowboarding, at Blackjack. An even larger operation is Indianhead Resort (☎ 800-346-3426) in Wakefield. Bessemer also has one of the best back-road trips in the UP. County Rd 513, a narrow county road, turns north off US 2 and heads past a US Forest Service ranger station. The road stretches only 13 miles but you pass by three pullouts leading to a half-dozen waterfalls, all connected by trails, and these trails are in turn linked to the North Country Scenic Trail. A USFS campground ($8) is found at the north end near Black River Harbor. Halfway there, turn right and go a mile to **Copper Peak Ski Hill**, the only international ski-flying hill in the Western Hemisphere. Chairlifts ($8) make the ride up to the 1782-foot top for an incredible view.

Ironwood has its own excellent waterfalls. The first thing to do is head west of town to the Michigan Welcome Center to pick up maps of local waterfalls. The best is **Superior**

Falls, approximately 15 miles west via US 2 and county roads. Here the Montreal River enters Lake Superior. You'll find many others in the two-state proximity. Ironwood shares with Hurley, Wisconsin, just over the border, the superb **Pines and Mines** mountain bike trail system; pick up detailed maps of these tough but rewarding trails at the Welcome Center. Just road tripping and no time to scout cascades? Downtown Iron Mountain has its own kitsch attraction, a 52-foot fiberglass **statue of Hiawatha**, the fictional hero of Henry Wadsworth Longfellow's famous poem.

Places to Stay & Eat Ironwood has a plethora of cheap motels, most of them with Finnish-style saunas. The ***Sandpiper Motel*** *(☎ 906-932-2000)* along US 2 is basic and cheap at around $35 per double. For more luxurious options, the best bet would be one of the ski resorts (see Things to See & Do). For eats, head for ***Joe's Pasty Shop*** *(116 Aurora St)* right downtown, a local tradition since 1946.

Getting There & Away Greyhound stops next to the Gogebic County Transit Station (☎ 906-932-2523), 285 E McLeod St. Heading east the bus stops at 8:25 pm for Iron Mountain ($23, 3 hours); the other scheduled bus requires a 4 am wake-up.

SAULT SAINTE MARIE

Founded in 1668, Sault Sainte Marie (pronounced 'Soo Saint Marie' and often called 'the Soo'), near the eastern end of the UP, is the oldest city in Michigan and the third oldest in the USA. It has a twin Soo on the Ontario side; see the Ontario Shore (Canada) chapter. Once the St Mary's Rapids, where Lakes Superior and Huron meet, had been tamed ('locked' is more apt) and commercial shipping could lock through, the city's future was cemented.

A Michigan Welcome Center awaits you as you come over the International Bridge.

Things to See & Do

The town is a popular tourist destination with loads of attractions; some are tacky, many are interesting and the best two are free. **Soo Locks Park** is at the end of Water St in the heart of downtown. It features an interpretive center and observation decks from which you can watch 1000-foot-long freighters being raised and lowered between the different lake levels. Just south

Soo locks in 1930

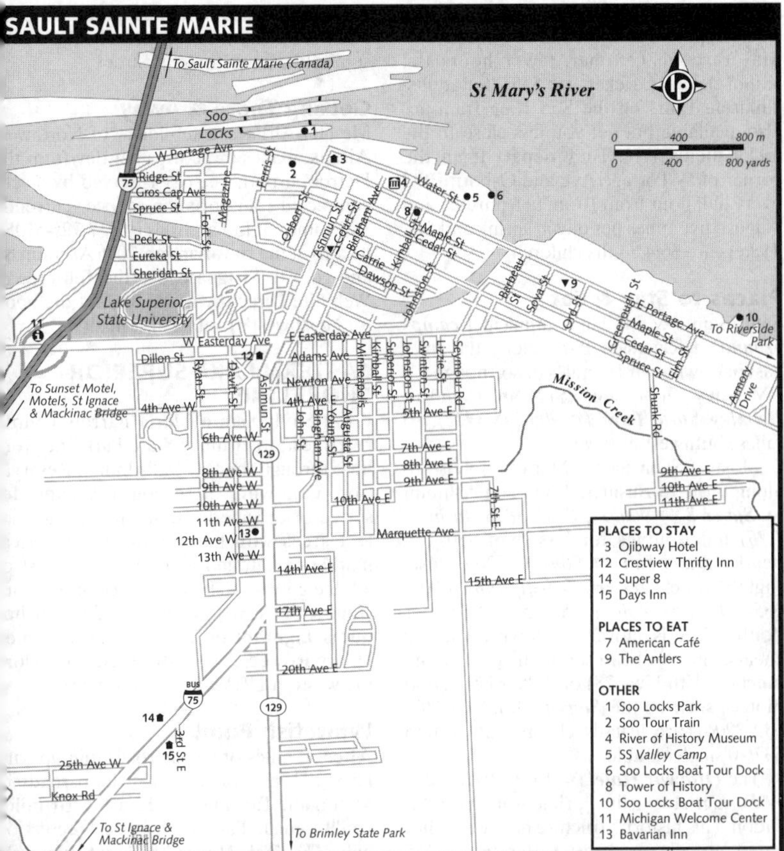

f the park is **Locks Park Walkway**, with displays that cover the city's 350-year history. If ou don't get your fill of locks history from ll this, head to the **River of History Museum** (☎ 906-632-1999), 209 E Portage Ave, where there's more; there are also exibits on the Ojibwa culture that was here rst. Hours are 10 am to 5 pm Monday to aturday, noon to 5 pm Sunday; $3/1 adults/hildren.

Ever popular is the SS *Valley Camp* ☎ 906-632-3658), a 550-foot-long freighter hat you can walk through. Most attention ere is drawn to the lifeboats recovered from the legendary *Edmund Fitzgerald* wreck. Hours are 9 am to 9 pm in peak season, 10 am to 6 pm lower season, May through August. Admission is $7/4 adults/children.

For a sweeping view of the locks, the city, and even the Soo's twin city across the St Mary's River, the 21-story **Tower of History** (☎ 906-632-3658), 326 E Portage Ave, has an observation deck, along with more historical displays. Hours are 10 am to 6 pm daily May through October; $3/2 adults/children.

Organized two-hour boat tours of the locks are available from a couple of locations east of downtown. Being dwarfed by the locks in your little boat is great fun. Tours depart regularly 9 am to 7 pm in mid-May through October, fewer hours the rest of the year. Tickets are $15/7 for adults/children. Tours on the Soo Tour Train are also available but get you less close to the locks themselves. They depart from the corner of W Portage Ave and Osborn Blvd every half hour from 10 am to 6 pm July and August, five times per day in spring and fall. Tickets are $6/4 adults/children.

Places to Stay & Eat

Sault Sainte Marie has a municipal ***campground*** in Riverside Park, along the river east of downtown 1½ miles or so, though it's RV-heavy. Good sites ($12) are found at ***Brimley State Park*** *(☎ 906-248-3422)*, 10 miles southwest of town.

Most of Sault Sainte Marie's motels are along the I-75 Business Loop and Ashmun St. ***Super 8*** *(☎ 906-632-8882, 3826 Business I-75)* has doubles for less than $50; the nearby ***Days Inn*** *(☎ 906-635-5200)* costs slightly more. ***Crestview Thrifty Inn*** *(☎ 906-635-5213, 1200 Ashmun St)* charges $54 per double but is closer to downtown. For cheaper motels, head south one exit (to the junction with Hwy 28) on I-75, where good motels, such as the ***Sunset Motel*** *(☎ 906-632-3906)*, are usually cheaper at around $37/40 single/double.

The ***Ojibway Hotel*** *(☎ 906-632-4100, 240 W Portage Ave)* is in a prime waterfront location. This historic structure has been renovated into a luxury beast, with rates of $115 single/double that are totally out of whack with the area, though the rooms are nice.

For dinner, head to a UP institution. ***The Antlers***, on Portage Ave, is the place to feast on giant hamburgers and specialties such as fried Cornish hen or foil-wrapped whitefish (main dishes from $6), and take in the hundreds of stuffed animals on the walls, all in a somewhat riotous atmosphere. This is no place for animal rights enthusiasts or those who crave silence. The ***American Café***, a few blocks south of Portage Ave on Ashmun, has been the place in the Soo for quality diner fare since 1902 (dishes from $4). It became so well known that in 1999 i[t] had to relocate to a bigger, sadly more anti[-]septic, location across the street.

Getting There & Away

Mesaba Airlines, a subsidiary of Northwes[t] Airlink, makes three trips per day from th[e] Detroit airport. The city is served by a sub[-]contracted transportation service (currentl[y] J&J Limo) of Indian Trails (☎ 517-725-5105)[;] it stops at the Bavarian Inn, 2006 Ashmun St and goes to St Ignace. See the Toll-Free & Web Site Directory at the back of the boo[k] for Northwest's contact information.

EASTERN LAKE SUPERIOR SHORELINE

From Sault Sainte Marie narrow count[ry] roads lead to Brimley State Park and fro[m] here through the Bay Mills Indian Reserva[-]tion. Following these you're tracing de[-]serted Lake Superior shoreline. A couple o[f] rest areas with bathrooms and historica[l] markers are found along the way. Best o[f] all, freighter-watch from a scenic lookou[t] (follow the signs) or the top of the **Pt Iro[-]quois Lighthouse**, the point from whic[h] Henry Rowe Schoolcraft set out to explor[e] the western UP. Watch out for deer!

Whitefish Point

After 30 miles or so, the roads join up wit[h] Hwy 123, one of the nicest loop roads i[n] Michigan. Turning north, after 10 mile[s] you'll come to Paradise, a modest recreatio[n] hub; ***The Fish House*** has great whitefish[.] Getting sidetracked is definitely in order.

Where Hwy 123 bears west, continu[e] north toward Whitefish Point. Eventuall[y] you'll come to the fascinating **Great Lake[s] Shipwreck Museum** (☎ 906-635-1742), dedi[-]cated to the 'Graveyard of the Great Lakes[.]' Among the exhibits is the bell from th[e] *Edmund Fitzgerald* wreck; a theater has [a] short film on the *Fitz*. Hours are 10 am t[o] 6 pm, mid-May through mid-October; $7/[?] adults/children. Outside is the Whitefis[h] Point Light Station, the oldest active ligh[t] on Lake Superior. Restored to its origina[l] state, it's open for tours.

The museum's location here at Whitefish Point is appropriate, since the bay it forms was a natural harbor for vessels trying to seek shelter from a storm. Owing to the spontaneous nature of Lake Superior, many didn't make it. Around the point are the scattered remains of nearly two dozen vessels, all comprising an underwater preserve. (The *Edmund Fitzgerald* did not actually go down here, though it was racing here to outrun the storm that sank the freighter on November 10, 1975.) Diving is possible but not for novices. Much less dangerous is bird-watching since the point is a natural stopover for migrating birds. Over 300 species can be seen here, including the endangered piping plover; there's even a viewing house.

Tahquamenon Falls

Returning to Hwy 123 and following it west, you'll eventually come to the top attraction in the eastern UP, **Tahquamenon Falls**. The Upper Falls in the Tahquamenon Falls State Park (☎ 906-492-3415) are 200 feet across with a 50-foot drop, making them the third-largest falls east of the Mississippi River. The Lower Falls are a series of smaller cascades best viewed by renting a boat and rowing across the river to an island. The large state park also has 176 campsites ($14) and great hiking, and there's a brew pub with excellent creative dishes right in the middle of it.

Another way to explore the falls is to take the 6½-hour **Toonerville** (☎ 888-778-7246) train and boat tour from Soo Junction, south of the falls along Hwy 28, east of Newberry. A narrow-gauge train travels 5 miles to the river, where you board a boat for a 21-mile trip to the park. One trip daily departs Soo Junction at 10:30 am mid-June through early October. Tickets cost $20/10 adults/children. A train-only tour is also available.

Lake Superior State Forest

To the west of Hwy 123 spreads a spiderweb of gravel county roads (in various states of repair), leading to the lakeshore and various flyspeck-isolated communities. Virtually all of the map is green – you're in the heart of the Lake Superior State Forest. Also here, some 25 miles west of Paradise, is **Muskallonge Lake State Park** (☎ 906-658-3338), a favorite of rock hunters searching for agates. The park sits on the former site of Deer Park, a 19th-century lumbering town; a few dock pilings in Lake Superior are all that remain. West of here on County Rd 58 you'll also find three rustic state forest campgrounds ($4). Even in high tourist season, these stretches are fairly devoid of people.

From here, most folks are probably going to head for Pictured Rocks National Lakeshore. County Rd 58 passes through the picturesque little bay community of **Grand Marais**, the eastern terminus of the park. Looking at a map, one would expect this isolated town – only one paved road runs the 25 miles to it – to be hanging on by its hope. Not so, it's doing perfectly well, thank you very much. A small **maritime museum** is near the Coast Guard station; times are flexible but in season it's usually open 1 to 4 pm weekends.

There are cheap motels here, including the ***Voyageur's Motel** (☎ 906-494-2389)*, a half-mile east of Hwy 77 on Wilson Rd, where doubles can be found for $38. ***Welker's** (☎ 906-494-2361)*, adjacent to the maritime museum, has similar rates but also offers a pool, whirlpool and sauna. Its restaurant serves a Sunday brunch. Otherwise, for food, you'll find more than you might imagine. The classic ***Westbay Diner*** has a retro diner-in-a-railway car look to it; it serves straightforward diner fare. Grand Marais also has a good ***brew pub***. For the most practical option, buy some smoked fish at the local fish market and hit the beach.

If you are headed south toward Hwy 28 from Tahquamenon Falls, **Newberry** doesn't look like much at first glance but does have a couple of museums and inexpensive motels, and it is a central spot for exploring this region. The local visitors' information center, at the junction of Hwys 28 and 123, will even give you a bunch of discount coupons for local businesses.

PICTURED ROCKS NATIONAL LAKESHORE

The crown jewel to the Upper Peninsula may be the Pictured Rocks National Lakeshore, a 110-sq-mile national park between Munising and Grand Marais famed for its colored sandstone bluffs with freakish rock formations. The cliffs rise some 200 feet over the water; some of them have caverns nearly 6 acres large. The artist's-palette geology comes from red Cambrian sandstone sedimentation stained with mineral oxides. A set of enormous dunes is also found on the east end of the park, near Grand Marais.

Information

Stop in at the Hiawatha National Forest and Pictured Rocks Visitor Information Center (☎ 906-387-3700), on the corner of Hwy 28 and County Rd 58, for maps, backcountry permits and other details. This is not the same as the Munising Falls Interpretive Center a few miles east. The Grand Sable Visitor Center 3 miles west of Grand Marais is open summers and can also issue permits. Another visitors' center at Miner's Castle cannot issue permits.

Things to See & Do

Munising is the usual gateway to the park. Most people view the 200-foot cliffs on a two-hour tour with Pictured Rock Boat Cruise (☎ 906-387-2379), which departs on the hour in summer from downtown Munising ($2 per person). Even air tours ($15 to $30) are available, from Pictured Rock Air Tours (☎ 906-222-8367). If you want to drive the park yourself, keep in mind that it's a long drive between Munising and Grand Marais along a mostly unpaved road – passable but teeth-chattering. This condition worsens significantly in periods of wet weather.

The most scenic backpacking adventure in the state is the **Lakeshore-North Country Trail**, a four- to six-day, 43-mile trek between Grand Marais and Munising through the heart of the park. It's part of the North Country National Scenic Trail. Most other trails – there are around a dozen – are short, typically a mile or two. Great day hikes include Miners Falls and Chapel Falls, the latter a bit longer at 3 miles.

Kayaking and canoeing are popular on three of the park's lakes, but the rivers are generally too shallow. Overnight sea kayaking along Lake Superior is possible for those with the necessary skills and equipment, but an entrance permit must be purchased. The offshore portion of the park is protected as an underwater preserve. Wrecks lie in pristine condition thanks to the primevally icy waters. The

Lake Superior from within Pictured Rocks National Lakeshore

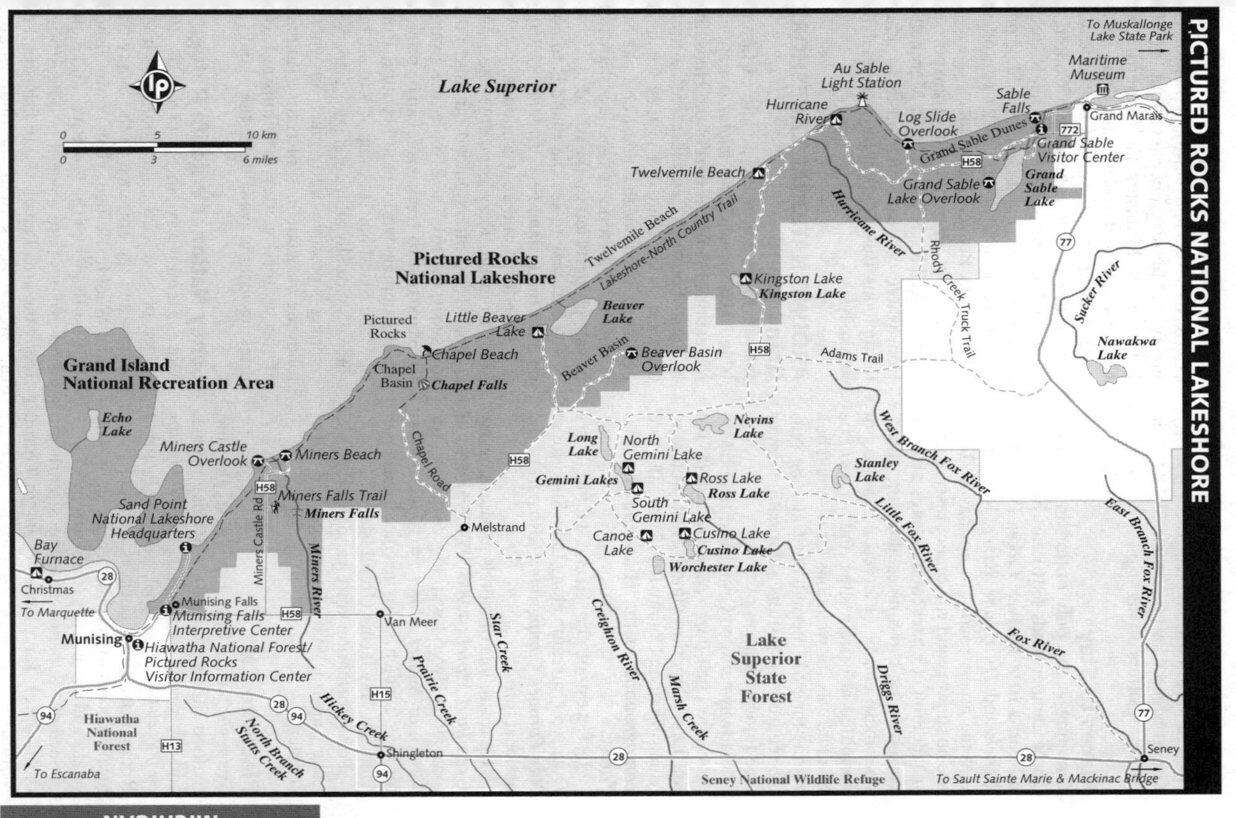
PICTURED ROCKS NATIONAL LAKESHORE
Lake Superior
0 5 10 km
0 3 6 miles
Pictured Rocks National Lakeshore
Grand Island National Recreation Area
Echo Lake
Miners Castle Overlook
Miners Beach
Sand Point National Lakeshore Headquarters
Miners Falls Trail
Miners Falls
Miners Castle Rd
Miners River
Bay Furnace
Christmas
To Marquette
Munising Falls
Munising Falls Interpretive Center
Munising
Hiawatha National Forest/ Pictured Rocks Visitor Information Center
Hiawatha National Forest
To Escanaba
North Branch Stutts Creek
Hickey Creek
Shingleton
Van Meer
Prairie Creek
Star Creek
Melstrand
Chapel Road
Pictured Rocks
Chapel Basin
Chapel Beach
Chapel Falls
Little Beaver Lake
Beaver Lake
Beaver Basin
Beaver Basin Overlook
Twelvemile Beach
Lakeshore-North Country Trail
Kingston Lake
Adams Trail
Long Lake
North Gemini Lake
Gemini Lakes
South Gemini Lake
Canoe Lake
Nevins Lake
Ross Lake
Cusino Lake
Worchester Lake
Creighton River
Marsh Creek
Lake Superior State Forest
Driggs River
Stanley Lake
Little Fox River
West Branch Fox River
Fox River
East Branch Fox River
Hurricane River
Au Sable Light Station
Log Slide Overlook
Grand Sable Dunes
Grand Sable Lake Overlook
Grand Sable Lake
Sable Falls
Grand Sable Visitor Center
Rhody Creek Truck Trail
Maritime Museum
Grand Marais
To Muskallonge Lake State Park
Sucker River
Nawakwa Lake
Seney
Seney National Wildlife Refuge
To Sault Sainte Marie & Mackinac Bridge
H58
H15
H13
28
94
77
772

visitors' information centers have information on regulations (see Information). Grand Island Charters (☎ 906-387-4477) in Munising offers diving trips.

Places to Stay

Camping is the only option in the area. Three campgrounds ($10) can be reached by car: ***Little Beaver Lake***, ***Twelvemile Beach*** and ***Hurricane River***. Remember that the access roads are not paved. There are no showers and you cannot reserve sites. In addition, 13 backcountry sites are dispersed every 2 to 5 miles along the shoreline; these can be reserved. Fires are not permitted at certain sites, and you *will* be fined heavily for violations (as it should be). A one-time $15 permit must also be purchased from the visitors' information center (see Information).

Halfway between Grand Marais and Munising are a half-dozen ***campgrounds*** ($7) of the Lake Superior State Forest. South of Munising along County Rd 13 are still more ***campgrounds***, in the Hiawatha National Forest.

Just west of the Grand Island Ferry Dock, you can camp along Lake Superior at ***Bay Furnace Campground***, also part of the national forest.

There are lots of motels in Munising; try ***Greenland Motel*** *(☎ 906-387-3396)*, east of town along Hwy 58, with singles/doubles for $30/35, or ***Sunset Motel*** *(☎ 906-387-4574)* for $45/50, which is also in a nice location on Munising Bay facing Grand Island.

For information on Grand Marais, see Lake Superior State Forest, earlier in the chapter.

Places to Eat

Sydney's has a full slate of steaks and seafood (items from $5), a Sunday brunch and the rowdy Shark Bar. The ***Navigator*** *(☎ 906-494-4423)*, a block from the Pictured Rocks Boat Tours dock, is a casual place locally known for its fish specials, along with steaks and sandwiches (dishes from $6).

See Lake Superior State Forest, earlier in the chapter, for places to eat in Grand Marais.

Getting There & Away

ALTRAN (☎ 906-387-4845), 530 E Munising Ave in Munising, operates a shuttle ($10) between the Munising Falls Interpretive Center and Grand Sable Visitor Center; this is what backpackers use. The shuttle leaves the Munising Falls Interpretive Center at 10 am and runs on unpaved County Rd 58; it returns via Hwy 77 and Hwy 28 at 11:45 pm. It will *not* deviate or stop to let you off at Chapel Falls, Beaver Basin, etc.

Your only intercity bus transport is another ALTRAN bus ($5) to Marquette from where you can catch buses to other destinations. Buses depart three times daily weekdays.

AROUND NATIONAL LAKESHORE

Grand Island

Just off Munising in the middle of Grand Island Harbor is **Grand Island**, a national recreation area that is part of the Hiawatha National Forest ($2 entrance fee). Attractions per se are limited. The East Channel lighthouse is one of the oldest on Lake Superior, but it's on one of the few shards of private property left on the island.

The best way to see the island is to hop on the Grand Island Ferry (☎ 906-387-3503, $12 roundtrip) and rent a mountain bike ($10) from the ferry company. The same company also offers guided bus and boat tours ($10 to $16). The 21-mile ride around the island on two-track roads can be broken up by camping overnight at beautiful Trout Bay. The island has six campsites in all, but since it's virtually all federal land, dispersed camping is possible pretty much anywhere, following all guidelines, of course (inquire at the visitors' center in Munising). No drinking water is available on the island.

Seney National Wildlife Refuge

More Hemingway lore surrounds the village of Seney, 25 miles south of Grand Marais, and the entrance to the Seney National Wildlife Refuge. Hemingway fished the East Branch of the Fox River and many of his exploits here made it into his stories. Today the area Papa loved to fish is part of the 96,000 acres of a national wildlife

efuge. The refuge has variegated ecosys-
ems with more than 250 species of fauna
lone. Miles and miles of footpath, bikeway
nd water trail are to be found in the interi-
rs; with everyone focused on the national
akeshore, this place can be deserted.
ressed for time, you can take a quick 7-
nile self-guided auto tour. A visitor center
☎ 906-586-4983) is located south of Seney
long Hwy 77 and has wildlife exhibits and
slide show. Canoes, kayaks, rafts, mountain
ikes and camping gear can be rented at
orthland Outfitters (☎ 906-586-9801),
outh of the visitors' center in Germfask.

ARQUETTE

pop 22,000

rom Munising, Hwy 28 heads west and
kirts Lake Superior as a beautiful stretch of
ighway with lots of beaches, roadside parks
nd rest areas where you can pull over and
njoy the scenery. Within 45 miles, you
each Marquette, a historic mining center
nd the largest city in the UP.

Stop at the excellent Michigan Welcome
enter (☎ 906-249-9066), an impressive log
odge on US 41/28 as it enters the city, and
ick up brochures on area hiking trails and
aterfalls. *Marquette Monthly* is a free
onthly paper that lists entertainment
ptions.

hings to See & Do

re shipping is still a major industry. The
pper ore dock along Lakeshore Blvd regu-
rly greets ore-ferrying leviathans. Check
e *Mining Journal* newspaper, which pub-
shes ship arrivals.

The **Marquette County Historical
useum** (☎ 906-226-3571) is downtown at
3 N Front St. Permanent displays include
emorabilia from logging, shipping and Eu-
opean settlement of the area. Hours are
) am to 5 pm weekdays. Admission is $3.
hipping is the focus at the **Marquette Mar-
ime Museum** (☎ 906-226-2006) along
akeshore Blvd. It's a small place but filled
ith interesting exhibits. Hours are 10 am to
pm daily, June through late September; $3.

The 5-acre **Superior Dome** athletic
omplex on the campus of Northern Michigan University is the largest wooden dome in the world, designed especially for heavy snowfall.

Outdoor activities abound in Marquette. Panoramic views of the city are enjoyed on the easy **Sugarloaf Mountain Trail** or the harder, wilderness-like **Hogsback Mountain Trail**. Both trails are reached from Hwy 550, just north of the city. Sugarloaf Mountain also has a ski hill, one of two in the area. Catch the sunset from the high bluffs at **Presque Isle Park** in the city – there's a lovely loop drive and a large deer herd (and, it's said, moose). You don't have to hike to the top of **Mt Marquette** south of town off US 41, but it'll take your breath away as if you jogged up. Another ski hill is here.

Marquette is the site of a dog-sled race in February; it's a multi-day festival that draws huge numbers of people. For information, call the welcome center (see Information).

Places to Stay

The ***Marquette Tourist Park*** *(☎ 906-228-0465)* is just north of town on Hwy 550 and has sites from $6. Or, head 15 miles south to Gwinn to camp, hike and fish at ***Anderson Lake State Forest Campground*** ($6).

Marquette is the perfect place to stay put for a few days to explore the central UP. Affordable motels include ***Value Host Motor Inn*** *(☎ 906-225-5000)*, on the US 41 bypass, where doubles cost $36 a night. Three miles south of the downtown area at 2090 US 41 (also US 28) is the ***Birchmont Motel*** *(☎ 906-228-7538)*, with rooms from $40 to $48. Close to the Mt Marquette scenic drive is the ***Tiroler Hof Inn*** *(☎ 906-226-7516, 1880 US 41)*, a lodge that belongs in the Alps, on a great secluded spot. Singles/doubles are $45/55. There's also ***Cedar Motor Inn*** *(☎ 906-228-2280)*, ***Super 8 Motel*** *(☎ 906-228-8100)* and lots more motels along US 41/28 in Negaunee and Ishpeming.

The most upscale lodging in Marquette is the ***Landmark Inn*** *(☎ 906-228-2580, 230 Front St)*, a renovated 1930s hotel with a sauna and whirlpool. Three dining rooms are also on site; the Sky Room Restaurant has a gourmet five-course dinner. Attractive rooms cost $85 single/double.

Places to Eat

The best pasties (meat pies) in town are at ***Jean Kay's Pasties & Subs***, at Presque Isle St and Center St. Espresso and vegetarian dishes are enjoyed at ***Sweet Water Café*** *(517 N Third St)*. Both can feed you well for under $6. ***Wahlstrom's Family Restaurant*** *(5045 US 41 South)* has home-style food and a cheap lunch buffet ($6). Pick up smoked fish at the waterfront at ***Thill's Fish House*** (look for the enormous iron-ore loading dock); this is a real-deal Great Lakes fish market, with items such as smoked whitefish sausage and whitefish livers.

The ***New York Deli and Italian Place*** *(102 W Washington St)* has over 60 soups and great deli food – you can even get chopped chicken livers (items from $5). ***Szechuan*** *(1031 N 3rd)* has Chinese and Thai food, along with a weekend brunch (dishes from $5).

Good food and handcrafted beer are found at the ***Vierling Saloon*** *(119 S Front St)*, a renovated 1880s pub that's absolutely packed every night for dinner. At night, the pub at the ***Landmark Inn*** hops just a few blocks up Front St. The local favorite for supper clubs is the ***Northwoods*** *(☎ 906-228-4343)*, 3 miles west on US 41 (28), following the signs. In a log building, it's got great steaks and a Tuesday night buffet (main dishes from $8).

Getting There & Around

The bus station (☎ 906-228-8393) is at 145 Spring St. Greyhound connecting service goes to and from Calumet ($21) and Escanaba ($15). Departures are late-night either way.

You can also get to Munising via a shuttle bus (see Pictured Rocks National Lakeshore).

Marqtran (☎ 906-225-1112) operates local buses (80¢). The Trowbridge Park line runs to Northern Michigan University.

MICHIGAN

AROUND MARQUETTE

Ishpeming & Negaunee

A handful of museums are found in the Marquette area, and the most interesting are in the neighboring towns of Negaunee and Ishpeming. The **Michigan Iron Industry Museum** (☎ 906-475-7857), on Hwy 492, 3 miles east of Negaunee, includes audiovisual displays and a reconstructed mine shaft. Hours are 9:30 am to 4:30 pm daily May through October; free.

The **National Ski Hall of Fame** (☎ 906-485-6323), right on US 41/28 in Ishpeming, the birthplace of US ski jumping, is dedicated to the history of skiing, from sk fashion right through the US Army 10th Mountain Division's action in WWII. After you finish at the ski museum, head over to Suicide Bowl and check out the ski jumps. Hours are 10 am to 6 pm weekdays, 10 am to 5 pm Saturday, noon to 5 pm Sunday May through late September, reduced hours the rest of the year. Admission is $3.

Ishpeming's secondary tourist destination is more tongue-in-cheek but no less interesting. Da Yoopers Tourist Tra (☎ 800-628-9978) is kind of a gift shop-cum museum, dedicated to the spirit of Yooperdom. Da Yoopers is a hilarious UP ban whose songs are all about what it means to be a denizen of the UP. They've gotten s popular in Michigan, Minnesota and Wisconsin that they've now opened their ow haven for everyone who secretly wants t be a Yooper. This is the number-one place i Michigan for kitschy-cool souvenirs.

Van Riper State Park

As you head west or north, keep your eye peeled for moose. Michigan in the 198 undertook a moose-relocation plan, usin moose from Ontario. In half a dozen spo west of Marquette – in some of the dense wilderness in the Midwest – herds were e tablished. Van Riper State Park, approx mately 40 miles west of Marquette, was or site. A moose information center is at th park. This park is also close to a wilderne area with excellent backcountry recreatio Admission is $4.

Big Bay

Northwest of Marquette along Hwy 550 the unpaved County Rd 510, there is acce to a number of waterfalls. After 25 or miles, the road gives out and you've reache the most rugged part of the already rugge

P – the Huron Mountains – and the little ›wn of Big Bay. A couple of lighthouses 'e in the vicinity but the Huron Mountains e the big draw. Outdoor access is virtually ılimited but this is a wild place with few ›ople, so don't venture out too far into the lls if you don't know what you're doing.

Big Bay is home to a few of Michigan's ost appealing high-end B&B choices. The ***hunder Bay Inn*** *(☎ 906-345-9376)* on Hwy 50 has a famous pub and dining room – ey were added especially for the 1959 mmy Stewart movie *Anatomy of a 'urder*. Another historic inn, the ***Big Bay oint Lighthouse*** *(☎ 906-345-9957, 3 Light-ouse Rd)* is more expensive, but it's a real ghthouse and has indescribably good ews from its seven rooms. Rates start at)5. To limit gawkers, tours are $2.

IOUGHTON & HANCOCK

hese two riverside sister cities are at the picenter of Finnish culture – the dominant nmigrant group in most communities – in ıe UP. They're also charming, bustling and iendly. Numerous national magazines ave rated them very highly for their liv-ɔility quotients and it's not hard to see hy, winters notwithstanding.

The Keweenaw Peninsula Tourism Office ☎ 800-338-7982) is at 326 Shelden Ave.

hings to See & Do

he **AE Seaman Mineral Museum** (☎ 906-37-3027) is on the campus of Michigan Tech niversity, east of downtown Houghton. he official state mineral museum, it's got ver 20,000 natural crystals, rocks and fossils ı its collection. Upper Peninsula copper ıd iron ore are detailed. The museum is ɔused on the 5th floor of the Electrical nergy Resources Center. Hours are 9 am 4:30 pm weekdays. It's also open noon to pm Saturday, May through October; $4/ ee adults/children. Go to the Hamar ouse Counseling Center reception desk rst for a free parking pass; it's a block outheast of the museum.

Houghton is also a departure point for e ferry to Isle Royale National Park (see le Royale National Park's Getting There & Away section, later in this chapter) from the headquarters downtown. Besides the trip to the park, the *Ranger III* ferry has evening tours ($13/5 adults/children) from 6 to 8:30 pm, mid-June through mid-September.

In Hancock the Finnish flag flies on street corners and the street signs are bilingual. Hancock is home to the US's only Finnish-American college – **Suomi College**. The Finnish-American Heritage Center (☎ 906-487-7367) is at 601 Quincy St on campus and has a museum, art gallery and Finnish-American archives. Fin-Pro is a downtown shop specializing in Finnish products, including famous Helo sauna products.

The most popular draw in Hancock is the **Quincy Mine Hoist** (☎ 906-482-5569) north of town along US 41. The hoist was the largest ever, at 880 tons; it required a four-story structure to house it. Tours of the mine and above-ground facilities are available. Hours are 10 am to 5 pm, noon to 5 pm Sunday, mid-May to mid-October. Full tours cost $13/7 adults/children, tours of the hoist only cost $8/3 adults/children.

Places to Stay

Both cities have excellent cheap options. In Houghton, the ***Downtowner Motel*** *(☎ 906-482-4421, 110 Shelden Ave)* is as its name says, in the heart of things. It's got decent rooms worth the $40/45 single/double rate.

The ***Charleston House Inn*** *(☎ 906-482-7790, 918 College Ave)* has elegant rooms in an early-20th-century home. Rates are $95 single/double.

Across the river, the ***Best Western Copper Crown Motel*** *(☎ 906-482-6111, 235 Hancock Ave)* is also in the heart of the downtown area and has good singles/ doubles from $45.

Places to Eat

The ***Northern Lights*** sits atop the Best Western-Franklin Square Motel in downtown Houghton and has fine water views. ***Marie's*** *(518 Shelden Ave)* offers Greek and Mediterranean-influenced dishes, with a few vegetarian options (choices from $5). Nearby, the Douglas House is a grand historic structure dating from 1888. Once a hotel, it's now a residential structure, but the downstairs still houses a popular saloon and ***Armando's***, an Italian eatery (items from $6). The ***Library***, off Shelden Ave at Portage St, is a brew pub with excellent food (from $6). But most popular is ***Suomi Home Bakery & Restaurant*** *(54 Huron St)*, a half-block south of Shelden Ave; here you'll find dozens of locals and genuine Finnish food. It's a real UP experience.

In Hancock, ***Kaleva*** is a diner with standard stick-to-your-ribs fare with a few Finnish-influenced items. North of downtown Hancock (follow the signs off US 41), the ***Keweenaw Co-op*** *(☎ 906-482-2030, 1306 Ethel Ave)* is a godsend for travelers. It's got organic produce, gourmet deli items, fresh-baked breads and a huge assortment of cheese. If you're heading to Isle Royale, stock up here.

Getting There & Away

Greyhound stops in Houghton at the City Transit Center (☎ 906-483-2370), 326 Shelden Ave, and in Hancock next to Monticello Grocery Store at the corner of Quincy and Franklin Sts. You have to flag the bus down on the main road in Hancock. A bus leaves Houghton for Marquette at 9:30 pm ($20, 2 hours); one for Calumet leaves at 5:30 am ($8, ½ hour).

CALUMET

In a region of copper towns, Calumet was king. The share of Calumet Mining Company rose from $1 to $75 in one year (1865–66) and a thriving company town rose for the nearly 60,000 workers (it has maybe 7000 now). The architecture of the downtown district and nearby Laurium is the UP's best preserved.

A visitors' center is found south of town along US 41; it's got loads of maps and brochures, including one on local architecture.

The Greyhound connecting service stops at Superior Cab (☎ 906-337-5515), at the corner of 6th and Elm Sts. To Marquette ($21) takes 1½ hours.

Things to See & Do

Two blocks west of US 41, **Coppertown US** (☎ 906-337-4354) was once the mine pattern shop (a mold-making room). Fasc nating displays recreate Calumet's boor town rise in copper mining. Hours are 10 a to 5 pm Monday to Saturday, June throu October (Sunday also July and August $3/1 adults/children.

Calumet is one of the UP's top spots f an architectural **walking tour**. Pick up a fr brochure from the visitors' center. The hig light is the amazing Calumet Theat (☎ 906-337-2610), 340 6th St, an orna edifice opened in 1900, funded by mon collected from the boomtown's 70 or saloons. At its opening, it was the grand thing to ever happen to the UP and i copper wealth. Today it hosts theater a musical performances. Tours are giv 11 am to 2 pm Tuesday to Saturday, M through September; $3/2 adults/childre Other highlights include the Red Jack Fire Station, which now houses the UP Fi fighters Memorial Museum, and a saloon 322 6th St which still serves drinks a doesn't look as if much has changed in interior since the old mining days.

Places to Stay & Eat

Rooms for $45 and less can be found at couple of places, including the ***Northga Motel*** *(☎ 906-337-1000)* on US 41 a ha mile north of town. ***AmericInn*** *(☎ 800-63 3444, 5101 S 6th St)* has higher rates.

Laurium, across US 41 from Calum was where the well-to-do built their hom It's now a haven for B&Bs, including t ***Laurium Manor Inn*** *(☎ 906-337-2549)*, 45-room mansion with 17 guest roon some with private balcony and firepla Rooms start at $55 and include a full buf breakfast. Tours are available for those n staying at the inn.

Downtown along 5th St, ***Thurner Bake*** has fresh baked goods and homemade sou and pasties. A few blocks away the ***Ev green Inn*** is in a historic building and h good daily specials (dishes from $4) such hot turkey and pasties. Two miles north ɔwn on US 41 the ***Old Country Haus*** has ɟerman food, a fairly substantial soup and alad bar, and a popular Sunday brunch. A ifferent ethnic cuisine is featured every Satrday night (entrées from $5).

:OPPER HARBOR

:opper Harbor is a departure point for the erry to Isle Royale National Park, but it's a vorthy destination in its own right. You'll nd a historic park and two of the most cenic drives in the UP.

'hings to See & Do

rockaway Mountain Drive stretches for early 10 miles between Copper Harbor nd Eagle Harbor, the highest point reachng 800 feet, which makes it the highest desgnated scenic drive above sea level etween the Rockies and the Alleghanies. If ou take this road, do it from the east, and ıen loop back along the shore route folɔwing Hwy 26, another scenic gem.

East of Copper Harbor a few miles is **Fort Vilkins Historic Complex State Park** (☎ 906-89-4215). This park is on the site of a miliıry post built in 1844. Nineteen restored uildings are populated by period-garbed ocents offering living history lessons. An nnual Civil War encampment is loads of ın. It's open 8 am to dusk, mid-May ırough mid-October; $4.

Opposite the fort complex is a pullout 'ith scenic views of the **Copper Harbor ighthouse**, which is unfortunately inaccesble since roads cross private lands. Boat ɔurs ($11/6 adults/children) depart the owntown dock hourly 10 am to 5 pm daily summer and last about 1½ hours. More ɔpular sunset cruises ($14/7 adults/chilren) are also offered. Reservations are a ɔod idea for the latter tour; call the ticket ffice at ☎ 906-289-4966.

The tip of the Keweenaw Peninsula east f Copper Harbor is rough and undeveloped nd, owned mostly by a paper company. It's chnically open for exploration provided ɔu respect the company's rights. Keweenaw dventure Company (☎ 906-289-4303) in opper Harbor can fill you in on the details as well as rent mountain bikes and kayaks; it also offers kayaking tours ($25). The offshore portion of the peninsula from Copper Harbor to Eagle River makes up the Keweenaw Bottomland Preserve, the resting site of numerous shipwrecks preserved by the icy water. Among others, A Superior Divers' Center (☎ 906-289-3483) in Copper Harbor has charters and rentals.

Places to Stay & Eat

There's ***camping*** ($14) in Fort Wilkins Historic Complex State Park. Loads of motels and cabin resorts line the highways in all directions. A cheap motel with a lovely, isolated setting is the ***Norland Motel*** *(☎ 906-289-4815)*, east of the Fort Wilkins complex. Singles/doubles cost $33/37. The rustic ***Keweenaw Mountain Lodge*** *(☎ 906-289-4403)*, high above the town, dates from the 1930s and has higher prices for its lodge and motel rooms. If you want a lodge room, book way ahead.

For food, most motels have a dining room. ***Jamsen's Fish Market*** on the dock of the Isle Royale ferry has good smoked fish. The best food – with a great view – is at the ***Harbor Haus Restaurant***, with good whitefish and trout, steaks, prime rib and a few German entrées (main dishes from $7). A close rival is the ***Mariner North***, with huge sandwiches and an enormous salad bar (main dishes from $6). A Friday seafood buffet and Saturday prime rib buffet are also popular. If you arrive cold, tired and hungry in the early morning hours, the ***Pines Restaurant*** will be open, serving great cinnamon rolls.

AROUND COPPER HARBOR

Hwy 26 stretches west of Copper Harbor for approximately 26 miles and takes in some eye-catching big lake scenery. The two lovely towns of **Eagle Harbor** and **Eagle River** are along the way. Both are great fun to just poke around in for an afternoon. Eagle Harbor has a great beach and lighthouse museum ($1).

For a sybaritic night's rest, the ***Sand Hills Lighthouse Inn*** *(☎ 906-337-1744)* is west of

Eagle River. Housed in the largest and last manned lighthouse on the Great Lakes (1917), it has eight lovely rooms from $125.

In Delaware, southwest of Copper Harbor, a little more than 10 miles away, is a 19th-century copper mine, which now offers underground tours. Take a jacket. Hours are 10 am to 6 pm July and August, until 5 pm otherwise May to October; $8/4 adults/children.

ISLE ROYALE NATIONAL PARK

Isle Royale (pronounced 'royal') National Park is a 210-sq-mile island in Lake Superior (the largest in the lake, in fact) famous for its populations of moose and wolves. The flora and fauna are diverse enough for it to be designated a World Biosphere Reserve. It can be reached by either ferry or floatplane from Houghton or Copper Harbor, both on the Keweenaw Peninsula. Another ferry operation runs two boats from the Minnesota North Shore

Orientation & Information

Windigo is on the southwest end of the island and has an information center, store and marina. This is where one ferry from

ISLE ROYALE NATIONAL PARK

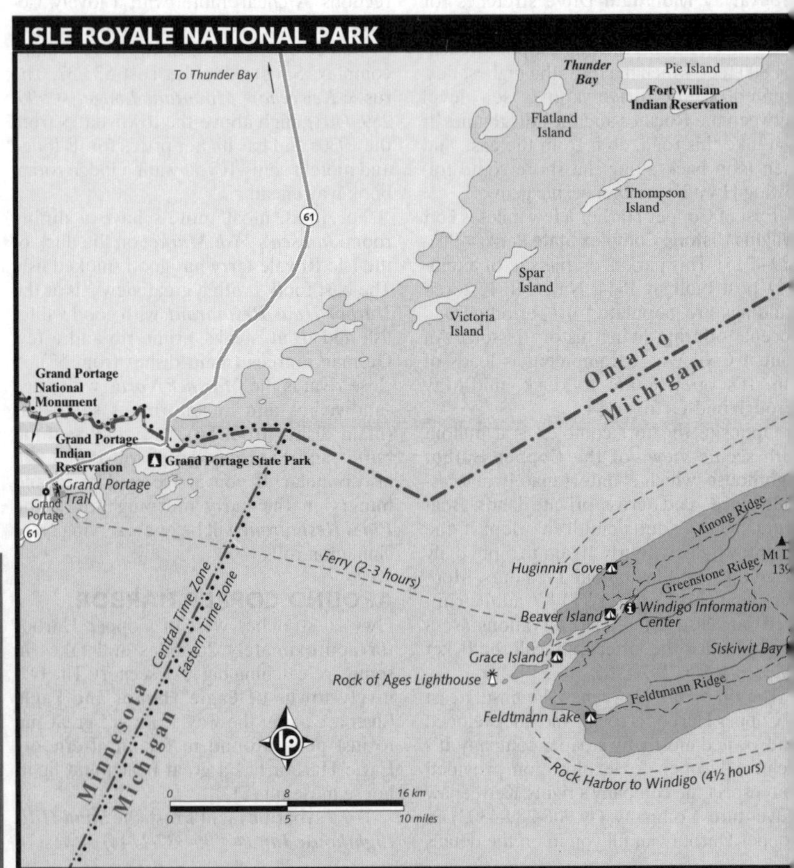

rand Portage, Minnesota, arrives and eparts. Rock Harbor is on the other side of e island and also has a spartan lodge and staurant.

The National Park Service headquarters r Isle Royale (☎ 906-482-0984, www ps.gov/isro) is at 800 E Lakeshore Drive Houghton. There are also information enters on the island, at Windigo (open June) to early September) and Rock Harbor pen mid-May to late September). The Veb site has detailed information about the ark and getting there. There is a fee ($4 per erson per night) to visit or hike and camp on the island. The park is closed from October 15 to April 15.

Dangers & Annoyances A particularly virulent species of tapeworm lingers in these waters. It cannot be killed chemically, so check with the park officials to make sure your filter is sufficiently advanced to remove it (.4-micron filter), or boil water for a minimum of two minutes. Black flies can really be horrible in summer; a face-net wouldn't be a bad idea. Obviously, be absolutely sure you know what you're doing if you plan to

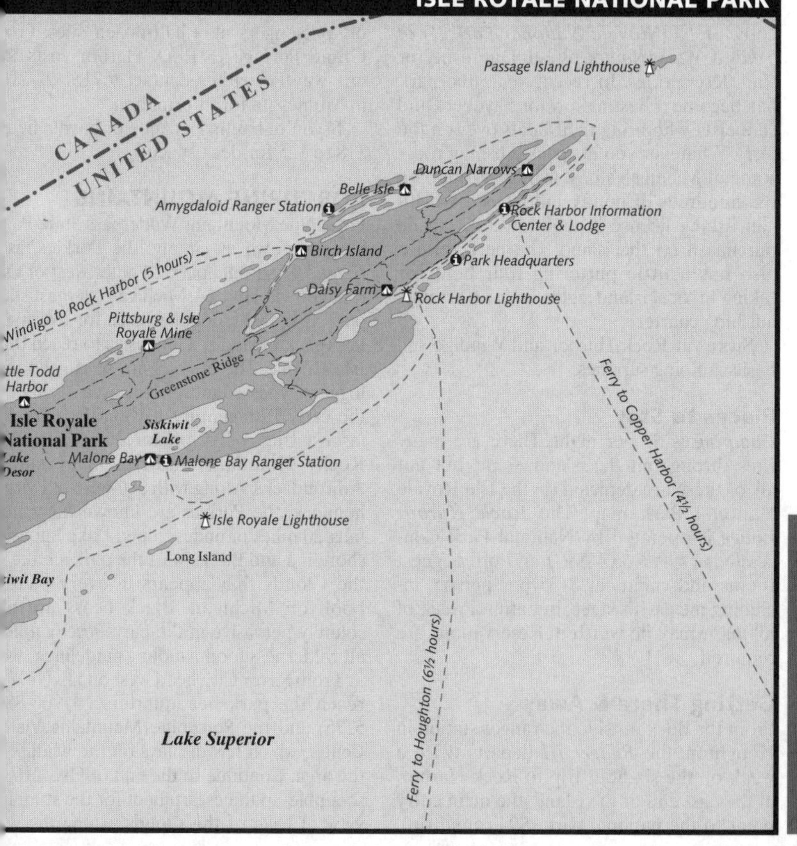

strike off for a week or two of backcountry living.

Activities

Isle Royale is totally free of vehicles, roads, McDonald's, rush-hour traffic – you get the picture. It is laced with 165 miles of hiking trails that connect dozens of campgrounds along Lake Superior and on inland lakes. Most backpackers spend five or more days hiking the park; the 40-mile **Greenstone Ridge Trail** is the most popular route. You must be totally prepared for this wilderness adventure, with a tent, camping stove, sleeping bag, food and water filter. Be prepared to share a campsite. Beyond that, hiking options are absolutely unlimited. Pick up a copy of *Isle Royale National Park: Foot Trails & Water Routes*, by Jim DuFresne, for trail descriptions. In recent years the park has become a destination for kayakers and canoeists, who bring their boats over on the ferry. Whatever you do, pack a fishing rod – some of Michigan's best fishing is found on the hundreds of ponds and lakes; a Michigan fishing license is required and can be purchased on the island. The park service also has a little puttering tour boat for taking in local island sights and can arrange a fishing charter.

Stores at Rock Harbor and Windigo sell basic camping supplies.

Places to Stay

Camping is $4 per night. There are many sites throughout the island; some, but not all, of these are depicted on the Isle Royale National Park map. The ***Rock Harbor Lodge*** is operated by National Park Concessions *(☎ 906-337-4993)* and offers guest rooms and cabins at $135 per person, including meals. It's steep, but after a week of hiking it may be worth it. Reservations are required.

Getting There & Away

From the dock outside the ranger station in Houghton, the *Ranger III* departs twice a week on the six-hour trip to Rock Harbor, at the east end of the island, the main entry point to the national park ($94 roundtrip). Near the dock in Houghton is Isle Royal Seaplane Service (☎ 906-482-8850), whic will fly you there in 20 minutes ($21 roundtrip). Or head 50 miles up the Kewee naw Peninsula to Copper Harbor (a beaut ful drive) and you can jump on the *Isl Royale Queen* (☎ 906-289-4437). The boa trip from here is shorter (4 hours) and little cheaper ($80 roundtrip), but the boa is smaller. If Lake Superior is rough, they' be passing out barf bags like sack lunches.

From Grand Portage, Minnesota, tw other ferries operate. The *Wenonah* stops a Windigo, at the west end of the island. Th round trip is $64 ($37 if it's a same da return). The *Voyageur II* is a great optio since it circumnavigates the island, droppin off passengers at a half-dozen sites. Fro Grand Portage to Rock Harbor costs $5 one-way. For either, contact ☎ 715-392-21(in Minnesota for information.

If you're hauling a canoe or kayak, figu $18 to $25 for deck space.

PORCUPINE MOUNTAINS

Porcupine Mountains Wilderness State Par better known as simply 'the Porkies,' is rugged 94-sq-mile park 20 miles west of O tonagon via Hwy 64. Michigan's largest sta park, it is also a popular place for overnig backpacking and is a lot easier to reach tha Isle Royale. The Porkies are so rugged th loggers bypassed most of the area's timber the early 19th century, leaving the park th largest tract of virgin forest between th Rocky Mountains and New York state Adirondacks. Along with 300-year-old virg hemlock, the Porkies are known for wate falls, 20 miles of undeveloped Lake Superi shoreline and the view of the park's Lake the Clouds that appears in every pictu book on Michigan. Black bears are a solutely pervasive in the park; *strictly* follo all wilderness food handling guidelines.

From Silver City, head west on Hwy 107 reach the park headquarters (☎ 906-88 5275) and the **Porcupine Mountains Visit Center**, which has displays on the wildlife the area. Continue to the end of Hwy 107 scramble up the escarpment for the stunni view of **Lake of the Clouds**. Along the w ou pass ***Union Bay Campground***, a huge, 9-site facility on Lake Superior ($14 a night). ypass it if you can and camp at the much ore scenic ***Presque Isle Campground*** ($9) r one of the small outpost campgrounds long S Boundary Rd ($6). There are also 16 ***alk-in cabins*** ($40) in the park, but most are served a year in advance. For lodging infor-ation call the park headquarters.

The Porkies feature a 90-mile trail system nking the walk-in cabins and backcountry camping areas. One of the most popular walks is the 16-mile **Lake Superior Trail**; one of the most scenic in the park is 9-mile **Big Carp River Trail**, which begins above Lake of the Clouds and ends at Lake Superior. Pick up a copy of *Michigan's Porcupine Mountains Wilderness State Park*, by Jim DuFresne, for trail descriptions. A back-country permit costs $6 per night for a party of four. You also need a vehicle entry permit ($4 a day, $20 annual pass).

Ontario Shore (Canada)

Don't forget that Lake Huron doesn't end with Michigan. From Sault Sainte Marie, Ontario, south to Windsor, Ontario, across from Detroit, the Canadian shoreline bends for 1025km and passes some top-notch shoreline beauty. The only major city is Sudbury, which is covered in detail in Lonely Planet's *Canada* book, as is Toronto, a short drive and possible day trip from th Lake Huron shore.

For information on crossing the US Canada border, see Border Crossings in th Getting There & Away chapter.

Highlights

- Sault Sainte Marie, aka the Soo, known for its lock between Lakes Huron and Superior and as departure point for a great train ride into the Canadian wilderness
- Midland & Penetanguishene, side-by-side towns with two reconstructions of native Indian sites in the former, and a great naval port reconstruction in the latter
- Lovely Bruce Peninsula, 65km that include two national parks and an excellent section of the Bruce Trail, a UNESCO World Biosphere Reserve
- Manitoulin Island, populated in large part by native Indians, the world's largest freshwater island and a popular summer destination

SAULT SAINTE MARIE

• pop 81,000

The Canadian Soo is technically larger tha its Michigan twin (see the Sault Sainte Mar map in the Upper Peninsula chapter), b that's hardly ever apparent. Most attractio are found in a compact downtown zone. F this reason and because inexpensive accon modations are available, it's not uncommc for travelers to hang out here for a spell.

Information

To the right of the International Bridge is a Ontario Visitors Center, open daily in th summer, with any information you need. Th Sault Sainte Marie Chamber of Commer (☎ 705-949-7152) is at 334 Bay St downtow The Log-In Café is in the Ramada Inn at 2 Great Northern Rd and has Internet acce for about $4 per half-hour.

Things to See & Do

Like its Michigan neighbor, Sault Sain Marie offers a chance to view a lock syste up close. As you cross the Internation Bridge, you pass over **Parks Canada National Historic Site – Canadian Lock** (☎ 70 941-6205), an interpretive museum on th engineering and construction of the Can dian Sault lock. Hours are 9 am to 8 p weekdays, noon to 8 pm weekends mi June through early September, reduc hours the rest of the year; $2/85¢ adults/ch dren. An up-close and personal look at th locks comes via the *Chief Shingwauk* to boat, run by Lock Tours Canada (☎ 70 253-9850). Two-hour cruises depart fo times daily mid-June through mid-Septe ber, fewer times in October. Fare is $17 adults/children.

The lock may be the most popular sight, ut another popular draw here is the all-day **gawa Canyon Train Tour** (☎ 705-946-7300). eparting from near the boat tour dock, the ain winds 365km through the Canadian hield wilderness and spectacular Agawa anyon. Special overnight trains also run ear-round. Regular tours depart at 8 am aily early June through mid-October. Fare $52/16 adults/children.

Sault Sainte Marie has many other attracons, among them the free **Art Gallery of lgoma** (☎ 705-949-9067), 10 East St, with onthly exhibitions of local and regional rtists. It's open weekdays from 9 am to pm. Nearly 3km east of the International ridge is the **Canadian Bushplane Heritage entre** (☎ 705-945-6242), 50 Pim St, a nique, fun museum devoted to bush-plane ying and fighting forest fires. Hours are am to 9 pm daily June through September, educed schedule the rest of the year; $5/1 lults/children.

laces to Stay & Eat

ummertime dorm rooms cost $18 at ***Sault ollege** (☎ 705-759-6700, 443 Northern Ave)*. here's always a cheap bed at the central ***HI lgonquin Hotel** (☎ 705-253-2311, 864 ueen St E)*, a hostel with beds for $19/21 embers/nonmembers. Budget lodging ptions can also be found along both Hwy 7 N (Great Northern Rd) and Hwy 17 E eading toward Sudbury. Among the eaper options to the north, the ***Bel Air lotel** (☎ 705-945-7950, 398 Pim St)* has ngles/doubles for $49/53. Downtown prices se precipitously. The motel with the best cation is the ***Days Inn** (☎ 705-759-8200, 20 Bay St)*, right downtown, with singles/ oubles from $90/100.

A good place to feed your face is the ***oney Garlic** (☎ 705-256-1732, 625 Hwy 17)* in the Wellington Square Mall. For $6 unch) and $10 (dinner) you can attack the 0-item buffet. Everything from sushi to ish kebab is offered.

Downtown, most dining is a bit more exensive though there are a few cheap diners nd coffee shops with less pricey food. ***Cesira's** (☎ 705-949-0600, 133 Spring St)* has good homemade Italian with fairly inexpensive lunches. If money is no object, ***A Thymely Manner** (☎ 705-759-3262, 531 Albert St E)* has creative continental cuisine using fresh regional ingredients (entrées from $20). It's perennially listed in *Where to Eat in Canada*.

Getting There & Away

The bus station (☎ 705-949-4711) is near the corner of Brock and Queen Sts. Ontario Northland (☎ 800-461-8558) and Greyhound (☎ 705-949-4711) have routes in and out. All the way around the lake to Owen Sound would take 12 hours and cost $140. To get to Detroit or Chicago, you have to take a bus to the Michigan side from the city bus terminal on the corner of Queen and Dennis Sts.

NORTH CHANNEL

East of Sault Sainte Marie, North Channel lies between the Ontario mainland and big Manitoulin Island. It's got a dozen diminutive villages and a few good vistas.

St Joseph Island

Roughly 50km east of Sault Sainte Marie is a turnoff of Hwy 17 south to St Joseph Island, the third-largest freshwater island in the world. Very rural, it's used mostly by fishers and tourists visiting **Fort St Joseph National Historic Site**, ruins of a British fort dating from the turn of the 18th century. Docents in period costume explain the site. A large bird sanctuary surrounds the fort. Hours are 10 am to 5 pm daily, mid-May weekends through early October. Admission is $2/1 adults/children. The island also has a museum, campgrounds and a couple of motels.

Manitoulin Island

Heading east on mainland Hwy 17 just before McKerrow, Hwy 6 branches south toward Manitoulin Island, the largest freshwater island in the world, home to a large Native American population and lots of farms. The island is approximately 140km long and 40km wide, with over 100 lakes.

ONTARIO SHORE (CANADA)

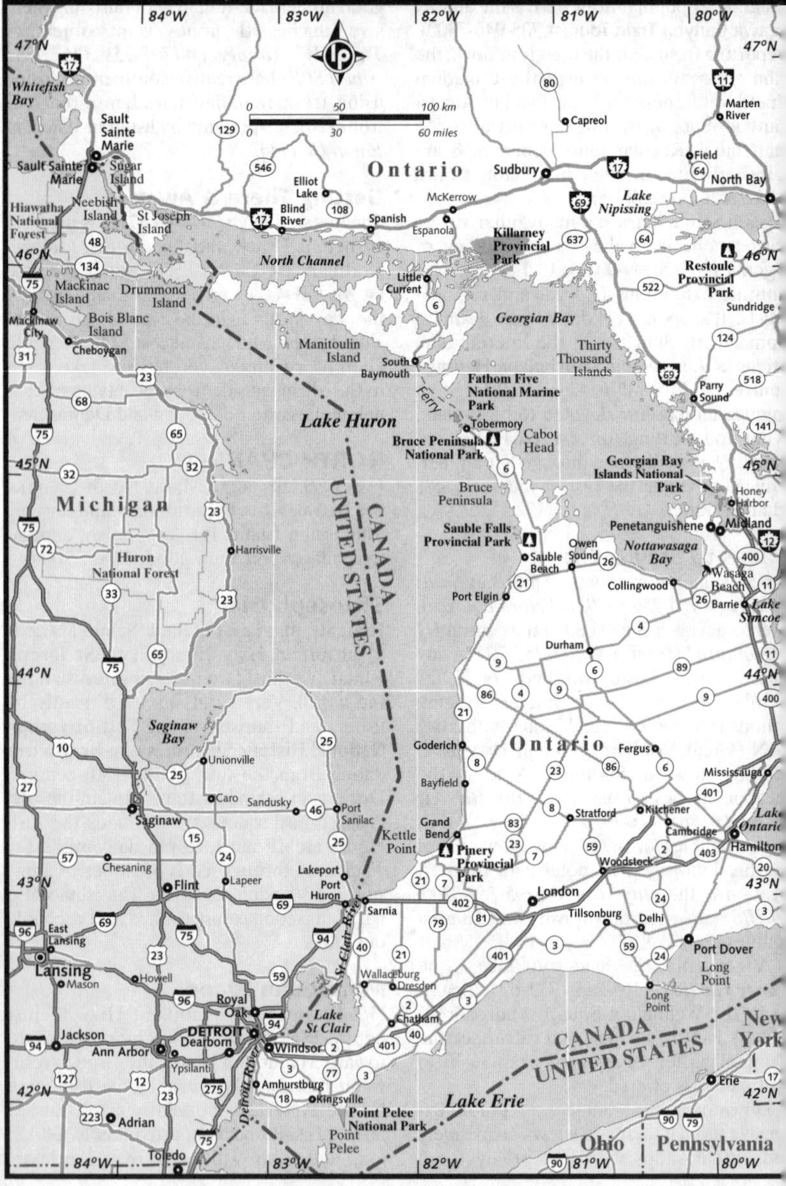
84°W
83°W
82°W
81°W
80°W
47°N
46°N
45°N
44°N
43°N
42°N
0
50
100 km
0
30
60 miles
Ontario
Michigan
Whitefish Bay
Sault Sainte Marie
Sault Sainte Marie
Sugar Island
Neebish Island
St Joseph Island
Hiawatha National Forest
Mackinac Island
Drummond Island
Mackinaw City
Bois Blanc Island
Cheboygan
Elliot Lake
Blind River
Spanish
McKerrow
Espanola
Sudbury
Capreol
Marten River
Field
North Bay
Lake Nipissing
Killarney Provincial Park
Restoule Provincial Park
Sundridge
North Channel
Little Current
Georgian Bay
Manitoulin Island
South Baymouth
Thirty Thousand Islands
Fathom Five National Marine Park
Ferry
Parry Sound
Lake Huron
Tobermory
Bruce Peninsula National Park
Cabot Head
Georgian Bay Islands National Park
Honey Harbor
Bruce Peninsula
Penetanguishene
Midland
Sauble Falls Provincial Park
Sauble Beach
Owen Sound
Nottawasaga Bay
Wasaga Beach
Collingwood
Barrie
Lake Simcoe
Port Elgin
Durham
CANADA
UNITED STATES
Huron National Forest
Harrisville
Saginaw Bay
Unionville
Caro
Sandusky
Port Sanilac
Saginaw
Goderich
Bayfield
Fergus
Mississauga
Kitchener
Cambridge
Stratford
Hamilton
Lake Ontario
Grand Bend
Kettle Point
Pinery Provincial Park
Woodstock
London
Chesaning
Flint
Lapeer
Lakeport
Port Huron
Sarnia
St Clair River
Tillsonburg
Delhi
Port Dover
Long Point
Long Point
East Lansing
Lansing
Mason
Howell
Royal Oak
Wallaceburg
Dresden
Chatham
Lake St Clair
DETROIT
Dearborn
Windsor
Jackson
Ann Arbor
Ypsilanti
Detroit River
Amhurstburg
Kingsville
Point Pelee National Park
Point Pelee
Adrian
Toledo
Lake Erie
Erie
New York
Ohio
Pennsylvania

hing is good, as is boating – **Baie Finn**, a km fjord in the North Channel, has pure ite quartzite cliffs.

The best thing to do is head immediately **Little Current**, where there is a year-round rist information center (☎ 705-368-3021). other seasonal office is in South Bayuth, where the ferry lands. Little Current has a museum and several good trails hin 20km of town. A handful of other seums are found on the island.

Unfortunately, the closest Greyhound ses come to the island is Espanola, 5km ith of Hwy 17; it leaves you some 45km m Little Current. The best way to visit s area is with a car. See Bruce Peninsula, er in this chapter, for ferry details to the nd. Once on the island, you can rent a ycle in Little Current, but if you arrive on ferry, you've got to get there from South ymouth, 63km away.

ORGIAN BAY & LAKELANDS

uth of Sudbury, the road follows the yawn Georgian Bay some 350km to Owen und, passing through the regions known Muskoka (near Parry Sound) and ronia (basically the peninsula sticking t into Georgian Bay west of the Georgian y Islands National Park).

llarney Provincial Park

uth of Sudbury, Hwy 637 heads west to at many people consider Ontario's best rk. One of the province's three wilderness rks, it's famed for its beauty (the famed oup of Seven – artists famous for their le and landscape subject matter – painted re) and its paddling. The only way to get und the interiors is by foot, ski, canoe or yak. It's so popular that reservations are a y good idea. There is a campground ($11 $20) at the park headquarters (☎ 705-7-2900, 800-668-7275) at Lake George d one in Killarney village; you can also ke off into the 75km of portages.

rry Sound

op 6310

rry Sound is the largest town on the long etch from the bottom of Georgian Bay to Sudbury. It's known as much for being the home of ice hockey legend Bobby Orr (of Boston Bruins fame) as it is for the scenery of the 30,000 Islands area, the highest density of islands in the world. An information center is found south of town along Hwy 69.

East of downtown is the **West Parry Sound Museum** (☎ 705-746-5365) with art and historical displays. Hours are 10 am to 6 pm daily in summer (Tuesday to Sunday the rest of the year); $4. Even better is the adjacent 96-foot observation tower with splendid Georgian Bay views. Two boat companies, the Island Queen (☎ 800-506-2628) and Mu Chippewa (☎ 888-283-5870) operate tours of the 30,000 Islands. Fares are $14 to $17 for the two- to three-hour cruise.

Plenty of inexpensive lodging options are found in town. ***Town & Country Motel*** *(☎ 705-746-8671, 7 Joseph St)*, north of downtown, has furniture handmade on Manitoulin Island. Singles/doubles start at $42.

For food, downtown's ***Alcatraz*** looks like just another sports pub, but it's got an extensive menu with good ribs and steaks (from $6). ***Bay St Cafe***, on the harbor, is open seasonally with seafood and steaks.

Greyhound and Ontario Northland make runs north and south. To Sault Sainte Marie takes seven hours and costs $74; to get to Midland ($28; 6 hours) you'll have to transfer in Barrie, south of Midland, and it takes most of a day.

Georgian Bay Islands National Park

This national park is a group of 59 islands organized into two sections. It's home to the largest diversity of amphibians and reptiles in Canada. It's also popular with boaters of all types. **Beausoleil Island** is the central feature of the park. Access is by water taxi ($25 to $35 one-way) only and these operate out of Honey Harbour, which also has a park service headquarters (☎ 705-756-2415). A day use fee is $3/2 adults/children; camping costs $11 to $15.

PMCL (☎ 705-526-0161) is at 476 Bay St and makes runs along the shore west to Owen Sound ($22); some buses would require a transfer in Barrie.

Midland & Penetanguishene

These side-by-side cities have lots of attractions, centering much on the Georgian Bay 30,000 Islands region. Boat tours launch from both Midland and Penetanguishene (around $15/7 adults/children). A short walk from downtown Midland is **Huronia Museum & Huron Indian Village** (☎ 705-526-2844), a 3-acre reconstruction of an Indian village with extensive anthropological exhibits. Hours are 9 am to 6 pm daily July 1 to early September, reduced hours the rest of the year; $4. Midland also has **Sainte-Marie among the Hurons** (☎ 705-526-7838), east of town on Hwy 12, a reconstruction of a 17th-century Jesuit mission (Ontario's first European community), with an attached museum. A nearby shrine commemorates six Jesuit martyrs. A restaurant with themed menus is on site. Hours are 10 am to 5 pm April through October; $10/7 adults/children. Nearby is the **Wye Marsh Wildlife Centre** (☎ 705-526-7809), a 150-acre hands-on nature center with wildlife presentations and 5 miles of trails. Hours are 10 am to 6 pm daily late June to early September, reduced hours at other times; $5. Canoeing is also available.

Nearby Penetanguishene has the excellent **Discovery Harbour** (☎ 705-549-8064), a recreated 19th-century naval base with two replica schooners. Archaeological surveying is ongoing at the site and educational sailing tours are offered. A theater offers regular performances in summer. Hours are 10 am to 5 pm daily early July to September, with reduced hours in May and June; $6.

Places to Stay & Eat The east-west Yonge St in Midland has a number of cheaper motels, including the ***Park Villa Motel*** *(☎ 705-526-2219, 751 Yonge St W)*, which has singles/doubles from $45. King St, the main north-south street in Midland, has lots of good eateries, including the ***King's Buffet*** *(815 King St)*, with an enormous Chinese buffet. ***King Cellarman's Ale House*** *(337 King St)* has pasta, steak and British-influenced menu items, along with Celtic music on Thursday.

Wasaga Beach

This is a chain of connected beaches 14k in all, purportedly the longest freshwat beach in the world, with a provincial park the middle. You'll find lots of cottages a casual resorts. People from Toronto esca here since it's the closest resort to the city

The local chamber of commerce (☎ 70 429-1407) is at 550 River Rd W and has li ings of all local lodging. You'll need th help if you come on a weekend.

From the north, you'll probably have transfer buses in Barrie. Buses also trav eastward from Owen Sound to get he Buses travel right along River Rd W.

OWEN SOUND

• pop 20,000

Owen Sound is the largest city in the regi and no matter which direction you cor from it's likely you will at least drive throu It's ensconced in a snug little sound, s rounded on three sides by the Niagara E carpment. Lots of good hiking trails are the area; three waterfalls can be visited.

The visitors' information center (☎ 51 371-9833) is at 1155 1st Ave W. It's got so very good brochures on historic walki tours.

The bus station (☎ 519-376-5375) is 1020 3rd Ave E. Routes east aboard PM lines are pretty straightforward, but to to Sarnia you'll have to go to the inla town of London first.

Things to See & Do

The **Tom Thomson Memorial Galle** (☎ 519-376-1932) is at 840 1st Ave W. Tho son, a member of the legendary Group Seven, grew up in Owen Sound and w deeply affected by the natural landsca The gallery has Canada's third-largest c lection of Thomson's work and also h other Group of Seven works. Hours a 10 am to 5 pm Monday to Saturday, noon 5 pm Sunday; free.

The **Owen Sound Marine Rail Museu** (☎ 519-371-3333) is next to the visitors' formation center and has various exhib on steamer ships and freight trains that tablished the town. Hours are 10 am to 5 p uesday to Saturday, 10 am to 4 pm Sunday; dmission is free but that may change. earby the **Owen Sound Mill Dam Fish adder**, Ontario's first fish ladder, allows out and salmon to access spawning ounds upstream in the Sydenham River.

The three-day **Summerfolk Music Festi-al** is held in mid- or late August and draws uge crowds.

laces to Stay & Eat

arrison Park (☎ 519-371-9734) in town as campsites for $14. Some cheaper motels n be found along 9th Ave, including the *avellers Motel (☎ 519-376-2680, 740 9th ve E)*, which has doubles from $45. The *rey Heron (229 9th St E)* is a casual eatery ith a super menu ranging from burgers to lectic contemporary cuisine (items from), including some vegetarian options.

RUCE PENINSULA

there is a must-do on the Canadian Lake uron drive, it is arguably this 99km detour to the tip to quaint little Tobermory, king in two national parks (not to mention o provincial parks) along the way. From obermory you can either backtrack and ntinue south along Lake Huron, or head ck toward the North Channel via a ferry Manitoulin Island; it's popular, so make a servation (see Getting There & Away, low). Unfortunately, as of October 1999 ere was no public transport from Owen und up the peninsula and officials were t confident that was likely to change.

ruce Peninsula National Park

t the northern tip of the peninsula, Bruce ninsula park headquarters (☎ 519-596-33, 596-2263 for reservations) has infor-ation on camping and hiking.

Several chunks of land make up the ruce Peninsula National Park. Most pular for short trips is the network of ils near **Cyprus Lake**; trails lead one way another to several geologic formations. e gem of the park is its portion of the **uce Trail**, an epic hike over 800km all the y to Niagara Falls tracing a World Bio-here Reserve, the Niagara Escarpment. The segment in the park traces the shoreline and links with the Cyprus Lake trails.

Fathom Five National Marine Park

The pellucid waters around the peninsula's end surround an archipelago of 20 islands and contain 140 species of fish and nearly two dozen shipwrecks, all of which comprise this national park.

The most popular way to explore the park is via **boat tours**, mostly using glass-bottom boats. Several companies operate out of the harbor and charge $14 to $18; one has a $10 sunset cruise to Cave Point along the shoreline. Try True North II (☎ 519-596-2600), Seaview III (☎ 519-596-2950) or Great Blue Heron (☎ 519-596-2999).

Most popular is **Flowerpot Island**, a rugged island popular as a day hike (wear good shoes and take sunscreen; $3 day-use fee). The same boat tour companies will also zip you out to Flowerpot Island in an inflatable boat.

Diving is excellent here, and there are numerous charter operators with lessons and rentals, including GS Watersports (☎ 519-596-2200) at the harbor in Tobermory. One of the most popular sites is the caves, or Grotto, on the peninsula's eastern side. All divers must register at the park headquarters.

Places to Stay & Eat

Camping costs $18 at the ***Cyprus Lake Campground*** 10 miles south of Tobermory and can be reserved for an additional fee of $9. Backcountry camping is possible; you must have a permit before venturing out. It's possible to camp ($14) on Flowerpot Island with prior reservations (☎ 519-596-2503).

Tobermory has a dozen lodging options. Among the cheapest are ***Cedar Vista*** *(☎ 519-236-2395)* and ***Peacock Villa*** *(☎ 519-596-2242)*, both of which have singles/doubles from around $45. The ***Harbourside*** *(☎ 519-596-2422)* has more luxurious options.

Most restaurants in Tobermory are of the steak-and-seafood variety, including the ***Lighthouse*** and ***Collin's Harbour Restaurant***, both with main dishes from $7; the latter has an excellent garlic shrimp dish. ***Crow's Nest*** is a coffee shop and pub with less expensive sandwiches.

Getting There & Away

The MS *Chi-Cheemaun* (the 'Big Canoe' in Ojibwa) sails between Tobermory and South Baymouth on Manitoulin Island, a trip of just under two hours. Trips generally depart early May through mid-October. In summer there may be as many as four trips daily. These are very popular crossings so book early (☎ 800-265-3163). Fares are $12/6 adults/children one-way, or $20/10 for a walk-on, same day return. Vehicles cost $25 to $53.

HURON SHORE

From Owen Sound south to Sarnia are a half dozen lakefront communities and a few good provincial parks.

Sauble Beach

• pop 900

Sauble Beach is a popular resort area where the Bruce Peninsula joins the lakeshore. Dozens of motel, resort and cottage operations line the shoreline (cottages are usually cheapest). North of the village is the excellent ***Sauble Falls Provincial Park*** *(☎ 519-422-1952, 800-668-7275 for reservations)*, which has campsites for $16 and up. Reservations are a good idea.

Port Elgin

• pop 6990

Port Elgin, another resort community, is popular for canoeing along the Saugeen and Rankin Rivers. A different type of attraction altogether is the nuclear plant about 10km south; free tours are offered.

Goderich

• pop 7500

The Canada Company founded this town as the terminus of the Huron Road (Hwy 8), which stretches from Guelph to Lake Huron. It has the largest harbor on the Canadian side of Lake Huron; the town boasts a gorgeous, lengthy promenade along its waterfront – sunsets along here are legendary. Its central square is lovely well, with streets radiating out spokelike.

The **Huron Historic Gaol & Governo House** (☎ 519-524-6971), 181 Victoria St has an eerie octagonal building that serv as the local jail from 1842 to 1972, alo with the house of the warden. The jail w designed as a model of humanitarian inca ceration; judged from a contemporary pe spective, you make up your mind. Hours a 10 am to 4:30 pm daily mid-May to ear September, lesser times otherwise. T **Huron County Museum** (☎ 519-524-2686) less interesting but has some fun hands- exhibits detailing European settlement the county. A combination ticket is $7 adults/children.

Bayfield

• pop 790

It's easy to miss Bayfield, just off t highway. If you've got the money it's de nitely worth a stop for some of the loveli historic inns and B&Bs in a very untouris atmosphere. The local restaurants are exce lent as well. ***The Little Inn of Bayfie*** *(☎ 519-565-1832)* is Ontario's oldest conti uously operated inn, with rooms starting $115 a night.

Grand Bend

• pop 970

Grand Bend is yet another resort town th really packs the crowds in on some wee ends. It's a much more boisterous crow than that which frequents chi-chi Bayfie to the north. **Pinery Provincial Park** ($7) a **Ipperwash Provincial Park** are south town. Pinery Park is among the provinc most densely forested coastal areas. The are 1000 campsites here ($17 to $22 plus entrance fee) and lots of trails. A bit farth south at Kettle Point are some intrigui geological formations.

SARNIA

• pop 124,000

The largest Canadian Lake Huron ci Sarnia sits across from Port Huron, Mic gan, and in the center of Canada's oil ref ing region. Sarnia is busy and full

CHARLES COOK

ıe *Bernice D* at Sturgeon Point Lighthouse (MI)

CHARLES COOK

oll down the dunes at Sleeping Bear Dunes National Lakeshore (MI).

LEE FOSTER

ɪrcupine Mountains (aka 'the Porkies'), Lake of the Clouds (MI)

THOMAS HUHTI

THOMAS HUHTI

THOMAS HUHTI

ıchigan's cities are a study in contrasts: Battle Creek, Lansing and Detroit.

CHARLES COOK

Leave your log barrel at home, Long Slide Falls (WI)

CHARLES COOK

A tunnel – Wisconsin style

CHARLES COOK

Fun at Summerfest, a 10-day Wisconsin musical affair

WISCONSIN DELLS VISITOR & CONVENTION BUREAU

The Zen side of the Wisconsin Dells

ard-working residents and offers a couple f decent sights.

An Ontario Travel Centre (☎ 519-344-403) is just off Hwy 402 west of town. It's ot more information than the Sarnia local isitors' office nearby.

hings to See & Do

Near the harbor, **Centennial Park** has a romenade and Great Lakes model, and hip watching is prime. Downtown at the Bayside Mall, 150 N Christina St, **Gallery ambton** (☎ 519-336-8127) has permanent lisplays that include Group of Seven and other Canadian artists. Hours are 10 am to :30 pm Monday to Wednesday and Saturday, 10 am to 9 pm Thursday and Friday; free.

Three blocks north in an old Victorian nansion, **Discovery House Museum** (☎ 519-32-1556) has a room-size working model of 920s Sarnia along with various nautical nd industrial displays. Hours are 9 am to pm Tuesday to Friday, 1 to 5 pm Saturday; 4/2 adults/children.

laces to Stay & Eat

The ***Chipican Motel*** *(☎ 519-336-4153, 1144 N Christina St)* has cheap doubles from $44. N London Rd has more cheap lodging. Close o downtown the Tudor-style ***Drawbridge nn*** *(☎ 519-337-7571, 283 N Christina St)* has lecidedly more luxurious rooms and prices.

Right downtown, the ***New Trish Inn***, ront and Lochiel Sts, is a bright, airy place vith straight-up Canadian food with some reative specials (from $4).

Getting There & Away

Buses depart regularly for London and Toronto and are your main mode of transport if you want to get to the Lake Huron hore, probably via Owen Sound. Greyound buses stop along Christina St S, south of the mall. VIA Rail (☎ 800-361-1235) is at 25 Green St, with regular departures to Toronto and Chicago.

SARNIA TO WINDSOR

Out of Sarnia, forsake the boredom of Hwy 40 heading south and opt for the smaller Hwy 33, better known as the **St Clair Parkway**, which hugs the shoreline for 30 or so miles and passes by no fewer than 22 parks, seven boardwalks and numerous gardens. East of Wallaceburg 8 miles is Dresden, site of **Uncle Tom's Cabin Historic Site** (☎ 519-683-2978). This was the home of Reverend Josiah Henson, whose early life inspired Harriet Beecher Stowe to write *Uncle Tom's Cabin*. Hours are 10 am to 4 pm Tuesday to Saturday, noon to 4 pm Sunday May 15 through October 15; $5/3 adults/children.

From here you'll probably have to pass through Chatham, which is home to the **Chatham Cultural Centre** (☎ 519-354-8338), 75 William St N, a museum, art gallery and theater. Hours are 1 to 5 pm weekdays.

WINDSOR

Windsor sits across the Detroit River from its US counterpart. Like Detroit, the city has auto manufacturing (and other industry) as its economic linchpin. Unlike Detroit, its riverfront is well planned and attractive, much of it left to green space. It is one of the busiest entry and exit points along the US–Canada border and is popular with US day-trippers visiting the city's casinos (when the exchange rate is favorable). Both the Ambassador Bridge (US$2.25) and Detroit–Windsor Tunnel (US$2) link the cities, the tunnel leading into the heart of Windsor.

Windsor sites appear on the Downtown Detroit and Detroit & Dearborn maps, in the Southern Michigan chapter.

Orientation & Information

The Windsor Tunnel drops you onto Riverside Drive, a major artery, near Goyeau St. One block west of Goyeau St is Ouellette, the other main street. Head four blocks south on Goyeau St to an Ontario Travel Center (☎ 519-973-1338).

Things to See & Do

Windsor has three lovely parks along the river. At the north end of downtown along Riverside Drive is **Dieppe Gardens – Udine Fountain**. Try a boat tour of the Detroit River aboard the *Pride of Windsor*

(☎ 800-706-2607; $10 to $60). To the west along Riverside Drive is the **Windsor Sculpture Garden**, a great 'art gallery without walls,' as it's called. To the east of downtown is **Coventry Gardens & Peace Fountain**. This floating fountain is one of the largest in the world and presents water displays. On the way to the gardens stop in at the **Canadian Club Distillery** (☎ 519-561-5499) for a free tour (reservations are a good idea).

The **Art Gallery of Windsor** (☎ 519-969-6111) is at 3100 Howard Ave, in the Devonshire Mall, and has exhibits on Canadian contemporary and historic art. Hours are 10 am to 7 pm Tuesday to Friday, 10 am to 5 pm Saturday and noon to 5 pm Sunday; free.

Detroit and Windsor co-host the International Freedom Festival, held at the end of June and in early July to celebrate Canada Day and Independence Day. Lots of events take place in both cities.

Places to Stay & Eat

In summer the ***University of Windsor*** *(☎ 519-253-3000, ext 3276)*, west of downtown near the Ambassador Bridge, offers dorm beds from $31. Budget motel lodging can be found south of town along either Dougall Ave, Huron Church Rd (Hwy 3) or Howard Ave. The ***Ivy Rose Inn*** *(☎ 519-966-1700, 2885 Howard Ave)* is at the higher end of the budget lodgings in the area, with singles/doubles from around $55, but you get more amenities.

Downtown, Ouellette Ave and its environs have just about all the eating choices you need. ***Basil Court*** *(327 Ouellette Ave)* serves good Thai and daily specials (from $6). Nearby and across the street are a number of coffee shops, some with inexpensive meals. For more substantial fare, ***Casa Blanca*** *(☎ 519-253-1172, 345 Victoria St)* has excellent Italian fare (main dishes from $10) in a cozy Victorian atmosphere.

Getting There & Away

The bus station (☎ 519-245-7575) is off the corner of Ouellette Ave and Chatham St. Many departures head east toward Toronto; to get to the Lake Huron shore you'll have to go through London one way or another. The VIA Rail station (☎ 519-256-5511) is about 3km east of downtown near the corner of Walker and Wyandotte Sts. There are frequent trains to Toronto via London.

Wisconsin

Facts about Wisconsin

Around the country and beyond, Wisconsin is associated with green pastures and cows. The dairyland image is based on fact, but the state is hardly so one-dimensional. It quietly attracts millions of annual vacationers and is a major Midwestern destination. Many visitors never even see a dairy farm.

The state defies easy categorization. The economy is multifaceted, with sectors such as computer manufacturing buttressing the traditional family farm. Wisconsin's landscapes range from wild Lake Superior islands and tracts of lake-filled forests to the ever-changing vistas along the Mississippi River. Door County, on Lake Michigan contributes shores reminiscent of those along the ocean. Outdoor activities of every type are possible – and very popular.

Milwaukee is the state's largest city and is its arts, manufacturing and financial center. Madison, the state's second in size, is the capital and home to the University of Wisconsin. Neither is a sprawling metropolis, but they share a relaxed sophistication.

Wisconsin's nickname, the Badger State comes from a term applied to lead miners at the beginning of the 19th century who burrowed into the state's northern hillsides. Consequently, residents affectionately refer to themselves as badgers.

Wisconsin Facts

Nickname Badger State

Population 5,122,900 (18th largest)

Area 56,154 sq miles (26th largest)

Admitted to Union May 29, 1848 (30th state)

Road Information Call ☎ 800-762-3947

Road Rules All drivers and passengers are required to wear seatbelts. Children to age four are required to be in a child safety seat. Motorcyclists are not required to wear helmets, but their passengers under age 18 are.

Taxes State sales tax is 5.5%. Some towns also add accommodations tax.

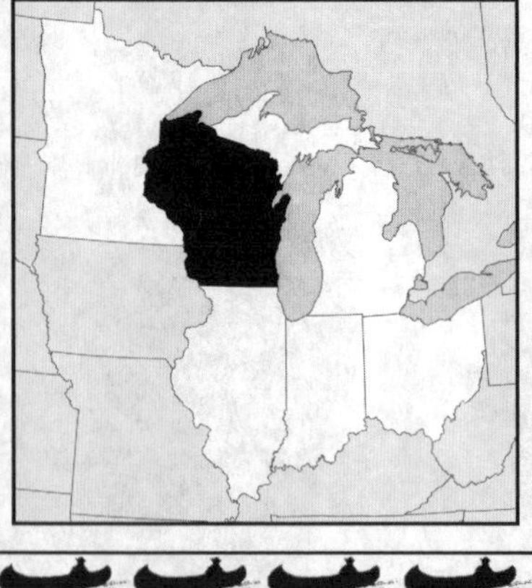

History

When the first Europeans arrived, there were Siouan-speaking Winnebago around the Green Bay area, but most of the land was occupied by Algonquian people, who lived mainly by hunting, fishing and an annual harvest of wild rice.

In 1634, French explorer Jean Nicolet landed near Green Bay, where a trading post was opened in 1648. It was soon followed by another on the Mississippi River though it was 25 years before the inland routes between these outposts were fully explored. French Jesuit missions were established in the 1660s around Ashland and on nearby Madeline Island in the Apostle group, and soon after, south of Green Bay at what is now De Pere. However, France's claims to the territory passed first to the British and then to the new USA.

A lead-mining boom in the 1820s spurred development, bringing many immigrants from nearby states to work in the mines. By the 1830s, most of the region's Indian tribes had been marginalized or pushed westward through a combination of internal disputes, the increasing number of white settlers, US

WISCONSIN
CANADA
UNITED STATES
Lake Superior
Minnesota
Michigan
Wisconsin
Isle Royale National Park
Apostle Islands National Lakeshore
Madeline Island
Chequamegon Bay
Keweenaw Peninsula
Keweenaw Bay
Duluth
Superior
Bayfield
La Pointe
Hurley
Eastern Time
Central Time
Lac Vieux Desert
Brule River
Rhinelander
Lake Nokomis
Wausau
Eau Claire
Chippewa Falls
La Crosse
Rochester
Stevens Point
Wisconsin Rapids
Green Bay
Appleton
Oshkosh
Lake Winnebago
Fond du Lac
Sheboygan
Manitowoc
Two Rivers
Sturgeon Bay
Washington Island
Marinette
Peshtigo
Lake Michigan
West Bend
Cedarburg
MILWAUKEE
Waukesha
Madison
Racine
Kenosha
Janesville
Beloit
Rockford
CHICAGO
Illinois
Iowa
Minnesota
Waterloo
Cedar Rapids
To Des Moines
To Minneapolis
Prairie du Chien
Dodgeville
Mineral Point
Spring Green
Wisconsin Dells
Lake Wisconsin
Castle Rock Lake
Lake Poygan
Lake Dubay
Big Eau Pleine Reservoir
Lake Chippewa
Mississippi River
Wisconsin River
Kickapoo River
Rock River
Chippewa River
St Croix River
St Louis River
Wolf River
Menominee River
Antigo
Langlade
Laona
Wabeno
Lakewood
Niagara
Rapid River
Grand Island
Pelican Lake
Basswood Lake
Vermillion Lake
Birch Lake
Boulder Lake
Island Lake
93°W
91°W
89°W
87°W
47°N
45°N
43°N
0 40 80 km
0 25 50 miles

government policy and disastrous treaty signings. The Native Americans' last attempt at staving off virtual elimination from the region occurred in 1832 along the Mississippi in the land of the Fox and Sauk Nations.

The Sauk, led by Black Hawk, refused to accept relocation across the river into Iowa. A series of bloody skirmishes culminated in the Battle of Bad Axe, perhaps the sorriest tale in the state's history. It ended with most of Sauk's followers, including old men, women and children, being slaughtered by US soldiers. After that lethal encounter there was little to impede further white settlement and development.

Following statehood and the Civil War, there was massive immigration to the state, much of it from Germany and Scandinavia. Even today, more than half the population has German ancestry.

Wisconsin was known early on for its beer, butter, cheese and paper. In the 20th century, production of agricultural equipment grew into a major and diverse specialized machinery-manufacturing industry. Food processing is also significant, and tourism has become increasingly important.

Geography

Wisconsin can be divided into five geographic regions. The Superior lowland rings the northernmost area. South from there is the Superior upland, a mostly forested plateau that is less than 1500 feet above sea level but is the source of the state's main rivers, such as the Wisconsin, Menomonee, Wolf and St Croix, which generally flow to the south. This largely undeveloped area is Wisconsin's beloved outdoor-recreation region.

The bulk of the state's agricultural lands lie across the flat central plain. The western uplands of the southwest escaped the ice-age glaciers and are characterized by rugged terrain, including scenic gorges cut by the rivers. The lowlands of the south and southeast are covered in fertile glacial 'drift' interspersed with lakes; the central portion is classic Wisconsin dairyland, and the main cities – Milwaukee and Madison – are in the southeast.

The often beautiful Wisconsin River runs north-south for 430 miles, and the Mississippi edges the western border. The state has hundreds of waterfalls, mostly in the thinly populated northeast and northwest.

National Parks & Protected Areas

The beautiful Apostle Islands National Lakeshore preserves 21 Lake Superior islands in their natural state. Two national forests, Chequamegon and Nicolet, cover much of the north. Both offer tremendous outdoor recreational opportunities. Ranger offices listed in the text supply information and maps.

There are 59 state-managed parks, forests and recreation areas. All state parks offer camping. For reservations at any park or forest, call ☎ 888-947-2757, or visit www.dnr.state.wi.us. You can reserve a campsite with a Visa or MasterCard from 11 months to 48 hours prior to arrival. For information, check the Web site or contact the Wisconsin Department of Natural Resources, Parks and Recreation (☎ 608-266-2181), PO Box 7921, Madison, WI 53707-7921.

A vehicle permit available at any state park costs $5/18 per day/year for residents, $7/25 for others. Permits are valid at all state parks, and the day pass is also valid the next day. Camping costs about $10.

The Ice Age Trail, still under development, meanders across the state atop the end moraines of the last glacier. The longer, completed segments are found in state and national forests and parks. Good sections are marked in Kettle Moraine State Forest (north and south units). Offices there can supply further information.

Government & Politics

Politically, the state leans slightly toward the Republican party, especially when it comes to federal elections. When electing governors, voters seem to flip parties with nearly each four-year election. Democratic strength comes from Milwaukee and Madison, Republican from rural Wisconsin.

Since the early 20th century, the state has consistently been at the forefront of socially progressive reforms. Wisconsin set a precedent in developing laws mandating workers' compensation for injured employees and a minimum wage. It has long been associated with farmers' cooperatives. Wisconsin was the first state to eliminate the death penalty and the first to require seat belts.

Current governor, Republican Tommy Thompson, is no Jesse Ventura but he does take an annual jaunt around the state on a Harley, which certainly separates him from the majority of elected officials.

Arts

Milwaukee is a leading cultural center, with a nationally regarded symphony and ballet and more than one opera company. Madison also has an active, high-quality performing-arts calendar. Both cities have excellent visual art galleries.

The state department of tourism produces an annual guide to Wisconsin's 250 arts and crafts fairs.

Those with an interest in architecture will find Wisconsin a bonanza. Throughout the state – which was home to world-renowned innovator Frank Lloyd Wright – there is a keen sense of preservation, and many towns have restored their Main St districts. Historic sites protecting 19th-century architecture are abundant, and Milwaukee has some eye-catching contemporary structures.

Ride the Rails

Wisconsinites love to get out on two wheels. Whether it's dashing around central Madison or taking curves along the Mississippi, residents of all ages can be seen out bicycling. This is serious recreation here, from lone mountain bikers on hilltops to entire families cruising valleys.

The Wisconsin Department of Tourism has mapped out road, mountain and trail routes across the state and publishes them, along with listings on cycling events, in the annual *Biking Guide*. Superb and most popular are Wisconsin's 24 state rail trails, former railroad lines now paved over and dedicated to bicyclists and roller skaters. They average about 30 miles in length but vary dramatically. All provide access to great rides without worry of traffic, yet with services nearby.

Three good examples are the Military Ridge Trail, 40 miles from Verona to Dodgeville; the Mountain Bay Trail, 90 miles from Wausau to Green Bay; and the Bearskin–Hiawatha, 24 miles from Minocqua to Tomahawk.

For access points and information, visit major tourist offices or contact state parks. Day or season permits ($3 and $10, respectively) are required for riders over age 16.

G ASKEVOLD

Innovative use of the rails in 1911

Wright's highly influential work can be seen in Racine, Madison, Spring Green, Richland Center and Mirror Lake State Park.

Information

The Wisconsin Department of Tourism office (☎ 608-266-2161, 800-432-8747 for guides, ☎ 800-372-2737 for information, www.tourism.state.wi.us) is at 123 Washington St, Madison, WI 53707. Twelve Wisconsin Travel Information Centers are around the state's perimeter. Most towns have a chamber of commerce.

Visitors should note that tourist areas are busy through July and most of August, particularly on weekends. Wisconsin Dells, Door County and Bayfield are consistently chockablock with tourists, and arriving without reservations can be frustrating, time consuming and expensive. The entire northland area, with its countless summer resorts, also gets a steady flow of visitors. Campers with no aversion to the rustic can generally find spots in the state and national forests.

The state's telephone area codes are filling up much more quickly than anticipated. The existing code regions may be changed before the next edition of this book.

Special Events

January

American Birkebeiner – Cable; North America's largest Nordic ski race

World Championship Snowmobile Derby – Eagle River; the things almost fly

May to September

Big Top Chautauqua – near Bayfield; region's top summer event; concerts, theater and a musical take place under a tent

July

Experimental Aircraft Fly-In – Oshkosh; attracts some 300,000 aeronautics enthusiasts late in the month

August

Wisconsin State Fair – Milwaukee; one of the country's biggest and best state fairs

County fairs, much the same as the state fair but in miniature and in a more rural, less hectic setting, are held throughout the summer across the state. Virtually every region has one, with concerts, tractor pulls, livestock competitions, plenty of food and some amusement rides. They're always well attended and a good opportunity to mix with the locals.

Food & Drinks

Cheese, generally mild, is plentiful across the state, as is fresh and smoked fish. Milwaukee is famous for beer, and the brewing tradition and passion continues. Unbeknownst to many, Wisconsin has an active wine industry; rather than being centered in a certain region, the vintners are actually scattered across the state from the northwest to the southeast.

Cranberries are an important niche produce, and Door County grows a lot of fruit, notably cherries and apples. The Wasau area produces very high-quality

LIBRARY OF CONGRESS

Rural Wisconsin, 1941

ginseng. You could go home younger than when you left.

For more information on Wisconsin delicacies, see 'Wisconsin Is Full of Brats' and 'Roiling Boils' in the Eastern & Northern Wisconsin chapter, and 'Custard Custom' in the Southern Wisconsin chapter.

Getting There & Around

Milwaukee and Duluth have major airports with linking flights across the country. Within the state, public transportation is not extensive. Greyhound buses serve the major urban centers and some of the smaller lakeland resort towns in and around Rhinelander. Badger Bus Lines offers frequent service between Madison and Milwaukee.

Amtrak connects many towns on its run from Chicago to the Twin Cities, including Milwaukee and Wisconsin Dells. Its bus service links Milwaukee with Green Bay.

I-94 runs north from Chicago to Milwaukee and then cuts across the state to Minnesota. Major highways link all the cities. Except on holiday weekends and the usual Friday night trek north from Milwaukee, roads are rarely congested (summer weekends in Door County are an exception).

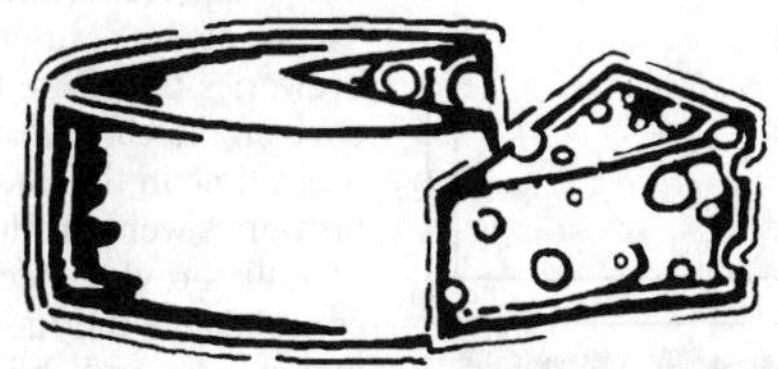

Southern Wisconsin

Even though most of the population resides here, this part of the state has some of the prettiest landscapes, particularly in the hilly southwest, which missed the flattening effect of the last ice age. Farther east is the Mississippi River. Madison is a fine stop, and there are must-sees throughout the region for Frank Lloyd Wright fans. To the north is Wisconsin Dells, one of the state's major attractions. On Lake Michigan is Milwaukee, a mid-size city with charm and character, smiling quietly in the shadow of Chicago.

Highlights

- The famous beer-brewing traditions of Milwaukee
- Crazy Wisconsin Dells' tourist thing
- Frank Lloyd Wright buildings in Madison, Spring Green and Racine
- A hike or bike ride around the glacial features of Kettle Moraine State Forest
- Bird-watching at Horicon Marsh

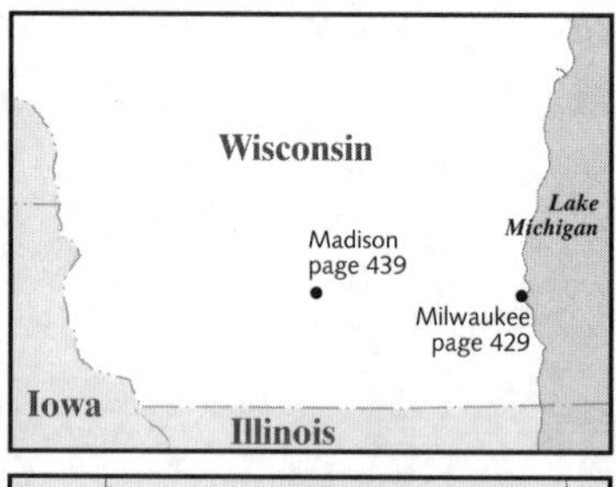

MILWAUKEE

• pop 610,700

The city of Milwaukee has managed to nurture the assets of urban America and yet avoid the pitfalls: It's friendly yet cosmopolitan; modern yet historic; sizable yet safe. Beaches and parks trim the architecturally varied edges of downtown around Lake Michigan. The compact and walkable central district, with its reclaimed riverfront, is vibrant night and day. Various nearby neighborhoods, each with a distinct history and atmosphere, add to the mix.

History

The lakeside location where the Milwaukee, Menomonee and Kinnickinnic Rivers flow into Lake Michigan was instrumental in the city's development. Long used by Native Americans, the spot became a French Canadian fur-trading post in 1818, established by Solomon Juneau. In 1846 the villages of Juneautown, Kilbourntown and Walker's Point amalgamated to form Milwaukee, with Juneau serving as the city's first mayor.

The effects of the influx of German settlers from that time through the late 19th century remain evident in the city's restaurants and assortment of mansions and baronial residences from the industrial heyday. These early residents started the small breweries that were to have a lasting influence on the character of Milwaukee – there was a time in the late 19th century when 80 breweries were producing. The introduction of bulk brewing technology in the 1890s consolidated the individual brewers into a major industry. Schlitz, 'the beer that made

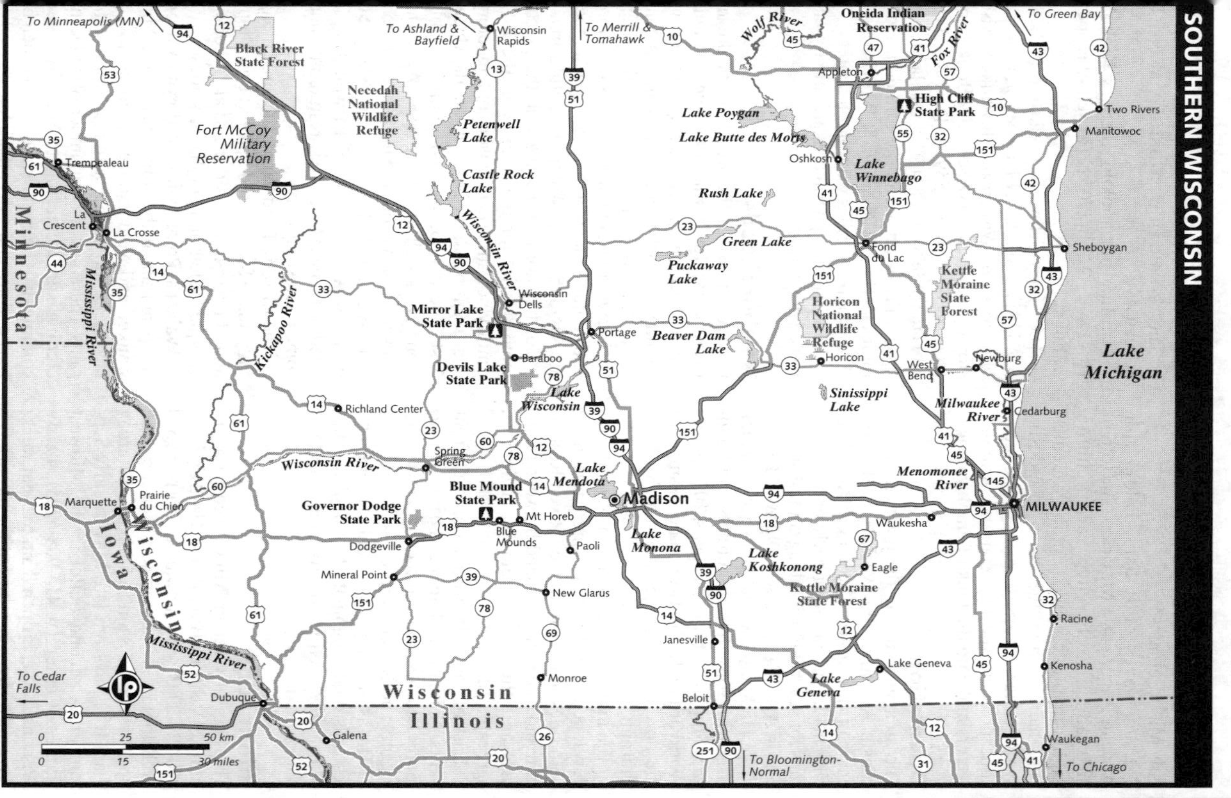
SOUTHERN WISCONSIN
To Minneapolis (MN)
Black River State Forest
To Ashland & Bayfield
Wisconsin Rapids
To Merrill & Tomahawk
Wolf River
Oneida Indian Reservation
Fox River
To Green Bay
Appleton
High Cliff State Park
Two Rivers
Manitowoc
Necedah National Wildlife Refuge
Petenwell Lake
Fort McCoy Military Reservation
Trempealeau
Lake Poygan
Lake Butte des Morts
Oshkosh
Lake Winnebago
Castle Rock Lake
Rush Lake
La Crescent
La Crosse
Wisconsin River
Green Lake
Fond du Lac
Sheboygan
Minnesota
Mississippi River
Puckaway Lake
Kettle Moraine State Forest
Kickapoo River
Wisconsin Dells
Mirror Lake State Park
Horicon National Wildlife Refuge
Portage
Beaver Dam Lake
Horicon
Lake Michigan
Baraboo
Devils Lake State Park
West Bend
Newburg
Lake Wisconsin
Sinissippi Lake
Richland Center
Milwaukee River
Cedarburg
Spring Green
Wisconsin River
Lake Mendota
Menomonee River
Blue Mound State Park
Madison
MILWAUKEE
Marquette
Prairie du Chien
Governor Dodge State Park
Mt Horeb
Blue Mounds
Waukesha
Iowa
Wisconsin
Dodgeville
Lake Monona
Paoli
Lake Koshkonong
Eagle
Mineral Point
New Glarus
Kettle Moraine State Forest
Racine
Janesville
Mississippi River
Lake Geneva
Kenosha
To Cedar Falls
Monroe
Lake Geneva
Dubuque
Wisconsin
Beloit
Illinois
Galena
0 25 50 km
0 15 30 miles
To Bloomington-Normal
Waukegan
To Chicago

Milwaukee famous,' as well as Pabst and Miller, were all based here at one time, but only Miller remains.

Later waves of Italians, Poles, Irish, African Americans, Mexicans and others have added to the city's varied culture. Light manufacturing, notably medical equipment, is now the principal industry. White-collar occupations in government, education and the financial and insurance sectors make up the bulk of employment.

Orientation

The area surrounding the junction of Wisconsin Ave and Old World 3rd St is the heart of downtown. The Grand Ave shopping mall, incorporating early architecture, runs for several blocks along central W Wisconsin Ave. Wander down Old World 3rd St to W Highland Ave, an old-style shopping strip with some fine restaurants and buildings. Stop at historic Usinger's, 1030 N Old World 3rd St, for bratwurst and a sample of the dozens of sausages that they've been churning out since 1880.

The inspired Riverwalk is a system of redeveloped downtown walking paths along both sides of the Milwaukee River. Restaurant and pub patios wedged between buildings and the water create a distinctive, agreeable cityscape.

East of the core are pleasant lakefront parks. N Lincoln Memorial Drive leads to sandy beaches and parkland popular with joggers and Rollerbladers.

The astonishing list of quality events and festivals could dominate this book's entire Milwaukee section. Try to take in at least one of them.

Information

The helpful Greater Milwaukee Convention & Visitors Bureau (☎ 414-273-7222, 800-231-0903, www.milwaukee.org) is at 510 W Kilbourn Ave in the convention center, open weekdays 8 am to 5 pm and Saturday 9 am to 2 pm from late May to early September. A second outlet in the Midwest Express Center (☎ 414-908-6205), 400 W Wisconsin Ave, is open 8 am to 5 pm weekdays only. There is a third at the airport. For assistance finding hotel accommodations, call ☎ 800-554-1448.

The downtown post office is at 606 E Juneau Ave.

For Internet hookup, there is Kinko's (☎ 414-272-2730), 1703 N Farwell Ave, open 24 hours.

The Harry Schwartz Bookshop (☎ 414-332-1181) is at 2559 N Downer St, near the University of Wisconsin–Milwaukee. Also stop by one of the HW Schwartz Bookshops (☎ 414-332-1181), 2559 N Downer Ave, and (☎ 414-963-3111), 4093 N Oakland Ave.

The Froedtert Memorial Lutheran Hospital (☎ 414-259-2606), 9200 W Wisconsin Ave, is about 5 miles west of the center.

Laws against jaywalking are strictly enforced downtown.

Neighborhoods

Covering most of the west side of downtown, **West Town–Kilbourntown** contains much of the more recent development including the convention centers and, in contrast, Old World 3rd St. East of the river, **East Town–Juneautown** reveals its age more and contains many of the city's premier theaters and the lively Water St nightlife area.

Farther north is **Yankee Hill**, the prestigious district for the wealthy in the 19th century, now interspersed with contemporary apartment buildings. North again, the **Upper East Side** is good for restaurants, notably along N Farwell and N Prospect Aves. The University of Wisconsin–Milwaukee is here.

Easygoing, Italian-flavored **Brady St** between Astor St and N Farwell Ave, is lined with bakeries, cafés, restaurants and some interesting stores.

The **Historic Third Ward**, anchored along Milwaukee St south of I-794, has tony shops and old warehouses redone as art galleries, antique outlets and graphic-arts houses.

Walker's Point, south of downtown on the peninsula at the confluence of the Milwaukee and Menomonee Rivers, is now a largely Latino district with plentiful restaurants. There are also a number of clubs, including some catering to the city's gay community. The main streets in the neighborhood are 2nd, 5th and 6th Sts.

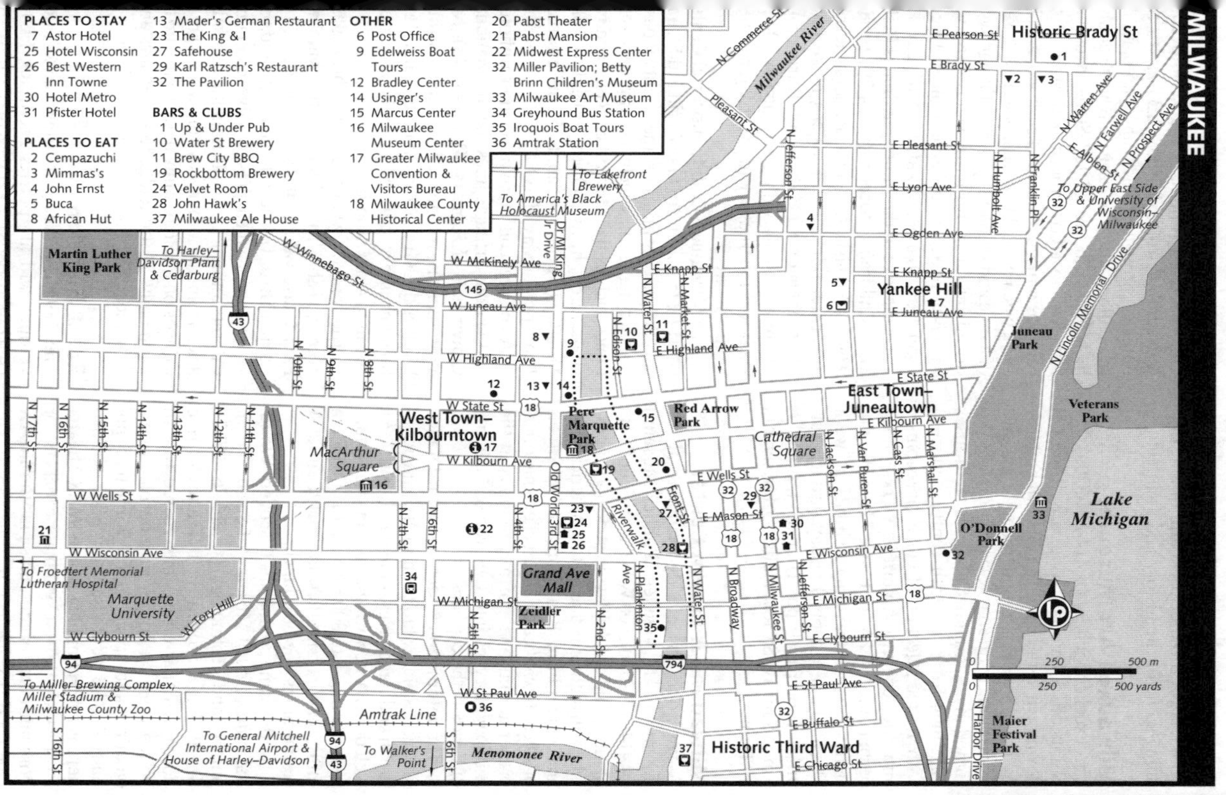
MILWAUKEE
PLACES TO STAY
7 Astor Hotel
25 Hotel Wisconsin
26 Best Western Inn Towne
30 Hotel Metro
31 Pfister Hotel
PLACES TO EAT
2 Cempazuchi
3 Mimmas's
4 John Ernst
5 Buca
8 African Hut
13 Mader's German Restaurant
23 The King & I
27 Safehouse
29 Karl Ratzsch's Restaurant
32 The Pavilion
BARS & CLUBS
1 Up & Under Pub
10 Water St Brewery
11 Brew City BBQ
19 Rockbottom Brewery
24 Velvet Room
28 John Hawk's
37 Milwaukee Ale House
OTHER
6 Post Office
9 Edelweiss Boat Tours
12 Bradley Center
14 Usinger's
15 Marcus Center
16 Milwaukee Museum Center
17 Greater Milwaukee Convention & Visitors Bureau
18 Milwaukee County Historical Center
20 Pabst Theater
21 Pabst Mansion
22 Midwest Express Center
32 Miller Pavilion; Betty Brinn Children's Museum
33 Milwaukee Art Museum
34 Greyhound Bus Station
35 Iroquois Boat Tours
36 Amtrak Station

The CVB has self-guided walking tour booklets on these districts and others, outlining some of the history and architecture.

Milwaukee Art Museum

This excellent gallery (☎ 414-224-3200), 750 N Lincoln Memorial Drive, is well located downtown at the lake. The modern building by Eero Saarinen is undergoing a massive expansion, with an eye-catching wing designed by Santiago Calatrava. It houses paintings from the 15th century onward, with a good selection of postimpressionism and 20th-century American works and a permanent display on Frank Lloyd Wright. It has various traveling exhibits as well. Open 10 am to 5 pm Tuesday through Saturday (noon to 9 pm Thursday), noon to 5 pm Sunday; $5 for adults, $3 for seniors and students.

Milwaukee Museum Center

A few hours can quickly evaporate at the downtown **Milwaukee Public Museum** (☎ 414-278-2700), 800 W Wells St. Four floors of nicely laid out displays include popular exhibits on dinosaurs and Native American life, and a great bison-hunt diorama. The Streets of Old Milwaukee is an excellent historical presentation; one portion to note is the window glimpses into the everyday city life of various ethnic groups.

The international sections, with detailed life scenes and exhibits on such countries as Japan and Papua New Guinea, are also very well done. A new wing exhibiting butterflies is to open in late 2000. Open 9 am to 5 pm daily; $6/5/4 adults/seniors/students. A restaurant is open for lunch.

In the same complex is **Discovery World**, the James Lovell Museum of Science, Economics and Technology (☎ 414-765-0777), 815 N James Lovell St. It features three floors of hands-on exhibits geared toward young visitors. Topics include electricity, weather and space. Open 9 am to 5 pm daily; $5/4/3 adults/seniors/children. Also here is the **Humphrey Dome IMAX Theater** (☎ 414-319-4629). Combination tickets for both museums or museums plus the IMAX cinema are available.

Other Museums

One-of-a-kind **America's Black Holocaus Museum** (☎ 414-264-2500), 2233 N 4th St outlines through artifacts and photograph the chilling story of racism, lynchings an mob justice in the United States. Museum founder James Cameron, an African American, was himself a victim of such violence in 1930, when he and two friends were accuse of a rape and murder. They were dragged ou of jail into a mob of thousands. His tw friends were beaten and hanged; he survived Open 9 am to 5 pm Monday to Saturday; $5

By the lake in the Miller Pavilion is **Bett Brinn Children's Museum** (☎ 414-291-0888) 929 E Wisconsin Ave, a participatory learning center full of fun. Kids can make toys create their own TV show and learn abou the human body with giant models. Ope 9 am to 5 pm Tuesday to Saturday, noon to 5 pm Sunday; $4.

The **Milwaukee County Historical Cente** (☎ 414-273-8288), 910 Old World 3rd St, ha two floors of exhibits on the county's past Subject matter has included approachable topics such as the Milwaukee River and regional circus history. Open 9:30 am to 5 pm Monday to Friday, 10 am to 5 pm Saturday 1 to 5 pm Sunday; free.

A colorful collection of costumes, photo and various artifacts lines the **Internationa Clown Hall of Fame** (☎ 414-319-0848), 16 W Wisconsin Ave, suite LL700, on the lowe level in the Grand Ave Mall. Regular performances are part of the appeal. Ope 10 am to 4 pm Monday to Friday.

The 'wonder what those are' three glas domes, visible from I-94, are the **Mitchel Park Conservatory** (☎ 414-649-9830), 524 S Layton Blvd. The desert, the jungle and th show dome, which presents five changin exhibits annually, provide miniature sanctuaries from the urban environment – grea escapes on a cold or rainy day. Open 9 am to 5 pm daily; $4 for adults, $3 for seniors an kids under 18.

Pabst Mansion

The 1893 residence of brew master, developer and art patron Frederick Pabs (☎ 414-931-0808), 2000 W Wisconsin Ave, i considered one of the masterpieces of American Flemish Renaissance architecture. It is a sumptuous place, and you don't need a course in history or architecture to appreciate the craftsmanship throughout the 37 rooms. It was recognized immediately as the pinnacle among the mansions created along what was known as Grand Ave, for its grand homes. Now operated by Wisconsin Heritages, Inc, it's open from 10 am to 3:30 pm Tuesday to Saturday, noon to 3:30 pm Sunday; $7/3 adults/kids.

Breweries

Connoisseurs might dismiss the bland beers churned out by the big-name national breweries, but hundreds of beer drinkers line up daily at the mega **Miller Brewing complex** (☎ 414-931-2337), 4251 W State St, responsible for such popular brands as Lite and High Life. The free one-hour tour features a slick promotional slide show followed by visits to the original chilling caves and bottling and distribution areas, which give you a good idea of how much of this stuff is swilled daily. The generous tasting session in the historic inn features three of the many brands produced, often including one of the Leinenkugel brews, from a former small, independent brewery in Chippewa Falls. Frequent tours are offered 10 am to 3:30 pm Monday to Saturday from June through September, less often from October to May. Call for tour schedule details; the frequency varies with demand.

Two of the newer microbreweries offer similar tours, but without the walking. **Sprecher Brewing** (☎ 414-964-2739), 701 W Glendale Ave, 5 miles north of downtown off Hwy 43, offers tours ($2) and tastings (with music) at 4 pm Friday and 1, 2 and 3 pm Saturday. There may be weekday tours in summer; regardless, call for reservations.

The **Lakefront Brewery** (☎ 414-372-8800), 1872 N Commerce St, gives $3 tours at 5:30 pm Friday and 1:30, 2:30, 3:30 pm Saturday.

Also note there are brew pubs on N Water St (see Entertainment), and each has someone who will talk beer if you're serious.

Harley-Davidson Sights

When the three Davidson brothers and their friend William Harley built three motorcycles in a wooden shed here in 1903, they could never have imagined they were giving birth not only to the world's most famous motorcycles, but also to a legend. The distinctive style and sound of their bikes continues to gain converts every year.

Aficionados may be interested in the free one-hour tours at the **power-train plant** (☎ 414-535-3666), 1700 W Capitol Drive, about 20 minutes from downtown. This plant manufactures engines and transmissions, which together constitute the power-train of the machine. The tour is somewhat more technical than many people would expect (there are no flashy body parts, assembled bikes or painting and finishing at the plant); it includes a video and a stroll among the machines stamping out engine and transmission parts. The lobby has some classic bikes to view, as does the employee parking lot. No open-toed shoes, high heels, or children under 12 are permitted. Tours begin at 9:30 and 11 am and 1 pm daily from June through August, and at the same hours Monday, Wednesday and Friday from September through May.

The home office is also in Milwaukee, but the final assembly and painting plants are in York, Pennsylvania, and Kansas City, Missouri.

For shopping there is the **House of Harley-Davidson** (☎ 414-282-2211), 6221 W Layton Ave off I-43, a huge dealership with clothing, collectibles and bikes. Closer to the parts plant is **Milwaukee Harley-Davidson** (☎ 414-461-9044), 11310 Silver Spring Rd, with 27,000 sq feet of hog happiness.

Milwaukee County Zoo

About 12 minutes west of town off I-94, the Milwaukee Zoo (☎ 414-771-3040), 10001 W Bluemound Rd, is a clever patchwork of foreign and domestic environments, each seemingly integrated with the next. Thus, predator and prey enclosures sit side-by-side, separated only by moats. Among the segments are polar bears, big cats and an African savanna.

Special features include the seal and sea lion show, birds of prey performance and the heritage farm, with dairy cows, exhibits and a petting zoo. Both a minitrain and a tram are available to help whisk visitors around the sizable grounds. Open 9 am to 5 pm daily from May through September, until 4:30 pm the rest of the year; $8/7/6 adults/seniors/kids.

Organized Tours

Walking Tours Nonprofit Historic Milwaukee (☎ 414-277-7795) leads a series of informative and entertaining Saturday and Sunday walks outlining history and architecture around various neighborhoods. The focus varies from the River St 'bad girls of beer town' to church and cathedral gargoyles. Most tours are offered from June to October, but there is something going on all year. Call to see what is coming up and where to meet; $5/2 adults/students.

Bus Tours Grayline (☎ 414-271-0996, 800-998-2325) has a year-round 1½-hour orientation tour ($20). There's free pickup from downtown hotels with advance reservations. A number of longer specialized tours are available to large groups but not individuals.

Cruises The *Iroquois* (☎ 414-384-8606) tools around the harbor and shipping docks twice daily from June to early September. Boats depart from the dock on the west side of the river between Clybourn and Michigan Sts; $10 adults, $7 kids 12 to 17, $5 kids under 12.

The comfortable, glass-encased *Edelweiss* (☎ 414-272-3769) does two-hour lunch ($32) and dinner ($60) cruises along the Milwaukee River and out into Lake Michigan. The dock is on the west side of the river at W Highland Ave.

Riverwalk Boat Tours (☎ 414-283-9999) runs fun weekend river cruises from June to October, stopping at three brew pubs on the three-hour trip. Departures are from Pere Marquette Park, at the corner of Old World 3rd St and State St; $10.

Special Events

It's impossible to include all the events. In summer there is a different ethnic festival almost every week. The following list contains some of the most popular ones. All the ethnic festivals are held at Maier Festival Park, known as the Summerfest grounds, on the lakeshore southeast of downtown at the foot of E Chicago St, within walking distance of the Milwaukee Art Museum. Each of these festivals features food, games, dancing and lots of music.

June–July

Bastille Days – a free French festival in East Town (☎ 414-271-7400)

Festa Italiana (☎ 414-223-2193)

German Fest (☎ 414-464-9444)

Great Circus Parade – a huge, 19th-century–style horse and wagon parade along three miles of downtown streets, including Kilbourn and Wisconsin Aves, preceded by a week of activities (☎ 414-223-2193)

Summerfest – a 10-day musical love affair, with dozens of concerts by big-name and lesser-known acts, drawing close to a million visitors annually from far and wide (☎ 414-273-3378)

August

Irish Fest (☎ 414-476-3378)

PrideFest – held at Henry Maier Festival Park, a time for the gay, lesbian, bisexual and transgender community to strut its stuff (☎ 414-272-3378)

Wisconsin State Fair – held annually since 1855, one of the nation's biggest, and many say best, state fairs, with hundreds of vendors and concessions, agricultural shows and competitions, concerts and fireworks; participants at the livestock (cows, pigs, etc) and food (pies, cheeses, maple syrup, etc) judging take their commitment very seriously. 8100 W Greenfield Ave, west of town off I-94

Places to Stay

Budget The ***Wisconsin State Fair Park*** *(☎ 414-266-7000, 800-844-3247, 8100 W Greenfield Ave)* has 128 RV-only sites starting at $20 for electric, $40 for full hookup; reservations are advised. For camping, head southwest to Kettle Moraine State Forest (see the North of Milwaukee section, later in this chapter).

The quiet, easygoing HI ***Red Barn Hostel*** *(☎ 414-529-3299, 6750 W Loomis Rd, Greendale)* is 12 miles southwest of town, west of I-94, near the crossroads of Root River Parkway. It's accessible by city bus: Take the No 10 bus south on Wisconsin Ave to 35 St, then the No 35 bus south to Loomis Rd, and walk 10 minutes west. The hostel is open May to October; a bed costs $11/14 members/nonmembers. Even if you're driving, call for directions; if you miss it, you can't turn around for miles. The hostel really is in an old barn – notice the stone walls – but is well equipped. If a group hasn't booked in, it won't be busy at all.

There's another HI hostel north of town in Newburg (see North of Milwaukee, later).

In summer, the University of Wisconsin's ***Sandburg Halls*** *(☎ 414-229-4065, 3400 N Maryland Ave)* offer simple rooms at $26/35 single/double, but they need a deposit a week before your arrival.

On Howell Ave, south of town near the airport, are some name-brand lodgings. Cheapest is reliable ***Motel 6*** *(☎ 414-482-4414, fax 414-482-1089, 5037 S Howell)* at $40/46 single/double. Another in this chain *(☎ 414-786-7337, fax 414-789-0510, 20300 W Bluemound Rd, Brookfield)* is 15 minutes west of town and is cheaper by $5.

Super 8 *(☎ 414-481-8488, fax 414-481-8086, 5252 S Howell Ave)*, 5 miles from downtown, has rooms for $62/67. Northwest of downtown, ***Baymont Inn & Suites*** *(☎ 414-535-1300, 800-428-3438, fax 414-535-1724, 5442 N Lovers Lane Rd)* has rooms for $50/65. There are other motels nearby on the same street.

Mid-Range The ***Best Western Inn Towne*** *(☎ 414-224-8400, fax 414-224-8696, 710 Old World 3rd St)*, right in the heart of downtown, is a bargain with rooms starting at $80 in the July–August peak season.

Next door, the ***Hotel Wisconsin*** *(☎ 414-271-4900, fax 414-271-9998, 720 Old World 3rd St)* is a delightful throwback in every way to the 1950s, with small, older rooms starting at $50 and newer ones with fluctuating prices starting at $89 in July and August, less off-season. The lobby, with its old pictures, and the bar and little restaurant are living museums.

The traditional ***Astor Hotel*** *(☎ 414-271-6370, 800-224-8400, fax 414-271-6370, 924 E Juneau Ave)* has doubles starting at $87 (more on weekends). The popular restaurant has a lively street patio.

Top End The downtown ***Hotel Metro*** *(☎ 414-272-1937, 800-448-8355, fax 414-223-1158, www.hotelmetro.com, 411 E Mason St)* is a perfect renovation of a 1937 Art Deco building. Well appointed, distinctively designed rooms range from $145 to $245. You won't have to go far to eat, as the dining room is highly regarded.

Pfister Hotel *(☎ 414-273-8222, fax 414-273-5025, www.pfister-hotel.com, 424 E Wisconsin Ave)* is a grand old hotel built in 1893 that makes endless pfabulous wordplays on its name. Singles/doubles start at $150 and rise to $244. The old wing is nicest.

Places to Eat

For a relatively small city, Milwaukee has a lot of good food, ranging from the traditional to a tasty ethnic assortment.

Downtown ***The Pavilion*** *(☎ 414-765-0990)*, in a great location in the Miller Pavilion, by the lake at the foot of E Wisconsin Ave, serves basic American food well ($8 to $18) but rounds out the menu with Italian,

Custard Custom

Frozen custard is a Milwaukee (and by extension, Wisconsin) food craze, if not addiction. Specialty stands, stores and aficionados with bliss in hand are seen scattered all over town. The frosty treat, available in a range of flavors and often a special of the day, is not unlike ice cream, but is creamier and smoother still. When asked the difference, devotees, between ecstatic lip smacks, make remarks such as, 'Oh, it's way worse for you,' 'It's *really* bad,' and 'rich, plus eggs.' Everybody has a favorite outlet, but the uninitiated will find any sample worth licking. Since 1942, Leon's, at 3131 S 27th St, has topped many people's lists. Kopp's, with numerous outlets around town, is another top-ranked dealer.

Mexican, steak and fish dishes. Open until 10 pm Monday through Thursday, 24 hours Friday and Saturday, until 8 pm Sunday.

Clever ***Safehouse*** *(☎ 414-271-2007, 779 N Front St)*, downtown by the river, is marked simply with a door indicating an import-export business. It's an inexpensive sandwich-burger restaurant like no other. Opening the door leads diners into the world of espionage. Take a look over your shoulder and slip inside; it's a lot of fun.

The ***African Hut*** *(☎ 414-765-1110, 1107 Old World 3rd St)*, is a small, inexpensive storefront restaurant with a worthy menu of authentic meat and vegetarian African dishes. Spicy peanut stew ($8) comes with rice and vegetables such as okra or collard greens. Closed Sunday. ***The King & I*** *(☎ 414-276-4181, 823 N 2nd St)* serves Thai specialties, from familiar noodle dishes (pad Thai, $10) to extensive seafood offerings (sautéed shrimp with chili and coconut milk, $14).

Moving upscale, German fare is readily available. ***Karl Ratzsch's Restaurant*** *(☎ 414-276-2720, 320 E Mason St)* has been maintaining the European heritage since 1904; note that it doesn't serve lunch. Arch-competitor ***Mader's German Restaurant*** *(☎ 414-271-3377, 1037 Old World 3rd St)* is two years older. Both have lots of heavy wood, rows of beer steins and attentive service. Main courses are about $20.

Also fairly dressy and in the same price range is ***John Ernst*** *(☎ 414-273-1878, 600 E Ogden Ave)*, opened in 1878, making it the oldest restaurant in the city. The classic Old World dining room serves steaks, seafood, more German meals and a good-value fish fry every Friday night. It's closed Monday.

Buca *(☎ 414-224-8672, 1233 N Van Buren St)* is a casual and inexpensive Italian restaurant.

See Entertainment for pub grub to complete the early German influence.

Brady St & Upper East Side ***Mimma's*** *(☎ 414-271-7337, 1307 E Brady St)*, open for dinner only, is a classy, expensive, European-like restaurant serving fine Italian fare.

More Italian food is on Oakland Ave northeast of Brady. The ***Oakland Trattoria*** *(☎ 414-964-2850, 2856 N Oakland Ave)*, with pizzas and pastas ($9 to $12), has a comfortable neighborhood feel.

The more formal ***Cempazuchi*** *(☎ 414-291-5233, 1205 E Brady St)* serves the little-known side of Mexican cuisine, that of complex sauces, multiflavored salads and lots of seafood; no Tex-Mex border foods here. These classically inspired dishes are in the $16 range. It's closed Monday, open for dinner only Sunday.

A local institution, ***Ma Fischer's*** *(☎ 414-271-7424, 2214 N Farwell Ave)* is billed as a family restaurant but has been catering to *every* kind of person 24 hours a day, seven days a week, since 1947. The all-encompassing menu delivers solid value, if not gourmet subtlety. The home-style Greek-inspired dinners ($7) are good.

Maharaja *(☎ 414-276-2250, 1550 N Farwell Ave)* is a pleasant Indian restaurant with good food. Lunch is a buffet; at dinner most dishes are about $10, the prix fixe vegetarian combination for two is $25. The bread and vegetable selections are particularly impressive.

Tiny ***Abu's*** *(☎ 414-277-0485, 1978 N Farwell Ave)* serves excellent Middle Eastern pecialties amid simple, modest decor. Various combination platters that include sides of hummus, baba ganoush and tabbouleh are all under $10 and very good. Closed Sunday.

Walker's Point South of town a few blocks (over the 6th St bridge and too far to walk), on S 5th and 6th Sts in the Latin enclave of Walker's Point, are about 10 Mexican restaurants. The good, low-priced food and unpretentious atmosphere draw crowds on weekend nights.

The trendiest is boisterous ***La Fuente*** *(☎ 414-271-8595, 625 S 5th St)*, with a comfortable outdoor patio to complement the broad menu. Finger-food standards such as burritos and tacos are bolstered by authentic plates such as enchiladas and mole dishes, as well as various seafood dishes in the $12 range. Expect a full house.

Pedrano's *(600 S 6th St)*, open daily and until 3 am Friday and Saturday, is a plain, homey place where a solid meal is yours for less than $7. Numerous other worthy establishments are within walking distance.

Elsewhere in Milwaukee In addition to beer, custard and German fare, the city has another gastronomic weakness: the Friday fish fry. This tradition is followed across the city and throughout the state, but nothing can compare to the way it's done at the ***American Serb Memorial Hall*** *(☎ 414-545-6030, 5101 W Oklahoma Ave)*, at the corner of 53rd St southwest of downtown. From noon to 9 pm, the dining room satisfies armies of regulars with all-you-can-eat baked cod.

Entertainment

The weekly *Shepherd Express* tabloid is a good source for events and club information.

Performing Arts Evening enjoyment goes far beyond distinguishing ale from lager – the city is among the national leaders in support of cultural institutions. The top venue is the ***Marcus Center*** *(☎ 414-273-7121, 929 N Water St)*, home to the ballet, symphony, opera and various other concerts and theater productions. The ***Pabst Theater*** *(☎ 414-286-3663)*, a Victorian gem from 1895 at 144 E Wells St, presents a range of theatrical and musical performances.

The ***Milwaukee Symphony*** *(☎ 414-291-7605, 800-291-7605)* is very highly regarded. Its season is from September to June.

Not a lot of American cities can boast more than one opera company. Of several here, the most prestigious, founded in 1932, is ***Florentine Opera of Milwaukee*** *(☎ 414-291-5700)*, with performances from October to May.

Skylight Opera Theatre *(☎ 414-291-7811, 158 N Broadway)* does both classic and more modern opera among its varied musical presentations.

Present Music *(☎ 414-271-0711)* showcases contemporary composers.

The ***Milwaukee Ballet*** *(☎ 414-643-7677)*, also with a fall and winter season, is considered one of the country's best.

Bars The beer legacy ensures you don't go thirsty in this town – and there is a quenching array of brew available. N Water St at E State St has more than a dozen bars and restaurants. The following two brew their own and are worth sampling. Downtown on the river is the popular ***Rockbottom Brewery*** *(☎ 414-276-3030, 740 N Plankinton Ave)*, for drinks, pool games and meals; the ***Water St Brewery*** *(☎ 414-272-1195, 1101 N Water St)* has a full menu.

Across the street, ***Brew City BBQ*** is popular for its beer selection and cheap barbecue meals. On the east side of the river, the more sedate ***John Hawk's*** *(100 E Wisconsin Ave)* in the basement but with a deck by the water, is a 'British' pub with a big choice of beers, fish fries and live jazz on Saturday.

On the Upper East Side, the very German ***Von Trier*** *(☎ 414-272-1775, 2235 N Farwell Ave)* has 20-plus beers on tap, a beer garden and good German snacks. In the Historic Third Ward, the ***Milwaukee Ale House*** *(☎ 414-226-2337, 233 N Water St)* pours six of its own brews and serves substantial hamburgers and sandwiches.

The Dubliner *(☎ 414-672-5488, 922 S 2nd St)* has Irish beers, whiskeys and Celtic music.

Cozy ***At Random*** *(2501 S Delaware Ave)*, a bar designed for lovers, serves no beer but shakes and stirs all manner of cocktails. It's southeast of downtown about halfway to the airport.

Dance Clubs Live bands pack the small dance floor at ***BBC Bar & Grill*** *(☎ 414-272-7263, 2022 E North Ave)*, which has disco on Wednesday, swing on Thursday, funk on weekends. ***La Cage*** *(801 S 2nd St)*, in Walker's Point, draws a gay and straight crowd at its multiple bars and dance floors.

Live Music ***Up & Under Pub*** *(1216 E Brady St)* is a well-established place for a range of good music, including frequent blues bands, with varying cover charges. The cool ***Velvet Room*** *(☎ 414-319-1190, 730 Old World 3rd St)*, in central downtown, is known for martinis and cocktails but also has live jazz some nights. ***Big Dogs*** *(☎ 414-645-9013, 3062 S 13th St)* is a blues bar southwest of downtown, below Marquette University.

Spectator Sports

The Milwaukee Brewers (☎ 414-933-9000, 800-933-7890) play major league baseball in the National League. A new stadium, Miller Park, is being constructed to replace County Stadium; the new park (next to the old one) will have a retractable roof. Tickets are almost always available and range from $5 to $20. The pregame tailgate parties and concession bratwurst are local sources of pride.

The NBA's Milwaukee Bucks (☎ 414-227-0500) shoot hoops at the Bradley Center, 1001 N 4th St. Other than at courtside, tickets are usually available throughout the season for $14 to $40.

Getting There & Away

Air General Mitchell International Airport is at 5300 S Howell Ave, south of downtown about 8 miles. Milwaukee-based Midwest Express (☎ 800-452-2022) is regularly voted one of America's best airlines. The other major airlines operating at Mitchell are Air Canada, Continental, Delta, KLM, Lufthansa, Northwest, TWA and Unite (see the Toll-Free & Web Site Directory fo phone numbers).

Bus The bus station, 606 N 7th St at th corner of Michigan St, is convenientl central. Greyhound (☎ 414-272-6688) has 1 daily buses to Chicago ($14, 2 hours), four day to Minneapolis ($50, 6 hours express) and five daily to Madison ($11). The Dulut bus travels via Green Bay and the Uppe Peninsula ($70, 12 hours). Across the street Badger Bus Lines (☎ 414-276-7490), 635 N 7th St, goes to Madison six times daily ($12 1½ hours).

Train The Amtrak station (☎ 414-271 0840), downtown at 433 W St Paul Ave has six trains a day to and from Chicag ($19, 1½ hours), and the daily *Empire Builder* stops here on its Chicago–Seattle route. To Minneapolis the fare ranges from $47 to $86.

Getting Around

To/From the Airport Limousine Service (☎ 800-236-5450) operates an airport shuttle van to and from hotels. Call for reservation for the $9 trip.

American United (☎ 414-220-5000) charges $25 to the airport from downtown, a trip that, if all goes well, takes 20 minutes.

Bus The Milwaukee County Transit System (☎ 414-344-6711) provides efficient loca bus service ($1.35). It also offers the cheap PrimeCo Shuttle from downtown to Maier Festival Park for the various summer ethnic festivals. Call for schedule and routes.

An excellent way to get around is the Milwaukee Loop, a downtown circuit on a trolley-like bus that runs Wednesday through Sunday in summer from late May to early September. An all-day, on-and-off pass is just $1, and trolleys run every 20 minutes. Call the transit number for information.

Car Avis (☎ 800-331-1212) has four offices including one at the airport and another downtown at 916 E State St. Thrifty (☎ 414-

224-8981) also has a downtown office at 830 N 4th St. Here and elsewhere, prices are comparable. A one-day mid-size car costs about $30 plus the usual extras (insurance, gas) at Avis.

AROUND MILWAUKEE

Within easy day-trip distance are a varied group of destinations, some of which could be combined to make an invigorating outing.

North of Milwaukee

Twenty minutes up US 43 is **Cedarburg**, an atmospheric, low-key tourist village featuring an award-winning historic main street. Antiques shops, galleries and quaint B&Bs nestle together on well-preserved Washington Ave. Stop by the **General Store Museum**, at the corner of Spring and Washington Sts, with its fine collection of antique general-store products, packaging, signs and more. Tourist information is also offered here. Open 10 am to 4 pm Monday to Friday, 10 am to 3 pm Saturday and from 11 am to 3 pm Sunday.

The **Lizard Mounds**, some 20 mounds in various geometric and zoomorphic shapes that were built between 500 and 1000 AD, are a part of the Washington County Parks System (☎ 414-335-4445). The large earthen mounds, now covered in grass, are similar to others found throughout the Midwest. They're about 2 miles north of West Bend off Hwy 33. From Milwaukee, take Hwy 45 to Hwy 33.

In nearby Newburg, the HI ***Wellspring Center*** *(☎ 414-675-6755, 4382 Hickory Rd)* is a small hostel often used for retreats. It's open all year, but call ahead. A night's stay costs $15.

There's good walking and cross-country skiing close by in **Kettle Moraine State Forest** (northern unit, take Hwy 45 to Hwy 67). Its visitors' center (☎ 414-626-2116), on Hwy 67 near Dundee, has details on the glacial features and trails. Camping is possible all year, but July and August are busy. Rates are $8 to $12, and state park stickers are valid for entry.

South & West of Milwaukee

On the Lake Michigan shore 30 miles south of Milwaukee on Hwy 32, **Racine** is an unremarkable industrial town. The key visitor attraction is the **Administration Building of the Johnson Wax Company** at 14th and Franklin Sts, designed by Frank Lloyd Wright. The main office, dating from 1939, is a magnificent space, with tall, flared columns. The research tower, also Wright designed, was added in 1950. It all needs to be seen from the inside, so take one of the free guided tours, generally offered 10 am to 2:15 pm Tuesday to Friday (and Saturday from late May to early September). Tours must be booked in advance (☎ 262-260-2154), and the schedule is subject to change; call ahead to be sure. While you're in Racine, stop by Dover Flag & Map travel store (☎ 414-632-3133), 323 Main St.

Southwest on I-43, then south on Hwy 12 is pretty **Lake Geneva**, which, like its European counterpart, presents a manicured shoreline and obvious evidence of wealth. You may see a vehicle from Illinois at the side of the lake, its occupant busy on a cell phone. Relaxing boat tours depart from the 1933 Riviera Pavilion for trips around this focal point of the southern resorts. The imposing lakeside building, where big bands once played, is at the foot of Main St (Hwy 50) at the junction of Wrigley Drive.

The well-treed lakeside, interspersed with beaches and piers, can be stunning when the fall colors are at their height. A 21-mile recreation trail encircles the shoreline. Broad St by the lake, and more so, Main St, have some fine restaurants.

About 40 miles southwest of Milwaukee, 2 miles south of Eagle, **Old World Wisconsin** (☎ 262-594-6300) is a first-rate state historic site. On 600 acres with 65 original buildings, the costumed interpreters representing numerous ethnic groups bring 19th-century Wisconsin to life; 10 am to 4 pm, 5 pm on weekends, May 1 to October 31. Food is available. Admission is $11/10/6 adults/seniors/children. From Milwaukee, head west on Hwy 18, then south on Hwy 67.

Adjacent hilly, glaciated limestone **Kettle Moraine State Forest** (☎ 262-594-6200), southern unit, off Hwy 67, has a good system of walking, biking and skiing trails by bluffs and meadows. There is also camping ($8) available all year; the usual season is June to October, and July and August are the busy season.

MADISON

• pop 191,262

Wonderfully situated on a narrow isthmus between two lakes, Madison is a pleasing combination of small state capital and lively college town. It consistently takes honors and mentions for qualities such as best small city, nicest place to raise a family, best place for a woman to live, even most enlightened town. Heck, the people even seem better-looking and more fit than in most places.

There's a lot to take in, what with the museums, arts, restaurants, stately buildings and the University of Wisconsin campus. For visitors, an added bonus is that much of the city is compact and walkable, and most of the rest can be reached by bicycle. It's certainly no hardship to settle in and spend a few days here.

Orientation

The massive state capitol marks the center of town. Keep an eye on it, because the diagonal streets that flare off it at angles to the central grid are confusing to newcomers. One of those diagonals, State St, off-limits to cars but open to buses, pedestrians and bicyclists, is the city's heart, a lengthy strip of stores, bars, cafés, restaurants and museums running from the capitol west to the extensive grounds of the University of Wisconsin.

Lake Mendota marks the northern edge of the core, Lake Monona the southern. The campus marks the western edge of downtown. On the east side, Williamson St, known as Willy St, extends the downtown through a mix of shops, restaurants, counterculture and residential neighborhoods.

The airport lies northeast of downtown near I-90/94. Hwy 12/14 edges along the southwestern limits of town, Hwy 12/18 along the southeastern.

Information

The Visitors Bureau (☎ 608-255-2537, 800 373-6376, www.visitmadison.com), 615 E Washington Ave, five blocks from centra Capitol Square, is open weekdays 9 am t 4:30 pm.

In the other direction, near the square, i the excellent Wisconsin Department o Tourism (☎ 608-266-6162, 800-372-2737) 201 W Washington Ave, offering informa tion on any place in the state. It's open 8 ar to 5 pm weekdays from May to Novembe (until 4:30 pm November to May) and Sat urday 8 am to noon from June to October.

The post office is at 215 Martin Luthe King Jr Blvd in the Municipal Building.

The Madison Public Library (☎ 608-266 6300), 201 W Mifflin St, offers Interne access. Visit Canterbury Booksellers (☎ 608 258-9911), 315 W Gorham St and Universit Book Store (☎ 608-257-3784), 711 State St.

Meriter Hospital (☎ 608-267-6000), 30 W Washington Ave, is central.

State Capitol

At the hub of town is this grand govern ment center, with its imposing white granit dome, surrounded by Capitol Square. Th magnificent interior, which includes th Wisconsin Supreme Court and impressiv stained glass, murals and woodwork shoul not be missed. There's no more incongruou a sight than a pizza delivery guy struttin through the palatial hallways at lunch. Fre guided tours are available on the hour (af ternoons only on Sunday) from the infor mation desk in the ground-floor foye (☎ 608-266-0382). Entrances are on all fou sides. From the foyer, walk up to th outdoor observation deck, too.

Museums

The four-floor **State Historical Museu** (☎ 608-264-6555), 30 N Carroll St beside th square, offers thorough coverage of Wiscon sin's past. Exhibits include excellent dis plays on the state's Native America nations, the fur trade, immigration, lumber ing and farming. Open from 10 am to 5 pr Tuesday through Saturday, noon to 5 pr

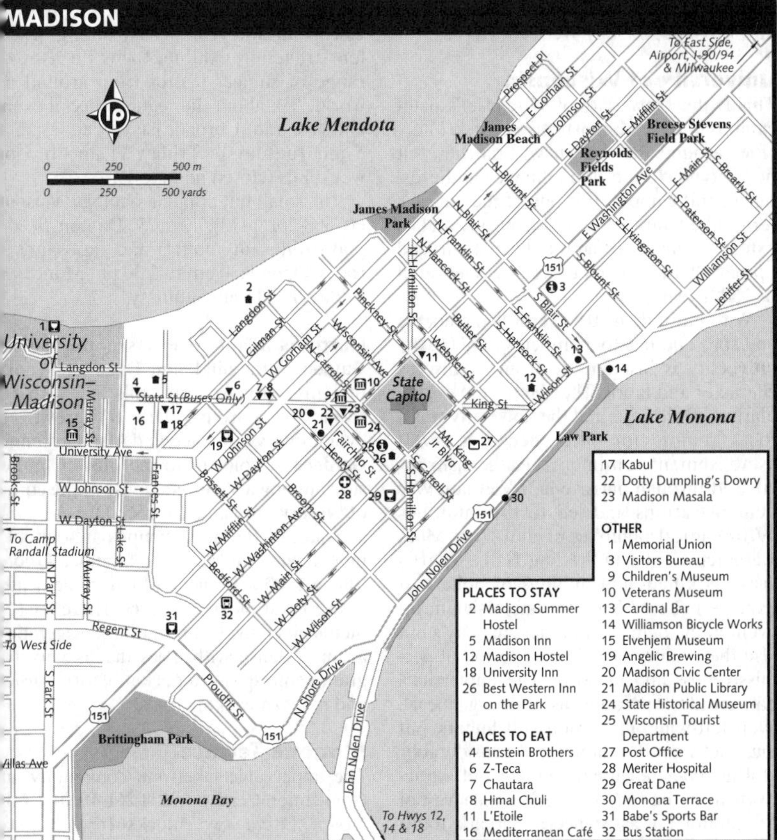

unday; $2 suggested donation (free for Visconsinites).

Across the street, the **Veterans Museum** (☎ 608-264-6086), 30 W Mifflin St, is worth a visit. Its thoughtful displays outline all the wars the USA has been involved in, and it even has a piece of the Berlin Wall. Other exhibits detail the role of women and civilians during wartime with varied artifacts and media, such as radio clips, ensuring the information isn't dry. Open 9 am to 4:30 pm daily (closed Sunday and holidays from September to April); free.

The interactive **Children's Museum** (☎ 608-256-6445), 100 State St, provides participatory displays and various activities linking learning and play for young children. Open 9 am to 4 pm Tuesday to Sunday; $4.

The Madison Civic Center, 211 State St, is a performance venue that includes the **Madison Art Center** (☎ 608-257-0158), housing modern and contemporary visual art. Its three galleries feature nontraditional, often challenging exhibitions. Open 11 am to 5 pm Tuesday through Thursday,

11 am to 9 pm Friday, 10 am to 9 pm Saturday, 1 to 5 pm Sunday; free.

University of Wisconsin

This is the University of Wisconsin's main campus and its administrative center. Many cities around the state have branches, but none come close to the influence and prestige of this campus. It is one of the nation's top-ranked universities academically, and its extensive sports programs keep their end up as well. In 1999 the university celebrated its 150th year.

With more than 40,000 enrolled students and staff and faculty numbering 17,000, the university is inseparable from Madison's character and fabric. The 1960s were particularly volatile here, and the university was a focal point for the decade's anti-establishment sentiments. Radicalism increased through massive anti-Vietnam War demonstrations and led to the infamous 1970 political bombing of the Army Math Research Center in Sterling Hall. A physicist was killed, and millions of dollars of damage inflicted. This became a significant event in the demise of not just the city's but also the country's celebrated period of permissiveness and idealism. The university's nationwide reputation as a strong liberal, even left-wing, institution still lingers, but mass activism has diminished considerably.

The 900-acre campus spreads out attractively from the end of State St, a mile west of the capitol. For assistance, a map and tours, call the Campus Assistance and Visitor Center (☎ 608-265-2400), 716 Langdon St, in the Red Gym building.

Even without a particular destination, a stroll through the campus is time well spent. The casual visitor could do worse than following the 1½-mile **Lakeshore Path** along the edge of Lake Mendota west from Memorial Union (at the end of Park St by the lake) to Picnic Point, a narrow green peninsula jutting into the lake, offering fine picnicking and views.

Museums The top-rate **Elvehjem Art Museum** (☎ 698-263-2246), 800 University Ave, has a permanent collection spanning from antiquity to the present, emphasizir European and American painting. Exce lent traveling exhibits focus on a broa range of subject matter from around tł world. Ask about the regular special even and live radio broadcasts. Open 9 am 5 pm Tuesday to Friday, 11 am to 5 pı weekends (closed holidays); free.

The small but popular **Geology Museu** (☎ 608-262-1412), 1215 W Dayton St, di plays dinosaur models and thousands rocks. Open 8:30 am to 3:30 pm Monday Friday, 9 to 11 am Saturday.

Gardens Plant lovers, see the **Botar Garden** on the hill below Birge Hall (nor of University Ave on Mills St), with 8(species from around the world growing evolutionary sequence, and **Alan Centenni Gardens**, a colorful formal flower garde surrounding a Victorian house at the corn of Observatory and Babcock Drives.

South of the main campus area about mile down S Mills St is the fabulous **Arbor tum**, a 1200-acre patch of nature dedicate to preservation and research. There are se ments given over to rare prairie vegetatio an area dense with lilacs that is very fr grant come spring, a pocket of virgin fore and miles of walking trails.

Monona Terrace

The impeccable lakefront Community ar Convention Center (☎ 608-261-4000), 1 Joh Nolen Drive two blocks from Capit Square, opened in 1997, 59 years after Fran Lloyd Wright designed it. Politics, cost ove runs, WWII and local opposition to the buil ing and the man delayed the project un 1992, when Madisonians finally passed a nancing and construction referendum. Th low building, with arched windows and rooftop garden overlooking Lake Monon links, rather than separates, the lake and cit

See the Wright display in the gift sho and the photos of him and his work b Pedro Guerro down the corridor. Tours ar given from the gift shop at 11 am and 1 p daily for $2 (free on Monday and Tuesday The building is open 9 am to 5 pm daily, th rooftop until midnight.

'irst Unitarian Meeting House

/right fans should also visit the striking tri-ngular church (☎ 608-233-9774) at 900 Jniversity Bay Drive west of downtown. Take University Ave from downtown to ıst past the university campus and turn orth on University Bay Drive.) Wright de-ıgned it in 1946 and himself was a member f the First Unitarians. The church, listed on ıe National Register of Historic Places, is pen most days, and visitors are welcome at unday services. Tours of about an hour are ffered 1 to 4 pm weekdays, 9 am to noon aturday ($3).

ctivities

'icycling is excellent in town and around ıe lakes. Williamson Bicycle Works (☎ 608-52-5292), 601 Williamson St by Lake Ionroe at the foot of Blair St, rents bikes nd Rollerblades. Get a route map at the isitors bureau. Carl's Paddlin' Canoe and ayak (☎ 608-284-0300), 617 Williamson St, ents by the day or longer.

pecial Events

Iadison enjoys a large number of special vents during the year. Contact the visitors ureau for listings and information.

uly

ane County Fair – The urbane gives way to simple country fun; fairgrounds are at the Dane County Expo Center, 1919 Expo Way, south of town about 2½ miles (☎ 608-224-0500).

ugust

adison Blues Festival – At the end of the month, this festival (☎ 608-836-8999, www.madison blues.com) draws fans from around the state to Olin Park, south of downtown on Lake Monona off John Nolin Drive. Tickets are available through Ticketmaster (☎ 608-255-4646) and at the Madison Civic Center box office (☎ 608-266-9055), 211 State St.

ear-Round

rmer's Market – Walking is nearly impossible at this crowded, colorful Saturday morning market at Capitol Square, with vendors selling bountiful produce and other goodies. Live music is often on hand, too.

Places to Stay

Budget The convenient new HI ***Madison Hostel*** *(☎ 608-441-0144, 608-282-9031, ⓔ madisonhostel@yahoo.com, 141 S Butler St)* is a short walk from the state capitol, in an overhauled three-story brick building on a residential street. To reach a live person, call the first number from 9 to 11 am or 5 to 9 pm. Rates are $14/17 members/nonmembers for dorms; a private single/double $27/30.

Langdon Hall *(☎ 608-251-8841, 126 Langdon St)*, a central student residence, rents rooms from the last week of May until mid-August. There is a week minimum, but the week's rate is only $63. Washrooms are down the hall, and some rooms require sharing. Meals are also available.

Moderately priced motels can be found off I-90/94, Hwy 12/18 and along Washington Ave. Eight miles south off I-90, ***Motel 6*** *(☎ 608-221-0415, fax 608-221-0970, 6402 E Broadway)* is a deal at $35/41 in summer.

East of the center, ***Select Inn*** *(☎ 608-249-1815)*, off the interstate at 4858 Hayes Rd, has rooms for $40 to $55.

Mid-Range Six miles northeast of downtown, ***Econo Lodge*** *(☎ 608-241-4171, 4726 E Washington Ave)* is reliable and includes a simple breakfast for $54/62 in summer.

The ***University Inn*** *(☎ 608-257-4881, 800-279-4881, 441 N Frances St)* is a small hotel charging $65/75 single/double weekdays in July and August, $99 weekends. By September, prices drop and the weekend premium disappears. It's just a block from the campus and steps to State St.

The straightforward ***Madison Inn*** *(☎ 608-257-4391, 601 Langdon St)*, beside the university, is a good, lesser-known option at $70 to $85. The ***Best Western Inn on the Park*** *(☎ 608-257-8811, 800-279-8811, fax 608-257-5995, 22 S Carroll St)* is right beside the state capitol. Features include a pool and restaurant. In summer, prices start at $70/80 and rise to $125.

Off I-90, ***Days Inn*** *(☎ 608-223-1800, fax 608-223-1374, 4402 E Broadway Service Rd)*, with an indoor pool, charges $100/110 dropping almost 40% after September. At the ***Comfort Inn*** *(☎ 608-244-6265,* *fax 608-244-1293, 4822 E Washington Ave)* rates are $100/120 single/double. The complimentary continental breakfast buffet is a cut above.

Places to Eat

There's almost too much good eating here; decision making when you're hungry is no fun. The multitude of quality ethnic options is heaped atop solid American offerings.

Budget There are budget options aplenty on State St, where many eateries have outdoor tables. ***Einstein Brothers*** *(☎ 608-257-9828, 652 State St)* cranks out eye-opening coffee and bagels until 3 pm daily.

The friendly ***Mediterranean Café*** *(☎ 608-251-8510, 625 State St)* offers tasty, filling Middle Eastern standards such as shawarma and falafel plates for a wallet-friendly $6.

From its tiny kitchen, ***Himal Chuli*** *(☎ 608-251-9225, 318 State St)* cooks up excellent Nepali meals. Meatless or not, plates often include dahl, rice, curry and flat breads with a satisfying blend of spices. Everything is under $8. ***Chautara*** *(☎ 608-251-3626, 334 State St)* is the same owners' newer, spiffier incarnation with a more elaborate menu and higher prices.

At ***Z-Teca*** *(☎ 608-280-8720, 548 State St)*, Mexican fast food meets contemporary high-tech design with simple, sparse decor and stainless steel tables. Huge burritos are made to your specifications without lard, and vegetarian options are offered. Prices are low even for Mexican beer.

It's hard to ignore the local favorite, ***Dotty Dumpling's Dowry*** *(☎ 608-255-3175, 116 Fairchild St)*, a few steps from State St. A range of hefty hamburgers (including buffalo burgers) and other sandwiches (all about $6) are served with beer in and around the unique decor of airplanes, fish and posters.

For nicely done Afghani food in more of a traditional dining room, there's ***Kabul*** *(☎ 608-256-6322, 521 State St)*, where kebabs and other favorites are in the $10 range.

A new addition to the international range of eating options is the mouthwatering bargain Indo-Pakistani fare at ***Madiso Masala*** *(☎ 608-287-1599, 115 State St* serving vegetarian, fish and lamb dishes in cozy, narrow storefront setting.

Sedately cool ***Michelangelo's*** *(☎ 608-25 5299, 114 State St)*, near the Children Museum, is perfect for coffee, smoothi and sweets. It's open early until late dail On one recent visit the staff kept a lost wa of $80 until the grateful student returne for it, so give 'em a tip.

The many food carts seen around tow specifically around the capitol or at the un versity end of State St, dole out stunning tasty, mainly ethnic meals at rock botto prices.

Mid-Range Since the 1950s, ***Smokey*** *(☎ 608-233-2120, 3005 University Ave)* h been *the* place for steak. Entrées cost $16 $20. Closed Sunday and Tuesday.

L'Etoile *(☎ 608-251-0500, 25 N Pickney S* is an expensive contemporary-continent dining room with a heralded reputation. Th chef incorporates local produce wheneve possible. Entrées cost $20 to $28.

Entertainment

State St, near the university, obviously h several bars. Walk by them to the terrace the ***Memorial Union*** *(800 Langdon St* Lighthearted, mixed crowds – everybo from students to families – start collecting late afternoon at the lake-edge patio Thur day through Saturday from April to Se tember. Crowds build until about 9:30 pr when the free live music begins. If the ba tender asks for student or member ID, get free day pass inside the union. In po weather, the action moves indoors to t cavernous main hall. Food is available at t cafeteria.

For dancing, the ***Cardinal Bar*** *(☎ 60 251-0080, 418 E Wilson St)* is a favorite, wi different types of music almost night Popular pubs include ***Great Dane*** *(☎ 60 284-0000, 123 W Doty St)* and ***Angel Brewing*** *(☎ 608-257-2707, 322 W Johns St)*, both of which brew their own. T latter also has live music. ***Harmony B*** *(☎ 608-249-4333, 2201 Atwood Ave)* is eighborhood place northeast of the center ith live weekend blues.

The *Madison Civic Center* (☎ *608-266-055, 211 State St)* is a mecca for the perrming arts as the home of the local mphony, traveling Broadway shows and arious concerts and productions through ie year.

pectator Sports

hrough autumn, the UW Badgers play ollege football Saturday at the campus amp Randall Stadium (☎ 608-262-1866), t the west end of W Dayton St north of Ionroe St. Games are usually sold out, esecially for games against Big 10 opponents, hen the stadium noise and chaos reach ltimate proportions.

Basketball and hockey are played at the ohl Center (☎ 608-262-1400), on campus t the corner of W Dayton St and Frances t. The ticket office is here, too.

etting There & Away

ane County Regional Airport is northeast f downtown off Hwy 113. Major airlines flying in and out of Madison include American, Midwest Express, and United (see the Toll-Free Directory for phone numbers). Taxi fare to downtown is about $13 and the ride takes from 15 to 25 minutes.

The Greyhound bus station (☎ 608-257-3050) is centrally located at 2 S Bedford St. There are about five buses a day (some express) for the Twin Cities for $38. Milwaukee gets six runs, at $10 for the 90-minute trip. Badger Bus Lines (☎ 608-255-6771) also services Milwaukee from the same depot ($12).

WEST OF MADISON

Mt Horeb

• pop 4182

Twenty miles west of Madison on Hwy 18 is this agreeable little town with a commodious Main St edged with antiques shops and gift retailers, many proffering troll carvings, a local quirk taken from Scandinavian folklore and now well out of hand. A good number of these and the decorative ones around town come from the **Wooden Chicken** workshop, 219 E Main St, with erratic business hours.

Badger Behavior

Wisconsin has two football teams to go nuts over. Besides the Green Bay Packers, the U of W Badgers generate passion and overindulgence. You'll know it's a game-day Saturday when everyone in the downtown area is wearing red. The restaurants, bars and parking lots will be busy starting early in the morning, with Bloody Marys and bratwurst fueling the excitement. By close to game time the atmosphere is electric, and driving anywhere downtown is strongly discouraged.

Although the in-stadium antics, chaos and violence have been tamed since the 1980s (armed deputies are well in evidence and aren't shy about making arrests), the noise and vulgar student chants remain undiminished. The Bucky Badger mascot is a favorite, and the halftime show featuring the university's impressive marching band maintains fan momentum.

The 'fifth quarter' is a local tradition: After the game, none of the 70,000 or so spectators leave. Win or lose, the music blares, the marching band cranks out polkas and everyone sings and dances in a frenetic finale.

Tickets are generally available except for games against Michigan, Ohio State, Penn State or other perennial rivals also within the Big 10. Archrival Minnesota really heightens the intensity.

Scalping is illegal, but people selling tickets are usually on hand at the field or perhaps the night before in one of the student pubs around the campus.

Popular bars for watching the game include Babe's Sports Bar, close to the corner of Regent St and W Washington Ave (look for the old train sitting beside the restored depot), or the Big 10 Pub, 1330 Regent St.

To many visitors the real highlight is the **Mustard Museum** (☎ 608-437-3986), 111 E Main St, an astounding collection born of one man's ridiculously intense passion, which has touched fame if not the sublime. Try to get on a tour. Admission, samples and humor are free. Open 10 am to 5 pm daily. Afterward, enjoy something Norwegian or Swedish at ***Shubert's Café and Bakery***, across the street. It's well known for its Swedish rye bread. You might also sample the meatballs or one of the sweet pastries.

Toward Blue Mounds is **Cave of the Mounds National Natural Landmark** (☎ 608-437-3038), a limestone cave complex with fascinating formations. Tours are $10 and run all year, but the schedule varies.

Minutes away on County Rd JG, **Little Norway** (☎ 608-437-8211) is an original mid-1800s Norwegian farmstead complete with antiques and crafts and a fine example of a wooden Norse church. Open 9 am to 5 pm daily from May through October (until 7 pm in July and August); $7/6/3 adults/seniors/children.

Spring Green

• pop 1283

Forty miles west of Madison on Hwy 14, Spring Green sits amid lovely countryside. It makes an excellent base for exploring the outstanding architecture and pastoral geography of the area. Architect Frank Lloyd Wright, who for many years lived just down the road, has had a lasting impact on its style. Even Spring Green's central M&I Bank, on Jefferson St, is obviously Wright-influenced. Many of the area's buildings were in fact designed by Wright students and associates. Don't leave town without visiting the free **Calliope Center**, on Hwy 14 by the motels, for a guaranteed smile at these shiny circus-music makers.

Taliesin Head 3 miles south of Spring Green on Hwy 23 to reach Taliesin, Wright's home for most of his life and the site of his architectural school, which lives on.

There are several Wright buildings here; the house was built in 1903, the Hillside Home School in 1932, and the Frank Lloy Wright Visitor Center (☎ 608-588-7900), de signed as a restaurant, in 1953. From May October there's a wide range of instructiv guided tours covering various parts of th complex ($10 to $60). It's also open in Apr and November, but with diminished servic

For information and reservations, whic are required for the more lengthy detaile tours and presentations, contact the Visit Center in advance. Either the basic tour the $15, 90-minute walking tour (no rese vation needed) is a good introduction. Fa should pick up a copy of the Wisconsi Wright tour pamphlet here, which is als available at most tourist offices. It lists th state's Wright buildings and gives address and contacts. Consider lunch at the center good café.

Places to Stay & Eat There are a half-doze motels strung along Hwy 14 north of tow several of which were designed by Wright ap prentices. Two such are the recommende ***Usonian Inn*** *(☎ 608-588-2323, 877-876-642* or the ***Prairie House*** *(☎ 608-588-2088, 80 588-2088)*, both charging around $60 for double in July and August, less otherwis Downtown also has a B&B, the ***Hill*** *(☎ 608-588-7751, hillstbb@exepc.com, 3 W Hill St)*, with rooms for $70 to $80. Sou on Hwy 23, near Taliesin, Tower Hill Sta Park (☎ 608-588-2116) has good, bas ***camping*** ($9 to $13) and walking trails.

The ***Post House***, on Jefferson St, is goo for any meal.

Richland Center

Wright was actually born 27 miles northwe of Spring Green in the town of Richlan Center. The AD German Warehouse (☎ 60 647-2808), 300 S Church St, was designed Wright in 1915 and is the only remainin example of his work from that decade. It notable for its geometric concrete decor tions. Tours ($5) are offered by appointme only, from May to October.

House on the Rock

South of Taliesin on Hwy 23 is House on th Rock (☎ 608-935-3639), one of the busie attractions in the state. It accommodates huge crowds in summer.

The strange 'house,' one man's obsession, incorporates its surroundings, but any likeness to Wright's work and subtlety ends here. It was built atop a column of rock and has become a sprawling monument to the imagination. But it's the content, incorporating collections of assorted objects and wonderments, that overwhelms. There are carousels, music machines, street scenes, model ships, folk art objects and more. It's kitsch with class, whimsy extraordinaire for kids of all ages and not at all underdone.

Open 9 am to 7 pm daily from mid-March to the end of October (until 8 pm from late May to early September). There is also a Christmas season from November to January – call for details. Admission is high but it takes three to five hours to see it all! Even the washrooms have things to ogle. $16 for adults, $10 for kids seven to 12, $4 for kids four to six, free for kids under three.

Farther south is huge **Governor Dodge State Park** (☎ 608-935-2315), with a network of trails running by waterfalls, through woodlands and canyons, to cliff viewpoints.

Dodgeville

• pop 4200

Stepping back in time, Dodgeville's mid-19th-century downtown is a National Historic District. Among Iowa St's preserved storefronts are several standard restaurants. Six miles east off of Hwy 18/151, HI ***Folklore Village Farm*** *(☎ 608-924-4000, 3210 County BB)*, has dorm beds for $12. The main attraction, though, is the folklore group's regular musical nights, with dancing and much joviality; it's good fun, and you don't have to be a guest of the hostel to attend. There's good cycling nearby.

Seven miles south of Dodgeville and about the same size is **Mineral Point**, known as the birthplace of Wisconsin. In 1836 the

Architecture & Landscape – Scenic Drive

Head west out of Madison on Hwy 14 for a trip through the rolling green hills and pastures that inspired the brilliant innovations of architect Frank Lloyd Wright. After 40 miles you'll reach Spring Green. Turn south on Hwy 23 for 3 miles to reach Taliesin, Wright's home and workshop. On the way, enjoy the roadside glimpses of the meandering Wisconsin River.

Continuing south you'll reach Governor Dodge State Park, with its network of trails, quiet surroundings and countryside views. It's a perfect stop if you'd like to get out and stretch your legs. Farther still on Hwy 23 is Dodgeville, with an old-fashioned downtown that makes for a pleasing place to stop for lunch or coffee.

Head south out of Dodgeville to the architectural splendors of Mineral Point. Then, for an altogether different building style, head east on Hwy 39, edged by green dairy pastures, into the town of New Glarus with its decidedly Swiss look. From here Hwy 69 winds north, linking to Hwy 18, which leads back to Madison. This is a fine, easy drive through a gentle valley with some quaint towns along the way. Arts and craft shops are abundant. Paoli, with its restored mill and numerous weekend-browser shops, is a good stop.

Territory of Wisconsin was proclaimed here, and the first governor, Colonel Henry Dodge, was inaugurated. The early-19th-century town is a limestone and sandstone architectural gem. Many of the preserved buildings were constructed by immigrants from Cornwall, England, who arrived beginning in the 1830s to work the newly discovered lead mines. A highlight is the restored Cornish **Pendarvis State Historic Site** (☎ 608-987-2122), where costumed interpreters outline the days of the early mining camps, as well as the lasting Cornish influence. Open 9 am to 5 pm daily from May to November.

Southwestern River Valleys

Scenic Hwy 60, which you can pick up in Spring Green where it temporarily merges with Hwy 14, meanders west through Richland County and into hilly Crawford County, with the lovely Wisconsin and Kickapoo Rivers and Valleys. There is some excellent canoeing, cycling and hiking in this quiet region. From Hwy 60 you can pick up Hwy 18 and head into Prairie du Chien.

ALONG THE MISSISSIPPI

The Mississippi River forms most of Wisconsin's western border, and alongside it run some of the most scenic sections of the Great River Rd – the designated route that follows the river from Minnesota to the Gulf of Mexico. (In Wisconsin, it's Hwy 35.)

Prairie du Chien

• pop 5600

This old river town was founded as a French fur-trading post in 1673 and named for the prairie dogs once prevalent in the area.

Today, central Black Hawk and Main Sts are somewhat bedraggled strips of shops and second-rate bars. But the sumptuous **Villa Louis** mansion (☎ 608-326-2721), 521 North Villa Louis Rd, reveals a different life. It was built for a successful fur trader in 1870 on St Feriole Island, at the historic river area near Water St, and now houses an outstanding collection of Victorian furnishings. Open 9 am to 5 pm from May to October; $5.

This island area is primarily open park land, but there are two other components t the historic complex. The **Astor Fur Trad Museum** and the **Museum of Prairie d Chien** provide further insights into th times. They are open the same hours as th Villa. The grounds are always open an make a pleasant waterfront setting for stroll.

The **Prairie du Chien Museum at Fo Crawford** (☎ 608-326-6960), south of dowr town at 717 S Beaumont Rd, is in a restore medical hospital from 1816. It detail medical history with equipment and materi als from the 19th century. Open 9 am t 5 pm from May to October.

Marquette Rd and Hwys 18 and 35 hav the usual chain motels and restaurants.

The hilly riverside, where the final alte cation in the bloody Black Hawk War wa fought, is very pretty as you head north ou of town. Historic markers tell part of th story of the war, which ended with th Battle of Bad Ax, in which Indian me women and children were massacred a they tried to flee across the Mississippi.

Across the river in Marquette and sout in Dubuque, casinos housed in replic paddle wheelers offer summer river cruise that are inexpensive or free – if you ca resist the temptation to gamble.

La Crosse

• pop 51,000

Farther north on Hwy 35, La Crosse is a fi riverside city with an historic downtown. Th visitors bureau (☎ 608-782-2366, 877-56 3522) is at 410 E Veterans Memorial Driv in Riverside Park. This parkland runs alor the river west off Front St, a couple of block to the east of downtown. The bureau is ope 10 am to 6 pm daily in summer; the upstai office remains open weekdays all year. Th **Riverside USA Museum** is also in this buil ing, with displays focusing on the history La Crosse and the importance of the Missi sippi to the region. Open 10 am to 5 pm dai from late May to early September; free.

At 111 S 3rd St, the **world's largest si pack** is at Heileman Brewery (☎ 608-78 2337). Free tours of the brewery are offere om 10 am to 4 pm Monday to Saturday, l am to 3 pm Sunday from June to ugust, 11 am to 3 pm Tuesday to Saturday om September to May.

From **Grandad Bluff** there are sweeping ews of the river. To get there drive along lain St east until it becomes Bliss Rd. ollow Bliss up the hill and turn right (east) 1 Grandad Bluff Rd.

The *La Crosse Queen* (☎ 608-784-8523) oes sightseeing and meal cruises. The boat ock is at the west end of State St in Riverde Park. The 90-minute sightseeing cruise osts $10/9/5 adults/seniors/children. The oat operates from May to near the end of ctober.

The *Julia Belle Swain* (☎ 800-815-1005), aving from the same dock area, does onead two-day river excursions as well as local uises. The two-day excursion with meals is 209 per adult double occupancy, $99 per iild. They have an office and gift shop at 00 Main St.

Both paddle wheelers operate from May near the end of October.

Rose St north of downtown has numerus inns and motels.

When hunger strikes head to ***Fayze'e*** *35 S 4th St)*, a bustling restaurant and kery known for sandwiches, soups and eat bread. Also downtown on and around earby Pearl St are several pubs.

For more upriver attractions, see the outheastern Minnesota chapter.

pper Mississippi River ational Wildlife Refuge

orth of La Crosse off Hwy 35 between nalaska and Trempealeau, this wildlife fuge includes 200,000 acres of backwaters ad islands, preserving habitat for birds, fish ad other animals. The area is visited by milons of anglers annually. Bird-watching is ccellent. Popular sport fish are walleye, ss and crappies. State fishing licenses are quired. For licenses, fishing and boat unches or rentals, contact the La Crosse isitors Bureau. Boaters and canoeists unmiliar with the river should be aware that e backwaters can be convoluted and consing; ask for advice before setting out.

BARABOO

• pop 9200

Baraboo is northwest of Madison along Hwy 12, 10 miles south of Wisconsin Dells. It's a small, quiet town on the Wisconsin River with three significant reasons for a visit: the Circus World Museum, the International Crane Foundation, and the Midcontinent Railway. A new chamber of commerce (☎ 608-356-8333, 800-227-2266) was in the works during research.

Baraboo was once the winter home of the Ringling Brothers Circus. The **Circus World Museum** (☎ 608-356-8341), 426 Water St (Hwy 113), close to Broadway St downtown, is on the original site and preserves a collection of circus wagons, posters and equipment from the heyday of the touring big tops. It's open 11 am to 5 pm from September to April; $3. From May to September it's open 9 am to 6 pm and admission rises to $12, including performances by clowns, animals and acrobats. From the middle of July to the middle of August it stays open until 9 pm and presents evening shows.

North of town off Hwy 12, the **International Crane Foundation** (☎ 608-356-9462), 11376 Shady Lane Rd, is devoted to promoting and preserving some of the world's largest bird species. This is one of the few places in the world where endangered whooping cranes can be observed. The lovely grounds are open 9 am to 5 pm daily from May through October; $7/6/4 adults/seniors/kids under 12.

Four miles west of town in North Freedom is the **Midcontinent Railway** (☎ 608-522-4261, 800-930-1385), with 7-mile steam-train rides and a collection of historic rolling stock. It operates from late May to early September. Tickets are $9/8/6 adults/seniors/children. The 50-mile trip through the Baraboo River Valley on the former Chicago & North Western Railroad line, from 1903, offers rail buffs a bit of nostalgia.

Among numerous motels, the ***Spinning Wheel*** *(☎ 608-356-3933, 800-360-5003, 809 8th St)*, on Hwy 33, stands out and is reasonable at $60 weekends, $50 weekdays in season from June to September. Excellent

THOMAS HUHTI

The Midcontinent Railway in the Baraboo River Valley

Devil's Lake State Park is south of town (see Wisconsin Dells).

Several diners are scattered around the central blocks surrounding the county courthouse. Browse along Broadway, Ash St and 3rd, 4th and 5th Aves.

WISCONSIN DELLS

• pop 2400

Along with Door County and the Apostle Islands, this is one of the state's best-known, most-visited areas, but it is an altogether different experience. Despite the unspoiled natural appeal of the scenic sandstone formations carved out by the Wisconsin River, the Dells has become primarily a mind-numbing megacenter of artificial, touristy diversions, led by family theme parks, super miniature golf courses and elaborate water slides.

The concentration of instant fun lures thousands from adjacent states and beyond. But it is a very short season – you can barely reserve a bed from June to late August, and then they're begging you to take on Indeed, many places close shortly after th kids get back to the books.

Information

The Dells Visitor Bureau (☎ 608-254-808 800-223-3557, www.wisdells.com), 701 S perior St, is well organized, well informe and well equipped. It's open 8 am to 9 p daily from late May to early September; th rest of the year it's open 8 am to 5 pm dai

The hefty *Wisconsin Dells* promotion magazine, as well as other brochures, ofte includes discount coupons for attractio and restaurants. In addition, 10 major attra tions offer discount combination ticket Look for their booths around town, marke with huge triangular signs indicating 35% o

Natural Sites

To appreciate the town's original attractio take one of the **river trips**. Since the la 19th century, visitors have admired the co voluted sandstone formations and cragg bluffs along this 15-mile stretch of the Wi consin River. It is now interrupted by a da in the center of town, so vessels cruise eith the Upper or Lower Dells. Dells Boat Tou (☎ 608-254-8555) is the big operator, wi trips running from April to early Novemb and continuously all day in summer. Th Lower Dells trip ($12) is one hour, th Upper Dells ($16) two hours, and becau of the different topography, the Upp Dells trip allows a stop to let visitors wand around a couple of rock formations. If yc can't take both trips ($20), this is recom mended. Also consider the sunset wine-an cheese trip ($23). The fall colors ac another dimension.

Another popular trip is with the **Origin Wisconsin Ducks** (☎ 608-254-8751), 18 Wisconsin Dells Parkway, aboard WW amphibian crafts known as ducks ($1 1 hour). Part of the tour goes through su rounding woodland, and then you spla into the river for the rest. Kids love it, b you don't see as much of the river.

Horse-drawn carts tour a mile throu rocky gorges for 30 minutes at **Lost Cany** (☎ 608-253-2781), $6/3 adults/children. Th

JOHN ELK III
bert Frost's trees (MN)

JOHN ELK III
Split Rock Lighthouse perches 130 feet above Lake Superior (MN).

JOHN ELK III
e Minnesota sunset on Lake Wobegon

JOHN ELK III
nooth sailing through Duluth (MN)

JOHN ELK III
Historic water towers (MN)

RICHARD CUMMINS

RICHARD CUMMINS

A sun-kissed Victorian, Nicollet Island, and pretty purple pasqueflowers at Lake Harriet (MN)

JOHN ELK III

Über pop-art at the Minneapolis Sculpture Garden (MN)

RICHARD CUMMINS

'Round and 'round they go at the Minnesota State Fair.

RICHARD CUMMINS

Minny's downtown reflection

Ideas Given Harmonious Presence

With his books, speeches and range of building designs, Frank Lloyd Wright (1867–1959) was and remains a major influence on contemporary architecture. His often-employed low, horizontal style, incorporating the surrounding landscape as an element, foreshadowed the environmentally sensitive, nature-conscious designs made common in the 1960s.

His imaginative use of wood, brick, stone, texture and shapes are distinctive characteristics. The interiors of Wright buildings are appealing, with their relaxing use of natural light and outdoor scenery, coupled with a subtle feeling of spaciousness.

Some of his best known projects are in New York, Chicago and California, but many important examples of Wright's work can be viewed and visited in Wisconsin, his home state. See the Madison, Racine and Wisconsin Dells sections.

anyon is south of town on Canyon Rd, just ff I-90/94 between Lake Delton and Wisonsin Dells.

The other way to see some area beauty is o hike the trails at **Mirror Lake** or especially **evil's Lake** State Parks, off Hwy 12 south f the Dells. The latter has 500-foot bluffs round its lake. Nature lovers, don't miss valking **Palfrey's Glen**, a state-administered rimeval rocky gorge about 4 miles east of Devil's Lake off Solum Lane from Hwy 113. You need a state park vehicle sticker annual or day) to enter, but there is no ther fee.

The downtown visitors' center has a heet on other area hiking trails. Mushroom-shaped **Stand Rock**, on County Rd N north of town, is the Dells' most amous landmark. It's on Native American and but can be visited for $3. A 90-minute dance show is performed nightly in summer or a separate admission fee.

Nature Safaris (☎ 800-328-0995) specializes in natural tours of the area, including Devil's Lake.

Other Attractions

The dramatic array of touristy sites is joltingly atypical of low-key Wisconsin. The **Tommy Bartlett Thrill Show** (☎ 608-254-2525), 560 Wisconsin Dells Parkway, is a favorite. The $11 show includes waterskiing, juggling, dancing, acrobatics and daredevil acts. The **Rick Wilcox** magic show (☎ 608-254-5511), on Wisconsin Dells Parkway, also delivers. Admission is $17 to $21 for adults, $12 to $16 for kids age five to 12.

Hours can be spent at the central go-cart, miniature golf and water parks. (A day at the last obviates a motel pool.) Broadway and Wisconsin Dells Parkway are lined with the full range. Go-cart places charge about $5, miniature golf courses about $7, water parks in the range of $18 to $25 for a day pass.

Also see the **HH Bennett Studio & History Center** (☎ 608-253-3523), 215 Broadway, a state historic site outlining this photographer's work from the late 19th century, which brought the Dells to the world's attention.

Parson's Indian Trading Post, 370 Wisconsin Dells Parkway, is as much museum as store – great for browsing. Prices range from just a few bucks for souvenirs to hundreds of dollars for authentic Native American artifacts.

Places to Stay

For camping, book at ***Devil's Lake State Park*** *(☎ 608-356-8301)* south of Baraboo, but beware – it's deservedly one of the state's most popular parks, and is regularly full. A second choice is ***Mirror Lake State Park*** *(☎ 608-254-2333)* although the lake often gets a lot of algae growth.

Mirror Lake also has the ***Seth Peterson Cottage*** *(☎ 608-254-6551, E9982 Fern Dell Rd, Lake Delton)*, a 1958 Frank Lloyd Wright cottage available for rent if you can

THOMAS HUHTI

One of Wisconsin Dells' kitschy and cute attractions

book far enough ahead – and have deep enough pockets. It's enchanting in winter. The one-bedroom cottage sleeps four and goes for $225. Inexpensive tours ($2) are offered from 1 to 4 pm on the second Sunday of each month.

There are numerous commercial campgrounds geared to RV traffic. Several can be found along Hwy 12, both north and south of town.

Despite countless feature-packed motels and incredible resorts that virtually guarantee kids' unswerving devotion, lodging gets *very* tight from June through late August, and prices soar accordingly, averaging more than $100 for motels and $175 for resorts. Budget places start at $75. All the national chains are represented in the area.

An exception is the ***Finch Motel*** *(☎ 608-253-4342, 811 Oak St)*. It's central, clean and friendly, and prices start at $40 mid-week even in peak season. Of course, there's no pool, garden or other extras. Also a relative bargain is the enormous ***Gables Motel*** *(☎ 608-253-3831, 822 Oak St)* with a pool and even plastic palm trees. Rooms cost $7 to $90 in season, $30 to $60 off-season. Othe modest places can be found on Vine St.

For a B&B, try Victorian ***Terrace Hil*** *(☎ 608-253-9363, @ terrace.hill@maqs.ne 922 River Rd)*, a short walk to town, ye quiet. A standard room is $65 in season fo two.

The ***Wilderness Hotel*** *(☎ 608-253-972 800-867-9453, www.wildernessresort.com 511 E Adams St)* sits on a golf cours and has a mammoth indoor-outdoor wate park. Rates start at $135. The ***Polynesia Resort*** *(☎ 608-254-2883, 800-272-5642, ww .dellspolynesian.com, 857 N Frontage Rd* offers yet more but is costlier still, wit prices starting at $170 in July and August.

Places to Eat

Food is generally pricey. ***Dell Haus*** *(12 Broadway)* is a good, basic, low-cost plac for breakfast, sandwiches and full meals The spaghetti dinner is $7. ***Monk's*** *(☎ 608 254-2955, 220 Broadway)* is a big, clean ba you can take the kids to for delectable ham urgers ($5). Of the many all-you-can-eat inner buffets, each about $14, try the one at ıe ***Chula Vista*** resort *(☎ 608-254-8366, 031 River Rd)*. It's prepared on weekends ı June and daily through July and August.

For fine dining, moderately priced ***Del-ar*** *(☎ 608-253-1861, 800 Wisconsin Dells arkway)* has been broiling steaks and rilling seafood since 1943.

ietting There & Away

Greyhound buses stop at the Burger King t the west end of Broadway.

The Amtrak station (☎ 608-254-7706) is entral, by the Broadway bridge on La Crosse St behind the visitor bureau. There is ne daily eastbound train for Milwaukee nd Chicago and one westbound for St Paul.

IORICON MARSH

ust north of the town of Horicon, off Hwy 3, is the vast Horicon Marsh, abutted to the orth by the Horicon National Wildlife Refuge. Both are expanses of flat grasslands and waterways ideally suited to bird life. The area is best known for the 200,000 Canada geese that drop by on their spring (March, April and May) and autumn (September and October) migrations. But there are many species of waterfowl, heron and egret, as well as deer and small mammals.

The Horicon Marsh Parkway is a 50-mile auto-tour route that encircles the area, following state and country highways through many area towns and allowing access to displays, placards, bird-watching sites and viewpoints. For marsh information, the Service Center (☎ 920-387-7860) is a few miles north of Horicon on Hwy 28; the parkway can be accessed from here. From downtown Horicon, pontoon boat tours run through the marsh or canoes can be rented.

For cyclists, the Wild Goose State Trail is a 34-mile surfaced path running along the western edge of the marsh and then northeast to Fond du Lac. One access point is west of Horicon on County Rd 33 by the airport.

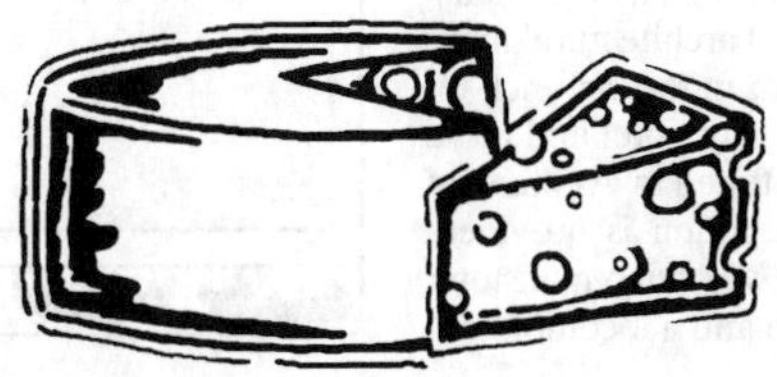

Eastern & Northern Wisconsin

Eastern Wisconsin

This portion of the state is characterized primarily by mid-size industrial and manufacturing towns that most vacationers tend to shun. But many of these centers offer unexpected sights. Examples are the fascinating aviation history revealed at the Experimental Aircraft Association Museum in Oshkosh and the master illusionist's props shown at the Houdini Historical Center in Appleton. For many Midwest residents, gentle Door County needs little introduction; it's an immensely popular resort area. Green Bay is the state's third-largest city and boasts the famous Packers football team. North of here the land becomes noticeably more rugged and offers white waters, fishing and quiet walking trails.

In most towns and villages on the Door Peninsula and in rural eastern and northern Wisconsin, the highway runs right through town, doubling as Main St.

FOND DU LAC

• pop 37,757

Fond du Lac sits amid flat farmland at the shore of Lake Winnebago. The north end of Main St ends at redeveloped Lakeside Park with the Lookout Lighthouse, which allows for views of the state's largest lake.

For information, the CVB (☎ 920-923-3010, 800-937-9123, www.fdl.com) is in a little strip mall off Main St at the entrance to Lakeside Park. It's open weekdays 9 am to 5 pm and Saturday 9 am to 1 pm from late May to early September.

A novel way of seeing the city's good assortment of historical and architectural highlights is via an audio tour in the car. Pick up the map at the CVB or any hotel and drive the route with the radio tuned in. At many of the sites an audio description is provided. Suggested stops include Victorian mansions, a cathedral, a lighthouse and a locomotive.

Highlights

- Taking in the Apostle Islands wilderness on awesome Lake Superior
- Kayaking the white water of the lakelands
- Absorbing the atmosphere at the legendary Green Bay Packers' home turf
- Snowmobiling in the northlands around Eagle, with its vast trail network
- Relaxing along Door County's seashore-like perimeter
- Sampling a local taste treat, the Wisconsin brat
- Camping in quiet, secluded Rock Island State Park

The 12-room 1856 **Octagon House** ☎ 920-922-1608), 276 Linden St, is on the 'ational Register of Historic Places. It was uilt as a fort and later used as a station on ıe Underground Railroad. Visitors will nd out about some of the house's secret iding places. Call for schedule; $8.

Rooms at the ***Econo Lodge*** *(☎ 920-923-020, 649 W Johnson St)* range from $30 a ouble from September through April to 70 a double on summer weekends. Extras ıclude a free breakfast and indoor pool. everal restaurants are on Main St.

)SHKOSH

pop 50,000

)n the west side of Lake Winnebago,)shkosh is best known as part of the brand ame Oshkosh B'gosh, the cute country-ɔok kids' clothing line.

The CVB (☎ 920-236-5250, 800-876-5250, /ww.oshkosh.org) is at 2 N Main St at the 'ox River in the convention center. It's open am to 5 pm Monday to Friday. The door is round the back, away from Main St.

There are not many compelling reasons ɔ follow the long route from US 41 into lowntown. One is the very good **Oshkosh 'ublic Museum** (☎ 920-424-4731), 1331 \lgoma Blvd at the north end of down-ɔwn, which tells the story of when this was Sawdust City,' the world's lumber capital in he 19th century. The fur trade, exploration, nd modernization are all covered also.)pen daily, but call for hours, especially in vinter; free.

Access to Lake Winnebago is generally imited by development and private prop-:rty around its circumference, but boat ruises are offered from the dock at the lowntown Pioneer Inn Resort and Marina ☎ 920-233-1980), 1000 Pioneer Drive.

Oshkosh B'gosh, along with 59 other com-ɔanies, has an outlet in the huge Horizon)utlet Center, south of town on US 41.

Across the highway, the **Experimental \ircraft Association Museum** (☎ 920-426-1800) has a fabulous and extensive collec-ion of winged things, from spacecraft, nilitary planes and the historic to the weird and wonderful. Check out the Wright flyer, for which the pilot had to lie on the wing and work the controls. Other eye-catchers are the *Baby Bird*, which is only 11 feet long, and the Aerocar, which looks like an original Volkswagon bug with wings. Budget a couple of hours minimum, and make time for the train shuttle to the outdoor exhibits, where visitors can pay to ride antique planes. It's open 8:30 to 5 pm Monday to Saturday, 11 am to 5 pm Sunday; $8/7/6 adults/seniors/kids.

In late July the huge Oshkosh air show, known as the **Experimental Aircraft Fly-In**, features hundreds of historic planes and experimental aircraft. This is one of the state's premier events, attracting visitors from across the US and Canada. Book accommodations well in advance; the CVB can help.

Places to Stay & Eat

The ***Circle R Campground*** *(☎ 920-235-8909)* south of town (exit US 41 at County Rd N and look for signs) is a real find. It's got RV sites ($19), tent sites through a cornfield ($15), an intriguing homespun museum with farm implements and various vehicles and a small live-animal collection including a donkey and various birds, and it's just minutes to town.

Super 8 *(☎ 920-426-2855, fax 920-426-5488)* is off US 41 north of the aircraft museum on W South Park Ave. Rooms are $47/55 in June, July and August. The other chain hotels have locations along US 41 as well.

Friar Tuck's *(☎ 920-231-9555, 1651 W South Park)*, near US 41, serves good low-priced sandwiches all day every day.

Though most restaurants are at the highway, downtown is ***Lara's*** *(☎ 920-233-4440, 715 N Main St)*, which is worth the trip. It has a spacious, comfortable dining room with a range of well-prepared Mexican standards and interesting traditional dishes for about $10 or less. Open daily (for dinner only on Sunday).

A second option where you can't go wrong is the ***Granary*** *(☎ 920-233-3929, 50 W 6th St)*, in a restored 19th-century flour mill. Lunch features burgers and sandwiches; dinner has

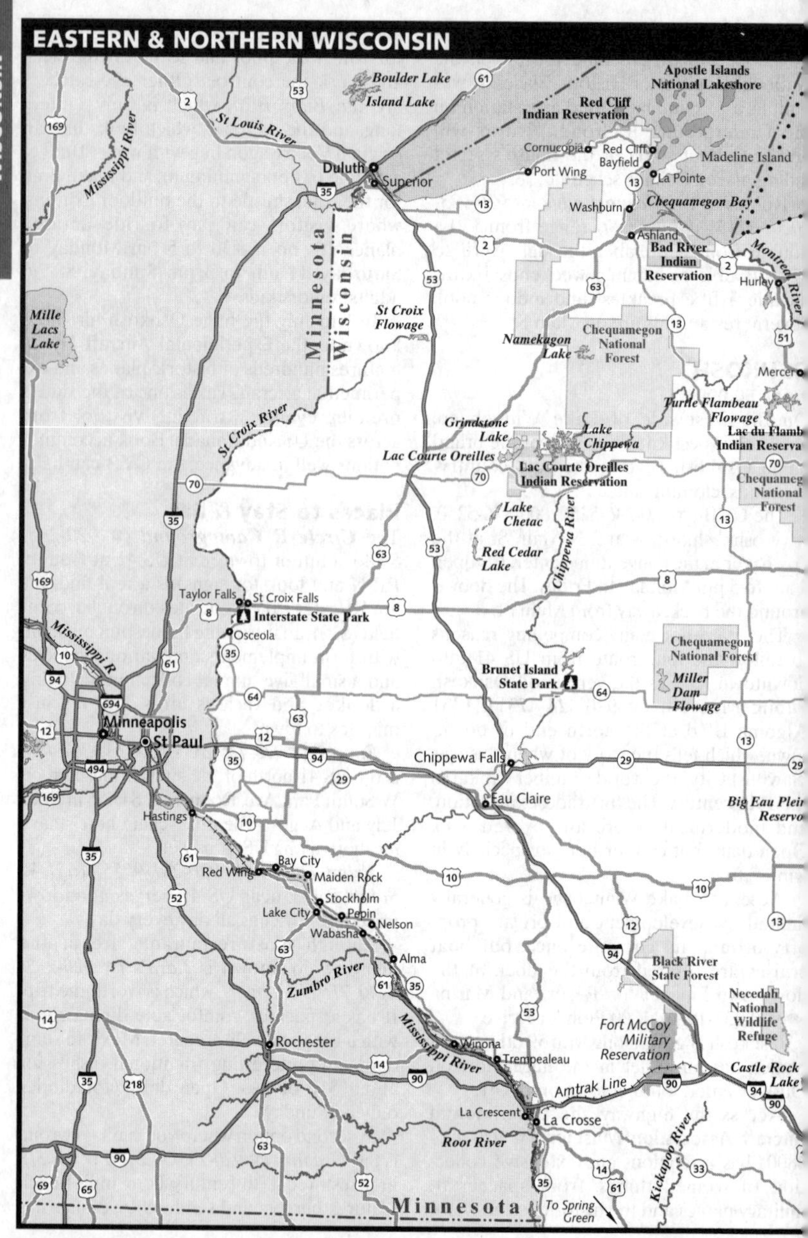
EASTERN & NORTHERN WISCONSIN
Boulder Lake
Island Lake
St Louis River
Mississippi River
Duluth
Superior
Apostle Islands National Lakeshore
Red Cliff Indian Reservation
Cornucopia
Red Cliff
Bayfield
Port Wing
Madeline Island
La Pointe
Chequamegon Bay
Washburn
Ashland
Bad River Indian Reservation
Montreal River
Hurley
Minnesota
Wisconsin
Mille Lacs Lake
St Croix Flowage
Namekagon Lake
Chequamegon National Forest
Mercer
Turtle Flambeau Flowage
Lac du Flamb
Indian Reserva
St Croix River
Grindstone Lake
Lake Chippewa
Lac Courte Oreilles
Lac Courte Oreilles Indian Reservation
Chequameg National Forest
Lake Chetac
Red Cedar Lake
Chippewa River
Taylor Falls
St Croix Falls
Interstate State Park
Osceola
Mississippi R
Chequamegon National Forest
Miller Dam Flowage
Brunet Island State Park
Minneapolis
St Paul
Chippewa Falls
Eau Claire
Big Eau Pleir Reservo
Hastings
Red Wing
Bay City
Maiden Rock
Stockholm
Lake City
Pepin
Nelson
Wabasha
Alma
Zumbro River
Black River State Forest
Necedah National Wildlife Refuge
Fort McCoy Military Reservation
Rochester
Winona
Trempealeau
Mississippi River
Castle Rock Lake
Amtrak Line
La Crescent
La Crosse
Root River
Kickapoo River
Minnesota
To Spring Green

EASTERN & NORTHERN WISCONSIN

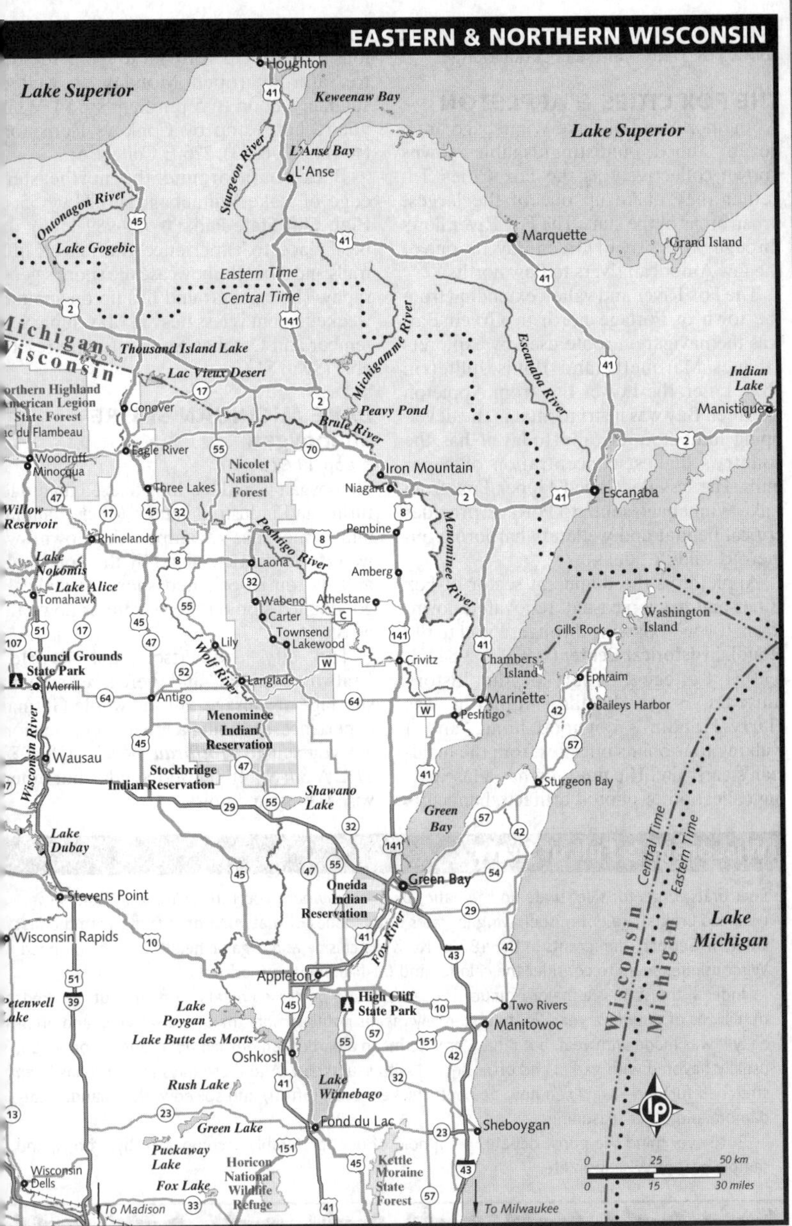

steaks, ribs, seafood and pastas averaging about $18. There's also a cocktail lounge.

THE FOX CITIES & APPLETON

At the north end of Lake Winnebago are a dozen almost indistinguishable towns known collectively as the Fox Cities. Together they make up one of the largest urban areas of the state. The Fox River flows through on its way to Green Bay; it's one of the few American rivers to flow north.

The Fox River and valley, extending from the town of Portage north to Green Bay, was the navigation route used by explorers Jacques Marquette and Louis Jolliet in 1673. Later, the Lower Fox from Appleton to Green Bay was instrumental in the developing lumber trade, and today it has the country's highest concentration of paper mills. The less developed Upper Fox, from Lake Winnebago south to Portage, provides critical habitat and wetlands, harboring numerous wildlife zones.

Appleton is the dominant sector of Fox Cities and has a pleasant, renovated downtown. If you're passing through, a visit to the **Houdini Historical Center** (☎ 920-733-8445), 330 E College St, part of the history museum, is worthwhile. Appleton was Harry Houdini's boyhood home, and a walking tour points out sites from the magician's early life. The museum has a fascinating collection of photos, artifacts, handcuffs and a video on some of Houdini's miracu lous exploits. Open 10 am to 5 pm Tuesda to Saturday (open Monday as well i summer), noon to 5 pm Sunday; $4. Whil you're here, stop by Conkeys Bookstor (☎ 414-735-6223), 226 E College St.

Back south around the northeaster edge of Lake Winnebago, off Hwy 55, i **High Cliff State Park** (☎ 920-989-1106), th best place to experience the lake. Cliff trails and a beach showcase the shore's geog raphy. The campground fills up on summe weekends, but is less busy in May, June, Sep tember and October. Some sites are reserv able ($9 to $13).

LAKE MICHIGAN SHORE

Sheboygan

• pop 49,676

Sheboygan is, and has long been, a manufac turing and industrial center. Much plannin and money has revamped the downtow waterfront district, edged by the boardwal and its tourist-oriented shops. It makes good lunch stop on the way up or down th coast.

The city calls itself the 'World' Bratwurst Capital,' and there's certainly n shortage of sausage. For the whole Germa experience, including a great beer selectior get yourself to ***Hoffbrau*** *(☎ 920-458-415 1132 N 8th St)*. It's closed Sunday but other wise is busy and noisy.

Wisconsin Is Full of Brats

Beer brats, brats for sale, brats on the patio, brats everywhere you turn. Wisconsin's brats (pronounced brahts) are not misbehaving ingrates but varieties of bratwurst originating with the first wave of German immigrants in the 1820s. Nouvelle cuisine and organic health food be damned, Wisconsinites seem to consider the calorie- and fat-filled brats a food staple.

Indeed, the state is a major producer of sausage and processed meats, grinding out hundreds of millions of pounds a year. 'Bratwurst' really means nothing more than fried sausage, and originally it was made with veal, but it has come to mean a barbecued or fried pork sausage on a bun, usually flavored with garlic, and often served with sauerkraut. And these days the term has been stretched further – brats can now be beef, chicken, even tofu (!) and spiced with coriander, cardamom and other seasonings.

But never mind the purist debate; get a hold of one, preferably accompanied by a brew, and sample part of Wisconsin life.

Bratwurst Days, held the first weekend in ugust, bring in 100,000 people for brats nd beer. Things get started Friday evening nd go all the following Saturday, when ere is a parade. Most events take place utdoors in Felton Park. For more details, ontact the CVB at ☎ 800-457-9497.

South of town, Kohler–Andrae State ark (☎ 920-451-4080), with camping, pro-ects a great stretch of beach and a delicate une area.

Manitowoc

pop 32,520

f you're headed for Michigan, you may be nterested in the SS *Badger* (☎ 888-643-779, www.ssbadger.com), the car ferry that ails from Manitowoc to Ludington, Michi-an, in four hours, thus eliminating the need o drive around the lake. It operates daily rom mid-May through late October. A one-way trip is $39/36/18 adults/seniors/kids and 47/27 car/motorcycle (with a 20% discount n the 12:30 am boat). Note that Wisconsin, which is on central time, is an hour behind Michigan, on eastern time. The ferry termi-al is central, at the foot (eastern end) of ranklin St on the waterfront.

The Wisconsin Maritime Museum ☎ 920-684-0218), 75 Maritime Drive, has he Midwest's largest maritime collection. wo floors outline topics such as Great akes shipping and shipbuilding with nodels, artifacts and equipment. In addition o the varied displays, visitors can tour the JSS *Cobia* submarine. Open 9 am to 6 pm daily (from noon only on Sunday from Sep-ember through April).

Two Rivers

• pop 13,030

A few miles north up Hwy 42 (which winds ll the way up the Door Peninsula) is Two Rivers, which claims the ice-cream sundae was invented here: The story goes that hocolate sauce was poured over ice cream t the local soda fountain in 1881 at the cost of 5¢ – but only on Sunday.

Historic Washington House (☎ 920-793-2490, 888-857-3529) at the corner of 17th nd Jefferson Sts, has a replica of that original ice-cream parlor and serves more than a dozen different sundaes. Other rooms reveal different aspects of the town's social past, with exhibits ranging from antique toys and a player piano to a dentist's office. Open 9 am to 5 pm daily; a donation is requested. The lobby doubles as the town's Visitor Information Center.

Those with an interest in printing should not miss the **Hamilton Wood Type Museum** (☎ 800-228-6416) across the street. This one-of-a-kind collection displays all the vintage equipment used in the manufacture of wood type, beginning with its introduction in the 19th century. Open 9 am to 5 pm Monday through Saturday, from 1 to 5 pm Sunday; free.

Historic Rogers St, 2102 Jackson St in the East Twin River downtown, is on the National Register of Historic Places. It preserves the original French Canadian fishing village established here in the 1840s.

North by the shore along County Rd O is **Point Beach State Forest** (☎ 920-794-7480), 3000 acres of forest edged by sandy beach, all presided over by Rawley Point Lighthouse. Before the lighthouse was built in 1853, some 26 ships hit the shoals offshore. There are 11 miles of trails around the woods and dunes and a medium-size campground. Admission is $4.

The area around Two Rivers is *much* cheaper than Door County; motel rooms cost $35/40 single/double in June, July and August, and you usually don't need to reserve ahead of time. Look along Hwy 42 in and around town.

GREEN BAY

• pop 100,000

Founded in the 1660s as a fur-trading post, Green Bay boomed as a Lake Michigan port and later as a Midwestern railroad terminus.

Processing and packing agricultural products became a major industry during the late 19th century and gave name to the city's legendary football team (see 'Pack Attack').

For visitors, the city can be neatly compartmentalized into two sections, each with a small concentration of sites, hotels and restaurants. One is the central downtown area, based at Walnut and Washington Sts on the eastern edge of the Fox River. The other is southwest of here on and around Lombardi Ave by Lambeau Field, the football stadium.

Green Bay is not a place in which most visitors are likely to linger, but football features aside, there are several fine specialty museums.

Information

The visitors' center (☎ 920-494-9507, 888-867-3342, www.greenbaywi.com) is in the back of the domed arena beside the Don Hutson Center, off Oneida St. This is beside Lambeau Field just south of Lombardi Ave and southwest of downtown. Hours are 8 am to 7 pm Monday to Friday, 9 am to 2 pm Saturday and Sunday.

Football Sights

The Green Bay Packers are the area's major tourist attraction. All day long, cars drive up to and around **Lambeau Field** (☎ 888-442-7225), 855 Lombardi Ave, and awestruck visitors take snapshots in front of the unmistakable green-and-yellow throwback of a stadium. Tours are given every half hour from 9:30 am to 4:30 pm from June through August, but not on game days or the days before and after. The 1½-hour tour includes the field, press box and sky boxes. Tickets are first come, first served; $8/6/5 adult/senior/kids.

Next door, the **Green Bay Packer Hall of Fame** (☎ 920-499-4281), appropriately located on Lombardi Ave, is packed with memorabilia and has football movies, interactive exhibits, even casts of players' hands. In summer, people are lined up before it opens. Hours are 10 am to 5 pm daily (until 6 pm June through August); $8/6/5. The gift shop stocks an array of souvenirs, jerseys and a comprehensive selection of written Packer lore. Around back is the Don Hutson Center, the indoor practice and training facility.

For the insatiable, the **Packers Pro Shop** (☎ 920-496-5717), 1265 Lombardi Ave, open daily, also has a varied selection of all things Packer – from key rings to street-size sigr stating Packers Fan Parking Only.

National Railroad Museum

The rail museum (☎ 920-437-7623), 2285 Broadway, features some of the bigge steam and diesel locomotives ever to ha freight into Green Bay's vast yards. Ther are about 75 pieces of rolling stock, a hug model layout, films and changing exhibit From May through October, antique trai rides are offered on a narrow-gauge lin around the 30-acre grounds. Open all yea 9 am to 5 pm daily (closed weekends fror September through April); $6/5/4 adult seniors/kids or $18 per family.

Neville Museum

The Neville Museum (☎ 920-448-4460), 21 Museum Place beside the Fox River at th Dousman St bridge, houses two floors th chronicle the region's ancient and moder history. Another section displays contemp rary art – mainly paintings from around th state. Temporary shows, sometimes qui raw and controversial, are also mounte Open 9 am to 4 pm Tuesday to Saturda (until 9 pm Wednesday), noon to 4 pr Sunday; $3 donation suggested.

Oneida Nation Museum

This museum (☎ 920-869-2768), 7 miles wes of town on the Oneida Reservation on E Rd (call for directions) outlines the histor of the Oneida – the People of the Standin Stone – originally from New York State an part of the Iroquois confederacy but drive west by the increasing numbers of white se tlers in the 18th century, and by the feder government. The museum houses artifact crafts and provides details on Oneid culture, past and present. There's also traditional-style longhouse. The museum open Tuesday to Sunday from June t September, Tuesday to Friday from Octobe to May; call for hours; $2.

Heritage Hill State Historical Par

South of downtown, off Hwy 172 at Webste St, Heritage Hill (☎ 920-448-5150, 800-721 5150) is a 40-acre living museum reflectin

Pack Attack

The National Football League's Packers are not so much a team as a phenomenon. They dominate the minds and hearts of sports fans across the state and beyond. How else explain why otherwise normal adults would put on wedge-shaped, yellow-orange hats and willingly call themselves cheeseheads...in public and on national television?! But then again, the fans may as well have a nickname, because that's how the team got its. The Packers were sponsored by a meat-packing company when first formed way back in 1919, making them one of the oldest professional football teams in the country.

Contemporary professional sports is a world of mega dollars in major cities. Green Bay is the archetypal small-market town, the Packers a team not bought and sold by millionaire tycoons but actually owned publicly by Wisconsinite fans. Lambeau Field, named after the team's founder, has been the team's home since 1957, making it the longest serving arena in the NFL. Although the stadium has been expanded, every seat has been sold out for every game since 1960.

From the beginning, the Packers have been more than competitive, with a dozen championships under their belts. They are the only team to have won three consecutive NFL titles twice (1929–31 and 1965–67), earning the city the right to proclaim itself Titletown. They triumphed at the first two Superbowls (1966 and '67) and again in 1996.

Among the team's legends is Vince Lombardi, coach and mentor from 1959 to 1967. Best known for hard-edged, competitive statements such as 'Winning isn't everything, it's the only thing' and 'Hurt is in the mind,' this complex, charismatic man also said, 'If people can't find work, whether it's their fault or not, you've got to help them, clothe them and house them properly.'

On game days, tailgate parties start in the stadium parking lot four hours before kickoff. You can't get a ticket through the box office, but commercial agencies can sell you one. Try TicketKing (☎ 920-405-1000, 800-992-7328) or Event USA (☎ 888-997-2253).

ortheast Wisconsin from the late 18th entury to the turn of the 20th century. Cosumed workers and reconstructed buildings ring the periods to life. Open 10 am to 5 pm laily from late May to early September (call bout extended weekend hours in July and August); $6/5/4 adults/seniors/children.

Places to Stay

Away from the action, ***Motel 6*** *(☎ 494-6730, fax 920-494-0474, 1614 Shawano Ave)* is the best value, at $34/40. It's just under 3 miles to Lambeau Field, off US 41, northwest of downtown at exit 169.

The stadium area has several options. Cheapest is the ***Road Star Inn*** *(☎ 920-497-7666, 1941 True Lane)*, across from the football field. Singles/doubles start at $36/42, but don't expect any extras.

Days Inn *(☎ 920-498-8088, 800-329-7466, fax 920-498-8492, 1978 Holmgren Way)*, a block from the stadium, has an indoor pool and provides a continental breakfast. Summer rates range from $50 to $90 a double, depending on conventions or other events.

In the center is the ***Best Western Washington St Inn*** *(☎ 920-437-8771, 800-252-2952, fax 920-437-3839, 321 S Washington St)*, with an indoor pool, saunas and free breakfast. Rates range from $50/60 to $85/90 single/double, depending on season and conventions.

Places to Eat

Kroll's *(☎ 920-497-1111, 1990 S Ridge Rd)*, on the west side of Lambeau Field, has been a local institution since 1936, and the large, arcing booth seats certainly reflect earlier eras. It's a low-priced family restaurant with a short, straightforward menu featuring sandwiches and fried fish. The most popular dishes are the perch and grilled chicken. You can also try bluegill, a respected pan fish in Wisconsin that rarely shows up in restaurants. Everything is less than $10. Open daily for lunch and dinner.

A few doors closer to Lombardi Ave, the casual ***Fifty Yard Line*** is a spacious sports bar with inexpensive standard food and lots of TVs for those not across the street at the game. Nearby, next to the stadium in the Best Western, is ***Bay City Smokehaus*** *(780 Packer Drive)* for moderately priced ribs, beer and blues. Barbecued chicken and beef are also offered, and there's a good Sunday brunch.

Downtown, N Washington St has a strip of eateries by the Port Plaza Mall. The low-cost ***Oxford Café & Pub*** *(217 N Washington St)*, does a good job on the usual sandwich fare and has some above-average salads – try the raspberry walnut version ($5).

Titletown Brewing Co (☎ 920-437-2337) on Dousman St at the corner of Broadway, across the bridge from Main St downtown, is a brew pub and restaurant in a former railway station. Lunches average $7, dinners $13, and include pesto pasta, steak, and cornmeal-coated trout with black beans. They always have five regular brews and a seasonal one on tap.

For special occasions, residents choose ***Chanterelles*** *(☎ 920-469-3200, 2638 Bay Settlement Rd)*, near the Weidner Centre, a theater complex. This dressy, elegant dining room offers seafood, an assortment of pastas and a couple of vegetarian choices for $15 to $20.

Getting There & Away

The Greyhound station (☎ 920-432-4883), 800 Cedar St, is at the corner of Main St, west of downtown. There are four runs daily to Milwaukee ($19) and three to Madison ($26) and Minneapolis ($55). On weekends the station is open only for arrivals and departures.

DOOR COUNTY

Extending some 60 miles into Lake Michigan, the Door Peninsula, with 250 miles of picturesque coastline flanked by cherry orchards and interspersed with small 19th-century villages, is one of the Midwest's top vacation destinations. The boat-filled harbors are reminiscent of Cape Cod, and the blend of gentility and nature also draws comparisons to New England.

Peak season is from July through Labor Day (the first Monday in September). The summer season includes May and June; the off-season is from October to May.

Despite the ever-increasing traffic and ongoing condominium developments, the Door, as it's called, remains largely unspoiled by commercial excess. There is no neon, no over-the-top go-cart tracks or the like. Nearly all the lodgings and restaurants are independents, and if they're not historic they're usually designed in keeping with architectural tradition.

Visitors usually make a loop up and down the peninsula on Hwys 57 and 42, stopping at some of the towns and state parks along the way and perhaps taking a ferry to the small islands at the north tip. Many people enjoy making the rounds of the lighthouses. There are no public buses so you'll need your own transportation. Bicycling is popular in the parks and towns and rentals are often available. In winter there are miles of Nordic ski trails.

The most attractive – and active – part of the peninsula begins north of Sturgeon Bay and most of the sites lie on the western shoreline, the bay side. The numerous small roads linking the east and west sides reveal the unchanged rural farmlands of the peninsula.

Wisconsin is the nation's fourth-biggest producer of cherries, and 95% of them come from Door County. The region also produces much of the state's considerable apple crop. The white cherry blossoms blooming around the middle of May, and the pink apple blossoms, unraveling about a week later, are a major spring attraction, but they don't last long – only about a week or two for each. Conveniently, many of the orchards are alongside Hwy 42. In fall, the thinned crowds and changing leaves create an altogether different atmosphere.

Every effort should be made to savor some, if not all, of the peninsula's gastronomic delights. The fresh and dried cherries are scrumptious (dried cherries are a ocal specialty), as are the juices and ciders hat may be pressed from one of the many pple varieties. Superb smoked fish – almon, lake trout and whitefish – is available at local retail outlets particularly round Gills Rock.

Many restaurants host outdoor Scandiavian 'fish boils,' a fun tradition good for he whole family (see 'Roiling Boils'). The hamber of commerce in Sturgeon Bay has stings and a schedule for these casual vening dinner events. You could also look the *Door County Official Vacation Guidebook*, available at tourist offices.

Accommodations are expensive and scarce in high summer. Campgrounds can reduce costs, but they too are very busy. (Most of the private campgrounds are open from about mid-May to mid-October.) All lodging should be booked in advance, especially on summer weekends and for any special events. Note that nearly all cottages and resorts have a one-week minimum in July and most of August. The best choices of accommodations are on the west coast. Prices drop markedly by September. Be prepared for heavy traffic on holiday weekends.

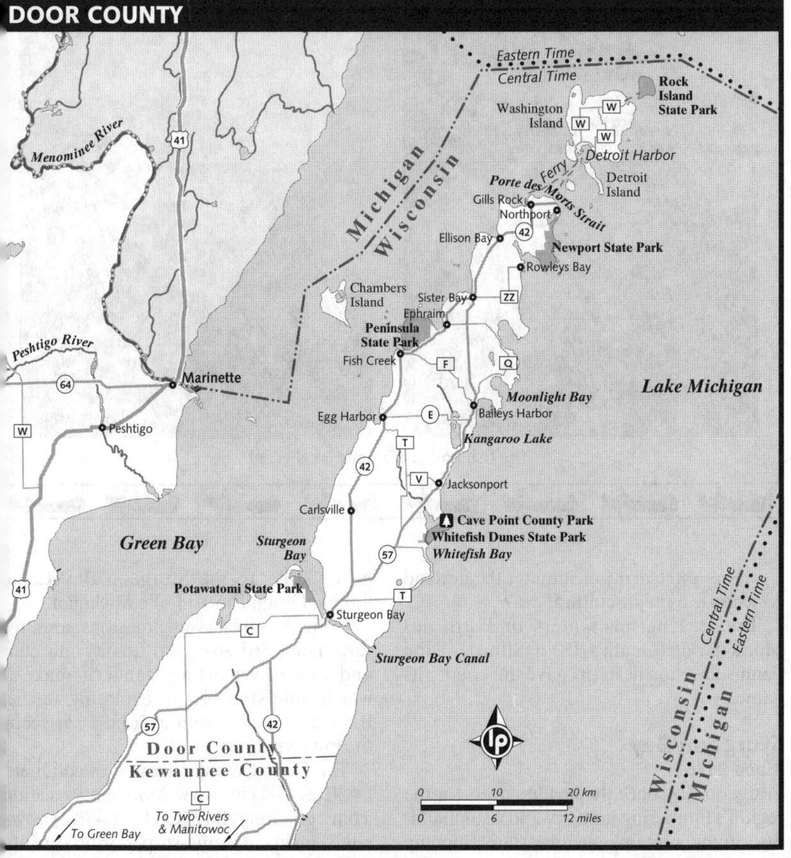

Roiling Boils

The fish boil is a well-entrenched Scandinavian tradition that is as much a social event as a meal. Chopped whitefish, potatoes, onions and sometimes carrots are all dumped into a large cauldron, which is being brought to a boil over an open wood fire. When everything is cooked, a bell is rung announcing time for boil over. That is when the cameras come out and the sudden intake of breath by the spectators is heard.

The attendants pour kerosene onto the fire, deftly making sure not to singe their eyebrows. The heat of the instant inferno boils the cauldron to overflowing, taking with it any boiled-off grease and fat from the soupy mix. The contents are then scooped out with a net and are ready to serve. In addition to the all-you-can-eat boiled contents and drinks, there is salad, bread and, to top it off, cherry pie.

All of this is done outdoors, and the casual, festive air is well suited to the summer weather and mingling of people on holiday. At about $14, a fish boil should be on your to-do list.

MARK LIGHTBODY

MARK LIGHTBODY

The fish boil, a dramatic local event

A top-notch array of summer theater and concerts is a major cultural draw.

The treacherous waters of Porte des Morts Strait (Death's Door Strait), at the peninsula's northern tip, gave the county its name.

Sturgeon Bay

• pop 9176

Sturgeon Bay, once the headquarters for the region's lumbering industry and a shipbuilding center, remains an important shipping port thanks to the Sturgeon Bay Canal linking Green Bay to Lake Michigan.

With the preserved limestone architecture along 3rd Ave, two quality museums and the busy working canal, it makes a worthwhile stop before exploring further. Indeed, you can use it as a base for seeing the entire peninsula.

The Door County chamber of commerce (☎ 920-743-4456, www.doorcountyvacation.com), on Green Bay Rd (Hwy 47/52) as you enter town, is a one-stop resource cente with information on activities, events, bicycling and accommodations for the peninsula. It's open 8:30 am to 4:30 pm weekdays, 10 am to 4 pm weekends June through October. There is also a useful free phone link to listed lodgings in all the towns (available 24 hours).

Museums The **Door County Historical Museum** (☎ 920-743-5809), 18 N 4th St (corner of Michigan), outlines all aspects of the peninsula's history. Open 10 am to 4:30 pm daily from May 1 to October 31; free.

The waterfront **Maritime Museum** (☎ 920-743-5958), 120 N Madison Ave at the south edge of the drawbridge, details the area's boat-building and fishing history. Open 9 am to 6 pm daily; $5.

Places to Stay & Eat Lodging is more plentiful here than anywhere else in Door County, though most visitors prefer to stay farther up the peninsula. Accommodations range from standard motels to gracious Victorian B&Bs, and much of it is pricey. If you arrive on the peninsula and find most accommodations full, you might have good luck finding a vacancy here; the chamber of commerce can help.

Among the lowest-priced motels in the county are the ***Nightengale*** *(☎ 920-743-7633, 1547 Egg Harbor Rd)*, starting at $54 for two in June, July and August, and the ***Cherryland*** *(☎ 920-743-3289, 1309 Green Bay Rd)*, starting at $65, with a pleasant garden and indoor whirlpool.

Restaurants also are abundant. The ***Pudgy Seagull***, at the corner of 3rd Ave and Michigan St, is the perfect low-cost, basic, good-anytime-for-any-meal type of place, a spoon without the greasy.

Bayou *(☎ 920-743-3033, 50 3rd St S)*, open for dinner only, is a fine place for a night out. The menu, complemented by a thoughtful wine list, features Southern dishes, primarily seafood, including shrimp, catfish and a tasty jambalaya with rice and beans. Entrées cost $12 to $18.

Potawatomi State Park

Potawatomi (☎ 920-746-2890), across the canal from Sturgeon Bay, is a good camping park (the northern loop sites are larger and more private) with an observation tower perched on a 150-foot bluff and several short trails. There is no beach along the rocky, cliff-edged shoreline. Reservations are recommended through July and August and for all long weekends during the warmer months, although the park also offers winter camping. Sites cost $10 to $13.

Carlsville

The main attraction in Carlsville is the Door Peninsula Winery (☎ 920-743-7431) on Hwy 42. Visitors can tour the facilities for free year-round and sample the fruit wines, such as cherry, plum and apple, for which the region is well known. This winery also now produces its own more traditional grape wines. Open at 9 am daily year-round (closing time depends on traffic, weather, season and other factors).

Egg Harbor

• pop 183

Egg Harbor is the first of the string of bayside communities. Unfortunately, Main St here gets egg on its face relative to the next three towns northward: It's a long strip of pseudo-historic tourist shops without much appeal.

An exception to the contrived atmosphere is the authentic 19th-century bar ***Shipwrecked*** *(☎ 888-868-2767, 7791 Egg Harbor Rd)*, the county's best brew pub. There are about six fine beers, from a crisp blond to a unique wheat-and-cherry ale. Pub food is available at the bar and on the patio. Full meals, $12 to $16, are served in the dining room. The broad menu includes chicken, steak and seafood. The Friday fish fry is good.

As Al Capone once did, visitors can hang their hats upstairs from Shipwrecked's pub in the ***Upper Deck Inn*** *(☎ 920-868-2767, 888-868-2767)*. Nightly rates in the modernized rooms start at $70, less after late August.

Camp-Tel *(☎ 920-868-3278)* is a family campground north of town on Hwy 42. Sites are $18 to $23.

The ***Lull-Abi Motel*** *(☎ 920-868-3135, 7928 Egg Harbor Rd)* costs $75 during peak season, $50 in spring and fall.

There are several first-class resorts here, including the small ***Egg Harbor Lodge*** *(☎ 414-868-3215, www.eggharborlodge.com)*, overlooking the bay. It has all the amenities, including a putting green and tennis courts. No kids or pets are allowed. Peak season rates range from $120 to twice that.

Fish Creek

• pop 200

This little village typifies the region. There are few overwhelming attractions, but its pretty harborside location, scattered 19th-century homes and inns, and streets of tourist-oriented shops and galleries are ideal for strolling. Evenings bring a special ambience, with many establishments trimmed in white lights.

Alexander Noble House, 4167 Main St, is the oldest house in its original location (built in 1875) and is now the town museum. It's also on the National Register of Historic Places. Tours are offered from 1 to 4 pm daily in summer.

South of town half a mile on Hwy 42 is **Lautenbach's Orchard Country** winery (☎ 920-868-3479), where very good dry and semisweet cherry wines can be sampled and purchased. Open 10 am to 5 pm daily all year, with free tours offered through July and August at 11 am and 1 and 3 pm. You can challenge the amazing cherry pit-spitting records on a measured runway.

The **Peninsula Players** (☎ 920-868-3287) put on a series of comedies from June to mid-October in a garden setting. This is the country's oldest resident professional summer theater, begun in 1934. The theater is on Peninsula Players Rd, south of town off Hwy 42.

Between Fish Creek and Ephraim on Hwy 42, the **Skyway** (☎ 920-854-9938), an old-style, 1950s movie drive-in, makes for a fun and maybe nostalgic evening. Call for schedule and film information.

Places to Stay & Eat A camping option if the state park is full, ***Path of Pines*** *(☎ 920-868-3332)*, on County Rd F, has sites for $18 to $20, and each has water and power.

Julie's Park Café and Motel *(☎ 920-869-2999, 4020 Hwy 42)*, by the park entrance, provides quality lodging and meals at good prices. Rooms start at $75 from June 25 to the third week of August and drop to $40 in the off-season. The restaurant patio is the best place in town for breakfast, and the varied dinner menu is a good bet, too. Nightly $9 dinner specials (eg, vegetarian on Monday, ribs on Saturday) can't be beat.

The classic place to stay (and eat) is the casually upmarket ***White Gull Inn*** *(☎ 920-868-3517, www.whitegullinn.com)*, centrally located on Main St and built in 1896. Its antique-filled rooms start at $102 in the lodge and spiral to over $200 for the cottages, which can sleep up to eight. All meals are available, including fish boils.

Peninsula State Park

With its location and features, Peninsula State Park (☎ 920-868-3258) is one of the busiest, most popular parks not only in the state but, justifiably, in the entire Midwest.

Bike trails wind through the park, and an excellent series of walking trails lead to various highlights. Bicycles can be rented at Edge of the Park Rental (☎ 920-868-3344) near the park gate on Hwy 42 for an hour to a week. Among the top draws are the restored Eagle Bluff Lighthouse (tours available) and the 75-foot tower affording views over Nicolet Bay. Other assets are the bluffs, cliffs and abundant deer. Don't miss a walk, cycle or drive along Sunset Trail, a shoreline road, as the sun goes down over the bay. The **American Folklore Theatre** (AFT; ☎ 920-868-9999) has put on a lighthearted musical summer program since 1970 at the 700-seat park venue.

Despite the nearly 500 sites, about 100 with electricity, camping reservations are essential for summer weekends and holidays. Rates are $10 to $15.

Ephraim

• pop 261

With its postcard-perfect sweep of beach, moored sailboats and waterfront mai treet punctuated with the spires of the Moravian and Lutheran churches, Ephraim s the prettiest village in the county. That plus its lodging and dining possibilities make this a fine place to stop for a few days. But it's not cheap.

The village was founded in 1853 as a Moravian community and retains some noteworthy visible history. **Moravia St**, up the hill behind Water St, has the 19th-century churches and the 1880 Pioneer Schoolhouse. Down at the water, on Anderson Lane north of the center, is **Anderson's Store and Dock**, an ever-evolving town mainstay. The dock was originally the warehouse for goods such as farm produce and fish; later it became a movie theater. Today it is as much a signpost as anything, as it's covered with the names of people who have visited. Anderson was one of the town's original Scandinavian inhabitants.

There are more than a dozen art galleries, most on Water St.

The *Stiletto* (☎ 920-854-7245), a catamaran, does 75-minute trips around the bay and shoreline for $19; catch it at the South Shore Pier, off the main street. Also here is the Ephraim Sailing Center (☎ 920-854-4336), which rents sailboats, kayaks and canoes.

The **Fyr Bal Festival** (☎ 920-854-4989), held in the middle of June, is a three-day event based on the traditional Norwegian summer-welcoming ceremony. Concerts, dances, a bonfire and more mark the occasion and satisfy the Norse gods.

The **Midsummer's Music Festival** (☎ 920-854-1833) celebrates the solstice with chamber music performances in the Hardy Gallery. AFT performs at the Village Hall in September and October after their summer season in the state park.

Places to Stay Most economical are the three rooms in the house at ***Billerbeck's*** *(☎ 920-854-2528, 9864 Hidden Spring Rd)*, at just $30 with shared bath. It's south of the center, near the beach.

The ***HarborSide*** motel *(☎ 920-854-4134, fax 920-854-6876, @ schuder@maildoorcounty-wi.com, 9986 Water St)*, on Hwy 42, has 17 simple but clean rooms and is within walking distance of the center. Rooms are $83 single/double in peak season but drop to as low as $50 otherwise.

A comfortable, historic hostelry is the ***Hillside Hotel*** *(☎ 920-854-2417, 800-423-7023)*, which has offered beds and breakfast since 1890. The 100-foot veranda, with rocking chairs overlooking the beach and the bay, certainly helps to ease any lingering work-related tensions. Rooms are in the $100 range.

If money is not an issue, it's hard to top the grand, century-old ***Edgewater Resort*** *(☎ 920-854-2734)*. It's the dominating but gracious and stately complex in the center of town, on Water St overlooking the bay. All the modern comforts blend with the historic at this classic inn. Rooms range from $120 to $250 in July and August.

Places to Eat For breakfast, there is the ***Old Post Office*** *(☎ 920-854-4034, 10040 Water St)*, beside the Edgewater Resort. Fruit pancakes and all the standards are served beside large windows framing the bay. Fish boils are fired up at dinner (call for reservations); it's not open for lunch.

Leroy's Coffee Bar *(9922 Water St)*, a shady, cozy spot half hidden from the road, is open early to late for excellent coffee and a sweet or muffin.

The appealing ***Summer Kitchen*** *(☎ 920-854-2131)*, at the north end of town on Hwy 42, is swathed in flowers and umbrellas, luring in the hungry from May to October. Lunches include a fine chicken-cashew salad or burgers for $8. Among the complete dinners, at about twice that price, are pecan whitefish or pastas.

Sister Bay

• pop 675

Another attractive village, Sister Bay is especially enticing if you arrive with an appetite. The main street is a smorgasbord of some of the most diverse restaurants on Hwy 42 (called Bay Shore Drive in town). Some modestly priced lodging can also be found here.

Century Farm Motel *(☎ 920-854-4069)*, south of Sister Bay at 10068 Hwy 57, rents cottages starting at $45. ***Edge of Town Motel*** *(☎ 920-854-2012)*, north of the center on Hwy 42, has 10 rooms for $60 in July and August and is open all year.

South of town, ***Carroll House*** is great for breakfast, which is served from 7 am to closing at 1 pm.

Sister Bay Café *(☎ 920-854-2429, 611 Bay Shore Drive)* is an immensely popular Norwegian restaurant with good prices for all three meals. The menu contains American standards and an assortment of Norwegian, Swedish and Danish items. Norwegian-style open-faced sandwiches are $7 at lunch; try the cream cheese topped with herring and cucumber on a slice of dark rye. The farmers' *lapskaus* (a stew) with crackers is good value. Oslo chicken with loganberries (not unlike cranberries) or whitefish at dinner is about $14.

Al Johnson's Swedish Restaurant *(☎ 920-854-2626, 704 Bay Shore Drive)* is perhaps the best-known restaurant in Door County. With goats wandering over the grass roof, it's no wonder! Menu items such as Swedish pancakes, pickled herring and a fruit soup add to the American family-restaurant standards replicated here. Although the selection is notably extensive, what really differentiates the restaurant is the Scandinavian decor and the wait staff in their lovely, colorful, traditional garb.

For some uncommon spice on the Door, head to ***La Puerto*** *(☎ 902-854-4513, 10961 N Hwy 42)*, a casual cantina with Tex-Mex favorites for less than $8. Open daily in summer, closed Tuesday in fall and open weekends only in winter.

Ellison Bay

In tiny Ellison Bay, the **Pioneer Store**, cluttered with a wide range of supplies, goods and more, is almost as much a museum as a general store, but it also has basic groceries and some locally produced foods, such as cheese and jams.

The casual ***Viking Grill*** *(☎ 920-854-2998)* on Hwy 42 is said to be where the local fish-boil tradition began, back in 1939. They serve it up every day ($13) from 4 pm until about 9 pm in peak season, at picnic tables in a gardenlike setting or indoors if the weather isn't cooperating.

Some people make a point of visiting many of the area's state and county parks and tourism publications list them all. Two not worth the considerable effort of locating and reaching are Ellison Bluff and Door Bluff Headlands county parks. They are more for landscape conservation than visitors. Neither affords much of a view, and the latter lacks even a table or outhouse.

Gills Rock & Northport

There isn't much here other than the two Washington Island ferry terminals. But do stop in one of the three smoked-fish shops. Charlie's (☎ 920-854-2972) is near the dock in Gills Rock on Hwy 42; the trout is especially supreme. It's open 10 am to 5 pm daily from May to October, weekends only from November to April.

Mike's Bikes is at Northport by the dock for those wanting to cycle Washington Island.

Washington Island

• pop 650

With few attractions and limited facilities there is little to do here, and therein lies the appeal. Pick up a map at the visitors' center near the ferry terminal.

As throughout Door County, debate continues over increasing development and condo construction. For now, visitor numbers are relatively low, with many vacationers actually cottage owners or long-term renters. The 6-mile by 6-mile island has only 650 residents, mainly of Scandinavian descent, and even with boatloads of visitors you won't see a crowd anywhere.

Day-trippers can see many island highlights in about five hours. The Ridges, on the northern part of the island by the Rock Island ferry landing, is an undeveloped preserve with sand dunes, woods and a walking trail.

Oddly, there is no real village or area of concentrated facilities – another indication of the island's slow pace. Most of the commercial establishments lie by the ferry terminal or stretched along Main Rd from there.

The **Jackson Harbor Maritime Museum**, by the ferry dock and with a collection of maritime bric-a-brac, resembles a hastily planned garage sale yet is very interesting to browse. There are all kinds of fishing supplies, equipment, nets, a boat or two and a video on the area's commercial fishery. Open 10:30 am to 4:30 pm daily in July and August, and on weekends from Memorial Day through September; $1.

The log **Jacobsen Museum**, on the south shore of Little Lake on the island's northwestern tip, has a collection of local artifacts from Native American inhabitants and early Scandinavian settlers. There is also a restored log cabin, circa 1930, with authentic furniture. It's open daily 10 am to 4 pm from late May through mid-October; $1.

The **Farm Museum**, on Jackson Harbor Rd east of Main Rd, has a log home, various original buildings and a collection of farm implements. The animal-petting area is popular with kids. Open daily from mid-June to mid-October.

Places to Stay & Eat For spending the night, choices range from camping to motels, inns and cottages. ***Island Camping*** *(☎ 920-847-2622)*, on Eagle Side Rd 5 miles from the ferry terminal, has tent and electric sites for $18 and $21, respectively. There are also five lodge rooms available at just $35/40 single/double.

Gibson's resort *(☎ 920-847-2225)*, at West Harbor, is reasonably priced with two-bedroom housekeeping cottages for $60 a night, $300 a week. Rooms start at $20 for a single. It's open all year and has some boats available for guest rental.

The ***Bitter End Motel*** *(☎ 920-847-2242, 800-400-0208)* is on Main Rd and is open all year. The rooms in the addition built in the mid-1990s are modern and comfortable, even offering HBO.

For a meal, try ***KK Fiske*** on Main Rd, which features island fish specialties: whitefish and 'lawyers,' which are burbot, bottom-feeders similar to catfish. They also make pizza and fruit pies. Another choice a little farther up the road is the ***Cellar Restaurant at Karly's***, with a bit of everything on the menu and an outdoor patio, which goes well with a beer in hand.

Mann's, also on Main Rd, is a grocery store with a deli and baked goods.

Getting There & Around There are two ferries to Washington Island. The passenger-only boat (☎ 920-847-2039) departs Gills Rock from the middle of June to early September for $8/4 adults/children and $3 per bike, roundtrip. There are four or five trips per day in each direction.

The Washington Ferry Line (☎ 920-847-2546, 800-223-2094) runs all year from the Northpoint Pier and takes vehicles. In peak season trips depart nearly hourly; they become as infrequent as twice daily in the dead of winter. In summer, arriving at least an hour ahead of schedule is advisable. Roundtrip rates are $8/4 adults/kids, $17 per car, $3 per bike.

Once on the island, there are several options for getting around other than taking your car. The island is small and flat, so bicycling is popular and rentals ($5 per hour) are available at the ferry landing on the mainland or on the island from Harbor Bike Rental, near the ferry dock.

Hanlin's Moped Rental (☎ 920-847-2251), on Lobdell Rd by the ferry terminal on the island, rents mopeds by the hour ($22 for the first hour, $13 each additional hour) and is open daily from June to September.

Vi's Taxi (☎ 920-847-2283) offers a 1½-hour narrated tour (the per-person rate decreases with the number of people you have, but for two would be $8.50 each) or will go wherever you wish. The Cherry Train (☎ 920-847-2039) is a little trolley that makes a 90-minute tootle around the island's main sites from mid-May to mid-October. Tickets are $6. The train picks up passengers at both ferry landings.

Rock Island State Park

Off the northeastern tip of Washington Island, a 15-minute ferry ride away, is Rock Island, a wooded oasis of shoreline, peace and tranquility. The entire island is state parkland, and no vehicles, not even bicycles, are permitted, making for a vacation within a holiday.

For those not overnighting on Washington Island, three hours will allow some walking, a picnic and maybe a swim or a look at the lighthouse. With a full day (recommended), more of the history and trails can be enjoyed, more lake breezes and vistas absorbed.

Sites include the **Potawatomi Lighthouse**, Wisconsin's oldest, with tours at 11 am and 3 pm on summer Fridays ($3); the dolomite cliffs it sits atop; the **CH Thordason** estate complex, now on the National Register of Historic Places and open daily (free); and the fabulous crescent sand beach.

Walking trails meander the 900 acres; the longest, at 5 miles, skirts the island's perimeter.

The ferry (☎ 920-847-2252) departs Jackson Harbor on Washington Island from the end of May to the middle of October. Through July and August trips go every hour, dropping to three daily in the shoulder seasons. Roundtrip fare is $7.

Rustic ***campsites*** *(☎ 920-847-2235)*, by the beach just a short walk from the ferry dock, cost $8 on weekdays, $10 on weekends for state residents ($2 more for all others). There are a couple more remote, private walk-in sites, too. All can be booked, and reservations should certainly be made throughout the summer and are essential on weekends and holidays. There is drinking water on the island, and pit toilets, but that's it – there's nothing else. Pick up a map at the booth by the dock as you arrive.

Eastern Door County

The eastern edge of the county, dubbed the quiet side, is less visited and less costly. Little-developed **Newport State Park** (☎ 920-854-2500) at the northwestern edge of the peninsula, features a fine blend of rocky cliffs, sand beaches, forest and wetlands. There are 30 miles of good trails and basic, isolated backpack campsites – and no other comforts. For serious outdoor enthusiasts this is a highlight of the county. The usual park entry fees apply ($5 resident, $7 nonresident), but they're waived if you have the seasonal sticker. Overnight camping is $10, and some sites can be reserved.

North of low-key Baileys Harbor, around Moonlight Bay on County Rd Q, the still working **Cana Island Light** is accessible by a narrow stone pathway from the mainland. The adjacent house can be visited 10 am to 5 pm daily for a small fee. On the way to the light on County Rd Q is the 1000-acre **Ridges Sanctuary**, with a walking path.

The fish boil at the ***Square Rigger Galley*** *(☎ 920-823-2408)* in Jacksonport includes a few amenities, such as corn on the cob and even better, someone extracting the fish bones for you.

South of town, **Whitefish Dunes State Park** (☎ 920-823-2400) has a spectacular beach (beware of rip tides) and 14 miles of trails and dune sandscapes but no camping. Entry is $5 for residents, $7 for nonresidents, free with a seasonal sticker. At adjacent, free **Cave Point County Park**, with picnic tables, watch the waves explode into the caves beneath the shoreline cliffs.

NORTH OF GREEN BAY

At Green Bay almost all the northbound traffic turns right and goes into Door County. Turning left and following Hwy 41/141 leads to a quiet, off-the-beaten-path wooded region of white water. The water comes in two forms – on the rivers, mainly the Peshtigo, ideal for kayak and raft adventures, and in the forests as waterfalls, ideal for peaceful sightseeing, walking and picnicking. Because of its rocky landscapes, forests, falls and lack of crowds, the region is sometimes referred to as 'Wisconsin's Canadian wilderness.'

The main road here isn't busy, and the secondary roads have virtually no traffic at all. Even in midsummer you can have some parks almost to yourself. The area has the most trout streams in the state, and the High Falls Flowage, on the Peshtigo River northwest of Crivitz, has excellent bass fishing.

Crivitz

• pop 996

Halfway from Green Bay to the Michigan border, tiny Crivitz is the local metropolis with a couple of restaurants, a pub or two nd several motels. The Crivitz Area Museum Complex (☎ 715-854-3278) outlines the lumbering history of the county. It's open noon to 4 pm Wednesday to Saturday from late May to early September. In winter an excellent cross-country ski trail system is maintained.

Two miles south of town, the ***Peshtigo River Campground*** *(☎ 715-854-2986)* is busy with people here to take the 'tubing shuttle' and gently float down a placid section of the river. It's ideal for families or anyone needing a slow, lazy day cooled by the river. Campsites cost $14 to $18, open from May to October.

The ***Bonnie Bell Motel*** *(☎ 715-854-7395)* on Hwy 141 is a modest, inexpensive place. They are open year-round, but call ahead, as they do close down at certain intervals.

The interesting portion of the Peshtigo River lies northwest of town, to High Falls Flowage and Reservoir and beyond. Despite numerous casual resorts and kayak outfitters found along Parkway Rd, which follows the Peshtigo River between County Rd A northwest and County Rd C, the area is largely undeveloped. ***Popps Resort*** *(☎ 715-757-2791, fax 715-757-3511)* has motel units, cabins and boat rentals all at moderate prices. On weekends a two-night minimum is in effect.

Athelstane

The route north up Hwy 141 from Crivitz and then west on little-traveled County Rd C through Athelstane also provides access to the white-water outfitters. The **Peshtigo River** west on County Rd C in this area is a turbulent, frothy, rapid-filled stretch of water considered to be among the most challenging in the Midwest.

Wildman Whitewater Ranch *(☎ 715-757-2938, www.wildmanranch.com)*, on the Roaring Rapids section of the river, is an adventure resort designed as an Old West town. They offer camping ($7 per person), basic cabins ($50) for up to five people through to amenity-packed chalets ($200) for up to six people. Kids should be at least 12 years old to raft.

Raft rentals are $20 for a half day and there are guided day trips for $36 per person. All equipment can be rented, including wetsuits and sleeping bags. Weekend reservations are always a good idea and highly recommended at holidays. All day-trippers should bring extra clothes.

Another established resort is ***Kosir's*** *(☎ 715-757-3431, 715-757-3358, www.kosirs.com)*, also with camping ($5 per person) and cabins, for which there is a two-day minimum ($157 for up to four people) on Friday and Saturday night in July and August. Weekdays are $65. They offer rafts or one-person yaks, a cross between a raft and a kayak. Basic guided trips on the Peshtigo cost $19 weekdays, $21 weekends. Kosir's also does a trip farther north, on the Menomonee River ($38), which is even rougher and wilder. Minimum age on that trip is 16.

The area white-water season is from April or May through September, depending on the weather.

Amberg & Pembine Area

The numerous county parks in and around these two towns all have picturesque, unspoiled waterfalls. You could make a fine day going from one to the next, taking pictures and walking trails. Many are close to Hwy 141, but watch closely for the signs. Three good ones are Dave's Falls, Twelve Foot Falls and, close to Pembine, Long Slide Falls.

Northern Wisconsin

The northern third of the state is primarily a thinly populated region of forests and lakes. This is the land where rest room doors are marked 'Bucks' and 'Does.' The lakelands portion in particular is a busy resort area appreciated for camping and fishing in summer, skiing and snowmobiling in winter. The entire region has plenty of Ma-and-Pa motels, resorts and cottages scattered among small, logging- and tourism-oriented towns. Scenic Hwy 70 cuts east-west from Hwy 51 through the northwestern portion.

The town of Merrill on Hwy 51 marks the region's southern edge. It has the excellent **Council Grounds State Park** (☎ 715-536-8773), once used as a meeting place for Chippewa (Ojibway) bands. There's a beach, trails and original pine forest. Most of the original white pines of the area floated down the Wisconsin River and virtually built much of the Midwest. Have breakfast or lunch at ***Skipper's*** *(812 E First St)*, a small-town classic.

Continuing north is the lakelands; east are the north woods.

Public transportation through the region is sketchy. Greyhound serves Antigo, Rhinelander and Minocqua from Chicago, Milwaukee and Green Bay once a day in each direction.

NORTH WOODS

The **Nicolet National Forest** is a huge wooded God's country ideal for outdoor ac tivities, summer and winter. For informatio and booklets on trails, camping and sites visit the ranger stations in Lakewood o Laona (on Hwy 32), Eagle River (on Hw 45) or Florence (on Hwy 141 near the Mich igan border). The headquarters is i Rhinelander (☎ 715-362-1300), on Hwy 1 northeast of Merrill.

Entrance to some areas and features i free; many require a day pass or annua permit ($10). Hiking, biking, skiing an snowmobiling provide access to wildernes regions where wildlife is plentiful. Som sections have suggested driving tours. Inex

The North Woods – Scenic Drive

Head east on Hwy 64 out of Merrill to Antigo, the largest town in the area and a good place to gas up and get any other required supplies. From Antigo go northeast on Hwy 52 to Lily. This quiet route presents an eye-pleasing mix of forest, farms and gentle hills. From Lily head south on Hwy 55, which edges the Wolf River, to Langlade, at the edge of the forest and known for its river-trip outfitters. From Langlade Hwy 64 east leads to tiny County Rd T, east of Langlade. You are now definitely in the north woods. The farms are gone and timberland flora and fauna are all around. Evergreens such as pine and hemlock are abundant. The vast Nicolet National Forest, covering an area running north to Michigan, protects much of the land. Take narrow, winding, almost deserted County Rd T north to Townsend, just north of Lakewood on Hwy 32 in the heart of the forest. Bald eagles may be seen, especially around the rivers and lakes.

From here take Hwy 32 north through Wabeno to tiny Laona, with its wood mills and surrounding lakes. From here head back west out of the forest on Hwy 8, providing still-pleasant driving but with noticeably more traffic, to Rhinelander. Or turn north from Hwy 8 onto Hwy 45 before Rhinelander and head to Three Lakes. Both are much busier resort towns than the ones you'll have driven through.

The entire route is between 100 and 150 miles but will take longer than imagined, as the narrow roads won't allow high speeds and the landscape encourages an easy pace.

LIBRARY OF CONGRESS

›ensive, rustic camping is almost always ıvailable in the forest, even at the peak of ›ummer.

›ntigo

• pop 8276

:ast on Hwy 64 from Merrill, Antigo is ınlike most of the quaint pit stops in this dis-rict. It is a real town in both size and ameni-ies and has all the franchises to prove it. The ›ntigo area chamber of commerce (☎ 715-›23-4134, fax 715-623-4135), open 8:30 am to ›:30 pm weekdays, has district information.

Anglers definitely should stop for a tour weekdays only) at the north-end **Mepps** actory (☎ 715-623-2382), 626 Center St, vhere all the famous lures are put together ›y hand. Look for the Sheldon's Inc build-ng. If you hit a squirrel on the way over, hey'll buy the tail. But don't swerve delib-›rately – it's worth only 16¢.

Greyhound (☎ 715-623-6464) buses from ınd to Chicago via Green Bay stop at Vagner Shell Oil, 709 S Superior.

.anglade

Though nothing more than a crossroads, .anglade, at the edge of Nicolet Forest, ›erves as base for the area's excellent **white-vater adventures** on the Wolf River. Novices and families can take rubber rafts; hose looking for excitement can navigate ›ougher areas in canoes and kayaks. Nu-nerous outfitters offer rentals, guided trips ›r accommodations. The trout fishing is also ›enowned.

An excellent place is ***Bear Paw Outdoor ›dventure Resort*** *(☎ 715-882-3502, www bearpaw.com)*, with a top-notch staff and a ›ange of river trips, or you can design your ›wn. They run white-water courses from ›ate May to early September and have a ›ystem of bike trails. Lodging varies from ›ampsites ($15) to rustic cabins ($22) to ›eluxe digs ($90).

Buettner's Wild Wolf Inn *(☎ 715-882-›186)*, on Hwy 55 6½ miles south of the ›unction with Hwy 64, has lodging in its ›ustic inn, plus more modern rooms in a ›notel 6 miles north on Hwy 55 (both $43 ›or a double bed). Raft trips cost $7 to $25.

For more indulgence, book the fabulous ***Wolf River Lodge*** *(☎ 715-882-2182, www .wolfriverlodge.com, N2119 Taylor Rd)*, south on County Rd P in White Lake, which has been making nature accessible since 1919. Rates range from $80 for comfortable rooms in the large, classic stone-and-hemlock country lodge to $160 for the well-appointed private one- and two-bedroom cabins.

Lakewood & Vicinity

Lakewood has several pubs, restaurants, a grocery store and gift shops.

The rejuvenating 15-minute walk around **Cathedral Pines**, a virgin stand of white pine and hemlock at the north edge of town, is a great respite. More white water can be found eastward, on the Peshtigo River near Crivitz and Athelstane (see those sections, earlier, for more information).

North on Hwy 32, a mile south of **Carter**, is a 0.6-mile forest walking trail to the top of McCaslin Mountain and an overlook. Back on Hwy 32, farther north, is Wabeno and its free **Logging Museum**, with an operational historic log hauler. The museum is open 11 am to 4 pm Monday to Thursday, 10 am to 5 pm Friday and Saturday, 10 am to 4 pm Sunday from late May to early September. Click a pic beside the statue of Larry the Log Roller and have a refreshment across the street, where there are a couple of modest restaurants and an ice-cream stand.

Tiny **Laona**, in the middle of the forest, is a classic small lumber town. It's surrounded by gorgeous country and lined with more Appalachian-like hole-in-the-wall bars than anything else. These tend to be on the rough-and-ready side, but they certainly do offer character.

The **Camp Five** (☎ 715-674-3414) museum complex with a working steam train, the *Lumberjack Special*, is a good site. It's a quarter mile west of Laona by the junction of Hwy 32 and Hwy 8. You board the train to get to the museum area, which includes a logging museum, blacksmith shop, small nature center and farm animals kids can pet and feed. Open 11 am to 4 pm, Monday to Saturday from mid-June to the end of August. The train departs on the hour from 11 am to 2 pm. Tickets for the whole package cost $14 for adults, $9 for kids 13 to 17, $5 for kids younger than that. There are fall color trips on Saturday in late September and early October.

Places to Stay & Eat In Laona, a surprise is the pleasant, little-used HI ***hostel*** *(☎ 715-674-2615, 5397 Hwy 8)*, which makes a good base for exploring the area. Beds cost $12, and canoes are available for rent. For a bite and some conversation, stroll over to the homey ***Club House***, also on Hwy 8.

Waubee Lodge *(☎ 715-276-6069, 800-492-8233, fax 715-276-3133, www.waubeelodge.com)*, 6 miles east of Lakewood on County Rd F, has modest nightly motel units, weekly cottages and a supper club.

The main street in Lakewood (Hwy 32) is good when hunger strikes. Among the choices, ***Al & Linda's Pour Haus*** *(☎ 715-276-6637)* is worth a stop.

LAKELANDS

From Merrill, take meandering Hwy 107 to **Tomahawk**, with the big, annual YesterFest, a historical and ethnic festival held in mid-August. For details call the chamber of commerce (☎ 715-453-5334). All renegades from the 1960s will smile at menu names such as avocado-da-vida sandwich, served at the excellent ***Uncommon Grounds Café*** *(111 W Wisconsin St)*.

Rhinelander

• pop 7427

Despite being the north woods' largest town, Rhinelander gets booked solid on summer weekends. Check in at the Hwy 8 west visitors' center (☎ 715-365-7464, 800-236-4386, www.ci.rhinelander.wi.us) for maps and more. It has an excellent booklet on off-road biking in the area and another for a 16-mile self-guided auto tour of sites related to the forestry industry, which is so vital to the northern half of the state. Open 8 am to 5 pm weekdays, 9 am to noon Saturday.

The indoor-outdoor **Rhinelander Logging Museum** provides a look at the industry's past. It's in Pioneer Park, a few blocks southeast of the downtown core, south of Lincol[n] St off Baird Ave. Open 10 am to 5 pm fro[m] late May to early September; free.

Raise a glass under the tent at Rhinelander's **Oktoberfest**.

The ***Claridge Motor Inn*** *(☎ 715-362-7100, 800-427-1377, fax 715-362-3883, 70 N Stevens St)*, at $61/66 single/double i[n] summer, is a good value. The ***Downtowne Motel*** *(☎ 715-362-7171, 800-634-6324, 15 N Anderson)* is friendly and about half tha[t] price.

Downtown Brown St has numerou[s] restaurants.

Three Lakes

This neat, pretty resort town makes a goo[d] place for a break. With the **world's larges[t] chain of lakes** (20) and national forests t[o] the east and west, it's a vacation hub. Th[e] main street is Superior St, a continuation o[f] Hwy 45. The Information Bureau (☎ 715-546-3344, 800-972-6103, www.threelake[s].com), near the corner of Nelson St, ca[n]

Foamy Fun

An unexpected quirk of the lakelands region is its passion for waterskiing. Tomahawk, Rhinelander, Three Lakes, Conover and other towns present regular summer shows, either free or at low cost. Seemingly out of a 1950s time warp, the somewhat corny performances feature all the jumps, acrobatics and smiling faces you've once seen on TV. But you can't be cynical about all these good-looking kids – and they are kids, starting at age eight or so and going to about 20 – doing something so well and obviously enjoying it so much. On the shore or dock, with some popular hit song blaring, there's often some bump and grind thrown in too – from the guys! Many skiers go on to become professionals at Disney World and the like. The enthusiasm and lack of slick perfectionism make for an entertaining, old-fashioned hour of innocence and fun. There are some darn fine tricks, too.

elp with accommodations. Much of these re weekly cottage rentals.

The downtown ***Oneida Village Inn*** *☎ 715-546-3373, 800-374-7443, 1785 Su-erior St)* has moderate rooms. Superior St lined with eateries and gift shops. Drop by he downtown ***Three Lakes Winery*** *(☎ 800-44-5434, 6971 Gogebie St)* for a bottle of heir unique sweet yet astringently tart ranberry wine.

There's good **bird-watching** at Thunder Aarsh, 3 miles north on Hwy 45. The **Na-ional Forest Scenic Byway** is a highlight rive to Eagle Lake; get a map at the Infor-nation Bureau or the ranger station in Rhinelander or Eagle River.

Eagle River

pop 1374

he north country playground is perhaps est represented here. With an array of ourist services and activities and events or all seasons, there is something for every-ne. Restaurants and accommodations are lentiful.

The visitors' center (☎ 715-479-6400, 800-59-6315, www.eagleriver.org) at the corner f Maple St and Silver Lake Rd is informa-ve. It's open 10 am to 5 pm daily.

Spend an hour at **Carl's Wood Art Auseum** (☎ 715-479-1883), 1230 Sundstein Rd, if you have any appreciation of wood or 'himsy. It's open 9 am to 5 pm Monday to aturday, 10 am to 4 pm Sunday from late Aay to mid-October.

Hawk's Nest Outfitters (☎ 715-542-2300) as kayak, canoe and tube excursions and entals.

Events to watch for include the mid-August **muskie fishing open**; the **Cranberry est** at fall harvest (usually early October), ith enlightening tours given about this ajor Wisconsin fruit; and the **World Cham-ionship Snowmobile Derby** in January (call e Derby Race Track at ☎ 715-479-9711 for nformation and seat reservations). There is lso the **US1 Select Snow Cross Race**, another ajor snowmobile race, in December.

For lodging, the best value is ***White Eagle Aotel*** *(☎ 715-479-4426, 800-782-6488)*, on Hwy 70 west, with doubles for $55 in July and August, $50 or less the rest of the year. ***Riverdale Resort*** *(☎ 715-479-4373, 800-530-0019, 5012 Hwy 70 west)* has cottages and motel units on the Eagle River. Rooms start at $50 a day; cottages $70/340 a day/week.

There are numerous diners in the center. At dinner try ***Sprang's***, an Italian eatery on Hwy 70 west, with a pseudo-alpine look. They've packed in the hungry since 1972.

Woodruff & Minocqua

• pop 4500 (combined)

These twin towns are also busy vacation centers but without the woodsy atmos-phere. Get local, forest, hiking and bicycling information at the Minocqua Chamber of Commerce (☎ 715-356-5266, 800-446-6784, www.minocqua.org), on US 51 south. It's open 8 am to 5 pm weekdays, 9 am to 3 pm Saturday. See good-time **Scheer's Lumber-jack Shows** (☎ 715-356-4050) with climbing, sawing, chopping and more, 2 miles north of Minocqua. The $6 shows run at 7:30 pm from mid-June to the end of August on Tuesday, Thursday and Saturday. There are also 2 pm matinees on Wednesday, Thurs-day and Friday.

Northern Highland American Legion Na-tional Forest is more than a mouthful for a green, lake-filled, camping and fishing para-dise. Come winter, the Nordic skiing is ex-cellent. See the Woodruff ranger station (☎ 715-356-5211), 8770 County Rd J, for advice and maps.

Eat at rustic, logging camp-style ***Paul Bunyan Meals***, a popular family restaurant on US 51, with buffets for all three meals ($10 at dinner).

Greyhound buses (☎ 715-356-9009) stop at the Hardee's Restaurant at the corner of Hwy 51 and Hwy 70. This is the end of the line for buses in northern Wisconsin.

Lac du Flambeau

Stop at the Ojibwe Museum and Cultural Center (☎ 715-588-3333), 603 Peace Pipe, where displays include canoes, art, crafts and clothing. Open 10 am to 4 pm Monday to Saturday from May to October.

Just north of the Cultural Center in the Indian Bowl, traditional singing and dancing are performed Tuesday evening from the last Tuesday in June to the third Tuesday in August; $5. Take insect repellent.

Out of town on the Lac du Flambeau Indian reservation, check out Waswagoning (☎ 715-588-2104), a re-creation of a traditional village open 10 am to 4 pm Tuesday to Saturday from mid-June to the end of September.

Mercer

If possible, catch the loon-calling contest on **Loon Day**, at the beginning of August in the attractive little loon capital of Wisconsin. For information, call the Mercer chamber of commerce (☎ 715-476-2389), on Hwy 51 south of downtown (just look for the giant loon).

The nearby **Turtle Flambeau Flowage** is a magnificent protected water wilderness area created by the damming of the Turtle and Flambeau Rivers. The rivers and lakes are a canoe tripper's delight, with abundant wildlife, notably loons and eagles, and great fishing. And no portages! Sections of the Flambeau River provide white water ideal for kayaking. Lodges and campsites provid[e] access, while outfitters can put trip package[s] together. Try Hawk's Nest Outfitters (☎ 715[-]476-0077, 800-688-7471) 3 miles south o[f] Mercer on Hwy 51. Access and informatio[n] are also available in the towns of Manitow[ish] Waters, Springstead and Butternut[.] Good maps are necessary.

If Heaven Has a Soundtrack

Anybody who has spent time in America's north woods agrees: The mesmerizing call of the loon breaking the silence on a warm, still summer night is a thing of ineffable beauty.

The health of the loon population indicates the health of its habitat, and the Turtle Flambeau Flowage area is one of this waterfowl's last American breeding areas. Essential to the loons are relatively pollution-free lakes and minimal human encroachment into their habitat. But the present population of 2500 faces ever diminishing numbers because of an increase in the number of recreationists. Never disturb the loons unnecessarily (it's illegal) and their enchanting wails, tremolos, yodels, hoots and cries will always be linked to vacation memories. To become more involved, contact Loon Watch (☎ 715-682-4531, ext 201), Northland College, Ashland, WI 54806.

LAKE SUPERIOR & THE APOSTLE ISLANDS

Wisconsin's northwest corner, abuttin[g] Lake Superior, is presided over by [a] glaciated coastline crowned by the un[-]spoiled Apostle Islands.

From the south or the east, you com[e] through little-known **Hurley**, which doesn['t] deserve the visitor neglect. The former iron mining center long had a reputation as [a] drinking, gambling and prostitution cente[r.] Even today, legendary Silver St has [a] wayward pioneer feel about it, with its ques[-]tionably named 'gentlemen's clubs[.'] However, there are some interesting minin[g] sites, the ***Iron Nugget*** restaurant-cum[-]museum and, nearby, the historic town o[f] Montreal, plus waterfalls and canoeing. I[n] winter, mounds of snow make ideal skiin[g] and snowmobiling.

Ashland

• pop 8695

Ashland, marked with a large iron-or[e] loading dock but laudably preserving larg[e] segments of shoreline, makes a good sto[p.] The Northern Great Lakes Visitor Cente[r] (☎ 715-685-9983), 3 miles west of town o[n] Hwy 2, has tourist information, an observa[-]tion tower and exhibits on the region. Ope[n] daily all year, hours vary.

The **Historical Museum** (☎ 715-682[-]4911), 522 Chapple Ave in a forme[r] mansion, explains the transport termin[al] history.

Quiet ***Prentice Park,*** west off Hwy 2 a[t] Turner Rd, with artesian water, trails and [a] deer paddock, is a real discovery at $5 fo[r] a tent site. ***Crest Motel*** *(☎ 715-682-6603)*, o[n] Hwy 2 west of the center, has great views an[d] rooms for $40. ***Hotel Chequamegon*** *(☎ 71[5-]682-9095, 800-946-5555, www.hotelc.com*

010 Lake Shore Drive W), is a finely restored waterfront inn with rooms starting at $90.

The brew pub in the restored ***Depot*** estaurant complex, centrally located on 3rd Ave W, is an excellent place for an econom-ical meal and a pint. The relaxed ***Black Cat Coffee House*** *(211 Chapple St)* is perfect for breakfast and lunch.

Bayfield

pop 800

With its narrow, winding streets, Victorian-era buildings and vistas of the lake and islands, this is one of the state's finest villages. It is also the access point for the lovely Apostle Islands.

A bustling (and growing) resort town, it gets extremely busy in July and August. Both accommodations and boat tours should be booked in advance, particularly for weekends. Quadruple this warning during the late-summer Apple Festival. Rates drop sharply by September.

The chamber of commerce (☎ 715-779-335, www.bayfield.org), on Manypenny Ave at Broad St, is open 9 am to 5 pm Monday to Saturday. Storefront outfitters renting kayaks and bikes and leading kayak trips can easily be found on the main streets.

Things to See & Do To learn a little history, the **Heritage Museum**, on Broad St north of Rittenhouse Ave, has a collection of area and marine artifacts. It's open 1 to 4 pm Tuesday to Saturday from late May to early September. The **Cooperage**, the historic warehouse where barrels were once crafted for shipping fish, is worth a brief visit. It's across the road from the ferry dock. Both are free.

A drive up the hill behind town on Washington Ave leads to area **orchards**, primarily apple but also cherry, which have retail stands.

The area gets a lot of snow in winter. Activities include downhill and cross-country skiing, dog sledding and snowmobiling. The chamber of commerce can provide details, or you can try the outfitters.

Special Events The Big Top Chautauqua (☎ 715-373-5552, 888-244-8368) is the region's top summer event. Begun in 1986, the series of concerts, some theater and a major musical run from the end of May to mid-September. All performances are under a canvas tent, carrying on this American tradition. There is a show nearly every night, as well as weekly radio broadcasts well known across the state and heard around the country. The site is 3 miles south of town off Hwy 13 at the base of Mt Ashwabay. Tickets range from $12 to $18, less for kids. A free shuttle bus runs from Bayfield for every show.

Organized Tours A cruise around the islands is on nearly everyone's list. Apostle Islands Cruise Service (☎ 715-779-3925, 800-323-7619), based at the central City Dock at the foot of Rittenhouse Ave (Hwy 13), has a trip for any interest.

The Grand Tour is a three-hour voyage that skims around many of the 22 islands, although most remain a fair distance away. You get some narrated history and a look at two lighthouses and shoreline erosion features at Devils Island. The tour runs once a day from May 15 to October 10 and sells out ($23) in summer. Try to get on the upper deck (bring sun protection).

A good option is the Islander tour, which breezes around the inner islands and allows for a stop at either Stockton or Manitou Island. An island visit, even if brief, is a more complete experience than the simple cruise, which can be repetitious. This nearly four-hour trip ($23) runs once daily from mid-June to early September.

Other variations include sailing on the wooden schooner *Zeeto* ($42), a lighthouse cruise or a close-up evening spin around the Squaw Bay caves ($23 each).

The cruise service also operates **water taxis** (☎ 715-779-5153) for those wishing to camp or kayak in the national park. It's not cheap, but each fare is good for up to six passengers, roundtrip. Some examples are Basswood Island for $76, Long Island for $125, Bear Island for $196. Day hikers should ask about possible discounts with hourly waiting costs.

Trek & Trail (☎ 800-354-8735) with a store on Rittenhouse Ave at Broad St, is an outfitter and tour operator. They rent sea kayaks for four hours ($20) to several days. They also offer a range of trips, kayaking courses, truck shuttles to put-in points and even dog sledding around the islands in winter. The sea cave trips (with kayaking lesson), at $90, provide access to one of the park's most photographed areas.

Places to Stay For campers, ***Dalrymple Park Campground***, a mile north of town on Hwy 13, has green, quiet, basic lakeside campsites starting at $10. Fully developed ***Apostle Islands View*** *(☎ 715-779-5524)*, a half-mile south on Hwy 13 (follow signs up the hill), is the best for RVs, charging $16 to $22 for a site with full hookups.

There are numerous B&Bs averaging $55 to $75, and less expensive guest houses. ***Kinney's Guest Rooms*** *(☎ 715-779-3980)*, on Old Military Rd about eight blocks from the center, charges $30 to $60, depending on bath facilities and the market for its three rooms.

The ***Seagull Bay*** motel *(☎ 715-779-5558, www.seagullbay.com)*, on the corner of Hwy 13 and 7th St, is a good choice. Rates are fair, at $35/60 in the low/high season for the standard rooms, each with a lake view. Kitchen units and a cottage are also available.

The ***Isaac Wing House*** *(☎ 715-779-3907, 888-320-5468, 17 S 1st St)*, in the heart of town, has several guest rooms, each with a separate sleeping area. It's clean, tastefully decorated, air-conditioned and has some character. Rates are $70 to $90 a double, with some rooms sleeping six people.

By far the classiest and most expensive accommodations are at ***Old Rittenhouse Inn*** *(☎ 715-779-5111, www.rittenhouseinn.com)*, an elegant Victorian manor at the corner of Rittenhouse and 3rd Sts. Rooms start at $120 in summer.

Places to Eat After walking up the lawn, it's guaranteed the interior of ***Greunke's Inn*** *(☎ 715-779-5480, 17 Rittenhouse Ave)* will bring surprise and a smile in equal measure. This is absolutely the best place for breakfast and is also popular for the $12 fish boils Thursday through Sunday in summer. Sandwiches and burgers make up the lunch menu.

Coffee Island Express *(☎ 715-779-7010)*, at the corner of S Broad and Manypenny Ave, is a tiny, laid-back place to unwind, read a paper and wait for the freshly made soup, salad or sandwich to arrive. There are dozens of coffees, teas and smoothies to choose from, and a few outdoor tables. Everything is under $6.

For mouthwatering fresh or smoked fish, don't miss either ***Bay Fisheries*** or the ***Fish House*** outlets. They have herring, trout and whitefish at great prices. Both are on Wilson Ave by the Coast Guard building. ***Maggie's*** *(257 Manypenny Ave)* is a good place for an evening drink, with burgers and pizza available.

Moving upscale, the ***Old Rittenhouse Inn*** dining room, with an historic air, is great for a splurge. The prix fixe dinner ($45) may feature duck, fish or venison. Lunch entrées are $10.

A local specialty is sautéed whitefish livers, listed on many a menu.

Getting There & Around Bay Area Rural Transit (BART; ☎ 715-682-9664) is a nifty little bus service traveling between Red Cliff and Ashland with stops at Bayfield and Washburn. Bayfield to Ashland is $2.10 with eight trips a day on weekdays. It'll stop at any street corner and runs all year.

Trek & Trail (☎ 800-354-8735), in the center of town on Rittenhouse Ave, rents bikes at $5/hour, $20/day.

Apostle Islands National Lakeshore

The Apostle Island archipelago, sprinkled off the point of the Bayfield County peninsula, is one of Wisconsin's premier blessings. The red-edged, emerald isles set against Superior's blue hues are an immensely appealing yet accessible escape.

There are 22 islands, 21 of which are protected as part of Apostle Islands National Lakeshore; Madeline Island is the exception. There is also a mainland portion on the lakeshore that edges along the shoreline fo

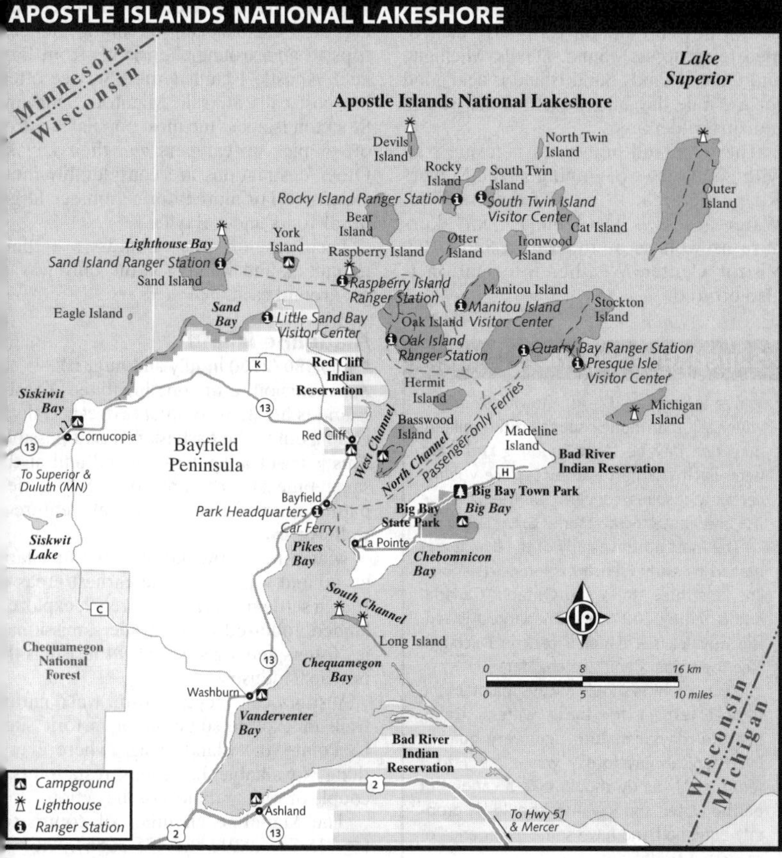

2 miles north of Bayfield, but it has no amping.

The visitor center at park headquarters ☎ 715-779-3397), 410 Washington Ave in ayfield, is open 8 am to 5 pm daily from Iay through October and weekdays only ntil 4:30 pm the rest of the year. It provides ll the information and advice needed for isiting, kayaking and hiking the islands, 17 f which have campsites. The necessary $15 ermits required to camp for one to 14 days re sold at the center, and you can book a ampsite here as well.

Kayaking is popular in the park, though this is a potentially dangerous area for an inaugural trip. Even swimming spots should be chosen carefully. Before beginning any long paddles, check the weather with a ranger. Also, wearing wet or dry suits is recommended.

Park highlights include the naturally carved sandstone formations and caves along the mainland shore near Meyers Rd and on Sand and Devils Islands; the trails on Oak and Stockton Islands; the many bears on Bear Island and the solitude on all of them. The lighthouses are a major attraction, with free tours on Raspberry (scheduled ferry access), Sand, Devils, Michigan and Outer Islands. Sand Island is also good for a 2-mile day hike. Much of the islands remains wilderness.

The mainland unit has a lakeside trail with good views beginning at the Meyers Rd picnic area, 18 miles from Bayfield. Water access is available for kayakers here as well as at the Little Sand Bay Visitor Center. Weather information is also offered.

Superlative Superior

You're looking at 10% of the world's freshwater. All that money spent on the military may one day be standing on guard right here. Earth's largest lake by surface volume certainly inspires concern for the way we use and abuse the awesome Great Lakes.

The most northwesterly of the five, it was named by early French explorers. Its shoreline laps three states and Ontario, Canada, and is fed by 200 rivers. The largest island, Isle Royale, is a national park in Michigan (see the Upper Peninsula chapter).

Recreationists should always maintain the utmost respect for these waters. Calm, peaceful days can turn ugly very quickly. Even typical, day-to-day waves are 1 to 4 feet high. Nobody should take a canoe out on the water, and kayakers should be properly equipped and have some experience or go with a guide.

Here is some food for thought: Superior's highest wave was recorded at 31 feet, the average temperature is 40° F and the average depth is 489 feet. No wonder so many drowning victims are never found. The lake is responsible for 350 known shipwrecks and has claimed at least a thousand lives. And for a little more perspective, consider that a drop of water entering the lake remains for about 191 years before heading toward the ocean.

Getting There & Around Various companies offer seasonal charter, sailing and ferr trips to and around the islands from Bay field. Apostle Islands Cruise Service offer low-cost calls at Oak, Manitou, Sand an Stockton Islands (the most popular) to dro off or pick up campers *and* their kayak Other destinations are considerably mor expensive. For more information, see Orga nized Tours under Bayfield.

Facilities on the islands are bar minimum, and walking is the only way t get around each.

Madeline Island

• pop 180 (2500 in July and August)

An excursion to the one inhabited Apostl Island is highly recommended, especially getting out to the park islands isn't possibl This is an ideal spot to unwind and at th same time absorb some of the Apostle natural charms. Even a one-day venture well worthwhile.

Madeline is the largest in the islan group and was one of the earliest areas c Indian settlement. In 1659, French explore landed, followed by fur traders, missiona ies, fishers and loggers. Today tourism is th principal industry.

Visitors can bicycle, swim, walk natur trails or explore some minor historic site **La Pointe**, the island village where every thing is walkable, has shops, restaurants, couple of sites and most of the action.

The Madeline chamber of commerc (☎ 715-747-2801, 888-475-3386), with a office on Middle Rd in La Pointe, is ope 8 am to 4 pm Tuesday to Saturday from Ma to October, the same hours on Monda Wednesday and Friday the rest of the yea

Things to See & Do The palisaded **Made line Island Historical Museum** (☎ 715-74 2415), just off the main street in tow outlines the island's history, detailin Ojibway culture, the fur trade and develo ment. Open 10 am to 4 pm from late May t October (until 6 pm in July and August); $

Generally ignored, La Pointe **India Cemetery**, on the road behind the yac ub, reveals some decaying but still in-guing Ojibway burial houses meant to d the deceased's four-day journey to the terlife. It's off Old Fort Rd, near the MI olf Club.

Big Bay State Park has a beach and a fine ooded walking trail by the lakeside sand-one formations. Bog Lake Outfitters ; 715-747-2685) rents canoes and kayaks r a paddle around the **Madeline Lagoon** the superb beach at Big Bay Town Park, f Big Bay Rd.

A walk on the **Capser Trail**, among tower-g pines, ferns and forget-me-nots, reveals e island's character long before the age of alty and private property signs. It's near wn; get a map from the Madeline chamber commerce.

aces to Stay Campers have two good oices, both 7 miles from town. Popular ***ig Bay State Park*** *(☎ 715-747-6425)* often ts booked up. Sites are $10 on weekdays, 2 on weekends, and none have electricity. ***ig Bay Town Park***, along Big Bay Rd, has first come, first served sites. They aren't as ce as the state park's, but the beach is ex-llent. Rates are $10/13 tent/RV site. Look r flora and fauna at the adjacent lagoon.

In La Pointe, small, central ***Madeline land Motel*** *(☎ 715-747-3000)*, on Main St ar the ferry, has clean, spacious rooms nong the best priced on the island at out $85 in July and August, including con-nental breakfast. The ***Island Inn*** *(☎ 715-7-2000, fax 715-747-6155)*, down the eet, has rustic country style, with wood-neled rooms and birch-bark furniture, for 0 in summer. It's a short walk to the ferry t quiet, as it's off the main drag.

Much of the rest of the lodging consists pricey B&Bs or cottages, often with ree-day or longer minimums. The amber of commerce can help locate a eekly booking; expect to pay $800 or ore.

aces to Eat La Pointe options are nu-erous and cover all budgets. The ***Island ifé***, on the main street at Middle Rd, has a pleasant, resorty, screened-in porch on the outside and an unexpected Middle-Eastern tentlike interior. It's open for all meals and includes some Mexican items among the sandwiches (around $7). Dinner entrées, mainly featuring fish, are $12 to $16.

The ***Harbor Dining Room***, a couple of doors from the ferry landing, has a fine waterfront setting at which to eat lake trout or whitefish entrées ($13).

If you've forsaken the trip to Europe and are vacationing hard, make reservations for dinner at the ***Clubhouse*** *(☎ 715-747-2612)*, on Old Fort Rd by the golf course (they'll pick you up from the ferry dock). You'll get a sophisticated, contemporary meal based on traditional classics but enlivened with local produce, game or fish perfectly pre-pared. The wine list has 300 international wines.

Tom's Burned Down Café, on Middle Rd and seemingly lifted from the Florida Keys, is a funky, open-sided bar and eatery that gets better the longer you stay. You might catch some live music and can't miss the metalworks scattered about.

Getting There & Around The Madeline Island Ferry (☎ 715-747-2051) runs from Bayfield to La Pointe except during freeze-up, about January to March. One-way fares for the 25-minute cruise are $4/2 adults/kids, $8 for a car. Departures are at least every hour from late June to early September, less frequent otherwise.

Motion to Go (☎ 715-747-6585), on Middle Rd, rents bikes for $6/22 an hour/day and mopeds for $12/50 an hour/day. The ferry company offers two-hour bus tours for $9, including a visit to the state park.

HIGHWAY 13 WEST

This is a fine drive around the Lake Superior shore west of Bayfield. It passes the Ojibway community of **Red Cliff** and the mainland segment of the national lake-shore. The road continues to tiny **Cornucopia**, which looks like a seaside village and has great sunsets, then runs on through a timeless countryside of forest and farm.

It then joins US 2 for the final few miles into the port of **Superior**. East of town, see the falls and cascades at **Amnicon State Park**. In **Patison State Park**, south of town, Big Manitou Falls, with a 165-foot vertical drop, are the state's highest. In Superior, which is often booked solid in summer, tour the SS *Meteor* ore freighter (☎ 715-392-5742 The ship is moored off Barker's Island; tak Barker's Island Rd off Hwy 2/53 just sout of the visitor center. A tour is $5. Rig across the border on Hwy 53 is Dulut Minnesota (see the Central & Norther Minnesota chapter).

Minnesota

Facts about Minnesota

Long ago the Sioux Indians called one of this region's major rivers *minisota*, meaning sky-tinted waters. In the 'land of 10,000 lakes' (actually thousands more), the name is equally if not more apt today. Millions of annual vacationers seek out the waters for the wealth of outdoor recreation. It's said there is one boat for every six residents and that more than 2 million Minnesotans fish. In addition to all the water, forests, with all their recreational possibilities, cover 35% of the state.

Minnesota Facts

Nickname Gopher State

Population 4,609,500 (20th largest)

Area 84,068 sq miles (12th largest)

Admitted to Union May 11, 1858 (32nd state)

Road Information Call ☎ 800-542-0220

Road Rules Drivers, front-seat passengers and all children ages four to 10 must wear seat belts. Children under age four must be in car seats. Motorcyclists are not required to wear helmets.

Taxes State sales tax is 6.5%. Cities and towns levy their own hotel tax, usually about 3%.

The Midwest's largest state also offers excellent cultural opportunities and gastronomic pleasures within the Twin Cities of Minneapolis–St Paul. Other regions and towns provide engaging historical sites, spectacular scenery and year-round activities. The readily observed self-effacing Minnesota humor is found everywhere. It's not unusual to see phrases like 'almost famous' at a restaurant or 'pretty good service' at an outfitter's, or to hear 'land of blond hair and blue ears' in one of many references to the snowy winters.

Most of the population is of Scandinavian (especially Norwegian and Swedish) or German background. Cities and towns, though, have increasingly diverse ethnicities, with significant numbers of other Europeans, Asians, African Americans and Latin Americans.

Minnesota is a prosperous state with a balanced economy of agriculture, forestry, mining, manufacturing and a strong information and services sector. It has an educated citizenry, a flashy governor and no end of potential for economic growth. The one major hurdle is how to develop while maintaining the qualities that visitors and residents currently enjoy.

Residents sometimes refer to their state as Minnesnowta, and they have a point. Although it doesn't always, it can snow as early as October and as late as May. Residents in the central and northern regions shovel many feet per season. Drivers should be prepared and well informed if blizzards have been forecast. If you're traveling in winter, build delays into your agenda.

History

The Minnesota area was primarily inhabited by eastern bands of the Sioux nation when the first French explorers and trappers arrived in the 17th century. Starting in the early 18th century, Anishinabe bands (also called Ojibway or Chippewa) of the Algonquian nation moved into northea

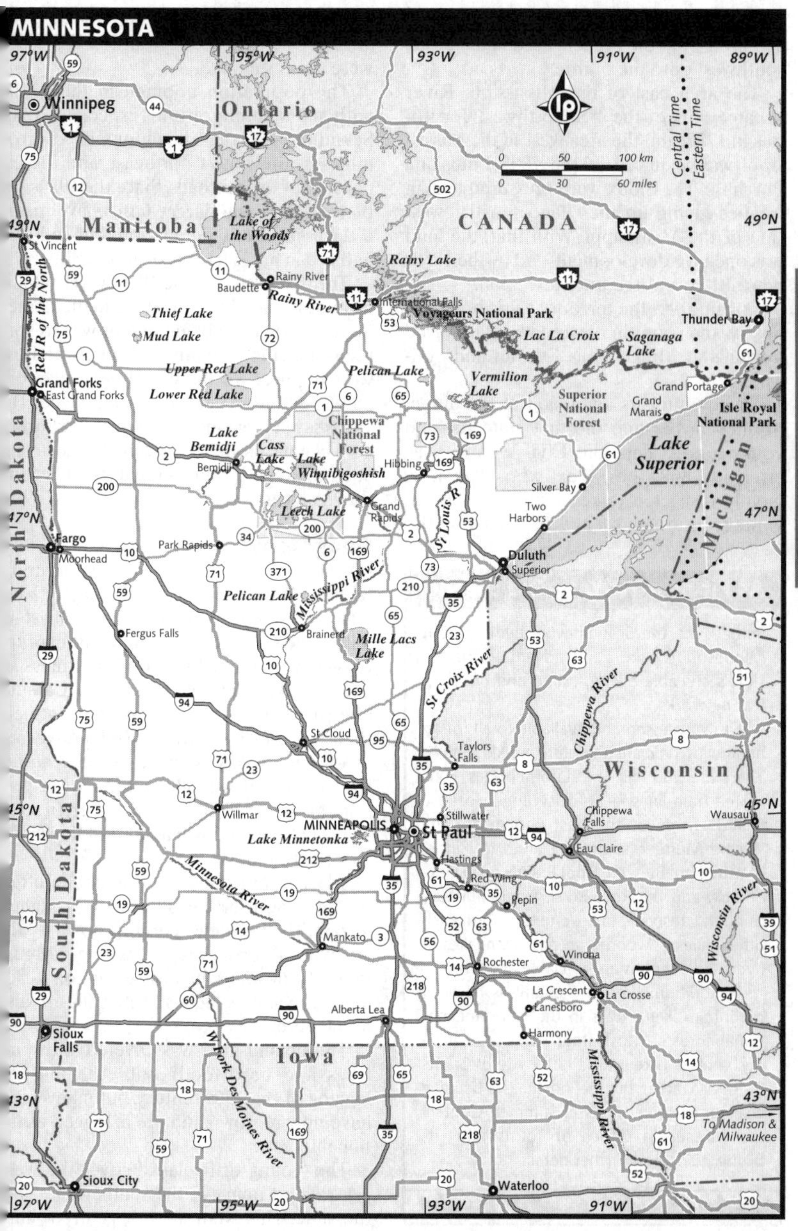
MINNESOTA
97°W
95°W
93°W
91°W
89°W
Winnipeg
Ontario
Central Time
Eastern Time
0
50
100 km
0
30
60 miles
Manitoba
Lake of the Woods
CANADA
49°N
St Vincent
Rainy Lake
Rainy River
Baudette
Rainy River
International Falls
Voyageurs National Park
Lac La Croix
Saganaga Lake
Thunder Bay
Thief Lake
Mud Lake
Red R of the North
Upper Red Lake
Lower Red Lake
Pelican Lake
Vermilion Lake
Grand Portage
Grand Forks
East Grand Forks
Superior National Forest
Grand Marais
Isle Royal National Park
Chippewa National Forest
Lake Bemidji
Cass Lake
Lake Winnibigoshish
Bemidji
Hibbing
Lake Superior
Michigan
Silver Bay
Two Harbors
Grand Rapids
Leech Lake
St Louis R
47°N
Fargo
Moorhead
Park Rapids
Duluth
Superior
North Dakota
Pelican Lake
Mississippi River
Fergus Falls
Brainerd
Mille Lacs Lake
St Croix River
Chippewa River
St Cloud
Taylors Falls
Wisconsin
Willmar
Stillwater
45°N
Chippewa Falls
Wausau
MINNEAPOLIS
St Paul
Lake Minnetonka
Eau Claire
Hastings
Minnesota River
Red Wing
Pepin
South Dakota
Wisconsin River
Mankato
Rochester
Winona
La Crescent
La Crosse
Lanesboro
Alberta Lea
Harmony
Sioux Falls
Iowa
W Fork Des Moines River
Mississippi River
43°N
To Madison & Milwaukee
Sioux City
Waterloo

Minnesota and, armed with guns they had acquired from the French, pushed the Sioux southwest onto the prairie.

The area east of the Mississippi River became part of the US Northwest Territories in 1787, and the area west of the Mississippi was acquired in the 1803 Louisiana Purchase. The Sioux were pressured to sign treaties giving up their lands on the west side of the Mississippi. With that, the land was open for development, and by the 1850s new settlers poured into the region.

Logging was the territory's first boom industry, and soon there were water-powered sawmills at Minneapolis, St Paul and Stillwater.

Shortly after its admission to the union, Minnesota became the first state to send volunteers to fight the Civil War. A year later, in 1862, the Sioux, who were now largely restricted to reservations, took advantage of the absence of many of the fighting-age men to launch an uprising. Bu after a series of bloody battles, the Siou were again subdued.

The population boomed in the 1880s with mass immigration (especially fron Scandinavia), the development of iro mines in the state's northeast, and the ex pansion of the railroads. Since the 1920s, de pleted forests and larger farms have mean a declining rural population, but industr and urban areas have grown steadily.

The depression of the 1930s was brutal i Minnesota, and like elsewhere in the Unite States, it took the beginning of war to spu recovery. Huge amounts of timber and or were required for the WWII military effor and those industries were modernized. Th 1950s saw a large increase in manufacturing with chemicals, heavy machinery, electroni equipment and, later, computers all becom ing significant.

As Fit as a 78-Year-Old Swede

Perhaps it's the Scandinavian heritage, but Minnesotans take good advantage of the state's enviable hiking, skiing and bicycling trail networks.

Easily accessed and available to all for an hour or a day are the state's biking trails. There are 360 miles of state rail trails, converted train lines ideal for cycling. Most are paved. Three of the best known are the Willard Munger, south of Duluth to Hinckley; the Paul Bunyan, from Brainerd to Hackensack; and the Root River, from Fountain, through Lansboro, to beyond Rushford. Each offers miles of wooded scenery with lakes or rivers. Bike rentals are available at all three.

In addition, there are countless miles of mountain-biking trails in the state and national forests. Most state parks also have designated bike trails. Lutsen and Giants Ridge ski areas, in the northeast, become challenging bike parks in summer. Contact the Minnesota Office of Tourism for its biking guide and further details.

Geography

Minnesota has three main geographi regions. The Superior upland, largely lake filled forest, covers the entire northeaster half of the state. This is a continuation of th rugged Canadian Shield, a vast mass o ancient rock that covers much of Canada The shield is the first part of the continen that was permanently raised above se level. The rocky surface is only thinl covered in soil, if at all, and the lower por tions are generally filled with water. In som shield regions, as much as 40% of the land i covered in water.

Glaciers did not have a dramatic effe on this region, leaving it the state's roughes terrain. The northeast corner, known as 'th arrowhead' for its shape, has Eagle Moun tain, Minnesota's highest elevation (230 feet). The state's highest waterfalls are als found here.

The upland area was covered with pin trees and hardwoods until the massiv logging of the 19th century, but many area have now regrown and are managed as na tional forests.

The 'young drift plains' cover the wes central and much of the southern areas c the state. This is an area of gently rollin ch agricultural land. Crops and pastures ıake it the state's most productive farmnd. Within this area, the portions littered ith glacial moraines are hillier, with lots of kes; the area south of Detroit Lakes is an xample. To the west lies the Great Plains.

The state's southeastern corner is classed driftless area (meaning it missed the flatning effects of the last ice-age glaciers). The nd known as the bluff country is an appealg mix of rivers and streams, rocky outcrops, eep valleys and towering bluffs. Most resients live in or near this green, undulating gion south of the Twin Cities and edged by e Mississippi. That mighty river begins its urney at Lake Itasca. Other important vers are the Red, Minnesota and St Croix. bout 5% of the land is covered in lakes.

Iational Parks & Protected Areas

Indeveloped Voyageurs, in the far north on e border with Canada, is the lone national ark in Minnesota, although there are two ational monuments: Grand Portage, in the ortheastern arrowhead and also on the order, and Pipestone, in the far southwest. 1 addition, there are two fabulous, huge, ild national forests, Chippewa and Suerior, both in the north. Each of these has stablished campsites and trails for hiking, iking, skiing and more. Superior contains e vast Boundary Waters Canoe Area Vilderness.

Minnesota has an excellent system of 68 ate parks. A permit costing $4/day, $20/ ear is required to enter. Camping reservaons (☎ 800-246-2267) can be made for any ate park from three to 90 days in advance sing a credit card. Some sites are held on a rst come, first served basis. Sites range om $8 to $15. Cabins can also be booked, eir rates and types vary from $36 to $150. n average cabin, good for four people, ight include a shower, cooking facilities nd bedding for about $80.

Camping and recreation are also possible the 57 state forests. Some of these areas re free, others charge minimal fees. The amping season, whether in public parks or private campgrounds, is generally from Iay to October, with only late June, July and August being busy. Some places permit winter camping, but expect diminished or minimal services.

For further information, see the visitors' centers and ranger stations listed in the text or get in touch with the Department of Natural Resources (☎ 888-646-6367, www.dnr.state.mn.us), 500 Lafayette Rd, St Paul, MN 55155-4040.

Government & Politics

Through its early years the state was a Republican stronghold. Since about 1930, both parties have been elected fairly equally, although the fame of noted Democrats such as Eugene McCarthy, Hubert Humphrey and Walter Mondale may make it seem otherwise. In recent decades, both parties within the state have become somewhat distinct from their national counterparts, the Democrats aligning with farm-labor (Hubert Humphrey came from the Democratic-Farm-Labor Party, a descendant of the original Farm-Labor Party) and the Republicans frequently running as independents.

Since 1998, the Reform Party governor Jesse Ventura, a former pro wrestler, has broken all the molds with his outspoken, freewheeling, straightforward approach. Whether it will work twice is unknown (he's up for reelection in 2002), but people certainly have noticed the breath of fresh air. The Midwest, often considered staid and conservative by East and West Coast observers, can now lay claim to the first politician who is also available as a plastic action figure.

Arts

The Twin Cities dominate the state's cultural activities and attractions and do so in grand fashion. The Minneapolis Institute of Arts is the state's premier art museum, and the Walker Art Center has an excellent collection of modern art with a renowned outdoor sculpture garden.

Minneapolis and St Paul have a very active theater scene, including the Guthrie Theater, nationally recognized for its highquality productions. The acclaimed St Paul Chamber Orchestra and Minneapolis Symphony Orchestra are supplemented by the well-regarded Minnesota Opera. Clubs in and around the downtown run the gamut of first-class nightlife, featuring jazz, blues, comedy, dinner theater and more.

Minnesota native Garrison Keillor hosts live broadcasts of his immensely popular weekly radio show, *A Prairie Home Companion*, from the Fitzgerald Theater in St Paul. His often humorous tales, which have been compiled into enjoyable books, are great for getting a crash course on revealing aspects of the Minnesota psyche and culture (see Literature in Facts about the Great Lakes).

Duluth, to the northeast, has its own cultural institutions, such as the art museums and performance halls of the Depot and the Duluth–Superior Symphony Orchestra. Well-supported and well-attended summer theater is found across the state in towns such as Bemidji and Lanesboro.

There is much preserved 19th-century architecture in addition to some striking contemporary design in the Twin Cities.

Information

The Minnesota Office of Tourism (☎ 651-296-5029, 800-657-3700, www.exploreminnesota.com) is at 121 E 7th Place, St Paul, MN 55101. It operates 12 Travel Information Centers (TICs) around the state, mostly at busy state boundary crossings. They are all open year-round, except the one at Grand Portage, near the Ontario border, which is open May through October. Local chambers of commerce and Convention & Visitors' Bureaus are ubiquitous.

Special Events

January

John Beargrease Sled Dog Marathon – a famous, grueling race running between Duluth and Grand Marais

Winter Carnival – in St Paul, featuring ice sculptures and other frigid festivities

August

Bayfront Blues Festival – held in Duluth

Minneapolis Aquatennial – a 10-day water-based event, with boat races at the suburban lakes

Minnesota State Fair – held in St Paul

Native American Powwows – take place in sever central Minnesota communities, such as thos around Leech Lake

WE Fest – a major country music event in Detro Lakes

Food & Drinks

Fish is very popular, especially walleye, lak trout and whitefish, which turn up on menu across the state. Friday fish fries are foun everywhere. Widely available is wild ric grown in the north and served in a variet of ways, including delicious soup. It crunchy texture and slightly nutty flavo add distinction to any dish.

The German and Scandinavian back ground of much of the population is some times evident. Beer and bratwurst ar staples of many casual get-togethers an happy hours. Among the Swedish plates yo may see offered in restaurants are *lefse* (thin potato pancake served with butter an sugar) and meatballs. Herring and oper faced sandwiches, often featuring fish, ar also standards. Lutefisk, cod that has bee soaked in lye and later boiled, is not a common as it once was. *Kringgle* is a co feecake served at Easter and Christmas.

Dinners in restaurants generally cos between $10 and $20 anywhere in the stat In the Twin Cities, where cuisines fror around the world (notably Asia) are avai able, it's possible (but not necessary) to ru up bills three times that. Although region or idiosyncratic foods are not readily avai able, some of the state's best restaurant found in the Twin Cities, offer Midwester cuisine, which uses fresh, local ingredien and produce, including game (venisor pheasant), fish (trout, whitefish, walleye) wild rice, local mushrooms, blueberries an cranberries. There may also be some Nativ American influence, such as buffalo meat.

Getting There & Around

The Twin Cities airport, just 9 miles fror either town, is a major Midwest termina Most Midwestern cities can be reache from there in about an hour. Canada i linked directly as well.

Amtrak passes through on its *Empire Builder* route from Chicago to Seattle. The main stops include Winona, Red Wing, Detroit Lakes and Minneapolis–St Paul. Amtrak's bus service makes a run from St Paul to Duluth.

Greyhound connects most major cities and runs north through the center of the state, covering many of the lakeland towns. Jefferson Bus Lines covers the southeast, including Rochester and Winona. Lorenz Bus Lines connects the Twin Cities to Grand Rapids and heads into the Iron Range, with stops including Hibbing and Virginia.

The state is well-served by interstates, with I-90 and I-94 crossing east-west. Going north-south, I-35 links the Twin Cities and Duluth. Hwy 61, of Bob Dylan fame, is a well-known scenic route on the eastern edge of the state.

Southeastern Minnesota

Minneapolis–St Paul

• pop 2.3 million

Commonly known as the Twin Cities, the sprawling Minneapolis–St Paul metropolitan area is the financial, commercial and cultural center of the state. Known more as a congenial place to live than a compelling tourist destination, it's pure US heartland – industrious, prosperous and heavily into sports and shopping. But the Twin Cities also have more theaters, dance companies and concert venues per person than anywhere except New York. Together they boast a formidable list of galleries and museums, and to top it off, they have a wide array of American and ethnic eateries.

Midwest visitors can easily spend a few days exploring the sites of the clean, safe, central cores and neighborhoods. Minneapolis is the state's largest city; St Paul is the capital.

HISTORY

French trappers and fur traders were the first Europeans in the area, and Belgian missionary Louis Hennepin preached to Indians here in 1680. Fort d'Huillier was established in 1700 in Mankato, about an hour's drive to the southwest. Zebulon Pike explored to the upper reaches of the Mississippi in 1804, a year after the USA acquired the region as part of the Louisiana Purchase. Fort Snelling, the most remote outpost of the USA's Northwest Territories, was built in 1820.

The first flour mills were built along the river in the 1820s, using the power of the St Anthony waterfall. Starting in the mid-19th century, Minneapolis grew as a processing center for wheat from the prairies and timber from the north. For a time the falls were the highest navigable point on the Mississippi and a natural terminus for river traffic. In the late 19th century, an important

Highlights

- The history and art of the Twin Cities' museums
- Crisscrossing the Mississippi for views, pretty villages and eagle-watching
- Bicycling the southeast's ancient bluff country
- Enjoying a meal amid the charm of Lanesboro

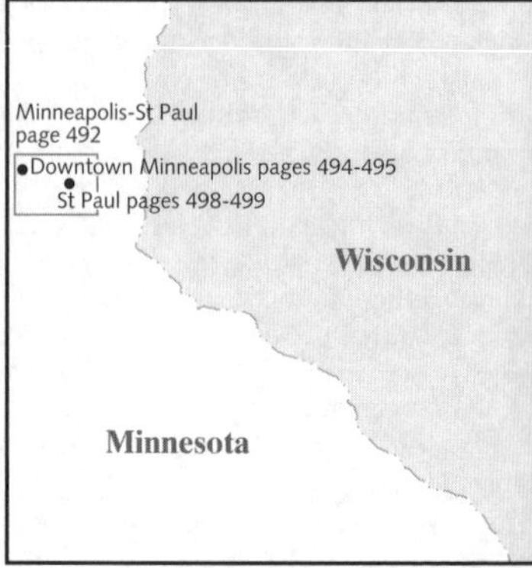

ailroad bridge at the falls contributed to apid industrial growth, which was fueled by nmigration. Even today, St Paul has a more ierman and Irish heritage, while Minneap-lis is still noticeably Nordic.

ORIENTATION

'he Twin Cities form a metropolis on both ides of the generally hidden Mississippi River. Development patterns have meant he waterway is not often visible, but ecent thinking suggests a new apprecia-ion for and focus on the river may be orthcoming.

On the west side, downtown Minneapolis – he heart of the two cities – is a modern grid f high-rise buildings. Pedestrian-only Nicol-et Mall is the bustling, 12-block-long main hopping and eating street in the very con-emporary downtown. An extensive network f enclosed overhead walkways, called kyways, links much of the center. St Paul has hem too, but the system is not as widespread. 'aken together, there are about five miles of kyways. They are wonderful in winter but an leave the surface streets somewhat de-erted. In summer most people prefer to be out on the sidewalks. Either tourist office can upply maps of both networks.

In Minneapolis the skyways connect many prominent downtown buildings. Among them are the IDS Building, with its eye-catching Crystal Court, on Nicollet at S 8th St; the Norwest Tower, on Marquette Ave at 7th St S; and the Hubert H Humphrey Metrodome, a few blocks southeast, with its air-supported roof.

The Warehouse District, just northwest of the center, has the Twin Cities' most concentrated nightlife. Most of the major arts halls are also on this side of the river.

Downtown living has really caught on, and central Minneapolis is now one of the nation's booming residential markets. That can only mean a still more lively and vital core. The Mississippi River area, to the east of the center, and Loring Park, to the south, are two districts with ongoing in-fill housing developments (or, developments built in underused areas).

Downtown St Paul is 10 miles to the east on I-94. Smaller and quieter, it has retained more of its historic character, although construction continues to add to its numerous high-rise buildings and enclosed skyways. The main artery is 7th St.

Both central areas include many good attractions and are well served by local buses.

RICHARD CUMMINS

Minneapolis, home of the first flour mills

SOUTHEASTERN MINNESOTA

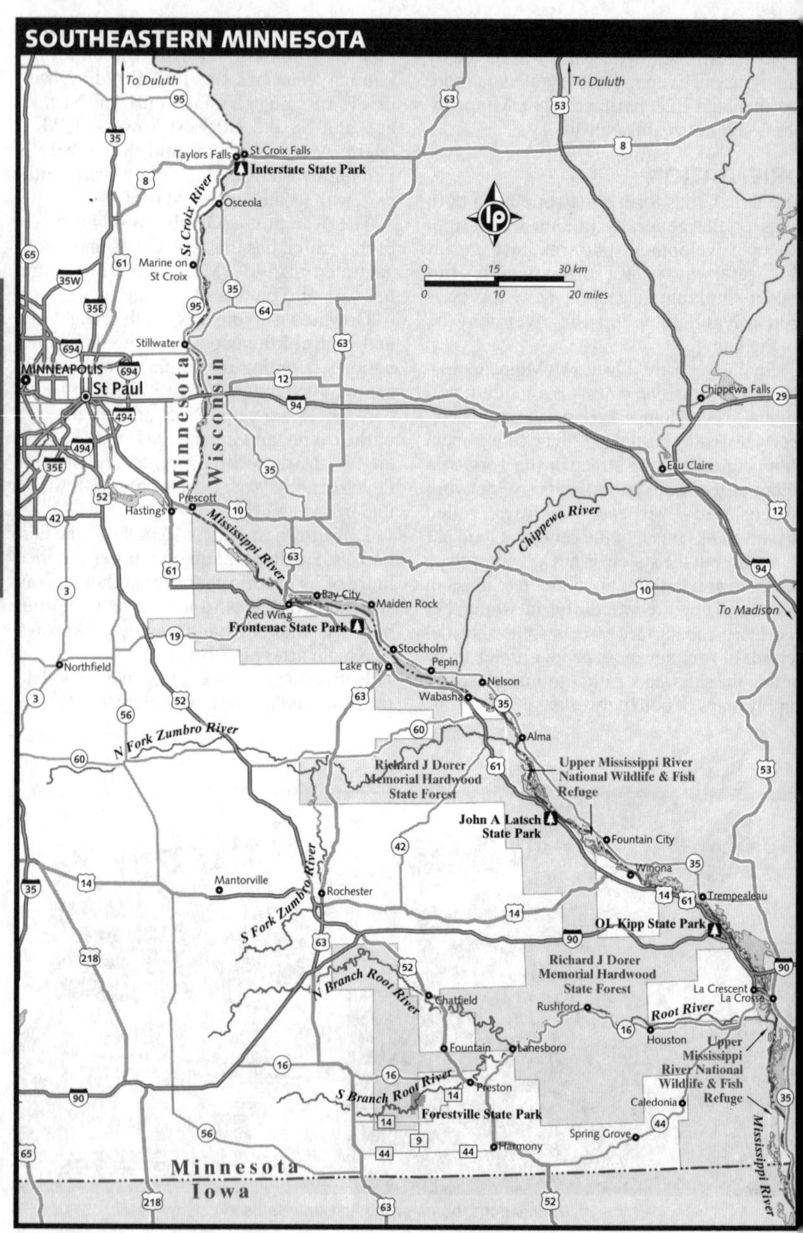

Note that in 'Minny' the directional street designations come after the street name, eg, 7th St S. In St Paul, they usually come before, eg, W 5th St.

In either city, but especially Minneapolis, downtown parking is costly – and scarce. Use the central parking complexes known as ramps, which are well marked with street signs.

Suburbs sprawl in every direction, interspersed with lakes and parks, for which you really need a car (beware: on the highways the locals drive very fast.

INFORMATION

Tourist Offices

The Greater Minneapolis Convention & Visitors Association (☎ 612-348-4700, 888-676-5757, fax 612-335-5841, www.minneapolis.org) is at 4000 Multifoods Tower, 33 6th St S downtown. It's open 8 am to 5 pm Monday to Friday.

For walk-in tourist information, the better bet is the visitors' center (☎ 612-335-5827) at street level in the City Center complex at the corner of Nicollet Mall and 7th St S. The door is opposite Dayton's department store. It's open 10 am to 7 pm weekdays, 10 am to 6 pm Saturday, noon to 5 pm Sunday. For further information on the city, try the Downtown Council's Web site at www.downtownmpls.com, with parking, retail and event information.

The very helpful St Paul CVB (☎ 651-265-4900, 800-627-6101, fax 651-265-4999, www.stpaulcvb.org) is at 175 W Kellogg Blvd, though it's open only 8:30 am to 5 pm Monday to Friday. It's in the huge River-Centre convention complex, which also has the Wilkins Auditorium and the sports arena.

Money

The main branch of the Norwest Bank (☎ 612-667-7990) is at the southwest corner of 6th St and Marquette Ave in Minneapolis. They can exchange foreign currency.

Post & Communications

General-delivery mail goes to the main post office in Minneapolis, 1st St S and Marquette Ave, by the river. The address is 100 S 1st St, Minneapolis, MN 55401-9998. It's open Monday to Friday 7 am to 11 pm, Saturday 9 am to 1 pm.

Note that the Minneapolis and environs telephone area code is ☎ 612 or 763. For the St Paul area, it's ☎ 651. To call from one side of the Twin Cities to the other, include the area code *without* prefacing it with a ☎ 1. It is not considered a long-distance call.

Bookstores

Vast Barnes & Noble (☎ 612-371-4443) is at 801 Nicollet Mall at 8th St, kitty-corner from Dayton's department store. The University of Minnesota has two locations, the east-bank store (☎ 612-626-1896) at 231 Pillsbury Drive SE and the St Paul branch, at 1420 Eckles Ave. Also in St Paul, Ruminator books (☎ 651-699-0587), at 1648 Grand Ave, is famous for taking that name after selling its former one, the Hungry Mind, to a 'dot-com' company. One of the oldest bookstores in the country, the feminist-oriented Amazon Bookstore (☎ 612-338-6560), which sued Amazon.com over the similarity in names, is at 4432 Chicago Ave S in Minneapolis. The Minnesota Women's press runs a small feminist bookstore (☎ 651-646-3968) at 771 Raymond Ave in St Paul.

Other choices include Brother's Touch (☎ 612-377-6279) at 2327 Hennepin, Once Upon a Crime (☎ 612-870-3785) 604 W 26th St and Micawbers (☎ 651-646-5506) at 2238 Carter Ave in St Paul.

The Map Store (☎ 651-227-6277), in the World Trade Center at 30 E 7th St, St Paul, has everything from canoe to country maps. There's also Books for Travel (☎ 651-225-8006) at 857 Grand Ave in St Paul. Corner stores and gas stations sell city and district maps.

Libraries

The Minneapolis Public Library (☎ 612-869-8863), 300 Nicollet Mall between 3rd and 4th Sts, has Internet access. It's open 9 am to 9 pm Monday to Thursday, 9 am to 6 pm Friday, 10 am to 6 pm Saturday. The building also houses the Minneapolis Planetarium.

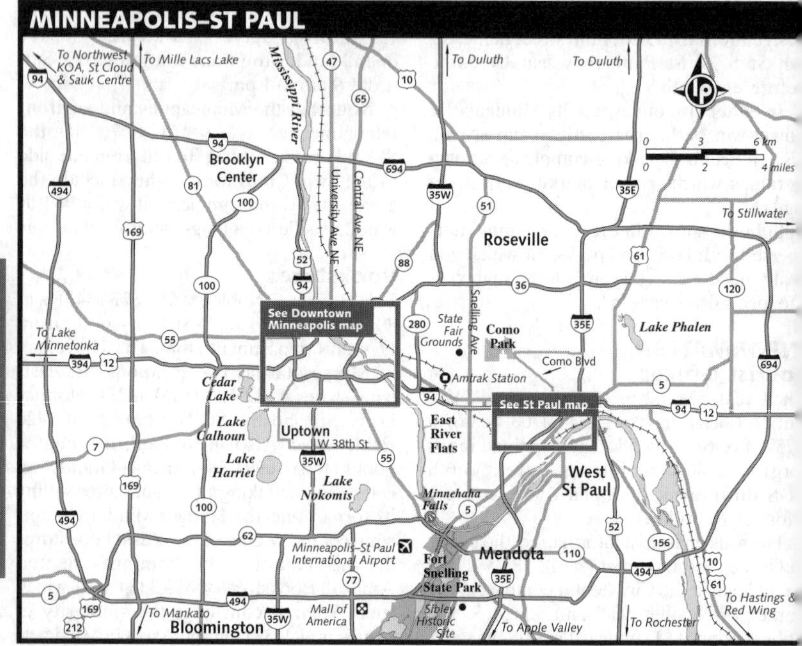

Medical Services

In Minneapolis, Hennepin County General Hospital (☎ 612-347-2121) is at 701 Park Ave S near the Metrodome. In St Paul, United Hospital (☎ 651-220-8000) is at 333 N Smith Ave between Kellogg and Grand Sts.

Gay & Lesbian Travelers

The Out Front Helpline (☎ 612-822-8661) serves the Twin Cities' gay, lesbian and bisexual community.

For venues and events, check the free weekly, *Focus Point*, and *Minnesota Women's Free Press* (www.womenspress.com), a free biweekly. See the Bookstores section, earlier in this chapter, for information about the Free Press bookstore and Amazon Feminist Press.

MINNEAPOLIS Neighborhoods

Heading up Groveland Terrace, west of Loring Park and just south of the Walker Art Center, leads to **Lowry Hill**, with a fine view, where scraping together the rent is not an issue: Groveland Terrace and especially Mt Curve Ave have been home to monied Minnesotans since the 19th century. The grand residences display all manner of architectural styles.

Following Hennepin Ave south leads to **Uptown**, a busy area of shops and restaurants southwest of downtown Minneapolis. This is a varied district centered around the corner of Hennepin Ave S and Lake St, with good places to eat and some upmarket shops. Numerous bookstores and cinemas and a few well-known nightspots all blend into a lively mix. It stays active until the wee hours. Lake Calhoun is west along Lake St W.

Across downtown, by the Mississippi, a small part of the University of Minnesota is on the west side of the river in the **West Bank**. The area is best known for its theater district, at the corner of 4th St S and Riverside Ave, although that label may be tretching it, even for marketing planners: There are only a couple of theaters, which do draw evening visitors, but the area seems to be sliding a bit, especially at the Five Corners section, around Cedar Ave S and 4th St S. There are a couple of major camping and outdoor stores and several restaurant-pubs with outdoor seating where Washington Ave S and 15th Ave S collide.

The **East Bank**, based around the corner of Washington Ave SE and Oak St SE, is a studenty ghetto now becoming more mixed. There are good eateries and some hotels in the vicinity. Indeed, it's now calling itself **Stadium Village**. With the Metrodome just west down Washington Ave, area businesses get especially busy on game and event days. The university's Weisman Art Museum is here, too.

North of the campus, above University Ave, is **Dinkytown**, based at 14th Ave SE and 4th St SE, an area dense with bleary-eyed students at cafés. A few cheap places to eat and several bookstores round out this small commercial area.

Also see Summit–Selby Neighborhood, below.

Walker Art Center & Sculpture Garden

The center (☎ 612-375-7600) is at attractive Loring Park, a few blocks west of the south end of Nicollet Mall on Vineland Place. From the park, a very sculptural pedestrian bridge crosses I-94 to the center's door.

Inside is a strong permanent collection of 20th-century art and photography (including big-name US painters and some great US pop art). There are also temporary exhibitions and performance spaces. Roy Lichtenstein, Georgia O'Keeffe and Mark Rothko are among the painters represented. Open 10 am to 5 pm Monday to Saturday (until 8 pm Thursday), 11 am to 5 pm Sunday; $4 (free on Thursday).

Across from the Walker Art Center is the Sculpture Garden, some seven acres studded with imaginative contemporary works; admission is free.

Minneapolis Institute of Arts

This sizable three-story gallery (☎ 612-870-3131), 2400 3rd Ave S, south of downtown, is a veritable history of art, especially of American and European painting. Many world heavyweights are represented, such as Georgio de Chirico, Jasper Johns, Pablo Picasso and Andy Warhol. There is also an excellent African section. Don't miss the American West collection either. Open 10 am to 5 pm Tuesday to Saturday (until 9 pm Thursday), noon to 5 pm Sunday; free ($5 for special exhibits).

American Swedish Institute

This superb Romanesque mansion (☎ 612-871-4907), 2600 Park Ave, tells the story of America's Swedes. It houses artifacts and antiques from the time when Minneapolis had a bigger Swedish population than most cities in Sweden. Open noon to 4 pm Tuesday to Saturday (until 8 pm Wednesday), 1 to 5 pm Sunday; $4/3 adults/children.

Minneapolis Planetarium

The Minneapolis Planetarium (☎ 612-630-6150), 300 Nicollet Mall between 3rd and 4th Sts, presents regular star shows and some special events, such as a summer solstice celebration.

Mississippi Mile

On the north edge of downtown at the foot of Portland Ave, Mississippi Mile encompasses the **St Anthony Falls Historic District**. The worthwhile 2-mile self-guided recreation and heritage trail (1 mile per riverside) provides interesting history and the city's best access to the banks of Old Man River. It seems miles from downtown Minneapolis' bustle.

St Anthony Falls was the power source for the area's early mills and was later fitted with locks so river traffic could continue upstream. The car-free Stone Arch Bridge gives a good view of this much-modified watercourse. Of the 29 dams on the river from Minnesota to the Gulf of Mexico, the lock and dam here are the farthest north.

On the north side of the river, Main St in the southwest section of the **Old St Anthony**

DOWNTOWN MINNEAPOLIS

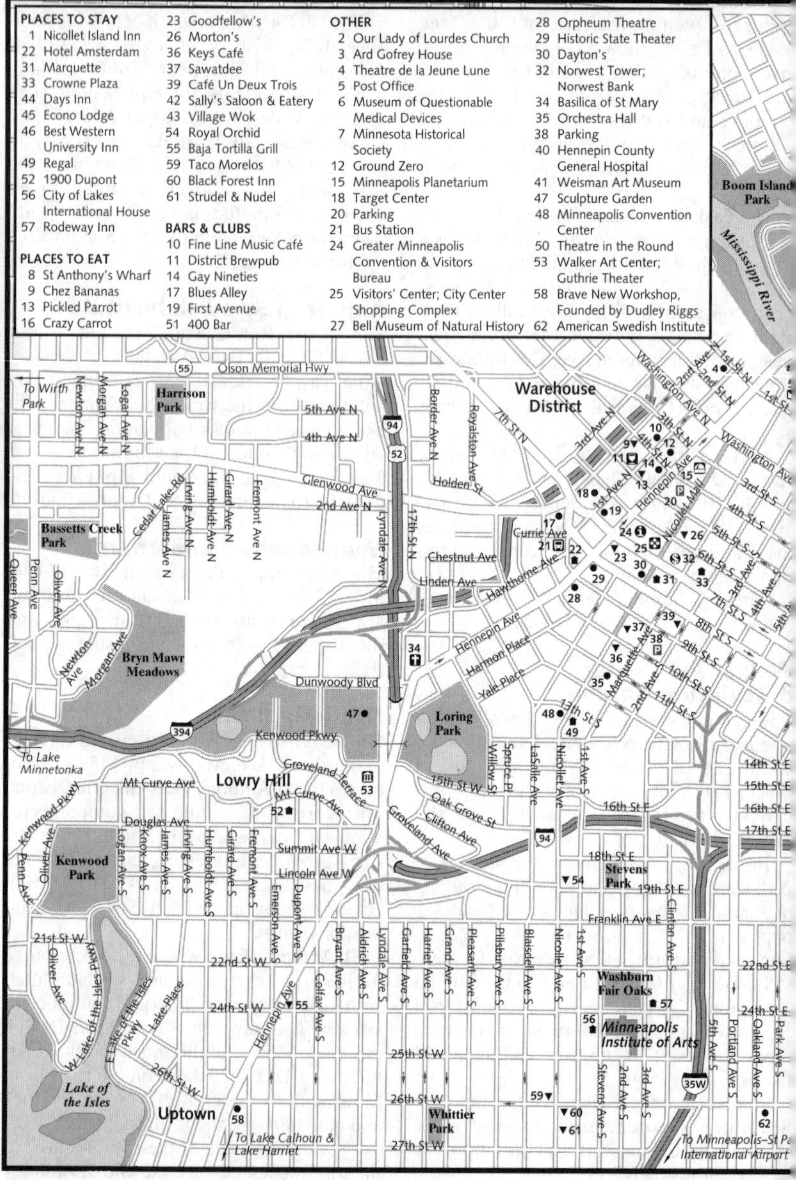
PLACES TO STAY
1 Nicollet Island Inn
22 Hotel Amsterdam
31 Marquette
33 Crowne Plaza
44 Days Inn
45 Econo Lodge
46 Best Western University Inn
49 Regal
52 1900 Dupont
56 City of Lakes International House
57 Rodeway Inn
PLACES TO EAT
8 St Anthony's Wharf
9 Chez Bananas
13 Pickled Parrot
16 Crazy Carrot
23 Goodfellow's
26 Morton's
36 Keys Café
37 Sawatdee
39 Café Un Deux Trois
42 Sally's Saloon & Eatery
43 Village Wok
54 Royal Orchid
55 Baja Tortilla Grill
59 Taco Morelos
60 Black Forest Inn
61 Strudel & Nudel
BARS & CLUBS
10 Fine Line Music Café
11 District Brewpub
14 Gay Nineties
17 Blues Alley
19 First Avenue
51 400 Bar
OTHER
2 Our Lady of Lourdes Church
3 Ard Gofrey House
4 Theatre de la Jeune Lune
5 Post Office
6 Museum of Questionable Medical Devices
7 Minnesota Historical Society
12 Ground Zero
15 Minneapolis Planetarium
18 Target Center
20 Parking
21 Bus Station
24 Greater Minneapolis Convention & Visitors Bureau
25 Visitors' Center; City Center Shopping Complex
27 Bell Museum of Natural History
28 Orpheum Theatre
29 Historic State Theater
30 Dayton's
32 Norwest Tower; Norwest Bank
34 Basilica of St Mary
35 Orchestra Hall
38 Parking
40 Hennepin County General Hospital
41 Weisman Art Museum
47 Sculpture Garden
48 Minneapolis Convention Center
50 Theatre in the Round
53 Walker Art Center; Guthrie Theater
58 Brave New Workshop, Founded by Dudley Riggs
62 American Swedish Institute
Boom Island Park
Mississippi River
Warehouse District
Harrison Park
Bassetts Creek Park
Bryn Mawr Meadows
Loring Park
Lowry Hill
Kenwood Park
Stevens Park
Washburn Fair Oaks
Minneapolis Institute of Arts
Lake of the Isles
Uptown
Whittier Park
Olson Memorial Hwy
Glenwood Ave
Hennepin Ave
Nicollet Mall
Dunwoody Blvd
Kenwood Pkwy
Franklin Ave E
To Wirth Park
To Lake Minnetonka
To Lake Calhoun & Lake Harriet
To Minneapolis–St Pa
International Airport

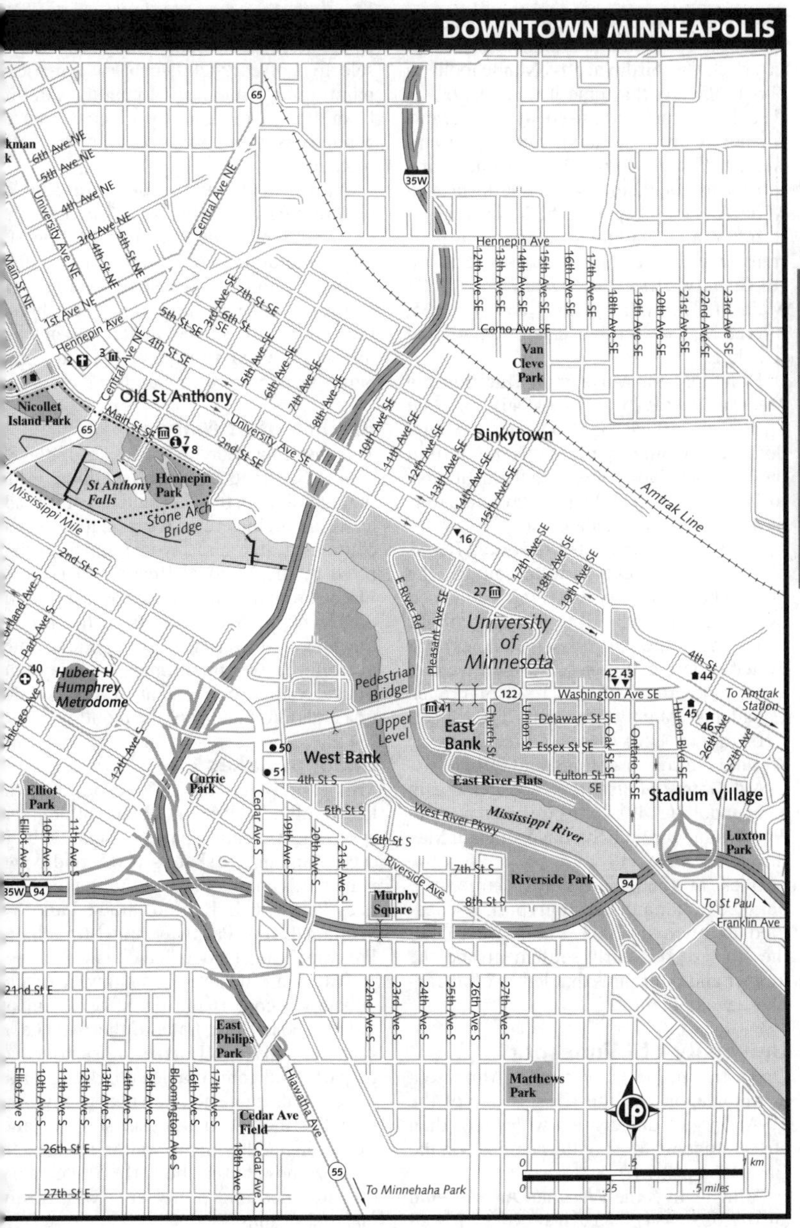
DOWNTOWN MINNEAPOLIS
Old St Anthony
Dinkytown
University of Minnesota
Nicollet Island Park
St Anthony Falls
Hennepin Park
Stone Arch Bridge
Hubert H Humphrey Metrodome
Van Cleve Park
Pedestrian Bridge
Upper Level
East Bank
West Bank
East River Flats
Mississippi River
Stadium Village
Luxton Park
Riverside Park
Murphy Square
Currie Park
Elliot Park
East Philips Park
Matthews Park
Cedar Ave Field
Amtrak Line
To Amtrak Station
To St Paul
To Minnehaha Park
Washington Ave SE
University Ave SE
Hennepin Ave
Como Ave SE
Hiawatha Ave
Riverside Ave
Cedar Ave S
Franklin Ave
West River Pkwy
Mississippi Mile

district has a stretch of redeveloped buildings housing shops, restaurants and bars. This was, in effect, the birthplace of Minneapolis in about 1850. At that time it was part of the Red River cart trail, used by immigrants (mainly Scottish settlers) traveling toward western Canada from what became Manitoba; some of them headed south through Minnesota to this spot on the Mississippi.

Information and tours along the heritage trail are available at the Minnesota Historical Society office (☎ 612-627-5433), 125 Main St. The walking tours are about $5, offered May to October; call for details and schedule.

Don't miss the **Museum of Questionable Medical Devices** (☎ 612-379-4046), 201 Main St, displaying stacks of wacky quackery. And don't be too smug – some of this stuff is from the 1980s and '90s! Open 5 to 9 pm Tuesday to Thursday, noon to 9 pm Friday and Saturday, noon to 5 pm Sunday; free.

On Prince St behind the reworked Riverplace building is **Our Lady of Lourdes**, the oldest church in town (1857). It's still used by the descendants of the French Catholic community, and *tortieres* (meat pies) are available here daily. These inexpensive pies are a popular traditional food of French Canadians. (Many of the early French settlers in the USA arrived via Quebec.) Around the corner at Bank and Ortman Sts is **Ard Gofrey House**, the oldest house in Minneapolis (1849). Tours are given noon to 3 pm Friday through Sunday from late May through September.

Back at the riverfront, a large new heritage center and mill-ruins park is scheduled to open in 2002. Plans are to tell the story of this early settlement and the lumber and flour mills that led to Minneapolis' development.

University of Minnesota

Downstream, the University of Minnesota at Minneapolis, by the river, is one of the USA's largest universities, with more than 50,000 students. Most of the campus is in the East Bank district.

A highlight is the **Weisman Art Museum** (☎ 612-625-9494), 333 River Rd E. It's an angular, irregular, stainless-steel structure by architect Frank Gehry. Exhibits include a selection of early-20th–century American painting and regularly changing exhibits from around the country. Open 10 am to 5 pm Tuesday to Friday, 11 am to 5 pm weekends; free.

Also on campus the **Bell Museum of Natural History** (☎ 612-624-7083), at the corner of University Ave and 17th Ave SE displays dioramas of Minnesota's wildlife among exhibits on the state's geographic features. Changing shows present a broad range of natural subject matter. Open 9 am to 5 pm Tuesday to Friday, 10 am to 5 pm Saturday, noon to 5 pm Sunday; $3.

Basilica of St Mary

This inspiring church (☎ 612-333-1381), 88 17th St N, with its 200-foot-high dome, is the oldest basilica in the US (built in 1913; 'basilica' is an architectural term relating to the church's design and layout) and is recognized by the National Register of Historic Places. From downtown, the basilica is south on Hennepin Ave across from the Loring Playhouse, which is near Loring Park. Tours are offered by appointment Tuesday and Thursday afternoons and at 10:30 am on the first and third Sunday of the month.

Chain of Lakes

Minneapolis has the unique boast of 22 lakes within its city limits. Many offer green space and recreation paths popular with bicyclists and in-line skaters. If you're driving, main roads linking the lakes are Lake of the Isles Parkway, E Lake Calhoun Parkway, William Berry Parkway and Minnehaha Parkway, but get a detailed city map.

Within a mile or two southwest of the downtown core is the oasislike Chain of Lakes. Cedar Lake, Lake of the Isles, Lake Calhoun and Lake Harriet are surrounded by parks and comfortable suburbs. The last three are all connected by a bike trail. Other activities include boating in summer and ice-skating and skiing in winter. It's hard to visualize now, but in the early 20th century this groomed and pretty area was mostly malarial swamp.

Who Needs Facts? This Is Romance

Throughout the Twin Cities area and beyond, the traveler keeps coming across references to Hiawatha. The explanation behind them is nearly as vague as our hazy recollections of the familiar name.

We know the name thanks to *The Song of Hiawatha*, one of the most famous works by Henry Wadsworth Longfellow. This epic poem from 1855 recounts the triumphs and tragedies of the Ojibway–Chippewa leader Hiawatha and his wife, Minnehaha. The sympathetic narrative hails the wise and true ways of the continent's native peoples and the loss of innocence with the coming of the Europeans.

While the spirit of the poem still resonates, a few points could use clarification. Longfellow never visited this area. Rather, as he did for his Acadian poem, *Evangeline*, he gathered research by reading the work of explorers and other writers. Hiawatha was actually an Iroquois Confederacy leader in the 16th century who came from somewhere in the New York–Quebec region. The model for Longfellow's tale was likely a legendary Ojibway figure named Nanabozho.

Nevertheless, the story of Minnehaha Falls, although not perfect history, has served to protect an inspiring spot of natural beauty within a modern city.

Outdoor activities at **Wirth Park**, just west of downtown, run the gamut. **Thomas Beach**, on Lake Calhoun, is popular for swimming. Calhoun is the largest of the inner-city lakes and entices good-size crowds on warm summer weekends. Canoes can be rented. A restored streetcar shuttles passengers the mile to Lake Harriet from May to October; catch it by the water pump across from the band shell on the west side of Lake Calhoun.

Summer concerts are regularly scheduled at the conspicuous castlelike band shell on Lake Harriet. There's another beach at Lake Nokomis.

Also visit **Minnehaha Park**, south of downtown, off Hiawatha Ave (Hwy 55), one block south of Minnehaha Parkway. The highlight is lovely 50-foot-high Minnehaha Falls, made famous by Longfellow's narrative poem *Song of Hiawatha*, published in 1855. Though Longfellow never actually visited, his romantic historic tale of the Indian leader and his wife, Minnehaha, remains an American favorite. The 'laughing waters' and their gorge are visited by a half million people annually.

Also in the park is **Minnehaha Depot**, the embellished train station of 1875, now a small, free museum.

Call the Parks Board (☎ 612-661-4875) for full recreation information.

ST PAUL

Science Museum of Minnesota

The brand new, enlarged science museum (☎ 651-221-9444), 120 W Kellogg Blvd, has expanded exhibits on dinosaurs, fossils and other favorites but also a new Mississippi River display (with views of the river) and a new hands-on human body gallery. There is also a 3-D laser show and an Omnitheater screen (like an IMAX, but in a dome shape arching above and around the viewers). Open daily (call for seasonal hour variations); $5/4 adults/children ($9/6 with Omnitheater). There's parking and food outlets at the building.

Children's Museum

Young kids will also like the interactive displays here (☎ 651-225-6000), 10 W 7th St. Games and activities are designed for fun and education. Open 9 am to 5 pm daily (until 9 pm Thursday); $6, $4 for kids under three.

State Capitol

On a hill northwest of downtown, the Cass Gilbert–designed government center (☎ 651-297-3521), 75 Constitution Ave, is absolutely luscious indoors and out, from the golden horses on its giant dome down. The sheer, eye-filling splendor rivals the cathedrals of Europe. Pick up a guide

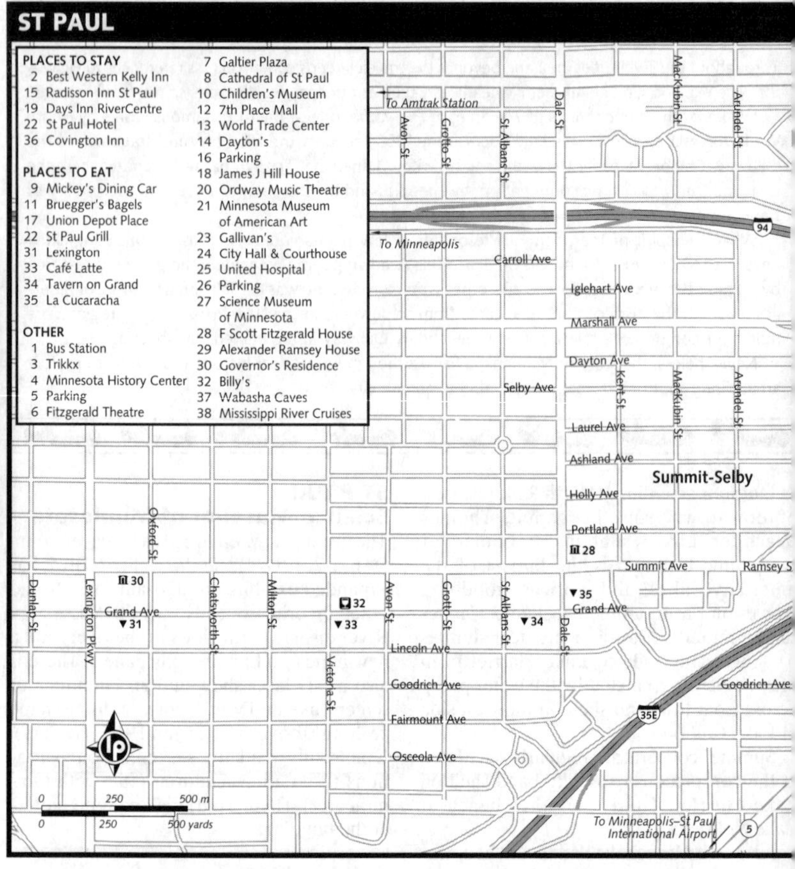

booklet in the lobby or take one of the free hourly tours, which include a rooftop stroll otherwise off-limits. The capitol also proffers good views of downtown and the cathedral. Open 9 am to 5 pm weekdays, 10 am to 4 pm Saturday, 1 to 4 pm Sunday.

Minnesota History Center

From the capitol, walk southwest across parkland to this excellent history museum and research center (☎ 651-296-6126), 345 Kellogg Blvd W at the corner of John Ireland Blvd. Interesting, varied displays ranging from early African American city life to Minnesota in winter are spread ove[r] the 3rd level. See the 10-foot, Minnesota built sailboat that made it across the At[lantic] Ocean in 1979. Also listen to th[e] exhibit of loon calls, especially if you'r[e] heading north. Other sections are on nativ[e] people and state history. Open 10 am t[o] 5 pm Wednesday to Saturday (until 8 pm Tuesday), noon to 5 pm Sunday; free.

Cathedral of St Paul

Perched on another hill nearby, at 239 Selb[y] Ave at Summit Ave, the dominating cathe[dral] is the mother church for Catholics o[f]

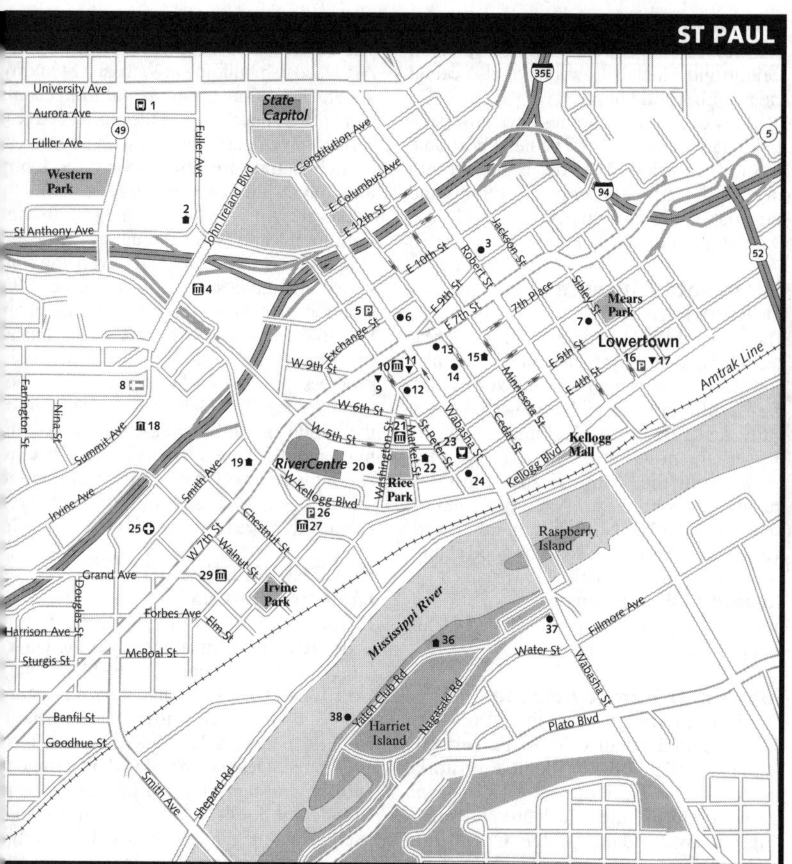

he Twin Cities. The lower level has a small nuseum. The interior, with a capacity for 000, was first used in 1915 and contains ome fine murals, glass and stonework.)pen 7:30 am to 5:30 pm daily (until 4 pm 'riday), except holidays. Tours are offered Aonday, Wednesday and Friday at 1 pm; lonations accepted.

ummit–Selby Neighborhood

'he cathedral marks the edge of this very ttractive area. This once wealthy 19th-entury district, now socioeconomically and thnically mixed, is well worth a stroll. Follow Summit Ave to Lexington St along its fine string of Victorian houses.

The palatial **James J Hill House** (☎ 651-297-2555), 240 Summit Ave, a railroad magnate's mansion, is open for tours Wednesday to Saturday ($5; call first).

The **Governor's Residence**, (☎ 651-297-8177), 1006 Summit Ave, is a 1912 English Tudor mansion with 20 rooms; visitors see only the functional lower-level sections. Don't expect to have a few words with Jesse – he's gone for the weekend. Tours are offered 1 to 3 pm Friday from May to October; free (bring a picture ID).

Writer F Scott Fitzgerald once lived at 599 Summit Ave, and authors Garrison Keillor and Sinclair Lewis have also called the neighborhood home.

Many of the area's homes have now been divided into apartments. The neighborhood, now also known as 'The Hill,' is blessed with an intriguing array of shops, restaurants and bars based along Selby Ave, Grand Ave, Dale St and Lexington Parkway.

Minnesota Museum of American Art

The turreted 1902 Landmark Center (☎ 651-292-4355), facing Rice Park at 75 W 5th St downtown, is a former federal court building. At different times it has housed the post office and FBI offices. The fine rooms and offices are now hung with art, featuring works from the 19th and 20th centuries, mainly by lesser-known American painters, many of them Minnesotans and other Midwesterners. There are also some good changing contemporary exhibits. Downstairs is the **Schubert Club Museum**, with a vast collection of keyboard instruments. Open 11 am to 4 pm Tuesday to Sunday; free.

Alexander Ramsey House

The Ramsey state historic site (☎ 651-296-0100), 265 S Exchange St, is the perfectly preserved 1872 home of the first territorial governor. The gracious Victorian mansion has period furnishings, much fine craftsmanship and costumed interpreters. Open 10 am to 3 pm Tuesday to Saturday, 1 to 3 pm Sunday from May to January (call for exact dates); $5.

Como Zoo & Park

It will never rival the world-class Minnesota Zoo, but Como (☎ 651-487-8229) at the corner of Midway Parkway and Kaufman Drive northwest of the capitol, remains a favorite local attraction. Animals include the big cats, wolves and gorillas. Open 10 am to 6 pm daily from April to September, until 4 pm the rest of the year; free.

While here, take a stroll through Como Park and see the glass-domed conservatory and Japanese garden.

Other Attractions

The **City Hall and Courthouse** is the 20-stor Art Deco–ish building at Wabasha St and W 4th St. The 30-foot sculpture out front claim a qualified superlative as the world's larges carved onyx figure. Visitors with an intere in architecture are able to view the lobb weekdays 8 am to 4:30 pm; free.

Lowertown is a historic area of forme warehouses and factories built at the beginning of the 20th century and now being converted into studios and live-work spaces. It' based around Mears Park at 5th and Sible Sts. Some restaurants have opened, but a this point the area remains a work i progress and doesn't live up to the promotional billing. The Galtier Plaza building, a the corner of 6th St and Jackson St, is stunning, and there are a couple of fine places t eat in the redone Union Depot train statio on Kellogg Blvd at Sibley St. What the are now needs more than anything else is peopl

SOUTHERN SUBURBS

Mall of America

In the southern suburb of Bloomingtor about 10 miles from either city, is the USA' largest shopping center (☎ 612-883-8800) with theaters, restaurants, bars and mor than 500 stores, all under one enormou roof. It opened in 1992 and has been bus ever since. Despite the abundant publicit and the constant ebb and flow of cars an shoppers, it doesn't dramatically distinguis itself from megamalls across the countr That is, other than statistics claiming th mall gets more visitors than the Gran Canyon or Disney World.

For the most part, the stores and th goods are all familiar, but at least you ca get the things on your list without shufflin from mall to mall all over town. On th other hand, you aren't likely to find muc that's unique, or to deal with a small, independent retailer. Prices are also pretty standard. Anchor stores are Bloomingdale Macy's, Nordstrom and Sears. Retail hour are 10 am to 9:30 pm Monday to Saturda 11 am to 7 pm Sunday.

Special features are Knott's Cam Snoopy amusement park and Underwate

Vorld aquarium. The former (☎ 612-883-:600) is a boisterous collage of rides, performances and games. Entry is free; tickets or individual activities or passes for most $21) are sold. At the aquarium visitors valk through a glass tunnel to view sharks, urtles and much more; $8/6 adults/children.

The 4th floor is given over to restaurants ınd bars. They are what might be expected – niddle of the road.

The mall is at I-494 and 24th Ave, just east of the intersection of I-494 and Hwy 77, and is well served by local buses. Drivers should watch for signs. Shoppers arrive from miles around, including from surrounding states. Although the parking areas get congested, there is almost always ample oom for browsing once inside.

ort Snelling State Park

ust east of the mall, at the junction of the Mississippi and Minnesota Rivers (at the orner of Hwys 5 and 55), is historic Fort Snelling, the state's oldest structure (☎ 612-'26-1171). The fort was established in the early 19th century as a frontier outpost in he remote Northwest Territories. Now guides in period dress show restored buildings and displays of frontier life. Open .0 am to 5 pm Monday to Saturday, noon to pm Sunday, May to October; $5. Take the Fort Snelling exit off Hwy 5 or 55.

ibley Historic Site

South across the confluence of the rivers, he Sibley Historic Site (☎ 651-452-1596), .357 Sibley Memorial Hwy (Hwy 13), off -494, preserves two stone houses from the tate's oldest white settlement. One belonged to Henry Sibley, a fur company nanager, the other to a French fur trader, ean Faribault. They now chronicle Minneota's early development. Open 10 am to pm Tuesday to Saturday, noon to 5 pm Sunday, from May 1 to October 31; admission varies but is inexpensive.

Minnesota Zoo

The nationally respected zoo (☎ 612-432-'000), in the suburb of Apple Valley, 20 niles south of town (follow the signs off I-35E), has naturalistic habitats for its 400-plus species, with an emphasis on cold-climate creatures such as beavers, cougars and wolves. It contains 2000 animals in innovative outdoor and indoor enclosures, and for that some animal experts consider it to be one of the country's top 10 zoos. The dolphin shows and marine center and 3-D IMAX cinema are additional features.

Open 9 am to 6 pm Monday to Saturday, 9 am to 8 pm Sunday, from April through early September. From September to April, hours drop to 9 am to 4 pm daily. $8/4 adults/children; the IMAX costs extra, but combination tickets offer some reduction. A visit takes several hours minimum.

LAKE MINNETONKA

It's with good reason that Minneapolis is referred to as the City of Lakes, although the entire region surrounding the Twin Cities is dotted with bodies of water. About 20 minutes west of Minneapolis on I-394 is the largest of them all, Lake Minnetonka. A side trip to the popular old resort towns of Wayzata and Excelsior makes for a quick, easy getaway from the big city bustle. A relaxed afternoon can be spent poking around the waterfront shops, sipping a caffe latte and maybe taking a cruise out on the water. The area oozes money. The lake is lined with mansions and retreats owned by some of the most prominent Twin City names, and slips rimming the shore are graced by impressive boats. Much of the surrounding landscape is leafy green, and parks are numerous.

In Excelsior, on the lake's southern shore, Water St is lined with antique and specialty stores aimed at the idle visitor. There are restaurants and a bakery too. Hwy 101 east around the lake to Wayzata affords some good vistas.

On the north side of the lake, in Wayzata, stroll along Lake St or hop on the free Towne Trolley, which putters around downtown. Boutiques, galleries, cafés and restaurants are plentiful, and the beach is never far away. At the west end of Lake St is the Depot, a former trolley station now housing the chamber of commerce. The adjacent park has the tour boat dock; tours run from late May to early September.

The restored *Minnehaha* steamboat (☎ 612-474-4801) from 1906 shuttles back and forth between the two towns on summer weekends and holidays, taking about an hour each way. Another option is the *Lady of the Lake* (☎ 612-929-1209), an old paddle wheeler, which does 90-minute narrated trips out of Excelsior Tuesday, Thursday and Sunday. Call for the schedule.

South of Excelsior in Chanhassen is the **Chanhassen Dinner Theatre** (☎ 612-934-1525), the largest dinner-theater complex in the country, with multiple stages and a good reputation. Musicals and comedies make up most of the agenda year-round. Prices range from $28 to $60 for dinner and show, depending on day of the week. Matinees are cheaper.

ORGANIZED TOURS

Reliable Gray Line (☎ 612-469-5020) offers a total of six different city and area tours. The nearly four-hour Twin City highlight bus trip is $19. There are various convenient departure points, including hotels in both downtowns. Call for the closest stop. A six-hour version includes a river cruise ($28). Others go farther afield – say, to Stillwater.

Metro Connections (☎ 612-333-8687) has a comprehensive 3½-hour narrated bus trip in and around both downtowns and out to the Mall of America, the local lakes and city landmarks ($20). Both companies operate all year.

Mississippi River Cruises (☎ 651-227-1100) has been offering quality on-the-water trips aboard paddle wheeler look-alikes since 1969. The basic two-hour trip is $10 and is offered from late May to early September. Lunch and dinner cruises are an option. Each city has a central, convenient departure dock, but call for detailed directions.

For the unique Down in History Tours (☎ 651-292-1220), at the Wabasha Caves, 215 Wabasha St S, costumed, storytelling guides bring alive the cities' gangster era. See a cave once used as a nightclub, as well as various crime sites ($4). Call for schedule and variations.

SPECIAL EVENTS

To the uninitiated, the colorfully fragran wheeling and dealing on Nicollet Mall a noon on summer Thursdays comes as a rev elation. Laden fruit and vegetable stall between 5th and 10th Sts are surrounded by customers pouring from the central offic towers. A sense of a joyous rite seems t pervade the street, with glorious gladiola everywhere. It creates a bit of pure urba magic. This inner-city farmers' market oper ates here through summer into October. I also takes place on Saturday from aroun 9 am to mid-afternoon.

The granddaddy event is the **Minnesot State Fair** (☎ 651-642-2200) a 10-day extrav aganza at the end of August that bring people to the Minnesota State Fairground off Hwy 51, from miles around. Annual at tendance is now at 1 million, including visi tors from surrounding states. The fair, firs held in 1859, features a spectrum of attrac tions, from agricultural exhibits and con tests to top-name concerts to food t carnival rides of all sorts. To give some ide of the irreverent sense of fun, look n farther than the 1999 promotion that fea tured the bronze hand of an athlete holdin a flaming corn dog as though it were th original Olympic torch. This 'Corndogu Eturnus' symbol may become a permanen emblem. Admission costs $6/5/4 adults seniors/children.

At the same time but extending throug most of September is America's largest Re naissance Festival (☎ 612-445-7361), hel weekends, with jousting, equestrian event knights in armor, Renaissance music an food. Most activities are outdoors. It's hel in Shakopee, southwest of Minneapolis. Th entrance is 2 miles south of Hwy 41, of Hwy 169 south.

Other events include:

January

Winter Carnival – at various downtown St Pau locations, with ice sculptures and other frigid fes tivities (☎ 651-223-4700)

May

Festival of Nations – a multicultural event a RiverCentre, St Paul (☎ 651-647-0191)

uly

Taste of Minnesota – a food festival held at the State Capitol grounds (☎ 651-228-0018)

innesota Fringe Theatre Festival – performances take place at Loring Park through the end of August (☎ 612-823-6005)

win Cities Ribfest – a three-day outdoor munch, usually under tents on Nicollet Mall, celebrating Minnesotans' love of ribs with competitive comparisons (☎ 612-673-0990)

ugust

inneapolis Aquatennial – 10 days of boat races, parades, concerts and water shows at the city lakes (Calhoun, Nokomis as well as others), downtown and on the Mississippi River (☎ 612-331-8371)

ctober

ktoberfest – a German festival in the St Anthony Historic District (☎ 612-673-5123) at St Anthony Main

LACES TO STAY

he closest campground is ***Northwest KOA*** *☎ 612-420-2255)*, 15 miles northwest at I-94 xit 213, with tent sites ($18), hookups ($24) nd cabins ($35). Open May to October.

inneapolis

udget ***Kaz's Home Hostel*** *(☎ 612-822-286)* is in a residential area 5 miles south of inneapolis on a city bus route. It's closed uring the day; call for reservations and ddress. There are two beds at $12 per erson including kitchen use.

Independent hostel ***City of Lakes International House*** *(☎ 612-871-3210, 2400 tevens Ave S)*, off 24th St W south of downown Minneapolis, beside the Institute of rts, is a friendly backpackers' hostel. orm beds are $17, private rooms $34, with heets included. It's open all year but reserations are recommended in summer. The ffice is open mornings and evenings but here's usually somebody around to let you n or answer the phone.

The busy ***Hotel Amsterdam*** *(☎ 612-288-459, 800-649-9500, 830 Hennepin Ave)* is a mall, European-style gay-friendly downown hotel ($30/35 single/double and up). t's in the center of activity by the Warehouse District. Unfortunately, it represents the only budget hotel in Minneapolis.

Forty minutes south of downtown, in Lakeville, is ***Motel 6*** *(☎ 612-469-1900)*, off I-35 at Hwy 70, at $42/48 June to September.

Mid-Range Motels can be found surrounding both cities around the expressways. One grouping is south of town, around I-494 near the airport. ***Super 8 Motel*** *(☎ 612-888-8800, fax 612-888-3469, 7800 2nd Ave S)* costs $67/74 mid-May to October. There are numerous places in Bloomington; both 78th St E and 80th St E have many hotels and motels. Another area of concentrated motels is Brooklyn Center, north of the city where I-694 meets I-94.

The straightforward ***Rodeway Inn*** *(☎ 612-871-2000, fax 612-874-7276, 2335 3rd Ave S)*, south of downtown across from the Institute of Arts, charges $70 single/double and has a restaurant and a downtown shuttle.

The handy East Bank area – near the university, close to the Metrodome and an easy drive to downtown – has several moderately priced choices. ***Best Western University Inn*** *(☎ 612-379-2312, fax 612-378-2382, 800-528-1234, 2600 University Ave SE)* offers an indoor pool and breakfast. Rates range from $70 to $90.

Econo Lodge *(☎ 612-331-6000, 2500 University Ave SE)* is a good value at $75 a double from May to October, and it has a pool and a coffee shop.

Rooms at the ***Comfort Inn*** *(☎ 612-560-7464, 1600 James Circle N)* are about $75, higher for special events and less in winter. Take exit 34 off I-494. West from here on I-694 will lead to still more of the familiar chain motels.

Days Inn *(☎ 612-623-3999, fax 612-331-2152, 2407 University Ave SE)* has parking, a restaurant and includes breakfast. Rates are $80/90 in summer, dropping to $65/75 in the off-season. Special events and weekends always mean higher rates.

AmericInn *(☎ 612-566-7500, fax 612-566-7500, 2050 Freeway Blvd)* is about 10 minutes from downtown. Rates start at $90 from May to October, $80 otherwise, but go up on weekends and holidays. They have an indoor pool. Take exit 34 off I-494; the motel is north of the interstate.

Top End The B&B ***1900 Dupont*** *(☎ 612-374-1973, fax 612-377-6047, 1900 Dupont Ave S)* is in Lowry Hill, within walking distance of downtown ($90 to $100 double).

Among many central business-class hotels is the ***Regal*** *(☎ 612-332-6000, 800-522-8856, @ reservations@regalmpls.com, 1313 Nicollet Mall)*, at 13th St S. Weekend specials begin at $99.

The ***Nicollet Island Inn*** *(☎ 612-331-1800, fax 612-331-6528, 95 Merriam St)*, by Mississippi Mile, is a unique renovated factory from 1893 with 24 rooms and a well-established restaurant. Rates start at $125; ask about deluxe B&B packages.

The ***Marquette*** *(☎ 612-333-4545, 800-328-4782, fax 612-288-2188, 710 Marquette Ave)* is in the landmark IDS Building, in the heart of downtown on Nicollet Mall. This is class, from the amenity-packed rooms to the lounges and fitness facilities. Rates start at $190 during the week at this corporate-oriented hotel. Weekend B&B specials for two start at $119.

Also in the vicinity is the comparable ***Crowne Plaza*** *(☎ 612-338-2288, 800-556-7827, fax 612-673-1157, 618 2nd Ave S)* at the corner of 7th St.

St Paul

Mid-Range & Top End The central ***Days Inn RiverCentre*** *(☎ 651-292-8929, fax 651-292-1749, 175 W 7th St)*, formerly known as the Days Inn Civic Center, is inexpensive, at $65 per double. Prices could rise following ongoing renovations.

North of the center, the ***Best Western Kelly Inn*** *(☎ 651-227-8711, 161 St Anthony Ave)* has rooms starting at $90/100 single/double.

The more expensive ***Radisson Inn St Paul*** *(☎ 651-291-8800, 411 Minnesota St)* is very central, on the Town Square and attached to the skyway system. Don't confuse it with the slightly more upmarket Radisson Hotel St Paul, of the same chain, a few blocks away on E Kellogg Blvd.

The comfortable ***Covington Inn*** *(☎ 651-227-4288, www.covingtoninn.com)*, a B&B on Pier 1 off Yacht Club Rd on Harriet Island, provides a novel, nautical urban getaway. The inn and café have been fashioned out of a river towboat (like a tugboat but it can't push). Rates from June to October range from $135 to $195, dropping by $30 from November to May.

The esteemed ***St Paul Hotel*** *(☎ 651-292-9292, 800-292-9292, fax 651-228-9506, www.stpaulhotel.com, 350 Market St)*, is a classy five-star business hotel built in 1910. Rooms start at $170 and rise stratospherically for the elite suites. Weekend romance specials, at $200, may win a heart.

PLACES TO EAT

Minneapolis

City Center In the center, you don't need to look much beyond Nicollet Mall between 5th and 11th Sts S, which caters to thousands of shoppers and workers. ***Keys Café*** *(☎ 612-339-6399, 1007 Nicollet Mall)*, begun in 1973, serves up laden plates at reasonable prices. Omelets, burgers, sandwiches, salads etc, are all under $8. ***Sawatdee***, at 10th St, is a favorite for Thai dishes at about $10.

Café Un Deux Trois *(☎ 612-673-0686, 11-9th St S)*, in the Foshay Tower, is a local favorite. It has the look of a traditional Parisian bistro and a menu with both the classic fare (mussels, steak frites) and some contemporary additions (various fish and pastas). Most dishes are $12 to $16. They don't serve lunch on weekends.

Stairs lead way down into the darkened sanctuary of famous ***Morton's*** *(☎ 612-673-9700, 555 Nicollet Mall)*. Diners come for serious steak or not at all. Most of these prime, perfectly aged cuts are in the $3[illegible] range and the sides are extra.

Art Deco ***Goodfellow's*** *(☎ 612-332-4800, 40 S 7th St)* is ranked as not only one of the city's best, but also among the nation's top restaurants. Contemporary Midwest cuisine is served in an elegant setting. The wine list is renowned. Closed Sundays.

Nicollet Ave Nicollet Ave, known as Eat St, is a gold mine for the hungry, offering a varied abundance of low-cost places scattered along more than a dozen blocks south f downtown. ***Strudel & Nudel*** *(☎ 612-874-113, 2605 Nicollet Ave S)* is good for break-ıst. ***Royal Orchid*** *(1835 Nicollet Ave S)* as good, authentic Thai food at budget rices. Dressier ***Black Forest Inn*** *(☎ 612-872-812)*, at the corner of Nicollet Ave S and 6th St W, with an alluring patio, draws an lder crowd for schnitzels and the like, with ntrées in the $10 to $14 range. ***Taco Morelos*** *☎ 612-870-0053, 14 26th St W)* serves real-eal Mexican. The *pollo mole* (chicken with picy chocolate sauce) with rice, piping hot ortillas, salad and corn chips is a great meal or $10. There are also Middle Eastern, Viet-amese and many other ethnic restaurants.

ptown ***Baja Tortilla Grill*** *(☎ 612-893-556)*, Hennepin Ave S at 24th St W, serves n amazing vegetable burrito (less than $5) nd a range of Mexican dishes.

Famous Dave's *(☎ 612-822-9900, 3001 Iennepin Ave S)* is known equally for bar-ecued ribs, live blues and Chicago street-cene design. There's no cover if you're aving dinner. Meals are in the $15 range.

Immensely popular ***Figlio's*** *(☎ 612-822-688, 3001 Hennepin Ave S)*, in Calhoun quare, is a classy bistro serving pastas and izza at low prices. Most entrées are $8 to 14. It remains open into the wee hours and ne people-watching is good.

Aississippi Mile On the Main St waterfront trip is ***St Anthony's Wharf*** *(☎ 612-378-7058)*, casual seafood place perfectly situated for n after-dinner stroll by the river. Meals are bout $20 without wine. Open daily.

Varehouse District Within the celebra-ory atmosphere here and all the drinking stablishments, the ***Pickled Parrot*** *(26 5th St I)* is often packed for its American stan-ards and Southwestern plates and salsas.

Well-entrenched ***Chez Bananas*** *(☎ 612-32-0673, 119 4th St N)*, with its trademark lastic toys at the table, serves good Carib-ean cuisine, with entrées such as lime-eanut chicken. Most dishes are $8 to $14.

Dinkytown There are more cafés here han you can shake a stir stick at, but you can also get a hit of smart food at ***Crazy Carrot***, at the corner 14th Ave SE and 4th St SE, specializing in juices and smoothies.

East Bank There's a mixed crowd on the large patio at ***Sally's Saloon & Eatery*** *(712 Washington Ave SE)* for generous portions of burgers, sandwiches and spicy meats brought sizzling to the table (all under $10). ***Village Wok*** *(610 Washington Ave SE)* is a good Chinese restaurant with a huge menu and items mainly under $8.

St Paul

Downtown The classic, cramped, some-what bedraggled ***Mickey's Dining Car*** *(☎ 651-222-5633)*, W 7th St at St Peter St, dishes up basic American favorites 24 hours a day. It's busy with area workers at lunch; otherwise the clientele is an assortment of street people kept in line by the warm staff's experience.

Bustling ***Bruegger's Bagels*** *(☎ 651-225-4363, 1 W 7th Place)* has all manner of bagel sandwiches and soups under $5. Open daily from 6:30 am. The coffee's good, too.

The cavernous renovated train station, now called Union Depot Place, at the edge of Lowertown has Greek ***Christo's***, with an $8 lunch buffet. Also here, ***Leeann Chin*** *(☎ 651-224-8814, 105 Union Place)* is a deluxe Chinese buffet ($14). The upscale, white tablecloth setting reflects the quality of the food. Open daily.

At the top end of the spectrum is the ***St Paul Grill*** *(☎ 612-224-7455, 350 Market St)*, in the St Paul Hotel. The gracious dining room is renowned for its excellent beef and seafood. Expect to pay about $30 (not in-cluding wine). Also here and more casual – and less costly – ***The Café***, specializes in American and Midwest-influenced pastas and fish.

Grand Ave The best hunting grounds in town are around Grand Ave. Ethnic eater-ies abound (Ethiopian, Greek, Vietnamese and more) on and around Grand between Dale and Victoria Sts in this busy, friendly, casual neighborhood. All restaurants listed are open daily.

Café Latte *(850 Grand Ave)* is popular for low-cost soups, sandwiches, pastries and coffee.

La Cucaracha *(36 Dale St)* has been serving Mexican food in a multihued cantina setting since 1964. Almost all the standards and more are offered at $10 or less.

The ***Tavern on Grand*** *(656 Grand Ave)*, with a real tavern atmosphere, is famous for its bargain walleye. Lunches are $9, complete dinners $12 to $14, depending on whether you order one or two fillets.

The ***Lexington*** *(☎ 651-222-5878, 1096 Grand Ave)*, has been *the* place to celebrate in the Hill since 1935. It's comfortably elegant with soft lighting and wood paneling. Entrées on the traditional beef and fish menu are in the $25 range. Chateaubriand for two is $60.

ENTERTAINMENT

The Twin Cities are famous for their range of performing arts, with dozens of fine theaters, dance companies and classical music groups. With 100,000 students and a sizable gay community, the Twin Cities also offer an active bar scene. This was the spawning ground for fondly regarded proto-grunge bands Hüsker Dü, Soul Asylum and the Replacements, and for the artist once again known as Prince.

For listings, see the daily *Minneapolis Star Tribune* or the free and very thorough weekly papers, *City Pages* and *Pulse*. Ticketmaster (☎ 612-989-5151) sells tickets for most major events.

Performing Arts

The quantity and quality that could go under this heading give credence to Minneapolis' self-dubbed moniker, 'Mini-Apple.' In particular, look for events at these venues (all in Minneapolis unless otherwise noted):

Brave New Workshop (☎ 612-332-6620, 2605 Hennepin Ave) – an established Uptown venue for musical comedy, revue and satire, founded by Dudley Riggs

Historic Orpheum Theatre (☎ 612-339-7007, 91 Hennepin Ave) – presenting musicals, Broadwa shows, and other major productions

Historic State Theater (☎ 612-339-7007, 805 Hennepin Ave) – another venue for Broadwa shows and touring acts

Guthrie Theater (☎ 612-377-2224, 725 Vinelan Place) – quality classical and contemporar music performances

Orchestra Hall (☎ 612-371-5656, 1111 Nicolle Ave) – with superb acoustics, a great venue fo recitals and concerts by the acclaimed Minnesota Symphony Orchestra

Ordway Music Theater (☎ 651-224-4222, 34 Washington St, St Paul) – home of the St Pau Chamber Orchestra and the Minnesota Stat Opera

Theatre de la Jeune Lune (☎ 612-333-6200, 105 1s St N) – features experimental French-America collaborations

Theatre in the Round (☎ 612-333-3010, 245 Ceda Ave) – comedies and dramas year round

Fitzgerald Theatre (☎ 651-290-1221, 10 East Exchange St) – has the live broadcasts of Garriso Keillor's *Prairie Home Companion* radio sho among its various presentations. Call for detail

Bars & Clubs

Minneapolis The most happening area i the Twin Cities without question is th Warehouse District in Minneapolis, wit many varied drinking and dancing spots. It' totally jammed weekend nights. Some club have cover charges – the price varies depending on who's playing.

First Avenue *(☎ 612-332-1775, 701 1s Ave N)* once featured Prince's Purple Rai band and is now a large dance club wit some live performances. ***Fine Line Musi Café*** *(☎ 612-338-8100, 318 1st Ave N)* is small venue with assorted live jazz, blue and rock. ***District Brewpub***, on 1st Ave N near 5th St N, is popular for talking an mingling.

Gay Nineties *(☎ 612-333-7755, 408 Hennepin Ave)* has dancing, dining, drag show and a gay and straight clientele. There' good blues at ***Blues Alley*** *(☎ 612-333-1327 15 Glenwood Ave)*.

Long-standing ***Ground Zero*** *(☎ 612-378 5115, 15 4th St N)*, popular with young gay nd straights, features theme nights with echno and dance, plus local bands on Vednesday.

Toward the campus, for eclectic live nusic, check out the student-oriented bands t ***400 Bar*** *(☎ 612-332-2903)*, on 4th St S at Cedar Ave.

t Paul Downtown, ***Gallivan's*** *(354 Vabasha St)* is a friendly piano bar busy vith the after-work crowd. Also downtown s the ***Great Waters Brewing Co*** *(426 St Peter St)*, at the corner of W 7th Place. They ull a good number of their own beers, from ale lagers to dark stouts. Try the Brown rout. The flowered, fenced-in patio is a fine lace to sit and sip for a while. Live music is dded Thursday to Saturday nights.

Trikkx *(☎ 651-224-0703, 490 N Robert St)* s a favorite gay club. Away from the center, ***Billy's***, at the corner Grand Ave and Victoia St, draws a good-looking crowd of 20-nd 30-somethings for beer and burgers nder the umbrellas.

The ***Dakota Bar & Grill*** *(☎ 651-642-442, 1021 E Bandana Blvd)*, located in the Bandana Square shopping mall, is a slick, vell-established jazz and dinner club about 10-minute drive northwest from downown St Paul. Call for directions.

South of town, the top floor at ***Mall of America*** has assorted bars.

SPECTATOR SPORTS

The Hubert H Humphrey Metrodome HHH Metrodome), in sports-mad Minneapolis on Chicago Ave between 5th and 6th Sts, is home to the Vikings pro football team ☎ 612-333-8828). Ask Minnesotans which wo teams are their favorites and you'll ear, 'The Vikings and whoever is playing he Packers.' Vikings tickets range from $20 o $60 but are always sold out. Scalpers round the stadium offer tickets at inflated rices (which is technically illegal).

The University of Minnesota Gophers ☎ 612-625-5000), who also play at the Metrodome, aren't quite as popular but raw crowds and devotion (see 'Gophers Go for It'). Tickets ($11 or $23) are available for most games but disappear for matches against Wisconsin and Ohio State.

Tickets ($4 to $20) are always available for the Twins major-league baseball team (☎ 612-375-7444), which also plays at the HHH Metrodome, but the seats will be situated pretty high in the stadium.

The Timberwolves pro basketball team plays at the Target Center (☎ 612-337-3865), 600 1st Ave N. Most games have some tickets available but not at courtside.

Hockey is huge in Minnesota, but after a minor scandal its pro team, the North Stars, packed off to Dallas. A new NHL team, the Wild, will start play in a new St Paul arena at RiverCentre in late 2000.

SHOPPING

Minneapolis is considered one of the top five retail centers in the USA. And that is not including the Mall of America or other

Gophers Go for It

While overshadowed by the Vikings in town, the U of M Gophers football team generates a lot of press and passion. The team is regularly ranked in the top 25 across the country.

Despite the team's rabid following, the only time tickets sell out other than during playoffs is when the Gophers play Ohio State or the Wisconsin Badgers. There is a lot of bad blood between the Gophers and the Badgers, but it's nothing like the hatred the fans seem to harbor. It's the same, in reverse, in Madison, Wisconsin.

Friday nights before game day is the 'Rally at Sally's,' a bash at the campus student bar (☎ 612-331-3231), 712 Washington Ave SE. It's a pretty big deal, with highlight films shown and a lot of enthusiasm exhibited. Saturday prior to the game, the tailgate party at the Metrodome attracts large crowds, with the university marching band intensifying the already high energy.

If you need additional information, contact the Gophers Media Department at ☎ 612-624-6004.

suburban markets. The city has hundreds of stores, many of them concentrated along Nicollet Mall. Dayton's department stores, based in the city, have a branch at the corner of Nicollet and 7th St. Another is at 411 Cedar St in St Paul. Gavidae Common complex, off Nicollet between 6th and 7th Sts, has 50 quality, name shops wedged between branches of Neiman Marcus and Saks Fifth Avenue. Across the street, the modern City Center has another 70 stores, including Marshall's and Victoria's Secret.

GETTING THERE & AWAY

Air

Minneapolis–St Paul International Airport (MSP) is a major regional hub, home of Northwest Airlines (☎ 612-726-2111), which, in conjunction with KLM, operates several direct flights from Europe, including from London and Amsterdam. Most other flights from Europe are routed through Amsterdam. For Asian connections, Osaka, Japan, is the major hub. Iceland Air (☎ 800-223-5500) flies to and from London, Glasgow and Stockhom.

Other important carriers are American Airlines, Air Canada, Delta and United; see the Toll-Free & Web Site Directory at the back of the book for contact information.

The airport is between the two cities but south 9 miles at I-494 and Hwy 5, adjacent to the Mall of America.

Bus

Downtown Minneapolis has a central, spiffy new bus terminal (☎ 612-371-3323) with attached parking ramp on Hawthorne Ave at the corner of 9th St N across from the Orpheum Theatre. It's two blocks from the Target Center. Both Greyhound and Jefferson Lines, which runs south to Rochester, use it.

In St Paul, the bus station (☎ 615-222-0509) is at 166 W University Ave.

From either station, there are frequent buses to Milwaukee ($49, 6 hours) and Chicago ($63, 9 to 11 hours). Greyhound also runs through the lakelands to Rhinelander and to Duluth.

Train

The Amtrak station (☎ 651-644-1127), 73 Transfer Rd off University Ave SE, is in S Paul, about 5 miles to each downtown Once-daily trains go southeast to Milwaukee and Chicago and west to the wester USA. To Milwaukee the fare ranges fron $40 to $86, almost the same as going t Chicago. St Louis connections are made i Chicago.

GETTING AROUND

To/From the Airport

Airport Express Shuttles (☎ 612-827-7777 go to and from downtown Minneapolis ($11 and St Paul ($9). It connects to all majo hotels, and no reservations are required.

Airport Taxi (☎ 612-544-0000) charge $21 to or from Minneapolis.

Bus

Metropolitan Council Transit Operation (MCTO; ☎ 612-373-3333) runs local buse throughout the metropolitan area ($1; $1.5 during rush hour: Monday to Friday 6 t 9 am and 3:30 to 6:30 pm). Express bus N 94 links the Twin Cities downtown cores. I downtown Minneapolis, catch it on 6th S (going east) at Marquette St; in downtow St Paul, catch it on Minnesota St (goin north) at 6th St.

The Arts & Eats Express is a van operated by MCTO ($1; $1.50 during rush hour) which scurries around Minneapolis's Nicollet Ave and the downtown theater and hote district. Call for details; it's a great, easy wa to do the town.

Trolley

Both cities have limited, visitor-oriente trolley systems. Both are excellent ways o getting about. In Minneapolis, River Cit Trolley (☎ 651-223-5600) does a 65-minut loop around downtown and the Mississip Mile for $8 or $10 hop-on, hop-off for th whole day. There are 20 stops. Pick it up at th Minneapolis Convention Center at Nicolle Ave and 13th St S or Walker Art Center. I runs 10 am to 4 pm weekdays, 10 am to 5 pm weekends, from early May to late October.

In St Paul, the Capital City Trolley (☎ 651-771-8639) circulates through downtown, stopping at major sites and stores weekdays for just 50¢. Call for details and stop locations.

Car & Motorcycle

In Minneapolis, Budget (☎ 612-727-2000) is at 229 10th St S; in St Paul (☎ 651-727-2000) it's at E 8th and Jackson Sts. Rates for a compact Ford Escort are $45/day with unlimited mileage.

Midwest Motorcycle (☎ 612-525-1015), 15 Washington Ave N, rents Harley-Davidsons at $45/hour, $200/day. Now's your chance – or you can hire a driver (you'll have to unless you have a motorcyclist's license).

Auto-Delivery (☎ 612-323-3311) is a drive-away company based in Anoka, a northern suburb.

St Croix River Valley

The storied St Croix River begins its journey in Wisconsin's northwest corner south of Superior. It widens as it reaches Minnesota and flows southward for 150 miles, forming the boundary between the two states. Finally, just south of the Twin Cities at Prescott, it merges with the Mississippi. Classed as a National Scenic Riverway, it is the world's only river protected along its entirety.

The northern section, above Stillwater, is federally designated wild and scenic and is good for canoeists. The lower, wider sector is recreational. A county bike trail covers much of the route. The riverway headquarters for information (☎ 715-483-3284) is on Hamilton St beside the river just north of downtown in St Croix Falls, Wisconsin. A second office for the lower river area (☎ 651-430-1938) is at Stillwater.

During the 18th and early 19th centuries, Ojibway and Dakota Indians used the waterway. Explorers, fur traders, lumberers and settlers followed. In the valley, the booming lumber days before and around the turn of the 20th century brought much wealth and development. Today, many of these historic buildings have been revitalized as shops, inns and museums. Their charm, together with the river itself and the waterside state parks, make for a fine day or two of discovery. For more information contact www.uwrf.edu/scvta.

In the summer, visit during the week if possible. Though considerably less known by out-of-state visitors than the nearby Mississippi area, the small towns can get crowded easily.

STILLWATER

• pop 14,000

Stillwater, on the lower St Croix, is the largest of the river's communities. It's a busy 19th-century logging town with a lot of visible history, including the can't-miss church spires and courthouse cupola. The stores, restaurants, galleries, antiques outlets and antiquarian bookshops now ensconced in the old buildings attract good-size crowds on summer weekends.

Stroll the quiet side streets, where many of the Victorian houses are on the National Register of Historic Places.

Stillwater is known as the birthplace of Minnesota; territorial authorities met here in 1848 to petition Congress to form the Minnesota Territory.

For town and valley information visit the chamber of commerce (☎ 651-439-7700, www.stillwaterchamber.com), 423 S Main St in the Brick Alley Building, open 9 am to 4 pm weekdays. Pick up their parking guide, walking tour brochure and list of events, including the Oktoberfest celebrations, which despite the name are in September.

At the north end of town is the **Depot**, 601 N Main St, the restored train station now housing the Logging and Railroad Museum. It's not expansive but is worth a look, and it's free.

Also here is the gorgeous **Minnesota Zephyr** (☎ 651-430-3000, 800-992-6100), an elegant 1940s-era dining train that makes 3½-hour trips along the valley and includes

The St Croix River Valley – Scenic Drive

The 60-mile St Croix River Valley runs between Hastings on the Minnesota side just south of the Twin Cities (Prescott on the Wisconsin side) to Taylors Falls (St Croix Falls on the Wisconsin side). Its delightful blend of culture, history and scenery have led to comparisons with the Rhine Valley.

Due east of St Paul on Hwy 36 is Stillwater. From there turn north on Hwy 95 and head up the valley. Look for the small waysides along the limestone hills edging the road where you can pull over for views of the river. You'll pass woodlands and then arrive at picturesque little Marine on St Croix. Drive through William O'Brien State Park, with its mix of hardwood trees, wetlands and green fields. North of the park, head east over the St Croix River to Osceola, in Wisconsin. It's a good place to stretch your legs and eat lunch.

From Osceola you can either cross back to Minnesota and head north on Hwy 95 or continue north in Wisconsin on Hwy 35. Hwy 95 is closer to the river and provides more glimpses of the water. The landscape rolls gently, and farms are mixed in alongside the woods. When you reach Hwy 8, turn east (off Hwy 95) or west (off Hwy 35) and head to Taylors Falls. The stretch of road just south of Taylors Falls descends appreciably, providing excellent views of the river and its cliffs.

If you choose to head up Hwy 35, you pass right by Interstate State Park, with its rocky glacial gorges and sweeping river vistas; consider stopping for a hike or to take in the view. You'll also reach the park on the Minnesota side after turning east on Hwy 8.

LIBRARY OF CONGRESS

MINNESOTA

a five-course meal for $64. Dress is semi-formal. In July and August a midday and box lunch tour is added at $20/13 adults/children.

River cruises depart from the Municipal Docks to the south of Nelson St by the river, behind the chamber of commerce.

The **Stillwater Trolley** (☎ 651-430-0352) putters around the narrow, hilly streets of town for 45 minutes offering a narrated tour that covers more than obvious main thoroughfare sites. It departs from the Freight-house Restaurant (at the chamber of commerce) regularly from May to October.

The **Washington County Courthouse**, on 3rd St, just south of Pine St is the oldest in the state (built in 1867) and contains an old sheriff's office and jail.

MARINE ON ST CROIX

• pop 600

Picture-perfect Marine looks as if it ha[s] been airlifted from a country road in Ne[w] Hampshire. The **Stone House Museum**, open 2 to 5 pm weekends from July 4 t[o] Labor Day, traces the settlers' story and ha[s] a Swedish-style kitchen on display. Als[o] take a peek at the classic general store. Bot[h] are on Hwy 95.

The ***Voyageur Café***, on the main street, i[s] very comfortable, and one of the excellen[t] salads, such as the grilled chicken ($7), is [a] complete meal. After exploring the village, [a] walk in the 700-acre **Lee and Rose Natur[e] Preserve** showcases the undeveloped side o[f] the valley's personality with rolling hills an[d] ɔwers. The Apple River, across in Wiscon-n, is renowned for its tubing.

VILLIAM O'BRIEN STATE PARK

lwy 95 splits this Minnesota park (☎ 651-33-0500), just north of Marine on St Croix. he riverside offers canoeing and trails with iews of a couple of islands (they're not part f the park). The larger inland section has amping and more miles of trails which are ood for hiking or skiing.

SCEOLA

dged by the river bluffs, Osceola is a pretty Visconsin town whose numerous restau-ants and shops make a good break. ascade Falls in Mill Pond Park is a local eauty spot, and the whole place looks es-ecially captivating in autumn.

From the old depot, 114 Depot Rd, 90-ninute vintage train trips aboard the Osceola & St Croix River Railway (☎ 651-28-0263) slice through the rugged valley to Aarine on St Croix and back. It operates on eekends and holidays only from the end of Aay to late October. Fares are $12/11/7 dults/seniors/children. Ask about special vent trips and the autumn leaf watchers.

AYLORS FALLS

pop 700

Attractive Taylors Falls, east on Hwy 8 off Iwy 61 or Hwy 95, marks the upper limit of arge boat navigation on the St Croix. The ompact central area of town contains estaurants, antiques shops, gift shops, everal B&Bs and a motel or two.

Folsom House (☎ 651-465-5535) 272 W Government St on top of Angelic Hill, is the ormer home of lumber baron and state enator William Folsom. This state historic ite reflects the life and times of the area's ell-to-do in the mid-1850s. The site is open to 4:30 pm daily from late May to mid-October.

Glorious **Interstate State Park** (☎ 715-465-711), off Hwy 8 as you head toward town, ontains rocky cliffs and a deep gorge known s the Dalles, where the river knifes between ne two states. Glacial potholes and rock for-nations are Dalles highlights. There are bluff-edge hiking trails through the woods, and **boat tours** operate from the gates of the park. Seven-mile, 1⅓-hour cruises ($9) operate three times daily. Three-mile, 30-minute trips ($7) are offered once a day. All operate from late May to mid-October.

Across the bridge, the Wisconsin side of Interstate Park (☎ 715-483-3747) is perhaps more spectacular, with great river vistas along the cliff sides affording views of rock climbers and the tour boats. Other assets are camping and canoe rentals.

Back on the Minnesota side about 1½ miles downstream is the park's campground, more hiking trails and canoe rentals. The latter should be seriously considered: A great two- to three-hour drifting trip down to Osceola is $25 and includes the return shuttle.

South of the Twin Cities

From Stillwater or St Paul, the journey south on Hwy 95 along the St Croix leads to the Mississippi River. Along the way is the town of Afton, which has preserved its center with stores and places for a meal or drink. There are boat cruises, too. The river-side Afton State Park, south of town on Hwy 21, has trails and camping. A bike trail runs to Hudson, Wisconsin, about halfway to Stillwater.

At Hastings is the confluence of the St Croix and Mississippi Rivers. Vermilion Falls is a local attraction, as is the Victorian archi-tecture, notably in a condensed downtown two-block area classed a historic district.

MISSISSIPPI RIVER AREA

From the Twin Cities southward, the Missis-sippi, one of America's natural and cultural treasures, divides Minnesota and Wisconsin. On the west side Hwy 61, and on the east Hwy 35, both often edging along the water's banks, are designated as the Great River Rd, the scenic route that follows the river all the way down its course. The drive, with stops at numerous picturesque towns and viewpoints, makes a rewarding experience.

Each side has its more impressive sections. Generally, there are more villages on the Wisconsin side. The Minnesota side is higher, with more expansive views, and the trip is quicker.

There's a broad range of places to stay and many things to do, from watching bald eagles to hiking to visiting paddle wheeler museums. Most of the chambers of commerce are closed weekends.

Red Wing

• pop 15,000

On Hwy 61, Red Wing, with a restored downtown, is the area's gateway. The name is taken from Hoopoohoosha, a Sioux chief whose emblem was a swan's wing dyed red. The town was incorporated in 1853 and shortly after became the world's largest wheat-shipping port, soon enjoying wealth and wielding political and cultural clout. Today it is best known for its Red Wing stoneware and rugged Red Wing footwear.

The **Depot**, down at the river at the foot of Plum St, is the Amtrak and Greyhound terminal. There are buses daily to St Paul, La Crosse and Chicago, with stops en route. The chamber of commerce (☎ 651-38 4719, 800-762-9516) is also here, open wee days 8 am to 5 pm.

Things to See & Do West of the cente see the **Pottery District**, on Old West Ma St just north off Hwy 61, where pottery still made and there are restaurants and th Bierstube sports bar and brew pub. I summer you may see classic river stean boats at the dock on their trips from Ne Orleans.

The **Goodhue County Museum** (☎ 65 388-6024), 1166 Oak St, outlines region history from the time of the Dakota (Siou through the development of river con merce. Open 10 am to 5 pm Tuesday t Friday, 1 to 5 pm weekends.

The restored 1910 **Sheldon Theat** (☎ 651-385-3667, 800-899-5759), 3rd St East Ave, presents a year-round lineup quality plays.

The **Cannon Valley Bike Trail** meande for 20 miles alongside the Cannon Riv westbound to Cannon Falls. The trailhead just west of the Pottery District on Old We Main St. In Welch, about halfway ther

Old Man River – The Mississippi

Around the world the simple mention of the name 'Mississippi' conjures images as varied, wondrous, fanciful and moving as the most American of rivers itself. But most people don't know that the mighty waterway begins its journey to the Gulf of Mexico in northwestern Minnesota. Indeed, there are more miles of Mississippi in this state than any other.

Henry Schoolcraft was the first European to see the source, when Ojibway chief Ozawindib and his tribe members led Schoolcraft to it in 1832. Their word for it was *Gichiziibbi*, great river. The shallow, creeklike beginning, flowing north within Lake Itasca State Park, now draws half a million visitors a year.

But all the statistics are noteworthy. It's one of the major rivers of North America and the second-longest in the US. Only the Missouri, one of its tributaries, is longer. Together the two constitute the third-longest river system in the world, after the Nile and the Amazon. The Mississippi drains an enormous area covering 31 states and parts of Canada. Among its 100 tributaries are other legendary rivers, including the Illinois, the St Croix and the Ohio.

Through generations, the waters affectionately known as Old Man River have carried natives, explorers, missionaries, traders, pioneers, fishers, blues musicians, gamblers and tourists. Farm products, commercial goods, raw materials, barges, canoes and paddle wheelers have all flowed with the river. Today much of it is protected and the Great River Rd, winding along both sides of its course through Minnesota, Wisconsin and Illinois, reveals abundant history and beauty.

ubes can be rented to gently float downstream. The river continues to Northfield.

At the west end of town off Hwy 61/63 is **Barn Bluff**. Watch for the trailhead for the path that leads to great views over the river. On the other side of the road, a little farther along, Skyline Drive rises up to Memorial Park lookout atop **Sorin's Bluff**, also a great vantage point.

Places to Stay & Eat For camping, there is the very good ***Frontenac State Park*** *(☎ 651-396-6157)*, south of town about 10 miles on Hwy 61, with trails and a great river view. It's open all year but camping is from May to October only.

The ***St James Hotel*** *(☎ 651-388-2846, 800-252-1875, www.st-james-hotel.com, 406 Main St)* is the classy old lady in town, with tastefully renovated rooms. Among the eating areas are the intimate lower-level dining room, with original limestone, and the more relaxed upstairs pub. Rates vary with the room, day and season. The small rooms (still elegant) start at $75, the larger standard rooms start at $95.

The ***Treasure Island Resort*** *(☎ 651-388-6300, 800-222-7077)* is a Caribbean-theme hotel complex based around a casino northwest of town on Sturgeon Lake Rd, which runs east off Hwy 19 and north off Hwy 61. Standard rooms are $65 Sunday to Thursday, $89 Friday and Saturday from late May to early September; they're lower in the off-season.

Hwy 61, especially west of town, has a few of chain motels and eateries. Downtown, at the colorful ***Blue Plate Café*** *(☎ 651-388-7573, 416 W 3rd St)*, you get the personal touch, with good food for under $10 at any meal. Try the blue-corn chicken. Open 8 am to 8 pm daily.

Liberty's *(☎ 651-388-8877)*, at the central corner of W 3rd and Plum Sts, serves all the diner standards but in surroundings a cut above the typical diner. Open 8 am to 11 pm daily.

Southward on the River

The best part of the valley begins south of Red Wing. On the Minnesota side Lake City is bland at best, but there are outstanding views of Lake Pepin, a wide spot in the river. Wisconsin has more sites of interest.

Maiden Rock to Nelson In Red Wing, cross the river on Hwy 63, and downstream on Hwy 35 is **Maiden Rock**, with views from its 400-foot Indian legend namesake. It's said a young woman jumped to avoid her selected marriage partner.

Between here and tiny **Stockholm** (population 69) is a great stretch, as the road travels right beneath the towering bluffs. Stockholm has a few craft outlets and camping. The ***Star Café*** is a fine place for lunch or dinner.

To the south, **Pepin** has a busy little waterfront with some tourist shops and a restaurant. At the Pepin Historical Museum, on the highway, learn about Laura Ingalls Wilder, a local author who wrote a series of popular children's books about her life, inspiring the *Little House on the Prairie* TV series. On County Rd CC, 7 miles north of town, is a reconstructed log cabin at her birthplace. In town are motels, B&Bs and a campground at the river.

In **Nelson**, stop at the cheese factory, where they also make sandwiches. ***Beth's Twin Bluffs Café*** packs in locals.

Wabasha Cross back to Minnesota for a side trip to Wabasha (population 2400), founded in the 1830s and possibly the oldest town in the state, with a nice historic downtown devoid of national franchises. The chamber of commerce (☎ 800-565-4158) is at 154 Pembroke Ave, open 11 am to 4 pm weekdays. In the back see the American Bald Eagle Center.

Eagles are abundant here from November to March, feeding on fish. There is an observation deck at the foot of Pembroke Ave at the river. Guides are on hand Sunday afternoon to discuss these national symbols.

Two miles west of town on Hwy 60 is the private **Arrowhead Bluffs Museum** (☎ 651-565-3829), with a collection of Native American artifacts, mounted wildlife and guns (the operators are also hunting consultants).

Open 10 am to 6 pm daily from May through December.

Try the ***Rivertown Café***, on Pembroke Ave, for a taste of small-town America (straightforward nonspicy dishes, homemade pies and other standards). More food and a good night's sleep await at the traditional ***Anderson House Hotel*** *(☎ 800-535-5467, 333 W Main St)*.

Alma to La Crescent On the Wisconsin side again, Hwy 35 is very scenic to **Alma**, a winsome little town. Buena Vista Park, way up the hill, provides a grand lookout. Drive to it by turning off Hwy 35 at County Rd E (at the southern end of town) and following the signs.

Lock and Dam 4, at the riverfront in the middle of town, has an observation platform from which to see riverboats and barges. At Rieck's Lake Park, at the north edge of town on Hwy 35, tundra swans can be seen in October and November, egrets and herons in spring.

With a B&B, hotel, motels, shops and a few places for a bite, Alma makes a handy respite. Moderately priced ***Hillcrest Motel & Cabins*** *(☎ 608-685-3511)* north of town on Hwy 35, is open all year.

At **Fountain City** a must-visit is the unbelievable but true Rock in the House, where a 55-ton boulder crashed down the hillside into a house, and the residents just left it there and live as is! Park beside the road and go take a look. The room with the rock has been transformed into a sort of museum, with lots of press coverage on display. There may not be anyone around, but the door is usually open; have a peek and put a small donation in the box.

Merrick State Park *(☎ 608-687-4936)*, just north of Fountain City on Hwy 35, isn't special but does have camping from April until snowfall (with only limited facilities past October 15).

Cross the river (for the last time) to **Winona**, a former port with a strong Polish presence. The downtown has more than a dozen buildings, including houses and churches, on the National Register of Historic Places; many are on 2nd and 3rd Sts. The chamber of commerce (☎ 507-452-2272), at 67 Main St, is closed weekends.

Aboard the Wilkie Steamboat Center, at the foot of Center St, the Grand Salon is quite a piece of work. The lower deck is a museum about the riverboats, open 11 am to 4 pm Wednesday to Sunday. They make a good, brief visit; $3. Landlubbers will find impressive views extending for 20 miles from Garvin Heights Park, on Garvin Heights Rd south off Hwy 61.

A room at ***Days Inn*** *(☎ 507-454-6930, fax 507-454-7917)*, on Hwy 61 north of downtown, is $50. Numerous less costly independent motels can be found on Hwy 61 in both directions. The ***Jefferson Pub & Grill*** is at the historic waterfront area at the foot of Center St.

From Winona south to **La Crescent**, Hwy 61 provides endless superlative views of the river, with sections of bare, layered limestone, sandbars and marshes flanked by green, irregularly shaped hills. It's wonderful that Old Man River can still look this untamed. Apple country surrounds La Crescent; County Rd 6 is pretty at blossom time.

WEST OF THE RIVER

The region of southeastern Minnesota west of the river has its own charms and variety.

Northfield

• pop 15,000

Northfield is a pleasant college town south of St Paul on Hwy 3 with a well-restored late-19th-century downtown bisected by the Cannon River. Division St, with far more cafés than it has a right to, makes a good lunch stop. The Jesse James gang was foiled in a bank robbery here in 1876, and related sites make the most of this bit of notoriety. The annual reenactment and associated activities the weekend after Labor Day (the first Monday in September) are good fun.

The chamber of commerce (☎ 507-645-5604, 800-658-2548) is at 500 Water St S. Pick up the Outlaw Trail pamphlet, which provides details on the attempted heist and allows latter-day investigators to follow the bad guys' tracks. They also have a walking guide to the central historic district.

The **Northfield Historical Bank Site and Museum** (☎ 507-645-9268), 408 Division St, exhibits more evidence, such as some original guns and the safe Jesse et al tried to rob. Open 10 am to 4 pm Tuesday to Saturday, from 1 to 4 pm Sunday.

Mantorville

pop 870

This tiny, tourist-oriented village southeast of Northfield and several miles west of Rochester on Hwy 14 was once a stagecoach stop and retains enough 1850s-era limestone buildings to be placed on the National Register of Historic Places. Other than on summer weekends, traffic is light.

The small Dodge County Historical Museum (☎ 507-635-5508), on Main St near 6th St, provides background on the area. Open noon to 4 pm Tuesday to Saturday from May to October, 10 am to 4 pm Tuesday, Friday and Saturday from October to May; $2.

The old **Opera House** (☎ 507-635-5420) on 5th St stages great goofball melodramas on weekend evenings from May to October for $5.

To spend the night, forget the new motel and call at the ***Grand Old Mansion*** *(☎ 507-635-3231)*, on 4th St at Main St, for some historic atmosphere. It's open all year, with rooms for $43 to $64, depending on choice of the mansion, the old schoolhouse or the log cabin.

A meal at the richly period-decorated ***Hubbard House*** *(☎ 507-635-2331)*, from 1854, completes the package. It's on Main St at 5th St, with an extensive, moderately priced menu. Closed Mondays.

Rochester

• pop 71,000

The small city of Rochester is the largest in far southern Minnesota, and while it's a good place to live, it doesn't hold much appeal for visitors. Despite that, the numerous hotels and motels do sell out in summer, especially when an event is on. An example is the Gold Rush Days antiques show and sale the third week of August.

Broadway (intersecting at Center St) is the main street, but the central core has few restaurants or attractions. The CVB (☎ 507-288-4331, 800-634-8277), 150 S Broadway St, is in the Radisson Hotel. It's open weekdays; the hotel desk can provide a map if the CVB is closed.

Things to See Rochester is home to the famed **Mayo Clinic** (☎ 507-284-2511), which attracts medical patients and practitioners from around the USA and the world. A look-see, even for the healthy, is instructive. This was the world's first and remains its largest private medical facility. Free morning tours and a film outline the Mayo brothers' story and describe how the clinic developed its cutting-edge reputation. The extensive art collection, found throughout the complex, ranges from pre-Columbian pottery to paintings by Miró and Warhol. Get information and pick up the self-guided tour booklet in the Mayo Building, main floor, 200 1st St SE. For those with a keen interest, free tours of the art collection are offered once daily Tuesday to Thursday.

The **Mayowood Mansion** (☎ 507-282-9447), 3720 Mayowood Rd SW, southwest of downtown at Mayowood Lake on the Zumbro River, is the former home of three generations of Mayos, including doctors Charles H and Charles W. The 40-room country estate proves how successful and prominent the clinic's founding family became. Heads of state from around the world were guests at the mansion. Tours are given Tuesday through Sunday; call for details.

Places to Stay & Eat Most accommodations and restaurants are on the feeder highways around the edges. Nearly all motels provide shuttle services to the downtown Mayo Clinic.

The ***Deluxe Motel*** *(☎ 507-289-2161, 209 17th Ave SW)*, west of downtown, is the cheapest, at $31. ***Motel 6*** *(☎ 507-282-6625, 2107 W Frontage St)*, northwest of the center beside Hwy 52, is a few dollars more.

The ***Days Inn Downtown*** *(☎ 507-282-3801)* is very central, at the corner of Center

St and 1st Ave NW. Room rates range from $50 to $70 a double. There's a coffee shop on site.

Find your way along with knowledgeable locals to ***Daube's*** *(14 SW 3rd St)*, near Broadway, a German bakery and café. They bake fine bread and pastries and open at 7 am Monday to Saturday.

If you like beef, hoof over to ***Michael's*** *(since 1951; ☎ 507-288-2020)*, at the Centerplace Galleria complex on Broadway (ask for directions). You won't be disappointed. The seafood and Greek specialties are also good. Entrées are about $15. Closed Sundays.

HISTORIC BLUFF COUNTRY

The southeastern corner of the state is a peaceful blend of green hills, narrow winding rivers, rocky limestone bluffs and state forests. The topography, rugged and driftless (meaning it escaped the flattening effects of the last ice age), is ideal for outdoor activities. The Root and Zumbro Rivers are good canoeing waters, there are several designated bike trails and the area is superb for carefree driving in autumn, with roads meandering through brilliant colors. Several of the attractive towns have good services and are centers for the regional Amish community. A fine two or three days can be spent slowly exploring this region of ancient lands and old ways.

Harmony

• pop 1080

Though very small, Harmony is one of the prime regional visitor destinations. Aside from some attractions of its own, it makes a good base for further forays around Bluff Country. Hwy 52 becomes Main St in town.

North and east of town are about 150 traditional Old Order **Amish** families. Their horse-drawn carriages (or the evidence of them) are often seen. From Main St, several people run tours around the Amish country, including a farm visit, using either a minibus or your own car. Trips are offered all year but never on Sundays. A tour of a little over two hours with Amish Country Tours (☎ 507-886-2303, 800-278-8327), departing from the Depot on Main St, is $10.

Two miles south from town on Hwy 13 and then 2 miles west on Niagara Cave R is commercial **Niagara Cave** (☎ 507-886-6606), which is unique for having a 60-foc waterfall and very high chambers among it impressive formations. Open 9:30 am t 5:30 pm daily from May through Septem ber, weekends only in April and Octobe: $8/7/5 adults/seniors/kids.

The 18-mile **Harmony–Preston** pave bike trail runs north to Preston, where i connects to the terrific **Root River Stat Trail**. The latter 36-mile trail links Fountai through Lanesboro to beyond Rushforc See the Lanesboro section for more on th Root River trail.

A couple of small museums, antiques an gift shops and Amish craft outlets round ou the local offerings.

Places to Stay & Eat Central ***Slim Bunkhouse*** *(☎ 507-886-3116)*, at the corne of 1st and 2nd Aves NW, two blocks west c Main St, is operated by the town wood carver and has rooms for $35 a double – steal. Otherwise, there is the ***Country Lodg Motel*** *(☎ 507-886-2515, 800-870-1710)*, o Hwy 52, with breakfast. Prices range fror $43 to $85, depending on season and roon

Two good restaurants steps from eac other on Main St are worlds apart. Th ***Harmony House*** *(☎ 507-886-4612)* i packed with locals fitting steak sandwiche and inexpensive grilled-cheese sandwiche in among the chatter; the ***Intrepid Travele*** *(☎ 507-886-2891)* has moderately price smoked salmon wraps, European wine an beer with classical music accompanimen closed Wednesday.

Lanesboro

• pop 860

If bluffs yield jewels, this is one. Lanesboro i a dandy little town graced by the Root Rive and fine historic houses backdropped b limestone outcroppings. It offers all the serv ices a traveler requires, and it makes a grea starting point for the area's outdoor activitie

The Lanesboro Visitor Center (☎ 507 467-2696, 800-944-2670) is in the old trai depot, 100 Milwaukee Rd, downtown. It

pen 9 am to 5 pm Monday, Tuesday, Thurs-
lay and Friday, 10 am to 4 pm Wednesday,
aturday and Sunday.

Almost everything in town is on the main
lrag, Parkway Ave. The main concentration
f businesses is at its north end.

Outfitters right here rent bikes, canoes, ubes and kayaks and provide shuttle services. A four-hour canoe rental including free huttle costs $25 to $30. The paved Root River State Trail in either direction provides yclists with a memorable scenic ride. It ollows an abandoned railroad bed, and lans are to extend it west to Houston. It enerally runs downhill from Fountain, but s quite level and provides fine views of the alley and bluffs along the Root River. Wild urkeys, hawks, turkey vultures and deer are ommon.

Come nightfall, if you still have energy to burn, inquire about the occasional Sunday night barn dances and regular free concerts in Sylvan Park. The dances are held at the Sons of Norway Hall beside the community center at the south end of Parkway Ave. Sylvan Park is also on Parkway Ave, closer to downtown.

The respected Commonweal Theatre Company (☎ 800-657-7025) performs a popular summer season of generally light productions. Their theater is in the heart of downtown on Parkway Ave.

Winding Hwy 16 east from here to Rushford, edging along the bluffs and river, is particularly scenic. From Rushford, with a fine setting but not much else, the road continues to La Crescent, on the Mississippi River.

MINNESOTA

Into the Bluff Country – Scenic Drive

LIBRARY OF CONGRESS

Leave Rochester on Hwy 52 south. From Chatfield to Preston the traffic thins and the softly rolling hills present a mix of dairy pastures and cornfields. Just before dropping down into Preston turn off Hwy 52 onto Hwy 16 east. In a few miles head south on County Rd 11. Then take County Rd 118, a narrow gravel road, into the woods and rocky bluffs of Forestville State Park (☎ 507-352-5111). Here, if you make a brief stop, you can park the car, walk across the bridge and be transported into an 1890s village, complete with costumed interpreters. Be prepared to be made part of the story.

Back in the car, continue on County Rd 118 eastbound to County Rd 5. Head south across the Root River and watch for the signs to Mystery Cave, still within the state park. You can take a tour ($7) of the cave (☎ 507-937-3251), one of the region's fascinating limestone features, with pools, passageways and interesting formations. The park is open Tuesday to Sunday from late May to early September and has camping.

From the cave, take County Rd 14 to County Rd 9; head south to County Rd 44, then west to Harmony. This is a relatively flat stretch of agricultural land. From Harmony drive north on Hwy 52 to pretty Hwy 16 east. Aim for Lanesboro and you're back into the more rugged, rocky bluff lands.

Places to Stay & Eat From May to October there is cheap tent and RV camping right in town at Sylvan Park, on Parkway Ave on the way into the center from Hwy 16. Or head east 3 miles on Hwy 16 to ***Eagle Cliff Campground*** *(☎ 507-467-2598)*, which many use as a tubing, canoeing or cycling base. Rentals are available.

Lodging includes a strong list of motels and B&Bs, even a hostel. The ***Old Barn Resort*** *(☎ 507-467-2512, 800-552-2512)*, on the bike trail and river, has camping, hostel beds ($11) sports rentals, a pool and a bar and restaurant. It's 7 miles from town; call for directions. Elsewhere, prices range from $35 to $100, with $60 being the average. A bit out of downtown is ***A Guest Haus Motel*** *(☎ 507-467-3512)*, Parkway S at Hwy 16 open all year, with rooms for $45 to $50 in summer.

Downtown is ***Brewster's Red Hotel*** *(☎ 507-467-2999, 106 Parkway Ave)*, with six mid-priced rooms.

Food is equally plentiful, ranging from basic diner, café and pub fare, to sausages at ***Das Wurst Haus*** and upmarket contemporary at ***Mrs B's***. All can be found at the small downtown strip along Parkway Ave.

Central & Northern Minnesota

Wooded and lake-filled, this area of the state is synonymous with outdoor activities and summer fun. State and national forests cover much of the territory, providing a full range of natural and active pursuits. Campsites and cottages abound, and almost everybody is fishing crazy. Autumn brings fall festivals, stunning color and fewer tourists. In winter, snowmobiling, skiing (mainly Nordic) and ice fishing take over. Year-round resorts and Native American–managed casinos are scattered throughout the region.

Central Minnesota has been made famous by author and broadcaster Garrison Keillor and his tales from the fictitious town of Lake Wobegon. North of Bemidji the population thins, the land flattens and the vegetation becomes less lush. The captivating Iron Range district, with a totally different topography and history from the rest of the state, forms a large tract in the central eastern region.

The northeastern corner of the state is presided over by majestic Lake Superior, beginning at the inviting city of Duluth, and the incredible lake-filled forests of the Boundary Waters.

Highlights

- Exploring the fascinating landscapes and mining stories of the Iron Range
- Hiking cliffs and trails of state parks along Lake Superior's stunning shore
- Canoeing the tranquil lakes of the Boundary Waters Canoe Area Wilderness
- Casting for walleye and muskie in the north woods
- Wading across the source of the great Mississippi River in Itasca State Park
- Stepping into the early fur-trading days at Grand Portage National Monument

MINNESOTA

Central Minnesota

MILLE LACS LAKE

The lakelands begin at this large, circular body of water also known as 'the walleye factory.' It's said more walleye hatch here than at all the state's hatcheries combined. But with an average depth of just 20 feet and plenty of weeds, the lake produces copious amounts of bass, pike and muskie, too. In winter, the lake is speckled with up to 5000 ice-fishing huts.

Hwy 169 is the main road running past the west side of the lake. At the lake's southwestern corner **Mille Lacs Kathio State Park** (☎ 320-532-3523) is excellent, offering

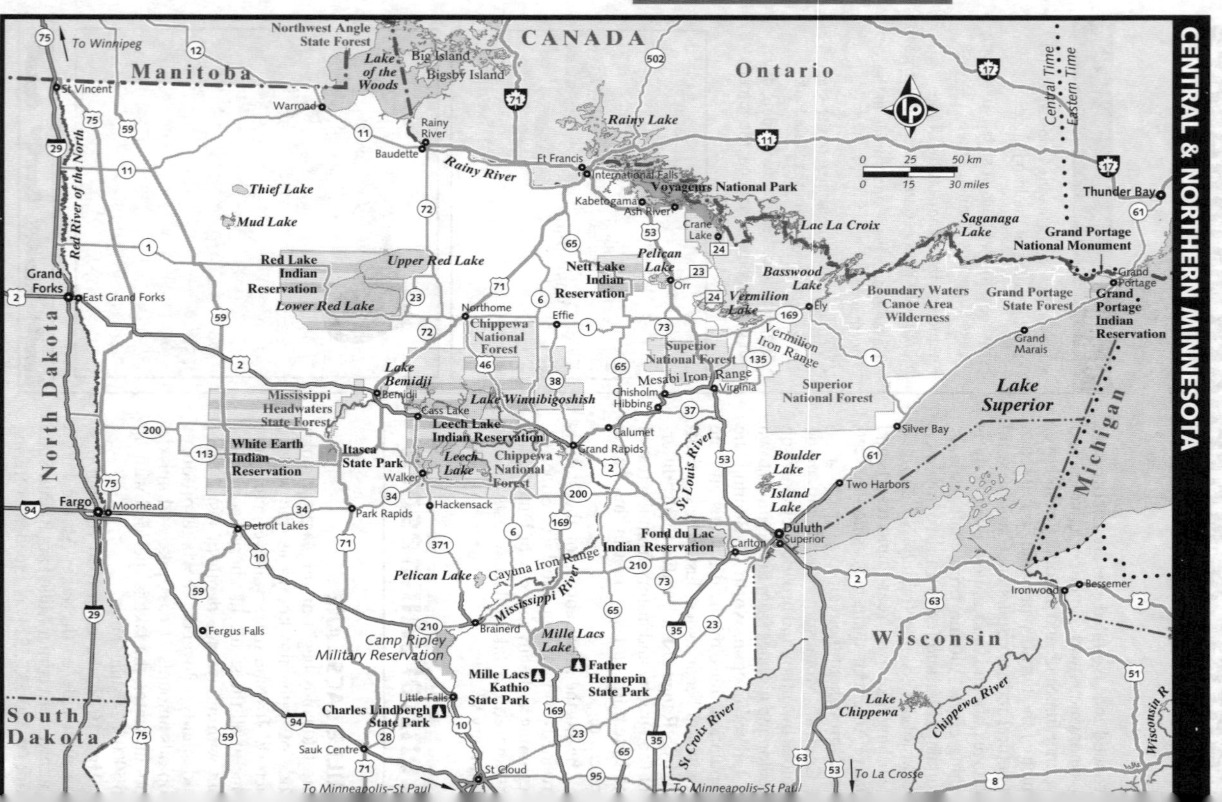
MINNESOTA
CENTRAL & NORTHERN MINNESOTA
CANADA
Ontario
Manitoba
North Dakota
South Dakota
Wisconsin
Michigan
To Winnipeg
Northwest Angle State Forest
Lake of the Woods
Big Island
Bigsby Island
St Vincent
Warroad
Rainy River
Baudette
Rainy River
Ft Francis
International Falls
Rainy Lake
Voyageurs National Park
Kabetogama
Ash River
Crane Lake
Lac La Croix
Saganaga Lake
Grand Portage National Monument
Grand Portage
Central Time
Eastern Time
Thunder Bay
0 25 50 km
0 15 30 miles
Red River of the North
Thief Lake
Mud Lake
Red Lake Indian Reservation
Upper Red Lake
Lower Red Lake
Grand Forks
East Grand Forks
Nett Lake Indian Reservation
Pelican Lake
Orr
Basswood Lake
Vermilion Lake
Ely
Boundary Waters Canoe Area Wilderness
Grand Portage State Forest
Grand Portage Indian Reservation
Grand Marais
Northome
Effie
Chippewa National Forest
Vermilion Iron Range
Superior National Forest
Mesabi Iron Range
Virginia
Chisholm
Hibbing
Superior National Forest
Lake Superior
Lake Bemidji
Bemidji
Lake Winnibigoshish
Mississippi Headwaters State Forest
Cass Lake
Leech Lake Indian Reservation
Calumet
Grand Rapids
St Louis River
Boulder Lake
Silver Bay
White Earth Indian Reservation
Itasca State Park
Leech Lake
Chippewa National Forest
Walker
Island Lake
Two Harbors
Fargo
Moorhead
Hackensack
Park Rapids
Detroit Lakes
Fond du Lac Indian Reservation
Duluth
Superior
Carlton
Cayuna Iron Range
Pelican Lake
Mississippi River
Ironwood
Bessemer
Fergus Falls
Brainerd
Camp Ripley Military Reservation
Mille Lacs Lake
Mille Lacs Kathio State Park
Father Hennepin State Park
Little Falls
Charles Lindbergh State Park
Sauk Centre
St Cloud
St Croix River
Lake Chippewa
Chippewa River
Wisconsin R
To Minneapolis–St Paul
To Minneapolis–St Paul
To La Crosse

amping, cabins, hiking trails, canoe rentals nd small lakes to explore. **Father Hennepin tate Park** (☎ 320-676-8763), on the southastern edge of the lake, has a popular each; indeed, it is the quickest cool place to each for sweltering Twin City folks.

North up Hwy 169 is the good **Mille Lacs ndian Museum** (☎ 320-532-3632), which utlines the historic and current resident)jibway culture. Open 10 am to 5 pm daily rom mid-May through October; $4. A retored 1930s trading post sells crafts and ooks.

Near the museum is the large Ojibway Grand Casino gambling center and hotel omplex.

At some point each summer is the mayfly courge, the few days when these flying nsects, though harmless, are *everywhere*. They hatch, mate and die not even bothering to eat.

The town of Garrison, west of the lake on Hwy 18, has a couple of coffee shops and a giant roadside monument to the beloved walleye.

BRAINERD

• pop 12, 000

Sprawling Brainerd is the central lakelands' argest entrepôt and commercial center. Relative to its smaller, prettier north counterparts it seems congested, busy and not overly attractive. For more north-woods ambience, it's best to continue north on Hwy 371 to Nisswa and beyond. But if you're ooking for golf courses, amusement parks, water slides or other commercial family-fun attractions, look no farther. Many are found north of town along Hwy 371.

Brainerd hosts the immensely popular **NHRA/Winston Nationals** drag races in mid-August at its International Raceway. This is the state's ultimate motorsports event, and the town is booked solid over the three days. For information, call the chamber of commerce (☎ 218-829-2838, 800-450-2838). Other races occur through the summer.

Often ignored, **Crow Wing State Park** (☎ 218-829-8022), 9 miles south on Hwy 371, has camping, hiking, Indian history and good views of the Mississippi and Crow Wing Rivers. Crosby, northeast on Hwy 210, is a bit of an antiques center.

NISSWA

• pop 1390

Tiny Nisswa, on the 'going up north' boat and trailer route along Hwy 371, has become a minor tourist center of a different sort. The one main street hosting a plethora of gift shops has been done up in quasi-pioneer style to good effect. There's a chamber of commerce cabin on Main St at Nisswa Ave.

At the Depot Complex in the former train station is a history exhibit; across the street a modest Pioneer Village has been recreated. They're at the corner of Main St and Nisswa Ave; both are free.

Much of the activity surrounds the fabulous **Paul Bunyan State Trail**, a rail trail for cycling and in-line skating. It runs about 100 miles from Brainerd (actually neighboring Baxter) to Bemidji. So far the first 50 miles (to Hackensack) are paved, and Nisswa has become a major access point. Route map booklets are available at the chamber of commerce cabin. The lake and forest scenery is grand, with more than 20 lakes along the trail. Bunyan Bike (☎ 218-568-8422) rents bicycles and provides a shuttle service: Call them and they will deliver the bikes, and they'll pick you up or drop you off anywhere along the route, allowing you one-way trips.

Every Wednesday afternoon since 1965, from early June to mid-August, the zoom of **turtle races** has been heard behind the chamber of commerce cabin. Turtle selection begins at 1 pm and they're off and dashing by 2 pm.

Motel Nisswa *(☎ 218-963-7611)*, on Hwy 371 near the turn-off into town, is functional and very central. The ***Adirondack Café***, in the middle of the Main St retail strip, serves excellent coffees and sweets and is an agreeable place to plan the day.

Greyhound buses stop at the chamber of commerce en route between Brainerd and Bemidji and beyond.

WALKER

• pop 950

This attractive little town on large Leech Lake makes a good stop. It bills itself as the

MINNESOTA

Lewis & Lindbergh – A Literary & Historical Scenic Drive

Fans of literature and history may wish to take a meandering route from the Twin Cities toward the north country. Northwest of St Cloud along I-94 is **Sauk Centre**, a town of 7000, in the middle of dairy country that was the childhood home of Nobel Prize–winning novelist Sinclair Lewis. He was born here in 1885. As is the case with two other famous central Minnesotans, Judy Garland and Bob Dylan (see boxed text 'Bob Dylan's Boyhood'), Lewis and his work were not always appreciated by the hometown residents (and in some cases they're still not).

His 1920 novel, *Main Street*, made his reputation, but the portrayal of small-town America based on Sauk Centre characters and events was less than flattering, and many residents never got over the indignation. Of course, he *did* name the town Gopher Prairie.

Downtown, the main streets haven't changed much since those first published descriptions. Just off the interstate on Main St is the Sinclair Lewis Interpretive Center, with a biographical video and some first editions. Information on Lewis-related sites around town is also available. For example, the restored Palmer House Hotel, downtown at No 500 on what is now called Sinclair Lewis Ave, is where the young Lewis once worked as a desk clerk.

A short walk away is the Sinclair Lewis Boyhood Home (☎ 320-632-3154), 812 Sinclair Lewis Ave, now on the National Register of Historic Places. It has some period furnishings and personal effects. It's open from late May to early September.

After much European travel, Lewis returned to Sauk Centre later in life. His grave is in the Greenwood Cemetery, east of the center on Sinclair Lewis Ave. Among his other realistic, satirical books, which are often critical of American society, are *Babbitt* (1922), *Arrowsmith* (1925) and *It Can't Happen Here* (1935). Much of his writing is based on his Midwest experiences.

For the return to Hwy 371 north, avoid retracing the interstate and take Hwy 28 northeast to Little Falls. It meanders past farms and cornfields interspersed with sections of meadows and marshes. A couple of roadside turnouts beside lakes can be used for picnicking. The eastern end runs alongside the Swan River, which flows into the Mississippi at Little Falls. Aviator Charles Lindbergh grew up on a farm here. **Charles Lindbergh State Park** (☎ 320-616-2525), in addition to offering campsites and preserving a bucolic Mississippi River bank, has an interpretive center on Charles Jr, the aviation innovator. Parts of his first plane are on display.

From here Hwy 371 continues north. Halfway to Brainerd is the **Camp Ripley Military Reservation**, the country's largest National Guard training facility. The Minnesota Military Museum (☎ 320-632-7374), on the grounds, outlines the role Minnesotans have played in America's conflicts since 1858.

LIBRARY OF CONGRESS

JS muskie capital: Historically, the fish have)een plentiful, and catches have always been ıumerous here. In the vicinity are countless esorts and the Chippewa National Forest. Hwy 371/200 becomes Main St n town, and most of the ervices are stretched along ıere.

At the east end of downtown (although it feels like he south end) on Hwy 371/200 is the chamber of commerce (☎ 218-547-1313, 800-833-1118, www.leech-lake.com), open weekdays 9 am to 6 pm, Saturday 10 am to 3 pm. It provides local and area advice. The Chippewa National Forest offices (☎ 218-547-1044) at the chamber of commerce and in the town of Cass Lake, to the ıorth, have information on hiking, canoeing ınd camping.

Adjacent to the chamber of commerce ıre the Wildlife and Indian Museum, the Old School House and Cass County Museum. All are open from early June to September. They house small collections relating the area's past, and all three can be visited for $3/1 adults/children. The Indian museum contains a wildlife diorama, depictions of early-20th–century Indian life and a raditional canoe. The log schoolhouse was ıctually in service until 1937, and the Cass history museum has some Indian beadwork ınd artifacts on logging and homesteading.

Drop in at the Walker Drug Store on Main St and get a wooden postcard.

Cajun Fest, at the Moondance Fairgrounds, is three days of music at the end of August.

Places to Stay & Eat

South of town and then west on Hwy 200 is he exceptional ***Stony Point Campground*** n the Kabekona State Forest, with perhaps he most appealing location on all of Leech Lake. Sites are $16 for tents, $23 with power. It's very busy on holiday weekends but is otherwise not bad.

Muskie Mythology

Throughout Minnesota, fishing is a quasi-religion. Where else can you see newspaper features regularly listing what's biting which bait where? You can't go into any commercial establishment – gas station, restaurant, hardware store, tourist office – without seeing stunning stuffed specimens overhead. It seems taxidermy, at best a quirky hobby in most of the world, must be taught in school here.

Walleye, bass, pike and trout aside, it is the muskellunge that is revered above all, the stuff of true glory and lore. The muskie is one of the largest American freshwater fish species and is unquestionably the most ferocious. The world-record muskie weighed in at 70lb, so potential size is another appeal.

The sight of a large, flipping, obviously upset muskie, with its jaws full of jagged, chomping teeth, is enough to create instant respect, awe and sometimes terror. There are tales of people landing a muskie and then in utter panic jumping overboard, of fishers who fear for their lives firing a bullet into the catch and going down with the ship. Other anglers cast a million times, watching lunkers approach the lure only to veer away. More time is spent with nothing to show for it fishing muskies than any other fish.

You may hear stories about out-of-state muskie anglers. Two tourists in a rented boat were having a great outing, and after landing a few were debating how they could find the same weedy bay the next day. One said, 'I'll scratch an X in the bottom of the boat.' The other replied sarcastically, 'Oh, that's brilliant. What if we don't get the same boat?'

Chase Motor Inn *(☎ 218-547-2882, 800-772-6769)*, downtown by the city dock at the end of 5th St, has rooms starting at $58 and cottages on the water starting at $80.

The suitably named ***Lakeview Inn*** *(☎ 218-547-1212, 800-252-5073)* is a decent place with moderate prices at the south edge of town on Hwy 371/200.

For a munch, the ***Outdoorsman Café***, in the middle of Main St with a log façade, is a perfect blend of appropriate woodsy character and hearty standard meals. Two-leveled ***Giuliana's***, in the center of town on Main St is a good Italian restaurant, pub and ice-cream parlor. Most meals are under $12, and they come with bread and salad.

The ***Café Zona Rosa***, at the corner of Front St W and 5th St, is a casual spot with an outdoor patio for Mexican lunches and dinners. It's also a good place for an evening beer.

DETROIT LAKES

• pop 7150

To the west along Hwy 34 the woods suddenly vanish, the sky seems to rise and nearly flat fields are lined with rows of canola, hay, corn and other grains. Park Rapids, with its wide main street with cars parked up the middle and historic street lamps, has a definite Western flavor. In early July there's even a rodeo.

Detroit Lakes, however, is the center of another green lake district, the last in western Minnesota before the plains and combine thrashers really take over. The mile-long beach downtown on Little Detroit Lake is an old resort strip that entices visitors from the Dakotas and beyond. West Lake Drive follows it. Family resorts and campgrounds are numerous on the 400-odd lakes within 25 miles.

The chamber of commerce (☎ 218-847-9202, 800-542-3992, @ dlchamber@lakesnet.net) is at 700 Washington Ave.

The **Tamarac National Wildlife Refuge**, less than 30 minutes north, is a major bird sanctuary with a visitor center. The three-day **WE Fest**, held each August, is one of the USA's largest country music events and draws big-name performers.

Old motels and quaint cabins sit side-by-side on West Lake Drive across from the lakefront beach. Try cute ***Fairyland Cottages*** *(☎ 218-847-9991)*, a real throwback. In July and August rentals usually require a minimum stay of a week and go for $300. ***Capri Motel*** *(☎ 218-847-4458, 800-772-2775)* is at 1334 Washington Ave, with rooms for $46 for two people. On weekends in July and August there is a three-day minimum. There are also cabins for rent.

By the way, if you're continuing to Fargo, North Dakota, because of the influence of the film Fargo, don't bother. It was filmed in Minnesota, although no one seems to know exactly where. (Despite rumors, it was not Brainerd.)

ITASCA STATE PARK

Northwest of Walker, Itasca (☎ 218-266-2100), Minnesota's oldest state park, is immensely popular, encompassing some of the best northern scenery in the state. It contains the official headwaters of the mighty Mississippi, one of the largest remaining stands of old-growth pine forest in Minnesota and some Indian sites. It's home to deer, foxes, bears, loons and eagles. Activities include canoeing, biking, hiking and cross-country skiing. Needless to say, it is one of the state's most-visited parks.

Things to See & Do

A scenic circular 15-mile drive, including 10 miles through what's known as the wilderness zone, circumnavigates Lake Itasca and leads past many sites and trailheads.

After a stroll through the woods you can wade across the Mississippi at its source, 1475 feet above sea level. The information center provides excellent background on the storied river.

The sandy beach by Brower Inn snack bar is a great place to swim after some summer exertion. And the grove of 200-year-old red pine and 300-year-old white pine feels like a natural church.

Itasca Sports Rental (☎ 218-266-2150), open all summer at Lake Itasca's North Arm, has bikes, canoes, rowboats and fishing gear at reasonable prices. Boats can also be ented at other lakes within the park, but ook them at Itasca.

Itasca Tours runs daily 90-minute aturalist-led boat tours on Lake Itasca rom near Douglas Lodge.

Does this park have it all, or what?

laces to Stay & Eat

he prime camping season is May 15 to)ctober, but the two campgrounds (☎ 800-46-2267) remain open all year with limited menities. In summer, don't show up vithout reservations. ***Bear Paw Camp-round***, the smaller of the two, is desirable ecause it has lake views and a few walk-in ites. Rates are $12 for a basic site, $14 with lectricity.

The immaculate, comfortable log-design II ***Mississippi Headwaters Hostel*** *(☎ 218-66-3415, fax 218-266-3451,* ⓔ *itascamn@ol.com)* offers dorm beds ($15/18 nembers/nonmembers) and some family ooms. Private rooms ($24/35 single/double, r $45/60 for peak weekends) are also availble. Often it's nearly empty, but sometimes t's nearly full with various organized roups. It's open most of the year, but call irst, especially in March and April, to heck. The location is perfect – on the North Arm, with bike and other rentals nearby.

If you want a little rustic luxury, try the enerable ***Douglas Lodge*** *(☎ 800-246-267)*, run by the park, with lodge rooms tarting at $47 a double. There are also arious cabins around the park, starting at 75. Some have fireplaces and cooking facilties, and sizes vary; some accommodate ight people. Cabins can be booked one ear in advance, and early reservations are ecommended.

The lodge dining room offers simple neat-and-potato meals but they're a good alue, at $10 or less.

BEMIDJI

• pop 11,000

On the western edge of the Chippewa National Forest, neat and tidy Bemidji is an old lumber town with a well-preserved lowntown. This, together with the arching parkland waterfront marked with a giant statue of legendary logger Paul Bunyan and his faithful blue ox, Babe, make Bemidji, 'first city of the Mississippi,' an appealing stop. And that's with no real attractions. Rather, it acts as a hub for the surrounding vacationland.

The chamber of commerce and CVB (☎ 218-751-3541, 800-458-2223, www.bemidji.org), on Paul Bunyan Drive (County Rd 21) at 4th St NW beside the statues, displays

Feats to Match the Feet

It's difficult to determine which is taller, the tales of their legendary exploits, or the statue of woodsman Paul Bunyan and Babe the blue ox. For over a century, these stories of the colossal have been heard from coast to coast: Paul scooped out the Great Lakes when Babe was thirsty and needed water bowls. Ole, the Norwegian blacksmith, opened the mines in the iron ranges when Babe required shoes.

The first written records appeared in newspaper stories in 1910 based on a lumberjack's accounts, and books followed. They told of Babe pulling forests of logs, mountains, even fogs, and of the monumental breakfasts that Paul consumed.

In Bemidji, see the bright lakeside statue of the pair. Inside the chamber of commerce and CVB next door is a whimsical collection of oversize personal effects. Across the state and beyond are Paul Bunyan–themed restaurants, museum artifacts, bike trails and more, all commemorating this captivating figure. The folk hero also lives on in numerous children's books.

LIBRARY OF CONGRESS

MINNESOTA

some of Paul's former possessions, such as his toothbrush. It's open weekdays 8 am to 6 pm, Saturday 9 am to 6 pm, Sunday noon to 5 pm.

Morrell's Trading Post, across the street, has genuine Indian crafts, along with a wide assortment of souvenirs. The Woolen Mills factory store, on 3rd St, makes and sells quality north-woods woolens. They've got sweaters, Hudson Bay blankets (the all-wool, white-with-colored-stripes blankets first used in the early fur trade days) and more.

Activities

Kayaks, canoes, sailboats, Windsurfers and mountain bikes can all be rented at the waterfront at the Bemidji State University campus north of downtown off County Rd 21.

Bicyclists, ask about the Paul Bunyan State Trail (see the Nisswa section), which ends its approximately 100-mile path a Lake Bemidji State Park. Riders can als pedal the Great River Rd (County Rd 2 along the Mississippi to Itasca State Park.

Hikers should consider exploring th trails of Buena Vista State Forest, which a the name indicates lead to good views. Th forest is just south of Black Duck Stat Forest, about 12 miles north of town o Hwy 71 or County Rd 15.

The Bemidji area gets piles of snow, wit reliable amounts from the end of Novembe right through to April. With that kind o season, hibernation has given way to well-ingrained ski culture. For downhill enthusiasts, the Buena Vista Ski Area (☎ 218 243-2231), about 12 miles north on Hwy 71 has 15 runs, some set up for snowboarders The chalet rents equipment.

Sweep That Rock Out of the House!

Out of the public eye, in quiet arenas around the state surrounded by heaps of snow, a small but fiercely devoted group of Minnesotans gathers on winter evenings to throw rocks and sweep ice.

The ancient sport of curling, founded in Scotland hundreds of years ago, continues a marginal, often belittled existence in the frozen wastes of Canada, Scandinavia, Western Europe and the USA. It's played by 15,000 people across the US snowbelt, and the Midwest is its American home.

Even recently obtained Olympic status has failed to raise the profile of this most democratic sport. It's played by all ages, men and women, often in mixed teams. You don't need independent wealth or tons of expensive gear. A healthy respect for tradition and the game's well-mannered etiquette, combined with a competitive spirit, are the essentials.

The game of sliding 42lb of highly polished granite across pebbled ice to a target (house) looks simple, but it actually comes with its own vocabulary, strategies and practised techniques. There are four people to a team, two teams in the game. The game is broken into 'ends' (kind of like innings in baseball), each of which is over after each team has shot eight stones (two per player). There are 10 ends in a standard game. Teams alternate sliding the stones down the 'sheet' (the ice) to the house with a swing of the arm and slide of the feet. Once a shot is made, the opposing team decides how to react. They can attempt to bash it out, use it as a guard for one of their own or ignore it. Rocks remaining in the house score one point each.

Participants from the Dakotas to Wisconsin or farther drive for miles on icy roads to partake in tournaments called bonspiels. The St Paul curling club is the largest in the country, but rinks can be found in Duluth and small communities across the state, such as Mapleton, which bills itself as the southern curling capital.

Visitors will generally be welcome at any club to watch a game and to appreciate that a bit of a workout followed by the customary postgame chat and drinks is a fine, civilized way to pass a snowy night.

The local Nordic club maintains about 100 miles of cross-country trails and organizes numerous group events and races.

Also in winter, the active Bemidji Curling Club welcomes visitors and public viewing.

Places to Stay

For camping, ***Lake Bemidji State Park*** *(☎ 218-755-3843)* is about 8 miles north of town on County Rd 20 at the top of the lake, with a beach and trails.

Several modest but comfortable motels can be found south of town. Friendly ***Paul Bunyan Motel*** *(☎ 218-751-1314, 800-848-3788)*, 915 Paul Bunyan Drive NE, with its own little beach, starts at $38 for rooms on the street, $56 for those by the lake, less after September. (Despite the motel name, the beds are normal, not giant-size.) The ***Lakeside***, next door and with the same phone number, is similar.

North of town, ***Bel Air Motel*** *(☎ 218-751-3222, 800-798-3222, 1350 Paul Bunyan Drive NW)* is a small place with large rooms good for families. In July the price for two adults and two kids ranges from $55 to $65. Nearby is ***Super 8*** *(☎ 218-751-8481, 1815 Paul Bunyan Drive NW)* at $46/50 single/double.

Places to Eat

After tooling through many central lakelands towns, Bemidji is a veritable cornucopia at mealtime – it even has its own brew pub. That is partially the influence of Bemidji State University, north of downtown.

The ***Coachman Café*** *(509 Beltrami Ave NW)* is the local favorite for cheap breakfasts, excellent cinnamon rolls or coffee cake. Everything is made from scratch, even the salad dressing. It's open daily.

The vintage 1932 ***Rite Maid Café***, in the center of town on Paul Bunyan Drive, is a basic diner. It closes in late afternoon and doesn't open on Sunday.

The Union Square complex, across from the lake in the middle of town, has a small array of eateries and a bar. ***Great Wall*** has a Chinese buffet. In adjacent Union Station, ***1st City Brewery*** is recommended. The burgers ($6) are especially good, but it also serves pizza, steaks, pastas and more. Any of the half-dozen house-brews are worth trying; if you can't make up your mind, get the sample tray. Arrive early – it gets busy.

Moving upscale is the casually classy ***Tutto Bene*** *(300 Beltrami Ave NW)*, with Italian specialties, a romantic outdoor patio and an espresso bar.

There's a ***bakery*** on Minnesota Ave.

Entertainment

The ***Paul Bunyan Playhouse*** *(☎ 218-751-7270, 314 Beltrami Ave)* is Minnesota's oldest professional summer theater. The season runs from mid-June through August, with shows at 8 pm Wednesday through Sunday.

The ***Stats*** is a busy sports bar in Union Square. Young locals drink at ***Mort's Hard Times Saloon***, on 3rd St NW just up from Paul Bunyan Drive along the lake.

Getting There & Away

Greyhound stops here on its route connecting the state's northern and southern cities. There's one a day in each direction. The depot is at the south end of town at the U-Haul building, which is behind the Bonanza restaurant on Paul Bunyan Drive.

CASS LAKE

East of Bemidji on Hwy 2, tiny Cass Lake houses the Chippewa National Forest headquarters (☎ 218-335-8600, ⓔ chippewa/r9_chippewa@fs.fed.us) in a splendid three-story Finnish log building from the early 20th century. They have a wealth of pamphlets, maps and advice to offer.

Cass Lake is one in a chain of eight lakes, all renowned for fishing, and is surrounded by three dozen resorts. Much of the land around Cass and Leech Lakes is on the Leech Lake Indian Reservation.

The Anishinabe people celebrate several **powwows** through the summer, which are open to the public. Area chambers of commerce will have details. These colorful events feature elaborate costumes and traditional drumming, singing and dancing. Often some Native American foods, such as bannock and buffalo, and crafts are for sale. Visitors might like to know that 'powwow' was an East Coast Indian term applied by early white explorer-pioneers to any type of Indian gathering. Indigenous peoples across the continent subsequently adopted the name for their contemporary cultural celebrations.

CHIPPEWA NATIONAL FOREST AREA

Minnesota's original pine forests were almost totally eliminated by logging in the late 19th and early 20th centuries, but natural regrowth and commercial replanting now cover a third of the state. The lovely Chippewa, one of the largest segments, was the first national forest established east of the Mississippi. The 1036-sq-mile forest is a mixed-use area with managed woodlands, water catchments, Indian reservations, bald eagle habitats and abundant recreational opportunities. With 1300 lakes, 23 campgrounds and extensive hiking or biking trails, as well as various canoe routes, there's no shortage of activities to enjoy. In winter skiers and snowmobilers take to the woods.

For information about the forest headquarters, see the Cass Lake and Walker sections. Camping reservations can be made for some of the established campgrounds (☎ 877-444-6777). Four hundred backcountry sites, known as dispersed campsites, are free, and no permits are required. Campgrounds are open mid-May to mid-September, although some can be used out of season without the services.

The forest has the highest concentration of bald eagles in the lower 48 states, plentiful deer (be careful driving at night), moose, ospreys, loons and good fishing. Ask about bear precautions.

Other highlights include the **Lost 40**, a 100-acre section of forest containing hundred-year-old red and white pines near the town of Northome on Hwy 71. Scenic County Rd 10, east of Cass Lake, leads to campgrounds and **Camp Rabideau**, a Civilian Conservation Corps (CCC) encampment from the depression-era work program; it has 15 buildings on the National Register of Historic Places, an interpretive center, a picnic area and walking trails, but no camping.

GRAND RAPIDS

• pop 8000

On the east side of the forest, Grand Rapids is another old lumber town, with the enormous Blandin Paper Mill and some defunct open-pit mines nearby. A few attractions make it OK for a brief visit. Hwy 169 south is the commercial strip, with all the usual chains.

The chamber of commerce (☎ 218-326-1251, 800-472-6366, www.grandmn.com), at 1 NW 3rd St in the old railroad depot, operates weekdays 8 am to 6 pm, Saturday 9 am to 5 pm, Sunday 11 am to 3 pm. In winter it's closed on weekends. There is also 24-hour accommodations information.

Village Bookstore (☎ 218-326-9458) is a fine stop-off at 201 NW 4th St, suite 105.

Things to See & Do

Judy Garland (née Frances Gumm) was born here in 1922 and lived here for four years. A number of sites revolve around her life. The **Itasca Heritage Center** (☎ 218-326-6431), at the corner of Hwy 169 and 4th St (Hwy 2), is

Judy Garland, a well-known child of Grand Rapids

in the old Central School – just follow the yellow brick road in from the street. It includes a good little history museum with a collection of Garland artifacts, including her ruby slippers and photos tracing her life. Open 9:30 am to 5 pm Monday to Friday, 9:30 am to 4 pm Saturday; Sunday from late May to early September it's open 11 am to 4 pm; $4.

The **Children's Museum & Oz Exhibit** (☎ 218-326-1900), 19 NE 4th St downtown, is two museums in one. One section is an area where kids can make crafts; the other has more fun *Wizard of Oz* memorabilia. Open 10 am to 5 pm Monday to Saturday, noon to 5 pm Sunday; $3. Combination discounts are sold for it and the **Garland Birthplace Historic House** (☎ 218-327-9726), just south of town on Hwy 169. The house is decorated as it was when Judy lived there and offers details on the family's life. The gift shop has some interesting items, such as tapes, films and photographs. Open 10 am to 5 pm daily all year (on summer Sundays it's open in the evening only); $3.

Three miles south of town, the **Forest History Center** (☎ 218-327-4482), off Hwy 169 south, is a reconstructed logging camp, complete with lumberjacks and floating cook shack. These drifting kitchens went downstream to mills with the logs and the lumbermen. Trails border the Mississippi. It's open from late May to mid-October, but the main building stays open most winter weekends. For that summer season, hours are Monday to Saturday 10 am to 5 pm, Sunday noon to 5 pm; $5/4/3 adults/seniors/children.

For those driving north, Hwy 38 to Effie is a 47-mile National Scenic Byway that traverses undeveloped wooded lakelands.

Activities

The Mesabi Trail, a recreational and bike path heading northeast from Grand Rapids all the way to Ely, on the border of Boundary Waters Canoe Area, is scheduled to open sometime in 2002. This will be a fabulous route through the Iron Range and then up into Superior National Forest to Ely.

Special Events

The chamber of commerce can supply details on these and other events.

June

Judy Garland festival – for true fans, a festival held the last week of the month

August

White Oak Rendezvous – a reenactment on the first weekend of the month of the 1798 Northwest Company fur trading post rendezvous, at which fur traders collected to deliver their goods and socialize; with a thousand participants in costume and 200 tents, the rendezvous brings the period to life (☎ 218-246-9393)

Places to Stay

The ***Schoolcraft State Park*** *(☎ 218-247-7215)* has 30 rustic campsites along the Mississippi, open from May to October. It's west of town, south off Hwy 2.

The ***Itascan Motel*** *(☎ 218-326-3489, 800-842-7733, fax 218-327-2290, 610 S Pokegama Ave)*, on Hwy 169 south, is a good, clean place with great prices, at $38 double. Kitchenettes are available.

Farther out but always dependable is ***Super 8*** *(☎ 218-327-1108, fax 218-327-1108 exit 105, 1702 S Pokegama Ave)*. Rooms are $50 single/double with continental breakfast.

The grandest place to lay your head is the ***Sawmill Inn*** *(☎ 218-326-8501, 800-235-6455, 2301 S Pokegama Ave)*, with a lobby that looks straight out of a lakeside resort, complete with chunky furniture and stuffed animal heads. It's a spacious, well designed, good-value lodge, with rooms starting at $56 and rising to $78 at poolside on summer weekends.

More modest motels can be found along Hwy 2 east and west of town.

Places to Eat

First choice come mealtime should be the ***First Grade*** café, on the ground floor of the Itasca Heritage Center, in the old Central School at the corner of Hwy 169 and 4th St (Hwy 2). Excellent, well-prepared breakfasts, lunches and baked snacks are freshly made every day. The chicken pita with salad ($6) is a true bargain. Start with the mushroom wild rice soup. It's great to get away with eating in the classroom, too. Open 7 am to 4 pm (Sunday 10 am to 2 pm).

New China *(214 NW 1st Ave)* lays out a fair daily buffet for the smile-making price of $5 for lunch, $7 for dinner. There is a broad à la carte menu too.

Getting There & Away

The bus depot is at Vanity Cleaners, close to the Children's Museum, at the corner of Hwy 169 and 1st Ave NE. Lorenz Bus Service (☎ 612-784-7196, 800-784-3611) runs to Hibbing and Virginia on the Iron Trail and south to the Twin Cities. Buses run weekdays only.

IRON RANGE

An area of red-tinged scrubby hills rather than mountains, Minnesota's Iron Range district consists primarily of the Mesabi and Vermilion Ranges, running north and south of Hwy 169 from roughly Grand Rapids east to Ely. The lesser Cayuna and Gogebic Ranges (the latter in Wisconsin) complete the productive zone.

Iron was discovered here in the late 19th century by the Merrit brothers, who noticed the reddish, sandy dust under an uprooted tree. It can be said without hyperbole that the readily accessible rich ore deposits changed history. European immigrants poured into the region; thousands of Austrians, Cornish, Czechs, Finns, Germans, Italians, Poles, Serbians, Slovaks and others arrived, ready to risk everything for a new life. Their labors made the steel that made the rise of US industry possible.

At one time 70% of the nation's iron ore was extracted from the vast open-pit mines here. This was the raw product used to construct the country's buildings, bridges and machinery. Meeting the demands for WWII took a tremendous toll. When the high-quality ore was almost exhausted, the region developed techniques to use low-grade ore and taconite. This innovation has saved the local industry, albeit in a considerably scaled-back form. Overseas sources have cut dramatically into markets, too.

Visitors can see working mines and numerous related sites all along Hwy 169, which is known as the Iron Trail in this area. Though the earth has been violently pillaged and huge open pits and denuded hills are often in evidence, the entire district has taken on a unique, sparse beauty and inspires an awe all its own. The multicolored, layered mounds and enormous holes filled with rainwater, forming their own lakelands, are fascinating landscapes. The toil and history that created them are equally intriguing and make an enthralling, very human story.

Most of the attractions on the Iron Trail and nearby are seasonal, generally open from late May to early September.

Calumet

East of Grand Rapids, at Calumet, stop at the **Hill Annex Mine State Park** (☎ 218-247-7215) for a great introduction to the whole region. The excellent free museum details the history; tours of the former pit mine indicate the scale of these operations. The ore was so rich here that it hardly needed processing. Open 9:30 am to 6 pm daily from late May to early September. The 1½-hour bus tours ($6/4 adults/children) run hourly from 10 am to 4 pm.

Hibbing

• pop 18,000

As the largest Iron Trail town, Hibbing has some more-than-adequate services and interesting attractions. The visitors' center (☎ 218-262-4166), E 211 Howard Ave, is open 9 am to 3 pm Monday to Saturday from late May to early September, 10 am to 4 pm weekdays the rest of the year.

Things to See & Do The **Hull Rust Mahoning Mine**, the world's largest open-pit iron mine, 3 miles north of town taking E 3rd Ave is a must. A viewpoint presents a free and amazing panorama of this 3-mile-long mine complex, still in operation. Massive trucks and machinery become dinky toys, dwarfed by the awesome water-filled basins, which have been producing for more than a hundred years. A display room has a video

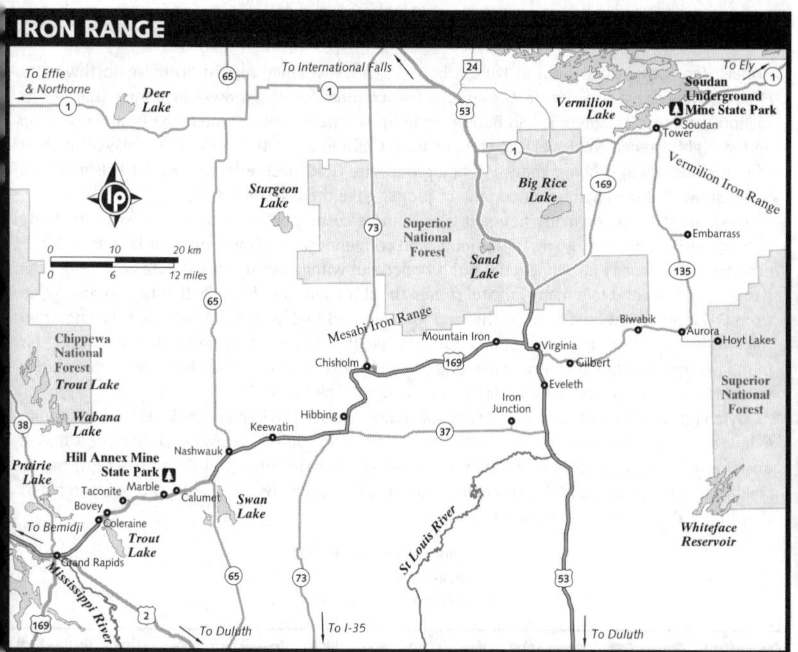

and some information. The mine shuts down periodically, depending on world markets. It's open May 15 to September 30, 9 am to 5 pm.

The **Hibbing Taconite Co**, operating on the pit's northern perimeter, offers tours Wednesday and Thursday from mid-June to mid-August for $5. Book reservations through the Ironworld Discovery Center in Chisholm.

The **Greyhound Bus Origin Museum** (☎ 218-263-5814), 1201 Greyhound Blvd, is north of town on the way to Hull Rust. The famous bus company started in Hibbing in 1914, carrying miners to the pit. The museum tells the company story with models, posters and a bus collection. Open 9 am to 5 pm Monday to Saturday from mid-May through September; $3/1 adults/kids.

The **Historical Museum** (☎ 218-263-8522), at the corner of 23rd St and E 5th Ave, depicts through models and artifacts the area's mining and logging history. Open 10:30 am to 4:30 pm Monday to Saturday from mid-May to mid-October.

Bob Dylan lived at 2425 E 7th Ave as a child and teenager, but the house is now home to other residents. The Hibbing Public Library, near 24th St and E 5th Ave, has a small display of Dylan-related items.

Howard Street Booksellers (☎ 218-262-5206) is worth a stop at 115 East Howard St.

Places to Stay North of town up County Rd 5 is ***McCarthy Beach State Park*** *(☎ 218-254-2411)*, with two lakes, sandy swimming, mature pines and trails.

South of downtown, where Hwy 169 meets Hwy 37, is the reliable ***Days Inn*** *(☎ 218-263-8306)*. Rates are $48/52 single/double and include a good continental breakfast. Also here is ***Super 8*** *(☎ 218-263-8982, E 1411 40th St)*, with rooms at $55/62.

Close to the center is ***Hibbing Park Hotel*** *(☎ 218-262-3481, 800-262-3481, fax 218-262-1906, E 1402 Howard St)*, a comfortable place with a pool, bar and restaurant. Rates are $65/75 in summer.

Bob Dylan's Boyhood

Robert Zimmerman was born in Duluth in 1941, but his family moved 50 miles northwest to Hibbing when he was seven. It was an area known more for its narrow-mindedness than for its folkloric or musical traditions, and Bob never fit in. He spent a lot of time in the local music shop and at night listened to black radio stations from Chicago and Little Rock, which played the sort of music nobody in Hibbing knew. His first group, the Golden Chords, wowed the kids in a local talent show, but the chamber of commerce judges gave them second prize.

From an early age he made frequent trips to more cosmopolitan Minneapolis, where he hung around the student area, going to jazz joints and coffeehouses and meeting musicians. In 1959 he entered the university in Minneapolis but dropped out within a year. At that time he adopted the name Bob Dylan and told many fanciful stories about his early life, typically that he was an orphan from Oklahoma, that he'd been on the road for years and that he knew Woody Guthrie and other folk musicians. These stories were none too credible, but they were Dylan's way of disowning his mundane, middle-class origins and creating a worldly image. One acquaintance commented, 'He talked like he had smoked a lot of dope, and I could tell he hadn't.'

Dylan hit New York's Greenwich Village folk scene in early 1961 and never looked back, though a few songs do mention 'the North Country.' His 1965 album *Highway 61 Revisited* makes obscure references to northern Minnesota's most scenic road, though it doesn't suggest happy childhood memories: God tells Abraham to kill his son out on Hwy 61, and a promoter suggests that the next world war could be easily done:

'We'll just put some bleachers
out in the sun
and have it on Highway 61.'

Places to Eat At the corner of Howard St and E 6th Ave, ***Zimmy's*** (☎ 218-262-6145) is a popular lunch and dinner spot with an all-purpose burgers-to-steaks menu and all manner of easy-to-down drinks. Downtown, ***China Buffet*** *(☎ 218-263-6324, 116 E Howard St)* spreads out a decent buffet daily ($4.25 for lunch, $7 for dinner), and it's open until 10 pm. ***Grandma's in the Park*** *(☎ 218-262-3481, 1402 E Howard St)*, in the Hibbing Park Hotel out by the highway, is busy with a large menu of sandwiches, chicken and full-meal standards under $12.

Chisholm

• pop 5290

Chisholm has no mine, but there are two important mine sites. Also here on the west side of town is the impressive 85-foot statue of an iron miner, the country's third-largest freestanding memorial.

The chamber of commerce (☎ 218-254-3600, 800-422-0806) is at 10 NW 2nd St.

Things to See & Do Visible from the statue is the **Ironworld Discovery Center** (☎ 218-254-3321, 800-372-6437), on Hwy 169, a huge theme park and living museum revealing the area's rich industrial and ethnic mosaic. Exhibits, foods, costumes, music and crafts present the cultural side while a restored trolley, pit mine and interpretive center focus on industry.

Each day different activities and special shows are presented. In addition, there are major themes or festivals, often ethnically based, scheduled throughout the summer. Listen for the hopping button-box accordion festival, with everything from Cajun to Polish styles. Open 9:30 am to 5 pm daily from mid-June to mid-September (sometimes open later for special events)

$8/7/6/30 adult/senior/student/family. Expect to spend several hours minimum.

The **Minnesota Museum of Mining** (☎ 218-254-5543), 719 NE 2nd St, despite looking a little neglected, is a good site where you can wander amid a hodgepodge of mining-related articles. The lawn is littered with heavy equipment. Inside are simulated storefronts from the late 19th century, rock samples, digging equipment, some interesting old photographs and plenty more. There's even an old bus, from the forerunner of Greyhound, Mesabi Transport Ltd. Open 10 am to 5 pm from late May to early September; $3.

Downtown, the **Classic Car Museum** (☎ 218-254-4201), 305 W Lake St, has a fine collection of 36 cars, including a 1913 Model T, a '41 Chevy convertible and a '65 T-Bird, as well as scooters, gas pumps and other memorabilia. At $5/3 adult/child it's a bargain for car lovers. Open 9 am to 5 pm daily from late May to early September.

Places to Stay & Eat There's camping at ***KO Campground*** *(☎ 218-254-7414)*, in the Museum of Mining complex, for $13 or $15 with full hookups. It's officially open from May to October, but it's a pretty easy-going place and they'll likely let you set up almost anytime.

When hunger strikes go where everybody else does – to homey ***Helen's Diner*** *(12 Lake St)*. Basic breakfasts and lunches are served. There's a bakery across the street. For dinner, you're best off in Hibbing.

Eastern Iron Trail

It was the iron first discovered in **Mountain Iron** that touched off the region's development. Two blocks north of historic Main St, remnants can be seen of the original streets from the turn of the 20th century. Farther north another block or two is Minntac Mine Overlook, a National Historic Landmark with views over the giant, still-operating US Steel Minntac taconite mine. Tours are given on summer Fridays, with buses departing from the Senior Citizen Center (☎ 218-749-7299) on Main St in the heart town. The center has a tourist information desk.

South of Hwy 169, west of town, is the ***West 2 Rivers*** recreation area and campground (☎ 218-735-8831) for RVs and tents. There's a beach. RV sites are $11, basic tent sites away from the main campground are $5.

A few miles east is the considerably larger town of **Virginia**, where along Chestnut St several eateries, including a couple of Chinese restaurants, and some places for a beer can be found. The chamber of commerce (☎ 218-741-2717, 800-777-8497), 403 N 1st St, provides local and district information.

East of town off Hwy 135 is free **Mineview in the Sky**, an overlook with an information center atop granting spectacular views of the 3-mile-long, multicolored Rouchleau open pit. The truck on display provides added perspective. The modest Virginia Heritage Museum (☎ 218-741-1136), 9th Ave N, has artifacts, photographs and postcards relating to logging and mining.

For overnighting there is the downtown ***Lakeshore Motor Inn*** *(☎ 218-741-3360, 800-569-8131, 404 N 6th St)*, at $35/42 single/double. Good, basic ***camping*** can be found 30 miles north at Pfeiffer Lake (☎ 218-229-3371) in the Superior National Forest on USFS 256 off Hwy 1.

Detouring south of the Iron Trail on Hwy 53, Eveleth has the revamped **United States Hockey Hall of Fame** (☎ 218-744-5167), 801 Hat Trick Ave, and, downtown, the world's largest hockey stick. The museum showcases American players and Olympic teams. It's open daily all year for $3.50.

Toward the eastern end of the ranges, tiny, tidy alpine-themed **Biwabik** has the region's top resort, the imposing hillside ***Biwabik Lodge*** *(☎ 218-865-4588, 800-383-3183)*. A golf course and Giant's Ridge downhill ski resort are five minutes away. Prices are very reasonable, starting at $60 in summer, $45 for fall specials.

Just east of **Aurora** is the free Active Mine View taconite mine appearing like a colossal gravel pit with seemingly miniature trucks maneuvering about. It's about 1½ miles off Main St, east along 3rd Ave N, and is open 9 am to 7 pm daily. LTV Steel Mining (☎ 218-229-2245, 218-229-2614), a massive taconite operation, offers tours Tuesday and Friday from May to September, departing from City Hall. Call for times and reservations. For spending the night, the ***Forest Garden*** *(☎ 218-229-3676, 413 S Main St)* is reasonably priced, at $40/45.

Farther east is **Hoyt Lakes**, on the edge of Superior National Forest. It's the easternmost of the iron mining communities. Near the two adjacent lakes you'll find camping, swimming and numerous forest trails. It's known especially for the miles of snowmobiling trails. Three miles north is the Longyear Drill Site, the remains of an exploratory mine drilling operation from 1890. This was the humble start of today's multinational Longyear Exploration Company.

Northern Iron Trail

From just west of Aurora, Hwy 135 winds its way north toward huge Vermilion Lake. Off Hwy 135, about halfway to Tower from Aurora, is the tiny village of **Embarrass**, with the vestiges of an original Finnish pioneer settlement. At one time, before the 1950s and the taconite mine developments, the village was almost 100% Finnish. (This entire section of Minnesota was home to many early immigrants from Finland.) Today there is a mix of people reflecting the many nationalities that were represented in the influx of iron miners in the 1950s.

Tours of the old farmsteads, sauna (a Finnish tradition), an unusual 'housebarn' and other structures, some of which are on the National Register of Historic Places, are offered (from late May to early September); stop at the Embarrass Visitor Center (no phone), at the corner of Hwy 135 and County Rd 21, open daily in summer.

Embarrass is also known for its frigid temperatures, with a low of -57°F recorded here in January 1996. There's a restaurant near the main intersection for a snack before heading on, or a campground if you want to linger. Incidentally, the town got is name from a nearby river whose name was derived from a French word describing obstacles (such as logs) in the water.

There's something different at the las stop on the Iron Range mining tour. Withi a state park (☎ 218-753-2245), **Soudan** ha the region's only underground mine. Tour ($6) take visitors a half mile below th surface for a train ride to experience wha many of the earliest ore miners lived. Thi mine remained active until 1963. The park i open 9 am to 6 pm daily from late May t early September. A park permit is require but there are miles of walking trails and visitors center, too.

Beautiful, island-studded **Vermilion Lak** is at the southern edge of the Boundar Waters area. The town of Cook (with ranger station), on Hwy 53, acts as gateway to the west end of the lake, which i 8 miles away. Roads connect to variou points around Lake Vermilion and north.

Tower, which is right on the lake, on th southern shore, is another gateway to th wilderness. From just east of Tower you ca drive north up County Rd 77 to Moccasi Point. Canoeists can put in here and paddl north to the Trout Lake portage. Cross th portage and you're into the Boundar Waters.

Northeastern Minnesota

DULUTH

• pop 85,000

At the westernmost end of the Great Lake Duluth has successfully made a transformation from a strictly industrial port town int a partly funky and happening resort town But together with its Wisconsin neighbo Superior, it remains one of the busiest port in the country, with more than 40 miles o wharf and waterfront and sailors on leav downtown.

French explorer Daniel Greysolon, Sieu Dulhut, brokered a peace agreement her in 1679 with the Ojibway and Sioux nation which enabled French adventurers t develop the fur trade. Duluth grew as

ıipping point for timber and, later, for iron ɾe from Minnesota's Iron Range. It now andles huge quantities of grain as well.

Today Duluth's heavy industries have een downsized, and some former factories nd freight depots house restaurants and ntertainment venues. Service industries, ducation and medicine have picked up the mployment slack. The combination of a ritty industrial history, a dramatic lakeside ɔcation, a working port and a revitalized ɩty center makes Duluth a captivating lace to stop.

Orientation

Superior St is the main downtown street, but most of the visitor activity is based around bustling Canal Park Drive, the walkable restored waterfront.

Going up Lake Superior toward Two Harbors is known as 'eastbound,' although it seems north and is technically northeast.

Information

The Duluth CVB (☎ 218-722-4011, 800-438-5884, www.visitduluth.com), 100 Lake Place Drive, near the clock tower, is open 8:30 am to

5 pm, weekdays year-round. The Summer Visitor Center (☎ 218-722-6024), on Harbor Drive beside the Vista tour boat dock, is open daily in summer. Walking guide pamphlets are available on downtown art and architecture.

The post office, open 8:30 am to 4:30 pm Monday to Friday, is in the US courthouse, by the water fountain at the corner of 1st St and 5th Ave W.

Carlson Books (☎ 218-722-8447), 206 E Superior St, is a magazine and used-book store to get lost in. Some visitors think it's one of the best sites in town. Also try Northern Lights (☎ 218-722-5267) at 307 Canal Park Drive.

St Luke's Hospital (☎ 218-726-5555) is at 915 E 1st St.

Canal Park Waterfront District

In addition to its distinctive atmosphere and lakeside views, Duluth has numerous attractions, many in its waterfront area. The area is based on Canal Park Drive and Lake Ave south of downtown, over the bridge spanning I-35.

The **Lakewalk** is a recreational path that skirts the area and runs east along the water. The tourist office has a pamphlet guide to the collection of contemporary waterfront art, about a dozen large works, mainly sculptures.

The engineering marvel **Aerial Lift Bridge**, on Lake Ave, rises to let ships through to the port. It was built in 1905 and completely overhauled in 1986. Huge blocks of concrete act as counterweights when the bridge is raised. Its innovative design and operation have earned it entry into the National Register of Historic Places. There is enough boat traffic that summer visitors easily have the opportunity to see it in operation.

Beside the bridge is the excellent **Maritime Visitors Center** (☎ 218-727-2497), on Lake Ave, with captivating exhibits on shipping, wrecks and the Great Lakes. It also has a schedule for the bridge lifts and marine traffic. Or call the boat-watchers' hot line (☎ 218-722-6489) to find out when the big ones come and go. They pass within feet of here. The center is open 10 am to 9 pm daily from late May to early September, otherwise till 4:30 pm (from mid-December to April it's open only Friday t Sunday); free.

Docked along Harbor Drive, the ***Williar A Irvin***, a 610-foot Great Lakes freighte can be boarded. The ship delivered iron an coal around the region for 40 years. Inte esting hour-long tours ($6.50) are offere from May through October, and the include a self-guided look around the *Lak Superior* tug, moored alongside. The ship open 9 am to 6 pm daily (until 8 pm Frida and Saturday) in June, July and August. I May, September and October hours ar 10 am to 4 pm. In late October watch out fc the Halloween Ship of Ghouls, a scary, fu special put on aboard the ship by the un versity theater department.

Visiting the tugboat alone is $3. A comb nation ticket, including the OMNIMA cinema across the street, is $10. Nearby o Harbor Drive is the massive Duluth Ente tainment Convention Center (DECC which contains convention and perfo mance halls.

Look for the **Great Lakes Aquariu** (☎ 218-525-2265) near the DECC o Harbor Drive.

Ore Docks Observation

In keeping with the shipping theme b farther south along the waterfront, at S perior St and 35th Ave W, the iron-or railway docks can be viewed. Here the ship are loaded with ore and taconite from dock extending 2000 feet into the harbor. Th busy piers load and unload all manner cargo – salt, coal, limestone and more. Oth goods are shipped from the Wisconsin sid of the port facilities, in Superior.

The Depot

Back toward the city, in the fine old tra station at 506 Michigan St, is this museu and arts center (☎ 218-727-8025), ope daily. Within the complex, the **Children Museum** has hands-on activities. The **Louis Historical Museum** has exhibits c Native Americans, fur traders, loggers an others who played a role in local histor With almost full-size re-creations, the Dep Square display accurately represents som

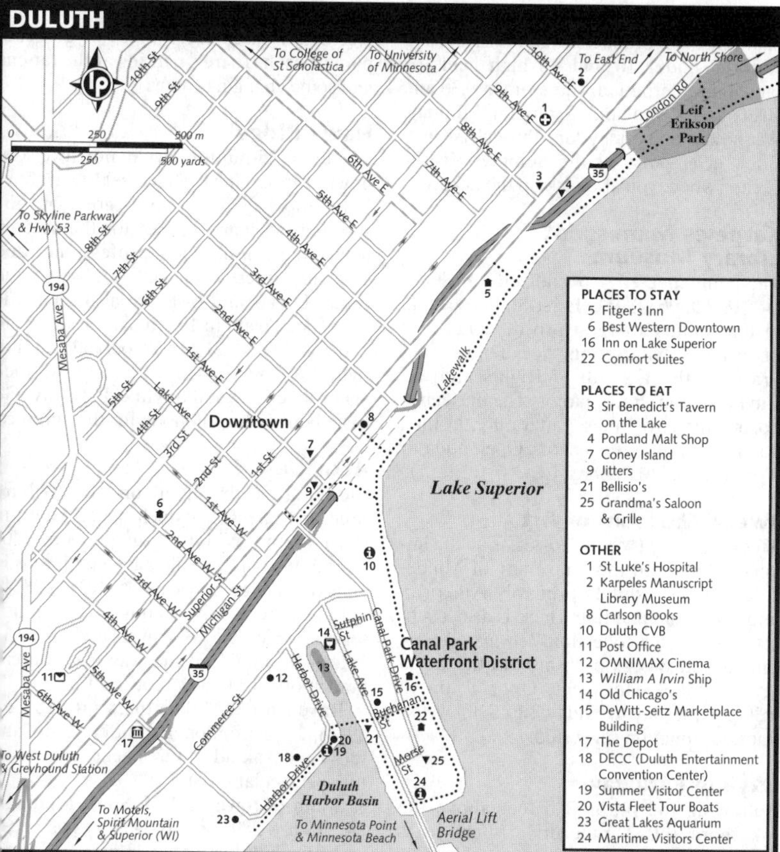

uildings and a streetscape of the city circa 910. Best of all is the **Lake Superior Rail-** **oad Museum**, with a great collection of old ocomotives and historic equipment. Ad- nission is $8/5 adults/children, which gets ou in to all three.

The **Art Institute**, with contemporary orks and performance venues, is also here. t's home to the Duluth–Superior Sym- hony Orchestra and theater productions.

lensheen

Iore upscale history is visible at this expan- ve Jacobean mansion (☎ 218-726-8910), 3300 London Rd, 5 miles east of downtown. The 39 rooms of the gracious estate, built in 1908, feature original furnishings. The mani- cured grounds and lakeside setting help put the former home of Chester A Congden on the National Register of Historic Places. The house is open 9:30 am to 4 pm daily from May 1 to October 31, Friday to Sunday only the rest of the year (call for hours).

Lake Superior Paper Industries

Free one-hour tours are offered of the paper-making process at the mill (☎ 218-628-5100), 100 N Central Ave, in West Duluth. The speed (and noise!) at which this high-tech plant spins out product is mind-boggling. No children under 10 and no high heels or sandals are permitted. Tours run at 9:30 am, 10:30 am, 1 pm and 3 pm on Monday, Wednesday and Friday, June through August. Book in advance at the Summer Visitor Center, where you also pick up the tickets.

Karpeles Manuscript Library Museum

This unexpected specialized museum (☎ 218-728-0630), 902 E 1st St, houses one of the country's largest private collections of original manuscripts. See handwritten drafts of the US Bill of Rights and the Emancipation Proclamation. The museum's documents cover music, literature, history, science and other endeavors. Open noon to 4 pm Tuesday to Sunday; free.

Tweed Museum of Art

This art gallery (☎ 218-726-8222), at 10 University Drive on the University of Minnesota campus, exhibits primarily American and European painting. There is also a substantial ceramic collection. Ten major exhibitions with works from around the world are mounted each year. Open 9 am to 4:30 pm Tuesday to Friday, 1 to 5 pm weekends; $2 donation suggested.

Skyline Parkway

Following the bluffs 700 feet above the lakeshore, this 27-mile drive offers vistas (when it's not foggy) of the city and harbor. Much of this residential road is now lined with trees and houses, so it's not worthwhile following it straight through, but some segments are grand. Get to the First United Methodist Church, known as the Copper Top, at the corner of Skyline and Mesaba Ave for a fine vantage point. Another lovely spot is the Enger Tower, in green Enger Park, adjacent to Central Park, off the parkway east of Mesaba Ave.

Minnesota Point

Follow Lake Ave south across the Aerial Lift Bridge to this residential district. Stretching along the north side of the narrow peninsula all the way to Park Point Recreation Area are 5 miles of gorgeous public beach. There's parking at the far end and some changing rooms.

Hawk Ridge

About a 15-minute drive northwest of downtown is Hawk Ridge, 600 feet above Lake Superior. The view is great but the spot is particularly known for the autumn hawk migration, when professional and amateur birders come out to observe and count. Eagles and owls are also seen. The site is open 6 am to 10 pm daily. Exit I-35 at 21st Ave E; take 21st to Woodland and turn right; turn right again at Suively Rd, then again at Glenwood/Skyline Parkway. Go east about 1 mile and look for the entrance

Activities

Bicycling is excellent on the Willard Munger State Trail, which begins south of town at the Willard Munger Inn, 7402 Grand Ave. The 75-mile paved path runs to Hinckley. Diamondback's (☎ 218-624-4814), at the inn, rents bikes and has a bus shuttle service, which allows you to cycle 5 or 1[illegible] miles – downhill all the way! Or you can branch off to rougher mountain-bike trails.

Raven Moon Adventures (☎ 218-724-8914), 1632 London Rd, offers half- and full-day kayak adventures near town or u[illegible] the spectacular coast.

South of town on I-35, Spirit Mountain (☎ 218-628-2891, 800-642-6377) has excellent downhill skiing, with 23 runs and a dedicated snowboarding area. There are also cross-country trails.

The North Shore Trail up the Lake Superior shoreline provides snowmobilers with an amazing 153 miles of winter wonderland. Even within city limits there are miles of trails.

Visitors can pop in to the DECC, 32[illegible] Harbor Drive, for a glimpse of a game at the Duluth Curling Club (☎ 218-727-1851) from October through the winter.

Organized Tours

Vista (☎ 218-722-6218) has a fleet fo[illegible] harbor tours ($9, 2 hours) and lunch [illegible]

dinner cruises. Trips run from mid-May to mid-October from the Harbor Drive docks by the *William Irvin*. You can buy tickets at the Summer Visitor Center.

The North Shore Scenic Railroad (☎ 218-722-1273) has three trip options from the Depot. The 90-minute ride is $9; the full six-hour narrated excursion to Two Harbors along the lake is $17. The latter includes some history and a two-hour stop in Two Harbors. Ride the rails from late May to early September.

A fourth rail option is a trip along the St Louis River aboard the Lake Superior and Mississippi Railroad (☎ 218-624-7549). These trains depart west (south) of town off I-35. The historic route on vintage equipment is mostly a nature trip, during which waterfowl may be seen along the river. It runs summer weekends only. The 12-mile, 1½-hour trip costs $7/6/5 adults/seniors/children.

For a self-guided walking tour of a portion of Duluth's historic East End, pick up the folder at the Visitors Bureau. It outlines two dozen noteworthy houses from the early 20th century along Superior and 1st Sts. When the lumber, railroad, iron ore and shipping industries were at their peak a lot of wealth was generated, and this area was where many prominent citizens chose to live and build.

Special Events

For events without telephone numbers, call the CVB for information.

January

John Beargrease Sled Dog Marathon – called the most grueling race in the lower 48 states, with 20 dog teams departing Canal Park for the 330-mile, three-day course to Grand Portage; there are numerous related events and activities in town and along the way (☎ 218-722-7631)

August

Duluth International Folk Festival – around the first week of the month at Leif Erikson Park (east along the shore, a fast 15-minute walk from downtown along the Lakewalk Trail), a full day of traditional music and dance from the city's ethnic groups, such as Mexicans and Native Americans, with some folk and blues singers too, plus lots of crafts and food

Bayfront Blues Festival – one of the Midwest's largest annual music events, held mid-month, featuring more than 20 performances over three days at Bayfront Park, on the lake south of Canal Park; there are also club events (☎ 715-394-6831)

September

Northshore In-Line Marathon – held mid-month, the country's biggest in-line skating race, with more than 2000 participants racing along a 26-mile route winding up the Lake Superior shoreline

Places to Stay

This is a *very* busy place in summer, and lodgings are generally full. There was a time you could slip over to Superior, Wisconsin, but the jig is up on that, and it's usually booked solid too. Definitely reserve in advance. Note that even most area campgrounds get full.

Budget Twenty miles south off I-35 exit 242, ***Jay Cooke State Park*** *(☎ 218-384-4610)* is a lovely forested area where campsites cost $12 to $15.

Spirit Mountain *(☎ 218-628-2891)* is a ski area with campsites 10 miles south of town at I-35 exit 244. Sites cost $15 to $22. It's geared toward RVs, but there are a few tent sites; the best are the walk-ins.

The small, year-round home hostel ***Hillside Hostel International*** *(☎ 218-726-0610, 1223 W 4th St)* has room for just a few people. Call Greg, the congenial owner, to check on availability before walking up the hill. He's usually able to carve out a space for you somewhere. Rates are $15 per person, and the porch alone is worth nearly that.

The pretty ***College of St Scholastica*** *(☎ 218-723-6000, 218-723-6483, Residential Building Services, 1200 Kenwood Ave)* is the best-kept secret in town. The second phone number is useful only during office hours on weekdays. This highly regarded coed Benedictine liberal arts college has two comfortable guest rooms available year-round. The single is $22, the double $44, each with private bath. In addition, there are dorms available for the 10 weeks prior to August 15. Each of these simple rooms with twin beds is $28, less for students, regardless of

MINNESOTA

how many people use it. Ask whether the cafeteria is open. The No 12 Kenwood bus from downtown passes the college. All rooms are in Somers Hall, where there is a 24-hour attendant.

Motel 6 *(☎ 218-723-1123)* is minutes south of town on I-35 ($36/41). London Rd, east of downtown, has a couple of inexpensive motels. West of downtown are some more motels.

Mid-Range & Top End In town, the ***Buena Vista*** *(☎ 218-722-7796, 800-569-8124, 1144 Mesaba Ave)* is an older place providing a good value with fine rooms and a superlative location – minutes from the center and featuring a spectacular view of the city and lake. In midsummer rates are $55/60 single/double ($10 more for lake-view rooms) and drop to as low as $35 midweek in winter. There is also a well-known glass-sided dining room offering all three meals. Dinners range from $12 to $15, Mexican to seafood.

The ***Chalet Motel*** *(☎ 218-728-4238, 800-235-2957, 1801 London Rd)* with the alpine look charges $50 to $80 in summer.

Best Western Downtown *(☎ 218-727-6851, 131 2nd Ave W)* is in the central core, just seven blocks from Canal Park. It's relatively small, with 45 rooms for $55 to $85 in summer, with the higher end charged on weekends and for special events.

In Canal Park, ***Comfort Suites*** *(☎ 218-727-1378, 800-228-5150, fax 218-727-1947, www.duluth.com/comfortsuites, 408 Canal Park Drive)* balances price, location and features in an honest package. The lake is on one side, the action of Canal Park on the other. Rooms start at $109 in summer, $79 in winter.

Nearby ***Inn on Lake Superior*** *(☎ 218-726-1111, 888-668-4352, fax 218-727-3976, www.duluth.com/iols, 350 Canal Park Drive)* also has poolside or lakeside rooms, at slightly higher prices.

More interesting and plush, with a blend of modern and antique furnishings, is ***Fitger's Inn*** *(☎ 218-722-8826, 800-726-2982, www.fitgers.com, 600 E Superior St)*, in a thoughtfully restored former brewery. This is a first rate-hotel with all the amenities and attentive service. Rooms start at $90 (costlier with lake views) and rise to $250 for the whirlpool suites. Prices decline by about 15% from November to April.

Places to Eat

Downtown, ***Jitters*** *(102 W Superior St)* serves up bagels, sandwich wraps and great coffees. ***Coney Island*** *(107 E Superior St)* is the city's classic greasy-spoon diner and has been serving its cheapest breakfasts since 1921.

Most of Duluth's restaurants are in one of two concentrated districts. Down on the waterfront near the Aerial Lift Bridge there's a clutch of eateries covering all price categories. Most are in the restored commercial spaces on Canal Park Drive and Lake Ave. Many are owned by the same family, but who can complain when both standards and costs are noteworthy? Locals and tourists flock to one such, the casual ***Grandma's Saloon & Grill*** *(☎ 218-727-4192)*, at the corner of Canal Park Drive and Morse St. Filling favorites such as plates of pasta or hefty sandwiches cost about $8, steaks $15. Try to grab one of the upper deck tables overlooking the bridge.

In the DeWitt–Seitz Marketplace building, ***Taste of Saigon*** *(☎ 218-727-1598, 394 Lake Ave S)* offers inexpensive Vietnamese food, including a choice of vegetarian dishes. Try the vegetable mocdoc (a pasta) with lemongrass. Served with a large bowl of rice it's a spicy meal for just $5.50. In the same complex, ***Amazing Grace*** *(☎ 218-722-6775)* is a comfortable café with excellent sandwiches, and folk music at night.

You won't see families or teenagers at ***Bellisio's*** *(☎ 218-727-4921)*, at the corner of Lake Ave and Buchanan St. With its good food and sedate patio, it is single-handedly providing the area with an elevated tone. Lunches at this Italian eatery run $10, dinner entrées about $20. An order of bruschetta and a plate or two of mussels marinara from the appetizer menu together with a bottle from the extensive wine list makes a fine bit of romantic class on the cheap.

A second, less hectic dining district is based at the renovated Fitger's brewery complex, 600 E Superior St. ***Fitger's Brewhouse***

Grille (☎ *218-726-1392)* makes its own beer and has the usual pub fare. ***Chi Chi's*** *(☎ 218-727-09790)*, a pseudo-Mexican chain, is mentioned not for the adequate food but for having one of the most spectacular patios anywhere. A block to the west, ***Sir Benedict's Tavern on the Lake***, at the corner of E Superior St and 8th Ave E, is a popular place for its jaw-stretching sandwiches ($5 to $6), varied beer selection and unobstructed lake views.

Across the street in the park by the water, summer sees a constant stream at the substantial brick-and-stone ***Portland Malt Shop*** for fabulous ice creams.

Entertainment

The Minnesota Ballet, Duluth–Superior Symphony Orchestra and Duluth Playhouse theatrical group all perform at the ***Depot*** *(☎ 218-727-8025)*, 506 Michigan St.

The ***Duluth/Superior Entertainment League*** *(☎ 218-722-2000)* presents major productions such as *Cats* at the DECC, 327 Harbor Drive, bringing in audiences from around northern Minnesota and Wisconsin.

Old Chicago's *(327 Lake Ave S)*, a pub in the waterfront district, is raucous on summer nights, serving beer and pizza. ***Fitger's*** (see Places to Eat) has some fine homemade brew and, often, live music in the Tap Room.

Folk and blues musicians, young singer-songwriters and poets are often heard at the ***Amazing Grace Bakery*** coffeehouse *(☎ 218-722-6775, 394 Lake Ave S)*, in the DeWitt-Seitz Marketplace building.

Getting There & Away

Duluth International Airport, 6 miles northwest of downtown off Hwy 53, provides service to major US cities and has some international flights. Northwest Airlines (☎ 218-727-8791) is a principal carrier.

The Greyhound station (☎ 218-722-5591), 4426 Grand Ave by the corner of N 45th Ave W, is several miles west of downtown. From the station any city bus going east on Grand Ave leads to downtown. There are almost a dozen buses daily to St Paul ($20, 3 hours) and connections to Milwaukee ($70, 10 to 11 hours). There is one bus daily to Ashland and one to International Falls. Grand Marais and Thunder Bay, Ontario, are served four times a week.

Getting Around

Call the Duluth Transit Authority (☎ 218-722-7283) for local bus routes and schedules.

The visitor-oriented Port Town Trolley (50¢), which operates from late May to early September, is all most people will need. The minitrain on wheels tools down Superior St, along the waterfront and Canal Park and back every half hour all day.

Budget (☎ 218-727-7685) is one of several car-rental outfits at the airport. Rates are about $30 per day, with 150 free miles and 17 cents per after that.

Diamond (☎ 218-727-8868) is a major cab company. The airport trip is about $12.

WHITE WATER SOUTH OF DULUTH

Despite some of the world's best canoeing, Minnesota doesn't have a lot of fast-flowing white-water excitement. Wisconsin is better known for that. The boundary waters and the St Croix, Zumbro, Root and Mississippi Rivers all generally offer flat waters. But this is decidedly not the case along the **St Louis River**, about 20 miles south of Duluth near Carlton.

Superior Whitewater (☎ 218-384-4637) runs 2½-hour wet-and-wild inflatable-raft trips down the rapids daily from May through September. The cost is $35, and participants must be at least 12 years old. For those seeking an extra kick, try the two-person inflatable kayaks known as rubber duckies. These challenging trips go for $49.

Early in the season the waters are faster, but of course, colder. The office is on Hwy 210 just east of Carlton. Reservations are suggested for holiday weekends. Nearby Jay Cooke State Park (☎ 218-384-4610) offers bicycling and walking trails and camping.

LAKE SUPERIOR'S NORTH SHORE

North of Duluth, Superior St, London Rd or the Skyline Parkway lead to Hwy 61, which presents 150 miles of history and dramatic shoreline topography. This is one of the most impressive strips of asphalt in the state, if not the Midwest, with enough to see and do alongside to force even type A personalities to linger. Unfortunately, so many do that area accommodations get *completely* booked in summer. Make reservations, and that includes at the glistening pearls of the state park string highlighting the route. Their wonderful trails and spectacular waterfalls are regional highlights. Remember, a park day-pass is good the next day, too, and at any park. For camping information and reservations call the state parks' central line (☎ 800-246-2267). Don't forget you must reserve a minimum of three days in advance.

Lodges, cabins and motels are numerous. Look for the smoked fish and wild rice outlets. Note that the region is spectacular in fall, too.

Two Harbors

• pop 3650

Since the 19th century, this has been the last real town until Grand Marais, and it has all the services. There's a central chamber of commerce (☎ 218-834-2600, 800-777-7384, www.twoharbors.com/chamber) on 7th Ave open 9 am to 4 pm weekdays. Two miles up Hwy 61, the major RJ Houle Information Center (☎ 218-834-4005, 800-554-2116) has details on accommodations along Hwy 61. It's open daily in summer.

Hwy 61 becomes 7th Ave, the main street in town.

Things to See & Do All the sites are on Waterfront Drive at 1st Ave, by the lake. The **Depot Museum** has exhibits on the iron ore trains (which still run). The North Shore Scenic Railroad, from Duluth, pulls in to the station here. The restored tugboat *Edna G*, the last coal-fired tug on the Great Lakes, can be toured. Around the bay is the Two Harbors Lighthouse, also called the Agate Bay Lighthouse. Though not necessary for ship safety, it still operates and can be toured for $2.50. It's open daily from May to September, but if you find someone there at any time, they'll likely let you in for a look.

The massive, omnipresent iron ore docks ship taconite from the Iron Range to the blast furnaces of steel mills around the lakes

Superior Hiking Trail In addition to the fabulous state parks, the long-distance Superior Hiking Trail merits special mention So far 220 miles of the eventual 300 between Minnesota and Canada have been completed, running along the high ridges paralleling much of the shoreline. The trail has been called one of the best in the world. You can walk for an hour or two weeks. Designated campsites are first come, first served Relatively expensive lodge-to-lodge hiking i possible, but make reservations in advance.

Access points to the trail are found al along Hwy 61, and many of them offe special features, such as falls, rock formation and wildlife viewing, or grand panoramas Visit the information office in Two Harbor (☎ 218-834-2700), 731 7th Ave, for suggeste day trips to peaks, falls and other sites. Cal Superior Shuttle (☎ 218-834-5511), 960 Hw 61 east, for details on its weekend trai service, which allows for one-way hikes. The drop off and pick up at trailheads. Trail information is sometimes available at visitors bureaus and state parks all along Hwy 61.

Places to Stay & Eat The ***Burlington Ba Campground*** *(☎ 218-834-2021)* at the eas end of town on Hwy 61, is on the lake an has electric sites and full hookup sites. It' not geared toward campers with tents.

There are several independent mote and the pricier ***AmericInn*** *(☎ 218-834 3000)*. The latter, in town on Hwy 61, has pool, sauna, free light breakfast and room starting at $90.

For a bite in town, stop at ***Vanilla Bea Bakery & Café***, on 7th Ave, for deliciou coffee, a fresh muffin or pastry or a full mea If it's late afternoon, the ***Black Woods Ba & Grill***, also on 7th Ave, has a good happ hour and you can stay for a dinner of rib chicken or pasta.

Two miles east on Hwy 61, stop at ***Betty Pies*** for a delicious homemade slice c sandwich lunch. The sweet pies are s popular there's a toll-free reservation hot line (☎ 877- 269-7494)!

Along Hwy 61

With five captivatingly scenic waterfalls, a river gorge and lakeside setting, time passes all too quickly at **Gooseberry Falls State Park** (☎ 218-834-3855). The wooded trails away from the falls are practically deserted. There are 70 campsites and opportunities for winter sports, too.

Minutes beyond is **Split Rock Lighthouse State Park** (☎ 218-226-6377), with the archetypal lighthouse perched photogenically 130 feet atop a rock cliff. A state historic site preserves the light and grounds as they were in the 1920s. The light and history center are open 9 am to 5 pm daily from mid-May to mid-October; and then the center only noon to 4 pm Friday to Sunday (closed Thanksgiving weekend, the month of December and Easter weekend). Admission is $5. Trails lead to the beach below and along the cliff tops. There is backcountry and kayak camping.

At **Beaver River**, cruises aboard the *Grampa Woo* (☎ 218-226-4100) skim along the Superior shoreline by the cliffs and Split Rock Lighthouse for two hours from late June to Labor Day ($18).

The massive Northshore Mining complex at Silver Bay presents a visual blemish, but alas, work must be done. Just east, watch carefully for the signs to **Palisade Head**. The road, too narrow and windy for trailers or large campers, leads to cliffs with fabulous views. It's considered among the best rock-climbing sites in Minnesota, but picnicking will do nicely too. On clear days, Wisconsin's Apostle Islands can be spotted.

Another 2 miles and you have to stop again at fabulous **Tettegouche State Park** (☎ 218-226-6365), with absolutely idyllic swimming at the mouth of the serpentine Baptism River. This is like a movie set for Shangri-La. There's kayaking, camping and excellent trails leading over the rugged hills to four small, isolated lakes. High Falls, possibly Minnesota's highest waterfall, tumbles here (Grand Portage State Park claims its falls are the highest).

Temperence River State Park (☎ 218-663-7476) features the cascading river churning through a dramatic rocky gorge and the area's second-largest campground, with 55 sites. Open all year, the North Shore Commercial Fishing Museum (☎ 218-663-7804), at Tofte (just east of the park), has displays about Superior and the fishers.

In the **Lutsen Mountains**, a gondola leads to the peak of Moose Mountain and the Lutsen Mountain Bike Park (☎ 800-360-7666), with 50 miles of trails, including some *serious* ones, lift service and rentals. The downhill skiing is excellent.

Places to Stay & Eat Beyond the Silver Creek Cliff tunnel are the cute brown housekeeping cabins by the water at ***Erickson's Goosebury Cabins*** *(☎ 218-834-3873)*. Rates start at a reasonable $40.

The ***Inn at Beaver Bay*** *(☎ 800-226-4351)* is a modest roadside hostelry with rooms from $40.

Cascade Lodge *(☎ 218-387-1112, 800-322-9543, www.cascadelodgemn.com)* is another admirable inn nestled beside Cascade River State Park. The lodge is open all year and can suggest seasonal activities. Basic rooms begin at $70 and rise for deluxe cabins.

The year-round ***Lutsen Resort & Sea Villas*** *(☎ 218-663-7212, 800-258-8736, www.lutsenresort.com)* is a venerable lodge with a range of rooms and cottages by the lake. The impressive wood-paneled lobby and dining room reflect its 1885 beginnings. Rooms in the Cliff House begin at a very reasonable $50 and climb to hundreds for complete condos. Minimum stays may be in effect. The renowned Superior National Golf Course is across the street.

About 5 miles east of Gooseberry Falls State Park is the ***Mediera Marketplace***, where you can get a sweet and cappuccino or chicken with wild rice. Climb the stairs out back for a view of Split Rock Lighthouse.

Grand Marais

• pop 1170

About 110 miles from Duluth, this agreeable lakeside town makes a good base for exploring the rest of Hwy 61, Superior National Forest and the Boundary Waters Canoe Area Wilderness.

The Visitor Information Center (☎ 218-387-2524, 888-922-5000, www.grandmarais-mn.com) is at 13 N Broadway St. For more information and the permits required to enter the Boundary Waters wilderness, go to the Gunflint Ranger Station (☎ 218-387-1750, www.bwcaw.org), just south of town on Hwy 61. It's open daily from May 1 to September 30 and less regularly the rest of the year.

Grand Marais is more a supply and service center than a tourist destination, so there aren't many sites. Art appreciators should stroll over to the **Arrowhead Center for the Arts** (☎ 218-387-1284), 2nd St at 3rd Ave W, which houses the Grand Marais Playhouse. They have a year-round theater schedule and a good reputation. Also here is the Art Colony, with a range of activities, workshops, concerts and shows.

Outfitters rent equipment and organize trips. Cascade Kayaks (☎ 218-387-2360), on Broadway near Hwy 61, leads kayak trips of varying lengths, and rents equipment. See the Gunflint Trail and Boundary Waters sections for more outfitters.

Places to Stay Enormous, never-full ***Municipal Camping*** *(☎ 218-387-1712, 800-998-0959)*, at the south edge of town, is a pleasant RV and tent godsend by the water, but it's costly: $22 for tents, $28 for RVs. It's open May 1 to mid-October. Campers get pool discounts. From the campground there is a trail to Sweethearts Bluff. There is also rustic camping in Superior National Forest and Pat Bayle State Forest, north and west of Grand Marais.

The casual, friendly ***East Bay Hotel*** *(☎ 800-414-2807)*, downtown at the end of Wisconsin St on the lake, has a range of rooms, from basic in the 1946 section to modern in the 1994 addition. Prices start as low as $26 and rise to $90, and there is a restaurant and hot tub.

Among several motels is the small, white, downtown ***Seawall*** *(☎ 218-387-2095, 800-245-5806)*, at $60; closed in winter. Others include the ***Sandgren Motel*** *(☎ 218-387-2975, 800-796-2975)*, $45 to $65, and the ***Harbor Inn*** *(☎ 218-387-1191, 800-595-4566, @ harborinn@boreal.org)*. All three are on Hwy 61 in the small central area of town. There are also a couple out of sight up the start of the Gunflint Trail.

Places to Eat The ***Blue Water Café***, Wisconsin St at 1st Ave, open 6 am to 9 pm daily, is *the* all-purpose place and is full of locals at breakfast.

Line up for a warm 'skizzle' at ***World's Best Donuts***, at the corner of Broadway Ave and Wisconsin St, and put a hometown pin on the map.

For a burger and shake with a side of nostalgia, look no further than ***Leon's***, on Wisconsin St near Broadway Ave, with its glistening tiles, chrome and mirrors.

The ***Gunflint Tavern***, on Wisconsin St near 2nd St, is open daily from noon to midnight. Various well-prepared dinners ($14) come with a tasty organic salad and a delightfully dressed up sorbet. Sandwiches are offered at lunch.

To the Canadian Border

The one exceptional stop on this uneventful segment of Hwy 61 is **Judge CR Magney State Park** (☎ 218-0387-2929), with camping, hiking and a series of waterfalls along the Brule River. Walk to Devil's Kettle, where half the river disappears.

Nature ends abruptly at the imposing 24-hour ***Grand Portage Lodge & Casino*** complex *(☎ 218-475-2401)*, with good rooms for $60. Ask about hiking or skiing from the trail center on County Rd 17. The Rendezvous Powwow, in mid-August, is a major event.

Hwy 61 continues to **Grand Portage National Monument**, near the Canadian border. There is no town (gas is available), but the historic site where the early voyageurs had to carry their canoes around the Pigeon River rapids as they traveled to and from Lake Superior is a great stop. This was the center of a far-flung trading empire, and the recon structed 1788 trading post is highly recommended. The interpreter's retelling of the voyageur 'romance' is alone worth the price of admission. The original 8½-mile portage can be hiked today. The site is open daily, but the historic buildings are open only from mid-May to mid-October. Admission is $2.

Near the historic site are two boat services (☎ 715-392-2100) for Michigan's **Isle Royale National Park** in Lake Superior (see the Upper Peninsula chapter). The day-tripper runs from mid-June to mid-September, the overnighter from May through October. Ask for directions to the docks; they're not well marked.

Right on the mountainous border is **Grand Portage State Park**, for day use only. It rivals Tettegouche State Park for the claim to the state's highest waterfall.

GUNFLINT TRAIL

The 63-mile paved Gunflint Trail, County Rd 12, runs inland from Grand Marais through the Superior National Forest wilderness, with canoe-trip outfitters, a few lodges and their restaurants along the way. The Gunflint Trail Association (☎ 800-338-6932, www.gunflint-trail.com) can help with information and accommodations. The area is made for camping and exploring by canoe (or cross-country skis in winter). Aside from the Ely area, the Gunflint provides the best access to Boundary Waters Canoe Area Wilderness. Tofte, off Hwy 61, is another access point.

At the north end of the trail, HI ***Spirit of the Land Island Hostel*** *(☎ 218-388-2241)*, on an island in Sea Gull Lake, has bunk beds ($16 to $18) and canoe rentals. Reservations are recommended; call first from Grand Marais to arrange boat transport to the island once you get to the end of the road.

For interior trips see Bear Track Outfitting (☎ 218-387-1162, 800-795-8068) on the south edge of Grand Marais on Hwy 61. This quality company can furnish all equipment, supplies, route planning and advice. Another choice, also on Hwy 61 in Grand Marais, but on the other side of the road, is Wilderness Waters Outfitters (☎ 218-387-2525, 800-325-5842).

BOUNDARY WATERS CANOE AREA WILDERNESS

The 15,000 unspoiled sq miles of the BWCAW, within the northern third of Superior National Forest, unquestionably represent one of the world's finest canoeing regions. With 1500 miles of canoe routes connected by generally short portages, hundreds of clean lakes, and rich, diverse wildlife, it's a nature lover's dream. The largest US wilderness zone east of the Rockies, the federally managed region stretches along the Canadian border, connecting with Ontario's wilderness Quetico Provincial Park.

Canoeing is the dominant activity; motorboats are permitted only in designated areas. There are some sections for hiking.

Camping is free in the national forest, except at established campgrounds, but permits are required to enter the BWCAW. They cost $10 per person per trip. In summer, each access point uses a daily quota system. Permits for a given entry point can be reserved (☎ 877-550-6777) from May 15 to September 30 for $9. Reservations are taken beginning January 15.

Ranger stations and access points are scattered around the BWCAW perimeter (see the Grand Marais and Ely sections). The former provide maps, information and permits. Information is also available at www.bwcaw.org. By mail, contact Superior National Forest, 8901 Grand Ave Place, Duluth, MN 55808-4399.

Permits are also available at some outfitters, resorts and fishing shops. For information on resorts and outfitters, contact visitors' centers in such places as Ely and Grand Marais.

Animals to look for include loons, deer, moose, beavers and bears. Get advice on bears before setting out – some precautions are necessary, and all food must be hung in trees. Become acquainted with the regulations; for example, cans and bottles are banned. Use can easily become abuse of the diminishing wilderness. Camping within the BWCAW is at designated sites only. Each has a basic latrine. Also it is essential to purchase

Howl of the Wolf Heard Again

The wolf, loved or hated, best represents the American wilderness. Ranchlands aside, the wolf has historically avoided human settlement, always retreating from development. Through legend, superstition, folklore and scientific observation, this animal, more than any other, has long been linked to the country's wild areas – the lakelands, forests and mountains. Only where large predators exist can true wilderness be preserved.

Wolves are an intricate part of the natural ecosystem, both maintaining and reflecting its health. By weeding out the sick, injured and weak of its prey, wolves keep other populations vital. By checking the growth of coyote populations they help maintain rodent numbers, which in turn support other animals such as hawks and eagles.

But this often misunderstood symbol of the wilderness almost disappeared from the Midwest. Bounties were paid until the1960s, and by the mid-1970s wolves were on endangered lists across their limited range in Minnesota, Wisconsin and upper Michigan. Since then a recovery program has meant a sharp upturn in their numbers. There are now about 2100 wolves in northeastern Minnesota, and the population rises annually. These wild packs, feeding mainly on deer, are the largest grouping of wolves east of the Rockies. Today fortunate campers and canoeists may once again hear their haunting howl.

a detailed map at a ranger office or outfitter before setting out.

The region is busiest on weekends from July through mid-August. September, when the bugs are gone, traffic has diminished and the weather is still warm, is an ideal time for a trip.

You can do it all yourself, get fully or partially equipped at an outfitter or let the pros run the whole show. See the Gunflint Trail and Ely sections for outfitters.

ELY

• pop 3970

Hilly Ely (pronounced **Ee**-lee) is a small, engaging north-woods town of traditional wood-frame facades and seemingly dozens of outfitters, all punctuated by the neon glow of bars and storefronts on E Sheridan St. The charming spell is broken only by the ludicrous-looking new buildings of the national fast-food franchises. Ely is the main BWCAW access point and supply center.

The chamber of commerce (☎ 218-365-6123, 800-777-7281, www.ely.org), 1600 E Sheridan St, is open 9 am to 6 pm daily (Sunday noon to 4 pm) from June to early September, 9 am to 5 pm weekdays from early September to late May.

For camping and canoeing details, get in touch with the Kawishiwi Ranger Station (☎ 218-365-7681, 877-444-6777), 118 S 4th E which can help with trip suggestions, advise you on 'no-trace' environmental camping and issue permits.

Things to See & Do

The ace **International Wolf Center** (☎ 218-365-4695), 1396 Hwy 169 east of downtown is an educational headquarters offering exhibits, films and the chance to see the live wolves living on the premises. The Wolf Mythology presentation is excellent. The center has on- and off-site activities, including wolf howls and wolf-viewing trips. Open 9:30 am to 5:30 pm daily from May through October, 10 am to 5 pm Friday to Sunday from November through April; $5.50.

The **Dorothy Molter Museum** (☎ 218-365-4451), on Hwy 169 east, between the chamber of commerce and the wolf center tells the story of an idiosyncratic city woman who came to these woods in 1930 and never left. She was the last resident of the BWCAW. Her intriguing life and times are revealed in the original cabins. Open 10 am to 6 pm daily from late May to early September; $3. Don't forget to get a root beer.

The **Ely–Winton Museum** (☎ 218-365-3226), in the east end of the main Vermilion College building, on Camp St near the chamber of commerce, outlines the town's and area's past; $2. A combination ticket ($8) is available for all three sites.

Take a look at the splendid nature photography work of Jim Brandenburg at the Brandenburg Gallery, above the store at 105 N Central Ave. He has done a lot of work in the north woods in between international assignments for *National Geographic*.

For a real Minnesotan experience based on its Scandinavian roots, get relaxed and clean over at the **Ely Steam Bath** (☎ 218-365-6728), on Harvey St by the corner of 1st Ave. For decades miners, loggers, hunters, campers, canoeists, and others have soaked up steam and small talk. There are male, female and couple sections, or the larger group room, open to both men and women, in the Finnish tradition. The hours are odd: Wednesday and Friday it's open 4 to 8:30 pm, Saturday 2 to 8:30 pm. Walk over to check. There are towels and showers, and you can get in and out of the steam as much as you like.

Activities

Outdoor outfitters are found all over town and beyond. There are guided canoe trips ranging from a day to weeks. Canoe rentals range from $25 to $35 per day. Packages with equipment and food are about $65 per day. Some operators offer winter Nordic ski packages and dog-sled and winter-camping trips. Ice fishing and snowmobiling are also major, well-organized activities.

East of town on Hwy 169 is the Hidden Valley Recreation Area which is good for mountain biking and walking. The road continues in to the BWCAW.

Places to Stay

Lodging, including campgrounds, sells out in July and August. Arrive early in the day or reserve ahead of time. The chamber of commerce bends over backward to locate vacancies and match your preferences – even if you've left it to the last minute and come in panicky. With 500 lakes within a 20-mile radius, area lodges are plentiful, but many have three-day minimums.

Fall Lake *(☎ 218-365-2963)*, 6 miles east of town on Hwy 169 (also called Fernberg Rd) in Superior National Forest, has camping ($8 to $12) and swimming.

The small, basic ***Four Star Motel*** *(☎ 218-365-3140, 1145 E Sheridan St)*, open summer only, has singles for $32. ***Budget Host*** *(☎ 218-365-3237, fax 218-365-3099, 1047 E Sheridan St)* is open all year and has a sauna. Rates are $50/60.

At slightly higher cost is ***Paddle Inn*** *(☎ 218-365-6036, 800-270-2245, 1314 E Sheridan St)*, one of the larger local inns.

Lodge and resort cabin rates are in the ballpark of $125 a night, $800 a week in peak summer season. There are dozens of them, and most are family owned and operated. They generally offer housekeeping cabins with a lakeside location geared toward vacationers interested in fishing and swimming. Some are small and rustic, others deluxe, with all the modern conveniences and even satellite TV connections. Call the chamber of commerce to get a list. The standard season is mid-May to October; June through August is busiest.

Places to Eat

Northern Grounds *(117 N Central Ave)* is a comfortable big-city café with bagels, cappuccinos, sandwiches and the like. It opens at 6:30 am.

For the basic breakfast special and meals under $5, ***Britton's Café*** *(5 Chapman St)*, away from the tourists, can't be beat. The ***Chocolate Moose***, at the corner of Sheridan St and Central Ave, with a fine deck, could be the busiest place in town. It sells a lot of pizza, although walleye, buffalo steaks ($16) and burgers ($4) are offered.

Down the street, ***Ely Steak House*** *(216 Sheridan St)* is good for fish and steak dinners ($20) and has the best lounge for a quiet drink.

Far Northern Minnesota

West out of Ely, Hwy 169 leads to Hwy 53, which runs north to Canada. The east side is flanked by the Kabetogama State Forest, itself adjacent to Voyageurs National Park. Orr is the largest town en route and is a supply center of sorts. Various park access points are reached off Hwy 53. Heading this way from the Grand Rapids and central Minnesota area, Hwy 73 is the main route, but Hwy 6, while slower, is the more scenic option.

VOYAGEURS NATIONAL PARK

Voyageurs protects a rough, rugged northwoods landscape between Minnesota and Ontario. Big waters are the essential characteristic: some 30 glacial lakes, four of them huge, cover a considerable percentage of the park. Nearly all access is by boat. Five hundred islands, bays, beaches and simple campsites are the basic ingredients. Rocky outcrops, bogs, and mixed woods are others.

The area that was to become the international border between the USA and Canada was first known to the Ojibway. In the 17th century, French Canadian fur traders, or voyageurs, began exploring the Great Lakes and northern rivers by canoe. The park covers part of their customary waterway. Later, European trappers, lumberers and miners followed. The area remains largely unchanged, and although resorts dot the landscape, traffic is far lighter than in the vacation zones to the south.

The park is best and most commonly explored by motorboat. All boaters should have navigational charts. Until recently, the waters were considered mostly too wide and too rough for canoeing, although the small interior lakes are fine for that. This attitude is changing somewhat, as serious paddlers seeking new challenges are arriving in greater numbers. More significant is the increased popularity of safer, drier kayaks. But Voyageurs remains no place for novices. If you're seeking wildlife, flat waters and forest camping, the Superior National Forest and Boundary Waters Canoe Area Wilderness are likely where you'll want to be.

If you're without a boat, within Voyageurs the park has two cruise services (see Access Points & Services) and offers free use of boats on some of the 26 interior lakes. There are also several mainland trails. The park is always open, but winter ice limits accessibility. In winter, skiers and snowmobilers explore the frozen park.

Those boating to Canadian waters should inquire at the ranger stations about immigration requirements, fishing licenses and other regulations.

Orientation & Information

Four communities provide access to the park. From south to north on Hwy 53, they are Crane Lake, Ash River, Kabetogama and International Falls–Rainy Lake. Each of the four has an information office. Only the last is open all year. Information is also online at www.nps.gov/voya.

These areas have outfitters, rentals and services, plus some smaller lakes for canoeing. The access roads offer camping and lodges on or near Rainy Lake and are often used by those putting in their own boats. There is a long hiking trail on the Kabetogama Peninsula that's accessible by water taxi from Ash River and a shorter one northwest of Kabetogama.

Access Points & Services

Reached along County Rd 23 from Orr, **Crane Lake** has a small ranger station (☎ 218-993-2481) open from May to September. The Visitor Bureau (☎ 218-993-2901, 800-362-7405, www.cranelake.org) is at 7238 Handberg Rd. The lakeside village has a private campground, outfitters, houseboat rentals and numerous lodges. Resorts here and elsewhere charge from $400 to as much as $700 a week. Day rates start around $60.

Anderson's Canoe Outfitters (☎ 800-777-7186), 7255 Crane Lake Rd, rents equipment, including kayaks, and has shuttles to various lakes and access points in remote Boundary Waters and Quetico areas.

Ash River has a full park visitors' center (☎ 218-374-3221), open daily from May to early September. There are two short trails nearby and a couple of lodges in the village. For camping there is the Ash River Campground (☎ 218-757-3489), in the Kabetogama State Forest, on County Rd 129 just before entering town, plus a couple of other campgrounds in town. All are open May to October.

Larger **Kabetogama** has about two dozen establishments split among lodges, resorts, campgrounds and outfitters. Call ☎ 800-524-9085 for accommodations assistance. The park visitors' center (☎ 218-875-2111) is open daily from May to September. It operates all-day and evening cruises and two-hour guided canoe paddles. Call for reservations.

Most resorts rent by the week, with rates ranging from $300 to $800. Accommodations range from simple lodge rooms to cabins of varying sizes and amenities to luxurious suites. When available, daily rates run from about $40 to $125 or more.

A good inexpensive resort is ***Driftwood Lodge*** *(☎ 218-875-3841, 888-816-1529, 10012 Gappa Rd)*. It has plain but very nice rustic housekeeping cabins starting at $300 a week in July and August. There are also larger, more costly cabins.

Another good place, with a wide variety of options, is ***Watson's Harmony Beach*** *(☎ 218-875-2811, 10002 Gappa Rd)*. Here rooms in the lodge go for $35/45 single/double. Cottages range from $90 a night and $450 a week to $150 a night and $725 a week. Meals are available. Watson's also has camping at $18 a night.

Both places are easily found just off County Rd 122 beside Kabetogama Lake.

Twelve miles east of International Falls, on Hwy 11 at **Rainy Lake**, is the main park office (☎ 218-286-5258). It's open all year but closed Monday and Tuesday from October to May. This is the best place for information. Park headquarters (☎ 218-283-9821) is at 3131 Hwy 53, International Falls, but it's more administrative than tourist-oriented. There is no park campground here, but private accommodations of all types are nearby. Ranger-led programs include guided walks, canoe trips and nature observation. A range of boat tours (☎ 218-286-5470) is offered, from two-hour eagle watches to eight-hour day trips. Call for details and reservations.

INTERNATIONAL FALLS & THE CANADIAN BORDER

International Falls maintains the international tradition of uninspiring border towns. Though busy in summer for a town of 8300, it is nowhere near the tourist mecca of many of the resort towns to the south and east. The town boasts two nationally known figures: Tammy Faye Bakker and Chicago Bear football star Bronko Nagurski grew up here.

With nearly all the lodgings and eateries on the feeder roads, the three-block downtown doesn't warrant much attention. A

A Taste of History

The region around Rainy Lake and Lake of the Woods (on both sides of the border) is well known for growing wild rice, which is actually a wetland grass. Native Americans have harvested it in northern Minnesota since long before European arrival. Traditionally, the seeds are collected in late summer by gently whacking the stalks over a slow-moving canoe. It is then dried and sorted by hand.

Today, the rice is also commercially grown and separated and processed by machine. This cultivated version is known as paddy rice. Aficionados say that the true wild rice tastes better and is worth the extra cost. It also employs many Indians in a time-honored practice.

Both kinds of rice can be purchased at roadside stands in the area and sampled at regional restaurants. The long, black-and-white grains have a delicious, slightly nutty flavor.

MINNESOTA

couple of specialized sites, the friendly residents and low prices justify a brief stop.

The CVB (☎ 218-283-9400, 800-325-5766, www.rainylake.org), 301 2nd Ave, is right by the international bridge to Fort Francis, Ontario. Hours are 8 am to 5 pm weekdays. For statewide information, visit the Minnesota Tourism Office (☎ 218-285-7623) at 200 4th St.

Things to See & Do

Paper manufacturer **Boise Cascade** (☎ 218-285-5011), which produces the pervading smell of sulfur or money (depending on your point of view), offers eye-opening free tours of its plant. This high-tech operation is one of the largest, fastest paper-making plants in the world. The walk, which has been rated as one of the country's best industrial tours, is offered at 8:30 and 11 am and 1:30 pm weekdays from June 1 to August 31. Meet at the CVB at the corner of 2nd St and 4th Ave. No children under 10 and no open-toed shoes are allowed.

Grand Mound History Center (☎ 218-285-3332), 17 miles west on Hwy 11, is the site of the state's largest prehistoric burial mounds. Though the state once had 2000 similar, although smaller, mounds, there is little evidence of them left today. Thorough interpretive exhibits outline the history of the Middle Woodland natives who lived in the area between 200 BC and 800 AD. Take insect repellant to walk to the overgrown mound where 5000 bodies were buried over 1200 years. Open 10 am to 5 pm Thursday to Saturday, Sunday noon to 5 pm from June to early September, weekends only through October; $3/2/1.50 adults/seniors/children.

The **Bronko Nagurski Museum** (☎ 218-283-4316), 214 6th Ave, honors the local legend who some say was the greatest football player of all time. He played for the Minnesota Gophers and for the NFL's Chicago Bears in the 1930s. Sharing the premises is the **Koochiching Museum**, with artifacts and exhibits on area history. Both are open 9 am to 5 pm daily from late May to mid-October, weekdays only the rest of the year; $3.

After dark watch for the **northern lights** (aurora borealis), which are frequently seen in summer.

Ranier is a small community 2 miles east where Rainy Lake empties into the Rainy River. The lift bridge allows the heavy rail traffic to cross between Canada and the USA. Hwy 11 east continues to Voyageurs National Park.

Hwy 11 westbound from International Falls leads through forest to Lake of the Woods, bordering Ontario and Manitoba. The island-filled lake has great fishing and is a popular summer cottage area. The border crossing near Warroad is open 24 hours.

Places to Stay

The ***Hilltop Motel*** *(☎ 218-283-2505, 800-322-6681, ❷ hilltop@norshore.net, 2002 2nd Ave W)*, on Hwy 52 south, is a fine, family-run motel with immaculate rooms and modest prices. Some units are individual cabins at $33/36.

Budget Host Inn *(☎ 218-283-2577, 800-880-2577, fax 218-285-3688)*, five blocks west of Smokey Bear Park on Hwy 11-17 west of town, is about $5 more and close to shopping malls.

Super 8 *(☎ 218-283-8811, 2326 US 53)* is larger, has more features and offers suites and efficiencies. Standard rooms cost $44/50.

Places to Eat

For a low-cost, home-style meal the ***Shorelunch Café*** *(☎ 218-285-7483, 1523 US 53 South)* is recommended. Have the bargain walleye dinner with wild rice soup ($8). It opens for breakfast at 5:30 am.

A second popular choice is ***Barney's*** (☎ 218-283-3333), five blocks west of town on Hwy 11, an all-purpose place with its own bakery and where you can also get a drink. It's open daily 5 am to 10 pm. Meals from the extensive, modestly priced menu include roast beef and fish.

Downtown, ***Coffee Landing*** *(☎ 218-283-8316, 444 3rd St)* roasts its own beans on the premises.

Getting There & Away

Greyhound serves the city once a day using the Budget Host Inn (☎ 218-283-2577) as a depot. It's less than half a mile west of downtown on Hwy 11-71. The bus travels south to Virginia, Duluth ($30) and the Twin Cities, departing at 8:30 am. There is no transport to Canada, but the Grey Goose bus line goes from Fort Francis, Ontario, to Winnipeg, Manitoba.

NORTHWEST ANGLE

Jutting into Lake of the Woods from Canada's Manitoba, with no road connection from the US, is Minnesota's oddball territory, the Northwest Angle. Figuring out and then surveying and marking the Minnesota–Canada border began more than 200 years ago, and this is the result.

In 1783, after the American Revolution, British and American negotiators came up with a concept for determining the border. Unfortunately, it was based on the notion that the Mississippi would always be America's western edge and that the river went north to Lake of the Woods. When these assumptions proved false, a new British–American team in 1818 changed the border to a point straight down from the northwest tip of Lake of the Woods to the 49th parallel. That left this wooded, lonely chunk of land, which is now mostly state forest.

Controversy continues. Canadian and American politicians are wrestling over fishing and resort regulations in the area. Isolated American lodge owners on the Angle claim they are bearing the brunt of the dispute and losing business because of it and have threatened to secede from the USA and join Canada if they don't get some attention, respect and more than a sympathetic ear.

Toll-Free & Web Site Directory

For toll-free number information, call ☎ 800-555-1212.

Accommodations

The listings for this book give the local phone and fax numbers where available. They also include toll-free numbers and Web site or email addresses when available for independent properties that are not affiliated with a group or chain.

Listed here are the toll-free telephone numbers for the lodging chains included in this book. The Web addresses are also included, because usually you can make reservations at these sites and they often have special Web-only deals.

Baymont Inns ☎ 800-301-0200
www.baymontinns.com

Best Inn ☎ 800-237-8466
www.bestinn.com

Best Western ☎ 800-528-1234
www.bestwestern.com

Clarion ☎ 800-252-7466
www.clarioninn.com

Comfort Inn ☎ 800-228-5150
www.comfortinn.com

Courtyard by Marriott ☎ 800-321-2211
www.courtyard.com

Days Inn ☎ 800-325-2525
www.daysinn.com

Doubletree ☎ 800-222-8733
www.douletreehotels.com

Drury Inns ☎ 800-325-8300
www.drury-inn.com

Fairfield Inn by Marriott ☎ 800-228-2800
www.marriott.com

Four Seasons ☎ 800-332-3442
www.fourseasons.com

Hampton Inns ☎ 800-426-7866
www.hampton-inn.com

Hilton ☎ 800-445-8667
www.hilton.com

Hyatt ☎ 800-233-1234
www.hyatt.com

Inter-Continental ☎ 800-327-0200
www.interconti.com

Knights Inn ☎ 800-843-5644
www.knightsinn.com

Marriott ☎ 800-228-9290
www.marriott.com

Motel 6 ☎ 800-466-8356
www.motel6.com

Quality Inn ☎ 800-228-5151
www.qualityinn.com

Ramada ☎ 800-228-2828
www.ramada.com

Red Roof Inn ☎ 800-843-7663
www.redroof.com

Sheraton ☎ 800-325-3535
www.sheraton.com

Travelodge ☎ 800-255-3050
www.travelodge.com

Airlines (Domestic)

Following are the primary domestic airlines serving the Great Lakes region.

Access Air ☎ 888-422-2377
www.accessair.com

Air Canada/Air Ontario ☎ 800-776-3000
www.aircanada.ca

AirTran ☎ 800-825-8538
www.airtran.com

America West Airlines ☎ 800-235-9292
www.americawest.com

American & American Eagle Airlines ☎ 800-433-7300
www.aa.com

American Trans Air ☎ 800-435-9282
www.ata.com

Continental ☎ 800-523-3273
www.continental.com

Delta Air Lines ☎ 800-221-1212
www.delta-air.com

Midwest Express ☎ 800-452-2022
www.midwestexpress.com

Northwest Airlines ☎ 800-225-2525
www.nwa.com

Pro Air ☎ 800-939-9551
www.proair.com

outhwest Airlines ☎ 800-435-9792
www.southwest.com
'WA ☎ 800-221-2000
www.twa.com
Jnited ☎ 800-241-6522
www.ual.com
JS Airways ☎ 800-428-4322
www.usairways.com

irlines (International)

ollowing are the primary international carers serving the Great Lakes region.

ir Canada ☎ 888-247-2262
www.aircanada.ca
ir France ☎ 800-321-4538
www.airfrance.com
litalia ☎ 800-223-5730
www.alitaliausa.com
British Airways ☎ 800-247-9297
www.british-airways.com
Canadian Airlines ☎ 800-426-7000
www.cdnair.ca
Delta Air Lines ☎ 800-241-4141
www.delta-air.com
beria ☎ 800-772-4642
www.iberia.com
celand Air ☎ 800-223-5500
www.icelandair.com
apan Airlines (JAL) ☎ 800-525-3663
www.jal.co.jp
KLM ☎ 800-374-7747
www.klm.nl
ufthansa ☎ 800-645-3880
www.lufthansa.com
Mexicana Airlines ☎ 800-531-7921
www.mexicana.com.mx
Northwest Airlines ☎ 800-447-4747
www.nwa.com
abena ☎ 800-955-2000
www.sabena.com
SAS ☎ 800-221-2350
www.scandinavian.net
wissair ☎ 800-221-4750
www.swissair.com
'WA ☎ 800-892-4141
www.twa.com
Jnited ☎ 800-538-2929
www.ual.com
Virgin Atlantic ☎ 800-862-8621
www.virgin-atlantic.com

Car-Rental Agencies

Advantage ☎ 800-777-5500
www.arac.com
Alamo ☎ 800-327-9633
www.alamo.com
Avis ☎ 800-331-1212
www.avis.com
Budget ☎ 800-527-0700
www.budget.com
CruiseAmerica (RV rental) ☎ 800-327-7799
www.cruiseamerica.com
Dollar ☎ 800-800-4000
www.dollar.com
Enterprise ☎ 800-736-8222
www.enterprise.com
Hertz ☎ 800-654-3131
www.hertz.com
National
(Domestic) ☎ 800-227-7368
(International) ☎ 800-227-3876
(TDD) ☎ 800-328-6323
www.nationalcar.com
Rent-a-Wreck ☎ 800-535-1391
www.rentawreck.com
Thrifty ☎ 800-367-2277
www.thrifty.com

Money

Western Union ☎ 800-325-6000
www.westernunion.com

State & Federal Resources

Illinois
www.state.il.us/
Indiana
www.state.in.us/
Ohio
www.state.oh.us/
Michigan
www.state.mi.us/
Minnesota
www.state.mn.us/
Wisconsin
www.state.wi.us/
US Forest Service ☎ 800-280-2267
www.fs.fed.us
US Postal Service ☎ 800-275-8777
www.usps.com

Transportation

AAA ☎ 800-272-2155
www.aaa.com
Road service & towing (members only) ☎ 800-222-4357

Amtrak ☎ 800-872-7245
www.amtrak.com

Green Tortoise ☎ 800-867-8647
www.greentortoise.com

Greyhound ☎ 800-231-2222
www.greyhound.com

Lakefront Trailways ☎ 800-638-633
www.lakefrontlines.com

SuperShuttle ☎ 800-258-382
www.supershuttle.com

Travel Agencies

Council Travel ☎ 800-226-862
www.counciltravel.com

STA ☎ 800-777-011
www.statravel.com

Travel CUTS
www.travelcuts.com

Index

Abbreviations

IA – Iowa
IL – Illinois
IN – Indiana
KY – Kentucky
MI – Michigan
MN – Minnesota
MO – Missouri
OH – Ohio
Ont – Ontario, Canada
WI – Wisconsin

Text

Bold indicates maps.

Bold indicates maps.

D

Bold indicates maps.

Bold indicates maps.

Bold indicates maps.

Bold indicates maps.

Bold indicates maps.

Bold indicates maps.

Bold indicates maps.

Bold indicates maps.

Boxed Text

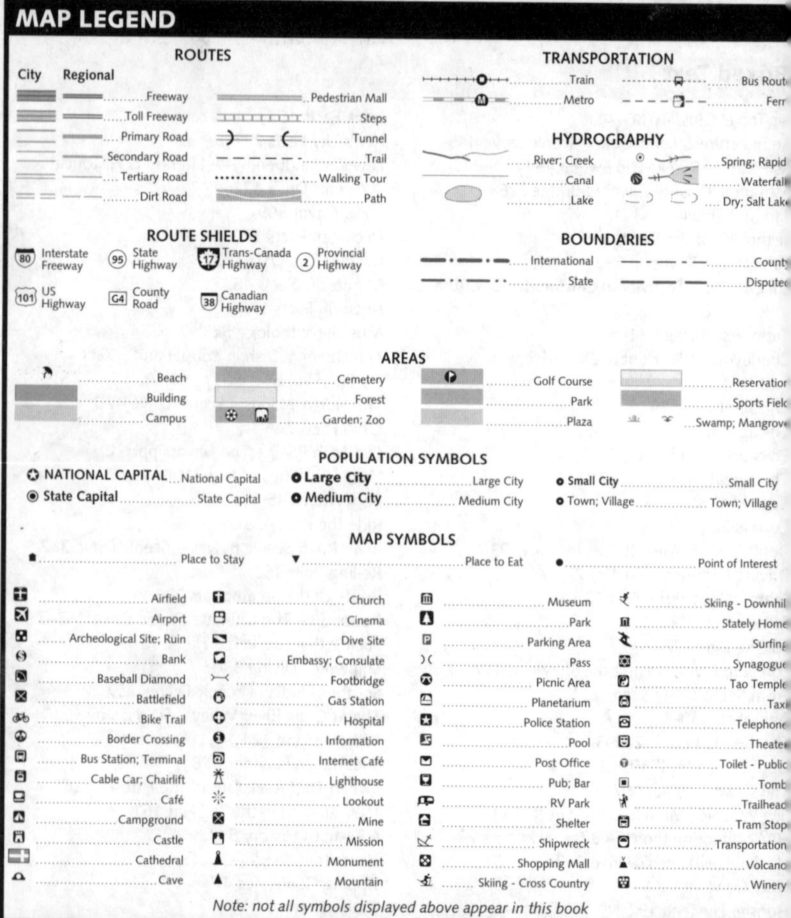

LONELY PLANET OFFICES

Australia
PO Box 617, Hawthorn 3122, Victoria
☎ 03 9819 1877 fax 03 9819 6459
email talk2us@lonelyplanet.com.au

USA
150 Linden Street, Oakland, California 94607
☎ 510 893 8555, TOLL FREE 800 275 8555
fax 510 893 8572
email info@lonelyplanet.com

UK
10A Spring Place, London NW5 3BH
☎ 020 7428 4800 fax 020 7428 4828
email go@lonelyplanet.co.uk

France
1 rue du Dahomey, 75011 Paris
☎ 01 55 25 33 00 fax 01 55 25 33 01
www.lonelyplanet.fr

World Wide Web: www.lonelyplanet.com ***or*** **AOL keyword: lp**
Lonely Planet Images: lpi@lonelyplanet.com.au